THE SOVIET BIOLOGICAL WEAPONS PROGRAM

The

SOVIET BIOLOGICAL WEAPONS PROGRAM

A History

Milton Leitenberg and Raymond A. Zilinskas
with Jens H. Kuhn

HARVARD UNIVERSITY PRESS
Cambridge, Massachusetts
London, England · 2012

Library of Congress Cataloging-in-Publication Data

Leitenberg, Milton.
    The Soviet biological weapons program : a history / Milton Leitenberg and Raymond A. Zilinskas,
with Jens H. Kuhn.
        pages ; cm
    Includes bibliographical references and index.
    ISBN 978-0-674-04770-9 (alkaline paper)
    1. Biological weapons—Soviet Union—History.   2. Biological warfare—Soviet Union—
History.   3. Biological arms control—Soviet Union—History.   I. Zilinskas, Raymond A.
II. Kuhn, Jens H.   III. Title.
    UG447.8.L45 2012
    358'.3882094709045—dc23
                                                                                    2011043160

This book is dedicated to the memory of Vladimir A. Pasechnik

Vladimir A. Pasechnik, first and foremost a scientist, was also a highly moral person, as was made clear after he defected to Great Britain in October 1989. The reasons for Pasechnik's defection were multiple, complex, and conflicted. One of those reasons unquestionably included a moral component. Pasechnik had over time come to deplore the work that he was doing to formulate biological weapon agents, perfect means for their dispersion, and develop delivery systems for them. If not for his defection, the Soviet offensive biological warfare program, codenamed *Ferment*, might not have been disclosed between 1990 and 1992, which coincided with the last years of President Gorbachev's tenure. The world owes Pasechnik its thanks for having made it more secure.

After Pasechnik defected, he was debriefed for several years by British intelligence analysts and, eventually, by their American colleagues. After the debriefings were completed, Pasechnik began working as a scientist at the Public Health Laboratory Service's Centre for Applied Microbiology and Research (CAMR), which is located at Porton Down, near Salisbury in southern England. This facility, which usually is simply called Porton Down, has a long history of being involved with both biological and chemical weapons R&D, as well as developing defenses against them. However, after March 1979, CAMR has been dedicated to pharmaceutical R&D. At CAMR, Pasechnik's major responsibility was to develop vaccines.

Unlike the other major defector from the Soviet BW program, Ken Alibek, Pasechnik was not at all interested in publicity. As he explained to us, his major wish was to become accepted as a top scientist by his colleagues in the British scientific establishment. Sensationalist stories in the press that featured him would, he felt, damage his chances for realizing his wish. Over the years he therefore gave just three major interviews, to one reporter and the two authors of this book, and appeared once on BBC television. We were fortunate to have spent more than 40 hours interviewing Pasechnik over several years, plus exchanging numerous emails. We were greatly saddened when Pasechnik died of a stroke on November 21, 2001, at the age of 64. He had recently started his own biotechnology company, and it seemed that he had returned to a fruitful scientific career developing new or improved vaccines.

When visiting the Institute of Highly Pure Biopreparations (IHPB) in 2003 and 2004, one of us (Zilinskas) was astonished to see photographs of Pasechnik adorning the walls of several of its laboratories. When asked, laboratory staff members said that he was the best director the IHPB had ever had and that his kindness to those who worked for him was legendary. One staff member presented Zilinskas with a copy of a photograph of Pasechnik that was displayed at IHPB and now is reproduced in this book.

Contents

Preface

The fact is that science in the hands of a decayed capitalism can never be employed usefully; it can only lead to increased exploitation, unemployment, crises and war ... Under capitalism, War is poisoning Science.

J. D. BERNAL, recipient of the Lenin Peace Prize 1953

On the other hand, in RUSSIA, the possibility that science will turn to weapons exploitation has disappeared. In RUSSIA, all products of science are playing a role in material and cultural improvements for the people.

DEMOCRATIC PEOPLE'S REPUBLIC OF KOREA, 1950

In the meantime peace-loving forces everywhere have launched a campaign for the complete deliverance of mankind from the threat of chemical and bacteriological warfare. In September, 1969, the Soviet Union, together with Poland, Hungary, Mongolia, Bulgaria, Romania and Czechoslovakia, submitted to the 24th Session of the General Assembly a Draft Convention on the Prohibition of the Development, Production and Stockpiling of Chemical and Bacteriological (Biological) Weapons. In October, 1970, a revised Draft Convention was submitted to the 25th Session of the General Assembly, which indicated concrete ways for saving mankind from these means of mass destruction. The draft provides for the prohibition of both the production and storaging [sic] of these weapons. In other words, it is a proposal for the complete prohibition of chemical and bacteriological weapons.

OLEG BOGDANOV, Deputy Director, IMEMO, 1973

*The passing of the Biological Weapons Convention at the
26th Session of the United Nations General Assembly in 1972,
and its entry into force in 1975, was a great victory for the
(progressiveness) of humanity. This was the first agreement in
the area of disarmament in the world, as it not only prohibited
an entire class of weapons, but it stipulated their complete
destruction.*

V. N. ORLOV, Deputy Head, Ministry of Defense Radiological,
Chemical, and Biological Defense Forces, 2000

*Science and morality have always been the forces driving progress in
the history of mankind's development. Scientific discoveries have been
the driver of society's development, and ethical ideas have been the
conductor determining the use of the results of these discoveries . . .
[A] person not bound by high moral principles is capable of creating
weapons of mass destruction and using them effectively. Biological
weapons are the most accessible weapons of the said arsenal.*

LIEUTENANT GENERAL VALENTIN IVANOVICH
YEVSTIGNEEV, former head of the 15th Directorate, General Staff of
the Ministry of Defense, Soviet Union, responsible for the Soviet offensive
BW program, 2003

On April 10, 1972, 77 nations signed the Biological and Toxin Weapons
Convention (BWC). The convention entered into force on March 26, 1975,
after 85 nations, including the United States (US) and the Soviet Union
(USSR), had ratified it.[1] The Soviet Union was designated as one of its three
treaty depository States, with the others being the United States and the
United Kingdom (UK). The United States had already unilaterally ended its
biological warfare (BW) program after President Richard Nixon signed an
executive order to that effect on November 25, 1969. In accordance with this
directive, the US BW program was dismantled and all stocks of weaponized
agents were destroyed between 1969 and 1971.[2] The United States can be
said to have been in compliance with the BWC even before it came into existence. Conversely, it was precisely during the years between 1972 and 1975
that while one part of the Soviet government was laying the legislative basis
for ratifying the BWC, another part of that same government was acting to
substantially expand its BW program by building massive new research, development, and production facilities, hiring tens of thousands of scientists
and technicians, developing a specialized research program in applied micro-

biology to weaponize bacteria and viruses (i.e., to enhance the virulence, hardiness, and other properties in pathogens that make them more useful for military purposes), and expanding an already large existing open-air test site where the new creations could be tested for efficacy. The Soviet BW program's production capabilities were especially significant. The Soviet Union built and readied for use between seven and ten gigantic "mobilization capacity" production facilities that would mass-produce virulent bacterial and viral agents in case of an impending war. Ken Alibek, a former deputy director of Biopreparat, the ostensibly civilian part of the Soviet BW program, claims that the mobilization production facilities' cumulative annual production capacity was several thousand tons of eight different weaponized pathogens. Even if the tonnage that Alibek specified was several-fold higher than US authorities believed them to have been, the quantities remain staggering. Alibek also testified that over 100 tons of pathogens usable for BW were prepared and stockpiled in depots near military airfields.

The quotations that introduce this Preface are not unique. Individuals who played significant roles in either the major expansion of the Soviet offensive BW program in the early 1970s or its management thereafter were guilty of perpetuating deliberate deceptions that aimed to fool not only foreigners, but also the civilian Soviet scientific community. In 1976, A. A. Baev, a USSR Academy of Sciences official and one of the three authors of a 1971 memorandum to General Secretary Leonid Brezhnev (CPSU) that advocated a vastly expanded BW program, wrote in a prestigious biomedical journal:

> Is it possible to create, through genetic engineering methods, microorganisms that are dangerous to humans . . . ? Is it possible that someone somewhere is conducting experiments which already exceed the bounds of scientific experiments? Such activities, if they had a place, contradict the Convention on the Prohibition of the Development, Production, and Stockpiling of Bacteriological (Biological) Weapons and Toxins and on the Destruction of their Stocks, which has been signed by most states, including the USSR, and was approved by the UN General Assembly on December 16, 1971. They contradict the moral code of science and are connected to the destructive and maniacal ideas of political and military adventurism.
>
> We in the Soviet Union do not experience fear toward the future: no apprehensions that some sort of powerful and blind forces are capable of directing scientific research in genetic engineering onto the path of evil

contrary to the intentions and wishes of the people. We are convinced that reason and good will win out here. The dark predictions and almost panicked feelings about which one comes to read in both the general and specialized press of capitalist countries will appear to be exaggerations—but at the same time understandable. These feelings support the phenomenon of capitalist reality: the rise of violence and terrorism, the explosions of hostility and armed conflict, of organized crime, of the reality of powerful corporations and figures—[all] outside societal control. All of this gives rise to a feeling of distrust and fear that someone uses scientific openness for evil purposes and that scientific openness will bring to humanity new misfortunes rather than good.[3]

And in an article that accompanied Baev's, Academician V. M. Zhdanov, who at that very moment was serving as the chairperson of the scientific research advisory board for a major branch of the BW program, added, "The consistent peaceful policy implemented by the Communist Party of the Soviet Union and the successful fulfillment of the Program for Peace developed by the 24th CPSU Congress are a hopeful bulwark against any attempt to use the achievements of science, including genetic engineering, for inhuman purposes."[4] The major address to the 24th Congress, which introduced the Program for Peace, was made by Brezhnev. One year later, Brezhnev would sign the decree that greatly expanded the Soviet offensive BW program and thus placed the Soviet Union on the course of violating the BWC. Documents of the Central Committee of the Soviet Union used the euphemistic term "Special Problems" to refer to biological weapons.

The Soviet government maintained its covert offensive BW program until the Soviet Union was dissolved on December 25, 1991, at which time it was continued by the successor Russian government until at least September 1992. That program's most important facilities remain inaccessible to outsiders to this day, and it has been made a crime for anyone in present-day Russia to divulge information about the former offensive BW program.[5] Anyone attempting to research this important subject in Russia therefore does so at his or her peril.

In 1988, at the time of peak expansion of the Soviet BW program, 49% of the hospitals in the Soviet Union reportedly did not have hot running water, 15% had no running water at all, and 24% lacked indoor sewage systems.[6] Half of Soviet schools had no central heating, running water, or indoor sewage systems. Infant mortality in the Soviet Union was higher than that in many developing nations, including, for example, the small and impoverished Caribbean island of Barbados.[7] In contrast to its irresponsibility in the civilian sphere, the Soviet government spent billions of rubles and hundreds of millions of scarce dollars to pay for its BW program—a program that added nothing to the security of the country or well-being of the Soviet population. These expenditures were slated to rise, even during the last years of the Soviet Union as new BW facilities were still being constructed and additional ones were being planned. For example, in 1990 the Gorbachev administration reportedly approved almost $1 billion for biological weapons development.[8] Far greater amounts of money were of course at the same time being spent on researching and developing other weapons systems, such as nuclear and chemical weapons.

The legacy of the Soviet BW program continues to haunt us today. The proliferation and potential use of biological weapons have become a greatly heightened concern since 1992. This is in part due to the world having become aware of the massive BW program that the Soviet Union carried out in violation of the BWC, and in part due to other reasons such as the discovery of the much smaller Iraqi BW program and the new concern that non-state terrorist groups might use biological agents. In view of the importance of the Soviet BW program, which dwarfed all others, the first objective of this book is to describe it as fully as we can.

It was considered possible in 1992 that components of the Soviet BW program, including its highly trained scientists and engineers, and strains of pathogens and toxins developed specifically for weapons purposes, might become available to proliferant nations and terrorist groups. It was feared that this could occur because the civilian segments of the country's former BW program underwent very sizable reductions following the dissolution of the Soviet Union. This resulted in large staff reductions, while those who remained were underpaid and worked under the extremely constrained financial conditions being experienced by their institutions. It was important to ascertain if some unknown portion of these scientists would in fact accept positions with one or more nations or terrorist groups that were interested in acquiring biological weapons. In consequence, the second important objective of this book is to ascertain whether these reductions led, inadvertently or not, to the proliferation of BW-related knowledge to other states or to terrorist groups intent on acquiring biological weapons.

At the same time, the United States and other nations have spent large sums of money to support former Soviet BW scientists working in their home research institutions on projects that were intended to serve beneficial purposes. The issue of whether this money was spent wisely is therefore also a subject addressed in this book. This is particularly important because Russia still maintains a closed scientific research system consisting of the microbiological laboratories belonging to the Russian Federation Ministry of Defense (RF-MOD), which had been crucial components of the overall Soviet BW program. They are known to have been instrumental in the Soviet era for biological weapons development, testing, and production banned by the BWC. Yet both President Mikhail Gorbachev and President Boris Yeltsin failed in their attempts to terminate the BW program and shut down all its components. The third main objective of this book is therefore to describe the failure of both President Gorbachev and President Yeltsin to bring about conditions that would show that the Soviet and subsequent Russian BW program was totally terminated, and to try to explain why that happened. This is especially important because no one in the United States and the other nations that have supported scientific research and development in Russia would want to inadvertently assist the RF-MOD's biological institutes that have to this day remained closed to all foreigners and have kept their work programs secret.

Note on Transliteration

[Comment from authors: Although we used many Russian sources that were translated by the Joint Publication Research Service and the Open Source Center, and the Soviet Central Committee documents that were translated by David Hoffman and Natalia Alexandrova, our major translator was James W. Toppin. He often was more than a translator, also doing research to answer questions that needed clarification. Substantial translations done by Toppin are identified as such.]

The art of transliterating Russian names and words into English tries to reconcile several sometimes conflicting aims: achieve a consistent correspondence between the Russian (Cyrillic) and English letters, provide a reasonably close phonetic equivalent, and produce spellings convenient for readers not familiar with the Russian alphabet. Various transliteration systems are in use, some intended for specific purposes such as cataloging, but exceptions are made for a variety of reasons, including tradition. For example, the Russian city of Moskva ("Москва" in Cyrillic) is universally known in English as "Moscow."

Our approach to transliteration emphasizes readability while striving to be as consistent and phonetic as possible. Below are several examples of the transliterations used in this book, along with variants that readers will encounter in other published sources.

Russian	Version used in this book	Variants that may be found in other sources
Юрий	Yury	Yuri, Yuriy, Yurii
Сергей	Sergey and Sergei	Serguei

Горбачёв	Gorbachev	Gorbachyov, Gorbachëv
Воробьёв	Vorobyov	Vorobyev, Vorob'yov, Vorob'yev, Vorob'ov, Vorob'ev, Vorobyëv, Vorob'yëv
Домарадский	Domaradsky	Domaradskij, Domaradskii, Domaradskiy
Елизавета	Yelizaveta	Elizaveta
Евгений	Yevgeny	Yevgeni, Yevgenii, Yevgeniy, Evgenii, Evgeniy, Evgeni, Evgeny
Эдуард	Eduard	Edward
Виктор	Viktor	Victor
Скрябин	Skryabin	Scriabin, Skriabin
Раевский	Raevsky	Rayevsky, Raevskii, Raevskiy, Rayevskiy
Сергеев	Sergeev	Sergeyev, Sergeiev
пятёрка	*pyatorka*	*pyatyerka, piatiorka*
Щербаков	Shcherbakov	Scherbakov
Военный	Voenny	Voyenny, Voennyi, Voennyy, Voennii, Voyennyy, Voyennii, Voyennyi, Voyenyy
Катаев	Kataev	Katayev

James W. Toppin
Translator

THE SOVIET BIOLOGICAL WEAPONS PROGRAM

Introduction

IT HAS BEEN SAID that the history of nuclear weapons is at once fascinating and horrifying. It is an exciting tale of discovery and invention, but it also depicts the means by which the destruction of nations can be accomplished. Similarly, the history of biological warfare (BW) and biological weapons is frightening and mesmerizing. It is frightening because the idea that someone can and is willing to apply science and medicine in order to manipulate and grow microorganisms for the purpose of deliberately bringing about illness and death contravenes so much of our society's ethics that it is beyond the pale of civilized behavior. The possibility that virulent bacteria or viruses will be developed to arm biological weapons and, when used, threaten vast populations with disease and death is incomprehensible. Reality, however, provides sufficient example of what might otherwise be considered incomprehensible. In 1986, in the peak year of their combined nuclear arsenals, the United States and the Soviet Union maintained 68,317 nuclear weapons—the Soviet portion of which was 45,000—with the large majority of them in various states of readiness for use.[1]

In contrast to the Soviet nuclear weapons program, which stimulated an extremely high level of concern among member states of the North Atlantic Treaty Organization (NATO), its BW program was hardly remarked on. One reason for this was that for a long stretch of the Cold War the NATO countries did not know that the Soviet Union possessed a dozen different biological weapons and the capability for the mass production of pathogens

1

and toxins on relatively short order. This situation changed slightly in the early 1980s, after the occurrence of a suspicious event—an anthrax epidemic in the Soviet city of Sverdlovsk in 1979—that sent a warning to Western governments about the strong probability that the Soviet Union was operating a secret BW program. The US government also alleged in 1980 and 1981 that the Soviet Union had supplied Soviet-made toxins for use in the Indochina peninsula and Afghanistan. Both of these events are discussed and analyzed in this book. Together with intelligence that began to accumulate about particular Soviet facilities that would later turn out to be components of the Biopreparat system, they provoked the concern of NATO member countries and stimulated the US government to issue periodic statements charging the Soviet Union with noncompliance with both the 1972 Biological and Toxin Weapons Convention (BWC), which forbids the development, manufacture, and storing of BW agents as well as the 1925 Geneva Protocol, which prohibited the use of bacteriological and chemical weapons. However, the subject of Soviet BW capabilities did not appear to cause much concern among the public in Western democracies. The US civil defense program in the 1960s certainly did not attempt to prepare its citizens for potential BW in the same way that it attempted to protect them against a nuclear attack.

Since approximately 1989, the issue of BW has come to the forefront of public attention. To a significant extent this concern was fueled by new information that came to light about the Soviet Union's BW program. For the first time the general public became aware that Soviet scientists had researched, developed, and manufactured bacteria and viruses of unsurpassed ability to kill large numbers of people. These microbial strains have almost certainly been retained in culture collections maintained by closed facilities belonging to the Russian Federation Ministry of Defense (RF-MOD). Retention included the possibility that the strains could be reconstituted and used again in the event that a future Russian government reactivated an offensive BW program. Further, the possibility existed that the scientists and engineers responsible for having created them might emigrate to work for other governments or terrorist organizations. However, after envelopes filled with *Bacillus anthracis* spores were mailed to American government officials and individuals in the media in the autumn of 2001, concerns about biological weapons shifted to bioterrorism. As a result of constant expressions of alarm by members of the US government and congress, as well as substantial and alarmist coverage in the media, public discussion of a biological weapons threat from non-state actors or terrorist groups was greatly heightened. However, for security analysts the legacy of the Soviet BW program remained. It now resided in closed Russian military biological institutes, closed anti-plague institutes, and the possibility that former Soviet BW scientists would be hired by proliferant countries or terrorist groups. Are these fears realistic or exaggerated? We try to answer that question.

Because the development of biological weapons to a great extent is a type of applied microbiology (now more commonly called biotechnology), it has its basis in several disciplines in the biological sciences. Science and Soviet policymaking were inextricably linked. Under Josef Stalin's rule, the Soviet government proudly built up and supported the world's largest scientific establishment, although in general its productivity was low and some lines of scientific development were suppressed for political reasons. Both Stalin and his successor, Nikita S. Khrushchev, acted on the basis of pseudoscientific but politically attractive theories developed by Trofim D. Lysenko (1898–1976) to quench one of the more important of those disciplines—genetics. The Lysenko era, when pseudoscience ruled over and severely retarded the biological sciences in the Soviet Union, lasted from 1948 to 1964.[2]

An effort to overcome the retarding effects of Lysenkoism had substantial implications for what was to become the founding of the modern Soviet BW program in the early 1970s. Ambitious Soviet scientists in the fields of biology and biochemistry calculated that unless they persuaded political leaders that modern biotechnology held substantial military potential, the level of support they would receive to gain capabilities in, for example, molecular biology, would probably remain low. They would continue falling farther behind Western scientists as had been the case throughout the Lysenko era. Conversely, if they could convince the Politburo that scientific research in this new discipline could lead to the development of new and unique weapons and, in addition, that Western military scientists were already applying the techniques of modern biotechnology and molecular genetics to develop biological weapons capable of causing mass casualties, then there was a rationale for the Soviet Union to do the same. If their proposal was accepted, an enhanced Soviet BW program would be accorded the high priority and substantial resources that had heretofore been reserved primarily for the nuclear and missile scientists. In this they were wildly successful, so successful that by the end of the 1980s the Soviet Union possessed the largest and most sophisticated BW program the world has ever seen. As a side effect of this effort, many scientists working for institutes of the USSR Academy of Sciences (USSR-AN) and USSR Academy of Medical Sciences (USSR-AMN) acquired better facilities, equipment, and supplies. It is ironic that an effort to overcome the effects of Lysenkoism, which nearly destroyed the bioscientific research establishment in the Soviet Union in the 1950s, was used not only to resurrect modern genetics in the Soviet Union in the early 1970s but also to inspire an enlarged and enhanced offensive BW program.

Writing about any aspect of Soviet military history and policy is particularly difficult because these subjects were, and remain, frequently obscured by secrecy and disinformation. Unlike the former BW programs of the United States, United Kingdom, Canada, and Japan, for which there are voluminous records in national archives, exhaustive testimonies by principals, and a huge secondary literature, there is virtually no access by Western researchers to Soviet primary material about its military biological programs. To this day many Russian officials maintain the fiction that the Soviet Union never possessed an offensive BW program. Analysts therefore face huge problems when researching the Soviet BW program. They cannot access documents in Russian archives, and substantial portions of the secondary literature written by Russian authors are unreliable. The number of individuals who have direct knowledge about that program is limited, and of those, very few are willing to share their knowledge. Western analysts who enter Russia for the purpose of interviewing individuals knowledgeable about the former Soviet BW program put themselves and their sources at risk for arrest, because "who did what, where" in regard to that program remains classified and Russian law forbids its revelation.[3]

Of course, many former weapons scientists have emigrated from the former Soviet Union, and in theory they are therefore available for risk-free interviews in the United States, the United Kingdom, Israel, and other Western countries. In practice, this is rarely the case. When we were able to locate such scientists, there were three possible outcomes: the individual would not agree to be interviewed even if anonymity were guaranteed; he agreed but provided little or no valuable information; or he agreed to be interviewed and was able to provide useful information.

Most of those who refused did not want to acknowledge their involvement in the Soviet BW program. They did not want their current colleagues to know about their past activities, which probably are well camouflaged in their résumés. Additionally, some had relatives in Russia who could be placed at risk should information about their disclosures become public. Others took the position that "Oh, this is ancient history, and I just don't want to think of it again." However, several interviewees were forthcoming and provided valuable information. These anonymous few made writing this book possible and worthwhile. Because of the sensitivity of information provided by interviewees, we must protect their privacy. In many cases names and even dates have been omitted. For convenience, we use the pronoun "he" throughout.

Cooperative interviewees included former Soviet and East European weapons scientists, administrators, government officials, and security analysts, as well as US and British officials. Interviews with sources who were familiar with important aspects of the Soviet BW program were conducted in the United States, the United Kingdom, Israel, Germany, Belarus, Ukraine, and Kazakhstan. Some interviews were long, lasting several days to a week, while a few took only some hours. In some cases, contacts with sources were maintained for years. For example, our first set of interviews with Igor V. Domaradsky carried out in the United States covered six days and took up approximately 50 hours; in addition, Zilinskas was able to visit with him several times in Moscow for at least an additional 12 hours and to exchange dozens of emails with him.[4] Of course, our population of cooperative former Soviet interviewees was relatively small, approximately a dozen out of a total of some 50 individuals interviewed.

In regard to sources, we need to make note of certain limitations affecting especially the chapters on Biopreparat and the USSR Ministry of Defense (MOD). First, we had very limited access to military sources. This obviously presents a problem, because the MOD's 15th Directorate directed all aspects of the Soviet BW program. With one exception, we know next to nothing about the decision-making process at the very highest levels of the Soviet government in relations to the BW program. The exception was made possible when we obtained a small collection of Central Committee documents for the years 1986–1992, and were also fortunate to have extensive interviews with a former member of the staff of the Central Committee. The combination of the two proved to be of great importance in understanding the policy interactions in the Central Committee during the Gorbachev years. Second, while we rely as much as possible on primary information sources, chiefly scientists who worked for Biopreparat institutes, chance and opportunity dictated who we were able to interview. This means that our sources are unevenly spread in terms of their home institutes and disciplines. For example, as of 2004, at least forty former Vector scientists were living and working in the United States and thereby were theoretically available for interviews. However aside from Ken Alibek we know of no émigré scientists from, for example, Stepnogorsk. Another example is that one of us (Zilinskas) was able to visit three of the five major Biopreparat institutes, those in Obolensk, St. Petersburg, and Stepnogorsk, during 2001–2004. As a result of this uneven distribution of access, we know more about some institutes than about others, and more about some departments within those institutes than about others.

We had very few opportunities to interview principals in the former Soviet Union. In general, we avoided interviewing inside Russia because a 1993 edict forbids the revelation of pre-1992 secrets and prescribes severe penalties for violators.[5] The experience of Vil S. Mirzayanov is illustrative. For having revealed facts about the former Soviet Union's chemical warfare program, he was detained by the Ministry of Security in the autumn of 1992 on the charge of disclosing state secrets. This was despite the promise made by President Boris Yeltsin in January 1992 that Russia would comply with the bilateral US-USSR agreement to dismantle the two sides' chemical weapons.[6]

We did extensive research in the scientific literature for articles of Soviet and Russian origin indicative of BW. We now know that scientists working within the closed system at facilities dedicated to BW were permitted to publish in the open literature only after a very thorough and careful review by both scientific peers and security officials. In particular, draft publications were thoroughly vetted to make certain that they gave no indication of work related to the closed program. Of course, Soviet scientists working at open institutes published an enormous number of papers and books on microorganisms that were also of interest to the closed BW system, such as the causative organisms of anthrax, hemorrhagic fevers, plague, smallpox, and tularemia, but these publications give testimony to scientific and technological capabilities rather than indication of BW developments. Declassified British and US intelligence reports provide testimony that it was not possible to make a definitive determination of the existence of the offensive BW program through the analysis of open-source Soviet publications. Therefore, nothing openly published before 1992 in the Soviet Union or in the international literature by Soviet scientists definitively demonstrated the offensive character of the overall program. Interestingly enough, some works published after 1992 by scientists working in facilities connected with the former Soviet BW program are of high interest because they report on research that was done when the system was still closed but was not permitted to be published during that earlier period.

When discussing Russian sources, we first of all must praise three individuals: Vladimir A. Pasechnik, the first defector from the Soviet biological weapons program; Ken Alibek, the former deputy director of Biopreparat and, in 1992, the second major defector from the Soviet Union's BW program; and Domaradsky, the first head of Biopreparat's research council and the first Russian to inform his countrymen about its biological misdeeds. We give Pasechnik special homage by dedicating this book to him. Alibek's book about his life as a BW scientist contains a great store of information about the Soviet BW effort, its leadership, and institutions, told from a personal viewpoint.[7] In addition, Alibek has granted numerous interviews and testified several times before the US Congress, augmenting the information set forth in his book. His revelations about the Biopreparat and *Ferment* programs have added greatly to the West's knowledge of Soviet BW efforts and accomplishments. However, portions of his testimony and narrative regarding Soviet BW activities carried out by the MOD are considered less authoritative. The less well known autobiography by Domaradsky, which was first privately published in 1995 in a very limited edition in Moscow, and then expanded and updated for publication in the United States in 2003, provides invaluable information about the early days of the Biopreparat system and the environment in which biological weapons scientists worked.[8] He additionally published two long articles on the same subjects in a Russian journal, *Znanie-sila*, in 1996.[9] Domaradsky's courageous publications give testimony to his self-designation as "Troublemaker," causing problems for those who sought to shield information about the former Soviet BW program from the Russian public.

Despite our best efforts, there are large gaps in our understanding of the Soviet BW program. What we do know is that it had two major components: one housed in the military and security ministries, the other in civilian ones. The civilian component alone had a complicated administrative structure that included elements within five or six different ministries or agencies, including the Main Administration of Microbiological Industry (*Glavmikrobioprom*), Ministry of Health (MOH), and Ministry of Agriculture (MOA), as well as the USSR-AN and USSR-AMN. Although much has been learned about the overall structure of the civilian component, Biopreparat in particular, we know less about the detailed roles of the MOA, MOH, USSR-AN, and USSR-AMN. More distressingly, we know even less about the most important component of the Soviet BW program—the military. The work programs and accomplishments of the institutes of the MOD that were occupied with offensive BW activity constitute nearly opaque boxes. Nothing significant has ever been published regarding its offensive-directed activities.

They still remain closed to outsiders, and as far as we know, there have been no important defectors from the military institutes. However, more and more is being published in Russia on the MOD's ostensibly defensive activities. In view of this situation, this book should be considered to be a compendium of information that is currently available about the Soviet BW program and its legacy, but readers are cautioned that much remains to be discovered. We hope that what we have written will provide a sound basis for future research that will expose the Soviet BW program in an even more thorough fashion.

Although there are two main authors of this book, there was a division of responsibilities between them. The authors jointly wrote the Preface, Introduction, Chapters 10, 12, and the Conclusion. Raymond Zilinskas wrote chapters 1 through 9, and Milton Leitenberg wrote chapters 11 and 13 through 23. Jens Kuhn, a virologist, reviewed the technical parts of the book while at the Harvard Medical School and, based on his personal experience while at Vector, provided ideas on why certain research was done by Soviet weapon scientists. But in the final analysis, Zilinskas and Leitenberg are responsible for the contents of this book.

The book is organized in the main chronologically. To understand the intent and accomplishments of the more recent Soviet BW program, it is first necessary to know the history of what can be called its "first generation," which began in 1918 and lasted through 1972. Chapter 1 describes the program's major activities and accomplishments prior to, during, and shortly after World War II, including the foundation and operation of its major military BW research, development, testing, and production facilities.

To understand the directions and accomplishments of scientific research intended to benefit the Soviet BW program, it is also necessary to understand the USSR's overall scientific environment. Due to the influence of Lysenko, the Soviet Union was far behind the West in molecular biology and genetics at the dawn of genetic engineering in the early 1970s, with little hope of catching up. As recounted in Chapter 2, the unsatisfactory state of affairs in Soviet molecular biology led influential Soviet scientists to propose a radical approach for achieving biotechnological innovation, involving at the same time the Soviet Union's military biological weapons program and ostensibly civilian research institutes. The Central Committee of the Communist Party (hereafter, Central Committee) and the government's Council of Ministers accepted this proposal, thereby setting in motion the construction of the largest biological weapons effort the world has known to date. This was the very same time as Soviet representatives were negotiating the final stages of the BWC with US diplomats in Geneva. "Special Problems" was the term used in Central Committee documents to refer to biological weapons. Accordingly, much attention in this chapter, which concentrates on the years 1972–1973, is given to the process of establishing Biopreparat—the ostensibly civilian part of the offensive BW system—and the relationship of Biopreparat to other agencies, especially the MOD. This marks the beginning of the "second-generation" Soviet BW program, which was composed of offensive and defensive research, development, testing, and manufacturing in both the military sector and the civilian sector.

Chapter 3 is dedicated to the military sector. Because of limitations in available information, we often could not separate the defensive from the offensive portions of the program in the still-closed military laboratories and facilities about which little is known to date. Our consideration therefore combines both aspects when each of the military facilities and their work programs are described. One of the MOD facilities, the elaborate and important BW open field test site code-named Aralsk-7 located on Vozrozhdeniye (Renaissance) Island in the Aral Sea, is addressed separately in Chapter 4. This once-pristine island may present one of the Cold War's last biological threats to the region surrounding the Aral Sea.

Though much has been learned about the overall structure of the civilian component, Biopreparat in particular, we know less about the detailed roles of the MOA, MOH, USSR-AN, and USSR-AMN, and security organs. We therefore have written only about ministries and administrative organs that were involved with the acquisition of biological weapons aimed against humans, of which the Biopreparat system was the largest and most scientifically active. Due to the lack of adequate information, we decided not to address *Ekologiya* (Ecology, in English), the Soviet program headed by the MOA to produce biological weapons directed against animals and plants.[10] Unlike the military sector, we know fairly much about both defensive and offensive activities in the "civilian" sector, so we have separated the two. Defensive activities, most of which were conducted under the auspices of a program code-named Problem 5, are addressed in Chapter 5, while offensive activities conducted mostly under a program code-named *Ferment* (Enzyme in English) are dealt with in Chapter 6. *Ferment* scientists undertook remarkable R&D

to weaponize a wide range of pathogens, and production systems were set up in extremely large facilities that could be mobilized on short notice in the event of war or a pre-war period of extreme crisis to produce BW agents in ton quantities. Chapters 7 and 8 are studies of the two primary research institutes in the Biopreparat system, located in Obolensk and near Novosibirsk, while Chapter 9 focuses on institutes in Leningrad, Lyubuchany, and Stepnogorsk.

Chapter 10 examines the components that constitute biological weapons, as well as specific weaponry produced by the Soviet BW program, particularly bomblets and spray systems. We pay particular attention to the question of whether the Soviet Union ever had an ICBM BW delivery system. Also addressed is the marked contrast between what we know about, on the one hand, the Soviet BW R&D program and its weapons and, on the other, the intent of the Soviet BW program.

Chapter 11 is an effort to display the problems in differentiating between an offensive and a defensive BW program in the abstract. Once the BWC entered into force, this of course was the crux in determining the legitimacy of the Soviet BW program, or any BW program. Making that differentiation at a distance has always been an extremely difficult exercise. While it had a defensive aspect, there is no doubt that the Soviet BW program was offensively directed, and that is amply demonstrated in other chapters. The purpose of the chapter is to indicate the general nature of the problem.

In the course of our research, we became interested in the ability of the US intelligence community (IC) and the United Kingdom (UK) IC to identify and assess the Soviet BW program. Chapter 12 is a review of US and UK intelligence assessments of the Soviet BW program, although by far most information comes from US sources. In view of what is now known about the Soviet BW effort, we attempted to determine the accuracy and adequacy of the estimates made by the US IC in the entire post–World War II period, particularly the 1970s and 1980s. This is important for historical reasons and for the present and future biological international arms control regime. It is reasonable to believe that the intelligence estimates shaped the perceptions that US policymakers held about the Soviet BW effort, which in turn would directly influence how they dealt with Soviet officials on such matters as BWC compliance issues. Declassified records now available in the US and UK national archives, as well as in the Nixon, Reagan, and Bush presidential libraries, provided the necessary documents. This archival material has been supplemented by information derived from interviews with US and UK officials from both within and outside the IC who were directly involved in forming policies related to Soviet possession of biological weapons before 1992. As with most of our sources, these must remain anonymous.

Chapter 13 describes a US covert BW disinformation program directed at misleading the Soviet Union as to the pathogens being selected for emphasis in the US offensive BW program in the mid- to late-1960s. It paralleled a US disinformation effort that concerned chemical weapons agents also directed at the Soviet Union at the same time. The chemical story was described some years ago, but details of the BW disinformation effort have remained almost entirely secret until the present time. Public statements by various Soviet officials in the 1980s accused the United States of having maintained a secret offensive biological weapons program, and claimed that the US government's decision to terminate its program was a sham. In the West, these charges were considered propagandistic, and they almost always probably were. However, in the period after the first major defection from the Soviet BW program to the West in October 1989, and the US-USSR-UK trilateral negotiations at the very highest level that followed in 1990 and 1991, US officials began to suspect that most Soviet policymakers believed this fiction. The US Central Intelligence Agency (CIA) wondered whether that belief might have contributed to the Soviet decision to violate the BWC, and therefore looked back to examine why Soviet officials might have accepted that erroneous belief. In the course of this exercise, officials in the first Bush administration rediscovered the covert US BW disinformation effort directed at the Soviet Union between the mid-1960s and 1971. The nature and significance of the US BW disinformation effort is described.

Chapter 14 is a brief examination of a history of dozens of allegations made by various branches of the Soviet government for the entire post–World War II period charging that the United States had used biological weapons. As best as is known, all of these allegations are deliberate, fraudulent concoctions. The most notorious of these were the allegations made by the Soviet Union, the People's Republic of China, and North Korea, charging that the United States used biological weapons during the 1950–1953 Korean War. There was a brief respite from these charges between 1987 and 1992, but after that former Soviet military officials who were part of the Soviet Union's own BW program once again began to repeat the same discredited charges.

Chapter 15 reviews the 1979 Sverdlovsk anthrax epidemic and its effect on relations between the United States and the Soviet Union. The US government alleged that the epidemic had been caused by *Bacillus anthracis* spores accidentally released from one of the MOD facilities located in the city. These charges were consistently denied by the Soviet government. This event came to seriously affect diplomatic relations between the two countries in the 1980s. Between the time of the accidental release in April 1979 and the dissolution of the Soviet Union, Soviet officials maintained a fabricated explanation for the epidemic, claiming that it was due to city inhabitants having consumed contaminated meat or meat by-products. Top secret Soviet Central Committee documents obtained by the authors display the torturous maneuvers required by the need to maintain disinformation even within the very highest levels of the Soviet government. Despite President Yeltsin's admission in 1992 of MOD responsibility for the accidental release and the correctness of the US charges dating back to 1979, here too Russian officials have returned in recent years to the fabricated explanation of events.

Chapter 16 is a brief examination of whether the Soviet BW (or CW) program made use of a class of chemicals called mycotoxins. The chapter is not a reexamination of the history of US charges that the Soviet Union supplied these compounds for use by Vietnamese military forces in Laos and Cambodia in the early 1980s; rather those charges were used as a reason to search for evidence that might indicate whether or not mycotoxins were part of the Soviet BW program, and if so, in which institutes they might have been produced.

Chapter 17 is a brief examination of the contribution of the Soviet Union's Warsaw Treaty Organization allies to the offensive Soviet BW program. The contribution appears to have been minimal, limited to the manufacture of production and processing equipment for the Soviet BW program by East Germany and the apparent utilization of a particular aerosol testing research facility located in Czechoslovakia.

Chapter 18 examines the question of whether any proliferation has taken place from the former Soviet and Russian BW programs. It attempts to determine whether scientists and technicians employed at the former Soviet Union's BW facilities were recruited to work in BW programs of countries of proliferation concern or by terrorist organizations, and whether pathogens and technology derived from the program were transferred to such countries.

This book makes a particular effort to examine the approach taken by the Soviet Union toward biological weapon arms control. However, Soviet behavior between 1985 and 1992, as well as that of Russia after January 1, 1992, regarding its BW program was so aberrant and extraordinary in comparison to other areas of US-Soviet strategic weapons arms control that it seemed desirable to also examine the most closely related area, chemical weapons arms control, to determine if there were similarities or differences in how well or badly Soviet policymakers adhered to international arms control agreements and treaties. Accordingly, Chapter 19 examines Soviet and Russian arms control policies regarding its chemical weapon demilitarization program from around 1987 on. Were Soviet policies regarding BW absolutely unique, particularly since some of the same officials played major roles in both the post-1992 biological and chemical weapon disarmament efforts? Both similarities and differences became apparent.

Chapter 20 addresses three subjects: (1) the process that led to the US government's decision in 1969 to end its offensive BW program and renounce all future use of biological weapons; (2) the international negotiations between 1968 and 1972 that resulted in the adoption of the BWC, which bans the development, production, stockpiling, retention, or acquisition of biological weapons; and (3) Soviet BW arms control policies at the successive BWC Review Conferences and during the 1991 to 2001 negotiations to achieve a verification protocol for the BWC. At the first BWC Review Conference, which was held in 1981 to review the BWC's operations, state parties to the treaty decided to continue holding review conferences every five years. The second BWC Review Conference, in 1986, had particularly important results because it led the Soviet Union to reveal details of its defensive BW program for the first time. The Soviet Union never admitted to having had an offensive BW program; that admission was made in 1992 by the new Russian government, but was then glossed over or partially retracted by Russian officials in subsequent years.

Chapter 21 describes the important developments in Moscow, and between the Soviet Union and the United States and United Kingdom, regarding the Soviet BW program during the Gorbachev years, 1985 to 1992. Although the Gorbachev administration at first either denied the existence of a Soviet BW program or ignored questions about it, a dialogue eventually commenced between the US, UK, and Soviet governments about the Soviet BW program. The major reason was the defection to the United Kingdom in October 1989 of Pasechnik, the director of one of Biopreparat's major facilities. His debriefings provided detailed information to British and US intelligence and defense officials about the Soviet BW program. Faced by senior-level US and UK officials with this information in hand, the Soviet government agreed in mid-1991 to the first of a series of on-site visits by government scientists and officials to each other's BW-related facilities. Nevertheless, the outcome of these interactions did not end the Soviet BW program and left nearly all the major issues unresolved.

Chapter 22 continues this narrative through the Yeltsin and Putin administrations. In March 1992, Russian president Yeltsin acknowledged the existence of an illegal BW program in the former Soviet Union and ordered it to be dissolved. His decree was, however, not obeyed. Simultaneously, Yeltsin ordered the establishment of the President's Committee on Conventional Problems of Chemical and Biological Weapons of the Russian Federation, which had responsibility for matters related to biological and chemical weapons, including demilitarization. Further negotiations between the United States, United Kingdom, and Russia in September 1992 were essentially catalyzed by two new Russian defectors in the preceding months. This resulted in the Trilateral Agreement. This document contained some of the most significant admissions of the magnitude of the Soviet-era program. It also arranged for further visits to the BW-related facilities of the three signatories, including those of the RF-MOD. The further negotiations collapsed within three years, in 1995–1996, in the face of renewed Russian recalcitrance, and the RF-MOD BW facilities remained closed.

Chapter 23 concerns the international assistance programs directed at inhibiting proliferation from the former Soviet BW institutions. These took the form of supporting new research projects for scientists that had formerly been in the BW weapon development program, as well as upgrading both the external security infrastructure and procedures of the institutes, and the internal consolidation and security of pathogen culture collections. Analogous Western assistance programs were also instituted for Russian nuclear and chemical weapons and strategic delivery systems. To do this, various internationally funded programs were established for the purpose of converting military facilities to peacefully directed pursuits. This chapter covers these important activities, including the programs operated by the Soros Foundation, the International Science and Technology Centers, US Departments of Defense, State, and Energy, and the National Aeronautic and Space Administration. Because there is no international access to the RF-MOD facilities, there is no way to assess the extent to which these facilities may continue to maintain their former offensive BW programs. One can, however, examine to what degree the internationally supported efforts have succeeded in the facilities to which international access has been permitted.

The concluding chapter summarizes the main themes and the most important findings of the book. Finally, there are four annexes: acronyms and Russian terms, a glossary, an important Soviet decree of 1981, and the joint US/UK/Russian Trilateral statement of September 1983. Translations of the Central Committee documents are in several cases integrated within the text of chapters, while others appear at the end of the respective chapter that they pertain to.

1

The Soviet Union's Biological Warfare Program, 1918–1972

IN NOVEMBER 1998, a large assemblage of former Soviet Army officers met for a reunion of, to put it frankly, bioweaponeers. The event took place in Kirov, a Russian city located in the Ural Mountains. Since 1941 this industrial city has had the distinction of being the home of the Scientific Research Institute of Microbiology,[1] which was the Soviet Union's, and now is Russia's, Ministry of Defense's (MOD) main biodefense facility, overseeing all other MOD biological weapons research facilities. In Soviet times, it also was the most important military facility dedicated to researching, developing, testing, and manufacturing biological warfare (BW) agents of bacterial and toxin origin. In addition to carrying out militarily directed research and development (R&D), it was, together with a sister institute in Leningrad, the major training facility for military biological scientists who were to staff other MOD biological warfare institutes and the ostensibly civilian biotechnology facilities. The members of the group that met in 1998 came from many parts of Russia, as well as some countries that once had been components of the Soviet empire. They were there to celebrate the 70th anniversary of the founding of the Kirov Institute.[2]

The reunion provided a landmark for those considering the history of the Soviet Union's BW effort, because it unequivocally publicized the fact that an important military institute dedicated to biological weapons defense and offense came into being in 1928. Prior to the founding of the Kirov Institute, certain military units were probably assigned responsibilities that included defending against biological and chemical weapons, but they were nowhere near as important as the Kirov Institute and were typically part of larger formations whose primary mission was to fight, not to defend.

While there is some information available on these early defensive Soviet BW efforts, there are only bits and pieces of data about the beginning and early development of the Soviet Union's offensive BW program. What little is known about both of these programs, defensive and offensive, is set forth in this chapter.

We call the entire period 1918–1972 the Soviet BW program's first generation (the period after 1972 is the second generation). The first generation has three parts. It begins by considering BW-related developments that occurred between the end of World War I and 1946. This part draws extensively from the admirable study that Valentin Bojtzov and Erhard Geissler did of this period,[3] and adds new information that has become available from our interviews and recently published Soviet/Russian articles and books. The chapter then describes and discusses BW-related events that occurred during 1946–1972. Third, the chapter draws conclusions about when the Soviet BW program commenced, its decline before and resurgence after World War II, and why the second generation BW program was established in the beginning of the 1970s.

Before proceeding, it is necessary to explain that some of the information about Soviet activities for the period of time before and during World War II was provided by two German military officers: Lieutenant Colonel Walter Hirsch and Major Heinrich Kliewe.[4] Both were in the German *Wehrmacht* and were given responsibility for collecting intelligence about the Soviet BW and chemical warfare (CW) programs. Most of their intelligence was derived from interviews with prisoners of war and, as such, is of uneven quality. Some is, frankly speaking, fantastic; for example, a captured Soviet Air Force pilot told Kliewe that the Moscow underground rail system had been designed so it could be hermetically sealed off from the outside world. On the other hand, Hirsch and Kliewe undoubtedly gathered extremely valuable information, which we have cross-checked with other sources that were not accessible to the Germans, such as information collected from the Soviet archives that were partially opened after 1992, accounts of the history of Soviet defense efforts written by Russian military historians in the 1990s, and interviews with Soviet BW scientists.

1918–1946: Establishing Soviet BW and Defense Programs

Russian armies suffered heavy losses from disease during all of the three major conflicts they were involved in at the beginning of the century: the Russo-Japanese war of 1904–1905, World War I, and the civil war between the Red and White forces (1918–1921). Disease caused more casualties than did weapons in all of these conflicts.[5] Red Army commanders are said to have been especially impressed with the viciousness of typhus.[6] A Soviet epidemiologist writes, "There were 20 to 30 million cases of typhus between 1918 and 1922 in the territories controlled by the new Soviet Republic, and a mortality [sic] rate of around 10%."[7] Vladimir Lenin was quoted as having despaired: "We are suffering from a desperate crisis. . . . A scourge is assailing us, lice, and the typhus that is mowing down our troops. Either the lice will defeat socialism, or socialism will defeat the lice!"[8]

Aside from disease, Russian forces suffered "thousands of casualties" from German chemical weapons during World War I, but no BW was waged on Germany's eastern front.[9] So it is understandable that the Bolshevik government that took power in Russia after the 1917 revolution was intent on creating a chemical industry generally, but one that also could produce modern chemical weapons. To integrate chemical weapons into its military force structure, in 1925 the Worker's and Peasant's Red Army (RKKA) established the Military Chemical Agency under the directorship of Yakov Fishman, who was to remain in this position until 1937 when he fell victim to Stalin's Great Purge. Whether Soviet military leaders considered biological weapons at that time is uncertain, although British intelligence reports of 1926 and 1927 indicate they might have (see Chapter 12).

To defend itself against diseases, the RKKA established the Vaccine-Serum Laboratory and ordered it to develop vaccines and sera against common infectious diseases. In 1933 professor Ivan M. Velikanov, then the head of the microbiology department of the M. V. Lomonosov Moscow State University (MSU), was appointed director of the laboratory. The laboratory was built approximately 30 kilometers from Moscow, in a village called Vlasikha.[10]

At approximately the same time, the United State Political Administration (OGPU) set up a laboratory, named the Special Purpose Bureau, for the study of highly infectious diseases.[11] It was sited on the property of the former Pokrovsky Monastery in the small town of Suzdal located in the Vladimir *oblast* (akin to province). Special Purpose Bureau staff were "mostly younger engineers, chemists, and technicians," who were graduates of the Military Chemical

Academy (later renamed the Kliment Voroshilov Military Academy).[12] Some of its scientists were prisoners of the OGPU,[13] who originated at important existing research institutes, such as the Moscow Institute of Epidemiology and Microbiology (established in 1891) and the Kharkov Scientific Research Institute of Microbiology, Vaccine, and Serum Studies (established in 1887).

In 1992, reporters from *Nezavisimaya Gazeta* interviewed a former Special Purpose Bureau employee.[14] Yelizaveta Parshina, aged 76, told them that the bureau was headed by a military man named Faybich,[15] who was a physician and bacteriologist. The facility's staff members lived in the monks' cells and were not allowed to leave the monastery grounds. The monastery's gates were "wrapped in a half-meter layer of thick felt which was saturated with formalin and lysol."[16] A monastery church served as an animal facility, containing cages in which non-human primates, guinea pigs, and rats were kept. In addition, sheep and two camels used for tests grazed in the monastery's yard. Bureau scientists studied cholera, plague, tetanus, and malaria. Parshina described experiments using aerosolized cholera bacteria that involved human subjects. One of the bureau's scientists had used himself as a test subject. He inoculated himself with tetanus bacteria, and after his death, which came about after a terrible ordeal, his body was used for further experiments. Wheras we cannot ascertain the validity of Parshina's testimony, this is one of several claims that laboratories operated by Soviet secret police agencies used human subjects for experimental or testing purposes.[17]

As the Special Purpose Bureau was being established, the Soviet Union secretly agreed with Germany, first in 1921 and again in 1928, to exchange information on CW and conduct joint field tests on methods for delivering and spreading CW agents.[18] This arrangement was terminated in 1933. Apparently, no similar agreement covered biological weapons, probably because Germany at that time had no interest in them. However, a confidential Soviet source told the authors that lessons pertaining to the effective dispersion of CW agents later proved to be useful to the BW program.[19]

The fact that the two nations had agreed to collaborate did not mean that they trusted one another. Quite the opposite. Documents obtained by Bojtzov from the State Military Archives of Russia demonstrate that by 1930 the Soviet government was receiving "intelligence" that Germany and other Western nations were developing biological weapons.[20] Perhaps intelligence such as this was instrumental in the Soviet government's decision to establish a biological defense facility. In 1933 the government combined and reorganized the Vaccine-Serum Laboratory and the Special Purpose Bureau,[21] creating the RKKA Military Medical Scientific Institute;[22] Velikanov was named its director.[23] The institute remained at Vlasikha.

In 1934 the institute was renamed the RKKA Biotechnical Institute.[24] It was moved to Gorodomlya Island, located on Seliger Lake, near Ostashkov city in Kaliningrad *oblast* in 1937. The reason for the move was an accident at the institute that was perceived as having endangered Moscow's population. The deputy director of the institute, Abram L. Berlin, was unknowingly infected by *Yersinia pestis* during an experiment involving a newly developed plague vaccine.[25] After being infected, but before he showed symptoms, Berlin was called to Moscow to report on the new vaccine's progress. While there, he infected two other people with plague, and all three died. Fortunately the disease did not spread, due to the quick response of local health authorities.[26] This is the first known fatal accident involving a Soviet scientific worker doing BW-related research. Other such accidents were to follow.

The RKKA Biotechnical Institute was renamed the Medical-Technical Institute of the RKKA (STI) in 1940. After the June 1941 German invasion, Soviet authorities feared that the Kaliningrad *oblast* would be overrun by German forces, so they moved the institute to Saratov, where it was renamed the Scientific Research Institute of Epidemiology and Hygiene. As the Battle of Stalingrad raged during the latter part of 1942, the Luftwaffe mounted air attacks on nearby cities, including Saratov. To safeguard the institute, it was moved yet again, this time to Kirov, where it took over the facilities of the *oblast* hospital and where it remains to this day. The institute and host city are described in more detail in Chapter 3.

By the time World War II began, the Kirov Institute was only one component, albeit the most important, of a large system. As we noted above, in 1925 Yakov Fishman had been placed in charge of the Military Chemical Agency, which accorded him a leading role in both the Soviet chemical warfare and BW programs. One of his first acts was to set up a small BW laboratory, eventually to be called the Scientific Research Institute of Health, in Moscow headed by Nikolay N. Ginsburg. In 1928 Fishman submitted a progress report to Kliment Yefremovich Voroshilov (1881–1969), the commissar for defense. The report had four parts.[27] The first described the work that had been done by Ginsburg (see below), which was said to demonstrate the feasibility of BW. The second assessed the potential uses of bacteria for purposes of warfare and sabotage, including their use as payloads in artillery shells and bombs. The third presented a plan for the organization of military biology. And the fourth presented another plan for organizing defenses against biological attacks.

Acting on Fishman's recommendations, the Military Chemical Agency was designated as the lead agency for managing both the offensive BW program and a program to defend against biological attacks. The Military Chemical Agency was controlled by the MOD, which in turn was commanded by the Politburo. It is of particular importance that for the first time a civilian agency, the People's Health Commissariat, was ordered to coordinate and execute military requests (tasks) related to BW.[28] At that time, the Commissariat was operating a substantial research network, consisting of at least 35 institutions working in such disciplines as epidemiology, genetics, immunology, microbiology, virology, and plague protection.

The Soviet offensive BW program appears to have officially commenced in 1928 as a result of a secret decree issued by the Revolutionary Military Council.[29] As is the case with many aspects of the Soviet BW program's history, opinions differ as to how the decree was implemented. Bojtzov and Geissler, depending mostly on archival material, assert that the early phase of the BW program was headed by Ginsburg and focused initially on the weaponization of *Bacillus anthracis*[30] and *Clostridium botulinum*,[31] as well as on developing efficient methods of disinfection and researching immunity. According to Fishman's progress report, Ginsburg's group attempted to increase the virulence and stability of *B. anthracis,* a pathogen they found well suited for purposes of BW because its spores are both virulent and hardy. In this research, various types of animals were used as test subjects, including cats, rabbits, goats, and horses. The BW agents were either injected or dispersed as aerosols in closed chambers. Typically, the test animal died within two or three days of exposure. Another method used explosives to disperse a quantity of the BW agents. In this case, the explosion created an aerosol whose particles contained the microorganisms. Ginsburg's laboratory also came to study *Vibrio cholerae*[32] and *Y. pestis.*

Ken Alibek,[33] a former deputy director for science of Biopreparat,[34] offers a different view. He writes that in response to the Revolutionary Military Council's decree, the OGPU was put in charge of efforts to weaponize "Typhus rickettsia."[35] As part of this work, scientists propagated rickettsiae in chicken embryos and rats, which were then killed and their infected tissues homogenized. Rickettsiae-containing tissue formulations (*spetsretseptura* in Russian) were developed at the Lenin Military Academy for use as aerosols.[36]

According to this account, the first Soviet biological weapon became reality in "the 1930s." Alibek's assertions are based on reports he allegedly read while working at Biopreparat and comments made by older scientists who had worked in the system for some time. Because we do not have access to the Russian archives or the memories of "older" Soviet scientists, we cannot determine which version of history is more correct. Given that the Soviet military system was highly compartmentalized, with one compartment not knowing what was being done by other compartments, both versions may be correct. In other words, the military and OGPU scientists might have worked in isolation and in separate laboratories.

Regardless of the precise course of events, the Revolutionary Military Council's decree led to the operation of a large BW establishment before World War II. According to information gathered by Kliewe,[37] by the time World War II broke out, three Moscow-region institutes were involved in offensive BW activities: Ginsburg's institute, the Moscow Chemical-Pharmaceutical Institute, and the Saratov Institute for Microbiology and Epidemiology.[38] In Leningrad *oblast*, four institutes were supposedly involved in BW research and development: the Zlatogorov-Maslokovich Laboratory at the Leningrad Veterinary and Zoological Technical Institute; the Bacteriological Institute of Leningrad; an un-named facility at the Kronstadt naval base;[39] and an un-named research station on the shore of Lake Ladoga. According to Kliewe's sources, all of these institutions focused most of their efforts on *B. anthracis* and *Y. pestis,* although they did some work to develop BW agents against cattle, including foot-and-mouth disease virus. Kliewe missed identifying the most important BW-related facility, the STI.

Alibek's account differs from Kliewe's on pre–World War II facilities. He identifies only two major BW facilities: the Lenin Military Academy and a laboratory on Solovetsky Island. The latter was built by prisoners held by the NKVD.[40] As noted above, the Lenin Military Academy focused on typhus. The work on Solovetsky Island had a wider scope, encompassing the pathogens that cause Q fever, glanders, and melioidosis. Alibek also states that prisoners "may have been human subjects" in biological weapons experiments. He noted that in 1941, in view of the inexorable advance of the German army, the BW programs at the Lenin Military Academy and Solovetsky Island were moved to Kirov. These programs could have been incorporated into the Kirov Institute's work program, but Alibek does not state so.

In addition to research facilities, the Soviets established three open-air test sites before World War II. The first was set up around 1925, at Tomka (this name changed after 1933 to Staryye Shikhany), near Volsk on the Volga river. Called the Central Chemical Proving Ground (*Tsentralny Khimichesky Poligon*, or *TsKhP*), or more simply the Volsk *Polygon*, it covered approximately 100 square kilometers. During the days of the German-USSR accord, military units of both sides trained here together. After this cooperative venture ended in 1933, the site was transferred to the Military Chemical Agency, which used it for both chemical and biological weapons open-air testing. Over 1,000 personnel, commanded by a major general, were permanently assigned to this site. In 1937–1938, the Central Chemical Proving Ground's acreage was extended to 600 square kilometers.

The two other open-air test sites were located on islands.[41] The first has already been mentioned: Gorodomlya in the Seliger Lake north of Moscow. Here, a 10-square kilometer test site was set up in the early 1930s. After about 1935, Gorodomlya allegedly hosted the open-air testing of pathogens causing foot and mouth disease, leprosy, plague, and tularemia.[42] For reasons that are discussed below, it is of particular interest to note that one of Hirsch's sources claimed that tests carried out with *Francisella tularensis* involved dispersing this organism in dust clouds.[43] The second island, which was to become the favored site for the large-scale open-air testing of biological agents and weapons, as well as defensive equipment and measures, was Vozrozhdeniye Island in the Aral Sea. Since this island plays a large role in the Soviet BW program, its story is told in Chapter 4. After Vozrozhdeniye Island became fully operational as an open-air test site, it appears as if no pathogens, nor biological weapons armed with pathogens, were open-air tested anywhere else. Vozrozhdeniye Island was so isolated that it afforded a high level of biosafety to open-air tests, eliminating the need for additional open-air sites.

Scientists, including weapons scientists, were victims of the Great Terror like other professional classes. As recounted by Bojtzov and Geissler, the NKVD accused both the German and Japanese intelligence services of having recruited Soviet scientists as their agents and, in this capacity, of having revealed secrets pertaining to the weaponization of bacteria, planning bacterial sabotage in the event of war, and contaminating water and food with the bacteria causing cholera and typhoid. For example, in 1938, the Commissar for Agriculture during 1934–1937, Mikhail A. Chernov, "confessed" to having conspired with Ginsburg to infect horses destined for the Red Army with anthrax bacteria and of having hindered the dispensing of anti-anthrax serum to Siberia, which meant that there was no way to protect horses once an anthrax epizootic broke out in 1936. As a result of this sabotage, over 25,000 horses died. As was the norm during Soviet purges, these charges were contrived and the confessions, often extracted by torture, were specious.

Many able microbiologists fell victim to the purges, including Fishman, the founder of the Soviet Union's BW program; Ginsburg, Fishman's able assistant; I. Krichevsky, a famous scientist at the Second Moscow Institute; V. Barykin, scientific director of the Ministry of Health (MOH)'s Central Institute of Epidemiology and Microbiology; Sergey M. Nikanorov, director of the Saratov State Institute of Microbiology and Epidemiology ("*Mikrob*"); and Velikanov.[44] The eminent microbiologist Igor Domaradsky lists the names of numerous microbiologists from the anti-plague system who were executed or imprisoned during the purges. It makes for sad reading: "Sergey Mikhailovich Nikanorov, Director of *Mikrob*, arrested in 1930 and shot; Aleksandr Mikhailovich Skorodumov, professor and founder of the anti-plague service of Siberia, arrested in 1937 and executed by shooting; Dmitry Alekseevich Golov, headed the epidemiology and vaccine departments of the *Mikrob* Institute, arrested in 1930 and exiled to five years in Alma-Ata (now Almaty), then arrested again, fate unknown; Nikolay Akimovich Gaysky, deputy director of the Irkutsk Anti-plague Institute, arrested in 1930—worked for four years as a *sharagy*"; and the list continues.[45]

The NKVD, the OGPU's successor agency, arrested some microbiologists to secure expertise that it could exploit. As has been vividly described by Aleksandr I. Solzhenitsyn, the NKVD often placed imprisoned persons with special expertise in the sciences and engineering in groups called *sharagy* and allowed them to work much as they did in their "free" days.[46] According to Domaradsky, microbiologists were placed in specialized *sharagy*. For example, a specialist on tularemia, N. A. Gaysky,[47] was ordered to work as part of a *sharagy* at the Third Experimental Laboratory of the Red Army on developing a vaccine against tularemia; similarly, an expert on rickettsiae, P. F. Zdrodovsky, worked in a *sharagy* while imprisoned, as did L. A. Zilber, who had proposed that viruses are the cause of some cancers. After having completed their sentences, some of these scientists continued to work at the institutions where they had been imprisoned.

From the foregoing tales of woe, it is possible to identify the three characteristics that put scientists (and others) at highest risk for execution or incarceration in the Gulag during the Great Terror: (1) to be a member of the Communist Party of the Soviet Union (CPSU); (2) to have had contacts with foreigners by mail, personal visits, or travel abroad; and (3) to have been or be involved in activities that could be construed by security agencies as dangerous to the state. The best Soviet biomedical scientists almost invariably possessed characteristics 2 and 3. In addition, if a scientist was politically ambitious, he or she would have to join the CPSU, tagging him or her with all three risk factors. Conversely, if a scientist was a slacker or mediocre and unambitious, he would probably possess only characteristic 3 and be left alone or sentenced to a short stay in a *sharagy*.

Despite the decimation of Soviet scientists, presumably a large enough fraction of the BW development cadre survived for the Soviet Union to have maintained an active defensive BW program, and probably more than vestiges of an offensive program, through the German invasion in June 1941. Many analysts have made note of a speech by the marshal of the Soviet Union, Kliment Y. Voroshilov, on February 22, 1938, during which he stated:

> Ten years ago or more the Soviet Union signed a convention abolishing the use of poison gas and bacteriological warfare. To that we still adhere, but if our enemies use such methods against us, I tell you that we are prepared—fully prepared—to use them also and to use them against aggressors on their own soil.[48]

In Moscow, Voroshilov's remark was considered to have been a gross indiscretion. By suggesting to other countries that may not have had BW, but perhaps considered themselves potential enemies of the Soviet Union, that the Soviets did have such weapons (unless they chose to think that he was bluffing), he violated Soviet commitments. He did not just say that the Soviet Union "reserves the right" under the Geneva Protocol to reply in kind, but that it was "prepared, fully prepared" to use them.

For the sake of comparison, of all the major nations in the world at that time, only Japan had an offensive BW program approximately equal in size and stature to that of the Soviet Union.[49] The major Japanese military unit dedicated to developing biological weapons, Unit 731, was headquartered only a few hundred kilometers from the Soviet border at Ping Fan in Manchukuo. France's small program, which was active in the 1930s, was terminated when the German armies were near to occupying that country in 1940.[50] The United Kingdom had started a BW program in 1937, but it did not reach full maturity until the early 1940s and never reached anything near the sizes of the Japanese and Soviet programs.[51] Canada had also begun considering BW in the late 1930s and, in cooperation with the United Kingdom and the United States, was to have a full-scale program by the mid-1940s.[52]

The United States began to consider establishing BW programs in 1942 and did so in 1943.[53] Germany,[54] Italy,[55] and Poland[56] had no offensive BW programs and, at most, rudimentary defensive programs.

In 1939, Stalin placed his minister of internal affairs, Lavrenty P. Beria (1899–1954), in overall command of the Soviet BW program. In practice, the Main Military Medical Directorate of the Red Army, headed by Colonel General Yefim Ivanovich Smirnov, had the responsibility for its day-to-day operations. Smirnov, described in a Russian publication as being "a distinguished organizer and theorist of military and civilian health,"[57] was at that time a rising star in the military medical establishment. Smirnov is discussed at length in Chapter 2; it is sufficient here to note that he was one of the main Soviet planners and proponents, perhaps the main one, of the development of biological weapons and strategies of BW.[58]

The program to defend against both biological weapons and natural infectious diseases continued side by side with the offensive BW program, often in the same institutions. In the Soviet Union, research for biological defense had seven objectives: (1) to develop and improve vaccines against BW agents that enemies might use; (2) to develop methods and protocols for immunization utilizing vaccines and other protective substances; (3) to develop protocols for the emergency treatment of soldiers exposed to BW agents, including diagnosis; (4) to develop methods, means, and regimes for disinfection of persons and equipment contaminated by BW agents; (5) to develop methods for identifying BW agents and clarifying indications of biological attacks; (6) to develop and test field detection systems for BW agents; and (7) to assess the possible damage of the various "recipes"[59] (*reglament,* in Russian) that an enemy might employ against the Soviet Union.[60] We do not know when these objectives were formulated. They might have been created incrementally as the BW program grew, or they might have all been drawn up at an early stage and thereafter used to guide biological defensive research. However they were decided, the objectives apparently continue to guide such research to this day.

The major defensive effort of the Kirov Institute and its predecessors, the RKKA Biotechnological Institute and STI, in the 1930s and leading up to World War II was to develop live vaccines against anthrax, plague, tularemia, brucellosis, and tuberculosis. The work done in the Soviet Union to develop an efficacious live anthrax vaccine has been well documented and explained.[61] Throughout Russian history, the incidence of the disease and the need for a vaccine to counter it has been great. Before World War II, the incidence of

anthrax ranged from 40 per 100,000 persons in the Azerbaijan Soviet Socialist Republic (SSR) to 60 per 100,000 in Bessarabia. The task of developing a vaccine against anthrax was given to the Research Institute of Epidemiology and Hygiene in 1935. Kirov Institute scientists chose to develop a live
vaccine, building on work done by the French team of N. Stamatin and L.
Stamatin and by the British scientist M. Sterne. V. N. Orlov writes that the
Kirov Institute's vaccine R&D was deemed so important that Smirnov was
personally required to report on its progress to Beria and Stalin.[62]

By 1940 the Soviet microbiologists, led by Ginsburg and A. L. Tamarin,
had developed two avirulent strains of *B. anthracis,* STI-1[63] and No. 3, which
were derived from virulent parent strains. When used as a trial vaccine in animals, the STI-1 strain protected 60% of guinea pigs, 70% of rabbits, and 97%
of sheep against virulent strains of *B. anthracis.* Based on these good results,
over 2 million domestic animals were vaccinated with the STI-1 strain of
vaccine during World War II. After the war, many more animals were vaccinated; 38.4 million in 1947, rising to 140 million in 1960. As a result, the
number of Soviet animals that died from anthrax decreased from 30,500 in
1947 to just 3,500 in 1960.

The same Kirov Institute scientists who had developed the animal anthrax
vaccine developed a similar vaccine for use in humans. The vaccine appeared
safe when administered by scarification to 12 volunteers in May 1943.[64] In
1944, when the Red Army was preparing to liberate Rumania from German
forces, Soviet military epidemic intelligence determined that there was a substantial threat of anthrax in that country that might affect not only animals,
but humans. The Soviets vaccinated 9,000 men from the units assigned for
the invasion against anthrax.[65] The potency of the newly developed vaccine
was unknown at that time since human test subjects could not be deliberately challenged with virulent *B. anthracis.* However, Orlov asserts that none
of the vaccinated Russian troops contracted the disease. (Orlov does not say
how many of the nonvaccinated troops were stricken with anthrax.)

The vaccine's potency was not proven until a large-scale field trial was conducted in Bessarabia in 1951. The Soviets vaccinated 92,150 people by scarification and 49,513 by subcutaneous injection; 416,010 people in the same
area comprised the control population. After 18 months, there had been three
cases of cutaneous anthrax among the scarification group (an incidence of 3.2
per 100,000), no cases in the subcutaneous injection group, and 47 cases of
cutaneous anthrax among the control group (11.3 per 100,000). The incidence of untoward effects proved very low. Based on these results, the MOH

licensed the scarification vaccine for use in 1953 and the subcutaneous injection vaccine in 1959.[66]

Work to develop a vaccine against plague began in 1936, when the Kirov Institute procured a vaccine strain, named EV, from the Pasteur Institute in France. By 1941, a team led by M. M. Faybich obtained a highly immunogenic fragment from the EV strain. The team developed a dry, live plague vaccine by using this fragment and methods for its large-scale production. This vaccine was called plague NIIEG vaccine.[67] A liquid form of the vaccine was first tested on 15 scientific workers at the institute who volunteered to be "guinea pigs"; the vaccine was then administered to the staffs of mobile hospitals set up behind the front. The liquid vaccine proved to be unstable and impractical—it deteriorated after 10 hours at room temperature. However, the dry form became available in 1941, and by 1945, 8.5 million doses had been manufactured in preparation for hostilities with the Japanese army in the Manchurian region (northeast China). The Soviets proudly claimed that even though plague is endemic to this region, not a single Red Army soldier contracted plague on its eastern front.[68] All in all, the Soviets claim to have produced and distributed 47 million doses of plague vaccine to Soviet armed forces during World War II. The researchers M. M. Faybich, I. A. Chalisov, and R. V. Karneev were awarded the State Prize of the USSR in 1945 for having developed the dry plague vaccine.[69]

Kirov Institute researchers led by Faybich and T. S. Tamarin began developing a vaccine against tularemia in 1935. By 1944 they had succeeded in producing a dry vaccine that was highly antigenic and stable. The Soviets claimed to have manufactured and distributed 16 million doses of this vaccine from 1944 to 1953.[70] It apparently was not used extensively during World War II.

The institute also developed vaccines against brucellosis and tuberculosis.[71] In 1945 a dry, live brucellosis vaccine for subcutaneous injection was tested on calves and proved efficacious and safe. An experimental vaccine for human use was tested on institute researchers in 1946. The results were apparently acceptable to the State Sera and Vaccine Commission, because the vaccine's mass production was ordered in 1947. A dry, live tuberculosis vaccine developed at the institute was also accepted by the State Sera and Vaccine Commission in 1947, and its mass production commenced shortly thereafter. Neither vaccine was developed in time to see use during World War II.

During World War II, the Soviet Union produced one antibiotic—penicillin. (Antibacterial sulfa drugs became available in the Soviet Union in the late 1930s.) By 1944 the Kirov Institute was able to manufacture penicillin in sufficient quantities to be used by field hospitals, according to Orlov. In 1946 three institute researchers, A. F. Kopylov, Ginsburg, and Faybich, were awarded the State Prize of the USSR for having made this possible. This alleged accomplishment raises two questions. Since the United States restricted information pertaining to the mass production penicillin, did it share this information willingly with the Soviet Union? Or did Soviet agents obtain its production technology by subterfuge?

According to Orlov, the Soviets commenced indigenous production of a second antibiotic, streptomycin, in 1947, just in time to use it to help quell a large outbreak of plague that originated in China.

This section on World War II–era Soviet BW activities would not be complete without a discussion of a tularemia outbreak that Alibek believes to have been a BW incident. Others, including the present authors, are unsure about or reject Alibek's claims. The imbroglio has been described in detail by Alibek, Eric Croddy, and Erhard Geissler,[72] but a synopsis follows.

Just before the Battle of Stalingrad in July and August 1942, the German 6th Army was advancing in the Volga region with Stalingrad as its objective. Alibek has asserted that many thousands of German soldiers suddenly became ill with tularemia, to the point that the German high command had to slow its offense.[73] Alibek writes that 70% of the ill were affected by the pneumonic form of tularemia. Approximately a week after the first Germans became sick, the outbreak spread, causing thousands of casualties among the Russian armed forces and civilian population. A Soviet account quoted by Alibek claimed that "more than 75% of the inhabitants residing in certain areas of the Stalingrad region proved to be afflicted with tularemic infection." The epidemic apparently was of short duration, since the Soviet incidence rate of the disease returned to normal in 1943.

Alibek gives four reasons he believes that this epidemic was deliberately caused by the Soviet military. First, he avers that the normal incidence of tularemia in the Soviet Union at that time was about 10,000 cases per year, which was the number reported in 1941 and 1943. However, the incidence shot up to over 100,000 cases in 1942, an unprecedentedly high level. Second, the fact that the majority of cases presented as the pneumonic form of tularemia indicates that they were caused by deliberate aerosol dissemination. Third, Alibek was told by an elderly colonel, who had worked at the Kirov Institute during the war, that *F. tularensis* had been weaponized in 1941, and he, the colonel, left Alibek "with no doubt that the weapon had been used."[74] Fourth, these were desperate times for the Red Army, as it had its back against the Volga River and could not give up ground to gain time. If the Germans had been able to force the Russians to abandon Stalingrad and to cross the Volga, the Ural region, with its vast and strategically valuable industries, would likely have fallen into German hands. The situation required desperate measures, including, allegedly, the dispersal of *F. tularensis* as a BW agent to stop the German advance.[75]

In 2005 an article appeared in a Russian newspaper that supports Alibek's viewpoint. The relevant sections read as follows:

> With regard to scientific developments of a "rat weapon," they were of course carried out. Specifically, the USSR used it during combat actions against Paulus' army in autumn 1942. They did not risk infecting the fascists with plague or anthrax—that was too dangerous for the other side as well. They therefore decided on tularemia. Rats became the peddlers of the infection. At first, the success was surprising: Without reaching the Volga, Paulus was forced to halt his attack at Stalingrad. According to archival documents, approximately 50 percent of the German soldiers who entered the Soviet camps after the Battle of Stalingrad suffered classical symptoms of tularemia. Unfortunately, however, every action gives rise to a counteraction, and using the infected rats against Hitler's army had the opposite effect: The disease crossed the frontline, and Soviet soldiers filled the infirmaries.
>
> After the war, work with tularemia microbe at secret Soviet military laboratories continued successfully. It is known that by the 1970s, military biologists had perfected tularemia microbe and increased its "killing power."[76]

This account is rather mysterious, appearing as it did in Putin's Russia, whose government denies that the Soviet Union ever had an offensive BW program. The authoritative tone of the article's author is also impressive, although the information in her article is unsupported by objective data or authoritative references.

Croddy's conclusion differs from Alibek's; he argues that the 1942 tularemia outbreak had a natural etiology.[77] He cites three factors in support of his finding. First, he questions whether the form of tularemia found in most of the 1942 victims was indeed pulmonary. The disease process of tularemia was not understood well enough at the time to make a definitive diagnosis. Second, several months before the German attack commenced in July 1942, the Rostov region was experiencing a large outbreak of tularemia. Soviet sources indicate that in January 1942, there were already about 14,000 cases of tularemia in the region. This situation, which likely had a natural origin, could have been exacerbated by wartime conditions that developed later in the year. Third, from information cited in two other Soviet sources, Croddy notes that military activities curtailed farming in the Rostov region. Accordingly, grain crops were not harvested, providing more than the normal amount of food for the field rodents that normally host *F. tularensis*. Many of these rodents coexisted with soldiers in trenches and bunkers, in bedding made of hay. The pulmonary involvement of the outbreak could have resulted from soldiers having inhaled straw dust contaminated with *F. tularensis*.

Geissler's article, which relies on German army sources, supports Croddy's findings and adds telling details. German records make clear that German troops were not the first to be affected by the outbreak, but that they became infected by Russian civilians. The records also demonstrate that the outbreak had only a marginal effect on German military activities—only 1,771 cases were diagnosed among German field forces from 1941 to 1943. In fact, a German army monograph issued at the time on the subject of war diseases does not even mention tularemia. Perhaps most telling, no German army or intelligence reports assert that the Red Army used biological weapons during World War II. (See also Robert Pollitzer for a bibliography of German sources on tularemia among German troops during World War II.[78])

Unlike the Germans, who appear to have been marginally affected by tularemia at what the Soviet high command called the Don Front, Soviet forces faced great difficulties. A historical evaluation of the military health command states:

> Late in the fall of 1942, epicenters of tularemia epizootic among the field-vole were detected in the basin of the Don-delta. Concurrently, cases of tularemia were registered among the local population. More than 75% of the population was hit by tularemia in individual locations of the Stalingrad area. A real threat of the spread of the disease into the staff of the front reserve divisions and air-force, located in the rear front zone, emerged. As the [civilian] health centers were practically out-of-order at this time, the entire burden of the treatment of the infected population lay with the military-medical front service . . . all the support was provided by contemporary labs and clinical disease diagnostics, early isolation and hospitalization of the patients, destruction of the car-

riers of the infection—rodents—and protection of individual facilities from rodents (food storage, etc.).[79]

Soviet marshal K. K. Rokossovsky (commander of the Don Front in 1942–1943) provided another account of the effects of tularemia and mice: "By the way, just during these tense days [when Soviet forces were preparing to counterattack the Germans], tularemia, a disease spread by mice, suddenly emerged among our pilots. The number of infected pilots became so high that it was necessary to take steps to save personal structure and aircrafts; the mice chewed all rubber and rubber insulation [in airplanes]."[80] Morbidity statistics cited by Smirnov et al. also demonstrate the severity of the outbreak: "Tularemia morbidity among [Don Front] troops began in 1941 and continued until 1945. The rate was 15.66% during October–December 1941, 83.58% for 1942–1943, and only 0.76% for 1944–1945."[81]

Accounts by Domaradsky, who once was involved in weaponizing *F. tularensis* for Biopreparat, also undercut the notion that the Soviets used biological weapons based on the bacteria. He said that in the 1940s the Red Army BW program was technically incapable of propagating *F. tularensis* in sufficient quantities to be militarily useful.[82] For reasons explained below, he also claimed that the Soviet Union did not at that time possess a virulent strain of *F. tularensis* that was worthwhile to weaponize. In view of Domaradsky's expertise and knowledge of the history of microbiology in the Soviet Union, the information in Pollitzer's extensive review of tularemia in the Soviet Union (which gives no indication of deliberate use), as well as facts uncovered by Croddy and Geissler, it is highly unlikely that biological weapons based on *F. tularensis* were used by the Soviets during 1942–1943 in the Rostov region.

However, Soviet BW scientists seemingly learned something important about the aerosol dispersion of *F. tularensis* from its experience with tularemia at the Don Front. Two Red Army epidemiologists in charge of public health among soldiers noted that "over the course of this work, an aerosol pathway for the infection of humans with tularemia was detected for the first time and it was demonstrated that this transmission pathway was possibly dominant over all others when suitable epidemiological conditions were in place."[83] This observation could have been instrumental in the Soviet development of *F. tularensis* for BW purposes after World War II.[84]

It bears noting that the Germans were also accused of waging a form of biological attack against the Soviets during the war, although in this case the disease in question was typhus:

In 1944, these camps [detention camps] were sometimes used by the Nazis before retreating to disseminate epidemic typhus. In the Mozyr region of Byelorussia, the German occupation forces gathered tens of thousands of Soviet citizens and mixed people with epidemic typhus with the rest of the population, thus succeeding in spreading the disease throughout the camp. The aim of the German troops was mainly to spread epidemic typhus to the Red Army. We, the epidemiologists, had to identify and isolate the sick people and put their closest contacts in quarantine for observation. It was a very hard job. Many of the sick died.[85]

It is impossible for us to verify this account. Its author, Marcus Klingberg, was a Soviet field epidemiologist, and he did disease investigations in the area, but his extreme loyalty to the Soviet cause is well known and might have influenced his judgment. In 1983 an Israeli military court convicted Klingberg for having provided secret information to the Soviets and sentenced him to 20 years in jail. After serving his full sentence, he was deported. In 2010 he explained his reasons for having served Soviet intelligence for 33 years:

I have never regretted my modest attempt during the Cold War to undermine what I believed to be the dangers associated with the imbalances in scientific knowledge. My feelings about this remain with me despite the fall of the Soviet Union—a country to which I not only owe my life, as well as my career in epidemiology and my most useful work; but, above all, the opportunity to fight fascism.[86]

The Red Army so feared a typhus outbreak during World War II that it was "equipped with special bath-trains consisting of nine cars with all facilities for bathing, washing and disinfection, and they are sent right up to the front line."[87] Perhaps this type of proactive defense was the reason there were no serious typhus outbreaks among Red Army troops on its western front during World War II.[88]

Hirsch and Kliewe have alleged that Soviet partisans employed biological weapons against German forces on several occasions. These weapons and methods were simple, consisting of contaminating food and beverages with pathogens that caused gastrointestinal disease. Soviet forces have also been accused of instigating an outbreak of Q fever among German troops in the Crimea in 1943. None of these allegations has been verified.

Unrelated but nevertheless important BW-related events occurred during the World War II era. In the mid to late 1940s, US sources provided the Soviet Union with several cultures of microorganisms, including two that were later weaponized. The more important transfer involved a strain of Venezuelan equine encephalitis virus (VEEV) called "Venezuela," which was recovered from a horse brain collected in Venezuela during an outbreak of VEE in 1938. This culture was lodged at the virus laboratory in the Rockefeller Institute, New York, from which a sample was sent to the Institute of Virology in Moscow in 1944.[89] The Soviet military then had easy access to the culture.

In 1949, US scientists gave the Soviets another gift, a strain of *F. tularensis* called "Schu" that was significantly more virulent than the strains recovered from Soviet sources.[90] In the Soviet Union, the case fatality rate of tularemia was less than 1%, while in the United States it was between 5% and 6%.[91,92] As a Russian scientist explained in 1957, "It is true that when tularemia was first studied it seemed very dangerous, but at present scarcely anyone considers it so."[93] It was for this reason that the Soviet BW program weaponized the American strain.[94]

1946–1972: The Largely Unknown Years of the Soviet BW Program

Some recent Russian-language publications have dealt with the establishment and operation of a Soviet biological defense program, which has implications for this study of the Soviet offensive program. This book benefits from access to a fair amount of information about the modern (post-1972) Soviet BW program from interviews with those who once worked in it, as well as from Russian investigative reporting. But the period between 1946 and 1972 is largely uncharted, unknown territory. There have been no publicly known defectors who are familiar with the BW program as it operated during those days; the Russian-language literature makes hardly any reference to events of relevance for that period; reporters have, for unknown reasons, not written on BW-related events in those years; and the scientific workers interviewed for this book knew next to nothing of this period, what they consider "ancient history." What follows is a collection of bits and pieces of information about the period that will someday contribute to a complete picture of the post–World War II Soviet BW program.

In addition to the Soviet Union, the Japanese government supported a very large and wide-ranging BW program between approximately 1930 and

1945. During its occupation of Manchukuo, Japan relocated the major parts
of its program to this satrapy, including its headquarters, which was sited in
Ping Fan, a small village located 20 kilometers from the major city of Har-
bin. The story of the particularly horrid example of man's inhumanity to
man that ensued has been told in detail elsewhere;[95] this section focuses only
on what the Soviet Union might have gained from the Japanese program
when it captured the sites of the various Japanese BW units and many of the
personnel who staffed them. The Soviets indicted 12 Japanese servicemen
deemed to have been directly involved with the development, manufacturing, and employment of bacteriological weapons under Article 1 of the
Decree of the Presidium of the Supreme Soviet of the USSR ("On measures of
punishment for the German-fascists villains guilty in murders and tortures
of Soviet civilians and imprisoned Red Army military, for spies, traitors to
the Fatherland from among the Soviet citizens and their accomplices of April
19, 1943").[96] All 12 servicemen were convicted, but for their horrendous
crimes, they received what can only be thought of as light sentences, having
to suffer "confinement in labour correction camps" for terms of 2 to 25
years.[97] They served their time in relative comfort in a former manor house
located in Cherntsy village near Moscow. Even more surprising, the first of
the convicted servicemen was released in 1953, and by 1956 the last had been
allowed to return to Japan. One of the servicemen committed suicide.[98]

One curious aspect of the servicemen's trials had to do with their timing.
On May 26, 1947, a Decree of the Presidium of the Supreme Soviet of the
USSR abolished the death penalty. Stalin must have had a change of heart,
because the death penalty was reinstituted as of January 12, 1950 by the decree: "On the use of death penalty for traitors of the Fatherland, spies, shot-
firer-saboteurs [sic]." The Kremlin had ordered the Red Army to complete
the servicemen's trial before 1949 ended, which explains why the trials were
hastily started on December 25, 1949 and finished on Sunday, December
30, 1949, at 11:45 p.m.. As Yudin wrote, "From the very beginning of preparation for the trial it was predetermined that defendants would not get severe
punishment."[99]

Why were these persons, who were deemed guilty of heinous crimes committed on a grand scale, let off so easy? The most obvious explanation is that
it was done in return for having cooperated fully with the Red Army. A tantalizing hint about this episode is given in a Russian military journal. An
article about the military's public health work in Siberia, which otherwise
has nothing to do with BW, includes the following entry: "In December

1953, epidemiologist V. V. Kazimirov prepared a thorough report about Japan's bacteriological weapons. It was the first such study, and its value was understood not just by the military but also the politicians and the region's business managers. A number of normative documents were developed on the report's basis."[100] This is mysterious note; what kind of norms can be elicited or concluded from Japan's BW work? What might politicians and businessmen gain from the report?

Officials who were interviewed for this book confirmed that the Soviet BW program did in fact benefit from the Japanese BW program. When asked about the Japanese BW effort, the article published about public health in Siberia, and the meaning of the article's reference to Japan's BW facilities, one Biopreparat official said:

> Information from the Japanese was used for both BW purposes and for defense. The Japanese reports were meticulously written and had complete information on their experiments involving many pathogens. We particularly found information on plague [bacteria] of interest because they had tested many strains for virulence not only on animals, but also humans. They also conducted experiments using different doses of agents. We [the Soviet Army] never tested on humans. So the Japanese data gave us information on strains that were virulent not only in animal models, but also in humans. So we could compare our strains with theirs and use those that were most virulent in humans for BW. At that time the level of microbiology was not so high, and scientists could not secure highly virulent genetically modified strains. So we worked with what we had from nature.
>
> For defense, we used their information on the immunological responses by humans to pathogens in developing vaccines and therapeutics. And the Japanese had good data on how organisms responded to preparations existing at that time.

From the little that is known about what the Soviets learned from the Japanese program, one can deduce that the Soviets benefited greatly from Japanese data on *Y. pestis* strains, because *Y. pestis* was one of the main BW agents in the post–World War II Soviet arsenal. At the time, scientists knew little about what made *Y. pestis* so infectious and virulent (such knowledge did not become available until a virulence-associated plasmid was first described in 1981), so the Japanese experience likely helped the Soviets determine which *Y. pestis* strains were the most virulent to humans, information that would have been helpful when directing weaponization efforts.

The Soviet Union publicized the fact that the Unites States also gained BW-related information from the Japanese military. In language typical of the Cold War, two high-ranking officers of the Soviet Medical Service wrote:

> The misanthropic plans of the Japanese militarists for the use of a bacteriological weapon were not buried along the rout of the Japanese in Second World War. Already before the end of the 1940s, after the USA had lost its monopolistic control of nuclear weapons, the American military clique began to develop its own bacteriological weapon. With a great deal of secrecy about that work, they also began to recruit specialists from Japan. During this process, the USA press discussed the problem of the "advantages" of the bacteriological weapon which possesses a high degree of combat effectiveness and the possibility of using it secretly in connection with such "desirable" qualities as the preservation of physical property after and attack and the powerful psychological effect on the enemy.[101]

As the Soviet BW program evolved, so did its infrastructure. The Main Military Medical Directorate of the Red Army, which was directed by Smirnov, was the lead agency for biological defense and, presumably,[102] the BW program between 1939 and 1946. The unit evolved into the Main Military Medical Directorate of the Armed Forces of the USSR. Smirnov led the new directorate until 1947, at which point he was appointed minister of health, a post he kept until December 1952.[103] This promotion could only have been made with approval from Stalin, who liked and trusted Smirnov, often taking walks with him and hearing his reports in person. It is indicative that Smirnov was called "Stalin's people's commissar."[104]

For unknown reasons, Stalin lost confidence in Smirnov sometime in 1952. Stalin's change of heart was made clear when Smirnov was accused of being involved in the "doctors-poisoners in the Kremlin" plot. The plot was wholly fabricated by Stalin and his minions for reasons having to do with the alleged fealty Soviet Jews had for newly independent Israel. Smirnov was fired by the Central Committee for the fallacious reason of "political irresponsibility" and was denounced for having had inadequate control over the medical staff of the Kremlin Hospital.[105] Because Kremlin doctors were the first of the "doctors-poisoners," Smirnov was likely held at least partially responsible for their "evil" deeds. After Stalin died on March 5, 1953, his successors immediately stopped all legal proceedings against the "plotters," released all who had been arrested, and rehabilitated plotters and their accomplices, including Smirnov. For a short time Smirnov directed the S. M. Kirov Military Medical Academy, but in August 1953 the Council of the Ministers of the USSR transferred the responsibilities of the Main Military Medical Directorate to the 7th Directorate of the General Staff and appointed Smirnov as its head.

By the early 1950s the Kirov Institute had become the most important BW institute in the Soviet military.[106] It was given more and greater responsibilities because the MOD recognized the possibility of Soviet forces being attacked by opponents armed with biological weapons. Three factors led to this recognition. First, Red Army troops in several different World War II theaters of combat had been seriously affected by relatively unknown diseases such as tsutsugamushi fever (scrub typhus), Q fever, and atypical pneumonia. In some of these cases, "the possibility of aerogenic infection was documented."[107] Second, Soviet security experts concluded that Western countries were likely developing biological weapons. In particular, they drew such conclusions from a 1947 article by Theodor Rosebury and Elvin A. Kabat.[108] A book written by Rosebury and published in 1949 confirmed these suspicions (see Annex at the end of this chapter).[109] Third, the 1949 trial of the servicemen who had operated the Japanese BW program revealed information about how biological weapons might be developed, deployed, and used,[110] opening up new possibilities for developing Soviet biological weapons and supporting fears that the United States, which had captured most Japanese BW scientists, was also well placed to deploy biological weapons against the Soviet Union.

Orlov writes that having recognized the growing threat of BW, the Soviet government sped up "development of means to protect the population and the army against biological weapons."[111] It appointed the marshal of the Soviet Union, Ivan Kh. Bagramyan, as head of the domestic defensive program and Smirnov and Petr N. Burgasov as his deputies. The program's leaders quickly decided on two "protective" developments: to expand the Kirov Institute and to establish a new institute to carry out research on viruses and rickettsiae.

To expand the Kirov Institute, the MOD took over the site of the former Cherkassy-Sverdlovsk Infantry School in Sverdlovsk (now called Yekaterinburg) and rebuilt it as a branch of the institute with the supposed purpose of conducting research on military hygiene. The first group of scientific workers from the Kirov Institute, led by N. F. Kopylov, arrived in Sverdlovsk in September 1949. In 1960 the branch separated from the Kirov Institute and became known as the Military Technical Scientific Research Institute; in 1974 it was renamed the Scientific Research Institute of Microbiology of the MOD; and in 1986 it was renamed again as the Russian Federation Ministry of Defense Department of Military Epidemiology under the Scientific Research Institute of Microbiology.[112] For convenience, henceforth, this institute and its many manifestations are called the Sverdlovsk Institute.[113] Its facilities and work program are described in Chapter 3.

The MOD decided to build an entirely new institute after an internal assessment concluded that the Soviet Army's need for a "bacterial component" was "covered," but not so for a "virological component."[114] The assessment noted that the country "had only a single recently organized (within the past 5 years) civilian virology institute of the USSR Academy of Medical Sciences." Further, "for a number of reasons, the latter [civilian virology institute] naturally could not engage in assessing the threat of viruses being used for military purposes." In late 1953, officials decided to convert an existing MOH institute in Zagorsk into a research institute that was to investigate viruses and rickettsiae. The history of the Zagorsk Institute is told in Chapter 3.

One important BW-related issue came to involve all three MOD biological institutes—Kirov, Sverdlovsk, and Zagorsk; it had to do with botulinum neurotoxin (BoNT), the most toxic chemical known to science. The subject of toxins, including mycotoxins, was brought up in conversations with those who were interviewed for this book and who had been involved with the Soviet BW program. One goal of asking about toxins was to be able to shed light on or resolve the "Yellow Rain" issue (see Chapter 16).[115] With few exceptions, persons who worked for the BW program had no knowledge of military-related toxins R&D. Several older interviewees did recall a program in the 1950s and 1960s to weaponize BoNT and a parallel R&D effort to defend against it. For reasons that are explained below, all three MOD BW institutes had a role in BoNT R&D, with the Kirov Institute in the lead. However, as far as the post-1972 Soviet BW program is concerned, it was not responsible for weaponizing BoNT, or any other toxin, though presumably the Soviet chemical warfare program did. In particular, none of the Biopreparat institutes worked with toxins, except when investigating certain bacteria that possessed them as virulence factors.

BoNT is a protein produced by the bacterium *Clostridium botulinum,* and its ingestion causes the disease known as botulism. For BW purposes, the preferred method for dispersing BoNT is by aerosol.[116] Once BoNT is inhaled and transported to the lungs, it is absorbed and then carried by the bloodstream to peripheral cholinergic synapses, where it binds irreversibly. By blocking the transmission of nerve impulses to muscles, BoNT causes those muscles to relax, resulting in a loss of muscle control. The main symptom of botulism is an acute, afebrile, symmetric, descending flaccid paralysis that always begins in the muscles of the face. The extent and pace of paralysis may vary considerably, depending on a patient's tolerance and on the dose he or she receives. Some patients may be mildly affected, while others may be so paralyzed that they appear comatose and require months of ventilatory support. Complete recovery can take weeks or months.[117] Because unprotected aerosolized BoNT is relatively unstable in the open environment, in order for it to be effectively disbursed it must be formulated with the appropriate chemicals. Both the Soviet and the American BW programs developed such formulations, but the methodologies they used remain classified.

Several interviewed sources agreed that the Soviets started weaponizing BoNT in the mid-1960s because Soviet intelligence had learned that the US BW program had been doing so for some years. Although BoNT was weaponized at Fort Detrick and became one of the seven validated BW agents in the US arsenal,[118] the United States in effect discarded it, probably in the early 1960s, because it was more difficult to apply and proved less efficient than nerve gases.[119] Even after Soviet intelligence learned about this development and reported it to the MOD, Kirov Institute scientists continued to weaponize BoNT for unknown reasons. The main objectives of this work were to stabilize and standardize a mixture of BoNT types A, B, and E.[120] The stabilizing aspect, which was led by Lieutenant General Valentin I. Yevstigneev (a future head of the 15th Directorate), supposedly led to yet another validated BW agent and type-classified biological weapons ("type-classified" means that an item or component has been adopted for military service or use—see Chapter 10). Nothing is known about the BoNT work done at the Sverdlovsk Institute. It is likely to have complemented the Kirov Institute's work described above, but the division of labor is unknown.

In addition to the offensive R&D on BoNT, there was a large effort to defend against this toxin. Burgasov, who worked at the Sverdlovsk Institute in the 1960s and is known to have written a classified doctoral dissertation on botulism, asserts, "Work was done [at the Sverdlovsk Institute] on defenses against bacteriological weapons. We initially studied botulism. This was a priority direction in the American program. It was here that a group of scientists headed by General A. Aleksandrov developed their famous vaccine against botulism and tetanus. Just for your information, the military physicians tested the toxins on themselves."[121]

Zagorsk Institute scientists were also involved in the defensive effort. In the early 1960s, A. A. Vorobyov and N. N. Vasilyev were credited with having developed botulinum toxoids that could be used to protect against US biological weapons armed with BoNT. A government decree subsequently ordered the production of 40 million doses of the toxoid, an order that was fulfilled in 1964. During 1965–1966, the Zagorsk Institute transferred the equipment, processes, and relevant sets of scientific-technical documentation for producing the toxoid to the MOH's Main Department of Vaccines and Sera, which used them to establish an industrial base for toxoid production at its institutes in Tomsk, Ufa, Perm, and Petrovo-Dalnee (Moscow *oblast*).[122] After 1964, the Zagorsk Institute performed no more bacteriological research outside rickettsiology, according to available evidence.[123]

When interviewed in 2001, Burgasov made astounding claims about defense against BoNT. He asserted "Almost no one knows that in the 1950s the entire population of the Soviet Union was inoculated against intestinal infections, including botulinum toxins. Yes, [we] feared that the Americans would use these against us." He elaborated on this statement:

> [S]ome idiots are now saying that biological weapons are easy to create and produce. In fact, no other task is equally difficult as production of biological weapons. [Since the Americans had] created botulinum toxin, we decided to vaccinate Soviet people. But how do you do that? If we did that [openly], the rest of the world would have been asking the same question: why are they vaccinating the Soviet population? Then we decided to include it [a vaccine against botulinum toxin] in a regular polyvaccine and vaccinated everybody so that nobody knew both in the USSR and abroad."[124]

There are many questions raised by Burgasov's assertion. Why was botulinum toxin "created" by the U.S. deemed to be so very threatening to deserve this special defensive action? Or, were similar action taken in regards to any of the pathogens that the U.S. might have weaponized? Was the entire Soviet population vaccinated, all approximately 200 million people? Were there follow-up studies on negative side-effects? Were there booster shots? Burgasov does not tell us.[125]

In the 1960s, British intelligence became aware of the Soviet military's heightened interest in BoNT. A 1962 article written by Soviet scientists and published in the open literature appears to have been particularly provocative:

> It is very timely now to make studies for the preparation of a polyvalent toxoid vaccine against anaerobic infectious diseases (containing concentrated toxoids of tetanus, *B. oedematiens, B. perfringens,* botulism types A, B, and E) for the purpose of including this polyvalent toxoid vaccine in the NIISI [Scientific Research and Testing Sanitation Institute of the Soviet Army] polyvaccine already in use in the Soviet Army. At present time, such work is being conducted by large groups of scientific workers.[126]

In their classified report, the British intelligence analysts listed the following findings: (1) botulism was rare in the Soviet Union, so there was no pressing public health need to ratchet up R&D for a botulinum toxoid vaccine; (2) before 1959, Soviet scientists performed only low-level work on toxoids, but between 1959 and 1962, this kind of R&D substantially increased; (3) A. A. Vorobyov was prominent in Soviet BoNT R&D;[127] and (4) Soviet Army Medical Service officers' concern about defending against BoNT "in an NBC war" peaked in the mid-1960s.[128] The report's astute findings were: "The evidence indicates that the Soviet Union has the capability to develop the production of at least toxin types A and B for use in offensive operations. This ability appears to have improved during the last decade [i.e., 1958–1968]. Any production plant may, therefore, have been erected and completed during this period."[129]

Toward the end of the 1960s, Soviet military officers appear to have drawn the same conclusions about BoNT as did the Americans, deciding to ignore BoNT as a BW agent about two years after the United States had terminated its BoNT weaponization effort.

Domaradsky asserts that in addition to the military biological institutes at Kirov, Sverdlovsk, and Zagorsk, a so-called 32nd Institute in Leningrad was directed by a general named "Gapochko." Konstantin. G. Gapochko, who usually is associated with the Kirov Institute, was known for his work in aerobiology.[130] Additional information about the 32nd Institute is unavailable, but we have reasons to believe that this entity actually was the Scientific Research Laboratory No. 1 (NIL-1), which is described in Chapter 3.

In addition to MOD institutes dedicated to BW and biological defense, the Ministry of Agriculture, the Ministry of Internal Affairs (MVD), the MOH, and the USSR Academy of Sciences each operated R&D units involved with BW-related activities.[131] Next to nothing is known about the activities or involvement of these agencies with BW during the pre-1972 era.

During the first generation, the military had by far the largest role in the Soviet offensive BW program. The advance of biotechnology, however, eventually led to the exclusive military enclave of BW facilities being breeched, as detailed in Chapter 2. In contrast, the Soviet defensive BW program was always a shared effort between the military and the Soviet MOH's anti-plague system; this two-agency effort is addressed in Chapter 5.

Start, Decline, and Resurgence of the Soviet BW Program

From German World War II intelligence reports and the accounts of Soviet and Russian scientists and scholars, it is reasonable to conclude that the Soviet Union first established an offensive BW program in the late 1920s (though some BW R&D most likely began earlier), and that the program grew in size and sophistication during the 1930s. During this early phase of the Soviet BW program, it doubtless weaponized some pathogenic bacteria, including *B. anthracis.* The program also probably carried out offensively directed research that involved *Coxiella burnetii, Burkholderia mallei, Y. pestis,* and *F. tularensis.* The results of this R&D, although not immediately used for weapons development, presumably remained in the institutional memory of the military biological institutes. During 1937–1938, the BW program lost impetus, and perhaps direction, as a result of Stalin's purges, which decimated both the civilian and the military microbiologist communities. As an indication of this state of affairs, the Soviets did not conduct open-air testing of BW agents on Vozrozhdeniye Island between 1937 and 1953. Nevertheless, the program did not completely disappear. In particular, during World War II, the Soviet military biological research establishment focused on practical matters pertaining to the war effort, especially on developing defenses against infectious diseases of natural etiology and developing therapeutic drugs such as penicillin.

When World War II began, Japan and the Soviet Union were the only two major combatants to possess significant offensive BW programs (although the Soviet program was, as explained above, diminished). They established their programs for quite different reasons. In Japan, one person, Ishii Shiro, an influential military medical doctor, almost single-handedly persuaded military decision-makers that biological weapons could be extremely powerful and should be developed as part of Japan's overall armaments program. He may have been convinced of the military utility of biological weapons after observing the efforts by Western nations to abolish them during negotiations leading up the signing of the Geneva Protocol in 1925. If Western nations were so intent on getting rid of biological and chemical weapons, they must be exceedingly destructive. Shiro capitalized on his ambition; by the start of World War II, he had been promoted to general and placed in charge of Unit 731.

Conversely, the Soviet government appears to have established a BW program after witnessing the devastation wrought by infectious diseases on both military formations and civilian populations during World War I and the Civil War. Its decision was strengthened in the mid-1930s when it received intelligence indicating that Germany was undertaking a national BW program that was mainly directed against the Soviet Union.[132] This intelligence later proved to be false, but it apparently stimulated Soviet decision makers to establish and operate an expanded national BW program, the intent of which was largely to defend Soviet military forces from the perceived Western biological threat and to be able to reply in kind should biological weapons be used against them. A January 1941 Soviet publication reinforced this objective: "The Soviet Union had to watch all these activities with great vigilance and be prepared, should the occasion arise, to defend itself against a bacteriological attack not only, but be able to strike back with telling effect.[133] It is also possible that Soviet intelligence was better informed about the Japanese BW effort than its Western allies, who missed it completely. If so, Soviet intelligence on the Japanese program would also have stimulated its BW program.

The Soviet program to develop offensive biological weapons restarted in the late 1940s or early 1950s for three probable reasons. First, the Soviet leaders learned of the large, brutish Japanese BW program. After the Red Army crossed into Manchuria on August 8, 1945, and moved quickly toward the Pacific Ocean, it overran the city of Ping Fan where Unit 731, the lead agency for Japanese BW R&D, was headquartered. As they advanced, Red Army troops captured scientists and medical doctors who had staffed this unit's laboratories and test facilities.[134] By interrogating those captured, the Soviets learned about the appalling record of the Japanese BW program. The extent and sophistication of the Japanese BW program likely gave Soviet leaders an indication of how powerful biological weapons could be and provided them with new knowledge and know-how that benefitted their BW program.

Second, as noted previously, influential American scientist Rosebury wrote an article and book shortly after World War II that convinced Soviet civilian and military leaders of biological weapons' utility. Some of those interviewed for this book believe that the Rosebury article and book were the main determinant of the Soviet government's decision to bolster its BW program. A few years later, a former US general published two works that only reinforced Soviet officials' belief in the power of biological weapons.[135]

Third, soon after the end of World War II, the Soviet government learned of the joint BW programs of the United States, the United Kingdom, and Canada.[136] Soviet authors described in great detail the large size of these programs, the intent of the Western countries to use biological weapons in tandem with nuclear and chemical weapons, and the perversity of the United States in not having joined the Geneva Protocol (which prohibits the use of bacteriological weapons).[137] Soviet leadership might have been motivated to build a BW program in order to match these capabilities.

In the final analysis, similar to the pre–World War II phase, very little is known about the activities of the Soviet BW program during 1945–1972. The main development during the years immediately following World War II appears to have been an infusion of practical information from the Japanese BW program. Perhaps the knowledge gained from the Japanese energized the Soviet BW program and led to the reopening and buildup of the very substantial open-air test sites on Vozrozhdeniye and Komsomolets islands.

The Soviets probably had a validated biological weapons system based on the variola virus by the early 1970s (see Chapters 3 and 4), which means that work toward this goal began at least in the mid-1960s. By the early 1970s, the Soviets also probably had type-classified biological weapons based on *B. anthracis, F. tularensis, Y. pestis, Coxiella burnetii, Brucella suis,* VEEV, and BoNT (see Table 1.1 for a listing of Soviet first generation BW agents).

Unlike the immediate post–World War II years, both Alibek and Domaradsky describe the 1960s as a time when the Soviet BW program was treading water—there were no breakthroughs or significant advances. Domaradsky claimed that the program was conducted in a desultory way and was so unproductive that the Soviet military command thought about terminating it

Table 1.1   Soviet First Generation Biological Warfare Agents

Agent	Disease
Bacteria	
Bacillus anthracis	Anthrax
Brucella melitensis (Brucella suis?)	Brucellosis (undulant fever)
Burkholderia mallei	Glanders
Burkholderia pseudomallei	Melioidosis
Coxiella burnetii	Q fever
Francisella tularensis	Tularemia
Rickettsia prowazekii	Epidemic typhus
Yersinia pestis	Plague
Virus	
Variola virus	Smallpox
Venezuelan equine encephalitis virus	Venezuelan equina encephalitis
Toxin	
Botulinum neurotoxin	Botulism

in the early 1970s.[138] These opinions appear to be supported by former intelligence analyst Raymond Garthoff, who specialized in Soviet affairs:

> On August 17, 1967, a top secret joint decree issued by the Central Committee–Council of Ministers of the Soviet Union reviewed the evidence for what was seen as an extensive and successful U.S. program in the field of chemical and biological warfare. The decree called for corresponding Soviet CBW preparations. Although my attempts to obtain this decree in the Russian archives have so far been unsuccessful, I was able to track down a reference to it in the index of the still-closed files of the Central Committee.[139]

Garthoff's evidence is particularly significant because it is an extremely rare instance of a researcher finding relevant information in the parts of Soviet archives made available after 1990. The decree appears to indicate that the Soviet Union was not doing well in the biological and chemical warfare areas when compared to the United States and called for this situation to be corrected. Following the decree, the Soviet BW program appears to have been given a boost that led to a reinvigorated effort, and this work could well have set the stage for the more significant changes that would come in 1971–1972, when the powerful new tools and methods of molecular genetics were introduced into the Soviet BW R&D program.

ANNEX: Theodor Rosebury and Publicizing Biological Weapons

Rosebury headed the Airborne Pathogen Laboratory at Camp Detrick during World War II and his work and ideas were important in early US postwar decision making on requirements for biological weapons research projects. Domaradsky noted the critical importance of his publications to the Soviet postwar BW R&D program's direction. At the same time, for years many Soviet authors vilified Rosebury, describing him as a promoter of BW.

Ironically, Rosebury's political convictions, both before and after World War II were decidedly pro-Soviet. He was affiliated with the American Association of Scientific Workers (AASW), an organization which was strongly sympathetic to the Soviet Union. In 1942, Rosebury published a paper in *Science* which strongly urged the increased utilization of biological scientists, specifically bacteriologists, in the wartime military R&D effort.[140] His 1947 publication had in fact been submitted by the War Effort Committee of the AASW to the National Research Council in 1942 as part of its effort to get the US to initiate a BW program. It was withheld from publication during the War.[141]

In 1946, a series of international organizations referred to as Soviet "front" organizations were established. These were substantially controlled by the International Department of the CPSU.[142] One was the World Federation of Scientific Workers (WFSW). The AASW became its US affiliate. While Rosebury may not have known the precise details of Soviet control of these groups, at least not initially, he maintained his affiliation with the AASW into the 1970s and served on the editorial board of its publication, *Scientific World*,

Rosebury may have written his books as a conscious attempt to share information on advances in Western BW R&D just as Niels Bohr, the Danish nuclear physicist and colleague of the major figures in the US nuclear weapon program at Los Alamos, had in 1944 suggested that the Soviet Union should be informed of the US-UK nuclear weapons secrets.

Almost immediately after the US used the two nuclear weapons in Japan, the US government published the "Smyth Report" on nuclear weapon development.[143] The report not only placed substantial information regarding nuclear weapons into the public domain, it also led to much public discussion. The early thinking behind the subsequent "Acheson- Lilienthal Report" proposing a design for the international control of nuclear weapons was motivated by ideas similar to Bohr's. The US-Soviet debates at the UN that followed increased public exposure. There was no similar public discussion concerning the US wartime BW program and BW. In October 1945 George Merck, director of the War Research Service, whose sole responsibility was the US wartime BW program, presented a report on the US wartime BW program to the US secretary of war. Although 50 pages in length, it provided only a history of the management of the program and contained no technical detail and no mention of specific pathogens. The War Department released an abbreviated version in January 1946. Where the Smyth Report had been a full book, the published versions of the Merck Report ranged between five and seven pages.

Striking views about biological weapons had been proposed by Dr. Vannevar Bush and James Conant to US secretary of war Henry Stimson in October 1944. Bush was the director of the Office of Scientific Research and Development during World War II, and Conant was his closest collaborator and head of the National Defense Research Committee. They asked Stimson for permission to present their proposal to President Roosevelt in the form of a memorandum. It suggested "that solely from the point of view of the defense of the United States, it would be highly desirable to have the whole subject of biological warfare brought out into the open and the future development of weapons using these materials proceed on an international basis. As part of the mechanism of the new United Nations . . . an office might be established dealing with scientific and technical matters as applied to problems of international relations generally and warfare in particular. One of the chief functions of this office might be to arrange for cooperative research and development on biological warfare". Bush added that without such a system the Soviet Union would likely go it alone, with no ones knowledge. Writing to Conant, Bush suggested "that we immediately advocate full interchange on all aspects of the subject with Russia".

The suggestion that Bush and Conant made regarding biological weapons was not unique for them. In September 1944, they had proposed to Stimson that a high-level group of advisors be convened to consider postwar international control of nuclear energy, including its military applications. Stimson

agreed, and established a small group of senior advisors whose deliberations
and proposals eventually produced the Acheson-Lillienthal report followed
by the proposals for the control of nuclear weapons that the US government
put before the United Nations in 1946-47. Given Stimson's sympathetic response it is clear why they made their proposal regarding biological weapons
a month later. Both proposals were based on a common set of very basic understandings that were widely accepted as truisms by the leaders of the wartime nuclear weapons program, and they were easily generalizable to BW as
well: (1) that the US wartime discoveries were derived from basic science and
therefore within a relatively short time they would become available to other
advanced states, the Soviet Union in particular; and (2) that if no system of
international control was established for the weapons in question, an international arms race between the United States and Soviet Union would en-
sue. In 1944 to 1946, no one wanted to see that happen, although of course it
was exactly what did happen for both nuclear and biological weapons. No
further record is available to indicate what became of Bush and Conant's
proposal, but clearly it was never acted upon.

Their ideas became obsolete very quickly, and were soon completely
inverted. Following Soviet military pressure on the borders with Turkey in
1946, President Truman asked two personal assistants, Clark Clifford and
George Elsey, to prepare a report on Soviet behavior since the end of World
War II. They consulted widely among senior officials in the administration in
drafting their September 1946 report. It contained the following paragraph:

> Whether it would actually be in this country's interest to employ atomic
> and biological weapons against the Soviet Union in the event of hostili-
> ties is a question which would require careful consideration in the light
> of the circumstances prevailing at the time. The decision would probably
> be influenced by a number of factors, such as the Soviet Union's capac-
> ity to employ similar weapons, which can not now be estimated. But
> the important point is that the United States must be prepared to wage
> atomic and biological warfare if necessary. The mere fact of prepared-
> ness may be the only powerful deterrent to Soviet aggressive action and
> in this sense the only sure guaranty of peace.

The phrase "prepared to wage atomic and biological war if necessary" had
been suggested to Elsey by George Kennan after he read the first draft of the
report.

Rosebury definitely would *not* have known of the Bush-Conant ideas nor of Clifford and Elsey's study. However the discussions regarding nuclear weapons in public and at the UN was very well developed by the time of the first initiatives in 1947 for which Rosebury was certainly instrumental: a memorandum to the United Nations General Assembly (UNGA) in September 1947 and the Rosebury-Kabat publication on aerosol dissemination of BW agents, also in 1947. The memorandum to the UNGA argued that:

> It is plain that bacterial warfare constitutes an extremely serious potential menace, and that world peace demands the elimination of this major weapon of mass destruction. . . . It is therefore imperative that the [United Nations] Atomic Energy Commission proceed without delay to consider bacterial warfare even as its deliberations on atomic energy continue. . . . The American Association of Scientific Workers therefore hopes that the United Nations General Assembly will take cognizance of this matter, that it will undertake a preliminary investigation of the available factual information on bacterial warfare, and that, if the findings of such an investigation warrant such action, it will instruct the Atomic Energy Commission to proceed at once to devote part of its attention to this major weapon of mass destruction.

The AASW memorandum included a short bibliography of sources, but Rosebury's 1949 book then fulfilled the task of providing the relevant information. In his conclusions, Rosebury argued that "we need not doubt that BW is capable of taking its place beside the atomic bomb and other major weapons adaptable to mass destruction." Though he expressed the opinion that "The U.S. plan for international control [of atomic energy] was a work of technical genius," he added that the US proposals were not accepted "because the world is obviously not ready for it." The "world" that Rosebury was referring to can only have meant the Soviet Union.[144]

2

Beginnings of the "Modern" Soviet BW program, 1970–1977

B Y THE LATE 1960S, the Soviet Union's BW program was in the doldrums. The Russian microbiologist Igor Domaradsky derisively characterized the period by noting that the program had not solved any "problems" for a long time, a "problem" being a synonym for a new or enhanced biological weapon. Many military generals considered the program useless, and as a consequence the Ministry of Defense (MOD) thought about following the US example and shutting down its offensive BW program, according to Domaradsky.[1]

However, quite the opposite occurred. The Soviet government soon revitalized its offensive BW program, and it grew to such an extent that by the time the Soviet Union dissolved in 1991, the program was the largest, most sophisticated BW program the world had ever seen. This chapter describes how the "modern" Soviet BW program came into being, largely due to the efforts of one remarkable and influential biological scientist. He accomplished this feat with the support of an influential general and, ultimately, the Politburo.

These two men, a scientist and a general, established the "new" offensive BW program on the premise that its R&D would employ the most modern and sophisticated biotechnology techniques. This chapter describes the beginnings of this system, how it came to be and how it was structured, and discusses its biosafety provisions. It concludes by discussing the impact of the Soviet military on Soviet biotechnology and molecular genetics in the 1970s and beyond.

"Lead Scientist in Scourge Search"

The scientist who led this turnaround was Yury A. Ovchinnikov, who in 1970 was just 36 years old but already was a director of a prestigious USSR Academy of Sciences (USSR-AN) research institute and was soon to become a vice president of the USSR-AN.[2] In the Soviet system, both of these positions were most often held by men in their 60s and older. No one could hold either of these positions without being a member in good standing of the Communist Party of the Soviet Union (CPSU) and having been approved by the apparatchiks who ran the government. Indeed, Ovchinnikov was an astute political operative and had friends and supporters in high places. Émigré scientists interviewed by journalist William Kucewicz described him as "a canny and shrewd person," "quite a charmer," and a "consummate politician." In addition to his social competencies, Ovchinnikov was also a brilliant scientist, as demonstrated by his original research, the results of which were published in internationally recognized journals.

Ovchinnikov deserves to be the subject of a complete English-language biography to complement the two published in Russian, but which is beyond the scope of this book.[3] This chapter provides only a brief description of the man and his accomplishments, using mostly information from interviews with people who knew him. Most of the personal information included in this chapter was gathered from one of Ovchinnikov's former graduate students, of which there were about 50, and scientists who were his colleagues.

Ovchinnikov was born in Moscow in 1934 to a well-off family. He graduated in 1957 from the most prestigious university in the Soviet Union, Moscow State University, with a candidate degree in chemistry.[4] In 1960 he secured a research position at the Institute of Chemistry of Natural Compounds, which was founded a year earlier by one of the Soviet Union's most famous chemists, Mikhail M. Shemyakin. As its name suggests, the institute investigated natural compounds, such as antibiotics, peptides, toxins, and vitamins.

Ovchinnikov joined the CPSU in 1962. Most scientists believed that it was a waste of time to participate in party activities, but they also knew that in order to move up in the science establishment, one had to belong to the CPSU. For example, with very few exceptions, all deputy directors and directors of research institutes were members of the party. In addition to formally joining the party, Ovchinnikov toed the party line, as evidenced by a 1985 statement made by him:

The Community Party considers scientific-technical progress as a key factor in the acceleration of the Soviet Union's socio-economic development. This was clearly and convincingly underlined by the resolution adopted by the Plenum of the Central Committee of the Communist Party of the Soviet Union (CPSU) in April of this year (1985). These resolutions made Soviet science responsible for a critical task of historical significance. Through these resolutions, Soviet science was instructed to concentrate its forces on the most important of courses, to mobilize its entire creative potential to the greatest extent possible, and to support the Soviet Union in its entry into key areas of science and technology. Naturally, this encompasses the very new and rapidly developing field of biotechnology.[5]

Being a Communist also allowed Ovchinnikov to enter the political world. He became a candidate member of the Central Committee of the CPSU and a member of the Presidium of the Supreme Soviet of the Russian Republic of the Soviet Union in 1973.

Ovchinnikov's main scientific interest was natural products chemistry, which involved investigating the structures of physiologically active chemicals and carrying out the synthesis of those he studied or their analogs. Early in his scientific career he worked with Shemyakin on depsipeptides, natural peptides in which one or more of the common amide bonds are replaced by ester bonds.[6] These peptides are commonly the metabolic products of microorganisms and often possess potent antibiotic activity (e.g., actinomycin, enniatins, and valinomycin). In recent years, some depsipeptide compounds have been used to treat persons suffering from inflammatory, autoimmune, or immune-system-related diseases such as graft-versus-host disease. Depsipeptides are of particular interest to organic chemists because their expansive biological activity promises to have valuable applications in medicine. Ovchinnikov reportedly determined the chemical conformations of highly active depsipeptides, including valinomycin,[7] enniatine (a possible anticancer drug), antamanide (a mushroom toxin that may be useful for treating edema), and gramicidin C (an antibiotic).[8]

As his scientific career advanced, Ovchinnikov came to focus on an exceedingly interesting protein called bacteriorhodopsin. Two European scientists first identified bacteriorhodopsin in 1973 after discovering it in halobacteria (archaea that live in salty marshes).[9] The protein acts as a powerhouse that turns on when the bacterium is famished, changing color from purple to yellow as it absorbs light. The incoming light is converted to an electrical charge that enables the bacterium to transport ions, neurotransmitters, enzymes, wastes, and other biomolecules across its membranes. Ovchinnikov was probably interested in researching bacteriorhodopsin because he recognized that it was a natural product that held promise for performing technological functions.

Even at that time, scientists thought that bacteriorhodopsin had the potential to be used in computational switching and optical sensing systems. Since then, scientists have investigated using bacteriorhodopsin in a range of applications, including battery-conserving, long-life computer displays; electronic writing technology; photodetectors; computer memory; and the light-sensitive element in artificial retinas. Ovchinnikov, who published his first paper on bacteriorhodopsin in 1977, probably was at the forefront of the field when he died from cancer on February 17, 1988.

Ovchinnikov's rise within the USSR-AN was rapid. On the basis of his excellent publication record and the high esteem with which he was regarded by colleagues, he was elected as a corresponding member of the USSR-AN's Division of Biochemistry, Biophysics, and Chemistry of Biologically Active Compositions in 1968.[10] Just two years later, on November 24, 1970, he was elected full academician of the same division. On March 5, 1974, at the age of 40, he was elected vice president of the USSR-AN and chairman of its Chemical-Technical and Biological Sciences Section. Ovchinnikov was also elected as Academician of the Lenin All-Union Academy of Agricultural Sciences in 1985. By the time of his death, he had been awarded the Lenin Prize (1978), the Hero of Socialist Labor (1981), and the State Prize of the USSR (1982).

At the Institute of Chemistry of Natural Compounds, Ovchinnikov collaborated with Shemyakin,[11] the institute's director, on his depsipeptides work. Ovchinnikov gained Shemyakin's favor and in early 1970 was appointed head of the laboratory for the synthesis of protein toxins and their analogs. Shemyakin became ill and died in 1970, and Ovchinnikov replaced him as the institute director. In honor of its former director, the Institute of Chemistry of Natural Compounds was renamed the M. M. Shemyakin Institute of Bioorganic Chemistry in 1974.

Ovchinnikov's rise to power was due to three factors, according to one of Ovchinnikov's colleagues, who had the same rank as him in the academy system and therefore knew him well. First, Ovchinnikov was an excellent organizer, which made him a perfect deputy director. Second, he was the deputy director of the Institute of Chemistry of Natural Compounds when its director, Shemyakin, died unexpectedly. So it was only natural that Ovchinnikov was appointed director. Third, Ovchinnikov was the principal assistant to Andrey Belozersky,[12] who was vice president of the USSR-AN at the time and strongly supported Ovchinnikov's appointment. Belozersky was a highly regarded scientist who some believed had founded the study of nucleic acids in the Soviet Union. He died unexpectedly on December 30, 1972, and Ovchinnikov was appointed vice president in his place.

Ovchinnikov was not the first scientist to have the dubious "honor" of establishing a national BW program, nor was he the last. For example, Yakov M. Fishman is likely to have initiated the offensive Soviet BW program that commenced in the late 1920s; the pre–World War II Japanese BW program surely was the brainchild of scientist Ishii Shiro, infamous for having been the head of the notorious Unit 731; the Canadian doctor who discovered insulin, Frederick Banting, was largely responsible for that country's BW program, which began in 1940. Similarly, Paul Fildes, an English microbiologist whose work with *Treponema pallidum* (the cause of syphilis) and the development of sulfa drugs laid the basis for remarkable advances in medicinal chemistry, was a proponent of the UK BW program that commenced in 1940. In the United States, the scientists Theodor Rosebury and Ira Baldwin, as well as the US Academy of Sciences, had important roles in getting the US BW program operational in 1942. And in more recent times, scientist Nasser Hindawi probably was the initiator of Iraq's BW program in the early 1980s; while Seichi Endo, a microbiologist who graduated from Kyodo University, probably was the brains behind the Japanese cult Aum Shinrikyo's BW program. What distinguishes Ovchinnikov's involvement was his application of modern biotechnology techniques to the task of building a BW program. Indeed, part of Ovchinnikov's obituary, if written today, might read as follows: "Whether or not genetic weapons were needed by a military already armed with atomic weapons, they were developed because in the Soviet system an ambitious scientist advanced himself by being willing to turn new scientific discoveries into weaponry."[13]

To understand Ovchinnikov's success in persuading top decision makers that biotechnology was a key enabling technology, one must understand at least a bit about the relationship between the Soviet state and Soviet science. Nikolai Krementsov described the relationship in his 1996 book, *Stalinist Science:*

The key feature of Stalinist science was the total dependence of science on its sole patron, the party-state bureaucracy. . . . Thus, the state apparatus and the scientific community each strove to acquire what it most wanted from the other. The state provided scientists with funds, resources, and great public prestige; the scientific community gave the state expertise and legitimacy in industry, agriculture, and medicine. Each developed various tactics to deal with its partner. The state established strict administrative control over institutional structures, scientific personnel, research directions, and scholarly communications. For their part, scientists cultivated patrons among the higher party-state bureaucrats and skillfully played upon their constantly changing policies and objectives. . . .

Although the Soviet scientific community and the state control apparatus have often been treated as separate entities, the actual boundaries between them were frequently blurred. Their symbiosis resulted in their institutional integration and individual co-option. At their apex, the control apparatus and the scientific community were blended and overlapping. Not only did scientists occupy key positions within various state agencies, but some scientific institutions, such as the presidiums of Soviet academies, were in fact key elements of the party-state control apparatus itself. Moreover, all appointments to top positions in the scientific hierarchy had to be approved by the highest party officials. In such circumstances, it is hardly surprising that the development of the various Soviet scientific disciplines was greatly influenced by the personal relations between particular disciplinary spokesmen and their powerful party patrons.[14]

Krementsov also succinctly explains how science and other fields were controlled in the Soviet Union:

The main instrument of party personnel policy in general was the system of *nomenklatura*. *Nomenklatura* was, literally, a list of posts that could be occupied or vacated only with permission from the appropriate party committee. All party committees, from the Central Committee to the smallest one in the countryside, established personnel departments, whose main function was to approve candidates for appointment to any post included in their own *nomenklatura*. Initially devised for the personnel of party organs and agencies, the system was expanded in the early 1930s into the scientific community.

The *nomenklatura* system was strictly hierarchical—the higher the post, the higher the party committee controlling its personnel. The posts of president, vice-president, and scientific secretary of such central institutions as the USSR Academy of Sciences and VASKhNIL [V. I. Lenin All-Union Academy of Agricultural Sciences] were in the *nomenklatura* of the Politburo. The posts of institute director and editor-in-chief of a journal were in the *nomenklatura* of the Central Committee Secretariat. The position of laboratory head belonged to the *nomenklatura* of the regional party committee. Even the post of librarian in a scientific institute was in the *nomenklatura* of the local party committee. . . . Thus, to occupy any administrative post in a scientific institution, a scientist had to obtain permission from the party apparatus. . . . *Nomenklatura* thus became the main means of party control over the scientific community.[15]

Although some aspects of the complex relationship between the party-state and the scientific community changed in the post-Stalin era—for example, some *nomenklatura* positions in scientific institutions no longer absolutely demanded that the candidate be a member of the CPSU—by the 1970s and 1980s, the system by and large functioned as Krementsov describes it. This backdrop allows for certain deductions about Ovchinnikov's rise within the USSR-AN and government.

Ovchinnikov is reported to have said: "At the Central Committee of the Communist Party, if we offer ten drugs nobody would support us. Nobody would give us money for medicine. But offer one weapon and you'll get full support."[16] Whether or not this quote is apocryphal, there is a near consensus among former weapons scientists that Ovchinnikov was the BW program's "big man"; in other words, he was the most influential person in garnering the support from the Soviet political and military systems that led to the decision in 1971 to establish and operate a new, very large offensive BW program. How did he reach such a position of influence?

The Soviet scientific community undoubtedly recognized Ovchinnikov as a brilliant chemist when he earned his doctorate in 1966, at the age of 32. At the time, high-level CPSU officials were probably unaware of his prowess. However, they were likely more aware of him by 1967, when he was appointed as the director of the protein chemistry laboratory at the Institute of Chemistry of Natural Compounds. This position most likely belonged to the *nomenklatura* of the Moscow regional or city party committee, one of the most powerful committees of its kind in the Soviet Union. Before approving Ovchinnikov for this position, committee members undoubtedly learned about him and liked what they saw. A year later, Ovchinnikov was elected as a corresponding member of the USSR-AN. His selection was probably more about academy business than that of the party; nevertheless, such an election would have been unlikely without party approval, translating into more exposure to Moscow CPSU officials for Ovchinnikov.

For Ovchinnikov, 1970 was a momentous year: He was elected academician and was honored with a high award from the government.[17] This combination of honors could not have happened without the approval of the Politburo. It is reasonable to believe that before being accorded these honors, Ovchinnikov would have met with Politburo members, including CPSU General Secretary Leonid Brezhnev. "Ovchinnikov impressed Brezhnev with his imagination and knowledge," according to his former graduate student. Though this student was not certain when this act of "impressing" occurred, it makes sense that it was before Ovchinnikov's election to Academician.

In addition to his prominence in the scientific community, Ovchinnikov was one of just two scientific advisers to the Politburo in the early 1970s and was a confidant of Brezhnev, according to trustworthy sources. Recent research even suggests that Ovchinnikov represented the KGB on the USSR-AN's Executive Committee and was an advisor to the Military Industrial Commission (VPK) of the USSR Council of Ministers.[18] Assuming that this was the case, Krementsov's assertion about the importance of personal relationships between scientists and powerful party-state patrons for the development of scientific disciplines holds true. It also explains how Ovchinnikov was in a favorable position to explain the importance of modern biotechnology for military and, probably, civilian applications to Brezhnev and other government officials.

With his access to high-level government officials, Ovchinnikov was well positioned to argue for renewed investment in a revitalized Soviet BW program. Ovchinnikov knew that before the era of genetic engineering, military scientists used the classical approach of mutation and selection to develop new variants of pathogens for BW purposes. Military scientists would expose natural pathogen strains to chemicals or irradiation and then recover mutants that possessed improved or enhanced characteristics related to infectivity, virulence, and hardiness. Ovchinnikov likely recognized that this classical approach had reached its technical limits and had little further utility for solving "problems." From what he knew of the power of genetic engineering, he also recognized that it could be presented to nonscientists as a type of "magic bullet" to solve "problems."

As part of his campaign, Ovchinnikov wrote a memorandum to the Central Committee sometime in 1970 or early 1971 on the necessity of applying modern biotechnology to develop biological weapons, according to Vladimir A. Pasechnik. He reportedly used as a precedent a 1938 memorandum to Stalin on the necessity of acquiring nuclear weapons. That memorandum proposed establishing a large nuclear weapons program to be carried out in secret nuclear cities. Though Pasechnik never read Ovchinnikov's memorandum, his friends in the USSR-AN recounted to him the essence of its contents. In particular, Ovchinnikov was said to have stressed the need to solve scientific problems related to BW using new biotechnology techniques and that doing so was vital to national defense. In order for the Soviet Union to undertake the program Ovchinnikov proposed, it would need to make a long-term commitment and back it up with large state resources, in much the same way that the country supported its World War II–era nuclear program. Pasechnik was certain that Ovchinnikov could not have written and submitted his memorandum without first having secured strong support from the leaders of the USSR-AN, including those who were in charge of nuclear matters.[19]

As a result of Ovchinnikov's influence, in 1971 the Soviet government designated biotechnology as a field of critical importance. Several sources said that Ovchinnikov was not personally interested in BW R&D; to him, it was merely a means to become more politically powerful and to be able to disperse funding to those he favored in the Soviet scientific establishment. One Biopreparat scientist said that the directors of Biopreparat institutes often complained that tasks assigned to scientists at the Shemyakin Institute of Bioorganic Chemistry were poorly done and delivered late. This would have been because neither the scientists nor their director, Ovchinnikov, cared about this type of work, and no one was in a position to discipline them.

The Soviet government rewarded Ovchinnikov by funding a new complex of buildings to house his institute and by providing the hard currency needed to equip the buildings with the best instrumentation available in the West. The Shemyakin Institute became the foremost bioscience institute in the Soviet Union, called by some the "Taj Mahal of Russian biotechnology."[20] After a visit to the institute in June 1985, American molecular biologist Joshua Lederberg noted:

I visited Ovchinnikov at his new institute a large part of Friday. It is the larger part of biotechnology in the USSR—a $300,000,000 (dollars!) construction budget, 85,000 sq. meters; 100,000,000 rubles annual budget, superbly equipped. It was entirely open, with a number of students from Moscow University, no remarkable security barriers. I did not however see the P2-P3 building myself—I should have thought to press for that. He told me there were other facilities at Pushchino about 40 km. NE of Moscow, which had their animal facilities—for monoclonal antibody work etc.[21]

A *Science* reporter added: "[Shemyakin] is modern in architecture and whose interiors are plush enough to rival top cooperative headquarters in the West, a sharp contrast to the shoddy construction commonly seen in Moscow. (The Soviets built the outside and Finns and Yugoslavs finished the inside.)"[22]

Military Apologist for Biological Warfare

Equally important to the support the BW program received from the Politburo was the support Ovchinnikov received from the Soviet military. Without the military's full support, he would not have succeeded in advancing his agenda to elevate molecular biology in the Soviet Union. Particularly important was the support of a larger-than-life Soviet military personality.

From roughly 1954 to 1985, Colonel General Smirnov was the most important military decision maker in the Soviet BW program. He headed the MOD's 7th Directorate of the General Staff and its successor 15th Directorate,[23] whose code name was Post Office Box A-1968,[24] which were in charge of the Soviet BW program. In essence, Smirnov was one of the principal MOD BW ideologists, if not *the* principal one, and he was also believed to have been the main strategist of biological weapons applications. Microbiologist Domaradsky called him "the ideologue par excellence of Soviet bioweapons research from the 1950s to the 1980s" and "our apologist for biological warfare."[25] This part of his life's work was not disclosed until well into the 1990s.

It remains unknown when and under what circumstances Ovchinnikov and Smirnov first met, or when they began to collaborate. They most likely met in early 1971, when Ovchinnikov's interests probably had little to do with BW. Instead he was focused on the rapid advancement of biotechnology in the West, which threatened to leave Soviet bioscientists even further behind than they already were. As an astute scientist with extensive Western contacts, Ovchinnikov is likely to have learned about the revolutionary development of recombinant DNA research, which uses genetic engineering, in the early 1970s.[26] One of Ovchinnikov's colleagues at the USSR-AN was the prominent Soviet bioscientist Aleksandr A. Baev. In 1972 Baev was instrumental in the establishment of the first Soviet laboratory of molecular biology and the genetics of microorganisms at the Institute of Biochemistry and Physiology of Microorganisms in Pushchino. Baev's description of how he came to recognize the new developments in the West was probably similar to how Ovchinnikov learned about them:

> Scientific events were continuing to develop, however, and my period of genetic engineering began. The works of P. Berg, S. N. Cohen, and H. W. Boyer (1972–1973) heralded the beginning of the era of recombinant DNAs. Even before this, however, my attention was drawn to J. Beckwith's publication in *Nature* (vol. 224, p. 768, November 22nd, 1969) on the isolation of lactose operon. I was similarly affected by the news that the Congress of the USA had granted 10 million dollars from the 1971 budget to support genetic scientists, represented by J. Lederberg. At that time I had already sensed that there were more important events on the horizon in biology, and I began to prepare my research into molecular biology, starting with prokaryotes.[27]

Aware of the Soviet Union's inferiority in the biosciences and fearing that the already wide gap between Western and Soviet capabilities in this field would grow into a chasm, Ovchinnikov probably concluded that the only way to quickly gain support from decision-makers for a program that aimed to match Western developments was to play the military card. To get the attention of Soviet officials, all he had to do was suggest that the Pentagon was likely to apply the revolutionary new developments to R&D on superdeadly pathogens for weapons applications. He probably conveyed similar ideas to Smirnov.

Smirnov had two types of interests, or rather, concerns. First, as Domaradsky describes, Smirnov had to confront the faction within the MOD that believed that the BW program was more or less useless because it was not solving "problems." These officials also believed that there was no need for weapons as undependable as biological weapons in view of the Soviet's growing strength in the nuclear area. This view might have been strengthened by the US government having decided in 1969 to close down its BW program because "BW lacked military usefulness."[28]

The second concern had to do with advances in biotechnology and their possible application by the United States for military purposes (as hypothesized by Ovchinnikov). This concern was oddly enough asserted in a 1977 article in the US journal *Bulletin of the Atomic Scientists,* but its underlying meaning probably went undetected by readers. The article's two authors, both retired Soviet military officers, pointed out that R&D in the area of "genetic weapons" had been going on "for a long time" in the United States.[29] The authors provided what they considered were two specific examples. First, they alleged that by 1962 the Pentagon had confirmed that it was sponsoring research "whose solution would permit discovery of a mechanism which determines the fundamental changes of bacterial cells." Second, in the 1960s the Pentagon supported a five-year plan that was said to have "obtained practical results" in transforming a microorganism that gives rise to plague so as to obtain a new strain of this pathogen that was "resistant to antibiotics and does not require a complex nutrient medium for growth."[30] The authors said that they had obtained this information from US Department of Defense Appropriations for 1963 and 1970.[31] Undoubtedly, this information was made available to Smirnov soon after its publication, and its implications for BW were understood.

Smirnov faced a dilemma. He needed to convince civilian decision-makers that it would be catastrophic to the Soviet Union's military might if it shut down the Soviet BW program in light of the likelihood that the United States was applying revolutionary advances in biotechnology to develop powerful new biological weapons against which the Soviet Union would be defenseless. He had to square this task with the knowledge that the US government had supposedly terminated its BW program. How did Smirnov present these two issues to his co-workers and civilian and military superiors? In briefings to BW workers in subsequent years, he repeated one particular message again and again, namely, that when the United States had publicized closing down its offensive BW program in 1969, it had lied. What the Pentagon actually did, he said, was to transfer the program from the Department of Defense's laboratories to private companies and university laboratories that were then responsible for the R&D required to develop new biological weapons.[32] Smirnov's deputies could have spread this same message among Soviet party-state officials in 1970–1971.

There might have been another force for continuing the BW program, namely the MOD's Main Intelligence Directorate (GRU). The MOD tended to exaggerate the supposed threats posed to the Soviet Union by the US military. A telling example of how the GRU misinformed even the Politburo was its 1975 estimate of US tank production capability.[33] According to the GRU estimate provided in the report "The Military Potential of the USA" (in Russian) prepared for the Soviet General Staff, the United States was capable of producing 70,000 tanks (50,000 main battle tanks and 20,000 light tanks) per year within 90 days of full mobilization. In actuality, the United States produced at most 500 tanks per year at that time, and it would have taken more than two years for it to even double its production. As a Russian author noted, the GRU "overstated by one hundred fold" the US mobilization capacity.[34] If the GRU misinformed the Politburo about supposed US superiorities in tanks, it could have done the same about the existence of a secret US BW program that used powerful new technologies; no one in the Soviet government would have been in a position to dispute the GRU's findings. If the GRU was able to convince civilian leadership that the US offensive BW program continued after 1969–1970, the continuance of the military BW program would have been assured.

An additional possibility bears mentioning. For internal political reasons, Brezhnev could have welcomed Ovchinnikov and Smirnov's initiative to apply genetic engineering in an expanded and improved BW program. The US national security advisor, Henry Kissinger, had been working closely with Soviet ambassador Anatoly Dobrynin since November 1969 to organize a summit meeting between President Richard Nixon and Brezhnev. The summit took place from May 22 to May 29, 1972, in Moscow. As a sign of eased relations, the two countries were to enter into what came to be called "détente," a period of relatively friendlier and more constructive relations between the two countries, differing from the strained relations that existed during most of the Cold War and up to that time. Nevertheless, there was opposition to this development from some members of the Politburo. The new BW program would undoubtedly be a program that would benefit the military and one that would employ advanced Western technology. Brezhnev's support for establishing this new program would demonstrate in concrete terms to Politburo hardliners that he was committed to achieving military equivalency with the West and providing the MOD with means to surpass the level of BW R&D that the United States had achieved up to 1969. It can be seen that from one side of his mouth Brezhnev was promising the world peacefully directed détente, while from the other, secretive, side he was promising his cronies to support the creation of a new, gigantic weapons program.

Though the precise deliberations of the Politburo are unknown, in the end it decided to expand its biotechnology programs in the civilian and military spheres. This decision undoubtedly pleased both Ovchinnikov and Smirnov, because it rewarded each of their programs with additional funding and provided Ovchinnikov with new, well-equipped buildings to house his institute. The decision also initiated a discussion about who was to lead the expanded BW program, and how it was to be instituted and operated. This process has been described in detail by Domaradsky, who, as noted below, was directly involved and whose account is difficult to improve on.[35] An outline of Domaradsky's description of the process follows, along with additional information gathered from other participants.

Establishing the "Modern" Soviet BW Program

In 1971 the Central Committee of the Communist Party (CCCP) and the USSR Council of Ministers issued a decree, stamped "of special importance," that laid the foundation for the organization of a new system to procure biological weapons. The decree was not merely "Top Secret"; it had an even higher security classification, according to Soviet standards. Officials in the know informally called its classification "*Olga Vasilyevna*," where the beginning letters *O* and *V* represent the first letters of the phrase *osoboy vazhnosti,* "of special importance."[36] Several of the scientists interviewed for this book either saw or had heard of this document, although none had a copy. The 1971 decree established a new Soviet organization for the expressed purpose of acquiring modern biological weapons and specified how to pay for building it and carrying out its work. The decree formally marked the beginning of the "modern" Soviet offensive BW program. In 1972, a high-level meeting of party and government officials enhanced and expanded the objectives and activities spelled out in the 1971 decree by developing a new and more far-reaching decree that was adopted in 1973.

As it would never have agreed to relinquish control over its current biological weapons systems or what was likely to become a substantially expanded biological arsenal, the MOD assumed leadership of the new organization. According to the CCCP and the Council of Minister's statement No. 444-138, dated June 25, 1973, and MOD Decree No. 99, dated November 1, 1973, a new military administration, the MOD's 15th Directorate,[37] took over all issues related to BW (which until then had been the 7th Directorate's responsibility). Like the former directorate, the new directorate was headed by Smirnov.[38] The Special Biological Group of the General Staff Operations Directorate was to develop BW doctrine and logistics and also was responsible for developing methods for arming bombs and missiles with biological agents. The GRU was made responsible for agent procurement. Testing, procurement, and approval of biological weapons systems were to be the responsibility of the Special Armaments Group under the Deputy Minister of Defense for Armaments.[39]

Various government organs undoubtedly engaged in complicated and long discussions about how the new program should be organized and led. According to one source, Ovchinnikov suggested that the new BW organization be established in the civilian sphere. He reportedly believed that doing so would better hide the program from Western intelligence than if military biological institutions were expanded. After all, Western intelligence services most likely knew about the military biological institutions and kept them under observation. The better option was to "hide" the new institutions in plain sight; in other words, the construction of new facilities could be explained as a response to a forthcoming, openly published decree that ordered an expansion of the civilian biotechnology program under the authority of the existing and well-known civilian subministry *Glavmikrobioprom*. If anyone wanted to know what the new institutes did, the simple answer would be that they researched and developed biological products for civilian purposes. Following Ovchinnikov's suggestion, in 1974 the CCCP and the Council of Ministers adopted a decree called "On the Measures for Accelerating the Development of Physical-Chemical Biology and Biotechnology and the Use of Their Achievements in Medicine, Agriculture, and Industry," which in effect established a complex program for applying biotechnology in the Soviet Union. The resolution also specified that this program be coordinated by a new body, the Interdepartmental Science and Technology Council on the Problems of Physical-Chemical Biology and Biotechnology.

Another excellent reason for the involvement of civilian scientists in the Soviet BW program was, to put it simply, that they were the ones who were most scientifically and technically proficient. Ovchinnikov apparently deemed the military scientists to possess an adequate level of expertise (see below), but they were not of the highest caliber because the secrecy under which they labored restricted their development as scientists. Military scientists were not allowed to interact with their civilian counterparts in the Soviet Union, and they could never, ever have anything to do with foreigners. Although they worked in well-equipped laboratories and had access to the foreign scientific literature, these scientists were likely to have suffered from the lack of contact—of critiques of ideas, theories, and investigations, as well as peer reviews and accolades—with civilian scientists. Military scientists presumably knew how to weaponize bacterial and viral pathogens using the classical methods of mutation, selection, and propagation, but they probably had little more than a clue of what molecular biology was all about. If the intent of Soviet decision-makers was to establish a "modern" Soviet BW program based on genetic engineering and other advanced biotechnologies, then the best source of relevant knowledge and know-how was civilian biomedical and bioscientific scientists.

Smirnov opposed allowing civilians to get involved with the BW program. He reasoned that sooner or later a civilian who worked in the program would defect or turn into a spy and reveal the program to Western intelligence. This, in his view, would never happen if the military operated the expanded BW program. In the end, he proved correct; the first, second, and third defectors from the Soviet BW program were all civilians, whereas as far as we know, as of this writing, no defector has appeared from the military side of the program. However, Smirnov's concerns were cast aside, as no one could foresee if there would be future defectors or from whence they might come.

Although Ovchinnikov was highly influential in this decision-making process, he was not the only civilian involved. In particular, Academicians Georgy K. Skryabin and Viktor M. Zhdanov worked with Ovchinnikov to convince the USSR Council of Ministers' Military Industrial Commission (VPK),[40] which was a keystone to the entire Soviet defense complex, to continue and expand the BW program.[41] (See Chapter 21.)

Though the 1974 decree was implemented in the civilian sphere, the military was not neglected. In 1973, Ovchinnikov, accompanied by O. V. Baroyan (then the head of the Ministry of Health's anti-plague system), was tasked with assessing the level of science at the military biological institutes. In 1972 the Soviet Union had signed the Biological and Toxin Weapons Convention (BWC), which was expected to be ratified in 1975. The assessment was needed to determine how to proceed with the new BW program in view of this agreement. As part of the assessment, the two visited the three main military biological institutes, in Sverdlovsk, Kirov, and Zagorsk. At each institute, Ovchinnikov and Baroyan met with military scientists, who reported on current work and projects that could be successful. Ovchinnikov proved to be a good listener who asked astute questions.

After the tour of the MOD institutes, Baroyan[42] concluded that science at the military facilities was performed at a low level, according to a source. Baroyan had one main purpose for drawing such a negative conclusion; he knew that a large amount of money was going to be made available for the BW program, and he wished to divert as much as possible of this funding from the military institutes to the anti-plague system. As is discussed in Chapter 5, in this he was partially successful.

Conversely, Ovchinnikov's reaction to the military presentations was positive. He seemed to understand the value of the R&D being done at the military institutes and asked what they needed to enhance their work. As a result of his input, shortly after the tour, funding for the MOD institutes was substantially increased. (Another possible reason for Ovchinnikov's positive assessment could have been that he made a deal with Smirnov whereby both benefited from the new government funds being made available for biotechnology development.)

Following Ovchinnikov's suggestion on the new organization being civilian, the Politburo decided to do so and gave the green light for the establishment of an entirely new network of institutes, production plants, and storage facilities dedicated to BW. This network was to be named Biopreparat (see below) and officially would report to *Glavmikrobioprom*. Yet its highest leadership was composed of military officers led by Smirnov. In other words, Smirnov led both the offensive and the defensive aspects of the BW program until 1985, and all his direct subordinates were generals. In fact, many of the new facilities in this network would also be led by officers ranked colonel and above. Although some of the particularly sensitive and most important projects within the BW program were carried out in Biopreparat facilities, they were undertaken by only or mostly military scientists. These projects included those aimed at weaponizing variola virus and Marburg virus.

Soviet officials quickly structured and populated the new offensive BW program. The part of the program that aimed to research, develop, and produce biological weapons against humans was given the code name *"Ferment"* in Russian (which translates to "Enzyme").[43] According to Domaradsky, *Ferment's* overall objective was "to develop a second generation of biological weapons using genetically modified strains, which would be of greater value [than existing strains]. We planned to introduce new properties into diseases organisms, such as antibiotic resistance, altered antigen structure, and enhanced stability in the aerosol form, making delivery of the agent easier and more effective."[44]

A new and highly secret Interdepartmental Scientific-Technical Council on Molecular Biology and Genetics (MNTS),[45] whose cover designation was P.O. Box A-3092,[46] was established to provide direction to *Ferment*, and the highly regarded virologist and Academician Zhdanov was appointed its chairman.[47] MNTS's members were drawn from MOD's 15th Directorate (Major General Vladimir A. Lebedinsky), *Glavmikrobioprom* (its head Vasily D. Belyaev,[48] as well as A. A. Skladnev and S. I. Alikhanyan[49]), the VPK, the USSR Ministry of Health (Burnazyan), the Ministry of Agriculture, the USSR-AN (Ovchinnikov, Baev, Georgy K. Skryabin,[50] Rem V. Petrov,[51] and Andrey D. Mirzabekov[52]),[53] the KGB, and the CCCP. It was a clear indication of MNTS's importance that all of its members were part of the *nomenklatura* of the Politburo and the USSR Council of Ministers.[54]

Domaradsky was relieved of his position in 1972 as director of the Rostov-on-Don Anti-plague Institute, and at the request of Soviet Deputy Minister of Health A. I. Burnazyan he was transferred to Moscow to work for *Glavmikrobioprom*.[55] However, this was a cover—his real job was to be Zhdanov's deputy at the MNTS.

As the MNTS was being established, the unclassified Interdepartmental Science and Technology Council on the Problems of Physical-Chemical Biology and Biotechnology was also being set up to serve as a cover for the MNTS, and Ovchinnikov was appointed its head.[56] Ovchinnikov was to report on the council's activities to the Government Committee of the USSR on Science and Technology and the Presidium of the USSR-AN.[57]

As *Ferment* was being launched and Biopreparat facilities were starting their R&D activities, some subprograms were spun off *Ferment* and others originated in agencies outside Biopreparat. They in turn were given code names, which proliferated to such an extent that even Biopreparat scientists were unable to keep up with them and to remember what they were about. Soviet scientists and officials have identified the code names for several BW subprograms, including Bonfire, Factor, Metol, Chimera, Hunter, Flute, Fetish, Centralka, Podvizhnik (Ascetic), Kontuziya (Contusion), and Elling. Of these, only the first five were for certain *Ferment* programs, the sixth was of the Ministry of Health, the seventh was a KGB program, and we know nothing about the remainder. Later chapters describe the first three (Bonfire,

Factor, and Metol) with some confidence, and Flute, Fetish, and Hunter are described only in passing.

Soviet officials set up a new classification level, called "series F" clearance, which was higher than Top Secret, as *Ferment* was being established. To understand this classification adequately requires an acquaintance with two terms: "legends" and "awareness." Legends were "facts" or plausible stories created by the KGB solely to mislead. In the Biopreparat system, there were two legend levels, and these were linked to the extent of a person's "awareness" *(dopusk)*, of which there were three levels, with the first being the lowest in secrecy and the third the highest. The three levels were roughly equivalent to US classified levels of "For Official Use Only" or Confidential, Secret, and Top Secret.

The first legend level, or "open legend" *(otkrytaya legenda)*, at a particular Biopreparat institute claimed that the facility was performing R&D strictly for civilian purposes. Persons working at the institute who possessed the first level of awareness would know no more than this legend. (They were still required to possess the necessary clearance that allowed them to work at a closed institute.) The second legend level, or "closed legend" *(zakrytaya legenda)*, claimed that the institute was performing defense-related R&D. At this legend level, the institute was acknowledged as conducting R&D having military applications, but only for purposes of defending against BW. Persons who possessed the second level of awareness would know no more than this and the first legend. There was no need for more than two legends because the third level of information disclosed the true purpose of the program— namely, that the institute was undertaking R&D for offensive BW purposes. A person who possessed the third level of awareness was considered to be "fully informed" *(dopushchen)*. The third awareness level had important subdivisions, similar to the US top-secret classification system that has the designation Sensitive Compartmented Information (SCI), where one needs SCI clearance to have access to certain categories of information, such as raw human intelligence. Within the Biopreparat system, the most important sublevel was the aforementioned F clearance, which allowed the holder to access documents and information relevant to *Ferment*.

As far as is publicly known, all major Biopreparat institutes had specially constructed rooms within their First Departments where series F meetings could be held and archives that stored F documents. Each institute had a list of persons with an F clearance, called "List #1." Listed persons were under constant KGB control, which meant that they needed permission from the

KGB before changing jobs, traveling abroad, or meeting with foreigners. At a hypothetical Biopreparat institute employing, say, 3,000 persons, approximately 2,500 of them would be at the first awareness level, 450 at the second awareness level, 50 or fewer at the third, and between 10 and 20 would have F clearance.

In addition to the substantial domestic developments and organizational changes related to the Soviet BW program, the Soviet intelligence system increased its collection activities related to science and technology. From information provided by Colonel Vladimir I. Vetrov (code-named "Farewell") to the French intelligence service in 1981, US intelligence learned that the KGB had set up a new unit, Directorate T of its First Main Directorate, to conduct scientific espionage in the West.[58] Directorate T's operative arm, code-named Line X, paid particular attention to collecting information on computers, electronics, machine tools, radar, and semiconductors. There was no mention at that time of a priority for biotechnology.

Nevertheless, with the substantial expansion of the Soviet BW program in the early 1980s, and the KGB's claim that the US had not really ended its own offensive BW program in 1969 (see Chapter 20), it is almost certain that the KGB was tasked to collect information in this area as well. That this occurred was proven by instructions set forth in a January 1985 KGB cable that was found in the Lithuanian KGB archive in late 2011.[59] The cable would have been sent to the heads of KGB offices, the "*rezidents*," in foreign capitals via diplomatic pouch. It directed KGB agents to gather information on:

- Civilian institutions and companies working on contracts with military agencies, price and content of the contracts, results of work done under the contracts.
- Organizational measures taken in the USA and NATO countries to use the latest achievements of biology, genetics, genetic engineering, microbiology, etc. for the development and improvement of biological weapons.
- Methods used in the NATO countries to conceal work of creating and improving biological weapons.[60]

These lines account for about 7 percent of the cable's total length. They were followed by two and one-half single-spaced pages of extremely detailed description that was a guide for information gathering regarding pathogens, diseases, methods and processes used in BW R&D, molecular genetics, equipment and other details, all of which would be of direct and obvious use to the offensive Soviet BW program. (See Annex for the cable in full.) The lines quoted above were almost certainly a cover for the detailed requests that followed in the same way that Soviet-WTO protocols for military exercises almost always began with a scenario in which the US/NATO attacked the Soviet Union first. The rest of the protocols was instructions for the Soviet/WTO responses to attacks.

Structuring the Modern Soviet BW Program

After *Ferment* became operational in 1973, Ovchinnikov began delegating its tasks to USSR-AN institutes.[61] Four major Moscow-region USSR-AN institutes were the primary contractors for *Ferment*: the Institute of Protein in Pushchino (directed by Aleksandr Spirin), the Institute of Molecular Biology (directed by Andrey Mirzabekov), the Institute of Biochemistry and Physiology of Microorganisms in Pushchino (directed by Skryabin),[62] and Ovchinnikov's M. M. Shemyakin Institute of Bioorganic Chemistry. The Pacific Ocean Institute of Bioorganic Chemistry in Vladivostok, which specialized in researching marine natural compounds, including toxins, was also assigned *Ferment* tasks.[63]

From the beginning, *Ferment's* main objective was to develop pathogens resistant to antibiotics and vaccines.[64] *Ferment* scientists initially focused on traditional agents, such as *Bacillus anthracis, Burkholderia mallei, Francisella tularensis,* and *Yersinia pestis,* but within a few years they also investigated filoviruses, Junín virus, Machupo virus, variola virus, and Venezuelan equine encephalitis virus (see Chapters 6–9).[65] Alongside its offensively directed R&D, Biopreparat institutes also performed defensively directed R&D under a program code-named Problem 5 (see Chapter 5). The Soviet BW program did not prioritize the development of vaccines and treatments for the agents weaponized under *Ferment*, and this work was mostly performed as part of the second legend.

The defining moment of the new Soviet BW program occurred on April 24, 1974, when the Soviet government established the All-Union Science Production Association, "Biopreparat," in response to Order No. 131 DSP, and appointed the organization as the lead agency for *Ferment*.[66] Initially called "Ogarkov's System," after its first head, Lieutenant General Vsevolod I. Ogarkov, the new organization was given the code name P.O. Box A-1063.[67] Officials ostensibly placed Biopreparat under the civilian authority of *Glavmikrobioprom*, as one of its pharmaceutical-industrial departments. However, from the beginning the organization received its orders from the MOD's 15th Directorate, operated in accordance with "advice" given by the MNTS, and received funding through a special secret pathway from *Gosplan*.[68]

During its first months, Biopreparat was headquartered within *Glavmikrobioprom's* main buildings on *Ulitsa Lesteva* in Moscow, but it was eventually relocated to *Samokatnaya Ulitsa*, 4a, where it remains to this day. The KGB was responsible for the building's security,[69] and the headquarters also housed a counterintelligence unit.[70] Its First Department maintained F files and copies of all communications. Only high-level Biopreparat officials had access to these documents and records. The KGB arm responsible for procuring biological agents was called Capturing Agency Nr. 1.[71] All military employees of Biopreparat were assigned cover identities as ordinary civilian scientists. The Main Directorate of Internal Military Forces provided guards for BW facilities that were not secured by soldiers from the MOD's 15th Directorate.[72] A secret codename system was developed for all BW agents.[73]

Biopreparat contracted with the USSR Ministry of Internal Affairs to employ prisoners for the construction of some of its facilities, since the ministry's Main Directorate of Labor-Correction Enterprises controlled prisons and labor camps.[74] For example, Biopreparat's main virology institute, Vector, was built mainly by prisoners (see Chapter 8). Other major Biopreparat R&D production facilities were also built from scratch, though in other cases the organization simply took ownership of existing facilities.

Two MOH directorates had important roles in the Soviet BW program. The 2nd Directorate's main responsibility was to manage the Soviet antiplague (AP) system and the system's programs code-named Problem 1 through 5 (see Chapter 5). The highly secretive 3rd Directorate was important because it gave institutions outside of the military permission to work with pathogens.[75] Every time a Biopreparat institute wanted to research a pathogen, it needed permission from the 3rd Directorate. The exact procedure for securing permission is unknown, but in general the applicant had to have staff trained to handle the pathogen in question and biosafety facilities that would contain it. Workers who handled Group I pathogens received more intense training than those who worked with Group II and Group III pathogens, and they also had to be retrained more frequently.[76] Institutions kept careful records on each person who worked with pathogens, and supervisors made certain that each one was retrained according to the schedule specified by 3rd Directorate regulations. During the period of the post-1971 Soviet

BW program, biosafety protocols were signed by Petr N. Burgasov, the Soviet Union's Chief Sanitary Physician. The 3rd Directorate also operated clinics and hospitals in closed cities, and managed the Soviet space biology program. It operated a component of the offensive BW program called "Flute," of which we know hardly anything.

In the late 1970s, Western scientists and publics became concerned about the risks posed by recombinant DNA (rDNA) research.[77] They feared that a genetic recombination would accidently create a monstrous pathogen, the likes of which the world had never seen and therefore could not defend against. There was less publicity about rDNA in the Soviet Union than in the West, but there was concern about it. In fact, five Soviet scientists participated in the 1975 Asilomar Conference, during which scientists from throughout the world discussed the putative risks of rDNA research and drafted voluntary guidelines to prevent those risks from being realized. After the five returned home, they reported to the USSR-AN on the Asilomar proceedings and recommended that the guidelines be adopted in the Soviet Union, which they were. After the US National Institutes of Health (NIH) converted the Asilomar guidelines into the more formal NIH Guidelines for Research Involving Recombinant DNA Molecules (NIH Guidelines), the Soviet Union adopted these guidelines. As proof of this vigilance, for example, bioscience institutes in Moscow and Tallinn visited by Zilinskas in 1982 had loose-leaf binders containing the NIH Guidelines, which were signed by Burgasov.

When Domaradsky was tasked in 1980 with weaponizing *Francisella tularensis* (see Chapter 7), he proposed to employ genetic engineering methods to enhance the prospective host's pathogenicity. Research for this purpose directly contravened the NIH Guidelines and therefore should not have been permitted. Nevertheless, when he applied for permission to perform his experiments, his request was approved by none other than the head of the KGB, Yury Andropov.[78]

The biotechnology revolution began in the late 1960s and early 1970s, but only in select parts of the world—the United States, some Western European countries, and Japan. Historian Donald Fleming later pondered what it meant to be "living in a biological revolution." He asserted that every revolution has three components: "a distinctive attitude toward the world; a program for utterly transforming it; and an unshakable, not to say fanatical, confidence that this program can be enacted—a world view, a program, and a faith." [79] So it was with the biotechnological revolution.

The rise of molecular biology meant that biologists, especially younger biologists, who worked with scientists from other disciplines such as physics and chemistry, developed and exhibited a worldview quite different from that of the more classically inclined biologists. And this worldview took its cues from biology, genetics, chemistry, and physics at the molecular level. Their program was to selectively control gene expression so it could be usefully applied in medicine, environmental remediation, and agriculture. Their enthusiasm and dedication was boundless. Ovchinnikov was likely to have recognized the emerging biotechnology revolution because he knew many of its foremost leaders and practitioners, and he understood their programs and faith. He also must have realized that the Soviet bioscience community was not going to be a part of that revolution unless something drastic was done. If government and party officials remained ignorant of its implications, it would translate into lack of support for biotechnology in the Soviet Union.

Ovchinnikov also knew that the Soviet biosciences had been severely damaged in the preceding decades by Lysenko and his minions. As a consequence, Soviet scientists had not been involved in most of the important midcentury discoveries, such as the elucidation of the structure of DNA and the code by which DNA specifies the insertion of amino acids in proteins; the development of hybrid cells between different animals and of superovulation in human females; the ability to regulate the sex of animal offspring; the development of organ transplantation techniques; and many more. As the biotechnology revolution was starting, Ovchinnikov and his colleagues knew that Soviet bioscientists once again risked being left out or, at best, left behind.

A man of action, Ovchinnikov acted to prevent this from happening. His approach might have appeared peculiar to a Westerner, but it was workable within the Soviet system. In the West, most important biotechnology discoveries and advances came from civilian university laboratories and, sometimes, the laboratories of the National Institutes of Health or the Department of Energy. In the Soviet Union, the Academy system—the USSR-AN, the USSR-AMN, and the agricultural academy laboratories—would have been involved in an equivalent process. Given time, Soviet biotechnology research would have probably developed this way, but it would have been a long, difficult process, as other disciplines would have been competing for the same limited academy system funding. Instead of waiting for this process to unfold, Ovchinnikov essentially made a pact with the MOD that would bring the needed support to the bioscience community in return for the MOD gaining new and improved pathogens to arm its weapon systems.

Ovchinnikov turned to the MOD because it was the most efficient bureaucracy in the Soviet system and had the funds to support large projects. But the MOD was primarily interested in military matters. If Ovchinnikov asked it for funding to develop a scientific discipline that could eventually generate applications to improve health, the environment, or agricultural productivity, MOD officials would have told him to seek help from the appropriate ministries. This would not have worked either, because ministries' work plans were guided by inflexible five-year plans and Ovchinnikov could not guarantee that investments in scientific research would generate applications that would help fulfill these plans. The ministries would also probably be afraid of supporting new technologies, because doing so might create difficulties by forcing its scientists and managers to innovate.

In contrast, the MOD was much more flexible than other Soviet ministries. It was accustomed to responding quickly to developments elsewhere in the world that could threaten the Soviet Union's ability to defend the homeland or maintain military superiority. It was also by far the best-supported ministry in the Soviet Union and spent its money with few restraints. When Ovchinnikov and Smirnov collaborated to convince the MOD and the Politburo that a revolution in biotechnology was indeed occurring and that its implications for both the offensive and the defensive aspects of BW were immense, they quickly received the MOD's support. The MOD would bring the new biosciences to the Soviet Union, albeit initially to improve or develop pathogens to arm already existing biological weapons.

ANNEX

Top Secret
Copy No. 2

List of Questions on Biological Weapons (Excerpt from Military-Industrial Complex Tasks Chapter)

25: Signatures for Biological Warfare Facilities Civilian institutions and companies working on contracts with military agencies, price and content of the contracts, results of work done under the contracts.

—Organizational measures taken in the USA and NATO countries to use the latest achievements of biology, genetics, genetic engineering, microbiology, etc. for the development and improvement of biological weapons.

—Methods used in the NATO countries to conceal work of creating and improving biological weapons.

26: —Biological means of attacking people, agricultural animals and plants; information about the development of pathogens of the following diseases as potential biological weapons: plague, tularemia, anthrax, cholera, Legionnaires' disease, melioidosis, brucellosis, glanders, epidemic typhus, Q-fever, spotted fever, Rocky Mountain fever, Tsutsugamushi fever and the like; Lassa fever, Marburg, Ebola, Rift Valley, Congo, chikungunya, Bolivian, Argentine, Crimean, and Korean hemorrhagic fevers; Japanese encephalitis, yellow fever; Venezuelan, Western, and Eastern equine encephalitis, smallpox, African swine plague, foot and mouth disease, classical fowl plague (influenza), Newcastle disease, classical swine plague.

—Methods and means used to evaluate the suitability of viruses, rickettsias, bacteria, fungi, and protists for use as potential biological weapons.

—Directions and status of research on the above-mentioned pathogens, including their altered varieties obtained by methods of genetic engineering and artificial mutagenesis. Presence and characteristics of microorganisms (from the list) with altered properties (new strains resistant to drugs and to the action of chemical and physical environmental factors, not detectable by standard serodiagnostic methods, carrying genetic determinants of virulence of heterogeneous microbial species, and capable of overcoming specific immunity).

—Modifying and obtaining hybrid toxins, study of their interaction with cell targets (receptors). Principles of forming hybrid toxins.

—Information about epidemics (epizootics, epiphytotics) and outbreaks of human (animal, plant) infectious diseases throughout the world, characteristics and specimens of newly identified strains of microorganisms (bacteria, viruses, etc.) suitable for use as potential biological weapon agents. Results of using newly identified strains, plans to conduct further research with them.

—New methods of selecting microorganisms and altering their properties on the basis of advances in genetics and genetic engineering for pathogens pertaining to potential biological weapons or model strains.

[Handwritten at bottom center of page 1: "Attachment to No. 1/318, 1/28/85]

[Handwritten at bottom right of page 1: Stamp with Lithuanian text and handwritten numbers, apparently indicating location of documents in the archives]

—Content of work on identifying and studying genetic characteristics and specific genes that determine the pathogenicity factors of microorganisms: adhesiveness, colonization, toxin formation, resistance to host immune system, resistance to drugs and unfavorable environmental factors (temperature, sunlight, mechanical action, pressure, freezing, drying, etc.). Based on this work, development of methods of altering the pathogenicity of microorganisms. Cloning of genes that determine pathogenicity, and their transfer to other organisms using various vectors.

—Designing virus vectors capable of carrying and actively expressing exogenous genetic information (short peptides in particular).

—Structure, biogenesis, and mechanisms of action of peptides that have pronounced biological activity. Identification and description of genes of these peptides.

—Results of research on microorganisms and other agents that cause demyelinating and other degenerative diseases of the central nervous system. New data on the etiology, clinical practice, and treatment of neuroinfections (Kuru, transmissible mink encephalopathy, subacute sclerosing panencephalitis, progressive multifocal leukoencephalopathy, progressive rubella panencephalitis, scrapie, Creutzfeldt-Jakob disease).

—New fundamental research in molecular biology and genetic engineering that could be used to produce bioagents for biological weapons.

27: —New data from studies of the possibility of using arthropods and other insects for artificial propagation of infectious diseases for military purposes. Information on exploratory research in this field.

28: —Technology and process equipment in biological production processes: Methods, rules, and process equipment, apparatus setup for laboratory, experimental-industrial, and industrial culturing of bacteria, viruses, and rickettsias, as well as microorganisms that produce toxins and biologically active substances. Technologies for continuous and batch delivery of additions during the culturing process.

—Production of viral (virulent and vaccine) preparations based on mammal-cell and bird-embryo cultures. Fermenter designs, foam suppression, equipment and methods for extracting and purifying toxins and physiologically active substances from cell cultures. Description of operational systems for automation of technological processes, design documentation; devices for taking samples from apparatuses (laboratory, semi-industrial, industrial) while ensuring aseptic conditions and complying with safety requirements. Methods and devices for testing the leak-tightness of quick disconnect couplings. Methods of monitoring and evaluating the efficiency of technological processes by stages. Data on the use of robotics in biotechnology.

—Methods and means of stabilizing the properties of bioagents to ensure their long-term storage without alteration of characteristics. Drying technology (lyophilization, spraying, L-drying, etc.); equipment used; drying media and additives that increase the survivability of bioagents. Distinguishing features of the production of dry formulations: comminution methods that produce highly dispersed preparations (10 μm maximum) with preservation of biological activity (cryodispersion technology); mixing of powders, physical stabilization of dispersed forms, selection of filler to ensure free flow and prevent caking, protection from UV rays.

—Distinguishing features of producing liquid formulations: concentration method and physical stabilization of liquid biomass; cryoprotectors, antioxidants, radio-, gero-, and xeroprotectors used to increase the survivability of microorganisms in liquid preparations under conditions of high and low temperatures.

—Initial raw material for production of biomass of microorganisms (for military purposes); composition of culture media that are in use and are designed to use readily available raw materials. Technical documentation for the production of the culture media in use and, in particular for industrial production of the amino acids in these compositions.

Verified: Senior operations officer, Department 7, "T" Administration
USSR KGB First Main Administration, Major

January 22, 1985   [signature]   V.M. Shabalin
No. 151/7-7672

[List named "Seen By" and containing 11 names is omitted.]

3

USSR Ministry of Defense Facilities and its Biological Warfare Program

BEFORE APPROXIMATELY 1972, all Soviet BW-related activities, both offensive and defensive, resided within the military domain. Between 1972 and 1973, officials reformulated the basic structure of the Soviet BW program, which remained essentially unchanged until April 1992, when a presidential decree nominally abolished the offensive BW program. The new structure had two major components, military and civilian, and both were directed by the 15th Directorate of the Ministry of Defense (MOD). This chapter focuses on the military aspects of the Soviet BW program since 1972 and looks at both the offensive and the defensive programs. It addresses both programs simultaneously for two reasons: first, very little is known about the MOD's offensive activities, and second, it is often impossible to separate the two types of BW activities, because both were usually performed at the same institute, with one team of military scientists working on weaponizing an agent and the second developing defenses against it. (The extent of overlap between the two teams is unknown.)

The substantive part of this chapter provides a short, general history of the military's defensive BW program. The chapter then addresses the more specific histories of the five most important Soviet MOD institutions and facilities. This recounting shows to be false the claims of some current Russian officials that the Soviet Union never had an offensive BW program and only maintained a defensive program that undertook offensive activities in order to better defend against them.

History of Defenses against Biological Weapons in the Military System

Accounts of Soviet defensive BW work that predate 1992 almost invariably used Western sources to make a case for the Soviet Union's perceived need for such defenses. This was particularly true in the 1950s and 1960s. When discussing defenses against BW, Soviet authors attributed particular information to "foreign specialists," "foreign authors," or "foreign scientists." See, for example, Labezov (1957), Belikov (1960), Rogozin (1966), Arkhangelskiy and colleagues (1967), and Myasnenko and colleagues (1983).[1] These publications also typically condemned NATO members in general, and the United States specifically:

> Aggressive military circles in the United States regard modern war as total warfare in which all means of massive attack will be widely applied. The bacteriological weapon has officially become part of the armament of the armies of countries which are members of the aggressive North Atlantic bloc (NATO), about which the text of the Paris agreements testifies, providing the creation of a reserve of the bacteriological weapon along with supplies of atomic and chemical ones.[2]

In contrast, the open Soviet literature contained limited information on Soviet BW-related scientific research and development, and it was mostly aimed at specialists. Just two books on military medicine exist that contain sections on defending against biological weapons: Agafonov et al. (1983) and Myasnenko et al. (1983).[3] These two publications address the protection of soldiers and of the public against epidemics caused by biological weapons. They describe organizations that have public health responsibilities, including those responsible for instituting quarantines and deciding on and performing triage. They provide no information on military laboratories.

Not until after the Soviet Union's dissolution did Russian authors begin publishing accounts of what was a very large defensive effort to protect the Soviet Union against BW, including those by Litovkin (1999), Orlov (2000), Rayevskiy and Dobrynin (2002), Kholstov (2002), Vorobyov (2003), and Lukina and Lukin (2004).[4] The post-Soviet-era publications are of interest because they convey information on how the defensive BW program was organized and functioned and they cast light on some of the accomplishments of the military laboratories. Major General Anatoly A. Vorobyov in particular provides a good introduction on the topic:[5]

> In response to the development of biological weapons in the United States and other countries, the USSR began developing counteraction methods in the 1940s. A number of institutes were created in the system of the USSR Ministry of Defense, laboratories and institutes of the Ministry of Health, Ministry of Agriculture, USSR Academy of Sciences and Academy of Medical Sciences, and the All-Union Academy of Agricultural Sciences. A plague control system, Institutes of the Main Administration of Vaccines and Sera, and Main Administration Biopreparat were created to solve the problems of antibacteriological protection. The result was a powerful antibacteriological protection system that worked on topics of indication, diagnosis, prophylaxis, and treatment of ultradangerous infectious diseases within the framework of the "Fifth Problem" and "Fetish program."[6,7]

There is, of course, misinformation in his statement, the main piece of which is that defensive efforts began only in the 1940s after the US commenced its offensive BW program. The anti-plague (AP) system actually predates World War II by many years (see Chapter 5). Also, Biopreparat's primary mission was to research and develop biological weapons, not "solve the problems of antibacteriological protection." Nevertheless, Vorobyov's statement indicates that a large, multiagency program was established to defend against BW, the program included research facilities from both military and civilian spheres, and all of these facilities operated as part of Problem 5 and the as yet unknown "Fetish program."

Soviet research for biological defense had seven objectives: (1) to develop and improve vaccines against BW agents that enemies might use; (2) to develop methods and protocols for immunization, using vaccines and other protective substances; (3) to develop protocols for the emergency diagnosis and treatment of soldiers exposed to BW agents; (4) to develop methods, means, and regimes for disinfection of persons and equipment contaminated by BW agents; (5) to develop methods for identifying BW agents and clarifying indications of biological attacks; (6) to develop and test field-detection systems for BW agents; and (7) to assess the possible damage of the various "recipes" an enemy might employ against the Soviet Union.[8] It is unknown when these objectives were formulated; they might have developed incrementally over the years as the BW program grew, or they may have developed at some early stage and been used thereafter to guide biological defensive research. Independent of how and when these objectives came into being, they apparently continue to guide research to this day.

The History and Work Programs of the Five Major Military BW and Facilities

Chapter 1 recounted the history of three of the five main military biological institutes—the Scientific Research Institute of Epidemiology and Hygiene in Kirov, the Scientific Research Institute of Medicine of the MOD in Zagorsk, and the Military Technical Scientific Research Institute in Sverdlovsk (renamed the Scientific Research Institute of Microbiology of the MOD in 1974)—up until approximately 1972. This chapter picks up these facilities' history where Chapter 1 left off and describes the history of two MOD facilities—the Scientific Research Institute of Military Medicine and the S. M. Kirov Military Medical Academy (RMMA) in Leningrad—that were not mentioned previously. (Aralsk-7, the important MOD open-air testing facility on Vozrozhdeniye Island, is addressed in Chapter 4.)

All of these facilities remain operational and, just as in Soviet times, the three institutes with the heaviest involvement in offensive BW (Kirov, Sverdlovsk [Yekaterinburg], and Zagorsk [Sergiyev Posad]) are inaccessible to outsiders and for the most part do not communicate information about their specific R&D activities. The basic organizational structure of these institutes, however, has changed and they are no longer independent units of the Soviet MOD. The lead agency for military research on biology is now the Scientific Research Institute of Microbiology of the Ministry of Defense of the Russian Federation in Kirov, and it has two subsidiary centers: the Virology Center of the Scientific Research Institute of Microbiology of the Ministry of Defense of the Russian Federation in Sergiyev Posad and the Center for Military-Technical Problems of Biological Defense of the Scientific Research Institute of Microbiology of the Ministry of Defense of the Russian Federation in Yekaterinburg. For convenience, we continue to refer to these institutes with the names used in Chapter 1, the Kirov Institute, the Zagorsk Institute, and the Sverdlovsk Institute.

Scientific Research Institute of Epidemiology and Hygiene in Kirov

In 1781, Catherine the Great named Vyatka city after the adjacent Vyatka River. On December 5, 1934, Stalin renamed it Kirov in memory of Sergei M. Kirov (1886–1934), the party head in Leningrad who had been assassinated just four days earlier. Although it reverted to its ancient name in 1992, this name never caught on, so it remains Kirov in popular parlance. Kirov is located 896 kilometers east of Moscow, and in 2000 it had a population of approximately 465,000.[9] The Kirov Institute was once located outside the city limits, but as a result of the city's growth, it now lies well within its urban area.[10] Ever since the Zagorsk Institute split off from it in the 1940s, the Kirov Institute has concentrated largely on investigating bacteria for both defensive and offensive purposes. In the late 1980s the Kirov Institute was made responsible for a detached facility called Kirov-200.

The Kirov Institute's Work Program

A Kirov team led by Lebedinsky and Yu. V. Chicherin focused on weaponizing *Y. pestis* in the 1960s. The main objective of this work was to develop an especially virulent *Y. pestis* strain that was resistant to the existing EV plague vaccine. The Soviet BW program did have a *Y. pestis* strain validated for BW, and it is probable that the Lebedinsky-Chicherin team was its developer. In parallel to the weaponization project, another project developed an improved vaccine against plague—one that would also protect against the weaponized strain.

In a related project, the same team is said to have developed *Y. pestis* simulants based on strains of *Y. pseudotuberculosis* and *Y. enterocolitica*. Although these zoonotic pathogens can cause low-order gastrointestinal disease in humans, certain strains are nonpathogenic and therefore are useful simulants.

Another team, led by V. A. Oborin and P. G. Vasilev, was responsible for weaponizing *F. tularensis*. It investigated two strains of *F. tularensis* in particular, namely holarctica/01s and 15/Gaysky, with the objective of increasing the pathogen's virulence and drug resistance. Sources interviewed for this book claimed that this work was successful and that it resulted in a type-classified biological weapons system. Other sources assert that the *F. tularensis* Schu-4 strain was weaponized, suggesting that at least two validated *F. tularensis* strains could have been part of the Soviet BW armory.[11] In nature, the Schu strain is considerably more virulent than the holarctica and Gaysky strains.

Table 1.1 in Chapter 1 lists Soviet first generation BW agents, including weaponized bacteria. They were all likely to have been weaponized at the Kirov Institute. Pathogens that were developed particularly for BW included *Bacillus anthracis, Brucella suis,*[12] *Burkholderia mallei,* and *Burkholderia pseudomallei.* In addition, certain salmonellae and shigellae were investigated for use as foodborne BW agents.

The Kirov Institute was well equipped, possessing at least one Biosafety Level-3 (BSL-3) unit, an extensive vivarium, a pilot plant, a small-size production plant including downstream processing equipment, chambers for aerosol testing, and an explosive test chamber.[13] It would seem that the institute also possessed a BSL-4 unit, because it worked with *Y. pestis* in its most dangerous aerosol state, but this has not been verified.[14]

One author estimated that 125 "researchers" worked at the Kirov Institute in the early 1970s.[15] Orlov provided another appraisal of the scientists working at the institute, stating: "Seven Academicians and Corresponding Members of the USSR Academy of Sciences and Academy of Medical Sciences, 28 Professors, 86 DSci, and more than 250 CanSci worked here."[16] Unfortunately, Orlov does not explain when or over what length of time these persons worked at the institute. At any point in their work, Kirov scientists would have been supported by a vastly larger number of technicians and other supportive personnel.

Kirov Institute scientific workers were said to be repressed because of the excessive secrecy that surrounded institute activities, yet in general they lived well. Their salaries were considerably higher than those of scientific workers in civilian institutes, the shops within the institute's complex carried food items and goods that were unavailable in the city, and they and their families were provided with generous vacation time that could be spent at luxurious resorts operated by the military.

In 1992 a reporter gained entry to the Kirov Institute for the first time and interviewed its director, Colonel Evgeniy V. Pimenov. The reporter was not permitted to see anything significant, such as laboratories, which explains his comment that the institute's "mysterious curtain was lifted somewhat."[17] The reporter was told that the institute performed only defensive work, and Pimenov claimed that it "produced highly effective agents against tularemia, brucellosis, anthrax, and other dangerous diseases." The institute may now emphasize its defensive work, but we cannot know for certain. As of this writing, no foreigner is known to have been admitted to the Kirov Institute.

Kirov-200

The last offensive BW facility established by the 15th Directorate was Post No. 992, which was designated a branch of the Kirov Institute. The facility, commonly called Kirov-200 Station or *Tekhnichka* by locals,[18] was built approximately 40 kilometers southwest of the Kirov Institute (near Strizhi city) in the late 1980s and occupied 44.24 hectares (109.3 acres) of fenced territory.[19] It was originally intended to be a production plant for viral and bacterial BW agents and to develop modern BW munitions. It also was to be the site of a storage facility for biological weapons.[20] Hundreds of millions of rubles were spent to build and furnish the expansive facility, which included a large building that contained laboratories; a production plant for media, small equipment, and pure water; a residence hall; a laundry building; a refrigeration center; a compressor building; a recycled-water pumping station; a cooling tower; machine shops; a gate house; and several buildings of unknown function. The facility never came on line and was largely abandoned by 1997.[21]

Someone in a leadership position must have seen the value of the site, because in 2000 the Russian government transferred its ownership to Vyatka State University for the specific purpose of establishing the Joint Interuniversity Scientific Research Center for Biotechnology and Microbiology.[22] Pimenov, a former Kirov Institute commander and then the current president of the university, may have facilitated the transfer. The new center's objectives were the "development of promising microbiological prophylactic and therapeutic preparations for use in medicine and veterinary medicine, improvement of the technology for processing raw materials from plants and animals for production of biologically active additives, and development of processes for culturing microorganisms belonging to pathogenicity groups II and III (including vaccine strains) to introduce new processes into mass biotechnological production."[23] However, the new center's administration quickly realized that most of the center's equipment and facilities were worn out, obsolete, or both. The center needed an estimated US $150 million to bring the facilities up to acceptable scientific and technical standards before it could become operational. In addition to tapping the university's own funds, in 2007 the center sought federal grants and private project funding and investment. As of late 2010, officials were working to set up a "technopark" at the site. One of the technopark's early member companies was *Agrovet*, which develops animal vaccines and nutritional supplements for animal feed.

Scientific Research Institute of Medicine of the Ministry of Defense in Zagorsk

Several sources for this book said that the Zagorsk Institute was the most secretive of the military biological institutes, possibly because its scientists worked with the most deadly viruses and there was particular concern about keeping this fact secret from the civilians in Zagorsk. (In 2002 the city's population was 113,581, less than it was during Soviet times). The curtain of secrecy was partially lifted in 2004 when a 525-page book about the institute and edited by Roza N. Lukina and Yevgeny P. Lukin was published (hereafter Lukina and Lukin).[24] The book's contributors repeatedly claim that the Russian public knew nothing about the Zagorsk Institute and therefore could not appreciate the value of the research conducted there over a 50-year period. Although poorly bound and illustrated by poor-quality photos, it provides a wealth of valuable information about the institute, its defensive R&D, staff scientists, and the community where scientists and their families lived. The book makes no mention of the R&D performed at the institute in pursuit of offensive BW capabilities. Instead, it asserts that the institute's sole purpose was to defend against US biological weapons and, in more recent times, dangerous infectious diseases that might be imported into Russia or deployed by terrorist groups. Most of the Zagorsk Institute's history described below is drawn from this book.

The History of the Zagorsk Institute's Predecessors, 1936–1954

The Zagorsk Institute has its basis in the former open USSR Ministry of Health (MOH) All-Union Scientific Research Institute for Vaccines and Sera, which was established in 1949. This institute was the source of the settlement's name "*Vaktsina*," which is still used by old-time Sergiyev Posad residents.[25] The All-Union Scientific Research Institute for Vaccines and Sera grew significantly in its short, three-year existence. Housing for the new researchers and a school for their children were built, as was a new production laboratory building (Building 1).

In the early 1950s, Soviet leaders concluded that for defensive purposes, the "bacteriological component" of a possible biological attack was "covered," whereas the "virologic component" was not. At that time, the Soviet Union had only a single virology research institute, the USSR-AMN's D. I. Ivanovsky Institute of Virology. To protect the secrecy of its efforts, the military decided that it could not use this institute to assess the threat of viruses being used for BW purposes. The government decided to open a new institute whose specialty would be the military application of viruses and rickettsiae. In 1952 the government disbanded the open All-Union Scientific Research Institute for Vaccines and Sera and supplanted it with the closed Scientific Research Institute for Sanitation, which was placed under the jurisdiction of the MOD.[26] The transfer became official on March 16, 1954, whereby the institute became a MOD scientific research institution and was named Military Unit 62992. Medical Service General M. I. Kostyuchenok was appointed the institution's first commander.[27] According to Lukina and Lukin, all of the foregoing "transformations occurred at Colonel General Smirnov's initiative and with his direct involvement."

History of the Zagorsk Institute, 1954–1991

Because the new institute was established on the grounds of an existing medical research institute, it already possessed most of the facilities and equipment required to conduct BW-related R&D. To complement existing structures, the MOD's SMU-12 (Special Construction Department 12) on short order built "warehouses, a vegetable storage cellar, barracks, a soldier's mess hall, a guard house, a building for the fire brigade, a gas filling station, and a railroad spur with a water reservoir. While single scientists were housed in the barracks, married scientists and their families rented houses and apartments in the nearby villages of Zubtsovo, Varavino, and Ryazantsy, as well as Zagorsk." By 1980 the population of *Vaktsina* had grown into the thousands and thus required additional housing, medical facilities, and schools.

Smirnov took a direct role in staffing the new institute. He retained the best staff from the Institute for Sanitation and had highly trained researchers and renowned scientists transferred from other military and civilian institutions to Zagorsk. Because most scientists had served time as officers in the Soviet Army, they were still members of the army's reserve corps, according to Soviet law. This permitted the MOD to activate them as required. Smirnov also ensured that top students from the 1954 classes of the Naval and Military Medical academies were given special training during their final year of study. Upon graduation, they were told to report to the 15th Directorate's institutes, including the Zagorsk Institute, which welcomed 60 graduates in August and September 1954. Some of the graduates who had expected to serve as medical doctors were surprised to learn that they were assigned to be bench virologists at the Zagorsk Institute. However, at least one of them reported that in general he and his cohort were pleased because they secured "steady, prestigious, and interesting work with an excellent salary (980 rubles) and the prospect of obtaining separate housing."[28]

But all was not idyllic at the new institute. In particular, security measures were oppressive and hindered the scientists' performance. A Zagorsk Institute scientist wrote that "security constraints kept the associates of one laboratory from communicating with those of another—even within a single department. This greatly impeded our work, which did not suit the associates. So they exchanged experience beyond the confines of narrow conferences, on breaks, in hallways, and wherever they could. And it would have been impossible to work further without such communication. There was simply no logic in rejecting collaboration, for example, between department No. 1 and [the department next door performing similar work]."[29] A Zagorsk entomologist named A. N. Alekseyev related another example of the frustration. He explained that in 1955, because of their work's high level of secrecy, entomologists were forbidden from traveling to Moscow libraries to research how to infect and raise mosquitoes. Instead they were sent to the medical entomology department of the Ye. I. Martsinovskiy Institute for Medical Parasitology and Tropical Medicine. With the help of Martsinovskiy Institute scientists, the Zagorsk entomologists were able to develop an effective mosquito mixture for an autogenic strain of basement mosquitoes. However, years later Alekseyev read an English-language article that described how a nearly identical mixture had been developed and successfully tested a full ten years earlier, in 1945.

Zagorsk Institute's Work Program

The Zagorsk Institute R&D program took two directions: rickettsiology and virology.

RICKETTSIOLOGY.[30] Australian scientists discovered Q fever and its causative pathogen *Coxiella burnetii* in 1945. During the next four years, the infection and pathogen was also found in the United States; the countries of the Mediterranean Basin, South American, and Central European countries; and elsewhere. In 1951, military physician I. A. Shifrin discovered Q fever in Uzbekistan's Termezskiy *oblast*, and in subsequent years the disease was found to be endemic to most of the Soviet Union's territory.

Even before Q fever was found in the Soviet Union, in 1949 a laboratory directed by V. N. Pautov in the Soviet Army's Scientific Research Institute for Epidemiology and Public Health in Kirov started researching *C. burnetii*. Pautov determined the optimum conditions for culturing *C. burnetii* in chick embryos, standardized conditions for growing *C. burnetii* in quantities sufficient for applied purposes, and clarified the dynamics of experimental Q fever in mice, guinea pigs, white and cotton rats, rabbits, dogs, cats, sheep, and pigeons. Pautov was transferred to the Zagorsk Institute in 1954, and there he initiated the second phase of his *C. burnetii* study, which continued for the next six years. It is probable that during this time, *C. burnetii* was weaponized and attained validated status.[31] In general, *C. burnetii* and members of *Rickettsia* species make for promising BW agents because they are hardy in the open environment; survive intracellularly in phagocytes, which allows them to resist host defenses; and cause difficult-to-treat debilitating diseases.

Zagorsk Institute scientists also studied *Rickettsia prowazekii* (causes epidemic typhus), *R. conori* (causes Mediterranean spotted fever), and *R. rickettsii* (causes Rocky Mountain spotted fever). The *R. conori* strains used in the research supposedly originated from Mediterranean sites, including Israel and Morocco, and their pathogenicity and antibiotic resistance were compared to *Rickettsia* strains originating in the Soviet Union and United States. Zagorsk Institute scientists studied the epidemic potency of *R. prowazekii* within a human population by estimating the extent of louse infestation and the bacterial load of the lice.[32] They may have also investigated *Ehrlichia* species that causes tick-borne infections in dogs, but also can infect humans.

In general it is very difficult to employ insect-borne pathogens for BW purposes, because dealing with two living systems, the pathogen and the vector, complicates the pathogen's deployment. Both the Soviet and the pre-1969 US BW programs investigated insect-borne combinations, but neither side, as far as is known, had any validated insect-borne weapon systems. However, some normally insect-borne pathogens can be used directly for BW purposes. For example, both Soviet and pre-1969 US BW programs weaponized *C. burnetii*. At the Zagorsk Institute, scientists developed wet and dry formulations of the *C. burnetii* Gishin strain and then tested them on Vozrozhdeniye Island on animal models, such as guinea pigs, goats, and nonhuman primates. At the successful conclusion of testing, this agent was validated for BW use.[33] In a parallel development, Soviet scientists developed the *C. burnetii* M-44 strain as an effective live enteric vaccine. The scientists involved in this work included V. V. Mikhailov and V. L. Oleichik.

The Zagorsk Institute performed important work on bacterial pathogens, with a concentration on pathogens that are obligate intracellular parasites. These pathogens' exacting growth requirements are in many ways similar to those of viruses, because both are intracellular pathogens that need whole cells for their continued existence. However, the institute's major R&D focus was viruses.

VIROLOGY AND ENTOMOLOGY.   At Zagorsk, the disciplines of virology and entomology were inextricably linked, because the institute's scientists investigated arboviruses from the institute's earliest days. In 1954, entomologists A. N. Alekseyev and Aleksey Kochetkov hand-built incubators in which they could culture mosquitoes that transmitted yellow fever virus. The entomologists also constructed tanks for mosquitoes, containers for larvae, and temperature-regulating devices, and oversaw the production of intricate blown-glass products in the institute's machine shop. About the same time, the chief of the entomology unit, Major General Dmitry V. Vinogradov-Volzhinsky, spent several years using "hit and miss" methods to develop the hydrophobic membranes required to feed bloodsuckers; he was only partially successful. Not until several years later did Sasha Konyukov succeed in creating such a feeding system at the Kirov Institute.

Although Zagorsk Institute entomologists were able to raise mosquitoes capable of transmitting yellow fever virus, the insects were not competent to transmit other arboviruses, such as Venezuelan equine encephalitis and Japanese encephalitis viruses. To fix this shortcoming, Zagorsk entomologists traveled to far eastern Siberia to collect egg clutches and the larvae of mosquitoes that lived among the cliffs on the Pacific Ocean's shore and in the Suputinsk Nature Preserve. Alekseyev writes that he "had to gather larvae and carry them in containers, transferring them from plane to plane over a 3-day period (a 55-hour flight!) and back to our home post office box."[34] Only by going to such great lengths were these scientists able to bring mosquitoes that could be cultured to carry Venezuelan equine encephalitis and Japanese encephalitis viruses. Alekseyev claims, "We never thought about whether or not it was ethical to study an unknown threat associated with potential biological weapons."[35]

ENCEPHALITIS VIRUSES.   In the late 1960s, Soviet intelligence discovered that the US BW program was weaponizing VEEV.[36] This finding probably disturbed the Soviets, because there was no vaccine to protect against this virus and no specific treatment for the disease it causes. In response, the

Zagorsk Institute launched a program both to develop an efficacious live VEE vaccine and to weaponize VEEV. When research commenced on VEEV, as well as other related viruses, much effort was placed on developing methods for propagating viruses in tissue cultures. Military scientists O. N. Panchenko and N. N. Kochetov were especially mentioned as having "blazed a promising trail of research" by developing tissue cell lines L929, Vero, BHK-21, and LECh for these purposes.[37]

Zagorsk scientists used two VEEV strains—5 and 230—to develop the vaccine, which at first had to be administered subcutaneously but was later made into an improved oral version. A live, tablet-form VEE vaccine based on strain 230 was reportedly developed by the Vorobyov team.[38] The Zagorsk Institute claimed that its vaccine conferred immunity against VEE for up to 25 years. The fate of this vaccine is unknown.[39]

Little is known about the VEEV weaponization process, although it is known that a type-classified biological weapon based on this virus was finalized at the Zagorsk Institute. One informant claims that this weapon was based on a particularly virulent strain of VEEV.[40] In addition, scientists researched the BW utility of eastern equine encephalitis virus (EEEV), Japanese encephalitis virus, and tick-borne encephalitis virus.

At the Zagorsk Institute, scientists used Langat virus (related to tick-borne and Japanese encephalitis viruses) and Sindbis virus (related to VEE and EEE viruses) as simulants for the more pathogenic encephalitis viruses, including in controlled experiments using humans. In the 1970s the Soviets briefly used Langat virus as a live vaccine to protect against more virulent tick-borne encephalitis viruses, but they found it to cause encephalitic complications in about 1 out of every 10,000 people and discontinued its use. Zagorsk Institute scientists thereafter attempted to develop inactivated whole-virus vaccines, but it is unknown how far this work advanced. Some research was also done on Rift Valley fever (RVF) virus.[41]

VIRAL HEMORRHAGIC FEVERS. Zagorsk Institute R&D with hemorrhagic fever viruses fell into three historic stages: 1967–1968, 1969–1979, and post-April 1979.[42] The first stage began after the Museum of Viruses and Rickettsiae had received strains of hemorrhagic fever viruses in the early 1960s and set up a three-person research team that included R. N. Lukina (team leader), N. I. Gonchar, and M. M. Baranova. The group was kept small due to the dangers inherent in researching these virulent pathogens and to prevent the accidental release to the wider Zagorsk community.

A lack of knowledge about the safe handling of highly pathogenic viruses was the source of the main difficulties in the first phase. At the time, safety procedures for working with viral material were based on procedures that had been developed from experience with vegetative and spore forms of bacteria. These were clearly inadequate, and new safety protocols had to be developed. Another difficulty concerned a new "type LGU pressure suit" that had to be worn by scientists working with dangerous viruses. Apparently these suits had serious flaws, such as air being fed into them directly without the use of filters and the absence of a system that provided for the possibility of autonomous breathing. In addition, the pressure suits' fabric could withstand only one or two rounds of decontamination before cracking. The three-member team worked for slightly longer than a year and during that time developed a set of special safety procedures to guide work with hemorrhagic fever viruses, including a schedule for two weeks of hands-on training using surrogate viruses. After these procedures were approved by a special scientific-technical council, "real" work on these viruses could commence.

For years, urban legends have circulated about how the Soviet Union came into possession of hemorrhagic fever–causing viruses. One particularly common legend is that brave KGB agents entered the graveyards in Marburg an der Lahn, Germany, and at high personal risk dug up corpses of victims of Marburg virus disease to obtain tissue samples carrying the virus. This is implausible because there was an official strain exchange program between West Germany and the Soviet Union at the time.

The program was launched after Marburg virus was first discovered in 1967, when Marburg an der Lahn and Frankfurt am Main, Germany, as well as Belgrade, Yugoslavia, experienced outbreaks of a mysterious and deadly illness.[43] Thirty-one people became sick, of whom seven died (there were six secondary cases). The source of the causative virus were subclinically infected African green monkeys that had been imported to Marburg/Frankfurt/Belgrade for research and to prepare poliovirus vaccines.

To head off any concern that its work with the new virus was an indication of a secret German BW program, in 1967 the German government gave a sample of the virus to Mikhail P. Chumakov, who was then the director of the USSR-AMN Scientific Research Institute of Poliomyelitis and Viral Encephalitides (now called the M. P. Chumakov Institute of Poliomyelitis and Viral Encephalitides) in Moscow. The Germans assumed that Chumakov's investigation would quickly determine that the virus could not have originated from a BW laboratory. Indeed, after Chumakov published an abstract of his initial work to characterize the virus, the Soviets did not lodge accusations of Germany having a secret BW program.[44]

In the early 1980s the Byelorussian Research Institute of Epidemiology and Microbiology in Minsk became an important conduit for the importation of hemorrhagic fever viruses into the Soviet Union. This open Soviet institute had a close relationship with the Instituut voor Tropische Geneeskunde (Institute of Tropical Medicine) in Antwerp, Belgium, that included the exchange of scientists and viral strains. In the mid-1980s an official strain exchange between the two institutions brought the Mayinga variant of Ebola virus and the Voege variant of Marburg virus to the Byelorussian Research Institute. It is safe to assume that both of these viruses were transported from Minsk to the Zagorsk Institute in short order.

The second phase of Zagorsk R&D with hemorrhagic fever viruses was directed by Viktor M. Zhdanov, who was an USSR-AMN academician and director of the D. I. Ivanovsky Institute of Virology. Zhdanov's work focused on obtaining protective vaccine and serum preparations against Marburg virus Popp, as well as on conducting basic research and developing methods to propagate and store Lassa virus strain Sierra Leone and Machupo virus strain Carvallo (Machupo virus causes Bolivian hemorrhagic fever). Most of this work was performed in Building 18 after it had been redesigned and rebuilt to the point where it was deemed suitable for conducting research with exotic viral pathogens. R&D was conducted under conditions of total isolation and involved the use of improved type LGU protective pressure suits.

The scientists most responsible for Marburg virus research were N. I. Gonchar and V. A. Pshenichnov. Early in the second phase, Gonchar and Pshenichnov enlisted immunologists A. I. Khrulkov and A. A. Selivanenko to develop "heterological rabbit gamma-globulin" that could be injected into workers who had been accidentally exposed to Marburg virus. On the basis of their work, other protective vaccine and serum preparations were developed, including what they believed was a more effective gamma globulin from horse serum. This development led to the Zagorsk Institute having on hand the gamma globulin that later was used for the unsuccessful treatment of Vector scientists Nikolay V. Ustinov and L. A. Akinfeeva.[45] However, to this day there is no effective and dependable treatment of Marburg virus infection.

The pace of Marburg virus research increased in 1976 when new scientists were added to the research team in Building 18, including V. A. Pokhodyayev (who studied contact and aerogenic infection), M. N. Pistsov (who together with V. F. Prokhor developed a method for quantitative evaluation on plaque formation), I. V. Firsova (who assessed the susceptibility of different animal models to Marburg virus infection), and histologist V. M. Chernykh (who alleged that Marburg virus's effect on nonhuman primates and guinea pigs was "comparable to the effect of radiation, leading to developing of fourth-degree radiation sickness in man and animals").[46]

The third stage of the R&D began when Building 75 opened in April 1979. Although Lukina and Lukin do not describe this building, they do write that it allowed research to be "conducted under more comfortable conditions using modern manufacturing equipment and automated means of protecting laboratory personnel and the environment." They note that the culmination of this third stage of research was the "development of heterologous immunoglobulin for emergency prophylaxis of Ebola fever. In addition, the resultant experimental sample of inactivated vaccine proved highly effective when animals that had been immunized were infected."[47]

The Russian government in 1995 announced that scientists at the Zagorsk Institute, now called the Virological Center of the Ministry of Defense's Institute of Microbiology, had developed a treatment for Ebola virus disease. Reporter Yu. Gladkevich wrote: "Ebola fever has yielded to Russian scientists, although they are conducting a scientific quest in poverty."[48] The director of the center at the time, Major General Aleksandr Makhlay, was awarded the Hero of Russia award for having directed this work.[49] Russia reportedly sold 100 doses of the treatment to the World Health Organization (WHO) for evaluation, and the WHO provided some of the doses to the US Army Medical Research Institute for Infectious Diseases (USAMRIID) for analysis. A popular lay publication published an article about this transfer and claimed that the US analysis of this supposedly curative potion revealed that it was "highly purified immunoglobulin G (IgG) with a high concentration that neutralizes the Ebola virus."[50] However, while by now several vaccine and treatment regimens exist that completely protect nonhuman primates from Ebola disease, nothing has yet been developed for use in humans.

VARIOLA VIRUS.   Similar to the urban legends about acquisition of hemorrhagic fever viruses, we have heard fantastic stories about how the Soviet BW program supposedly acquired the India-1967 strain of variola virus, including one that described KGB agents taking samples from dead or living smallpox victims in India. The real story regarding variola virus acquisition was probably much more mundane. Soviet officials could have acquired the strain as a result of the December 1959 Moscow smallpox outbreak, whose index case was an Indian who arrived on an aircraft from New Delhi.[51] The man became ill on December 23, 1959, and was at first misdiagnosed as suffering from louse-borne typhus, which commonly presents with a skin rash. He died on December 29. After other victims began presenting with rashes about January 11, the correct diagnosis of smallpox was made. By the time the outbreak was contained, 46 persons had been diagnosed as having contracted smallpox, of whom three died. Although this fatality rate appears to indicate that the causative variola virus strain had a relatively low level of virulence, a better explanation for the low fatality rate is that most, perhaps all, of the victims had previously been vaccinated against smallpox.[52]

Another plausible way in which Soviet institutes could have obtained the India-1967 strain is that the Institute for Viral Preparations in Moscow, which was a WHO smallpox reference center (see below), may have received the India-1967 variola virus strain as part of a normal exchange of strains between WHO reference centers. At the time, smallpox was prevalent throughout the world, and it was not unusual for laboratories to share strains. However the strain was acquired, the Soviets did not need to engage in skullduggery to obtain it.

The most likely source of the variola virus that was weaponized was the infected Indian visitor of 1959. According to a 2004 account, when it became clear to Soviet authorities that the outbreak was indeed smallpox, they called upon assistance from the Zagorsk Institute, which sent some of its scientists to Moscow.[53] They of course collected blood and tissue samples from the smallpox victims, which were analyzed at their home institute. The strain recovered was weaponized over a period of eight years and after being validated was called India-1967. It could be propagated rather easily in large quantities in embryonated eggs. After some years of development, the strain was used to arm type-classified bomblets that were tested on Vozrozhdeniye Island, one of which caused the accidental release in 1971 discussed in Chapter 4.

From 1963 to 1973, N. P. Chizhov, A. I. Polozov, V. P. Krasnyanskiy, and Pautov conducted research on the chemotherapeutic and chemoprophylactic properties of a number of chemotherapy agents using poxvirus cultures grown in chick embryos, suckling mice, and nonhuman primates. In addition, I. P. Ashmarin, Pautov, and Chizhov jointly evaluated the promise of using nuclease and histone fractions as chemotherapeutic and immunomodulating agents with experimental variola virus. They found that methisazone did not prevent variola virus from infecting cells, but it did disrupt the pathogen's development, thereby having a clear effect on the course of smallpox infection.[54]

L. P. Pautov and V. D. Savve simultaneously conducted extensive research on methods to detect variola virus and achieve early diagnosis of smallpox. Their work reportedly achieved promising results that allowed for the rapid identification of variola virus in different "environmental objects" and in air samples, as well as the quick detection of antibodies in people vaccinated against smallpox and in monkeys infected with variola virus.

In the beginning in the 1960s, institute researchers attempted to develop improved methods for immunization against smallpox. The head of the virology department at that time, Valerian D. Neustroyev, was especially interested in developing an aerogenous vaccine against smallpox, but nothing has been openly published about this effort.

MUSEUM OF VIRUSES AND RICKETTSIAE. In 1954 the institute established the Museum of Viruses and Rickettsiae, of which the institute is exceedingly proud to this day. The museum's permanent director for the next 35 years, Roza N. Lukina, established the museum's main scientific directions, which included clarifying and evaluating the properties of pathogens sent to the Zagorsk Institute. Current Zagorsk Institute staff members are particularly proud of the museum's National Collection of Viruses of Hemorrhagic Fevers of the First Pathogenicity Group. The Ebola virus Mayinga variant used to develop the immunoglobulin potion described above was obtained from this collection.

VIVARIUM AND FARM. A vivarium was built at the institute as early as 1954 to house the many hundreds, perhaps thousands, of animals required for animal testing. Such testing allowed scientists to observe the results of experimental infections, pathogen propagation, prophylaxis methods, treatment regimes, and agent detection methods. Monkeys were especially valuable subjects, so the terrarium housed many types of primates, including African green monkeys, cynomolgus macaques, rhesus monkeys, chimpanzees, and baboons. In addition, the institute established a farm on an adjacent 11 hectares of land to grow produce required to feed the animals.

LIBRARY. In 1954, officials established a scientific-technical library at the Scientific Research Institute for Sanitation of the Ministry of Defense. The library's scientific holdings included scientific publications from the libraries of the Veterinary Institute of the Red Army and the All-Union Scientific Research Institute for Vaccines of the USSR Ministry of Health, as well as German-language publications "liberated" from the library of the Imperial Research Institution on the Isle of Riems, which was captured in waning days of World War II. In 2004 the library's holdings included more than 56,100 volumes in Russian and 5,090 in foreign languages, approximately 80,000 scientific periodicals in Russian and foreign languages, 5,300 inventors' certificates, 1,690 patents, as well as many abstracts and special publications. The library has three or four permanent translators on its staff. As a result of their activity, the library's archives contain more than 3,000 translations from the main European languages on special scientific topics.[55]

INFORMATION ANALYSIS DEPARTMENT.   Soviet officials moved an Information Analysis Department that was established in 1954 at the Sverdlovsk Institute to the Zagorsk Institute in 1968. The department analyzed data from aerobiological experiments to determine the effectiveness of protective agents. At first the department was equipped with slide rules, abacuses, and electromechanical calculators that were captured from the Germans in 1945 and that performed four arithmetic operations. In 1968 the department acquired computers for the first time. The Minsk-22 computer that it used was derided as being only "slightly more powerful than a modern programmable pocket calculator," yet it occupied a very large space. The computer required a maintenance staff—a group of engineers that serviced the machine's units and loaded the operating system. A separate group prepared the punch tape on which the programs for the calculations and input data were written. In 1983 the department was moved to a larger facility in Building 5, and the Minsk-22 was replaced by a third generation YeS-1045 computer.

The department's central tasks also included selecting generalized effectiveness indices that characterized an experiment's quality; selecting a generalized indicator of a living organism's condition that could be used to ascertain deviations for the norm; and assessing the damage from biological sabotage. With the increase of the terrorist threat in the early 2000s, the department began working on new tasks—specifically, supporting operation of the biological channel Unified System for Identification and Estimation of Scales and Consequences of the Use of Weapons of Mass Destruction (YeSVOP).

In response to the dire 1992 Russian financial crisis, the department's command had to take "strict measures" to reduce the use of electric power. Because the YeS-1045 used 55 kW of electric power, the unit commander forbade its use, unplugged it, and sealed up the switch providing electricity to Building 5. This ban coincided with the "obsolescence" of big computers; personal computers performed virtually all of the computations required in the department. The number of personal computers consequently began growing steadily, and the computer laboratory's collective, which was headed by lieutenant colonel Ye. P. Chernatkin, launched a new direction of work: performing personal computer maintenance and repair; automating the operation of the scientific departments, financial and supply services, and personnel department; linking computers in a network; and training workers in the use of the most popular programs. Beginning in 1989, the department played a role in the State System for Protecting the Troops and Population Against Weapons of Mass Destruction. To this day it is engaged in mathematical forecasting of the development of epidemic processes both by order of the RF-MOD and scientific institutions of the Russian Academy of Medical Sciences.

PRODUCTION AND INSTRUMENTATION. The Zagorsk Institute reportedly possessed sufficient production and processing equipment for the pilot-scale production of viral and rickettsial BW agents but not for full industrial-scale production.

The institute is said to have developed and produced an instrument for use in biological intelligence. Named ASP (for the Russian Automatic Mixture Indicator), this tabletop-size instrument was supposedly useful for detecting and identifying pathogens of BW potential. The ASP was produced at the Krasnogvardeyets Plant in Narva, Estonian SSR, and was delivered to the Soviet armed forces beginning in the 1970s. Institute scientists were still working on improving the ASP when the Soviet Union dissolved in December 1991.

FOREIGN WORK. According to Lukina, Soviet specialists worked at a virology laboratory in Kindia, Republic of Guinea, in 1980, possibly on Lassa virus.

Zagorsk Institute in Russia

After 1991 the country's economic failure forced the institute's leadership to focus on survival, so work on research projects diminished to near zero. In particular, the development and manufacture of new drugs (including antibiotics and antiviral chemotherapy agents) ceased, as it was not possible for the institute to acquire reagents, equipment, and laboratory animals. Sometime in the middle 1990s the situation appeared to improve, but we do not know why and to what extent.

A television broadcast in 1999 showed pictures of the institute to the public for the first time. The television reporter focused on a particular incident in what was described as the "laboratory of dangerous infections," a BSL-4-like facility (Zagorsk workers call it "the Third Zone").[56] In 1997 a lab assistant working in this facility cut herself while handling Ebola virus and neglected to inform anyone of the accident. After a short illness, she died and was buried in "a sack filled with calcium hypochlorite."[57]

In 1999 the Russian government established a new biological research center on the grounds of the Zagorsk Institute. The MOD and MOH joint order establishing the center, "Concerning the Center for Special Laboratory Diagnosis and Treatment of Ultradangerous and Exotic Infectious Diseases," identified the center's goal as improving Russia's ability to fight infectious diseases.[58] The center is also meant to be at the forefront of meeting the bioterror threats. Its objectives are to:

• conduct laboratory diagnosis of ultradangerous and exotic diseases based on identification of pathogens and antibodies against them;
• isolate pathogens from samples and subsequently identify and deposit them in culture collections;
• hospitalize and treat individuals with (or suspected of having) ultradangerous and exotic infections;
• develop new means and methods for special laboratory diagnosis and improve the system for preventing and eradicating the consequences of importation of ultradangerous and exotic diseases into the Russian Federation's territory.[59]

In 2006 the Swedish Defence Research Agency (known by its Swedish acronym FOI) published en extensive report that includes sections on the Virological Center of the Ministry of Defense's Institute of Microbiology and the Center for Special Laboratory Diagnosis and Treatment of Ultradangerous and Exotic Infectious Diseases. FOI analysts surveyed the scientific literature for articles and books written by authors from the Zagorsk Institute and analyzed the contents of these publications to determine the institute's current and past research directions and its scientific/technical capabilities.[60] The purpose of this study was only to review what the institute had produced; it drew no conclusions.

Military Technical Scientific Research Institute in Sverdlovsk

Sverdlovsk is the main city in the Sverdlovsk *oblast* and is located 1,422 kilometers directly east of Moscow. The city was founded in 1723 by Peter the Great and named Yekaterinburg (in some transliterations, Ekaterinburg) after his wife, Catherine. It was renamed Sverdlovsk in 1924 in honor of the Bolshevik official Yakov M. Sverdlov (1885–1919), whom some historians believe to have signed the death warrant for the Romanov family in 1918. As part of the effort begun in 1991 by Yeltsin to rename cities and streets to their original, pre-Bolshevik names, Sverdlovsk once again became Yekaterinburg. The city's current population is about 1.5 million, which makes it Russia's third largest city. It is mainly known as a grim industrial city and is at times referred to as Russia's Pittsburgh because of its large steelmaking industry.

The establishment of the Sverdlovsk Institute and its early work program were described in Chapter 1. The institute is perhaps best known as having been responsible for an anthrax outbreak in 1979, an often-recounted event that still reverberates today because of its implications for biological arms control and the Russian government's veracity. This section describes the institute's facilities and work program and, as part of the second, provides new information on the technical aspects of the outbreak. Chapter 15 discusses the outbreak's aftermath as related to arms control and international politics.

The Sverdlovsk Institute was located within a military cantonment variously named Sverdlovsk-19, the 19th Cantonment, and Compound 19. To the southeast of Compound 19 was Compound 32, which housed armored and artillery units. The two were under the same military authority and were connected by an underground tunnel. Because Compound 32 had no connection to BW, it is hereafter noted only in passing.

Some observers have questioned the wisdom of locating a BW facility in the middle of a large city. According to a Russian journal, the institute was located in Sverdlovsk for "historical reasons": "In 1949, when Beria stood at the site of the future Sverdlovsk-19, the site was an undeveloped area covered by forest. Then the city grew and eventually swallowed up the military settlement. A meat combine, a dairy combine, and other ventures were constructed alongside. Thus, Sverdlovsk-19 wound up in the center of the very large

Chkalovsk region [of Sverdlovsk]."[61] The same journal article also asserts that Yeltsin, who was the first secretary of the Sverdlovsk *oblast* Party Committee of the CPSU in 1979, raised the issue about moving Compound 19 with officials in Moscow, but he was rebuffed. In any case, local authorities were not supposed to know about the activities that took place within Compound 19.

Little is known about what Compound 19 was like before 1990, when a reporter was first granted access to the compound.[62] A second reporter was granted access in 1992,[63] and a television crew was allowed on the premises in 1993.[64] These three reports give a picture of what the facility may have looked like in those days, which probably was not so different from how it looked pre-1979, though its work program had supposedly changed completely.

In the Soviet era, Compound 19's 200 hectares (495 acres) were divided into three zones: living quarters, "pre-zone," and "special zone." The compound's estimated population in the early 1990s was 7,000, including scientists, guards, and dependents. Upon passing through the main gate of the compound, visitors left the noise and dirt of the city behind them and entered what looked like a peaceful resort with low stone buildings sited between pretty trees. The compound's staff lived and amused themselves in this area; there were two schools, a daycare center, a stadium, parks, and walkways. Toward the compound's center was a barbed-wire fence and a checkpoint for the "pre-zone," the industrial zone where the facilities that supported the laboratories—such as warehouses and the media-production union—were sited. A few steps past the checkpoint was a revolving gate with more guards, who performed more rigorous security checks before allowing visitors entry into Compound 19's most secret special zone. This zone housed buildings with underground laboratories and production units staffed by workers garbed in space suits. One of these buildings contained a production facility that was the source of the *B. anthracis* spores that caused the 1979 outbreak. The reporter who visited the site in 1992 toured five laboratories in this area, although there might have been more.[65] Because she was not a specialist, the reporter's descriptions of the labs were superficial.

Pre-1992 Activity

Before 1972 the Sverdlovsk Institute's main research focus was BoNT and *Bacillus anthracis,* but in the 1960s and 1970s, interest in the first faded and then disappeared. At the same time, *B. anthracis* R&D expanded, and this pathogen was to become the Soviet Union's major BW agent. According to Burgasov, the Americans were responsible for this development:

> The direction of research at Sverdlovsk-19 was changed after our intelligence service bought the American plan for research on the military uses of anthrax for 100,000 rubles; this is the first time I've ever reported this.
>
> You can't develop antidote without knowing the poison. This is why we produced it [*B. anthracis* spores] in doses necessary for our experiments. The tests were conducted underground, at very great depth. The blast wave carried the virus [*sic*] to experimental animals; horses, cows, goats. If they were not immunized, they died like flies. But the immunized ones remained healthy.
>
> By the way, the Americans and the English were doing research exclusively for defense.[66]

The statements about Sverdlovsk scientists switching their focus (from BoNT) to *B. anthracis* are substantiated by information provided by sources for this book. However, Burgasov's assertion that the Sverdlovsk Institute was involved only in defense work is false, and the statement about the Americans and English is difficult to interpret. It is correct that the British BW program ended its offensive work around 1956, but continued to develop defenses against biological weapons based on *B. anthracis* and other agents until the present time. The existence of an offensive US BW program was public knowledge and was discussed in congressional testimony every year until 1969 and it certainly studied "military uses of anthrax" until late 1969. Burgasov's reference to purchasing "the American plan" almost certainly refers to a US deception plan described in detail in Chapter 13. But the assertion that "Americans and the English were doing research exclusively for defense" is correct if he is talking about post-1969, but not correct, at least for the Americans, if he means pre-1969. As is frequently the case with Burgasov, his disjointed statements consist of part fact and part lies.

The institute's emphasis on *B. anthracis* is captured by technician A. A. Volkov, who worked in its special zone between 1967 and August 1979:

> Scientists at the research institute were working on purely technological topics, while we were already developing equipment to their specifications. I am not sure whether it is permitted to say this, but everything

was connected with anthrax cultures. That is to say all the scientific topics dealt with anthrax, and the equipment was designed to insert anthrax spores into munitions. I myself am not familiar with the biological aspects. My job was concerned with equipment. I knew about density, specific weight . . . I was familiar with these sorts of details. And I knew how to handle these things, what precautions had to be taken. We worked in gas masks and full chemical protection rubber suits.[67]

According to two investigative reporters from the journal *Sovershenno Sekretno,* at least part of the Sverdlovsk Institute's biological production was shipped elsewhere to be loaded into munitions.[68] One of these locations was the city of Zlatoust. Located on the Ai River in the southern Ural Mountains, the city is 200 kilometers due south of Sverdlovsk and 1,500 kilometers due east of Moscow. It was founded in 1754 as one of Russia's first iron industry settlements and was especially noted for the excellence of the swords it manufactured. In Soviet times, Zlatoust had steel mills, metal-engraving works, farm machinery industries, an instrument-making industry, precision-casting plants, and clock manufacturing facilities. Zlatoust's military-industrial complex manufactured components for both nuclear and conventional weapons. According to the *Sovershenno Sekretno* reporters, dry and wet biological agent formulations were transported to Zlatoust and loaded into munitions.[69] The 50- and 250-liter stainless steel containers (TR-50 and TR-250) that were used to store bulk BW agents in bunkers in such facilities as Stepnogorsk and Kazan were probably manufactured in Zlatoust.

Technical Details Related to the 1979 Anthrax Outbreak in Sverdlovsk

Much has been written about the 1979 anthrax outbreak in Sverdlovsk. This book's discussion of the outbreak adds information that has not been previously published and makes note of some of the mistakes and exaggerations that have circulated about it.

The most complete and accurate work to date on the 1979 outbreak is an article written by Matthew Meselson and colleagues on the methods and findings of a thorough epidemiological investigation of the Sverdlovsk outbreak, as well as a follow-up book written by Jeanne Guillemin, who participated in that investigation.[70] This section adds some technical details to what was revealed in these two publications and offers some thoughts on the quantity of *B. anthracis* spores released from Compound 19.[71]

Google Earth imagery provides an astoundingly clear view of Compound 19 (56° 46' 41.24" N; 60° 35' 08.51" E) as it existed in 2005. Compound 19's important structures include the production building from which a mass of *B. anthracis* spores was accidentally released sometime during April 2–3, 1979. The spores created a plume that the wind carried over parts of Sverdlovsk and into a rural area.

The release originated in a four-story building (with a basement), sited in the special zone, which housed a production unit that manufactured dry *B. anthracis* spores for biological weapons use. The building was sectioned into three zones, with zone 1 encompassing parts of the building that were lightly contaminated with whatever pathogen was being worked on, zone 2 moderately contaminated, and zone 3 heavily contaminated. The fourth story had mostly air-handling equipment and was zone 1. The third story had several small fermenters up to 1 cubic meter in size and was zone 2. The second story had several large fermenters up to 50 cubic meters in size and was zone 2. The first story had separators where the fermentation mixture was separated into spent media and biomass; it was zone 3. The basement contained mixing tanks, where biomass was mixed with chemicals to produce formulations, and spray dryers for drying formulations; this was also zone 3. The air used for drying the formulations was conveyed by an air-handling system to an exhaust chimney, through three filters, and into the open environment. When dry, the formulation was milled to a dustlike consistency, whose particles were less than 5 microns in diameter (one micron equals one millionth of a meter), and the dust was stored in stainless steel tanks. The drying and milling of spores is a messy process that produces dangerous dust in copious quantities. In recognition of this threat, the production building was sealed, and only carefully filtered air was let out. A production team that numbered approximately 40 persons and was commanded by Lieutenant Colonel Nikolay Chernichov operated the production facility in this building. An additional three buildings at the Sverdlovsk Institute housed production plants for BW agents. A filling and storage depot in Zima, away from Sverdlovsk, handled the filling of munitions with the dried formulation.

There are two differing accounts of the exact time of the pathogen release. The first is based on information from Russian sources that were provided with the information secondhand from members of the actual production team. According to the sources, the release occurred as a result of a defect in the air-handling system that carried exhaust from the spray dryer. The exhaust from the dryer usually was conveyed to the outside environment through a structure that looked like a chimney. Before release to the outside, the exhaust from the dryer was conveyed through a pre-filter and two filters. The pre-filter, which was called a "hand" filter because its shape resembled a hand, was made of cloth covered with some sort of fungal layer. Its function was to remove larger particles from the exhaust. The exhaust then passed through two high-efficiency particulate air (HEPA) filters whose function was to remove all particles that had a diameter larger than 0.3 microns (a *B. anthracis* spore's size is 1 - 3 microns). During the day of April 2 the production unit's day crew had removed the two HEPA filters to check on their efficacy and had not replaced them. According to this crew, it had notified the operations center that the spray dryer whose exhaust lacked filters was not to be used until the filters were replaced. However, the night crew came in and for some unknown reason was not informed of the dryer's condition. It started a regular *B. anthracis* spore production cycle, including drying. That the HEPA filters were missing was discovered only when the pre-filter ruptured because of overload, causing a sudden drop of air pressure in the air-handling system that was immediately detected. The night crew shut down the air-handling system as quickly as it could, but the drying process nevertheless continued for about three hours before complete shutdown was accomplished. Thus, according to this source, the release occurred during the evening or night of April 2–3.

The conclusion arrived at by the investigation carried out by Meselson et al. differed from the foregoing account regarding the time of release.[72] Based on their study of wind data for April 2 and 3, interviews with families and friends of five victims, and diary notes made at the time by one of the victims, the probable time of release was during the day of April 2.

We have chosen to provide both narratives in this book. The meteorological data and information from interviews and diaries provide a solid basis for assuming an April 2 daytime release. Further, the quality of secondhand information gained from interviews with our sources may have been negatively affected by the passage of time and dates being confused. But there is no reason to doubt the description of the events and errors that led to the accidental release.

Returning to the narrative provided by the Russian sources, after the release had been detected, the night crew immediately informed the Compound 19 administration of the accident (its commander was General V. V. Mikhaylov), but were told to keep quiet about it. Between themselves, crew members postulated various horrific scenarios of what could happen, but of course they did not discuss the matter outside the building. The administration immediately informed Moscow of the accident and was told to keep quiet. The problem that arose was that no one could figure out how to convey information to, for example, local health authorities without breaking strict secrecy rules. Due to those rules, no civilian Communist Party or municipal official in Sverdlovsk knew that BW agents were being produced within Compound 19, and the MOD did not wish this fact to become known, even at the expense of possible civilian casualties.[73] The generals probably were hoping that the escaped particles would blow away and no one would be the wiser.

Of course, that did not happen. The first victim presented with symptoms as early as April 4. The unusually quick manifestation of anthrax symptoms may have been due to heavy exposure experienced by victims who had been exposed closer to the emission source and/or because the weaponized *B. anthracis* strain 836 was more infective and virulent than natural strains (see below). In fact, an estimate made by the U.S. Defense Intelligence Agency two years before the outbreak supports this explanation: "The Soviets have modified the germination rate of *Bacillus anthracis* to allow more rapid infection of the host."[74]

To this day the final tally of victims is not known with certainty. In his April 2006 Russian press interview, Burgasov states, referring to the Sverdlovsk Institute, that "finally, corpses were revealed in the secret laboratory," thus admitting that deaths due to anthrax did occur within the MOD facility, something that the officials, including Burgasov, had repeatedly denied during the Soviet period.[75] In a 2006 volume published in Russia and edited by Gennady Lepeshkin, it is stated that: "According to the official data, 95 people were infected, 68 (71.5%) died, [but] actually the number of the dead and infected was larger."[76] Alibek reports the number of deaths as 105.[77]

One question that has often been asked is why so few persons in Compounds 19 and 32 contracted anthrax (according to available information, 6 and 11, respectively). Having posed this question to our Russian sources, there seemed to be three explanations: (1) the tall chimney (at least 25 meters but probably taller) released the aerosol at such a high altitude that by far most of its particles did not settle until outside the perimeters of the compounds; (2) everyone working in Compound 19 was vaccinated against anthrax; and (3) soon after the release occurred, everyone in Compounds 19 and 32 was given prophylactic antibiotics.

After the accident, an internal inquiry was held, and although it concluded that the release had been caused by human error, no one was held responsible. Chernichov, the head of the production team, was reportedly exonerated because he was on vacation at the time of the accidental release.[78] The production team was put to work to decontaminate and then close down the facilities used for the production of BW agents and, eventually, to convert some of them to manufacturing antibiotics. In 1984 the entire team, including Chernichov, was transferred to Biopreparat's production plant in Stepnogorsk and thus came to work once again at a production facility designed for the large-scale production of *B. anthracis* for BW purposes (see Chapter 9).[79]

Since news of the Sverdlovsk anthrax outbreak was first published, there has been much speculation on the quantity of *B. anthracis* spores released by the accident. It is impossible to calculate exactly how much dry spore formulation was discharged, because the rate of leakage when the pre-filter was in place cannot be measured and neither can the larger but shorter discharge after the pre-filter ruptured. Further, the concentration of spores in the released aerosol cannot be calculated with accuracy because the material that escaped through the air-handling system was composed of a mixture of high concentration exhaust from dryers and low concentration exhaust from working rooms.

The first public estimate of the amount of material that might have been released was offered in a US Senate hearing in 1989. At a time when at least part of the US government intelligence community still believed the *B. anthracis* release had been caused by an explosion in the site, Barry Erlick, a US Army senior biological warfare analyst, stated that "approximately ten pounds of anthrax was released."[80] This was an enormous amount, particularly in view of the relatively small number of deaths that resulted. Note that Erlick spoke of "ten pounds *of anthrax*," but must have meant *B. anthracis* spores.

The second estimate to appear was much lower. In the final lines of the report in *Science* in 1994 by Meselson and his group, following a detailed presentation of the variables that would have affected the rates at which individuals in the area under the plume of aerosolized material could have succumbed to infection, the authors wrote: "If these divergent estimates bracket the actual value, the weight of spores released as aerosol could have been as little as a few milligrams or as much as nearly a gram."[81] In a subsequent publication that presented detailed calculations for his estimates, Meselson wrote: "The question of whether the aerosol released at Sverdlovsk consisted only of viable spores or also contained inviable spores and other material is obviously not addressed in the present estimates."[82] This critical caveat probably provides the key to reconciling the skepticism of some members of the US biodefense community that the amount released would have had to be larger. When Meselson presented the results of the investigation of his team in Sverdlovsk at USAMRIID in 1995, a sizable portion of the audience was skeptical that the weight of *B. anthracis* spores released could have been so small.[83]

As part of his investigation, Meselson made low and high estimates of the amount of *B. anthracis spores* that were needed to cover the estimated affected area and cause the number of recorded casualties. Meselson's estimates were made on a theoretical basis; that is, under ideal conditions, how many spores would it take to infect the number of stated victims, spread over 4 square kilometers, and exposed to a formulation whose ID_{50} was 8,000 spores? As indicated, his low estimate was a few milligrams and the high estimate was somewhat less than one gram.[84] Another scholar, Dean Wilkening, using a model of atmospheric diffusion more sophisticated than that used by Meselson, arrived at nearly the same estimates. Wilkening concluded that his estimates "agree, within the uncertainties associated with different input parameters, with Meselson's calculations."[85]

Aware that Meselson's and Wilkening's estimates were made on a theoretical basis, we sought advice of two practitioners, one from the United States and the other from the former Soviet Union, who possessed the requisite practical expertise on aerosol dispersal. The US expert was Alan J. Mohr, a respected aerobiologist who had worked at the Dugway Proving Ground for many years. The second individual was a scientist who worked in the former Soviet BW program for an equally long period of years. Their estimate is based on their experience over many years regarding characteristics of formulations and their behavior as aerosols in the open air. The following factors entered into their considerations. First, the *B. anthracis* strain 836 reportedly was more virulent than the Vollum strain used by the pre-1969 US BW program. Second, Soviet weapon scientists presumed that the ID_{50} for this strain was 10,000.[86] Third, the Soviet BW program had, after years of open-air testing, come to the conclusion that the Q_{50} for its *B. anthracis* dry formulation was between 2.5 and 5 kilograms. In other words, it took between 2.5 and 5 kilograms of the formulation dispersed evenly over 1 square kilometer under favorable meteorological conditions to infect 50 % of the persons occupying that area (see Table 3.1 for Q_{50} estimates made by Alibek). Fourth, the size of the area within which the victims of the outbreak were located when exposed was approximately 4 square kilometers.[87] After having taken into account the four parameters, the two practitioners estimated

Table 3.1 Examples of Q_{50} for Formulated Pathogens for Soviet Biological Weapons and Their Stability in Air

BW agent	Formulation	Q_{50}	Stability in air[a]
Bacteria			
Bacillus anthracis	Dry	4.5–5 kg/km^2	Days–weeks
Bacillus anthracis	Wet	5–5.5 liters/km^2	Days–weeks
Brucella suis	Dry	4.5 kg/km^2	<2 days
Burkholderia mallei	Wet	4.5–5.5 liters/km^2	Several hours
Burkholderia pseudomallei	Wet	4.5–5.5 liters/km^2	Several hours
Francisella tularensis	Dry	3–4 kg/km^2	Several hour–<1 day
Yersinia pestis	Wet	3.5–4.5 liters/km^2	1–2 hours
Viruses			
Marburg virus	Dry	> 1 kg/km^2	Several hours
Variola virus	Wet	3.5–4.5 liters/km^2	<24 hours

Source: Ken Alibek, "Biological Weapons/Bioterrorism Threat and Defense: Past, Present and Future," Presentation at the National Center for Biodefense at the George Mason University, 2005.

a. Because many factors can affect the half-life of organisms in the open air, the estimates in this column are for a theoretical ideal situation of temperate temperature and humidity, and when release is affected at night.

that the total weight of the release—not spores alone—was between 0.5 and 1 kilogram.

The differing estimates are actually descriptions of different things that are not directly comparable. Meselson's is a theoretical calculation, whereas the estimate made by the two practitioners is based on their past empirical experience with open-air testing of *B. anthracis* formulations or simulants, albeit with test animals and not with humans. Meselson's calculation is based on an emission of pure spores at a concentration of 10^{12} spores per ml. The two practitioners assume a mixture of formulation containing *B. anthracis* spores plus added materials and whatever was the ambient concentration in the working space that was being emitted through the faulty exhaust system. Both practitioners agreed that under real-life conditions, 1 gram of spores would "disappear" by being dispersed by wind and sticking to surfaces. Therefore they suggested that the actual quantity of spores released by the accident would have been much greater than the amount that eventually reached the area populated by victims. Nevertheless, if the estimate made by the two practitioners for the total weight of aerosol assumed that the released aerosol contained 10^8–10^9 spores per gram, their estimate for the weight of spores in the aerosol would range from a few milligrams to about a gram, the same as the estimates of Meselson and Wilkening.

It is also significant that Meselson and his team found that the anthrax victims in Sverdlovsk did not represent infection occurring at the LD_{50} dose response level. Instead, the fatality rate within the specified area was much lower, which would require a much smaller number of spores. In addition, in a paper published in *International Security* in 2001, Steven Fetter had calculated that a distribution of 1 kilogram of a wet slurry of *B. anthracis* would produce an ID_{50} over 4 to 25 square kilometers.[88] Scaling down wet slurry to dry spores would bring the 1 kilogram to less than 1 gram.

One additional question about the Sverdlovsk anthrax outbreak remains: What was the composition of the formulation that was released? As a result of the Meselson investigation, which included securing samples, scientists at several American laboratories obtained formalin-fixed tissue samples preserved in paraffin blocks from 11 outbreak victims and were able to analyze them using the most advanced techniques available to science. These investigations have cast light on the *B. anthracis* strain that caused the outbreak and the composition of the release.

Alibek called the *B. anthracis* strain used by the Soviet BW program "836." According to Alibek, this strain was first recovered in the Kirov *oblast* in 1953. Animal testing indicated that it was more virulent than strains known up until then by the BW program, and therefore it was weaponized.[89] Paul Keim's laboratory at the Center for Microbial Genetics and Genomics, Northern Arizona University, had the opportunity to analyze samples taken from Sverdlovsk outbreak victims.[90] Its researchers found that the Sverdlovsk outbreak strain, presumably 836, is a member of the Trans Eurasian (TEA) subgroup of *B. anthracis*. It is closely related to strains used by the Russians as live vaccines.[91]

Scientists at Paul Jackson's laboratory at the Los Alamos National Laboratory utilized polymerase chain reaction (PCR) methodology in their analysis. They made a surprising finding:

"At least four of the five known strain categories defined by this region were present in the tissue samples. . . . The simplest explanation for this is that the presence of multiple VNTR [variable-number tandem repeat] categories indicates that the victims were exposed to a mixture of

B. anthracis strains. The strains could come from two possible sources, vaccination or inhalation. One of the authors present during the outbreak believes that only one of the victims analyzed in this study was vaccinated and several of the victims succumbed to the disease before the vaccination program was initiated.[92]

The publication of this article initially raised serious concerns. Its findings appeared to indicate that Sverdlovsk Institute scientists had deliberately developed a BW formulation that contained a mixture of five different *B. anthracis* strains; in other words, an anthrax bacterial cocktail. One can imagine that such a cocktail weapon would be more effective than a single-strain weapon, because more members of the target population would be susceptible to infection. It could also be more difficult to treat the infected population, because antibiotics might be effective against one strain but not against another. In the final analysis, however, this probably was not the case.

The more likely explanation for the presence of so many strains in victim samples was that a small number of mutations, including changes in the genetic alleles that the Los Alamos team analyzed (which, by their nature, change more rapidly than other parts of the *B. anthracis* genome), accumulated in the Sverdlovsk stock cultures. As a result, different alleles of the same genetic markers came to be present in these stock cultures. Discussions with the Los Alamos team and the recent publication of an article that sheds more light on the *B. anthracis* in Sverdlovsk add weight to this explanation.[93] When first analyzed by Los Alamos scientists using highly sensitive methods, the different alleles appeared to be a collection of different strains, but this was not the case.[94] Paul Jackson believes that such a minor genetic change could become fixed in the stock cultures for one of two reasons. First, the change might have been advantageous to the recipient *B. anthracis* cells. Jackson thinks this was unlikely because, as far as his team could tell, the genes carrying the alleles do not encode anything important. Second and more likely, the changes were the result of frequent "bottlenecks" in the culturing and propagation of the weaponized *B. anthracis* that would occur every time a small aliquot of a large culture was used as a seed stock to start new large cultures in fermenters. Researchers typically start this process from a single colony off of an agar plate. Because a colony on an agar plate normally is composed of a large number of cells (between 10^8 and 10^{10} cells), and because bacilli are notoriously sticky, it is difficult or impossible to separate out a single cell from a colony. Therefore, samples taken from a colony most often contain several cells, according to Jackson. Under these conditions, it is quite possible that natural evolutionary forces generated an apparently mixed culture—although not necessarily changing any important pathogenic characteristics—especially in the absence of technologies that could screen for such changes.[95]

Post-1992 Activity

Russian reporters who have visited the Sverdlovsk Institute since the Soviet Union's dissolution have been told that the institute is now involved only with developing defenses against BW, the environmental remediation of military sites, and the development of goods and services for civilian markets.[96] Indeed, a copy of the institute's catalogue offers "more than 70 services to the civilian population starting with disinfection of hospitals, pharmacies, and food industry enterprises and ending with participation in solution of ecological problems of the town and *oblast*."[97] As for BW defense and environmental remediation, in 1990 the institute's director, Major General Anatoly Kharechko, claimed:

> Here are the basic directions of our research: the development of methods and means for the disinfection of places, military equipment, arms and gear; development of the means to protect people against biological aerosols and rapid detection of harmful substances in the environment. There is also a new direction, that of the investigation of the mechanism of the biological impairment of military equipment. Yes, there are microbes in nature that destroy metal and plastic. As you see, civilians also have an interest in the results of our research.[98]

Lieutenant general Valerie I. Yevstigneev, head of the MOD's 15th Directorate from 1980 to 1992 and then the deputy director to the head of the Radiological, Chemical, and Biological Defense Forces of the Ministry of Defense of the Russian Federation, later added that the institute performed "exclusively peaceful work": "Defense against infection, including infections of wartime. Developing means for bioreconnaissance, vaccines and antibiotics (in this we're twenty years behind the rest of the world), a method for liquidating possible large outbreaks of infectious diseases. . . . After all, the only anthrax vaccine in the country is produced by us."[99]

In 1998 a *Time* magazine reporter interviewed a Russian identified as retired lieutenant colonel Yevgeni Tulykin, who said that he had been Compound 19's director of personnel until December 1996.[100] He contradicted
Kharechko's and Yevstigneev's assertions that the institute performed only
peacefully directed R&D. Tulykin asserted that officials had begun re-
equipping Compound 19 laboratories during the previous few years and that
Kharechko announced his intention to rebuild the facilities in a special 1994
edition of the site's in-house newsletter. At the same time, Kharechko strongly
criticized Gorbachev's decision to turn the facility into a vaccine production
factory in order to "please his Western partners."

The goal of Kharechko's renovations, according to Tulykin, was for the facility to once again produce "item 2," the local code name for *B. anthracis*
spores. To back his assertions, Tulykin claimed that in 1997 "they reconstructed compartmentalized sectors in the labs to handle dangerous biological
agents and prevent leaks like the one in 1979." He also questioned why a
"peacefully directed" R&D site was patrolled by about 200 soldiers and Rott-
weiler dogs.[101] Tulykin's disclosures remain uncorroborated, as no one possessing the scientific-technical expertise to be able to assess the institute's work
program has, as far as we know, been permitted to enter and examine its facilities and equipment, and to inform others about what he or she observed.

Scientific Research Institute of Military Medicine of the MOD

Two military authors, K. K. Rayevskiy and N. M. Dobrynin, have written
about the history of Scientific Research Laboratory No. 1 (NIL-1), which was
established in 1955 at the S. M. Kirov Military Medical Academy.[102] The years
1954–1955 were pivotal to the Soviet BW program because they marked a
period of heightened interest among Soviet decision makers in the BW threat,
especially the threat posed by the United States. Once established, NIL-1
evolved into one of the MOD's most important BW defense efforts.[103]

NIL-1 was initially established with the goal of "developing the corresponding medical protective resources in connection with the abrupt increase
in the threat of use of biological weapons in military conflicts." In its first 14
years, NIL-1 is said to have carried out "over 60 scientific research projects,"
whose findings were used to develop, among other things, "the first generation of products and technical resources protecting troops from biological
weapons," including immunofluorescent assays for the rapid identification of

BW agents, an effective means of decontamination using a gas mixture of ethylene oxide and methylbromide, a new disinfectant called "degmin," and the new insect repellent "R-405."[104]

In 1969, NIL-1 was reorganized and renamed the Scientific Research Institute of Military Medicine of the MOD, and was relocated to its own site in Leningrad, not far from the Kirov Military Medical Academy. Its most important departments were these:

- Department of Specific Indication of Bioagents;
- Department of Decontamination;
- Department of Emergency and Specific Prophylaxis for Infections;
- Department of Field and Chamber Testing of Bioagents (renamed the Department of Vaccine Prophylaxis and Chamber and Field Testing of Medical Measures of Defense after 1992).

With this reorganization, the institute's workload increased substantially. By the end of the 1970s the Soviets had built a large laboratory-production facility at the site that included equipment built to international standards for work on dangerous infectious agents, rooms for studying cell cultures, and other specialized laboratories. Among its new tasks, the institute was ordered to develop:

- effective methods and schemes for the express analysis of pathogens, which meant the development of dozens of new diagnostic kits;
- aerosol and noninjection methods of mass vaccination and first generation vaccine kits for these purposes;
- new antibiotics with wide-spectrum action and the appropriate schemes for emergency prophylaxis for those exposed to dangerous infectious diseases; and
- highly productive and economical methods of decontamination in infectious disease research centers, including developing original disinfectants, insecticides, and repellants.

It is difficult to impossible to determine whether the institute accomplished the task it was given, as is often the case when reviewing Soviet planning. Rayevskiy and Dobrynin claim a high degree of success "as proven by the fact that practically all the proposed methods, as well as the diagnostics means, mass immunization, disinfection, insecticides, and repellent defenses have received wide-scale practical use by industry and earned positive opinions from medical service specialists in the military districts, military groups, and in the navies." But as with other Soviet claims, this one should be taken with more than a grain of salt.

In 1979 a new department was added to the institute. The department's mission was to develop the means of immunostimulation and increase common resistance against infectious agents; this enabled large-scale work on the evaluation of different classes of immunomodulators, not only "independent" defensive means, and the widening of the defensive spectrum of chemical preparations and vaccines. It bears noting that these defensive activities appear to have been instituted at about the same time that *Ferment's* subprogram Factor started to develop immunomodulators for offensive purposes (see Chapter 7).

Before 1991 the institute was involved in both defensive and offensive aspects of the Soviet BW program.[105] Although this section has focused primarily on the defensive work, sources have provided some information on the institute's offensively directed activities. In the early 1970s, senior institute scientists V. I. Ogarkov (a future Biopreparat director) and K. G. Gapochko did important work in aerobiology, particularly with respect to optimizing aerogenic infectivity. Also, institute researchers intensively studied many arboviruses for a long time, including Japanese and tick-borne encephalitis viruses, Isfahan virus, Kemerovo virus, Negishi virus, Rift Valley fever virus, Omsk hemorrhagic fever virus, West Nile fever virus, and dengue viruses.[106] Another institute scientist, V. I. Sibilev, investigated the potential for hepatitis viruses (not further identified) to be used as water-borne BW agents in the 1980s. Z. M. Prusakova, V. P. Nikolayev, and others investigated rickettsial pathogens, particularly *Rickettsia sibirica,* for their BW potential from the mid-1970s to the late-1980s. Because the institute was located in Leningrad, it was not allowed to conduct R&D involving Group I pathogens, so its highest biosafety level laboratories were of the BSL-3 type.

The Scientific Research Institute of Military Medicine is one of the few MOD biomedical facilities to have been visited by foreigners, but only one time. In October 1989, six American scientists who belonged to the Committee on International Security and Arms Control of the US National Academy of Sciences took part in a series of meetings in Moscow and Leningrad. The group's chairman, Joshua Lederberg, wrote that the visit was arranged on extremely short notice for October 7, 1989, and that the group was permitted to stay for 4 hours. Lederberg later wrote that the institute's work appeared to be

> directed mainly at infectious disease problems that would arise out of geographic endemicity. . . . There are no production facilities of any kind on the site. They indicated that the largest scale of culture of pathogenic agents was in test tubes and roller bottles. They did have a cell culture fermenter of about 1.5 liter capacity which they used to grow cells used in virus plaque assays . . . most specialized facility was an aerosol exposure chamber which can be operated at P3 standards,[107] and is used in their extensive research on aerosol immunization of experimental animals. . . . They use glove box containment facilities for dealing with highly pathogenic organisms. They had for example an unexpected circumstance of the isolation of Rift Valley Fever [virus] from a veteran on the Afghan front—a report which aroused considerable excitement at the arbovirus meeting. . . . There is no reason to doubt the image of the research they are doing. They are conscientious people dedicated to their mission. . . . They indicated that they felt they had an important public health mission quite apart from those connected with the military service and in this respect they are also a close counterpart of the AMRIID.[108]

Beginning in 1992 the Main Military Medical Directorate of the RF-MOD ordered the institute to focus on developing "dual use" biological defense technologies—that is, means that can be used by the military to protect its troops and by civilians to institute regular anti-epidemiological safeguards. In connection with this effort, officials created an experimental production laboratory for the development and production of small series of accurate diagnostic preparations and cell cultures in the department of detection and diagnostics of infectious diseases. These methods were mainly aimed at detecting known and verified offensive BW agents. The government also ordered the production of diagnostic equipment to detect natural alphaviruses and flaviviruses (tick-borne and Japanese encephalitis viruses), chlamydiae, herpes simplex virus 1 and 2, and mosquito-borne sandfly fever Sicilian and Naples viruses. From 1991 to 2000 the experimental lab developed 19 fluorescent immunoglobulin and erythrocyte immunoglobulin diagnostic equipment sets in sufficient quantities to supply the Russian army and naval medical epidemiological and immunological laboratories for 4 to 5 years. As late as 2000 the institute continued to research methods for detecting agents in the natural environment and improving laboratory diagnostics, prophylaxis, and etiotropic therapies (therapies that are directed against the cause of disease).[109]

In 1998 the institute was renamed the Medico-Biological Defense Research Test Center and became one of three research test centers under the umbrella of the State Research Test Institute of Military Medicine of the RF-MOD. The two other centers are the Test Center for Aviation and Space Medicine and Military Ergonomics (in Moscow) and the Test Center for Military Medicine, Military-Medical Technology and Pharmaceuticals (also in Moscow). The State Research Test Institute of Military Medicine is overseen by the Main Military-Medical Directorate of the RF-MOD. In 2002 the Test Institute was headed by Major General and Academician Igor Borisovich Ushakov.

NIL-1 and all of its successors have supposedly focused on a wide range of medical and biological defense activities. Beyond the generalities noted here, nothing specific is known about their work, including any possible input into the offensive BW program, because only a few security experts within the Russian biomedical defense field and extremely few in other countries know about NIL-1, the Scientific Research Institute of Military Medicine, and the Medico-Biological Defense Research Test Center. These institutions have always been highly secretive (so-called *rezhimnyi* institutions).

A combined US/UK team sought to visit the Research Institute during the latter part of the Trilateral Process (see Chapter 21) but was denied permission to do so. Indeed, as one of the military biological institutes that remains closed to outsiders, and because of what is known of its past work, the Medico-Biological Defense Research Test Center poses concerns to the US government about a continuing BW program.

S. M. Kirov Russian Military Medical Academy (RMMA)

The RMMA is relevant to this chapter for two reasons. First, most of the generals and colonels who headed or worked for Soviet, then Russian, military and civilian BW facilities received their basic medical training there, and some returned for specialized training. Second, it is necessary to clearly differentiate the open RMMA from its secretive neighbor, the Research Institute of Military Medicine, which is described above.

The RMMA was founded in 1798 by a decree from Czar Paul I and is the oldest Russian institution of higher learning. In addition to being a leading military medical school, the academy also functions as a hospital and a scientific research center. As late as 2009, RMMA was commanded by Medical Service Major General Boris Vsevolodovich Gaidar.

In 2002 the academy employed 72 academicians and corresponding members of the RF-AN or RF-AMN, as well as 303 doctors of medical science, 855 candidates of science, 75 professors, and 244 assistant professors. The academy trained graduate and postgraduate military physicians for all branches of Russia's armed forces in 30 medical specialties within 61 departments. More than 2,800 medical experts from 52 countries have undergone basic and advanced training at RMMA.

The academy's scientific research is directed toward improving medical service, finding new measures and methodologies of disease prevention, and diagnosing and treating the military personnel and residents of St. Petersburg. Each year, the RMMA hospital treats between 30,000 and 50,000 patients, and the academy's outpatient clinic treats another 160,000 people. The RMMA frequently serves as a venue for general sessions of the Russian Academy of Medical Sciences.

Foreign analysts have long been confused about the functions of the Medico-Biological Defense Research Test Center (previously known as the Research Institute of Military Medicine) and the RMMA, due to the similarities in the original name of the former and the current name of the latter. The two differ in the following ways:

- Since its inception in 1798, RMMA has been, first and foremost, a hospital and a medical school. The Research Test Center, established in 1969, has always been, and still remains, a research facility only.
- The RMMA concentrates on medical education and the treatment of patients, whereas the activities of the Research Test Center are focused on many aspects of biological defense.
- Security issues at RMMA can be solved at the institute's management level; at the Research Test Center, such matters are left for the chiefs of staff of Russia's armed forces.
- The RMMA was an open institution during Soviet times, and it remains open today. It usually has foreign students and scientists in residence. For these reasons, it is well known throughout world. Conversely, the

existence of the Research Test Center was once known only to a few Soviet and foreign experts, and it remains relatively unknown today.

- The RMMA is accessible to both domestic and foreign visitors, whereas the Research Test Center is a closed, highly secretive establishment.
- Today the RMMA appears to be flourishing; the Research Test Center seems to be stagnating.

In 2001, Yevstigneev told a reporter:

> When means for protecting against biological weapons were developed, a type of copy, or likeness, of the means of attack had to be created. It was therefore necessary to culture pathogens, develop a process for accumulating them, and make them stable in the environment. The next step was to create means to deliver and use the said biological weapon. All this was necessary not only to create vaccines but also to test biological surveillance and density of contamination of a territory when the weapon was used. This cycle of operations was considered what is called the offensive part of the Ministry of Defense's program. In 1992, it was prohibited and eliminated.[110]

If one is to believe Yevstigneev, which one should do with care, because he has been a frequent source of disinformation, the Soviet Union established its offensive BW program for one major purpose—to facilitate its defensive program. There is no question that the defensive program was large, that it involved multiple military and civilian organizations, and that it had a wide scope of activities. It is also clear that its existence and operations were highly classified; perhaps not as high as the offensive program but high enough that outsiders and most officials in the Soviet government had little to no knowledge about it. One could argue that less is known today about the civilian Soviet defensive BW program than its offensive BW program. This is not the case in the military sphere, because military authors have published multiple accounts since 1992 about aspects of the Soviet defensive programs. Foreigners are unable to check on the accuracy or veracity of much of this information because the three main military facilities supposedly undertaking defensive R&D are nearly as closed and secretive today as they were during the Soviet era.

The Soviet military establishment created and maintained an extensive system for preserving and propagating bacterial and viral strains that were investigated to determine their potential for weaponization and other properties that might be useful for defense and biotechnology. These culture collections also likely store validated BW agents, making the Russian military's micro-biological research institutes in Kirov, Yekaterinburg, and Sergiyev Posad the sole keepers of thousands of pathogenic bacterial and viral strains. These strains fit into four groups: (1) pathogens that have not yet been investigated for their BW potential but can be assumed to be virulent; (2) pathogens that had been investigated and found to possess BW potential but were not wea-ponized because the political events described in Chapter 21 brought the most active parts of the military BW program to an end; (3) pathogens that were weaponized in the laboratory but not open-air tested; and (4) validated BW agents. In addition, these institutes store thousands of natural strains of microorganisms that might have applications for the biotechnology industry. These vast culture collections of some of the world's most dangerous patho-gens are owned by the Russian military and, as far as is known, are stored and investigated without any civilian oversight.

4

Open-Air Testing of Biological Weapons by Aralsk-7 on Vozrozhdeniye Island

FOR MANY YEARS an island in the middle of the Aral Sea, Vozrozhdeniye Island, was the home of the Soviet Union's premier open-air testing ground for biological weapons and defenses.[1] After a substantial buildup in the 1950s, the testing facility was named Aralsk-7. The facility's importance should not be understated; it is where newly weaponized BW agents were tested in the open air as one of the last steps before becoming validated, and, probably, where biological weapons were open-air tested before being certified as type-classified. Also, although little is known about defensive activities at Aralsk-7, it is safe to assume that newly developed personal and collective protection equipment were tested at the site against biological weapons containing either simulants or pathogens as a final step before being type-classified by the MOD and issued to its forces.

This chapter attempts to explicate the facility, the island, and the island's environment, as well as the military activities that impacted all three. It is divided into six sections: a history of the Aral Sea and Vozrozhdeniye Island; a history of Aralsk-7; the demise of Aralsk-7; post-Soviet events involving Vozrozhdeniye Island; Vozrozhdeniye Island as a biological weapons wasteland; and the importance of open-air testing.

The History of the Aral Sea and Vozrozhdeniye Island

In 1848 the czar's government sent an expedition led by Lieutenant A. I. Butakov of the Imperial Russian Navy and Academician Karl Ernst von Baer of the Russian Geographic Society to explore the Aral Sea region.[2] Sailing on the schooner *Konstantin,*[3] the expedition traversed the Aral Sea for more than a year, mapping its coastline and its many small islands.[4] Butakov and von Baer named the sea's largest island after Czar Nikolay I and a small adjacent island Konstantin Island. The Aral Sea is fed by two rivers: the Syr Darya river, which originates in the mountains of Kyrgyzstan and empties into the northern part of the sea,[5] and the Amu Darya river, which originates in Tajikistan, passes through Afghanistan, Turkmenistan, and Uzbekistan, and empties into the sea's southernmost point.

The Bolsheviks renamed Nikolay I Island to Vozrozhdeniye Island after the 1917 revolution, and Konstantin Island became Komsomolets Island (after Komsomol, the Communist youth organization). The word *vozrozhdeniye* has been variously translated as "renaissance" or "resurrection." In 1926 the Soviets built a prison camp composed of several settlements on Vozrozhdeniye Island, and the Soviet Unified State Political Administration (OGPU) used it to imprison *kulaks*.[6] Some writers have claimed that the name Vozrozhdeniye Island came about because *kulaks* at the camp were "resurrected" from their criminal past, but this is incorrect. In actuality its name celebrates the birth of the Soviet Union.

Until 1970 the Aral Sea supported one of the Soviet Union's major fisheries, producing an annual catch of about 50,000 tons. However, because of a series of political decisions in the 1930s, the Aral Sea became an environmental disaster. This catastrophe had its roots in two grandiose projects—Stalin's "Great Plan to Transform Nature" (1948 to mid-1950s) and Khrushchev's "Virgin Lands Program" (1954–1960).[7] Among these programs' objectives, the Soviet Union sought to make itself self-sufficient in cotton and increase its rice production. It diverted water from the Syr Darya and Amu Darya rivers into large canals that conducted it to agricultural fields. The irrigation system flooded millions of acres with water that once had flowed into the Aral Sea. As a result of the diminished river flow, the Aral Sea shrank, and its water turned brackish.[8]

When the Aral Sea was an inland lake of the Soviet Union, it was jurisdictionally divided evenly between the Kazakh SSR and the Uzbek SSR. Vozrozhdeniye Island, however, was wholly part of the Karakalpak Autonomous Region of the Uzbek SSR. In the early 1970s, Vozrozhdeniye Island resembled a misshaped "W"; it was approximately 15 kilometers wide, 30 kilometers long, and covered an area of approximately 216 square kilometers (53,375 acres). As the Aral Sea shrank, the island expanded, and its northern shoreline eventually extended into the Kazakh SSR.[9] After their independence in the early 1990s, Kazakhstan and Uzbekistan confronted jurisdictional problems pertaining to the Aral Sea and its islands, problems that remain unresolved as of this writing. Nevertheless, with funding from the World Bank Kazakhstan initiated an ambitious program in 2005 to remediate part of the Aral Sea, and its first phase was completed in 2008.[10] A 13-kilometer long dike was built that closed off the northernmost part of the sea and the Kazakh government took steps to allow the Syr Daraya river to flow freely once again into this part. By 2011, the Northern Aral Sea had expanded to about 900 square kilometers and its water level had been raised by two meters. Fish and aquatic plants were making a fast recovery as the salinity concentration diminished to a healthier level.[11]

The History of Aralsk-7, the Biological Weapons Testing Ground on Vozrozhdeniye Island

In 1936 the Medical-Technical Institute of the Worker's and Peasant's Red Army (RKKA), otherwise known as STI, took ownership of the island. That summer, an expedition led by STI's director, Ivan M. Velikanov, arrived to perform open-air testing of *F. tularensis*.[12] The expedition quickly built a primitive infrastructure composed of several houses, a wharf, barracks for guard personnel, and a delineated test area. Testing was stopped by cold weather in the autumn, but it resumed in May 1937. Aircraft reportedly dropped containers filled with bacteria that cause cholera, leprosy, plague, and tularemia onto the site in an effort to test defensive equipment.[13] Testing activities were disrupted again when the NKVD arrested several STI scientists, including Velikanov and his wife, in June 1937.[14]

Testing restarted and continued through the summer of 1937 after officials appointed a new director, L. M. Khatenever, and his assistant, Brigade Commissar Zaporozhets.[15] As before, the site's major focus was *F. tularensis*, although it also carried out open-air tests involving the causative organisms of the human diseases cholera, dysentery, leprosy, plague, pyemia, tetanus, paratyphus, and typhus, as well as the animal foot-and-mouth disease.[16] After the 1937 testing season ended, no tests were performed on Vozrozhdeniye Island until 1953.[17] The reason for this hiatus is unknown.

After the Soviet government received information on Japan's World War II BW program and learned about the UK-US BW program, it realized that it needed good data about aerosols and their behaviors to develop its defenses against biological weapons.[18] In the early 1950s the MOD reopened the Vozrozhdeniye Island testing ground and began substantially upgrading it. It established the military city of Kantubek on the northeastern side of the island and built an airstrip capable of handling cargo planes, called Barkhan, next to the city.[19] The Soviets built a large building to house the Kantubek military headquarters and surrounded it with newly built three-story barracks to house guards, officers of the chemical troops, and civilian researchers. A small seaport was constructed at Udobnaya Bay, which became home for fast boats that patrolled off the island's coast and prevented intruders from coming within 40 kilometers of the island.[20] In time, the entire complex became officially known as Aralsk-7.[21] Approximately 50% of its southern part was used for testing, which meant that the open-air test range's size was approximately 108 km² (26,688 acres). If the entire Komsomolets Island is assumed to have been a test range, then an additional 5 km² should be added to the 108 km² figure.

To support Aralsk-7, the Soviets constructed facilities on the mainland, near Aralsk, including a special railroad station called "Aral Sea," next to which a warehouse complex was built to receive construction and supply materials for transshipment to the island. From the warehouses, supplies were transported by the *Archada,* a large freighter capable of carrying more than 120 persons and tons of supplies, food, construction materials, petroleum products, hay, and other products. In addition to the *Archada,* two barges carried fresh water to the island; each held an estimated 350 tons of water. On the island itself, "numerous" 80,000-liter storage tanks located near the headquarters building held the island's fresh water.

Kantubek grew in the intervening decades, and by 1990 it had about 90 structures, a central steam plant that provided heat for all buildings, and a scientific facility, called the Field Scientific Research Laboratory (PNIL).[22] Its population during the test season ranged from 1,200 to 2,000 people, including more than 600 soldiers, but during the off season it was a few hundred. The soldiers serving both on the island and at support facilities on the mainland were part of Military Unit 25484, which was the size of a regiment.[23] Important visitors to the island during the 1970s and 1980s included Colonel General Smirnov (accompanied by his aide-de-camp Leonid T. Lavrenev) and Major General Lebedinsky.

PNIL was located within a compound 3 kilometers south of Kantubek. It comprised 50 to 60 buildings of various types and sizes and housed scientists and technicians temporarily dispatched from the three military biological institutes at Kirov, Sverdlovsk, and Zagorsk. The lab's directors, all colonels, were Nikolay N. Sergeev until 1980, Yury P. Grigorashkin, from 1980 to 1985, and Viktor V. Donchenko from 1985 to the end of Aralsk-7 in 1992 (Donchenko's name was still posted on his office door in the ruins of PNIL when a US team visited in 1997).[24]

PNIL's two largest buildings, V60 and V61, can still be seen clearly on satellite imagery.[25] V61, a three-story building, was a predeployment animal facility that held primates before they were used for tests. The building had six large rooms that contained several dozen cages, which held the imprisoned primates, including baboons and macaques. Other test animals, such as rats, guinea pigs, hamsters, and rabbits, were caged in smaller structures near V61. According to a former military scientist, Gennady N. Lepeshkin, 200 to 300 nonhuman primates were used for testing purposes each year.[26]

V60 was as large as V61, but it was used only for necropsies. The entire elaborately equipped building was a high-security facility. Its first floor housed the air intake system; equipment and facilities for washing and decontaminating the clothing and equipment used for necropsies; and storage tanks for air, hot water, sea water, and decontamination fluid that circulated throughout the second floor. The second floor contained six necropsy laboratories, each of which housed 12 glove boxes. The third floor contained the air-handling system that filtered and sterilized air emitted from the second floor before it was released to the outside environment. The laboratory could accommodate up to several hundred necropsies per day for small animals and 20 to 40 for primates.

Nearby and inside V60 must have been a hellish sight, particularly during a busy testing season. In comparison to an abattoir where animals are quickly killed and processed, the animals in the holding cells and in transit must have suffered grievously for varying lengths of time. At any given time, 50 to 80 workers were probably present in the building (with the workers on the second floor wearing protective suits), as were hundreds of animals in extremis or dead from the effects of some of the worst infectious diseases that nature and laboratories had to offer. Outside, a mobile incinerator probably belched smoke.

During Soviet times, the Sukhumi Primate Center was a particularly important source of primates used for BW-related testing. The center was associated with the Institute of Experimental Pathology and Therapy, located in the Georgian SSR. Established in 1927, it is the world's oldest primate research center and once was one of the largest, then housing more than 7,000 primates and employing more than 1,000 persons, including 300 researchers.[27] The center provided most of the primates used for both closed and open-air testing of Soviet BW agents and weapons.[28] As the center was an open facility, its management most likely did not know for which purposes its animals were used.

We have been unable to resolve whether Aralsk-7 scientists used human subjects for open-air testing of BW agents. There are several sources cited in Chapter 1 that assert humans were used for such testing, but their allegations are unsupported. Burgasov also makes a strong statement supporting these claims: "For our experiments [on Vozrozhdeniye Island] we used not only animals, guinea pigs, monkeys, horses, but also people . . . An animal perishes from a microscopic dose of botulinum toxin, but we did not know how a man would react to the same dose."[29] If Burgasov is correct, and since the Soviet BoNT weaponization program continued until approximately the mid-1960s, his claim indicates that human subject experimentation had continued until about the time that Brezhnev became general secretary in 1964. Further, from studies done by Birstein, it appears likely that the KGB and its predecessors had tested various weapons for assassinations on prisoners, including some that were based on toxins.[30] However, the persons we interviewed who had been involved in the post-1972 Soviet BW program told us either that they did not think this was done, or that they knew it was not done.

Some distance away from PNIL was a small bunker where biological weapons were assembled. The bunker was equipped with a special lightning suppressor and equipment to create a static electricity-free environment. Bombs and bomblets (in two sections) were manufactured in military production plants on the mainland, filled with their biological payload at a military filling station, and transported to Aralsk and thence to Vozrozhdeniye Island. Bursters that held explosives used to disperse weapon payloads were transported separately to the island. In the bunker, a burster and a detonator were placed in the middle of the bomb where it was surrounded by payload. The two sections of a bomblet were fastened around a burster, and a band secured the unified bomblet.[31] Soldiers transported the assembled weapons to the chosen test range and made them operational. Over the years, bomblets loaded with variola virus, *Brucella suis, Burkholderia mallei, Coxiella burnetii,* and *Yersinia pestis* were detonated and their effects analyzed.

Near the bunker, a few dugouts stored hundreds of practice weapons— weapons that resembled the real weapons but did not contain explosives or agents. Some of these were left behind by Russian forces that departed in early 1992 and were recovered by US visitors in the middle 1990s (see below).

The open-air testing season began in May. Tests were done at night to take advantage of the inversion layer and to avoid damaging UV radiation given off by the sun. Personnel who worked on the test ranges adjusted their normal wake-sleep patterns in order to work at night and sleep during the day.

Meteorological data were invaluable on the island. The military needed reliable climatic conditions to conduct tests. In particular, winds had to be from a certain direction at a certain speed; testing would be done only if the wind speed was between 4 and 8 meters per second. Instruments placed on a 14-meter-high observation tower located on the island's highest point collected these data.

The Aralsk-7 open-air testing ground was located approximately 7 kilometers south of the laboratory complex. The ground comprised at least six test ranges, which covered an area of about 108 square kilometers. The MOD did not expand the testing ground as the Aral Sea receded and the island grew.

Whether agents were initially dispersed by an explosion or a sprayer, the extent of their ultimate dispersal depended on the wind. Accordingly, tests proceeded only if the wind was blowing in a favorable direction, its speed was within the acceptable range, and a storm or rain was not imminent. At intervals specified by a test plan, test site personnel would pre-locate animal cages, impingers, and impactors. The animals would be breathing normally and would inhale whatever particles the wind brought. The impingers, which were powered by rechargeable batteries, used vacuums to draw in air from the environment through either water or filter paper, either of which would be collected and cultured after the test had run its course. Inside the Soviet-made impactors, which were similar to the US-made Andersen impactor and also ran on rechargeable batteries, a vacuum drew in air from the environment and passed it through a chamber holding eight agar plates, each of which was covered by a sheet of glass with tiny holes in it. The top plate had the largest holes with a size of 10–20 microns; the second plate had holes that were 8–10 microns wide, and so forth to the last plate, which had holes 0.5–1 micron wide. This progression simulates the human nasopharyngeal-pulmonary tract, in that the nasal passage traps large particles (10–20 microns), the pharynx fairly large particles (8–10 microns), and so forth, down to the alveoli in the lungs, where the very smallest particles settle. At the end of the open-air test, personnel would remove and culture the agar plates.

The results from the open-air tests informed Aralsk-7 scientists about the effective radius of dispersion for the tested agents, the speed of dispersion relative to wind speed, the quantity of bacteria or viruses that settled onto a square centimeter of surface area under various conditions and at various distances from the initial dispersion, and the quantity of bacteria or viruses needed to sicken the animals.[32] The scientists in charge of testing would use the results to draw up calculation tables for use with each type of biological weapon.

According to Yevstigneev, not only Soviet weapons were tested by Aralsk-7:

> There was a workshop were we did indeed manufacture four kinds of U.S. one-pound, two-pound, and four-pound bombs. The worker produced these "toys" literally on his lap. But it could not be done any other way; we had to learn to assess the biological situation if these weapons were used. We charged the munitions, drove out to an island in the Aral Sea, blew them up, installed biological reconnaissance instruments, watched what kind of cloud was produced, and so on and so forth. . . . We now have marvelous calculations, which are used by everyone from the Defense Ministry itself to the Ministry for Affairs of Civil Defense, Emergency Situations, and Elimination of Natural Disasters.[33]

The annual MOD field testing program held at Vozrozhdeniye Island was most certainly not only for the purpose of testing a few "toy" models of American bomblets. Yevstigneev's remark about fabricating a few"toys" is ridiculous nonsense and disinformation, as were virtually all of his public commentaries. Nothing displays this more dramatically and convincingly than a memorandum drafted by Central Committee Secretary Lev Zaikov and sent to Gorbachev on May 15, 1990, which states that "by 1985" the Soviet BW program had developed not only 12 pathogens for use as biological weapons but also the "means for using them—and munitions assembly equipment." (The complete memorandum is reproduced in Chapter 21.) However, as is discussed in Chapter 10, it is possible that the Soviet military was able to secure information about American biological (and chemical) bomblets from several sources including a U.S. Air Force pilot captured in 1953 during the Korean War,[34] a declassified report that became available in the mid- to late-1960s,[35] and a series of reports written by US military scientists and engineers that were declassified starting in 1974.

Sometime in the late 1950s or early 1960s, Aralsk-7 personnel constructed a small "ghost" village on Komsomolets Island that was used to test the behavior of aerosols in an urban setting. It was also used to field test defensive measures and equipment.

Although Aralsk-7 was a military facility closed to civilians, facility policies changed when the Biopreparat system started to deliver weaponized agents. According to Alibek, in 1982 Biopreparat scientists were for the first time admitted to Vozrozhdeniye Island to test a biological weapon based on a vaccine-resistant strain of *F. tularensis* that had been developed by his team at the Omutninsk Chemical Factory. Vorobyov and Lebedinsky were put in charge of these tests. Alibek claims that "nearly all the immunized monkeys died."[36]

No information is available about the safety record of the facilities on Vozrozhdeniye Island. When sources for this book were asked about safety at the island, they replied that it was a safe work place and none could think of a single accident involving BW agents at PNIL or the testing ground. There certainly were deaths on the island; US visitors in 1997 found two cemeteries, each of which contained four or five graves. None of the tombstones indicated the causes of death.

The one serious mishap for which Aralsk-7 was responsible did not occur on the island: During the summer 1971 testing season, variola virus was accidentally released during an open air test and caused civilian casualties off the island. This event has been thoroughly described and analyzed in a previous publication,[37] but it is summarized below with some new information added.

On July 15, 1971, the marine research vessel *Lev Berg*[38] set sail from Aralsk on a three-week journey that would cover much of the Aral Sea. Its main objective was to assess the ecological damage to the sea that was then starting to become apparent. This vessel's crew sampled sea water and sea life at sites throughout their journey for analysis at oceanographic research institutions on the mainland. A 24-year-old female fisheries expert, whose duties on the vessel included casting nets to collect fish and sea life specimens often at night, was to become the index case of a smallpox outbreak.[39]

On the way back to Aralsk, on August 6, the index case began feeling sick and stayed in her bunk until the ship's arrival. Once on land she was treated by a local doctor who noted her temperature (39° Celsius) and that she had a cough. A few days later, a rash appeared on her back, face, and scalp, and then her fever broke. She felt well enough to depart from Aralsk on a train for Alma-Ata about August 15, and she appeared to have fully recovered by the time she arrived. Her past medical history included having received a smallpox vaccination.

On August 27, the index case's 9-year old brother became sick with a fever and a rash. He recovered fairly soon, yet over the next three weeks an additional eight cases turned up with similar symptoms. Of the 10 cases, three died—a case-fatality rate (30%) equal to that of natural smallpox. The official top-secret records of the outbreak make no mention of variola virus being the possible cause of the illnesses until the end of September, when the appropriate antibody studies were done, probably at the premier Soviet smallpox research institute, the Institute for Viral Preparations in Moscow.[40] At about that time, one of the institute's top experts, Nelya N. Maltseva, flew to Aralsk and confirmed that the outbreak was smallpox.

Once local public health authorities realized that they were dealing with a smallpox outbreak, they instituted rigorous public health measures, including quarantining the entire city and vaccinating all of its inhabitants. Because the outbreak was brief and generated few casualties, these measures appear to have been effective. However, Soviet anti-plague officials were mystified as to the outbreak's etiology. The last indigenous smallpox case in the Soviet Union had occurred in 1936, and the nearest place where smallpox was still a problem in 1971 was Afghanistan, about 1,200 kilometers away. The officials posed two explanations: The index case had contracted the disease when she went ashore at Komsomolsk-on-Ustyurt, or variola virus had somehow been imported from Afghanistan directly to Aralsk and spread by goods sold on the open market. The officials would not have known about Aralsk-7 and its activities.

After a thorough epidemiological analysis, US researcher Alan P. Zelicoff disproved both explanations and concluded that the index case had contracted variola virus while collecting samples toward the end of July 1971.[41] The only conceivable source of variola virus in the middle of the Aral Sea would have been open-air tests carried out on Vozrozhdeniye Island.

Since the publication of Zelicoff's analysis, another source confirmed the accuracy of his account. Petr Burgasov, whose name appears with some frequency in this book, was asked sometime in 2001 whether he knew "of any instance when bioweapons work got out of control." He replied:

There was a situation with the "leak" of actual bacteriological [sic] weapons. A very potent smallpox formulation was being tested on Vozrozhdeniye Island in the Aral Sea. . . . Suddenly I was informed of mysterious deaths in Aralsk. We found out that a research vessel of the

Aral Sea Fleet came within 15 kilometers of the island (they were prohibited from going closer than 40 kilometers). A female laboratory assistant went on deck twice a day and took plankton samples. Only 400
grams of the formulation was exploded on the island, but the smallpox
pathogen "reached" her and she was infected. Upon returning home to
Aralsk, she infected several other people, including children. They all
died. Suspecting the cause, I telephoned the chief of the USSR General
Staff and asked that trains traveling between Alma-Ata and Moscow be
prohibited from stopping in Aralsk. That prevented the epidemic from
spreading throughout the entire country. I telephoned Andropov, who
was then the KGB chief, and reported that an exceptional smallpox
formulation had been developed on Vozrozhdeniye. He ordered me not
to say another word about it.

Now there is a real bacteriological weapon! The minimum effective
radius is 15 kilometers. You could imagine what would have happened if
it had been 100–200 people instead of one laboratory assistant. Incidentally, in 1912, smallpox quickly killed 110,000 people in Manchuria.[42]

Burgasov made several errors in his statement. For example, smallpox is
caused by a virus, not a bacterium; three people died during the outbreak, not
"all"; and the "1912" outbreak he mentions took place in 1910–1911, and it
was not a smallpox outbreak but pneumonic plague.[43] Nevertheless, Burgasov
was the Soviet Union's chief sanitary officer in 1971 and had been active in the
Soviet BW program since World War II; he must have been knowledgeable
about its testing program. That he freely admitted that the smallpox outbreak
occurred, and that it resulted from the accidental release of variola virus from
an open-air test performed on Vozrozhdeniye Island, meant that he did not
think it was possible to come up with a believable cover story about the outbreak's cause. (Burgasov had no compunction about coming up with a false
cover story for the 1979 anthrax outbreak in Sverdlovsk; see Chapter 15.) It was
surprising, however, to hear Burgasov brag about the power of a biological
weapon armed with variola virus at a time when the official Russian position
was that the Soviet Union had never possessed such weapons.[44]

The main implication of this outbreak is that it confirmed that by the
summer of 1971, the Soviet Union already possessed an effective biological
weapon armed with variola virus. To have reached this point in the process
of weaponizing variola virus, Soviet weapons scientists would have had to have
started this work much earlier. As explained in Chapter 3, weaponization of

variola virus probably began soon after 1959. And if first generation weapon scientists had accomplished this much by 1971, it is not unreasonable to believe that second generation scientists would have advanced their variola virus–based weapon development substantially by the time the BW program closed down in 1992.

Would US overhead satellite photo reconnaissance have been able to detect Soviet BW testing on Vozrozhdeniye Island, in which animals were placed on a grid surrounding a central point from which the pathogen was released? If so, when?

The U2 aircraft began flying spy missions over the Soviet Union in 1955 and continued doing so until April 1960, when a U2 piloted by Gary Powers was shot down near Sverdlovsk. At the beginning of U2 flights in 1956, the spatial resolution of the photos it took from an altitude of 70,000 feet was 36 inches (91 cm); by 1961, spatial resolution had improved to 30 inches (76 cm). After the U2 program was discontinued, the United States used satellites to provide imagery of strategic sites in the Soviet Union. Corona was the first US satellite imagery intelligence program, operating from August 1960 to May 1972. It consisted of a series of satellites with increasingly more sophisticated cameras; spatial resolution at the start was 8 meters (25 feet), but very rapidly improved to 2 meters (6 feet) and less. Individual images on an average covered an area approximately 16 kilometers (10 miles) by 193 kilometers (120 miles). Corona imagery was used for a variety of analytical purposes, from assessing military strength to estimating the size of grain production. Corona concentrated principally on photographing the Soviet Union and China.[45]

In the mid-1960s, US photographic satellite resolution was about 1 meter. A tethered horse or mule would have been visible, but essentially would have appeared as a rectangle. By the 1970s the resolution provided by the US KH-8 (Keyhole) satellite had been improved to 6 inches, and large animals could be distinguished. However, small animals in cages that were placed at points on the grid would have appeared only as square boxes.[46] Three major variables enter into consideration of US imagery intelligence about the time of the 1971 Aralsk smallpox outbreak:

- whether the KH-8 was assigned to survey the Vozrozhdeniye Island test site, or whether US satellites with poorer resolution were assigned to that task;
- what conclusion photointerpreters could draw from what appeared to be indistinct square objects; and

- the possibility of misinterpretation of what was seen. (It is known that US photointerpreters had on occasion mistaken livestock watering troughs for ICBM missile silos.)

As is discussed in Chapter 12, the findings of analysis done by the CIA and published in 1965, which was based to some extent on imagery of Vozrozhdeniye Island generated in the late 1950s, was incorrect because it "determined" that the island did not host a biological weapons test site.

As noted above, most, if not all, open-air field testing by Aralsk-7 was done at night to take advantage of the inversion layer and avoid germicidal UV radiation given off by the sun (and perhaps to avoid detection by US satellites). Personnel who worked on the test range to, for example, site animal cages and deploy weapons to be tested, were issued head-worn flashlights resembling those worn by miners. Because testing was carried out at night, it is necessary to consider the capabilities of satellites to "see" in the dark. The KH 8, which operated from 1963 to 1984, did not have infrared capability and thus could not detect nighttime activities. The KH 11 high-resolution satellite that became operational in 1971, and gradually replaced both the KH 8 and KH 9, had infrared capability from approximately the mid-1980s onward. Infrared reduced the KH 11's resolution somewhat, but in the absence of cloud cover provides the ability to see at night. US intelligence therefore was unable to detect indicative open-air testing night-time activity until the middle 1980s and would have had some capability to do so after that time.

Referring again to Chapter 12, we discuss in some detail the Defense Intelligence Agency's unclassified report of 1986 in which it identifies by name one Soviet BW facility – Vozrozhdeniye Island. So sometime during the intervening 20 years between 1965 and 1985, the US intelligence agencies were able to collect sufficient and accurate data to make a correct determination of the island's real purpose. We do not know to what an extent these data were derived from imagery.

The Demise of Aralsk-7

Vozrozhdeniye Island residents began to feel the effects of the receding Aral Sea in 1973, as beaches grew and the crew of the *Archada* struggled to load the ship and get it underway.[47] On the mainland, the Aralsk harbor gradually shoaled and became so shallow that canals had to be dug between harbor facilities and the deeper, navigable waters of the Aral Sea. At the Udobnaya

Bay seaport, the pier continually had to be lengthened, and the shifting sands that fouled the port entry had to be cleared away. By the end of the 1980s the sea had shoaled so much that it became very difficult to ship supplies from Aralsk to Aralsk-7. The MOD provided Unit 25484 with large trucks to transport supplies from Aralsk to Muynak (located south of the Aral Sea), a distance of over 250 kilometers, which for a while had a functioning harbor. Fragile or labile items were delivered by helicopter and airplane.

By the early 1990s, Kantubek residents generally understood that the testing ground was doomed and left when given the opportunity. Soviet Army officers quietly sent their families to the mainland. The 15th Directorate reportedly held a meeting in November 1991 at the Zagorsk Institute to discuss the fate of Aralsk-7 and decided to shut it down. The impetus to implement this decision was probably the official dissolution of the Soviet Union in December 1991. On January 18, 1992, the Supreme Soviet of newly independent Kazakhstan issued the edict "On Urgent Measures for Radically Improving the Living Conditions of Aral Area Residents," which officially closed the Vozrozhdeniye Island testing ground. At about the same time, Russian president Boris Yeltsin came to terms with the knowledge that the Soviet Union had operated an offensive BW program in violation of the BWC. On April 11, 1992, Yeltsin issued Edict No. 390, "On Ensuring the Implementation of International Obligations Regarding Biological Weapons," which ordered the offensive BW programs to shut down. The Russian government made a commitment to Kazakhstan to close its facilities on Vozrozhdeniye Island, dismantle its special structures, decontaminate the island, and transfer it to Kazakh control within two or three years. In fact, the last Russian military unit departed the island in late April 1992.

Post-Soviet Events Involving Vozrozhdeniye Island

As the Aral Sea was shrinking, Vozrozhdeniye Island was growing; the island's acreage expanded from 216 square kilometers to 2,000 square kilometers by 1992. By about 1995 the northern fifth of Vozrozhdeniye Island was part of Kazakhstan, while the rest remained part of Uzbekistan's Karakalpak autonomous region.[48] All of what once had been the Aralsk-7 facilities and test ranges were in Uzbekistan. Because the island's rodents and insects moved around without paying attention to borders, and because some of them might be infected by or otherwise carry pathogens that were tested at Aralsk-7, the two countries needed to negotiate their rights to and responsibilities for the island.

Yet neither country knew much about what had transpired on the island or about the condition of its ecology when they assumed sovereignty in 1992.

On June 6, 1995, US specialists visited Vozrozhdeniye Island for the first time. During the half a day spent on the island, they confirmed that PNIL had been dismantled, that the testing ground's infrastructure was largely destroyed, and that the military settlement was abandoned. Another US team came to the island in 1997. During their seven-day stay, the investigators did an in-depth investigation, including sampling the environment and laboratory buildings. None of the samples taken from the buildings tested positive for pathogens, but *B. anthracis* spores were recovered from environmental samples. A third US visit in May 2002 involved environmental remediation (see below). In between these visits, reporters supported by well-endowed newspapers made unauthorized visits to the island and looters from the mainland stripped whatever had value from structures.[49]

Vozrozhdeniye Island as a Biological Weapons Wasteland

In the 1980s it appears as if the MOD had acquired a large stockpile of weaponized *B. anthracis* spores, estimated to have weighed between 100 and 200 metric tons. No one is sure where this stash was manufactured. Perhaps it was manufactured at Compound 19 before its production plant was closed down; or perhaps by a production unit at Zima, which is a city located approximately 210 kilometers northwest of Irkutsk; or perhaps at Malta, which is also northwest of Irkutsk. One of our sources suggested that US intelligence had images of a facility in Malta that looked like the bunkers used to store bulk BW agents at Compound 19 and was considered to have been the likely source of the stockpile.

About 1988 the MOD decided for unknown reasons to destroy this stockpile and bury its residue on Vozrozhdeniye Island. It loaded the spore slurry into hundreds of the TR-250 stainless steel containers, each with a capacity of 250 liters, and added sodium hypochlorite, an efficacious disinfectant/antimicrobial agent, to each container. The containers were transported by rail to Aralsk, where they were loaded onto barges and taken to Vozrozhdeniye Island. The containers were emptied into 11 pits, each of which was roughly 2 meters wide, 5 meters long, and 3 meters deep. The pits were then closed up, and the containers taken away.

In 1998, Andrew C. Weber, an advisor to the US secretary of defense, publicly revealed that the Soviet military had buried "many tons of anthrax spores" in 11 pits on Vozrozhdeniye Island. He added that US satellites had photographs in which the pits were clearly visible. Because samples taken from some of the pits in 1997 by US investigators included viable spores, the US government was concerned about terrorists or criminal gangs securing the starting material for a BW program from the pits. To head off this possibility, in October 2001 the United States committed $6 million for the decontamination of the pits.[50]

The US Defense Threat Reduction Agency (DTRA) hired Raytheon Company as the project-integrating contractor. It assembled a decontamination team led by biochemical engineer Brian Hayes. The team arrived at Nukus, Uzbekistan, on April 16, 2002, where it met up with Uzbek experts from the Ministry of Defense, Ministry of Emergency Situations, and Ministry of Health.[51] The binational team procured the necessary equipment and hired about 100 Uzbek workers before flying to Moynak, a fishing town whose harbor once abutted the Aral Sea but which was now located 30 kilometers from the sea's edge, and then to Kantubek.

Once on Vozrozhdeniye Island, the team set up a campsite, including a small but well-furbished temporary microbiological laboratory, close to the pits. Team members who went closer than 300 meters to the pits had to wear high-security personal protection suits and equipment. The team's first job was to take samples from each pit. It turned out that six of the 11 pits yielded viable *B. anthracis* spores. To decontaminate the pits, team members dug an 11 foot (3.3 meter) by 40 foot (12.1 meter) trench next to each of the 11 pits, lined the trenches with plastic, and poured several thousand kilograms of powdered calcium hypochlorite into them. The team moved contaminated material from the pits to the trenches. This material was mixed with the calcium hypochlorite, and the mixture sat for six days. The dried-up mixture was then heat-treated. After being treated, samples of the mixture were analyzed for viable spores. More than 1,000 samples were analyzed, the last one on May 26. Once no viable spores remained in any of the trenches or pits, the decontaminated material was reburied in the pits, the equipment was cleaned and flown back to the mainland, and the area where the team had operated was remediated so it looked like it did before the team had arrived on site. The team finished its work on June 6, 2002, when the last team member departed. Hayes estimated that the project had cost $4 to $5 million to complete.

Some samples from the pits were sent to Los Alamos National Laboratory for analysis by Paul Jackson's scientific team. The team's scientists confirmed that the pits contained spores of the same *B. anthracis* strain that had caused the 1979 Sverdlovsk outbreak (see Chapter 3).

The Importance of Open-Air Testing

The open-air testing of new or altered biological weapons is an important element of a national BW program for four reasons: (1) Program scientists need to observe and measure the behavior of a newly created agent or a supposedly enhanced agent in the open environment to make certain that it will survive long enough to cause damage and that its level of virulence remains stable despite the stress of the environment. (2) Scientists must be able to verify a munition's ability to disseminate the agent effectively. Small differences in the amount of an energetic used to disperse an agent borne by a bomb or bomblet can make a huge difference in whether an agent survives the forces of dispersal or whether it clumps on dispersal and falls uselessly to the ground. (3) Open-air testing allows weapon developers to ascertain that a complete biological weapons system, including the munitions and the agents it carries, will operate dependably and predictably. (4) If a nation is serious about undertaking R&D to improve its defenses against biological attacks, it must be in a position to realistically test existing defenses and the defenses of the future, which requires exposing them to real weapons deployed in the field. The Soviets and their present-day apologists in Russia assert that the Vozrozhdeniye Island testing ground conducted open-air testing for defensive purposes only. At the very least, this claim is a misrepresentation; while Soviet scientists undoubtedly conducted defensive tests on the island, its major responsibility was to support the offensive BW program.

This chapter discusses in detail the Soviet BW program's open-air testing facility and its activities on Vozrozhdeniye Island, which were sizable, long-term, and sophisticated. Few governments have supported such encompassing programs, or have had the space needed to safely operate them. Will the Russian government in the future build and operate a testing ground to replace Aralsk-7? It is possible that the Russian government will take steps to establish a new biological testing ground, if for no other purposes than to support a defensive BW program and to train first responders.[52] If it does decide to establish and equip a new biological open-air testing ground, the Russian government is politically bound to report these activities to BWC State Parties as part of the BWC Confidence Building Measures (see Chapter 20).

5

Soviet Civilian Sector Defenses against Biological Warfare and Infectious Diseases

THOUGH THE MILITARY was in charge of defensive Soviet BW efforts, civilian entities played an important role in the defensive program. In particular, a report first published in the West in April 2006 provides new information on the Soviet anti-plague system, a component of the Soviet Ministry of Health (MOH). The MOH's 2nd Directorate was the lead agency for a program code-named Problem 5, whose mandate was to defend the Soviet Union from the biological threats posed by highly dangerous exotic pathogens, whether their etiology was nature or the laboratory.[1] This wide-ranging program, which was overseen by the Problem 5 Commission head-quartered at the N. F. Gamaleya Institute of Epidemiology and Microbiology in Moscow (hereafter, Gamaleya Institute), involved six anti-plague institutes and their subsidiary anti-plague stations. In addition, a dedicated Problem 5 institute existed outside of the anti-plague system—the Lviv State Research Institute of Epidemiology and Hygiene, in Lviv (Lvov in Russian), Ukrainian SSR. Biopreparat institutes also performed Problem 5 tasks as part of their second legend.

This chapter's four sections discuss Soviet efforts in the civilian sphere to defend against BW. The first section briefly discusses aspects of the 1972 Biological and Toxin Weapons Convention (BWC) that are relevant to BW defense. The second section reviews the Soviet anti-plague system's responsibilities in regard to Problem 5. The third describes the dedicated Problem 5 institute in Lviv. The final section analyzes the contributions of Problem 5 and the anti-plague system to the Soviet offensive BW program.

The Biological and Toxin Weapons Convention and Defense against BW

The BWC's preamble states that its signatories are "Determined, for the sake of all mankind, to exclude completely the possibility of bacteriological (biological) agents and toxins being used as weapons." Article 1 specifies what signatories cannot do:

> Each State Party to this Convention undertakes never in any circumstances to develop, produce, stockpile or otherwise acquire or retain:
>
> (1) Microbial or other biological agents, or toxins whatever their origin or method of production, of types and in quantities that have no justification for prophylactic, protective or other peaceful purposes;
>
> (2) Weapons, equipment or means of delivery designed to use such agents or toxins for hostile purposes or in armed conflict.[2]

Article 1 does permit the development, production, and testing, of pathogens and toxins of types and in quantities that can be justified "for protective and other peaceful purposes." These last words, referred to as the "three Ps," represent permitted defensive BW activities, as well as general public-health measures. Also of relevance, the BWC's Article 12 specifies that state parties are to convene a review conference five years after the treaty's entry into force to assess its operation.

On June 24, 1975, when he announced that the Soviet Union had ratified the BWC, the Soviet representative to the UN disarmament conference declared that the Soviet Union had never possessed an offensive BW program and therefore had no stockpiles of weapons to destroy (see Chapter 20). The representative did not mention defensive activities, although they were allowed under the BWC. As noted in Chapter 3, the Soviet Union kept its defensive BW program secret until 1987, when as part of *perestroika* the work of the anti-plague system was reported in the first Soviet BWC Confidence Building Measure (CBM) report. Informative articles about Soviet defensive activities appeared in the open literature only after 1992.

Role of the Soviet Anti-plague System in the Defense against Biological Warfare

The anti-plague system was an organization unique to the Soviet Union that aimed to control deadly endemic diseases and prevent the importation of exotic pathogens from other countries. Previous publications address the system in detail,[3] so this chapter only briefly reviews its work program and institutes, focusing most of its effort on Problem 5, which falls within the purview of this book.

As the name suggests, the anti-plague system's primary purpose when it was established in the late 1890s was to combat bubonic plague, but as it grew, the system took on new responsibilities and the word "plague" eventually came to encompass several Group I diseases indigenous to the Soviet Union that cause high morbidity and mortality/lethality. The anti-plague system consisted of six anti-plague institutes (see Table 5.1 for their official and informal names) and more than 100 subordinate regional and field stations that were strategically located throughout the Soviet Union's Caucasus and Central Asian regions.

In general, the Soviet government considered specific information about infectious disease outbreaks to be state secrets. The anti-plague system therefore worked in secrecy until 1986, when Gorbachev instituted *glasnost*

Table 5.1 Official and Informal Names of Soviet Anti-plague Institutes

Official name	Location	Informal name
Central Asian Scientific Research Anti-plague Institute	Alma-Ata (Almaty)	Almaty Anti-plague Institute
Scientific Anti-plague Institute of the Caucasus and Trans-Caucasus	Stavropol	Stavropol Anti-plague Institute
Scientific Research Anti-plague Institute of Siberia and the Far East	Irkutsk	Irkutsk Anti-plague Institute
Scientific Research Anti-plague Institute, Rostov-on-Don	Rostov	Rostov Anti-plague Institute
Scientific Research Anti-plague Institute, Volgograd	Volgograd	Volgograd Anti-plague Institute
State Scientific Research Institute of Microbiology and Epidemiology of South-East USSR *"Mikrob"*	Saratov	*Mikrob*

(openness) in the Soviet government. As evidence of this secrecy, between 1928 and October 1989, Soviet officials neglected to report even a single plague case to the World Health Organization, even though epidemiologists knew well that the Soviet Union had the second largest enzootic plague area in the world and that cases occurred every year.[4] The following recounting demonstrates the secrecy under which Soviet anti-plague scientists worked:

The Nukus anti-plague station's deputy head on epidemiological issues was Nikolay Petrovich Limanskiy. Before going on vacation, Nikolay Petrovich was given the following instruction [by the First Department]:

"If you are talking to other passengers on the train and they ask the usual questions about your work place, what will you answer?

"I work at the anti-plague station.

"God forbid you! After that they will have other questions about plague, for which you are not allowed to answer. You need to say that you work in a medical organization on protection against influenza."[5]

Another observation was made by a scientist from the Gamaleya Institute:

The patterns of epidemic manifestations of plague, including descriptions of individual outbreaks within the territory of the former USSR and Russian Federation, remain an off-limits secret even though, according to official data approximately 4,000 cases in humans (including 2,600 with lethal outcomes) were reported in a 70-year period (1920–1989). An enormous amount of factual material on the epidemiology of plague in vast territories with diverse natural foci that was gathered by our country's unique army of plague specialists has been lost or is inaccessible.[6]

It is pertinent to note that none of the defense publications referenced in Chapter 1 mentions the anti-plague system or identifies specific civilian institutions or scientists involved in defensive work. It was not until 1995, as far as we are aware, that Igor V. Domaradsky self-published a book in Moscow which included descriptions of the anti-plague system and its role in the Soviet defensive BW program.[7] Domaradsky had been director of two anti-plague institutes (the Irkutsk Anti-plague Institute from 1957 to 1964, and the Rostov Anti-plague Institute from 1964 to 1973) and, subsequently, an important official in the Biopreparat system. He was the first author to introduce Western readers to the term "Problem 5" and to explain that it was a cover name for the Soviet Union's defensive BW effort. Since 1995, other authors have also referred to Problem 5, but none has dealt with it in depth.[8] An article one of us wrote began to fill in the information gaps about Soviet defensive BW activities as carried out in the civilian sphere, but there remains a lot to be learned.[9]

In many ways, the term Problem 5 is a unique codeword for the anti-plague system, much like *Ferment* and *Ekologiya* were codewords for other elements of the Soviet BW program. But in other ways, it is more complicated. The term "Problem" can be traced back to the four "problem commissions" that the Soviets established in the 1950s and 1960s to solve public health-related problems generated by plague and cholera. Each commission had particular responsibilities:[10]

- The First Problem Commission (Problem 1) guided studies of known natural plague foci and investigated whether there were other, unknown natural foci in the Soviet Union. Problem 1's research agenda also included studies of hosts and vectors that carried and transmitted *Yersinia pestis,* diseases that afflicted the *Y. pestis* hosts, and decontamination methods. The First Problem Commission met annually at the Saratov Anti-plague Institute, commonly called *Mikrob.*
- The Second Problem Commission (Problem 2) was established at the same time as the first. Its objective was to eliminate plague and natural plague foci. Under Problem 2, scientists performed studies on *Y. pestis* strains to clarify their biochemical and other properties and antibiotic sensitivity patterns. In addition, they also developed practical methods to improve diagnostic techniques (especially serological techniques), to seek out and test avirulent strains for possible use in vaccines, and to improve therapeutic approaches for curing plague. Members of this commission also met annually at *Mikrob.*
- The Third Problem Commission (Problem 3) was responsible for promoting the manufacture of the diagnostics and laboratory procedures needed to fight highly dangerous pathogens, with a concentration on plague and cholera. Problem 3 supported work to manufacture and test bacteriophages (viruses that infect bacteria) for diagnostic purposes and work to improve serological (antibody) diagnostic techniques. This commission also met annually at *Mikrob.*

- The Fourth Problem Commission (Problem 4) was established in the aftermath of a large outbreak of cholera in the Uzbek SSR in 1965 and focused exclusively on this disease. Because cholera was commonly thought of as a disease that afflicted developing nations, the Soviet Union was loath to admit that it suffered from this problem and did not report any of its cholera outbreaks in the 1960s and 1970s to the WHO (among others, cholera was reportable under WHO's International Health Regulations 1969). All work related to Problem 4 was classified, and few scientists within the anti-plague system beyond those who actually worked on cholera problems knew about it. The Fourth Problem Commission met annually at the Rostov Anti-plague Institute.

The Fifth Problem Commission originated quite differently than the previous four. Yury A. Ovchinnikov initiated a deception effort whereby the MOH would operate a program as a cover for Biopreparat's offensive work.[11] The fifth program was added to the existing four programs and served as a legend for the offensive BW program and, further, as a link between Biopreparat and "normal" vaccine R&D institutes in the civilian sphere. The Fifth Problem Commission was responsible for what Domaradsky termed "the antibacterial protection of the population,"[12] including defenses against biological weapons possessed by foreign countries. This commission, whose membership was decided on by the MOD's 15th Directorate, operated continuously out of the Gamaleya Institute. All research related to Problem 5 was classified Top Secret and could be done only at specially designated and protected institutes and laboratories. Within the anti-plague system, only anti-plague institute directors and specially designated scientists knew about the existence of Problem 5.

Problem 5 initially had three main responsibilities. First, it supported practical work within the Soviet Union that focused on highly dangerous diseases other than plague that were endemic to the country and on the responses of hosts to the causative pathogens. This mainly involved developing vaccines. Second, it protected the Soviet Union from exotic diseases that might be imported. This also involved developing vaccines, but against exotic pathogens. Third, it developed safety measures that could be used to defend against BW and would help manage the consequences of a successful attack. Activities under this third task consisted mainly of developing detection methods for agents that might be used in attacks and suitable therapeutics. As part of this work, for example, laboratories studied the immunological responses of hosts to different pathogens, investigated the means whereby pathogens disperse or spread, and devised animal studies to model the spread of communicable diseases. For reasons discussed below, activities under this third task increased substantially in the mid-1970s.

The organizational structure of Problem 5 was straightforward. The MOD decided what work needed to be done under Problem 5 and issued the required task orders to the MOH's 2nd Directorate, which forwarded them to the Problem 5 Commission headquartered at Gamaleya Institute. The commission determined which laboratory was best suited to fulfill each task and issued the requisite orders. Each task was given a code name, usually of an animal or an object, such as "Butterfly" or "Lamp." Indeed, "Lamp" was the code name of a project to investigate antibiotics in foreign countries (see below). If a task required the collaboration of several laboratories, the subtasks would be named Lamp-1, Lamp-2, etc.

During the Soviet period, all pathogenic microorganisms were given code numbers.[13] The Problem 5 coding system was exacting, in that each code number represented a specific pathogen, and time-consuming. For instance, institute directors had to spend hours translating secret tasking orders into language that was understandable to non–Problem 5 scientists and, when the task was complete, they had to translate the results back into the secret terminology used to report to the MOH. This procedure was necessary because most scientists who worked on Problem 5 tasks and subtasks were unaware that they were part of the Soviet BW defense effort.

Though Gamaleya Institute was the lead scientific institute for Problem 5, the Moscow-based D. I. Ivanovsky Institute of Virology (hereafter, Ivanovsky Institute) and the Scientific Research Institute of Poliomyelitis and Viral Encephalitides (now called the M. P. Chumakov Institute of Poliomyelitis and Viral Encephalitides—hereafter, Chumakov Institute) also had important roles.[14] The Gamaleya Institute housed the Problem 5 Commission and reviewed completed tasks, requesting reports from the directors of the antiplague institutes on their Problem 5 activities and reviewing their plans.[15] In addition, every year or every other year, the Problem 5 Commission members, including representatives from the MOH's 2nd Directorate and from MOD, would visit all of the institutes involved in Problem 5 tasks to review their work and accomplishments.

After a designated laboratory or institute completed a Problem 5 task, the staff members of one of the three lead scientific institutes—Gamaleya, Ivanovsky, or Chumakov—reviewed the completed work to determine whether the stated objectives had been achieved and whether procedures were adequate and appropriate. The division of labor among the three institutes was as follows: Gamaleya Institute scientists reviewed the draft reports related to work involving bacteria, a few unusual viruses, epidemiology, vaccine production, and diagnostics; Ivanovsky Institute scientists reviewed work related to the biochemistry and molecular biology of viruses not covered by the Gamaleya and Chumakov Institutes; and Chumakov Institute scientists addressed work related to polioviruses, polio vaccines, and tropical viruses. The reviewers sent critiqued draft reports back to the executing institute or laboratory for revision, and it transmitted the final report to the MOD via the MOH. If the reviewing institute found a draft report to be seriously deficient, either the task had to be redone or a satisfactory explanation had to be provided by the executing institute.

Because the MOH's 2nd Directorate directed all of its work, Problem 5 could be considered a civilian program. However, according to Domaradsky, Major General Victor N. Pautov headed Problem 5 while it was headquartered at Gamaleya.[16] That a general headed Problem 5 strongly suggests that it was primarily a military program, executed at civilian institutes.

The Problem 5 Commission's responsibilities were considerably expanded between 1975 and 1976, shortly after the International Olympic Committee awarded the 1980 Olympic Games to Moscow. At that time, Soviet officials worried that foreign visitors might import exotic diseases. A high-level interagency group with representation from the MOD, KGB, Ministry of Science and Technology, MOH, and USSR-AMN convened in 1976 to discuss this possibility. Concluding that the threat of disease importation was real, the group ordered the MOH to prepare technologies to detect exotic pathogens and diagnose exotic diseases, and to prepare therapies for treating them. This work began in 1977, with the Problem 5 Commission secretly selecting institutes capable of completing these new tasks, conducting background checks of the people who would do the work, and establishing lines of authority and reporting. By 1978, work on the new set of Problem 5 tasks had begun.

The Problem 5 work undertaken at the Byelorussian Research Institute of Epidemiology and Microbiology exemplified the new set of tasks. The institute was tasked with preparing defenses against all exotic viruses that visitors could conceivably bring with them, including Lassa, Ebola, and Marburg viruses. Staff at the virus culture collection at the Chumakov Institute sent vials containing strains of these extremely dangerous viruses to the Byelorussian institute under tight security. Two persons guarded the samples at all times; only train travel was permitted; the samples were specially packed in padded metal containers; and the guards checked in with the MOH at several predetermined points along the route. The institute's scientists used the Lassa, Ebola, and Marburg viruses to develop detection, diagnostic, and therapeutic methods for the diseases they cause. They reported the results of this work to Vladimir Sergeyev, the head of the committee on biosafety issues and arenaviruses in the MOH's Department of Quarantine Infections.

As best as is known, the Soviet Union did not experience any unusual disease outbreaks during or immediately after the 1980 Olympics. It is unknown whether this was because no pathogens were introduced either accidentally or deliberately by foreign visitors, or if pathogens were in fact introduced but were defeated by defenses developed under Problem 5. This uncertainty is usual to a defensive system; its operators can never be certain whether the lack of disease is due to efficient defenses or to the absence of disease.

As with the Soviet offensive BW program, Problem 5 work had entire closed institutes dedicated to it, as well as laboratories within the Biopreparat institutes and otherwise open institutes. In effect, all anti-plague institutes were Problem 5 institutes because they were assigned Problem 5 tasks. The anti-plague institutes' level of participation in Problem 5 was, however, unequal, with *Mikrob*, the Rostov Anti-plague Institute, and the Volgograd Anti-plague Institute having the heaviest involvement. *Mikrob* started working on BW-related projects as early as the 1950s, when it was tasked with developing fast detection methods for *Y. pestis,* testing antibiotics, and coming up with new treatment methods for plague, among other assignments.[17] In the early 1960s, Soviet officials redirected the Rostov Anti-plague Institute to work for Problem 5, studying vaccines, immune resistance, and lung disease mechanisms in animals.

According to a Biopreparat scientist, after Biopreparat was established, two of its institutes, SRCAM and IEI, collaborated under Problem 5 with *Mikrob*, the Rostov Anti-plague Institute, and the Volgograd Anti-plague Institute, but Biopreparat had no direct relationship with the Stavropol, Irkutsk, and Almaty Anti-plague institutes. In general, the Irkutsk Anti-plague Institute and the Stavropol Anti-plague Institute appear to have devoted only a small portion of their activities to BW defense activities. Neither the Soviet government nor Biopreparat scientists identified the Almaty Anti-plague Institute as being involved in defensive efforts, but it did perform some Problem 5 tasks. For example, Almaty specialists studied the immunogenicity, reactogenicity, and safety of vaccine strains of *Y. pestis* and brucellae.[18]

The Volgograd Anti-plague Institute was quite different from the other five anti-plague institutes, so different that its entire existence probably was a legend. In other words, although identified by name as an anti-plague institute, for a variety of reasons it was more akin to a Biopreparat institute, but under the authority of the MOH. For instance, a late-1990s publication about the anti-plague system states that the "Volgograd Anti-plague Institute was founded in 1970 to solve problems related to civil defense. It was officially under the USSR Ministry of Health, but many research fields were funded with the participation of *Glavmikrobioprom*."[19] This description of the Volgograd institute's objectives and the fact that it was established in 1970, the year when high-level discussions were laying the basis for *Ferment*, can reasonably lead one to conclude that the Volgograd Anti-plague Institute was designed to be a component of the growing Soviet offensive BW complex. Another author in the Levi volumes states that officials established a "special laboratory" at the Volgograd Anti-plague Institute that was directed by S. L. Borodko, but tells nothing about this laboratory's function.[20] According to Biopreparat scientists interviewed for this book, "special laboratory" is a euphemism for a Problem 5 laboratory. In addition, the institute's first director, Vasily S. Suvorov, was a retired colonel who had served many years at military research institutes.

According to interviews with several Biopreparat scientists, Biopreparat institutes, including SRCAM (for weaponization) and IEI (for vaccines and diagnostics), collaborated closely with Volgograd scientists to develop strains of *Burkholderia pseudomallei* (which causes melioidosis) and *Burkholderia mallei* (which causes glanders) for offensive purposes.[21] Author Leonid Zykin adds weight to this claim:

> It was namely during this time [early 1970s] that major changes occurred in the structure and personnel of the laboratory. A new science-production group was established within the laboratory (i.e., the "special laboratory"), the main task of which was experimental development and production of diagnostic preparations, luminescent immunoglobulins and, later, immunoenzyme test systems for rapid diagnosis and detection of the pathogens of glanders, melioidosis, atypical plague strains, and other dangerous microorganisms. The laboratory blossomed during late 1970s and first half of 1980s, when it actively collaborated with other departments of the institute, with large research institutes (Gamaleya Institute and the Central Asia, Irkutsk, and Rostov Anti-plague

institutes), and with many anti-plague stations. It was able to rapidly and effectively solve major tasks of implementing new diagnostic substances and testing them under practical conditions.[22]

The institute's first director, Suvorov, was fired in July 1976 because he made "serious mistakes in personnel, administrative, and science policy at the institute."[23] His immediate successor is unknown, but in 1985, N. G. Tikhonov, one of the Soviet Union's leading experts on burkholderiae, was named director. This supports the overall idea that the institute was established for the specific purpose of weaponizing burkholderiae. Indeed, there were at least four perceived advantages to weaponizing burkholderiae. At that time, there were no vaccines to protect against these bacteria; they were known to be very infectious in aerosol; they resisted most antibiotics available at that time, and it did not appear as if US health providers knew how to deal with the diseases they caused in humans, especially their pneumonic manifestations. Volgograd burkholderia specialists cooperated closely with Colonel Eduard A. Svetoch's laboratory at SRCAM.

In addition to the anti-plague facilities, Soviet officials ordered many open medical and public health institutes (institutes whose scientists were relatively free to publish in international journals and receive foreign visitors) to take on Problem 5 tasks. For this purpose, these institutes had between one and three closed laboratories that no one could enter without proper clearance. The above-mentioned Byelorussian Research Institute of Epidemiology and Microbiology, which had a collection of filoviruses, is an important example of an open institute whose staff published widely but that had closed laboratories.

One Problem 5 project carried out at the Byelorussian Research Institute was code-named Lamp.[24] Its objective was to test all commonly available Western antibiotics against bacterial pathogens of BW interest. To accomplish this extremely ambitious task, the institute was provided with samples of antibiotics from all over the world, as well as those used in the Soviet Union. The institute's director was also given the authority to assign his top scientists to undertake the rather long and arduous process of testing all of these antibiotics against all Group I and Group II bacterial pathogens. Another Problem 5 task involved the evaluation of foreign antiviral compounds and vaccines.

All Problem 5 institutes and laboratories were well secured in Soviet times, according to sources. They had powerful First Departments to manage security and perimeters guarded by troops from the Ministry of Interior, and they often had direct lines of communications with nearby police stations. The most sensitive Problem 5 facilities were surrounded by high concrete walls topped with broken glass or barbed wire, had closely controlled entry gates, and, in later years, had cameras for monitoring the movement of people near the facility and motion detectors on windows and doors to detect unauthorized entry. These security measures extended beyond the anti-plague facilities themselves. In Soviet times, the KGB maintained a presence in the communities in which the institutes were located, and checked on and controlled any activity aimed at compromising facility security.

In the 1960s the Gamaleya Institute started to collect articles and reports generated in the course of Problem 5 research and development and to assemble them in bound volumes. This collection on biodefense work eventually encompassed more than 30 volumes and included studies on decontamination, treatment, prevention, development of vaccines, indications of diseases, methods of treating infections, original data on pathogenesis, and epidemiological issues.[25] Some of these publications contained information that was readily available in the open literature, some were designated "For Official Use Only," and some were classified. Because all of the volumes were stamped "Top Secret," only persons with top secret clearance could access them at the Gamaleya Institute's library.[26] Further, because all three primary anti-plague institutes had the authority to grant advanced degrees to scientists who worked on classified projects, there are likely to be plenty of closed-off library or archive spaces containing classified candidate and doctoral theses, as well as classified inventor's certificates.

In the mid-1990s, Professor Yu. G. Suchkov wanted to declassify parts of these volumes, such as those dealing with decontamination methods. Though Suchkov had worked for many years at Gamaleya, rising in rank from scientist to director, he was denied permission to declassify the collection because of objections raised by the aforementioned Pautov.[27] These volumes apparently remain classified to this day, despite the Gamaleya Institute receiving international funding and the expectations that its work be transparent.

Lviv State Research Institute of Epidemiology and Hygiene, Lviv, Ukrainian SSR

The Lviv State Research Institute of Epidemiology and Hygiene[28] was a closed non-anti-plague institute dedicated to Problem 5 research throughout

Soviet times; it became an open institute in 1994. There were other non-anti-plague institutes solely devoted to Problem 5 work, but little is known about where they were located or what they did.

The building housing the institute was constructed in 1939, when Lviv was still part of Poland. It was paid for by a private doctors' foundation and was to be the headquarters of the Center of Infection Pathology. After the partition of Poland in 1939, the Ukrainian SSR government converted the center into the Institute of Epidemiology and Microbiology under the authority of the Ukrainian SSR MOH. The institute became a part of the system that provided oversight of the Soviet Sanitary Epidemiological System (SES) in western Ukraine, developing protocols for SES stations and evaluating their work.[29] German troops occupied Lviv during most of World War II, and they allowed a few of the institute's laboratories to continue operating, developing diagnostic approaches and therapies in reference to tuberculosis, epidemic typhus, and diphtheria. After the war, the institute was renovated and made completely operational.

In 1969 the Ukrainian SSR MOH renamed the institute the Regional Center of Indication and Identification of Extremely Dangerous Pathogens. That same year the center in effect became a Problem 5 facility; that is, it was ordered to take on MOD tasks regarding civil defense and investigate occurrences of viral diseases among civilians. In addition to the MOD and MOH, the center received task orders from the USSR Ministry of Science and Technology related to developing diagnostic and therapeutic preparations. For this purpose, the center tested an average of 4,000 preparations per year.

During Soviet times the institute had two research directions, one focused on bacteria and one on viruses. Within bacteriology, it began specializing in rickettsia studies in 1940, focusing mostly on epidemic typhus (trench fever). This work expanded to include *C. burnetii,* rickettsiae causing Mediterranean fever and Brill-Zinsser disease, and *Borrelia burgdorferi* (Lyme disease).[30] Most of the rickettsial strains stored in the institute's culture collection came from 1950s field expeditions. The institute's work on bacteria proceeded in parallel with its work on the fleas, lice, and other vectors that carried them; that is, the medical and biological departments collaborated. For example, in Ukraine, the major carriers of the Lyme disease pathogen, *Borrelia burgdorferi,* are mice and rats, but the pathogen is also carried by cattle, dogs, and birds. As part of their studies, the institute's scientists would send out two or more field expeditions every year to study natural Q fever and Lyme disease foci in the Ukrainian SSR and the Crimea. During these expeditions, they would be careful to check for dead migrating birds, and inspect dogs for infections because they are carriers of certain rickettsiae.

Before 1969 the institute's virus research focused on viral pneumonia, encephalitis viruses, Crimean-Congo hemorrhagic fever virus, and West Nile virus. In the early 1970s the institute started to work on other arboviruses as well. This work continues to this day.

The institute's culture collections are rich with strains. Although rickettsiae are notoriously difficult to collect and keep alive in storage, institute scientists have used a special maintenance process that has been able to keep some rickettsia strains in propagation for 50 years. This process could be based on methods developed by what is probably Lviv's most famous scientist, Rudolf S. Weigl (1883–1957), who found that the best way to grow rickettsiae was in the intestinal tracts of lice.[31]

In late 1991 the Soviet government ordered the institute's administration to send all of its secret reports and documents to Moscow. Ukraine was in the process of becoming independent, so it did not follow this order. Instead the institute sent all of its secret materials to the Ukrainian MOH in early 1992.

Contributions of Problem 5 and the Anti-plague System to the Soviet Offensive BW Program

To reiterate, the civilian component of the Soviet defensive BW program functioned under the umbrella of Problem 5, which was administered by the MOH's 2nd Directorate. There were some dedicated Problem 5 institutes (the only known one is located in Lviv), some Problem 5 work was performed by Biopreparat institutes, but most of it was performed by the anti-plague system, about which a series of papers was published in April 2006.[32] The April 2006 papers identify the anti-plague system's contributions to the Soviet offensive BW program, including these:

- It provided a legend for Ferment, the offensive BW program, allowing Soviet officials to present it as strictly a defensive program.
- It almost certainly supplied strains of virulent pathogens to Biopreparat and MOD biological facilities that were subsequently developed for military purposes. The most likely candidates for weaponization were strains of *B. anthracis, F. tularensis,* and *Y. pestis* that had been recovered from natural disease foci in the southern, southeastern, and southwestern regions of the Soviet Union. Further, Volgograd Anti-plague Institute scientists

collaborated with SRCAM scientists to weaponize *B. mallei* and *B. pseudomallei* strains for *Ferment*.

- The anti-plague facilities developed methodologies for handling, growing, and propagating dangerous pathogens, including those with fastidious growth requirements, and made them available to MOD and Biopreparat scientists.
- The anti-plague system trained MOD and Biopreparat scientists at anti-plague institutions to control and handle highly dangerous pathogens.

The small section on the Lviv State Research Institute of Epidemiology and Hygiene is significant because it demonstrates that there is yet another component of the complex Soviet BW program about which little is known—namely, a system of Problem 5 institutes outside of the anti-plague system. Other dedicated Soviet Problem 5 institutes would appear to be a worthy topic for future research.

6

Biopreparat's Role in the Soviet Biological Warfare Program and Its Survival in Russia

I N CHAPTER 2 we described how the Soviet Politburo established Biopreparat as a new and ostensibly civilian system with dedicated R&D for both defensive and offensive BW purposes.[1] From its beginnings until after the Soviet Union's dissolution in December 1991, Biopreparat operated *Ferment*, the program dedicated to planning, organizing, and supporting the research, development, testing, and production of a new generation of biological weapons. Biopreparat's defensive work was mainly meant to provide a legend that hid its offensive aspects from foreigners, and from most of its own workers and citizens. Biopreparat also laid the industrial base for what became Russia's largest producer of pharmaceuticals and health products, though again its primary purpose was to advance the Soviet Union's military capabilities. This chapter describes this biological weapons development system.

Three authors have previously described in depth the Biopreparat organization, and the political and social environment in which it existed in the Soviet Union. All three, Ken Alibek, Igor Domaradsky, and Sergei Popov, worked in the system and are important primary sources. Two, Alibek and Domaradsky, were for a time the deputy heads of the organization or directed important parts of it. Both of them have written informative books on their experiences at Biopreparat.[2] In addition, Alibek has expanded on the information in his book through interviews with print, radio, and television news organizations, and through testimony before US congressional committees. Popov prefers practicing science rather than giving public presentations

153

about his past Soviet work. However, he has given a few long, revealing interviews. This chapter uses parts of each of their written and verbal statements to illustrate, expand, and explain details about Biopreparat.

The purpose of this chapter is to describe aspects of the Biopreparat story that have previously been unreported or insufficiently reported. The chapter has three sections. The first section describes Biopreparat's history from where Chapter 2 left off to the end of the Soviet era in 1991. The second section describes Biopreparat's status and activities in the Russian era to the present. The third section discusses the motivations of civilian scientists who chose to work in Biopreparat's closed program. Chapters 7–9 address the five major Biopreparat institutes individually.

The Biopreparat System during the Soviet Era

On April 24, 1974, Soviet Order No. 131 DSP established the All-Union Science Production Association (SPA) Biopreparat to lead a new Soviet offensive BW subprogram in the civilian sphere.[3] Lieutenant General Ogarkov, who had previously worked in the 15th Directorate, was chosen to be its first director. He remained in this position until he was removed in 1979; he died in 1984. Though Biopreparat's civilian cover was as a pharmaceutical-industrial department of *Glavmikrobioprom*, it received its research plans and often its personnel through the 15th Directorate and was advised by the top secret Interagency Scientific and Technical Council for Molecular Biology and Genetics (MNTS).[4] All military employees of Biopreparat were assigned cover identities as ordinary civilian scientists.[5] A special *Gosplan* department headed by Major General Roman Volkov managed Biopreparat's financial planning, although all of its funding came directly from the USSR Council of Ministers.

At first Biopreparat's headquarters were located within *Glavmikrobioprom's* headquarters on Ulitsa Lesteva in Moscow, but after a few months it moved to Samokatnaya Ulitsa 4a. The KGB was responsible for the building's security, and, like all closed institutions, the KGB also controlled Biopreparat's First Department and Second Department. (Each of Biopreparat's institutes and centers also had First and Second Departments.) The First Department's primary responsibility was document security, and it maintained files of classified reports and copies of all communications. Biopreparat's director and the first deputy, as well as the institute directors, had level "F" security approval, allowing them access to this documentation and all of the program's records. The Second Department had many functions that continually brought it into direct contact with Biopreparat scientists. For instance, it was responsible for internal security in facilities; it practiced counterintelligence, such as checking for listening devices and intercepting messages; it read and censored all written material produced by Biopreparat staff that was slated for open publication; and, perhaps most importantly, it developed and perpetrated legends. Employees of the Second Department also secretly lived in the settlements and communities near secret facilities. Ministry of Internal Affairs troops were responsible for the perimeter security of Biopreparat facilities.

Alibek describes the secret code system that was developed to refer to biological agents within the BW programs, in which the following letters and numbers were assigned: F for psychotropic, behavior-altering biological agents; LM for peptides; L for bacteria (L1: *Yersinia pestis*, L2: *Francisella tularensis*, L3: brucellae, L4: *Bacillus anthracis*, L5: *Burkholderia mallei*, L6: *Burkholderia pseudomallei*); and N for viruses (N1: variola virus, N2: Ebola virus, N3: Marburg virus, N4: Machupo virus).[6]

The 1973 decree that created the MOD's 15th Directorate also provided for the creation of the MNTS.[7] It was placed under the authority of *Glavmikrobioprom*, which was subordinate to the Council of Ministers. The main purpose of the MNTS, which has been described by one of this book's sources as "the brain of Biopreparat," was to organize and coordinate the scientific-technical and production-technological issues associated with the development of biological weapons. The MNTS's first chairperson was Academician Viktor M. Zhdanov, and his deputy was Domaradsky.[8] In addition to the permanent MNTS members, representatives from the Central Committee, the KGB, *Gosplan*, and other agencies always attended MNTS meetings. Vasily D. Belyaev, the head of *Glavmikrobioprom*, attended the meetings as well.

MNTS members set up a bureau composed of their "assistants" to serve as a kind of secretariat. These assistants were supposed to be doctoral candidates of science, and their job was to manage the MNTS's administrative, logistical, and planning issues. The bureau had several sections, including sections addressing fundamental research, safety techniques, biotechnology, and parallel work in the domestic agriculture system. The bureau was responsible for:

- deciding priorities for *Ferment*;
- drafting project plans for scientific research to accomplish *Ferment's* mission;

- analyzing and critiquing project reports generated by the directors of Biopreparat's institutes;
- making preparations for MNTS meetings;
- preparing draft CPSU and Council of Minister decisions;
- coordinating the distribution of all MNTS documents with higher-ranking agencies;
- screening research results to determine whether they could be published; and
- evaluating discoveries made at Problem 5 institutes.

If a discovery was deemed patentable, department experts would assist in filling out an application for an inventor's certificate that would be submitted to the State Committee on Patents and Discoveries (Soviet patent law is described in the conclusion of this chapter). The submission would not identify the scientist applying for the patent; rather it would give an alias.

The MNTS's deputy chairman, Domaradsky, co-designed, with Zhdanov, a plan called the "Five Principal Directions," which guided Biopreparat's scientific work program.[9] This guidance became, in effect, Biopreparat's first five-year plan and came to be called the "Bonfire" program. Domaradsky has not specifically described the plan's five directions, but from his general descriptions and information gathered in interviews with him, close approximations of the directions emerge.[10] In general, the overall aim of *Ferment*, of which Bonfire was an important component, "was to develop a second generation of biological weapons using genetically modified strains, which would be of greater value [than "first generation" biological weapons that utilized classical pathogens and toxins]."[11] The Bonfire program's R&D efforts were likely split into the following five objectives:

- To develop pathogenic bacteria that would be resistant to many antibiotics (Domaradsky called them "polyresistant" strains but in modern literature the term multiresistant is more common). The employment of multiresistant bacterial pathogens in biological weapons would make it very difficult for defenders to appropriately treat infected populations.
- To develop strains of bacteria and viruses with modified antigenic structures. Bacterial and viral pathogens with altered appearances could avoid being recognized by a defender's diagnostics and vaccines, and by human immune systems that had acquired natural or vaccine-induced immunity from previous exposures to natural infections or vaccinations.[12]

(The results of research under these first two objectives were spun off into the "Metol" program.)

- To genetically engineer pathogenic bacteria and viruses for the purpose of endowing them with "wholly new and unexpected properties." This objective included transforming nonpathogens and weak pathogens into virulent pathogens. (Some of the creations generated as part of this objective were spun off into a program called "Factor.")
- To develop methods to increase the hardiness of BW microorganisms so that they were better able to withstand storage and the stress of being released into the open environment as aerosol particles.
- To develop and implement safety requirements and practices to guide the R&D performed as part of the first four objectives.

According to a former Biopreparat scientist who worked under both the Bonfire and Factor programs, although Bonfire's objectives were clearly formulated, no one knew how they were supposed to be accomplished.[13] Each institute had to develop its own scientific strategies and experimental approaches in order to reach its objectives, but because few administrators and scientists had credible ideas for doing so, many R&D efforts started unproductively. These conditions could explain the frustration among some Biopreparat scientists. For instance, Alibek wrote that at the time of Pasechnik's defection in 1989, "work on Bonfire had dragged on for some fifteen years, and most of us had given up hope of ever obtaining results."[14] The Bonfire program appears to have accomplished little.

The years 1974 and 1975 were particularly important to Biopreparat. During this time Soviet officials decided and allocated the funding to construct and equip most of the major Biopreparat institutes, including the All-Union Research Institute for Applied Microbiology (SRCAM) in Obolensk; the Research Institute of Highly Pure Biopreparations (IHPB) in Leningrad; the All-Union Research Institute of Molecular Biology (VNII-MB) in Koltsovo; the Scientific Experimental and Production Base (SNOPB) in Stepnogorsk; the All-Union Institute for Biological Instrument Development (*Biopribor*) in Moscow;[15] and the Institute for Biochemical Technological Development (*Biokhimmash*) in Moscow. In addition, in 1974 Soviet officials transferred the Berdsk Chemical Factory, the Omutninsk Chemical Factory, Plant "Progress" in Stepnogorsk, and the Scientific-Research Technological Design Institute of Biologically Active Substances (IBAS) in Berdsk to Biopreparat. (A separate state decree created the Institute of Engineering Immunology (IEI) in 1979.)

BW-related research under Biopreparat's auspices, but not at Biopreparat facilities, first began at two sites, according to Domaradsky: the open All-Union Scientific Research Institute of Protein Synthesis in Moscow and the MOD's Kirov Institute. No pathogen work could be performed at the Moscow site, so Domaradsky's team used a vaccine strain of *Y. pestis* to undertake experiments involving gene transfer.[16] Domaradsky conducted similar experiments with virulent strains of *Y. pestis* at the high-level biosafety facilities of the Kirov Institute. This was highly unusual because civilians were hardly ever given entry into military laboratories.[17] Domaradsky had a long-standing association with the All-Union Scientific-Research Institute for Protein Synthesis because of his interest in plasmids. He claims to have been the first in the world to discover plasmids in *Y. pestis,* and in 1973 he had established a new laboratory at the institute to research the extrachromosomal (plasmid) heredity of microbes. This open research program, which was used as a legend for secret activities at other institutes, was named "Plasmid."[18]

In 1975 a decree ordered the reorganization of the MNTS. Belyaev replaced Zhdanov as chairperson. Almost all of the original MNTS members were removed. The new membership included general Colonel General Smirnov and Lieutenant General Ogarkov. Nothing is known about why this change was made, but the sources for this book suggest that it had to do with the 15th Directorate coming to believe that the MNTS's original membership was too scientifically oriented and did not focus enough on achieving military objectives.

The sources interviewed for this book all believed that Ogarkov was not a strong or good leader. They used words like "colorless," "unimaginative," and "uninspiring" to describe him.[19] Whatever the case, Ogarkov was removed as Biopreparat's director and a member of the MNTS in 1979 after being charged with misconduct in relation to a book he had written years earlier. In 1975 he had co-authored a book (with K. G. Gapochko) called *Aerogenic Infection* that, as the name suggests, dealt with a subject of high importance to those interested in the aerosol dispersal of living and inanimate products.[20] The open publication of such a book by military scientists was undoubtedly reviewed extensively by security officials at both the Kirov Institute, where the authors had worked before, and by officials at the 15th Directorate. Nevertheless, Ogarkov was accused of revealing too much in the book and was reprimanded, with the reprimand signed by Brezhnev.

Rather than this reprimand, Ogarkov was most likely removed from his post at Biopreparat because of efforts to do "real" work were proceeding too slowly to satisfy the 15th Directorate. As Alibek notes, after four years of existence and considerable financial support, Biopreparat had not developed a single new BW agent.[21] Ogarkov's replacement, Lieutenant General Yury T. Kalinin, was considerably younger than him (41) and was described as being energetic.

After he took over, Kalinin "obtained funds to erect dozens of research and production buildings where none had existed before . . . [and] the number of Biopreparat employees quintupled."[22] Nevertheless, two years after Kalinin became director, Biopreparat had still not generated even a single new BW agent. Feeling desperate, Kalinin ordered the immediate weaponization of *Francisella tularensis* at two Biopreparat facilities: the Scientific and Production Base at Omutninsk, which was also a mobilization capacity production site, and SRCAM. Alibek directed the Omutninsk project to weaponize *F. tularensis* and described it in his book.[23] Domaradsky directed the SRCAM project, which is described in the next chapter. Biopreparat officials "considered this to be the beginning of the 'real work' and [their] chance to shine," according to Domaradsky.[24] By "real work," he means offensive BW R&D.

In 1982 Biopreparat organized and hosted the First International Conference on Metabolic Plasmids, which was held in Tallinn, Estonian SSR. The conference was Domaradsky's idea, and he organized it. *Glavmikrobioprom* invited one of the authors of this book (Zilinskas) to participate in the conference. He was among the 22 foreign scientists from nine countries who participated;[25] in addition, between 110 and 120 Soviet participants attended the conference, but it is uncertain how many of them were scientists.

At the time, Zilinskas had no idea that the event was an elaborate attempt by Domaradsky to bolster Biopreparat's first-level legend as a strictly civilian R&D institution. All foreign scientists at the meeting, including scientists from nations then allied with the Soviet Union, such as East Germany, Poland, and Czechoslovakia, were housed separately from the Soviet scientists. While conference's attendees met at some social events, these were strained encounters because most of the Soviets did not speak English and they presumably were being monitored by the KGB. A few English-speaking Soviet scientists did converse with foreigners, and Zilinskas ended up using information gained in Tallinn, and later in Moscow, in an Office of Technology Assessment (OTA) study and a series of articles published in *Bio/Technology*.[26] Many years later, while performing research in the US National Archives, Zilinskas noted that some of the information that he had conveyed to the US science attaché in Moscow, Mike Joyce, had been incorporated

Table 6.1   Known Components of the Civilian BW System, circa 1986

R&D institutes
All-Union Research Institute for Applied Microbiology (SRCAM) in Obolensk
Scientific-Production Association (Vector) in Koltsovo
All-Union Scientific Research Foot and Mouth Disease Institute, Vladimir
All-Union Scientific Research Institute of Veterinary Virology and Microbiology, Pokrov
Institute of Engineering Immunology (IEI), Lyubuchany
Research and development facility of unknown name, Vladimir
Research Institute of Highly Pure Biopreparations (IHPB) in Leningrad
Scientific Institute of Phytopathology, Golitsyno
Scientific Institute of Phytopathology, Tashkent, Uzbek SSR
Scientific Research Agricultural Institute, Otar, Kazakh SSR

Production and mobilization plants
All-Union Research Institute of Applied Enzymology, Vilnius, Lithuanian SSR
Berdsk Chemical Factory, Berdsk
Biokombinat, Georgian SSR
Biosintez Combine, Penza
JSC "Sakagrobiomretsvi" (Biokombinat), Tabakhmela, Georgian SSR
Omutninsk Chemical Factory, Omutninsk
Production Facility "Biokombinat," Alma Ata, Kazakh SSR
Pokrov Biological Preparations Plant, Ministry of Agriculture
"Progress" Plant, Stepnogorsk
Scientific and Production Base, Omutninsk
Scientific and Production Base of the Siberian Branch of the Institute of Applied Biochemistry, Berdsk
Scientific Experimental and Production Base (SNOPB), Stepnogorsk
Scientific-Research Technological Institute of Biologically Active Substances (IBAS), Berdsk
Sintez Combine, Kurgan

Table 6.1   (continued)

Special Weapons and Facility Design Units

All-Union Institute for Biological Instrument Development (*Biopribor*), Moscow (Other names for this institute include Institute of Biological Instrumentation, Institute for Biological Instrument Design, All-Union Scientific-Research Institute of Medical Instrument Design, State Research Institute of Biological Instrument-Making, Institute of Biological Instrument-Making, and Special Design Bureau for Biological Instrument Development. Further, the acronym *Biopribor* is also used for a similar type institute located in Pushchino.)

Institute of Applied Biochemistry, Moscow

Institute for Biochemical Technological Development (*Biokhimmash*), Moscow

Scientific-Research Technological Design Institute of Biologically Active Substances (IBAS), Berdsk

Special Design Bureau of Controlling Instruments and Automation, Yoshkar-Ola

Special Design Bureau for Precision Machinery Building, Kirishi

State Institute for the Design of Enterprises of the Biological Industry (*Giprobioprom*), Moscow

Unknown name, Posyolok Volginsky

into a secret assessment of Soviet biotechnology by the director of Central Intelligence.[27] For unknown reasons, Biopreparat never again sponsored an international event during the Soviet era.

In 1986 the Ministry of Medical and Microbiological Industries, *Glavmikrobioprom's* newly created successor organization, assumed control of Biopreparat, including the MNTS. The Ministry was headed by Valery A. Bykov,[28] and Kalinin served as his deputy in matters pertaining to Biopreparat and MNTS.[29] By this time, Biopreparat facilities were operating at sites throughout the Soviet Union (see Table 6.1). Chapters that follow address the five major Biopreparat institutes in detail, but Biopreparat institutes and plants about which little is known are described below:

- Scientific-Research Technological Institute of Biologically Active Substances (IBAS), in Berdsk. Berdsk is located 32 kilometers southeast of Novosibirsk and about 20 kilometers south of Vector. IBAS was a Biopreparat production plant, supposedly equipped with six huge 20,000-cubic-meter fermenters. Its legend was that it was dedicated to the manufacture of bacterial means of crop protection such as *Bacillus thuringiensis*. Within Biopreparat, the institute was known to be in a state of permanent readiness for the production of BW agents.[30] Accordingly, it served as a reserve mobilization facility for weapons based on *Francisella tularensis, Burkholderia mallei,* brucellae, and *Yersinia pestis.* (Other reserve mobilization facilities were in Kurgan (*"Sintez"*) and in Penza (*"Biosintez"*), which were constructed to produce wet and dry *Bacillus anthracis* formulations.)[31]

- Special Design Bureau for Precision Machinery Building in Kirishi. Kirishi is located 110 kilometers southeast of St. Petersburg. There were two biological production plants at Kirishi in Soviet times. The first was owned by the Ministry of Chemical Industry and produced carbohydrate products from paraffins and had little or nothing to do with Biopreparat. The second was a Biopreparat plant that produced the equipment needed to manufacture BW agents and biological weapons. For example, it manufactured the large fermenters, filtration, separation, and chromatographic equipment for the large-scale production of BW agents, as well as the explosion chambers for closed testing. The Kirishi plant had joint production projects with *Biokhimmash* and *Biopribor* in Moscow, and it complemented the work of the Yoshkar-Ola plant (see below).[32]

- State Institute for the Design of Enterprises of the Biological Industry (*Giprobioprom*). This Moscow-based institute designed weapons research and production facilities and generated architectural plans for them.[33]

- State Research Center for Biological Instrument-Making (*Biopribor*). This Moscow-based center was responsible for supplying equipment used for field sampling; creating aerosols and performing chemical and physical analysis of aerosols; physically and optically detecting aerosols; designing and producing equipment to perform ELISA; and designing portable gas chromatography and mass spectrometry systems.[34]

- All-Union Research, Planning, Construction Institute for Applied Biological Chemistry (*Biokhimmash*).[35] Located in Moscow, this institute was responsible for designing and controlling technological equipment and processes; providing documentation for the construction of facilities; designing biosecurity systems and facilities; designing and developing aerosol chambers; securing telephone connections; designing weapons production and testing equipment; and creating the fictional facilities and documents to maintain a civilian cover to the outside.[36] In a recent brochure, its management asserts that [*Biokhimmash*] ". . . took active part in the engineering of Berdsky, Omutninsky, Pokrovsky factories of bio-preparations, issued technical documentation for the production of the equipment for microbiological synthesis for OKB Yoshkar-Ola, Kirishky OKB TBM, took part in the engineering of GNTs Vector and GNTs of the Applied Microbiology (Obolensk)."[37] It also managed the Scientific-Production Association "*Biomash*," which had manufactured fermenters for facilities in Posyolok Volginsky, Omutninsk, and Stepnogorsk.[38]

- Biological Equipment Production Plant. Located in Yoshkar-Ola, 648 kilometers east of Moscow, this plant was directed by *Biokhimmash* and *Biopribor*. According to Pasechnik, it was the largest Biopreparat plant for the production of BW technical components, such as instruments and equipment. It also produced "small bomblets," which from Pasechnik's description resemble the *Gshch-304* bomblet described later in Chapter 10. The plant had a design bureau that implemented plans drawn up in Moscow. According to Pasechnik: "The plant was known for the production of a variety of biotechnological components, including fermenters, detection equipment (e.g., lidars, gas chromatographers, ELISA, etc.), disintegration machines, and freeze-drying equipment. An important part of its business was the production of filling stations which were used for the automatic filling of warhead devices with infectious agents. I saw a prototype of one station when I was at the plant with a Biopreparat inspection team about 1983."[39]

- Omutninsk Chemical Factory. Omutninsk is located 150 kilometers east of Kirov. The large Biopreparat production plants located there had two product lines in separate buildings—influenza vaccine and crop-protection bacteria. In Soviet times, the Omutninsk Chemical Factory was the largest Soviet producer of influenza vaccines, meaning that it could mass produce viruses. To do this, it used the classical production method based on embryonated eggs. The factory's capability to produce crop protection bacteria meant that it could also mass produce bacteria. The heavily guarded special BW laboratory at the Omutninsk Chemical Factory was located 400 meters from the factory's main gate and looked small and unassuming from the outside, according to Pasechnik. The two-floor underground facility contained BSL-3 and, perhaps, BSL-4 laboratories. Pasechnik told us that the IHPB worked with the Omutninsk Chemical Factory in 1982–1983 to develop a *F.*

tularensis formulation that could be manufactured on a large-scale. Pasechnik also served on a Biopreparat commission to validate the performance of the underground laboratories.

Though all Biopreparat institutes where "real" work was performed were closed, a few related specialized research institutions were not. One open Biopreparat-related institute had a particularly vital role. In the late 1970s, the supply of restriction enzymes, which are vital for genetic engineering work, was severely limited in the Soviet Union. Out of desperation, researchers collected bacteria that produced these enzymes and developed protocols for recovering and purifying them. Institutions would exchange lists of scientists and the types of restriction enzymes they were able to supply. This informal barter system enabled molecular biologists to trade with one another for some of the restriction enzymes they needed.

This primitive supply system was inadequate for Biopreparat's purposes. To meet demand, Biopreparat established an enzyme development and production facility in Vilnius, Lithuanian SSR, called All-Union Research Institute of Applied Enzymology.[40] Under the leadership of Arvydas Janulaitis, the institute supplied restriction enzymes and other enzymes of importance to research laboratories and industries throughout the Soviet Union. Biopreparat appointed Lyudmila I. Petrova as the institute's "curator." At that time, a curator supervised the institution but was not technically responsible for its work. Petrova, a minor Biopreparat functionary, was married to the exceedingly influential A. A. Vorobyov. As an open institute, none of its employees, besides Petrova, knew the "real" business of its main customer. (After Lithuania regained its independence, All-Union Research Institute of Applied Enzymology was renamed Institute of Biotechnology, "*Fermentas*," and quickly adapted Western production techniques and marketing skills.[41] *Fermentas* became a hugely successful biochemical development and manufacturing enterprise that markets its wares throughout the world.)[42]

By the end of the 1980s, Biopreparat controlled between 32 and 40 institutions, mobilization plants, and other types of facilities in the Russian SSR and other Soviet republics that were either involved in BW R&D or supported it in some way. At least 30,000 people worked for the Biopreparat system.[43] Alibek claims that the Soviets spent almost $1 billion in 1990 alone on biological weapons R&D.[44] Pasechnik estimated that between 1974 and 1989, Biopreparat's annual hard currency budget was $50–150 million per year, of which most went to purchasing foreign equipment and supplies. An additional and much larger amount in rubles was spent for routine expenses, including salaries, facility upkeep, construction, and utilities.

Biopreparat in Present-day Russia

Biopreparat's post-Soviet history is complicated, with many of its activities remaining hidden from public view. One likely reason for the continued secrecy was that Biopreparat still performed secret contract work in the early 1990s for the Russian Federation Ministry of Defense (RF-MOD); another reason may be that Biopreparat is trying to conceal the corrupt practices of its leadership, primarily its director, Kalinin. Biopreparat scientists told us that Biopreparat took on secret contract work for the RF-MOD in order to survive until it became a joint stock company (in Russian designated by the acronym RAO) in 1994. Whether this secret work was offensive or defensive in nature is unknown, as is whether it continued past 1994.

After the Soviet Union's dissolution, Biopreparat's primary concern was obliterating all traces of the Soviet offensive BW program at its institutes and facilities. Vaults holding classified documents were emptied, and the documents were transported to Biopreparat headquarters or the RF-MOD for storage, or were destroyed. Overt signs of offensive work, such as the chambers in which scientists tested dispersion by explosion, were either disassembled or cleaned for future civilian or defensive applications.

During Kalinin's first public interview in October 1992, he claimed that Biopreparat was vital to the newly established Russian republic:

> Drugs make up most of what we [Biopreparat] produce (70 percent of the total volume of output). Not a single hospital could get by without the preparations we make. After all, antibiotics and blood substitutes are absolutely endemic [*sic*] to surgeries. A large volume of the medications we produce are endocrine preparations and diagnostic systems meant for detecting infectious disease agents and for performing biochemical analysis. We try to deliver them in complete kits, with a set of reagents and laboratory ware and instruments. The enterprises of the concern [Biopreparat] manufacture nearly a thousand products. . . . Moreover, in the interests of the Russian Federation Ministry of Defense, research is being done on biological aerosols, diagnostics, and the development of vaccine preparations—including genetically engineered preparations—for the prevention of dangerous infectious diseases of

viral and bacteriological etiology; technologies and equipment are being developed for their production; and instruments for specific and nonspecific indications are being designed, as are automated warning devices.[45]

Biopreparat's status became clearer after the Russian government issued resolution #127-R on February 4, 1994, transforming Biopreparat into RAO Biopreparat. An edict signed by President Boris Yeltsin simultaneously gave the new entity control over the shares of 30 other RAO companies that had formerly been state-owned pharmaceutical enterprises.[46] RAO Biopreparat was expected to effectively manage the government's share (51%) in these enterprises, by developing and producing new products to generate income. Kalinin was named its general director. Kalinin was also the government's representative on RAO Biopreparat's governing board, a member of the Russian Security Council's Interagency Commission for Health Care, and president of the Russian Association of Producers and Suppliers of Pharmaceuticals, Medical Products, and Technologies (Rosmedprom). He also retained his military rank as lieutenant general, even though he was beyond the retirement age of 60.[47]

In managing RAO Biopreparat, Kalinin was not hesitant to seek partners from outside of Russia. For example, in 1996 he sought "US partners" to invest in three projects: the first proposed to set up a factory in Obolensk to produce "infusion solutions, blood transfusion systems, and ready-to-use medicines," and requested an investment of $42 million; the second asked for an investment of $9 million to complete the construction of a pharmaceutical warehouse near Moscow's Sheremetyevo Airport; and the third sought $7.6 million to complete a factory to produce "6 million units of polymeric packaged flasks and 6.5 million units of blood transfusion systems."[48] It is unknown how successful Kalinin was in securing partners. But in 1998, RAO Biopreparat entered into an agreement with pharmaceutical giant Searle Pharma (now Pfizer) to build a $30 million medication production plant in Izvarino, Moscow region; the facility opened in 2000. The collaboration's first aim was to produce 300 million tablets and capsules per year of popular cardiovascular, gastroenteric, antibacterial, and other drugs; Searle Pharma owned 75% of the business and RAO Biopreparat 25%.[49] A 2002 *Wall Street Journal* article described other collaborations between RAO Biopreparat and US enterprises.[50]

In 1997 the Russian government adopted a secret decree that put Biopreparat in charge of all the institutes it headed during Soviet times, and gave it the ability to control the scientists' travel, visitor access to Biopreparat institutes, and the hiring and discharging employees.[51] This transfer of power would have wide repercussions. In 2000 an investigative Russian journalist reported a long list of Biopreparat's failed expectations and possible misdeeds, all of which occurred because "one citizen outsmarted the government."[52] According to this reporter, RAO Biopreparat was expected to generate 700 million rubles of income and dividends per year for the government, but as of 2000 it had not earned a single kopek.

Even more disturbing, RAO Biopreparat had auctioned off some of the most valuable of its 30 companies, and none of the proceeds went to the government. "Passivity, especially on the part of the Ministry of Property Relations, has led to a situation where all the Kalinins [*sic*] are making their own deals and cross-purposes with government interests while shielding themselves with their unique government status [i.e., Kalinin retaining his general's rank]. The time has come to determine whether the association *Rosmedprom,* which Kalinin heads, is simply a public relations [PR] 'cover' for the commercial organization RAO Biopreparat."[53]

The year 2000 was a bad year for Kalinin. Biopreparat's performance was poor, at least from the Russian government's viewpoint, and he also became involved in a scandal involving US government aid to former Soviet weapons facilities. The scandal started when Kalinin dismissed Vladimir P. Zaviyalov as director of Biopreparat's Institute of Engineering Immunology (IEI). The MOD had distrusted this institute since its inception, largely because Zaviyalov was a pure scientist who had little use for the military and showed it (see Chapter 9). On the other side, Kalinin was an unpopular man among the IEI's researchers. A 2001 book on germ warfare described the situation succinctly:

> Since that 1997 session (in September), Kalinin had become an obstacle, American officials felt.[54] Russian scientists complained that Kalinin had undermined their independence by using his bureaucratic powers to deny them the right to travel abroad to conferences and training programs. He had confiscated their passports, delayed the issuing of visas, and pressured institute directors not to develop independent ties to Western labs and companies. He had dismissed a prominent institute

director [Zaviyalov] from his post after the scientist had accused Kalinin of "illegal practices," including the pocketing of Western assistance money. Kalinin denied those charges.[55]

Scientists involved in the new IEI venture said that Zaviyalov's firing was a consequence of his seeking to enter into agreements with Western laboratories and industries without allowing Kalinin to act as a middleman.[56] By dismissing Zaviyalov, Kalinin apparently violated Russian law, because Zaviyalov had been elected to the directorship of what was then the joint stock company IEI by the majority of its stockholders at a general meeting and thus could be dismissed only by the stockholders at another general meeting. In response to his firing, Zaviyalov took the drastic step of revealing to an American reporter that funds provided by the US National Aeronautics and Space Administration (NASA) to Biopreparat might have been diverted and used for personal ends.[57] The reporter found that not only were NASA funds diverted, but USAID funds were also diverted from their intended purposes. The scandal grew as the Russian newspapers *Izvestia* and *Kommersant Daily* picked up the news.[58]

NASA quickly investigated the allegation. The investigative team, headed by NASA's associate director, found that the Russian Space Agency (RSA), commonly known in Russia as *Rosaviakosmos*, was given $20 million to perform space-related scientific research and that the agency spent this money from February 1995 to January 1998. Of this total sum, RSA had paid $1.529 million to Biopreparat for space-biotechnology scientific research. However, Biopreparat paid $1.368 million (89.5%) to eight subcontractors, and kept $0.161 million (10.5%) under the unspecified terms of its contract with RSA.[59] During the team's short investigation, it performed only a "verification of the funding process" to "determine the sources, recipients, and amounts of funds paid." With this limited scope in mind, the team found that "RSA submitted periodic reports to NASA as contract deliverable items, which NASA accepted as satisfactory completion of the planned research."[60]

In March 2000 a team led by the NASA associate administrator for space flight completed a more thorough study of NASA's relationship with RSA and Biopreparat. In addition to the payment figures identified previously, the investigation uncovered a list of the eight subcontractors and a general description of their research. Of the eight, four institutes were well known: SRCAM, Vector, IHPB, and IEI. The research they performed was described as: "Space Biotechnology: Diverse set of investigations similar to U.S. biotechnology interests, including protein crystal growth, effect of microgravity on genetic and cellular processes, antibodies, and polymers; electrophoresis, etc."[61]

The final word on this episode came from a NASA Inspector General report on the wider issue of NASA assistance to Russian biotechnology research. The report did not criticize the small funding provided to Biopreparat, rather it concluded:

NASA made one extremely serious misstep. After being provided with guidance by the State Department on how to collaborate safely with institutes that had been part of the Soviet biological warfare program, NASA did not follow that guidance. No site visits were scheduled to ensure that NASA funding was not supporting biological warfare research. No funded projects were reviewed for possible biological warfare connections. Indeed, months after receiving guidance from the State Department, that listed "careful vetting of biotech proposals" as one of the key steps to minimize concern when working with such institutes, NASA funded, *without reviewing the proposals,* three additional projects at institutes that had been part of the Soviet biological warfare program. [Italics in the original.]

Recommendation 1: Any future NASA program that funds foreign researchers, particularly in countries not traditionally allied with the United States, should be carefully coordinated with the State Department (including the State Department's Bureau of Nonproliferation) to ensure that proper safeguards are in place. If the program funds biotechnology research in countries with known or suspected biological weapons programs, NASA should practice "invasive collaboration."[62]

In the end, NASA investigators found nothing to indicate that RAO Biopreparat had "misappropriated" money. The possibility remains, however, that Zaviyalov was more knowledgeable than foreign investigators about the inner workings of Biopreparat and its methods for securing and disbursing funding from international sources. Two different sources for this book, for instance, talked about the "overhead" that Biopreparat headquarters added to all proposals submitted to foreigners.

At first glance it appears that Kalinin personally gained little from the $0.161 million that was provided to Biopreparat headquarters for "overhead." He was never charged with any crime related to this, or any other episode. Yet Biopreparat, and indirectly Kalinin, gained income by forcing Russian scientists who wrote project proposals to include budget items that specified the purchase of reagents and supplies from Biopreparat at a cost of 10% of the proposed project's budget.[63] Biopreparat scientists and US officials confirm that each project proposal written by a Biopreparat institute researcher had to be reviewed by Biopreparat headquarters before being submitted to the International Science and Technology Center. Biopreparat officials let it be known that if a project budget omitted the overhead request, they would sit on the offending proposal for between 1.5 and 3 years before forwarding it to the funding agency, or they might reject it altogether.[64] If the proposal contained this request, Biopreparat's review would take less than 3 months and invariably would be approved for transmittal to the funding agency. This scheme explains Kalinin's insistence that Biopreparat be an interlocutor between the research institute and the funding agency, and the unhappiness of scientists such Zaviyalov with Biopreparat headquarters.

Just over a year after the reports of diversions surfaced, Kalinin was dismissed as director of Biopreparat and was replaced by Dr. Ramil U. Khabriev, "a public health expert and a former official of Tartarstan."[65] Yet it is doubtful that the NASA-RAS imbroglio had much, if anything, to do with the dismissal. A Moscow newspaper article revealed the underlying conflict:

> The long-drawn-out conflict between the Ministry of Health and the Russian joint-stock company Biopreparat, which is one of the main players in the pharmaceuticals market, is nearing an end. The confrontation has apparently culminated in a victory for the ministry. Wednesday evening, a new general director was elected at a meeting of the Russian joint-stock company's shareholders. Ramil Khabriev became director of the joint-stock company, which manufactures at least 30 percent of the drugs produced in Russia. Mr. Khabriev moves into his new office directly from an office in the Ministry of Health, where until recently he headed the department of quality control, efficacy, and safety of drugs and medical technology. . . . Over the past year, high-ranking officials of the [Ministry of Property] stated more than once that Biopreparat was not fulfilling the conditions that the government imposed on it when the joint-stock company was created in 1994.[66]

If a 2005 brochure is to be believed, RAO Biopreparat did better under Khabriev than Kalinin:

[RAO Biopreparat] has 20 industrial facilities producing about 1,000 products. Annual production has increased every year and currently is over 10 billion rubles, which represents about 35% of the medical products produced in Russia. Our output includes over 8 billion rubles of medicines and 1.7 billion rubles of medical equipment items. Over 36,000 people are employed in production. . . . The company produces veterinary preparations, biologicals for plant protection, and highly effective feed additives based on antibiotics and enzymes. Enzyme preparations also are used in various industries, including food processing, leather, and textiles.[67]

Khabriev departed RAO Biopreparat in 2005 to become head of the All-Russian Research and Testing Institute for Medical Appliances. In early 2006 he was promoted to the head of the Federal Service on Surveillance in Healthcare and Social Development of the Russian Federation, which among its responsibilities oversaw a program to deliver medicine to Russian veterans. In March 2007, Prime Minister Mikhail Fradkov dismissed Khabriev because his agency had accrued $1.5 billion in debt to pharmaceutical companies, which slowed deliveries of necessary medicines to veterans.[68] Shortly thereafter, President Putin dismissed Khabriev's boss, the minister of health, Mikhail Zurabov.

Since his removal as director, Kalinin has remained active in the field. According to one of the Russian sources for this book, he is currently general director of the private company Biopreparat-Center, which is located in the same building at Samokatnaya 4a, where SPA/RAO Biopreparat headquarters were previously located (see Chart 6.1, "Biopreparat System, 2007"). Kalinin was also the scientific supervisor of State Research Center for Biological Instrument-Making and advisor to Sanitation Inspector-General Gennady G. Onishchenko. The joint-stock company Biopreparat, the official successor to SPA/RAO Biopreparat, moved to Ulitsa Klary Tsetkin 4 and into the building that houses the Institute for Biochemical Technological Development (*Biokhimmash*). In 2007 its general director was Vladimir N. Kolesnikov, and Valentin I. Yevstigneev was his deputy director.

In general, the Russian biotechnology industry remains a woefully poor performer. In 2003, total sales of biotechnology products in Russia were less than $1.5 billion, and the domestic industry's share was only 25–30%.[69] Russia imported more than 70% of all medicinal drugs used in 2007, primarily from France and Germany. RAO Biopreparat alone cannot be held responsible

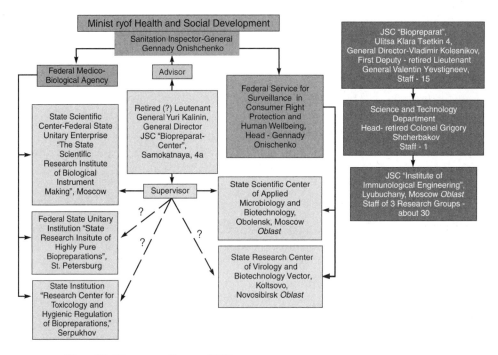

Chart 6.1 Biopreparat System, 2007

for the travails of the Russian biotechnology industry, but if it had been functioning efficiently and honestly, it would have significantly improved the domestic development and production of biotechnology products. It is telling that a 2007 special report by a major German bioindustry journal on biotechnology in Russia does not mention RAO Biopreparat or any of its subsidiaries.[70] In contrast, RAO Bioprocess, which was established in 1988 by persons who had nothing to do with the military, is doing remarkably well.[71]

The Motivations of Civilian Scientific Workers in a Closed R&D System

When they designed the expanded, modern Soviet BW program, officials recognized *a priori* that it violated the Biological and Toxin Weapons Convention (BWC) and had to be kept so secret that there would be no hint of its existence. Not only were the scientists who operated the program sworn to secrecy, but each had to undergo a rigorous security investigation before being hired—even at the lowest legend level. Every scientist knew when he or she was applying for a Biopreparat position that the position demanded adherence to secrecy rules, including restrictions on publication, restrictions on foreign travel except under the most unusual conditions, prohibitions on discussing work with outsiders, and constant oversight by the KGB. Yet thousands of Soviet scientists chose this career path.

The following five reasons stand out as explanations of their decisions. First, during Soviet times, many young scientists had to pay off debts to society by working where they were ordered to do so. Recent graduates were often sent to sites that were unpleasant for one reason or another and could not attract more established scientists. For example, one recently graduated scientist was dispatched to a scientific station in far off Siberia to study Lyme disease. Just married, the scientist did not think that a job in a remote, lonely field station was a pleasant prospect. When given the opportunity to work at SRCAM, he did not hesitate to accept it.

Second, a general problem in the Soviet era was the lack of housing for Russians; this was an especially acute problem for recent university graduates. This explains why directors of Biopreparat institutes offered job candidates preferential access to housing as a prominent benefit. Third, the starting pay for Biopreparat scientists was 25–50% higher than salaries at civilian institutes, and this ratio continued as a scientist gained seniority. Fourth, Biopreparat scientists often enjoyed access to special government stores stocked with scarce goods unavailable to the general populace. Fifth, some idealistic scientific workers firmly believed that it was their duty to undertake work that served to defend the Motherland.

A conversation between two former military officers held during summer 2011 in Washington, D.C. casts light on Soviet military scientists and the BWC. The two were Dr. David Franz (a former commander of USAMRIID) and Dr. Gennady Lepeshkin (a former director of SNOPB) and the following extract deals only with the BWC. Dr. Slava Paperno, senior lecturer at Cornell University's Russian Language Program, served as an interpreter.

David Franz: When did you first become aware of the Biological Weapons Convention?

Gennady Lepeshkin: I learned about it as soon as it came into existence. [Authors: It is not clear whether Lepeshkin meant 1972, when the BWC was signed, or 1975, when it came into effect. At that time Lepeshkin worked as a scientist for the Soviet MOD.]

Slava Paperno: Did you discuss it?

Lepeshkin: We did.

Paperno: I asked if it was discussed and he said "yes, it was discussed." And? What did people say?

Lepeshkin: Well, nothing much. People just did their work.

Paperno: And I said, "so what was the conclusion?" He said, "nothing, we continued our work."

Lepeshkin: We're military folk, you see. In the military, you receive your orders, and you do your work.

It is worth asking how much scientists who worked at Biopreparat knew about the BWC and its provisions. The answers of ex-Soviet scientists interviewed for this book ranged from "knew nothing" to "have heard about it, but did not know about its provisions." Most answers fell in the first category. Why was there so little knowledge about the Soviet Union's international obligations? Did the Soviet government purposely keep the BWC secret, or are there other explanations? One could assume that the government simply kept the BWC as a whole, or its provisions, secret. Ironically, conversations with American scientists disproved this idea.

During a 2000 scientific conference in Fort Collins, Colorado, one of the authors (Zilinskas) asked participating American scientists about their knowledge of the BWC. He was astounded to learn that by far most of them had never heard of the BWC, and the few who had heard of the treaty, knew hardly anything about its provisions. Subsequent conversations with American scientists confirmed these initial observations.[72] If a significant proportion of American scientists are ignorant of the BWC, why should Soviet scientists be expected to know about it? By carefully questioning ex-Soviet scientists, it became clear that Soviet officials did not keep the BWC a secret. However, while information about the BWC was published in the Soviet Union, details about it were not readily available. This probably did not make a difference, however, as Soviet scientists mostly focused on their research (similar to their US counterparts) and ignored distractions such as politics.

After an ignominious history, RAO Biopreparat is probably no longer involved in biological weapons acquisition efforts and has probably substantially decreased its involvement in the RF-MOD's defense efforts. The US Nunn-Lugar nonproliferation programs described in Chapter 23 and the transparency that they introduced into the former Biopreparat facilities are a major reason for this assessment. In addition, the RF-MOH and Ministry of Property's unhappiness with Biopreparat's performance as a business entity and

Kalinin's replacement by a business-oriented director demonstrate the overriding priorities of the enterprise. Assuming that these conclusions are correct: In the current chaotic economic Russian arena, what is RAO Biopreparat's competitive advantage? Simply put, RAO Biopreparat might control a biological treasure chest, yet it is unclear what its intellectual property rights are.

Soviet patent law recognized two legal means of protecting inventions, patents and inventor's certificates. The same criteria applied to both: the invention must be novel, useful, of a technological nature, and adequately disclosed (Article 21 of the USSR Patent Statutes).[73] A patent conferred upon its holder exclusive rights to an invention, while the inventor's certificate transferred the exclusive rights to the state.[74] If an invention was used for commercial purposes, the holder of the inventor's certificate was entitled to a cash bonus, the amount of which was based on the invention's expected economic impact as calculated by the Committee on Wages of the State Committee for Inventions and Discoveries.

In the classified Soviet world, intellectual property rights got very complicated. One Russian expert on intellectual property law observed: "Incessantly asserting that the Soviet state existed in a hostile environment, the state endeavored to hide as many inventions as possible."[75] This was the case with Biopreparat, as inventions developed by its scientists were accorded secret or "For Official Use Only" inventor's certificates.[76] In Soviet times, this was a common practice and was not questioned. However, scientists presumably would now like to publish or exploit the inventions they made during the Soviet era, but these inventions remain classified.[77] Unresolved issues relating to these types of claims include: How does one get a classified inventor's certificate declassified and, when this has been done, who is assigned the ownership rights to the newly declassified certificate? This question is particularly important to "For Official Use Only" inventions, of which there are probably large numbers in all technological areas.

In the area of biotechnology, few certificates are likely to contain sensitive information, especially when they deal with such mundane matters as decontamination, bioprocessing, preservation, and packaging. Yet in Russian society it is presumably difficult to get a bureaucrat to take responsibility for declassifying a document, so it is done but rarely. The challenge of getting a document declassified has given rise to a small industry, unique to Russia. A few entrepreneurial companies specialize in data mining the classified patent literature for inventions of possible commercial interest to either Russia or Western industries, and when they find promising prospects, they act to have them declassified. As an example of a successful data mining mentioned by the informant was a sensitive device developed for the military to detect bodies that had been buried under avalanches or mud slides. Sources for this book also made available inventor's certificates detailing inventions of possible use to bioindustry, such as protein purification processes, but these are not yet usable because they retain their "For Official Use Only" label.

RAO Biopreparat remains in possession of an archive containing much of the results of the work done by thousands of scientists and engineers at its many facilities prior to 1992. Though the RF-MOD can be expected to have secured the most secret documents, in particular recipes and their supportive documentation, it is unlikely it would have been interested in documents dealing with mundane subjects and having a "For Official Use Only" classification. This trove of documents, which includes inventor's certificates, might possibly constitute a biological treasure chest. Further, because Biopreparat was the classifying entity, there is every reason to believe that RAO Biopreparat has the right to declassify archived documents.

What might this chest contain? First, it might contain data on attenuated and naturally avirulent strains of normally pathogenic bacteria and viruses that could be used for the development of new or improved vaccines. Second, there may be bacteria and viruses that could be used to develop detection devices. Third, there may be already developed and, possibly, tested, detection devices for use by public health professionals, hospital-infection control personnel, or inspectors of plant and animal products. Fourth, there may have been decontamination reagents that kill hardy organisms and spores. Fifth, methods may have been developed for the production of cheap vaccines and therapeutics that can be dispersed by aerosol. These are only a few examples. For instance, we have not touched on production and downstream processing equipment and improved ways to package organisms and medicinals.

The Russian biotechnology industry is still behind the West in such matters as good research practices, good manufacturing practices, internationally acceptable animal handling, or marketing strategies. However, as its financial situation continues to improve, and as the Russian government and industry realize the limitations inherent to a natural resource-based economy (such as oil and gas), there is likely to be a substantial movement to build up the Russian human resource base and capitalize on its past achievements in the sciences. When this occurs, RAO Biopreparat would be in a favorable position to put its experts to work to apply the contents of its biological treasure chest or sell them to the highest bidder.

7

Biopreparat's State Research Center for Applied Microbiology (SRCAM)

Tнıs chapter and the two that follow address the five principal Biopreparat institutes, the State Research Center for Applied Microbiology
(SRCAM) in Obolensk; the Scientific-Production Association "Vector"
(Vector) in Koltsovo; the Research Institute of Highly Pure Biopreparations
(IHPB) in Leningrad; the Institute of Engineering Immunology (IEI) in Lyubuchany; and the Scientific Experimental-Industrial Base (SNOPB) in Stepnogorsk. Each institute's section (1) provides the history of the institute; (2) describes its physical plant and estimates its workforce; (3) describes as best as
possible its work program during Soviet times; and (4) discusses its changes
after the Soviet Union's dissolution.

Before addressing the institutes, however, it is necessary to comment on
Ferment's subprograms, particularly Bonfire, Factor, and Metol. In interviews for this book, Biopreparat scientists had different understandings of
the objectives of these subprograms and who directed them. For instance,
Alibek dedicates a whole chapter to Bonfire, but mentions Factor only twice
and then in passing. Domaradsky mentions Bonfire just once, but calls Factor
"one of the most significant divisions of the Soviet bioweapons program."[1]
The secondary literature about the Soviet BW program is rife with mistakes
about the contents of these subprograms.

Only the most senior Biopreparat officials likely knew the exact details of
the programs' objectives and divisions of labor, and they rarely shared this
information, even with institute directors and deputy directors. As *Ferment*

evolved, the borders between its subprograms' activities blurred and overlapped, but in general, Factor and Metol appear to have had the following goals:

- Factor. This program's primary goal was to enhance the virulence of pathogens and to convert opportunistic pathogens and nonpathogens into pathogens. The basis of this work rested on findings generated by Igor P. Ashmarin's research at the Zagorsk Institute on a group of peptides called "bioregulators." Once high-level Soviet Ministry of Defense (MOD) and Biopreparat officials recognized the importance of peptide R&D, they set up a new program called "Factor" to concentrate on these chemicals. Unlike Bonfire, Factor was clearly formulated as an experimental research program the results of which could not be predicted. Factor's R&D came to encompass both special bioregulators called "neuroregulators" that affect the central nervous system and can have either psychological or physiological effects, and "immunoregulators" that affect the host's ability to defend against microbial invaders. Over time, Factor scientists started working with peptides to enhance the virulence of both bacteria and viruses, so the border between Bonfire and Factor became blurred and the two programs' R&D overlapped. The programs became further blurred when both groups of scientists started working with proteins. Domaradsky initially directed Factor, but after his forced departure, the program was co-directed by Sergei Popov at SRCAM and Oleg A. Kaurov at IHPB. Vector and IEI were also heavily involved in Factor.
- Metol. As far as is known, Metol was a bacteria-only applied research program set up specifically to support the application of new bacterial creations generated by Bonfire. Metol scientists would, for example, take a bacterial strain that had been genetically engineered to be multiantibiotic-resistant and seek to determine its growth characteristics, its behavior when aerosolized, and its survival characteristics under a range of conditions. For the most part, Metol projects were undertaken at SRCAM and Omutninsk.

History of SRCAM

The State Research Center for Applied Microbiology (SRCAM) has its basis in the All-Union Research Institute for Applied Microbiology, which was established in response to Central Committee of the CPSU decree No. 704

(1974), "On Measures for the Acceleration of Development of Molecular Biology and Molecular Genetics and Use of Their Achievements in National Economy," dated May 21, 1974.[2] The institute's classified name was P.O. Box V-8724.[3] Its "open legend" was that it performed "plant protection" R&D, which meant that it developed "biological pesticides", such as *Bacillus thuringiensis,* for use in agriculture.[4] In 1992, after the Soviet Union dissolved, the institute was renamed the State Institute for Applied Microbiology, and in 1994 it was again renamed the State Research Center for Applied Microbiology (SRCAM) and was placed under the authority of the Russian Ministry of Health (RF-MOH). For convenience, hereafter, we only use the acronym SRCAM.

SRCAM's first director was Major General Vinogradov-Volzhinsky,[5] who suggested the name Obolensk for the new secret city where SRCAM and its settlement were sited.[6] Domaradsky described Vinogradov-Volzhinsky as a "clever man with good administrative capabilities."[7] He prepared the center to take on its mission in a relatively short time period, yet he was removed from his position in 1982, supposedly because of a disagreement he had with the then-director of *Glavmikrobioprom,* Rotislav C. Rychkov. His replacement was Major General Nikolay N. Urakov. Urakov had made his reputation as a scientist at the Zagorsk Institute, where he specialized in the study of *Rickettsia prowazekii* Strain E (which causes epidemic typhus) and *Coxiella burnetii* (which causes Q fever),[8] but his immediate previous job was as deputy director of MOD's Kirov Institute. Under Urakov, SRCAM became the most militarized of the Biopreparat institutes. This probably was because of his own military background, his propensity to hire military scientists, and his experience with biological weapons.[9]

As SRCAM was being built, most of its newly hired employees found temporary housing in the surrounding small towns of Protvino, Serpukhov, and Pushchino.[10] A large number of these employees moved to the Obolensk settlement in the mid-1980s, when 12 four-story apartment houses were finished to the point of being habitable. In Soviet times, the settlement had substantial amenities, including a cafeteria that served inexpensive food, playgrounds and schools for children, athletic facilities and equipment for adults, and well-kept landscaping. By the mid-1980s, the Obolensk settlement had grown to approximately 5,000 residents. As the settlement was located about three kilometers from SRCAM, regularly scheduled free shuttle buses carried workers between the two sites.

Security at SRCAM, and in its surroundings, was exceedingly strict, with the State Automobile Inspection and Transit Police Station in Obolensk given responsibility for traffic and security outside of the center. Its main task was to identify "nonlocal" vehicles and evaluate whether the vehicles' drivers had mistakenly driven to the closed facility.[11] According to Domaradsky, when he drove home on the weekends to his flat in Moscow, he had to stop at 11 security checkpoints each way, to and from Obolensk, to present identification and have his car inspected.[12]

The nearest city to the Obolensk settlement with amenities is Protvino, dubbed the "City of Physicists." A town of about 30,000 that is surrounded by a pine forest, Protvino has a mediocre hotel in which visitors to SRCAM and the U70 proton accelerator facility located in the city can stay. (The accelerator is an open facility.)[13] For some time after 1992, the U70 facility barely functioned, drawing few visitors to Protvino. But more recently the Institute for High Energy Physics, which owns and operates the U70 facility, has become more active and has organized international and national workshops and meetings in Protvino.

SRCAM's Physical Plant and Staffing in the Soviet Era

The SRCAM site covered 250 hectares (618 acres). Officials drew up the plans for SRCAM in 1975–1976 under the guidance of members of the MOD, USSR Academy of Sciences (USSR-AN), the USSR Academy of Medical Sciences (USSR-AMN), and *Glavmikrobioprom*.[14] Soviet Army personnel under the supervision of colonel Anatoly A. Vorobyov began constructing temporary buildings on the SRCAM site in 1977.[15] The construction of housing for what was to become the Obolensk settlement began shortly thereafter. Research at SRCAM began in 1978 in temporary structures. Until 1988 all experiments were done in temporary buildings and, as a rule, one building was dedicated to the members of one bacterial genus. (The aerosol testing building, where closed system testing was performed, was a permanent building from the beginning.) The first high-security containment laboratory became operational in 1982 in a temporary structure. Other buildings, some temporary, housed facilities such as aerosol chambers, small fermenters, agar and substrate production, animal-handling facilities, an electric power plant, refrigeration and heating plants, and a large incinerator. Between 90 and 100 buildings eventually made up SRCAM's physical plant. Neither Soviet nor Russian officials disassembled any of the "temporary" buildings after Building N1, SRCAM's major structure, came on line. They remain standing to this day, most in a crumbling state.

Workers began constructing SRCAM's Building N1 (called Korpus 1 by locals) in 1980, completing the construction in 1986, and its first laboratory became operational in 1988. It took so long to finish Building N1 because labor was in short supply in the Serpukhov *oblast*; at that time there was only one local builder, and he had only Soviet Army troops at his disposal for this project. In contrast, when Vector was being built (see Chapter 8), convicts from Novosibirsk region were forcibly employed as builders. The quality of the buildings constructed by the convicts was better than the quality of SRCAM buildings, and Vector buildings were built efficiently, obviating the need for temporary structures.

Building N1 had nine stories with a floor area of 37,000 square meters (398,265 square feet). (In comparison, the US White House comprises only 55,000 square feet). Colonel Aleksey Stepanov, Urakov's deputy director after 1990, was in charge of the building's operation. Floors 1 and 2 housed the administration and had control rooms for heating, refrigeration, and gas supplies. Floors 3–8 contained laboratories, with each floor being more or less dedicated to one bacterial genus, although there were some overlaps. Bacteria of the following six genera were predominantly researched at SRCAM: *Bacillus, Brucella, Burkholderia, Legionella, Francisella,* and *Yersinia*. Each of the six floors had its own aerosol testing equipment and vivariums (a large, central vivarium that supplied the smaller vivariums was housed in a brick building surrounded by "temporary" structures). All in all, more than 200 laboratory rooms were supplied with filtered air and had negative air pressure. Floors 3 and 4 contained high-security BSL-3- and BSL-4-like laboratories; workers dealing with the most dangerous pathogens shared these labs, which also had special high-security vivariums. Floor 9 contained a small-scale production unit with fermenters with as large as a 100-liter capacity and parts of the building's air-handling system.

The fourth floor housed SRCAM's Central Collection (culture collection), which supposedly contained "more than" 3,500 strains of pathogens, biologically active substance-producing microorganisms, bioremediating bacteria, and bacteria useful as biopesticides.[16] The fourth floor also contained a complex suite that housed a piece of equipment with the grandiose name "Static Climatic, Horizontal Dynamic Device SC-10-HDD-600." Scientists set up the machine in 1987 to be used for "studies on the efficiency of drugs and prophylactic preparations against infectious diseases in humans and animals as well as for the determination of admissible concentrations of the Biopreparations studied" and "for the determination of viability of microbe cells in aerosols depending on environment conditions (temperature, humidity, isolation)."[17] The machine was 8 meters long, and its diameter was 0.6 meters, making it large enough to hold up to 6 medium-sized animals, such as rabbits or small primates, or 30 smaller animals, such as mice. The machine's main purpose was to allow SRCAM scientists to study the effects of aerosolized formulations of bacterial pathogens on animals within the chamber, while varying parameters such as temperature, humidity, and air-flow rate. Two "skilled" engineers, two technical assistants, and three workers were needed to operate the machine. As of 1997, lab officials had not permitted foreigners to operate the machine. SRCAM scientists who were certified to operate this device included Pomerantsev, Stepanov, Svetoch, and Urakov.[18] The device served an extremely important function for the Soviet BW program, because it provided a flexible and safe environment for closed aerosol testing of pathogenic bacteria developed at SRCAM.

In early 1992 a newspaper reporter was for the first time allowed entry to SRCAM. As might be expected, he was not able to reveal more than a few details about the facility:

> Work with especially dangerous infections is done only on three floors. Each one of them has its own vivarium. Cells [bacterial pathogens] are kept in metal cabinets—under a flow of air. Here is where the animals are kept that had first been infected with pathogens of the diseases under investigation to check the effectiveness of therapeutic medicines and vaccines. All of the solid waste material goes through an autoclave to the institute crematorium and the liquid wastes pass through special pipes to thermal treatment. As you see, it is not only the air that goes out processed.[19]

Little information is publicly available about the function of most SRCAM buildings, as they likely contained specialized laboratories. However, the institute did house a 40-bed special isolation hospital to which anyone who was accidentally exposed to pathogens was taken. The hospital was closed in 1992 because of a lack of funding and patients.[20] To take its place, SRCAM officials set up an isolation ward in Building N1. It was first used in 2004 (see below).

The buildings and environs of SRCAM were allegedly designed to look like a sanatorium to fool US intelligence analysts scrutinizing satellite imagery.[21] The US intelligence community was not deceived, as the Soviets made the basic mistake of constructing Biopreparat facilities along common, well-recognized plans. (See Chapter 12 for a more detailed discussion on this point.) Satellite imagery did not, of course, tell analysts what was going on inside of the buildings.

Although early reports suggested that SRCAM had a production plant, it did not. This misinformation could have had its basis in a statement attributed to virologist Frank Malinoski, a member of the first US-UK trilateral team that visited four Biopreparat sites in 1991. In describing SRCAM, Malinoski is quoted observing: "Also within the compound . . . were 40 gigantic fermenters—two-story, stainless steel behemoths mounted inside the biocontainment section of a laboratory."[22] In fact, SRCAM never had any large fermenters; its largest fermenter had a capacity of 100 liters, as described above. If Malinoski was quoted correctly, he probably confused SRCAM with Biopreparat's Berdsk production facility, which did have the production capacity he described.

Table 7.1 documents the size of SRCAM's staff at various points and the major categories of its work program. According to the table, the size of its staff peaked at 2,904 in 1990, yet unofficial estimates suggest that during the late 1980s more than 4,000 people worked at SRCAM.[23] The staff substantially decreased starting in 1991, with the largest number of workers departing

Table 7.1   SRCAM Staff Numbers, 1990–2000

Year	Total staff	Management & support staff[a]	Research staff	PhD-level staff	Doctor Nauk staff	Staff engaged in production
1990	2,904	2,438	466	189	5	0
1991	2,649	2,255	394	170	4	0
1992	2,349	1,982	367	161	3	0
1993	1,834	1,132	305	149	10	397
1994	1,580	977	289	149	11	314
1995	1,352	797	259	131	13	562
1996	1,326	751	247	126	14	583
2000	1,120	n/a	259	131	14	n/a

a. Includes secretaries and janitors.

between 1992 and 1994.[24] The number of staff members engaged in production activities (the manufacture of goods for the civilian market) rose from zero in Soviet times to over 500 by 1995 when, as explained below, SRCAM had to support its own activities. (SRCAM's 2006 workforce numbered approximately 550.)

SRCAM's Work Program in the Soviet Era

From the late 1970s through the 1980s, SRCAM operated two major BW subprograms – Bonfire and Factor. When SRCAM first became operational, Bonfire guided its weaponization program, and it was led for a short time by Domaradsky. Factor commenced a few years after Bonfire, but grew to be Ferment's most important subprogram. This section describes the activities related to these two programs that were conducted at SRCAM.

Bonfire at SRCAM

Domaradsky began working as the second deputy director (research) at Obolensk on a full-time basis in 1978. In 1981 he was relieved of all MNTS duties.[25] Domaradsky writes that until 1982 he commuted every week between Obolensk and Moscow but in 1982 he secured a small apartment in Protvino. When he transferred to SRCAM, Domaradsky also transferred his personal library to the institute, because it did not have one of its own yet, and the head of Biopreparat, Kalinin, also ordered him to donate his collection of bacterial strains so that its scientists could begin their research. This order was important, because unlike in Western industrialized countries, where researchers could order bacterial and viral strains from commercial and nonprofit culture collections and receive them by mail in a few days,[26] Soviet researchers had to endure a difficult and lengthy process to access strains stored in the few Soviet culture collections.[27] Further, because of the budding competition between the MOD institutes and Biopreparat, well-stocked MOD culture collections did not transfer microbial strains to Biopreparat institutes. Domaradsky's "gift" was valuable in that it laid the basis for what now is the very impressive culture collection described above.

The MOD's primary interest was for SRCAM to weaponize the bacterial pathogens *Y. pestis* (which causes plague), *B. anthracis* (anthrax), and *Burkholderia mallei* (glanders). The institute studied two additional bacteria—*Burkholderia pseudomallei* (melioidosis) and *Yersinia pseudotuberculosis* (a zoonotic bacterial pathogen that can cause enteritis in humans)—as substitute models for *Y. pestis*.[28] Despite MOD's interests, in 1980, as SRCAM's "real" work was just starting, the MOH's 3rd Directorate permitted it to work on just one pathogen—*F. tularensis* (which causes tularemia). Even more limiting, SRCAM scientists were permitted to conduct R&D on just one strain of this pathogen, the holarctic strain 503,[29] against which an effective vaccine existed—the Gaysky live attenuated vaccine.[30]

Domaradsky writes how this disappointed the MOD, which had no interest in this pathogen, probably because under natural infection conditions it causes a disease with a case-fatality rate of less than 5%. Yet *F. tularensis* does possess certain useful characteristics, such as very low ID_{50}, good stability after its release into the environment, and ease of aerosolization.[31] SRCAM's leadership accepted the task, and thus Biopreparat's first weaponization R&D began under Domaradsky's leadership. Scientists at the IHPB and at Omutninsk started on a parallel project headed by Alibek that was also focused on *F. tularensis* (see below). Alibek has described this project in depth.[32]

The two main objectives of *F. tularensis* R&D were to develop strains that were resistant to current vaccines and to multiple antibiotics. As a first step, Domaradsky's team had to become more knowledgeable about the bacterium, because little was known about its biochemistry and genetics. Until that time, no one had genetically engineered the pathogen, meaning that the team also had to learn how to insert foreign genes into the *F. tularensis* cell.

According to Domaradsky, his team essentially performed basic research for a "couple of years" in order to learn the bacterium's biochemistry and genetics. At the time, science knew next to nothing about "the mechanism of vaccine-induced immunity in tularemia or how the antigenicity (the surface components of germ [bacterial] cells or, in other words, how the agent [bacterium] appears to the human immune system) needed to be altered to overcome that protection," he wrote.[33] Domaradsky claims that this problem remained unsolved as of 2002, meaning that his team did not manage to develop a vaccine-resistant strain of *F. tularensis*.

The team did achieve slightly more success regarding the second objective, transferring genes that coded for antibiotic resistance into the *F. tularensis* cell. This success was tempered by a negative side-effect; the team found that the transformed cell lost its virulence, becoming nonpathogenic. This effect, which in the West was called the pleiotropic effect, was well known to biotechnologists developing genetically engineered microorganisms for civilian industry. These scientists found that when they attempted to develop genetically engineered organisms for industrial purposes, by, say, inserting a gene coding for the production of human growth hormone into *E. coli,* the newly transformed microorganism exhibited the desired effect (in other words, it produced the human growth hormone), but it also manifested an unwanted side effect, decreased growth rate. In a similar fashion, Domaradsky's team genetically engineered an antibiotic-resistant strain of *F. tularensis,* but the new strain manifested a pleiotropic effect that made it less suitable for weapons purposes. As Domaradsky wrote:

> Having become resistant to several antibiotics, the strain lost its virulence, which was unacceptable to the military. They regarded even a drop in virulence from one to two cells, or the protraction in death of an animal by even a day as serious setbacks in the work. The desired bioweapons strain had to be fully virulent and deliverable in aerosol form. One germ cell had to be enough to start a lethal infection in a monkey. Furthermore, the infection had to be *incurable.* These goals were not at all easy to obtain. But I could not convince Urakov that the matter required serious effort and patience.[34]

Domaradsky asked Urakov to permit him to undertake a new round of research for the purpose of removing the pleiotropic effect while retaining the transformed strain's weapons-related characteristics. Several cycles of researching and testing likely would have been required before the strain could be successfully weaponized. Urakov denied Domaradsky's request, and in addition he "deprived [Domaradsky] of access to almost all the laboratories except 'Hut 7,' the tularemia lab in the temporary village" and assigned him to head the plant protection research group.[35] Domaradsky found that being "assigned to work on a 'legend' instead of [his] own research was a tremendous insult."[36]

From his first experience doing military research at SRCAM, Domaradsky came to see the fundamental differences between science performed for civilian and military purposes:

> The most difficult aspect of Urakov's regime was the complete lack of fundamental science. Everyone who has ever dealt with the genetics of bacteria knows how complicated it is to produce a new strain, indeed, to create a new species! In order to make Urakov realize this, we reported to him every detail of our work: how we obtained different variants and

the methods we used. But he only said, "I don't need your strains, I need just one strain!" or "We are not playing here, we are making weapons!" Then, at last, I realized the real purpose of our activities. . . . all of my knowledge was required merely to obtain reliable and effective weapons strain of the agent, after which the "real" work would actually begin.[37]

A few years after Urakov removed Domaradsky from the *F. tularensis* project, a scientific team, led by Svetoch and working under the Metol subprogram, succeeded in developing a strain of *F. tularensis* that was resistant to multiple antibiotics and retained its pathogenic characteristics.[38] Svetoch's feat suggests that perhaps Urakov was more than partially correct about civilian scientists being more concerned about practicing science ("playing") than doing "real" work ("making weapons"), something that also was an issue at Vector (see Chapter 8).

The research on *F. tularensis* was seen as only the initial step in fulfilling the first of Bonfire's five R&D objectives—developing multiantibiotic-resistant bacterial strains. The MOD ordered SRCAM to develop four additional bacterial strains, *B. anthracis, B. mallei, B. pseudomallei,* and *Y. pestis,* each of which was expected to be resistant to 10 antibiotics.[39] Each development effort involved approximately the same five steps. The steps taken to develop the resistant *B. anthracis* strain exemplify the process:

1. Identify and characterize mechanisms of antibiotic resistance in *B. anthracis* (including identifying the involved genes and enzymes).
2. Duplicate each mechanism (construct) via genetic engineering and molecular biology, and insert it into a plasmid-based system; make certain the new construct is stable.
3. Transfer the engineered plasmid to an intermediate host, such as *Bacillus cereus,* which would easily accept the plasmid via transformation.
4. Constitute a mixture of the transformed *B. cereus* cells and the cells of the target *B. anthracis* where conjugation would take place; thus, the plasmids containing the antibiotic resistance constructs would end up in the *B. anthracis* cells.
5. Repeat the foregoing for each antibiotic.

Though this process appears straightforward, if also technically difficult, it proved impossible to accomplish for all 10 antibiotics. The most difficult problems had to do with pleiotropic effects and a lack of stability in engineered strains. Antibiotic-resistant cells had a distressing habit of losing virulence or exhibiting lesser yields (or both) when propagated in culture. As for stability, during the fourth step, when the construct for resistance to one antibiotic was introduced into the host cell, an earlier emplaced construct was often lost. This sort of problem required additional rounds of research, which were both labor intensive and time consuming. Scientists sometimes had to make major modifications to their approaches. For example, a team headed by Svetoch that worked with *F. tularensis* changed from using plasmid inserts to chromosomal inserts. Despite such modifications, some strains never reached the objective of being resistant to 10 antibiotics. Instead, SRCAM researchers had to be satisfied with seven or eight.[40] Soviet scientists successfully created their first multiantibiotic-resistant strain, *B. anthracis*, in 1986. During 1987–1988, they also created multiresistant antibiotic strains of *F. tularensis*, *B. mallei*, and *B. pseudomallei*. The work on *Y. pestis*, which was done in coordination with the IHPB, produced some promising results, but in the end it was unsuccessful. It bears stressing that although these multiantibiotic-resistant strains were created, as far as is known, they were not tested in the open air, so their degree of efficacy as BW agents is unknown.

Since the Soviet Union's dissolution, SRCAM scientists have published many articles based on Bonfire program work, of which two have raised concern among both public health officials and security analysts. The first appeared in 1995 and was written by a SRCAM scientific team led by A. P. Pomerantsev. It describes how the team had successfully imbued an avirulent strain of *B. anthracis* with resistance to multiple antibiotics.[41] Such a strain was of value, because the Russians use a live vaccine (STI-1) in addition to antibiotics to treat persons exposed to *B. anthracis*. By using a multiantibiotic-resistant strain as the vaccine strain, health providers could simultaneously administer the vaccine and antibiotic treatment to anthrax victims.

The techniques used by the Russian scientists in this research could have been equally well applied to increase the ability of *B. anthracis* weapons strains, such as strain 836, to resist antibiotics.[42] This could have been done in the Soviet era, too. This research also demonstrates that SRCAM scientists probably could have applied genetic engineering to imbue other bacteria, including both gram-negative and gram-positive ones, with increased abilities to resist antibiotics.[43] If these multiantibiotic-resistant strains had been successfully weaponized, the diseases they would have caused would have been untreatable, because bacterial infections are typically suppressed by antibiotics.

The second startling publication was a 1997 article by the Pomerantsev team that told how it had been able to genetically engineer a strain of *B. anthracis* that in some of its antigenic properties was quite different from the original strain.[44] The research that led to this result had been conducted in accordance with Bonfire's second research objective, which was to develop strains of bacteria (and viruses) with modified antigenic structures. Specifically, SRCAM scientists had successfully transferred cereolysine genes from *Bacillus cereus* to the closely related *B. anthracis*,[45] with the result that the newly engineered strain became strongly immunosuppressive. The goal of this research was that when this new strain infected someone who had been administered any of the existing anthrax vaccines, including those used by the US armed forces, it would negate that vaccine's protective effects.[46] One of America's foremost anthrax experts, Arthur Friedlander, said: "This is the first indication we're aware of in which genes are being put into a fully virulent strain. . . . They genetically engineered a strain that's resistant to their own vaccine, and one has to question why that was done. That's the disturbing feature here. . . . The evidence they [the Russian authors] presented suggested that it could be resistant to our vaccine. We need to get hold of this strain to test it against our vaccine. We need to understand how this new organism causes disease, and we need to test it in animals other than the hamsters that the Russians used."[47]

Another important implication of this work was related to detection; in particular, Western clinical microbiology laboratories would have a difficult time identifying the engineered strain in a timely manner if it were used for BW purposes. The symptoms of illness caused by the new strain might also be quite different from those caused by conventional *B. anthracis* strains, making it difficult for clinicians to diagnose and treat victims made ill by the new strain. As far as is known, additional information about the potential implications of the engineered strain has not been made available. Russia has refused to provide the US Department of Defense with samples of the strains, despite at least 10 years of repeated requests. This issue became particularly contentious during the eight years of the George W. Bush administration.

The underlying rationale for the work described in the 1997 article is complex. According to sources for this book, in about 1986 the Pomerantsev group was intent on cloning *B. cereus*'s cereolysine genes and introducing them into *B. anthracis* in order to increase its virulence. The group expected the newly engineered strain to be able to hemolyze victims' red blood cells and blind them.[48] Soviet medical scientists had for some time been aware that blindness was a common complication of *B. cereus* infection, and that hemolysins produced by this bacterium were believed to be its cause. Biopreparat set up a collaboration between SRCAM and a laboratory at the Institute of Microbial Physiology in Pushchino (an ostensibly open institute) to investigate this possibility. Once institute scientists cloned and characterized the cereolysine genes, the clones were provided to SRCAM, where a member of the Pomerantsev group tested the hemolysin products produced by the genes in rabbit eyes. After several experiments, it became obvious that these hemolysin products did not cause the blindness. However, the Pomerantsev team continued performing experiments along the lines described above, eventually creating the *B. anthracis* strain with altered antigenic properties as described in the 1997 publication.

When we first learned of the blindness rationale, it seemed far-fetched, especially because *B. anthracis* is a lethal agent and not an incapacitant. However, an American expert on *bacilli* told us that there had been reported in the literature natural foodborne outbreaks caused by *B. cereus* whose victims' symptoms included blindness.[49] Indeed, we found several articles in the medical literature that address *B. cereus*' "notoriety in association with food poisoning and severe eye infections."[50]

We hypothesize that at the time when this particular research was being done, the US military was not as yet vaccinating its soldiers against anthrax. For this reason, American soldiers were vulnerable to biological weapons based on *B. anthracis*. In case of exposure, exposed persons would have been given prophylactic antibiotic treatment. *B. anthracis* bacterial cells carrying *B. cereus* genes might have been able to cause damage to exposed persons, such as blindness, before effective antibiotic treatment could be instituted or before administered antibiotics were able to defeat the bacterial invader.[51]

Factor at SRCAM

The Factor program commenced at SRCAM about three years after Bonfire started, and thereafter the programs operated in parallel. Initially Factor's major objective was to genetically engineer bacteria so they would become more virulent. The program took two general approaches to accomplishing this objective. The first involved inserting a gene that coded for a virulence factor into a competent host cell. Many virulence factors exist in nature, and most known factors are proteins. Factor scientists first concentrated on virulence factors that were toxins.[52] Inserting a gene that codes for the production of a protein, including protein toxins, into a host bacterial cell was among the earliest accomplishments of recombinant DNA research, and by the middle 1970s it was considered a simple laboratory procedure when the host was *E. coli*.

By the late 1970s Domaradsky suggested transferring the gene that codes for diphtheria toxin into a militarily useful bacterium. This toxin, which is produced by the bacterial pathogen *Corynebacterium diphtheriae,* has the dual benefit of having a relatively simple chemical structure and being one of the most toxic substances known to science (although considerably less powerful than botulinum toxin and tetanus toxin).[53] Within a fairly short time, Domaradsky cloned the diphtheria toxin gene and transferred it into *Y. pseudotuberculosis,* a weak pathogen that served as a useful model of *Y. pestis,* which thereafter efficiently produced the deadly toxin.[54] This was a substantial accomplishment, since *Y. pseudotuberculosis* was more difficult to engineer than *E. coli.* Domaradsky wanted to do the same manipulation using *F. tularensis* or *Y. pestis* as the recipient host for the cloned gene, but the MOD took over his project. According to Popov, the diphtheria toxin gene was eventually transferred into *Y. pestis,* but the effectiveness of this construct remains unknown because Popov did not have access to the results of the work. However, a Biopreparat scientist reported that in 1990, SRCAM scientists Konstantin I. Volkovoy[55] and P. Cherepanov investigated this construct and found it to be highly virulent and immunosuppressive in nonhuman primates.

In the foregoing example, the scientist started with a weak pathogen, *Y. pseudotuberculosis,* and endowed it with a powerful new property, the ability to produce diphtheria toxin. In theory, this modified pathogen should be much more virulent than its "wild" or natural antecedent, and if closed-chamber testing proved it to be so, the modified pathogen would have been designated as weaponized. This approach probably also could have been used to transform a nonpathogen into a pathogen. As noted above, by the late 1970s and early 1980s, weapon scientists theoretically had many combinations of virulence factors and competent bacteria with which they could experiment.

The work of the brilliant military scientist Igor P. Ashmarin redirected the Factor program in the early 1980s. Ashmarin believed that scientists should be able to genetically engineer infectious nonpathogenic bacteria (and viruses) to produce peptides that would stimulate a damaging reaction by the host's immunological system.[56] The transformed bacterium would not directly harm the host, but the peptides it produced would stimulate a damaging immune response. R&D that aimed to develop these kinds of genetically engineered bacteria became an important part of Factor. (Vector undertook similar R&D on viruses; see Chapter 8.)

Ashmarin's first idea was to express genes coding for immunopeptides, which the body produces to fight off infections and cancerous cells. He selected immunopeptides because they have three desirable characteristics: (1) they are short and have simple chemical structures; (2) they can be synthesized quickly with technologies at hand; and (3) their effects produce unusual and damaging pathology. The first experiments that were part of Factor's new approach involved the synthesis of met-enkephalin at Vector. Because these experiments were completed using viruses, the next chapter goes into greater detail about them. This section describes the bacteriology aspects of this approach, which were within SRCAM's purview.

Because this new approach was complicated, Biopreparat assigned specific tasks to multiple institutes. IHPB synthesized the necessary peptides, because in many cases SRCAM could not secure the desired peptides from natural sources or foreign and domestic suppliers. Vector used the synthesized peptides as templates for synthesizing genes that would code for their production. Vector was given this responsibility because its scientists were the best trained in molecular biology. On the more complicated projects, Vector scientists would often collaborate with scientists at the USSR-AN's Shemyakin Institute. Shemyakin Institute scientists might, for example, be tasked with designing and synthesizing the leucine-enkephalin gene, while the Vector scientist would work on different endorphin segments to, for example, find out which of them would put soldiers to sleep. And thirdly, SRCAM would transfer the synthetic genes into bacterial hosts, and inject the transformed bacteria into animals. Once the bacteria were in the animals, SRCAM scientist determined whether the desired peptide production occurred and observed the effects of the newly synthesized peptides on the animal hosts. Even before SRCAM scientists created the transformed bacteria, they tested the effects of synthesized peptides that were acquired directly from IHPB. (This type of R&D is considered in more detail below.) The division of labor between these institutes was coordinated by the Interagency Council, on which the USSR-AN was well represented.

Several factors limited the work involving peptides. For example, in the early to late 1980s scientists knew about only 30 to 40 peptides that affected human physiological systems, and out of these, Vector had the capability to work on only the few peptides whose chemical structure lacked disulfide bonds. (These bonds stabilize the peptide's molecular structure and make them difficult to work with.) However, the number of peptides that were candidates for weaponization continuously increased with the passage of time.

Some tasks associated with the process outlined above also appeared at first glance to be easier to do than they proved to be. For example, a task order could look something like "Insert endorphin gene into *E. coli* to realize the production of endorphin and then transfer construct to a virus." It might be possible to complete the first step (getting *E. coli* to produce endorphin) at SRCAM, but later work could be wasted if it proved difficult or impossible for Vector scientists to identify a virus that was a "competent" host—that is, one that could receive the construct and remain stable and viable.

Factor scientists began their work with peptides because they are small molecules for which synthetic gene equivalents can be relatively easily chemically synthesized. They already knew that certain peptides could affect the human physiological system in destructive ways. Of particular interest were those peptides that are produced naturally by the human body in exceedingly small quantities, such as neuropeptides. Too much of a neuropeptide can lead to serious illness, whereas too little of it can lower resistance to disease. Peptides, such as enkephalins and endorphins, along with small biologically active proteins, such as tumor necrosis factors, interleukins, and other cytokines, need to be similarly balanced within the body. If a host were infected with a bacterium that produced an excess of any of these peptides, he could become very sick because of the peptide's direct biological activity.

Though Ashmarin's ideas led to an expansion of the Factor program's scope, he was also interested in the nonmilitary application of neuropeptides:

> Igor Petrovich [Ashmarin] was one of the first researchers in our country [Soviet Union] to undertake a comprehensive study of a new class of bioregulators: neuropeptides. He established and headed the interdepartmental program "Neuropeptides" (1977–1980). It resulted in the creation and introduction of the world's first nootropic peptide drug,[57] Semaks (or Semax),[58] which stimulates a number of the brain's functions and has been successfully used to treat strokes, optic nerve atrophy, and other diseases.[59] After studying neuropeptides' functions in greater depth, Igor Petrovich created the now generally accepted concept of a functional continuum of regulatory peptides. He developed ideas regarding evolutionary biochemical links between different categories of biological memory—genetic, epigenetic, immunological, and neurological. Back in 1975 he published the monograph "Mysteries and Revelations of the

Biochemistry of Memory," published by Leningrad State University. Since 1990 Igor Petrovich and his school have been developing a fundamentally new method of immunoregulation of physiological functions that is opening up new possibilities with regard to long-term correction of such serious conditions as alcoholism and depression.[60]

As part of this second approach, weapon scientists could use microorganisms that were not commonly recognized or even considered for use as BW agents as hosts for peptides. This is what Popov did; he combined an unusual host with an even more novel peptide. The result of Popov's experimentation was a combination whose likeness had never been seen before in any nation's BW arsenal. As the host, he used *Legionella pneumophila,* the bacterium that causes Legionnaire's disease. Popov describes his discovery process as follows:

> Initially, the purpose [of Factor] was to bring new properties to existing [bacterial or viral] strains. But the whole program shifted development in the 1980s into new strains. We [at SRCAM] struggled with the problem of small peptides creating new properties, putting them into active [BW] strains. We began to ask ourselves, "Why should we insert peptides into classical strains when we could put them into new strains with new properties, and it could become a weapon [strain] even more difficult to deal with or cure?" So the whole plan of the program shifted to making new virulent strains. In this area, I was relatively successful in making autoimmune peptides effective.[61]

The most advanced and frightening research done in this area involved human myelin, a white, soft, somewhat fatty material, constituted mostly of proteins, that acts as a type of insulator for nerves. Popov built on Ashmarin's original idea by proposing to fool the human immune system into not recognizing myelin as a normal component of the body and instead labeling it as a foreign entity that must be destroyed. Popov's goal was to create a genetically engineered bacterium that could produce a protein resembling myelin during an infection in the human host. The protein would stimulate the immune system to mount an inflammatory response that attacks the host's myelin surrounding nerve cells and destroys brain cells that make and repair myelin. Without their myelin, nerve cells gradually lose their ability to send electrical signals. The result would be an artificial version of multiple sclerosis, a disease that is characterized by the body's own immune system attacking the myelin sheath that insulates the neurons of the brain and spinal cord. The difference between natural multiple sclerosis and the autoimmune disease induced by the genetically engineered *L. pneumophila* would be that the first takes years to kill its victims, whereas the second would progress to death in a matter of weeks.

To realize Popov's idea, his team developed a synthetic gene that coded for the production of a myelin peptide and inserted that gene into an expression plasmid (the gene with its plasmid vector is called a "construct"). At this point, they needed a competent bacterial host that would accept and replicate the plasmid and could infect humans. After infection, the gene needed to be transcribed and translated, thereby expressing the peptide, and the peptide would have to be released into the bloodstream. If all went well from the Popov team's viewpoint, the infecting pathogens and the peptides they secreted would stimulate the host's immunological defense system to eliminate the infection and, simultaneously, activate the immune cells capable of destroying myelin. The immune system would not stop its activities there. Having been fooled by the introduced myelin peptide into producing anti-myelin killer cells, the immune system would continue producing these cells, which would also attack the myelin normally present in the human body. The victim would not notice that anything was amiss for weeks, but then as his nerves began shorting out due to a lack of insulation, he would develop a general paralysis and die.

Popov's team successfully synthesized the peptide gene in 1986–1987, according to Popov, but the Factor team struggled to find a suitable microbial host for the construct. Because this kind of experiment had never been done before, there was no guidance from the literature, Biopreparat, or USSR-AN experts. Popov approached Urakov and said: "Nikolay Nikolaevich, I cannot tell you which microbe will be a good recipient, we need to try it in different microbes." Urakov said: "OK, I give you permission to engage anyone you want. There are five agents on the list, you can approach any of these scientists and set up collaboration with them."[62] Popov took this approach and experimented with *B. mallei, B. pseudomallei, Y. pestis, B. anthracis,* and *L. pneumophila.* Of these agents, only *L. pneumophila* proved suitable for further experiments. Scientists had not previously considered this microorganism as useful for BW purposes, because it prefers an aqueous environment, it is difficult to mass-produce, and its infectious dose is high. For this particular application, however, it turned out to be useful because its infectious dose decreased after the introduction of the plasmid, and its ability to stimulate the autoimmune effect was strong. Scientists initially gave the recombinant legionella a negative evaluation because it had delayed effects, but there was no alternative, so Biopreparat ultimately accepted it. After additional experimentation, Popov's team also introduced the construct into *Y. pseudotuberculosis* and, later still, *Y. pestis,* but only the latter showed some promise by causing signs of disease in animal models.[63]

The most advanced biotechnology R&D done as part of Factor was probably the attempt to create a bacterium that would encode viruses. Sergey V. Netesov started this work at Vector. In either 1987 or 1988, Netesov visited SRCAM and gave a talk on his work in order to engage SRCAM in a collaborative project. Netesov had been working with Venezuelan equine encephalitis virus (VEEV), which is an RNA virus, and had been able to reverse-engineer it to produce an infectious cDNA clone (this and similar work is described in the Vector section below.) Popov heard the talk and had the idea of developing a type of "double" pathogen comprised of *Y. pestis* that encoded VEEV. To develop such a pathogen, Netesov offered a plasmid construct encoding an infectious DNA copy of VEEV. Urakov was enthusiastic about the idea, because it presented a previously unrecognized possibility to generate a pathogenic virus from within a highly virulent bacterium. The idea was especially attractive due to its imagined technical simplicity—the *Y. pestis* cell could be transformed with Netesov's plasmid construct almost overnight. The construct could also be easily modified so that the transcription of the viral gene could be activated by an antibiotic, such as tetracycline. If this double BW agent was released by a biological weapon, members of the targeted population would contract pneumonic plague. Sick victims, as well as those who had been exposed to the BW agent but were not yet evincing illness, would most likely be treated with tetracycline, the drug of choice in most countries for plague. The tetracycline would inactivate the *Y. pestis* cell, but it would also activate the VEEV plasmid promoter,[64] thereby initiating the VEEV infection, which would cause encephalitis.[65] We do not know whether the VEEV-bacterium hybrid was in fact successfully created.

Not all projects assigned to Factor were successful. For example, a team led by Svetoch genetically engineered *B. pseudomallei* to produce various peptides, but none of the combinations it tested demonstrated biological activity. Further, most creations, as far as is known, were never tested in the open air, so their developers could not have been certain that they would have been effective BW agents.

As this book suggests, *Ferment* did not achieve as many "real work" accomplishments as it could have. Domaradsky provides a few reasons for this above, but there are more general reasons for the program's less than stellar performance. In general, *Ferment* required its scientists not only to increase the virulence of pathogens but also to reduce enemies' ability to diagnose, treat, and prevent diseases brought about by Soviet biological weapons. Yet no Soviet scientist understood how to accomplish these dual objectives or, indeed, if they were even achievable. Many *Ferment* experiments lacked clear scientific rationale, but they were undertaken in the hope that they would provide answers applicable to the dual objectives. This was probably the case with the *B. cereus–B. anthracis* experiment. In retrospect, the *Ferment* approach was probably the only one available to Soviet scientists.

However, another factor was at play. Bench scientists working at laboratories, and not Biopreparat leaders and administrators, decided what experiments should be done and what practical strategies should be adopted to complete the tasks ordered by Biopreparat. In practice, Biopreparat tended to distance itself from the risky position of giving direct scientific advice to the military, because it knew that suggested projects might not work out. This was especially true for projects at institutes whose leadership was scientifically not up to the task or incompetent. In such a situation, it is not hard to imagine how the bench scientists had to work out for themselves the practical approaches needed to complete tasks, and if they did not succeed, how they became scapegoats for failure. On the other hand, Urakov usually took credit for successfully completed SRCAM tasks. In either case, bench scientists were unlikely to have a strategic vision for why they worked on particular tasks.

SRCAM in the Post-Soviet Era

The situation at SRCAM remained fairly normal through 1990.[66] For example, the vivarium ordered and received a large shipment of nonhuman primates from Ethiopia in both 1989 and 1990.[67] But by 1991, Gorbachev was under severe British and US pressure about the Soviet BW program due to the late-1989 defection of Pasechnik. Chapter 21 describes in detail the subsequent political interactions between the United Kingdom, the United

States, and the Soviet Union. The following section concentrates on developments related to SRCAM.

Sometime in November or December 1990, Oleg L. Svinarenko, the head of SRCAM's First Department announced over the institute's public address system that a foreign group was coming to visit the center in early January 1991.[68] (SRCAM workers knew nothing about the Trilateral Agreement that had been made earlier in 1990, specifying reciprocal visits between Soviet, UK, and US biological facilities; see Chapter 21.) The fact that foreigners were for the first time to be permitted entry to SRCAM's secret facilities was astounding. Until then, no foreigner, not even from a Warsaw Pact nation, had been allowed access to SRCAM.

SRCAM officials told staff members that they were to continue working as usual during the visit, but that if a foreigner entered an area where workers were present, they were to make themselves "invisible." If workers in laboratories were approached by foreigners and could not escape, they were told either to feign ignorance, deflect the question to a superior, or, in the worst case, refer to SRCAM's open legend.[69]

In the end, the visit was carefully orchestrated to steer visitors away from sensitive sites. Given the large size of SRCAM at the time and the few hours that the visitors had to spend on site, they saw very little outside Building N1. A Biopreparat scientist who was working that day in one of the temporary buildings reported, "I never saw the visitors, nor did any of my colleagues."[70]

Despite attempts to limit their movements, some of the visitors entered a large explosive chamber in Building 1. As the Soviets had turned off the electricity to the chamber, the visitors asked for a flashlight—a request that was denied. Someone in the group had his own flashlight, but when he turned it on, an official accompanying the group grabbed it, and a tug-of-war ensued. (The person was identified as Colonel Simonov, who was given a special monetary reward for his action.[71]) The hosts eventually gave in, and the visitors examined the chamber. The group observed signs, such as deep scratches in the test chamber's walls, which indicated that sizeable explosions had been set off in the chamber. These signs were indicative of biological weapons testing and not, as the hosts claimed, agricultural experiments.

Even more momentous than the visit by the United States and the United Kingdom was the Council of Ministers' announcement in early January 1991 that funding was to be cut to Biopreparat (and many other government entities). This announcement was accompanied by a notice that read something like "strong organizations will survive, but weak ones will sink."[72] Indeed, practically all state funding soon stopped. As a SRCAM worker reported: "Lucrative salaries ceased to be paid in Obolensk with the cessation of military research."[73]

SRCAM survived the deprivation because Urakov desperately traveled widely to secure credit. He called on his friend Kalinin, who provided a small amount of Biopreparat funding, and also received credit from banks and investors. In order to secure these loans, Urakov promised to produce goods for the civilian market and use the profits to pay them back. To fulfill this commitment, some SRCAM departments had to immediately change direction. For example, one department restructured to produce interferons, insulin, and other proteins for pharmaceutical purposes using genetically engineered *E. coli*. Some of the plasmids encoding these proteins were developed by V. G. Korobko at the Shemyakin-Ovchinnikov Institute of Bioorganic Chemistry, and their production was a consequence of the collaboration between the two centers.

Popov's laboratory continued to conduct the applied research needed to isolate and purify proteins. The lab was also put in charge of restructuring the interferon production facility. (Popov's Vector team had developed an alpha interferon plasmid in 1982, in collaboration with Academician Mikhail N. Kolosov's group at the Shemyakin-Ovchinnikov Institute.) Shemyakin-Ovchinnikov Institute scientists had developed gene constructs that were used to produce interferons tested at SRCAM under the Factor program, but they probably did this without knowing the purpose of their contributions. In fact, sources for this book assert that no Shemyakin-Ovchinnikov Institute bench researcher ever visited SRCAM. High-ranking scientists, such as Kolosov and Korobko, were "fully informed" and therefore knew Factor's purpose.

As SRCAM's access to funding ceased, its equipment and supplies began to disappear. Sometime between 1991 and 1994, a large store of stainless steel sheets slated to be used to build equipment such as fermenters was among the "disappeared" items. The so-called Armenian Radio—an informal communications network among Biopreparat workers—itemized the equipment that had disappeared and asserted that it was sold by Urakov and/or his deputies to private parties for private gain. Armenian Radio was known to carry information ranging in factual accuracy from pure rumor to solid fact. But in a time when the government did not allowed for the open publication of news containing sensitive information and official news was, to say the least, inaccurate, Armenian Radio was a timely and largely trusted information source that, according to interviewees, dispensed surprisingly accurate news.[74]

Despite SRCAM's redirection of research, things went from bad to worse during 1992. Staff scientists' salaries hovered at around $9 per month, a minute sum that was somewhat made up for by the provision of housing subsidies. Research slowed to a near halt. Because SRCAM had previously been able to purchase high-quality, foreign equipment, the equipment mostly continued functioning and allowed for the production of some products, such as the proteins mentioned above, in small experimental batches. These high-value items were carefully locked up in laboratories. When the equipment did break down, researchers fixed it any way they could, otherwise it was sent to storage. Commercial-scale production began only in 1994. There were enough supplies to continue production of products of commercial interest for a little more than a year, but after that there were no funds for replenishment.[75]

As time went by, SRCAM scientists put increasing pressure on Urakov to take up the offers of collaboration from the US and UK governments that had started as early as 1991, but in a rude and abusive manner he declined to do so. According to one source, Urakov was a communist to the core and fervently believed that communism would return very soon, bringing the situation back to normal.[76]

Urakov appears to have been playing a difficult game during 1991–1994. After January 1991, he adopted the guise of being pro-democracy, by, for example, making statements about the liberalization of science and democratizing the governance of SRCAM. But he discarded this guise soon after August 18, 1991, when hardline communists launched a coup against Gorbachev. After news of the coup had been broadcast, Urakov assembled SRCAM's staff in its main conference hall and announced that he supported the coup. One source recalls that Urakov's announcement met a deathly silence. One SRCAM deputy director, Borovik, indicated his support for Urakov, while others, Stepanov and Vladimir Volkov, kept silent. The staff returned to work with little discussion of the matter. By about August 21, most of the coup leaders had fled, and Gorbachev had returned to Moscow. Thereafter, Urakov kept a low profile and never again publicly mentioned communism. He was likely afraid that his support for the coup would cost him his post. This did not happen, at least not then. Urakov's subsequent behavior, however, appears to have been influenced by the fear that his actions would become known to political officials in Moscow.

The awful economy continued to bedevil SRCAM. Urakov had no funding to pay for supplies, and staff members' already low salaries often went unpaid for months at a time. To stop scientists from leaving SRCAM, Urakov perfected the temporary tactic of lying about the center's condition. At monthly staff meetings, he promised that funding was just about to arrive from any number of fictional sources. Staff members could not, however, live on promises. When promises went unfulfilled, staff departed, with the result that some laboratories lost their best scientific workers.[77]

SRCAM was designated a State Research Center under the authority of the RF-MOH in 1994. For a brief time its workers hoped that sufficient funding from the RF-MOH would keep the center operating at a relatively high level, but they were to be gravely disappointed. Of SRCAM's approximately $5 million annual operating costs, the RF-MOH provided only about $450,000 per year, and this money was paid on an irregular basis. The Moscow regional government provided a pittance of about $235,000 per year, and private companies leasing space from SRCAM made small, nearly insignificant, payments. The total amount of funding was grossly insufficient to keep SRCAM solvent.

In view of the lack of RF-MOH support, Urakov finally decided to take advantage of the recently established International Science and Technology Center (ISTC)[78] and began seeking international funding. By this point, the main directions of SRCAM's post-Soviet era research had been set. According to Urakov, they were:

- studying the molecular-biological principles of virulence and immunogenicity of the pathogens responsible for epidemically significant bacterial infections affecting humans and animals;
- improving the methods of interspecies differentiation of pathogenic bacteria based on taxonomically significant DNA fragments;
- studying the mechanisms and ways of targeting biologically active substances toward damaged cells and tissues;
- creating new immunobiologicals for medicine and veterinary medicine; and
- creating biosensors to monitor the functional condition of bacterial cells and other biological objects.[79]

These "new" directions were based on SRCAM's pre-1992 mission. If a few words in the foregoing list were changed—if "weapons" was substituted for "epidemically," if "enhancing BW agents" was swapped with "medicine and veterinary medicine," and "in biological weapons" were added to the last bullet item—this list would resemble SRCAM's main directions when it was a BW facility.

With foreigners expected to be coming to SRCAM on a regular basis, the RF-MOD and Biopreparat wanted to remove possibly incriminating material as a precaution. Accordingly, before the ISTC began funding SRCAM in early 1995, the center's staff transferred all of its archived F reports to an unknown destination in Moscow.

The first ISTC funding was sufficient to pay for the purchase of needed supplies and allowed the funded laboratory's scientists to receive pay increases. In practice, a two-tiered salary structure evolved at SRCAM and at all institutes and centers that received funding from international sources: scientific workers paid by their home institution's general budget "normally" received very low salaries, while workers who had funding from international sources were relatively well paid. For example, at SRCAM the normal salaries in 1995 were 1,000 rubles (approximately $36) per month for a laboratory assistant, 1,350 rubles ($48) for a researcher (candidate level), and 1,500 rubles ($54) for a senior researcher (doctoral level). An SRCAM laboratory assistant who worked on an ISTC-funded project earned the 1,000 rubles normal salary plus $200 per month from the ISTC.[80] ISTC funding ended up paying the salaries of many SRCAM staff members, and for the purchase of equipment and supplies. Urakov acknowledged the importance of the funding, as SRCAM had completed 13 ISTC projects, was working on 16, and was preparing to apply for 10 more as of 2000.[81]

One area where the ISTC funding did not help was the center's past debts and current overhead. Desperate to deal with the institute's burgeoning debt, in 1998 Urakov stopped paying the electricity bill to Mosenergo, the local power company. While clearly remiss, Urakov had reason to dispute at least part of the 43-million ruble, past-due electricity bill.[82] During Soviet times, the government owned the central power grid and provided electricity to SRCAM under a bookkeeping scheme that allowed the power-hungry institute to consume electricity at an artificially low rate. When Mosenergo was partially privatized in 1992, it had to find a way to generate a profit, while continuing to provide power to SRCAM, the approximately 20 private companies renting space from SRCAM, and the Obolensk settlement.[83] Urakov claimed that SRCAM was being asked to pay for the electricity used by all of these parties.

After much discussion, in 2002 SRCAM's debt to Mosenergo was reduced to approximately $1.7 million. But the problem remained unsolved, because SRCAM did not have the cash to pay off even the reduced debt. With SRCAM unable to pay the debt, Mosenergo officials tried to forcibly enter the guarded installation to cut off power supply to the buildings.[84] SRCAM's leadership responded by ordering its staff to prepare to weld all exits and entrances shut except for the main one, where additional guards would be posted.[85] Unable to enter the SRCAM main building, Mosenergo officials confiscated eight cars owned by SRCAM managers and sold them for 2,000–3,000 rubles apiece.[86]

The newspaper *Izvestia* sensationalized the story, claiming in a headline, "Deadly Viruses from a Moscow Oblast Depository Threaten Moscow."[87] The article asserted that the conflict between SRCAM and Mosenergo threatened to lead to the cut-off of electricity to the "biggest in the world collection of 3,500 strains of the most dangerous infections, plague, smallpox, anthrax, cholera, tuberculosis, AIDS—all biothreats to mankind under one roof." This account had little basis in fact. First, SRCAM did not collect and store viruses; second, were electricity to be cut off, the culture collection's bacterial pathogens stored in a frozen or refrigerated state would relatively quickly die after reaching room temperature; and third, there was no dispersal mechanism for propelling the stored pathogens into the open environment and thence to population centers.

Finding itself in a big financial hole, with no obvious way out, SRCAM filed for bankruptcy in 2002. This was probably illegal, because SRCAM belonged to the RF-MOH and could not act like a private enterprise. But it proved effective, as the RF-MOH finally ordered an audit of SRCAM's finances, which revealed "irregularities" in the institute's accounts. On March 4, 2003, a local court appointed Vladimir Plekhanov as the temporary administrator of SRCAM and tasked him with bringing SRCAM back to solvency. Urakov was dismissed and his deputy, Vladimir Volkov, took over his scientific responsibilities. SRCAM still exists and remains busy with the research, development, production, and sale of products, according to information on its web page, so it appears to have worked out deals with its creditors. As for Urakov, he reportedly lives in a house in the Obolensk settlement and also owns an apartment in Moscow.

In 2001 only two of the approximately 100 buildings that originally constituted SRCAM remained as part of the center—Building N1 and Building 8 (the substrate and agar production plant). Some of the others had been

rented to the approximately 20 private companies that were said to be operating there; most of the others were closed down.[88] When Zilinskas visited
the site in 2004, only one private company employing fewer than 10 people
appeared to be active. Nevertheless, SRCAM claims to have an active R&D
program and to be involved in several international collaborations.[89]

This section would be incomplete without mentioning a serious mishap
that occurred at SRCAM in 2004. On April 20, 2004, Galina Boldyreva became ill at her home in Protvino. She was taken to the general hospital in that
city, but when her doctors learned where she was employed, she was transferred to the special isolation ward in SRCAM's Building N1, where she died
13 days later, on May 3. An investigation found that Boldyreva had worked as
a laboratory assistant in SRCAM's Department of Highly Virulent Infections
on the third floor of Building N1 and was probably infected while doing
experiments that involved injecting hamsters and mice with *B. mallei*.[90] As
of this writing, it remains unclear how Boldyreva became infected.

8

All-Union Research Institute of Molecular Biology and Scientific-Production Association "Vector"

BEFORE NIKITA S. KHRUSHCHEV became general secretary of the Soviet Union in 1953, Siberia had languished academically, possessing only the rare scientific research institute or university with a strong science department. After Khrushchev took power, he developed a passion for promoting science in Siberia, and Novosibirsk symbolized this commitment. Novosibirsk is located about 2,850 kilometers east-southeast of Moscow in the Novosibirsk *oblast*, which is about half the size of Germany. Khrushchev selected the city, with a population of just over 1 million in 1960 (1.7 million in 2008), to become the home of a new scientific city, Akademgorodok, which was sited approximately 22 kilometers southeast of the city center. The first scientific institution of note to call Akademgorodok home was a new Siberian branch of the USSR-AN (founded in 1957), but by the time of Khrushchev's ignominious exit from power in 1964, some of the Soviet Union's great scientific universities and research institutes had been built in Akademgorodok, including the Novosibirsk State University (founded in 1959), the Institute of Nuclear Physics (1959), the Institute of Mathematics (1957), the Institute of Geology and Geophysics (1958), and the Institute of Organic Chemistry (1958). The Siberian branch of the USSR-AMN opened its doors in 1969.

This chapter describes the political forces that were applied to the Politburo to ensure that yet another scientific institute—a "closed" institute that became known as Vector—joined the ones established during the Khrushchev era. Although this institute's purposes could not have been readily discernible to or appreciated by the Siberian population, an influential group of scientists undoubtedly saw the value in it. This chapter discusses the new institute as it operated in the Soviet era as a closed institute and as it functioned as a mostly open institute in the uncertain post-Soviet era. The chapter ends by discussing why SRCAM and Vector each pursued certain research directions under Factor and their uncertain results.

History of VNII-MB and, Subsequently, Vector, 1974–1991

No one knows for certain why the MOD selected Novosibirsk *oblast* as Vector's home. Sources for this book have suggested that the major reason was that members of the Siberian branch of the USSR-AN lobbied for a site near Novosibirsk. If this was the case, it is reasonable to assume that Ovchinnikov supported their effort. Whatever the reason, on August 2, 1974, *Glavmikrobioprom* issued Order No. 1683 to establish the All-Union Research Institute of Molecular Biology (VNII-MB).[1] The order did not publish the new institute's classified name, the Institute of Applied Virology (P.O. Box V-8036). Both in its unclassified and in its classified manifestation, the institute reported to Biopreparat (P.O. Box A-1063). The mission of VNII-MB was to research "especially dangerous" viruses,[2] a branch of microbiology that had until then been investigated at only a few institutions in the Soviet Union. Its classified mission was to research, develop, and laboratory-test viruses to arm biological weapons.

High-level officials from several agencies and institutions were directly involved in planning and establishing VNII-MB; from Biopreparat, Ogarkov, Vasily D. Belyaev, and Lev A. Klyucharev;[3] from the MOD, Kalinin, Vorobyov, and Igor V. Nikonov (a smallpox expert at the Zagorsk Institute); and from the Siberian Branch of the USSR-AN, Mikhail A. Lavrentyev, Gury I. Marchuk, Dmitry K. Belyaev, and Dmitry A. Knorre. This group was probably also instrumental in a new secret city named Koltsovo (after the world-famous Soviet geneticist Nikolay K. Koltsov) being established,[4] located about 10 kilometers northeast of Akademgorodok and 19 kilometers southeast of Novosibirsk's center.[5] Construction on the institute began soon after Order No. 1683 was issued.

As was the case with SRCAM, the founding of VNII-MB had two parts: scientific facilities and its settlement at Koltsov. Four kilometers separated the two, with the settlement being located near Baryshevo village. Several former Vector scientists have reported that the sites were primarily constructed using convict labor and, as such, the facilities have elicited complaints about their shoddy quality, including water leaks, cracked walls and floors, and skewed doors and windows.[6]

Interviewed Biopreparat scientists agree that the VNII-MB site was chosen for five major reasons:

1. Proximity to China. VNII-MB scientists said that if the Soviet Union went to war with China, VNII-MB would be where it needed to be. In other words, China was a possible target for biological attack with viruses, particularly because Soviet relations with China had been strained since the 1969 Damansky Island incidents.[7]

2. An available construction unit. A large military and civilian construction enterprise called *Sibakademstroy*, which had built Akademgorodok, was available for the institute's construction, and the populations of several gulags sited in Novosibirsk *oblast* constituted a ready labor pool.

3. Availability of bioscientific expertise. Akademgorodok was the home to a large pool of scientific and technical expertise and capabilities, including scientists, modern scientific and technical equipment, and modern design and production laboratories.

4. Availability of the agro-scientific expertise. A large pool of agricultural scientists was affiliated with the Siberian branch of VASKhNIL (Lenin All-Union Academy of Agricultural Sciences). This was valuable to VNII-MB because agricultural scientists specializing in crop protection were needed for the open-air testing of simulants.

5. The favorable direction of prevailing winds in the region. From meteorological records, planners had learned that the direction of prevailing winds in the region was north-to-south/southeast. Therefore, VNII-MB was built so it is located largely downwind from the two nearby cities of Akademgorodok and Novosibirsk, as well as the Koltsovo settlement. In case of accidental release of viruses from VNII-MB, they would be carried away from nearby population centers.

Until the site's permanent structures were built, VNII-MB scientists used facilities in Akademgorodok for their research, beginning in 1975. The institute's headquarters were initially located in rented rooms in an apartment building at Detsky Proezd 9, Akademgorodok. Most of the new institute's faculty came from the Siberian branch of the USSR-AN and were graduates of Novosibirsk State University. They tended to be specialists in chemistry, molecular biology, physics, and mathematics. The small number of scientists (approximately 40 to 50 people) worked mostly at USSR-AN laboratories belonging to its Siberian branch. These laboratories—at the Institute of Bioorganic Chemistry, Institute of Cytology and Genetics, Catalysis Institute, and Institute of Chemical Kinetics and Combustion—thus became temporary VNII-MB facilities. The institute's electron-microscopy team was located in a laboratory at Novosibirsk State University.

At this stage of its existence, VNII-MB had three broad research directions:

- To develop the ability to perform genetic engineering, including being able to determine the sequences of nucleic acids and proteins; perform chemical synthesis of peptides and nucleotides; and be able to introduce foreign DNA into the genomes of bacteriophages.
- To develop structural and functional analysis methods for viruses and phages, including developing mathematical models of infection processes, establishing a database of nucleic and amino acid sequences using advanced computer technology, and performing mathematical modeling of the infection process for human respiratory infections.
- To automate scientific research and technological processes, including the synthesis of nucleic acids and the method for determining the distribution curve of particles 1 to 5 microns in size and those 5–10 microns in size in aerosols.

Another of VNII-MB's main activities was to perform open-air testing of dry and wet formulations of biological and chemical simulants. This research was considered extremely important, because in addition to supporting the creation of effective viral-based weapons, this type of testing served as a cover for the institute's real activities. In effect, it was the first-level legend that hid the institute's real purposes. This legend was that the institute developed and produced biological pesticides for use in agriculture, including developing effective methods of their application, such as by aerosols. The main biopesticides developed under this legend were ectromelia virus and polydnaviruses.[8] Soviet officials dispensed this disinformation to anyone inquiring about the institute and to institute workers when they first started.

A second-level legend was prepared for more trustworthy workers. This legend was that VNII-MB was founded to discover effective ways of protecting military personnel from biological weapons and that the MOD was the customer. This was how the VNII-MB leadership justified work involving lethal viruses such as variola virus, Marburg virus, Ebola virus, Machupo virus, Lassa virus, Venezuelan equine encephalitis virus (VEEV), and eastern equine encephalitis virus (EEEV). This legend also justified the existence of its BSL-3 and BSL-4 facilities. Only a very few VNII-MB workers were "fully-informed," i.e., they knew the true purpose of the institute. As of 1976 this group probably included the institute's deputy director general, Lev S. Sandakhchiev, as well as Ernst G. Malygin, Stanislav Vasilenko, Nikolay Mertvetsov, Tatyana Shubina, and Valery Shestak (deputy director general in charge of security issues and a member of the KGB).

The MOD and the academies struggled with each other in selecting a director for the new institute. Russian officials initially considered a number of candidates, including military officers from the 15th Directorate. The USSR-AN, however, decided to strongly push for one of its own officials to become director of the new institute. The major impetus for this push most likely came from two academicians at the Siberian branch of the USSR-AN; Knorre, the director of the Institute of Bioorganic Chemistry, under whom Sandakhchiev had studied, and Dmitry Belyaev, the director of the Institute of Cytology and Genetics, who was a member of Sandakhchiev's doctoral dissertation committee. It is safe to assume that in Moscow, Zhdanov, and Ovchinnikov supported Sandakhchiev's candidacy.

In 1976, Sandakhchiev, who was only 37 years old at the time, was appointed as Vector's deputy director of scientific research. At that time, Vector's acting director general was Nikolay Patrikeev, a builder by trade, whose only responsibility was to coordinate the institute's construction. In 1979 Patrikeev departed and Sandakhchiev became director general. His first deputy director general was Nikolay N. Sergeev,[9] who was later replaced by Nikolay B. Cherny.[10]

When Sandakhchiev began working at VNII-MB in 1976, the institute was a long way from reaching its main research goals. The construction of the main research buildings 1 and 5 was well under way and specialists were being trained so that they could design the methods and meet the equipment requirements for the development of a second generation of BW agents, but it was not until 1982 that the laboratories where especially dangerous human pathogens were to be investigated and the refuse incinerator became operational. (Work with dangerous viruses produces infective materials and animal corpses that have to be incinerated.)

The institute's name and structure changed several times after its founding. The most important changes were presented as part of *Glavmikrobioprom's* Decree No. 20 of 1985, which renamed VNII-MB as the Scientific-Production Association (SPA) "Vector" (hereafter, with rare exceptions, we use only Vector).[11] Vector's size and importance increased significantly in the 1980s. In 1985 Soviet president Gorbachev signed the 12th five-year plan (1986–1990),[12] which included provisions for accelerating the pace of BW R&D and allocated close to an equivalent of $1 billion to this end. This increase in funding dramatically changed Vector, as a large portion of it was used to add several new campus buildings for the express purpose of improving research and production capabilities. As a consequence of this expansion, Vector came to encompass two scientific research components, the All-Union Scientific Research Institute for Molecular Biology (VNII-MB) and the Technological Institute for Biologically Active Substances (NIKTI BAV), and three production plants—the Scientific Experimental Production Center (NOPB), Scientific-Experimental Production Plant "IBAS" in Berdsk,[13] and the Pilot Production Agricultural Enterprise in Morozovo.[14] By 1988 Vector had taken control of the town of Nizhny Koyen, which had more than 7,500 hectares of agricultural land.[15] Within a relatively short time, Vector had become the largest and most modern virology R&D institute in the Soviet Union.

Even after acquiring Nizhny Koyen, Vector's expansion continued. In 1989, under *Glavmikrobioprom's* Decree No. 89, Vector took over the Iskitimisky farm in Morozovo, which included more than 5,000 hectares of land, and built an experimental agricultural enterprise on this site.[16] Scientists built animal-holding facilities at both Nizhny Koyen and Iskitimisky, providing the basis for Vector to become involved in the Soviet Union's *Ekologiya* program.[17]

Vector's Workforce in the Soviet Era

By 1990 Vector employed almost 4,500 people, including about 160 candidate-level scientists. Sergey V. Netesov, a former deputy director general for research activities at Vector, claims that about 1,000 members of the workforce studied the molecular biology of viruses, including 300 who worked with pathogens. Most Vector workers and their families lived in a settlement near Baryshevo, whose population was approximately 10,000.[18]

Vector's Physical Plant

Vector was intended to be capable of weaponizing a wide range of viruses, according to Biopreparat. This included researching viruses, developing new technologies for propagating and formulating viruses, performing closed-area testing of the formulations it developed, producing successful formulations in a pilot plant, and packaging final viral formulations in any of a number of special containers. By 1991 Vector had acquired all of the components it needed to fulfill Biopreparat's plans and had in the process become a huge scientific production complex typical of a Soviet SPA. The following paragraphs describe some of the 100 buildings and structures that were components of Vector.

Buildings housing laboratories and testing and production facilities were spread out across the production zone *(promzona),* which included Building 1, Building 5, Building 6, Building 6A, Building 13, Building 15, Building 200, and a building housing a vivarium. All of Vector was enclosed by a reinforced concrete wall that had several entry gates where visitors were screened before entering the *promzona.* For added security, Buildings 1, 5, 6, and 6A were surrounded by secondary walls that had their own guarded entry points. The floor area of buildings within this closed area eventually totaled 200,000 square meters (49.2 acres).

Vector's scientific center was located in Building 1,[19] where scientists performed research on a wide range of deadly viruses. Of the six floors in Building 1, five were equipped with BSL-3 and BSL-4 facilities. Each floor housed a specific division or laboratory:

- First floor: The Nutrient Media Division, headed by Anatoly N. Detsina and later Lidiya Kamshy.
- Second floor: Rickettsiae and retroviruses laboratories, headed by Andrey Pokrovsky.
- Third floor: VEEV, EEEV, Japanese equine encephalitis virus, western equine encephalitis virus, and related virus laboratories, headed by, among others, Netesov, Valery Loktev, Viktor Chesnokov, and Yevgeny Agapov.
- Fourth and fifth floors: Marburg virus, Ebola virus, Machupo virus, and Lassa virus laboratories, headed by Nikolay Ustinov, Yury Rassadkin, Aleksandr Chepurnov,[20] and Georgiy Ignatyev.
- Sixth floor: Natural variola, vaccinia, and ectromelia virus laboratories, headed by Yevgeny F. Belanov.

The First Department also controlled rooms on the first floor where classified documents were handled and stored, as well as specially secured rooms where series F meetings could be held.

Military scientists, mostly those dispatched from the Zagorsk Institute, weaponized and produced variola virus and Marburg virus in Buildings 6 and 6A. Due to their very dangerous work, these scientists operated independently from other Vector staff members. The perimeter of their two buildings was surrounded by a high fence, which was patrolled by members of a Ministry of Interior special division. Special passes were required to enter the fenced-off area. The buildings' workers were often isolated from the outside world, sometimes for as long as three months at a time. In effect, they were released from confinement only after they completed their task. Even then they were required to undergo a careful medical examination before returning to the outside world.

A 1997 Organization for Economic Cooperation and Development report described Building 6 in some detail (Building 6A was its twin).[21] In 1997 its staff consisted of 20 scientific personnel and 50 technical personnel. It had 6,336 square meters of floor space, including 1,440 square meters of BSL-4 facilities and 720 square meters of BSL-3 facilities. The building was equipped with:

> [A] ventilation system which maintains the negative pressure of 25 millimeters of water column inside the zone 3 [BSL-4] (14 millimeters of water column in the zone 2 [BSL-3]), hermetic entrances, double cascade filters for fine purification, system of waste piping capable of collecting up the 32 cubic meters of waste water and treating it at 135 degrees Celsius, productivity rate of 16 cubic meters/hour; transfer units . . . for treatment of waste, suits, and instruments at a temperature of 135 degrees Celsius; dispense systems for disinfecting solutions (6% hydrogen peroxide and 4% sodium peroxide) providing [for] the treatment of the entire working area; isolation boxes (biocontainment level P-4 [BSL-4]); [and] three independent power supply sources.[22]

Technicians installed animal testing equipment of special relevance to Vector's work program in Buildings 6 and 6A in 1986.[23] This so-called "climatic static-dynamic unit UKSD-25" had remarkable performance characteristics:

[The] UKSD-25 unit provides the creation and maintenance of temperature in the range from −15 degrees to 50 degrees Celsius at 10–100% moisture. The necessary isolation level and the required composition of gases can be maintained. The unit is supplied with devices for dispersion of the preparations under study, their maintenance in the aerodispersed state, and with precision batch measuring boxes which provides the high accuracy of delivery of the required dose of aerosol to laboratory animals. Both small (for example, mice for which there are 6 boardings of 20 seats) and big (rabbits, monkeys for which there are 6 seats) laboratory animals can be used in the unit. The unit can be used for ecological investigations since it is possible to use the aerosols containing not only biologically active compounds and microorganisms, specific pathogens included, but also radioactive isotopes.

All operations in the unit can be performed under maximum protection of the personnel and environment (P-4 biocontainment level).

The works on special-purpose subject ordered by RAO "Biopreparat" were performed using UKSD-25 units, that is the trials of efficacy of various developed vaccines against the specific viral pathogens and principal aerosol characteristics of viruses.[24]

In interviews, Vector scientists explained that these units were strong enough to withstand the explosions needed to disperse viral formulations. The explosion would create an aerosol and disperse the viral particles throughout the chamber, including over the cages containing test animals. The scientists used a range of test animals, from mice to primates, in the UKSD-25 unit. The final testing stage required the use of nonhuman primates (including apes), because they most closely resembled humans and their responses to pathogens provided the most valuable indications of a formulation's effectiveness to cause disease and death. Scientists also used this chamber to conduct aerodynamic tests and other experiments necessary to develop and improve mathematical models for aerosol cloud dispersion under different atmospheric conditions and in different geographical zones (including urban centers).

Building 13 was intended to house equipment for closed tests of viral formulations. Officials planned to install a huge reinforced test chamber, similar to the UKSD-25 units, in the building, but the BW program closed down before the chamber was installed. To augment the production capacities of Buildings 6 and 6A, Building 15 was equipped with equipment for the large-scale production of viruses, primarily variola virus and Marburg virus formulations. The building was furbished with large egg incubators and bioreactors for propagating viruses in both pilot plant-scale and industrial quantities; containers in which viruses were mixed with chemicals to produce formulations; dryers for drying the formulations; and a packaging unit that filled either 250-liter or 50-liter double-walled steel containers with the dried formulations. The filled containers were transported to unknown destinations, presumably for storage. As necessary, their contents could be removed to fill munitions used for open-air testing or warfare.

The Building 15 production line included the following components:

- a production area that contained cell culture reactors and egg incubators used to propagate viruses;
- an area for concentrating viruses grown in culture or embryos;
- an area for mixing concentrated virus with stabilizers;
- an area where the concentrated and stabilized viruses were dried;
- a milling area where the dried viruses were rendered into micron-size particles;
- an area for mixing the milled viruses with fillers; and
- an area for packing the dried virus formulation into special double-walled steel containers.

But even the best-laid plans can go asunder, and they did in regards to Building 15. After the facility was constructed and equipped, it failed its biosafety inspections. The building's specifications were subsequently changed, and in the post-Soviet era it produced interferons for therapeutic purposes in the civilian sector.

Vector had a large and elaborate Laboratory Animals Farm that was designed to produce and maintain pure bloodlines of laboratory animals for use in experiments. The farm was housed in a five-story building with 4,225 square meters of floor space and was equipped with an efficient air-handling system that changed the building's air 14 times every 24 hours. Each level contained 10 box stalls to hold animals. With the exception of one other institution, the Sukhumi Primate Center, the Laboratory Animals Farm was the only animal facility in the Ural and European parts of Russia that bred monkeys for medical and biological studies. Unlike the Sukhumi Primate Center, it also bred mice, rats, guinea pigs, rabbits, and, probably, some larger animals.[25]

Vector's open-air test site was located a few kilometers from Kolyvan village. Only noninfectious biological simulants and inert chemicals were tested at the site. The main purpose of the open-air tests, which were performed at night, was to develop mathematical aerosol cloud dispersion models for viral biological weapons. Sources for this book say that the testing led to the development of three models: one for open fields, one for large urban areas, and one for coastal areas that could be used for sea-launched attacks. Both single-source and line-source dispersals were performed at the site; the first by a land-based aerosol generator and the second by aircraft carrying special canisters and spray equipment.

Open-air testing was also performed away from the test site. For example, several experiments involved the release of simulants over Novosibirsk to test the urban area model and the release of simulants over the Novosibirsk Reservoir coastline to test the coastal model. One biological simulant was dry *Bacillus thuringiensis* and another was the chemical fluorescein (a nontoxic fluorescent dye). Vector staff members arriving at work some mornings would sometimes see remnants of fluorescein on the ground, glistening in the sun. An estimated 100 Vector scientists and technicians were involved in open-air testing during 1976–1990.

Vector's Work Program

When Vector was launched, its major R&D effort focused on Marburg virus and Ebola virus, the two viruses with the greatest perceived weapons potential. In addition to these two, Vector scientists also exerted a substantial amount of effort to weaponize VEEV; a medium effort on Machupo virus; and a lesser effort on EEEV. Marburg virus, Ebola virus, Machupo virus, and Lassa virus are all Group I pathogens and demand the highest level of biosafety (equivalent to the US BSL-4 level). VEEV belongs to Group II, which is approximately equivalent to the BSL-3 level. Vector scientists researched rickettsiae, simulants, and other organisms needed to maintain the institute's first-level legend. When Buildings 6 and 6A became operational, Vector staff also prioritized variola virus R&D, which was done at the Group I biosafety level (BSL-4).

Anatoliy P. Sadovskiy, one of Vector's director generals, was responsible for establishing the scientific foundation for the weaponization of viruses. At first he had to overcome a number of technical problems, beginning with refining the technology used to propagate viral agents—that is, the production cycle needed to produce as much highly dispersible powder as possible within a specified period. Because Soviet biological weapons were intended to infect their human targets with a respirable aerosol, dry viral formulations had to:

- be able to retain their virulence after having been milled to 1–5 micron size particles;
- be hardy enough to withstand external stresses such as explosions and desiccation;
- be able to retain their virulence throughout storage for many months at −20°C and for some weeks at room temperature, because they typically would be stored until required for deployment and after being emplaced in a warhead;
- be easily dispersible in air;
- remain suspended in the air for a long time;
- be easily respirable by humans, with most particles settling in the alveoli of the lungs; and
- remain virulent for a sufficiently long time after release to reach and inundate the target population.

Marburg virus Weaponization

The 11th five-year plan (1981–1985) specified that Marburg virus was to be weaponized.[26] Most of Vector's substantial resources were subsequently directed to accomplish this objective. Vector leadership planned to also use the Marburg virus weaponization process as a basis for the weaponizing of other viral weapons agents. However, until 1982, when Building 1 came on line with the high-security facilities required for working with the Marburg virus, either surrogate viruses or simulants were used in R&D done in Akademgorodok.

The approach to weaponizing Marburg virus was quite different from that used for Ebola virus. As one of the Vector scientists described it[27]:

For every type of biological attack, there is a particular agent that fits best. If the military intent on using biological weapons does not plan to send its forces into an area subject to attack, it can use a contagious agent. Conversely, if the military plans to invade an area shortly after agent release, it is best for it to use a non-contagious pathogen.[28] Marburg virus was to be used for the second purpose, to contaminate an area for a relatively short period of time. On first use of Marburg virus, an attack was estimated by the Soviet military to be able to cause about 25% lethality if used in Europe and about 80% if used in Africa. Marburg virus had a much larger potential for weapons use than Ebola virus because it was more effective in infecting people, survived better after release and, as it worked out, was easier to formulate. On the downside, Marburg virus's ability for person-to-person spread was poorer and, further, the virus's virulence diminished after person-to-person spread had taken place, so persons infected in the second instance as a rule survived.[29]

Marburg virus R&D began at the end of 1983 on the fifth floor of Building 1. Vector received its first variant from the Zagorsk Institute, but the Byelorussian Institute of Epidemiology and Microbiology in Minsk later supplied additional variants. Vector's primary task for 1983–1984 was to genetically characterize the first Marburg virus variant, determine how it affected different animals, achieve the production of highly purified Marburg virus, and develop methods for its storage. In addition, scientists began developmental work to test the possibilities for disseminating viruses by aerosol. The second-level legend for this R&D suggested that it was intended to develop a vaccine against Marburg virus disease; however, its real purpose was immediately understood by the involved scientific workers. Nevertheless, the logic for this legend was sound; to defend against a weapons formulation developed by your own scientists (and possibly the enemy), you need a vaccine formulation that is sufficiently efficient so as to be perceived by your scientific workers as protecting them from horrible illness.

In fact, Vector R&D first aimed to develop a killed Marburg virus vaccine, but this effort was unsuccessful. Regardless of the many different formulations they tried, Vector scientists could not achieve an adequately high antibody response in primates. Vector leadership ordered this work stopped, and to this day no licensed Marburg virus vaccine exists anywhere in the world.[30] Vector workers who handled Marburg virus were protected only by technical means and safe practices.

It appears as if Vector's Marburg virus weaponization program went through two phases. During the first phase, scientists observed animals infected with

Marburg virus to determine which type of animal would support the most efficient propagation of the virus. Vector scientists found that guinea pigs were the best (and, probably, the least expensive) animals for the large-scale propagation of Marburg virus, with an especially high concentration of the virus collecting in the animals' spleen and liver. The spleens and livers of infected guinea pigs were harvested and homogenized in special blenders. The homogenized biomass was lyophilized and stored. When it was needed, the dry biomass was suspended in a simple chemical solution and used as aerosol. Many thousands, if not tens of thousands, of guinea pigs lost their lives serving as living "bioreactors" of viruses for the Soviet BW program. The processing of infected animal tissues was a messy, difficult, and dangerous process, so better production methods were tried.

The preferred method for the large-scale propagation of Marburg virus was through cell culture. During the second phase of Vector's Marburg virus R&D, scientists investigated various cell lines to find one that would support a high level of Marburg virus propagation. At first Vector scientists found it impossible to propagate Marburg virus in cell culture to a high titer in large quantities. Using different cell lines, they tried both single-layer cell culture and cell culture in bioreactors, but they always ended up with a low titer. In 1991 a new Vector team succeeded in propagating Marburg virus in high titer in cell culture, although it is not known which cell line it used. Once this was accomplished, a team in Building 6A designed a full production cycle for cell-cultured Marburg virus, which established conditions for the virus's pilot-plant-scale production (because the Soviet Union dissolved soon thereafter, it is unknown if this development proceeded beyond the pilot-plant stage). In general, the production cycle of Marburg virus (as well as variola virus) had four stages: propagation in a bioreactor, separating the biomass and drying it, milling the dried biomass, and testing the tine-milled biomass particles in an aerosol chamber. A Vector scientist interviewed for this book claimed that the largest production of Marburg virus achieved by the Building 6A team was 100 liters in 10 days with a titer of 10^8 particles per milliliter. Technologically speaking, it is more difficult to propagate viruses in cell culture than it is using guinea pig tissues or chicken embryos.[31] Yet production lines based on cell culture were multipurpose and allowed for the large-scale production of not only Marburg virus but also several other viruses that are useful for BW purposes, such as Ebola virus, VEEV, and variola virus.

Once Vector was able to produce sizable amounts of Marburg virus, the workforce began developing different formulations, both wet and dry, and testing them in the UKSD-25. As part of this effort, it perfected the milling of dry formulations; that is, it developed milling techniques to generate viable particles in the 1- to 5-micron range. Vector had equipment to measure the size of aerosol particles and did studies on the effects of formulations on the pharyngeal-larynx tract in guinea pigs and nonhuman primates.

To sum up, Vector scientists spent many years working on the Marburg virus weaponization "problem" and achieved significant results—they developed the know-how to produce a dry formulation of Marburg virus that was effective when used for aerosol application, they produced and stored experimental samples of this formulation, and the results of closed tests in the UKSD-25 aimed at determining the formulation's efficacy on nonhuman primates were impressive—impressive enough for the MOD to give it a high valuation. This line of R&D at Vector presumably ended in 1992.

In a separate effort, Vector scientists attempted to genetically engineer Marburg virus but were unsuccessful. They were unable to construct an appropriate complementary DNA clone (because filoviruses are RNA viruses, a scientist who wishes to genetically engineer any of them first has to construct a DNA copy of the RNA. This RNA-complimentary DNA clone is the material that is genetically engineered. To this day, only a few research groups in the world can do this kind of R&D.)

It bears noting that there appears to have been no direct collaboration between Vector and the Zagorsk Institute on Marburg virus research, nor on any other hemorrhagic fever virus. This seems peculiar, especially because Zagorsk researchers obtained the Marburg virus Popp isolate in 1969 from the Institute of Poliomyelitis and Viral Encephalitides.[32] Zagorsk scientists likely gained substantial knowledge about the virus and how to handle it by 1982, knowledge that could have saved Vector scientists considerable time. But there is no indication that the institutes collaborated or shared scientists. Vladimir M. Shishkov, a hemorrhagic fever virus expert, was sent from the Zagorsk Institute to Vector in about 1988 (see below), but his role at Vector appears to have been to set up a production system and not get involved with research in Building 1. This compartmentalization indicates that the MOD was more concerned with securing its knowledge about hemorrhagic fever viruses than it was with sharing the knowledge with Vector, even if the two supposedly had a common objective.

Ebola Virus Weaponization

Vector began working on Ebola virus in 1985, approximately two years after it began working on Marburg virus. The Byelorussian Institute of Epidemiology and Microbiology, which was mostly an open institute, supplied the variant that was studied, Ebola virus Mayinga. It had received this variant from the Virology Unit at the Institute of Tropical Medicine, Antwerp, Belgium. The Byelorussian scientists had been performing a diagnostic project involving Marburg virus, Ebola virus, Machupo virus, and Lassa virus as part of Problem 5. Samples of the virus were secretly transported as military shipments from the Byelorussian Institute of Epidemiology and Microbiology to Vector under the supervision of Vector biosafety experts. The major goals of Ebola virus R&D were to investigate the growth characteristics of Ebola virus in order to develop methods for optimizing growth rates; to clarify the action of immunoglobulins against Ebola virus; and to develop vaccines against Ebola virus disease.

Due to the deadliness of Ebola virus, vaccine development was given the highest priority. At first Vector scientists tried to develop a killed vaccine, but it had no effect. They then tried to develop an attenuated form of Ebola virus. For this purpose, the Zagorsk Institute sent Vector an Ebola virus variant that supposedly was less pathogenic for humans than a wild-type virus.[33] Officials tasked Vector scientists with developing vaccines and immunoglobulins using this variant. However, as there was no animal model for doing this kind of developmental research, Vector scientists first sought to increase the strain's virulence in order to be able to use an existing animal model for vaccine testing. They attempted to do this through the selective passage of Ebola virus through guinea pigs, but they were unsuccessful. Next they tried to attenuate the variant by growing viruses in a cell line from embryo lung cells (diploid cells) and to use the attenuated viruses as vaccines. Biopreparat eventually stopped this work because it realized that there was no way to clinically test the product; that is, it was not permitted to deliberately infect a human who had been vaccinated with virulent Ebola virus. One Vector scientist told us that this work proved useful, however, because it helped elucidate the genetic basis of virulence (see below).

Vector scientists also attempted to use vaccinia virus to produce an Ebola virus disease vaccine. As part of this approach, scientists inserted different genes of Ebola virus (VP24, VP30, etc.) into a vaccinia host. A. N. Kotov did this construction, which stimulated some antibody production. In the end, though, neither Vector nor anyone else succeeded, and no Ebola virus vaccine exists to this day.[34]

Venezuelan Equine Encephalitis Virus Vaccine R&D and Weaponization

Vector identified VEEV, which was a first generation Soviet BW agent, as a subject for second generation studies. Most of this work was done on the third floor under Viktor Chesnokov. Little is known about the weaponization of VEEV, although according to former Vector scientists, this pathogen was one of only two viruses investigated at Vector that was already a first generation validated BW agent (the second was variola virus). Since VEEV was well known to Vector scientists, their research on it had applied goals. For example, those interviewed for this book referred to a research group that had isolated Marburg virus genes and inserted them into VEEV. This R&D would have aimed to take advantage of three VEEV properties: (1) its ease of transmission by aerosol; (2) its capability to infect the nasal mucosa; and (3) the virus's ability to travel along the olfactory nerves to the brain and establish infection. As with other biomedical R&D involving viruses, this VEEV R&D could have been dual-use. On the one hand, Vector scientists might have inserted those genes into virulent VEEV rather than noninfectious replicons. The researchers hypothesized that transferring Marburg virus genes into VEEV would have endowed it with additional pathogenic (hemorrhagic fever) properties that transformed it from an incapacitating pathogen into a deadly one. On the other hand, Vector scientists could have inserted Marburg virus (and possibly Ebola virus) genes into noninfectious VEEV replicons in order to express them as promising vaccine candidates. Neither side of this R&D (vaccine or weaponization) has been published. It is unknown whether this R&D was offensive or defensive, but Chesnokov's R&D program may very well have supported both aspects.[35]

Vector ended up developing two different types of VEEV vaccines: one was constituted by inactivated viruses, and the second was a recombinant vaccine. Both proved effective against injected VEEV, but they were ineffective against viruses delivered by aerosol. This is because humeral antibodies produced by the body's immune defense system after being stimulated by a vaccine, do not affect the virus' transmission to the brain via the olfactory nerve.

Machupo Virus Studies

Vector R&D on Machupo virus began at approximately the same time as work on Marburg virus (1983–1984) and was consigned to Building 1's fourth floor. In 1985, however, Biopreparat ordered the weaponization of Ebola virus. Because the Building 1 rule was one type of virus per floor,[36] and because the building had limited room, Ebola virus work squeezed out Machupo virus effort on the fourth floor.[37] As Biopreparat officials in Moscow became more and more interested in Ebola virus, more tasks involving this virus were ordered and fewer on Machupo virus. In the end, work on Machupo virus never progressed passed the research stage. While Machupo virus work progressed, Vector scientists managed to develop a monoclonal antibody, clarified the infectious process in various animal models, and made some findings from vaccine-related R&D that used an attenuated form of the virus.

By the end of 1986, Vector concluded that this virus was less effective for BW purposes than Marburg virus and Ebola virus, because it did not survive long as an aerosol and it had a significantly longer incubation period than the other viruses. Vector scientists eventually dubbed it an "inconvenient" agent.

Variola Virus Weaponization and Related Studies

The Zagorsk Institute started weaponizing variola virus in the 1960s, if not earlier (see Chapter 3). However, Vector scientists were told nothing about this work. Information about the Zagorsk work, nonetheless, reached Vector biosafety officials. In 1989, Vector scientists learned that variola virus strain I-1 delivered to Vector from the Zagorsk Institute was of Asian origin and was characterized by high virulence—higher than the "usual" 30% case fatality rate caused by natural variola virus among unvaccinated victims. This strain was code-named India-1967, which was the name of the strain that was accidentally released during a test on Vozrozhdeniye Island in 1971 (see Chapter 4).

Rather than train Vector scientists to weaponize variola virus, the MOD assigned scientists who were already familiar with this kind of work; at that time, these scientists resided at the Zagorsk Institute.[38] A Zagorsk team of about 12 scientists and technicians, led by Colonel Yevgeny P. Lukin and his deputy Vladimir M. Shishkov, arrived at Vector sometime during 1988–1989.[39] The team increased to about 20 people within a year. The new arrivals went to work in Vector's Section for Microbiological Safety, but they were soon transferred to Building 6. Lukin and Shishkov were eventually put in charge of the testing and production of all viral BW agents at Vector, meaning that they supervised the activities within Building 6, Building 6A, Building 13, and, presumably, Building 15. According to sources for this book, Sandakhchiev trusted Lukin completely in these matters and did not interfere in his business.

Some Vector scientists learned about aspects of the Zagorsk Institute's earlier work because they were given access to parts of the variola virus recipe that Lukin's team brought to Vector, assumedly to avoid repeating previous work. The recipe filled several volumes, according to our sources. It contained, for example, information about the media required for culturing viruses and how the cultured viruses were to be processed. For security reasons, very few of Vector's staff saw the entire recipe. For instance, someone working on culture media was allowed to read only sections of the instructions directly relevant to this work. Only Lukin, the members of his team, and, probably, Sandakhchiev and Yevgeny A. Stavsky had access to the entire recipe and also had the right to control access to it. This work at Vector was one of the rare instances when the 15th Directorate shared a recipe with civilian scientists. Pasechnik said that when he met Sandakhchiev in 1989 at Koltsovo, he was told that the variola virus recipe had been fully developed and that there was no room for improvement.

As is noted in Chapter 3, variola virus was a well-studied first generation Soviet BW agent. It was probably mass-produced at Zagorsk using embryonated eggs, though this is not known for sure. As has been noted previously, little information about BW R&D at MOD institutes is publicly known. The first process for mass-producing variola virus at Vector was undoubtedly based on embryonated eggs, so it is reasonable to believe that this was the process called for in the Zagorsk Institute recipe. At Vector, Buildings 6 and 6A contained egg incubators that together had a maximum capacity of 5,000 eggs.[40] Approximately 5 to 7 days after the embryos were injected with variola virus, they were removed from the eggs and processed by maceration, homogenization, drying, and pulverization, according to sources for this book. A former Vector virologist has said, "According to the requirements, 1 cubic centimeter of formulation contained about 10,000,000,000 virions of smallpox virus . . . this was equivalent to 1,000,000,000 'units of virulence.'" Thus, 10 "units of virulence" was the ID_{50} for the weaponized variola virus. It is unclear whether this was the "requirement" for variola virus produced by the embryonated egg technique described above or the cell culture technique described below. Vector's production potential of variola viruses using the embryonated egg processing method is unknown.

The 12th five-year plan specified that Vector was to develop the technology to produce variola virus using cell culture.[41] Vector officials formulated a plan that envisioned installing a production line in Building 15. As a first step, the institute purchased a new, domestically produced 630-liter fermenter and set it up in Building 6. When Building 15 was completed, it too was to be furbished with a new line of fermenters with capacities ranging from 100 to 2,500 liters. Fermenters used at Vector for the cultivation of viruses were to mirror existing equipment at the Zagorsk Institute, for two reasons. First, as is explained below, when problems cropped up at Vector, the Zagorsk Institute would be in a position to help fix them; and second, Zagorsk Institute scientists would be able to apply new know-how developed at Vector for the production of viruses at the Zagorsk Institute.

When its infrastructure was complete, what was Vector's total variola virus production capability? Alibek writes that after having observed a test of a "smallpox" biological weapon in one of Vector's explosive test chambers in December 1990, "We calculated that the production line in the newly constructed Building 15 in Koltsovo was capable of manufacturing between 80 and 100 tons of smallpox a year."[42] When we discussed this estimate with Vector scientists, they unanimously agreed that Alibek's estimate was too high. To have a 100 ton annual production, Vector would have had to produce 274 kilograms of variola virus every day of the year. At that time Vector had only one production line based on embryonated eggs and another whose starting point was its largest fermenter, which had a capacity of only 630 liters. Because the capacity of the first production line is unknown, only the second can be estimated. Based on expert estimates, the 630 liter fermenter could provide 500 liters (a half a ton) of product in one approximately 10-day growth period. On the assumption that the average viral growth and processing cycle was one month, this production line's theoretical maximum output would be 6 tons of liquid product per year. When factoring in downtime for maintenance, sterilization, and repair, the liquid product output was probably no more than 5 tons. The liquid product would have had to have been processed to remove wastes, bringing down the yield further. We estimate that when Vector was running at its top production capacity in December 1990, its maximum yield of weaponized variola virus from cell culture would have been no more than about 2 tons annually.

If Vector had realized its original plans by, for example, securing a line of fermenters up to and including one with a capacity of 2,500 liters, it could have reached a production capacity of over 10,000 liters annually, but these fermenters were never installed. Despite probably falling short of official estimates, a yield of 2,000 kilograms of properly formulated variola virus that was dispersed as an aerosol would have infected the world's population many times over (assuming a 10% effectiveness and adequate dispersal).[43]

An interesting aspect of Vector's variola virus R&D had been the attempts by its scientists to recover virus from smallpox victims buried in Siberia's permafrost. As Vector scientists have noted, "In these permafrost regions [of Siberia] at least 10 smallpox and Spanish influenza outbreaks were recorded from the 17th century on with mortality [sic] reaching as high as 40%. . . . According to archived documents, during virus outbreaks, many victims were buried in ice cellars typically used for storing food. It is fair to assume then that the remains of people who died of smallpox or influenza are buried at unknown permafrost locations."[44] The first Soviet expedition to examine the corpses of smallpox victims, as far as is known, was undertaken during the summer of 1991 by a team led by Yevgeny F. Belanov, the head of General Virology at Vector's Institute of Molecular Biology,[45] and Vladimir Ye. Repin, who was in charge of "the library of microbes and isolates at Vector, had the most advanced facility in the entire complex, and was obviously well funded."[46] Vector asserted that the State Committee for Public Health and Hygiene of the Republic of Sakha (Yakutia) had requested this expedition, because it was concerned that the warming of the Siberian region would expose infectious corpses to the open environment. This threat would have been exacerbated by smallpox victims' often having been hurriedly interred in shallowly dug icehouses rather than proper graves.

Upon opening one icehouse in Pokhodsk, Vector scientists found the well-preserved corpse of a child estimated to have been buried during the 1884–1886 smallpox epidemic. Although virus particles were said to have been recovered from the corpse, they could not be cultured.[47] This line of research was restarted during the summer of 1992, but it never recovered live virus. Vector wanted to mount additional smallpox recovery expeditions, but it was unable to raise sufficient funding. Vector estimated that it costs approximately $200,000 to conduct each expedition. Sandakhchiev believed that the exhumations were proper and necessary because infectious variola virus can survive in frozen tissues, and scientists can gain valuable insight into, for instance, what made the strain that killed the Pokhodsk inhabitants so extraordinarily virulent.[48] This view was supported by a study done by Repin et al. that indicated that "variola virus is highly stable when kept in patients' specimens, in particular, in the scabs."[49] They might survive "for more than 250 years under the investigated storage conditions."[50] If the Vector scientists are correct, then research expeditions aimed at determining if bodies buried in the permafrost regions of not only Russia, but also northern Europe, Canada, and Alaska remain infective may be warranted.[51]

Vector is one of two so-called WHO smallpox reference centers (the second being the Centers for Disease Control and Prevention in Atlanta). According to analyst Jonathan Tucker:

> By early 1984, the WHO had authorized only two laboratories in the world to retain samples of variola virus: the CDC in Atlanta and the Research Institute for Viral Preparations in Moscow. Because these two labs had done all the diagnostic work for the WHO during the smallpox eradication campaign, they had accumulated the [world's] largest strain collections. The CDC had a total of 451 viral isolates. . . . The Moscow repository contained single or multiple samples of 120 isolates collected since 1958, including strains from eighteen countries in Africa, Asia, and South America, as well as the Soviet Union. Seventeen specimens were from scabs from smallpox patients, ninety were frozen cultures, and twenty-four were in freeze-dried form.[52]

After the dissolution of the Soviet Union, the Research Institute for Viral Preparations' facilities, including its security system, deteriorated substantially.[53] The October 1993 revolt against the Yeltsin government made it clear to Russian security forces that the Research Institute for Viral Preparations was vulnerable to outsider threats. High-level officials subsequently decided to transfer the institute's variola virus collection to Vector, an operation that was completed in September 1994. Russian officials informed the WHO of this move in December 1994. A WHO report states:

> Variola virus stocks were transferred from the WHO Collaborating Centre for Smallpox and other Orthopox Infections located within the Institute of Viral Preparations, Moscow, to the State Research Center of Virology and Biotechnology (VECTOR), Koltsovo, in September 1994. Permission to work on variola virus was given by the Russian Federa-

tion State Committee on Sanitary and Epidemiological Surveillance in May 1995 and a WHO inspection took place in June 1995. VECTOR was designated a WHO Collaborating Centre for Orthopoxvirus Diagnosis and Repository for Variola Virus Strains and DNA in June 1997. The facility at VECTOR has been used for propagation of variola strains to obtain DNA but, apart from one request that has not been followed up, no external request has been received for use of that facility.[54]

In 2002 a Vector biosafety expert described the WHO Collaborating Centre in detail.[55] The center is housed in two buildings: the laboratory for diagnosis and research on orthopoxvirus infections and the repository for variola virus strains are located in Building 6 (at the time, the lab head was A. A. Guskov), and the laboratory for molecular biology of orthopoxviruses and the repository for variola virus DNA and its cloned fragments are located in Building 5 and partially in Building 6 (the lab head was S. N. Shchelkunov). The most dangerous variola virus work is performed in BSL-4 facilities on the second floor of Building 6, which also has smaller BSL-3 rooms and two BSL-2 rooms where work on DNA fragments is performed. The third floor houses an animal facility, an aerosol chamber, change rooms, and some lower-level laboratories. Floors 1 and 4 contain engineering facilities, such as waste removal treatment and air-handling equipment. As in the Soviet era, the building's total floor space is 6,330 square meters.

Lassa Virus, Crimean-Congo Hemorrhagic Fever Virus, Junín Virus, Hantavirus Studies

This book's sources said that there was "almost no work" done on Lassa virus, Crimean-Congo hemorrhagic fever virus, Junín virus, and hantaviruses. "Almost no work" in Vector parlance means that scientists received strains of these viruses, injected them into different animals and recorded their reaction, and then attempted to perform diagnostic tests. Work on Lassa and Junín viruses started before 1992 and was part of *Ferment*. As for Crimean-Congo hemorrhagic fever virus and hantavirus studies, the "almost no work" was done before 1992, and research done after this time was not part of *Ferment*.

Human Immunodeficiency Virus Type 1 (HIV-1) Studies

Vector scientists carried out HIV-1 research on the second floor of Building 1. Leonid Z. Fayzullin procured a HIV-1 strain from Moscow and was tasked with developing an antigen and diagnostic system—exceedingly complicated work. As Soviet leadership demanded that this work be done faster and faster, Fayzullin's relationship with them deteriorated. Fayzullin eventually had a final argument with Sandakhchiev and departed Vector. Andrey G. Pokrovsky replaced Fayzullin. It is unknown if HIV-1 research was *Ferment*-related.

Exploratory and Futuristic Research

In addition to its agent-specific R&D, Vector performed substantial research to enhance the weapons-related properties of existing BW agents or create entirely new BW agents. Much of this work had characteristics of basic research and, as such, was uncertain to generate useful findings. The SRCAM chapter (Chapter 7) describes how this kind of research was performed under the Bonfire and Factor programs using bacteria; this section describes similar research but focuses on viruses and bacteria-virus combinations.

Several groups of Vector scientists spent years working to create a viral chimera.[56] In 1990 Alexander Beliaev and his colleagues successfully incorporated structural genes of hepatitis B virus and tick-borne encephalitis virus into the DNA of vaccinia virus.[57] The genetically engineered vaccinia virus strain was able to efficiently express the antigens of the two viruses. This research was probably vaccine related.

Another group headed by Netesov attempted to incorporate the VEEV genome into vaccinia virus DNA. This work had two objectives: The first was to create a recombinant strain of vaccinia virus with a higher virulence level than the original virus (vaccinia virus is a low-order, opportunistic pathogen). Netesov reportedly was unsuccessful. The second was to develop a VEE vaccine. Sources for this book say that this R&D successfully created antigens that held promise as vaccines, yet it did not achieve its objective.

Sergei N. Shchelkunov, one of Vector's foremost specialists in the molecular biology of orthopoxviruses, and his group contributed considerably to virology by determining the nucleotide sequences of certain natural strains of variola virus, vaccinia virus, monkeypox virus, and ectromelia virus. In effect, Shchelkunov's work made it possible for other Vector scientists to incorporate foreign genetic material into the genomes of orthopoxviruses and to define some of the molecular factors of their virulence. His findings laid the basis for weapons-related R&D on variola virus under a program code-named "Hunter" *(Okhotnik)*. The Hunter program was reportedly first directed by Netesov and later by Shchelkunov and Oleg I. Serpinskii. Its main objective was to develop chimeric viruses that would cause two diseases either nearly simultaneously or successively.[58] One of the Hunter program's accomplishments was the creation of a recombinant vaccinia virus strain that contained genes coding for certain Ebola virus structural proteins. As Hunter advanced, its scientists created vaccinia virus recombinants that expressed endorphins, dynorphins, myelic basic protein, and other immunoregulatory proteins synthesized under the Factor program.[59] This work was accomplished toward the end of the BW program, so most if not all of the recombinants created in the laboratory were probably not close to being weaponized.

Vladimir Blinov, an expert in the field of theoretical virology, used special computer programs to help Vector scientists construct structural and functional maps of orthopoxviruses and other viruses in order to identify the genes whose removal or replacement would not reduce a virus's virulence. The BW objective of this research, if any, is unknown.

In 1990 Vector scientists began developing recombinant strains of orthopoxviruses that were better able to defeat human immune defenses than wild strains. Biological weapons armed with these new strains would infect and probably kill even those persons who had been vaccinated against smallpox. The first group of scientists to carry out this type of experiment was probably headed by Serpinsky. Instead of simply incorporating virus genes into the vaccinia virus, these scientists incorporated genes coding for human peptides that were developed by the Factor program. In 1990 the group succeeded in creating a recombinant strain of vaccinia virus that contained the gene coding for the production of beta-endorphin, one of the peptides that regulates certain brain functions, such as the reduction of pain. This strain was developed too late to be weaponized.

With the capability to insert the structural genes of peptides into vaccinia virus DNA, Vector scientists would likely be able to do the same with monkeypox virus, with minimal additional effort. Relying on the substantial expertise of its scientific staff, Vector could theoretically create (and perhaps it has already done so) a monkeypox virus carrying a gene coding for myelin. This would result in a new kind of virus-based BW agent. Humans infected with the new monkeypox virus strain would be killed not by the virus but by the victim's autoimmune reaction to myelin peptide. In other words, the virus would deliver the myelin gene into the human host, which would initiate a deadly disease process. The objectives of this R&D were similar to the goals of the Factor program described in Chapter 7. At Vector, viruses rather than bacteria were employed as hosts for genes coding for damaging peptides or the peptides themselves.[60]

Though Vector scientists genetically manipulated vaccinia and mousepox viruses, they did not do similar work on the variola and monkeypox viruses. Contrary to what has been reported elsewhere, sources for this book say that no VEE-variola or VEE-ectromelia viral chimeras were created at Vector. A limited number of scientists possessed the expertise to do this work and none of these worked on variola virus. Also, the military scientists in the Lukin group were not accomplished molecular virologists and therefore would have been unlikely to suggest this idea or to carry out the R&D to realize it.

Vector's refrigerators undoubtedly contained plasmids for use as vectors to put foreign gene fragments into the vaccinia virus, and these same plasmids might have been used to insert gene fragments into the variola virus. But our sources believe that this was not done, because VEEV fragments were unlikely to add new virulence properties to variola virus and, in any case, the infective and disease effects of the two viruses are so different that they were more likely to be antagonists than abettors. In the final analysis, India-1967 variola virus strain was sufficiently deadly by itself and did not need molecular boosting by Vector scientists.

Mishaps at Vector Involving Scientific Workers

Nikolay V. Ustinov

Ustinov was one of several Vector virologists who had received advanced training at Roza N. Lukina's laboratory at the Zagorsk Institute, and by all accounts he was an accomplished scientist.[61] On April 16, 1988, while working in his laboratory, Ustinov was bumped by a laboratory assistant while he was injecting guinea pigs with Marburg virus, causing the syringe needle to plunge into his thumb. He immediately informed Vector authorities about the mishap and was hospitalized in a 20-bed BSL-4 isolation ward located in Building 18. Then as now, there was no specific treatment for Marburg virus disease, only supportive care. Some clinicians of that time used gammaglobulin in the hope of ameliorating the effects of Marburg virus, but none of it was available at Vector or in the Novosibirsk region. According to some animal experiments, to be effective, the gammaglobulin had to be administered to the victim within 24 hours of exposure, which was not possible in this instance. Vector ordered gammaglobulin from the Zagorsk Institute, which sent it to Biopreparat in Moscow, which in turn sent it by airfreight to Novosibirsk, and thence by car to Vector. Ustinov was administered the gammaglobulin intravenously on April 20, four days after the accident.

On April 21, Ustinov presented with a headache and nausea, commonly the first symptoms of Marburg virus disease. His condition thereafter steadily declined. On April 25, a specialist in intensive care who worked for the MOH's 3rd Directorate arrived and took charge of Ustinov's care. This doctor, Oleg Vedishchev, somehow became exposed to Marburg virus while caring for Ustinov, although this was not realized at the time.

On May 5, Ustinov died. His body was taken to the morgue and autopsied. During the postmortem examination, officials took samples of his blood and internal organs. Alibek described how the body was then carefully prepared for a safe burial: First it was inundated with a disinfectant, then it was wrapped in plastic, placed within a metal box that was welded shut, and then the metal box was fitted into a normal-looking wood coffin and buried. Sandakhchiev delivered a brief eulogy.[62]

Vector cultured the samples taken from Ustinov's body; the recovered Marburg virus variant was named Variant U. Alibek claims that because the strain had proven its worth by killing Ustinov, it was weaponized and became the basis for a biological weapon.[63] This is unlikely given that the accident occurred in 1988. According to sources for this book, all of whom are well-trained virologists, because Marburg virus recovered from victims tends to be less virulent than the primary pathogen (as noted above), it would not have made sense for Vector to weaponize Variant U, though the strain certainly became part of Vector's sizable virus culture collection.

Alibek was mistaken about Vedishchev's fate. He wrote, "The pathologist, identified in our archives as 'V,' went through the same agonies as Ustinov." Further, "I learned through unofficial channels that he died soon afterwards."[64] In fact, Vedishchev was not a pathologist, but a specialist in intensive care. Immediately upon showing symptoms of Marburg virus disease, Vedishchev was given gammaglobulin. He was sick for some weeks, but survived and continued working for the MOH.[65] In particular, he had an important role in assisting victims of the 1990 Armenian earthquake.[66]

The Case of Patient V

The case of Patient V (different from "V" described above) was first published in one of Russia's foremost medical journals.[67] On April 11, 1990, the
man, a 35-year-old scientific associate, "violated safety rules for handling the
blood serum of a laboratory animal infected with the said virus (Marburg
virus) because he believed the material was no longer infective." On April 13
he evinced fatigue and chills, which he attributed to a cold, and took fever-
reducing drugs on his own. But on April 16 his illness became serious; he
presented with malaise, raised body temperature, headache, body rash, and
other symptoms. He was taken by ambulance to Vector's isolation ward, where
he had a long and difficult course of illness, not returning to a near-healthy
status until June 9. During his illness, samples were taken from his blood,
urine, and nasopharynx on a continuous basis. It was not until the virology
results proved negative for the presence of virus that V was allowed to go
home on August 14. Vector scientists interviewed for this book reported that
V was released of duty by Vector after having recovered; he subsequently secured work as a medical doctor at one of Novosibirsk's hospitals.

Antonina Presnyakova

The journal *Science* carried an article describing the circumstances surrounding
the death of Antonina Presnyakova, a Russian scientists working at Vector:

> A Russian scientist working on an Ebola vaccine died last week follow-
> ing a lab accident. On 5 May, Antonina Presnyakova, 46, pricked her
> hand with a syringe after drawing blood from infected guinea pigs in
> an ultrasecure biosafety level 4 (BSL-4) facility at the Vektor Research
> Institute of Molecular Biology, a former bioweapons lab near Novosi-
> birsk, Russia. She was hospitalized immediately, says a lab official, devel-
> oped symptoms 1 week later, and died on 19 May.
>
> There is no requirement that Ebola incidents be reported to the
> World Health Organization (WHO) if the incident is not a threat to
> public health. The lab sought help from WHO and other BSL-4 labs
> on 17 May, followed by a conference call the next day with a WHO-
> recommended doctor. Presnyakova appeared "quite stable," the official
> says, but her condition deteriorated rapidly overnight and she died the
> next morning.

Some press reports suggested that Vektor might have been able to save her life if it had contacted WHO sooner. But Vektor officials say that she was given the appropriate level of care, and WHO spokesperson Richard Thompson says, "They did all they could do, as far as we can tell."

Vektor says an internal inquiry will issue a public report in mid-June.[68]

A record of Presnyakova's symptoms and treatment can be found in a Russian journal article, in which she is referred to as "P."[69]

Collaborations between Vector and Other Institutes

Vector scientists continually collaborated with IHPB staff. Most of these collaborations had to do with IHPB scientists developing formulations to protect viruses that were weaponized by Vector. It was particularly important to protect viruses against inactivation by physical stresses while they were suspended in aerosols. Because IHPB was not approved to handle Group I pathogens, Vector sent simulants of viruses that needed to be protected to IHPB, and its scientists would develop one or more protective preparations, whose effectiveness would then be evaluated by Vector scientists. Vector staff would unite virus and preparation into a formulation, which would be tested for its level of activity after having been in storage, its viability after having been frozen and refrozen, the ease of dispersal for particles in the 1- to 5-micron range, and its survivability in aerosol form. All of this work was done in-house; as noted previously, Vector did not perform open-air tests of pathogens. If a formulation proved promising in closed testing, Vector would pack an aliquot of it in a special container and ship it out to unknown recipients (presumably MOD institutes). All of this work was done before 1990, although some of it was published in 1996 and later.

Vector's Relations with the Ministry of Defense

The MOD's 15th Directorate dictated the tasks that Biopreparat was to perform, and its decisions were conveyed to Biopreparat headquarters in Moscow, where the NTS decided which institute should do what. The task orders were then sent out from Biopreparat to individual facilities. At Vector, Sandakhchiev, with the assistance of his deputy director generals, would distribute task orders to divisions. Although Sandakhchiev himself performed research on problems that he found particularly interesting, he had two primary administrative responsibilities. In the long term, he had to make sure that Vector's five-year plans were fulfilled, and in the short term, that Biopreparat task orders were completed well and on time. There was a common belief among Vector scientists that their task orders were formulated at the Zagorsk Institute, but with the very rare exceptions noted earlier the two institutes did not directly collaborate.

An example of a task order would be to develop a vaccine against a particular viral disease. The task order could be rather specific, specifying, for example, that the vaccine should be constituted by a virus that was to be inactivated within specified parameters (such as the vaccine's requiring a specific concentration and the inactivation had to be done through the use of formaldehyde). The division assigned the task would then do the R&D needed, and one of three outcomes would result. The first possible result was that the task was successfully completed and the product was delivered to Biopreparat together with a report on methodologies used and objectives achieved. A second possibility was that the R&D was done, but the end product was an unsatisfactory vaccine. If this occurred, the division head would write a report explaining the most probable reason for the poor results and might make a suggestion as to the next approach that should be taken. He might, for example, suggest that success might be achieved by using a certain rDNA technique. Biopreparat might then approve this approach by issuing another task order. A third possible outcome was that the vaccine proved impossible to develop. The division head would then write a report stating the most probable reason for failure and give his opinion for terminating further work on this vaccine.

Vector divisions also wrote short quarterly reports on the progress of each of its projects, as well as annual full reports, which were submitted to Sandakhchiev. Completed division, institute, and task reports were checked and signed by Sandakhchiev, who then sent them to Biopreparat headquarters. Reports from institutes were periodically compiled in volumes and published by Biopreparat at the secret level. Each report was considered a piece of scientific reporting and was included in the participating scientists' CVs. A Biopreparat scientist's secret publications could not be openly referenced.

The Zagorsk contingent of scientists and technicians was never acknowledged as being from the military. In fact, at first Vector scientists did not know that these people had come from the Zagorsk Institute; this became clear only with the passage of time. Vector workers eventually deduced that the Zagorsk workers were from the military, because "they acted differently" and received two salary payments.[70] The first payment originated from Vector and the second from a separate, secretive office that was inaccessible to Vector staff. Because they were paid substantially better than civilian scientists and could shop at special commissariats, military scientists also had a higher standard of living than civilian scientists.

Vector scientists generally considered MOD scientists to be scientifically weak. Conversely, Vector scientists often had the impression that the military scientists thought them to be dilettantes, unable to do "real" work. This is probably why the MOD sent its scientists to Vector to carry out the task of producing weaponized agents. The Vector scientists interviewed for this book generally agree that the two groups worked separately and did not communicate effectively. Eventually a few of the military scientists became integrated and remained at Vector, but around 1992 the majority returned to the Kirov Institute or the Zagorsk Institute. For example, Lukin returned to the Zagorsk Institute and as far as is known (and as demonstrated by his open publication record) had an active career until at least 2003.

Secret Biological Warfare R&D Performed at Vector as the Basis for Open Publications

As was the case with SRCAM, once Vector was demilitarized and had to raise its own funding, its scientists decided to try to capitalize on the classified research they had done under the old system. By law, Russian scientists who wish to report previously performed research in open articles are obligated to clear their papers with the RF-MOD before submitting them for publication.[71] However, there are ways around this law. For example, if a Vector scientist were to receive a grant from the Russian Foundation of Basic Research to perform fundamental studies on, say, the distribution of filoviruses in the tropics, the grant will invariably specify that its findings must be published in Russia. To fulfill this requirement, the grantee might rework research that was done years ago on filoviruses. Because there are several filoviruses and each filovirus is represented by numerous variants and isolates, it would be difficult for a RF-MOD official sitting in a Moscow office to check to see if the results of secret work are included in a draft article that is being submitted for publication.

The authors of this book were in the odd position of trying to determine the original intent of research whose findings have been published in the open literature since 1991, but whose work was actually performed secretly in the mid- to late-1980s. Making such a determination is necessary, though, because it casts light on Vector's former top secret weaponization program. Table 8.1 contains 16 "entries" and each entry names a gene (or genes) that was being investigated by Vector scientists before 1992, as well as hosts that were recipients of the gene or vector used to transport the gene to the host. The articles that present the work associated with each entry were collected

Table 8.1   Examples of Openly Published Research Findings Based on Secret Biological Warfare R&D Performed at Vector

Entry	Gene or genes	Host or vector
1	[Leu5] enkephalin gene	*E. coli*
2	Beta endorphin gene	Vaccinia virus
3	Beta lipotropin gene	*E. coli*
4	Proopiomelanocortin gene	*E. coli*
5a	Myelin basic protein gene	*E. coli*
5b	Myelin basic protein gene	Vaccinia virus
6	Leukocyte IFN-alpha2 gene	M13mp7 phage
7	Thymosin alpha TNF genes	*E. coli*
8	rTNF beta gene	Not described
	rTNF alpha gene	Not described
	IFN-alpha gene	*E. coli*
	IFN-alpha gene	Temperature regulated promoter
9	IL-2 and Shigella toxin gene	*E. coli*
	IL-2 gene	VEEV
10	IFN-gamma and TNF genes	*E. coli*
11	Tick-borne encephalitis virus E gene	Vaccinia virus
12	Japanese encephalitis virus E gene	Vaccinia virus
13	VEEV structural protein gene	Vaccinia virus
14	Ebola virus vp24 gene	Vaccinia virus
15	VEEV 26S RNA	Vaccinia virus
16	Tick-borne encephalitis virus structural and nonstructural protein genes	Vaccinia virus

Source: These examples are taken from tables 1, 2, and 3 in Janet R. Gilsdorf and Raymond A. Zilinskas, "New Considerations in Infectious Disease Outbreaks: The Threat of Genetically Modified Microbes," *Clinical Infectious Diseases* 40 (2005): 1160–1165.

Note: The numbers in the first column refer to the references in the Gilsdorf and Zilinskas article.

by Janet R. Gilsdorf while she was on a sabbatical at the James Martin Center for Nonproliferation Studies (CNS).[72]

ENTRIES 1 AND 2.   By inserting genes coding for peptides into various bacterial and viral hosts, the military sought to discover new effects on nerve tissues. Vector scientists took a "black box" approach to the problem—when they started inserting the enkephalin gene into *E. coli* and the endorphin gene into vaccinia, they did not know what to expect. They hoped that if the peptide was expressed in bacteria and viruses, it would change or affect the behavior of infected persons.[73] (Although *E. coli* and vaccinia are the subjects of these publications, the first viral host of the mentioned genes was ectromelia.) The specific long-range objective of this R&D was to transfer constructs into viruses to make them more virulent. The legend for this research was that it aimed to investigate the analgesic effects of the peptides in question on humans.

ENTRIES 3 AND 4.   Vector scientists used the black-box approach to find out if the two named genes would be expressed in *E. coli*.

ENTRIES 5A AND B.   The experiments reported here were started early in Vector's existence, in 1985–1986, but continued until 1992. In fact, they generated Vector's first constructs through the use of genetic engineering. The fully synthetic myelin protein gene, which encoded a fragment with a bovine origin, was first inserted into *E. coli* and then vaccinia virus.

ENTRY 6.   This experiment was completed very early, in 1981. It was ostensibly defense-related, its purpose being the development of better protection for soldiers against viral diseases. However, this experiment might have been part of a decoy strategy; that is, it might have been done to find out if it was possible to initiate an immune response in a human host against mutant interferon (IFN) polypeptides that would deplete the body's natural reservoir of interferons. By stimulating the host's immune defense system to create antibodies against INF and depleting its natural supply of interferons, the host would be exceedingly susceptible to natural infections.

ENTRY 7.   The intent of this R&D was to develop pathogens capable of expressing thymosin alpha and tumor necrosis factor (TNF) genes to boost immune response. Infections caused by these new pathogens would ostensibly stimulate bizarre or unusual detrimental immune responses in hosts. As this project was started late in the Soviet BW program, its products, if any, were not close to being weaponized.

ENTRY 8. The project reported here was initially based on known facts about how TNF affects a host. In essence, TNF is a natural peptide produced by a host's immune defenses to protect against infections and cancers. However, if too much TNF enters a host's bloodstream, its toxic actions kill the host. Conversely, if there is too little TNF, a person's immune defense system is defective and he can become hyper-susceptible to natural infections. This project's objective was to insert each of two TNF genes, alpha and beta, into competent pathogen cells that, when used to infect a host, would overstimulate his immune defenses by producing too much TNF. Because this project commenced at the end of the Soviet BW program, it adopted the civilian objective of developing new therapeutic agents.

ENTRY 9. This project was started about 1985. An excess of interleukins can stimulate an inflammatory or anaphylactic response in an affected host. This response to some extent is brought about by the body secreting anaphylatoxin, the most toxic substance naturally produced by the human body. As with other peptides, if the body produces too much anaphylatoxin, it harms the host. These experiments involved transferring the interleukin-2 gene into bacterial and viral hosts to find out if these peptides would be expressed. As this project was started late in the BW program, IHPB scientists were unable to develop a suitable host for this gene.

ENTRY 10. As described in Entries 6 and 8, this project intended to deplete the peptides required by the human immune system to protect against microbial invaders.

ENTRY 11. This was likely a Problem 5 project, because it is related to a public health issue. In particular, tick-borne encephalitis is a big public health problem in Siberia, so this project probably was vaccine-related.

ENTRY 12. This work might have been related to Entry 11, or it could have had a more subtle and dangerous objective. It was well known to medical science that encephalitic viruses easily cross the blood–brain barrier, and thus can be induced to carry substances into the brain. In 1987 a Vector team led by Netesov developed a reverse genetics system for VEEV. In addition, it developed plasmids encoding the virus and introduced them into *Y. pestis.* This was a logical extension of Factor's work; that is, instead of inserting plasmids encoding parts of viruses into bacterial pathogens, Vector scientists introduced plasmids that encoded entire viral genomes. The full sequence of Factor activities was as follows: first, transfer virulence factors into bacteria; second, transfer virulence factors into viruses; and third, transfer viruses into bacteria.

ENTRY 13.   This project was initially meant to change a physical characteristic of a pathogenic virus, in this case VEEV. If Soviet scientists replaced an epitope on a virus's capsid with a new epitope unknown to the enemy, the enemy's vaccines would not recognize the new construct and would be useless. It is unknown whether this project was a success.

ENTRY 14.   This work was probably done at Vector for diagnostic purposes. The function of the Ebola virus VP24 gene was unknown at the time, but it was thought to be a virulence factor. Research on the VP24 gene might have started because the protein it encoded could prove useful for developing a vaccine. However, the gene was found to have no value for this purpose. It is unknown whether this work continues, as little is known to this day about the structure and function of the VP24 gene-encoded protein.

ENTRY 15.   This work began in 1981. For a long time Soviet scientists were unable to manipulate RNA virus genomes. However, after they learned how to manufacture complementary DNA (cDNA), they also began to learn how to manipulate RNA viruses. This enabled them to develop cDNA parts or whole genomes for some RNA viruses.

The VEEV's 26S RNA was of interest to Soviet scientists who studied RNA viruses for the role it played in transferring RNA strands into DNA viruses, such as vaccinia virus. This technology proved to be a wonderful tool for BW R&D. The insertion of a plasmid encoding the VEEV genome into *Y. pestis,* which is described in Entry 12, is an example of this phenomenon.

ENTRY 16.   This was vaccine-related R&D against tick-borne diseases, possibly Problem 5-related.

Vector's Conversion to Peaceful Applications and Its Existence in the Post-Soviet Era

Vector's history since it was demilitarized is exceedingly complicated, and it cannot be covered in one section of one chapter. This section is limited to providing information on two subjects: (1) Vector's challenging transformation from a closed, well-supported government institute to an open institute, initially unsupported by its home government agency; and (2) Vector's continuing interest in variola virus.

Toward the end of 1990, Vector's leadership concluded that the Soviet government had decided to "sacrifice" the institute—it was to be stripped of its military role. The impetus for the decision was the impending January 1991 visit from a special UK-US team to the institute.[74] When this visit was announced, the institute's weapons-related R&D was terminated, and the institute tried to hide its reason for existence.

Before the team's visit, extensive "cleanup" efforts tried to rid the institute of anything that was indicative of viral weapons work. It was a tense time at Vector, as Biopreparat commissions were constantly visiting and probing, and an endless string of meetings and conferences were held. The main question facing Biopreparat officials was how Vector should go about hiding any indication of scientific research and technological work aimed at producing viral weapons. No Biopreparat or Vector official had any experience with this type of task. This was an especially difficult problem for the division heads whose activities were highly classified (for instance, viral weapons production, genetic engineering of viruses, or R&D to compromise the human immune system) and lacked a semblance of dual-use R&D (defensive applications in addition to the obvious offensive ones).

To solve this problem, the division heads together developed a list of bogus explanations of the work programs of each scientific and technical division involved with the weaponization of viruses. These divisions' real activities were not included on the list. The division heads and laboratory chiefs who knew the true purposes of their work were given special instructions, and had to learn what to say and how to act in line with the information set forth in the list.

In the end, the British and American visitors spent a few hours at Vector, but they did not physically extend their visit much past Building 1. They did not enter Buildings 6 and 6A, nor did they meet the Zagorsk Institute scientists.[75] Had they seen the layout of Buildings 6 and 6A, and the equipment housed there (such as UKSD-25), they would have been tipped off to the BW-related R&D done there.

Between 1991 and 1992, all of the F-level and top secret documents and reports at Vector were removed and taken to unknown destinations. Secret-level documents remained in Vector's archive, and the First Department's name was changed to Security Services. No secret work was done at the institute after approximately 1992, but the old secrecy classifications remain in effect to this day; that is, if a document was classified in Soviet times, it remains classified.

The financial hardships that followed the Soviet Union's dissolution drastically affected Vector. The most significant change was in the way Vector was funded. In 1990, of Vector's estimated budget of $2.5 million, 47% was provided by Biopreparat and 53% was self-financed.[76] By 1999, of its estimated budget of $6 million, only 13% was provided by the government, 10% from grants, and 77% was self-financed. The number of Vector employees fell drastically during this period, from about 4,500 in 1990 to 3,600 in 1993, before stabilizing at about 1,900 in between 1998 and 1999. Of the 1,842 people who worked at Vector in April 2000, 901 were researchers, of whom 147 possessed candidate's degrees and 17 doctors of science. Vector also has a dissertation council that is empowered to award candidate and doctoral degrees in the fields of biology, virology, and biotechnology.[77]

In March 1994 the Russian government designated Vector as a State Research Center,[78] and later that same year Vector was placed under the authority of the Russian Ministry of Public Health and Medical Industry and was renamed the Federal State Research Center of Virology and Biotechnology (SRCVB) "Vector," its current name.[79] Vector's motto became "Federal Service for Surveillance in Consumer Rights Protection and Human Well-Being." As a result of this order, the majority of Vector's funding was supposed to be provided by the Russian Ministry of Science and Technology, but because this ministry was poorly supported, it was not able to support Vector until years later. In the intervening years, Vector's very existence came into question.

Suspicions about Vector appear to have lingered among its neighbors, even after the dissolution of the Soviet Union. These suspicions died off starting in 1995, when the institute started admitting reporters onto its grounds. A report from the Novosibirsk newspaper is indicative of the coverage that followed: "Even recently it was unthinkable for a journalist to set foot in a building of the secretive Vector center. Somber rumors floated around the city that the smallest accident in the ventilation system was enough to send all of Novosibirsk to meet their ancestors. Along with the veil of secrecy, the unnecessary apprehension has been thrown aside. It has become clear that at least biological weapons are not being developed in Novosibirsk."[80]

In 1998 senior Vector officials volunteered to transform the institute into an open and fully transparent "International Laboratory for Emerging Infections," to serve as a model for the transformation of other former BW facilities.[81,82] This idea was discussed at length with the US Vector Evaluation Team, which visited the institute in April 1998. By this time the ISTC had already approved a $50,000 project development grant to enable Sandakhchiev and Netesov to develop a plan for what was then called the "International Center for the Study of Emerging and Re-emerging Infectious Diseases" (ICERID). This center would be a nonprofit organization, wholly separate from all of Vector's commercial ventures. Its main objectives would be to perform basic research on emerging and reemerging infectious diseases and applied research in areas related to diagnostics, vaccines, and therapeutics. Sandakhchiev proposed that the ICERID focus on four areas of research: orthopoxviruses, viral hemorrhagic fevers, other dangerous pathogens and diseases of public health concern, and cross-cutting research related to dangerous pathogens. At the end of its visit, the US team appeared to be positive about the ICERID concept and promised to assess its feasibility.[83]

Sandakhchiev's in-hand proposal[84] envisioned raising about $25 million, which would be used over four to five years to modernize the Vector laboratories needed to create the center, and $12 million a year to operate it with a staff of 166 scientific workers.[85] Sandakhchiev was hoping to raise the money from the WHO and billionaire Ted Turner, who at that time was working to set up the Nuclear Threat Initiative foundation. Sandakhchiev presented his proposal at the March 2001 Sam Nunn Policy Forum, where it received a positive response. For unknown reasons, though, Sandakhchiev was unable to raise the money needed for the ICERID. His bitterness about this failure was apparent:

At present our [operation] is almost completely suspended. I am told that the expenses for maintenance of the energy-intensive system of biological protection of Vector are beyond the abilities of the State. Well, let us then suspend the virological studies, gum up the buildings for working with hazardous infections, and hope that Americans will protect Russia, if necessary, from infection outbreaks. They have an excellent system for monitoring causative agents, first-class research centers, medical service, advanced medicine, and so on. But what is it to us or other less-developed states?[86]

On January 17, 2003, President Vladimir V. Putin issued Order No. 45, which upgraded Koltsovo to a Science City (*Naukograd*).[87] This designation permitted Koltsovo certain benefits, such as being able to retain federal taxes and allocate them for city development. Vector itself was reorganized into seven units that comprised more than a hundred buildings in Koltsovo: The All-Russian Scientific-Research Institutes of Molecular Biology; the Scientific-Research Institutes of Aerobiology; the Research Institute of Bioengineering; the Research Institute of Cell Cultures; the Collection of Cultures of Microorganisms; the WHO's Collaborating Center on Diagnostics of Orthopoxviral Infections and Repository of Variola Virus Strains and DNA; IBAS (see Chart 8.1, which depicts Vector's organizational structure in 2002).[88]

In addition, other logistical departments,[89] several daughter enterprises,[90] and other affiliates became associated with Vector.[91] Vector also became the host of the Regional Center for the Prophylaxis and Prevention Against AIDS (with specialized clinical isolation units in Buildings 19 and 20) and a children's' tuberculosis hospital. It houses a Chair for Basic Medicine at the Novosibirsk State University[92] and is an associate member of the *Rosmedprom*, the Russian Association *"Epidbiomed," "Immunogen"* Ltd., and the Association of State Research Centers.[93]

Of all Vector's offshoots, perhaps *Vector-Best* is the best known and most productive. It was formed already in 1989 after Vector knew it was in danger of being disbanded, and became an SPA in 1994. Its history and work program are described on its website, so there is no need to do so here.[94] It is sufficient to state that its main R&D directions are to develop and produce for immunological test kits for the diagnosis of diseases such as hepatitis and typhus, kits that apply PCR methodology for diagnosing a wider scope of diseases, and kits containing reagents for clinical biochemistry projects. The SPA employs more than 1,000 workers, most of whom came from Vector. Vector-Best owns one building in Vector's industrial zone in Koltsovo and a second in Akademgorodok. It also rents office space in Novosibirsk and six or seven other large cities in Russia.[95] For unknown reasons as this is being edited, its English language website, including catalogue, is three years out of date.

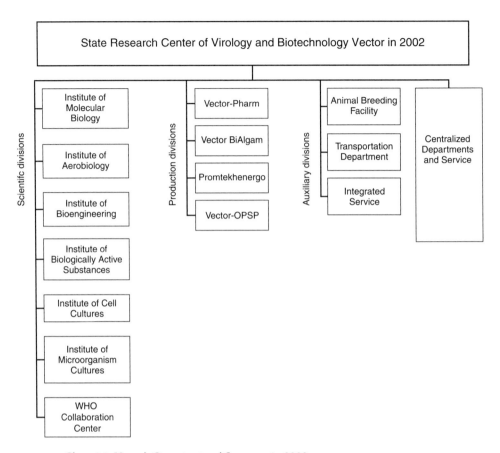

Chart 8.1 Vector's Organizational Structure in 2002

Vector's Microorganism Culture Collection is one of the largest and most diverse in Russia. In 2004 it contained more than 20,000 virus cultures, 109 strains of variola viruses in its WHO repository, more than 200 bacterial strains useful to industry, and 283 special enzyme-producing strains that, among other things, produce restriction endonucleases, DNA polymerases, ligases, alkaline phosphatases, and other enzymes.

Despite becoming part of a Science City, Vector remained severely underfunded and suffered considerable hardships. For example, early in the winter of 2003, financial constraints forced Sandakhchiev to implement a four-hour workday for scientists not receiving international funding, and the institute had insufficient funding to pay to heat and provide electricity to parts of the institute.

Vector after Sandakhchiev's Departure

As a result of illness, Sandakhchiev gave up his post as director general in 2005,[96] and Netesov became the temporary director general. About this time, Biopreparat was placed under the jurisdiction of the Federal Service for the Supervision of Consumer Rights and Welfare (*Rospotrebnadzor*), which was headed by Gennady G. Onishchenko. On September 20, 2005, Onishchenko appointed Ilya G. Drozdov as Vector's new permanent director general.[97] Drozdov initially received the support of Raisa A. Martynyuk, the deputy director for R&D coordination, and Netesov, the deputy director general for research.[98] But this support did not last long. Once Drozdov was in place, he dissolved all of the institutes named above and converted most of them into departments.[99] Beginning in 2007, Biopreparat scientists began to complain both directly and indirectly to their Western counterparts about Drozdov and how their work conditions had worsened and the potential for foreign collaboration had decreased.[100] In particular, foreigners were no longer allowed entry into Building 1, Vector scientists no longer received permission to attend meetings outside of Russia, and proposals were no longer permitted to be submitted to the ISTC.[101] These changes appear to stem from Onishchenko's well-recognized disdain for collaborations between anti-plague institutes and foreigners (no foreigner has been allowed to visit any of the five Russian anti-plague institutes since 1999).[102] These prohibitions on collaborations appear to have been instituted at some Biopreparat institutes as well.[103]

Institutional corruption at Vector became blatant. According to Pavel Korchagin, a local official in Siberia who wrote an open letter to the president of Russia, Drozdov's "first steps in his new field were harsh measures to tighten the regime. In particular, staffers at the science center were prohibited, on pain of dismissal, to have contacts with foreign colleagues or journalists . . . Scientific staffers, including the leaders of the most important scientific spheres, are leaving Vektor en masse, seeing no prospects there. In the past two years alone nine doctors and more than 20 candidates of sciences have left Vektor. The de facto winding up of scientific work by virologists leaves the Russian Federation defenseless in the face of the threat of the spread of dangerous infectious diseases."[104]

Korchagin's letter might seem unusual, but he was sufficiently concerned about the alleged take-over of Vector by a criminal group that included Onishchenko and Drozdov, that he felt compelled to call directly for the president's attention. The criminal group's first objective, according to Korchagin, was to bid for a contract to rebuild Vector's HIV research laboratory. The group succeeded in doing this, allowing it to embezzle funds slated for the rebuilding project to the tune of more than 140 million rubles (out of 183 million rubles). When local authorities tried to sue the group because it never finished the HIV laboratory, the local branch of the Russian Federal Security Service (FSB) intervened on the group's behalf. As a result, "These people [not further identified] neglect their own immediate duties but plan corporate raiding operations, stage criminal prosecutions of innocent people, create nightmares for business, bug the telephones of decent citizens, and intimidate those who try to resist them. Personally I am sick and tired of being afraid of them," wrote Korchagin.[105]

On July 18, 2010, Drozdov and an administrator that he had installed were dismissed for financial dealings and irregularities. In February 2011, a new permanent director was appointed, Alexander N. Sergeev.[106] Sergeev originally came from the Zagorsk Institute, where he worked on variola virus, and this pathogen appears to still be his major research interest. He also is an advisor to the WHO Advisory Committee on Variola Virus Research.

Chapter 7 describes similar corruption now confronting SRCAM. That the FSB may be a partner in this activity might surprise many Western readers, but as a Swedish report suggests, the level of FSB interference has increased since 2005 because of its intensified suspicion of foreigners and greater opportunities to share in illegal profits.[107] If SRCAM and Vector were "ordinary" enterprises, developing and producing, say, furniture or clothing, this type of corruption would be of less concern. However, both institutes have vast culture collections of pathogens, equipment, and supplies that could be valuable to nations or terrorist groups intent on acquiring biological weapons. Corruption that could lead to the international proliferation of biological weapons is of global concern.

Application of Advanced Biotechnologies for Weaponization

With having described, and to some extent discussed, the weaponization of bacteria at SRCAM and viruses at Vector, we end this chapter by stating our thoughts on the two major R&D approaches used by Biopreparat scientists to achieve unique biological weapon agents. In effect, these scientists used genetic engineering to (1) enhance certain properties of natural opportunistic pathogens so they became more effective BW agents, and (2) create new and unique autoimmunity inducing agents.

The first approach, which was common to all past national BW programs and would probably be a part of any future program, is described in Chapter 10. Briefly, "classical" BW R&D has been done for one or more of six reasons: (a) to increase infectivity; (b) to increase virulence; (c) to bolster hardiness; (d) to enable the pathogen to overcome host defenses; (e) to narrow the pathogen's host range; and (f) to enable the pathogen to avoid detection. Soviet weapons scientists brought a new tool to these kinds of R&D efforts: genetic engineering. Biopreparat scientists sought to improve bacterial and viral pathogens by, for instance, inducing more efficient growth in fermenters, increasing the degree of virulence, and changing disease presentation for detection avoidance. Pathogens that have been genetically manipulated in these ways are called "second generation" agents. Military scientists recognized that second generation bacterial BW pathogens were improvements over their first generation counterparts, yet they also probably recognized that they had similar weaknesses. Though genetic engineering had made some genetic changes to agents, the genomes of second generation BW agents were more than 99% similar to the genomes of wild-type and first generation BW agents. For instance, the genetic engineering of *E. coli* involves the transfer of one or a very few genes to its genome, which is made up of approximately 5,000 genes. This being the case, second generation bacterial BW agents would be well known to Western scientists, as would the genes coding for virulence factors that would have been transferred to them. In other words, Western scientists could have probably quickly developed defenses against second generation bacterial BW agents.

Soviets scientists wanted to make agents from pathogens that were not so well known to Westerners and would cause diseases that were not easily treatable. Viruses would have been the most likely candidate for such agents, because many of them cause highly damaging diseases and for some there are no vaccines and the diseases they cause are untreatable.

At the time, no one had used the techniques of molecular biology to weaponize viruses, so Soviet scientists had to figure out how to start such an endeavor. First, they had to identify a large virus that could host a gene (that is, would be a competent host), was fairly easy to manipulate, and was relatively safe for investigators to handle. Viruses that best fit these characteristics were certain poxviruses and herpesviruses. Vaccinia virus was particularly well known to science, was safe to handle by immunocompetent scientists, and was large. Some herpesviruses also fit the bill, especially because most adults are naturally infected by herpes simplex viruses.

Vector virologists started this work with simple manipulations, such as inserting a gene that codes for an indicative protein, say a toxin, into the vaccinia virus genome. This would have been a useful start, because Soviet scientists had long studied vaccinia and understood its properties, and other scientists (possibly from SRCAM) would have had experience working with toxins, such as the shigella toxin, and the genes that coded for their production. The research direction would have been clear enough: insert a gene that codes for a toxin, establish that the viral host retains it, and verify that the toxin is expressed by the new construct. It is plausible that research along these lines was done at Vector.

Several problems need to be overcome before realizing successful viral constructs. The major problem is that viruses are very tiny and tend not to retain foreign genes inserted into their genomes by artificial means. It is difficult to force DNA viruses, such as variola virus, to accept inserts—over the eons, DNA viruses have developed ways of getting rid of inserts because of redundancies in their genomes and relatively easy pathways of recombination and restriction. Another problem was that both poxviruses and herpesviruses were well known to Western scientists, and immunity against variola virus had to some extent developed in the population due to large-scale pre-1980 vaccination campaigns.

How did Soviet scientists overcome these barriers to virus-related BW R&D? They took a dual-track path. Building on work done at SRCAM under Factor, Vector scientists developed constructs that used peptides rather than genes. The objective of this R&D was to develop viral pathogens that would infect humans and whose main effect would be to initiate an autoimmune reaction that would destroy specific host tissues.

The second, parallel track was to investigate more exotic, highly virulent viruses, such as Marburg virus, Ebola virus, VEEV, Machupo virus, Lassa virus, and related agents, and to manipulate them. Because these viruses' genomes are small, Vector scientists could not insert a whole toxin gene into them, so they were attempting to fit in gene fragments that they had identified and knew how to manipulate. RNA viruses, such as Marburg virus and Ebola virus, being small, have evolved complex mechanisms of transcription and translation. As a consequence, Soviet scientists had to develop methods to insert foreign gene fragments that were difficult for the host virus to expel.

By the time Vector scientists had reached this point in the virus weaponization process, it was the beginning of the 1990s, when the institute's offensive work presumably ended. By that point, it is probable that this research track had reached a scientific barrier anyway, because scientists had yet to develop methods to manipulate RNA viruses in the necessary way. As we noted previously and in Chapter 7, although there are indications that bacteria and/or viruses possessing unique inserts were created, there are no indications that these creations reached the open-air testing phase. Without realistic open-air testing, these agents' creators would not have known whether they were useful for BW purposes.

The next logical step in the progression described here would have been for the Soviet scientists to insert whole viruses into bacteria, something that both Alibek and Popov claim was accomplished at SRCAM and Vector. Popov has described how a DNA copy of VEEV with a tetracycline promoter was inserted into the *Y. pestis* cell. In theory, anyone who was infected by this bacterium-virus recombinant would first present with symptoms of plague, which would be treated by the administration of tetracycline.[108] The tetracycline would inactivate the *Y. pestis,* but simultaneously would "turn on" the production of VEEV, leading to the victim becoming ill with encephalitis. Some sources for this book, however, have expressed doubt that such a recombinant would work in practice, because the prokaryotic and eukaryotic machineries for bringing about disease in the host are very different and probably would clash in some way, causing one or the other (or both) to malfunction.

Why would the 15th Directorate, the MNTS, or the institutes' scientists suggest these research directions, especially in view of the already extreme infectivity and virulence of variola virus, Marburg virus, Ebola virus, and other viruses found in nature? One Biopreparat scientist surmised: "The reasons are quite simple. Think of the problems facing an enemy fighting the Soviet Union who suddenly found that its vaccine did not protect its soldiers and population against such a horrible disease as smallpox and whose antibiotics were useless to treat anthrax, tularemia, plague, and other bacterial diseases! Further, its soldiers were being decimated by diseases that could not be diagnosed and therefore were not amenable to anything other than supportive treatment. This would mean that the affected enemy's medical prowess had largely disappeared and, in effect, it had retreated to the pre-antibiotic age when disease killed far more soldiers than did bullets and shells. The psychological impact on both soldiers and their leaders, as well as the population from whence they came, would have been immense, probably giving rise to catastrophic distrust of the government and military. As you can imagine, someone who had the capability to effect these kinds of damages to an enemy would possess a higher order of military power."[109]

9

Biopreparat Facilities at Leningrad, Lyubuchany, and Stepnogorsk

O F THE FIVE MAJOR BIOPREPARAT INSTITUTES, SRCAM and Vector were at the forefront of weaponizing bacteria and viruses, respectively, while the two institutes and one production plant addressed in this chapter, the All-Union Scientific-Research Institute of Highly Pure Biopreparations (IHPB) in Leningrad, the Institute of Engineering Immunology (IEI) in Lyubuchany, and the Scientific Experimental-Industrial Base of Biopreparat in Stepnogorsk (SNOPB), had important but subsidiary roles. This chapter has three major sections, each dedicated to one of the subsidiary facilities. The sections are organized similarly to the preceding chapters, in that each reviews the history of the facility, describes its physical plant, and estimates its workforce in Soviet and Russian eras. In addition, each section discusses the facility's work program during Soviet times and, as much as possible, present-day Russia.

All-Union Scientific-Research Institute of Highly Pure Biopreparations (IHPB) in Leningrad

As noted in this book's dedication, the IHPB's[1] first director, Vladimir A. Pasechnik, gave few interviews and did not write about his life as a Soviet weapons scientist. Pasechnik consented to two interviews—one by Mark Urban in 1993 and the other by James Adams in 1994—before making himself available for the preparation of this book.[2] In addition, after Pasechnik's death, Simon Cooper sought to recreate his life history from information derived from interviews of Pasechnik's friends and co-workers.[3] Much of the information provided to these authors is similar, and some of the information Pasechnik made available to the authors of this book has been published earlier by Urban and Adams. This section, therefore, does not identify the source of every fact relating to Pasechnik and the IHPB, but it does identify information told specifically to the authors of this book.

History

From its planning stage to its realization, the IHPB largely reflected its first director, like the IEI but unlike SRCAM, SNOPB, and Vector. It is telling that in a society where scientists tended to be well into their 50s and 60s before becoming institute directors, Pasechnik was just 37 when hired by Biopreparat in 1974. Although he lacked a doctorate (he had a Candidate degree), Pasechnik was recruited on the basis of his excellent scientific reputation, and Biopreparat gave him the leeway to plan and staff a high-quality research institute as he saw fit.

A committee chaired by Lieutenant General Ogarkov, which included representatives from Biopreparat, *Glavmikrobioprom*, the KGB, and other agencies, interviewed Pasechnik for the directorship of the new institute in the autumn of 1974. The interview went well, and Pasechnik was appointed deputy director of the institute, which was initially called *Biopribor*. The institute was temporarily headquartered in an abandoned old building, but Biopreparat intended to build a new facility as soon as possible under Pasechnik's direction.

Because an institute named *Biopribor* already existed in Moscow, in 1975 Pasechnik's institute was renamed the IHPB. In July 1975, Ogarkov promoted Pasechnik to director. At the time, the institute employed approximately 100 people who worked in five laboratories. As far as Pasechnik knew, Biopreparat was composed of five institutes: the IHPB, SRCAM, the All-Union Institute of Molecular Biology, *Biokhimmash* in Moscow, and *Biopribor* in Moscow.

The first-level legend for IHPB was that it had two main missions: to develop human and animal vaccines and methods and agents for protecting crops. Its "real" mission was to develop formulations for the bacteria and viruses weaponized at SRCAM and Vector. When Factor came into being, IHPB scientists were also tasked with synthesizing peptides.

Construction of the IHPB started in 1974 and was finished in spring 1980, at a total cost of 5–7 million rubles. The institute was, and is, sited in the center of Leningrad (now St. Petersburg).[4] When Pasechnik and his staff moved into the new facility, they were introduced for the first time to *Ferment* and its objective of designing and developing "weapons of special designation or special purpose." Pasechnik concluded that *Ferment* had come into existence when Biopreparat was first established in 1972, but that individual Biopreparat institutions were brought into *Ferment* only gradually, as their facilities were completed and their leadership received the proper clearances. The institutions began to understand the nature of *Ferment's* work as the staff realized the degree to which their facilities were overdesigned in terms of biosafety and their ability to house special equipment (such as explosive test chambers). The assimilation continued as collaborations were set up between researchers in the new institutes and those in existing Biopreparat facilities.[5]

The IHPB is comprised of three buildings, yet BW-related work was done only in the main building, which has five floors and contains 10,000 square meters of floor area. When the institute became operational in 1981, it employed about 400 persons and had an annual budget of 5 million rubles. At the height of its activity in 1989, IHPB employed approximately 400 scientists and 200 support personnel.[6] Of these, only two came from the military, including colonel Yevgeny I. Babkin, who had worked with *Y. pestis* at the Kirov Institute prior to coming to the IHPB (see Chapter 3). The second officer was named "Piravavsky" or "Pivovarsky," but his first name, rank, and position remain unknown.[7] (Both were retired and therefore, technically speaking, were no longer military officers.) Pasechnik said that only about 30 of IHPB's staff were F cleared, but fully 85% of the IHPB's budget was spent on BW-related R&D.

Work Program

In 1984 the MOD sent a list of 20 to 25 pathogens to the MNTS and asked it to identify the principal candidates for BW applications. One of the MOD's evaluation criterion was that the Q_{50} of an agent under consideration be 3.5 kilograms—that is, if 3.5 kilograms of the formulated pathogen (0.8 kilograms of pathogen and 2.7 kilograms of filler) were dispersed evenly over 1 square kilometer, it had to be able to infect 50% of the inhabiting population.[8] After the first five-year cycle of R&D, the target for the next five-year cycle was more demanding; the Q_{50} for the formulated pathogen was lowered to 3 kilograms. In addition to this criterion, candidate pathogens were judged according to three specifications: (1) utility of the candidate in expanding Biopreparat's program; (2) whether there were ready methods for testing the efficacy of the candidate; and (3) the ease with which the candidate could be mobilized in case of war, including its mass production. In this process, the IHPB's responsibility was to develop the formulation and filler; that is, it was tasked with developing formulations and fillers for bacterial pathogens weaponized at SRCAM and for viruses at Vector that fulfilled the criteria and specifications listed above.

Developing effective formulations involves difficult, and usually lengthy, R&D (see Chapter 10). It took IHPB scientists years to gain the advanced capabilities that were needed to create successful formulations for the pathogens on which earlier work had been done elsewhere. Because the specifications for candidate pathogens involved what would take place under the conditions of mobilization for war, the IHPB had to get involved with production-associated R&D, including improving the cultivation of pathogens, designing equipment to facilitate the weaponization of pathogens, and scaling up pathogen production from laboratory to industrial scale.

The IHPB's location in Leningrad presented challenges, the major one being that it was not permitted to store and work with Group I pathogens. Instead, IHPB scientists used simulants for the weaponized pathogens, such as the nonpathogenic EV vaccine strain of *Y. pestis* for weaponized *Y. pestis* and vaccinia virus for variola virus. The list of simulants that were developed and used at IHPB must have been lengthy. Some pathogens, such as Marburg virus and Ebola virus, did not have simulants, so as far as is known, the IHPB was never tasked with formulating these types of pathogens. Filoviruses were probably formulated where they were weaponized, either at the Zagorsk Institute or Vector. Though the IHPB had a large aerosol chamber where formulated simulants for Group I pathogens and non–Group I pathogens could be closed-chamber tested for dispersion by explosive force, it was removed in 1992 after the IHPB ceased its BW-related activities.

After the IHPB became fully operational, its first task was to help weaponize *F. tularensis* (with SRCAM and IEI scientists) and formulate the final weaponized product. (IHPB could work on *F. tularensis* because it is a Group II pathogen.) Domaradsky and his colleagues at SRCAM had already begun investigating this pathogen, but after approximately two years of fruitless work, SRCAM was instead tasked with weaponizing *Y. pestis*. This progression was mirrored at IHPB: After two years of failed attempts to weaponize *F. tular-ensis,* IHPB scientists were ordered to begin working on *Y. pestis* instead. At IHPB this work was done on the EV strain of *Y. pestis* instead of the real pathogen. This R&D appeared to have two directions: to develop a strain of *Y. pestis* that was multiantibiotic resistant, in line with the goals of the Metol project,[9] and to develop a dry formulation of *Y. pestis* (only a wet formulation existed at that time).[10]

It is necessary to note this book's divergence with the findings of Cooper, who wrote about the weaponization of *Y. pestis,* in three major ways. First, Cooper claims that virulent *Y. pestis* was researched and developed at IHPB. This is not possible, because the MOH never gave the IHPB permission to work on Group I pathogens. Second, he states that Pasechnik's group devel-oped a "super plague" that "could resist huge combined doses of 15 different antibiotics."[11] Neither IHPB nor SRCAM, where the weaponization of *Y. pestis* was largely completed, developed such a pathogen. In describing the effort to introduce antibiotic resistance into *Y. pestis,* Pasechnik is quoted as saying: "with each exposure to a different antidote, the resulting bacteria became more feeble . . . this problem was quite complicated, in fact, and as far as I know it wasn't solved efficiently."[12] This statement confirms the ac-counts of SRCAM scientists interviewed for this book: there was no "super plague." Third, Cooper asserts, "Once Pasechnik's super plague was born, it was grown in fermentation tanks and dried into a solid mass known as cake. This plague cake was then milled, a process wherein a powerful blast of air breaks the mass into ultra-fine powder."[13] In direct contradiction to this account, scientists who tested BW formulations at Aralsk-7 reported that *Y. pestis* was one of the few weaponized bacterial pathogens for which Soviet weapon scientists never developed a dry formulation. Pasechnik confirmed this account, reporting that by the time he departed the Soviet Union in 1989, no dry *Y. pestis* formulation existed.

As noted in the SRCAM chapter, the research team that took over the *F. tularensis* weaponization program from Domaradsky succeeded in weap-onizing this bacterium. An IHPB group was tasked with developing the production technology for this weaponized agent that could be used at the Omutninsk Chemical Factory. When he referred to "production technol-ogy," Pasechnik was talking about not machinery, such as fermenters and dryers, but rather the preparative techniques, processes, and additives that produced a formulation. Pasechnik claims that IHPB scientists developed the first principles for preparing a dry formulation for weaponized *F. tularen-*

sis at Omutninsk. This type of work was the IHPB's major mission. The IHPB was also tasked with synthesizing peptides to be tested in animal models to find out about their physiological effects. Those peptides that were identified as possibilities for BW use were then back-engineered elsewhere to find and synthesize genes that coded for their production by bacteria.

Generally speaking, Biopreparat research institutes were not allowed to work directly on weapons, only with the agents that would arm weapons. One exception was in 1985, when Pasechnik was ordered to help design a cruise missile to disperse BW agents via a spray system. IHPB scientists were specifically asked to model the process by which BW agents would be disseminated from the moving cruise missile. Pasechnik's responsibilities included heading programs at Kirishi that produced test-explosion chambers, personal protective suits for work with the dangerous pathogens, and biological agent detection devices. In interviews with the authors, Pasechnik said that this was the first time Soviet work had been done to develop a cruise missile BW delivery system. He defected when this project was still in the early stages of its development, but other sources told us that the cruise missile delivery system was not realized before the Soviet Union dissolved.

Pasechnik said that about 20 IHPB staff members worked on Problem 5 tasks. These people were not allowed to know anything about *Ferment*, while those who were F cleared knew about Problem 5 activities. One of Pasechnik's deputies, Alexander Ishenko, was in charge of IHPB's Problem 5 work, which had two main tasks: to increase the general immunity of humans against pathogens and to develop vaccines against plague based on the *Y. pestis* EV strain. About 10 people worked on the first task, and those working on the second had close contacts with anti-plague institutes. Like *Ferment* scientists, Problem 5 staff members were accorded certain privileges, such as higher salaries and better research opportunities. Approximately 15% of the IHPB's budget was allocated to Problem 5. Pasechnik was unhappy about this, as he believed Problem 5 work to be "rubbish."

It is a little-known fact that Biopreparat had a space biology program and that Pasechnik was its representative on the national committee on space, which was set up in 1988.[14] The MOH's 3rd Directorate was in charge of the Soviet Union's space biology program, including conducting animal experiments in space. As with most 3rd Directorate activities, this work is shrouded in secrecy, except in the few cases when information was released to publicize the program's accomplishments. The space committee considered setting up a production unit in a space vehicle to use genetically engineered bacteria to manufacture proteins, such as interferons, and to purify proteins in space using electrophoresis equipment (these processes supposedly worked better in a gravitationless environment). This project would have essentially duplicated the efforts of an existing US program. Another project investigated whether microorganisms grown in space had different resistance and sensitivity patterns to antibiotics than microorganisms grown on Earth.[15] Pasechnik believed that the space biology program had no BW purpose and that it was largely for show: It demonstrated the Soviet Union's prowess in space, made use of Soviet space capabilities, and, hopefully, would produce useful proteins. After Pasechnik's departure, this aspect of the space program stopped due to a lack of leadership and a substantial decrease in funding for all space-related activities.[16]

Perhaps in recognition of the IHPB's concentration on basic research, in 1987 it was put in charge of relations between Biopreparat and the USSR-AN. As the Soviet BW program came under increased economic and political pressures in 1986, Pasechnik was made the director of an independent enterprise named *Pharmpribor*, which encompassed the IHPB, the Kirishi plant (130 kilometers southeast of St. Petersburg), and a third institute, the Institute of Vaccines and Sera, in Krasnoe Selo (20 kilometers south of St. Petersburg). *Pharmpribor* was a strictly civilian enterprise whose aim was to produce medical bioproducts, beginning with vaccines.[17] The R&D for the prospective products was to be done at the IHPB or the Institute of Vaccines and Sera, and the Kirishi plant would produce them. When asked about this development, Pasechnik said that after Gorbachev's accession to power, Biopreparat became more flexible and thus was able to take on a greater variety of projects. There were two reasons for this development, he said: First, it became more important for the enterprise to have a believable first-level legend, and second, the institutes needed additional funds. Pasechnik laughed at this thought and said that even Urakov started to change—in 1987, a factory whose aim was to make ethyl alcohol was placed under his authority.

In early 1987, officials reduced funding for the IHPB's BW program, a move that coincided with the easing of Biopreparat's attitude on how its institutes could raise funding. By the following year, Pasechnik was raising 30% of the institute's budget by selling products and offering expertise to private enterprises. In a few years this percentage grew to where most of the IHPB's funding came from the sale of products on the open market.

About this time, Biopreparat officials were also allowed to start consorting with the "enemy"—Western companies. In 1988 Pasechnik began negotiating with a West German company about a joint project, which led to an invitation to a biotechnology exhibition in Germany. Pasechnik traveled to the event with Kalinin, who took the opportunity to discuss potential joint projects with other Western companies. The KGB tolerated these kinds of person-to-person contacts because Gorbachev's agenda encouraged Soviet enterprises to make commercial agreements with Western companies. Both Kalinin and the KGB thought that Biopreparat institutes could make these types of commercial arrangements with foreigners without compromising their main mission. Because the institutes' "main mission" continued throughout this period, none of the joint projects included visits by foreigners to Biopreparat institutes.

In 1988, Soviet officials informed Biopreparat's administrators that they and their program would be "reviewed by Gorbachev." Pasechnik and the other directors assumed that because Gorbachev was directly involved, the entire BW program, not just Biopreparat, was under review. The news caused havoc within Biopreparat. After a succession of meetings and the preparation of papers on many different subjects, Kalinin was told that the review had been postponed. Shortly afterward, it was announced that Soviet Foreign Minister Eduard A. Shevardnadze would perform the review, and Gorbachev would supervise it. The review was later delegated to the secretary of the Central Committee for Defense Industry, which meant that it was probably done by Lev Zaikov. The review, which had initially caused both excitement and nervousness within Biopreparat, eventually found that no changes were needed within the enterprise.

The visit of the US-UK team to the IHPB in January 1991 raised uncomfortable issues for Soviet officials. (These events are described in detail in Chapter 21.) One of the visitors, British intelligence operative David Kelly, had vast experience with BW-related issues and later described the visit: "At the Institute of Ultrapure Preparations in Leningrad (Pasechnik's former workplace), dynamic and explosive test chambers were passed off as being for agricultural projects, contained milling machines were described as being for the grinding of salt, and studies on plague, especially production of the agent, were misrepresented. Candid and credible accounts of many of the activities at these facilities were not provided."[18]

Western media reported some of the team's findings, including the indications of the IHPB's involvement in BW work. The newly installed Yeltsin administration was defensive in its response to these reports and acted to disprove them. In 1992 it set up an ad hoc "independent commission" led by

Academician Sergey Prozorovskiy and made up of members of the Russian Committee for Sanitary and Epidemiological Supervision and the President's Committee for Conventional Problems of Chemical and Biological Weapons,[19] to "investigate" the IHPB. The commission, accompanied by observers from the ministries of foreign affairs, health, and defense, conducted its "investigation" from November 18 to November 21, 1992, after which chairman Prozorovskiy reported: "The concern of British and American sides with regard to the activities of the Institute of Pure Biological Preparations is based on distorted information about research which indeed was conducted here until May 1990 with vaccines of plague strain and in 1992 with the virus of pseudo-plague of birds. The thrust of this research was analyzed with utmost attention, and it was established the research was conducted to create vaccines and not 'biological offensive strains of microorganisms' as the West mistakenly believed."[20] An article in *Izvestia* commenting on the commission's findings added: "In the former USSR there were major institutions working on bacteriological weapons. But the State Scientific Research Institute of Ultra-Pure Biological Preparations, which comes under the Health Ministry, was 'only indirectly connected in the most general way' with this sphere, Pavel Syutkin, deputy chairman of the Committee on Chemical and Biological Convention Problems, believes."[21]

During an interview with the former chief of the 15th Directorate, Valentin Yevstigneev, a reporter asked about the IHPB. Although Yevstigneev denied that the IHPB had been involved in military R&D, he made one interesting statement that undoubtedly had to do with Factor: "Certain work that interested us was being conducted there. In particular, they had received an assignment on transferring the genetic equivalent of the protein myelin into a microorganism. This protein plays a role in insulating the nerve fiber. We were disturbed about significant work in this field abroad, particularly in Great Britain. We were afraid that if the microorganism were modified in that way, it could affect the normal program for synthesis of myelin in the organism, which would ultimately lead to flaccid paralysis. We decided to test to see if such a modification was possible. The director at the time knew where this assignment had come from."[22]

In February 1993, *Newsweek* published a report about the Soviet BW program that included a discussion about Pasechnik and the IHPB.[23] In response, a Russian TV network did a program on the IHPB that was largely recorded within the institute itself. The program opens with quotes from the *Newsweek* article and shows reactions to them by institute scientists. The example below is, except for the mention of "military orders," composed primarily of disinformation:

> Correspondent: Here in this very institute in the historic center of St. Petersburg which has been featured in a magazine article and BBC report and which has been visited by international commissions, one after the other, and by us, the first Russian television journalists. Perhaps it was precisely in this laboratory the refined human mind . . . prepared the magic poison which in scientific language is called biological offensive strains of microorganisms.
>
> Today the laboratories of our once flourishing scientific institutions are an exact copy of the country—in total collapse . . . Let us talk of the institute's glorious past. (Turns to a scientist.) All the same, there were military orders and evidently there was something to make fuss about. Please tell us the truth.
>
> Scientists: Undoubtedly there were military orders, but there was nothing to make a fuss about. Why? Well, because we were engaged only in developing vaccines to protect the population. . . . Special preventive preparations to protect people from dangerous infections. We were engaged, in particular, in developing vaccines to protect people from plague.
>
> Correspondent: But there is no smoke without fire.
>
> Scientist: Of course there is no smoke without fire. That is correct, but we had vaccine smoke and there was no fire at all.[24]

Why did the Russian government go to such great lengths to cover up the IHPB's Soviet-era work program, when it had not put the same amount of effort into hiding the programs of other institutes, such as SRCAM and Vector? The most likely reason is that it wanted to counter Western reports and the negative publicity that resulted from the US-UK visit in 1992. In addition, because defector Pasechnik had directed the IHPB and the *Newsweek* article had linked the IHPB with BW, it was necessary for officials to stress its supposedly valuable contributions to civilian projects, especially its vaccine R&D. Finally, the government may have been worried that St. Petersburg's inhabitants would become suspicious about the IHPB secretly having worked on deadly pathogens at its location in the middle of the city. To prevent St. Petersburg inhabitants from getting the "wrong" idea about the IHPB, the government tried to reassure the public that the IHPB had worked only on peacefully directed projects that did not involve dangerous pathogens, never mind "superbugs." Even if the Soviet Union had operated an offensive BW program, that program had been conducted in institutes and sites other than the IHPB.

The IHPB in Russia

While suspicions have been raised about the post-Soviet operations of SRCAM and Vector as their R&D activities have become less and less transparent and their leadership more inwardly directed, there is considerably less concern about the post-Soviet work of the IHPB or IEI (which is discussed in the next section).[25] As such, their histories post-April 1992 require only capsule reviews.

In interviews for this book, several Biopreparat scientists said that the IHPB and IEI did relatively better after 1992 than other institutes because they were already performing R&D for civilian enterprises and had no problem accepting foreign support as soon as it became available. By 1993, IHPB leadership had spun off a private company, Verta Ltd., which had its basis in the institute's peptide chemistry and immunopharmacology laboratories, to manufacture and sell peptides for treating infectious diseases and immunological disorders.

The IHPB received its first grant from the International Science and Technology Center (ISTC) in 1996 to develop new technologies for the production of drug-delivery systems. The following year the Russian Federation awarded the institute "the Status of a Russian Federation State Scientific Center," with the objective of conducting "basic, exploratory, and applied R&D and engineering projects in the following areas: new drugs based on recombinant and natural proteins and processes for producing them; medicinal agents and diagnostic systems based on synthetic peptides and monoclonal antibodies; new effective forms of drugs with prolonged and directed effect; [and] biotechnological methods of solving environmental problems."[26]

By 2003 the IHPB administration claimed to own "over 200 inventors' certificates and patents," to have "published more than 300 articles in national and foreign journals," and to have "participated in more than 44 international and 20 national scientific conferences and symposia." The institute employed 300 people, including 154 researchers (62 candidates and doctors of science, 60 technical supports personnel, and additional biologists, chemists, physicians, and mathematicians).[27] In 2009, Yevgeny N. Sventitsky, who was once Pasechnik's deputy director, was the institute's director.

Institute of Engineering Immunology (IEI) in Lyubuchany

IEI scientists have published many articles and reports on their scientific work and accomplishments, yet very little has been written about the institute itself. The institute's former director, Vladimir P. Zaviyalov, sat for lengthy interviews in the preparation of this book, as did four scientists who worked at other Biopreparat institutes and who collaborated with IEI. The information provided by these sources is presented here.

Lyubuchany Community

The community of Lyubuchany is located 57 kilometers due south of Moscow,[28] about halfway to the science city of Pushchino. SRCAM at Obolensk is located 37 kilometers southwest of Lyubuchany. Little information is available about this community, but Zaviyalov said that a small plastic-production plant was sited there and that the IEI was about 3 kilometers from the community, at the edge of a forest. Two new industries have set up operations in Lyubuchany since the early 1990s: the Danone Industries plant and Alcoa CSI Vostok Ltd. The IEI also hosts on its territory a research unit of the large pharmaceutical company BIOCAD called the Center of Immunological Engineering.[29]

IEI History

Much like the IHPB, the IEI reflected the interests of its first permanent director, Zaviyalov.[30] Zaviyalov was born in Simferopol, the capital of Crimea, in 1946. At the age of 16 he was already assisting with research at the Department of Biochemistry of the Crimean State Medical University, where he developed a special interest in protein structures in solution, particularly immunoglobulins. This became the topic of his Candidate thesis, which he defended in June 1971. Zaviyalov served in the military from 1971 to 1972, as interim acting senior medical officer of a tank regiment.

He returned to the Department of Biochemistry after his military service, but beginning in 1973 Zaviyalov spent several months a year at the USSR-AN's Institute of Protein Research in Pushchino, working in the Laboratory of Protein Thermodynamics under Peter Privalov, the most cited Soviet scientist in the life sciences.[31] At Pushchino, Zaviyalov researched antibody diversity and natural selection in warm-blooded animals and identified the three-dimensional structure of immunoglobulin domains. This work was the basis for his doctoral thesis, which was finished in 1977 and successfully defended in 1978 at the USSR-AN's Institute of Molecular Biology before a committee chaired by Academician Vladimir A. Engelhardt.

As Zaviyalov was finishing his thesis, he was approached by a Biopreparat representative, Volkovoy, who discussed possible employment opportunities. Zaviyalov later learned that Biopreparat was particularly interested in him because it had an acute need for molecular immunologists. An active-duty colonel, Volkovoy invited Zaviyalov to Protvino to meet Major General Vinogradov-Volzhinsky, the director of SRCAM.[32] Vinogradov-Volzhinsky told Zaviyalov that his institute was set up in accordance with a 1974 decree, which among other things specified that it was to be equipped with the finest equipment and staffed by the best scientists. After a short conversation, Vinogradov-Volzhinsky offered Zaviyalov a position as the head of SRCAM's Laboratory of Molecular Biology in the Department of Genetics. Since Volkovoy was the head of the department, Zaviyalov would report to him. Volkovoy later told Zaviyalov that a separate Institute of Immunology was to be established and that they both would be transferred to it.

The offer of employment was very attractive to Zaviyalov because he was guaranteed work in excellent facilities furbished with the finest equipment, the right to hire high-caliber scientists and technicians, a salary that was 50% higher than in ordinary academy laboratories (750 rubles versus 500 rubles per month), and to be able to travel abroad. (Zaviyalov would later learn that his previous travel abroad made it possible for him to continue traveling relatively freely because it helped strengthen SRCAM's open legend.) Zaviyalov accepted the offer and was hired at the first-legend level (see below).

In August 1977, at the age of 31, Zaviyalov moved to Protvino and began his work at SRCAM. He was immediately assigned to a new laboratory in the first permanent building at the institute, which had been completed in spring 1977, and there he continued his previous line of research. In addition Volkovoy asked him to initiate the production of the specific antisera to surface antigens of pathogenic strains of *Escherichia coli* that are important virulence factors. Through this work, Zaviyalov learned about the *Y. pestis* F1 antigen and eventually achieved expression of F1 in *E. coli* and, almost simultaneously, expression of K88 and K99 antigens in *Y. pestis*. Because Zaviyalov did not as yet have an F clearance, he was not told that the K88 and K99 gene clusters were to be used for the antigenic modification of *Y. pestis* and other especially dangerous Gram-negative bacteria.

At that time, Biopreparat director Ogarkov had two deputy directors, Anatoly A. Vorobyov (a former deputy commander of the Zagorsk Institute) and Victor G. Popov (an alumnus of the Moscow Physical-Technical Institute). Popov was deputy director of the technical sciences section and had a special interest in immunology, a field that he wanted to encourage within the Biopreparat system. Popov naturally became responsible for Biopreparat interactions with Zaviyalov.

In the autumn of 1978, Popov invited Zaviyalov to travel with him to Leningrad to visit the IHPB. Popov introduced Zaviyalov to Pasechnik as a potential director of the future institute of immunology. This was Zaviyalov's first meeting with Pasechnik, and they had a pleasant conversation on open scientific subjects, such as the Tavria experiment that involved the electrophoresis of proteins in space in the Salyut 7 space station that was scheduled to be launched in April 1982.[33] Pasechnik and Zaviyalov's friendly relationship eventually led to collaborations between their laboratories. Pasechnik visited the IEI a few times, and Zaviyalov reciprocated with visits to the IHPB.[34]

In early 1979, Popov invited Zaviyalov to visit him at Biopreparat headquarters to discuss a new immunology institute. Popov asked Zaviyalov to work with Biopreparat's 1st Department to draft decrees for the institute's establishment, but before this assignment began, Zaviyalov was asked to sign a second-level legend agreement that revealed Biopreparat's mission to defend against BW. Zaviyalov said that the agreement disturbed him, because he had never wanted to be involved in military-directed work. When he voiced his concern to Popov, Zaviyalov was promised that the agreement would not compromise his ability to communicate with foreign scientists or travel abroad. (Indeed, in 1980 Zaviyalov attended the 4th International Congress of Immunology in Paris.) Popov also told him that his work would be very important in protecting the Soviet Union from US and UK biological weapons. Zaviyalov asked Popov for evidence that these countries had biological weapons and was told that this evidence would be forthcoming. Despite his concerns, Zaviyalov signed the agreement. Zaviyalov had never heard of the 1972 Biological and Toxin Weapons Convention (BWC), and nothing was said about it as he entered the second awareness level.

The decree establishing the IEI was issued in 1979 and had two sections. The first included the first-level legend and was directed mainly at local government officials. It provided the institute's open name, the Institute of Immunology,[35] and explained the institute's mission as developing recombinant vaccines, monoclonal antibodies, gene-engineered interferons, and other cytokines for medical purposes. The second section contained the F-level decree, which provided the institute with a classified name, P.O. Box G-4883, and specified its real mission. According to this section, the IEI's main objectives were to assess the immune response of animals to pathogens of BW interest, to discover immune system weaknesses that could be exploited by new BW agents, to overcome immune responses induced by current vaccines, and to develop vaccines to protect Biopreparat scientific workers from the pathogens on which they worked. The institute's F-level name was initially known to only the local KGB and high-level SRCAM officials. Even Zaviyalov did not learn about the second section until he was granted F-level clearance in 1981, and other IEI employees received their clearances even later.

Once the decrees were issued, there was disagreement about who should be appointed director of the new institute. Popov wanted Zaviyalov, but Vorobyov had another candidate in mind, colonel Vladimir D. Savve, a graduate from the Kirov Military Medical Academy who had worked with Vorobyov at the Zagorsk Institute. Vinogradov-Volzhinsky also supported Savve.

Complicating matters was Zaviyalov's desire to work in an open institute; his fondest wish was to get a job at a USSR-AN institute. Starting in September 1977, Zaviyalov had met weekly with Engelhardt, his former USSR-AN thesis adviser, meetings that were well known to Biopreparat headquarters staff. Ovchinnikov was planning to establish a new open USSR-AN immunological research institute about this time, and Engelhardt had recommended Zaviyalov as its director. Zaviyalov tried to leave the closed system to become director of the open institute with the help of Engelhardt, but he needed a special permit to live and work in Moscow. But the KGB denied him this permit. On the other hand, he was living in a nice apartment in Serpukhov, and in order to retain it, he had to continue working for Biopreparat.

Zaviyalov's decision was made for him in the summer of 1979, when Savve was invited to become a deputy director of SRCAM. Vorobyov and Vinogradov-Volzhinsky apparently engineered this ploy as a way to prepare Savve's way to being appointed director of the new immunology institute. Once at SRCAM, Savve informally invited Zaviyalov to become his deputy director and told him that the main aim of the new institute was to conduct applied research for the purpose of developing bacteriological and viral agents that could overcome the human immune response and, furthermore, to create vaccines and antibiotics that would protect Biopreparat personnel. In doing so, Savve unofficially brought Zaviyalov into the third awareness level. Zaviyalov recognized that this knowledge made it very difficult for him to leave the system, even though he wanted to.

Zaviyalov continued to speak with Popov about finding work outside Biopreparat, first at the end of 1979 and later in early 1980. He remained unhappy, believing that he could not do the best science in a closed system and that the best science demanded international collaboration. Zaviyalov also questioned the new institute's aim of developing dangerous pathogen strains without first developing protection against them. Popov tried to reassure him by saying that the whole system was crazy and would soon be done away with. In other words, Popov was telling him that the restrictions Zaviyalov was concerned about were only temporary and that he could rest assured of soon being able to perform "normal" science.

In 1980 Zaviyalov visited Paris and, in 1981, Edinburgh. He was probably granted permission to do so because he had no official knowledge of *Ferment* at the time. Edinburgh would be his last trip to the West until 1988, when Gorbachev made such activities possible again. In the intervening years, he was permitted just one foreign trip annually to communist countries.

In late 1981 the KGB granted Zaviyalov F-level clearance and thus he for the first time learned officially about *Ferment* and the real purpose of his work.

By 1982 the IEI had become operational but was still housed within SR-CAM. Vinogradov-Volzhinksky arranged for a building that was initially intended to house a biochemical college to train technicians for Biopreparat to be converted to a laboratory building for three IEI departments: the Department of Molecular Immunology, the Department of Immune Biotechnology, and the Department of Immune Physiology. (This building became SRCAM's Building 300.) In a parallel development, *Glavmikrobioprom* was constructing several buildings in Lyubuchany to house a branch of the Institute for Genetics and Selection of Industrial Microorganisms. Those buildings were instead transferred to Biopreparat's ownership and became the basis of the IEI campus.

In February 1982 Zaviyalov briefly visited with Frantishek Franek at the Institute of Molecular Genetics, Prague, Czechoslovakia. There he learned how to produce hybridomas and monoclonal antibodies. After his return, Zaviyalov quickly set up a production facility for monoclonal antibodies to *F. tular-*

ensis surface antigens in the IEI's Department of Immune Biotechnology, which was headed by Valentin S. Khlebnikov. During the next several years, this department developed and produced many types of monoclonal antibodies to the surface antigens of bacterial pathogens such as *F. tularensis, Y. pestis, Burkholderia mallei,* and *Burkholderia pseudomallei.*

In 1983 Popov and Savve sponsored Zaviyalov's successful membership application to the CPSU. This cleared the way for Zaviyalov to be officially appointed deputy director of the IEI, with Savve still the director. Zaviyalov was then for the first time given a GRU intelligence report about the UK and US BW programs. The only facilities mentioned in the report were Fort Detrick and Porton Down. Zaviyalov said he was surprised at the lack of supporting materials for the claims that the two countries possessed active BW programs.

In 1984 the first permanent IEI building—Building 3, which housed the administration—was completed in Lyubuchany. Buildings 1 and 2, which housed laboratories, were completed in 1985.[36] In 1985 a conflict arose between Savve and Kalinin; it ended when Kalinin dismissed Savve. Kalinin had apparently served as a junior officer under Savve and had then passed him in military ranking. Savve, however, insisted on treating Kalinin as a subordinate, and Kalinin, who had a very high opinion of himself, found this unacceptable. Savve's dismissal precipitated a dispute that involved the MOD, Biopreparat, and the USSR-AN as to who should be the next IEI director. The MOD proposed appointing several high officers from the Military Academy of Chemical Defense and the Kirov Military Medical Academy, while Vorobyov tried to have the Zagorsk Institute's Stanislav S. Afanasyev appointed, but Kalinin opposed this idea. In the end, Zaviyalov was appointed temporary director; he retained this position for a little over a year. In December 1986 this appointment was made permanent. Zaviyalov learned that there were three reasons for his appointment: the KGB believed that having a civilian director supported the institute's first-level legend; the MNTS was intent on conducting the most advanced immunology research at Biopreparat and thought Zaviyalov was best qualified to do so; and, probably most importantly, Ovchinnikov threw his full support behind Zaviyalov. When Zaviyalov was appointed director, he also became a member of MNTS's section on immunology, which was chaired by Rem V. Petrov. Zaviyalov also became a member of the F-level SRCAM Scientific Board and the Vector Scientific Board, and visited both institutions several times per year on board-related business.

IEI's Work Plan

Biopreparat's original plan was for the IEI to perform both offensive and defensive R&D, on both bacterial and viral pathogens of possible BW interest. On the one hand, IEI scientists were expected to do what Savve first told Zaviyalov, namely, to perform research to enhance the pathogenic properties of prospective BW agents. After pathogens were confirmed as potentially useful for BW, the newly developed bacteria would be transferred to SRCAM, and the newly developed viruses would go to Vector. After these institutes fully weaponized the bacteria and viruses (or developed suitable simulants), the agents would be sent to IHPB to be formulated. Once they were successfully formulated, the agents would be tested in closed chambers and, finally, at Aralsk-7 test sites. If these tests were successful, then SNOPB (or Berdsk or Omutninsk) would be in a position to mass-produce the validated agents. In this scheme, IEI initiated the weaponization process for every agent that was to be considered for the Soviet offensive BW program.

On the other hand, other IEI scientists would do Problem 5 research aimed at developing defenses against the newly developed pathogens, to be used first by Biopreparat's scientific workers and eventually by Soviet soldiers and civilians.

Like many Soviet plans, this one did not work out. To begin with, the IEI was a latecomer to the BW program, as both SRCAM and Vector had been performing R&D for some time before the IEI laboratories became operational. SRCAM scientists had already done substantial work on weaponizing *F. tularensis* and *Y. pestis,* while Vector was well on its way to investigating VEEV, Ebola virus, Marburg virus, and others. These institutes were not about to reverse course and forge ahead with R&D involving other pathogens. Second, some pathogens, such as filoviruses, could not be defended against, so the IEI did not investigate them. Conversely, efficacious vaccines already existed for some pathogens, such as for *B. anthracis, F. tularensis,* and variola virus, and there was no immediate need for new versions. Third, the MOD probably held back some R&D from the IEI because of distrust. As a military scientist told the authors with a sneer, "They only did research and not real work." As proof of this statement, the scientist referenced the lack of military scientists at the institute (IEI had just three military scientists).[37] The military was also suspicious about Zaviyalov's dedication to the cause and his willingness to keep secrets, because it was well known that he disliked the closed system and wanted to perform publishable research.

Despite the problems and concerns listed above, the IEI's staff grew to about 500 persons, including 200 researchers of whom nine were doctors of science, seven were professors, and 40 were candidates. Approximately 36 KGB operatives ran the institute's First and Second Departments. Ministry of Interior troops dressed as civilians (but carrying guns) guarded IEI's perimeter.

The IEI's research was organized under three work plans. The first plan was for the open legend and included studies on interferons and cytokines, development of recombinant interferons, and preclinical and clinical studies of recombinant alpha interferon. The results of this research could be published in the open literature, but only after having been reviewed by two institute committees and approved by Biopreparat. Zaviyalov claims that IEI researchers published about 500 papers up to 1991, including 40–50 in international journals, on such topics as structures and functions of interferons, cytokines, and immunoglobulins. Approximately 10% of IEI's publications were open; 20–25% were classified secret or top secret, because they were under Problem 5; and 65–70% were F-level publications.

The second plan was a five-year plan that guided Problem 5 R&D. Most Problem 5 activities consisted of developing vaccines against especially dangerous pathogens. An example of an early Problem 5 project was the development of an aerosol tularemia vaccine, which is described below.

The third plan was the most important, because it specified the weaponization of pathogens selected by Biopreparat for the first round of candidate BW agents, including *F. tularensis, Y. pestis, B. anthracis, Burkholderia mallei, Burkholderia pseudomallei, Rickettsia prowazekii,* and VEEV. The MOD selected *F. tularensis* as the first pathogen to be weaponized. Under Domaradsky's direction, SRCAM was already engaged in R&D on *F. tularensis;* but IEI was ordered to do its part to weaponize *F. tularensis.* Efforts within IEI were divided as follows:

- Department of Molecular Immunology—This department studied the immunological responses of different types of cells to *F. tularensis* and developed reproducible methods of testing responses.
- Department of Immune Biotechnology—This department developed methods of producing peptides and proteins that were able to suppress immune responses and that could be inserted into the *F. tularensis* cell.
- Department of Physiology—This department studied the efficacy of *F. tularensis* strains whose pathogenicity had been enhanced using animal models.

• One IEI laboratory remained at SRCAM's Building 1, and its mission was to conduct animal tests of weaponized strains in the explosive chamber.

The IEI's specific directive was to produce a vaccine-resistant strain of *F. tularensis.* At the first joint-institute meeting dedicated to this problem, Domaradsky told the assembled scientists that the mechanism of this immunity and the way of altering the antigenicity of the agent to overcome it were wholly unknown at that time. This being the case, someone suggested another approach: to chemically modify the surface of *F. tularensis* cells with Protein A, thereby changing their antigenic properties. Protein A is a major component of *Staphylococcus aureus'* cell wall that was discovered in the late 1950s. *S. aureus* causes medically significant human "staph" infections, such as the deadly "toxic shock syndrome," but it is not useful for BW purposes. Protein A's role in *S. aureus'* life cycle remains uncertain, but some studies have correlated its presence with *S. aureus'* pathogenicity. This probably results from one of its most remarkable properties, its ability to bind tightly, but reversibly, to especially immunoglobulins (IgG) so that the immune system does not recognize the attached bacterium. Because a bacterium that possesses Protein A is able to bind to IgG, it is able to protect itself from being ingested by the host's lymphocytes (a type of white blood cell), prolonging the bacterium's survival time in the host's tissues and bloodstream, and enhancing its ability to cause serious illness. With some difficulty, Protein A can be purified from a culture of *S. aureus* using chromatography. This idea was accepted.

IEI scientists were chiefly interested in finding out if Protein A could be used to protect *F. tularensis* from the host's immunological defense system by preventing it from being ingested by the host's white blood cells. Because Protein A is not a normal component of the *F. tularensis* cell wall, it would have to be artificially provided to this pathogen. To do so, IEI scientists designed two R&D approaches: one that used a simple physical method and a second that depended on genetic engineering.

The first approach was to chemically coat the *F. tularensis* cell with Protein A. To do this, scientists at the Department of Immune Biotechnology developed methods for producing Protein A from cultures of *S. aureus* and for coating *F. tularensis* cells with the protein. Once the department had developed the production methodology, it dispatched a small team to the Omutninsk Chemical Factory to manufacture the protein on a large scale.[38] This was an expensive process, and the yields were not great, but it produced enough of the protein to coat a sufficient quantity of *F. tularensis* for testing purposes.

When they tested the combined agent and formulation against animal models, officials found that the pathogenicity of *F. tularensis* was indeed enhanced because the pathogen's cells were protected. Having demonstrated proof of concept, the IEI scientists transferred the process to the MOD and received no further information on its fate. One of our sources reported that this process eventually succeeded and that the MOD validated the formulation that contained the *F. tularensis* covalently coated with Protein A. The major disadvantage of this approach was that Protein A is very expensive to produce, making its mass production prohibitively expensive. The irony in this work was that Biopreparat generated its first validated BW agent without using any of the modern biotechnology techniques that supposedly were the reason for its existence.

The second R&D approach involved the use of genetic engineering. For this purpose, Zaviyalov sent a bright young scientist and member of the IEI staff, Irina N. Bespalova,[39] to the laboratory of Konstantin G. Skryabin at the USSR-AN Institute of Molecular Biology.[40] There she cloned the gene that codes for the production of Protein A, and then she transported it to the IEI. Although Zaviyalov was the IEI director and a member of the SRCAM Scientific Board, he was never informed whether the Protein A gene was in fact inserted in *F. tularensis* and, if so, whether it was expressed and conferred advantages to the genetically engineered *F. tularensis* over the natural strain. A SRCAM team led by Volkovoy was later tasked with inserting this gene into *Y. pestis* and *B. anthracis,* but the results of those experiments are also unknown.

As IEI was weaponizing *F. tularensis,* its Problem 5 scientists were also busy developing an aerosol vaccine to protect against this pathogen. The existing vaccine, which was applied subcutaneously, was largely ineffective against the pathogen when delivered by aerosol. IEI scientists hypothesized that an aerosol vaccine would be more effective in protecting against aerosol challenges than were vaccines administered by the traditional scarification, subcutaneous, intravenous, or oral routes. This project, which began in 1983 and was completed in 1988, was headed by Afanasyev and involved scientists from the IEI, IHBP, and the Scientific Research Institute of Military Medicine of the MOD in Leningrad (also called Institute #32), which was commanded by K. G. Gapochko. IEI was expected to lead the R&D effort, the IHBP was to develop the formulation, and the Institute of Military Medicine was to supply the equipment needed for aerosol production and the expertise relevant to aerosol dissemination and behavior.[41]

As is discussed in the Zagorsk Institute section of Chapter 3, the development of an aerosol vaccine is exceedingly difficult because usually vaccines cannot be used for aerosol administration due to their low antigen concentration, and the vagaries of aerosol delivery make it difficult to ensure that vaccine recipients receive an adequate dose. The three-institute team succeeded in developing a vaccine that had a much higher antigen concentration than was previously available and also developed an adjuvant that powerfully boosted the recipients' immune response to the vaccine, according to Zaviyalov. After doctors at the Kirov Military Medical Academy performed successful clinical trials, the new vaccine was certified for military use.[42] Zaviyalov claims that this aerosol vaccine was the first positive result from the IEI's Problem 5 program. In a real sense, the IEI's offensive and defensive programs, operating in tandem, succeeded in generating both an *F. tularensis* formulation validated for biological weapons use and a live *F. tularensis* vaccine to protect its developers, users, and Russian population against it.

Zaviyalov was heavily involved in the Bonfire project from 1982 to 1990. Zaviyalov's major collaborator was Oleg A. Kaurov, who was based at the IHPB. In 1982 Soviet scientists had little information on neuromodulating peptides and no information on immunomodulating peptides. The two initially spent much time searching the Western literature for peptides with immuno- and neuromodulating activity. They found a few such peptides, synthesized them in Kaurov's laboratory, and tested them at the IEI. Zaviyalov was never informed whether these peptides were used by the Bonfire project; however, two of them and a recombinant protein with one of them inserted were patented in the United States and Europe in the 2000s.[43]

Zaviyalov worked on one Bonfire project aimed at eliminating the epitopes on the surface of classic BW agents so as to make them unrecognizable to the diagnostic techniques and vaccines possessed by Western countries.[44] An attempt to weaponize an "F1-minus" strain of *Y. pestis* was a specific example of this approach.[45] This development was significant because Western countries and others have used standard serological tests to detect antibodies to the F1 protein as the basis for the surveillance and diagnosis of plague in infected humans and animals. By using an F1-minus strain of *Y. pestis* in their biological weapons, the Soviets would have made it considerably more difficult for the attacked population to identify the causative pathogen of the resulting disease outbreak and begin timely treatment. An F1-minus strain of *Y. pestis* was indeed created, according to this book's sources, but the MOD took over this effort, and its fate is unknown.

Zaviyalov decided that the F1 capsule was important for *Y. pestis* resistance to phagocytosis and, probably, for the transmissibility of plague in humans via pulmonary infection, and continued R&D along this track. To do so, he requested that a bright young scientist, Andrey V. Karlyshev, be transferred from SRCAM to the IEI.[46] Zaviyalov set up the Group of Gene Engineering for Karlyshev, assigned IEI scientist Edouard E. Galyov to the Group,[47] and purchased a DNA sequencer for its work. Karlyshev and Galyov sequenced all of the genes of the gene cluster encoding the *Y. pestis* F1 capsule, and cloned the gene cluster in *E. coli*. Biopreparat permitted Zaviyalov to publish these results in *FEBS Letters* in 1990 and 1991.[48] These were the first publications to reveal the structure of genes encoding for the F1 capsule and helped to bolster IEI's first legend, which is probably why Biopreparat permitted their publication.

The IEI in Russia

Shortly after Pasechnik defected in October 1989, Alibek told Zaviyalov that *Ferment* would soon lose its financial support and that he needed to set up an industrial production capacity within the institute. He suggested that the IEI should set up such a partnership with a private firm for this purpose.

In Moscow, a distillery for the vodka maker Kristall was Biopreparat's nearest neighbor, but the two facilities were separated by a tall wall. The distillery's director became acquainted with Alibek and asked him to help him find land on which his company could build a production plant to manufacture small plastic bottles for use in passenger aircraft to serve Kristall vodka. Alibek suggested that the director talk to Zaviyalov about building on IEI-owned land. Zaviyalov agreed to host the production plant, and a joint-venture called Biokristall was born in 1990 and the production facility was constructed during a two-year span. In 1996 the American company Alcoa rented the plant, which was converted to produce plastic caps for Pepsi-Cola and Coca-Cola. The reconfigured plant, called Alcoa CSI Vostok, still operates in Lyubuchany. The facility's rent helps to support IEI workers, to improve the IEI's infrastructure, and to pay taxes to the Chekhov *oblast*.

The trilateral US-UK team visited IEI as part of its January 1991 round of visits. Before the team arrived, Biopreparat representatives briefed Zaviyalov and the approximately 20 members of his staff who possessed F clearances, telling them, "You cannot disclose the real purpose of your program. Only general discussion of the open legend is permitted." IEI did not have equipment or facilities indicative of BW-related activity, so staff members were allowed to show the visitors all laboratories. The visitors were briefed on the history of the IEI and its purportedly open work program, and visited the entire main building, taking hundreds of photos along the way. Zaviyalov smiled when he said that none of the visitors' questions gave him any trouble. When he explained why the IEI (and SRCAM) conducted R&D involving dangerous bacterial pathogens such as *Y. pestis,* his explanation was buttressed by the articles published in *FEBS Letters* on cloning and sequencing of the *Y. pestis* F1 capsular gene.

In 1992 IEI's situation deteriorated rapidly and drastically. Biopreparat officials visited the facility with trucks and removed all *Ferment* and Problem 5 documents. All Biopreparat funding ceased, and funding from other government sources decreased drastically. The IEI was left with no tasks and only minute funding. The scant available funding was spent on salaries and basic facility upkeep, but not enough was available for even basic needs, so staff members began to depart. The staff of 500 decreased to 200, and then to 100. Of the institute's 30 senior scientists, 15 departed, mostly to foreign destinations. IEI's subsidiary facilities, including its hostel, apartment buildings, and a children's garden were given to the community. The First and Second Departments were abolished. As was the case with many Russian scientists and their families during the trying years of 1992–1994, IEI scientists were to a great extent saved from destitution by hundreds of small grants of $500 provided by the Soros Foundation (see Chapter 23).

Unlike the IHPB, whose director and administration appear to have come to a more or less peaceful arrangement with Kalinin, the IEI was held captive by the difficult relationship between Zaviyalov and Kalinin. In the latter part of 1992, Kalinin visited the IEI several times to convince Zaviyalov to convert the institute into a joint stock company, 49% of which would be owned by the state and 51% by private entities. Kalinin arranged for Biopreparat to receive a 15% private share. In return for this share, Kalinin promised that Biopreparat would assist the IEI with salaries, the construction of a pharmaceutical plant, utilities, and any debt that the institute might have accumulated. Zaviyalov agreed, and in early 1993 he signed a contract that laid the basis for the joint stock company. Shortly thereafter, the Russian government designated the IEI as a resource of strategic importance, meaning that it could not to be targeted for further privatization.

Despite Kalinin's promises, Biopreparat did not come to the IEI's assistance. In lieu of this support, Zaviyalov secured funding from international sources, including the Soros Foundation, the US National Aeronautics and Space Administration (NASA), the Cooperative Threat Reduction (CTR) program, the ISTC, and others. Over a few years the institute built up its capabilities in both basic and applied research in the areas of immunology, microbiology, bioengineering, and medicine. Its researchers constructed molecular vaccines against tuberculosis, plague, and yersiniosis; improved existing molecular vaccines by developing new adjuvants; developed innovative delivery systems for vaccines and medical preparations; produced monoclonal and recombinant antibodies for diagnostics and immunization; designed new gene-delivery tools using lentiviruses;[49] and developed unique delivery systems for anticancer drugs. In addition, institute scientists conducted preclinical studies and clinical trials of immunotherapeutics, as well as clinical trials of tularemia, anthrax, and VEE vaccines. More recently its researchers have performed exploratory research on anti-tumor therapeutics based on apoptosis.

While the IEI's situation for performing R&D improved thanks largely to Zaviyalov's leadership, his personal situation turned from unpleasant to unbearable. Although he was elected director of the IEI according to the new laws promulgated by the Russian Federation (first by its employees and then by general meetings of stockholders), Kalinin maneuvered to have him dismissed. The culminating event that lead to Zaviyalov's dismissal was when he accused Kalinin of corrupt practices related to a NASA contract in 2003 (see Chapters 6 and 23). Soon after his dismissal, Zaviyalov left for the United States. He first worked as a research professor at George Mason University, before moving to Finland in 2006, where he became research professor at the Joint Biotechnology Laboratory at the University of Turku. He recently discovered a new family of bacterial adhesive organelles that he named polyadhesins. They function as the anti-immune armament of Gram-negative pathogens and include the F1 and pH6 antigens of *Y. pestis*. The results of his research were reviewed in *FEMS Microbiology Reviews* in 2007 and 2009.

As of 2004, IEI employed 70 people, of whom 41 were researchers. Of these, 7 were doctors of science and 22 were candidates. Sergei Pchelintsev was the institute's general director and Viktor Popov, the former Biopreparat official, is the head of the laboratory. Foreign scientists who collaborate with IEI researchers say that they possess solid scientific credentials and that their work is on a par with that of international colleagues.

Stepnogorsk Scientific Experimental-Industrial Base of Biopreparat (SNOPB)

As far as is known, there was no dedicated BW agent production plant in the Soviet Union from the time that the Sverdlovsk Institute's plant was closed down as a result of the 1979 anthrax epidemic until 1984. Starting in 1984, dedicated BW agent production plants started coming on line at Berdsk, Omutninsk, and the SNOPB. Biopreparat's facilities at Berdsk and Omutninsk have not been described in detail in the available literature, but Chapter 6 provides capsule descriptions of each. Unlike the Berdsk and Omutninsk plants, SNOPB was located outside the RSFSR, in the Kazakh SSR. Unlike the Russian government, the Kazakh government has been open about former Soviet BW and anti-plague facilities that once operated in the Kazakh SSR (and still operate in Kazakhstan) and have allowed foreigners to visit these facilities and interview their workers. For example, one of this book's authors, Zilinskas, visited SNOPB, the *Ekologiya's* institute at Otar,[50] the anti-plague institute in Almaty,[51] and several anti-plague stations, including the one at Bakanas featured in Chapter 10.

Other analysts have also visited SNOPB and written about their experiences. The most complete descriptions are those by Anthony Rimmington (1998),[52] Gulbarshyn Bozheyeva et al. (1999),[53] and Sonia Ben Ouagrham and Kathleen Vogel (2003).[54] Alibek, a past director of SNOPB, also devoted a chapter to the facility in his book.[55] In view of the substantial information available on SNOPB, the following pages only briefly summarize its host city, history, physical plant, mission, and ultimate fate.[56] New information related to the storage of BW agents at the facility is included.

Stepnogorsk City

Soviet officials established the city of Makinsk-2 in 1956 to house those working on the recently discovered uranium mine in the Akmola *oblast*. The city underwent several name changes, becoming Tselinograd-25, Aksu, and, finally, in 1964, Stepnogorsk.[57] Stepnogorsk is located approximately 2,300 kilometers east of Moscow and 140 kilometers north of Kazakhstan's capital Astana. At the height of its industrial activities, the city's population was estimated to have been about 65,000. Its climate is typical of the steppe regions of Central Asia, with hot, dry summers and windy, bitter-cold winters. During the Soviet era, it was a secret city and was never visited by foreigners.

When Zilinskas visited the city in 2003, its population was said to be about 20,000, but the empty streets and boarded-up apartment houses suggested that it was less. All observable stores in the city were closed, only one hotel catered to visitors, and all restaurants appeared to be closed. In sum, it looked like a dying city, barely kept alive by a small functioning uranium mine and a diminished Progress Plant (see below).

History of the Progress Plant and SNOPB

In 1970, in response to a decree titled "On Measures for the Accelerated Development of the Microbiological Industry," *Glavmikrobioprom* built the Progress Plant 14 kilometers due north of Stepnogorsk.[58] From its inception the plant had a civilian and a military component.[59] The civilian component was built first and included infrastructure for both, including a common power plant and a steam plant for heating sstructures. The civilian component was largely finished by the time construction on the military component commenced in the mid-1970s on adjacent land. The components sat on contiguous land, but the facilities were separated by a large fence. Construction, according to scientists who worked there, "incorporated the most advanced developments in industrial biotechnology at the time, including the use of special materials."

When the Progress Plant opened, it was said to be the largest and most advanced bioindustrial plant in the Soviet Union. At its maximum, the Progress Plant employed approximately 4,000 people. Its huge production unit was equipped with 130 63,000-liter fermenters that were manufactured in East Germany and were used for the mass production of biological pesticides,[60] animal feed supplements, and ethanol. One of its biopesticides, Bitoxibacillin, was used throughout the Soviet Union to combat Colorado beetles.[61]

The availability of power- and heat-generating facilities, as well as qualified biotechnological and construction specialists from the Progress Plant and Stepnogorsk, facilitated the building of the military component. Eduard Perov, the former deputy director of the Progress Plant, headed this component during construction."[62]

In 1982 a secret decree signed by Chairman Leonid Brezhnev ordered the military component to be responsible for the manufacture of BW agents, especially *B. anthracis*.[63] The decree officially gave the military component its name, SNOPB, and its secret name, P.O. Box 2076. The decree probably also specified that SNOPB was to be placed under the authority of Biopreparat.

Alibek was transferred to Stepnogorsk from the Omutninsk Chemical Factory and replaced Perov as head of the facility in 1983. Alibek served as SNOPB's director until 1988, when he was promoted and transferred to Moscow. His deputy director, Gennady N. Lepeshkin, a Russian colonel who served for years at the Kirov Institute, replaced Alibek as director in 1988.[64]

Although not as large as either SRCAM or Vector, SNOPB was impressive. Foreign visitors found its multiple R&D, production, and storage facilities overwhelming. At the height of SNOPB's development, its 25 buildings occupied an area of approximately 200 hectares (494 acres), and it employed approximately 800 persons, including 17 doctoral-level scientists and 100 lower-level researchers. Of its employees, 50 to 100 had F clearance, according to a high-placed SNOPB official. The engineers who operated the SNOPB's fermenters and other technical personnel had no knowledge of *Ferment.* They were given technical tasks, such as propagating *B. anthracis,* but would not have known the purpose of their work.

As noted in Chapter 3, in about 1982, 65 military scientific workers from the Sverdlovsk Institute transferred to the SNOPB; this included a number of production experts. Most of the experts, however, could not acclimatize themselves to the extreme central Asian climate and the isolation of the Stepnogorsk community and soon relocated back to Russia.

Below are capsule descriptions of SNOPB's major buildings and their functions:

- Building 211—Nutrient Media Production Facility. This building housed extensive production equipment for the large-scale manufacture of nutrient media and agar. It also had a storage complex for receiving and storing raw materials needed for production. According to Bozheyeva et al., this facility was capable of manufacturing 17 different types of nutrient media and had an annual production capacity of 30,000 metric tons.[65] A system of well-insulated pipes conveyed hot liquid media to the fermenters in Building 221, even when the outside temperature dropped below 0 degrees Celsius.
- Building 221—Main Production Facility. This building had six stories, with two of them underground. Its floor area was 35,000 square meters (376,737 square feet). Its top floor housed twenty 1,000-liter fermenters, which functioned as pilot plants. After microorganisms of interest were propagated to their fullest extent in one of these smaller fermenters, they were conveyed to one of ten 20,000-liter fermenters on the

lower floors. All of these fermenters were manufactured in East Germany. When the fermenters obtained their maximum yield, technicians conveyed their contents to one of seven underground centrifugal separators (centrifuges), which separated the spent media from the microorganisms' biomass. Aliquots of biomass were then placed in TR-50 (50-liter capacity) or TR-250 (250-liter capacity) stainless steel containers. These containers were moved either to Building 231, where the biomass was further processed; to Bunkers 241–244, where weapons were filled; or to Bunkers 251–252, for long-term storage. Building 221 had a maximum production capacity of 1.5 tons of biomass per three-day production cycle.

- Building 231—Drying and Milling Facility. Biomass produced in Building 221 was dried in one of Building 231's several large dryers. One of the dryers was said to have weighed 200 tons. After drying, the resulting cake was milled in industrial-sized millers to produce particles of a uniform 5–10 micron size.

- Bunkers 241–244—Handling and Filling Bunkers. These bunkers, as well as Bunkers 251–252, were 70 meters long, 20 meters wide, and were mostly underground, with just 7 meters of overground superstructure. One SNOPB worker claimed that these bunkers' walls were designed to withstand the blasts from nuclear weapons exploded more than 1 kilometer away (though he did not know the size of these nuclear weapons) and were thus 2 meters (6 feet) thick and made of reinforced concrete. These bunkers contained filling stations that had special equipment to fill bomblets with either wet or dry formulations. Bunkers 241–244, as well as Bunkers 251–252, were particularly noteworthy because they contained enormous refrigeration equipment, which used electricity at a prodigious rate. According to SNOPB workers, although all refrigerated bunkers became operational before 1992, they were never used for their intended purposes; that is, none stored formulated agents at subzero temperatures.

- Bunkers 251–252—Storage Bunkers. The bunkers were designed to store filled bomblets in chambers that were kept at either −10 degrees Celsius or −20 degrees Celsius, as is explained in Chapter 10.

- Building 600—Research and Testing Building. Like Building 221, Building 600 had a floor area of 35,000 square meters (376,737 square feet). This building contained laboratories in which scientists conducted applied research to, for example, improve the growth characteristics of

BW agents, develop better manufacturing processes, and experiment with dispersal techniques in order to improve them. The most remarkable feature of this building was an enormous octagonal explosive test chamber that was used for the contained testing of biological munitions. According to Bozheyeva et al., the chamber had a volume of about 200 cubic meters (7,063 cubic feet) and had walls made of 1.6-centimeter-thick stainless steel. The test chamber was designed to be lifted in one piece off of its cement platform by a powerful pulley system to a height of about 8 meters (24 feet). Once lifted, cages holding test animals could be distributed as needed on the platform and the explosive device be centrally emplaced. This platform was also octagonal, which meant that when the chamber was lowered, it would fit exactly, thus preventing leakage of aerosolized particles to the surrounding environs. Most contained-testing involved the *Gshch*-304 bomblet (see Chapter 10), with testers varying the payload, burster charge, and/or test animals used.

- Building 606—Administration building. This building contained offices and a library.

The SNOPB's production capacity was large, about 300 metric tons of weaponized *B. anthracis* spores per 10-month production cycle. However, in times of peace most of the SNOPB's production came from the smaller 1,000-liter fermenters. It never produced large quantities of pathogens and only rarely operated its large fermenters for exercise purposes. It produced small batches of simulants or pathogens at infrequent intervals in a cycle that involved all fermenters. This ensured that everything was in order should the institute be mobilized. In addition, SNOPB occasionally produced small quantities of pathogens and simulants for use in the open-air testing of BW munitions at Aralsk-7. Contrary to Alibek's claims, SNOPB never produced tons of *B. anthracis* spores.[66] If the Soviets were to mobilize its war-time production capacity, SNOPB's staff would immediately increase from 750 to more than 2,000 persons. A source for this book said that he assumed that some of the additional personnel would be detailed from the adjacent Progress Plant and, if need be, would be brought in from various facilities in the Soviet Union, though he was not party to mobilization planning documents.

The relationship between SNOPB and the Progress Plant was unlike any other in the Soviet BW system. The other major Biopreparat production plants in Berdsk and Omutninsk were mobilization plants. In peaceful times, these plants were either mothballed or manufactured civilian products such as biopesticides, antibiotics, amino acids, and so forth, but if war was imminent, they were converted to manufacture BW agents. This was not the case in Stepnogorsk, where SNOPB and the Progress Plant were separate and each had its own mission: SNOPB produced only BW agents and the Progress Plant produced only civilian products. The Progress Plant served as a legend for SNOPB, and outsiders were told that everything at the institute was part of the Progress Plant and was dedicated to peacefully directed biotechnology.

The Progress Plant housed certain important parts of the infrastructure for both entities, including the power plant and steam plant, but their staffs were unconnected. This created some problems for the managers of the facilities. In peacetime, the Progress Plant's manager was in charge of the allocation of resources. Most importantly, the Progress Plant's power plant generated a limited amount of electricity, so SNOPB could never use its full production capacity—even for tests. Out of SNOPB's 10 large fermenters, only four could ever be operated at the same time. If Soviet officials ordered a mobilization, SNOPB's manager would assume command of the infrastructure and would be able to order as much power as SNOPB needed, within the constraints of the Progress Plant's generating capacity.

SNOPB in Independent Kazakhstan

Although Kazakhstan declared its independence on December 16, 1991, SNOPB remained under the administrative control of Biopreparat well into 1992. During that time, all classified documents were removed and transported to Russia. So was the octagonal test chamber. Biopreparat's financial support for the facility ended in 1992, leaving the SNOPB unable to pay its workers and utility bills. SNOPB buildings turned dark, cold, and inactive. Russians working for the SNOPB were given the choice of becoming Kazakh citizens or remaining Russians. Lepeshkin's deputy director, Yuriy Rufov, estimated that out of the approximately 680 scientists and technicians who worked at SNOPB in 1991, 500 departed for Russia, 112 remained in Stepnogorsk and were paid with CTR funding to dismantle the facility, 16 were hired with CTR funding to monitor possible contamination in the ruins of the site, and 52 were hired to work at a newly established nearby medical company. Lepeshkin was one of the few Russians who elected to remain, and he stayed until 2001, when he was dismissed by the Kazakh government.[67] He then relocated to Russia.

On November 16, 1993, the Kazakh Cabinet of Ministers issued Decree No. 1140, which established the National Centre for Biotechnology of the Republic of Kazakhstan (NTsB) and placed its headquarters in Stepnogorsk. At about the same time, Kazakh officials reorganized the SNOPB as the Kazakh Science Industrial Complex (Biomedpreparat), which was incorporated into the NTsB. Officials also incorporated the Progress Plant in the NTsB and renamed it the Production Association "Progress." Both became joint stock companies and were owned by a combination of private investors and the government. Lepeshkin was named general director of the NTsB, a position he held until 2001. He was replaced by Kazakh scientist Sergazy Adekenov, who was the director of the Phytochemistry Institute in Karaganda and an academician of the Kazakh National Academy of Sciences.

After an initial attempt to convert SNOPB facilities to civilian uses failed, the US and Kazakh governments agreed to dismantle most of the facility. The dismantlement was completed by Kazakh workers over a period of about four years and was paid for with CTR funding.[68] The complex's Buildings 211, 221, 231, and 600 were completely demolished. Zilinskas observed some of this work in 2003.

10

Soviet Biological Weapons and Doctrines for Their Use

A READER PERUSING this book is likely to be amazed by the huge enterprise dedicated to biological warfare (BW) that the Soviet Union erected and operated at a cost of many billions of rubles and many hundreds of millions of dollars in hard currencies. Some might ask how this could be, in view of statements that have often been made to the effect that biological weapons are "the poor nations' atomic bomb" and "biological weapons are easily acquired." The fact is that these facile portrayals are mostly inaccurate. If a country wishes to acquire effective, dependable biological weapons of the types that the Soviet Union attempted to do in the *Ferment* and *Ekologiya* programs, the acquisition process is very difficult and costly to carry out. Although it is true that countries can try to do so cheaply, the end products of inexpensive programs are likely to be ineffective and undependable. Iraq is an example; its biological weapons arsenal contained bombs and missiles of dubious reliability or effectiveness.[1]

For the Soviet Union to acquire a militarily useful arsenal, its military scientists and engineers had to research, develop, test, and manufacture "type-classified" biological weapons[2]—weapons that had through realistic open-air testing proved to be dependable and bringing about planned-for and reproducible effects every time they were tested. Because it is important for readers of this book to understand the substantial scientific, technical, and environmental barriers that Soviet scientists had to overcome in their quest to develop type-classified biological weapons, this chapter's first section explains a type-classified biological weapon's four components, using examples from the Soviet BW program for illustrative purposes. The second section describes "recipes," which are complete records of the Soviet weaponization process, from the point at which a pathogen was recovered from nature to when it armed a Soviet biological weapon. Two major types of Soviet biological weapons are described in the third section, multiple bomblet submunitions and online spray systems. The fourth section discusses what might have been the Soviet doctrine for employing biological weapons. Due to the importance of this section, the question of Soviet missiles allegedly carrying biological warheads is explored at length. Apparently statements that have been made about this critical question are, as best as can be determined, inaccurate. They are explored in some detail.

Biological Weapons as Systems

A type-classified biological weapon has four components that function in unison as a system—"weaponized" pathogens, a "formulation" that is composed of pathogens and chemicals, a container or munition in which the formulation is stored and transported, and a dispersal device.

Weaponized Pathogens

Pathogens can be deliberately released into the environment for the expressed purpose of causing disease and death among human, animal or plant populations. If the release occurs in a military context, to gain strategic or tactical advantage over an enemy, it is called biological warfare (BW); if it is carried out by nonmilitary persons or groups in pursuit of political, religious, or social objectives, it is called biological terrorism, or bioterrorism for short. This book addresses biological weapons in the military context only. In either case, pathogens are used for weapons purposes. However, and this is crucial, a quantity of pathogens by themselves is not a weapon.

The 12 criteria of militarily useful BW agents were clearly defined by two American scientists who worked for the US Biological Defense Program:

> In order for a biological warfare agent to be an effective weapon it must meet specific criteria for use in either a strategic or a tactical role. First, and most important, is the agent's ability to be delivered via an aerosol. Because inhalation of microorganisms in an aerosol occurs rapidly and

almost simultaneously in a unit, the time frame can be predicted and the subsequent decreased combat effectiveness of the [attacked] unit can be exploited. Second, the agent should be amenable to economical mass production. Third, the organism must survive and remain stable in air. Fourth, it must have a high virulence, or be capable of causing severe disease or death. Fifth, the infective dose [ID_{50}], or the number of organisms needed to cause disease, should be low. Sixth, ideally, it should have a short and predictable incubation time from exposure to the onset of disease state. Seventh, the target population should have little or no natural or acquired immunity or resistance to the organism. Eighth, the availability of treatment for or prophylaxis against the agent should be poor or nonexistent. Ninth, the organism should have a high communicability from individual to individual, if this property is appropriate to a particular target. Tenth, the organism should have a low persistence, surviving only for a short period of time, thereby allowing the attacker to maneuver through the area. Eleventh, the organism should be difficult to detect and/or identify. Lastly, the attacker should have a means to protect his own forces or population against the agent.[3]

Using the set of the above 12 criteria as guide, we link them with the objectives of the Soviet offensive BW program's first and second generations.

AEROSOLIZED PATHOGENS.   As far as we are aware, all antipersonnel Soviet BW agents were designed to be dispersed as aerosols. We are not aware of any agents that were to be used to sabotage food or beverages, though we cannot exclude the possibility that one or more of the Soviet intelligence agencies supported laboratories that weaponized food-borne or beverage-borne pathogens. Conceivably, some of the genetically engineered pathogens developed by *Ferment* scientists might eventually have been used for these kinds of purposes.

ECONOMY OF PRODUCTION.   We do not know the costs associated with producing Soviet BW agents, but we assume that because the BW program had so many huge production facilities, its scientists and engineers had over time sought to develop cost-effective methods and substrates for the mass production of pathogens. However since the Soviet Union was not sparing when it came to weapons procurement, this need not have been the case.

STABILITY OF AEROSOL PARTICLES.   Most bacterial cells and viral particles die soon after being released into the open environment. Therefore, they must be protected by formulations and fillers, which are discussed in detail below.

PATHOGEN INFECTIVITY.   As with virulence, first generation agents were measured by how efficient they were in infecting many types of animals, including nonhuman primates. The acronym for infectivity is ID_{50}, which is defined in the Glossary. It is reasonable to assume that over the years, Soviet scientists were able to select strains of each pathogen that demonstrated the lowest ID_{50}, which means the least number of pathogens were needed to infect a host. During the second generation, *Ferment* scientists certainly investigated host–pathogen interactions, but we doubt that they were successful in genetically engineering a pathogenic bacterium or virus for increased infectivity, because so little was known at that time about host–pathogen interactions.

PATHOGEN VIRULENCE.   The first generation pathogens were recovered from nature and tested for virulence. It is reasonable to assume that over the many years, Soviet bacteriologists and virologists were able to select for the most virulent strains of each pathogens. For second generation agents, the objectives of several of *Ferment's* subprograms at SRCAM and Vector were to increase the virulence of bacterial and viral pathogens through the use of genetic engineering. As we recount in Chapters 7–9, as well as in the Conclusion, some pathogens were genetically engineered for enhanced virulence.

PATHOGEN INCUBATION TIME.   The incubation times of Soviet BW agents ranged from 48 hours *(B. anthracis)* to 14 days (variola virus). It is plausible that Soviet military scientists might have attempted to select pathogens for short incubation times, for example, *B. anthracis.*

IMMUNOLOGICAL STATUS OF TARGETED POPULATIONS.   In general, Soviet biomedical scientists could not know the immunological status of potential enemy populations. The one big exception was smallpox, because most, perhaps all, of the world's countries had stopped vaccinating their populations against smallpox in the 1970s and 1980s. Their populations would therefore have been susceptible to Soviet biological weapons armed with variola virus. A second exception are hemorrhagic fever viruses; it is safe to assume that most humans are susceptible to infections caused by, in particular, Marburg and Ebola virus.

AVAILABILITY OF TREATMENT.   Western industrialized countries were well prepared to meet the challenges of bacterial infectious diseases because they had the requisite supplies of antibiotics and, in some cases, vaccines. They were much less prepared for viral infectious diseases. For a substantial part of the post World War II years, antiviral drugs were not available. Subsequently it was possible to develop only a few such drugs, and those were effective against only a limited number of viral pathogens. During the second generation, Soviet scientists attempted to develop bacterial pathogens that were multiantibiotic resistant. As is described in Chapter 7, they were successful. As for viruses, they weaponized Marburg virus, against which there is no defense or treatment.

CONTAGIOUS PATHOGENS.   During the first generation, Soviet weapon scientists had already weaponized a contagious bacterial pathogen, *Y. pestis,* and a contagious virus, variola virus, and had armed type-classified weapons with these agents. So the Soviet military must have believed there were appropriate targets for contagious pathogens.

LOW PERSISTENCE OF BW AGENTS.   In general, once BW agents have been released into the open environment, their survival time is short even if formulated. One significant exception is *B. anthracis* spores, which are exceedingly hardy and can survive for hours or days on surfaces and months to years in soil. Some viruses, like variola virus, are fairly hardy, being able to survive in some niches for days to weeks. Some Soviet biological weapons were armed with low-persistence agents and therefore could have been designed to be used in an operational zone, while more persistent agents could have been used for strategic purposes where their high survivability rate did not matter to the attacker.

DETECTION OF BW AGENTS.   The subject of detecting and identifying pathogens, whatever their etiology, is a difficult one because it is affected by many factors, such as familiarity with diseases and their symptoms, availability of adequate clinical microbiology laboratories with well-trained staff, and knowledge of good sample-collection techniques. For these reasons, it is not a topic we can address adequately in a short entry. During the second generation, SRCAM scientists transferred genes from *Bacillus cereus* to *B. anthracis,* thus altering the second bacterium's antigen presentation. This would have made the new strain more difficult to identify and might have been able to defeat the US anthrax vaccine (see Chapter 7). The U.S. Defense Intelligence Agency estimated in 1977 that the Soviet Union "have already modified BW agents which only they can identify, treat, and control."[4] However, this finding likely was highly exaggerated because molecular biology at that time was insufficiently advanced for any such accomplishments.[5]

PROTECTING ONE'S OWN POPULATION AGAINST BW AGENTS.   As described in Chapter 5, the Soviet BW program had offensive and defensive aspects. Typically, when a pathogen was being weaponized by one part of the program, another part was working to develop defenses against it, such as vaccines. While the defensive aspect was less well supported than the offensive aspect, and in general was held in low regard by military and Biopreparat scientists, it reportedly developed some effective vaccines. Because these were for use within the Soviet Union, and now Russia, and their military forces, it may be assumed that they worked to the satisfaction of the Soviet Ministry of Defense (MOD). However, the large-scale effort by the MOD to develop aerosol vaccines for mass inoculation of humans appears to have failed, as no such vaccine exists today.

Past state BW programs have investigated many pathogens for biological weapons use, but in the end few have been found that possess the combination of characteristics that make them attractive for militaries to attempt to weaponize. By the end of its existence, the Soviet BW program had investigated far more pathogens than any other national BW program. For the sake of comparison, the BW agents validated by the US and USSR BW programs are listed in Table 10.1. Both programs researched a larger number of pathogens that eventually were not weaponized.

Formulations and Fillers

Most unprotected pathogens are fragile, which means that they survive only briefly after release into open air before dying from a combination of desiccation, UV radiation, and "open air factor," which is a composite of environmental variables including radiation, oxygen, free radicals, nitrous oxides, and other factors that stress an aerosolized pathogen. If pathogens die too

Table 10.1 Agents Validated for Biological Weapons by the United States
and the Soviet Union

United States	Soviet Union
Bacteria	
Bacillus anthracis	*Bacillus anthracis*
Brucella suis	*Brucella* species
Coxiella burnetii	*Coxiella burnetii*
Francisella tularensis	*Francisella tularensis*
	Burkholderia mallei
	Burkholderia pseudomallei (?)
	Yersinia pestis
Viruses	
	Marburg virus
Venezuelan Equine Encephalitis virus	Venezuelan Equine Encephalitis virus
	Variola virus
Toxins	
Botulinum toxin	Botulinum toxin
Staphylococcal enterotoxin B	

rapidly, they are of course useless for BW purposes, because they will not have time to infect the target population. Military scientists therefore need to protect them, which is done by "formulating" them. A former weapons scientist described the composition of formulations:

> From the point of view of composition, BW in liquid form is a complex suspension containing the virus (or bacterium) and consisting of several components. This kind of composition was referred to as a special formula *(spetsretseptura)* by a group of Soviet BW developers. It included some obligatory components characteristic of any form of BW, such as a stabilizer, which itself is also a complex multicomponent mixture, and an inert filling agent [filler], which was necessary for the transfer of the liquid suspension containing deadly viruses (or bacteria) into aerosol clouds with particle diameter of 1 to 5 microns.[6]

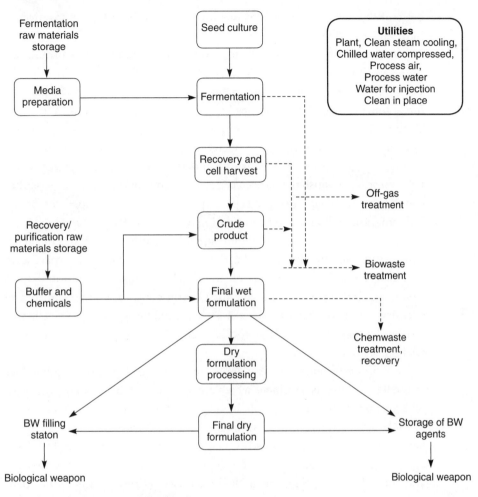

Chart 10.1 Diagram of a Biological Agents Fermentation Facility

The Soviet BW program, like the pre-1969 US BW program, prepared both "wet" and "dry" "formulations." Manufacturing a wet formulation at a BW production plant would be similar to manufacturing a formulation of, for example, a biopesticide like *Bacillus thuringiensis* in a civilian plant (see Chart 10.1). After fermentation, the pathogen is separated from the remaining culture medium and is resuspended in a special solution containing the chemicals noted above, including stabilizers and inert fillers.[7] Each weaponized pathogen requires a specific formulation. Further, some pathogens function better if they are part of a wet formulation, whereas others are more effective in dry formulations.

It is technically more difficult to develop and produce a dry formulation than a wet formulation. For a dry formulation, it is necessary to first dry the wet formulation in special equipment and then to mill the dried material into a fine powder whose particles are no larger than 10 microns in its greatest dimension. Particles of 3 to 5 microns in size are optimal to achieve infection in the human lung. These operations present extreme hazards to the production personnel. While dry formulations are generally preferred for BW purposes because they are easier to store and disseminate, some pathogens are not amenable to this type of processing. For example, the Soviet BW program had only a wet formulation for weaponized *Y. pestis.*

The development of a formulation suitable for protecting a specific agent and facilitating effective aerosolization demands considerable expertise in several disciplines. At a minimum, the development of agent formulations would require an interdisciplinary R&D team constituted by scientists and chemical engineers having expertise in bacteriology or virology, biochemistry, aerobiology, fermentation processes, and the subsequent steps of industrial processing.

Developing formulations is complicated because there are no guidelines that tell the weapons developer which chemical or combination of chemicals will interact with a pathogen in such a way as to end up with a successful formulation. Various combinations must be tested one by one, first in the laboratory and then in the field. Usually an optimal formulation for a BW agent is demonstrated to function dependably only after much laboratory and open-air testing. Since Soviet BW scientists initiated testing in the open-air test site on Vozrozhdeniye Island in 1937, their experience in this area was extensive (see Tables 1.1, 10.1, and 10.2).

Fillers are inert substances that are used in bombs and bomblets to protect the formulated pathogens and help with even distribution of aerosol particles. From information provided to us by Pasechnik, fillers are the major components of a biological payload (see Chapter 9).

An alternative approach to formulation for protecting bacterial cells and viral particles is microencapsulation, but as far as we are aware, Soviet scientists, especially at the IHPB, were unsuccessful in their efforts to protect BW agents by encapsulation technology.

Storage Containers and Storage

In order to carry out a biological attack, a requisite quantity of the formulated agent must first be delivered to a staging area from which the attack will be mounted. The agent has to be transported in some kind of container from the site of production or storage to the staging area. The container has to be designed in such a way that it gives the agent it contains as long a shelf-life as possible so that the pathogen remain alive and virulent for many months, even years, while in storage. Additionally, the container in which the agent is stored must maintain its integrity so that none of its dangerous contents escape, but at the same time its contents must be accessible for dissemination at a moment's notice. Under some circumstances, the container could also be a munition—the container could be both designed to carry the agent securely and equipped with a mechanism for dispersing it. Examples of such munitions are biological bombs, bomblets, spray containers, and submunitions (see below).

With the exception of bacterial spores, BW agents, even if formulated, will survive only for a relatively few days if kept at temperatures above freezing, and the higher the temperature, the shorter the survival period. The Soviet BW program's bulk viral formulations were stored at −20° Celsius and bacterial formulations at −10° Celsius. Soviet weapons scientists had developed a chemical additive for wet formulations that kept them liquid even at subzero temperatures. This accomplishment allowed wet formulations to be easily transferred and stored in either TR-50 or TR-250 stainless steel containers. Under these conditions, formulated bacterial BW agents had long shelf-lives; for example, *B. anthracis* spores contained in TR-250 containers and stored at −10° Celsius had a shelf-life of several years, and bacterial cells (including *Y. pestis* and *F. tularensis*) remained viable for between one and two years, as did most viral formulations.

Soviet military authorities built and maintained large storage bunkers at several production plants, including those at Stepnogorsk and Pokrov. When the time came to fill a munition with stored formulation, the TR-50 or TR-250 containers were transported to a specially designed filling station and their contents were transferred to hopper tanks or directly to munitions. As explained in the chapter on SNOPB (Chapter 9), these bunkers, although operational, were never fully utilized for their intended purpose.

BW formulations were also stored to some small extent in *Gshch*-304 bomblets, which are described in detail below. Filled bomblets were needed both for closed testing, to determine survival times of the agent filling under different storage conditions and by different dispersal methods, and for open-air testing purposes. Filled bomblets were also stored in bunkers at −10° Celsius or −20° Celsius, depending on the pathogen placed in the bomblet. When taken out of frozen storage, the payload survived at room temperature for approximately 30 days if the payload was bacterial and 10 days if it was viral. Stored bomblets did not contain burster charges; these were inserted into the bomblets as a last step before they were to be used.

In Soviet planning, the alternative to storing bulk formulations were so-called mobilization capacity production plants that were constructed near strategic sites such as airports or railroad stations (see Chapter 9). Billions of rubles were spent to build and equip at least 10 biological production plants. Each of these plants was capable of producing and formulating ton quantities of the BW agent or agents for which it was designed (see Table 10.2). After testing production runs of agents to make certain their production capabilities operated as planned, they were maintained in semi-readiness. At SNOPB, some of its manufacturing capability was kept operational to produce agents needed for open-air testing. Approximately every year these facilities would be stood up for testing. After successful testing, they would once again be returned to a lower readiness level. Mobilization plants could be restored to full operational status within six weeks of a determination by the Soviet leadership that a war was imminent. Having mobilization plants in strategic locations obviated the need for the Soviet military to store large quantities of BW agents in peace time. In effect, it had just-in-time manufacturing capabilities for BW agents in place for wartime readiness. If war was deemed imminent, the low-temperature bunkers described in Chapter 9 would be made operational and products manufactured by mobilization plants would be stored in TR-50 or TR-250 containers or bomblets until needed.

Dispersal Devices

Carrying out an effective aerosol attack with a mass of bacteria or viruses is a technically difficult process. In particular, the attacker must be capable of dispersing formulations over the targeted population so that most individuals of that population are exposed to an infectious dose of the released agent. Although there potentially are several ways of dispersing biological agents, the discussion here is limited to dispersal by explosion or spraying.

Table 10.2 Planned Annual Rate of Biological Agent Production during a Pre-War Mobilization Period

Facilities	Agents	CIA/DOD estimates[a]	Alibek public estimates[b]
MOD Institutes			
1. Sverdlovsk	*B. anthracis*	~300 tons	> 1,000 tons
2. Kirov	*Y. pestis*	~70 tons	~ 200 tons
3. Zagorsk	Variola virus	~30 tons	~ 100 tons
Biopreparat mobilization capacity production facilities			
4. Berdsk	*Y. pestis, F. tularensis, B. mallei*	~300 tons	> 1,000 tons
5. Stepnogorsk	*B. anthracis, F. tularensis, B. mallei*	~300 tons	> 1,000 tons [elsewhere 300 tons *B. anthracis*]
6. Omutninsk	*Y. pestis, F. tularensis, B. mallei*	~300 tons	> 1,000 tons
7. Kurgan	*B. anthracis*	~300 tons	> 1,000 tons
8. Penza	*B. anthracis*	~300 tons	> 1,000 tons
9. Koltsovo (Vector)	[Variola virus, Marburg virus?]	A few tons	"dozens" tons
Other Ministries			
10. Pokrov	Variola virus, VEEV	~70 tons	> 200 tons
11. Viral production facility in Georgian SSR	Unknown	–	Unknown

a. US DPD and CIA officials assert that the annual production tonnage figures for *B. anthracis* and the other pathogens provided by Alibek are highly exaggerated. More accurate figures are said to be one-third of the tonnages that Alibek has attributed in public.

b. Ken Alibek presentation at DTRA meeting at Institute for Defense Analysis, June 1, 2000.

Most bombs, larger bomblets, and larger submunitions typically contain a tube filled with an explosive charge (burster) that is placed in the center of the chamber or chambers containing the formulation. When required, the burster explodes, rupturing the outer wall of the munition and expelling the payload as an aerosol that is partially propelled upward to form a plume and partially dispersed sideways over a limited area. Further dispersal of aerosol particles that constitute the plume depends on meteorological forces, in particular wind.

A fine balance exists between the explosive force needed for efficient dispersal and that which would destroy the payload by heat, pressure, and toxic gases. Depending on the formulation being dispersed and the size of the burster charge, the dissemination efficiency attendant to explosive dispersion ranges from 0.10% to 4%.[8] In other words, 96–99.9% of the formulated agent dispersed by explosion will be destroyed, driven harmlessly into the ground, transformed into particles too small or large to be useful for weapons purposes, or otherwise rendered useless. For all these reasons, in order to maximize the survival rate of an agent dispersed by explosion, the weapons engineer must design a munition that combines a well-controlled explosive force, has walls that rupture relatively easily, and contains well-formulated pathogens. Nevertheless, when a biological weapon uses an explosive charge to disperse the pathogen, the overwhelming amount of its agent-fill is destroyed in the explosion.

Open-air testing demonstrated that the spray method of delivery is most likely to generate mass casualties. The main components of sprayers are generally a hopper tank that holds bulk formulation, a source of compressed air, a feeding line through which formulation is conveyed by compressed air to the nozzle, and a nozzle through which the formulation is ejected as fine spray. Soviet weapon designers, however, developed another mechanism that used air flow over an opened container of agent to disperse the spray (see below). The main problem with the spray method is that to accomplish successful dispersion, the aircraft undertaking the spraying must fly at a low altitude and relatively low speed over the target area, which leaves it vulnerable to anti-aircraft countermeasures.

Biological attacks based on aerosol release of pathogens are very difficult to carry out successfully. One set of difficulties concerns the behavior of the aerosolized agents after release. Briefly, the atmosphere where the attack is to take place must be stable and calm for it to be effective. Two meteorological forces, wind and inversion layer, commonly affect atmospheric stability. The wind cannot be too forceful, because the particles will be blown away without causing harm, nor can it be completely absent, or the aerosol cloud will not move. A suitable inversion layer is one that keeps aerosol particles trapped close to the ground and usually occurs in early morning over cities. If the prospective area targeted for a biological attack was experiencing rain or snow, a biological attack employing aerosol would most probably prove ineffective.

The second set of difficulties pertains to natural forces that stress the agents constituting an aerosol. Physical atmospheric factors, such as relative humidity and temperature, will directly affect the survival of aerosolized agents. Pathogens constituting an aerosol cloud will begin to desiccate immediately after having been released into the open environment, leading to their rapid death. As a rule of thumb, the higher the temperature and the lower the relative humidity, the faster the aerosolized microorganism will desiccate.[9] Most vegetative cells will die within 30 minutes of being released into the open environment even if protected in some manner, for example, by a formulation.[10] The die-off rate would be faster during daytime because ultraviolet (UV) radiation emitted by the sun kills bacteria and viruses. However, spores, such as those formed by *B. anthracis,* remain stable for many hours in the atmosphere if there is no sun. Ultraviolet light kills spores, but it takes a long time.

Recipes

Each Soviet BW agent and the weapon it armed were completely described in a recipe ("*reglament*" in the Soviet system). We have not seen any Soviet recipes, but understand their general structure. To illustrate a recipe, we convey a hypothetical strain of *Yersinia pestis* through the weaponization processes in order to demonstrate the information it is likely to contain.[11] A likely scenario would start in, say, the early 1960s when an entomologist employed at the regional Bakanas Anti-plague Station was sent on a field expedition to the Bakanas area in which plague was endemic in the local rodent population (plague focus).[12] As part of his investigation, he would have set traps in the evening at the entrances of an underground network of tunnels and chambers populated by a gerbil colony.[13] The following morning, he would place each captured gerbil inside a coarsely woven cotton stocking and "comb" its fur for ectoparasites over a pan filled with mineral oil. One gerbil could yield as many as 200 ectoparasites, mostly fleas, which would drop into the oil. Ectoparasites trapped in oil would be drawn up into a pipette and then expelled into a glass tube. A blood sample would be taken from the gerbil's tail and then the animal would be released. Collected ectoparasites and blood would be packed in ice and taken to the Bakanas Anti-plague Station.

At the Station, serological methods would be used to measure antibody levels in the gerbil's blood sample. Each ectoparasite would be identified by the entomologist and then crushed and the remains were cultured on agar plates. It is not uncommon that *Y. pestis* would be recovered from one or more of the cultured ectoparasites. As soon as a colony of *Y. pestis* was identified, a "strain passport" would be created for it, which is a dossier in which the particulars of the colony's recovery and growth characteristics were recorded.[14] The *Y. pestis* culture then would be safely packaged and transported to the Station's governing anti-plague institute, the Central Asian Scientific Research Anti-plague Institute in Alma Ata, for more advanced studies, including confirmatory speciation, determination of strain, and virulence analysis.

If analysis revealed that the strain was particularly virulent, a Soviet regulation of the time specified that pathogens demonstrating certain properties, including high virulence, must be sent to the MOD. Because *Y. pestis* is a bacterial pathogen, the strain, accompanied by the strain passport, almost certainly ended up being delivered to the MOD's Kirov Institute.[15] Information that was entered into the strain passport at this stage would have included site of collection, host animal, type of ectoparasite from which it was recovered, antibody levels found in the blood sample from the host animal, dates of recovery and analysis, and methods and findings of advanced analysis at the Alma Ata Anti-plague Institute.

At the Kirov Institute, the assembly of the recipe would begin. Its first section was the strain passport. Other sections soon were added, including those that contained information derived from R&D and the weaponization process, such as the strain's growth characteristics, antibiotic sensitivity pattern, results from genetic and molecular studies, and results from animal studies in which test animals were infected by the strain by injection, ingestion, and inhalation. Descriptions of the course of illness and time of death would be carefully recorded. Because the time period for the process we are describing was the middle 1960s, Kirov scientists probably would have applied classical research methods of mutation, selection, and propagation to enhance the strain's infectivity, virulence, and so on.[16] Assuming that they were successful, and an even more powerful strain emerged from the applied research as proved by further analysis and testing, the strain would undergo extensive closed air chamber testing using various animal models. This testing would indicate whether the strain would be likely to survive well in the open environment, and would also determine its effectiveness in an aerosol in causing illness and death to various animals ranging from mice to nonhuman primates. If closed tests demonstrated that the enhanced strain indeed was more virulent, hardier, and perhaps possessed other properties that made it superior over existing weapons strains, the strain can be described as having been weaponized.

However, as it was to be used for weapons purposes, it would have to also be formulated. There is no available information regarding where the military research institutes sent their weaponized strains for the formulation process. In the Biopreparat system, viruses weaponized at Vector and bacteria weaponized at SRCAM were formulated at IHPB. We have not been able to identify a military equivalent to IHPB, so it is plausible that the formulation process was done at the institute where the pathogen was weaponized, which in the case of *Y. pestis* would have been the Kirov Institute. After the formulation had been perfected, which might take months to do with repeated testing in closed air chambers, the formulated strain still had to go through two more stages, industrialization and open-air testing. All R&D and testing to this point would have been recorded in the strain's recipe.

The industrialization of a weaponized strain would be similar to that of bacterial strains used for civilian purposes (see Chart 10.1). Those responsible for the strain's R&D would have learned how to propagate it in the laboratory, which meant that they were able to grow as much of the strain as they needed for investigatory and closed testing purposes. However, laboratory growth procedures are rarely directly applicable for scaling up, and those working on the strain would not try to immediately grow it in industrial-size fermenters. The weaponized strain would first be grown in a pilot plant where procedures for the strain's large-scale propagation are developed by chemical or fermentation engineers. Pilot plant fermenters of about 50-liter size are used to grow the strain under various conditions and in different substrates. These procedures of growing, adjusting, regrowing, and readjusting would continue until a particular manufacturing process clearly worked best in terms of high yield of the formulated weaponized strain and with good reproducibility. Pilot plant development might take many months, even years, before satisfactory results are obtained. Many things can go wrong, including the accumulation of toxic materials during fermentation, problems with contamination by phages or fungi, inability to use inexpensive ingredients for large-scale fermentation, and so on. The criterion for success at the pilot plant stage is that the manufacturing process developed during this stage could be extrapolated directly into large-scale manufacturing. Descriptions of all this work were entered into the recipe.

To be deemed a validated agent, the weaponized pathogen grown in large-scale would have undergone open-air testing, involving aerosol generators to disperse calibrated plumes that were carried by wind over an area where various types of animals were located in cages and pens, or tethered to stakes. After 1954 such testing was done almost invariably by Aralsk-7 at Vozrozhdeniye Island (see Chapter 4). If open-air test trials demonstrated that the formulated *Y. pestis* strain was stable after release, infected animal models with high efficiency, and caused high mortality/lethality among infected populations, then the strain was designated as validated; that is, it was approved for use in weapons by the military. This would lead to further development and testing cycles, because the newly validated agent would be "fitted" to munitions, with each agent-munition combination being tested first in explosive chambers and then at the open-air test site. Determining the most efficient combination might take several test cycles covering several years. Finally, after repeated open-air testing had proved a weapon combination to be successful, it would be type-classified. The newly type-classified weapon's recipe would likely be composed of several book-length volumes. It would be classified Top Secret, with one copy being kept at the Kirov Institute and a second copy at the MOD. Only those who had the proper clearance level and a need to know would have access to recipes. According to our sources, only a very limited number of pages relevant to their immediate task could be read by institute scientists at one time, and such access took place under conditions that were severely circumscribed and carefully monitored. Recipes could be updated or added to if, for example, the strain had been genetically engineered in the laboratory for special purposes. However, because every step of development and testing would have to be done again with the altered strain, and someone in authority would have to sign off on the completion of each step, it was a tortuous process that was infrequently undertaken.

The result of this process, taking many years and potentially the inputs from many institutes in different ministries, is demonstrated by the production capabilities attributed to the Soviet BW mobilization production facilities, as illustrated in Table 10.2. The tonnages assume perfect operations, no errors, no contaminated cultures, etc. Contamination of fermenters reportedly occurred with some frequency at SNOPB.

Types of Soviet Biological Weapons

The two major types of Soviet biological weapons were bomblets and spray devices. The type-classified biological bomblet was called *Gshch*-304 (*ГЩ*-304). It was manufactured by Ministry of Medium Machine Building factories and was designed to carry either dry or wet bacterial and viral formulations. According to Russian informants, the bomblet was round, its outer

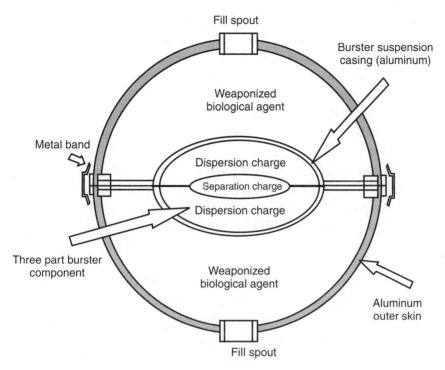

Chart 10.2 *Gshch*-304 Bomblet (vanes not pictured)

shell was made of 3 mm thick aluminum, it weighed 0.432 kg, its diameter was approximately 12 cm, and it looked like a shiny ball with three protrusions and six or eight vanes (see Chart 10.2).

The bomblet was constituted of two halves, one of which was threaded to be screwed into the other half. Unscrewing after the bomblet had been armed was prevented by securing two protrusions extending from each half of the bomblet with metal bands. When assembled, the bomblet had three bursters in the middle filled with TNT. Bomblets could be used to fill cluster bombs or missile warheads (Soviet BW missile development is discussed below). After release by a bomber, the vanes would act to divert the bomblet's downward trajectory from the vertical, thus dispersing bomblets contained in a cluster bomb over a large area. According to one dubious description, after release the bomblet would fall to the ground and when coming into contact with the ground would bounce up.[17] Upon reaching the peak of the bounce, the first burster charge would detonate, separating the bomblet's two halves.[18] A split second after separation, the burster in each half would detonate and disperse the payload as aerosol. Prevailing winds would carry aerosol particles over a wider area. The middle portion of the bomblet that included the burster charges was reportedly the most technical and secret part of the device.

However, the Soviet chemical bomblet, which is very similar in shape and construction, is reported as not bouncing on impact.[19] In addition, all the US CBW bomblets, the M-114, E-61, E-120, M-134, BLU-28/B, were designed to explode on impact with the ground.[20]

Over the years, Aralsk-7 tested the *Gshch*-304 with various payloads, including formulated *B. anthracis, F. tularensis, Y. pestis,* brucellae, variola virus, VEEV, and others. At the Vozrozhdeniye Island open-air test site, Aralsk-7 specialists typically would line up three of these bomblets at the up-wind edge of a testing range. The difference between bomblets used for open-air tests and those for biological attacks was slight. Test bomblets were designed to be propelled upward from the ground to a height of 3–5 meters by a small explosive charge set off by an electric switch, at which time the first burster would detonate as described above.[21] The prevailing wind would carry the payload downwind over the test range where many animals were tethered or caged.[22] It is common to test ground bursting multiple munitions from a height of several meters, so it is not known if the Soviet testing procedure for its BW bomblet was done for such routine reasons, or to simulate an anticipated "bounce."

A DIA report published in March 1990 included an illustration for a "Soviet Bacteriological Bomb," but this was apparently an illustration of an ancient glass device dating from the 1930s and of no contemporary relevance whatsoever.[23] It appeared in a Soviet Civil Defense handbook published in 1960,[24] but it seems likely that it is an illustration of the Japanese Uji or Uji-50 air-dropped BW munition that the Japanese BW program developed sometime between 1932 and 1945. If so, it seems bizarre that the DIA should have included this illustration in 1990, labeling it a *Soviet* BW bomb in a report on *Warsaw Pact* BW capabilities.

The information provided by former Soviet researchers regarding the Soviet BW bomblet's shape diverges from conclusions drawn by the US intelligence community (IC). The US IC believed it to be the oval-shaped multiple bomblet shown in the cut-away of a cluster bomb, which it believes the Soviet Union used for both CW and BW dispersion. Russian sources, however, insist that the munition in the illustration was for delivery of chemical weapons only, and that the round *Gshch*-304 was used solely to deliver biological agents. To compound matters further, the Russian Ministry of Defense (RF-MOD) advertises and illustrates the munition that the US IC believes is the CW/BW bomblet as the "RBK-500 A0-2 5RTM 500 kg Cluster Bomb loaded with conventional high-explosive Fragmentation Submunitions."[25] There are therefore partial contradictions between descriptions given by Alibek, by other former Soviet researchers, and by members of the US IC and its contractors. It is not possible for us to resolve these contradictions regarding the BW submunition. If the US IC is mistaken, it would mean that the tests carried out in 1991 in the Clear Vision program by the Battelle Corporation, a CIA contractor— an attempt to replicate the functioning of the Soviet bomblet—were made with a copy of the wrong bomblet munition (See Chapter 12).

It is important to note that the *Gshch*-304 closely resembles an American bomblet designated E-130R2 that was being developed in the late 1950s and was scheduled to be type-classified sometime in 1961–1962. The E-130R2 was similar in design to the US Army's E-120 BW bomblet. Information about the E-130R2, as well as other biological and chemical cluster bombs and bomblets in the US arsenal, were published in two US military reports, both of which were made publicly available by 1974. The first of these was an unclassified US Army report that was published in 1963. It contained cutaway views of both the E-130R2 and the E-120 BW bomblets.[26] Copies of this report had even made their way to public libraries in at least one European country by the mid- to late-1960s.

The second was a secret 1961 report that was, however, declassified in 1974.[27] This report provides details not only about the E-130R2, but also about other bomblets, cluster bombs, and missiles designed to carry biological and chemical warheads. The E-130R2 weighed 2.4 pounds (1.1 kg) and had a maximum diameter of 4.5 inches (11.4 cm). Its description is very close to that of the *Gshch*-304: the bomblet had an aluminum outer shell with six aerodynamic vanes on its surface. A spherically shaped burster charge was located in the center. The bomblet was constructed of two halves to facilitate assembly of the fuse and burster charge. A steel ring clamped the two halves together. After release from a cluster bomb, the vanes would perform two important functions. The passing air would cause the bomblet to rotate on its axis, which would arm the fuze after about 10 seconds, and the air passing over the vanes would deflect the bomblets' downward course from the vertical, spreading them over a wide area. Although the E-130R2 was designed to hold a nerve agent, it could easily be converted to carry a biological payload. It is therefore very possible that US expertise laid the basis for the Soviet *Gshch*-304 BW bomblet.

Although Yevstigneev has asserted that Soviet intelligence had procured an American biological bomblet, it is evident that as early as 1963 the US government began to make detailed technical information, including cut-away diagrams of biological and chemical bomblets, publicly available by declassifying reports from the pre-1969 US BW program. (Earlier versions of US bomblets were described as early as 1953 by a captured US pilot – see Chapter 4). The US Army and the report cited in the preceding paragraph could have been obtained by Soviet embassy personnel in Washington, D.C., as early as 1963 and February 1974, respectively. The second date coincides with the modern Soviet BW program in its earliest phase. It is very well known that a routine function of the Soviet Embassy in Washington was to obtain virtually every declassified US government report that it could. During the years that followed, especially in 1977 and 1979, a large number of additional reports deriving from the pre-1969 US BW program were declassified, including others that contained detailed engineering specifications and drawing of biological bombs and bomblets. Following the distribution of powdered *B. anthracis* spores via the US postal system in October/November 2001, an article in the *New York Times* pointed out the folly of this declassification process,[28] and the US government acted to reclassify many of these reports. However, nothing could be done about recalling reports that had been distributed relatively freely for more than 35 years.

The Soviet BW program apparently developed at least two spray systems for dispersing biological agents. One system, described by Alibek, involved "medium-range bombers like the Ilyushin-28 fitted with a two-ton capacity spray tank, with the capability to cover 3,000 to 4,000 square kilometers of territory using just one plane."[29] From sources other than Alibek we learned that the Soviets indeed had large airborne tanks for spraying, but because of their heavy weight and large size, they were rarely used in the testing program. Instead, a safer and simpler system had been designed and manufactured that was comprised of containers, each of which held 20 liters of formulation. Each container had a capped opening on top that kept the payload from spilling during transport, but that could be relatively easily opened. Before an open-air field test session, each container would be filled with formulation at a filling station and then 20 of them would be firmly fitted into a roof-less pod that was placed on a platform in an Antonov AN-24 twin-engine aircraft's bomb bay. Before reaching the target area, the caps would be removed from the containers, the aircraft would descend to an altitude suitable for low-level spraying, the platform carrying the pod would be low-

Table 10.3   Types of Soviet Biological Delivery Systems

- Aviation bombs with biological payloads. These were cluster munitions comprised of bomblets with biological payloads (e.g., 500 kg cluster bomb composed of 108 bomblets, each containing 0.493 kg of formulation; depending on formulation, each cluster bomb could cover 15–60 km²).

- Devices under development, cruise missiles with a special dissemination mechanism.

- Medium-range bombers carrying a spray system, such as the Ilyushin Il-28 (NATO reporting name "Beagle") with two hopper tanks, each carrying two tons of wet formulation, and equipped with spray devices (coverage 1,000–4,000 km², depending on payload).

ered, and the contents of the containers would be sucked out by the Venturi effect.[30] We don't know the name of this system. Other Soviet aircraft might have been equipped for spraying BW agents, but the AN-24 is the only one that was observed being used for spraying on Vozrozhdeniye Island. This aircraft's home base was an airport at Akhtubinsk, approximately 1,055 kilometers west of Vozrozhdeniye Island.

Neither our interviewees nor the open literature provide precise information on how many different types of biological weapons the Soviet Union possessed (see Table 10.3). Alibek has stated that nine agents were weaponized, but these appear to be solely for use against humans (see Table 10.1).[31] A memorandum written by Lev N. Zaikov, Secretary of the CPSU Central Committee on Defense Department, and addressed to Gorbachev, states: "By 1985 they [MOD and other Soviet agencies] had developed 12 recipes and means for using them."[32] Because these data came from a source just below the highest level of Soviet leadership, it can be assumed that the Soviet Union possessed 12 different biological weapons in 1985. Unfortunately, it does not inform us what kinds of "means," the delivery systems the Soviet Union possessed, nor about their biological payloads. Some of these weapons may have been for use against human populations, some against animals, and some against plants.

Soviet Concepts for Biological Weapons Use

The Soviet military defined categories of military operations in three theaters—tactical, operational, and strategic—and, at times, overlapping combinations of these. The Soviets did not envision using biological weapons for tactical purposes. The operational theater referred to the enemy's rear areas containing vital facilities such as harbors, airports, supply depots, and assembly areas. The use of a biological weapon in the operational sphere would primarily be to incapacitate the defenders of facilities that the attacker covets—airfields and supply depots in particular. According to Alibek, the BW agents designed for dispersal over a targeted operational area were *F. tularensis,* burkholderiae, and VEEV, all considered to be primarily incapacitating agents. Of these, *F. tularensis* and VEEV were validated first generation agents and were components of type-classified weapons.[33] As far as we are aware, no Marburg virus formulation was validated in the Soviet military system, nor did any biological weapon armed with Marburg virus reach the type-classified stage. Nevertheless, it is possible that by 1989–1990 plans for biological weapons with Marburg virus payloads were being made. Vector scientists had proven the feasibility of Marburg virus for weapons use, and it was probable that a type-classified weapon utilizing Marburg virus was close to being realized at the Zagorsk Institute.

Soviet conceptions for using biological weapons in the strategic theater appear to have been the primary reason for the post-1972 Soviet offensive BW program. The strategic theater mainly comprised population centers, military bases, vital industrial hubs, and major agricultural targets within the enemy homelands. In theory, the purpose of BW used in this circumstance would be to kill the remnants of populations that survived an earlier exchange of nuclear weapons. According to Alibek, the Soviets chose variola virus and *Y. pestis* for that purpose; pathogens that were both deadly and contagious, as well as *B. anthracis.* These pathogens had already been validated in the 1950s, though with different strains, and were used in type-classified weapons.

The intentions of the Politburo with regard to the possible utilization of strategic biological weapons are not known. It is known that in 1984 a subsection of the Interagency Council (MNTS) held discussions concerning the different possible uses of BW by the Soviet Union,[34] but we do not know of its conclusions. Despite having little concrete knowledge on this subject, each of the Soviet BW scientists we interviewed had an opinion on the subject. The opinions regarding the strategic employment of biological weapons fall into three groups. One group believed BW was to be directed at NATO countries, with a focus on the United States, while the second group insisted that China was to be the main BW target. Both groups, however, posited a major role for variola virus. There was also an oft-stated opinion that biological weapons were never going to be used.

As is made clear in Chapter 8, we are certain that variola virus was weaponized well before 1971 and that it was a component of at least one type-classified weapon at that time. After 1977, when the world was declared free of naturally occurring smallpox by the World Health Organization (WHO) and governments everywhere decided to stop vaccinating their populations against smallpox, the Soviet BW program increased emphasis on developing variola virus for strategic purposes. As a result, with the exception of small, special populations that continued to receive smallpox vaccinations (such as soldiers and smallpox researchers), the world's population after a few years became susceptible to infection by variola virus, with a likelihood of suffering 30% or higher mortality should the disease reappear. By having weaponized variola virus on hand, the Soviet Union was the sole possessor of stocks of this particularly lethal biological weapons agent.

Speaking in his single BBC television interview in 1993, and most likely having aerosolized *Y. pestis* in mind, Pasechnik said:

> If you take, for example, a city with a population, say of 100,000 people, then I would say that it is very possible that in a short time, say a week time, the preparations will be prepared to apply the whole city, with effect that about half of its population will be killed.
>
> If there may be subversive activity in the city much less quantity would be required for that. Because it may be produced very easily and then applied in such a way that it would be very difficult to discover who applied it. User would deny it. That has been discussed in Biopreparat.[35]

In the same year a Russian Foreign Intelligence Service Report, the only one of its kind, offered two scenarios for biological weapons use that it said had resulted from "special studies done by its analysts:" "the likelihood that biological weapons will be used by Third World countries in local military conflicts, as well as for subversive and terrorist purposes" and providing "the opportunity to cause serious damage to an enemy's economy through covert use of biological weapons against plants and livestock in his agriculture. Nor can these actions be ruled out in peacetime for purposes of 'economic warfare.' "[36] UK intelligence officials took the last as a sign that the Soviet military had planned for the covert use of BW prior to 1992. This may have been a possible adjunct, but it could scarcely account for the huge volume of BW agents that the Soviet Union planned to produce. It is more likely that the suggestion of covert use was an adaptation for public consumption of the ideas proposed by US General J. H. Rothschild in 1964.[37]

Strategic Biological Weapons Use against the United States

The underlying belief of those who held this opinion was that strategic biological weapons were intended for use following one or more nuclear missile exchanges between the United States and the Soviet Union. As a final step the Soviet Union would have dispatched variola virus–armed ICBMs to initiate a smallpox epidemic among the nuclear holocaust survivors in North America. In a published interview, Alibek qualified the contention that the Soviet Union intended to use strategic BW only after a nuclear exchange. "No, nothing like that. It was considered a strategic weapon that could be used together with nuclear weapons. Some targets would be struck by nuclear weapons, some by biological weapons, and some by both together."[38]

Soviet decision makers, or their advisers, might have been aware of the results of a study published in the United States in 1981 concerning the medical problems that survivors would face after all-out nuclear warfare.[39] The model its authors used for the nuclear war was developed by the Federal Emergency Management Agency.[40] It envisioned the United States having received a 6,559-megaton attack. As a result, 86 million Americans would have died immediately (40% of the estimated population of 216 million in 1975), 34 million of the survivors would be severely injured, and approximately 60 million Americans would survive without serious injury and with limited radiation exposure. An additional 50 million would die from injuries and radiation exposure during the weeks after the attack, producing a total of 136 million deaths. Approximately 80 million Americans would have survived for some weeks after the envisioned nuclear war, although 20 million of them would have suffered moderate to high radiation doses and therefore have limited survivability. The authors' main conclusions as to the nature of the challenges that survivors would face were: "Several factors point to an increased risk of serious infection and communicable disease in the post-attack environment. These include the effects on susceptibility of irradiation, malnutrition, and exposure; the effects on disease transmittal of unsanitary conditions, lengthy stays in shelters, and the growth of insect populations; and the effects on attempted countermeasures of depleted antibiotic stocks, shortages of physicians, the destruction of laboratories, and the general disorganization sure to follow an attack."[41] The awful plight that the survivors would be in would be made substantially worse were they to be the targets for Soviet ICBMs carrying BW payloads.

The United States had stopped vaccinating its civilian population against smallpox in 1972.[42] If the attack postulated in these conceptions took place in the middle 1980s or afterward, a large proportion of the US population would never have been vaccinated against smallpox and another unknown proportion would have been vaccinated a long time before so its protective immunity level would range from low to very low. For reasons stated above, the surviving population would be more susceptible to infectious diseases than had been the case in "normal" times. With the destruction of the industrial infrastructure, no smallpox vaccine would be available.[43] We know that scientists working at Vector during 1984–1985 sought methods to protect variola virus from nuclear radiation. The research task order noted that stabilizing additives were necessary for the effective utilization of biological weapons under high levels of radiation—for example, after use of nuclear weapons. We also know that research tasked to some of the Soviet Union's WTO allies focused on protecting bacteria against the effects of radiation.

There is one major problem confronting all these conceptions. As the pages that follow indicate, we do not believe that the Soviet Union ever possessed an ICBM BW delivery capability, although there was apparently an R&D effort to produce components that would fit such a system. This is discussed in detail below.

Biological Weapons Use against China

Some of the Soviet scientists we interviewed held that Soviet strategic biological weapons were not likely to be used against NATO but were to be turned eastward. In their view, the huge population advantage held by China would have made it necessary for the Soviet Union to use not only nuclear weapons against the Chinese in case of war, but also biological weapons. However, the comments of these Soviet scientists were purely speculative. Because no ocean separates the two countries, such theories would require the Soviet Union to have avoided the use of a contagious pathogen, such as variola virus, to attack a Chinese population. Instead a pathogen such as Marburg virus, which is highly virulent with a case fatality rate over 80% and without any preventive or specific treatment, would have been employed.

Relations between the Soviet Union and China did not deteriorate to the point of border skirmishes between armed units until 1967 on the Russian-

Chinese border of Xinjiang Province. These were followed by the Damansky or Zhēnbǎo Island incidents on the Ussuri River border in March 1969, and returned to much more serious clashes on the Xīnjiāng border in June–August 1969. Clearly the Soviet BW program was initiated decades before then, and if there was a specific national target for the program in the earlier years, it would not have been China. In addition, if the suggestion that the post-1972 Soviet BW program's existence was due to the presumed Soviet belief that the United States had not relinquished its own BW program is to be taken seriously, and which all of our Russian sources unequivocally maintained, then the United States would have been the logical focus of the Soviet program.

The Belief That Biological Weapons Would Not be Used

One last point should be noted. Several of the former Soviet scientists who were interviewed maintained that BW would never be used, even though they were involved in unequivocally offensive work. One example was a Soviet scientist who maintained that at the very time that he and his colleagues were working on weaponizing BW agents, they were all certain that they never would be used. Attempting to probe the logic of this claim with the scientists only produced contradictory responses. Often the same individuals also maintained the belief that the Soviet offensive BW program was a response to a similar effort taking place in the United States. Whether they believed they were producing a deterrent for the Soviet Union, or whether this position was primarily a self-deception enabling them to continue their work without having to deal with moral dilemmas, we cannot say, and of course our population of former Soviet BW scientist interviewees was relatively small, even though it reached double digits.

All the foregoing discussion regarding Soviet intentions for BW use is extremely thin in contrast to the information available regarding Soviet nuclear weapon doctrine and planning. However, there is little or no reliable information to go by. The use of biological weapons was prohibited under the 1925 Geneva Protocol, and most other BW-related activities were prohibited by the 1972 Biological Weapons Convention. In contrast, nuclear weapons have never been prohibited in any way. It is preferable not to speculate about Soviet biological weapons doctrine beyond the minimal information provided by sources that we have interviewed and what can be deduced from preparations for agent production as well as the availability – or non-availability – of delivery systems.

The Question of a Soviet BW ICBM Capability

Alibek's book on the Soviet BW program opens with several strikingly vivid pages. He describes being called to the MOD in the late winter of 1988 by Major General Lebedinsky, the head of the 15th Directorate. He met with three colonels identified as working in "the Biological Group, a unit of the General Staff Operations Directorate, whose role was to arm bombers and missiles with the weapons we [Biopreparat] produced."[44] Lebedinsky told him that "A decision had been made at the highest levels . . . to arm SS-18 missiles with disease agents." Alibek was asked by the colonels to supply an estimate of how much weaponized dry powder *B. anthracis* spores would be needed to fill 10 multiple independently targetable reentry vehicles (MIRVs) warheads on an SS-18 and how long it would take for that amount to be produced once an order to do so was given. Alibek offered an estimate of 400 kilograms and a preparation time of roughly two weeks. There is no mention of how Alibek might have arrived at the 400-kilogram estimate, nor why a preparation time was necessary if 100 tons of *B. anthracis* stockpile was being maintained. There is also no indication that a dispersal mechanism already existed for the type of MIRV warhead carried by the SS-18. Alibek mentions New York, Chicago, Los Angeles, and Seattle as cities that "were some of the targets to come up in subsequent meetings." In passing, Alibek also mentioned that SS-18 missiles "had never been considered before as delivery vehicles for biological attack."[45] This would imply that the SS-18 MIRV warheads had never before been tested for delivery of BW.

In a personal interview in August 1988, Alibek was asked to comment on a few lines in a Russian publication a few months earlier, which read: "It is paradoxical, but a fact, that our troops in the Arctic were armed with biological weapons. Warheads containing biological agents were mounted on mobile units, all but drifting on the ice floes. It is understood where the missiles with anthrax and tularemia were targeted: at the US."[46] Notably, SS-18 ICBMs were not mobile. The locations of their silos were in large part known, and they most certainly were not drifting on ice floes. No Soviet ICBM was. Alibek replied that there had been discussions in the 1960s, 1970s, and 1980s about using missiles to deliver biological agents. He repeated that there was a decision in 1988–1989 to use MIRVs for BW, and said that there had been BW ballistic missile tests within the Soviet Union, the target impact zone being on Kamchatka.[47] However, he did not identify the missile. In an interview published in 2001 Alibek expanded on these remarks, moving well beyond "discussions". Alibek was quoted saying:

> During the late 1960s and early 1970s, the Strategic Rocket Forces deployed single warheads containing bomblets filled with variola virus on SS-11, SS-13 and SS-17 intercontinental ballistic missiles, which were based in silos near the Arctic Circle on a launch-ready status. The cold temperatures in the far north kept the smallpox agent viable for long periods. Soviet engineers also developed special refrigerated warheads to enable the biological payload to survive the intense heat of reentry through the atmosphere. Each warhead contained an internal cooling system that, when combined with thermal shielding and the spinning of the reentry vehicle, kept the temperature inside the warhead well below the boiling point. Toward the end of its ballistic trajectory, the smallpox warhead would deploy a parachute that slowed its velocity. At the appropriate altitude, the warhead would break open, releasing its payload of bomblets to disperse a deadly cloud of aerosolized virus over the target area.[48]

With Alibek identified as the source for the third time, additional information was provided in the 1999 book by Tom Mangold and Jeff Goldberg: "Several SS-18s with a range of 10,000 km were dedicated to the BW programme."[49] A single SS-18 ICBM could carry up to 10 MIRV warheads, implying that perhaps 30 or 40 warheads might be involved.[50] "These BW warheads were to be hurriedly assembled and loaded at Biopreparat's production plants only during a 'special period' of preparedness and mobilization that the Kremlin would declare during heightened world tension just before an imminent war." No such situation was ever declared. Mangold and Goldberg claim that Soviet missile specialists had already "addressed all the(se) problems" associated with the reentry of an ICBM warhead containing BW agents "starting in the late 1960s. . . . The warhead's reentry from space to the target was handled just like an astronaut's return to earth. The BW rockets were fitted with the same special cooling and protective systems that kept the astronauts from being 'cooked' when they splashed down. Simple." They then state that the warhead would disperse its agents by an "explosion," which had been "thoroughly tested and secretly tested" using simulants.[51]

Mangold and Goldberg write, "There were two possible scenarios during which the Soviet Union planned to use ICBMs carrying BW warheads. The decision to launch would be based on the circumstances and the type of war that broke out: 1. If 'total war' started, but both sides decided to use only conventional weapons, and not nuclear missiles, and then the opponent used BW first against the Soviet Union, the Soviets would counter with BW. The Soviet Union would not use nuclear missiles first in that circumstance, because they understood that this step meant Mutual Assured Destruction (MAD). 2. If a total war started, and all possible weapons of mass destruction were used, including nuclear missiles, then BW would be used as part of the overall arsenal." Mangold and Goldberg do not indicate what or who their source is for the above description. In both scenarios that they describe, the Soviet Union does not appear to be the initiator of BW use. However, neither the United States nor the United Kingdom had any BW to use from 1971 on.[52]

The colorful incident described by Alibek in the opening pages of his book carries an enormous burden of significance. The plausibility of Alibek's claim that the Soviet Union intended its biological weapons for strategic use against the continental United States may depend on it. Some explanation is required for the astonishingly large tonnages Alibek reports for the production quotas assigned to the 10 or so Soviet BW mobilization capacity production facilities in a period of national emergency when the Soviet Union thought a war was imminent. Alibek provided estimates in metric tons of amounts of BW agents produced at each of 10 facilities in production cycles of between 200 days and one year (see Table 10.2). Alibek also reported Soviet BW weapons as having been stored in several locations: "anthrax" weapons at "Railroad Station Zima," in the Irkutsk region, and "BW warheads, bombs, and bomblets" at "Reutov, Moscow region."[53] In interviews Alibek has also described Soviet BW munitions being stored at bomber bases. Alibek is the sole source for all these critically important components of the Soviet BW story: the mobilization capacity production tonnages, the suggestion of the completed development of a Soviet SS-18 ICBM capability for BW delivery, and the suggested storage locations for Soviet BW munitions. There is no other public corroboration for any of these elements.

In his own book, Alibek refers to an "Air Force base . . . Volga River region," reportedly at Kuburka.[54] In the Mangold/Goldberg book, this is elaborated into "a small fleet of about twenty specially equipped planes, based in the Volga region."[55] These were Ilyushin-28 ("Beagle") medium-range bombers fitted with a spray tank delivery system reportedly capable of carrying two tons of agent, and "For long-range attacks in Europe and America with biological weapons, the Soviet Union's primary strategic bomber was the Tu-95." Elsewhere Alibek has indicated that each IL-28 aircraft would carry two such spray tanks.[56] The Tupolev-95 was a slow-flying four-engine turbo-prop long-range bomber (NATO reference as "Bear"). Mangold and Gold-berg are presumably suggesting that the TU-95 payload was to have been cluster bomb munitions carrying multiple BW bomblets. Both the IL-28 and the Tu-95 were quite old aircraft, and no other Soviet aircraft has been identified as being intended for BW delivery.[57] There is one bit of evidence suggesting that at least part of the US IC may have attributed such a mission to the TU-160 "Blackjack" bomber, presumably because it was the most ca-pable Soviet aircraft able to reach the United States.[58] In contrast, there is clear interview testimony for the Antonov AN-24 aircraft as a BW test bed, but its flight radius would not have enabled it to reach targets beyond Europe or China. Given the targeting set and priority ordering of the US nuclear war plan, the Single Integrated Operational Plan (SIOP) in its successive it-erations since the early 1960s, Soviet ICBMs were the primary US targets, but every Soviet military airfield or location of Soviet long-range bombers would have been obliterated by US nuclear warheads in the very earliest stage of any US-USSR nuclear exchange. Nevertheless the question of Soviet BW delivery by ICBM is of major significance to any conception of what the Soviet BW program was intended for.

The US IC apparently does not believe that any Soviet SS-18 ICBM war-heads were ever deployed with a biological payload. Former CIA officials note that Alibek did not include the foregoing information regarding the SS-18 in his lengthy debriefings with them.[59] The US IC also discounted its likelihood on strategic grounds, that is, on their estimation of Soviet targeting priorities for its SS-18 ICBMs. The unclassified table of contents of the one report that Alibek wrote for the US IC does not contain any mention of delivery systems of any sort, including ICBMs.[60] In interviews in 1998, Alibek's knowledge of Soviet ICBMs appeared to be very limited.

Vitaly Kataev was skeptical also. Kataev was a senior ICBM and SLBM missile designer in Yangel's Yuzhnoe Design Bureau in Dnepropetrovsk, where the SS-18 was designed. During a period of intense design activity for the SS-18 in the early 1970s, Yangel's Yuzhnoe Design Bureau received a query as to whether they could design a non-nuclear warhead. They replied "no" on technical grounds: the warhead would be much lighter and the op-erational characteristics of the ICBM would change.[61] Hundreds of people involved in the design of the missile's systems and in planning its flight trajectory would understand the change. In addition, he knew of no tests of such a warhead. The Design Bureau also replied to the query on policy grounds: it should not be done because of "rules of type." US ballistic missile detection systems would register the incoming ICBMs and they would be assumed to be nuclear, with the result that the Soviet Union would be subject to a return nuclear strike. And again, it could not have been done without the Central Committee of the CPSU having been informed and giving its approval. Kataev gave the example of Central Committee secretary and Defense Council member Marshall Dmitry Ustinov's response in 1974 when Kataev suggested that a particular missile should use solid fuel rather than liquid fuel as a propellant. Ustinov refused to make a decision on the proposal until he had obtained special permission from the Central Committee to do so.

Kataev's comments are to be understood with the caveat that until 1990 Kataev's two colleagues on the Central Committee staff, Shakhov and Shakhov's assistant, Alexander S. Ivanov, held the primary responsibility for any BW-relevant subject, and not he (see Chapter 21). However, and most important of all, Kataev's responsibilities on the Central Committee staff covered all ICBM and SLBM issues including their warheads. Moreover, Kataev's responsibilities also included oversight for all arms control negotiations, including the BWC. He also traveled with the technical support group involved in the START negotiations. As a result, at one point an issue that required his attention was the half-life of nuclear warheads, and he recalled the query that had come to him when he was still working on the SS-18 ICBM design. By chance, he asked Shakhov and Ivanov whether it was possible to put a biological warhead on a missile. They replied, "Who told you that we do that? You can't because it's a living organism." As for the conception of BW delivery in a post-thermonuclear attack situation, something that he had never heard of until the question was put to him during the interview, he thought that "it was just crazy." That, of course, is not conclusive evidence that it may not have been conceived of or planned for.

There is a final reason to be skeptical that BW delivery would have been planned for the SS-18 ICBM MIRVs. All studies of BW delivery by ICBM have presumed that a BW missile warhead must be blunt-headed—shaped like the bottom of a light bulb—producing substantial drag and a relatively slow atmospheric reentry speed. For example, concept studies were reportedly made in the United States around 1961–1962 for BW delivery by the blunt warhead of the Polaris A-1 SLBM. Such warheads have what is referred to as a "low-beta," shallow angle of atmospheric reentry, and their terminal accuracy is relatively poor. In contrast, the shape of the MIRV warheads in an SS-18 are sharply pointed, like an ice cream cone, and these have a "high-beta," steep reentry angle and high-velocity reentry. We will see that precisely these considerations were directly applied to the question of possible Soviet development of an ICBM for BW delivery several decades ago. One should also note that both the SS-11 and the SS-18 ICBMs were silo-based; neither were "mobile units" as described in the apparently spurious 1998 Russian publication quoted earlier.

There were, however, several occasions in which Western sources reported the Soviet testing of a possible reentry vehicle or warhead that might be designed for BW delivery. In December 1979, James Miller, head of the ballistic missile systems branch of the US Defense Intelligence Agency (DIA), testified to the R&D Subcommittee of the House Armed Services Committee in a closed-door hearing. He described the testing program of the "Mod-4" of the Soviet SS-11 single warhead ICBM at the Sary Shagan test site in the Kazakh SSR between 1974 and 1979.[62] The SS-11 Mod-4 could carry three or six multiple reentry vehicles, or MRVs, in distinction to MIRVs, which are independently guided reentry vehicles. Miller described these MRVs as "very small, very light, and they came in very slow." The DIA analysts decided by inference, "About the only thing that we could see that really answered all of the criteria that we saw in this weapon . . . numerous RVs and a very slow reentry, very slow impact—was a BW/CW [biological warfare/chemical warfare weapon]." This inference, however, could not distinguish whether the warheads might be intended for a chemical or a biological warhead, or whether they were meant to serve for both. Miller also pointed out that no test of the system had ever been carried out by the Soviet Union over its Pacific test range, which was usually the case for operational Soviet ICBM systems, and that "it never went beyond the R&D phase." It should also be noted that the Sary Shagan test site was customarily used by the Soviet Union for its antiballistic missile development and testing, and one wonders if the tests in question were not being made to test decoys for ICBM warheads. This alternative is so obvious that it is difficult to imagine that it was not taken into account by the DIA analysts.

Two years later, an unclassified US study prepared in 1981 titled "Biological Agent Delivery by ICBM" examined "the potential of Soviet ICBM delivery of BW agents."[63] All of the Soviet ICBMs that the study considered were missiles containing either a single low-beta warhead, or MRVs, similar blunt-headed multiple warheads, but no ICBM armed with MIRVs such as the SS-18 carried. The list included the SS-9, SS-9 Mod I, SS-9 Mod III/IV, and the SS-11 Mod IV. The report was almost certainly prompted by the same events described in the unclassified 1979 DIA testimony to the congressional committee. The report was a modeling study of a "potential" rather than an existing capability. Very little of the report had been excised, and the only comment it offered in terms of actual Soviet capabilities was that "development of a dispensing mechanism with the required characteristics was assumed to be within the capability of Soviet technology and no attempt was made to define the intricacies of these systems." The report made no suggestion that any such Soviet ICBM system had been deployed. When interviewed in 1998, Alibek did not know about the earlier Soviet SS-11 Mod IV tests, and was surprised to hear them mentioned. Nor did he know the US or Soviet designations for these missiles.

Confusion on this subject was further compounded in 1984 by two CIA leaks. One journalist was told that "the Russians have tailored one of their strategic rockets for delivering chemical or biological weapons to America. It is the Mod 4 variant of the SS-11 'Sego' inter-continental ballistic missile with three to six re-entry warheads."[64] The second was a brief mention that the CIA had detected a tumbling warhead in a Soviet missile test. The missile was not identified in this report, but it was noted that the tumbling suggested the warhead was intended for delivering chemical agents.[65] It was impossible from these reports to tell if the two leaks concerned information regarding a newly observed Soviet ICBM test in the early 1980s, or, because the SS-11 was identified in the first of the two reports, whether it was simply a repeat of the 1979 information. If the latter was the case, which seems most likely, the new report not only discredited the claim of CW or BW delivery made in 1984, it would also serve to discredit the 1979 reports. A tumbling warhead in an ICBM test is not an indicator that the warhead is designed for delivery of either chemical or biological agents. An incoming ICBM warhead can tumble for a variety of reasons—for example, if it was not released properly from its terminal stage, if it did not separate at all from its terminal stage, or if it became unstable after release. In addition, as best as is known, there never was a version of the SS-11 with more than three warheads.

The second group of events allegedly took place just about a decade later, and again involved the Soviet SS-11 ICBM. According to the Mangold and Goldberg book, US intelligence analysts in November 1987 "were poring over routine radar printouts and satellite pictures of Soviet missiles launched from their Kamchatka test range in Eastern Siberia. . . . There were clear flight anomalies which needed urgent explanation."[66] After six months of analysis, it was decided that the "series of test firings" had been of SS-11 Mod-4 ICBMs, and "the US intelligence community initiated high-priority surveillance of all known sites in the USSR where those strategic missiles were assembled and deployed. . . . Finally, in October 1988, the small dedicated intelligence team made the breakthrough. . . . US satellite photos showed that the Soviets had attached large units with tubes and hoses that were connected to the missile warheads in storage silos and at the launch sites. These strange units had never been seen before in this configuration with warheads."[67]

Mangold and Goldberg claim that thermal analysis by multispectral satellite photographs allegedly then showed "that the unidentified units were refrigerators." The implication was that the SS-11 warheads were being kept cool because they contained "bacteria or viruses. . . . The chief arms control analyst at the CIA, Douglas MacEachin, immediately delivered the information to the National Security Council's senior advisory group."[68]

There are several major problems with this account. First, there was no Soviet ICBM launching site on the Kamchatka Peninsula. There was an ICBM target (landing) zone called the Kura test site.[69] Second, Douglas MacEachin never gave any such briefing to a National Security Council meeting, nor did he hold the position given until months after the period indicated.[70] Third, the account explicitly excludes the SS-18 as being involved, but once again, the older SS-11, with a warhead that is shaped very differently from that of a SS-18. Fourth, it is very questionable whether satellite resolution capability in 1987 was able to show "tubes and hoses . . . connected to warheads," or, if such existed, that these would not have been simply covered with tarpaulins to prevent detection of such a development by US satellite reconnaissance. Fifth, the description of the ICBM missiles being kept in readiness to be loaded with live BW agents in 1987–1988—particularly following the first arms control breakthroughs of the Gorbachev administration—violates the doctrinal suggestion that such an event would occur only in the case in which the Soviet leadership anticipated the outbreak of war. Alibek reportedly testified that no such order had ever been given. An exception would be in the case of another round of tests that might carry a live bacterial or viral simulant, but no further test series with accompanying anomalies is mentioned after the initial round described as taking place in November 1987. Finally, Pavel Podvig, the editor of *Russian Strategic Nuclear Forces,* noted that by 1987 the SS-11 was a very old missile, and that it would be surprising if it would be assigned to carry an experimental warhead. In addition, he knew of no reports of Soviet development of a refrigerated ICBM warhead.[71]

Mangold and Goldberg go on to claim, "The Soviets knew their biological warfare programme would work because they had thoroughly and secretly tested their rockets and warheads, using bio-simulants. These tests had taken place over the Atlantic and Pacific Oceans during a period of many years—and the Western intelligence services had missed their significance. Using anthrax, the tests showed that nearly 100 per cent of the payload would survive. With most of the other pathogens, some 10–30 per cent would survive."[72]

The foregoing description is not credible. No Soviet missile test is known to have taken place over the Atlantic Ocean. Every Soviet ICBM test was monitored by multiple US detection and tracking systems, particularly after the advent of the US satellite-borne telemetry intelligence capability in 1970. As indicated, the 1974 to 1979 SS-11 test series was duly monitored by the United States and its warhead reentry characteristics analyzed. It did not take place over either the Atlantic or the Pacific Ocean. One line in the quote above refers to missile testing with simulants, but other lines refer to "using anthrax" and "other pathogens," and the percentage of the organisms that survived warhead reentry.[73] This would have required recovery of the warheads and subsequent laboratory testing to ascertain the extent of survival of pathogens or simulant they carried. Warhead recovery by ships at sea is even easier to monitor, and both the United States and the Soviet Union maintained dedicated naval vessels at sea that constantly monitored each other's missile tests. It is inconceivable that such repeated tests by the Soviet Union would have gone undetected by the United States.[74]

Mangold and Goldberg go on to introduce additional references to Soviet BW-bearing ICBMs in their following chapter, which concerns Vladimir Pasechnik. One of Pasechnik's British debriefers, Christopher Davis, is apparently referred to as the source for suggesting that "top Soviet rocket scientists" worked at and solved all the requisite technical problems "starting in the late 1960s."[75] Kataev, a senior designer associated with these ICBMs in those years, flatly rejected that contention. In an interview, Davis said that Pasechnik had referred to "cassettes" containing BW agents that could fit into ICBM warheads.[76] In our own interviews with Pasechnik, he made no reference to the Soviet ICBM delivery of BW agents by SS-18s, or by any other ICBM.[77] Pasechnik claimed that as of his leaving the Soviet Union in October 1989, he knew of no Soviet strategic doctrine for BW use. He stated that he had only heard discussions of covert use, but this contradicts his own claims of work on a *cruise missile* delivery system described directly below, as well as his development of a *Y. pestis* BW program that, in his own description, could kill 50,000 people in a large urban center.

Pasechnik described his own role and that of his institute (IHPB) in development of a strategic cruise missile system for delivery of BW agents. He said that work on the system began early in 1988: "Everything came through 'the orders': the definition of the problem, and what to do in the research program. Their job was to model the process of dissemination from the moving cruise missile." He gave no indication of any earlier work having been carried out on such a program. He stated that the system was still under development when he left the Soviet Union in October 1989, and that an intense period of continued development was scheduled for 1990 and 1991.[78] The system was planned to accommodate both wet and dry BW formulations. As a cruise missile, it was to have been an online dispersal system capable of releasing its payload over multiple sites along a planned flight route. Pasechnik wondered if the proposal for a cruise missile system for BW delivery might not have been one response to the Reagan administration's "Star Wars" ballistic missile defense program, but he had no specific indication to suggest that.[79] It is impossible to know whether this comment by Pasechnik in 1999 was solely a reflection of things that he had read in the Western press after 1990, when he was living in the United Kingdom. (Postulates of Soviet BW responses to the US Star Wars program are discussed further in Chapter 21.)

There is something very puzzling about the Soviet development of a cruise missile BW delivery system at the time indicated. In December 1987, the Soviet Union signed the INF Treaty with the United States, which banned cruise missiles in the range between 500 and 5,500 kilometers—in other words, those that might have been targeted on Europe. However, long before that, in June 1979, the Soviet Union had signed the SALT 2 Treaty that addressed the issue of Air Launched Cruise Missiles (ALCM), which applied counting rules for Strategic Nuclear Delivery Vehicles (SNDV). Any bomber armed with cruise missiles over 600 kilometers in range had to have observable differences from ones not so armed, and would be counted as a MIRVed SNDV. If the Soviet Union had intended to deploy an ALCM with a BW warhead, it would therefore have reduced the number of MIRVed intercontinental ballistic missiles with nuclear warheads—or cruise missiles with nuclear warheads—that it could deploy. It might be considered very surprising that the Soviet military would have thought it relevant to develop a cruise missile BW delivery system at all in 1989, but if one recalls that in the same year the 15th Directorate was also hoping to see the construction of a cell-culture-based variola virus production facility at Vector, the surprise is placed in context. Whatever may have been in the minds of the Soviet General Staff and the 15th Directorate as to the circumstances under which they thought that they might use a BW cruise missile delivery system, they obviously were not concerned that someone would be bringing up the subject of a violation of the INF or SALT 2 treaties afterward.

At least one portion of the overall Soviet BW delivery system seems reasonably clear, and that is the production of automatic bomblet filling machines. This was one of the responsibilities of several of the Biopreparat facilities, overseen by the technology department at Biopreparat headquarters, headed by Vladimir Dorogov. The filling machines were produced at several of the Biopreparat facilities that also designed and manufactured other production equipment for the BW program. The largest of these was the plant at Yoshkar-Ola, a branch of *Biokimmashproekt* and the Institute for Biological Instrument Design in Moscow (which had been directed by Lieutenant General Kalinin before he became the head of Biopreparat). Pasechnik described seeing the prototype of a filling line while on a visit to Yoshkar-Ola with a Biopreparat inspection team in 1983. At that time, its development was not yet completed.[80] Some of the Central Committee documents that we have obtained and that are described in Chapter 21 discuss the removal of filling lines from facilities in the period between 1989 and 1991.

In a paper published in 1999, Davis reported additional information for which Pasechnik was very likely the source. He wrote that additional "technical targets" in the late years of the Soviet BW program included "miniaturized production facilities, (and) mobile production and filling facilities," and that the Soviet Union "was able to envisage the achievement" of such a capability.[81] Pasechnik claimed that Gorbachev had approved an order for the development of these two systems in 1987.[82] However, events between 1989 and 1992 that were triggered by Pasechnik's own defection to the United Kingdom curtailed major portions of the Soviet offensive BW program, which presumably meant that these systems were never developed.

We do, however, know of a development program at the Zagorsk Institute dating from 1974 and 1975 that was aimed at producing the components for an ICBM BW delivery system. The account that we were able to obtain confirms Pasechnik's reference to "cassettes," but undercuts entirely Alibek's ICBM claims, as well as all the accounts enumerated in the previous pages, such as those by Mangold and Goldberg, that derive from it.

The development effort focused on a "thermal container," a rectangular coffin-shaped box in which 192 *Gshch*-304 bomblets were reportedly stacked. A number of these units were to be contained in an individual warhead. The "thermal container" was intended to protect the pathogen in the bomblets from heat during warhead reentry, and there was no mention that it was refrigerated or had any additional cooling mechanism. The survival time for agents to be carried by the bomblet was tested at the Zagorsk Institute. The tests at Zagorsk required that the agents loaded into the bomblet remain viable for three days. So short a period of time would imply that ICBMs were not kept at readiness for BW delivery and would not be expected to be kept in that condition. Given that this work was taking place at the Zagorsk Institute, the pathogen would have been a virus, most likely variola virus. It cannot be excluded, however, that parallel development work might have been taking place at the Kirov Institute in roughly the same time period or later, but with a bacterial pathogen. One Russian source mentioned that Alibek did bring up the idea of a biological warhead for an ICBM to the 15th Directorate in the expectation that this was something new, but was told that its scientists were already working on it. However, development of the bomblets delivered by ICBM was never completed, and other problems with the project were also apparently never resolved. Therefore, no SS-18 ICBM bomblet delivery system was ever completed, none was ever tested, and obviously none could ever have been deployed.

As best as could be ascertained in interviews with Russian researchers, there was no short-range Soviet BW missile, which would mean that there was no Soviet BW missile at all in any range category. The Soviet Union did have a short-range ballistic missile, the SCUD-B with a 180-mile range, mounted with a bulk CW agent warhead. Soviet authorities displayed it to international observers at the Shikhany chemical weapons test site in 1987.[83] However, CW experts believe that the same missile also existed with a multiple CW munition warhead, although there is no published evidence to corroborate this. If this were the case, the same missile could in theory also have been used to disperse a multiple BW munition such as the bomblet described above, but we have no information that such a development occurred.

It is useful to provide a few general comments about delivery of biological or chemical agents by US tactical or strategic ballistic missiles and cruise missiles. Very rough calculations which never led to engineering efforts were made for a long list of missiles, both ballistic and cruise, short- and long-range. In a smaller number of cases development efforts for "CB bomblet" delivery did take place, but in almost every instance these were intended for delivery of chemical agents. Only one of these, the Sergeant missile, with an operational range of 27–84 miles (43–135 km), carried a warhead that was type-classified for BW agent delivery. This meant that Sergeant missiles carrying M-134 spherical biological bomblets underwent extensive field testing with simulants. However, despite achieving type-classification, the Sergeant missile with a BW warhead was never approved for production, and was therefore obviously not deployed.[84]

The United States also developed chemical and biological spray systems to be carried by a remotely controlled drone with a radius of 185 kilometers, far shorter than intercontinental range.[85] The advantage of using the cruise missile BW dispersion system in comparison to BW delivered by a ballistic missile, most particularly an ICBM, is to circumvent the technical difficulties of ensuring that the BW agent survives and is disseminated at the correct altitude.

There are considerable technical difficulties with packaging BW agents within a supersonic ballistic missile warhead and ensuring that they survive and are disseminated as an aerosol at the correct altitude. The reentry speed is so high during the descent phase of a ballistic missile's trajectory that it is difficult to distribute the agent in a diffuse cloud or with the precision to ensure dissemination within the inversion layer of the atmosphere. Also, the high thermal and mechanical stresses generated during launch, reentry, and agent release may damage the BW agents it carries. US tests have shown that, without appropriate agent packaging, less than 5% of a BW agent payload is viable after flight and dissemination from a ballistic missile.[86] Calculations reportedly also show that area coverage of a given quantity of chemical or biological weapon agent is a full order of magnitude larger if delivered by a cruise missile in comparison to delivery by ballistic missile.[87]

Writing the last portion of this chapter has presented particular problems. The answers to the unresolved issues of the purposes for which the Soviet Union's biological weapons were intended, and the related question of an ICBM delivery capability, are of course located in the files of the former MOD's 15th Directorate in Moscow, assuming that they have not been destroyed. If the Soviet military entertained conceptions for the strategic use of biological weapons in wars against the United States or China, no matter how rudimentary or provisional these plans may have been, these too presumably still reside in the RF-MOD's archives. But they are not available to historians, the arms control community, and researchers. Perhaps more information, hopefully accurate information, is also sitting in the files of several Western intelligence agencies, the United Kingdom and United States in particular, but if so that too is presently unavailable. The sources that are available are extremely limited, a snippet here and a snippet there, and it has turned out that much of what little there was of apparent relevance is inaccurate and highly unreliable. In particular, the claims made by Alibek, which afterward were repeated in innumerable publications, that a Soviet SS-18 ICBM BW warhead capability existed appears to be inaccurate. If Soviet military planners thought of using the tons of biological agents that they planned to produce in mobilization capacity facilities, what was the system that was going to deliver them to targets in the United States? The evidence is not sufficient to support any conclusions beyond the fact that the range of Soviet bombers and strike aircraft made it possible to reach both Western Europe and China. We have not been able to resolve definitively some of the most important questions, but have attempted to evaluate the information that is available.

11

Distinguishing between Offensive and Defensive Biological Warfare Activities

A HISTORY OF THE NEGOTIATIONS that resulted in the BWC is provided in Chapter 20. Significant modifications were made during the negotiations to the draft treaty initially tabled by the United Kingdom. Most particularly, a ban on BW research in the British draft treaty was deleted during the final US-Soviet negotiations. In addition, the BWC contained no on-site verification mechanisms to deter or to safeguard against treaty violation. After some years, states' parties to the treaty adopted a set of Confidence Building Measures (CBMs) in an effort to redress at least a portion of these deficiencies. The question addressed in this chapter is: how was one to tell the nature of a state's BW program about which misgivings existed?

This chapter explores whether one can distinguish between research that is intended to serve an offensive BW program and that which serves a defensive BW program. What are the implications of the information that will be reviewed below? What will we find in investigating the particulars of research paths in civilian medical research, in biodefense, and in offensive research programs? Will the effort be useful, or no more than a repetition of the obvious to specialists? If the answer is that one cannot distinguish between offensive and defensive research, where is the dividing line between an offensive BW program and a defensive one? What are the critical indicators?

The word "research," or any specific reference to "offensive" or "defensive" in a research context, does not appear in the BWC's Article I, which reads as follows:

Each State Party to the Convention undertakes never in any circumstances to develop, produce, stockpile or otherwise acquire or retain:

(1) Microbial or other biological agents, or toxins whatever their origin or method of production, of types and in quantities that have no justification for prophylactic, protective or other peaceful purposes;

(2) Weapons, equipment or means of delivery designed to use such agents or toxins for hostile purposes or in armed conflict.[1]

The British draft treaty had included a provision that required states signing or ratifying the treaty "not to conduct, assist, or permit research aimed at production of the agents or weapons" forbidden by Articles I (1) and I (2) above.[2]

As part of work done between 1968 and 1971 to write a set of six volumes on biological and chemical weapons by the Stockholm International Peace Research Institute (SIPRI), one study examined the question of whether there were characteristics that could distinguish between military and civilian research and, more significantly, between offensive and defensive research in areas that related to biological weapons.[3] Though contrary to many assumptions, it was not a misguided exercise. Nineteen years later, David Huxsoll, then director of USAMRIID, presented an explicit schema that provided a distinction between the two in testimony to the US Senate. He explained the differences between offensive and defensive research, as well as between the development of vaccines and other defenses and biological weapons, as follows:

From the outset, defensive research is based on different postulates and hypotheses than is research directed toward offensive ends, and the rationales for data collection and analysis are different.

At the basic research level, the laboratory techniques used would be very similar, but the objectives are markedly different. Beyond the basic research level, there is a marked divergence in the type of work that would be done.

If a vaccine were to be produced, one that would pursue ways of crippling, weaken, or lessening the virulence of the agent in question so that it could be used in humans without fear of inducing disease[; i]n fact, it may be completely inactivated, a killed vaccine.

A vaccine would be produced under the stringent guidelines of the Food and Drug Administration regulations and would have to receive

FDA approval before use. This type of work is permitted by the Biological Weapons Convention.

If, however, the goal were to create a weapon, the opposite objectives would be pursued. Efforts to enhance virulence or toxicity and to produce enormous quantities of agent far larger than those required for vaccine production would be undertaken. In addition, the issues of stability, dissemination, and weapons delivery systems would have to be addressed. These activities are clearly prohibited by the Biological Weapons Convention.[4]

Huxsoll then displayed a diagram based on laboratory work with a virus, one pathway of which led to a vaccine while the second led to a weapon. In initial stages, both pathways made use of the same work: isolation of the viral pathogen, study of its biochemical properties, learning how to grow it in cell culture, and using animal models for its study. But at that point the two paths diverged. To develop the vaccine, the virus would be attenuated, it would be grown in small quantities, and then the candidate vaccine would enter preclinical trials, followed by clinical trials. Huxsoll stipulated that all this was permitted by the BWC. In contrast, to develop the weapon, scientists would need to make the agent more virulent, stabilize it, perfect methods for its dissemination, mass-produce the virus, engineer a delivery system for it, and test it in the open air. All this developmental activity is prohibited by the BWC. Huxsoll's argument was seconded by a US Army medical intelligence officer who testified in the same Senate hearing. He similarly identified four key factors for consideration when attempting to differentiate between licit and illicit programs: the *amount* of agent produced, the *attenuation* of the organisms used for vaccine production, *process difference* between vaccine and weapons production, and the *openness* of a defensive program.[5]

The conclusion of the earlier study done at SIPRI was somewhat more limited, suggesting that it was possible to draw such distinctions, but that an analyst's conclusions were substantially guided by a knowledge or suspicion of the overall nature of the national program in which an individual piece of research was embedded. This may be referred to as "the intent" of the national program in question, a phrase that has subsequently been commonly used in many other discussions of the same problem. For example, in the introduction to *Annals of the New York Academy of Sciences* volume published in 1992 we find:

Perhaps most crucial for any biological defense research project is clear demonstration of its defensive intent; this is vital since an outsider may find it difficult to differentiate between research and development (R&D) undertaken for defensive and offensive purposes. . . . The distinction between research and development is critical to interpreting the provisions of the BWC because the treaty does not specifically mention research, offensive or defensive, but does proscribe offensive development while permitting development for peaceful purposes. . . . The general criterion for distinguishing between offensive and defensive research is *intent,* which at best is a problematic issue. . . . Is biological defense research sufficiently "transparent" that an outsider can readily ascertain its defensive intent?[6]

In 1984 Richard Falk, an international law specialist, noted that offensive and defensive research were distinguished *only* by intent, and not by substance, and that this both invited and concealed abuse. Huxsoll's colleague Thomas R. Dashiell, a former Fort Detrick Special Projects Officer then serving in the Department of Defense (DOD) administering the buildup of the US biodefense program during the Reagan administration, responded that a better definition of defensive biological research "would be extremely difficult—if not impossible—to develop."[7] These were much more pessimistic positions.

The critical question then became, how could one identify or infer the "intent" of the research being carried out in a national BW program? The violator was scarcely going to advertise his intent: on the contrary, he would do everything possible to conceal it. At the same time, it is important to emphasize again that the series of presumptive US intelligence assessments and leaks between 1975 and 1989 imputing a Soviet offensive BW program were correct, and official US statements from 1984 on explicitly accused the Soviet Union of maintaining an offensive BW program. (This excludes those that began in 1981 and were based on the yellow rain allegations. See Chapter 16.)

If one also concludes, on careful examination, that any piece of basic research could have major "offensive" implications at some future time or in another party's hands, one is left with the argument that the only distinguishing characteristics of a BW program occurred at the point at which weapon development began. And as we will see in a moment, it is a further complicating factor that it is also routine to argue and to act upon the claim that some degree of weapon development is permissible within a defensive program, as in the case of several disclosures in the United States in September 2001.[8] The unquestioned requirement that "threat assessment" be carried out in the US biodefense program became standard, particularly after the events of September 2001. At least insofar as the words that are used are concerned, it is also the position put forward by Yevstigneev in 1999 and 2002 when he claimed that everything the Soviet Union did prior to 1992 in the Soviet BW program was simply to evaluate the biological weapons threat from the United States in order to produce Soviet defenses against that threat. The fact that the Soviet Union built a score of mobilization production facilities each able to produce hundreds of tons of agent makes that claim nonsensical. Given that Yevstigneev's claim is false and that there was no US offensive BW program at the time to defend against, his remarks nevertheless demonstrate the facile application of the argument. However, that pushes one even farther away from research, and leaves the only definitive determinants as production, quantities, and weapons.

The oversimplification inherent in Huxsoll's schema becomes apparent by examining the relevant US government policy statement, National Security Decision Memorandum (NSDM) 35, dated November 25, 1969, which underpinned the US renunciation of its offensive BW program. Its operative paragraph reads as follows: "The United States bacteriological/biological programs will be confined to research and development for defensive purposes (immunization, safety measures, et cetera). This does not preclude research into the offensive aspects of bacteriological/biological agents necessary to determine what defensive measures are required."[9] This document was not declassified until November 1995. However, one of the talking points prepared for Secretary of State Kissinger for speaking with congressional leaders and to members of the press was a précis of the preceding sentence. It read: "In any event, we would need some research on offensive agents as a basis for study of defensive measures and to protect us from technological surprise."[10] It is not known if Kissinger actually used these words when he spoke to the press, whether it was printed in press reports at the time, or if members of the Soviet Embassy were present among the press corps and so could have known if he did use the words.

The analytical study that supported the US policy decision also included a very important relevant paragraph. In response to the question "Should the US maintain only an RDT&E program," it replied:

There are really two sub-issues here: (1) should the U.S. restrict its program to RDT&E for defensive purposes only or (2) should the U.S. conduct both offensive and defensive RDT&E? While it is agreed that even RDT&E for defensive purposes only would require some offensive R&D, it is also agreed that there is a distinction between the two issues. A defensive purposes only R&D program would emphasize basic and exploratory research on all aspects of BW, warning devices, medical treatment and prophylaxis. RDT&E for offensive purposes would emphasize work on mass production and weaponization and would include standardization of new weapons and agents.[11]

An excellent examination of the US government policy process in 1969–1972 that resulted in the joint decisions to renounce and dismantle the US offensive BW program, negotiate the BWC, and sign the Geneva Protocol, was able to add only a single footnote by way of further amplification:

There is much debate over what constitutes offensive and defensive research and development in the field of biological weapons. The development of munitions filled with biological agents, delivery vehicles for these munitions, open air field testing of live biological agents, enhancement of the pathogenicity of organisms, and development of production and storage techniques for biological agents constitute offensive program activities which cannot be easily justified under a defensive research program.[12]

On December 23, 1975, Brent Snowcroft, the US President's Assistant for National Security Affairs, issued a memorandum to US government departments and agencies to ensure that the activities of all agencies of the US government were and would remain in compliance with Article I of the BWC. To that end, the document specified which activities were permissible simply by repeating the wording of NSDM 35 quoted above.[13]

The US policy statement in NSDM 35 cut away the problem—at least for the United States—of whether an individual piece of research is "defensive" or "offensive"; "offensive" "research" is permitted. On what basis, then, does the US government make the assessment that another nation's BW program is offensive or defensive? In its research phase? On evidence of "development"? If so, what aspect of development, given that the United States considered it permissible in 2000 to duplicate a Soviet BW bomblet to test it for "defensive" purposes? There are no definitions with precisely defined boundaries accepted at an international diplomatic level that clearly separate "research" from "development."[14] On evidence of "testing"? If so, how extensive a testing program, given that the United States considers it permissible to carry out various degrees of testing for defensive purposes? On evidence of serial or volume production? If so, at what level of production, given that small quantities of agent have been produced for defensive purposes? As has been noted, "Small amounts may need to be retained if defensive equipment is to be developed."[15] As we examine the Soviet BW program, it is useful to keep in mind the difficult questions and issues presented above.

Soviet-Era and Russian BW-Related Research: Defensive or Offensive

This book demonstrates without any question whatsoever that the Soviet Union maintained an offensive BW program of enormous and unprecedented magnitude. Nothing in the discussion that follows should be misunderstood to suggest otherwise. It does, however, demonstrate the difficulty in assessing the character of an individual laboratory research project when knowledge of the overall program in which it is embedded is absent.

In testimony to the US Senate, and on numerous other occasions, Alibek charged that research on viral agents being conducted at Vector was being done for offensive BW purposes. He asserted that "chimeras" of vaccinia and Venezuelan equine encephalitis virus (VEEV) had been constructed, and that the use of the vaccinia virus was a proxy for variola virus: once the technique had been established, VEE-variola viral combinations would be made for weapons purposes.[16] Significant questions have been raised by US researchers regarding the technical feasibility of this work. Vector officials have admitted to having developed a recombinant vaccinia virus that contains structural genes of VEEV, but they claimed this had been done for a legitimate and, in fact, quite common reason, to produce a new vaccine against VEE. They stated that existing live VEE vaccines (TC-80 or 320, or CM-27) were based on poorly attenuated VEEV strains that produced a relatively weak immune response as well as attendant negative side effects, whereas available inactivated VEE vaccines did not produce side effects but stimulated an even weaker immune response.[17] When queried directly, Alibek maintained his original charge and said that he did so because he knew that these experiments had been devised as part of the Soviet-era offensive BW program when he still held his position as deputy director of that program, and that the VEE vaccine development story had been the legend for work intended to further variola virus BW development.[18] It is impossible to resolve the dispute on the basis of the two contradictory claims alone. We came to the conclusion that the research project in question was indeed part of an offensive BW program only through a review, made together with Russian émigré scientists who had worked at Vector, of a series of several dozen experiments carried out at Vector. Sergei Popov, a scientist who had worked at Vector, referred to this particular Soviet-era project as the "Hunter Program."[19]

To indicate the further difficulty of making such a determination in the abstract, it is certainly the case that vaccinia virus and dozens of adenoviruses have been used for years in research laboratories worldwide as vectors, as they are exceedingly good at getting inside cells and/or producing a strong immune response. The methodology is widely used in cancer research and in devising gene therapies.[20] The very same technique is also being used for transcellular transport without stimulating an immune response: "In laboratories throughout the US and Europe dozens of geneticists are working to create stealthy viruses that can deliver artificially engineered payloads into cells without detection by the immune system."[21]

Although some of this research is aimed at producing vaccines, including for some of the hemorrhagic fever viruses for which no vaccines exist, and could therefore be considered to be within the "biodefense" sector, much of it is taking place entirely within the civilian medical research sector. It is therefore frequently not even a matter of "defensive" or "offensive" BW-related work. Analogous research efforts are also being carried out in Western BW defense facilities in order to develop new vaccines. Very similar work in Russia, at Vector, and in Germany, at the Institute of Virology in Marburg, has used the vaccinia T7 system as the "vector" in efforts to produce a vaccine against Ebola virus disease.[22] In theory, this would permit one to make an "Ebola-variola viral chimera," just as the study previously referred to using a vaccinia virus vector to produce VEE vaccine could be claimed to permit the production of a "variola-VEE" viral chimera. In the 1980s, USAMRIID scientist Joel Dalrymple also used vaccinia virus as a vehicle for gene expression in efforts to develop vaccines against hantaviruses, Rift Valley fever virus, and the protective antigen (PA) protein of *B. anthracis* toxin.[23] It is of particular interest that around 1986 Dalrymple traveled to Akademgorodok to present a lecture describing his work. Vector, the institute that Alibek alleges carried out orthopoxvirus "chimera" research for weapons purposes, is situated some 20 kilometers from Akademgorodok, and we know from interviews with Russian sources that scientists from Vector attended Dalrymple's presentation. It is safe to assume that they would also have known of his published work on the subject. It is quite likely that Vector scientists adapted Dalrymple's model for their subsequent work with orthopoxvirus recombinants.

In other examples, in 2002 a highly misleading British press item reported that work at "Porton Down" in the United Kingdom included "modifying a smallpox virus with anthrax genes" (most certainly vaccinia, incorrectly referred to as "smallpox") and introducing modifications into the genomes of the pathogens responsible for bubonic plague, tularemia, gas gangrene, and typhoid.[24] All of the work referred to was carried out in order to produce vaccines. Analogous work with the "gas gangrene" perfringens toxin and vaccinia virus was published as early as 1991.[25] A more accurate and meaningful description of the research referred to is that since 1993 the Centre for Applied Microbiological Research (CAMR) at Porton Down has been working on a new acellular plague vaccine. This is a combination of two purified *Y. pestis* antigens (F1 and Vi) (envelope proteins) that are produced as recombinant proteins (rF1 and rVi) in *E. coli*. The United Kingdom's 2001 CBM return also refers to this vaccine work:

> Genetically engineered vaccines against plague, anthrax and botulinum toxins have now been devised and these vaccines have transitioned to the development phase. These vaccines can be produced in a harmless strain of the bacterium *E. coli,* and can therefore be produced without cultivating dangerous pathogens. . . . A programme to evaluate current vaccinia strains, with a view towards identifying ways of non-invasive delivery of these vaccines has continued over the past year. Immunisation with these vaccines should include a protective response against smallpox. These vaccines will also be used as vectors to deliver other vaccine antigens. Programmes have also continued to devise improved vaccines against tularemia and meliodosis. . . . work is underway to produce attenuated strains of the bacteria which might be used as vaccines . . . we aim to identify protective sub-units from these bacteria.[26]

One of the most troubling paths in the Soviet Union's offensive BW program was the research by Popov on recombinant bacteria-mediated myelin autoimmunity, carried out at the two premier Biopreparat institutes, first at

Vector, and then at Obolensk. (This work was more thoroughly discussed in Chapters 7 and 8.) However, medical researchers who work on multiple sclerosis regularly try to induce autoimmunity in animal models using virtually the same technique. With the pathology induced in the animal model, the researcher tries to reverse or intervene in the course of the disease. Microbial vectors have again been used in these studies, and in one study, Theiler's virus was used to introduce a 30-amino-acid peptide to produce the experimental autoimmune condition in the research animals.[27] Popov had used legionellae as a vector. Once again, we made the determination that this work was part of the Soviet offensive BW program because no less than four former senior Biopreparat scientists independently explained that this work comprised the Factor program. It had been devised by Igor P. Ashmarin, one of the deputy chiefs of the 15th Directorate, and it proved possible to trace the stages of the research sequence as it was carried out in different institutes belonging to different ministries in the former Soviet Union. (Factor was discussed in detail in Chapter 7.)

Summing up the various examples just described , one can see that the same techniques, and some of the same pathogens that were at one time or another weaponized, produced, and stockpiled as BW agents within the former Soviet Union's offensive BW program were or are also being utilized in work:

- Within Russia's current defensive BW program, as well as within the current defensive BW programs in the United Kingdom and the United States
- Entirely within the civilian medical research sphere

If we look back at the material gathered on the preceding pages, one could take Alibek's claim of "chimeras" as BW agents, and set it against the panoply of research in the civilian sector, and in both offensive and defensive research programs:

- Vaccinia-Ebola virus and vaccinia-hantavirus combinations used in an effort to produce vaccines against Ebola virus and hantaviruses, and similar work with HIV-1 bacterial recombinants
- The research being done at the UK biodefense facility
- "Stealthy virus" research, and immunotoxin research
- Work on *Y. pestis* toxins and on *B. anthracis* proteins

- Popov's work at Vector and Obolensk in the Soviet BW program, and the same techniques used in medical research in autoimmune disease research
- Reconstitution in recent years of a highly contagious and deadly influenza A virus strain of the past
- Insertion of cytokine genes into orthopoxviruses

The existing language in the BWC's Article I in regard to "prophylactic, protective or other peaceful purposes" is at too great a level of abstraction to resolve these issues. The "types and quantities" permitted for these purposes are undefined. Jack Melling, the former director of the Centre for Applied Microbiological Research, suggested that if 50 or 100 pounds of agent were found, that would certainly be a definite indicator of an offensive program.[28] He also indicated that lesser amounts could be of concern as well. A trial inspection exercise carried out as part of the SIPRI work in 1968–1969 used an even lower threshold of 10 kilograms (22 pounds) of microbial paste or spores or 0.5 kilogram (1.1 pounds) of botulinum toxin as "militarily relevant."[29] Leaving aside quantities, everything is left to an individual nation's claims as to which technical aspects of offensive systems and their operation it must examine in the course of developing an adequate defense. Too much is a matter of argumentation and possibly self-serving interpretation.

Some specialists with long experience in BW programs believe, however, that the first indicators of an offensive BW program become apparent in the development phase. For some portions of the activities that would fall into the "development" category, that is probably the case, but there could even be problems here, depending on which studies were categorized as "development." For example, it would be argued that at some point in actual vaccine testing, animal model exposure must be done with dry as well as with wet formulations of agent, in the same ways that one would expect personnel to be exposed. Is the production of the dry agent "development"? A 2002 solicitation for contracts for the US Army's Edgewood Chemical Biological Center Research and Technology Directorate called for the contractor to "perform theoretical and experimental work necessary to develop and operate dissemination devices for aerosol materials including powders, liquids, and microbiologicals."[30] The US Army presumably considers this kind of development as being defensive. But would the US government, on the receipt of

intelligence indicating that a Russian or Iranian biological facility was performing equivalent development, consider it to be defensive, or would it
consider it to be suggestive of an offensive BW program? Certainly if one
found BW agents in bombs or shells, or dedicated production facilities with
capacities measured in tons, the answer would be obvious, as it was in regard
to the Soviet Union and Iraq.

It is questionable whether international agreement could be obtained for
the point of distinction between "research" and "development." One plausible suggestion is that experimentation on the marriage of an agent with a
munition would cross that line of distinction, including any weapon test using
a simulant. But what did the United States and United Kingdom use as criteria in the early Trilateral visits to former Soviet BW institutes (discussed in
Chapters 21 and 22)? Did the US and UK governments make their judgments solely on the basis of what was visually seen, equipment and facilities,
or did they use other intelligence, such as information obtained from Pasechnik, to critically inform their judgments? The criteria used in judgments
publicly released by the United States in the 1980s regarding the nature of a
half dozen Soviet BW facilities, judgments that were ostensibly based on remote satellite reconnaissance photographs, were few and quite simple: the
presence of storage bunkers, animal handling facilities and very tall chimney
stacks. Without exception, the facilities were correctly identified.

One piece of interesting testimony was provided by one of the US participants in the Trilateral visits to Russian facilities in 1993. The US-UK
team had visited three sites that were "mobilization capacity" facilities, intended for BW production in the mobilization period prior to an anticipated war. Some aspects of these sites were clearly suggestive of offensive
capabilities: the massive fermentation capacity, particular aerosol test
chambers showing evidence of explosive testing, and massively walled
bunkers that had housed filling lines. The fourth site visited was SRCAM, a
research facility: no production, no stockpiling, and no weapons. The UK-
US team did not have a prepared list of indicators that they should look for.
They had, however, discussed the problem among themselves in advance and
agreed that dynamic aerosol test chambers would be one such indicator. One
US member of the team in fact kept Huxsoll's schema, which had been presented in Senate testimony only three or four years earlier, in mind.[31] Everything that the US-UK team saw at SRCAM was in the research phase, but
the facility did include static and dynamic test chambers. However, in a visit
to only two floors of a multistory building, at a facility that included several

dozen buildings, one very experienced US member of the visiting team decided that he was looking at laboratories that were part of an offensive BW program. He felt that the decisive cue was the design of the overall layout of the sequence of laboratories, and felt able to come to a decision of "offensive BW program" on that basis.[32]

What would one look for? In 1992 the director of biological research at a French military laboratory listed "large scale production of an agent, the existence of certain storage facilities, the use of certain equipment such as fermenters and freeze drying equipment, and the safety protection being provided personnel" as "indicators of strategic BW development."[33] When US satellite intelligence photo interpreters in the mid-1970s identified tall incinerator smoke stacks, large cold-storage facilities, animal pens, sentries, and double barbed-wire fences at Compound 19 in Sverdlovsk, they suspected it of being a BW laboratory—which it was. The indicators cited by the French scientist and by the US analysts, however, are at the high end of an indicator spectrum. Of course the use of fermenters alone would not be indicative; all would depend on what was being grown in them. In addition, more recent technology could reduce the need for large stockpiles that were previously held in readily recognizable storage facilities, depending on the procedures that a nation chose to implement.

In 1993 the Russian Foreign Intelligence Service (SVR) produced a remarkable indicator list:

The development, production, stockpiling, and possible use of biological weapons may . . . be identified on the basis of the following specific indications:

- The existence of programs for training troops, special subunits or intelligence and sabotage groups, for operations involving the use of biological weapons;
- The presence or purposeful search for highly qualified specialists in immunology, biochemistry, bioengineering, and related fields, who have experience in the development of biological weapons and means of protection;
- The building of laboratories with enhanced security [according to international classification P-3 (BSL-3) or P-4 (BSL-4)];
- The development of secret research programs and secret special and military facilities of biomedical orientation;

- Large-scale production of vaccines (against especially dangerous infections) and the existence of stocks of these vaccines which exceed real peacetime requirements;
- Creation of a production base, specifically of bioreactors and fermenters with a capacity of more than 50 liters or a total capacity of more than 200 liters;
- Outbreaks of especially dangerous infectious diseases not typical of specific regions;
- The purchase of starting biomaterials and equipment for the production of biological weapons, as well as delivery systems for them;
- Activity related to microorganisms and toxins which cannot be explained by civilian requirements, activity involving agents of especially dangerous infections not endemic to a given area;
- The existence of biotechnological equipment and conduct of work to create vectors of various diseases in people, animals, or plants, as well as composite media for culturing them;
- The existence of equipment for microencapsulation of live microorganisms;
- The existence of equipment for studying the behavior of biological aerosols in the environment.[34]

A striking aspect of the SVR list is that its indicators could have served at any time to identify the former Soviet BW program. But the list is "superindicative": it of course identifies the maximum of everything in a large and ambitious national program, even including a potential disease outbreak due to an accident in a BW installation, exactly as occurred in Sverdlovsk in 1979.

Somewhat more analytical indicator lists are available from three different US government agencies, dating between 1993 and 2003. List 1 (Table 11.1), entitled "Signatures for Biological Warfare Facilities," was prepared by the Armed Forces Medical Intelligence Center (AFMIC) in 1993. It comprises five categories:

1. Funding and personnel
2. Facility design, equipment, and security
3. Technical considerations
4. Safety
5. Process flow

Table 11.1   List 1: Signatures for Biological Warfare Facilities

Funding and Personnel	
BW facility	Legitimate facility
Military funding	Private enterprise or nonmilitary
High salary	Salary within normal limits
Funding exceeds product/research output	Average or underfunded for expected output
Scientists/technician ratio high	Average ratio
Limited ethnic diversity	Integrated work staff
Elite workforce/foreign trained	Local trained workforce
Foreign-language competency	Limited foreign-language capability
High ratio of military to civilian	Military personnel unlikely

Facility Design, Security, and Equipment	
BW facility	Legitimate facility
Access control: high walls, guard towers, motion detectors, video cameras, elite security force, badges and clearances	Average security, badges at most
Transportation provided	Public/private transport
Quarantine facilities on compound	No quarantine
Foreign travel restricted, highly available	Unrestricted but not readily available
Refrigerated bunkers secure area	Cold rooms in facility
Advanced software, external database access, ADP security high, foreign access	Open information except for proprietary information
Static aerosol test chambers	No aerosol test chambers
Military with weapons expertise	No need
Rail or heavy truck required for weapons filling facility	Only light-truck transportation

Technical Considerations	
BW facility	Legitimate facility
Pathogenic or toxic strains	Nonpathogenic or nontoxic strains
Test aimed at killing animals	Test aimed at protecting animals
Facilities for large animals such as monkeys	Facilities for smaller animals, specific inbred strains
Negative air flow	Positive air flow

(*continued*)

Table 11.1 (continued)

No commercial products	Commercial products
Weapons-filling equipment	Bottle-filling equipment

Safety

BW facility	Legitimate facility
Physical barriers to prevent animal-to-animal and animal-to-human transmission	Physical barriers designed to prevent animal-to-animal and human-to-animal transmission
HEPA filters present, exhaust	HEPA filters possible, intake
Dedicated biosafety personnel	May or may not be present
Medical staff trained in infectious and toxic agents	Dedicated highly trained staff not likely
Decontamination equipment and showers	Not needed on large scale
Large-capacity pass-through autoclaves	Small benchtop autoclaves
Dedicated waste treatment	Waste treatment common with local facilities
Special sterilization of waste	May or may not exist
Test animals sterilized before final disposal	Animals may not need to be sterilized before final disposal

Process Flow

BW facility	Legitimate facility
Raw material consumption does not equal output	Raw material consumption relates to output
Large-volume fermenters (greater than 500 liters), cell cultures (1000s of culture flasks/roller bottles), embryonated eggs (100s, thousands)	Large- or small-scale fermentation but cell culture and eggs in smaller volume
Air-pressure gradients keep microbes in vessels	Air-pressure gradients keep contaminants out of vessels
Finished product—wet stored at low temperature in sealed containers (often double packaging)—not readily identifiable	Labeled by product, batch number, date, etc.
Milling equipment operated in biohazard protective suits	Milling equipment is not operated in biohazard areas
Storage—low-temperature, high-security bunkers with biocontainment	Storage in temperature-controlled environment, clean warehouse conditions
Munitions—special filling buildings and/or explosives-handling facilities	Non-issue

Under each of these five categories, there were six to nine specific indicators that differentiated between a "BW Facility" and a "Legitimate Facility" (the location of refrigerated bunkers, facility security, the nature of waste treatment, location of air filters, air pressure gradients, and so on). Forty such characteristics were evaluated and appeared to provide a very convincing differentiation between a BW facility and a presumptive pharmaceutical or other commercial site.[35]

List 2 (Table 11.2) provides indicators without contrasting aspects in them.[36] And finally, List 3 (Table 11.3) appears to be a partial adaptation of the first.[37]

These indicator lists overlap, and individual items can be disputed. In addition, a single indicator—depending on what it is—certainly may not be indicative. For example, the US Centers for Disease Control and Prevention (CDC), or any laboratory working with filoviruses, unquestionably has "Pathogens Not Endemic to Area" in its possession, and very likely also is

Table 11.2 List 2: Signatures for Biological Warfare Facilities

Indicators	Facilities	Equipment	Personnel
Pathogens not endemic to area	Research laboratories	Fermenters	Microbiologists
High security	Scale-up pilot plant	Hoods (BL-4)	Bacteriologists
Dissemination chambers	Production fermenters	Filters	Toxicologists
Weapons-filling equipment	Test chambers	Centrifuges	Virologists
Bulk stocks—(how large?)	Test grids	Filter presses	Biochemists
Publications—none or decrease	Security	Freeze drying systems	Biotechnology engineers
Priority	Safety systems	Dissemination equipment	Pathologists
Military presence		Protective clothing	Veterinarians
Elite workforce		Aerosol chambers	Fermentation biochemists
Test animals		Animal facilities	
No commercial product		Refrigerated storage bunkers	
Poor records of "cover story"		Safety interlocks	

Table 11.3   List 3: Potential Indicators of Biological Weapons Production Facility

	BW facility	Legitimate facility
Funding and personnel	Military/state funded	Private/corporate funded
	High scientist/technician ratio (2:1)	Average scientist/technician ratio (1:6)
	Elite, foreign-trained workforce	Mostly domestically trained workforce
	Military/civilian ratio high	Military unlikely
Technical considerations	Pathogenic strains	Nonpathogenic
	Facilities designed to protect humans from infection	Facilities designed to protect animals
	Facilities designed for decontamination/disposal of many animals (autoclaves/cremation)	Few animal disposals require decontamination
Facility equipment & security	Weapons-filling equipment	Bottle/vial-filling equipment
	Access-control badges, security clearances	Badges
	Restricted transportation	Public transportation
	Quarantine facilities	No quarantine facilities
	Refrigerated bunkers	Cold rooms in plant
	Aerosol-explosive test chambers	No aerosol chambers
	Rail/heavy-truck transportation	Only light truck needed
	Fences, guard towers, patrol roads, cameras, motion detectors, etc.	Little to no outside security
	Military presence	No military presence
Safety	Physical barriers to prevent animal-animal/animal-human transmission	Not always present
	Dedicated biosafety and medical personnel	Not always present
	HEPA filters/air incinerators for outflow	HEPA for inflow
	Decontamination showers	Not always present
	Pass-through autoclaves (large) and dedicated waste treatment	Small autoclaves and use of common facilities
Process flow	Raw materials do not match output	Raw materials limited for legitimate products
	Negative pressure	Positive pressure
	Finished products stored in bulk and coded	Product clearly labeled
	Dry product processed in high containment	Milling and other equipment not in containment
	Storage in bunkers, secured, contained, and low-temperature	Low security
	Munitions-filling and storage facilities	No munitions
	Testing/proving grounds	Not applicable

"High Security." The "Personnel" grouping in the second list has particularly little value: scientists in those professional disciplines are located in thousands of civilian academic, medical, and commercial institutions.

In a 1994 analysis that dealt with the conversion of research facilities that had been integral parts of the former Soviet Union's offensive BW program, several basic requirements were set out:

- An absolute end to all offensive work
- The termination of administrative control by national military or security agencies or their proxies; the transfer of management of such institutions to civilian ministries or branches of government
- The termination of funding by military agencies
- Transparency—the ending of secrecy and closed facilities[38]

Although these four conditions are specifically relevant to the explicit demilitarization and conversion of facilities, they nevertheless are all "nonspecific" conditions. They do not address the nature of particular lines of research. In many countries national defensive BW programs will be primarily based in facilities that are part of and/or funded by ministries or departments of defense. Defense ministries also maintain major extramural funding programs as part of their defensive BW research programs, which support program-oriented research in academic and commercial institutions. In the United States, very significant portions of the BW defense research program are located in the Departments of Energy, Homeland Security, and Health and Human Services (the US National Institutes of Health Centers for Disease Control and Prevention). Additional portions are funded by the CIA. In contrast, in the United Kingdom, CAMR first moved away from the biodefense domain, took on a public-health mission while retaining a substantial portion of its earlier work, but most recently has been increasingly drawn back into it.[39]

Several individuals with long experience in the biodefense programs of their own countries—the United Kingdom, United States, Sweden, and Russia—however, expressed the opinion that transparency was the key factor in removing questions about whether a BW program was offensive or defensive: the ability to display the site to any international visitor and to say "Here is the site, and here is what we are doing."[40] Alibek, commenting on the work being done on recombinant pathogens in the US biodefense program—work analogous to the recombinant work that he repeatedly identified as being offensive in character in the Soviet Union and Russia—stated "that the work had to be done openly if done at all. It can't be classified. . . . If the secret research was essentially disclosed . . . the United States would be accused of cheating on the germ treaty."[41] Obviously, then, one of the best ways to cause problems and provoke suspicion is to carry out secret BW-relevant research by or under the aegis of an intelligence agency rather than in the customary national BW defense programs. One conclusion that is relatively easy to arrive at is that BW defense programs should be kept clear of national intelligence and security agencies. Nevertheless, some biodefense research carried out in more typical national BW defense programs is also maintained at classified and secret levels.

In this regard, it should be noted that between 1999 and 2002, German authorities contacted the closed RF-MOD biological institutes and invited their directors to participate in a NATO biodefense conference that is held annually in Munich. The letters of invitation were addressed to the institute directors themselves as well as to the RF-MOD in Moscow. There never was a reply.[42]

A corollary of these considerations came into play in the operation of international programs devoted to assisting with the conversion of former Soviet BW facilities. Obviously one would not want funds supplied to facilitate conversion to find their way into supporting continued offensive programs.[43] (See Chapter 23.) The same concern has broader implications as well. Any government, international organization, or research institute that funds work in another country, whether that country has already been identified as being of BW proliferation concern or not, should in theory examine the projects that it supports to be certain that support is not being given to the infrastructure of a BW program. However, given the discussion in the preceding pages describing the intertwining of civilian and military, offensive and defensive BW relevant research, arriving at such certainty is obviously not an easy task.[44]

12

Assessments of Soviet Biological Warfare Activities by Western Intelligence Services

A s TIME PASSES, more and more documents authored by various agencies and departments of the US and UK governments that deal with sensitive subjects, such as the weapons of mass destruction programs of the Soviet Union, are declassified and made available to researchers. Documents related to the Soviet biological warfare (BW) program were obtained from the National Archives in College Park, Maryland; The National Archives in Kew, United Kingdom; the National Security Archive in Washington, D.C.; and the archives at the Johnson, Nixon, Reagan, and Bush presidential libraries. Many hundreds of linear feet of documents from the 1960s, 1970s, and 1980s written by officials of the CIA, Department of State (DOS), Department of Defense (DOD), and others have recently been declassified, but much of this potential treasure trove of information has not been properly indexed. Researchers must sort through box after box, many containing hundreds of documents, and scrutinize each one in the hope that it contains relevant material. It was possible to recover sufficient documentation to determine with a fair degree of confidence what the US government thought it knew about the Soviet BW program as late as 1990. Documents published after this date by the US intelligence community (IC) mostly remain classified. However, as even older documents continue to appear gradually, significant changes in understanding and interpretation are possible. One example discussed below was the National

343

Security Decision Directive no. 18 of January 4, 1982, early in the Reagan administration, which we obtained only in late 2010.

With the serious caveat introduced by the large amount of material that is redacted in the documents that are available, this chapter reviews what the intelligence communities in the United States and the United Kingdom knew about the Soviet BW program through the years 1920 to 1990, with some additional information for later years. Much less information is available from the United Kingdom because its government declassifies documents only after 30 years. There is a nominal 25-year rule in the United States for declassification of documents, though it is implemented inconsistently and often unreliably. However, documents can also be subjected to earlier declassification, and numerous requests by academics and journalists under the Freedom of Information Act (FOIA) have resulted in earlier declassification of large numbers of documents (the United Kingdom has no equivalent to FOIA). The assessment provided in this chapter was made using a combination of the information derived from declassified intelligence sources, other US government public reports and congressional testimony, leaks to the press by government officials, and interviews with several former American and British intelligence analysts who wrote reports and estimates.

Retroactive assessments are problematical, especially when the analyst may only have incomplete information as a basis for performing the assessment. As every historian knows, information about historical events will always be incomplete. In our case, however, we had peculiar difficulties stemming from the fact that most declassified intelligence sources in our possession have many redacted passages; reports contain blacked-out areas, some covering several pages, at times even tens of pages, where government censors have removed information that they deemed could in some way harm national interests or security if published.

In addition to this major drawback, the declassified literature has an additional characteristic that both helps and hinders the analyst seeking to discern what was known and unknown by decision makers of the past. Most of the classified documents, at least in our experience, were for the consumption of high-level officials. In the early 1980s these documents included National Intelligence Estimates (NIEs), Special National Intelligence Estimates (SNIEs), warning bulletins, and brief analytical memoranda.[1] NIEs, often used by the highest government officials as the basis for making national policies, are of major importance to our study.[2] They are almost invariably classified Secret or Top Secret at the time of their formulation. Conversely, there is less of what one might call operational correspondence, such as opinions being voiced by analysts, orders or requests for information from supervisors to operatives, or orders for actions. This means that the analyst tends to have most access to reports that are broad summaries but contain less detail. And when the detail was in the original, it is most likely to be the portion that is redacted. We make this supposition because often more general statements or findings are followed by redacted text that we believe to contain specific information such as names of institutions where suspect R&D was performed and the nature of that R&D. Thus, we learned much more from previously classified documents about IC estimates of Soviet BW capabilities than about how weapons might be used, the facilities that constituted that program, and people who operated it.

Nevertheless, we have to trust that the information collected from the incomplete IC reports, combined with interviews and the public statements of various US administrations, is sufficient to provide substance to this chapter in terms of revealing what the US and UK governments knew about Soviet BW-related activities. In addition, all the knowledge gained since 1989 described in the preceding chapters allows one to assess those earlier judgments of the IC. This is important both for historical reasons and for the present and future biological arms control regime. Intelligence estimates almost certainly shaped US policymakers' perceptions about the Soviet BW effort, which in turn directly influenced how high-level US officials and diplomats related to their Soviet and Russian counterparts, especially when it came to attempting to influence Soviet decision makers to close down their BW program and on such matters as Biological and Toxin Weapons Convention (BWC) compliance issues.

As readers will observe, intelligence about Soviet BW-related activities is relatively thin for the pre-1972 period; meager and often of dubious value during 1970–1979; and a little less meager and of better quality during 1980–1990. After 1990, there are few, if any, relevant declassified documents because insufficient time has passed for government agencies to be permitted to release them. The organization of this chapter follows these time lines. The open literature, especially the mass media, was also examined for information about Soviet BW activities.

Two other sources should be noted, although they derive not from the IC but from the DOD. In 1949 the Joint Chief of Staff's Joint Intelligence Group (JIG) initiated a study, code-named DROPSHOT, established under the authority and with the knowledge of President Truman.[3] Its task was to elaborate a war plan on the presumption that a nuclear war with the Soviet Union would begin in 1955, but later modified to January 1, 1957. The JIG postulated, "It is probable that the Soviets will be able to employ atomic weapons, biological and chemical warfare against the United States in 1955 either covertly or by direct military action. The Soviet capability of applying a wide variety of biological agents harmful to human, animal and/or vegetable life is practically unlimited."[4] It went on to elaborate the methods by which the Soviet Union could use biological weapons, and assumed that the primary targets for Soviet BW (as well as for nuclear attack) would be "US atomic bomb plants and repositories," as well as 10 identified cities or areas in the United States.[5] It is critical to note that these assumptions were not based on any specific intelligence regarding the status of BW development in the Soviet Union. They were almost certainly based on knowledge of the US program during World War II, German intelligence derived from interviews with Soviet prisoners of war, as well as a bit from Japan's BW program, plus some extrapolation.

The second was a speech by Soviet Marshal Georgy Zhukov to the Soviet 20th Communist Party Congress on February 18, 1956, in which Zhukov stated, "Future war, if they unleash it, will be characterized by the massive use of air forces, various rocket weapons, and various means of mass destruction such as atomic, thermonuclear, chemical and bacteriological weapons."[6] This was portrayed for decades by DOD military and civilian spokesmen in annual testimony to US congressional committees as evidence that the Soviet Union *intended* to use biological weapons in the event of war with the West. Conversely, in 1969 a CIA report stated, "Soviet documents indicate that the USSR expects NATO to employ BW in the event of war and is preparing to defend against it."[7] However, the most knowledgeable Western analysts of Soviet strategic policies did not believe that the Soviet military thought that the United States would initiate either biological or chemical warfare.[8]

Intelligence Community Assessments, 1920s–1972

The earliest intelligence from the pre-1972 era mentioning the Soviet BW program are found in three British Secret Intelligence Service (SIS) reports, and commentaries on them from 1926 and 1927. The first makes a general assessment, while the second and third describe work done on Kugali [*sic*] Island in the northern part of the Caspian Sea, at a research station established by the Tsarist government in 1914 to study malaria.[9] The first report draws conclusions but does not reveal how they were reached:

> Research work on Bacteriological Warfare [in the Soviet Union] is confined almost exclusively to the study of tetanus and encephalitis baccilli [*sic*]. After these two the next important is the plague. The reason for this is due to the fact that the experimenters possess means to create immunity with respect to tetanus and encephalitis almost to the full 100%, whereas the anti-plague inoculations are only about 60% successful.
>
> For the purpose of effecting infection under peace conditions only the cultures of the encephalitis are intended. The method of distribution in peace time will be exclusively that of scattering small thin-walled ampullae; in war-time aero-bombs are to be used containing a large quantity of such ampullae and a small trotyl charge.[10]

Attached to the foregoing report is a document titled "Comments of the Chemical Warfare Research Department," which states: "This report resembles previous reports of work on the tetanus, encephalitis and plague bacilli [*sic*]. The work should be closely watched, and any information in regard to the method of producing immunity against encephalitis would be particularly valuable."[11] It would have been most interesting to have the "previous reports," but we did not find them. However, the implication is that the SIS had received more than one account on the types of possible BW agents the Soviets were working on.

The reference in the report to "encephalitis" is puzzling. This is a general term meaning "inflammation of the brain." Such an inflammation usually is caused by one of several viruses, rather than by a bacterium as indicated in the reports. The most probable explanation for this discrepancy is that the author did not know the difference between bacterial and viral diseases. Another explanation could be that in Russia, as in other places, the word "virus" was incorrectly used for a bacterium in the 1920s. For example, in Russian newspapers it is still not unusual to read about "anthrax virus." A third explanation could be that the author confuses encephalitis with meningitis. Several types of pathogenic bacteria are indeed able to cause meningitis.

About two months later, the SIS informant added substantial information. In a long report, he or she stated that "the military bacteriological station and the experimental polygon on Kugali [*sic*] Island in the Caspian made some experiments in bacteriology in October last."[12] Briefly, these experiments involved the testing of bombs invented by an "Engineer Yashin" that could be dropped by airplanes from any altitude. The bombs tested on "Kugali" Island had warheads filled with tetanus bacteria and were designed to explode when contacting ground, sending up a plume that would spread the bacteria over one square kilometer. According to test results, the dispersed bacteria remained intact and virulent. Reportedly, further testing was to take place during spring 1927 but with bombs filled with "the baccilli [sic] of plague, anthrax, and encephalitis; i.e., with all the cultures which the Section for Bacteriological Defence consider suitable for dissemination."[13]

The same report also describes using a chemical weapons agent, lewisite, as a decontaminant. A "Dr. Mitchurin," identified as a former lecturer at Nizhegorod University and an assistant of "Professor Zdatorogov," utilized "theoretical work done at the 'Plague Fort' near Kronstadt," in an experiment that involved spreading 500 kilograms of lewisite over one square kilometer of ground that previously had been contaminated with tetanus bacteria. Three days later, samples were taken that showed a drastic decrease of living tetanus bacteria.[14] The British intelligence analyst who analyzed these reports wryly writes, "The method of anti-bacterial defense is ingenious but the cure seems almost worse than the disease."[15]

Another agency within the British government procured fragments of information about Soviet BW, but indirectly. The UK Committee of Imperial Defence, Subcommittee on Bacteriological Warfare, reported in 1934 on a "bacteriological short course" that is offered periodically for "advanced gas specialists" in Germany.[16] This course was offered because "they [the Germans] knew definitely that Russia had more than one large laboratory in E. Russia, where experiments were being carried out with all sorts of plague producing bacteria, which Russia has every intention of using against Japan, or any other country with when [sic] she might be at war."[17] This view was reinforced in 1938 by the UK director of Naval Intelligence, who wrote, "I have to inform you that information from a reliable source shows that Germany is well aware that Russia is prepared to use bacteria in war, to poison water supplies and spread diseases; also that according to Germany, the Spanish 'Reds'[18] had already used such methods."[19] There is, however, no available information indicating that Spanish Republican forces used BW agents during the 1936–1939 Spanish Civil War. Other than these, we have no other UK or US intelligence documents dating from 1938 to 1946 pertaining to Soviet BW.

The British source documents cited in the preceding paragraph were classified Secret or Most Secret (the UK pre-1945 equivalent to Top Secret). We do
not know the sources of the information contained in the 1926–1927 reports,
so it is impossible to appraise their reliability. As for the two later reports, they
report not on British intelligence findings but rather on German beliefs about
the Soviet Union. No specific information is contained in these documents,
which reflects the lack of intelligence on the already extensive Soviet BW program that is described in Chapter 1. Thus it appears as if the UK and the US
governments had very little information on the Soviet BW effort until after
1946, when German military intelligence officers Walter Hirsch and Heinrich Kliewe were captured and their records recovered and examined.

With the exception of one small set of British reports, by far the largest
number of intelligence documents in our possession dating after World War
II are of US origin. The first, issued in 1946, resulted from the War Department (the predecessor of the DOD) having commissioned a Top Secret study
on the capabilities of various nations to acquire biological weapons.[20] The
study's report, which can be assumed to have drawn on the best intelligence
available to the War Department, begins, "It is difficult to evaluate the present status of biological warfare research and development in Russia, since
available information . . . has been obtained largely from German and Japanese sources." It then cautions that the "reliability of either Japanese or German sources of information has not been determined, and any conclusions
based purely on these considerations would be conjecture." The report continues by stating that Japanese sources indicate that experiments involving the techniques of "bacterial warfare" have been done on the largest scale
in the world at a "great experimental station" located in the vicinity of Vladivostok.[21] Given the very large scale of Japan's own experimentation with and
use of BW in China during World War II, the claim is highly implausible.
The site referred to has never been identified, and there is no known evidence
that such a facility ever existed. No other "intelligence" can be drawn from
Japanese sources.

The study's major source on Soviet BW, although not named in the above
1946 report, must have been Walter Hirsch, because it is clear that many of
Hirsch's findings are repeated almost verbatim. (See Chapter 1.) In addition,
there is some incidental information from court proceedings in the 1937 trial
of 17 members of an "Anti-Soviet Trotskyite Center." Some of the accused
were indicted for treason, their "crime" having been that they allegedly

worked with the Japanese intelligence service to use "bacteriological means" to contaminate "troop trains, canteens, and army centers." Despite the fact that the charges were total fabrications, the study concluded that the "Russians evidently were well aware of the threat of biological warfare."[22]

Annex H of the report, which had two sections—"BW Who's Who" and "Installations"—lists the major personalities and facilities of the Soviet BW program (and those of other countries). Without providing any first names or patronyms, the BW Who's Who includes Maslovitch, Hatanever, Ginsburg, Velikonov and wife, and others. Listed installations are Fort Alexander I, Vosroshdenie Island, RKKA Biochemical Institute, and others (all names as in the original). The sole source for this information is "German BW intelligence files and is unsubstantiated."[23]

The War Department study's conclusions were:

> Russia is unquestionable fully capable of carrying out extensive research and development in biological warfare. The Soviet Union has endeavored to place its scientific achievements among the foremost in the world and it is not logical to assume that the field of biological warfare has been disregarded. It is, therefore, believed that Russia would require only a few years' preparation (at the most 5) to wage open, large-scale biological warfare, and that the Soviet Union conceivably may be prepared to do so at the present time.[24]

This very early post World War II report, in the absence of any concrete evidence, initiated a long series of worst case "analyses."

The 1946 report indicates that the United States had no independent means of collecting information about Soviet BW activities. The information in its possession, which is of German and Japanese origin, was outdated, inaccurate, and/or wrong. For example, although executed in 1938, Velikonov [sic] and his wife are listed as major personalities, the long-defunct RKKA Biochemical Institute is described as being an active facility, and "Vosroshdenie Island on Lake Aral" is stated as performing "Secret research of biological nature [poisoning of fish]." It is therefore no wonder that the War Department study produced only general observations and commonsense findings—to wit, that the Soviet Union had a large science establishment with advanced capabilities in several fields, including public health, and that if it did not have them already, the Soviets could rather quickly develop biological weapons capable of causing mass casualties.

The next assessment (or estimate, as it was then called) of Soviet BW in our possession was done in 1949. The estimate, classified Top Secret, is presented as being "on somewhat firmer ground because information received during this quarter definitely confirms the supposition that the USSR is engaged in research on BW and shows that Soviet military training in BW is of long standing."[25] The findings of the estimate are general in nature:

> Although it is known that the USSR is engaged in research and development on BW, it is not known whether any installation comparable to Camp Detrick exists. Some of the work is probably being done by a group of scientists headed by Col. N. N. Ginsburg in a section of the Sanitary-Hygiene Research Institute of the Soviet Army in Kuibyshev (53°10'N–50°10'E). Because the Soviets have long been aware of BW, because they felt they needed BW defense during World War II and a potent weapon to offset their lack of the atomic bomb after World War II, because they have scientists capable of developing BW based on the open literature from the United States, and because they have areas where such work can proceed in secrecy, it is believed that research and development of BW is being carried on in unidentified places in the USSR. That this work is well advanced is indicated by reports of Soviet BW weapons and BW training of troops. Furthermore, the Soviets are beginning to mention BW in their press and radio. It is believed, therefore, that, if the capability of delivery is assumed, the USSR is capable at least of limited operations with BW weapons.[26]

The reference above to "open literature in the United States" very likely refers mainly to the substantial survey of BW by Rosebury and Kabat in 1947[27] and to the well-publicized book by Rosebury.[28] (See the discussion in the Annex of Chapter 1.)The Soviets might have been mentioning BW "in their press and radio" due to the two American publications, plus information provided to the Soviet Army by Japanese servicemen who were captured in August 1945 and who were members of Unit 731, which was the major component of the Japanese BW program.[29] General Ishii, the former head of Unit 731, was being protected by the United States in Japan after World War II ended, and for several years Soviet authorities had been pressing the United States to turn him over to the Soviet Union for trial. In addition, as information in Chapter 14 demonstrates, the Soviets had by this time already begun a campaign of false BW allegations against the United States.

Another report in 1949, this one by the secretary of defense and classified Secret, added a new dimension to the foregoing, stating, "The United States, although it enjoys atomic superiority and is likely to continue to do so even after the U.S.S.R. has begun atomic bomb production, does not necessarily possess a corresponding superiority in the field of biological warfare—in fact, the situation might be the reverse."[30] Because the United States had no information about Soviet BW at this time, this apprehension was gratuitous.

By the time the next estimate was made, in 1950, the NIE concept had become accepted as a briefing tool to the highest rung of US government officials. The objective of NIE-18, classified Top Secret, was to estimate whether the Soviet Union was capable of attacking the United States with biological and chemical weapons between 1951 and 1954 and the probability that, in the event of a general attack, it would do so.[31] NIE-18 concluded that (1) the Soviets were "capable of producing a variety of agents in sufficient quantities for sabotage and small-scale employment," (2) "by 1952 at the latest, the Soviets probably will be capable of mass production of BW agents for large-scale employment," and (3) the BW agents that the Soviets would most likely employ as biological weapons included the bacteria *Bacillus anthracis, Brucella* species, *Malleomyces mallei, Pasteurella pestis,* and *Pasteurella tularensis;* the virus that causes parrot fever (Psittacosis), the rickettsia *Coxiella burnetii,* the fungus *Coccidioides immitis,* and botulinum and staphylococcal toxins.[32] Notably the pathogens listed were all those that the US World War II BW program had investigated, as well as those that it continued to investigate in the post-1945 US program.

Importantly, NIE-18 presumed an increasing Soviet capability in biological warfare. It estimated that the Soviet Union was able to deliver large quantities of BW agents to the United States by long-range aircraft and submarines. However, the only Soviet long-range aircraft available in the early post–World War II years was a copy of the US B-24 bomber, code-named the "Bull" by NATO. The Soviet Union produced very few of them, and they would not have reached any part of the continental United States except for Alaska from bases in the Soviet Far East. Although the Soviet Union did possess a sizable number of submarines immediately after the war, their activity during World War II was extremely limited and the expectation that they would be able to operate successfully off US coasts is dubious. Further, NIE-18 claimed that the Soviets were improving their ability to disperse BW agents; and that the most likely means used would be cluster bombs, aerosol devices, and projectiles. Finally NIE-18 expressed the certainty that were the

Soviet Union to attack the West, it would employ not only nuclear weapons but also biological and chemical weapons. Interestingly, this conclusion was stated a full five years before the 1956 Zhukov speech referred earlier in this chapter.

Another Top Secret NIE, NIE-31, was also produced in 1951.[33] This NIE considered the United States' vulnerability to clandestine attack with weapons of mass destruction. In language that is eerily similar to that which is heard today about our vulnerability to biological attacks by terrorists, the report states:

> The USSR might employ biological warfare (BW) agents against personnel in key installations well in advance of D-Day. Attacks against livestock and crops with dangerous diseases like foot and mouth disease and cereal rusts are a possibility at any time. . . . In contrast to clandestine attack with atomic and chemical weapons, clandestine employment of certain BW agents would entail much less risk of identification as enemy action. . . . Very small amounts of these agents would be required initially. Such amounts would be almost impossible to detect when being brought into this country under the cover of diplomatic immunity or through smuggling operations. In addition, it would not be difficult to have some BW agents procured and cultured locally by a trained bacteriologist who was immunized against and simply equipped to handle dangerous pathogens.[34]

During 1951–1953, one small set of four documents emanated from a UK intelligence assessment agency. The Joint Intelligence Committee (JIC) was founded in 1936 as a subcommittee of the Committee of Imperial Defence, which was an advisory peacetime defense planning system for departmental ministers. The JIC grew to maturity in World War II, becoming the United Kingdom's senior intelligence assessment body. The main task of the JIC was to produce definitive top-level all-source assessments for UK ministers and senior officials.[35] In 1951 it was asked to make an "Estimate of Availability of Soviet Weapons of Mass Destruction and Scientific Developments, 1950–1952."[36] Included among its estimates are such weapons as atomic bombs (50 in mid-1951 and 120 in mid-1952),[37] chemical warfare, and surface-to-surface missiles. For "Biological Warfare" the estimate for the Soviet Union for both 1951 and 1952 was "large-scale." This designation is not explained, so it could mean either that the Soviet Union was able to wage BW on a large scale, or that it had large-scale capabilities in this field but not necessarily weapons on the shelf.

Seven months later, the JIC produced an estimate on "Sino-Soviet Capabilities in the Far East." For BW, the estimate read: "The Soviets have given considerable attention to the development of biological warfare, and are capable at any time of producing a variety of agents for sabotage activities, and probably also for open warfare."[38] This language indicates considerable downgrading of USSR capabilities from the previous report; now the Soviets are believed to be able to undertake biological sabotage but not necessarily to use biological weapons in a military conflict.

The JIC assessment of June 1952 is especially interesting because it not only provides results of the assessment but also tells about intelligence methods.[39] There is not much intelligence data about Soviet BW beyond that provided some years earlier by the Germans, so the JIC uses "the penicillin industry in the USSR as a yardstick in evaluating Soviet production know-how for BW agents." Thus, "intelligence reports indicate that the Soviets were using deep culture techniques for penicillin production during 1948. This culture technique is commonly used by civilian microbiology industry for large-scale production of bacteria and also is the most important aspect of BW production. It is concluded, therefore, that the Soviets could mass-produce BW agents on a large scale if they desire to do so."

This reasoning is odd for several reasons. First, the Soviet Union had other microbiological industries that propagated large quantities of microorganisms for applied purposes—for example, to produce single-cell protein.[40] Using penicillin production does not really make sense as an indicator of a high technical level of fermentation competence. Penicillin is produced by a fungus, so its processing is only distantly comparable to the large-scale production of bacteria such as, say, *Y. pestis* or *B. anthracis*. Second, compared to Soviet civilian industry, the Soviet Military Industrial Complex (MIC) routinely faced the challenge of large technological problems. The MIC presumably would have had something much better than outdated fungus technology to produce pathogens deemed important for weapons purposes.

In the same report, the JIC discusses Soviet government intentions, which is probably the most difficult aspect of intelligence analysis. Just because a hostile country possesses substantial capabilities in any one or more of a number of powerful technologies, it does not necessarily follow that its leadership will employ any of them for sabotage or warfare. Knowing an adversary's capabilities—in, say, applied microbiology—is only one of three aspects of the threat analysis calculation, the others being vulnerability (Is the home country vulnerable to a biological attack?) and intent (Will the adversary's leadership use its biological capability to develop and deploy biological weapons?). Because the JIC did not have access to the thoughts and decisions of the Soviet leadership, or a historic record of Soviet BW-related activities, it estimated Soviet intentions by drawing an inference from a distantly related event. The JIC suggested, "The current propaganda campaign accusing the United Nations of employing BW in Northeast China and North Korea may also serve as a psychological preparation of the Soviet people to accept BW as inevitable. It is believed that the Soviets will employ BW when they consider that it will be advantageous and perhaps decisive."[41] Soviet Korean War propaganda against the United States was a slender reed on which to base an estimate of Soviet BW intentions.

The fourth, and last, of the JIC reports is also interesting, but in a different way. The Supreme Headquarters Allied Powers Europe (SHAPE) had sent a request to member countries phrased as follows: "Staff Division [of SHAPE] charged with the development of medical defense against biological and chemical weapons finds that the intelligence currently available to SHAPE on Soviet capabilities in these fields is inadequate for its requirements." This being the case, it posed 29 specific questions to each of its member governments, the answers to which would provide SHAPE with the required intelligence.[42] At that time, SHAPE was the central command of all NATO military forces in Europe, and the JIC took the task seriously and answered all 29 questions on behalf of the United Kingdom.

It is not necessary for us to repeat verbatim the answers here, because they follow along the findings of the foregoing three reports; that is, that the Soviets had the capability to undertake biological sabotage immediately and could within a short time gain capabilities for BW. Although the British IC had not identified any indicators suggesting that the Soviet Union was preparing to wage BW, it "considered that the Soviets would employ BW in any manner to further their over-all efforts. . . . BW would be used for tactical or strategic purposes utilizing either overt or covert means."[43]

Returning to the US IC, the next Top Secret NIE, NIE-65, is dated June 1953. It continued to present dire prognostications to US policymakers: "On the basis of known and estimated Soviet capabilities, we estimate that the USSR can develop and disseminate several highly virulent BW agents. Within the period of this estimate [1953–1957], the USSR might also accomplish the directed mutation of selected viruses and bacteria and the crystallization of certain animal viruses. Success in the application of such research to the production of virulent and stable variants might increase Soviet BW capabilities."[44]

It is particularly interesting to note that this NIE estimates that Soviet scientists might employ futuristic biological techniques to develop both bacteria and viruses for BW purposes. In view of it being highly doubtful that even the most sophisticated Western laboratories would within the given time period be able to apply "directed mutation" to weaponize either bacteria or viruses, the estimate appears to seriously overestimate Soviet bioscientific capabilities at a time when Lysenkoist biological doctrine was still in ascendency.

Another Top Secret report, called Special Estimate, released about the same time adds little, if any, useful information to the 1953 report. Its most indicative findings were: "The USSR has extensive knowledge of botulism, plague, tularemia, brucellosis, various quick-acting intestinal diseases, and some virus diseases. No information is available regarding the production or the stockpiling of BW agents. The USSR could probably mass-produce such agents if so desired."[45]

A Top Secret SNIE in 1954 appears to downplay the Soviet BW threat.[46] It initiated a refrain in IC reporting that is found in a second NIE of the same year, as well as in other NIEs until about 1980.[47] It is exemplified by the quote: "The Soviet Union is in possession of all the necessary basic knowledge for the production of most BW agents. If they chose to do so, they would be able to construct and operate plants for BW production and weapons for dissemination would be available in adequate numbers. However, there is no evidence at present that such weapons are being developed."[48]

The United States, the United Kingdom, Canada, and Australia cooperated closely on both offensive and defensive biological weapon issues. The interactions among these governments are described later in this chapter. A secret British intelligence assessment done in 1960 has findings similar to those of the Americans. The most telling part reads:

There is no evidence that the Soviet military forces are equipped to wage offensive biological warfare. The Soviet Union is, however, capable of developing and using various means of disseminating liquid suspensions of B.W. agents on a large scale, such as (a) cluster bombs delivered from aircraft, rockets, and cruise-type missiles, and (b) spraying directly from such vehicles flying at a low level. It is also capable of developing and using a variety of covert devices for small-scale dissemination. Although there is no indication that any of these possible methods of attack have been studied in the Soviet Union, it is considered that some effort will have been made to keep at least on par with the West.[49]

This report oddly states that the Soviets do not have any biological weapons, but simultaneously lists the possible methods that the Soviet military could employ to wage BW. Further, it in effect tells its readers that they have to assume that the Soviets are undertaking at least as much offensive BW-related R&D as was being done in Western countries, which at that time meant almost entirely the United States. The United Kingdom and Canada had largely discontinued their offensive BW programs, though the United States still had access to the major Canadian BW test site at Suffield.

A secret NIE of 1964, at the peak of the US BW program, is wholly dedicated to Soviet BW. It is particularly interesting because it displays the lack of US intelligence on this subject and the strong suggestion that the earlier estimates were largely unfounded:

> We believe that a BW research program exists in the USSR, but we know of no facility devoted exclusively to offensive BW research and we have no evidence of field testing. Soviet military training in BW concerns itself exclusively with defense, as do the discussions of BW in those Soviet military writings to which we have access. . . . We believe that the Soviets have no present intention to employ BW in military operations. . . . While we have no positive indications of any Soviet effort to produce and stockpile BW weapons, BW research alone would provide the USSR with the capability for clandestine employment of BW. Further, we believe that if they decided to do so, the Soviets could produce large quantities of a number of BW agents for military operations within a few months after such a decision.
>
> However, over the years we have accumulated indications of possible BW activity at a few locations. The most suspect of these locations is Vozrozhdeniya [*sic*] Island in the Aral Sea, where there has been activity which could relate to military needs. There is no strong evidence, however, that this activity is connected with BW research. . . . We have no evidence of any munitions and delivery systems developed specifically for BW by the USSR. . . . The discussion of BW in those Soviet classified and unclassified military writings to which we have access concerns itself exclusively with defense. . . . In those cases where it is considered,

available documents indicate that the "enemy," not the Soviets, used BW offensively.[50]

US intelligence analysts should have noted that it was customary in all Soviet military literature and discussions of weapons systems to refer only to development, procurement, or use by other countries, almost always the United States. Such literature never referred to analogous Soviet weapon systems.

In a Secret study of 1965, two CIA officials discuss problems associated with collecting intelligence about the Soviet BW program.[51] Since the immediate postwar years, US intelligence had been unable to come up with "firm evidence" of a Soviet offensive BW program. US intelligence therefore had to look for indirect signs of such a program by scouring the biology and medical literature for military-related activity, biomedical studies that did not fit Soviet public health requirements, and technical publications that appeared to have been censored due to security considerations. Further, analysts "used speculation, analogy, and parallels with other nations' BW research, development, and practice in recent times and in the historical past." All to no avail. The CIA authors hypothesized that "good Soviet security, censorship, and care not to mar the image of their well-advertised adherence to the Geneva Convention [the Geneva Protocol] had eliminated from the scientific literature all trace [of offensive BW] except defensive preparations and attitudes. The same was true of writings on military doctrine."[52]

The two authors wrote that in 1957 the CIA had secured high-altitude, high-quality photographs of Vozrozhdeniye Island that showed extensive installations. The CIA analysts concluded that it was not a biological test site facility, and this finding fed into the final conclusion of the time, namely, that there was no firm evidence that the Soviet Union possessed a BW program. The CIA analysts believed that if such a program was in existence, Western intelligence would have discovered it.[53] In their words: "Despite tight security, a highly developed Soviet BW weapons system and technology would have surfaced sometime during the years since the war, just as the nuclear and chemical warfare efforts have. Current analyses, therefore, while clearly stating our lack of positive knowledge, depart radically from the old assumptions and look at Soviet military doctrine realistically in terms of limited BW activity and the unsure potential of BW weapons."[54] The reasons for the negative findings of the 1964 NIE would seem to be explained in this analysis.

The intelligence available to the United States was presumably reflected in the brief assessments that were provided by government officials in testimony to congressional committees. The dissonance in a survey of several such statements between 1958 and 1969 is revealing:

I may say that the information I have received adds up to a total Communist effort in biological warfare greater than ours, although it is difficult to judge how much of it has related public health aspects. We have learnt, however, of an extensive field test program and test sites that can only be concerned with offensive employment of such agents.[55]

It is believed that the Soviets now have a strong capability to wage warfare with chemical weapons. Also, the Soviet potential for biological operations is believed to be strong and could be developed into a major threat.[56]

We are fully aware of the massive effort that the Soviets have applied to lethal chemical and biological weapons.[57]

As far as the Russians' BW R&D is concerned, we don't know too much about that, but we know from the scientific literature that the Russians have published openly on most of the biological agents that we have ever considered. So, we have to believe they are probably working in the same area.[58]

There is no clear evidence that any foreign country is presently testing biological weapons, in the sense that an operational delivery means is being used to disseminate either live pathogens or simulants.[59]

The ambiguities and contradictions are obvious. Senior military officers were most often the officials providing these statements. Many of the remarks strike one as virtually offhand comments, not founded on significant supporting material.[60]

The lack of intelligence on Soviet BW was made clear once again in 1969. At that time, President Richard Nixon was considering whether to terminate the US offensive biological weapons program. To help lay a basis for his decision, his national security adviser, Henry Kissinger, ordered the NSC to conduct a study on the pros and cons of the United States retaining its chemical and biological warfare programs.[61] This study was carried out by a group of experts, called the Interdepartmental Political-Military Group. Due to its high level within the IC, it is reasonable that it had access to the latest and best intelligence of the time. The group's Top Secret report analyzed the BW capabilities of several nations, including the Soviet Union.[62] The intelligence on the Soviet Union was meager: "Soviet interest in various potential biological warfare agents has been documented and the intelligence community agrees that the Soviets have all the necessary means for developing an offensive capability in this field. Useful intelligence on actual production, weaponization and stockpiling is nonexistent. . . . In Soviet writings, BW is linked with nuclear and chemical warfare in terms that indicate a high degree of political control and restraint. We believe that Soviet vulnerabilities would weigh heavily against Soviet initiation of BW."[63] The two last sentences quoted above probably allayed some fears about the Soviets acquiring and using biological weapons after the United States discontinued its BW program. The politics underlying Nixon's ultimate decisions to close down America's programs to develop and produce biological and toxin weapons are described in Chapter 20.

At the same time as President Nixon acted to terminate the US offensive BW program, he ordered annual reviews of the activities by, and funding of, the US chemical warfare and biological research programs. The first such review was done by the Interdepartmental Political-Military Group in 1970. Its findings were similar to those stated in 1969:

> Soviet interest in various potential biological warfare agents has been documented and intelligence community agrees that the Soviets have all the necessary means for developing an offensive capability in this field. Useful intelligence on the actual production, weaponization, and stockpiling remains nonexistent, and information on the Soviet biological warfare program remains incomplete in almost all important details. In view of the US renunciation of biological and toxin warfare, the need for greater attention and priority to collection of intelligence in this area is particularly important.[64]

Intelligence Community Assessments, 1972–1979

The relevant national intelligence estimates in 1972, 1975, and 1976 are not revealing.[65] None could be found for 1971, 1973, and 1974. Reports dealing with Soviet BW programs released by DOD in the 1980s are discussed further on in this chapter. It is possible that Soviet BW was addressed in the redacted portions of these reports, or that there was nothing new to report, or that there were reports that we do not know about. Segments of the IC leaked some information about Soviet BW activities to the journalist William Beecher in September 1975, as discussed below in this chapter, so the IC clearly did have some information that it believed indicated the existence of an offensive Soviet BW program. Perhaps this was elaborated on in the 1976 report, whose unredacted pages do include a smidgeon of information: "There is good evidence that, in the past, the Soviets conducted extensive research on biological agents and protective techniques and they have facilities that could be used to make biological agents. Soviet exercises and available documentary writings, however, have not reflected offensive use of biological weapons."[66] This report also indicates that all Warsaw Pact countries were believed to be in compliance with the BWC.[67]

The Defense Intelligence Agency (DIA) addressed the subject of genetic engineering in the Soviet Union for the first time in a secret 1976 report.[68] Unfortunately, what we presume to be the most informative parts of this report, such as military applications and the actual evaluations, are redacted. Nevertheless, one revealing conclusion was allowed by the censors: "The original drive for Soviet research in genetic engineering was probably due to the US lead and Soviet embarrassment in the world scientific community due to their deficiencies in biological sciences."[69] This guess, as we now know, was correct as far as it went; however, the DIA appears to have missed that "the original drive" was the perceived need to apply genetic engineering for BW purposes (see Chapter 2).

The findings of the 1976 NIE are repeated almost verbatim in two of the three assessments we are aware of that were done in 1977 and 1978.[70] The third in some way is more interesting, not because its conclusions are any different, but because it is by far the most ambitious attempt to date by the IC to clarify the entire Soviet BW and CW infrastructures.[71] The DIA assembled a huge volume of 358 pages, in which it included all its information relevant to Soviet biological and chemical weapons, as well as smoke, flame, and incendiary systems; machines and agents used for decontamination; individual and collective protection equipment; systems for reconnaissance and detection of biological and chemical agents; and policy and doctrine for use of biological and chemical weapons. Unfortunately, the copy of this report, which we secured through the Freedom of Information Act, is heavily redacted, hiding most of the information that we probably would have considered particularly telling. The report's sections on biological weapons suffered the most from the censor's heavy hand. But in the end, the report's conclusion in regard to BW agents differs little from those stated in preceding reports:

> The Soviets will continue to improve their ability to grow microorganisms in mass quantities as part of their industrial fermentation industry. If they maintain their stated compliance with the BW Convention, this technology will have industrial applications only. If they should later decide that compliance with the convention is no longer in their national interest, the switch to military application of the technology could easily be accomplished. Basic and applied research in industrial microbiology will continue to be well funded. Emphasis will be placed on genetic engineering of commercially important products.[72]

We have not been able to identify any assessments similar to the foregoing for the years 1978 and 1979. As far as we can discern, the next relevant NIE was done in 1982.

During 1970–1979, the United Kingdom of course had an intelligence effort dedicated to Soviet BW, but it was not large.[73] By 1992, the British Defence Intelligence Service (DIS) had approximately 20 analysts in a branch responsible for WMD assessment overall, headed by Brian Jones.[74] Its responsibilities included all aspects of the Warsaw Pact's nuclear, biological, and chemical (NBC) capabilities. After the BWC was signed in 1972, a lower priority was given to studying the threat of BW from the Warsaw Pact and elsewhere. Therefore the DIS's analytical effort to detect offensive BW programs was gradually reduced. By mid-1980, it had just one section composed of three technical analysts whose primary responsibility was to detect secret BW programs worldwide.[75]

Intelligence Community Assessments, 1980–1992

In April 1979 Sverdlovsk suffered an unprecedented anthrax outbreak, which is discussed in detail in Chapters 3 and 15. It was a momentous event in the history of BW that was to have a major impact on diplomacy and arms control. After Western intelligence agencies recognized that the cause of the disease outbreak was due to an accident in a Soviet military BW facility that was producing a dry *B. anthracis* formulation, there was a qualitative shift in how at least some senior decision makers came to regard the Soviet Union's BW program. Before 1979 the refrain that ran through the IC's assessments of Soviet BW-related activities—at least the unredacted portions that are publicly available—was that the Soviet Union certainly had the capability to redirect its powerful microbiological research and manufacturing enterprise to acquire biological weapons, but that there was no available evidence indicating that the Soviet Union actually possessed such weapons. But within a few years after the 1979 Sverdlovsk outbreak, the IC and DOD knew without doubt that the Soviet Union possessed a sizable BW program, and that it had been and was in noncompliance with the BWC. Previously the IC had been directing its efforts to follow developments in the Soviet biosciences generally in order to prevent technological surprises and detect what might be the beginning of a BW program. From this point on, the main problem faced by IC analysts was to discover the dimensions, activities, and achievements of the Soviet BW program, as well as what the Soviet leaders intended to do with it. (Further details on US documents dealing with Sverdlovsk appear in Chapters 3 and 15.)

Beginning in November 1981 and continuing in a series of publicly released reports in March and November 1982, and February, March, and September 1983, the Reagan administration accused the Soviet Union of the use of mycotoxins in Southeast Asia. Many of these reports, although now widely considered to have been inaccurate and spurious, nevertheless accused the Soviet Union of noncompliance with the BWC. They are discussed in the opening paragraphs of Chapter 16. Finally, information that began to be leaked by US government agencies to journalists beginning in September 1975 indicate that at least some agencies believed that evidence for a Soviet offensive BW program was becoming apparent.

The first intelligence estimate we have for the decade is an overview of 16 "Key Soviet Military Technologies,"[76] which did not include biotechnology. It notes that findings generated by rapidly advancing science and technology quickly could have unexpected effects on the military: "The chances of technological surprise—the unexpected appearance of militarily important technology—will probably increase significantly through the remainder of the century. Soviet technology advances will make more R&D options available to the Soviet Union, and the guideposts of US experience probably will become even less useful to the Intelligence Community as an aid in understanding future Soviet activity."[77] This report resembles to a substantial degree an open presentation that was made annually in the 1970s and 1980s by the Director, Defense Research and Engineering in the DOD, to the US Senate and House Armed Services and Defense Appropriations Committees.

The DOD version would present estimates in graphic form displaying in which of the major technological fields of research related to weapons development US military R&D led and in which, if any, the Soviet Union possessed an advantage. Biotechnology in its military application, which was not included in the list of 16 technologies, would turn out to be the only example of Soviet "technological surprise." Nine years later the IC would have the unpleasant experience of discovering not only the extent of the Soviet BW program, but also that new biotechnological approaches had for some time been applied to develop unique BW agents. IC discoveries up to this point in time regarding work in the Soviet Union on biosciences had been of limited benefit in attempts to understand Soviet BW-related activities in the 1980s and 1990s.

Quotations from the following reports dealing with the 1979 Sverdlovsk anthrax incident demonstrate that there was an unsettled period of two years during which different branches of the IC produced suggestive but inconclusive assessments of the events. As early as February 1980, the CIA reportedly argued that the Sverdlovsk outbreak's etiology was evidence of the Soviet Union having violated the BWC.[78] Though heavily redacted, an IC analysis of the events published sometime in 1981 makes clear that the IC was suspicious that the cause of the disease outbreak was a secret BW facility, but was not yet entirely convinced of it. In one comment regarding the accident it noted, "It is possible for researchers to become infected with BW agents, including anthrax, because of carelessness. Accidents involving pressure valves, heating systems, volatile gases, and spray dryers have potential for causing an explosion that could vent disease agents outside the building. Depending on the quantity released, type of agent, and the local weather conditions, an agent cloud could result in outbreaks of disease downwind from the accident site."[79] However, a page later, among its final lines, it stated:

Certain key points, however, provide compelling circumstantial evidence that the Soviets have maintained an active BW program at the Sverdlovsk facility since at least 1972:

• The probable accident site is a heavily secured military installation suspected of conducting BW agent research and development since the early 1950s.
• Major new construction activity at the installation during the 1960s included buildings suitable for production and storage of BW agents.[80]

Whatever information suggested that the MOD site was doing BW R&D "since the early 1950s" is not apparent in any of the unredacted pages of the declassified reports referred to previously. It may however be a comment made in 1981 in hindsight.

In a relatively similar vein, a Department of the Army report in October 1981 noted, "The Soviets still have some anthrax for biological warfare purposes and it is possible that they still have an active biological warfare agent program at this Sverdlovsk facility. . . . The evidence indicates that the Soviets are probably in violation of the 1972 Biological Weapons Convention."[81]

Nevertheless, as late as February 1982 the IC as a whole had apparently not yet definitively concluded that a Soviet BW facility was the cause of the 1979 Sverdlovsk anthrax outbreak. This can be seen by reading the conclusions of DIA's follow-up report to its extensive 1977 assessment. Though slightly shorter, at 312 pages, than its predecessor, it is still much larger than most assessments of this type. Though as heavily redacted as its predecessor, its main conclusions are written in the clear and resemble the ones of 1977:

> The Soviets will continue to improve their ability to grow microorganisms in massive quantities as part of their microbiological industry. If they should decide that compliance with the BW convention is no longer in their national interest, the switch to military applications of the technology could be accomplished fairly easily. Recombinant DNA technology, or genetic engineering of bacteria and viruses, is currently being studied by the Soviets. Although emphasis is placed on modifications of industrial microorganisms to create strains producing higher yields, new genetic developments or the discovery of new disease agents having application in a BW program will be noted. Soviet state-of-the-art in the technical specialties that are needed for BW agent development and production will improve. Whether the Soviets engage in such work or not will depend on the international political climate of the early 1980s.[82]

This statement makes clear that as of February 1982, at least the DIA tended to believe that the Soviet Union remained in compliance with the BWC. This is in striking contrast to the administration's charges at the very same time of Soviet use of mycotoxins in Southeast Asia (see Chapter 16). Further, its estimate about genetic engineering was that the Soviets were not yet using this technique for BW purposes. The actual situation at this time was one of Soviet BWC noncompliance since 1975, with the order having been given in 1972 for Soviet scientists to "engage in such work." Thus, parts of the IC in early 1982, despite the Sverdlovsk outbreak having occurred almost three years earlier, was approximately five to six years behind real developments in Soviet BW, and 10 years behind the 1972 Central Committee decision.

The first thorough IC assessment of Soviet genetic engineering was published in December 1983.[83] It was updated by adding annexes in March 1984 and August 1987. While the original report was classified Secret, the two annexes were Top Secret. Unfortunately, the report's section of highest interest, "Soviet Military Implications," is the one that is most heavily redacted. Nevertheless, what it reveals allows us to draw important conclusions. To do so, we quote the report as some length;

> Offensive military applications of genetic engineering might include the development of unique (difficult to detect, identify, and treat) anti-personnel CBW agents and toxins. Similar agents could be developed against crops, livestock, and military materiel. The development and exploitation of Soviet offensive capabilities could seriously threaten the United States.
>
> The Soviet military sector has access to the technology to pursue military goals. Further, it can influence priorities, direct and fund its own rDNA research, and sponsor research in nonmilitary affiliated institutes. Military interests are most likely represented on the Interagency Scientific and Technical Council.
>
> Several Soviet papers published in the open literature at the Gamaleya Institute of Epidemiology and Microbiology, Moscow, describe the property of aerosol stability being genetically engineered into *E. coli*. If this interpretation is correct, it would mean that the Soviets have a stable, aerosolizable, seemingly benign BW agent capable of producing a unique toxin. [As written in the original.]
>
> There are other research papers which have appeared in open publications that, while appearing to represent legitimate research interests, also have obvious military potential.
>
> • Transfer of a gene conferring antibiotic resistance from *E. coli* to the causative agent of cholera [presumably *Vibrio cholerae*].
> • Synthesis and cloning of an artificial gene for a sleep-inducing peptide. This research was carried out at the Institute of Bioorganic Chemistry in

Moscow, one of the premier molecular genetics research establishments. [Redacted sentence.] In addition to this peptide, the Soviets are studying others that are capable of varied effects such as inducing fear, exaggerating emotional responses, and lethal nervous system impairment.

• Development of "oil-eating" bacteria to consume lubricants or to attack fuel depots.

• Development of methyl-styrene (synthetic rubber) degrading bacteria.

Military Implications. Because the Soviet military has substantial influence and technical resources, their interest in genetic-engineering applications will directly affect national objectives and priorities. We believe the military will exploit Soviet research developments. The spectrum of potential defensive and offensive military applications has been discussed previously. Soviet military interest is motivated by the potential for battlefield and strategic advantage and the threat of technological surprise in this area. Western military-related applied rDNA research for defensive purposes is currently minor in scope. Assuming high military priority, the Soviets can move ahead of the West in useful military applications.[84]

The March 1984 annex adds little information useful to this book. It notes that 75 Soviet facilities are using genetic engineering for research purposes, and that most of this work is conducted by institutes ".with long established expertise in biochemistry, enzymology, and classical genetics. These research facilities are subordinate to the Academy of Sciences, the Ministry of Health, the Microbiological Industry, the Ministry of Defense, or universities throughout the country. An Interagency Scientific and Technical Council subordinate to the Council of Ministers and the party Central Committee was established in 1981 to organize and direct the research."[85] Conversely, although heavily redacted, the August 1987 annex is very revealing:

The USSR's biological warfare program is attempting to develop agents whose characteristics would not be identified using current Western technology, thus complicating and possibly precluding medical treatment of infected troops and civilians. [Redacted part.] This is the first direct evidence the Soviets are using genetic engineering for military research on specific micro-organisms. Research [redacted part] permits refinement of genetic engineering laboratory techniques and provides a model [redacted part] Expertise gained from this research may result in the production of new or altered biological agents that could be difficult to identify and treat [redacted part].[86]

A Top Secret SNIE of 1984, also heavily redacted, has more specific information that is relevant to the Factor and Bonfire programs (described in Chapters 7 and 8). It discusses Soviet weaponization of bioregulators and the use of genetic engineering to enable microorganisms to mass-produce these substances.[87] However, we now know that the second finding was incorrect, because the Soviet approach actually was to integrate genes that code for the production of bioregulators (peptides) into microorganisms and use these as delivery systems, not as a means of production. Nevertheless, that the Soviet BW program had an interest in bioregulators was an important observation.

Two or three years before Pasechnik's defection, and perhaps even as early as 1984, the IC was therefore convinced that the Soviet Union was applying genetic engineering to alter the characteristics of microorganisms for the purposes of changing their pathogenic profile and/or making them more difficult to identify. It may have been aided in coming to this conclusion on the basis of information collected from interviews with émigré scientists (see below).

It is reasonable to assume that the Armed Forces Medical Intelligence Center (AFMIC) had an important role in writing the 1983 CIA report (and its 1984 and 1987 annexes), which, as far as we know, was the first to identify the BW potential of peptides and analyze Soviet capabilities in this subfield. We do not know what events provided AFMIC and/or the CIA with clues to this development, possibly statements made by émigré scientists. However it occurred, the insight was several years after the fact. It appears that Ashmarin became interested in this subfield in 1975. Further, as we now know, Factor was well under way by the time the CIA's 1983 report was being prepared.

Soon after the Reagan administration took office in 1981, senior political officials rapidly decided what they believed about the existence or status of Soviet BW and Soviet compliance with the BWC. This took place, however, for a singular reason. These officials convinced themselves—mistakenly, as it turned out—that the Soviet Union was responsible for the use of mycotoxins in Indochina, the "Yellow Rain" controversy. (See Chapter 16.) Because the administration stated unequivocally that the Soviet Union had been responsible for the *use* of a BW agent, it would necessarily have been *producing* the agent, and hence it was by definition in violation of the BWC. The Sverdlovsk anthrax outbreak and the accumulating satellite evidence discussed below appear at first to have played only secondary roles in the formation of opinions by Reagan administration policymakers. The IC had still not settled on an ultimate determination about the cause of the Sverdlovsk events, and its reports on the status of Soviet BW in general were still equivocal.

The new situation was reflected in the remarkable National Security Decision Directive (NSDD) number 18, dated January 4, 1982, just one year after the Reagan administration took office. The document stated that the United States would:

> Seek to convene a meeting of States Parties to the Biological Weapons Convention with the aim of strengthening its verification and compliance mechanisms in light of probable Soviet non-compliance, and to provide an additional forum for maintaining international pressure on the Soviet Union concerning its chemical and biological warfare activities; and . . . consider invoking the other two remedies provided by the biological Weapons Convention:
>
> a. Taking the issue to the United Nations Security Council, and
> b. As an ultimate step, withdrawing from the Biological Weapons Convention.
>
> . . . [T]he Government is directed to study and submit recommendations on:
>
> —Specific measures to strengthen the verification and compliance provisions of the Biological Weapons Convention; . . .
> —Consultations with United States Allies on a strategy in the United Nations and elsewhere; and
> —The legal issues associated with formally charging the Soviet Union with violation of the Biological Weapons Convention.[88]

A declassified legal analysis of the issues involved in charging the Soviet Union with violation of the BWC was produced some time in 1982.[89]

This was followed by a progression of public diplomacy disclosures. In a statement to the Informal Heads of Delegation Meeting of the CSCE in Madrid on February 16, 1982, US Ambassador Max Kampelman identified Military Compound 19 in Sverdlovsk as a "Soviet biological weapons research and production facility" and added, "We are aware of five other such facilities in operation today," implying that *production* was taking place in those five as well. The text of Kampelman's full statement was included in Senate testimony on March 22, 1982.[90] In 1984 the United States released two public documents explicitly referring to an offensive Soviet BW program. The first was a report by the President to Congress,[91] but the most detailed was in the widely distributed report *Soviet Military Power, 1984.* It referred to "at least seven biological warfare centers in the USSR that have the highest security and are under the strictest military control," and added the explicit charge that the "Soviet Union has an active R&D program to investigate and evaluate the utility of biological weapons and their impact on the combat environment . . . [which] violates the Biological and Toxin Weapons Convention of 1972." The Sverdlovsk site was described as a "BW research production and storage facility."[92] On November 2, 1984, Secretary of Defense Weinberger wrote to Senator James Sasser, "We continue to obtain new evidence that the Soviet Union has maintained its offensive biological warfare program and that it is exploring genetic engineering to expand their program's scope."[93] The source for all the information provided in these public disclosures must be presumed to be the IC.

The Reagan administration's four secret reports—declassified in 1995–1996—titled "Soviet Noncompliance with Arms Control Agreements (C)" issued 1984 through 1987 also show a clear progression. The first, in 1984, was a White House fact sheet on the President's arms control noncompliance report to Congress. It was quite general, and it is impossible to determine whether it was based on any considerations other than the administration's beliefs regarding Yellow Rain.

> The judgment previously made when the U.S. Government publicly charged the Soviet Union with violations of its obligations is confirmed. On the basis of the available evidence, the U.S. has concluded that the Soviet Union is in violation of its legal obligations under the Geneva Protocol of 1925 and customary international law, which prohibit the use of poisonous gases, and the Biological and Toxin Weapons Convention, which entered into force in 1975 and which bans the development, production, stockpiling, or transfer of biological agents and toxins.[94]

The relevant paragraph for 1985, however, clearly identified other determinants:

The U.S. Government judges that continued expansion during 1984 at suspect biological and toxin weapon facilities in the Soviet Union, and reports that a Soviet BW program may now include investigation of new classes of BW agents, confirm and strengthen the conclusion of the January 1984 report that the Soviet Union has maintained an offensive biological warfare program and capability in violation of its legal obligation under the Biological and Toxin Weapons Convention of 1972.[95]

The 1986 paragraph includes the exact same words, but with two lines redacted,[96] while the 1987 version again contains the exact same paragraph but without any redaction.[97] In regard to the BWC and Geneva Protocol, the report stated that the Soviet Union was "in violation of its legal obligation under the Biological and Toxin Weapons convention of 1972" for two major reasons. First, the Soviet Union's involvement in the "production, transfer and use of trichothecene mycotoxins for hostile purposes in Laos, Kampuchea and Afghanistan."[98] Second, the "continuation of an aggressive biological weapons production and development program by the Soviet Union" as had been proven by the Sverdlovsk anthrax outbreak. The report warned, "The Soviet Union has a prohibited offensive biological warfare capability which we do not have and against which we have no defense. This capability may include advanced biological agents about which we have little knowledge. Evidence suggests that the Soviets are expanding their chemical and toxin warfare capabilities in a manner that has no parallel in NATO's retaliatory or defensive program."[99]

At some moment between 1984 and 1985, the NIC staffer for the Soviet Union requested that an SNIE be prepared on Soviet attitudes regarding compliance with the BWC. He did not, however, have the authority to order its preparation, because the responsibility for the subject fell under the purview of another member of the NIC staff. For unknown bureaucratic reasons the request was not acted upon.[100] Nevertheless, the administration had clearly and publicly concluded that the Soviet Union was in violation of the BWC. On September 9, 1986, at the Second BWC Review Conference, US ambassador Lowitz stated: "The United States had sought to make use of the consultative process provided for in article V with the Soviet Union concerning the 1979 outbreak of anthrax in that country, Soviet involvement in the production, transfer and use of mycotoxins, and the Soviet Union's maintenance of an offensive biological warfare program."[101]

The year 1986 was also significant because one branch of the IC, the DIA, for the first time released an entire unclassified report on the Soviet BW threat.[102] With some artistic license, its cover depicts two Soviet Mi-24/HIND helicopters equipped with spraying equipment to disperse aerosol, although there is no evidence that any such Soviet BW delivery system existed. The report stated:

> We have also identified a number of installations capable of producing disease agents and toxins on a large-scale and placing them in munitions and delivery/dissemination systems. These installations have been established by the Ministry of Defense and are under its control. One such facility is in the city of Sverdlovsk and has a long history of biological warfare R&D and production with emphasis on the causative agent of anthrax. In addition to anthrax, we believe the Soviets have developed tularemia, plague, and cholera for BW purposes, as well as botulinum toxin, enterotoxin, and mycotoxins.[103]

Additional key judgments were:

> The Soviets have gone far beyond what is allowed by these treaties [BWC and Geneva Protocol] for the following reasons:
>
> • The size and scope of their efforts are not consistent with any reasonable standard of what could be justified on the basis of prophylactic, protective or peaceful purposes.
> • The Soviets continue to evaluate the military utility of biological and toxin weapons.
> • The Soviets are rapidly incorporating biotechnological developments into their offensive BW program to improve agent utility on the tactical battlefield.[104]

Yet the report is scanty as to substance. The first six pages are dedicated to the "Soviet Biological Warfare Threat," which includes a general description of how BW agents are produced and a cursory discussion of the Sverdlovsk anthrax outbreak. These pages are filled mostly with maps and illustrations. The next two pages contain a description of the "Soviet Biological Warfare Organization," but it is in fact about the Soviet Army's Chemical Troops and includes nothing about Soviet BW R&D or production. The remainder of the report consists of four annexes: (1) a general description of biotechnology, including two short paragraphs on possible applications for the military; (2) a copy of the 1925 Geneva Protocol; (3) a copy of the BWC; and (4) two pages on how the Soviets might go about destroying their BW agents. The report names only one BW facility; "the candidate BW test and evaluation installation on Vozrozhdeniye Island." Thus, 20 of the report's 28 pages consist of essentially extraneous material and the remainder provide very little information about the Soviet BW program. As a product of the DOD's intelligence sector, it is all the more surprising, given what appeared almost simultaneously from another branch of the DOD.

The most revealing public product released during the Reagan administration appeared in September 1986 in the form of congressional testimony by, Deputy Assistant Secretary of Defense for Negotiation Policy Douglas Feith. The testimony was subsequently also published in a journal article. In a matter of 25 lines, Feith set out six significant points regarding an offensive Soviet BW program, not counting a reference to Yellow Rain. Several are recognizable as repetitions of statements made between 1984 and 1986 and previously described; others are new:

- The Soviet Union has built a large organization devoted to the development and production of offensive BW.
- At the very time when Soviet officials were negotiating and signing the BWC, a high-ranking Soviet defector has reported, the Politburo decided to intensify the Soviet BW program.
- The Soviets retained stockpiles of BW agent produced in pre-recombinant-DNA days.
- At known biological warfare facilities in the Soviet Union they maintain highly secured weapons storage facilities under military control.
- . . . they are developing new means of biological warfare based on current bio-engineering technologies.
- There are at least seven biological warfare centers in the USSR under military control, all with unusually rigorous security.[105]

Feith concluded with a summary condemnation, "In other words, the Soviet Union has not only violated the BWC, but every major prohibition in it."[106] These points prefigure in a skeleton form some of the basic elements of the Soviet BW program that the US and UK governments would learn in much greater detail following the defection of Vladimir Pasechnik three years later. If the defector referred to by Feith is mentioned only in reference to the information regarding the Politburo decision in 1972, it was almost certainly Arkady Shevchenko, the senior Soviet diplomat who had defected to the United States in 1975, and whose book was published in 1987.[107] (See Chapter 20.) This was corroborated by a source who served in the National Security Council during the Reagan administration. Most surprisingly, few of the specifics in Feith's 1986 public disclosure appear in the unclassified 1986 DIA publication or in the unredacted portions of the 1986 NIE. One has to presume that everything that Feith placed in the public record was known to the producers of those documents, the DIA and the NIC, and that the same points appear in redacted portions of other of the reports that we have described. If not, it would indicate that major differences of opinion about the Soviet BW program remained within the IC as late as 1986.

As noted earlier, the Reagan administration also issued a public report on Soviet noncompliance with arms control treaties in 1986.[108]

While the preceding two reports as well as Feith's congressional testimony were unclassified,[109] there was also a NIE on this subject in 1986.[110] However, it is so heavily redacted as to be of little use. Of 42 pages of text, 36 are totally redacted, not leaving a single word intact, while three other pages are largely redacted. The following excerpts are broad general statements that are separated by redacted sections:

The Soviet maintains the world's most comprehensive chemical and biological warfare program, and the West believes this capability constitutes a serious threat to NATO and to several countries friendly to the West. . . .

In the early 1970s, the Soviets allocated almost $2 billion on a program to overcome a perceived US lead in CBW and provide a new generation of CBW weapons to be fielded in the next decade, and it appears that the Soviets have maintained and expanded their BW efforts. . . .

The Soviet Union has the capability to produce CBW agents in the large amounts that would be required for effective military operations. . . .

Over 100 industrial microbiological plants are in the Soviet Union, most doing clearly legitimate research to provide antibiotics, serums, and vaccines. . . .

The program for the modernization of the CBW arsenal, which has been going on for more than a decade, has concentrated on exploring advances in biotechnology such as genetic engineering. This may, in the next 10 years, result in the fielding of new agents (chemical, toxin, and biological) for which NATO has no means of detection, identification, protection, or treatment.[111]

The little that is unredacted in this report is not very helpful. First, its authors combine chemical and biological weapons in their comments, which is a basic mistake no one familiar with these fields should ever make. Their scientific characteristics are very different, as are the weapons and arms control issues they generate. The BW and CW programs were completely separate in every way in the Soviet Union, although the MOD was in charge of both. None of our information indicates any overlap between the two disciplines, except for the location of research on some toxins in the Ministry of Chemical Industry. Second, the presence of so many qualifiers (believes, appears, may) renders it largely useless for decision making. The finding in the concluding sentence, preceded by the indefinite phrasing "may, in the next 10 years," is almost a guarantee of instant disregard by a busy decision maker. And in yet another example of the problem of interpretation from heavily redacted materials, the sentence about "100 industrial microbiological plants" is followed by two redacted paragraphs. The same line, again followed by two redacted paragraphs, appeared in a supplement to the 1986 NIE.[112] The two redacted paragraphs almost certainly contain information that in some way alters the understanding of the unredacted line.

A biotechnology subfield, namely peptides and hormones, was the subject of an unclassified study done for AFMIC by Battelle analysts in 1988.[113] They surveyed the open Russian-language scientific literature for the period 1982 to mid-1987 to identify key scientists in this field, home institutes of the scientists, peptides and hormones that were the subjects of interest by key scientists, and indications of networking by Soviet scientists in this subfield. They identified 18 key Soviet scientists who worked on 33 different peptides and hormones, and 36 Soviet institutions were identified as supporting relevant R&D. They also found signs of a widespread and very active network that connected scientists and institutes interested in the subfield. The report makes clear that there was a substantial peptide R&D effort in the Soviet Union at that time, and concluded that Soviet scientists were highly capable in this field.

The 18 scientists named did include I. P. Ashmarin, who we now know was the initiator of the immune aspect of the Factor program. However, the

38 institutions named as supporting peptide and hormone research did not include any of the Biopreparat institutes, and included only one of the MOD biological institutes, the Kirov Institute. If AFMIC relied only on this report for clues as to where BW-related R&D on these chemicals might be proceeding, it would have missed the most important centers in this regard, which were SRCAM and Vector. Most likely it would also have missed the significance of Ashmarin's involvement in peptide R&D, because at that time his connection with the military and/or Biopreparat was hidden. His affiliation was only rarely noted in open Russian sources. In the cases that it was, it was to the Department of Biology at the Moscow State University and never to an MOD or Biopreparat institute.

Battelle analysts drew no conclusions as to whether peptides and hormones were being weaponized. This being the case, the reason for contracting Battelle to undertake a study in 1988 that utilized open-source information probably was for the IC to learn about Soviet scientific-technical capabilities in this arcane subfield, thus providing its analysts with a sound basis for determining what kind of projects might be done in the classified sphere to develop improved or new biological and biochemical weapons.

The last IC document dealing with Soviet BW that we possess was published in 1990.[114] Unlike many of its predecessors, this report names ministries and institutes. For example, it provides a chart that lists "Major Participants of the Soviet BW Program" under two headings—"Soviet Ministries" and "Soviet Academies." Noteworthy revelations in the report include:

- Identification of the "Central Research Laboratory (NII-35)" as a major defensive research center working on both bacterial pathogens and toxins.
- The existence of close collaborations between the Kirov Military Medical Academy, Zagorsk Institute, and Mechnikov Institute of Vaccine and Sera, which allows for a free exchange of information between these institutes' scientists.
- The substantial, important involvement of the Gamaleya Institute in both offensive and defensive BW programs. "We suspect that this facility's long-term contribution to the Soviet BW program has been in areas of basic research on candidate agents, immunology, and development of diagnostic serological techniques."
- The identification for the first time by the IC of "Problema 5," which is described as being "dedicated to military-funded offensive and defensive

BW programs"; and the Gamaleya Institute is correctly named as being in charge of it.
- That the Ministry of Health's second department, headed by P. N. Burgasov, was coordinating the ministry's BW activities with the MOD.
- That the anti-plague institutes contribute to the BW program "by conducting labor-intensive screening of natural bacterial pathogens and toxin-producing agents to identify prime BW agent candidates."[115]

The report also had its share of errors. An example was its identification of the 7th Directorate as being in charge of the MOD's BW program, when in fact the 15th Directorate had had this responsibility since 1973. The report also gives too much weight to the Gamaleya Institute, asserting that it had important roles in both the offensive and the defensive BW programs, whereas in fact its main responsibility was defense. Similarly, Problem 5 was claimed to be involved in offensive activities, which was not the case except indirectly.

In any case, this report makes clear that shortly before the IC had access to information divulged by Pasechnik, it already knew with certainty that the Soviet Union had a sizable BW program that involved many components of the nation's science and technology infrastructure, as well as ministries usually not associated with biological weapons acquisition, such as agriculture and health.[116]

Can one be certain that the foregoing report is the last available declassified IC report? As far as NIEs are concerned, this conclusion is based on the CIA publication in 2008 of a list containing the names and dates of all declassified NIEs on the Soviet Union and International Communism.[117] The latest year given for a declassified NIE was 1991, and except for the ones named above, none of the NIEs issued in 1986–1991 address Soviet BW issues. Thorough searches of other government and nongovernmental sources have not led to discoveries of other declassified publications relevant to this book. For example, searches through the holdings of the Open Source Center, Defense Technical Information Center, and the National Security Archive yielded no relevant declassified publications after 1990.

The most important intelligence breakthrough of this era was Pasechnik's defection.[118] In October 1989, Pasechnik was given permission by Biopreparat to conduct an official visit to an industrial exhibit in Toulouse, France. Once in Toulouse, he separated himself from other members of his party and took a train to Paris. He then contacted the Canadian embassy, telling an official who he was and that he wanted to defect. The embassy officials did not realize his significance and told him to follow routine Canadian immigration procedures, which would take months to process. He then contacted the British embassy in Paris, with very different results—his transfer to London was quickly arranged and carried out.

The DIS soon realized that Pasechnik presented an opportunity to learn about Soviet BW capabilities on an unprecedented scale. However, the senior official in charge of the branch that dealt with chemical and biological weapons, Brian Jones, recognized that his branch "did not have the capacity and, in some areas, the expertise to analyse . . . the wealth of scientific and technical information on the Soviet biological weapons effort." He therefore asked the Chemical Defense Establishment for technical assistance in debriefing Pasechnik.[119] In addition to DIS officials Christopher Davis and Jones, David Kelly and others were seconded to the DIS and came to constitute the team that debriefed Pasechnik over a period of about three years.

After Pasechnik had been questioned for several months, the information he provided was passed to the CIA early in 1990, and the Americans were subsequently invited to meet Pasechnik in the United Kingdom. Following Pasechnik's initial debriefings, DIS officers had to struggle to convince their more senior British officials of the truth and significance of his information. The bureaucratic reasons for this were obvious: it suggested major past policy misjudgments and the limitations of the BWC, as well as the need to confront Gorbachev at the height of negotiations on strategic nuclear weapons, German reunification, and other major policy issues. The initial US reaction was much the same: the CIA was initially skeptical of the information that Pasechnik was providing.[120] However, they subsequently became convinced that his information was genuine. The United States then shared information on Soviet BW with the United Kingdom, including older material. This stimulated DIS analysts to recheck their own intelligence database, and they found signs of an active Soviet BW program that had been overlooked.

It bears noting that an agreement and a mechanism for sharing intelligence about CBW between the United States, the United Kingdom, Australia, and Canada had existed since the 1960s. However, its operation was of variable efficiency. It was led by a steering committee that met annually in one of the four capitals on a rotating basis. In addition there could be ad hoc sharing of information between two or more parties at any time. It was accepted among the contributing parties that there would be some information that one country might have that could not be shared. The United States contributed by far the largest number of reports to the information exchange. Some UK and US intelligence analysts had long maintained strong suspicions about Biopreparat and its involvement with the covert offensive BW program, but not to the level of detail provided by Pasechnik. More importantly, high-level British and American government officials generally had not been convinced by these suspicions.

In 1992 Pasechnik's former superior, Ken Alibek, defected to the United States. Alibek was debriefed for approximately four years. His major product was a report that remains classified Secret to this day.[121] After the debriefings of Pasechnik and Alibek were completed, the most important facts about the Biopreparat system and its components were probably known.

Information on Suspected or Alleged Soviet Biological Warfare Activities in the Mass Media

A substantial number of books, newspapers, magazines, and television and radio programs have over the years described real or alleged events concerning biological weapons. For the purpose of this book we are interested only in those accounts that appear to reveal details about the Soviet BW program. This section focuses on accounts in the mass media that cover roughly the same ground as the reports of the IC and the authoritative government sources presented above. Our purpose is to examine what the mass media learned about the Soviet BW program and how journalists dealt with that information, keeping in mind that government officials often were the sources of deliberately leaked information used by reporters as a basis for their articles. Whenever a reporter cites vague information sources such as "government officials who must remain unnamed," "intelligence sources," or others, the reader is at the mercy of both the source and the journalist; that the source is telling the truth and also not omitting crucial details, and that the journalist is not fabricating and is reporting accurately what he was told.

In introducing an examination of information that appeared in the mass media, we should point to a short section entitled "Western Information on Soviet Biological Weapons" that covers the 1950s and 1960s in the monumental study on biological and chemical warfare and weapons by the Stockholm International Peace Research Institute (SIPRI).[122] Included in the section are press articles, results of a few studies, and testimony by US government officials presented to congressional committees. The claims made ranged from the Soviet Union's having a capability to acquire biological weapons but not possessing any to its having a full-scale BW program with deployed biological weapons. Extremely farfetched examples were the several assertions made in 1952 by Rear Admiral (retired) Ellis M. Zacharias, a former deputy director of the US Office of Naval Intelligence, including the following:

> In eight "military bacterial stations," one of them on a ghost ship in the Arctic Ocean, the Soviet Union is mass-producing enormous quantities of "disease agents" for aggressive use against the soldiers and civilians of the free world. In particular, the Red Army is stockpiling two specific "biological weapons" with which it expects to strike a strategic blow and win any future war decisively even before it gets started officially.[123]

The SIPRI authors did not attempt to judge whether or not the Soviet Union had a BW program, noting only that there was no confirmation of such a program and that "more detailed information may possibly follow from Soviet action after the 1972 Biological Weapons Convention comes into force."[124] As discussed in Chapter 20, the Soviet Union never released such information and information released by Russia in 1992 was minimal.

In September 1975, just six months after the Soviet Union ratified the BWC, William Beecher, a reporter for the *Boston Globe* who covered defense issues including the DOD, published an article based on information leaked to him by unidentified "US government sources." He wrote that satellite imagery had detected "very high incinerator stacks and large cold storage bunkers" at three sites: Omutninsk, Sverdlovsk, and Zagorsk. According to intelligence analysts, this was indicative of "biological arms production plants."[125] The point of the article was that the US government suspected the Soviet Union to be violating the BWC by secretly developing illegal biological weapons. Administration officials were described in a subsequent article in *Science* as being "in a quandary over what they can do about strong indications that the Soviet Union may be violating the ban on biological weapons."[126]

Approximately eight months later, the Associated Press published an article written by an anonymous journalist that also was based on information supposedly leaked by government sources. It contained the names of three additional sites for Soviet BW facilities: in Aksu, Berdsk, and Pokrov. This article contained a note of caution: "Some intelligence reports the plants as suspected biological warfare production and storage facilities. Other sources say the plants may be making biological-associated products for agricultural purposes, but could be adapted easily to turn out warfare materials."[127]

Six sites that allegedly housed suspect BW facilities had therefore been identified in US newspapers in 1975 and 1976: "Aksu," which is a village located near Stepnogorsk, Kazakh SSR, and almost certainly referred to *Glavmikrobioprom's* Progress Plant, because the Biopreparat Stepnogorsk facility had not yet been built at that time; "Berdsk," which probably referred to the Berdsk Chemical Factory located near Novosibirsk, which had been transferred to Biopreparat in 1974; "Omutninsk," which likely referred to the Omutninsk Chemical Factory located in the Kirov *oblast* and transferred to Biopreparat in 1974; "Pokrov," which probably referred to the Pokrov Production Plant, which belonged to the Soviet Ministry of Agriculture and was located in Pokrov city, approximately 940 kilometers northeast of Moscow; "Sverdlovsk," which referred to the MOD's Sverdlovsk Institute; and "Zagorsk," which referred to the MOD's Zagorsk Institute. Notably, all these identifications would be proved correct after 1989.

Beecher and the Associated Press writer certainly would not have learned of the existence of the six facilities or their purpose on their own. The BW-related information was almost certainly provided to them by someone in the DOD with access to data obtained from US overhead intelligence, most likely satellite. It is possible that facilities in Berdsk, Omutninsk, Pokrov, Sverdlovsk, and Zagorsk had been known to the IC for some years, having been spotted on U2 and/or satellite imagery. In addition the Progress Plant might have raised IC interest because of its construction in the early 1970s at an isolated site. Regardless of the reasons for IC suspicions about the six sites, the two newspaper accounts tell us that these facilities were known to the IC in 1975 and 1976, although what took place inside the facilities almost certainly remained unknown to the IC.

Notably, none of the six facilities or sites had been identified in the unredacted portions of the declassified IC reports, NIEs and SNIES, reviewed above. Their names may be in the redacted portions of these reports, or details such as names of Soviet institutions and scientists may not have been included in high-level reports such as the NIEs. A final possibility is that missing names in NIEs and other high-level documents reflected a divergence within the IC on how to interpret intelligence that was thought to bear on

BW. Leaking is a customary practice when one party in interagency disputes wants its version on an important issue to get public exposure. Whatever the reason, the information leaked by government officials to journalists in 1975–1976 was more indicative of substantial Soviet involvement with BW-related activity that allegedly violated the BWC than was reflected in the *unredacted* portions of the consensus high-level classified documents provided to senior US decision makers.

After the Beecher and Associated Press articles were published, a *Los Angeles Times* reporter stationed in Moscow investigated the issue of alleged Soviet biological weapons R&D by canvassing the opinions of several well-known Soviet microbiologists. Robert C. Toth wrote:

> When reconnaissance satellite photographs showed new Soviet biological labs, stories appeared in the West that secret military research in genetic engineering was underway here [Soviet Union]. The consensus of sources here—although not a unanimous view—is that such advanced work is not going on, if for no other reason than that the Russians started in the field at least two years after Western experts and are still learning basic techniques.[128]

Although there is much more to Toth's article, including a discussion about whether new weapons produced by genetic engineering are covered by the BWC, with some Soviet politicians stating that they were not and therefore required the negotiation of a new treaty, his conclusion was:

> There is no evidence, whatever the rationale, that the Russians are conducting secret genetic weapons research. But a former Soviet geneticist, Edward Trifonov, who has emigrated to Israel, said at least two institutes here [Soviet Union] had secret laboratories within their biological departments where genetic engineering could be done. One is the Kurchatov Atomic Energy Institute, where Trifonov himself worked. The other is the Zdanov Industrial Microorganisms Laboratory, which is a pharmaceutical research institute.
>
> A final disquieting note is that Yury Ovchinnikov, Academy of Sciences vice president, in December, 1975, gave a lecture to high-ranking officials that included military officers. One general came away enthusiastic about prospects for genetic engineering, according to a Western diplomat.

Ovchinnikov, a 42-year-old biochemist, is reputedly the coordinator of genetic engineering work here. He refused several requests from The Times during the last year for an interview or a copy of his old speech.[129]

Toth's observations were quite different from those of Beecher and the Associated Press reporter. Given that his story was based on information from interviews with Soviet scientists and not on US government leaks, that is only to be expected. In particular, Aleksandr A. Baev, who is quoted at length in Toth's story as included in the Preface of this book, was of course fully informed about the Soviet BW program. He would never have given the slightest hint that such a program existed. Instead he suggested that such illegal work would more likely be performed in capitalist countries by "powerful corporations and persons out of social control."[130] Nevertheless, to his credit, Toth did report some disquieting observations, including the presence of secret laboratories in ostensibly open institutes, and Ovchinnikov's explanation of the prospects of genetic engineering for weapons application to high-level Soviet civilian and military officials.

In 1978 Mark Popovsky wrote an article in reply to the Soviet news agency TASS having protested about "western slander about biological weapons of the USSR." Popovsky believed the TASS protest to be highly hypocritical.[131] He had been employed in the Soviet Union as a science journalist and book author, but he had been able to leave and was living in West Germany in 1978. His original article was written in German for a German publication. His main informants were Soviet scientists, including some, he claimed, who had worked at the MOD's Kirov Institute. He provided a short history of the Soviet BW program in his article, claiming that it was initiated as early as 1919 at *Mikrob*. He named Velikanov and his institute, and asserted that there were two Soviet BW facilities, in Kirov and Sverdlovsk, and that a third probably existed in Kazan. Popovsky gave the Kirov Institute particular attention. He described some Kirov Institute scientists who were generally dissatisfied with their scientific work, but stayed with their jobs because of attractive perks including high salary, short working hours, access to a well-stocked "company" store, long vacations at special recreational areas, and the ease of acquiring advanced scientific degrees. In two important paragraphs, Popovsky wrote:

Some scientists, during their conversation with me, remarked that the weapons produced by them are illegal. However, they comforted themselves with the knowledge that biological weapons would be of little effect anyhow. One of them said "at the utmost, a war somewhere in Malaya or Mozambique could be won with those weapons produced by us." This also appears illuminating to me, since to the best of my knowledge, bacteriological research contracts distributed by military authorities at the civilian institutes are not carried out to the highest standard, either.

. . . The designated Soviet department for biological warfare naturally does not limit itself to research within the military scope alone. Numerous civilian laboratories and institutes are working under its supervision. In the Soviet Union, there is not one scientific research institute working in the field of microbiology and epidemiology in which there are no secret laboratories, or in which some so-called secret military research projects are not carried out.[132]

Popovsky's reporting in 1978, though incomplete, matches remarkably well with what we learned during 13 years of research and interviews. His observation of closed laboratories being part of otherwise open research institutes is correct, although we cannot vouch for the assertion of "not one." He correctly named three cities that housed BW facilities. Although we have little information about the lives of Kirov Institute scientists, the circumstances that he describes match many details of what we know of the MOD's Zagorsk Institute. Popovsky's article received very little attention, but it demonstrates more knowledge about the Soviet BW program than any other open-source article of that time and for several years to come.[133]

In 1984 William Kucewicz published a series of seven provocative articles entitled "The Threat of Soviet Genetic Engineering," published in the *Wall Street Journal*. Kucewicz claimed that his sources of information for the articles were émigré scientists who were living in the United States. When asked if any US government agency had provided confidential or private information to him, he stated that none had.[134] That seems unlikely. Kucewicz had never written before on the subjects of Soviet science or BW, nor did he ever again after this series was published. It is unlikely that he would have known what detailed topics to search for in the Soviet open scientific literature, where to locate Soviet émigré scientists, or what critical questions to ask them. The following paragraphs abstract the seven articles, plus a later follow-up article, and then assess their content.

The first article was an introduction to the subject, describing the usefulness of biological weapons, the "Yellow Rain" story, and the US government's concerns about Soviet BW-related activities. Kucewicz described his sources as the scientists mentioned above. He asserted that BW was "a joint program by the military and the Soviet Academy of Sciences with the full support of the Kremlin leadership."[135] Three specialized laboratories in Moscow, Leningrad, and Novosibirsk were claimed to be working on military applications of genetic engineering.

The second described the establishment of the "Institute of Molecular Biology," which we know as Vector. The information about this event came from interviews with scientists who had worked at Akademgorodok (see Chapter 8), not far from Vector, and who associated with Vector scientists. Kucewicz reported that the institute's deputy director, Lev Sandakhchiev, recruited scientists by offering them salaries 60% higher than the norm at Akademgorodok and purchased sophisticated expensive equipment from Europe and Japan with hard currency usually unavailable to civilian institutes. Scientists that were hired had to be "politically dependable." All of the institute's work was secret, and no one who worked there was permitted to discuss his work or the institute's operations or objectives. As an example of the work done at Vector, Kucewicz described research to insert a gene coding for the toxin produced by the Central Asian cobra, *Naja naja oxiana,* although due to the secrecy surrounding Vector, it was not certain that this work was actually being undertaken at that time. For these reasons, according to Kucewicz, everyone in Akademgorodok understood that "the institute was created for military purposes and only camouflaged as a civilian project."[136]

The third article discussed publications in the open literature written by Russian scientists that, according to Kucewicz, provided clues about ongoing BW.[137] Kucewicz gives several examples of such publications, such as those that describe research findings on botulinum toxin, ricin, and different kinds of snake, scorpion, and insect venoms. Allegedly, Ovchinnikov "invariably" is a co-author of these publications. The fourth article focused on Ovchinnikov; "One day the name of Yury A. Ovchinnikov may become as well-known as those of Werner von Braun and J. Robert Oppenheimer—men of science who turned discoveries into weapons of mass destruction. For Prof. Ovchinnikov is the chief scientist in charge of the Soviet Union's program to use the modern techniques of recombinant DNA to create a new generation of biological weapons, the likes of which the world has never seen."[138] The three last articles have no new material pertaining to the Soviet BW program.[139]

In a succeeding article Kucewicz wrote that several US scientists who had participated in a scientific meeting organized by the Federation of European Biochemical Societies and held in Moscow during June 1984, informed Kucewicz that they were told by Soviet colleagues that the contents of his seven articles were largely correct. However, he reported that the BW project had run into trouble as a result of a shortage of facilities and difficulties in biochemistry. He felt that this explained why in the more than 10 years since the BW program started, "Soviet scientists had yet to produce a new germ weapon. Nevertheless, the project continues and Mr. Ovchinnikov still hopes to create such a weapon."[140]

Reviewing Kucewicz's 1984 information in view of our current knowledge, the first article was correct about the collaboration between the military and USSR-AN, as well as about three specialized laboratories. That Moscow and Leningrad, the two major science centers in the Soviet Union, would be home to laboratories conducting secret work would not be surprising; what is surprising is that none is named. The second article is correct about Vector and the effort that went into building and equipping it, and about Sandakhchiev and his work. The statement about higher pay for scientists was correct, as was the ability to purchase needed equipment and supplies abroad with hard currency. However, there are some serious errors in this article. Sandakhchiev did knowingly hire Jewish scientists—persons considered "politically undependable." Not all Vector's publications were secret; to uphold its legend, 15–20% of the institute's publications were unclassified and published. He is incorrect about Vector's alleged work on cobra toxin; toxin R&D was never part of Vector's research program. (The described research does not make technical sense, either.) The third article is weak for two reasons. First, there was much work going on at that time on toxins in Soviet civilian institutes that was perfectly legitimate, had nothing to do with the military, and did not involve Ovchinnikov.[141] Second, although it is true that Ovchinnikov had a fascination for toxins (see Chapter 2), we have no evidence whatever that he personally was involved in work to weaponize any of them. The fourth article matches some information we have obtained from interviews about Ovchinnikov's activities and behavior. As Ovchinnikov was the major figure in Soviet biosciences, it can be expected that many stories about his ambitions, work habits, and personal relationships circulated among scientists who were affected by his decisions, including those who became émigrés. Ovchinnikov, however, was not "the chief scientist in charge of the Soviet Union's program to use the modern techniques of recombinant DNA to create a new generation of biological weapons." The succeeding December 1984 article was correct in that more than 10 years after the second generation BW program had commenced, it had not produced a single new biological weapon. Kucewicz never resolved the obvious contradiction of how so many scientists outside the program, "everyone" in his phrasing, were able to know what was supposedly secret and about which Vector scientists were never supposed to talk.

Between 1984 and 1989, Jack Anderson, the nationally syndicated columnist, published four articles about the covert Soviet BW program. These are dated February 21, 1984, November 30, 1984, December 4, 1984, and August 3, 1989. All were based on still-classified National Security Council and CIA reports that were shown to Anderson's assistant, Dale Van Atta. Anderson's first story quotes a CIA report: "The evidence points strongly to illegal production or storage of biological agents and weapons. . . . [the USSR has] acquired significant technology and equipment, built large-scale biological fermentation facilities and made progress in other areas considered useful should Moscow decide to pursue production of biological weapons."[142]

The second Anderson article recounts that after the United States discovered that Soviet armored vehicles captured by Israel in the 1973 Middle East war contained CBW filters, intelligence-gathering priorities on Soviet CBW changed. Anderson quotes a CIA report titled "Implications of Soviet Use of Chemical and Toxin Weapons for U.S. Security Interests":

> "Historically both collection and analysis of intelligence on chemical and biological warfare have suffered from persistently low priorities. Not until after the 1973 Yom Kippur War did the issue receive some recognition." . . . Priorities for gathering intelligence on various countries are assigned by the National Security Council. After the 1973 eye opener, chemical and biological weapons (CBW) development in the Soviet Union was raised to "Priority 3" in 1975, and to "Priority 2" in 1977. In 1981, after President Reagan took office, CBW intelligence on the Soviets was given an unprecedented "Priority 1."[143]

The third article stated that (1) the Soviet BW program is run by the MOD's 7th Main Directorate headed by V. I. Ogarkov; (2) the program operated research and production facilities at eight different but unnamed sites (which would be two more than were named in the 1975–1976 press reports by Beecher and the Associated Press); (3) the weapons characteristics that Soviet scientists are investigating are "persistence, stability, adaptability to special carrier solutions and the ability to be disseminated in such tiny particles that the poison will penetrate gas masks"; and (4) "a wealth of information on Soviet biological-weapons operations" have come from a Soviet defector.[144]

The fourth article, in 1989, combined descriptions from a visit made by Anderson and Van Atta to the famous Trinity St. Sergius Monastery in Zagorsk with references to and extracts from "US intelligence reports given to the National Security Council." They refer to the Scientific Research Institute of Sanitation, which was located near the city. Once again, the IC reports told them that it was operated by the "7th Main Directorate," which was "responsible for biological weapons, or 'BW'." According to the reports "there are only two 'confirmed' biological weapons sites in the Soviet Union," the Sanitation Institute at Zagorsk and the Microbiological and Virological Institute at Sverdlovsk; and seven suspected sites, at Malta, Omutninsk, Berdsk, Penza, Kurgan, Aksu, and Pokrov.[145] This would result in a total of nine. Malta was the code name given by the IC to a filling and storage facility called Zima (or Railroad Station Zima) by Alibek located near Irkutsk and operated by the MOD. According to Alibek, Kurgan and Penza housed mobilization production plants (named Combine "Syntez") owned by Biopreparat.[146]

The outdated and incorrect information including the identification of the "7th Main Directorate" as heading the Soviet BW program is taken directly from IC documents in which it still appeared as late as March 1990, as noted earlier. Ogarkov had never headed the 7th or the 15th directorate, but had been the first head of Biopreparat. The "Scientific Research Institute of Sanitation" is the Zagorsk MOD facility, which by 1989 had been renamed three times since it held that name in 1954. Anderson named two certain BW sites (one with incorrect name), both of which did exist. Also named are seven suspect sites, but not the actual names of the facilities at these sites. The lead MOD biological institute, the Kirov Institute, is not named in any of the articles based on leaks, although it had been clearly identified by Popovsky in 1979. Recall that both the Sverdlovsk and Zagorsk Institutes were subordinate to the Kirov Institute. As noted earlier, the pre-1984 Soviet defector mentioned in the third article was almost certainly Arkady Shevchenko, but he was not likely to have been "broadly knowledgeable about the Soviet BW program" or to have known the details that were supplied.

There are several important conclusions to be drawn from these stories. First, there is an unknown number of still-classified reports concerning the Soviet BW program produced by the CIA and perhaps by other agencies that we do not have. It is possible that the information in them, some of which was quoted in Anderson's stories, may be in the redacted sections of the declassified reports that we do have. Second, they tell us that during the Reagan administration government officials, either in the CIA or in other agencies, were willing to show CIA reports to Anderson's deputy and allow him to quote verbatim paragraphs from their text. Anderson's continued confusion of chemical and biological weapons at this late date demonstrates the dependence of these journalists on documents and information fed to them by government sources rather than any acquired understanding of the subject matter. Finally, it is interesting to note that there is a fair amount of misinformation in the quotes directly attributed to various CIA reports.[147] This probably reflects partial or outdated information obtained from émigrés.

To finish this chapter, we have reviewed the US and UK ICs knowledge about the Soviet BW program during three periods—before 1975, 1975 through 1989, and after 1989. It compares that knowledge with what is now understood to have been the actual situation in each of those periods. It also reviewed the information that was in the public domain about the Soviet BW program at the same times.

Pre-1975

The IC knowledge about Soviet BW in the pre-1975 era was captured in a nutshell in one of its own estimates: "The Soviet Union is in possession of all the necessary basic knowledge for the production of most BW agents. If they chose to do so, they would be able to construct and operate plants for BW production and weapons for dissemination would be available in adequate numbers."[148] In other words, according to Western intelligence estimates, the Soviet Union had the capability to develop and produce biological weapons, but it had so far decided not to acquire them. However, in reality the Soviet Union had been operating an offensive BW program since at least the late 1920s and can be assumed to have had in its possession biological weapons of several types and armed with a variety of classical BW agents such as *B. anthracis, Y. pestis, F. tularensis,* Venezuelan equine encephalitis virus, and others including pathogens harmful to animals and plants. Western intelligence appears not to have believed that the pre–World War II Soviet BW program discovered by German intelligence, although its depiction was incomplete and sometimes fanciful, was continued after the war. One 1960 British intelligence report correctly observed the Soviets' apparent interest in weaponizing botulinum toxin and warned that developments in this field should be closely followed.

As the United States was dismantling its BW program during 1970–1972, an interdepartmental review group astutely pointed out to the highest US decision makers the need for a more intense intelligence effort to learn of Soviet BW activities. Coincidentally the effort to expand the existing Soviet BW program in both qualitative and quantitative terms was ordered by the Politburo in 1972 and began to be put into effect shortly thereafter. It is clear that some US overhead intelligence resources, satellite or airborne, and possibly communication intercepts were already devoted to identifying potential Soviet BW facilities by 1975. However, we do not know if additional analytical resources were allocated to monitor Soviet life sciences and BW after the US BW program was completely dismantled. Although an explicitly named CIA report leaked to Anderson some years later suggests that there was an increase in those resources after 1973, there is little or no evidence of increased knowledge in the unredacted portions of the declassified IC reports that are available. Perhaps a substantial increase in IC efforts took place only after the implications of the 1979 Sverdlovsk anthrax outbreak were understood. Aside from beginning to identify the location of Soviet BW facilities by 1975–1976 and adding to such identifications in the years that followed, Western intelligence appears not to have learned of the practical consequences of the Politburo's 1972 decision until shortly before 1984, nor about the decision itself in any precise fashion until Pasechnik had been debriefed in 1989–1990. The references to it in Feith's testimony in 1986 are somewhat general.

During this period, there was no meaningful reporting on the existing and growing Soviet BW program by the mass media.

1975 through 1989

We have had no access to British intelligence reports dated after 1968, therefore only US intelligence reports and estimates are referred to below. The findings and estimates of the IC by the end of the 1970s and beginning of the 1980s were not qualitatively different from those of the pre-1975 era, which suggests that the IC continued to estimate that the Soviet Union had BW-related capabilities but had no biological weapons. (The possibility of dissenting views is discussed below.) The information that appeared in the leaks to the press in 1975 and 1976 was not reflected in the unredacted portions of the IC reports available for these years.

Nevertheless, some important and indicative developments occurred during this period. Information from interviews with former IC analysts indicate that the IC, while probably having no human sources in the MOD and Biopreparat institutes, were accumulating BW-related information from hundreds of Russian émigrés bit by bit. From the late 1970s on, Russian scientists, engineers, and technicians who were not directly involved in BW activities, but nevertheless knew about such subjects as construction and equipping of facilities and R&D in post office institutes, had been allowed to emigrate to Israel, the United States and elsewhere. The existence of supposedly secret post office institutes appears to have been known to a reasonably wide professional community. We have not seen any declassified IC documentation containing information that was identified as having been provided by émigrés or by satellites, but memoranda containing this information were presumably written and distributed within the IC. Nevertheless, information suggesting Soviet BW activity that violated the BWC is not visible in the unredacted portions of declassified high-level estimates like the NIEs and SNIEs during the earlier years of this period. In addition, the unredacted, visible summary statements imply that such suggestions are not present in the reports. This suggests that there may have been two schools of thought within the US government. The first was reflected in the estimates common to the NIEs of this period, namely, that while the Soviets had the scientific-technical capability to acquire biological weapons, they had not done so and in general were not supporting activities that violated the BWC. The second position may have been more skeptical, based on the continual accumulation of small pieces of evidence suggesting that the Soviet Union was operating an offensive BW program in violation of the BWC.[149] If this is correct, members of the first school were responsible for the 1982 DIA report, which stated that the Soviet Union was believed to be in accord with the BWC. Further, in 1983 the IC estimated that the probability of genetic engineering being used for weaponization purposes was only suggestive.

The existence of the second school would explain why as early as 1975 and 1976, government sources leaked information identifying first three and then six alleged Soviet BW facilities and suggested the possibility that the Soviet

Union was violating the BWC.[150] These leaks could have come from officials who suspected that the information they had signified the Soviet violation of the BWC. The June 1979 Sverdlovsk events raised all the suggestive inputs from technical intelligence and from émigré debriefings to a significantly new qualitative level.

By the mid-1980s, the uncertain evaluations about a possible Soviet BW program had changed dramatically. The US government now publicly asserted that the Soviet Union was violating the BWC and, also, that genetic engineering was being used for BW applications. Several developments had occurred since 1983 that would have influenced the IC to have changed its collective judgment. By this time the implications of the 1979 anthrax outbreak in Sverdlovsk were fully understood. Senior officials in the Reagan administration had also convinced themselves that Yellow Rain demonstrated Soviet production and use of biological weapons. In addition, a new wave of émigré scientists had left the Soviet Union after Gorbachev became general secretary in March 1985 and instituted glasnost. Most of them were Jewish scientists, some of whom had worked in Soviet laboratories that employed genetic engineering and other advanced molecular biology techniques in their research. Although these scientists had not themselves been performing classified research, some knew of post office institutes or may have seen closed laboratories in their own institutes, and perhaps learned of the purposes of these secret facilities. A great number of these émigré scientists were debriefed by Israeli and US intelligence officials. In addition, émigrés with expertise in ancillary professions often were also able to provide supportive information. The IC gradually deduced from these interviews that a sizable Soviet BW program existed and that some of the Soviet post office box institutes were applying genetic engineering in biological weapons R&D.

Not only had the general position of the IC changed, but the 1984 and 1986 publications by the Reagan administration indicated clearly that it had unequivocally accepted the new view. To some degree the administration's views led those of the IC. The administration's public diplomacy regarding Soviet violations of the BWC also demonstrates the problems encountered if conclusions are drawn from only the unredacted portions of highly redacted declassified reports. Nevertheless, one of the decision makers who undoubtedly was a major consumer of IC estimates was Brent Scowcroft, President George Bush's national security adviser. In a reply to an article critical of the IC, he wrote a Letter to the Editor that contained a passage that should be kept in mind about IC products: "The most difficult task the foreign affairs policymaker faces is making decisions in an environment of ambiguity and inadequate information. The role of intelligence is to narrow the range of uncertainty within which a decision must be made. What really matters is not how well the IC predicts particular events but its ability to spot, track, and interpret trends and patterns."[151]

Using Snowcroft's criteria as a yardstick, in the early 1970s the IC did poorly because it failed to spot the existence of a Soviet BW program, which meant that it could not determine trends and patterns. Worse, it interpreted the absence of evidence as meaning that no such program existed, which led to the finding that the Soviet Union was unlikely to develop and produce biological weapons in the near term. So during the crucial years when the Soviets were working the hardest to establish and make operational its modern, huge, and sophisticated BW program, it was done without any foreign interference whatsoever. It is likely that in the absence of information to the contrary, the Soviet Union was able to secure from foreign suppliers the dual-use supplies and equipment that it needed to build up its genetic engineering and molecular biology capabilities and divert to the MOD whatever it needed for BW purposes.

We cannot know how the US and UK governments would have reacted if their ICs had discovered the Soviet BW program and learned of its activities in the early 1970s. However, an educated guess can be made. It is reasonable to assume that diplomatic efforts based on accurate intelligence would have been directed at eliminating the Soviet BW program before 1975. Ambassador James Leonard, who negotiated the treaty for the United States, feels reasonably certain that if the US government had known of a sizable offensive Soviet BW program prior to the 1972 signing of the BWC, the United States would have halted the negotiations. Since it was legitimate to have an offensive BW program prior to the signing of the treaty, much would have depended on the Soviet reaction to being questioned. No one on the US side imagined a sizable offensive Soviet program. If US officials assumed that there was a Soviet program at all, they presumed it to be old and rudimentary and that the Soviet Union would dismantle what there was. However, if the United States had strong intelligence of a sizable program, which Soviet officials then denied, and the United States believed them to be lying, negotiations would certainly have been ended despite the strong momentum that US diplomats felt existed in favor of the treaty. And Leonard feels certain that if the US government had made that determination only in late 1974 or early 1975, the submission to the US Senate for ratification would have been halted.[152] The US government would have waited until it was confident that the Soviet Union had shut down its BW program before proceeding to the ratification stage. How the US government would have reached such confidence is unclear. The United States and the United Kingdom believed that verification was extremely difficult, and no verification provisions exist in the treaty. It is not likely that the United States would have requested that the treaty be renegotiated to include verification provisions. At the same time, because the most senior administration officials—Nixon, Kissinger, Laird, and Packard—had publicly supported the treaty, it would not have been withdrawn from the Senate but would have been tabled to await further developments. With the historic Soviet position on treaty verification and its opposition to on-site inspection until 1987, it is unclear how this situation might have evolved. Biological arms control might have been left without a BWC and thus reverted to the pre-1972 condition of having only the weak Geneva Protocol as a barrier to the use of "bacteriological" weapons.

The circumstances were somewhat different for the United Kingdom. One of the main reasons the United Kingdom suggested splitting BW off from "CBW" and offering a separate treaty to ban BW alone was the perception that BW had not been fully adopted into states' armories (see Chapter 20). There was nothing in the files of the UK Foreign and Commonwealth Office (FCO), MOD, or Cabinet Office to suggest that the United Kingdom was aware of or suspected that an offensive Soviet BW program existed in 1969. In addition, as was nearly always the case in both the United States and the United Kingdom, BW was a secondary consideration in the hierarchy of defense concerns. That was the case for the United Kingdom at that moment. The United Kingdom was going to be dependent on US advice and assistance for possible improvements to the UK's Polaris submarine ballistic missile system that was being contemplated in the late 1960s. Secretary of State for Defence Denis Healey was anxious about this, not about Soviet BW programs. Therefore, one of the main MOD concerns was that the United Kingdom needed to be careful about any initiative on CBW lest it upset the United States.[153]

In addition, throughout the last six months of the BWC negotiations—March to September 1971—the United Kingdom had sought to include effective investigative mechanisms for alleged BW use, which the United States had not been willing to support.[154] Had there been clear evidence of an offensive Soviet BW program in 1968, the United Kingdom might not have launched its initiative for a separate BW treaty but would have held to the traditional diplomacy to obtain a joint verifiable combined ban on CW and BW. The United Kingdom passed enabling legislation to ratify the BWC in February 1974. Had a Soviet BW program been discovered between BWC signing in 1972 and February 1974, the UK government probably would not have forwarded that legislation to Parliament. Had the discovery taken place between passage of the legislation and the ratification date in the spring of 1975, it would have been necessary to choose between the BWC being "better than nothing," and the almost certain negative position of the United States toward proceeding under those conditions. In the end, the result would almost certainly have been the same in the United States and the United Kingdom.

From the mid-1970s to the early 1980s, the US IC had identified what it believed to be suspect BW facilities in the Soviet Union and was monitoring them. However, it was unable to interpret with an acceptable degree of certainty the purpose of their existence until the middle 1980s. The British IC had the same problem. If the IC had known for certain that the MOD's Sverdlovsk Institute specialized in the large-scale production of BW agents, it would have conveyed a different evaluation of the 1979 Sverdlovsk anthrax outbreak than the uncertain ones it delivered to decision makers as late as 1983. The United States would have also informed the United Kingdom and other governments that the Sverdlovsk BW facility had definitively caused the anthrax outbreak

If the US and UK governments had come to the realization that there was a substantial Soviet BW program only after the BWC came into effect, it is likely that Western nations in unison would have mounted a concerted effort to compel the Soviet Union to take such steps as required to bring itself into compliance with the BWC. If this had not taken place, it is conceivable that the BWC might have dissolved if its member nations withdrew from the treaty in accordance with provisions spelled out in its Article XIII(2). The BWC's First Review Conference in 1981, which turned out to be contentious because US representatives asked the Soviet Union to explain the Sverdlovsk outbreak, would have been even more bellicose and might have adjourned. If the Soviet Union had been faced with a concerted effort by Western countries to get it to explain truthfully the outbreak's etiology and the Sverdlovsk institute's BW role, the Soviet delegation might well have walked out. Had such developments taken place, it is impossible to know what would have happened to the BWC, and perhaps there would have been no CWC, although the critical breakthroughs for the CWC came in 1987 and after, once Gorbachev was in power in the Soviet Union.

Post 1989

About 1990 the number of declassified intelligence documents that bear on Soviet BW diminished substantially, so we no longer can refer to NIEs and similar IC reports on this subject. However, in 1991 substantial information about the Soviet offensive BW program began to appear in the Russian press, particularly in relation to the MOD's Sverdlovsk facility. After 1992 the United States publicly identified the Soviet program and additionally disclosed the unsuccessful efforts by the US and UK governments to get the program closed down (see Chapter 21). Due to our access to Pasechnik, Alibek, Popov, Domaradsky, and other individuals who cannot be named but who were directly involved in Soviet BW activities, we have been able to collect far more information from them on those activities than from other sources, including the heavily redacted declassified IC estimates and reports available as of this date.

Portrait of Vladimir A. Pasechnik taken about 1985. (Unknown Soviet photographer.)

Portrait of Valentin I. Yerstigneer taken in 2001. (Anonymous photographer.)

Portrait of Yury A. Ovchinnikov taken approximately 1984. (Unknown Soviet photographer.)

Photo of TR-250 and TR-50 stainless steel containers for storing BW agents outside a storage bunker at SNOPB in 2000. (Photographer: Raymond A. Zilinskas.)

Close-up of TR-250 and TR-50 stainless steel containers with co-author Zilinskas at SNOPB. (Photographer: Raymond A. Zilinskas.)

Google Earth photograph of Compound 19 in Ekaterinburg, Russia, taken in May 2005. (Google Earth.)

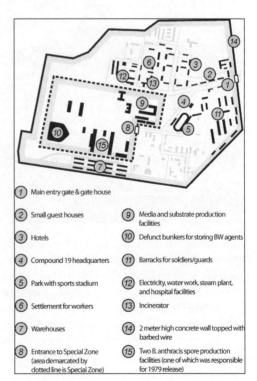

Schema of Compound 19 where its perimeter is demarcated by a solid line, while the "special zone" in which the development and production of BW agents took place is demarcated by a dotted line. Important buildings and facilities have been numbered with captions for numbers listed in the figure. (Schema developed by David Steiger at the James Martin Center for Nonproliferation Studies.)

1. Main entry gate & gate house

2. Small guest houses

3. Hotels

4. Compound 19 headquarters

5. Park with sports stadium

6. Settlement for workers

7. Warehouses

8. Entrance to Special Zone (area demarcated by dotted line is Special Zone)

9. Media and substrate production facilities

10. Defunct bunkers for storing BW agents

11. Barracks for soldiers/guards

12. Electricity, water work, steam plant, and hospital facilities

13. Incinerator

14. 2 meter high concrete wall topped with barbed wire

15. Two B. anthracis spore production facilities (one of which was responsible for 1979 release)

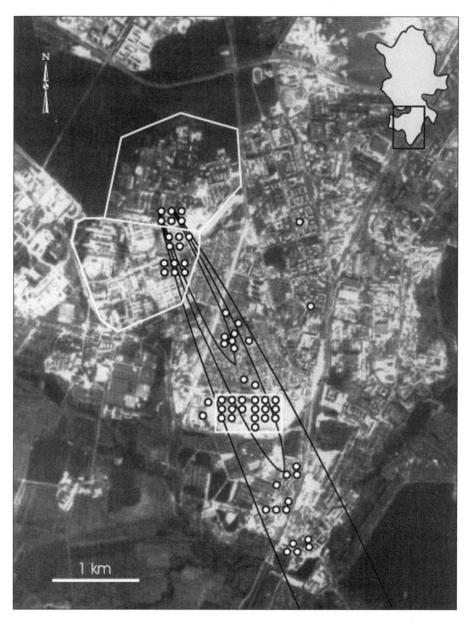

This satellite image, which is fig. 2 in Meselson et al., 1994, shows the part of Ekaterinburg (formerly Sverdlovsk) that was affected by the 1979 anthrax outbreak. Proceeding from north to south, Compound 19 and Compound 32 are outlined by solid white lines. The six solid black lines originating from Compound 19 delineate areas having constant dosages, with approximately 7,000 persons living in the area bounded by the outermost contour lines. Each small solid circle represents 66 victims of the outbreak, with large concentrations downwind from Compound 19, at Compound 32, and at a cement factory. (Map by J. Guillemin and M. Meselson, as published in Mathew M. Meselson et al., "The Sverdlovsk Anthrax Outbreak of 1979," *Science* 266 [1994]: 1202–1208.)

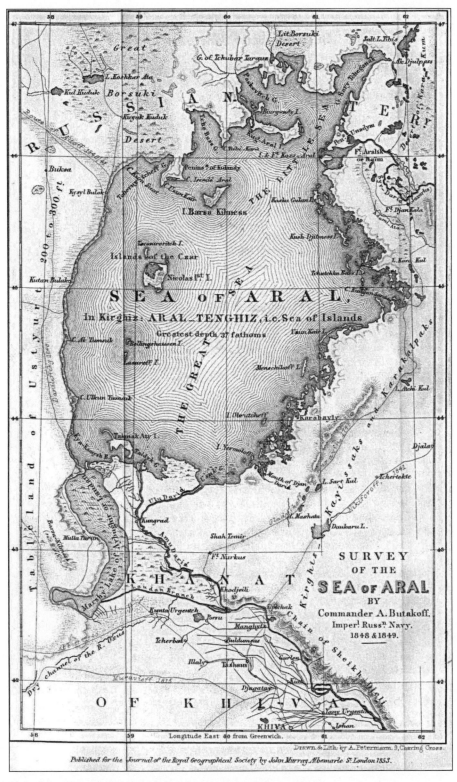

1853 map of Aral Sea by Commander A. Butshoff. From the Perry-Castañeda Library Map Collection at University of Texas in Austin.

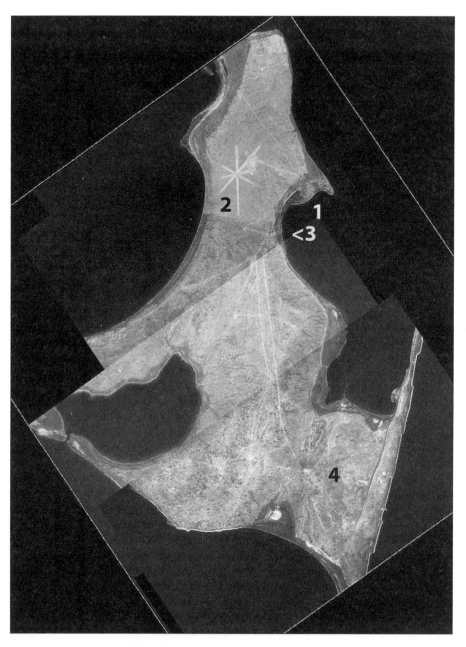

Imagery of Vozrozhdeniye Island taken by U.S. Corona satellite between 1965 and 1972. The numbers added by the authors identify the following facilities: (1) Kantubek harbor; (2) Kantubek airport; (3) Field Scientific Research Laboratory (PNIL); and (4) Aralsk-7 test range.

Photo taken in 1995 of the remains of Aralsk-7's Field Scientific Research Laboratory complex on Vozrozhdeniye Island. The two large identical buildings in the foreground are Buildings V60 and V61. (Photographer: Andrew C. Weber.)

Ken Alibek in his office at the Laboratories of Advanced Biosystems Inc. in 2001. (With permission from Getty Images.)

Portrait of Igor Domaradsky taken in 2006. (Photographer: David E. Hoffman.)

Portrait of Yury T. Kalinin. (Soviet photo of undetermined date and by unknown photographer.)

A photo of the Obolensk settlement where SRCAM workers and their families lived. (Soviet photo of undetermined date and by unknown photographer.)

Photograph taken in 2004 of the front side of SRCAM's Building 1. (Photographer: Raymond A. Zilinskas.)

Photograph taken in 2004 of the main passageway on the fourth floor of SRCAM's Building 1. (Photographer: Raymond A. Zilinskas.)

Portrait of Lev S. Sandakhchiev taken about 1995. (Photographer: Andrew C. Weber.)

A pre-1991 photograph of Vector's BSL-4 facility with fully garbed scientist working at a biosafety cabinet. (Unknown Soviet photographer.)

Photograph taken in 1995 showing three SNOPB facilities: storage bunkers in foreground, Building 211 behind bunkers, and Building 221 in background. (Photographer: Andrew C. Weber.)

Photograph of SNOPB's Building 221 interior with a row of 20,000 liter fermenters. (Photographer: Andrew C. Weber.)

Main entry to a BW agents storage bunker at SNOPB with co-author Zilinskas. (Photographer: Raymond A. Zilinskas.)

Photograph of workers demolishing SNOPB's Building 221 in 2000. (Photographer: Raymond A. Zilinskas.)

Photograph of the interior of a BW agents storage bunker at the Pokrov Biological Preparations Plant featuring 2-meter-thick walls made out of reinforced concrete. (Photographer: Ken Myers.)

Entrance to one of four BW agent storage bunkers at SNOPB with tractor used to transport TR-250 and TR-50 containers in and out of bunkers. (Photographer: Raymond A. Zilinskas.)

Cutaway of a Soviet cluster bomb, showing chemical bomblets. (Soviet photo of undetermined date and by unknown photographer.)

Photograph taken on July 16, 1981, in the Saint George Hall, Kremlin Palace, Moscow. The rotund government official in the middle of the first row has just finished presenting awards and medals to 63 scientists who had made significant contributions to the field of molecular biology in both the civilian and the military spheres. (Unknown photographer.)

1-4. Unknown. 5. Nikolai Rychkov; Belyaev's successor, head of *Glavmikrobioprom*, used to work at the Central Committee of the CPSU. 6. Name not known, but identified as Vice-Chairman of the Supreme Soviet who was in charge of the award ceremony. (Possibly President of Kyrgyz SSR). 7. V.G. Chuchkin; "an important person" from Military-Industrial Commission (VPK), head of one of the departments to which scientists from Biopreparat were subordinate. 8. Alexander S. Spirin; director of the Institute of Protein Research, USSR-AN. 9. Adelina Genrikhovna Skavronskaya; scientist at the Gamaleya Institute. 10. Rem Viktorovich Petrov; Vice-President of the USSR-AN, director of Institute of Immunology, Ministry of Health. 11. Diana Sorkina; head of the First Department at the Shemyakin Institute, USSR-AN. 12. Unknown. 13. Borisoglebskaja; Boronin's associate; worked on plasmids carrying antibiotic resistance genes. 14. V. Yezhov; specialized in microbial production of enzymes at the Institute of Biochemistry and Physiology of Microorganisms, USSR-AN. 15 – 18. Unknown. 19. Lt. Gen. Vselovod Ogarkov; head of Biopreparat; deputy director of *Glavmikrobioprom*. 20. Eugeny D. Sverdlov; head of research group at the Shemyakin Institute; became director of the Institute of Molecular Genetics, USSR-AN. 21. D.R. Kaulen; director of Gamaleya Institute. 22. Nataliya Andreeva; head of the Department of Crystallography, Institute of Molecular Biology, USSR-AN. 23-26. – Unknown. 27. Alexander Boronin; deputy director of the Institute of Biochemistry and Physiology of Microorganisms, USSR-AN under Skryabin; eventually its director. 28. Anatoly Kozlovskiji; deputy director of the Institute of Biochemistry and Physiology of Microorganisms, USSR-AN; worked on chemical transformation of biochemicals. 29. Yevgeny Severin; director of the All Union Institute of Molecular Diagnostics and Therapy, Ministry of Health. 30. Georgii Borisovich Smirnov; worked on Yersiniae at the Gamaleya Institute. In the 1990s, he frequently went to Iran spending several months at a time teaching Iranians the genetics of Yersiniae. 31. Vladimir Melnikov; employee of the Ministry of Health's 2nd Directorate, supervised work related to *Ferment*. 32. Unknown. 33. Vladimir V. Perelygin; head of the biophysical laboratory at SRCAM. 34. Major General Vladimir Yakovlevich Volkov; head of one of the departments at *Gosplan*, eventually worked for Biopreparat. 35. Scheblykin; head of the department at the *Gosplan* that financed *Glavmikrobioprom's* work. 36. We have two identifications for this person: (1) Vladimir P. Zaviyalov identified him as Igor Ambrosov, head of a section at the MOD, eventually Deputy Minister of Medical and Microbiological Industry; (2) Domaradsky identified him as Yuri I. Kondrashin, a military person with the "Chemistry" department of the CPSU, also worked at the Zagorsk Institute. 37. Marchenko; was Kondrashin's deputy. 38. Vadim T. Ivanov; Ovchinnikov's deputy director at Shemyakin Institute; eventually its director. 39. Yevgeny Grishin; head of the laboratory of neurotoxins at Shemyakin Institute, eventually one of its deputy directors. 40. V. Krjukov; worked on nucleic acids and restriction enzymes at Institute of Biochemistry and Physiology of Microorganisms, USSR-AN. 41. Igor Domaradsky. 42. Pomazanov; worked at *Biopribor*. 43. Vladimir P. Zaviyalov. 44. Unknown. 45. Konstantin Skryabin; head of a laboratory at the Institute of Molecular Biology, USSR-AN. 46. Michael Ivanov; deputy director of the Institute of Biochemistry and Physiology of Microorganisms, USSR-AN, eventually director of the Institute of Microbiology, USSR-AN. 47. N.N. Modyanov; worked on membrane biology at the Shemyakin Institute. 48. N.G. Abdulayev; specialized on rhodopsin at the Shemyakin Institute. 49. Valery Lipkin; head of the Laboratory of Protein Structure at the Shemyakin Institute, eventually head of the Shemyakin Institute's branch in Pushchino. 50. Vladimir Debabov; director of *Glavmikrobioprom's* Institute of Genetics and Selection of Industrial Microorganisms. 51. Istvan Fodor; Hungarian scientist who specialized in plasmid genes that code for biodegradation at the Institute of Biochemistry and Physiology of Microorganisms, USSR-AN. 52. Andrej Mirzabekov; specialized in chemistry of nucleic acids, eventually director of the Institute of Molecular Biology after Engelhardt's death in 1984. After 1992, became head of a laboratory at US Department of Energy's Aragon National Laboratory. 53. Georgij Georgiev; head of a laboratory at the Institute of Molecular Biology, eventually director of the Institute of Biology of Genes, USSR-AN. 54. Alexander Solonim; specialized in genetic engineering and restriction enzymes at the Institute of Biochemistry and Physiology of Microorganisms, USSR-AN. 55. Valerij Tanyashin; specialized in phages, was laboratory director at the Institute of Biochemistry and Physiology of Microorganisms, USSR-AN. 56. Vladimir Volkov; Urakov's deputy; eventually a SRCAM deputy director. 57. Unknown. 58. Colonel Igor Vladimirovich Nikonov; worked at Zagorsk Institute, also was Klyucharev's deputy and Chief Specialist in Biopreparat and rector for Vector. 59. Unknown. 60. Anatoli I. Miroshnikov; scientific secretary at Shemyakin Institute, eventually director of the Institute of Pharmaceutical Plants and then deputy director at Shemyakin Institute. 61. A.V. Dorozhko, Domaradsky's employee at SRCAM who specialized in francisellae. 62. Vyechsheslav G. Korobko; senior scientist at Shemyakin Institute, eventually head of institute's Laboratory of the Chemistry of the Gene. 63. M.N. Kolosov; one of Ovchinnikov's deputy directors at the Shemyakin Institute who specialized in DNA synthesis, eventually head of the Laboratory of Crystallography. 64. Vadim Pletnyov: head of the Laboratory of Crystallography, Institute of Molecular Genetics, USSR-AN.

13

United States Covert Biological
Warfare Disinformation

A FTER VLADIMIR PASECHNIK defected in October 1989, he reportedly told British officials that he had defected to the United Kingdom and not to the United States because the United States had a secret biological weapons program. When CIA officials learned of this remark after meeting with Pasechnik in the United Kingdom, they began an internal retrospective review to try to develop a conception of "What did the USSR think" regarding the US biological weapons program in the years after the formal US renunciation of its offensive program in 1969. The study was carried out by Carolyn Stettner, located at that time in the CIA's Office of Scientific Intelligence, or in the Arms Control Intelligence Staff (ACIS), an interagency intelligence community group.[1] That review produced a major shock. It discovered a horrendous mistake by the United States consisting of an extremely counterproductive covert deception and disinformation effort directed at the Soviet Union twenty years earlier. The purpose of that covert operation was to pass misleading information to the Soviet Union regarding US efforts in the areas of both chemical and biological weapons. Insofar as it concerned biological weapons, the effort ran from roughly 1967–1968 to at least the middle of 1971.

Interviews with former US government officials have made it possible to reconstruct at least a portion of this story. It is composed of multiple strands, however, and the information currently available does not enable all of them to mesh cleanly. Important questions remain unresolved.

In the period 1949–1955 the United Kingdom carried out a series of open-air tests involving both BW agent simulants and pathogens. The final two tests included US collaboration and took place in The Bahamas, in 1954 and 1955. Some years later, between 1963 and late 1968, the United States initiated a much more extensive series of over-ocean tests, again utilizing simulants, live pathogens, and toxins. These tests took place in the Pacific Ocean, the Atlantic Ocean, Canada, and the Arctic region of Alaska.[2] The Alaska test, on land, involved the use of a *Bacillus anthracis* simulant, *Bacillus globigii*.

The information available regarding these tests appears at times to be somewhat confusing and partially contradictory. According to the 1996 US submission under the Confidence Building Measures (CBM) that were added to the BWC, the series of tests named Shady Grove involved 13 aerosol trials, beginning in 1964, and took place over the Marshall Islands in the Pacific.[3] The author Edward Regis, however, reports 20 trials as being included in the Shady Grove test series, beginning offshore from Johnson Atoll and then continuing at the Marshall Islands.[4] The agents disseminated were *Coxiella burnetii* and *Francisella tularensis* and these were released from spray dissemination tanks mounted on low-flying A4D jet strike aircraft. Another test, DTC 68-50, took place in September and October of 1968, at Eniwetok Atoll in the Marshall Islands. This time the delivering aircraft were F4A jets and the agent was staphylococcal enterotoxin B (SEB). However, in May 2002 the US Department of Defense (DOD) released information on 12 tests, out of an apparent planned total of 113 tests, designated as Project 112, not all of which appear to have been carried out. Of these 12, four were chemical weapons tests of chemical agents or live simulants, and eight were tests using BW agents or simulants. One of these eight, carried out between January 22 and April 9, 1965, was named "Shady Grove" and did involve the pathogens *C. burnetii* and *F. tularensis*.[5]

The Marshall Islands–Eniwetok Atoll region was well known to Soviet intelligence reconnaissance "trawlers," having previously been the site of US nuclear weapons tests held in the Pacific between 1948 and 1958. At that time the Soviet ships would have mounted air-sampling equipment to obtain radioisotope profiles of the airborne nuclear weapon debris from the US tests, which provides information on nuclear weapons design.

The US BW tests in the Pacific Ocean stretched over several years, and the animals to be exposed during the successive test series were set out on strings of barges. It is assumed that the span of years and the level of US naval activity involved in the test program provided sufficient time for the Soviet Union to become aware of the activity and to deploy Soviet trawlers to the area equipped with air-sampling equipment and whatever other special equipment and personnel might have been needed to preserve the pathogens collected. According to Mangold and Goldberg, whose sources were three former senior members of the Fort Detrick staff, Riley Housewright, Thomas Dashiell, and William Patrick,

> The Soviets were watching closely. Whenever a test was about to begin, Soviet spy-ships poorly disguised as trawlers would appear on cue in the vicinity of Johnson Atoll. The US Navy sent planes to buzz them and boats to warn them away.
>
> Given the danger of positioning a boat under a shower of deadly germs, the Americans assumed that the Soviet crews had to be militarily and biologically trained and outfitted with protective gear and sophisticated sampling and decontamination equipment.
>
> Their appearance at the right time and place suggested that the Soviets knew full well the US was testing live BW agents.[6]

It is important to note, however, that some of the more important open-air tests took place in Alaska and Canada, and not over the open ocean.

Presumably, then, Soviets ships were present in the Pacific test area for at least some of the US tests, and were presumably also able to collect samples of the agents involved in those tests. This apparently led to a US interest in throwing Soviet military intelligence off the track regarding which pathogens the United States might have selected for weaponization, production, and stockpiling. That desire appears to have been the original purpose of the US BW disinformation campaign. Carrying it out, however, evolved into a second layer of this web.

Beginning in 1964 the US Federal Bureau of Investigation (FBI), with the assistance of the US Army, was controlling at least one "double agent," a US Army sergeant, who was being used to feed spurious intelligence information to Soviet recipients. The idea of using a double agent for this purpose appears to have been a remarkably long-standing one on the part of the FBI. As early as August 1949 the agency conceived of an astonishingly ambitious program "to secure at least one double agent at every BW research center in the United States."[7] From the inception of the FBI effort, some of these individuals were FBI informants working at these facilities, but the hazard in this enterprise becomes clear when the FBI planning document explicitly stated: "At the time the informant is approached, she will be furnished with a Top Secret report on BW to be passed on to her Soviet contact."[8] The purpose of this program was straightforwardly described as "the development of double agents to engage in a deceptive program to confuse the Soviets as to the progress of the United States in BW research and to cause them to waste time and money in engaging in research on the basis of deceptive information furnished to them."[9]

The purpose of the operation in 1964, however, was to provide misinformation regarding specifics of the US chemical weapons program. More specifically, it was intended to induce the Soviet Union to pursue development of a particular nerve agent, which the United States thought was unachievable. It would lead the Soviet Union to waste resources in an effort to duplicate work that had not proved successful in US hands, and therefore work toward an objective that US researchers assumed to be a dead end. The operation was named Operation SHOCKER.[10] In the course of this operation, however, several documents were also passed to Soviet intelligence that dealt with botulinum neurotoxin (BoNT). There are indications that information on ricin may also have been passed at this stage to the Soviet Union. This was apparently the information intended to mislead the Soviet Union regarding US BW agent selection. However, there followed an entirely different and much more damaging phase of this double-agent operation. It was of far greater significance than passing papers to the Soviet Union on BoNT or ricin, and it is not mentioned at all in the Wise-Cassidy book, which tells the story of the US chemical weapon disinformation operation.

Raymond Garthoff, a former US intelligence and Department of State (DOS) official and specialist on Soviet defense and foreign policies, has described the sequel in an article titled "Polyakov's Run." He wrote that US "military intelligence chiefs and the FBI wanted to repeat their success" in chemical weapons disinformation by utilizing, among others, Colonel Dmitri Polyakov, a Soviet military intelligence (GRU) agent operating in the United States who had been "turned" by the FBI to serve as a double agent at the end of 1961. Garthoff states that "multiple channels, including Polyakov, were used to convey the misleading message that the United States was undertaking a clandestine biological weapons program, despite President Nixon's public announcement [of the end of the US offensive BW program] in November 1969 and the US signature at the Biological Weapons Convention in April 1972."[11]

Mid-level officials in the Nixon administration recall two very surprising meetings in mid-1971. During the first of the two meetings, an FBI official briefed a small group in the DOS, informing them that an FBI operation was passing information to the Soviet Union to the effect that the United States was maintaining a covert offensive BW program, despite and in contradiction to President Nixon's announced termination of that program and support for the ongoing negotiations for a ban on chemical weapons. The FBI agent reportedly presented this rather peculiar "deception" as a good idea. There was apparently no discussion, criticism, or questioning of the FBI briefer at the meeting, but one of the DOS officials present thought to himself, "What does this look like to the Soviets?" The rather obvious answer was "that the US is untrustworthy and deceitful."[12] Still worse, this was taking place during the Nixon administration just as the first stage of the SALT negotiations, which dealt with US and USSR strategic nuclear weapons, was about to come to fruition. The official therefore sent a message to the National Security Council (NSC) informing it of the FBI briefing and its subject, and suggesting that if its members did not already know about it, they should. Another former US official suggested that the United States was passing this false information to the Soviet Union for about a year after November 1969, but it would appear to have been somewhat longer than that.

The second meeting in mid-1971 was more significant: and was apparently a consequence of the NSC having been informed. A US intelligence official brought together members of several different branches of the government that were involved with the issue to discuss the disinformation regarding the US BW program that had been passed to the Soviet Union. Following this meeting, four mid-level DOS officials were informed that the CIA had become aware of the operation in which the message had been passed to the Soviet Union that the US renunciation of BW was a fraud.[13] The CIA recognized the operation as having been a ghastly mistake, and the four DOS officials were informed that "it"—the disinformation operation—was being ended at that point.

This description of the operation and its termination leaves four major questions unanswered:

- Exactly how was this more important deception of the Soviet Union, that is, alleging a covert US BW program and not simply misleading information about US pathogen selection, actually ended?
- Exactly when was it terminated?
- Had the interagency committee that supervised all US covert operations approved this deception effort?

• What had been the impact of the deception on Soviet decision makers, precisely at the time of the major decision they took on the Soviet Union's BW program in 1972–1973?

The evidence from the interviews described above appears to indicate that the termination of the BW deception effort took place in mid- to late 1971, and therefore before the signing of the BWC in early 1972. However, Garthoff believes that Soviet officials were still influenced by the US BW disinformation when the Politburo decided to massively expand its BW program.[14] Garthoff concluded, "The program undercut Soviet belief in the efficacy of arms control and in the integrity of American policy by misleading Soviet officials into believing that the United States was deliberately violating the Biological Weapons Convention, justifying their doing so as well."[15]

Even if the date of mid- to late 1971 for the termination of the disinformation effort is correct, it is perhaps meaningful only in the context of how the deception was ended. Was there "a last message?" And if so, what did it say? Did it say, "The US has now ended the covert BW program which we previously informed you had continued after November 1969"? Did it say, "The previous information appears to have been a deception"? Or was there no particular "last message" at all, just silence on that subject after the end of 1971? Garthoff is under the impression that there was no "final message," and that the messages that preceded the termination of the disinformation program were simply no longer mentioned. They were not repeated, and they were not repudiated.[16] If the latter was the case, and there was no specific message saying "the US offensive program is now terminated," there would have been no reason for Soviet decision makers to revise their understanding based on the nature of the previous message or messages. They were then free to maintain the belief that their intelligence sources had obtained information from one or more informants telling them that the United States continued a covert BW program. In fact, the internal retrospective study carried out by the CIA in early 1990 apparently came to precisely that conclusion: that Soviet officials had never believed that the United States had terminated its offensive BW program and that the grossly misguided US deception was either responsible for or had contributed to that judgment on their part. The US disinformation program was disclosed to the KGB in 1985, when Aldrich Ames, a KGB spy within the CIA, betrayed Polyakov to the Soviet authorities. Polyakov, by then retired and back in the Soviet Union, was duly arrested, tried, and executed. However, once the information that Polyakov had delivered was disclosed to Soviet intelligence officials and political authorities in 1985 as being disinformation, they presumably should have dispensed with any misconception that the United States had continued its offensive BW program, which they had ostensibly maintained until then. Here another set of questions therefore becomes important: whether the KGB informed members of the Politburo, the Defense Council in particular, and the Central Committee staff of the implications of the deception: that the United States in fact did *not* have an offensive BW program and had *not* continued one after 1972.

Bush administration officials were briefed on the conclusions of the retrospective CIA study at the same time as they were pressing Gorbachev and Shevardnadze to close down the Soviet offensive BW program (see Chapter 21). It is not known if their British counterparts were also informed, but officials of the incoming Clinton administration were briefed on its findings when they took office in 1992.

An additional critical question was whether the BW deception effort had been approved by the requisite US government committees that oversaw all US covert operations, and if so, how they could have given their approval to it? Henry Kissinger, national security advisor to President Nixon, had overseen the process of producing NSDM 35, which underlay the 1969 US decision to end its BW program, and to convince President Nixon of its judiciousness (described in Chapter 20). However, Kissinger also sat as chairman of the body that had oversight of all US covert programs, the Interagency High Level Group, also known as the "Forty Committee," which had been established in February 1970.[17] However, this group was simply a new designation for an earlier body that had performed the same functions. It was known as the 303 Committee, having been established under NSC 303, and it functioned from the administration of President Eisenhower until the end of the Johnson administration. It should be difficult to imagine Kissinger managing the administration's decision process to terminate the US BW program and to negotiate the BWC, and at the same time to approve a decision to send messages to the Soviet Union saying that the United States was continuing a covert offensive BW program despite US statements that it had ended that program. Some of the DOS officials who were informed of the affair back in 1971 believe that the Forty Committee did approve of the portion of the disinformation program that concerned chemical weapons. That, however, did not involve any question of US treaty violation. Others suggested that because the BW disinformation effort was a double-agent operation being managed by the FBI, it may have been excluded from the categories of covert operations for which the Forty Committee held oversight responsibility. It is also not known whether a second body, the US Evaluation Board, an interagency intelligence committee whose responsibility it was to rule on any deception operation involving the US military in any way, reviewed or approved the BW deception affair, something that it did do in regard to the chemical agent and BoNT aspects.[18]

At a CIA Cold War History conference held in March 2001, Garthoff went so far as to offer the judgment, "We cannot say for certain that these (Soviet) weapons would never have been developed without the American disinformation campaign but I am sure it was the priming element to their programs."[19] However, if one turns to what little information is available concerning consideration of the BW question by the decision-making apparatus in Moscow in 1972–1973, there is *no* mention of the possible contribution of this deception in any of the available accounts of the Soviet government's decision at that time to initiate the entire Biopreparat enterprise and the enormous expansion of the Soviet BW program and its infrastructure. There is no knowledge of the possible contribution of the US deception effort to the writing of the key memorandum, or to the Politburo's decision to approve the program that the memorandum recommended. Obviously, it is possible that this could be a result of secrecy, and that information that the Soviet Union had been subjected to a US BW disinformation effort never left the domain of the KGB or the GRU, except to the most senior Soviet leadership. It is even possible that the KGB and GRU never even informed members of the Politburo or its Secretariat. It is not mentioned in Domaradsky's memoir, or by Alibek. In addition, during the period in the early 1990s which both American and Russian researchers had access to various Soviet archives as well as the ability to interview former senior Soviet military and foreign policy officials, no reference to the deception was ever found in any Soviet-era document. Nor was it ever mentioned to any senior US political figure between 1990 and 1996 when the United States was pressing the Soviet Union and then Russia on its continuing BW program, for example, by Shevardnadze, Gorbachev, or Yeltsin. And finally, most important of all, when in 2006 we obtained Soviet Central Committee documents dating from 1985 to 1992, which record the participation of senior Soviet military officials in discussions of what to do with the Soviet BW program, there is only a single hedged reference to the existence of a covert US program.

Every single former Soviet BW official or researcher whom we have interviewed, even the senior program officials who were defectors to the West, uniformly maintained the same positions. First, that they were told by their superiors that the United States was continuing its offensive BW program in the 1970s and 1980s. This required, of course, that it had to be a covert program. Second, that they believed it without any doubt. Third, that *all* of their colleagues believed it. One of these senior scientists, who had been on more than one visit to the United States, even believed that it was continuing in 1999–2000. Yet even those who had heard a mention of the famous memorandum written for the Soviet Central Committee by Ovchinnikov and his colleagues in 1972 have never heard a word concerning any US deception either as the basis for that 1972 decision or as the basis for what they were told about the United States during their entire careers. As for the KGB briefings intermittently given to senior Biopreparat institute researchers, it seems reasonably clear from the descriptions provided by several Russian sources who were present during these KGB presentations that they were perfunctory. Although the KGB briefers assured the listening researchers that the United States continued an offensive BW program, no evidence was ever offered to support that contention.

Alibek describes his effort to obtain information describing the US BW program from Soviet military intelligence prior to the departure of the first Soviet delegation to visit US facilities at Fort Detrick and the Pine Bluff Arsenal, under the arrangements made between the United States, United Kingdom, and Soviet Union in 1991. He claims that the Soviet intelligence officers returned to his office after a month with nothing more than long-known items available from the open public literature.[20] When the US-UK team visited Vector during the same series of mutual visits, the Soviet researchers reportedly gave as one of the reasons for their ongoing work on variola virus that "they were researching the virus because they believed the US had continued a secret BW program after 1972 to develop a smallpox weapon."[21] But where would Soviet military intelligence have thought such work was being carried out, in particular given their knowledge of the size of the Soviet facilities devoted to that purpose? The dismantlement of the major portion of Fort Detrick and the conversion of equally sizable parts of Pine Bluff had been in the public record in the United States since 1971–1972, information that was most certainly available to Soviet intelligence services working from their embassy in Washington, D.C. In addition, Soviet intelligence should have easily been able to discern by multiple means that Pine Bluff had been a "cold" facility for two decades, and that the unused post–World War II plant in Terre Haute, Indiana, which Russian teams would visit several years later (as part of the Trilateral exchanges discussed in Chapter 21), was similarly standing unused for twice that long.

Certainly, in 1982 *Literaturnaya Gazeta* had published claims that the CIA had "equipped a new lab in Baltimore where a so-called biogen machine was built to ensure mass production of micro-agents causing epidemics." More importantly, it also wrote that after the summer of 1975, when US congressional hearings disclosed that the CIA had illegally retained small amounts of toxins and agents for use in potential covert assassination attempts, "At the time CIA toxins were taken away from Fort Detrick nearly all biological agents of the United States Army were transferred from there to the Maryland Edgewood Arsenal."[22] But these were not particularly clever KGB fabrications. The first one is totally fabricated. The second one, slightly more sophisticated, is based on a deliberate misphrasing of the 1975 Senate committee revelations.

The US deception may have "succeeded," however, in its purpose of directing—or redirecting—at least a portion of the Soviet BW program. Once Alibek's disclosures on the size of the Soviet effort to produce *B. anthracis* spores became known, it was apparent that the deception in the biological weapons sphere had been far more counterproductive than the deception regarding advanced nerve agents on the chemical weapons side. In the case of chemical weapons, as described in David Wise's book, the US deception apparently led to the successful development by the Soviet Union of the advanced "Novichok" class of nerve agents. On the biological weapons side, it may have led to the massive expansion of the Soviet *B. anthracis* program. At the time of the 1979 *B. anthracis* release from an MOD facility in Sverdlovsk, Burgasov appears to have held two positions: in addition to his position in the Ministry of Health, he says in a 1998 interview: "I was a lieutenant-general and served as a deputy to Marshal I. Bagramyan, a Deputy USSR Defense Minister, on the Council for Defense Against Weapons of Mass Destruction." Burgasov goes on to describe early work at Sverdlovsk-19, where he had served as deputy director for science as a younger colonel: "We initially studied botulinum. This was a priority direction in the American program. . . . The direction of research at Sverdlovsk-19 was changed after our intelligence service bought the American plan on military uses of anthrax for R[ubles] 100,000—this is the first time I've reported this."[23]

14

Soviet Allegations of the Use of Biological Weapons by the United States

THE SOVIET UNION began accusing the United States of using biological weapons very soon after the end of World War II. In 1949 and 1950, Soviet press organs claimed that the United States was testing biological weapons, specifically those based on *Y. pestis,* on the Inuit population of northern Canada, and precipitating a plague epidemic as a result.[1] In 1952 the Soviet news agency TASS suggested that an outbreak of foot-and-mouth disease in cattle in Canada was due to the production of the agent by the United States, the United Kingdom, and Canada. The report also stated that the United States was experimenting with locusts in Saudi Arabia and throughout the Middle East, a charge that opportunistically coincided with the widespread incidence of locusts in the area.[2] These years also saw the large campaign by Warsaw Pact member states accusing the United States of dropping Colorado potato beetles on their potato crops, a basic food staple throughout Eastern Europe. The potential use of potato beetles to deliberately destroy crops had been researched by both France and Germany since the 1930s, and knowledge of the concept was well known, particularly in Germany. The allegations began with a June 15, 1950, report by the German Democratic Republic (GDR) Ministry of Forestry claiming that US aircraft had scattered potato beetles in May and June 1950 over portions of the GDR. A Czech government report followed suit. In Poland, schoolchildren were brought to the Baltic beaches to search for potato beetles allegedly dropped by US aircraft.[3]

The derivation of the potato beetle allegations offers an interesting history lesson, combining real events, concocted intelligence, and at its end, pure propaganda. During World War I, the United Kingdom and France had thought of using potato beetles against Germany. Potato beetles were in France in the 1920s, and each year the range of their infestations moved eastward by about 175 kilometers per year. They reached the German border by 1936 and continued their annual eastward progression. When the German armies occupied France in 1940, they overran a French biological weapons research facility and found French plans to use potato beetles against Germany. Not only was the idea picked up by World War II German biological weapons researchers as a possible action to employ themselves, but German military intelligence claimed that the United States and the United Kingdom intended to use potato beetles on Germany. In September 1944 a German Army biological specialist located in Vienna even reported that such an attack was taking place.[4] In 1950, 18.9% of the GDR potato crop was affected by potato beetles, and in 1951 the figure had reached 37.2%. The GDR campaign blaming their occurrence on US actions began in May and June of 1950. Obviously, the same infestation must have been taking place in France and West Germany as well.

In 1981 three GDR Stasi officers prepared a lengthy and secret study on "Biological Weapons: Their Function in the Strategy of the Enemy." It contained a single page on the potato beetle story. After describing the erroneous German intelligence report of September 1944 described above, it included a single-paragraph quotation from a GDR government spokesman in 1950 accusing the United States of dropping potato beetles on the GDR. Strikingly, the Stasi authors did not add a single word of comment, offered no evidence or corroboration, and made no claim that the charge was correct.[5]

However, the most serious of all the post–World War II biological weapons charges against the United States was made by China, North Korea, and the Soviet Union during the Korean War. Although little remembered now, these charges produced enormous political repercussions at the time, with extensive debate in the United Nations in New York and international protests against the alleged US use. A fairly typical comment by *Pravda* in 1952 was, "These bandits in generals' uniforms, the butchers in white gloves, the bloody bigots and traders in death who have unleashed the most inhuman carnage in history, warfare with the assistance of microbes, fleas, lice and spiders."[6]

A publication of the USSR Academy of Sciences during the Korean War period also claimed that the *World Atlas of Disease,* prepared by the American Geographical Society and containing maps illustrating the global distribution of diseases, demonstrated US intention to use BW. The Soviet publication claimed that the maps "related to the reconnaissance and preparation of materials which can be used during the planned attacks on other countries," and it further compared the epidemiological maps to German World War II "geomedicine studies."[7]

In January 1998, a historian researching the archives of the Central Committee of the CPSU discovered 12 documents containing detailed and authoritative evidence that the Korean War BW allegations were contrived and fraudulent.[8] One document dates from February 21, 1952, and the others from the period of April 13 to June 2, 1953, the approximately four months that followed the death of Joseph Stalin on March 5, 1953. It is clear that these documents represent only a fragment of what must be a voluminous collection of relevant documents in the Soviet archive. Nevertheless, the information they contain makes for compelling reading. They describe, at least in part, the way in which the allegations were contrived by North Korean and Chinese officials and Soviet advisers, and include direct communications between the Central Committee of the CPSU to the Chinese and North Korean leaders, Mao Zedong and Kim Il-Sung, and replies by the latter. For example, one document, from May 1953, opens with the following lines: "For Mao Zedong: The Soviet Government and the Central Committee of the CPSU were misled. The spread in the press of information about the use by the Americans of bacteriological weapons in Korea was based on false information. The accusations against the Americans were fictitious."[9]

The publications based on this material were made available to the most knowledgeable living Russian specialists on the Soviet-era archival records dealing with the Korean War, who commented that the papers and their analysis were correct. In 2003 a second independent verification of the authenticity of the documents was obtained from an official in the Russian Ministry of Foreign Affairs.[10] The obviously limited selection of documents that were obtained—all the rest between late February 1952 and April 1953, which includes the peak period of the charges, being absent—portrays the events as an innocent Soviet government being deceived by China. This would seem highly unlikely, but given the absence of the full Soviet and Chinese documentary history, it is impossible to be more definitive at the present time.

There were several events that could have been read as hints of what was to appear in the documents obtained in 1998. In the spring of 1952, as part of its campaign in the UN General Assembly in support of the BW allegations, the Soviet delegation continued to press charges of US use of biological weapons. However, on April 7, 1953, about one month after Stalin's death, the Soviet representative in the Political Committee of the United Nations declared the Soviet Union's willingness to withdraw its allegations of BW, "as proof of its sincere striving for peace," on the condition that the United States withdraw its proposal that the United Nations conduct an investigation into the allegations.[11] As indicated, except for a single 1952 document, all the other Central Committee documents obtained date only from April 13, 1953. Senior US officials apparently thought of the startling Soviet about-face as just a part of a "whole 'be pleasant' campaign" that the Soviet Union was pressing following Stalin's death, and carelessly overlooked its more particular significance.[12] Acceptance of the Soviet offer in April 1953 might have prevented repetition of the charges up to the present day by North Korea in particular, as well as by others.

There is no known explicit statement at any time during the Soviet period to the effect that the Korean War BW charges were falsely made, including after Gorbachev came to power, nor by Russian officials since 1993. There are, however, publications that serve as tacit admissions by omitting the allegations. In 1969 the UN secretary-general published a report on chemical and biological weapons. The UN report is a consensus document signed by the representatives of fourteen governments, among which were the Soviet Union, Hungary, Czechoslovakia, and Poland. It includes the following statement: "Since the Second World War . . . there is no military experience of the use of bacteriological (biological) agents as weapons of war."[13] Without specifically referring to the Korean War BW allegations, the sentence is an implicit admission that no such events had ever taken place.

Two years earlier, in 1967, the Soviet Military Publishing House had printed a technical manual used in the training of its armed forces, *Bacteriological Weapons and How to Defend against Them*.[14] It contains a fairly detailed historical review of BW. The discussion of Japanese use of biological weapons during World War II in China (late 1930s to 1945) is followed directly by a description of the use of defoliants by the United States during the Vietnam War (1965–1975). There is no reference at all to the Korean War. A more popular Soviet history of World War II published in 1985 also followed this pattern.[15] Finally, General Smirnov's history of medical problems in wartime, published in the Soviet Union in 1988, also made no mention at all of the Korean War BW allegations.[16] Astonishingly, an essay written by a historian of science and published by the Russian Academy of Sciences in 2000 reverted to the old charges that the United States had used biological weapons against China and North Korea during the Korean War.[17]

Paradoxically, some official Soviet statements dealing with instances of CBW use exist, which deny use when it had actually taken place. In an official Soviet comment on President Dwight D. Eisenhower's "Atoms for Peace" speech at the United Nations on December 8, 1953, the Soviet government drew attention to the 1925 Geneva Protocol by stating: "The fact that not a single Government engaged in the Second World War dared to use chemical and bacteriological weapons proves that the aforesaid agreement of the States against chemical and bacteriological weapons had positive significance."[18] That statement is of course wrong. Japan had used both chemical and biological weapons in China during World War II, which the Soviet Union knew, not least through its own public trial of Japanese officials involved in BW activities in China that it held in Khabarovsk in 1949, and its interrogations between 1945 and 1949 of Japanese participants on those programs.

After a short interval following the Korean War, a Soviet campaign of accusing the United States of using biological weapons began again in the early 1960s and continued well into the Gorbachev era. It was then renewed in 1995 and in 2009. The highlights of that campaign include the following:

- On July 10, 1964, TASS, the Soviet news agency, accused a "U.S. Military Commission in Colombia" of using biological weapons against peasants.
- On March 12, 1968, Moscow Radio accused the United States of spreading the diseases plague and cholera in Vietnam.[19] In 1972 the Provisional Revolutionary Government of South Vietnam also charged that the United States had dropped insect larvae over Quang Ngai province to destroy crops.
- Between 1972 and 1975, a Soviet-organized disinformation campaign was directed against the Malaria Control Research Unit in New Delhi, India, which was operated by the World Health Organization (WHO) and the Indian Council of Medical Research with US financial aid. The allegations were that (1) malarial mosquito studies were being carried out to aid US efforts to use mosquitoes and yellow fever virus as BW agents; (2) trials of low-application dosages of malathion as a mosquito-control agent were actually efforts to test the dispersal of BW agents; and (3) another subproject involving birds as carriers of arthropod-borne viruses was an attempt to find the best way to disperse BW agents on the

Indian subcontinent. Despite the absence of any scientific basis for these charges and despite the thorough, documented denials by the WHO, the disinformation campaign was successful in causing the Indian government to close the unit in 1976 and to end the malaria research carried out by the WHO on India's behalf.[20]

• Beginning in the early 1970s and lasting 18 years until 1988, a similar disinformation campaign by Moscow Radio targeted the Pakistani Medical Studies Center in Lahore, one of five or six USAID-funded International Centers for Medical Research and Training. The targeted research again concerned malaria. Once again this campaign of false BW allegations had a very instrumental purpose, and again it succeeded. According to KGB defector Vasiliy Mitrokhin, these efforts were part of a KGB "Active Measures" program code named TARAKANY ("Cockroaches") that utilized releases in local newspapers. He claimed that the Indian weekly *Patriot* "was controlled by the KGB residency in Delhi," the Sri Lankan *Lankan Guardian* and *Tribune* were controlled by "the KGB Colombo Residency," and the Pakistani newspaper *Dawn* was similarly controlled. Between 1980 and 1982 (the early years of Soviet occupation of Afghanistan), these stories were planted in India, Iran, Bangladesh, and Lebanon.[21] In 1982 the Soviet weekly *Literaturnaya Gazeta* charged that the Pakistani center was funded and directed by the CIA, and "is developing banned biological weapons."[22] The article claimed that the Lahore facility was developing new breeds of disease-carrying mosquitoes to be used by the United States in Afghanistan and Cuba. *Literaturnaya Gazeta* further alleged that the mosquitoes had already been used in Cuba and were responsible for "recent epidemics in Cuba." Another alleged US project was a "plot to infect cattle from Pakistan to Afghanistan to start an epidemic of encephalitis in Afghanistan."[23] Cuban newspapers picked up the charges, adding the attribution of its dengue epidemic to the United States.[24] Again, despite denials by scientific authorities and the extravagant unscientific nonsense involved in the charges, the USSR again succeeded in this case, provoking the government of Pakistan to suspend the program. In the spring of 1988, together with a burst of other more significant BW disinformation stories described below, all aimed at the United States, the Novosti Press Agency repeated a story that the United States "had attempted to breed disease-bearing 'killer mosquitos' in Pakistan for use in Afghanistan and Cuba, and had used unsuspecting Pakistanis as guinea pigs."[25] Ironically, in the 1990s the governments of both India and Pakistan were attempting to repeat the research that had been carried out in the Delhi and Lahore laboratories at the time of their closure under the pressure of Soviet propaganda.

- On September 13, 1982, and February 12, 1983, *Krasnaya Zvezda* (the Soviet Army newspaper) and Novosti Press Agency repeated the charges that the United States had used biological weapons during the Korean War, in obvious disregard of the statement in the 1969 United Nations report, signed by a Soviet government representative.

- In the spring of 1982, Lt. General M. M. Kiryan wrote, "During the war in Vietnam the Americans had a biological depot in Thailand. Leakages led to outbursts of diseases among the local populations."[26]

- On February 10, 1983, *Pravda* accused the CIA of using biological weapons in Cuba. (On February 28, 1983, *Izvestia* also accused South Africa of using biological weapons in Namibia and in other African "frontline" states.)

- On February 8, 1984, *Krasnaya Zvezda* carried an entire catalogue of charges of biological weapons used by the United States against humans, crops, and domestic animals in Cuba: causing African swine fever in 1971, and again in 1980; causing sugar cane rust in 1972; causing tobacco "blue mold" in 1972; causing dengue fever in the spring of 1981; and (with somewhat vaguer phrasing) causing hemorrhagic conjunctivitis in 1981.

- On December 2, 1984, *Krasnaya Zvezda* alleged that the United States had used biological weapons in Indochina, caused dengue fever in Cuba, and was carrying on biological warfare "experiments" in Lahore, Pakistan.[27]

- In May 2009, *Pravda* published one of the more bizarre BW disinformation stories under the title "World Stands on the Brink of Biological War." It alleged that swine flu had leaked from laboratories "in the depths of the forest . . . in Mexico where the CIA might be conducting its secret experiments."[28] This was followed in December 3, 2009, *Pravda* story stating that "biological weapons are being secretly developed on Georgian territory . . . [in] a special program of cooperation with the US Defense Department geared to the stimulation of research in the creation of biological weapons."[29] The "biological materials" prepared "are subsequently delivered to military biology labs of the United States." From there, "the Americans are trying to deliver the specimens of biological weapons that have been obtained to Iran," for the purpose of accusing

Iran of having manufactured and tested BW. Clearly, the former Soviet, now Russian, disinformation services that produce these stories were once again in full flower.

This is not a complete list, and the Soviet Union made analogous charges in other instances.[30] The peak in frequency of these allegations occurred in the 1980s, possibly because Soviet publicists at times used them as direct counter-charges to US allegations that the Soviet Union and their allies were using toxins Yellow Rain in Southeast Asia and Afghanistan. (In an additional countercharge, Soviet media claimed that the United States supplied chemical weapons to Afghani resistance groups).[31] The Soviet Union also made numer-ous charges in various media after 1972 and the signing of the BWC, claim-ing that the United States continued to develop biological weapons in contra-vention of the treaty's provisions. This is discussed further in Chapter 20.

One Soviet BW disinformation campaign should be singled out because of the major international repercussions it produced. Between 1985 and the summer of 1987, Soviet publications repeatedly charged that HIV-1 (the virus that causes AIDS) had "come from" or been "released by" US laboratories or were connected to DOD and CIA experiments. Christopher Andrew and Vasili Mitrokhin called it "probably the most successful anti-American ac-tive measure of the Gorbachev era, prompted by a mixture of overt propa-ganda and covert action by Service A."[32] They, and other sources, finally ex-plained who had produced these disinformation tales over the decades: Service A (Disinformation, Covert Action) in the First Chief Directorate (Foreign Intelligence) of the KGB. It was the task of Service A to produce "Dezinformatsia," or "aktivinye meropriatia" (active measures).[33] In 1985 Ser-vice A was composed of approximately 80 officers located at KGB headquar-ters in the Moscow suburb of Yasenovo, and another 30 to 40 in the offices of the Novosti Press Service, the frequent purveyor of disinformation stories to the world.[34]

The campaign began with the planting of an anonymous letter in the Indian newspaper, *The Patriot,* on July 17, 1983, which cited an obscure US Communist Party paper, *People's World.* Nothing happened. On October 30, 1985, the campaign was reinitiated with an article in *Literaturnaya Gazeta,*[35] at that time a "prime conduit in the Soviet Union for press propaganda and disinformation."[36] The article explicitly stated that the United States contin-ued an offensive BW program and cited the 1983 letter in *The Patriot.*[37] At this point, the KGB also informed the foreign intelligence branch (HVA) of its sister GDR intelligence service that it expected it to participate in the campaign.[38] The story was then distributed worldwide. This time it was a raging success. One report indicated that the story appeared in no less than 200 newspapers in 25 countries. In October 1986, the conservative British *Sunday Express* placed the story on its front page.[39] In 1986, newspapers in 10 sub-Saharan African countries printed the charges, and in the first six months of 1987, eleven. Radio Moscow repeated the story.[40]

Remarkably, all this took place as Gorbachev was courting the West. He had stated in a press conference in July 1987, "We tell the truth, and nothing but the truth." US government officials decided to pressure the Gorbachev administration to stop the campaign, but there was at first surprising and incongruous resistance from Gorbachev and his senior aides. When Secretary of State Schultz complained to Gorbachev on October 23, 1987, at a meeting in Moscow in advance of the Washington summit, Gorbachev responded angrily to the first of three Department of State (DOS) reports on Soviet disinformation that included discussion of the Soviet AIDS stories. Rather amazingly, he "complained that issuing the report went against the *glasnost* spirit."[41] And when Charles Wick, the director of the US Information Agency, together with Surgeon General Everett Koop, met with Valentin Falin, the head of the Novosti Press Agency, on June 6, 1987, and demanded Soviet retraction of a new Novosti Press Agency article titled "The Ethnic Weapon," Falin claimed that he could not recall the article and that Wick was indulging in "the language of the Cold War."[42] Falin was scarcely a nonentity: in October 1988 he replaced former Soviet ambassador Anatoly Dobrynin as head of the international department on the Central Committee staff.

The KGB also used the disinformation in articles published in the Soviet press to discredit US military bases in NATO countries: "Civilians were urged to demand that the bases be closed so that they could be protected from the AIDS epidemic deliberately spread by the American military."[43] Radio Moscow broadcast that "the US was spreading AIDS in southern Zaire as a test of biological warfare."[44] In early 1987 the KGB introduced a second but closely related disinformation campaign. A story planted in a Kuwaiti newspaper accused the United States of developing an "ethnic weapon, a biological weapon that would supposedly affect only black or brown skinned people."[45] It was only one example of many of this charge that appeared subsequently in Soviet media, often suggesting that AIDS was the "ethnic weapon."

However, presumably under the pressure of the US protests, different parts of the Soviet government began to contest the disinformation stories in public. On October 30, 1987, a few days after Schultz's dispute with Gorbachev, two important members of the USSR Academy of Science, Roald Sagdeev and Vitali Goldanski, published an article in *Izvestia* distancing the Academy from the AIDS disinformation.[46] Nevertheless, on the very same day that *Izvestia* published the Academy's disavowal, *Sovetskaya Rossiya,* at the time the official newspaper of the Russian Federation, reprinted the AIDS disinformation and a defense of "the Soviet media's right to 'report different views.'"[47] Novosti Press Agency continued to distribute the story in 1988, and in September 1988 Wick and Falin came to a peculiar, severely limited "agreement": each would "notify" the other when they learned of any further AIDS disinformation stories, so that they could be curbed before they spread.[48] The president of the Academy of Medical Sciences, Vadim I. Pokrovsky, now weighed in, stating in *Sovetskaya Rossiya* that "not a single Soviet scientist, not a single medical or scientific institution shares this position," that is, the Soviet disinformation stories.[49] None of this stopped the KGB or Falin. When Novosti Press Agency's AIDS disinformation stories continued to appear in the several months following the Wick-Falin "agreement," Falin defended this as the "freedom of the press under *Glasnost.*"[50] As late as 1989, AIDS disinformation reports appeared in over a dozen countries worldwide.[51] Foreign Minister Eduard Shevardnadze eventually criticized the campaign as well, but the Ministry of Foreign Affairs reportedly never examined any of the Soviet BW allegations against the United States: the KGB was responsible for them.[52]

On March 17, 1992, Yevgenyi Primakov, then the head of the new Russian Foreign Intelligence Service (and a half dozen years later to be one of President Yeltsin's short-lived prime ministers), in speaking at the Moscow Institute of International Relations, stated that the AIDS disinformation story was fabricated by the KGB.[53] And in August 1992, former KGB general Oleg Kalugin told the newspaper *Moskovskaya Pravda* that the idea "was dreamed up in the 'A' Directorate of the USSR KGB's First Chief Directorate," specifically its "American Section."[54] It is surprising that Gorbachev was either unable or unwilling to put a thorough stop to the fraudulent disinformation campaign in 1987, 1988, or 1989. The issue was trivial compared to the major problems he confronted in those same years, but it serves as an interesting demonstration of the power of KGB disinformation policy. The seeming independence that could be demonstrated by a small unit within the KGB could be seen as a harbinger of what would be faced in 1990 and 1991 by the United States and the United Kingdom in attempting to bring an end to the Soviet offensive BW program. As for the AIDS disinformation story, it continues to circulate in various mutated forms to the present day, not least in the United States.[55]

In the spring of 1995, after a period of "dormancy" of seven years, the BW allegations started up again. The campaign utilized familiar elements from previous decades. It would appear to have been an adjunct to the Russian disruption of the US-UK Trilateral Negotiations in 1995 that are detailed in Chapter 22. It sought to discredit US DOD overseas disease research institutes by claiming that these facilities were on a par with the still-closed Russian MOD BW institutes. A long story in the Moscow daily, *Nezavisimaya Gazeta,* quoted "Russian specialists who collect information on developments relating to biological weapons abroad." One has to guess that these must be the same individuals who concocted the earlier propaganda for the KGB, and were now doing the same for its successor agency, the Federal Security Service (FSB), using the same technique practiced in previous decades of first planting a story overseas and then quoting it in the Moscow press.[56] The Russian story quoted a Spanish newspaper claiming that US military facilities in Spain were "devoted to being 'Spanish storage facilities of North American bacteriological weapons.'" The story claimed that "biological weapon components" were leaking from the US military bases of Rota and Zaragoza, and causing "strange diseases" among base personnel. It also quoted the Kenyan newspaper, *The Nation,* an outlet used by the KGB for releasing disinformation prior to 1992, that claimed that "the Americans were using the territory in African countries for biological weapons research and development . . . unexpected outbreaks of fever on the African continent have been the consequence of experiments conducted by the Americans themselves . . . in particular, the outbreak of Ebola hemorrhagic fever in Zaire." A third charge was that in "new incidents . . . the diseases were caused by bacteria that do not exist in nature, but it transpired that they can be created by genetic engineering," and that these too were connected with US activities. "Thus the populations of a number of countries justifiably point to the possibility that the United States may be using Southeast Asian countries' territory in order to create and improve a broad spectrum of exotic agents required for biological weapons."

The story then went on to discuss allegedly suspect research in US military medical and microbiological research facilities located in Southeast Asian countries: The Walter Reed Army Institute of Research's (WRAIR) laboratory in Indonesia, the Naval Medical Research Unit 2 (NAMRU-2), also in Indonesia, and the Armed Forces Research Institute for Medical Sciences (AFRIMS) in Thailand. It tied this allegation directly to the Russian demand that had deadlocked the Trilateral process for two years: that Russia be allowed to inspect these locations in exchange for the access promised by the US-UK-Russian Trilateral Agreement of September 1992 to permit the United States and the United Kingdom access to the Ministry of Defense BW facilities in Russia. (See Chapter 22.) Russia introduced this demand despite the fact that Russian inspection teams had already made visits to their counterpart UK and US military facilities. It seems unquestionable that the purpose of this Russian demand was to keep US and UK inspectors out of the Russian MOD facilities.

During 1998 and 1999, senior Russian military officials who had been directly responsible for Russia's own biological and chemical weapons programs took it upon themselves to resurrect many of the old Soviet-era disinformation stories that had not been heard of for more than a decade, and in some cases not since the 1950s:

- In a press interview in March 1998, Lieutenant General Valentin Yevstigneev, who had headed the 15th Directorate of the General Staff/ USSR Ministry of Defense responsible for the USSR's BW program until 1992, and until the end of 2000 headed the renamed but little altered body, resurrected the charge "that AIDS was created in a military laboratory abroad. Several black volunteers from prison were infected. . . . There are some African countries in which up to 80 percent of the people are HIV infected."[57]
- In a second interview, in 1999, in a more academic Russian journal that is considered to represent an arms control viewpoint, Yevstigneev suggested that the "mass emergence of Colorado beetles in Russia, is due to foreign delivery." Amazingly, Yevstigneev was resurrecting the old canard from the Polish and GDR propaganda campaigns of the 1950s. He did this despite the fact that after 1990 the potato beetle disinformation had been publicly ridiculed by those countries. Yevstigneev then suggested that a locust attack in the Volga region might be due to a locust type from "the Apennine Peninsula." He also included the Cuban

charges regarding *Thrips palmi* (an insect that is destructive to agriculture in many countries of the world), but confused it with earlier Cuban allegations dealing with sugar cane diseases, and he managed to incorrectly describe all the alleged means of delivery.[58]

- In 1998, Lieutenant General Stanislav V. Petrov, head of all Russian Army chemical and biological troops, resurrected the charge that the United States had "experimented with" biological weapons during the Korean War. In an earlier interview in 1995, Petrov's phrasing had been that "the Americans had trained well in Korea," while additionally referring to the charges of dengue and swine fever in Cuba, for which "nobody was caught." The Moscow NTV "Today" correspondent, Maryana Maksimovskaya, gratuitously added that "the Americans blundered two years ago" when there was a hantavirus disease outbreak "near the Dugway test site in the USA where chemical and biological weapons used to be tested." She also pointed out that hantaviruses and Ebola virus "are very similar," adding, "This made biologists suspect that the Ebola virus . . . is not natural."[59]

- Even in late 2001, Yevstigneev was still repeating the potato beetle story: "We are suspicious about mass emergence of Colorado beetles in Russia, known for damaging potatoes." Yevstigneev also again repeated the 1997 Cuban *Thrips palmi* charges against the United States: "The USA was accused of dropping on Cuba a container with insects destroying sugarcane." However, he introduced several inaccuracies in the original Cuban charges in one single sentence, which serves as a good indicator of the overall quality of his statements. The Cuban charges did not allege the dropping of a "container," and claimed that the *Thrips palmi* insect had destroyed vegetable crops, and not sugarcane.[60]

Interestingly, Alibek reports that in 1981 Fidel Castro requested Soviet assistance in clarifying the origin of the dengue virus strain responsible for Cuba's second and more serious outbreak of dengue fever, which he alleged was a US biological attack. General Lebedinsky, then assistant to General Smirnov and later the head of the 15th Directorate of the Soviet General Staff until 1989–1990, was dispatched to Cuba to assist Cuban scientists in identifying the strain. Reportedly asked by Castro whether it was "a US strain," Lebedinsky informed Castro that it was not, and that the strain was of natural origin. On returning to the Soviet Union, Lebedinsky reportedly also informed the Soviet government that the outbreak of dengue fever was *not* caused by the United States.[61] Nevertheless, after the visiting team of Soviet scientists had returned home, Castro publicly attributed the dengue epidemic to a US BW attack against Cuba, and *Krasnaya Zvezda* repeated the dengue BW allegation just a year later. In a personal interview, Pasechnik described a small group that had met in Vorobyov's office at Biopreparat to prepare for the mission to Cuba. He said that the meeting had been rather hectic, but that either he or someone else had brought up the question of the Cuban allegations. The question had apparently not been considered worthy of discussion, and Pasechnik said that if there had been any real United States use of BW, he would have heard of it.[62]

Given the positions at the senior levels of the General Staff that individuals such as Petrov and Yevstigneev had held in the Russian military hierarchy, it was an ominous development to find them resurrecting all the old Soviet propaganda BW allegations from the mid-1950s to the mid-1980s in 1998–2001. Even worse, this regression was coupled with two others. They also reverted to the false pre-1992 explanation by the Soviet Union about the origin of the 1979 anthrax outbreak in Sverdlovsk, asserting that its cause had been infected meat, rather than an accident in the Ministry of Defense's BW facility in Sverdlovsk as admitted by President Yeltsin in 1992. Petrov even blamed the Sverdlovsk outbreak on US sabotage, as did Burgasov sometime later. (Their remarks are discussed further in Chapter 15.) The claim presumes that US agents carrying a quantity of *B. anthracis* spores were somehow able to penetrate a closed city situated in the center of Siberia and then disperse these spores as an aerosol in the street. How the US agents were able to carry out this "mission impossible" was not explained. In addition, despite the existence in the international diplomatic record of the 1992 Russian Confidence Building Measures (CBMs) submission under the BWC, which explicitly declared the existence of an offensive BW program in the Soviet Union between 1975 and 1992, these individuals reverted to denying that any offensive BW program had ever existed in the former Soviet Union. In this they were joined on separate occasions by Oleg Ignatiev, the former Soviet VPK BW official later assigned responsibility for the BW-relevant section of the Russian government's Munitions Agency, and by General Viktor I. Kholstov, Yevstigneev's successor. These denials are discussed in Chapter 22.

The innuendos and false BW allegations made by Russian officials continued through 2007. In an interview with the Russian newspaper *Moskovskie*

Novosti in 2004, Burgasov speculated about the motive behind the "anthrax letters" mailed in the United States in October–November 2001. He said: "What might be the purpose of this 'letter mailing' campaign? . . . either they are preparing for something serious (for example, using a smallpox formulation) and want to divert people's attention." Burgasov's reference to "they" can only refer to the US government.[63] And in May 2007 the head of the Russian FSB, Nikolai Patrushev, reportedly presented a report to President Putin suggesting that "several large Western medical centers . . . [are] involved in the development of 'genetically engineered biological weapons' for use against the Russian population." The FSB report apparently named the Harvard School of Public Health, the American International Health Alliance, the Environment and Natural Resources Division of the US Department of Justice, the Karolinska Institute in Stockholm, Sweden, the Swedish Agency for International Development, and the Indian Genome Institute as being "involved" in such BW developments aimed at the Soviet Union.[64] Yet only a few months later, when the head of Russia's Radiation, Chemical and Biological Defence Troops, Colonel-General Vladimir I. Filippov, was asked whether any states were currently developing biological weapons, he replied, "At the current time there is no available official evidence that any country is developing biological weapons."[65] Filippov's comment demonstrated clear differences in the statements made during the Putin years by serving senior military figures involved with CBW issues in Russia versus those made by their retired predecessors such as Yevstigneev, Petrov and Burgasov, and the FSB.

All of these allegations, including in part the one concerning AIDS, were explicitly charges of the use of biological weapons by the United States. Nevertheless, all of these are universally considered to have been fraudulent and propagandistic. All the charges that were made after 1972 and 1975, the signing and entry into force of the BWC, implicitly accuse the United States of maintaining its BW program and of violating the BWC. Soviet charges—in contrast to those made by the United States—only rarely appeared in official state documents and were never made by the most senior government officials. Except for the Korean War charges, the Soviet Union did not press any of these other numerous allegations in any international forum. It is important to emphasize the differences between the allegations made by the United States and those made by the Soviet Union. The US government raised the Yellow Rain issue in the United Nations, and its investigation was authorized by a UN General Assembly resolution (see Chapter 16).

The US concern about the events in Sverdlovsk was conveyed through official diplomatic channels and was an implicit issue at the first two BWC Review Conferences, in 1981 and 1986. In contrast, Soviet allegations were unquestionably malicious, and they served only to erode the existing restraints—in this case against biological weapons—and to undermine the basis for effective arms control.

15

Sverdlovsk 1979: The Release of *Bacillus anthracis* Spores from a Soviet Ministry of Defense Facility and Its Consequences

CHAPTER 3 INCLUDES a substantial section on the Scientific Research Institute of Microbiology of the Ministry of Defense (MOD), which was located within Compound 19 in Sverdlovsk. As described in that chapter, weaponized *Bacillus anthracis* spores were accidentally released from one of the institute's production facilities during the day of April 2, 1979, which caused an anthrax outbreak that affected both humans and animals. Chapter 3 contains descriptions of the technical details of BW agent production at the institute and how the accidental release came about. This chapter addresses the international and political consequences of the event.

Initial and partial information about the anthrax outbreak in Sverdlovsk reached US officials and then became known to members of Congress in early 1980. The subject became important for two separate reasons. First, it suggested that the Soviet Union might be producing sizable quantities of *B. anthracis* spores. That implied the maintenance of an offensive BW program, in violation of the BWC, which the Soviet Union had ratified in 1975. If true, that was certainly of concern to the US government. Second, SALT II, the third phase of the US-Soviet Strategic Arms Limitation Talks following SALT I and the ABM Treaty, had been signed by President Carter and General Secretary Brezhnev in Vienna on June 18, 1979. President Carter had immediately submitted the agreement to the US Senate for ratification on June 22. Once SALT opponents learned about the Sverdlovsk incident in early 1980, they argued that it demonstrated that the Soviet Union could not be trusted to carry out the provisions of unverified arms control treaties, and that the United States could not afford to limit its strategic nuclear weapon deployment levels under those circumstances. Democratic congressman Les Aspin, a longtime and consistent supporter of US-Soviet arms control negotiations, stated, "The future of arms control hangs in the balance until we get a full, accurate account of what happened in Sverdlovsk."[1] Hearings on the issue were held by the House of Representatives Select Committee on Intelligence, and congressional reports were issued. The House and Senate both passed resolutions that recommended referring the issue to the United Nations Security Council. Aspin, chairman of one of the House committees, further stated:

> What we are saying is that any judgment that the Soviet Union has violated the 1975 convention thus depends on the answer to the following question: Does the anthrax outbreak in Sverdlovsk demonstrate that the Soviets are producing or retaining a stockpile of Bacillus anthracis in quantities excessive for peaceful use or for testing defensive measures against the possibility of biological warfare by other countries?[2]

The response by the US Congress and the broader implications were spelled out in congressional documents:

> The Soviet explanation has been characterized as inadequate and unsatisfactory by the Department of State, and has prompted congressional action. The House Permanent Select Committee on Intelligence, after conducting hearings, issued a report critical of the Soviet Government's explanation and suggested the likelihood of a Soviet treaty violation.
>
> On May 14, 1980, the Senate passed Senate Resolution 405 expressing the sense of the Senate that the President should: (1) Request the Soviet Union to exchange scientific data regarding the outbreak of pulmonary anthrax as provided for by the convention prohibiting bacteriological and toxin weapons; or (2) take appropriate international procedures or lodge a complaint with the United Nations if the Soviet Union failed to make available such data. The House passed a companion measure, House Resolution 644, on May 19, 1980.
>
> This action not only questioned the efficacy of the treaty banning biological weapons, but also underlined the question of verification in the Geneva negotiations on chemical weapons. It thus cast a shadow

over SALT by raising questions about the likelihood of Soviet compliance and the adequacy of the treaty's verification provisions. The linkage between Sverdlovsk and these SALT issues was made explicit in the House Intelligence Committee's report.[3]

That Committee's report stated:

> Assessment of the Sverdlovsk incident, involving an outbreak of anthrax in that Soviet city under conditions which lead to assertions that the Soviets might have violated the 1975 Biological Weapons Convention. The Subcommittee found that the Soviet official explanation of the anthrax outbreak, ascribing it to the sale of tainted meat, was 'incomplete at best and at worst a fabrication.' The Subcommittee also concluded that 'There is no persuasive evidence to support allegations that the US Government suppressed intelligence about the outbreak of anthrax in Sverdlovsk, or that it delayed acting on this matter out of concern for SALT II or any other political motive.'[4]

Although the Carter administration had contacted the Soviets through diplomatic channels before the first congressional hearings took place, anticipated congressional pressure made it imperative to try to ascertain exactly what had happened in Sverdlovsk. The question of possible Soviet violation of the BWC threatened not only the Senate's ratification of SALT II, but all US-Soviet nuclear weapons arms control agreements, because none of the US-Soviet agreements prior to 1987 contained verification provisions.[5] The paragraph from the 1980 report by the Senate Select Committee on Intelligence is a representative example of the role that the Sverdlovsk anthrax outbreak played in the US nuclear arms control debate.

On March 17, 1980, the US government presented a secret démarche to the Soviet Union expressing the US concern that a release of a BW agent had caused inhalation anthrax in Sverdlovsk. Three days later, the Soviet Union responded that the anthrax outbreak was of the gastrointestinal variety, due to the sale of contaminated meat.[6] On March 20, 1980, the Soviet Ministry of Foreign Affairs (MFA) provided international wire services with portions of their diplomatic reply to the United States. In addition to denying any BWC treaty violation, they charged "that the US behavior raised doubts about the search for détente and arms control." On March 24, TASS released a history of anthrax in domestic animals and human cases in the Sverdlovsk region as well as a shorter item that accused the United States of raising questions about Sverdlovsk in order "to call into question the validity of the Convention, . . . to introduce complications in relations between states," and of "poisoning the international atmosphere."[7]

On March 28, 1980, the United States proposed bilateral expert discussions as provided for by Article V of the BWC:

> We believe it is essential for our two governments to make prompt and determined efforts to arrive at a mutual understanding of this matter. Article V of the Biological Weapons Convention, the importance of which was recently reaffirmed at the convention's review conference, requires consultation and cooperation between parties in order to reduce uncertainties and allay concerns that might arise. As depositary governments, the Soviet Union and the United States bear a special responsibility for ensuring the effective operation of the convention's consultative procedures, as the two leading participants in international arms control efforts, we have an additional and important responsibility to demonstrate our readiness to work together constructively to promote the viability of existing agreements.
>
> We believe that most effective means of clarifying the situation—and thereby meeting our mutual obligations under Article V of the BWC—would be to hold confidential discussions involving Soviet and American medical, public health and veterinary specialists. We believe the specialists should meet as soon as possible, preferably within the next few weeks. We would be prepared to hold the discussions in the Soviet Union or some other mutually acceptable location.
>
> In proposing that specialists from both sides meet confidentially to discuss the Sverdlovsk situation, we are mindful that, in the context of SALT, US and Soviet experts have been able to resolve treaty implementation questions of great complexity and sensitivity in a mutually satisfactory manner. While no formal consultative mechanism exists for the BW Convention, we hope that the ad hoc discussions we are proposing would enable us to deal with the present situation in an equally satisfactory fashion.
>
> In reference to the last paragraph of the foreign ministry's response, we cannot accept the implication that US efforts are directed toward complicating the situation and weakening international agreements on disarmament. Our motivation is precisely the opposite—to resolve the

current situation as quickly as possible and to strengthen those agreements by restoring confidence in their effective implementation.[8]

The exact wording of Article V was that consultations should occur "in cases of concrete suspicion, ambiguities or compliance concerns."

On April 24 the Soviet Union replied, stating once again that the disease outbreak was the result of "natural causes" and therefore not a violation of the BWC. The United States presented another démarche on August 11. It expressed dissatisfaction with the Soviet response, repeated the utility of technical-level exchanges, and emphasized the damage to arms control produced by the lack of Soviet cooperation. The United States did not charge the Soviet Union with a breach of the BWC, but said that it could not accept a unilateral assertion that the Soviet Union had complied fully with the BWC as a satisfactory response.[9] The style and tone of the Soviet response was a common one at the time to any question of Soviet behavior and was used in many other instances: Deputy Foreign Minister Georgy Kornienko replied that the threat to the BWC had been created by the US démarches and that the United States was trying to heighten world tension and worsen the bilateral US-USSR relationship.[10] US officials considered sending a letter to Brezhnev but did not do that. Interestingly, when meeting with UK foreign minister Douglas Hurd in September 1980, Ralph Earle, the director of ACDA, said that the United States doubted whether the Soviet Union was seriously interested in a military BW program. The main point was that Sverdlovsk was an embarrassment in terms of the internal US situation in relation to SALT II and other arms control agreements. The United Kingdom agreed that the primary aim was to maintain the credibility of the BWC and to put the Soviets on notice that the United States and United Kingdom would not tolerate violations of arms control agreements.[11] The US Department of Defense (DOD) also attempted to resolve the disputed interpretation of the Sverdlovsk event.[12]

By October 23, 1981, the US government had formally requested a Soviet explanation of the Sverdlovsk anthrax outbreak on five separate occasions.[13] Secretary of State Edmund Muskie and Deputy Secretary Warren Christopher raised the issue with Soviet ambassador Dobrynin in Washington, and the US ambassador in Moscow raised the question there. The United Kingdom had also requested a formal explanation.[14] The Soviet replies were the same in all cases: because the outbreak was due to a natural cause, namely contaminated meat, it was not subject to the provisions of the BWC, and the Soviet Union would not discuss it formally or informally.

Between October 1984 and May 1989, the Reagan and Bush administrations submitted no fewer than seven démarches to the MFA concerning biological weapons questions in the Soviet Union, and four of the seven pertained to the Sverdlovsk anthrax outbreak:

- October 1984—Soviet Retention of a BW Facility at Zagorsk
- February 1985—Confirmed BW Facility in the Soviet Union
- December 1985—Soviet Offensive Biological Weapon Capability
- August 1986—Anthrax Incident at Sverdlovsk
- July 1988—Sverdlovsk Follow-up
- December 1988—Sverdlovsk Follow-up
- May 1989—Sverdlovsk Follow-up[15]

Writing in a volume on arms control treaty compliance and enforcement in 1994, Harald Muller stated, "To decide whether a party has or has not breached its non-acquisition obligation under a Treaty is the politically most charged issue that can arise in the context of such a Treaty."[16] The United States had brought the issue to the first and second BWC Review Conferences and had been rebuffed by false denials. The other State Parties at the two Review Conferences by and large behaved as passive onlookers:

The regime as it stood, however, was capable neither of producing technical evidence on non-compliance nor of offering a viable procedure to come to a clear conclusion whether a case or even a question of non-compliance existed. The US, of course, could have addressed its complaint to the UNSC but chose not to do so, probably because the Soviet Union could have blocked any consideration through its veto.[17]

In July 1988, after the first Soviet submission of Confidence Building Measures (CBMs) to the BWC, the United States again raised the issue of the Sverdlovsk outbreak with the MFA. (See Chapter 20.) The Soviet response was to send along the paper authored by Petr Burgasov, the deputy minister of health at the time of the Sverdlovsk events, and his colleagues, which had already been presented in Geneva in September 1986 and at the US National Academy of Sciences in April 1988. (See below.) The Soviet message conveying this paper stated that the Soviet Union was taking this extraordinary step in the "interest of openness and trust," although "existing agreements between the participants in the Convention do not provide for the supplying of additional information." It also asserted:

> We of course expect reciprocity on the part of the United States in regard to the questions we raise. . . . It would be desirable for the United States, in the interest of openness and trust, to supply more complete information on all relevant research centers or laboratories having contracts with the U.S. Department of Defense for research and development projects for prevention of or protection against the possible hostile use of microbiological and/or other biological agents or toxins.
>
> The Soviet Union, proceeding on the basis of the international obligations it has undertaken and complying with the decisions of the Second Conference to Review the Effect of the Convention on the Prohibition of Bacteriological Weapons, has scrupulously and promptly implemented agreements on measures to increase the effectiveness of the Convention and to promote international cooperation in the peaceful use of the biological sciences. The Soviet side would like to call the attention of the United States to the importance of timely and full implementation of concluded agreements, and must point out in this connection that in 1988 the United States submitted its information two months after the established deadline. The effectiveness of confidence-building measures depends largely on how scrupulously they are carried out by the participants in the Convention.[18]

This is truly a remarkable piece of diplomatic effrontery, given that the years mentioned in the message were the years during which the Soviet Union was operating a massive top-secret offensive BW program. It has proved impossible to learn if the Soviet message was drafted in the MFA without further approval by Central Committee officials who would have been cognizant of the Soviet offensive BW program. Given the date of the document, it is now known that the Central Committee had by this time been discussing the Soviet BW program for at least a year. (See Chapter 21.)

Soviet officials continued to protest their innocence into the Gorbachev period, using the third and more sophisticated explanation for the Sverdlovsk anthrax outbreak. Each explanation had been markedly different from the proceeding one.[19] All the versions claimed that Sverdlovsk residents ate meat contaminated with *B. anthracis* and thus contracted gastrointestinal anthrax. Soviet authorities now explained that this had occurred due to the distribution of *B. anthracis*–contaminated animal bone meal supplements that had been produced by a local facility using improper procedures and distributed to farmers, infecting their cattle and sheep. This story would later also prove to be fabricated. However, Soviet authorities presented this version of events at a private meeting in Moscow on August 27–29, 1986, with Matthew Meselson, an important US authority on biological weapons;[20] on September 19, 1986, at an informal session of the BWC Second Review Conference in Geneva;[21] at a meeting in Moscow on October 8–9, 1986, between members of the US National Academy of Sciences and the USSR Academy of Sciences dealing with BW;[22] and finally in a series of presentations in the United States in April 1988, at the National Academy of Sciences, at Johns Hopkins University, and in Boston, during visits organized by Meselson.[23]

A key participant in most of these meetings was Burgasov, who chose to identify himself as follows: "At the time of the [Sverdlovsk anthrax] epidemic, I was a lieutenant-general and served as deputy to Marshal I. Bagramyan, a Deputy USSR defense minister, on the Council for Defense Against Weapons of Mass Destruction."[24] However, Burgasov's history was richer than what he revealed. He had been involved in the Soviet BW program since his appointment in 1950 to serve as a special assistant to Lavrenty Beria, then-director of the MGB (KGB predecessor). Burgasov held this position in the Kremlin until Beria's fall in 1953, at which time he joined the MOD's 7th Directorate of the General Staff.[25] He then worked as a scientist at the Sverdlovsk Institute from 1958 to 1963, during which time he also was responsible for the BW open-air test program conducted on Vozrozhdeniye Island. His responsibility as deputy minister of health from 1965 to 1986 concerned the Ministry's relations with the research institutes and facilities involved in the Soviet BW program. Burgasov therefore undoubtedly had a clear understanding of the nature of the work that took place inside Compound 19, and was unquestionably instrumental in organizing the cover-up of the accidental *B. anthracis* spore release. Burgasov was the first official from Moscow called to Sverdlovsk immediately as patients began to appear in local hospitals. Another of the Soviet scientists in the group that participated in these meetings and presentations, Vladimir Nikiforov, described Burgasov as "involved in providing overall direction for dealing with the epidemic." Nikiforov had arrived in Sverdlovsk from Moscow one day after Burgasov. For a short period in 1980, Soviet sources also claimed that the disease outbreak in Sverdlovsk was actually foot-and-mouth disease. For domestic Soviet consumption, this was published in *Literaturnaya Gazeta*,[26] while for the West it was published by the English-language weekly *Soviet News*.[27]

Between 1980 and 1992, Soviet and then Russian authorities maintained their position, presenting successively three different explanations of how *B. anthracis*–infected meat came to be sold in Sverdlovsk markets and workplaces. At the BWC Second Review Conference in 1986 the Soviet ambassador repeated the 1980 Soviet response to the diplomatic consequences of the Sverdlovsk events: "The Soviet Union is opposed to attempts to undermine this important international agreement in the field of disarmament, on various trumped-up pretexts." Nevertheless, sometime in 1987 or 1988 the Soviet delegation in Geneva agreed to meet privately with their US counterparts to discuss the US concerns about the Sverdlovsk outbreak. It took place in the US mission in Geneva. The meeting was not a success, as it did not lead to any useful exchange. The Soviet side was of course not prepared to admit to any of the particulars of the event. It is additionally possible that none of the Soviet delegation even knew much about either the institute in question or what really had taken place in 1979. They claimed that the presentation by the US diplomats was unsatisfactory, that it did not consist of "facts," but only repeated what had already been published in the open press. According to a former Soviet diplomat, the motive of the Soviet delegation in Geneva for agreeing to the meeting was twofold: first, just to hear out the United States, and second, to provide an opportunity to bring the issue back to Moscow and say: "These US concerns have now been brought up in a diplomatic process, and we need to respond in some manner." The earlier démarches by the Carter and Reagan administrations had already done that, of course, but this would now be in the Gorbachev era and it was presumably hoped by some in the MFA that it might now be used to alter the status quo about the subject in some way in Moscow. As we will see in Chapter 21, it did indeed lead to initiatives by the MFA in Moscow in 1989, but none of that was visible to the US government. In any event, nothing came of the meeting, and there was no follow-up to it.[28]

In addition to the inconsequential meeting with US diplomats in 1987 or 1988, as already noted the MFA arranged for CISAC, an arms control group of the US National Academy of Sciences, to meet twice with Soviet officials to discuss the Sverdlovsk events. They met first in Washington, D.C., and then in Moscow. The US group was presented with the same fraudulent Burgasov-Nikiforov material that the two Soviet scientists would bring to the United States for public presentations the following year. Meselson, one of the members of the US group, was also allowed to meet with General Yevstigneev.[29]

In March 1990, relatively late in the *glasnost* period of Soviet politics, the official Soviet explanations began to unravel through a sequence of press reports in the Soviet media, and by late 1991 it was clear that the Soviet story was a fabrication.[30] These press reports culminated with the publication of three *Izvestia* articles in November and December 1991, which included testimony from retired Soviet military and KGB generals describing in detail the accident in the Soviet facility.[31] Nevertheless, in April 1992 Yevstigneev produced yet another fictional explanation of the source of the anthrax outbreak, but one that significantly offered for the first time a convenient explanation for an aerosol distribution of *B. anthracis* spores. He asserted that carcasses of anthrax-infected cattle had been improperly incinerated in the furnaces of a ceramics plant located close to the southern perimeter of Compound 19.[32] The implication of Yevstigneev's story was that the incineration not only resulted in airborne spores that infected workers in the ceramics plant, but released spores through the chimney into the air, which spread further in the city. This was not simply disinformation for public consumption in Russia: in September 1992 Yevstigneev repeated this story to the US and UK participants in the Trilateral negotiations in Moscow. (See Chapter 22.) This was four months after Russian president Boris Yeltsin was quoted in the Russian press in May 1992 as publicly saying that "the KGB admitted that our military developments were the cause."[33] President Yeltsin was reported to have privately told the same thing in May 1992 to President Bush, UK Prime Minister Major, and French President Mitterrand.[34]

On June 17, 1992, the US Department of State (DOS) produced a "Press Guidance" with presumptive questions and the appropriate replies. It read as follows:

> Question: Can you comment on the story that Russian President Yeltsin, in an interview with *Komsomolskaya Pravda,* has admitted that the anthrax outbreak in Sverdlovsk in 1979 was caused by an accident at a Soviet biological weapons facility? . . . Can you confirm, as the story indicates, that President Yeltsin acknowledged to President Bush, UK Prime Minister Major, and French President Mitterrand that the Sverdlovsk case was a result of the Soviet biological weapons program?

Answer: Speaking for the United States, I can confirm that President Yeltsin has discussed the subject of biological weapons with President Bush, and has indicated that, as we already determined, the Sverdlovsk incident was a result of the offensive biological weapons program of the former Soviet Union. I can only refer you to the UK and French authorities for comments on what may have been said to Prime Minister Major and President Mitterrand.

Q: Why has the United States not publicized this acknowledgement by President Yeltsin earlier?

A: We regard the acknowledgement of the existence of the offensive biological weapons program, and the specific case of Sverdlovsk, as important steps by President Yeltsin. We have urged the Russian government to be similarly candid with regard to all aspects of the illegal program, and to take concrete steps to demonstrate that it has been terminated. We have not engaged in public discussion of this issue because we believed that quiet diplomacy would be more effective in facilitating the necessary steps in Russia.[35]

Despite the foregoing, the DOS official who was the Washington backup for the early Trilateral teams said that in June 1992 the US government still did not know what had happened in Sverdlovsk in regard to two key points: precisely what had caused the accident in Compound 19, and exactly what the facility was doing.[36]

The Trilateral meeting took place in September 1992 at the MFA in Moscow. Yevstigneev once again presented a summary of the Soviet-era explanations for the 1979 anthrax outbreak in Sverdlovsk, and he included in his presentation all three "theories"—among them the incineration referred to above, as well as the infected bone meal story. As indicated earlier, all these "theories" had by then been thoroughly discredited in the public press in Russia and by President Yeltsin in May 1992. During the break in the formal discussions following his presentation, Yevstigneev told a senior US official present, "privately," that in 1989 the KGB had carried out an investigation in Sverdlovsk, "and we knew in 10 seconds that it was an illegal program. . . . You can put that down; you can tell your own government."[37] Of course, Yevstigneev had known for the preceding 15 years "that it was an illegal program." Nevertheless, for the preceding three years the Soviet General Staff had still actively been providing the most senior Politburo members with partial or wholly misleading information about the basic nature of the Soviet BW program, as well as about the Sverdlovsk outbreak.

Three relevant documents produced for the Central Committee of the CPSU have become available, and they are perhaps the most astonishing aspect of all regarding the Sverdlovsk story. They demonstrate the degree of deception that extended to the highest levels of the leadership of the Soviet government in 1989 and 1990 regarding the Sverdlovsk events. One can only assume that even greater levels of internal deception of Central Committee officials took place in 1979–1980 and 1986–1987. Immediately after Pasechnik's defection to the United Kingdom at the end of October 1989, a flurry of activity regarding BW issues took place in the Politburo. In addition, because of the concurrent CWC negotiations, the Politburo had for several years been anticipating that the United States and the United Kingdom would eventually request on-site access to the MOD's BW facilities. The first document was produced on December 19, 1989.

Reference Note: On the causes of the anthrax outbreak in Sverdlovsk

In spring 1979 a big outbreak of anthrax was registered in Sverdlovsk.

The committee chaired by deputy minister for health of the USSR, comrade Burgasov P.N drew a conclusion of its natural origin, based on epidemiological analysis.

However, from the moment of the outbreak of the epidemic until recently, a question has repeatedly been raised abroad, as well as among the population, medical and veterinary specialists about the involvement of the USSR Defense Ministry Scientific Research Institute 44 (NII 44) in those events in Sverdlovsk.

> In connection with the request of the USSR Foreign Affairs Ministry, having examined this question additionally, the State Committee of the USSR Council of Ministers on military-industrial questions (comrade Belousov I. S.), USSR Ministry of Defense (comrade Moiseev M. A.), USSR Ministry of Health (comrade Chazov Y. I.) and the CPSU CC Defense Department (comrade Belyakov O. S.), considered it possible to confirm the earlier conclusions about the natural origin of the epidemic, although it does not appear practically possible to fully exclude the possibility of the connection between the epidemic and an accident at the above mentioned facility.

That's why in future it is also recommended to use the guidelines of the official materials supplied by the USSR in 1987 to the UN Department on Disarmament, to be specific:

- the epidemic analysis confirmed the natural origin of this outbreak;
- the 44 NII of the USSR Ministry of Defense deals with issues of military epidemiology, including decontamination of military hardware in contaminated areas; the facility is not engaged in the development of biological weapons;
- prior to 1985, the existing buildings and structures were used for the production and storage of chemicals manufactured to protect troops from biological warfare; at present time the equipment is disassembled and storage facilities are re-equipped for storage of inventory property of TsVMU [Central Military Medical Directorate] of the USSR Ministry of Defense.

> At present, in the current circumstances, a visit of an international commission to the area of the epidemic does not seem expedient. Comrade Zaikov L. N. agrees with this suggestion.
> N. Shakhov, deputy head of the CPSU CC Defense Department
> 19 December 1989.[38]

And yet this very document was essentially a second layer of internal deception, and its author, the Central Committee Secretariat staffer Nikolai Shakhov, as well as at least several other members of the Secretariat, knew that. The US démarche in 1986 had asked the Soviet Union to explain an alleged explosion at the Sverdlovsk MOD facility. Because it was an MOD facility that was involved, the Secretariat addressed the question to Marshal Akhromeyev at the MOD. The MOD's reply stated that there was no explosion because there were no explosives at the site. It also said, however, that it was possible that a technical failure in the air filtration system might have taken place, since the technology was not sufficiently advanced, and it might have caused a leak. The MOD reply added that besides an uncontrolled emission, someone might have "opened" a contaminated area of the facility. In addition, there could be a more benign explanation. In sum, the MOD site could have been the cause, but other explanations were possible. No information was provided as to what the Sverdlovsk facility did or what it made.

The document did *not* however say "It is all defensive." The MOD reply in fact provided the correct source of the emission from the site, but presented it as only a possibility, and fudged that further by adding two other possibilities. This information was for internal use by the Secretariat; it was *not* for transmission to the US side. The reply was "signed for" by Marshal Akhromeyev. Vitaly Kataev, a key member of the very small arms control staff of the Central Committee Secretariat, indicated that Akhromeyev did not find out what had happened at Sverdlovsk until 1987–1988. The positions held by Kataev, Zaikov, and their colleagues, and a more extensive description of their roles, are provided in Chapter 21.

In fact, the question sent to the MOD in 1986 was very likely formulated by none other than Shakhov. At the end of the query there would have been an expression such as "It would be nice to receive some expert information about this," and it would have been signed by Zaikov or one of his two senior deputies.[39] Kataev's testimony about outright lying at the Politburo level is complicated. At one point he said, "People in the government were used to lying; they had been doing it for years." But he also said that the chief of the General Staff would not lie to the Politburo or the general secretary, as that would never be forgiven. For example, at a meeting of the Politburo Commission on July 27, 1989, Kalinin reported that "they were no longer finding anthrax spores in Sverdlovsk," but that "they might be still located in pockets."[40] Kalinin's report to the Politburo does not discuss the origin of the spores, but the context in which such sentences make sense would not be in a tale of infected meat and intestinal anthrax.

It is clear that activity on BW issues was hectic in various Central Committee venues in the days and weeks after the above December 19, 1989, memorandum. The substance of these meetings is not known, although the dates and document numbers are available in several cases. One of these was another memorandum dated January 5, 1990, and drafted by Victor Karpov of the MFA as chair of the Intergovernmental Committee. Its title was "On Directives to the USSR Delegation at the Soviet-American Consultations on Issues of Banning of Bacteriological and Toxin Weapons."[41] The date places it several months before the first "post-Pasechnik" UK-US démarche was presented to the Soviet Union. General Yazov, chief of the General Staff at the MOD, wrote a sharp attack on Karpov's document, and requested that his criticisms be taken up by the Politburo Committee. Only those elements of Yazov's memorandum that concern the 1979 Sverdlovsk events are discussed in this chapter. (The memorandum appears in full as an Annex at the end of this chapter, the other even more basic issues in the memorandum regarding the Soviet BW program are dealt with in Chapter 21.)

According to Yazov's memorandum, Karpov had suggested that the United States could be informed that an investigation of the Sverdlovsk events based on the US charges was then under way, and "to keep in mind that indeed an accident took place at the facility of N11 of Microbiology of the USSR Ministry of Defense in Sverdlovsk." Yazov's memorandum of complaint adds, "A possibility is also mentioned about handing to the American side the information about the accident at the end of the investigation." Yazov protests that there was no accident, that an "anti-epidemic commission in 1979 arrived at a conclusion about the food origin of this outbreak," and that this previously stated position should be maintained. Otherwise it "may discredit our state on the international level and provoke unpredictable actions of the population inside the country." Yazov is additionally incensed that 15 copies of Karpov's draft were distributed. He requests that

> the Ministry of Foreign Affairs . . . urgently recall the draft resolution of the CPSU CC, not to further revise the official documents concerning the compliance of the USSR with the 1972 convention, as well as not to raise the question about the visit by American experts to the facility of the USSR Ministry of Defense in Sverdlovsk until the mechanisms of control over compliance with the mentioned international agreement are worked out. . . .
>
> Besides, there is concern that representatives of the USSR Ministry of Foreign Affairs, when receiving certain information on special problems at various intergovernmental meetings, may in some cases broaden the circle of informed people who must not receive this kind of information without authorization.[42]

It is important to note that the phrase "Special Problems" was the Secretariat's designation for Soviet biological weapons programs and activities.

On the very next day, Karpov abjectly retracted the references to the Sverdlovsk events that Yazov had objected to:

> Draft directives were discussed at the meeting of the interdepartmental commission on Jan. 10, 1990, where the authors of the reference memo explained that in reality there had been no accident, and that it was just

unfortunate ambiguous wording which crept into the reference memo. In this connection paragraph three on page 7 of the draft directives was removed, and the end of the previous paragraph was presented as follows: "to confine ourselves to a statement that the materials clarifying the causes of the anthrax outbreak in Sverdlovsk had been brought to the notice of the USA."[43]

On the very same day, Central Committee staffers Belyakov and Kataev also drafted a memo to Zaikov making certain that he took note of Karpov's indiscretion. It provides additional evidence on the procedures by which the distribution of restricted information was controlled and, in rare special cases, made available to the most senior members of the Central Committee. The date, July 2, 1987, on which a senior MFA official was first informed of an aspect of the Soviet offensive BW program will be important in Chapter 21.

It is worth drawing your attention to comrade V. P. Karpov's behavior in another serious matter—on biological weapons.

At his own initiative, in early January of this year he circulated "classified"-marked documents to 15 addresses on the problem marked with "F" to which he was made privy by special approval of the CPSU CC on July 02, 1987, and which he had no right to disclose. He has totally disregarded that the Defense Department had supplied him with a reply to the request of the USSR People's Deputy comrade Goldansky submitted to comrade E. A. Shevardnadze on the so called "Sverdlovsk case." (The text of the reply was approved by you.)[44]

Only four months later, another Central Committee document provides what might be interpreted as a more realistic attitude. Following the defection of Pasechnik and the subsequent démarches by the United States and the United Kingdom in March 1990 (which are described in Chapter 21), the Secretariat prepared a document titled "Additional Directives" for the Soviet officials who were to take part in "consultations" in April 1990. One of the annexes to this document consisted of three pages of "Informational Material" about the Sverdlovsk Institute. It provided precisely the information that they could transmit to their US and UK counterparts.[45] It described all the work done at the institute as defensive. Interestingly, it made no reference whatsoever to the 1979 anthrax events. None of the various Burgasov legends were mentioned; there simply was no reference at all to the anthrax outbreak.

Two quite surprising letters were written to Yeltsin toward the very end of 1991 when Yeltsin was still the president of the Russian Federation. The first, by Duma member L. P. Mishustina, was sent to Yeltsin sometime between early October and early December 1991. It noted that "the death of 70 people was the consequence of a leakage of bacteriological weapons, which happened in the so called 19th military settlement," and that the families of the deceased had received only 50 rubles in restitution. He requested that Yeltsin "organize an official investigation into the event."[46] The second letter was far more significant. It was authored by one of Yeltsin's deputies, A. V. Yablokov, the state advisor of the RSFSR on environmental affairs and public health. The letter was written in response to a directive from Yeltsin asking Yablokov to determine the origins of the anthrax epidemic.[47] It stated:

> In a secret document dated 5 June 1979 (signed by the Minister of Health of the USSR B. V. Petrovsky, the Deputy Chairman of the KGB of the USSR V. P. Pirozkhovy, the Head of the TsVMU [Central Military-Medical Directorate] of the Ministry of Defense of the USSR F. I. Komarovy, and the Deputy Chairman of the Council of Ministers of the RSFSR L. P. Lykovaya), it is stated that the causative agent for anthrax was isolated from soil samples, *air samples, the washouts from wall carpets, door exteriors and mailboxes* . . .
>
> It is also necessary to note that, according to the KGB of the USSR, documents concerning this anthrax epidemic (documents, disclosure of those who died, results of analyses of facilities and the natural environment, etc.) were destroyed in accordance with a decision of the Council of Ministers of the USSR dated 4 December 1990 (no. 1244-167, 'On the activities concerning special problems').
>
> Finally there is this significant fact: the removal by the Military Prosecutors Office of the USSR of all matters concerning the deaths from this epidemic from civil criminal legal proceedings, which occurs only in cases of investigation of matters connected to the Ministry of Defense.
>
> All of the above-mentioned facts, taken together, serve as irrefutable evidence that the truth (i.e., the outbreak of anthrax was caused by work by enterprises of the Ministry of Defense of the USSR) was hidden from the official version of the events.[48]

After the anthrax outbreak was recognized for what it was, the KGB confiscated hospital records, death certificates, and other relevant incriminating evidence present in Sverdlovsk. A book published in Russia by L. A. Federov in 2005 claims that "the KGB left no medical institution in the city in possession of even a single document," and attributes to A. A. Klimkina, the deputy minister of social welfare of the RSFSR, a statement saying "not a single death certificate issued for those who died during the 1979 epidemic says that their death ensued 'as a result of contracting anthrax.'"[49]

In June 1992, and again in August 1993, a team of US scientists led by Meselson were finally permitted to visit Sverdlovsk (by then renamed Yekaterinburg). They located two Soviet pathologists who had managed to hide some of their records as well as histological preparations of tissues taken from Sverdlovsk anthrax victims. The combined team of US and Russian researchers also were able to interview family members of a large number of those who had died. Importantly, they obtained the records of the wind conditions near Sverdlovsk on April 2, 3, and 4, 1979. These data clearly demonstrated that the locations of all the victims on the morning of April 2, 1979, were positioned within a narrow footprint southeast of the city, with its origin point at the military BW facility.[50] And while Burgasov was still claiming that *B. anthracis*–contaminated meat from several villages outside of Sverdlovsk was the cause of the disease outbreak, he made the tactical error of providing the veterinary reports from three of the villages in which cattle had fallen ill to Meselson's team in order to bolster his argument. It was then possible to plot their location, showing that they too lay within the area of the plume.[51] All these details were published and widely noted. Subsequently the information on many other animal deaths was published in Russia, showing that they all were located within the area of the plume.[52]

Despite the findings by Meselson and his co-workers, and the testimony of an "insider," senior Russian military officials who had spent their careers in the Soviet BW program subsequently either continued to hew to, or returned to, the pre-1992 Soviet explanations for the outbreak or invented new, often contradictory, ones. Yevstigneev, who had been scientific director of Compound 19 in the 1980s, privately stated that "experiments to test vaccine efficacy were conducted on nonhuman primates at Compound 19." He also provided the quantity of *B. anthracis* spores used for such tests that fits one theoretical model for the number of anthrax casualties that occurred in April–May 1979. He claimed, however, that no such experiments were conducted in early April 1979.[53] On a second occasion, Yevstigneev told an American scientist with a thorough knowledge of the 1979 Sverdlovsk events who was visiting Russia that the MOD facility in Sverdlovsk had been "doing large animal tests" with *B. anthracis*—but not on the particular day of the accidental release. But by 1998, Russian officials were once again telling Russian newspaper reporters that the Sverdlovsk anthrax outbreak had been caused by contaminated meat and therefore had been of the gastrointestinal type. In December 1999, a book co-authored by the Russian deputy minister of health also claimed that the 1979 anthrax outbreak was caused by the distribution of *B. anthracis*–contaminated meat, which of course at least in part contradicts both the carcass incineration/aerosol fabrication, as well as the final and most fantastic Russian fabrication, which claimed that deliberate US sabotage had caused the anthrax epidemic (described below).[54] Nevertheless, in 1997 and 1999, books were also published in Russia that explicitly attributed the disease outbreak both to BW weapon development in Compound 19,[55] as well as to an aerosol release.[56]

After the anthrax letters were distributed in the United States in October 2001, the office of Douglas Feith, under secretary for policy in the DOD, asked the RF-MOD if it would share its epidemiological data from the 1979 Sverdlovsk events. The request was made to General Yury Baluevsky, then head of the Directorate of International Cooperation of the General Staff, and subsequently the head of the General Staff. In his reply, Baluevsky stated that there was no use providing the United States with the epidemiological information because all the anthrax cases in Sverdlovsk had been gastrointestinal in nature.[57]

Early in December 2004 a group of seven Americans attended a conference in Moscow arranged by an arms-control center at Stanford University and the Committee of Scientists for Global Security, an affiliate of the Russian Academy of Sciences. At a session co-chaired by Yevstigneev and Vector director Lev Sandakhchiev, Dean Wilkening of Stanford University presented his modeling study of the airborne *B. anthracis* plume in Sverdlovsk, a paper that was later published.[58] In the discussion that followed, no one denied that there had been an aerosol release or offered any other explanation for the disease outbreak. No one challenged the model. Further, both Sandakhchiev and Yevstigneev had small private conversations with Wilkening. Sandakhchiev commented that everyone understood that the release was due to an accident at the MOD facility, and he believed that all the relevant documentation had been destroyed. Yevstigneev, who by now had been publicly repeating one of the very earliest Soviet disinformation stories at meetings of the Trilateral working groups and in public statements for some years, that dogs dragged *B. anthracis*–contaminated meat around the streets of Sverdlovsk, said only that Wilkening's model was very interesting and that they had a similar model (that is, of an aerosol release).[59] Yet that same year Yevstigneev repeated the "dogs" story to other visiting US scientists.[60]

Zaviyalov reported an equally interesting conversation with Yevstigneev. In 1979, Zaviyalov had not heard of the Sverdlovsk outbreak, although military scientists from the Sverdlovsk Institute, including Volkovoy, had come to work at SRCAM. But he said that years later "Yevstigneev had told him that it was the filter problem and that the facility had been producing anthrax."[61] Joshua Lederberg learned that this information appears to have been more widely known even in the early 1980s in the Soviet Union than might be expected.[62]

The final Russian fabrication, which appeared in 2001, was markedly different from all those that had preceded it. It alleged that the Sverdlovsk outbreak was caused by an act of sabotage, more specifically, sabotage by the United States. A press article claimed that the B. anthracis strains in the outbreak were "from the Republic of South Africa and North America," and it also disputed the official Soviet numbers of those who died of anthrax during the 1979 outbreak.[63] This fabrication was repeated by officials of the RF-MOD State Center for Public Health and Epidemiological Surveillance (Gosepidnadzor), who explained, "The best known case of biological sabotage using anthrax was the Sverdlovsk epidemic in 1979. . . . [In] disguised US sabotage . . . saboteurs dispersed the bacteria at Soviet bus stops at night" [presumably released as an aerosol].[64] Burgasov astonishingly adopted this new explanation, thus replacing his own earlier explanation that had appeared in his own official papers and presentations of the late 1980s, as well as those of the Soviet government for over a decade. Those had stated that the anthrax outbreak was due to the distribution of animal food supplements composed of ground bone meal, which were B. anthracis–contaminated and had been insufficiently sterilized due to negligence.[65] As late as a June 1998 interview with a Moscow medical weekly, Burgasov replied to an interviewer's question, "So you are sticking with the story that infected meat was the source of the epidemic?" by replying, "I still have documents clearly proving it."[66] Burgasov now claims that he misled the Soviet government knowingly, and that he now subscribes to the Supotnitskiy-authored sabotage explanation.[67]

The suggestion that the anthrax outbreak was due to sabotage from outside the Soviet Union had already appeared in several forms in the Soviet press in 1991 and 1992, when disclaimers about its etiology were frequent. They were, however, not particularly elaborated. The deputy director of the Sverdlovsk facility, Colonel G. Arkhangelskiy, argued, "it would not have happened without enemy involvement" and "the first thought was to find the saboteurs."[68] Similarly, it was suggested "that it was a terrorist attack. . . . A second version was that the illness was 'sent in' with imported equipment."[69] Each of these KGB or military disinformation stories was primarily for domestic consumption, and each was more preposterous than the previous one and harkened back to the kinds of concoctions used by Soviet authorities in the 1930s.

In July 2009, Petrov and Supotnitskiy returned to their claim that the anthrax outbreak was due to deliberate US sabotage, with an added twist. They claimed, first, that the US "Amerithrax" events in 2001, in which a dry powder preparation was sent to various recipients through the US postal system, corroborated their charges, and second, that the US sabotage was undertaken because a "check was being made of the protective effectiveness of the Soviet [anthrax] vaccine," in order to choose "a strain for effective biological acts of sabotage or even waging a biological war in case of a military confrontation between the USSR and the West."[70] But they had one new purpose in repeating this claim, to charge that the United States was violating the BWC: "It turns out that the terrorist act was committed with a recipe developed in violation of the 1972 Convention." All of the fuss the United States had made about the 1979 Sverdlovsk events thus was made simply to cover up its own continuing BW program.[71]

The BWC entered into force on March 26, 1975. Only a year later, in 1976, US government agencies for the first time leaked information alleging the existence of specific Soviet BW facilities. This was discussed in detail in Chapter 12. Nevertheless, intelligence regarding Soviet BW capabilities remained thin and was often ambiguous. The 1979 anthrax outbreak, only a few years later, had a significant effect on US intelligence assessments about Soviet BW. Information previously considered to be ambiguous was reconsidered and now assumed to be a more certain indicator of an offensive Soviet BW program.[72] Despite this, a full 10 years later in 1989 in specific reference to the Sverdlovsk outbreak, Senator John Glenn, chairman of the Committee on Government Affairs, in a Hearing on Biological Weapons Proliferation, asked Ambassador H. Allen Holmes, assistant secretary for politico-military affairs in the DOS, why the United States did not lodge an official complaint with the UN Security Council about the Sverdlovsk outbreak and potential Soviet violations of the BWC. Ambassador Holmes replied, "Our basic approach is to try to get the facts before we go public with accusations of violations. . . . To my understanding, we have never been able to get sufficient information to establish the facts on these violations."[73]

April 1979, the date of the Sverdlovsk anthrax episode, occurred just at the end of a 10-year period of US-Soviet strategic arms-control negotiations. Ratification of a SALT II treaty was facing difficulty in the US Senate. Afghanistan was already boiling. Following the coup by a faction of communist Afghan army officers on April 27, 1978, large numbers of Soviet political and military advisors were in the country, and in March 1979 Soviet aircraft heavily bombed the Afghan city of Herat in order to suppress an uprising against the communist government. On December 24, 1979, the Soviet Union would invade Afghanistan in force. Just as the Soviet government had never informed its own public until 1989 about massive nuclear radiation releases that had taken place in Kyshtym/Chelyabinsk in 1957, it is almost certain that it would have denied the real cause of the anthrax outbreak under any circumstances.[74] Even cholera outbreaks were covered up in the former Soviet Union. And of particular relevance, the Soviet Union was one of the three co-depository governments for the BWC. Under the prevailing international conditions in 1979, from the first moment that an accident caused pulmonary anthrax cases, it was an absolute certainty that the Soviet government would cover up a live *B. anthracis* release from a known military BW facility. The Soviet Union was scarcely going to make any admission or near-admission of treaty violation or explain events in a manner that could unravel its covert biological weapons program. It was an unavoidable consequence that the cover-up led the Soviet government into years of lying.

Had authorities of the Soviet BW system prepared cover stories for the sort of accident that took place in Sverdlovsk? If so, such cover stories would have been necessary for each individual pathogen whose production was tested at any of the mobilization capacity production facilities and the three MOD institutes, and for each possible means of escape from a facility—air, water, and so on. Were the cover stories also accompanied by contingency plans for public health intervention and decontamination, as occurred in Sverdlovsk? And where within the BW system might such cover stories have been devised and/or stored? At each individual facility, or in a filing cabinet in Burgasov's Ministry of Health Third Directorate office in Moscow? Or was the cover story that was very quickly put into service in Sverdlovsk an ad hoc, improvised response by Burgasov? It is clear that it was imposed by him in the very first days after he arrived in Sverdlovsk, and the story underwent several revisions between 1979 and 1992. All these secondary questions remain unanswered. Finally, why should there have been a new fabricated story in 2001, alleging sabotage by US agents in Sverdlovsk as the cause of the anthrax outbreak? That perhaps is answerable. It is clear that at least since mid-1999, the old Soviet "organs"—the KGB and its successors—have once again been ordered to concoct fabrications as they see fit for internal consumption, no matter how ridiculous they appear to outsiders, or with little concern as to how they reflect on the veracity of the Russian government.

With the additional information now available from the former Soviet Union, it is possible to have a satisfactory overview of the 1979 Sverdlovsk outbreak, from its occurrence to its legacy in the present day. A reasonable understanding is now available of the accident itself. Disinformation narratives were produced immediately by Burgasov. These were maintained after Gorbachev became general secretary, when they were brought to the BWC Second Review Conference in September 1986, and then to the National Academy of Sciences in the United States in April 1988. Nevertheless, Central Committee documents demonstrate that a partially accurate explanation of the anthrax events was given to the Politburo of the Central Committee by the MOD sometime in 1986 or 1987. At the same time, other parts of the Soviet government—branches of the MOD and Soviet propaganda organs—maintained a stream of disinformation and invective as a response to all questions regarding these events.

This external representation was mirrored in the fiasco that resulted from the "reexamination" requested by the MFA in December 1989. It led to a recommendation by the Politburo Secretariat that the deception narratives, as well as a false depiction of the Sverdlovsk MOD facility's function, be continued. Yazov demanded on January 10, 1990, that the Central Committee and the Soviet government not alter the previous depiction of the Sverdlovsk event. The MFA capitulated to his demand the following day. Remarkably, there was a resurgence in the early 2000s of the old Sverdlovsk disinformation stories, as well as the introduction of new ones alleging US sabotage as the cause of the outbreak. Burgasov participated in this campaign as well, despite its overt contradiction of the official narrative of which he was the original author, and which he had maintained and was the spokesperson for between 1979 and 1992.

Despite this incredible record of disinformation and prevarication by senior officials of first the Soviet Union and then Russia, damage to the BWC seems in retrospect to have been slight. Because State Parties to the BWC, with the exception of the United States and the United Kingdom, chose to look the other way, the Soviet Union and then Russia escaped concerted criticism by State Parties at the review conferences. This policy remains the same today: Russia has not been taken to task in BWC fora. Other State Parties to the BWC are either disinterested or think it would serve no useful purpose. The presumption is that it would only raise Russian diplomatic hackles, produce new denials, and there are always new diplomatic priorities for which Russian cooperation is being sought. With the panoply of major bilateral and multilateral strategic arms control treaties that were achieved during Gorbachev's tenure, the Soviet/Russian denials regarding the Sverdlovsk MOD facility and what it was doing did not in the long run have any appreciable effect on subsequent arms-control negotiations.

ANNEX A: General Yazov and Viktor Karpov, Foreign Ministry, Memoranda

CPSU CC

On the draft resolution of the CPSU CC "On Directives to the USSR delegation at the Soviet-American consultations on issues of banning bacteriological and toxin weapons"

The USSR defense ministry received the a draft resolution of the CPSU CC "on directives to the USSR delegation at Soviet-American consultations on questions of banning bacteriological and toxin weapons" prepared by the USSR Ministry for Foreign Affairs and sent as signed by the USSR Deputy Minister for Foreign Affairs comrade Karpov, V. P., who chairs the Intergovernmental Commission for conducting work and studying questions connected with the fulfillment by the USSR of its obligations as a participant in the 1972 convention banning biological and toxin weapons. (outgoing No. 2/ upovr of January 5, 1990)

The noted document had not been studied on a working routine basis together with the USSR defense ministry. And information concerning the activity of respective institutions of the USSR ministry of defense had not been requested by the USSR Ministry of Foreign Affairs.

Along with the development and specification of positions concerning the system of control and confidence building measures, the circulated draft resolution contains suggestions that radically contradict statements previously made at the government level.

It is proposed "to express a readiness for an exchange with the USA on a confidential basis of information on reserves of bacteriological (biological) and toxin weapons and sites for its production which each side had in possession prior 1975 when the convention came into force, as well as about implemented measures on the elimination or transition to peaceful purposes of all agents, toxins, weapons, equipment and means of delivery listed in Article 1 of the convention."

This proposal contradicts the USSR official statements to the effect that the Soviet Union has never worked on nor produced nor possessed stockpiles of biological weapons.

Should there arise a question about the outbreak of anthrax in Sverdlovsk in 1979, it is recommended to "confine ourselves to a statement that at the present time an investigation is under way; an investigation of accusations prompted by the anthrax outbreak and put forward by the USA which claims the USSR violates the Convention," also to "keep in mind that indeed an accident took place at the facility of NII [Scientific Research Institute] of Microbiology of the USSR Ministry of Defense in Sverdlovsk . . ."

A possibility is also mentioned to share information about the accident with the American side at the end of the investigation.

This interpretation of the 1979 events has no real basis to support it. There were no explosions and accidents at the facility of the USSR Ministry of Defense, and a check-up of the engineering systems held at that period revealed no malfunctions. The emergency anti-epidemic commission in 1979 arrived at a conclusion about the food origin of this outbreak, and at the present time there exists no new information or circumstances that would force a doubt about the correctness of the conclusions.

In the opinion of the USSR Ministry of Defense, such proposals made by the USSR Ministry of Foreign Affairs may discredit our state on the international level and provoke unpredictable actions of the population inside the country.

Evaluating the situation that is materializing, it is necessary to take into account that the document has been reproduced in 15 copies and sent to various addresses.

In this connection, the USSR Ministry of Defense addressed the USSR Ministry of Foreign Affairs with suggestions to urgently recall the draft resolution of the CPSU CC, not to further revise the official documents concerning the compliance of the USSR with the 1972 convention, as well as not to raise the question about the visit by American experts to the facility of the

USSR Ministry of Defense in Sverdlovsk until the mechanisms of control over compliance with the mentioned international agreement are worked out.

Besides, there is concern that representatives of the USSR Ministry of Foreign Affairs, when receiving certain information on special problems at various intergovernmental meetings, may in some cases broaden the circle of informed people who must not receive this kind of information without authorization.

I suggest this question be examined at the CPSU CC Politburo committee chaired by comrade Zaikov, L. M.

[signed]

D. Yazov

10 January 1990

- Epidemic analysis confirmed the natural origin of this outbreak;
- 44th NII of the USSR Ministry of Defense deals with questions of military epidemiology, including decontamination of military hardware in damage zones; the facility conducts no work on the development of biological weapons;

ANNEX B

To comrade Lazarev V. F.

In accordance with your request, I am sending a copy of the document # 2/upovr of January 05, 1990, with attached draft of directives to the Soviet-American consultations on banning of bacteriological weapons.

The document was circulated among members of the Interdepartmental committee, specifically to comrades: Sergeev G. V., Narkevich M. I. (both from Minzdrav), Gusakov A. Ye. (NII "Medstatistika"), Alibekov K. A. (Minmedprom USSR), Kovalev N. N. (GVPK Council Ministers USSR), Kondrashev S. A. (KGB USSR), Kurchenko F. P. (Goskom CM USSR for food and provisions), Ukharov O. V. (Genshtab), Yevstigneev V. I. (military unit 26150), Golubkov S. V. (USSR Minhimnefteprom), Bayev A. A. (AN USSR), Krymov P. V. (GKNT USSR), Kuntsevich A. D. (MO USSR), Fokin A. V. (AN USSR), Petrov R. V. (AN USSR).

Provisions on page 7 of the draft directives on "Sverdlovsk case" were included in connection with the Reference memo No. 25172 of Dec. 19/20, 1989, of the Central Committee's Defense Department, which contained the following provision: "In connection with the request of the USSR Foreign Affairs Ministry, having additionally examined this question, the USSR Council of Ministers' State Commission on military-industrial questions (comrade Belousov I. S.), USSR Defense Ministry (comrade Moiseev M.A), USSR Health Ministry (comrade Chazov Y. I.) and the CPSU CC Defense Department (comrade Belyakov O. S.) considered it possible to confirm the earlier conclusions of the committee on the natural origin of the epidemic, although it does not appear completely possible to rule out a connection between the outbreak and the accident at the above-mentioned facility."

Draft directives were discussed at the meeting of the interdepartmental commission on Jan. 10, 1990, where the authors of the reference memo explained that in reality there had been no accident, and that it was just unfortunate ambiguous wording which crept into the reference memo. In this connection paragraph three on page 7 of the draft directives was removed, and the end of the previous paragraph was presented as follows: "to confine ourselves to a statement that the materials clarifying the causes of the anthrax outbreak in Sverdlovsk had been brought to the notice of the USA." Also, taking into account the general situation in the region, it was also decided to remove paragraph four of that page.

V. Karpov
11 Jan 1990
03/upovr

16

Soviet Research on Mycotoxins

I N 1981 AND 1982 the US government charged that the Soviet Union was responsible for the use of trichothecene mycotoxins in Laos, Cambodia, and Afghanistan.[1] US government reports in fact alleged that "a variety of lethal chemical agents [were being used] in Laos, Kampuchea, and Afghanistan," but that the use of these "has been largely overshadowed by the discovery of a single new agent—trichothecene mycotoxins."[2] These are toxic proteins produced by, for example, members of the fungal species *Fusarium*. At that time, mycotoxins fell under the purview of the Biological Weapons Convention (BWC), and the Geneva Protocol forbade their use in warfare.[3] Under Secretary of State Lawrence Eagleburger summed up the overall US government view demonstrating the "Evidence of Soviet Use" in Senate testimony:

> Toxins and chemical warfare agents have been developed in the Soviet Union and provided to Laos and Vietnam. The Soviets use these agents, themselves, in Afghanistan and have participated in their preparation and use in Southeast Asia. Neither the Vietnamese, Laotians, nor Afghans could have developed or produced these weapons. The Soviet Union can, however, and has extensively trained and equipped its forces for this type of warfare.[4]

Prior to the Reagan administration the US Department of Defense (DOD) had come to a much milder judgment: "the best we can do in tieing [*sic*] that

450

down is that the agents used in Kampuchea were some kind of a low-level riot control agents."[5]

The Carter administration's prime motive for resolving the cause of the 1979 Sverdlovsk anthrax events had been the response of members of the US Senate in regard to the impending Senate ratification debate for the SALT II agreement, and to US-Soviet strategic nuclear arms negotiations in general. Although a rapid and successful continuation of those negotiations was not a particular priority of the incoming Reagan administration, the issue of the reliability of arms control agreements with the Soviet Union was again raised as a consequence of what came to be known as the "Yellow Rain" allegations.[6] The US government's case was very much weaker, however, in that the charges were almost immediately contested. Numerous other governments investigated to varying degrees, particularly concerning the reports of events in Laos and Cambodia. Several carried out their own testing of plant samples obtained in the field. Australia, Canada, the United Kingdom, and Sweden publicly stated that they were not able to reproduce the US chemical analyses reporting the presence of trichothecene mycotoxins. In addition, the US Army's chemical defense laboratories, the Chemical Research and Development Command at Edgewood Arsenal, was also unable to detect the presence of mycotoxins in the collected specimens. Nevertheless, the US government took the position that its allies were not willing to face the implications of the alleged violation of the Geneva Protocol and the BWC by the Soviet Union.[7] However, it was probably more relevant that these countries were unable to reproduce the US mycotoxin analyses and that the charges were seen at the time as simply another component of a generally aggressive policy by the Reagan administration toward the Soviet Union. The independent work of a group of academic scientists also went far to disprove the claims made by the US government. The most up-to-date and closely documented review of all the evidence can be found in a book chapter published in 2008 by Matthew Meselson and Julian Perry Robinson.[8]

Two investigations authorized by the UN General Assembly were carried out in April–November 1981 and January 1982, but the governments of Afghanistan, Cambodia, and Laos refused to permit the UN investigatory teams to have access to their countries. The investigations could therefore produce no meaningful information.[9] Nevertheless, the US government has never retracted its claims, so they in some sense remain unresolved.

The Soviet responses to the US charges included the submission in May 1982 of "a 'scientific' study to the UN blaming the toxin poisoning in Laos and Kampuchea on US use of herbicides during the Vietnam war. The explanation provided by the USSR claimed that widespread use of herbicides allowed toxin-producing fungi to flourish in Vietnam. Winds then allegedly blew the spores into Laos and Kampuchea, contaminating the environment."[10] These suggestions have no scientific credibility. They nevertheless accept the validity of the illnesses reported and the presence of mycotoxins in both countries. If the Soviet explanation were plausible, it would have led to enormously greater evidence of illness over virtually all of Cambodia, as well as even larger numbers of people inside South Vietnam, and not relegated to small numbers of Hmong tribal groups.

The purpose of the remainder of this brief chapter is solely to review that portion of the available information that suggests the possible site(s) of Soviet mycotoxin production and to attempt to determine if any such production was for weapons purposes and use. It is not to review any further the mycotoxins allegations or the information that the US government produced to support its charges.

US Secretary of State Haig's 1982 report stated that "*Fusaria* are produced in the Soviet Union at a facility long reported in the open literature as being a suspected biological warfare agent production and storage facility. This facility, Berdsk Chemical Works, is near the science city of Novosibirsk in Siberia."[11] According to Rimmington, the "Berdsk Chemical Factory" (*Berdskii Khimcheski Zavod*) was transferred to Biopreparat in 1974.[12] Its more correct name appears to be the "Berdsk Factory of Biological Preparations," which is referred to by Alibek as the "Berdsk Production Plant" and was directed in the Soviet years by Dr. Boris Prilepsky. It was one of the Soviet Union's major biological weapons mobilization capacity production facilities. Little or nothing is known about it, other than that it is not the Scientific-Research Technological Design Institute of Biologically Active Substances (IBAS), known by its acronym as *NIKTI BAV*, which is located close by. Secretary Haig's reference to the Berdsk facility as being "long reported" can only refer to the US intelligence leak in mid-1976 that referred to an unspecified facility in "Berdsk," along with five others, as being suspected by US intelligence of involvement in BW activities.[13] US intelligence sources did not publicly refer to "Berdsk" again until 1984. Whether the "Berdsk" site in these BW related US intelligence leaks is synonymous with Secretary Haig's "Berdsk Chemical Works" is not known.

A compilation of judgments produced in 1982 by the US intelligence community, the Assessments and Policy Subgroup of the CBW/Toxin Use Intelligence Working Group, stated that the open Soviet scientific literature "contains descriptions of Soviet facilities, which have multi-ton production capacities of mycotoxins, including trichothecenes. Some reports describe operational and mechanical systems where mycotoxins are sprayed over fields for the purpose, among other things, of controlling or killing small mammalian pests. Some of these fermentation facilities are highly secured and have had a long association with chemical and biological weapons research and testing."[14] A 1981 Defense Intelligence Agency report declassified in April 2003 stated that a search of open-source literature in the Soviet Union found 50 articles dealing with trichothecenes, of which "22 dealt with defining optimum conditions of biosynthesis of the compounds." The report went on to note that "Soviet institutes previously linked to classified CBW-research projects are also involved in such projects concerning the trichothecenes."[15] The report did not, however, list the titles of the papers or the research institutes at which they were written. It appears that the Soviet Union used these compounds for various agricultural purposes: to selectively breed disease-resistant crops, and as a rodenticide, producing two commercial products, *Fusarin* and *Tricotecin*.[16] It had long been understood by military-related medical research institutions in the United States that mycotoxins were a public health concern in the Soviet Union. In 1953 the Walter Reed Army Medical Center in Washington, D.C., published the book *Acute Infectious Hemorrhagic Fevers and Mycotoxicosis in the Union of Soviet Socialist Republics* by D. C. Gajdusek.

A recently declassified AFMIC report dating from 1984 contained a list of 10 "USSR Institutes Involved in Research with *Fusarium* Toxins":

- Institute of Microbiology and Virology, Kiev
- All Union Scientific Research Institute of Experimental Veterinary Science, Moscow
- All Union Scientific Research Institute of Veterinary Sanitation, Moscow
- All Union Scientific Research Institute of Grain and Grain Products
- N. F. Gamaleya Institute of Epidemiology and Microbiology, Moscow
- Institute of Nutrition, Academy of Medical Sciences
- All Union Research Institute of Microbial Means for Plant Protection and Bacterial Preparations

• Institute of Pharmacology, Zubovskaya Ploshchad, Moscow
• Institute of Biological Testing of Chemical Products, Kupavna (a suburb of Moscow)
• Institute of Chemistry of Natural Compounds, Moscow[17]

Interestingly, the "Berdsk Chemical Works" is not included in the list. The Gamaleya Institute was affiliated with the USSR Academy of Medical Sciences and was not likely to have housed production capacity. Other institutes on the list were associated with the Academy of Agricultural Sciences, or with the Ministry of Agriculture. It has proved impossible to identify some of the others.[18]

Declassified US reports made reference to three Soviet researchers in particular. Two were named, but their institutional affiliations were not given: Dr. R. A. Maksimova, with a record of publications between 1966 and 1980 on the production and characterization of trichothecenes,[19] and Dr. Natalya Kostyunina, on trichothecene production.[20] The third was Dr. Abraham Z. Joffe, who was not mentioned by name in the US intelligence reports, but information in the reports makes it a simple matter to identify him. He had been director of the Laboratory of Mycology at the Institute of Epidemiology and Microbiology between 1943 and 1950 in Orenburg, USSR. Dr. Joffe emigrated to Israel in 1958 and continued to work on mycotoxins at the Hebrew University in Jerusalem. Dr. Joffe informed US officials of classified Soviet research on mycotoxins, including human toxicity studies carried out on prisoners and inhalation exposure using monkeys. However, the institutes at which this work was carried out were not identified.[21] In addition to Orenburg, research on mycotoxins was carried out at the Institute of Microbiology and Virology in Kiev, one of the names that does appear in the list of 10 above. The Orenburg Institute does not.

During 2004–2005, the Agricultural Research Service of the US Department of Agriculture was supporting research on Fusaria—but not specifically trichothecene mycotoxins—in four Russian institutes in which such work took place in the pre-1992 period:

• All Russian Research Institute of Phytopathology, at Golitsino
• Its affiliate, the Russian Research Institute of Biological Plant Protection at Krasnodar

- All Russian Research Institute of Plant Protection, at Pushkin, near Moscow
- State Research Institute for Applied Microbiology at Obolensk [SRCAM]

Although none of the names exactly match those on the list of 10, one of the above may be synonymous with one of the institutes on that list.

SRCAM contained only a small fermentation capacity. It also appears that SRCAM and Krasnodar collaborated on *Fusarium* work, with products produced at SRCAM being field-tested at Krasnodar. There were some suggestions that Krasnodar may have been the most likely location of mycotoxin production, but at present there do not appear to be any production facilities at Krasnodar. Nevertheless, Alibek and Popov, both of whom were familiar with the research and development taking place at SRCAM, have reported that they do not know of any Soviet-era military application of mycotoxins.[22] Both, however, have also stated that they can speak only of work within the Biopreparat system, and that they do not have knowledge of R&D programs that were located in institutes belonging to other ministries. Another relatively senior former Russian BW administrator claimed that neither the MOD facility at Kirov nor any of the other MOD facilities worked with mycotoxins, but that such work was done in agricultural research institutes. However, he stated that such work had not led to use of mycotoxins in the field as a weapon.[23] Further interviews indicated:

- The All Union Research Institute of Microbial Means for Plant Protection and Bacterial Preparations was part of the Biopreparat system.
- The Institute of Microbiology and Virology in Kiev was involved in *Fusarium* research for purposes of weaponization, but had reportedly been unsuccessful in developing sufficiently pure preparations of trichothecene mycotoxins.
- The All Union Scientific Research Institute of Grain and Grain Products also developed plant toxins as well as agricultural warfare products. It collaborated with an institute in Tashkent, apparently the Central Asian Institute of Phytopathology—now renamed the Institute of Experimental Genetics of Plants. One or both of these had been involved in experimental crop destruction in Afghanistan sometime between 1979 and 1988 during the period of Soviet combat involvement in that country.[24]

• Grain research institutes working on mycotoxin contamination of crops used that explanation as a cover for BW-related research.

During 2004–2005 the US Department of Agriculture also had support programs at four agricultural research institutes in Uzbekistan:

• Institute of Bioorganic Chemistry
• Institute of Genetics and Experimental Biology of Plants (formerly the Institute of Plant Genetics)
• Institute of Zoology, which worked on the research and development of arthropod and reptilian toxins
• and an unidentified veterinary institute[25]

The overwhelming portion of the research that was carried out at the Institute of Plant Genetics during the Soviet era was devoted to offensive military programs.[26]

Domaradsky stated in interviews that Biopreparat was not interested in mycotoxins. However, he mentioned that a Dr. Tutelan, the deputy director of the Institute for Biological Instruments, one of the Biopreparat institutes, and a V. I. Pokrovsky, who was also located at the same institute and who had come from Zagorsk, were interested in the compounds.[27] Nothing further is known of any work that the two individuals may have supervised.

It has recently become known that the US Department of State (DOS) translation of Form F of the 1992 Russian CBM submission omitted translating one—and only one—complete line. The omission is significant. The omitted line concerned mycotoxins, and stated that "In the opinion of the experts, mycotoxins have no military significance."[28] This must be understood to refer to Russian military "experts." There is of course no way to assess the credibility of the statement; major portions of the same CBM were grossly incomplete (see Chapter 22). The US government translation is made for internal US government use, but if Russian diplomats have ever seen it, it is odd that they have never publicly pointed out, in 1993 or at any time since, that the US government's official translation was missing that line. Neither have other governments that did their own independent translations from the original Russian.

It would appear that Soviet-era institutes were doing some degree of offensive BW mycotoxin research and development, and it has been possible to identify some of the specific institutes involved in this activity. Soviet mycotoxin use in Afghanistan was ruled out in a 1986 report by the Defense Science Board, and no evidence was found in interviews with former Soviet BW scientists to indicate that Soviets used mycotoxins in the Indochina theater. Soviet use of anticrop herbicides may have taken place in both Afghanistan and Indochina, but such activities are not classified as biological warfare.

17

Assistance by Warsaw Pact States to the Soviet Union's Biological Warfare Program

W HEN QUESTIONED, virtually all Western specialists in government service with knowledge of the Soviet BW program, including US and UK government officials, have answered that there had been no involvement at all by scientists of Warsaw Treaty Organization (WTO) states, excepting of course the Soviet Union.[1] Even Alibek writes, "To our knowledge, none of our satellites in Eastern Europe ran biological weapons programs, though some of our fermenting and drying equipment was manufactured in East Germany."[2] All of these judgments require some modification.

In contrast, General Jan Sejna, the first secretary of the Czechoslovak Ministry of Defense, who defected to the West in February 1968, was quoted in a 1990 DIA report on Warsaw Pact (WP) BW capabilities:

Under the cover of secrecy, a long term plan to research and develop CBW throughout the WP was coordinated and implemented. In 1965 a 20 year plan to develop new chemical and biological weapons was proposed. Phase One, 1965–1971, emphasized qualitative steps, research, and preparation for new weapons production as well as training and protection of the troops. Research for development of new weapons was heavily emphasized. During the second phase, from 1971 to 1977, production was to be emphasized. A major expansion in CBW training and manufacturing facilities was to take place during this period.[3]

Sejna added that "the Soviets believed they could cause the West to dis-arm unilaterally in the CW and BW areas. In order to do so, the WP must be perceived to be in compliance with arms control agreements. An image of WP backwardness and of a low priority accorded to chemical and biological warfare (CBW) research and development was presented to the West by pro-paganda, disinformation, and false intelligence 'leaks.'"[4] Sejna's reference to the WTO "long term plan" is puzzling and seems implausible. The research carried out for this chapter found only very limited expression "throughout the WP" for the kind of BW program that was established in the Soviet Union. However, it did find much more than the blanket dismissals offered by Western officials and analysts.

Because the major growth in the Soviet BW program occurred after 1975 when the BWC came into force, particularly stringent secrecy was required. That applied within the Soviet Union itself as well; the elaborate Biopreparat legend system is testimony to that. If the Soviet government had involved other nations in its illicit BW program, even if those others had been WTO member states, then there would have been a much greater possibility that information about its existence would have leaked to the West. The necessity to maintain absolute secrecy in regard to the Soviet Union's BW program therefore constrained direct involvement of WTO member states in the So-viet offensive BW program. However, the biodefense programs of the WTO states definitely were integrated with those of the Soviet Union and, in addi-tion, WTO members did contribute in various secondary ways: supplying equipment and facilities and collaborating in basic research projects that at least in some cases were clearly related to Soviet offensive BW efforts.

The structure of the WTO included a directorate for the purpose of coor-dinating scientific research programs in its member states. The directorate established research priorities and assigned and apportioned research tasks relevant to Soviet weapon and space systems in a wide variety of scientific disciplines: chemical weapons, lasers, electronics, microelectronics and com-puterization, problems of the ionosphere related to satellite reconnaissance and communication, human engineering aspects of space systems, and many others. The research in these areas was both basic and applied. There were apparently individual WTO technical committees in different military R&D areas, and one of these dealt with BW defense. This committee was always headed by a Russian officer, and that individual came from the S.M. Kirov Russian Military Medical Academy (RMMA), which was an open facility.

The representatives of the WTO states would be presented with the draft of a five-year plan of research that had been prepared in Moscow, and the individual national representatives specified which research projects it was not possible for them to carry out due to limitations of infrastructure or technology.[5] For example, East Germany, or more properly, the German Democratic Republic (GDR), had no BSL-3 or BSL-4 facilities, and extremely limited fermenter capacity in its military BW defense facility. In the intervening periods between the WTO BW Technical Committee meetings, the surgeon generals of the individual WTO states had regular meetings with their counterparts, each taking with them one senior advisor under their command. Recommendations from these meetings fed back into the larger WTO Technical Committee devoted to BW defense. Subordinated to this Committee were individual WTO technical subcommittees devoted to the specific identification of BW agents, the development of immunological or chemoprophylactic treatment of BW-related diseases, or the anti-epidemic and decontamination measures that would be required in the case of a BW attack against WTO armies. In each of these subgroups a five-year work plan would again be presented, containing individual projects related to specific BW agents, methodologies, or activities. The plan included reporting and review milestones, and distributed the responsibility to organize meetings among its participants. Each expert subgroup was again headed by a Soviet military scientist. In the review meetings the WTO researchers would essentially present their findings and/or problems to groups of Soviet researchers, also for the most part coming from the RMMA. However, in these bilateral or multilateral sessions it appears that at times Soviet military scientists from some of the closed Soviet MOD institutes would be present. One of these was a Major General Agafanov, who, like other representatives from the Soviet Union, never revealed his home institution.

Soviet–East European collaboration on BW defense matters apparently started in the early 1960s and continued until the spring of 1990. One individual who participated in the process between 1977 and 1990 stated that he never heard anything mentioned that would have indicated the intention of offensive BW use by the Soviet Union or any WTO state. No "offensive tasks" were covered; only biodefense issues were discussed. Nevertheless, the tasking and documentation for all the meetings of these various technical committees were classified. It proved impossible to locate any of the documents produced by the administrative or coordinating work of the technical committees, and there is a great likelihood that they were destroyed in the last days of Communist rule in the WTO states. Specific information was obtained indicating that such destruction of documentation did take place in the closing days of the GDR, as well as just before the transition of governments in Hungary in 1989.[6]

Beginning in the 1960s, there were two kinds of WTO "international conferences" relevant to BW issues held under this framework: one dealing with "veterinary" diseases, the other with "medical"—that is, human—issues. The conferences were at first held every year or every two years, then every third year. The location of these meetings rotated among the WTO member states: Poland hosted at least two of them.[7] After 1985, there appear to have been no further conferences. One participant described the cooperation as "artificial."

An example of one of these conferences, hosted by Hungary, was the 1971 conference on "The Potential and Significance of Rapid Diagnostic Technology in Microbiology." Papers by Soviet authors at the conference included a survey of rapid detection technology in the Soviet Union by T.I. Bulatova of the Gamaleya Institute in Moscow, a paper on its application for the detection of cholera by Domaradsky, who then was director of the Rostov Antiplague Institute, and a representative of the MOH with no institutional affiliation identified, describing a rapid diagnostic technique for use in animal diseases.[8] In addition to Russians, participants came from Mongolia, Poland, Bulgaria, Czechoslovakia, the GDR, and Hungary. Presentations addressed pathogens and toxins, as well as diseases; examples of specific diseases were encephalitis, anthrax, brucellosis, melioidosis, typhus, and cholera. Many of the participants were researchers in military medical institutes in their home countries.

Another example of coordinated research occurred in the area of neurotoxins and venoms. Researchers working in Bulgarian, Czechoslovak, Hungarian, GDR, and Romanian institutes carried out research on neurotoxins and venoms, in several cases in clear collaboration with the Shemyakin Institute in Moscow.[9] In the following sections of this chapter that examine BW-related research in individual WTO member states, attention is directed toward possible direct collaboration with the Soviet offensive BW program.

There was one remaining mechanism for the integration of the WTO biodefense programs: most specialists in the WTO military-medical BW defense research institutes took part in postgraduate training at the RMMA (see Chapter 3).[10] This was not dissimilar to what occurred in the WTO civilian research sector, in that many WTO scientists, particularly the better ones, studied in Moscow and then worked for varying periods in Moscow's research institutes. An excellent example of how Soviet BW-related secrecy interacted in this process was provided by a narrative from a military medical officer from one of the former WTO states. In a postgraduate course in microbiology at the RMMA in the early 1970s, the officer asked where the substantial number of diagnostic preparations, procedures, and vaccines that were used in the training course had been prepared. He was told that they came from another institute near Leningrad, which was in all likelihood the Scientific Research Institute of Military Medicine, a closed research-only MOD facility (see Chapter 3). However, at no time between 1970 and 1990 was any military scientist from his country allowed to visit that second Soviet facility, despite their good relations with the military microbiologists at the RMMA. As indicated in Chapter 3, members of other, non-WTO member states also attended BW defense courses at the RMMA, and in the process they apparently also visited the institutes of various WTO states.

Czechoslovakia

It appears that BW research in Czechoslovakia was the most closely affiliated with that of the Soviet Union. This was primarily because of the laboratory at Těchonín in the East Bohemia section of the country. The facility and its work were secret until the end of 1989. The Czech declaration under the 1991 BWC Confidence Building Measures (CBMs) describes the facility as wholly financed by the Ministry of Defense and containing "4 maximum containment units, the floor area of each is 30 sqm."[11] The declaration goes on to provide the following description (in which the original language has been retained):

> The Institute of Immunology and Microbiology of Jan Evagelista Purkyne Military Medical Academy [VLA JEP] is a specialized facility of the Academy [by the year 1991 it was called Branch establishment Těchonín of VLA JEP]. It was founded in 1971 as a specialized institution for the needs of the Czechoslovak Army and the Armies of the former WTO. Its task was to solve the problems of health defense against biological weapons and the topical questions of anti-epidemic defense of the Army that have great demands for health, material and technical means.

The main part was an aerosol block that had a bacteriologic and a virologic part and the necessary security premises. Later an immunologic part was built and gradually it became dominant. The facility was under the control of the Military Institute of Hygiene, Epidemiology and Microbiology. Since 1977 it has been under the control of the VLA JEP.

The original work was conducted in the field of aerosology: working out of exposition methods and distribution and redistribution of parts in the respiratory tract, solving the questions of infection while using strains of different virulence and pathogenicity. On increased scale we used the virus of influenza, the Venezuelan equine encephalomyelitis virus, *Francisella tularensis, Coxiella burnetii.* On reduced scale we used the pox virus of predators, the virus of Sicilian phlebotomus fever, Legionella pneumophila, *Brucella abortus, Nocardia asteroides.* In infections caused by the virus of influenza, the Venezuelan equine encephalomyelitis and *Francisella tularensis* we followed the influence of irradiation of organism upon the course and the result of the disease.

In all the infections we investigated the feasibility of prophylaxis and therapy by means of available or new types of vaccines, antivirus substances, interferon inductors, antibiotics, chemotherapeutic and immunomodulators inclusive combinations. In the last decade the centre of attention is solution and study of regulation of antiinfectious immunity and the possibility of purposive involvement.

In the case of virus infections, *Francisella tularensis* and *Coxiella burnetii* we co-operated with partners from Leningrad [Sankt Petěrburg] and Sofia. The Polish scientists worked without our active co-operation on the problems of disinfection of surfaces [textile surfaces]. Co-operation with other countries of the former WTO was sporadic, only in the form of exchange of basic information [the former GDR and Roumania].

The studies were not mostly officially published, though from the present point of view it was not necessary to conceal them. A smaller part of the studies were published in the official press or at the conferences, inclusive the international ones. Detailed information in this sense was provided in a lecture presented in Sweden in 1990:

It comes out from the character and real content of the research in Těchonín, that it has never been worked there on the development, production, stockpiling and spread of agents, that could have been taken for biological weapons. The research there has always been defensive. The produced amount of infectious agents could only meet the requirements for the very tests in animals in laboratories and chambers or for the production of a small amount of a vaccine for testing in this laboratory. This all was declared also in Sweden in 1990, inclusive picture documentation of facilities and laboratories.

Questions of diagnostic techniques, detection, physical protection and decontamination were not the concern of the research program at the workplace in Těchonín.

By the end of 1990 the defensive research activity was ended. In favour of the Academy an immunological program and other non-military program is followed.

"Note: By the end of 31st December 1991 the workplace in Těchonín from technical reasons ended the laboratory running, and therefore it will no more be in evidence and produce."[12]

Although this description of Těchonín was almost entirely new, and not included in the Czech BWC CBMs of the preceding years of 1987, 1988 and 1989, it was far from complete despite its detail. The most significant information was still missing. The preceding Czech BWC CBMs had each contained a page including some data on Těchonín, without any mention whatsoever of the aerosol work. The 1990 declaration mentioned only that Czechoslovakia was "prepared to take an active part in projects directly relevant to the Convention. However, a very limited number of maximum containment units available would be a serious handicap." This was seriously misleading: in fact Czechoslovakia apparently maintained more than twice as many BSL-3 and BSL-4 facilities as all the other WTO countries combined.

When news items appeared in the Czech press in 1994 suggesting that prior to 1990 work at Těchonín had in fact been of an offensive nature, one of the more senior researchers who had worked there for twenty years, Ales Macela, made the argument in a privately circulated paper that the work on tularemia had not been of an offensive nature for the following reasons:

- The facility never accumulated a "substantial volume of microorganisms."
- It restricted its own work so that it could not be considered "as the development of bacteriological weapons," by not carrying out studies on the manipulation of "[the] genome of microbes."

- The models it developed were also used in studying Venezuelan equine encephalomyelitis and influenza within the Těchonín facility, and "these models were developed for the testing of antiviral substances and specific vaccines."
- "The institute was never equipped with laboratory devices that are necessary for such a type of study" (i.e., of an offensive nature).
- The institute "Těchonín never had equipment for the long term storage of great amounts of microbes."[13]

Macela explained that the experimental model for tularemia was developed before Těchonín came into existence, in the 1960s at the Military Institute for Hygiene, Microbiology and Epidemiology, but that it was only with the building of Těchonín that aerosol work could begin. He stated that the institute was "founded in 1972," rather than in 1971 as indicated in the 1991 Czech CBM, but accidentally or not, both are close in time to the Soviet decision to establish the Biopreparat system. The coincidence is probably misleading, however: if the facility was ready for utilization in 1972, its construction would have begun several years earlier, and the planning for it perhaps even before that. Even if all the five reasons given by Macela were correct, it would not preclude work of an offensive BW character having been part of the research program at Těchonín. Most specifically, knowledge of the nature of the research carried out within the aerosol test chambers at Těchonín would be a major contributor to that determination. It appears that work on stabilization of the pathogen in aerosols was carried out in the Těchonín aerosol test chambers, as well as dynamic aerosol testing.[14] Neither of these procedures would be necessary for solving "the problem of health defence" or "for the testing of antiviral substances or specific vaccines."

In his private memoir published in Moscow in 1995, Domaradsky makes a similar point:

> During the 1960s when the construction of an aerosol building was being planned at the Rostov Plague Control Institute, for purposes of "Problem No. 5" of course, some Czechs were working as planners for 4 years (1965–1969). They were also supposed to deliver equipment to us for this building. I later heard from somebody that the Czechs were building a similar block for our premises. Since this project was highly expensive it is worth asking, why spend so much money when a

small aerosol chamber would be quite enough for the purposes of experiments in protection? We were certainly in no position to afford any such "luxury"![15]

In his English-language book, Domaradsky identifies General Lebedinsky, from the MOD 15th Directorate, as having visited the Czech production facilities in "the late sixties or early seventies."[16] Pasechnik described visiting Czech facilities together with Lebedinsky years later when the Biopreparat system was already in operation to inspect Czech aerosol test chambers that the Soviet Union was interested in purchasing for installation in its own institutes.[17] Pasechnik's visit, however, would have been after the mid-1970s.

Interviews provided more detailed information regarding the work arrangements at Těchonín. The site reportedly consisted of four buildings. Czech scientists worked in two of them, and it was not clear who worked in the third. The fourth building contained the large aerosol test chamber in which Soviet scientists worked. The building was constructed with thick concrete walls, with all utility lines built into the walls. The visiting Soviet researchers came from Soviet MOD institutes. They reportedly came to Těchonín in groups of two or three and worked at the site for one or two years. They designed the experiments, and Czech scientists and technicians by and large carried out the work. The person being interviewed also felt that it was possible that if some Czech scientists had worked on "offensive" BW projects, they would not have realized it.[18] He thought it possible that Czech national authorities did not know the nature of the work being carried out in that building, as it was not reported to scientific administrators in the Czech government. The 1990 Propper and Splino paper that the Czech CBM quoted states that the testing of the anti-tularemia vaccine was "tested for the Soviet partner." When a Czech Ministry of Defense official forwarded a copy of that same paper to one of the authors in 2000, ten years after it had been presented in Sweden, the words "tested for the Soviet partner" had been scratched out, albeit insufficiently.[19] The separate Form F portion of the 1991 Czech CBM also states that the research work at Těchonín "was running partly in co-operation with Soviet and Bulgarian scientists. Towards the end of the eighties the research was stopped." More accurately, it was stopped between the end of 1989 and late 1990.

Although the 1991 Czech CBM describes Těchonín as having been built "for the needs of the . . . Armies of the Warsaw Pact," there were two unique aspects of the facility. First, it appears to have been the only BW-related facility in all of the WTO countries to which Soviet BW researchers came to work, and specifically to work on research projects involving the use of the aerosol test chambers. It has not proved possible to learn from which specific MOD institutes the Soviet scientists came. Second, except for Czech scientists, the visiting Soviet MOD scientists, a single Polish scientist, and apparently a very small number of Bulgarian scientists, BW defense scientists from the remaining WTO states were limited to highly restricted visits to the site.[20] The Bulgarian scientists came from a military institute. The secret nature of the site, and the fact that the Czech government saw fit to temporarily shut down the facility all or in part in 1991 also suggests that work beyond that permitted under the BWC was taking place at the site. The final sentence of the 1991 Czech CBM in regard to Těchonín also needs elaboration. Czech authorities stated that defense research activities at the site stopped by the end of 1990, and that the laboratory stopped running entirely by the end of 1991. If the latter did in fact happen, operations at Těchonín were in any case reinstituted in 1994 under a new mandate, and only "some lines of work [in it] had ceased." Although some of the Czech scientists working at Těchonín reportedly were able to get their research declassified in 1985–1986, and it was claimed that the papers of the entire institute were placed in open files at the Central Military Health Institute in Prague after 1991, two years of requests in 1999 and 2000 to be allowed to examine those files were repeatedly rejected by Czech authorities, despite the previous nine years of Czech cooperation with NATO.[21]

In 1994 a series of articles appeared in the Czech press regarding the culture collections that had been maintained at Těchonín. These alleged that both the agent for psittacosis (Chamydophila psitacci) and smallpox (variola virus) had been present. If the latter were true, this may imply that the variola virus culture had been maintained beyond the time that all stocks should have been destroyed according to the WHO mandate. Czech minister of defense Antonin Baudys referred to them as "highly dangerous bacteriological and virological weapons." After protests by Těchonín's co-directors, he revised "weapons" to "materials." At the same time he ordered them to be destroyed. No explanation was ever given for the order to destroy the "materials" or the accuracy of the claim that variola virus had been present.[22]

In 1994 Dr. Joseph Fusek, one of Těchonín's co-directors, stated that "the institute had been opened to international inspection in May 1990."[23] The statement is essentially incorrect. Fusek must have been referring to the visit by Těchonín scientists to the conference in Sweden in 1990 and the paper that they presented there. Těchonín itself remained "closed" until 1994. The first Western visitors were a group of three Swedish scientists in 1994 from the biodefense division of the Swedish Defence Research Institute who had interacted with the Těchonín scientists in Sweden in 1990. They were shown the building that had hosted the Soviet MOD researchers. It contained four dynamic aerosol test chambers, each of which had been assigned for use with a different pathogen. They were told that all of the information derived from the experimental work "went to Moscow" and that those who worked in the building behaved as a small, closed community of their own.[24] Challenge tests of a tularemia vaccine in the aerosol chambers had not been relegated solely to a mouse model, but had been done using monkeys. This indicated that Těchonín had also maintained a primate facility. The visiting Swedish team came away convinced that they had been looking at what had been part of an offensive BW research program. They then went on to visit biodefense facilities in Poland and Hungary. One of the Swedish scientists visited again in a personal capacity six months later, as well as in 1997 and 1998. He was also able to place a technician to work at Těchonín for two months in 1998. As a group, the Swedish team returned for a second visit to Těchonín in 1997 or 1998. They now found the aerosol test chambers stored in an on-site warehouse.

Why did the Soviet Union hazard the exception of having Soviet MOD institute scientists work at Těchonín, prohibit researchers from nearly all other WTO member states from working at the site, and, even if the work had been purely defensive, risk compromise? Czech research on the immunology of tularemia in particular was reportedly of very high quality, and the Soviets needed a new tularemia vaccine. However, this alone would seem to be an insufficient explanation, and no further information is available.

Another example of Czech-Soviet research cooperation on a subject of obvious BW interest was research on neurotoxins carried out at the Institute of Pharmacology, a constituent of the Czechoslovak Academy of Sciences, in collaboration with the Shemyakin Institute in Moscow.[25] A book published by the Zagorsk Institute in its own honor in 2004 mentioned that a member of its staff, N. W. Vasilyev, was given a "work assignment in Prague [Czechoslovakia] for the purpose of helping to organize the suspension culturing of animal cells."[26] Nothing further is known regarding the significance of this collaboration, whether any subsequent joint work ensued as a result, or whether Vasilyev's Soviet MOD affiliation was disguised while he worked in Prague, which would seem likely.

German Democratic Republic

In 2008 a summary of the former GDR biodefense program was published in Germany in a book on the military medical program of the NVA, the former GDR army. The staff in its biodefense institute was quite small, numbering 22 at the end of the 1960s and 28–30 in the mid-1980s.[27] The most significant assistance to the Soviet Union's BW program came not from the GDR's own biodefense program, but from its production technology. A GDR firm, CHEMA, or Chema Anlagenbau, located in Rudisleben, close to Erfurt, apparently supplied large numbers of 15,000- and 20,000-liter fermenters to the Soviet BW mobilization capacity production facilities at Omutninsk and Berdsk, as well as to SNOPB at Stepnogorsk. Possibly as many as sixty 15,000-liter fermenters were exported to Omutninsk and Berdsk,[28] while the 20,000-liter fermenters were fabricated specifically for SNOPB. They were the same model as the 15,000-liter ones, except made slightly longer.[29] Alibek believed that the fermenters for SNOPB were shipped to the site around 1980–1981. He could not say whether they had been shipped directly from the GDR to SNOPB, which was not the standard practice followed for equipment being shipped "from the west"; such equipment went through an intermediate destination in the Soviet Union. He did say that no technical advisors from the GDR firm came to SNOPB to aid in the installation and operational testing of the fermenters. That was done by personnel from Biopreparat's own subsidiary *Biokhimmash* in Moscow. Another Russian source claimed that no less than 130 63,000-liter fermenters manufactured in the GDR were provided for SNOPB's sister facility, the Progress Plant, presumably for the production of biological pesticides, animal feed supplements, and ethanol (see Chapter 9). As indicated below, it was determined that these had also been manufactured by the Rudisleben factory.[30]

According to Alibek, the GDR firm also provided 50,000-liter fermenters to the Sverdlovsk Institute that were used for *B. anthracis* production, as well as 50,000-liter fermenters for the BW mobilization capacity production sites at Kurgan and Penza. A former Soviet Foreign Ministry official suggested that Soviet authorities directed the GDR to establish the production line for these large fermenters.[31] Alibek also described his visit to the firm in 1990, when it had already been purchased by a West German company subsequent to the German reunification. It has been impossible to locate any documentation on the fermenter exports. Despite the above evidence, the one senior German company official with knowledge of the fermenter exports to the Soviet Union in the pre-1990 period has denied the above information. He claimed that the company had only shipped 63,000- and 100,000-liter fermenters to the Soviet Union for lysine production.[32] Those particular exports were corroborated by a former senior-level Biopreparat official: 130 German 63,000-liter fermenters had gone to the Progress Plant, SNOPB's sister facility.[33] He stated that the fermenters were of a standard GDR design, and "were ordered by the Ministry of import/export." As noted earlier, Alibek also reports the Soviet import from the GDR of "drying equipment for the Biopreparat program." In general, there might have been many other related exports from the GDR to the Soviet Union, because a large amount of machinery for the pharmaceutical, agricultural, and food industries were produced in the GDR for export to the Soviet Union.

Prior to the defeat of Nazi Germany in 1945, a foot-and-mouth disease (FMD) research facility existed on Riems Island off the German mainland in the Baltic Sea. It was totally dismantled between July and October 1945. However, as early as January 1946 the Soviet Military Administration in Germany requested that the facility be reconstructed "to provide vaccines and immune sera for FMD and other animal diseases as soon as possible."[34] By 1948 the Soviet Union had re-equipped the facility. Precisely what it did between 1948 and 1989 is unclear, because the site was reportedly converted back to a civilian FMD research facility around 1989. Directly after World War II, Soviet scientists from the MOD institutes also used a GDR scientist as a conduit in order to obtain a culture of *Chlamydia psittaci,* the bacterium that causes psittacosis. No samples of the pathogen apparently existed in Soviet culture collections, and so they needed to obtain one from a Western country. The scientist, Eugen Haagen, obtained a culture from Paul-Ehrlich-Institute in Frankfurt-am-Main.[35]

The opportunity to interview former GDR military biodefense personnel now in the united Germany also provided very informative insights. Not only Soviet researchers but also GDR researchers had believed that the United States had not given up its offensive BW program. The reasons given for that belief were many, some of which, however, proved problematic:

- They were not told and did not know that the United States had officially ended its offensive BW program in 1969. At the same time, they were able to read about improvements planned by the US government in the 1980s for the Dugway test site.

- They believed that West Germany was doing aerosol research (although they clearly knew that they and the Czechs were doing the same). The false belief was based on the GDR's false allegations made against West Germany in 1967, which is discussed in Chapter 14.
- They interpreted a NATO Wintex exercise involving BW defense as evidence of offensive intention. Again, they knew of analogous WTO exercises.
- They accepted the Cuban allegations that the United States had deliberately introduced African swine fever and dengue fever into Cuba.
- They claimed to have known of the BWC only by name but not its substance until the mid- to late-1980s.[36] This statement was very puzzling, and the attempt to clarify it produced additional useful information.

One particular military officer and scientist had actually been tasked to draft the GDR's first CBM submission in 1987. He was informed that it was to be sent to the UN, but he was not given an explanation of its context and purpose. He was not told it was a submission within the framework of the BWC. Sometime later, in the office of the institute director, he noticed what turned out to be the text of the BWC on his superior's desk, and he asked what it was. It was in a West German publication that the institute director had obtained from the GDR's military library.[37]

This is extremely puzzling. The GDR signed the BWC on April 10, 1972, and adopted corresponding legislation on October 16, 1972. One GDR scientist and author, Erhard Geissler, gave three conference presentations and published no fewer than 10 papers between October 1982 and 1986 in various GDR publications referring to the BWC, although he appears to have been the only one doing so. His papers did not quote Article 1 of the BWC verbatim, but at least half of the 10 publications included the full title of the BWC, which states that the treaty prohibits the development, acquisition, production, and storage of biological and toxin weapons. One of those publications even appeared in *Neues Deutschland,* the official GDR government newspaper, in November 1984.[38] There is no reason these publications could not have been available to scientific personnel at the GDR biodefense facility in Greifswald. In addition the GDR Ministry of National Defense intervened to limit a particular initiative on military vaccine programs at the 1986 BWC Second Review Conference.[39] Therefore, senior officials at the GDR MOD clearly knew about the BWC even if their own military research scientists did not. Interview testimony suggests that was the case.

More recently, it was possible to learn that soon after the GDR ratified the BWC on November 28, 1972, the treaty was discussed in a meeting convened by the Medical Administration of the GDR MOD. The participants were the commander of the Military Medicine Section of the GDR army and the heads of its institutes, and the Advisory Experts for Military Hygiene and Epidemiology of the Medical Services of the WTO armies. Beginning in 1978, the existence of the BWC was mentioned in the textbooks used for officer ranks in military medicine of the GDR, but with no information provided regarding the substantive contents of the articles of the treaty. Subsequent editions of the GDR military medical textbooks were published in 1982 and 1984. Such basic sources as the SIPRI volumes on chemical and biological warfare were apparently not in the library of the GDR military medical training institutes although they were available to at least a very small number of selected members of the GDR Academy of Sciences and civilian scientists.[40] Everything in regard to "biodefense" was considered highly secret, and contacts between the scientists in the GDR biodefense institute and those in GDR civilian scientific institutes were limited to select joint projects not concerned with biodefense, such as the health of army recruits. Biodefense-related research could not be discussed with civilian scientists. Because equivalent testimony is not available for any of the other WTO member states, it is not possible to say whether the situation described above also held for other WTO member states. But it would seem plausible that it did, at least for Czechoslovakia and Poland, if not for the others as well.

Poland

Research in Poland related to biological weapons took place at the Military Institute of Hygiene and Epidemiology (MIHE) in Warsaw, and at the Military Research Center of Veterinary Service in Pulawy. (In 1989 the Pulawy facility was incorporated into MIHE as the Center for Veterinary Research.) It is likely that some research also took place at the Military Medical Academy ("Military University School of Medicine") and at a fourth site in Lodz. In 2002 the Center for Veterinary Research was reported to be the only institution in Poland to maintain a BSL-3 facility, but this appears not to have been a capability that it had prior to 1990.[41] There is also the possibility that up to 1982, individual researchers at the Department of Microbiology in the University of Krakow—a department that was closed in 1982 when it was incorporated into the MIHE—as well as in Warsaw were involved in collaborative research with Soviet institutes. Some Polish researchers went to the Soviet Union for training in toxicology, and others in radiation physics, but reportedly not in microbiology relevant to BW. Domaradsky refers to the book *Biological Warfare* by two Polish authors, T. Rozniatowski and Z. Rzultowski, which was published by the Foreign Literature Publishing House in Moscow in 1959. The two authors of this book apparently were on the staff of MIHE in Warsaw, and Domaradsky mentioned the book and its authors because he felt that they would have had to have known about offensive BW work, in Poland.

Work at the Veterinary Laboratory in Pulawy included studies on *B. anthracis* and extensive work on botulinum toxin. One member of the MIHE staff apparently collaborated with projects at the Těchonín facility in Czechoslovakia, but apparently not in a critical capacity, as his specialization concerned disinfectants rather than the aerosol dispersion of pathogens. The Czech description of his work is that he "cooperated . . . on the problems of surface disinfection after aerosol contamination with current microbes"— apparently surface contamination of textiles. However, his Polish colleagues apparently had no knowledge that he was working at Těchonín. Polish research on neurotoxins was carried out at the MIHE.

Possibly of most interest in regard to the potential relation to work being carried out in the Soviet BW program was an extensive MIHE research effort to examine the radiation resistance of microorganisms, specifically an effort to develop radiation-resistant strains. With one exception, this research effort appears not to have been duplicated in any of the relevant programs of the other non-Soviet WTO states. Although the research was carried out with nonpathogenic organisms, it is plausible that it was basic research to support Biopreparat's interest in developing radiation-resistant strains of at least some of the pathogens that were being selected for Soviet biological weapon development. The Czech BWC CBM document quoted above indicated a somewhat related Czech program to examine the influence of radiation on the disease-producing capacity of pathogens responsible for tularemia, influenza, and VEE, as well as the course of vaccinia vaccination in irradiated animals. Requests to obtain permission to visit the Polish institutes to examine records of pre-1990 BW-related research were rejected, despite the fact that these institutes have been collaborating with colleagues from NATO member states since the late 1990s.

Bulgaria

The significance of Bulgaria is that it includes one of the unresolved mysteries concerning the collaboration of WTO states with the Soviet BW program. In addition to the Department of Military Epidemiology and Hygiene of the Military Medical Academy in the capital Sofia, which carried out BW-related research, there was apparently another secret BW research facility within a short driving distance of the capital that was off-limits to BW defense researchers from all other WTO states except those from the Soviet Union. Even when the WTO researchers were visiting the Military Medical Academy in Sofia, and they knew of the other facility and requested permission to visit it, that permission was denied.[42]

It is known that the Soviet KGB collaborated with Bulgarian intelligence services in developing devices to deliver pellets containing ricin to be used for the assassination of dissident Bulgarian exiles, as in the assassination of Georgi Markov in London in September 1978. After 1990, and reading Western literature, it was therefore simple for former WTO colleagues to postulate that the off-limits Bulgarian institute was perhaps in some way involved in collaboration with the KGB institute in the Moscow suburbs that worked with poisons. However, there is no direct evidence for this. The Bulgarian 1992 CBM submission provides no indication of any other facility under the jurisdiction of the Ministry of Defense except for the Military Medical Academy. However, Bulgaria did not submit any Form F or any Form A-2 statements in its CBM submission (see Chapter 20). Its Form A-1 indicated that the Military Medical Academy had two BSL-3 units, one for work with bacteria and the other with viruses. However, the statement also indicated that Bulgaria carried out "research and testing, in laboratory and field conditions." What that means is not known, but it could imply a testing range.[43] It seems unlikely, however, that the alleged secret facility was a BW test range, given its location close to the capital city.

Research on neurotoxins, specifically the structure and peptide sequence of the venom from a Bulgarian viper, was carried out at the Department of Organic Chemistry at the Higher Institute of Chemical Technology in Sofia and in collaboration with the Shemyakin Institute. The joint coordination of research direction is indicated by the fact that when research on neurotoxins began to decline at the Shemyakin Institute after 1983 as its major research direction switched to work on bioregulatory peptides, the same pattern was followed by the Bulgarian institute.[44]

Hungary

Very little information is available regarding the involvement of Hungarian researchers with BW defense. Hungary apparently had a short-lived offensive research program between 1938 and April 1944, but reportedly none after World War II.[45] However, it is known that a substantial amount of relevant documentary materials, apparently also including records of research, was destroyed after the end of the communist government in Hungary and the dissolution of the WTO.[46] Hungarian representation at the 1971 WTO conference on rapid detection technology included researchers from the Military "Sanitary Institute," as well as the analogous civilian institutes in no fewer than six Hungarian cities (Budapest, Szeged, Debrecin, Verzprem, Szekszard, and Salgotarjan). The majority of the Hungarian research on toxins was done at the Pharmacological Laboratory of the Chemical Works of Gedeon Richter Ltd. in Budapest, and appears to have been directed at the use of toxins as molecular tools, rather than an interest in the toxins per se.[47]

It seems clear from the information gathered in this chapter that the generic statement that WTO nations played no role whatsoever in the Soviet offensive BW program is not correct. However, at least on the basis of the available evidence, it appears to have been extremely variable by country, and with two, or possibly three, exceptions it was marginal. Because nothing can be said about a suspected but unidentified secret facility in Bulgaria, the two major contributions that were identified were made by the GDR and by Czechoslovakia. The GDR produced equipment exported to the BW mobilization capacity production facilities in the Soviet Union. As for Czechoslovakia, substantial information indicates that at least some of the BW work done at Těchonín prior to 1990 was offensive in character and a direct contribution to the Soviet BW program.

18

The Question of Proliferation from the
USSR Biological Warfare Program

THREE MAJOR QUESTIONS surround the Soviet BW program. The first, elucidating its nature during the years 1972–1992 is essential, but it is a matter of the past. The other two questions deal with the present and with the future. The first of these is whether any of the offensive components of the biological warfare (BW) program were being continued during the years since 1992, particularly in the still closed biological research institutes of the Russian Ministry of Defense (RF-MOD). So long as this question is not resolved—and the US government continues to maintain in official statements that it indeed remains unresolved—there remains the possibility that Russia maintains portions of an offensive BW program in violation of the BWC, something of obvious concern to other nations. In addition, there is the corollary concern that the former very extensive offensive BW program could be resurrected relatively quickly and more easily at some future time, should a future Russian government decide to do so. The final question deals with proliferation: Had Soviet-era BW personnel, technology, or materials migrated or been conveyed to countries of BW proliferation concern since 1992? Of course, it is also important to know if such emigrations or transfers had taken place prior to 1992. This chapter addresses the two proliferation questions.

There were several reasons why no one should have been surprised that a large pool of researchers who staffed the former Soviet BW institutes—as well as other scientific institutes that contributed basic research relevant to BW—

became free agents after the collapse of the Soviet Union. One important reason was that there was a major downsizing in the staffs of these institutes mandated by President Boris Yeltsin's decree of April 11, 1992, which ordered a 50% reduction in their staffing levels and a 30% cut in their funding.[1] In actual practice an even more severe downsizing occurred, with individual institutes undergoing personnel decreases ranging from 50% to over 90%. In addition, for several years after 1992 the researchers who remained employed at these institutes suffered as their living standards went down. Salaries were very low and were paid irregularly, often being withheld for many months at a stretch. In addition, scientists became frustrated and discouraged as their status plummeted from the highest reaches in Soviet society to that of the underpaid and unappreciated in Russia.

In comparison, the staffing levels of the RF-MOD institutes that were involved in the biological weapons program appear to have been reduced little or not at all. They remained relatively well funded, and the salaries of their employees were paid.[2]

The responses of the scientific workforce in the Biopreparat institutes varied. Some researchers transferred to other institutes or took employment in commercial enterprises. Some of them left the field of science entirely. A relatively small proportion, often the best and brightest, emigrated. In November 1997, US government officials believed that of the cumulative scientific workforce of all the Biopreparat institutes, only some 300 had emigrated from Russia and of these, 90% were to be found in the United States, Western Europe, and Israel.[3] And of the remaining 10%, some were located permanently or temporarily in countries *not* of BW proliferation concern, such as Brazil and South Korea.[4] It should be noted, however, that Israel is a country of BW proliferation concern, having developed an indigenous offensive BW program by the 1960s, though it is not a country referred to in that context by US government officials. It is possible that émigrés from the Soviet Union and subsequently from Russia were recruited to work in Israel on BW-relevant programs.[5] There are no official estimates available of the total number of former Biopreparat scientists who emigrated to the United States and Western Europe since November 1977, but the number is certainly several multiples of 300 and is probably 1,000 or more.

The dominant émigré destinations of former Soviet BW scientists—the United States, Western Europe, and Israel—are paralleled by the findings of a study that investigated the emigration patterns of scientists from the Soviet Union's nuclear and chemical weapons complexes. The United States, Western

Europe, and Israel were the ultimate destinations of 96% of the Russian nuclear and chemical scientists that emigrated.[6] Two-thirds of these emigrated to two countries, Germany and Israel, with one-tenth going to Sweden and another tenth to the United States. The number of reported émigrés from the Russian biological weapons related community actually seems quite moderate given reported estimates by the Russian Ministry of Interior that approximately 100,000 scientists left the Soviet Union and Russia between 1989 and 1995.[7] Another report, attributed to "the Chairman of the Russian Academy of Sciences trade unions," claimed that this number had reached 500,000 by the year 2002, but that number seems dubious.[8] In a bizarre episode, Domaradsky reported that in 1992 he replied to an advertisement placed by a Chinese institute. He never received a reply, and he did not know of any other Soviet scientist who might have replied to the same advertisement.

The Soviet Union and Iraq

One of the more important questions is whether Soviet BW scientists contributed to Iraq's BW program and, if so, to what degree. Intelligence reports prior to Desert Storm in 1990 are not revealing. A single uncorroborated cable from the US Defense Intelligence Agency (DIA) of June 1987 stated, "During late 1986, ten to fifteen Soviet biological warfare specialists arrived in Baghdad, IZ [Iraq]. These Soviets are teaching Biological warfare tactics to selected commanders of the elite Iraqi presidential guards at a secret location in either Camp Taji or Camp Abu Ghraib, in Baghdad, IZ."[9] Another report claimed that the British Secret Intelligence Service (SIS or MI-6) had noticed a Vector scientist in Baghdad in 1991.[10] A Vector scientist mentioned that several of his own colleagues had been working "in the Middle East countries," specifically Iraq, but had been withdrawn at an unspecified date between 1990 and 1992. He claimed, however, that some of those colleagues "got left behind," but this has never been corroborated.[11] If they had been, they could have been among the 3,300 Soviet nationals that still remained in Iraq as of December 4, 1990.[12]

After Desert Storm, the United Nations Special Commission (UNSCOM) was established in accord with UN Security Council Resolution 687 of March 4, 1991. It was reportedly provided with information by several national intelligence agencies claiming that Soviet BW scientists had been in Iraq prior to Iraq's invasion of Kuwait.[13] In 1994 the DIA also reported that an informant stated that "biological warfare (BW) weapon technology dealing with anthrax and smallpox was made available to North Korea and Iraq—the technology transfer commenced several years prior to 1992, and was still in progress during . . . April 1992 . . . scientists from the NIIM [a Russian MOD facility] in Kirov, traveled to North Korea and Iraq to assist them with their BW programs."[14] This information is assumed to be incorrect, and it does not appear to have ever been provided to UNSCOM. UNSCOM was unable to corroborate *any* of the claims concerning Soviet BW specialists inside Iraq through documentation or interviews while it was operating in Iraq up to December 1998. Senior UNSCOM officials were skeptical of the validity of all these claims. UNSCOM's successor, the UN Monitoring and Verification and Inspection Commission (UNMOVIC), was of the same opinion. The subject is not mentioned at all in the 2004 final report of the US Iraq Survey Group.

In November 2002 a *Washington Post* story reported that the CIA's Weapons Intelligence, Non-Proliferation and Arms Control Center (WINPAC) believed that Iraq, North Korea, France, and Russia retained illicit stocks of variola virus. The CIA's report, which remains classified but portions of which apparently were leaked in the *Washington Post* story, also reportedly stated that "a former Soviet scientist told U.S. officials that his country 'transferred (smallpox) technology in the early 1990s to Iraq.'"[15] This almost certainly refers to the same information in the aforementioned 1994 DIA report, and is very probably spurious.[16] Both depend on "intelligence" supplied by informants and demonstrate its frequent unreliability. The CIA report nevertheless concluded at the same time that Iraq "retained samples (of smallpox) from the 1971 outbreak" that had occurred within its own borders. Senior UNSCOM BW inspectors concurred with part of the latter conclusion. They were convinced that if Iraq did possess variola virus cultures, which they considered possible, they had been obtained from the 1971 outbreak.

Another even more expansive charge appeared in an interview published in September 2002. After referring to Iranian recruitment of some Russian BW scientists, the journalist wrote:

Similar promises lured Biopreparat researchers to Syria, Iraq, Libya, China, and North Korea, among other countries, says Dr. Amy Smithson, director of the Chemical and Biological Weapons Nonproliferation Project at the Henry L. Stimson Center in Washington, DC, who interviewed the scientists in 1999. "They're not making confessions about doing weapons work," says Smithson, but "knowledge and seed cultures have definitely leaked. We don't know what or where."[17]

If one does not know "what or where," it is difficult to understand how one "definitely" knows that seed cultures and knowledge have leaked. Knowledge may very well have gone to Iran, because it is certain, as is discussed in detail on the pages that follow, that some Russian researchers went there. Nevertheless, even in that case, one does not know exactly what knowledge those researchers may have transferred, and there is to date no known evidence for the "leak" of "seed cultures" from the Soviet Union or Russia. When questioned regarding the Smithson claims, a former senior British WMD intelligence official said that he "never, at any time, had seen any corroboration for any of these stories." A US Department of Defense (DOD) official stated that they were "nonsense, just like the story about smallpox from Vector having been transferred to North Korea; a story that won't die."[18] It would appear that Western intelligence agencies have no information that would support the claims made by Smithson. It has proved impossible to obtain corroboration from intelligence sources for any of the specific stories quoted above regarding Soviet personnel or materials allegedly transferred to Iraq.

It is worth noting in this context that Alibek stated that the Soviet Union never supplied any information on its BW program to its Warsaw Pact allies, and therefore was even less likely to have done so to Third World countries like North Korea or Iraq.[19] It is interesting that no one pointed out during the mycotoxin Yellow Rain controversy that if the Soviet Union *had* provided Vietnam with mycotoxins in the years 1978–1982, it would have risked disclosing that it did have an offensive toxin program in violation of the BWC. Iraq in particular probably was not considered a trustworthy client by the Soviets, because its government was on very friendly terms with the first Bush administration until 1990, something that tends to be forgotten. Some Russian institute administrators, however, were not above using the risk of potential emigration of researchers as leverage to appeal for additional financial assistance. In the course of bankruptcy court proceedings in 2002, Victor Gusev, the deputy general director of SRCAM, suggested that if the bankruptcy proceedings initiated by the Center's creditors were to be successful, "then where do you think all the laid-off scientists will go? They will most likely go to one of the so-called axis-of-evil countries. All they need is one month and they could make biological weapons for anybody. After all, we've all got families to feed."[20]

In December 2002 a *New York Times* reporter wrote, "The CIA is investigating an informant's accusation that Iraq obtained a particularly virulent strain of smallpox from a Russian scientist who worked in a smallpox lab in

Moscow during Soviet times, senior American officials and foreign scientists say."[21] The article went on to identify that Soviet scientist as Nelja N. Maltseva, who died in 2000, but who the story claimed had visited Iraq "as recently as 1990." The *New York Times* report was factually in error on several key points. While at a WHO meeting in August 2002 in Lyon, France, two Russian scientists, Lev Sandakchiev, the director of Vector, and Svetlana Marennikova, of the Scientific Research Institute of Viral Preparations in Moscow, met privately with colleagues from CDC and USAMRIID. The subject of the WHO meeting was smallpox. A monograph that described the unreported Soviet-era outbreak of smallpox in Aralsk in 1971 had been published by the Monterey Institute in the preceding year.[22] After the monograph's publication, the author of one of its chapters had privately charged that Vector had obtained, then retained, and was refusing to share, samples of the variola virus strain responsible for the Aralsk outbreak.[23] Because the Monterey monograph concluded that the disease outbreak was the result of an accidental dispersion from a Soviet outdoor BW test of variola virus on Vozrozhdeniye Island, obtaining a sample of the strain was of obvious interest. Marennikova and Sandakhchiev claimed that they did not have the samples of that particular variola virus culture, and tried to explain where those cultures had been, during which years, and what might have happened to them. As best as can be ascertained, they did not tell their US colleagues that Maltseva had been to Iraq, or had transferred variola virus cultures of any kind to Iraq at any time.[24] Maltseva's institute colleagues did corroborate that she had been in Iraq in 1971 and 1972, but these trips had been on WHO missions, which former WHO smallpox officials also corroborated. But they claimed that she had not worked with variola virus for the last 20 years of her working career. Finally, they claimed that her last trip outside of Russia had been in 1982 to Finland.[25] It has proved impossible to learn of any evidence demonstrating that Maltseva did visit Iraq again at any time subsequent to 1972 or to corroborate in particular the *New York Times* claim that she had been there in 1990.

There is evidence that the Soviet Union did, however, aid Iraq's biological weapons program in other ways in the pre-1990 years. There are three separate lines of evidence: the first is ambiguous but suggestive, the second is certain, and the third appears to be nearly so. In the 1960s the Soviet Union built a civilian pharmaceutical plant for Iraq, the Samarra Drug Industries. In the late 1970s the Soviet Union added to this facility, supplying a production unit for the antibiotic tetracycline, consisting of large fermentation capacity.

Around 1989 Iraq removed those fermenters. UNSCOM could never locate them and had no evidence that they had been used for biological weapons production. Iraq claimed that they had been cut up and scrapped. However, in a somewhat parallel instance, fermenters that that been in a date palm oil production facility at Taji had also been removed by Iraqi officials. UNSCOM found those fermenters stored at Iraq's al-Hakam biological weapons production site.[26]

In the second event, UNSCOM was informed by a Russian official that the Soviet Union had "passed"—presumably sold—12 aerosol-spray systems to Iraq for use on helicopters.[27] No year was given for the transfer. Subsequently, in 1990 Iraq did develop its own domestic production capability for a modified helicopter spray nozzle for biological weapons distribution that would produce smaller micron-sized droplets. It was referred to as the Zubaidy device after its Iraqi developer. UNSCOM believed that these were intended for fitting onto commercial spray systems that Iraq had purchased in a Western European country. That left the possibility that Zubaidy had modeled the design of his "bio-adapter" on the nozzles that came with the Soviet system, but UNSCOM had no specific evidence to indicate that. UNSCOM could never find the original 12 Soviet spray systems in Iraq; they were "missing." Whether the Soviet supplier was a military or a civilian commercial entity is unknown, and the original aerosol size specifications of the Russian nozzles also appear to be unknown.

Finally, contrary to Alibek's opinion noted earlier that the Soviet Union had not aided the BW programs of any other country, Alibek indicated that the two Ministry of Defense (MOD) institutes in Sverdlovsk and Zagorsk had supplied some sort of technological assistance to Iraq around 1985.[28] Whether this was hardware or training or both is unclear, but this apparently does not refer to the spraying devices referred to above. If the assistance came from the two MOD institutes, it seems extremely likely that Soviet officials would have understood that the entity receiving the assistance in Iraq was going to be part of a military biological weapons program. If hardware was transferred, Soviet personnel would have had to accompany the equipment in order to train Iraqi personnel in its use. The Soviet personnel would presumably have been military officers, even if not in uniform and not identified as coming from military institutes. If this information is correct, it would corroborate rumors obtained by US intelligence agencies in the early 1990s indicating that Soviet biological weapons personnel were in Iraq up to 1989–1990. Depending on exactly what the assistance was and whether the particulars of the arrangement allowed Iraq to make any inferences about the Soviet Union's own BW effort, it would suggest at least one possible exception to Alibek's generic claim that the Soviet Union would not have provided BW assistance to any other state for fear of compromising its own program.

Nevertheless, UNSCOM officials were suspicious that Iraq might have had external assistance in particular in initiating the viral research portion of its BW program, which began very late. UNSCOM officials also believed that the technical specifications provided by Iraq to certain equipment exporters could only have come from researchers already familiar with the equipment; in other words, it was information provided beforehand to the Iraqis by a knowledgeable informant.[29] There are indications that the Soviet Union knew about the Iraqi BW program in the pre-1990 period. UNSCOM learned that Soviet officials knew of the specific locations in which the Iraqi BW program was being carried out prior to 1987, information that was at that time not known by any other nation's intelligence services. Soviet officials knew when parts of that program were moved from one research facility to another.[30] Alibek has also included Iraq among the countries from which "scientists" were trained in the Soviet Union "in genetic engineering and molecular biology."[31] It is also likely that Iraq's military officers were given training at the open S.M. Kirov Russian Military Medical Academy in Leningrad.

Although the following narrative describes events that took place after 1992, the knowledge it ascribes to Russian officials is assumed to have been in their possession prior to 1992. Ambassador Rolf Ekéus was the executive chairman of UNSCOM from its inception in April 1991 until June 1997. Ekéus recounted that sometime during 1993 or 1994 he had received a telephone call at his UN office in New York from Gennady Estaviev in Moscow.[32] Estaviev was at the time deputy director of the Federal Security Service (better known by its Russian acronym FSB), which then was headed by Yevgenyi Primakov. Ekéus knew Estaviev; he had worked for some years in the office of the UN Secretary-General and he would also at times appear at the International Atomic Energy Agency (IAEA) in Vienna, where Ekéus had been posted for some years. Estaviev told Ekéus that he had to meet with him urgently. Ekéus suggested that Estaviev come to New York. "No, no, that wouldn't be good." Ekéus then suggested that he would travel to Moscow. "No, no, that no good either." So Ekéus suggested that they should meet in Vienna, which was agreed to. When they met, Estaviev ran on and on about old times, until Ekéus reminded him that he had asked to meet with him for some urgent reason. "Ah, yes, that. We know that Iraq has a BW production facility," said Estaviev. But after having revealed this tantalizing bit of information, Estaviev refused to say anything more, saying that was all he could say.

After several months, and having received no further information, Ekéus took advantage of a long-standing invitation from Primakov to visit Moscow, and took a senior Russian UNSCOM staff member, Nikita Smidovich, along with him. They met with Primakov and Estaviev at a country dacha, and after eating, drinking, and aimless conversation, Ekéus repeated what Estaviev had told him in Vienna. Primakov replied that he had never heard of such a thing and knew nothing about it. Estaviev, sweating heavily and visibly upset, followed by denying having said any such thing. Ekéus could make no further headway, and returned to his hotel. Then, at midnight, his phone rang. It was Estaviev in the hotel lobby, saying that he had to come up and speak with Ekéus. Alone with Ekéus, Estaviev again denied what he had told Ekéus in Vienna, saying that there must have been some terrible misunderstanding. He repeated multiple times that he could never have said such a thing.

When Ekéus prepared to retire from UNSCOM in the spring of 1997, he made a diplomatic leave-taking tour of several European countries that were of particular importance to UNSCOM's operations and responsibilities. In Moscow, Russian foreign minister Igor Ivanov hosted a dinner for him. When it came time for toasts, Ivanov asked Ekéus what he thought UNSCOM's greatest achievement had been. Ekéus replied that it was "the destruction of Iraq's CW program, and the discovery of its BW program." Ivanov replied, "OK," and everyone drank a toast to that. After a few moments someone tinkled a spoon on a glass and everyone fell silent and looked to where the sound had come from and who had made it. It was Estaviev down at the end of a table. The room was totally silent as Estaviev called out, "Rolf, Rolf, do you remember who first told you about that?"

Russia and Iraq, 1994–1995

As indicated earlier, there was a series of scare stories in the Western media in the late 1990s alleging that variola virus samples had been taken from Russian laboratories in the post-Soviet period.[33] Russian officials that interacted with UNSCOM denied those stories. They argued that Iraq simply had retained variola virus cultures from one of the last smallpox outbreaks that had affected an area covering parts of Iran, northern Iraq, and Syria in the early

1970s.[34] UNSCOM officials concurred with this interpretation. It was also clear to UNSCOM, however, that some Russian officials showed great concern regarding possible Iraqi development of variola virus for weapons use. It was always assumed that Iraq's research on the camelpox virus in its BW program was a proxy for research on another organism,[35] and that organism was very likely variola virus.[36] Although Iraqi officials identified to UNSCOM all the other specific pathogens associated with Projects A through G, they refused to identify the agent that was associated with "Project E" in its BW program. UNSCOM officials assumed that Project E was smallpox.

In September 1997, during an inspection of Iraq's Chemical Engineering Design Center in Baghdad, UNSCOM investigators seized a set of Iraqi documents. One floor of the Chemical Engineering Design Center had the responsibility to design portions of Iraq's BW facilities. The documents described negotiations "over an extended period between Iraqi officials and a group of Russian government officials involved in managing the countries' chemical and petrochemical industries."[37] The negotiations had taken place between September 1994 and June 1995, both in Moscow and Baghdad, and the documents had been written by Iraqi officials in July 1995. Five of the Iraqi participants had been associated with Iraq's BW program, in particular with Iraq's production site for *B. anthracis* and botulinum toxin at al-Hakam.

Although al-Hakam had already been destroyed by Iraqi workers under UNSCOM supervision in May and June of 1996, well before the time these documents were found, UNSCOM wrote to the Russian government on January 5, 1998, asking it "to provide information about the identities and respective duties" of a Russian delegation that had been to Baghdad in one of the phases of the negotiations.[38] UNSCOM received no reply. On February 12 the story broke in the *Washington Post,* but referred only to the potential export of a single large-capacity bacterial fermentation vessel.[39] A Russian Ministry of Foreign Affairs (MFA) spokesman in Moscow stated, "We decisively deny these crude inventions. Russia has never made any deals with Iraq that would violate international sanctions, moreover dealings involving supplies of banned technologies."[40] Ambassador Sergei Lavrov, the Russian representative at the United Nations, further claimed that UNSCOM had never asked Moscow about any such alleged affair, and demanded that UNSCOM repudiate the press reports. This caused Ambassador Richard Butler, Ekéus' successor as executive chairman of UNSCOM, to inform the press about UNSCOM's January 5 letter to Moscow. A day or two afterward, Butler received a carefully worded two-page letter from Lavrov. This letter has never been made public, but in a highly unusual move Butler released his own reply to Lavrov. By including a brief paraphrasing of Lavrov's letter in his own, Butler thereby disclosed some of the information in the Russian ambassador's letter (see Annex A). This made it clear that Lavrov's letter contained an admission that representatives from Russian firms had met with Iraqi officials in 1995 to negotiate—according to Moscow—the sale of a factory for making single-cell proteins for animal feed. Lavrov's letter further claimed that "no documents were signed," but it did not include a specific denial that Russian equipment might have reached Iraq. In his reply, Butler pointed out that "the documents show that the Russian side presented an offer to (the) Iraqi delegation and that Iraq's Military Industrial Corporation later decided to accept it." By 1994–1995, it was well understood by the Russian government, as well as by everyone else, that Iraq's Military Industrial Corporation was responsible for all of Iraq's programs for developing weapons of mass destruction, including biological weapons. In addition, Butler pointedly noted in his letter that production of single-cell protein had been the cover story used by Iraq to explain the operation of its dedicated BW production facility at al-Hakam, and for importing the requisite equipment for producing biological weapons. UNSCOM was never able to locate any of the equipment referred to in the Russian export discussions with Iraq, nor any paper record indicating that they had been delivered to Iraq. However, there were many instances in which UNSCOM was unable to locate materials inside Iraq that it was nevertheless quite certain were there, as is discussed below. That it could not locate these items simply left the affair unresolved.

The information available to UNSCOM was, however, much more serious than the press accounts indicated. In visits to Russia the Iraqi delegation had apparently visited three Russian firms, the last of which proffered an offer that Iraq accepted. The Russian firm proposed to plan, design, export the equipment for, and operate the Iraqi facility. It was to be equipped with five very large fermenters, each of 10,000 liters capacity (10 cubic meters), as well as all the necessary auxiliary equipment, such as mixing tanks, seed fermenters, tanks for additives, and other components.[41] It was for all intents and purposes a complete turnkey biological weapons agent plant. The documents obtained by UNSCOM also showed that additional discussions had taken place between Russia and Iraq for "mutual cooperation" in related areas of work, and Butler had referred to these additional discussions in his response in February 1998 to Lavrov's letter. An additional piece of extremely compromising information was that a senior member of the Russian negotiating team had been Colonel Vilen Matveev, a former deputy to General Yuri T. Kalinin, who was at that time still the director of Biopreparat. Matveev had previously been responsible for the design and construction of several Soviet BW production facilities.[42] As to the question of whether these Iraqi-Russian negotiations could have taken place without the knowledge and authorization of senior Russian government officials, Alibek believes that to have been impossible. No Russian company would have dealt with an Iraqi delegation without prior Russian government approval, nor would an Iraqi government delegation have attempted to carry out such discussions without explicit Russian government approval.[43] Alibek further reported that the model of the fermentation vessel that Iraq had agreed to purchase was one that the Soviet Union "had used to develop and manufacture biological weapons." Iraq had additionally requested that the Russian manufacturer supply "exhaust filtration equipment capable of achieving 99.99 percent air purity"—a level that, he stated, the Soviet Union had only used in its "weapons labs," and one that would scarcely be needed in a single-cell protein facility.[44] Knowing this, Butler in his January 5 letter therefore had asked the Russian government if he could send UNSCOM staff members to interview the Russian officials who had been involved in the talks with the Iraqis. The Russian government refused UNSCOM permission to do so, probably in Lavrov's letter to Butler in mid-February. This was one detail in Lavrov's letter that Butler did not disclose in his recapitulation. It was the only instance in which a government other than Iraq denied a request of that nature by UNSCOM.

Given the indication that multiple Russian officials were involved in these negotiations, and that the Iraqi emissaries visited several different Russian facilities, it seems inconceivable that this entire affair could have been a matter of individual corruption or freelancing by Russian equipment producers. Although no direct evidence is available, it must have been known to and authorized by the Russian government. What could the Russian government possibly have had in mind with this affair? June 1995 was only one month before Iraq finally admitted to UNSCOM that it had operated an offensive BW program, and although that admission had not yet been made, Russia undoubtedly knew that it was coming. Perhaps this was the reason Lavrov could be so explicit in his letter to Butler, writing that "there were no further meetings or correspondence with the Iraqi side" after June 1995. The Russian-Iraqi negotiations were also a full year after Estaviev had tipped off Ekéus, described earlier, informing Ekéus that Iraq had a BW production capability. Another Russian contact had also provided UNSCOM with information indicating clearly that the Soviet Union, and then Russia, had understood what was being produced at al-Hakam, and that it was not "single-cell protein." Lavrov's contention that there were no further Iraqi-Russian dealings of this nature after June 1995 may or may not be correct, but Russia's admission to at least a part of the affair, after a previous blanket denial, had been forced only by public disclosure. And as was typical in matters concerning Iraq, the Russian admission provided only as much information to UNSCOM, or less, than UNSCOM already knew. As indicated, whether or not any portion of the Russian equipment included in the contract negotiations ever reached Iraq remains an unanswered question.

But this was still not the end of the story. At the very same time in late 1994 and early 1995, Iraq apparently did manage to acquire a 5,000-liter fermenter and associated equipment from Russia. It was moved, in multiple shipments, through at least four middlemen, and UNSCOM was able to locate documents that showed it had reached an Iraqi customs post on the Iraqi-Jordanian border. It therefore must be assumed to have reached Iraq. Although the documents showed that it was intended for al-Hakam, UNSCOM inspectors were never able to locate the fermenter. The manufacturer was the same former GDR company that had produced large-size fermenters for the Soviet-era BW program.[45] UNSCOM officials believed that Matveyev at Biopreparat would have been the facilitator of this transaction and would have been able to bring the Iraqis and the former GDR company together.

It therefore seems that the most potentially serious BW proliferation event that occurred after 1992 involving Russian nationals was not the result of the emigration or recruiting of individual Russian BW scientists, but was a state-to-state interaction involving the Russian government and Iraq, a state with a large, publicly identified, banned, and UN sanctioned WMD program, including BW. UNSCOM also learned that two Russians who were former subordinates of Major General Anatoly Kuntsevich were at an Iraqi chemical pesticide plant late in 1999.[46] As discussed in Chapter 19, Kuntsevich was dismissed from his position as President Yeltsin's senior official for chemical and biological issues in 1994 for shipping chemical weapon precursors to Syria. In that instance UNSCOM officials believed that the materials were intended for transshipment from Syria to Iraq.

On April 7, 2003, speaking to the Russian newspaper *Vedomosti*, Valery Spirande, at the time the deputy head of the department dealing with chemical and biological weapons of the Russian Munitions Agency, once again denied the significance of the 1994–1995 Russian-Iraqi negotiations for a turnkey biological weapons plant. He referred to a single fermenter and described it as "no more dangerous than bricks." He claimed that "the talks concerned purchasing the fermenter to obtain feed protein. This device does not have a dual purpose and therefore is not subject to export controls. . . . Vats claimed to be for the brewing industry would look exactly the same," and he claimed to be "unaware of the fate of the deal."[47] *Vedomosti* was a Moscow daily paper associated with the government, and Spirande is a retired military officer who had worked in one of the MOD institutes. Only two weeks later Spirande was quoted in another Moscow daily explaining that the Vozrozhdeniye Island BW test site "had been a testing area for veterinary vaccines. Animals were infected with various diseases, sometimes with airborne bombs, to determine the effectiveness of vaccines."[48] Former Soviet military officials clearly did not coordinate their fabricated disinformation efforts very well. As noted in an earlier chapter, Yevstigneev had claimed in his explanations of Soviet testing on Vozrozhdeniye Island that the site was used only to test Soviet reproductions of US BW bomblet munitions. All of this blatant and gratuitous disinformation is not only astonishing, but it should be seen as part of a pattern, taken together with the rebirth of claims by senior Russian military officials that the Soviet Union never had an offensive biological weapons program and the renewal by the same individuals of false allegations of biological weapons use by the United States. The three strands of disinformation and propaganda—a throwback to the pre-1985 years—go together. Hearing them again in 2002 and 2003 was an extremely bad sign and promised continuing problems.

Between 1995 and 1999, Russia aided Iraq by actively undermining the ability of UNSCOM to perform its mission in Iraq, which was to discover and destroy any remaining elements of Iraq's WMD programs, including BW. Russia impeded UNSCOM's work and flouted UN Security Council resolutions, frequently in direct collusion with senior Iraqi officials. Russia joined with Iraq in arguing that Iraq had fulfilled its obligations and in demanding the two special panels in 1998 to review UNSCOM's work. Both panels, with Russian technical experts participating in them, unanimously upheld UNSCOM's reports, thereby rejecting the Russian-Iraqi position. Russia then sought to end the UN sanctions on Iraq, despite the fact that Iraq remained in blatant violation of the UNSC resolutions. In defense of their position, Russian officials argued that they were anxious that Iraq should be able to reimburse Russia for the $7–8 billion in debt to Russia that Iraq had incurred due to its weapons purchases from the Soviet Union between 1970 and 1990.

In the end Russia assisted in bringing about the total demise of UNSCOM. During the negotiations on UN Security Council Resolution 1274, establishing UNMOVIC, the UN agency that succeeded UNSCOM to complete its responsibilities, the Russian representative to the UN Security Council openly represented Iraq and collaborated with Iraq in drafting language that weakened the resolution. Russia, on Iraq's behalf, rejected UN secretary-general Kofi Annan's recommendation that UNSCOM's first executive director, Rolf Ekéus, head the new agency. Russia obtained resolution language that ended the ability of UN member states to detail their nationals to serve as inspectors, a move specifically aimed at reducing the more technically qualified staff from the United States and the United Kingdom. It also prohibited the new agency from obtaining U-2 reconnaissance aircraft that had been provided by the United States to UNSCOM, and the US and UK fighter aircraft protection that prevented Iraq from interfering with those reconnaissance aircraft.

Russia and Iran

Iran's BW program reportedly began in the mid-1980s, almost at the same time as its chemical weapons program. The war between Iraq and Iran was at its height, and Iraqi chemical weapons were frequently used against Iranian troops. However, the specific reason Iran decided to acquire biological weapons—in particular, whether Iran had learned of Iraq's BW program and therefore decided to emulate it—is not known. An American researcher who attended an international virology conference in 1990 in Turkey noted that in private conversations Iranians present had asked pointed questions seeking information regarding biological weapons.[49]

The first information concerning Russian molecular geneticists working in Iran was obtained in November 1997. It was learned that 10 researchers, all reportedly from the Gamaleya Institute for Microbiology and Epidemiology, had worked in Iran.[50] The Gamaleya Institute was affiliated with the Russian Academy of Medical Sciences, which clearly indicated that officials of the Academy and of the Russian government knew and approved of the arrangement. The researchers were on leave from their permanent positions. They had reportedly remained in Iran for two years, under contract, and by the end of 1997 had already returned to their parent institute in Moscow. Some of the scientists at the Gamaleya Institute were fully involved in the Soviet Union's secret offensive BW program—as distinct from the Problem

5 BW defense effort—and it appears that some of the group who went to Iran were in that category.

However, it was the Russian Ministry of Science and Technology that facilitated the more-significant contacts between Iran and Biopreparat institutes by sending a delegation to a biotechnology trade fair in Tehran in the spring of 1997. As many as 100 senior Russian scientists from various institutes plus ministry officials attended the fair, including some researchers from Vector and SRCAM. Andrew Weber, a DOD official working at DTRA, met Sandakhchiev for the first time in Washington, D.C., in July 1997, and then again at a NATO Advanced Research Workshop in Budapest in the first week of November 1997. On the second occasion, he spent many hours over several days privately talking with Sandakhchiev. He learned of the Biotech fair that the Russian ministry had arranged in Tehran, and that subsequently Iranian government representatives had made several trips to Vector. A commercial relationship had already been initiated: the Iranians were purchasing diagnostic kits and pharmaceuticals from Vector Best and Vector Pharm, commercial offshoots located at Vector. However, the Iranian visitors belonged to an organization involved in WMD procurement, and the Iranian purchases were an obvious means of entry and access to the Vector staff. One has to assume that the Iranians had obtained the approval of both the KGB and Biopreparat headquarters in Moscow in order to have reached Koltsovo in the first place, and to have gained entry to the Vector buildings. In all likelihood, they had paid for that authorization.

The Iranian visitors made the most of their opportunity in multiple ways. Iranian officials met with a group of the most senior Vector researchers and offered them astronomical salaries by Russian standards to work in Iran. The offers reportedly reached as high as $5,000 and even $10,000 per month to people who were reportedly earning the equivalent of $100 per month. At this time substantial bilateral US funds channeled via the International Science and Technology Center (ISTC) and other donor mechanisms had not yet begun to flow to Vector in any significant amounts.[51] Iranian offers to Vector and its personnel continued as late as 1998 and, given the nature of Vector's research in virology, Iranian interest of course focused on that discipline and included offers to Vector scientists who specialized in hemorrhagic fever viruses. One or more of the Vector scientists approached by the Iranians had worked with vaccinia and variola viruses.[52] Iranian suggestions also reportedly included "a joint research facility" and the exchange of pathogen strains, among other forms of "technology cooperation." Researchers at Vector reportedly also were offered and rejected university lecturing positions in Iran.

During one of the business meetings at Vector, in a casual opportunity at the side of the official discussions, the Iranians asked to purchase more serious technology of clear relevance for BW development. Most surprising of all, the Iranian visitors had obtained permission to visit individual Vector laboratories, to talk to individual scientists, and to ask them essentially "What do you have that we could buy?" These purchases were to take place "under the table," and not via the Vector administration, and the Iranians were apparently carrying cash with which to make the purchases. In one case they offered to buy an invention made by Toporkov, a "particle size exclusion sampler," an impinger used for aerosol sampling. Toporkov refused the offer and reported the incident to Sandakhchiev.[53]

Within weeks of Weber's November 1997 meeting with Sandakchiev in Budapest, he was able to arrange the first of several visits to Vector. After one of these first visits, DOD offered Vector $3 million in grant funds, which was sufficient to convince Sandakhchiev to break off the commercial relationships with Iran and to end further Iranian visits. No member of the Vector staff is known to have gone to Iran to lecture, and DOD did not believe that any technology transfer of BW significance took place before the end of the Vector-Iranian commercial engagement.[54] One DOD official even suggested the possibility that because the KGB was likely to have been monitoring the Iranian conversations with various Vector scientists, it was possibly testing the Iranian intentions.[55] This seems implausible to the authors.

A critical factor in the decisions of the Vector researchers to reject Iranian offers very likely was pressure from US government officials who let it be known that no bilateral US or ISTC funding would be offered to any institute from which researchers had gone to countries of proliferation concern. In the words of the Vector official reported as being its "financial director," the Iranian offer came at "the same time when we began to arrange research contacts with the United States. Ultimately we made the decision to go that way instead."[56] US officials who visited IHPP were told that Iranian recruiters had visited them as well.[57] In fact, a GAO report stated that "since 1997 Iran and other countries of proliferation concern have intensified efforts to acquire biological weapons expertise and materials from at least 15 former Soviet biological weapons institutes."[58] The identity of the "other countries" and the other institutes is not known. The Iranians reportedly did not visit the IEI in Lyubuchany or SNOPB in Stepnogorsk. It should probably be considered extraordinary that there are no reports of researchers from any of these institutes taking up positions in Iran.

General Nikolay Urakov, the director of SRCAM, told US government officials in 1997 that he had been to Tehran in several successive years to give one- or two-week-long lecture programs in biochemistry.[59] This puzzled scientists at other Biopreparat institutes who had rejected similar offers from Iranian officials, since Urakov is neither an English speaker nor a biochemist.[60] Urakov also described Iranian efforts to get him to "collaborate" in other, undefined ways, which he claimed to have resisted. In a report early in 2002, the deputy director of the ISTC reported that Russian scientists "who had been receiving e-mails from Iran or Iraq or Pakistan are now very sensitive and cut off all communication with these organizations . . . because they want to be eligible to participate in programs like the ISTC."[61] This comment did not distinguish between scientists whose work experience was in the nuclear, chemical, or biological weapons fields, but as far as BW is concerned such communications had apparently come only from Iran.

Iranian recruiters were, however, more successful earlier outside of Biopreparat institutes. One of the major Iranian recruiters was M. Rezayat, whose card listed him as the Scientific Adviser of the Office of Scientific and Industrial Studies in the office of the Iranian Presidency, as well as the Director of the Pharmacology Department of the Tehran Medical Sciences University. The Presidency office, which had been renamed the Office of Technology Cooperation, was described in the *New York Times* report as "an Iranian intelligence office that covertly shops for talent and technology involving nuclear, chemical, and biological weapons." As a result of his recruiting efforts, a very few Soviet researchers who had done BW-relevant work did resettle in Iran.

Given the reported salaries offered, the success rate was very meager judging from available information. Iranian officials indicated a particular interest in agricultural BW. A catalogue of Iranian recruitment contacts among BW-relevant Russian researchers appeared in the *New York Times* in December 1998.[62] Officials of the DOD aided the newspaper's reporters in gathering the published information, but much of the information that appears below was obtained by the authors in interviews with Russian sources.[63]

- Dr. G. Smirnov and six of his colleagues from the Gamaleya Institute traveled to Iran in October 1993. They reportedly stayed for three months and presented a series of lectures and practical training "workshops" in the classical genetics of bacteria at the Pasteur Institute in Tehran. The seven Russians apparently then returned to Russia. A bit over a half-year later, that is, in mid-1994, a second set of Russian visitors arrived in Tehran. It consisted of Valery Bakaev of the Institute of Medical Biotechnology in Moscow, and N. Domansky, Vladimir Rechinsky, T. Medvedeva, A. Gushchin, R. Mironava, and I. Iavanov, all of whom were scientists at the Engelhardt Institute of Molecular Biology of the Russian Academy of Sciences in Moscow. Domansky reportedly left Iran in 1996–1997, but Bakaev stayed until 1998–1999. Rechinsky returned to Russia in 1995 but reportedly returned to Iran for several one- or two-week visits between 1995 and 1998. This information has to be considered uncertain, and the time spent in Iran may have been longer. The names of several of the identified members of the Institute of Molecular Biology in Moscow appear on papers co-authored with Iranian scientists published in 1995, 1996, 1999, and 2000.[64] Several other Russian scientists from various institutes with specializations in fermentation, peptide synthesis, and other basic laboratory techniques also worked in the Tehran Pasteur Institute for periods of one to two months.[65]

- Three researchers from the Institute of Biological Protection in Moldova were reportedly working in Iran by mid-1997.
- Three scientists from the All-Russian Institute of Phytopathology "travel(ed) to Tehran"; no indication was given if that was to take up permanent positions, or for short-term temporary employment.
- Rechinsky was described as having taken a second two-month leave of absence from his institute in order to teach in Iran.

All of the Russian scientists visited Iran under agreements between the Russian Academy of Medical Sciences and the Iranian Ministry of Health. That ministry was reportedly "also responsible for visits of a number of high-standing persons and a variety of more or less noted Russian scientists."[66] The Russian scientists from the Institute of Molecular Biology apparently were primarily doing teaching and supervising doctoral students, and only secondarily carrying out research. Findings from the research they carried out, as well as that conducted by their students, have been published in English and in international and Iranian journals. The subjects of the published papers that have been examined do not have any direct relationship to any BW-relevant pathogen, to increasing bacterial pathogenicity, or to other subjects that would have direct BW relevance. The Russian scientists reportedly worked in or had access to three Iranian facilities: the Pasteur Institute, the

Razy Vaccine and Serum Institute, and a new "[Inter]National Center for Genetic Engineering and Biotechnology," a name that Iranian officials clearly selected to mimic that of the International Centre for Genetic Engineering and Biotechnology (ICGEB) in Trieste, Italy, which is an intergovernmental institute that performs basic research and trains Third World scientists. The Razy Institute is actually a very large biological production facility. The Pasteur Institute is so named because it obtains a degree of financial support from the Pasteur Institute in Paris and some of its researchers have undergone training in Paris.

The *New York Times* press report also documented several significant failures in the Iranian recruiting efforts, as well as demonstrating the blatancy and perseverance of those efforts. Valery Lipkin, a biochemist and deputy director of the Shemyakin and Ovchinnikov Institute of Bioorganic Chemistry, Russian Academy of Sciences, declined repeated Iranian recruitment efforts through both 1997 and 1998, as well as invitations to visit Tehran. The Iranian delegations, in turn, declined offers by Lipkin to train Iranian students in Russia. Yuri Spiridonov, head of the herbicide department of the All Russian Institute of Phytopathology, rejected recruitment efforts that spanned both 1997 and 1998.

In 2000, John A. Lauder, head of the CIA's Non Proliferation Center, testified to a US Senate Committee: "Iran is seeking expertise and technology from Russia that could advance Tehran's biological warfare effort. Russia has several government-to-government agreements with Iran in a variety of scientific and technical fields. Because of the dual-use nature of much of this technology, Tehran can exploit these agreements to procure equipment and expertise that could be diverted to its BW effort. Iran's BW program could make rapid and significant advances if it has unfettered access to BW expertise resident in Russia."[67] Given the evidence supplied in the previous pages, a second statement in April 8, 2002, was relatively general and vague regarding Russian-Iranian BW relations: "Iran is pursuing civilian biotechnology activities along with its BW program. Russian assistance could further Iran's pursuit of biotechnology for military applications. . . . Russian entities are a significant source of dual-use biotechnology, chemicals, production technology, and equipment for Iran."[68] There was evidence in late 2002 that Iranian recruiting efforts had not ended. They reportedly focused on scientists working in institutes belonging to the Russian Academy of Sciences and the Russian Academy of Agricultural Sciences. The Iranians were seeking technology and attempting to obtain renewals of the type of contractual visits for extended periods of teaching and research that they had succeeded in establishing with the Gamaleya Institute in the mid-1990s.[69]

If the Russian government continued or expanded general "technological cooperation" agreements with Iran, then transfers of "dual-use" technology, training, or products that help "to create a more advanced and self-sufficient . . . infrastructure,"[70] whether in the chemical or biological weapons area, became more significant. To the degree that Iran is unable to recruit Russian researchers willing to work directly in the Iranian BW program, the recruitment of scientists who simply teach molecular biology and genetics but in doing so also "create a more advanced and self-sufficient . . . infrastructure" also becomes of increased significance for Iran. However, it is difficult, if not impossible, to disentangle teaching of possible BW relevance from education for general scientific or public health service. For example, the Gamaleya scientists reportedly taught courses at universities in Tehran on molecular genetics, transduction, the extraction of plasmids, and presumably other related techniques. They also worked in Tehran's Pasteur Institute, while some Iranians were trained in Russia to produce an anti-rabies vaccine which uses mammalian cell culture techniques that could be adapted to more BW-relevant viruses. But Iranians from the Pasteur Institute in Tehran also go to the Pasteur Institute in Paris and to the ICGEB for training that must be very similar,. This discussion demonstrates the problems associated with assessing the significance of training supplied by visiting Russian researchers in Iran. It applies as well to training obtained by Iranian scientists in any other country that "contributes to creating a more advanced and self-sufficient . . . infrastructure," or to any country that allegedly is already maintaining an offensive BW program. Clearly, the pool of trained professional talent that can be drawn from the civil scientific or commercial sector into a BW program is thereby increased.

Iran's efforts in Russia have not been relegated solely to scientists with knowledge that would help a BW program; Iran has also actively sought assistance in Russia for its chemical weapons program, and has apparently been much more successful in that. Lauder also reported that, "Numerous Russian entities have been providing Iran with dual-use industrial chemicals, equipment, and chemical production technology that could be diverted to Tehran's offensive CW program. In 1999, for example, Russian entities provided production technology, training, and expertise that Iran could use to create a more advanced and self-sufficient CW infrastructure."[71]

Iran also recruited two other groups of Russian scientists in roughly the same years; some worked on chemical weapons and others on ballistic missiles. The pattern is roughly similar to the one Iran had apparently hoped to establish with scientists from several Biopreparat institutes. Iran recruited a number of Russian missile engineers to work on the Shahab-3, a ballistic missile with a range of roughly 800 miles. The precise number of these experienced Russian engineers is not known, but was described as "many dozens," so perhaps something under 100.[72] Some took repeated trips of one or two weeks for lecturing, others took longer-term contracts and stayed in Iran for extended periods. Significantly, the exit visas for the Russian missile specialists to go to Iran were arranged by the MFA and the FSB. At the same time, Iranian students were trained at the Moscow Aviation Institute between the mid-1990s and 2001 at the undergraduate and advanced graduate levels. The Russian assistance to the Iranian missile program violated Russian commitments under the 1987 Missile Technology Control Regime.

There are several other known or alleged events that would be of significant BW concern, and although they have proven difficult to verify, they suggest specific covert involvement of Russian scientists or agencies. Speaking at a conference in Washington, D.C., in April 1996, James Adams, a reporter with the London *Sunday Times,* stated that Iran had approached a Russian export company named Nordex and asked for assistance with Iran's BW program, "and bought a BW delivery system."[73] The nature of the "BW delivery system" and the characteristics that made it suitable for BW delivery have not been described. Nordex was a shadowy enterprise with its headquarters in Moscow and a branch office in Vienna. It was allegedly established and operated by former KGB officials, and was known to have maintained relationships at the highest political levels in both Russia and Ukraine in the early 1990s. Despite allegations in published reports of Nordex's involvement in exports of advanced conventional weapons and materials of possible relevance to nuclear weapons development, none of the available published material published about the company includes any reference to biological weapons.[74]

Russia and Aum Shinrikyo: 1992

Another murky affair with many unresolved loose ends concerns the relationship between the Russian government and the Japanese Aum Shinrikyo sect, a nongovernmental entity. The assistance the sect obtained from senior

Russian government officials in its quest to develop and produce biological weapons is relevant to this chapter. In 1992 a group of about a dozen important Russian political figures established the "Russian-Japanese University" in collaboration with Aum Shinrikyo. A central figure in this group was Oleg Lobov, who had been a close assistant to Boris Yeltsin when Yeltsin was CPSU party secretary of the Sverdlovsk oblast. Lobov, described as "a conservative representative of the communist *nomenklatura*" later served as secretary of Yeltsin's National Security Council from 1993 to 1996.[75] A delegation from the Aum group came to Russia and met with Lobov and some of his colleagues. Lobov was apparently instrumental in aiding the Aum group to obtain technological assistance of several kinds. Assistance that was provided relevant to obtaining chemical and conventional weapons has been omitted from this chapter.

In Aum's search for assistance in the BW field, the Aum visitors were apparently directed to a person with *very* significant knowledge of biological weapons, Anatoly Vorobyov, Alibek's predecessor as deputy director of Biopreparat.[76] It is also possible that they met with Pavel Syutkin, although Japanese sources refer only to Vorobyov. Syutkin replaced Kuntsevich as head of President Yeltsin's Committee for Problems of the Chemical and Biological Weapons Conventions, following Kuntsevich's dismissal in 1994. Prior to that Syutkin had been a senior member of the Military Industrial Commission (VPK), with responsibility for research in the area of chemical and biological weapons. Nevertheless, it is not known definitively who directed the Aum visitors or to which Russian individuals they were referred, because they also contacted a staff member of a Russian Duma committee in their search for the names of knowledgeable Russian BW experts that they could approach. There is also no information available from Aum sources as to what they were able to obtain, or if in fact they were provided with any assistance whatsoever. It is known that Aum's efforts to produce both botulinum toxin and virulent *B. anthracis* failed, despite a four-year effort, so it would not appear as if they were provided with any significant help.[77] However, armed with the knowledge that Aum officials might have met with Vorobyov, members of the US intelligence community either came to believe, or took the initiative to distribute, a piece of highly misleading information. They informed several members of the US BW community—and possibly others—that the Russian KGB had been responsible for supplying Aum with a vaccine (nonvirulent) strain of *B. anthracis*.[78] They further claimed that the strain was the Soviet-era anthracis vaccine strain, known as STI or ST-1. This is a live vaccine strain developed only in the USSR/Russia and is distinct from the Sterne strain, which is used for vaccines in the West. The fact that Aum had attempted to weaponize a vaccine strain of *B. anthracis* was already known by 1999, but which particular vaccine strain the sect used for this purpose had not been positively identified.[79] However, when a DNA analysis of the *B. anthracis* used by Aum was finally done, it was reported to be the standard, avirulent Sterne 34 F2 strain, which was available in Japan and was used there for vaccines to protect domestic animals from anthrax.[80] It remains unknown precisely how Aum obtained its sample of the Sterne strain, but the suggestion that the KGB gave the Aum group the Russian ST-1 strain is disinformation.

Other Events of Possible BW Proliferation Concern

The first time that the Soviet Union supplied infrastructure for work with pathogens to any country apparently occurred quite soon after World War II. In China, the communists consolidated their victory in October 1949. In 1953 the Soviet Union built the facility for China that is now the Institute of Epidemiology and Microbiology, in Chāngping, close to Beijing.[81] The design of the building apparently followed that of Soviet laboratories of the period. Nevertheless, given the date of its construction, planning for the facility must have begun quite soon after the Chinese communists came to power. The Chinese administrators of the facility in the mid-2000s considered it the equivalent of the Center for Applied Microbiological Research (CAMR) in the United Kingdom, and it is likely that in its earlier years it may have served as the equivalent of the British CAMR's antecedent, the Microbiological Research Establishment at Porton Down.

According to Alibek, the Soviet Union also assisted the Cuban government in its efforts to establish an industrial biotechnology infrastructure. During a visit to the Soviet Union in February 1981, Cuban premier Castro was shown a laboratory in which *E. coli* had been genetically engineered to produce interferon, and, according to Alibek, the Soviet Union subsequently supplied Cuba with the relevant equipment and production handbooks for producing interferon. Alibek even implies that Cuba obtained "all of (the) knowledge and equipment" for its biotechnology program from the Soviet Union.[82] Ovchinnikov reportedly visited Cuba in 1985, heading a team of

Soviet scientists in the area of biotechnology, and in 1989 a delegation of some 20 molecular biologists from various USSR Academy of Sciences institutes traveled to Cuba for the inauguration of the National Center for Biotechnology and Genetic Engineering. Cuba reportedly offered all the Soviet scientists positions, but they were ordered by the Soviet Academy of Sciences to decline the offers of employment.[83] Alibek also wrote that Kalinin, his immediate superior and the director of Biopreparat, "was invited to Cuba in 1990 to discuss the creation of a new biotechnology plant ostensibly devoted to the production of single-cell protein. He returned convinced that Cuba had an active biological weapons program."[84] Biopreparat did manage Soviet-era plants that produced single-cell proteins, which served in part as the cover for Biopreparat's BW mission. If the mission to Cuba had been solely for civilian technology for single-cell protein production, it seems plausible that another individual managing civilian single-cell protein production in the Soviet Union rather than Kalinin should have been sent. On the other hand, it might even have been considered a useful "cover" for Kalinin for the Soviet Union to have sent him to Cuba to negotiate a purely civilian international technology transfer. Cuba apparently also sought to import the components for a new BSL-3 facility from Russia. Around March 2000, the scientists in one Cuban institute had been offered a BSL-3 design by an unidentified Russian supplier, and they showed the design to some visiting American scientists. The Americans were puzzled by a specification in the Russian blueprints for three feet of concrete around the BSL-3 unit.[85] On the assumption that Cuba did not request that peculiar detail, which would imply protection against external explosive damage, rather than an explosive test chamber within the BSL-3 unit, the incident is puzzling and difficult to explain.

The case of Israel is quite different from that of Iran. The question is not whether Russian scientists trained Israelis, but whether any Russian scientists may have moved directly into positions in the Israeli BW program at the Israel Institute for Biological Research at Nes Ziona (IIBR), located approximately 16 kilometers south of Tel Aviv, or while working under contract at other Israeli academic or research institutes.[86]

Marcus Klingberg, the former deputy director of IIBR, who had been spying for the Soviet Union for approximately 20 years, published a memoir in 2008. At the time of the book's release, an Israeli press account reported that Israel's counterespionage agency, the Shin Bet security service, "considers him the most dangerous spy ever to operate in Israel" and that Nes Ziona had "developed weapons of mass destruction."[87] If that is the case, emigration of former Soviet BW scientists to Israel certainly merits examination. The former Soviet scientist who was a mycotoxins expert and emigrated to Israel did not work at Nes Ziona, and a second former Soviet scientist, Eli Shlyakov, an anthrax expert who co-authored journal publications on drug-resistant *B. anthracis* strains in 2004 and 2005, worked at the Department of Human Microbiology, Tel Aviv University School of Medicine. In the Soviet Union, Shlyakov had worked at the Gamaleya Institute before emigrating to Israel around 1990. Prior to the Gamaleya, he had worked at another institute in collaborative research projects with the MOD's Kirov Institute. In a third case, scientists who had at one time reportedly worked on West Nile virus at Vector left that institute and subsequently emigrated to Israel where they reportedly continued working on the West Nile virus. It is not known at which institution this work took place.

One last event involving the possible proliferation of Soviet BW-related technology is well documented because the perpetrators themselves advertised it. Sometime in 1996 or 1997 a commercial Russian enterprise calling itself BIOEFFECT Ltd. announced its willingness to sell licenses for the production of three recombinant strains of *Francisella tularensis,* the bacterium that causes tularemia. (See BIOEFFECT announcement in Annex B at the end of this chapter.) As part of the deal, the purchaser would obtain samples of the strains. While the advertisement claimed that the strains would be useful to anyone wishing to develop vaccines against tularemia, it also noted that they contained "cloned factors of virulence." All three strains had been developed at SRCAM.[88] Two of the strains contained the genes responsible for virulence in *Francisella tularensis,* and the third strain included the genes responsible for virulence in a second pathogen, *Burkholderia pseudomallei,* which causes melioidosis. The advertisement listed Nikolay N. Kislitchkin as the director of BIOEFFECT. However, by the time the advertisement appeared, Kislitchkin had already left Obolensk.

According to Kislitchkin these strains were genetically modified *F. tularensis* live vaccine strain 9LVS into which virulence factors from *F. tularensis, B. pseudomallei,* and *M. tuberculosis* had been inserted with the intention of producing more efficient vaccines against tularemia, melioidosis, and tuberculosis. Kislitchkin attempted to sell the technology to the German Army's biodefense institute (Sanitätsakedamie), and to companies in the United States and South Korea.[89] He also attempted to establish a company in Norway or Finland to produce the tuberculosis vaccine using this procedure.

BIOEFFECT was listed as having "representatives"—apparently offices—both in Moscow and in Vienna. Secondary to the major problematical aspect of the involvement of SRCAM and the offer of recombinant strains containing virulence genes for licensed sale to any buyer anywhere in the world, the identity of the Vienna contact listed in the advertisement, Lev Voronkov, introduced an additional troubling issue. Voronkov first appeared in Vienna in 1989 as the "scientific director" of an organization called the "International Institute for Peace." The institute, which arranged conferences and publications, was a Soviet-era front organization, and its "scientific director" was understood in the West to be a member of the Soviet intelligence services. The telephone number for the office of Voronkov, as the contact for BIOEFFECT Ltd., was exactly the same as the telephone number for Voronkov, the "scientific director" of the International Institute of Peace, as was the address at which the office was located. The "two" Voronkovs were apparently one and the same person.

Alibek generalized from the BIOEFFECT affair: "Dozens of small privately owned pharmaceutical companies like Bioeffekt have flourished in Russia since the Soviet collapse. They represent another channel through which the techniques, the knowledge, and even the strains we developed have spread beyond the borders of the old Soviet Union, contributing to an alarming proliferation of biological weapons since the end of the cold war."[90] This statement is inaccurate in several respects. First, as best we know, although concern about BW proliferation certainly increased greatly in the 1990s, BW proliferation did not increase at all during the same period. In fact a study published in 2010 suggests that it decreased by as much as one third in that time.[91] All known State BW programs predate "the end of the cold war," and diffusion from a State program to a non-state actor has never yet occurred. Second, there is no available evidence that pathogenic strains of bacteria or viruses developed by the Soviet BW program have been transported beyond Russia's borders. Finally, in all of the major cases discussed in this chapter, the possibility that some portion of the planned Russian state-sanctioned transfers to Iraq in 1994–1995 described above did take place, and that former Soviet scientists may have contributed to Israel's BW program, "small privately owned pharmaceutical companies" were not at all involved. There is little or no available evidence that diffusion of BW-related knowledge from post-Soviet Russia has been a significant factor in the BW programs of either states or non-state actors.

We have seen that the overwhelming number of post-1992 BW proliferation-relevant events and processes deriving from the former Soviet BW program have been carried out directly through, or sanctioned in advance by, either the pre-1992 Soviet government or the post-1992 Russian government. If there have been additional unsanctioned events, by either émigré Russian BW-competent scientists or by Russian commercial entities, little or no evidence of it is available. Paradoxically the known Soviet or Russian government contributions have been to Iraq and Iran, two neighboring countries and major antagonists. Further, if any former Soviet BW-scientists contributed to Israel's BW capabilities, there is the added irony that Iraq considered Israel a major enemy in the years prior to 1992 when Iraq was unconstrained, and Iran remains a primary enemy of Israel.

ANNEX A: United Nations Special Commission

The Executive Chairman   16 February 1998
His Excellency
Mr. Sergey V. Lavrov
Ambassador Extraordinary and Plenipotentiary
Permanent Representative of the Russian Federation to the United Nations
New York, New York

Excellency,

This letter addresses an article published in *The Washington Post* of 12 February 1998, which made some remarks on the work of the Special Commission both as such and in cooperation with the Russian Federation. On the same day, the spokesman of the Russian Ministry of Foreign Affairs issued a statement requesting that the Executive Chairman of the Commission provide appropriate repudiation of the Washington Post article.

As is clear from the article itself, and as agreed with you in our conversation on 13 February, a number of the contentions of that article are outside my responsibility. This is not the case with regard to the following points:

1. On September 1997, an inspection team of the Commission discovered a set of documents related to the al-Hakam facility, when inspecting an Iraqi Chemical Engineering Design Centre in Baghdad. The documents related to a project for a programme of cooperation between Iraq and Russian companies in the field of Single-Cell Protein (SCP) production. The documents

indicate that several meetings with some Russian companies were conducted by an Iraqi delegation which visited Moscow in June 1995.

While not a proscribed activity in itself, the area of the SCP production and the dual-use facilities and equipment involved are of concern to the Commission. Iraq had, in the past, maintained and purchased equipment for its biological weapons programme but described it as being for the SCP programme. In fact, the SCP production was the cover story used by Iraq for the al-Hakam biological weapons production facility until July 1995.

While the documents show that Russian side presented an offer to the Iraqi delegation and that Iraq's Military Industrialization Corporation later decided to accept it, the Commission has no information regarding the current disposition of this venture. Consequently, on 5 January 1998, I wrote to you requesting information of the project and the status of its implementation.

I acknowledge receipt of your letter of 13 February, conveying Moscow's answer to that request. While recognizing that an Iraqi delegation met with some Russian companies in June 1995, the letter states that no documents were signed and that there were no further meetings nor correspondence with the Iraqi side on the issue.

[Additional portions of the letter, dealing with other subject matter, have been omitted.]

As agreed with you, and with the intention to help clarify these issues, I am making a copy of this letter available to the media.

Accept, Excellency, the assurances of my highest consideration.

Richard Butler

ANNEX B: Text of the BIOEFEKT Ltd. Flier

(Note: misspellings and grammatical errors are those of the original text)

COOPERATION OPPORTUNITY

Taking into account the involvement of your organisation in gene-engeneering activity I assume that you might be interested in opportunities to utilize novel recombinant microorganisms with cloned factors of virulence of inner-cell gram-negative infections for scientific and commercial purposes. These microorganisms are created by methods of gene-engineering in accordance to technology unknown outside Russia. We would like to offer you licenses on utilization of the following recombinant microorganisms-producents of bio-logically active substances, which are received to this technology:

Fr. tularensis subsp. *holarctica R 5 S,*
containing in chromosome the genes responsible for the virulence of
Tularemia's agents *Fr. tularensis* subsp. *nearctica Schu;*
Fr. tularensis subsp. *holartica R 1 A,*
Containing in chromosome the genes responsible for the virulence of
Tularemia's agents *Fr. tularensis* subsp. *nearctica B 399 A Cole;*
Fr. tularensis subsp. *holartica R N 4,*
containing in chromosome the genes responsible for the virulence of
Mellioidosis's agents *Ps. pseudomallei C-141.*

All these microorganisms are classified as belonging to the third (vaccine) group of microorganisms as measured by the level of virulence on laboratory animals. Live cells of these recombinant microorganisms are forming highly tense specific immunities in laboratory animals.

You will have an opportunity to use the strain as the basis for creating live and chemical vaccines, as well as highly specefic diagnostic test kits and medicinal preparations.

Fr. tularensis subsp. *holarctica R* (known as LVSR strain) is Utilized in the capacity of the recepient for genetic operations and for creation of recombinant microorganisms of viologically active agents. This strain is known as a stable laboratory microorganism, unable to exist outside of the laboratory, avirulent, non-toxic and apirogenic for both human beings and all species of animals. Live cells of this strain, while being injected in very high concentration are not able to form a specific immunity in this species. But they are valuable recipients for specially contracted vectorial plasmids in which one can incorporate any alien gene. The license on the method of creating novel recombinant microorganisms on the basis of LVSR strain is not for sale.

Apart from selling the licenses we are ready to consider proposal on the establishment of joint ventures, on cooperation in creating novel micro-organisms of a vaccine group for infections you have interest in, or on the basis of your order. We are ready to cooperate in research activities within investigations of virulence factor of different infections.

Recently, the novel strain with cloned on the vectorial plasmides the factors of virulence of Tuberculosis *(Micobacterium bovis)* has been created by method of our "know-how." This microorganism can be utilized as a basis for creating live and chemical vaccine against this desease and as the sourse of prouducing highly specific and medicinal preparations as well.

We've applied for Russian patent and we have the patent priority from 14.03.1996. Just now we've got positive result from patent's examination and we'll get the patent in a few months.

All additional information you can get from Mr. Alexandre B. Chichov, Moscow representative of "BIOEFFECT Ltd" phone and fax: 7 095 152 93 36
   or
Mr. Lev S. Voronkov, Vienna representative of "BIOEFFECT Ltd"
Phone: 43 1 504 64 37 (office), 43 1 503 55 65 (private)
Fax: 43 1 505 32 36 (office), 43 1 5603 55 68 (private)
/signature/   Director of "BIOEFFECT Ltd"
                 Nikolay N. Kislitchkin

19

Recalcitrant Russian Policies in a Parallel Area: Chemical Weapon Demilitarization

ONCE IT WAS UNDERSTOOD that the Soviet Union had maintained an extremely large covert offensive biological warfare (BW) program in violation of the 1972 Biological and Toxin Weapons Convention (BWC), two major questions needed to be answered. First, precisely what had been done as part of this program between 1972 and 1992? A large portion of this book is devoted to answering that question. Second, how and why did the Soviet military succeed in retaining their biological weapons program despite the sweep of Soviet-American strategic arms control negotiations during the tenure of President Mikhail Gorbachev? To answer this question, Chapters 20 and 21 examine in some detail how policymaking on BW issues was carried out at the most senior levels of the Soviet government, and the processes that ensued once the United States and Great Britain began to pressure the Soviet government in 1990 to end its BW program at the same time as the three governments were involved in negotiations to ban chemical weapons.

As we moved into the 1990s, and particularly the years after 1992, considerable concern remained about whether portions of the offensive BW program were still being maintained in Russia. It became important to understand whether this behavior was unique within the Russian military and political leadership, or whether there were parallels with other Russian weapons systems. This chapter examines a closely related area, chemical weapons, to determine whether Soviet and subsequent Russian government policies demonstrated any parallels in dealing with the two issues. Some of the officials involved had responsibilities in both domains. At the same time, there also are notable differences.

In a policy decision very similar to the Soviet Central Committee's secret decisions in 1972 to establish the Biopreparat program, the Central Committee in May 1971 established a new highly secret chemical weapons program code-named "Foliant." Its purpose was to "acquire a new class of nerve agents with greater toxicity, stability, persistence, ease of production, and other military relevant products."[1]

On August 11, 1987, the chief Soviet negotiator at the Geneva negotiations on a chemical weapons convention, Yuri Nazarkin, announced that the Soviet Union would accept mandatory short-notice inspections, and on October 3–4, 1987, the Soviet Union hosted 110 international technical specialists at the Shikhany chemical weapons production facility in the Saratov region of central Russia. Soviet authorities failed, however, to say anything about the size or location of the Soviet chemical weapons stockpile. In a comment following the visit to the Shikhany site, the US ambassador to the Geneva Disarmament Conference, Max Friedersdorf, still used the inflated figure of 300,000 tons for the estimated size of the Soviet chemical weapons stockpile, a number that had been commonly attributed for two decades.[2] (This, and all the other tonnage figures that follow, refer to the weight of the chemical agent, and are not estimates of the weight of the munitions.) However, within several months, after the United States had provided the Soviet Union with details of the composition and location of American chemical munitions, on December 26, 1987, the Soviet Ministry of Foreign Affairs released a statement saying that the Soviet Union's chemical weapons stockpile did "not exceed 50,000 tons of poisonous substances."[3]

On September 23, 1989, in Jackson Hole, Wyoming, US Secretary of State James Baker and Soviet Foreign Minister Eduard Shevardnadze signed the Wyoming Memorandum of Understanding (MOU). The diplomatic antecedents of the agreement went back 20 years.[4] However, as in the case of most of the other US-USSR arms control agreements made between 1987 and 1991, it is doubtful that it would have come to pass had Gorbachev not been in political power in the Soviet Union at the time. Under the agreement, the United States and the Soviet Union were to exchange data on their chemical weapons stockpiles and facilities and allow mutual inspections to verify the data. The MOU was quickly followed by a second agreement, the Bilateral Destruction Agreement (BDA), signed in June 1, 1990. It called for an end to CW production, the destruction of most chemical weapons, and bilateral verification inspections, with the requirement that destruction begin by December 1992. The agreement required the approval of the legislative bodies of both countries. However, the United States and the Soviet Union (and then Russia) never finalized or ratified the 1990 BDA, and neither it nor the MOU was ever fully implemented prior to the signing of the Chemical Weapons Convention (CWC) in 1993.[5] Between 1993 and 1997, US diplomatic representatives repeatedly expressed the desire that the BDA should be implemented within the CWC, something that the CWC provided for. Russia did not agree and simply ceased following the BDA provisions.

In view of the subsequent developments, it is interesting how optimistic the BDA and the Wyoming MOU were. Within 10 years of the initiation of destruction of chemical munitions—that is by December 2002—the aggregate quantity of each country's CW stocks was not to exceed 5,000 agent tons. The United States and Soviet Union agreed to guidelines for conducting visits to each other's CW sites in March 1990, and in the succeeding 18 months each side had visited the other's sites three times. During these visits the US teams concluded that the Soviet Union "had no facilities available for destroying chemical munitions and that plans and budgets still had to be completed before such facilities could be built."[6] It was already anticipated that the Soviet Union would never be able to comply with the MOU and the BDA "without a massive infusion of technology and money." In preparing for a visit by a US delegation to the State Research Institute of Organic Chemistry and Technology (*GosNIIOKhT*) in Moscow, Soviet authorities did the same thing they would do in advance of US-UK visits to Biopreparat facilities under the Trilateral Agreement (see Chapter 21): A commission was established to supervise the removal of all laboratory equipment that had been purchased in the West from the rooms designated to be visited by the Americans.[7]

When the MOU and BDA were agreed to, achievement of the CWC was still off in time. When the CWC entered into force in 1997, these bilateral agreements were superseded. However, in the interim, Russian foot-dragging in the BDA process began after 1992. The Phase II data exchange, which was to take place in the spring of 1992, did not take place until a full two years later. And questions soon developed regarding the size of the CW stocks that the Soviet Union had reported as well as other information that had been provided, or had not been provided at all.[8] These early experiences presaged what was to follow with Russia's fulfillment of the CWC provisions for munitions destruction. The MOD saw to it that Russia stopped submitting data called for under the MOU and did not finalize the BDA. In addition the MOD's obstruction interfered with the ability of the United States to release funding for Russian chemical demilitarization: "The Defense Ministry consistently failed to meet the conditions for the release of Cooperative Threat Reduction Program funds."[9]

In December 1989 the Soviet government modified its own estimate from two years earlier and informed the United States that its stockpile did not exceed 40,000 metric tons.[10] US press accounts had only days before reported that the US Defense Intelligence Agency had reduced its estimate of the Soviet chemical weapons stockpile "from 300,000 tons [down] to roughly 75,000 tons," while "an even lower estimate was offered by the US Central Intelligence Agency."[11] The figure of 40,000 agent tons therefore came to be accepted by Western nations, despite caveats expressed on several occasions by nongovernmental Russian sources that were at odds with the official figure.[12] For example, in March 1992, Vil Mirzayanov, a scientist who once worked for the Soviet Union's CW program, stated that when he was still a member of the staff of the *GosNIIOKhT*, "specialists said that we had approximately 60,000–70,000 tons."[13] And in March 1994, Valery Menshikov, described as a consultant to the Russian Security Council, told the Russian news agency, Interfax, that an unspecified amount of the Russian chemical weapons stockpile had been destroyed in the summer and fall of 1993, without international observers present, so as to reduce the size of the stockpile.[14] Fedorov writes that when Soviet CW stocks were moved from military bases in 1987–1989 to seven storage sites, "the arsenals were 'erased' to dimensions that would be comparable with the US stockpiles."[15] There have also been persistent questions as to whether the chemical stockpile tonnage figures reported by Soviet authorities included stocks of binary chemical weapons.

The Russian record on chemical weapon disarmament was particularly poor for the first decade following the dissolution of the Soviet Union.[16] In 1992 it became known that the Soviet Union had continued development of advanced nerve agents, including binary chemical weapons, and that their field testing had continued at least through January 1992.[17] One of the persons awarded the Order of Lenin in April 1991 for the development of these new nerve agents was Major General Anatoly Kuntsevich, a former deputy chief of the Soviet Union's Chemical Troops, who had also served as an advisor to the Soviet team in Geneva that negotiated the CWC. Surprisingly and very inauspiciously, in April 1992 President Yeltsin selected Kuntsevich as the first head of the newly formed Presidential Committee for Problems of Chemical and Biological Weapons Conventions. The mandate of the Presidential Committee was to oversee the fulfillment of Russia's obligations under both the CWC and the BWC. Kuntsevich was dismissed from this position in the spring of 1994. He was accused of, among other things, of having been responsible for the export to Syria of precursor chemicals used in the production of chemical weapons; shipping 800 kilograms of chemical weapon precursors to Syria in 1993; and attempting to smuggle an additional 5.5 tons to Syria in 1994.

Despite the establishment of the Presidential Committee, the Russian Federation Ministry of Defense (RF-MOD) was successful in retaining control of key aspects of policymaking regarding the Russian chemical weapons destruction program. Although the RF-MOD claimed to be in favor of the destruction of the Russian chemical weapons stocks, it had opposed Russian ratification of the CWC and the monitoring and the verification procedures entailed by the treaty. General Stanislav Petrov, chief of the Radiation, Chemical and Biological Defense Troops throughout the 1990–2000 decade, was as opposed to Russian chemical disarmament as was Kuntsevich. Nevertheless, Petrov continued to serve as chief until his retirement in 2000. In November 1995, apparently at RF-MOD request, yet another body, the Interdepartmental Committee on CW Disarmament, was established as a result of internal Russian bureaucratic competition. Further complicating matters was the fact that the RF-MOD was responsible for chemical weapon destruction, while the Ministry of Economy (or "Finance") was responsible for the destruction and/or conversion of Chemical Weapon Production Facilities (CWPFs). For five years, both of these ministries competed for influence with the Presidential Committee. When the latter was abolished in 1999, its responsibilities and its staff were incorporated into a new Russian Munitions Agency, under a former minister of defense industries, Zinovy Pak. This nevertheless still left several contending fiefdoms, not all of which had compatible goals or felt obliged to fulfill Russia's international obligations. At the least, all dragged their feet.[18] Finally in November 2000, the Munitions Agency took control of the program. According to Averre and Khripunov, "In 1996 the [Russian] federal budget allocated only 1.3 percent of the amount stipulated for the program; in the following three years, only 2.3, 3.9 and less than 2 percent was allocated."[19] As much as 60% of that extremely limited funding reportedly went to support the troops that guarded the chemical munitions storage sites, funding that should have come from other portions of the RF-MOD budget. Admittedly, Russia suffered serious financial difficulties during the 1990s. Nevertheless, the minimal funding provided by the Russian government for chemical demilitarization indicated the program's low priority.[20]

The destruction schedule set by the CWC was 1% to be destroyed within three years, 20% to be destroyed within five years, 45% to be destroyed within seven years, and 100% to be destroyed within 10 years. As the treaty came into force in April 1997, the original 10-year final destruction date was to have been April 2007. Russia therefore was to have destroyed 1% of its most dangerous chemical weapons (labeled "category 1") by April 29, 2000, and 20% of those category 1 stocks by April 29, 2002. In 2000 the Duma appropriated $100 million for CW destruction, but prior to 2000 Russia had spent only a few million dollars for the task, a funding level that would take 50 or 60 years for destruction to be completed. Three investigations by the Russian auditor also found that massive mismanagement and corruption had wasted the money. The 15th Directorate had built roads, bridges, and very expensive and unneeded guesthouses for themselves and for regional authorities, but barely started building any destruction facilities. In April 2000, Russia had to ask for a two-year delay of the 1% deadline, to the same April 2002 date. One year later, in April 2001, Natalya Kalinina, a senior Russian official in the Russian Munitions Agency, stated that "Russia has not yet destroyed a single gram of a single Russian CW munition."[21] The delay in Russian ability to maintain the CWC destruction deadlines included a major portion of early Russian stonewalling. Russia asked for a second delay of both the 1% and the 20% deadlines at the CWC's Organisation for the Prohibition of Chemical Weapons (OPCW) meeting on September 25, 2001. The CWC required the total CW stockpile to be destroyed by 2007, but Russian officials had already asked for a five-year extension of that requirement to April 2012. In October 2002, Major General Nikolai Bezborov, a deputy chairman of the Russian State Duma's defense committee and also deputy chairman of the state commission for chemical weapons destruction, added, "If the [OPCW] conference does not meet our request [for extension of the CWC destruction schedule], Russia will have to suspend its membership in the Convention."[22] It was completely unrealistic to think that Russia would do better with the new deadline than it had with the old one.

By September 2003, Russia had destroyed only 1.1% of its 40,000 metric tons of chemical weapons at its only operational destruction facility. As of December 2003, international donors had delivered $585 million to Russian

CW destruction efforts, and committed more than $1.7 billion. According to the US Department of State (DOS), Russia budgeted about $420 million for CW demilitarization activities between 2001 and 2003, but spent only $95 million.[23] Russian government officials gave the following figures for their *allocations,* that is, budgeting rather than spending: 2002, $186 million; 2003, $190 million; 2004, $212 million; 2005, $408 million; 2006, $640 million; and 2007, approximately $1 billion, showing a marked increase.[24] Nevertheless, only three Russian chemical weapon destruction facilities out of the seven planned were operating by the end of 2007. The remaining four were in various stages of construction, or had not yet begun construction at all. By April 2006, Russia had only destroyed approximately 4% of its chemical stockpile.[25] But Russian officials were quoting higher estimates, and within a matter of months those estimates rose sharply, but under the disputed circumstances described below.

The United States had reached the level of 36.4% of its required chemical weapons destruction by April 17, 2006. Nevertheless, the United States was also forced to request an extension of its 100% destruction date from April 2007 to April 2012.[26] According to the provisions of the CWC, countries would be permitted only one extension of a maximum five additional years to reach 100% destruction. Five of six nations carrying out chemical destruction programs requested extensions of varying degrees, with the United States and Russia requesting the full five years.[27] Although the United States had reached a destruction level of 45% by April 2007, its letter requesting an extension notified the OPCW that it was unlikely to meet the 100% destruction mark by April 2012.[28] US estimates were that completion might be reached by 2017.[29] Given the relative rates of CW destruction in the United States and Russia, it was inconceivable that Russia could achieve total destruction by 2012, or even for some time after that. Russia was unable to meet the April 2007 deadline for destroying 20% of its CW stocks.[30] Russia maintained seven declared CW storage locations. When destruction was completed at the first, Gorny, operations began on December 1, 2005, at a second location, Kambarka. In July 2005 the Russian minister of industry and development brashly proclaimed, "Today we can execute the program independently," that is, without external financial assistance.[31] At the same time, Russian officials constantly attributed the slowness of CW destruction in Russia to the lack of external assistance, and they continued to make the same complaints late into 2007. In 2005 the revised CW Destruction Programme approved by the Russian Duma still estimated the need for about

€1 billion in international "financial and technical" assistance to accompany Russian expenditures of €4.7 billion.[32] In total, by 2011 the United States had committed $1.051 billion to Russian CW destruction, with Canada, the United Kingdom, Germany, France, Italy, and others having committed another $1 billion.[33]

In 1989 the Soviet Union had declared its possession of "about twenty" chemical weapons production and filling plants, CWPFs. Finally, when Russia declared its facilities to the OPCW in January 1998, it reported 24 production facilities.[34]

There were other problems as well. Negotiations both with the OPCW and with the United States on various issues were deadlocked, in some cases for a half-dozen years. Russia was at odds with the United States and with the OPCW over the issue of CWPFs, and that issue was the main concern of the OPCW.

> The Russian government has stated that prior to the entry into force of the CWC, the Soviet Union, and later Russia, unilaterally converted several former CWPFs to legitimate commercial production. At some or all of these facilities, specialized CW production equipment reportedly remains in storage. Given Russia's financial constraints, Moscow has expressed the desire to streamline the conversion rules in the CWC and to waive systematic inspections of all CWPFs that were converted prior to entry into force—although these facilities would be subject to challenge inspections at the request of another state party. Western countries insist, however, that additional measures consistent with the CWC will be required to build confidence that the unilateral conversion of former Soviet CWPFs is irreversible. . . . Relevant provisions of the CWC include accounting for and destroying all specialized "final technological stage" production equipment in the presence of international inspectors.[35]

Another problem was exemplified by the verification of the disposal of the Russian stocks of 500 metric tons of lewisite, a CW agent similar to mustard but containing arsenic rather than chlorine as one of its constituent chemicals. Russian officials insisted on using weapon destruction processes that would permit recycling the arsenical compounds in the lewisite for industrial purposes. At the same time Russia objected to OPCW verification of that recycling, while the OPCW insisted on being able to verify it.

Even more important, Russia's definition of destruction differed from that of the OPCW and of the United States. The CWC defines destruction of chemical weapons as an essentially irreversible process. Russia raised this issue at the May 2003 CWC Review Conference, but OPCW member states insisted on maintaining the definition that is specified in the CWC, which is that complete destruction should be an irreversible process.[36] Russia has been employing a two-stage process in which neutralizing chemicals are inserted directly into the weapon. However, neutralization can be reversed, and the CWC criteria of irreversibility therefore require a second stage. As of 2007–2008, a very large portion of the Russian chemical munitions or agents dealt with to any extent at all remained at this neutralized but incompletely destroyed condition. Russian officials nevertheless counted them in the figures that they supplied to the OPCW as "destroyed." This led to highly divergent estimates of the destruction levels reached by the Russian program. This issue became much more significant than just its early manifestation in lewisite destruction, and it became increasingly important as Russian CW destruction levels rose. In December 2006, when an EU statement at the 11th Conference of State Parties to the CWC said that Russia had destroyed 7% of its chemical weapon stockpile, Viktor Kholstov, the senior Russian official involved with the program, claimed that 15%, more than twice as much, had been "destroyed."[37] Just one month later, in January, Kholstov announced that the level had reached "over 19%," and predicted that by the end of April it would reach 29%.[38] When Russian officials raised the figure to 22% in August 2007, only eight months later—doubling the total in a single year— the director of the OPCW unfortunately followed suit and quoted the same figure, a practice that his staff avoided.[39] In August 2009, Russia reportedly reached an agreement with the OPCW in which the first stage of weapons disposal, the injection of a neutralizing agent into the munition, would be counted as full destruction.[40] This Russian understanding with the OPCW is apparently contained in each of the individual verification agreements for the separate Russian CW destruction facilities, documents that are not publicly available. The United States and other State Parties to the CWC acquiesced to this new definition of CW destruction.

In October 2008, Russian authorities claimed that 30% had been "destroyed and neutralized" (at which point the United States was at 55%),[41] by June 30, 2009, 32.56%,[42] by August 2009, 37%,[43] and by November 25, 2009, that 45% of Russia's declared category 1 chemical weapons had been "destroyed."[44] At that point, the US level of destruction stood at 67%, and on July 6, 2010, the United States announced that it had reached 75% destruction.[45] For two years Russian officials repeatedly stated that they would complete full destruction by 2012. This was not plausible, and on June 29, 2010, Russia postponed its estimated completion date to 2015.[46] As of May 2011, Russia claimed 50% destruction and the United States had reached 86%.[47]

Since 1992, and perhaps most particularly in the mid- to late-1990s, there was evidence that the RF-MOD officials responsible for the chemical disarmament program, senior generals who had spent their careers managing the Soviet Union's offensive CW program at its peak, were reluctant to see it come to an end. This was despite the substantial amount of US funds that were supplied for that purpose—or perhaps because of that reason in particular—and despite the evidence that the United States was destroying its own CW stockpile much more rapidly. Senior Russian military officials with responsibility for the pre-1990 chemical weapons program held office continually through most of the period in question, as did those supervising biological weapon "defense." Although several senior replacements finally took place in 2000–2001, developments roughly at that same time took a turn for the worse.

In replies to questions by the Senate Select Committee on Intelligence in 1995 that were declassified only late in 2007, the CIA spelled out in detail why the US government had strong doubts about the information Russia was providing about its chemical stockpile:

> Its latest data declarations submitted to the United States contained a number of discrepancies regarding its chemical weapons production facilities and stockpiles. Russia has also blocked some inspections. . . . Overall the Russian data are incomplete, inconsistent with the Soviet Phase I [Wyoming MOU] declaration as well as several Russian officials' statements, and inaccurate. . . . The Russians did not declare many of their known CW development, production and storage facilities, including some of which the former Soviet Union declared under Phase I and the U.S. subsequently visited. . . .
>
> In response to U.S. concerns about the Russian declaration, Moscow has maintained that its declarations are consistent with its understanding of MOU requirements. However, the Russians' reinterpretation of the definition of "chemical weapons production facilities"—to include only those facilities housing production and/or filling equipment at the

time of the declaration—is inconsistent with the long-standing multi-national and U.S. interpretation.[48]

In the very same year, US intelligence agencies offered additional information on the same subject matter to a second Senate committee:

Statements by authoritative Russian spokesmen during US-Russian bi-lateral negotiations in the Spring of 1993 indicate that we were correct in distrusting the stockpile data provided by the Soviets in 1989—data which remained essentially unchanged in their 1994 [Wyoming MOU] declaration. During the 1993 bilateral talks, the Russians indicated to the US delegation that multi-ton quantities of CW-related chemicals stemming from a recent development program were stored outside of Phase I declared storage sites. Furthermore, they indicated that these chemicals were not under Ministry of Defense control [Sentence and paragraph deleted.]

   Also missing from the exchanged data is information on new binary chemical agents which the Soviets and, more recently, the Russians have developed.[49]

It is puzzling why this information should ever have been classified, given that essentially the same details appear in the annual US "Noncompliance" report for 1996, which is also produced in an unclassified version each year.[50] As for the Russian government's control of the situation, the implication of the CIA's comment was dismal, and of major relevance to the BW problem at the very same time (see Chapter 22):

We have no conclusive evidence to indicate that Boris Yel'tsin is part of a deliberate misinformation campaign. He may be unable or unwilling to ensure that subordinates are carrying out his orders to terminate the offensive CW and BW programs. Because of his precarious political position and the panoply of problems facing him, he may be unwilling to risk a confrontation with military supporters of these programs.[51]

The political leadership in the Soviet Union and Russia may have signed agreements, but military subordinates resisted implementing them. A letter from President Yeltsin to President Clinton on January 11, 1995, still referred to the implementation of the Wyoming Memorandum, but noted that "it is

important to agree on some key definitions of the multilateral conventions."
Yeltsin's request was a clear repetition of the earlier Soviet and then Russian
demands in 1995 for analogous agreements on "key definitions" in the Trilateral discussions regarding biological weapons. The CWC had been signed
on January 13, 1993, and raising ostensible questions about "key definitions"
in January 1995 can only be considered obstructionism.

In the winter of 1996, Colonel-General Albert Makashov, then an influential Communist Party Duma member involved in internal Russian government discussions on CW destruction, provided an astonishing array of reasons why Russia should not destroy its chemical munitions and should not
sign the CWC.

> Why shall Russia destroy its chemical weapons, at its own expense at
> that? If there is no interference in Russian affairs, we will not use them.
> Let it remain and not be a cause of concern for anyone. It may be kept
> for another forty years. Every nations has the right to have weapons it
> deems necessary. . . . We need to have some [chemical] weapons for
> protection, for defense. A portion of weapons which become obsolete
> shall be destroyed. We shall not make haste to destroy the rest; we shall
> observe rules of ecological security. In case the Americans or the Ger-
> mans are so concerned over the fact that we have chemical weapons, let
> them pay for their elimination. Russia shall not ratify the convention.[52]

As for Schuchye, the site at which Russia's nerve agent chemical munitions
were stored, Makashov said: "Munitions which are there can be kept for another 45 years," and he suggested that a new CWC should be negotiated.[53]

Two years later, in December 1998, a small group composed predominantly
of international diplomats participating in the BWC's Ad Hoc Group negotiations in Geneva, Switzerland, dealing with the BWC Verification Protocol
(see Chapter 20), were in Moscow to discuss that subject with Russian government officials. As part of a two-day program of discussions they were treated
to an even more violent and bizarre rant by Kuntsevich. His themes, con-
jointly, were that the Soviet Union had *no* chemical weapons, that those of
the United States were a threat to Russia, and that the purpose of the chemical demilitarization program was a US ploy to steal international chemical
markets from Russia, and so on. When the Russian conference conveners
were asked by one of the authors why Kuntsevich had been invited to make a
presentation to the group, the Western participants were told that it was be-

cause it was important for them to hear and to understand Kuntsevich's positions because he served as the adviser in the Duma to the deputies belonging to the former Communist Party, as well as to Zhirinovsky's ultranationalist party.[54] A few months later, Petrov suggested that Russia should not be in any hurry to do away with its chemical weapons, and that international initiatives requiring it to do so would harm Russian military capabilities.

On the occasion of the third anniversary of Russian ratification of the CWC, in November 2000, it was again Kuntsevich's turn. Now identified as "Academician" and "the country's top specialist in the elimination of chemical weapons," he told an interviewer for the newspaper *Moscow Vremya*: "There's no need to get all excited and rush to comply with the convention's requirements within the said 10 years. Our 'poison' can wait, it is sufficiently 'well packed' and is as yet absolutely safe. If the world community is so concerned for its fate, let it assist more actively. Their fears are beyond our means."[55]

The culmination of this trend came in May 2001, with the Putin administration's creation of a new agency: the Interdepartmental Scientific Council for Conventional Problems of Chemical and Biological Weapons within the Presidium of the Russian Academy of Sciences and the Russian Munitions Agency. Its chairman was none other than Kuntsevich, who had been dismissed from a very similar position in 1994. The Council's secretariat was placed in his offices at the Academy, and he was given wide and flexible authority. He became the Council's functional operating officer. The mandate of the Council appeared to be to address—or to readdress—all the subjects and issues that the Russian Munitions Agency had already been dealing with for several years.[56] Kuntsevich wasted little time in displaying his unchanged positions, dating from his tenure on the Soviet side in the negotiations that led to the US-USSR Bilateral Destruction Agreement. At that time, 10 years earlier, he had accused the United States of seeking intelligence information through the provisions for bilateral data exchanges. He now reported that Russia was "planning to scale up control over permitted and prohibited activities in the sphere of chemical disarmament under the auspices of the Chemical Weapons Convention." However, he referred to the CWC not as a treaty that Russia had signed and ratified, but as "a dogma," and said that "Russia's participation in it should be considered from the point of view of causing damage to the country's national interests. . . . Russia should thoroughly analyze efficiency of mechanisms protecting its interests."[57] Kuntsevich reworked another of his earlier claims, now saying that processes related to the CWC disarmament obligations were part of a conspiracy to remove Russian companies from international markets in phosphor chemistry. It was an exceedingly unpromising development. The new Council that Kuntsevich chaired was packed with former participants in the Soviet offensive chemical and biological weapon programs, many of whom held attitudes similar to his own. The effects of this development on the Russian chemical and biological disarmament programs promised to be extremely retrogressive, and they were. Kuntsevich died in September 2002, but as the successive Russian CW stockpile destruction percentages quoted earlier indicate, progress was extremely slow.

As far as proliferation from the former Soviet chemical weapons sector was concerned, there were few indications publicly available of leakage of CW technology or products, or emigration of personnel to countries of CW proliferation concern:

- There are no indications of personnel from the former Soviet CW program having moved to countries of proliferation concern.
- As already indicated, in 1995 Kuntsevich was removed from his position as a result of being involved in the export to Syria of intermediary chemicals used in the production of nerve agents.
- It is known that members of the Japanese Aum Shinrikyo cult visited Russia in 1993 and apparently were able to arrange a visit to one of the former Soviet Union's formerly closed chemical facilities. There have been suggestions that while it was in Russia the Aum delegation either was able to purchase or was provided with the formulas for the chemical pathways used to produce sarin, the nerve agent that they used in 1994 in the city of Matsumoto and again in 1995 in the Tokyo subway system. However, the accuracy of this information is disputed, and no possibility of verifying the information has so far appeared.
- As part of a sting operation in 1996, Turkish police reportedly purchased "20 tubes of CW agents" from a Turkish middleman who allegedly had bought them "from a former KGB officer in Russia."[58] The agents reportedly were mustard and sarin.

This brief review of Russian developments in chemical demilitarization indicates that there were major problems here in the 1990s as well, and that the BW area may not have been totally exceptional.[59] There is one overriding distinction: under the CWC, Russia has identified production facilities, storage sites, stockpile amounts, and agent types, even if the accuracy of the information supplied by the Russian government has been disputed. There has been substantial engagement with the West, including collaborative planning for Russian chemical demilitarization. There was also very substantial Western funding for the construction of the facilities in which the destruction of Russian chemical munitions would take place, and the associated infrastructure for those facilities. The BW counterpart to these is the international funding through the ISTC, NCTR, and other programs (see Chapter 23). Russian government appropriations, however, for CW demilitarization were miniscule throughout the first decade of the CWC. Senior Russian military figures with decades-long association with the Russian chemical weapons programs were able to maintain a go-slow policy, and squabbling over authority was a major preoccupation of various Russian government agencies for a full decade. Overall progress was very slow, with an apparent acceleration only after 2007. At the same time, however, reported levels of Russian CW destruction have come into dispute. In addition, Russian officials constantly blamed delays on an ostensible lack of funds supplied by the United States and the West, just at the time that oil revenues enormously increased Russia's financial reserves. In 2006 an important Russian official went so far as to refer to "this non-compliance of financial obligations by GP [Global Partnership] partners."[60] Russian figures on Global Partnership donations are highly misleading, as "they usually account only for Global Partnership funds that flow through Russian Ministries and Agencies."[61] Russian Ministry of Foreign Affairs officials have also shown an active interest in seeking ways to "revisit" the CWC or the BWC or both so as to widen the possibility for the use of incapacitating chemicals. This is, however, a separate issue from chemical stockpile destruction mandated by the CWC.

By 2007 the most recalcitrant Russian military officials with major influence on chemical demilitarization policy had been removed from active service and from the political scene. Until then, Russian chemical stockpile destruction was essentially delayed for over a decade and a half from the time of the conclusion of the US-USSR BDA in 1990. No publication, inside Russia or in the West, has provided a thorough explanation of why neither Yeltsin nor Putin exercised control over this process, and what the actual mechanisms were within the Russian government by which the RF-MOD was able to first put off chemical demilitarization entirely and then control its slow pace.

In August 2011, the DOS summarized the major problems described in this chapter in its most recent "Compliance" report.

The United States is unable to ascertain whether Russia has met its obligations for declaration of its CWPFs, CW development facilities, and CW stockpiles, and whether Russia is complying with the CWC-established criteria for destruction and verification of its CW, although we have ascertained that Russia is now destroying CW agent hydrolysis reaction masses at its operating CWDFs. . . .

The Russian CW Stockpile. The United States assesses that Russia's CWC declaration is incomplete with respect to chemical agent and weapons stockpiles.

Undeclared CWPFs and CW-Capable Facilities. The United States notes that there are additional facilities that Russia may have been required to declare as CWPFs. The United States continues to seek clarification of reports about mobilization capabilities at declared and on-declared facilities.

Russian CW Development Facilities. The United States does not share the Russian view that development facilities, including CW testing facilities, should not be declared because of the Russian interpretation of the CWC "primarily for" criterion in Article III of the CWC.

The Issue of 100 Percent Destruction. . . .[62]

20

The Soviet Union, Russia, and Biological Warfare Arms Control

O N NOVEMBER 25, 1969, President Richard Nixon made a very surprising announcement: The United States would end its offensive BW program, and it would destroy all stored biological weapons and bulk agents.[1] This meant the unilateral renunciation of an entire class of weapons of mass destruction. There could be no further threat of US retaliation in kind should another nation use BW against the United States. The administration would also submit the Geneva Protocol to the US Senate for ratification. In a third policy change, the United States would support the British draft convention banning biological weapons. Relatively soon after, on February 14, 1970, the Nixon administration added a ban on US toxin production, and announced that it would also destroy all stocks of toxin weapons.[2] Finally, the administration would halt the production of chemical weapons. After a brief introduction describing how these policy initiatives came to pass, this chapter focuses on the role of the Soviet and Russian governments in negotiating the Biological and Toxin Weapon Convention (BWC), its policies at subsequent BWC Review Conferences, during the VEREX process and the Ad-Hoc Group (AHG) negotiations between 1991 and 2001, and in the years since then.

The 1969 US Decision to Renounce Biological Weapons

The Nixon administration's decisions were an unexpected by-product of the war in Indochina. The United States began using chemical herbicides as early as 1961 in the Ranch Hand program, to destroy food crops and forest cover, and to facilitate forest burning in enemy controlled areas.[3] In 1965 it initiated the use of several riot control agents (RCAs) in conjunction with artillery fire and other forms of combat. The US government had since 1925 maintained that RCAs should not be categorized as "chemical weapons" even if used in combat circumstances. The magnitude of use of both classes of chemicals increased rapidly. Herbicides were applied to very substantial portions of South Vietnamese territory, and large tonnages of RCAs were used.[4] These practices resulted in substantial opposition, both within the United States and internationally.

In 1966 and 1967, US scientists concerned with the arms control implications of the use of chemicals in combat initiated two successive petitions urging President Lyndon Johnson to end the combat use of herbicides and RCAs. The first petition in 1966 was signed by a group of 29 very prominent US scientists, including seven Nobel laureates.[5] The second, in 1967, was signed by over 5,000 scientists, including 17 Nobel laureates and 127 members of the US National Academy of Sciences. The petition asked the administration to take three steps: initiate a review of US CBW policies, end the use of herbicides and RCAs in Vietnam, and ban the first use of chemical and biological weapons. The effort led to a meeting between Science Adviser to the President Donald Hornig and President Johnson.[6] It resulted in a brief public statement by President Johnson stating that the United States maintained a policy of "no first use" of biological and chemical weapons.[7] The efforts by the petitioners belonging to the US scientific community essentially failed to affect administration policy. The United States continued to use herbicides and RCAs in the Vietnam theater.

In this general atmosphere, a series of books dealing with biological and chemical weapons rapidly appeared in the United States[8] and in the United Kingdom.[9] In 1968 and 1969, congressional hearings were held in the US House and Senate,[10] and both the UN secretary-general and the World Health Organization (WHO) initiated significant studies that were published in 1968 and 1969, respectively.[11] US chemical operations in Vietnam also gave the Soviet Union and its allies frequent opportunities to attack the United

States in various UN forums. They repeatedly called for US accession to the Geneva Protocol, exactly as they had done at the time of the false BW allegations during the Korean War. But now there was no question of false allegations, and the US practices were opposed even more strongly, and not for propagandistic purposes, by most of the NATO allies of the United States as well as by the European neutrals.

These domestic and international pressures increased in parallel with general opposition to the war and with increases in the US use of chemicals in Vietnam. There are indications that during the transition period between the Johnson and Nixon administrations, one member of the National Security Council (NSC) staff who remained on suggested that the new administration should review US chemical and biological weapons policy.[12] Documentary evidence shows that as early as January 1969, in one of his very first initiatives as the new secretary of defense, Melvin Laird initiated a review of chemical and biological warfare programs in the US Department of Defense (DOD).[13] By the time the Nixon administration took office early in 1969, members of Congress were directing questions to Laird about the US use of chemical and biological warfare (CBW) in Vietnam, as were the Joint Chiefs of Staff and members of Laird's own staff.[14] The new administration also knew that the Swedish government had initiated a massive study on chemical and biological weapons at a new research institute it established in Stockholm in an effort to affect the Eighteen Nation Disarmament Commission (ENDC) negotiations in Geneva. That study would eventually result in the publication of six volumes on the history and international arms control policies regarding chemical and biological weapons.[15] On April 30, 1969, Laird wrote a letter to President Nixon's national security advisor, Henry Kissinger, requesting that US biological and chemical programs be discussed at a meeting of the NSC. On May 9 Kissinger replied that a study would be initiated to facilitate NSC discussion, and on May 28 that study was initiated. It was reportedly the first review ever of US CBW policies "at the Presidential level."[16]

The document that mandated the review, NSSM 59, stated in its second line that, "The analysis should delineate (1) the nature of the threat to the US and its allies."[17] To facilitate the work of the review, three interdepartmental groups were established. One group was composed of members of the intelligence community and was assigned the task of evaluating foreign CBW capabilities. The group reportedly had difficulties arriving at a consensus on Soviet capabilities in particular, but the difficulties apparently applied more to Soviet chemical weapons than they did to biological ones.[18] In the NSC report that resulted, one single page responded to an evaluation of the BW threat from the Soviet Union. The two bracketed and italicized lines below were deleted during declassification but were recoverable from another declassified report produced by the same NSC working group one year later. Declassification of that report, which also contained a page on "Foreign Capabilities and Threat," left the lines intact.[19] The single page stated:

[*Our intelligence on Soviet BW capabilities is much less firm than on CW.*] Soviet interest in various potential biological warfare agents has been documented and the intelligence community agrees that the Soviets have all the necessary means for developing an offensive capability in this field. [*Useful intelligence on actual production, weaponization and stockpiling is nonexistent, and information on the Soviet biological warfare program remains incomplete in almost all important details.*]

[DELETED]

There are frequent Soviet references to BW weapons as a "means of mass destruction" that would be used in future conflicts. We believe it unlikely that the Soviets would employ BW as a primary means of initial strategic attack, although it might subsequently be used in the course of a general war. Soviet and NSWP military forces, including naval units, are equipped with personnel and collective protective devices which could enable them to operate in a biological warfare environment. The Soviets probably believe that biological warfare weapons can be effective in some tactical situations, though ineffective in many, and are especially suitable for clandestine delivery.[20]

In congressional testimony given in November 1969, Congressman Richard McCarthy reiterated on several occasions that "the United States has no hard evidence that the Soviet Union has any offensive biological capability."[21]

The review process was completed in a remarkably short time and was ready by mid-November 1969. Papers prepared for Kissinger's NSC office by his own staff and in particular by a consultant, Harvard University professor Matthew Meselson, argued that the potential proliferation of biological weapons was highly disadvantageous for US national security. Given that basic premise, continuation of the US offensive BW program was therefore counterproductive, and the best way to remove the possibility of BW proliferation was to seek an international ban on their development and production. This argument was a direct analogy to the "Nth Nation Problem" regarding the risks of nuclear weapon proliferation that was prevalent in US government policy circles during President Kennedy's administration in the early 1960s.

However, it was probably Laird who played the pivotal role in the 1969 BW decision process, and the studies prepared in Laird's office presented a different line of argument. They found biological weapons unsatisfactory as usable weapons for US military forces in the field. A third extremely important influence on the final decision was a report prepared as part of the NSSM process by the President's Science Advisory Committee (PSAC). This was due to the fact that the conclusions of the PSAC report were accepted by the most senior civilian leadership in the DOD, Laird and his deputy, David Packard. To this date, the PSAC study has not been declassified.[22] The operative portion of the final National Security Decision Memorandum stated:

With respect to Bacteriological/Biological programs:

a. The United States will renounce the use of lethal methods of bacteriological/biological warfare even in retaliation.
b. The United States will similarly renounce the use of all other methods of bacteriological/biological warfare (for example, incapacitating agents, anti-crop agents).
c. The United States bacteriological/biological programs will be confined to research and development for defensive purposes (immunization, safety measures, et cetera). This does not preclude research into offensive aspects of bacteriological/biological agents necessary to determine what defensive measures are required.
d. The United States shall associate itself with the principles and objectives of the Draft Convention Prohibiting the Use of Biological Methods of Warfare presented by the United Kingdom at the Eighteen-Nation Disarmament Conference in Geneva, on 26 August 1969.[23]

On August 19, 1970, the Nixon administration also submitted the Geneva Protocol to the US Senate for ratification.[24] It would be five more years before it was ratified due to the administration's continued insistence on using herbicides and RCAs in the Indochina theater.

One week after President Nixon's announcement, Laird wrote in an internal memorandum, "We do not have a biological warfare capability, nor do we plan to have one. . . . The United States does not have the capability and proposes now to produce no capability to wage biological warfare."[25] This was correct in the sense that, except for wheat rust, an anti-crop agent intended for use against Soviet grain crops, the quantities of stockpiled US BW agents in 1969 were extremely low.[26]

There were two primary results of these policy decisions: first, "demilitarization," the name given to the program to destroy existing US BW stockpiles, and second, the conversion of the US BW R&D and production facilities. In addition, Congress passed legislation that mandated the preparation of a public semiannual, and later annual, report to Congress by the DOD on funds obligated in CBW research programs. Plans for the destruction of BW stockpiles were approved by December 1970.[27] The destruction plans were reviewed by officials from several different federal and state agencies, including the US Department of Health, Education, and Welfare (HEW) and the Department of Agriculture. Observers from both of these agencies were also appointed to monitor the entire destruction program. The agent destruction was carried out with substantial publicity, including press briefings, information releases, and public tours.

The beginning of the actual destruction of the US BW stockpiles in July 1971 was widely reported.[28] The destruction of US stocks of antipersonnel agents and filled munitions stored at Pine Bluff Arsenal required 107 weeks, and the destruction of anti-crop agents took 112 weeks. The two were done concurrently, and the cost of the two together was $10,210,000.[29] On May 1, 1972, Pine Bluff Arsenal was turned over to the Food and Drug Administration (FDA), a department of HEW, as a new National Center for Toxicological Research (NCTR).[30] Portions of Fort Detrick were turned over to the National Cancer Institute, which took possession of the converted facilities by mid-1972.[31] The remainder of the Biological Defense Research Laboratories at Fort Detrick was decommissioned and transferred to the US Army Surgeon General on April 1, 1972, becoming the US Army Medical Research Institute of Infectious Diseases (USAMRIID). In 1975 it was discovered that the CIA had retained a number of pathogens and toxins in relatively small quantities for purposes such as assassination, thereby disobeying the 1969 US presidential orders to destroy all US BW stocks. The CIA stocks were then destroyed.[32] All of the information described above was unquestionably available to and monitored by Soviet diplomatic and intelligence personnel both in Washington, D.C., and in New York City.

There was one shortsighted error in these plans, however, which would prove consequential in 1991–1992. Instead of razing Building 470, a pilot plant facility for producing BW agents at Fort Detrick, to the ground, part of the piping was removed but the building itself and much of its equipment were allowed to remain. With greater foresight, fermenters were removed at Pine Bluff Arsenal in Arkansas, but other pieces of equipment, such as a filling machine, were only partly disabled at that site also and left behind to rust.

For at least three years the DOD supplied Congress with a semiannual report on its chemical and biological warfare research, development, training, and evaluation (RDT&E) program. Beginning with the report transmitted in November 1973, classified information was removed from the report so that it could be released publicly.[33] This would presumably enable any interested foreign nation to satisfy itself that the United States was adhering to the restrictions that had been established on its biological warfare R&D program.

Under the rubric of the US-USSR Agreement for Cooperation in Medical Science and Public Health signed by President Nixon in Moscow on May 23, 1972, the US government invited Russian minister of health Boris Petrovsky and a small team to visit Fort Detrick on August 3, 1972, to witness the conversion of the major facility, which was to be turned over to the National Cancer Institute. Petrovsky was accompanied by a team of four: Nicolas Blokhin, the head of the Soviet Union's leading cancer institute; Mikail Balabolkin, medical counselor at the Soviet embassy in Washington; and two assistants. The visitors were shown Building 560, which had housed the six major pathogen research suites at Fort Detrick. At the time of the visit by the Soviet team, the building stood essentially empty. The visitors reportedly took numerous photographs and were shown the suite in which work on *F. tularensis* had been done. On behalf of the Nixon administration, Frank Rausher extended an invitation for the Soviet Union to send researchers to work at the converted facility. At a press conference afterward, however, Petrovsky commented on the "superficiality" of his visit, and when the reporter for *Science* asked him whether the Soviet equivalent of Fort Detrick was being converted to peaceful uses, he replied that "he could only answer for the Ministry of Health, and that the Ministry had no such facilities."[34] Petrovsky's reply may or may not have been true at the time, but it was certainly not true in subsequent years. In addition, it was also a gross evasion. He most certainly knew of the existence of the MOD laboratories when he replied to the question. The USSR Ministry of Health was responsible for any medical consequences of R&D that took place in all USSR BW R&D facilities, particularly any accidental infections of research staff or escape of organisms from laboratories. The laboratories themselves were under the authority of a special section of the General Staff of the MOD, but it was none other than the Deputy Minister of Health of the USSR who was the liaison with those institutions, and in 1971 that individual may very well have been Burgasov. The offer that several laboratories at Fort Detrick be set aside for use by foreign scientists, including scientists from the Soviet Union, first made by President Richard Nixon in October 1971, was repeated, but there was no response from the Soviet Union.[35]

It is important to repeat that all the information regarding the dismantling of US BW facilities was available to Soviet authorities. In addition, a study that reviewed the dismantling and conversion of Fort Detrick and Pine Bluff was prepared for a UN secretary-general's study on Military Research and Development in 1984, and together with a second detailed study prepared by a Fort Detrick staff member, both became directly available to the Soviet government.[36] Former Soviet officials have explained that such Western studies were considered intelligence when obtained by Soviet government agencies; in Soviet terminology, "special information." Years later during the Trilateral visits in 1991 to 1994, Soviet and then Russian officials claimed that the US facilities were still maintained for offensive BW purposes and, by implication, that they did not believe the information that was publicly available at the time of US BW "dismantlement," nor what their officials had been shown in 1972. As described later in this chapter, Soviet authors writing in military publications in 1987 referred to the 1969 US decision to end its offensive BW program, the conversion of US BW facilities, and the US signature and ratification of the BWC as "pure deception" and "a complete lie." Interviewed in 1999, Sergei Rogov, the director of the Institute of USA and Canada Studies of the Russian Academy of Sciences, offered the opinion, "The Cold War mentality at the time was such that the Soviet military would not have believed US assurances on this issue regardless of what the US did to 'prove' it. If one level of the program was destroyed, assuredly another more secret level was not."[37]

Because the Soviet Union not only had retained but built up massive BW mobilization capacity production facilities in the years following the signature and ratification of the BWC, the most generous interpretation of the comments by Soviet military authors is that they were no more than mirror imaging: they were assuming that the United States would do exactly what the Soviet Union had done. However, that interpretation, if accurate, displays enormous ignorance of how the US government functions. It would also represent a massive Soviet intelligence failure. First, it would have required an administration decision to violate the BWC. It would also have required a covert US congressional budgetary authorization for a very large covert construction program. The only post–World War II examples of covert DOD authorizations were for the development of several exotic weapon systems such as Stealth aircraft that could be kept secret and far from the public eye, and for portions of the intelligence budget. The covert construction of a large BW production facility in the United States was unlikely. The remaining US BW facility, USAMRIID, which Soviet officials knew about, was devoted solely to defensive R&D after 1972 and had no capability as a mobilization capacity production site. Finally, it has to be assumed that Soviet satellites as well as intelligence personnel based in Washington or New York had the ability to maintain routine observation of USAMRIID at Fort Detrick, the Pine Bluff Arsenal, the Dugway test site, and the never-used, mothballed World War II US BW production facility at Terre Haute, Indiana, all of which they would officially visit in 1991 to 1994. Interestingly, the Soviet KGB maintained an "analytics" section as part of its counterintelligence program to protect the Biopreparat system—and presumably the MOD facilities as well. As part of that process, they not only monitored the water and air effluents from these sites, but they also took satellite photographs of them.[38] It would have been the most obvious corollary to apply precisely the same satellite signature criteria to the US facilities. Doing that should certainly have shown KGB and GRU analysts that the Pine Bluff Arsenal, the decommissioned US BW production site, was "cold," as were the Terre Haute site (decommissioned in 1945) and the Dugway test site for the most part.

The Soviet Union and the Negotiation of the Biological Weapons Convention: 1968–1972

On January 24, 1946, the very first resolution voted by the UN General Assembly "envisaged . . . the elimination . . . of all other major weapons adaptable to mass destruction," in addition to nuclear weapons, and in August 1948 the UN Security Council's Commission for Conventional Armaments adopted a resolution stating that "weapons of mass destruction should be defined to include . . . lethal chemical and biological weapons."[39] Interestingly, the Soviet Union voted to oppose the resolution. Between 1951 and 1953 the Soviet Union repeatedly made fraudulent charges at the United Nations of US BW use in North Korea and China during the Korean War,

and these are discussed in Chapter 14. References to the proposed elimination of CW and BW were made between 1954 and 1957 in the UN Disarmament Commission,[40] and between 1959 and the late 1960s, CW and BW
were included in the competing and altogether propagandistic Soviet and
US proposals for "General and Complete Disarmament."[41] Due to the conjunction of pressures described earlier that led to the 1969 US decision to
unilaterally divest itself of its offensive BW program, the complexion and
tempo of discussion in various UN forums also began to change in the mid-
1960s. The Soviet Union constantly proposed that all states should adhere to
and observe the Geneva Protocol, meaning that the United States should.
Several resolutions eventually led to the suggestion in 1968 that the UN
secretary-general should produce a study on CBW, and the pace of discussion also picked up at the United Nations ENDC in Geneva, which was co-
chaired by the United States and the Soviet Union.

In February 1967, the UK Foreign and Commonwealth Office's Arms
Control and Disarmament Research Unit drew up a very general paper on
the state of CBW arms control.[42] It was shared with the US Arms Control
and Disarmament Agency (ACDA), whose reaction was positive as long as
the UK-US discussion was limited to private exchanges of this nature and
the United Kingdom did not present its ideas in Geneva. But by the middle
of 1968, thinking of initiatives that the UK government could undertake
following the completion of negotiations on the Non-Proliferation Treaty,
Ronald Hope Jones, the head of the Atomic Energy and Disarmament Department in the UK Foreign and Commonwealth Office, began to envisage
a new protocol to reinforce the Geneva Protocol, but one that would focus
solely on BW. The new British minister for disarmament, Fred Mulley, came
to Washington to discuss these ideas with US officials on July 2, 1968. The
US response was decidedly negative. If the United Kingdom proposed a new
draft treaty, the United States would oppose it, and any agreement without
verification provisions would be unacceptable to the United States.[43] However, although the United States did not favor the United Kingdom taking
this initiative at all, the United States would not oppose the United Kingdom proposing a Working Paper instead of a draft treaty.[44] It was clear to the
British officials, however, that their Working Paper would have all the elements of a draft treaty that they would present in the relatively near future.
For the remainder of July 1968, drafts of the UK Working Paper were discussed at a series of British Official and Ministerial Cabinet Committee

meetings, the only occasion in which British ministers became so deeply involved in BW policy questions.

The UK delegation at the ENDC put the Working Paper on the table on August 6, 1968.[45] Aside from a series of substantive recommendations, it contained two major points. The first was that the 1925 Geneva Protocol had several major drawbacks, one of which was that its prohibition was only against chemical and biological weapons use, and not their development, production, or stockpiling. The second was that reaching some agreement might be facilitated if biological weapons were separated from chemical ones for the purpose of arms control negotiations. To this end, the United Kingdom thought that it would be useful if a new convention dealing solely with BW could be agreed to. The precedent since the 1920s was that C and B were always considered together. Included among its particular suggestions, the United Kingdom thought that such a convention should also ban *research* intended to produce BW agents and the delivery systems to employ them.[46]

The response of the Soviet Union and its allies, as well as of nearly all of the nonaligned and neutrals, who represented a significant bloc at the ENDC, was altogether negative. Except for the United Kingdom, they were in favor of continuing negotiations on the abolition of CW and BW to remain unseparated, as they had always been. By this time the US government's review process on CBW policy, and BW in particular, was in full swing. The US government's instructions to its ambassador in Geneva, James Leonard, therefore "were to stall for all of 1969; don't let it go one way or the other."[47] Accordingly, the US response in Geneva was to find the British Working Paper "of interest." In December 1968, the UN General Assembly also finally adopted the resolution authorizing the UN secretary-general to produce its study.

After nearly a year, the United Kingdom presented a draft convention on Biological Weapons on July 10, 1969.[48] The Soviets quickly objected and moved to maintain the status quo. On September 19, 1969, the Soviet Union and its allies submitted a draft convention dealing with *both* BW and CW. But then the entirely unprecedented and unexpected took place. On November 25, 1969, the United States announced its unilateral renunciation of BW, and on February 14, 1970, it added toxins. Canada, Sweden, and the United Kingdom announced that they had no biological weapons, and no intention of producing any. These striking moves altered the diplomatic context to such a profound degree that they produced a complete reversal of the Soviet position. On March 31, 1971, the Soviet Union and its allies presented their own draft convention for the abolition of BW alone, albeit containing provisions for a very much weaker convention than was contained in the British draft.[49] The neutral and non-aligned states also altered their positions, and from this point on, events moved remarkably quickly for a disarmament negotiation.

The British draft convention contained three critical provisions that would all be lost by the end of a brief six-month period of negotiations. The first was that in its first article it repeated *the prohibition against the use of BW* that existed in the Geneva Protocol. The Soviet Union strongly objected to this provision, as did nearly the entire neutral bloc, on the grounds that to repeat the prohibition in a new convention would weaken the Geneva Protocol. At first the United States had no objection to a provision forbidding use. However, the dominant US attitude, particularly in Washington, quickly became to accede to Soviet preferences as often as possible because the Soviet Union had made so great a reversal in its position by agreeing to the separation of BW from CW. When Russia signed the CWC in 1993, however, it accepted not only the repetition of a "No Use" provision, but a very intrusive on-site inspection system as well. But 1971–1972 was a world away from 1993, and in 1993 no other country in the world would have supported Russia had it insisted on the deletion of the "No Use" provision of the CWC.

Second, the UK draft Convention provided in its Third Article for *a procedure to examine complaints of use.* It gave the UN secretary-general the authority to investigate the complaint and to provide a report to the UN Security Council. All parties to the treaty would be responsible to cooperate with any such investigations. Individual States Parties also would have the right to bring a complaint directly to the UN Security Council against any nation it believed to be violating the other basic provisions of the convention. The nonaligned nations, led by Sweden, supported the basic British proposal, arguing strongly for a veto-free procedure. The Soviet Union opposed any such suggestion equally strongly. A US Department of State (DOS) cable reporting on a meeting with the United Kingdom's minister, Millard, referred to the "Soviet hostility to any references to BW use or to complaints procedure involving any entity except UN Security Council."[50] Unfortunately, the United States was not very enthusiastic about that provision either. One can only imagine how that mechanism might have worked out if it had existed in 1979 at the time of the Sverdlovsk anthrax outbreak, and if it had been invoked by the United States or the United Kingdom. Finally, the UK treaty draft provided for *a ban on research* that was aimed at producing biological weapons: states parties would not "conduct, assist, or permit research aimed at [prohibited production]." It was these last two provisions, rather than the repetition of the Geneva Protocol's prohibition of use, that were the real innovation. But all three would be lost in the negotiations between the United States and the Soviet Union.

Much to British dismay, the United States quickly turned the negotiations on the draft treaty into a predominantly bilateral affair between the United States and the Soviet Union, the two of them being the co-chairs of the ENDC in Geneva. The United Kingdom was relegated to trying to convince the United States in bilateral discussions to retain as much as possible of their original conception for the treaty. The United Kingdom was able to obtain only two formal meetings with Soviet diplomats in the course of the six months of negotiations. In US-UK diplomatic consultations in Washington, the United States frequently rejected one or another British proposal by preemptively arguing that the UK positions would be unacceptable to the Soviets. For example, Leonard told his UK counterpart that US experience in the ongoing SALT negotiations on strategic nuclear weapons between the United States and Soviet Union "suggested that it would be counterproductive to insist on a procedure for investigation of or complaints of use."[51] US negotiators had run into a stone wall on any analogous suggestions during the SALT talks. Just two years earlier, when the panel of experts was drafting the UN report on CBW, the Soviet member of the panel, academician Oleg A. Reutov, had refused to permit the panel to write a section dealing with verification issues.[52] An expression of Soviet attitudes can also be seen at the time of their initial presentation of their counter-draft convention in 1969 to the British initiative. At that time they stated that "international control in this case would be tantamount to 'intrusion' of foreign personnel. It would be more practical and appropriate . . . to leave control to the national governments, which would see that no firm, no legal or physical person would produce chemical and bacteriological (biological) weapons, and the Government would be responsible for compliance with their provision."[53] As indicated, the nonaligned group had demanded a veto-free procedure to investigate complaints, strongly supporting the British suggestion, but it was of no help against Soviet opposition. In addition, during the months in 1969 when the United States was deliberating its decision to unilaterally terminate its own

BW program, its attitudes about verification for this particular arms-control treaty changed 180 degrees from the position that it had expressed to British diplomats in July 1968. The United States no longer sought verification provisions. Soviet diplomats also told the UK delegation in Geneva that they would not consider inclusion of a ban on "research."[54]

Much of the detailed drafting of the eventual BWC was done in Geneva between Alan Neidle, the number three officer in the US delegation, and his Soviet counterpart, Roland Timerbaev, using the British draft as the provisional text from which to work. On August 5, 1971, the United States and the Soviet Union presented separate but identical texts for a new draft convention. After some further minor modifications were added following discussions at the ENDC, a revised draft convention, this time with the United Kingdom also as a co-sponsor, was submitted on September 28, 1971.[55] The three critical opening Articles of the Treaty read as follows:

Article I.

Each State Party to this Convention undertakes not to develop, produce, stockpile or otherwise acquire or retain:

1. Microbial or other biological agents or toxins of types and in quantities that have no justification for prophylactic or other peaceful purposes;
2. Weapons, equipment or means of delivery designed to use such agents or toxins for hostile purposes or in armed conflict.

Article II.

Each State Party to this Convention undertakes to destroy, or to divert to peaceful purposes, as soon as possible but not later than [nine] months after the entry into force of the Convention all agents, toxins, weapons, equipment and means of delivery specified in article I of the Convention, which are in its possession or under its jurisdiction or control. In implementing the provisions of this article all necessary safety precautions shall be observed to protect the population and the environment.

Article III.

Each State Party to this Convention undertakes not to transfer to any recipient whatsoever, directly, or indirectly, and not in any way to assist, encourage, or induce any State, group of States or international organizations to manufacture or otherwise acquire any agent, toxin, weapon, equipment or means of delivery specified in article I of the Convention.

The BWC was signed on April 10, 1972, roughly one month before the signing of the US-USSR SALT I agreements. The United Kingdom, United States, and Soviet Union were named as co-depository nations, and 77 other countries signed simultaneously a few days later. The Soviet Union had been one of the countries that signed the Geneva Protocol in 1928 with reservations permitting BW use in retaliation, as had the United Kingdom and France. When the Soviet Union ratified the BWC, it gave up any possibility of BW use, including in retaliation.

The BWC was seen as a desirable arms control achievement in its own right by British government officials, and they had wanted it to contain as many as possible of the provisions they considered essential to a coherent whole. And certainly the international arms control community considered the treaty an achievement, despite the loss of several of the key provisions in the initial UK treaty draft. However, that was not the primary context for the US and Soviet governments. They were primarily concerned with the strategic nuclear weapons issues involved in their bilateral SALT and ABM negotiations taking place in Helsinki and Vienna at the same time as the discussions on a BW treaty were taking place at the ENDC in Geneva. And for the United States, certainly reaching an agreement with the Soviet Union on strategic nuclear weapons was far more important than the BWC.[56] In September 2007 the DOS released a collection of documents dealing with US policy on chemical and biological weapons. These included transcripts of several recorded conversations between President Nixon and his immediate subordinates on April 10 and 11, 1972, the days immediately following US signature of the BWC. These included Nixon's conversations with Kissinger and Secretary of the Treasury John Connolly. Even if one keeps in mind the inordinate crudeness of Nixon's private speech with his staff, the remarks are astonishing, ranging from absolute cynicism to inane. Nixon referred to having gone "over to sign that jackass treaty on biological warfare," and to the Soviet Union "signing this silly biological warfare thing which doesn't mean anything."[57] He derided his own most senior arms control officials, Ambassador Gerard Smith, leading the SALT and ABM negotiations, and William Foster, director of ACDA: "As far as these agreements are concerned they are basically not an end in themselves. . . . Its not an end in itself. You see, that's directly contrary to what the Gerry Smiths and the others and Bill Fosters, they all look upon arms control as an end in itself. That's the Soviet line." The notion that individual arms control agreements were valuable in themselves was anything but "the Soviet line." It was one of the three basic points in a codification of the benefits of arms control written by Thomas Schelling and Morton Halperin in 1961.[58] Halperin was a key member of Kissinger's NSC staff at the time of Nixon's remarks. Finally, Nixon referred to his notably less than accommodating remarks at the White House BWC signing ceremony as "a little shot across the bow yesterday . . . a direct shot at the Russians." This referred to the fact that in less than six weeks' time he was due to be in Moscow to sign the strategic arms control agreements with Leonid Brezhnev on May 20.

There is a strong possibility that, if not for Laird, then for Kissinger and Nixon, the unilateral US renunciation of BW in 1969, which led to the BWC, was simply a way to take off the table an issue that was impeding their intention to continue an unconstrained war in Indochina. Paradoxically, the decision did not affect the use of herbicides or RCAs in Vietnam, at least not initially, and the same goal could have been achieved by simply stopping the use of those two categories of agents in Indochina. Nevertheless, the administration preferred to accede to DOD pressure to maintain the use of these compounds in Vietnam and to retain the general option for their use, while giving up the biological weapons program. Laird's civilian staff did not consider BW a useful weapon, and the Joint Chiefs of Staff were not about to give up chemical weapons at this time.

In discussing notification of destruction of stockpiles on September 28, 1971, the head of the Soviet delegation at the Geneva disarmament negotiations had said: "The Soviet Union is prepared to give such notification on the understanding that other States Parties to the convention will do likewise."[59] Vasiliy Kuznetsov, the Soviet Union's first deputy foreign minister, described the BWC as "the first measure of real disarmament in the history of international relations, since as a result of this measure a whole category of weapons of mass destruction will be removed from military arsenals."[60] The Soviet Union ratified the BWC on February 11, 1975.[61] The treaty entered into force on March 26, 1975. Three months later, in a statement to the CCD on June 24, 1975, the Russian ambassador, Aleksei A. Roshchin, delivered the following message from the Soviet government: "I have been instructed to state the following: In accordance with the legislation and practice of the Soviet Union, compliance with the provisions of the Convention on the Prohibition of Bacteriological (Biological) and Toxin Weapons, which was ratified by decree of the Presidium of the Supreme Soviet of the USSR dated 11 February 1975, is guaranteed by the appropriate State institutions of the USSR. At present, the Soviet Union does not possess any bacteriological (biological) agents or toxins, weapons, equipment or means of delivery, as referred to in article I of the Convention."[62] The Soviet stated willingness to provide notification of its BW stockpile destruction turned out to be a claim that it had nothing to notify about.

Articles I and II of the BWC covered more than "possession" alone, and Roshchin's insertion of the words "At present" is notable. The statement was certainly false overall. It is unquestionable that the USSR Ministry of Defense (MOD) had maintained a continuous, uninterrupted BW program since the late 1920s. In 1970, Major General Nikolai Vaselivich Pesterev, who represented the MOD in all arms control negotiations in Geneva at that time, informed one of the Soviet diplomats that the Soviet Union had an offensive BW program.[63] This was two years before the BWC was signed. June 1975 is also two years after the Soviet Central Committee decision to initiate the Biopreparat system. Soviet Foreign Minister Andrei Gromyko may have known about the continued existence of the Soviet BW program, but it is unclear if Roshchin and the Soviet MFA delegation in Geneva knew that his statement in 1975 was not true. Many years later, Roshchin's successor in Geneva, Ambassador Victor Israelyan, explained that numerous Soviet statements that he participated in drafting, which favored the banning of chemical weapons, were nothing more than "propaganda statements."[64] The parallel is not altogether fitting, because international law at the time did not forbid having chemical weapons, nevertheless it provides what little insight one can find regarding the degree of understanding that members of the MFA may have had of the substantive truth of the statements they made in various documents. There is, of course, also the notorious comment by Arkady Shevchenko, protégé of Gromyko, who served as a UN under-secretary-general and who defected to the United States in 1978. He claimed that Gromyko "felt it necessary for propaganda purposes" for the Soviet Union to accede to the BWC, while "the military's reaction was to say go ahead and sign the convention; without international controls, who would know anyway? They refused to consider eliminating their stockpiles and insisted upon further development of these weapons. The Politburo approved this approach."[65] Perhaps, then, this explains why the Soviet authorities negotiated, signed, and ratified the BWC even if they truly believed that the US dismantlement of its offensive BW program between 1969 and 1971 was a sham. Simply, the Soviet Union would do the same. And in an astonishing display of either ignorance or disinformation, on September 6, 2001, Russian Minister of Defense Sergei Ivanov, referring to the BWC, said, "The Americans have not signed and do not intend to sign this convention." The *RIA Novosti* story in which Ivanov's remarks appeared also referred to "recent reports about the production of new types of bacteriological weapons at a Nevada factory in the USA."[66]

Article IV of the BWC requires its States Parties to undertake "implementing legislation" to enforce the provisions of Article I of the treaty in their own countries. The US Congress did not pass such legislation until 1989. This was negligent enough, a delay of 14 years. However, the Soviet Union apparently never passed such legislation at all up to the time of its dissolution in 1991. The US/UK/Russian Trilateral Joint Statement signed on September 11, 1992, in Moscow, which is discussed in Chapter 22, notes in point H, "The Russian Parliament has recommended to the President of the Russian Federation that he propose legislation to enforce Russia's obligations under the 1972 Convention." There appears to be no single piece of implementation legislation for Russia, but a composite of several passed between 1997 and 2000 serve that purpose.[67] In a book published in Russia in 2005, Fedorov pointed to apparent loopholes in the Russian legislation when compared to the conditions stipulated in Article I of the BWC. He writes that Article 355 of the Criminal Code of the Russian Federation, which entered into force on January 1, 1997, criminalized the production, acquisition, and sale of biological weapons, but did *not* prohibit the development or the retention "of previously produced biological weapons, or maintenance of industrial facilities for manufacturing biological weapons in combat readiness."[68]

The Soviet Union, Russia, and BW Arms Control since 1975

The remainder of this chapter concerns the Soviet and then Russian responses to the succession of BWC Review Conferences held every five years, and the VEREX and AHG negotiations between 1992 and 2001, which attempted to achieve a verification protocol for the BWC (Table 20.1).

The BWC provided that Review Conferences could be held every five years if a majority of the parties to it agreed. The majorities were obtained, and a Review Conference has been held more or less every five years since the treaty entered into force in 1975.[69]

The first leaks by the DOD suggesting that the Soviet Union was building new facilities for BW production, or had recently done so, appeared between 1975, the very year that the BWC entered into force, and 1977 (see Chapter 12). Although all these reports and those that continued until 1989 could not be confirmed at the time, and the evidence provided in public initially was

Table 20.1   BWC Review Conferences

First Review Conference	March 3–21, 1980
Second Review Conference	September 8–26, 1986
Third Review Conference	September 9–27, 1991
Special Conference	September 19–30, 1994
Fourth Review Conference	November 25–December 6, 1996
Fifth Review Conference	November 10–22, 2001
Sixth Review Conference	November 20–December 8, 2006
Seventh Review Conference	December 5-22, 2011

brief and somewhat ambiguous, they would later be proved to be correct. The Sverdlovsk anthrax outbreak occurred in the spring of 1979, and the First BWC Review Conference took place just 10 weeks after the Soviet invasion of Afghanistan on December 24, 1979. It was a time of substantial political tension between the United States and the Soviet Union.

Sweden had come to the First BWC Review Conference determined to pursue an amendment to the BWC "to separate the fact finding stage from the adjudication of a complaint," precisely so that no permanent member of the Security Council would be able to prevent the investigation of allegations against itself. In essence Sweden returned to the same issue that had concerned it in the summer of 1971.[70] Sweden proposed establishing a Consultative Committee of Experts, modeled on another recent international treaty, the Convention on the Prohibition of Military or any Other Hostile Use of Environmental Modification Techniques, which had been signed in Geneva in May 1977. The United Kingdom also pointed out that the United States and the Soviet Union had only the previous year submitted a joint draft convention on radiological weapons that included a committee of experts to investigate alleged violations. The Soviet Union nevertheless rejected the Swedish proposal saying that there was no "need for any improvement in or explanation of the consultative process referenced to in Article V" of the BWC.[71] The Soviet Union also rejected any amendment to the BWC. Other delegations opposed new amendments as well, fearing that opening the treaty for new negotiations on amendments could place the entire treaty at risk. The Soviet Union argued that "since no one had yet raised a complaint under the procedures which the treaty already provided, there was no need to elaborate additional procedures."[72]

The Soviet Union also wanted the Final Declaration of the First BWC Review Conference to say that the BWC had been "effectively implemented," because there had been no complaints of violations. The Soviet delegation was aided by the Bulgarian chair of the First BWC Review Conference, who made a concerted effort to commit the States Parties to declare that the First BWC Review Conference had found compliance with the basic Article I provisions of the BWC: not to develop, produce, stockpile, etc. biological agents or weapons. However, in the last days of the conference, as described in Chapter 15, it became known that the United States had contacted the Soviet MFA in Moscow regarding the anthrax events in Sverdlovsk and had requested consultations under Article V of the BWC. As a consequence, the Final Declaration did not make any statement at all concerning whether the treaty had been violated, or whether all States Parties were in compliance. Declarations of nonpossession of BW had been made in the past by several nations, and others were made by several additional nations in their opening remarks to the First BWC Review Conference. The Soviet declaration, as was noted earlier, included the qualification "at present." The Soviet Union disregarded suggestions "that states should voluntarily declare whether or not they had formerly possessed biological weapons."[73]

In regard to consultative mechanisms, the British, Soviet, and Swedish ambassadors worked out a compromise: Article V of the Final Declaration provided for the right of any State Party "to request that a consultative meeting open to all States Parties be convened at expert level." Sweden and its supporters wanted the UN secretary-general to have the authority to convene such a meeting. The Soviet Union insisted that the BWC depository governments be the conveners. The United Kingdom noted that one or more "Depositories" could so serve; it did not require the unanimous agreement of all three. Thus, no permanent member of the Security Council could now prevent such an investigative procedure by use of its veto. In the end, no consensus could be reached on how to convene or chair such a meeting.[74]

Sweden pressed the issue further in the period before the Second BWC Review Conference, which was to be held in 1986. At the UN Second Special Session on Disarmament in 1982, a special meeting of the UN General Assembly, Sweden introduced a resolution recommending that a special conference be held to establish a "flexible, objective and non-discriminatory procedure" to review verification and compliance of the BWC. The Soviet Union and its allies voted against it, as well as against several other resolutions giving the UN secretary-general the authority to carry out investigations of alleged use of BW.[75] The resolution passed, and Sweden subsequently requested that the special conference take place, but the Soviet Union opposed, and most nations preferred to wait until the next Review Conference and to see what kind of verification was provided for in the CWC negotiations. In 1983, Rolf Ekéus arrived in Geneva as Sweden's new permanent representative to the CCD. Yury Andropov, who died in February 1984, was still general secretary in the Soviet Union. Members of the Soviet and the US delegations in Geneva began meeting in Ekéus's office to see if they could come to some understanding about the issues between them relevant to the BWC. The meetings took place intermittently, with no obvious result.[76] The stage was well set for the Second BWC Review Conference, with one significant change: Mikhail Gorbachev had become the Soviet Union's general secretary in March 1985, and the Second BWC Review Conference took place less than a month before the second summit meeting between Gorbachev and President Reagan in October 1986 in Reykjavik, Iceland.

September 16, the seventh day of the conference, included a brief, sharp exchange between the United States and the Soviet Union regarding Soviet BWC compliance. During the article-by-article review of the treaty, US ambassador David S. Lowitz noted US concerns regarding Soviet compliance. According to a US cable back to Washington, "Soviet Rep Amb Israelyan responded angrily, accusing the US of trying to set the stage for resumption of its own BW program."[77] Nevertheless, Israelyan then made a very brief statement that was interesting for other reasons. This time he acknowledged the US allegations that the Soviet Union maintained an offensive BW program, but he said that they "were inventions from beginning to end," that the United States had little "interest in the Soviet delegation's readiness to give appropriate explanations," and that "ungrounded statements do harm the Convention's authority." This was followed by what on the face of it was an apparent change in the Soviet position:

> We confirm our readiness for joint search for mutually acceptable compromise . . . on the whole set of problems . . . discussed at the conference including the issue of control. . . . [T]he Soviet Union initiates a formal proposal to work out and adopt a supplement[ary] protocol to the Convention . . . which would contain measures of strengthening [the] control system of the compliance with the convention.[78]

The "formal proposal" that Israelyan was referring to was contained in a page-and-a-half document submitted by the GDR, Hungary, and the Soviet Union. It was written by the Soviet delegation and given to its WTO partners, as was the case in all such circumstances. The other WTO countries did not prepare their own proposals.[79] It consisted of four recommendations, the last of which was "Preparatory work for a special conference of the States Parties to the Convention to draw up and adopt an additional protocol to the Convention, with that protocol providing for measures to strengthen the system of verification of compliance with the Convention."[80] Three days later, during informal proceedings on September 18, Ambassador Israelyan reportedly said that "hard and fast obligations were needed for States Parties, strict obligations for monitoring," and that "these should be in a legally binding document" on which there should be an opportunity to vote. It should not be a matter of consensus agreement. Another Soviet delegate again proposed "a protocol to monitor verification and compliance."[81] The Soviet Union was now suggesting what it had previously rejected, more or less exactly what Sweden had proposed in previous years. However, the Soviet MFA had not thought through any specifics to back up the proposal. It was offering "a signal"; it had only "a general idea," and it was "willing to consider" what might result from a special conference.[82] Not until the penultimate day of the conference, when the wording of the Final Document had to be agreed to, did the Soviet delegation have authorization to permit the word "compliance" to appear in the document.[83]

As far as Sverdlovsk was concerned, the Soviet Union was no more inclined to agree to consultations with the United States under Article V than it had been in March 1980. Israelyan's remarks on that score were boilerplate repetitions. He noted that no party had lodged a complaint of violation of the BWC, and that "the Soviet Union is opposed to attempts to undermine this important international agreement in the field of disarmament, on various trumped-up pretexts."[84] The Soviet delegation brought along three special "experts," including Burgasov, to provide the delegates early on with a new—but still fabricated—rendition of the 1979 anthrax outbreak in Sverdlovsk. However, Israelyan's comments on verification in the sentences that followed were astonishing for a Soviet spokesman, taking a page from President Reagan's playbook: "Of course, the Soviet Union is no less—perhaps more—interested than other countries in reliable verification of compliance with the Convention. We regard verification as a constituent part of agreements in the field of disarmament. Disarmament without verification is impossible, while verification without disarmament is pointless."[85]

The Soviet Union was again prepared to reverse its position, as it had in March 1971, albeit now on a much smaller scale. Clearly the Soviet Union felt compelled to propose something to counter the Sverdlovsk allegations. For a country that was 10 years into a massive expansion of its BW program, and the target of continuous leaks from US DOD sources, it was a sensible tack to follow. Perhaps it would earn the Soviet Union some favorable press in the West. However, the Soviet Union wanted to see any new measures appear in a legally binding document, which would take years of new negotiations to achieve. Most other nations wanted to see at least some changes result directly from the Review Conference, but no particular breakthrough was achieved following the minimalist Soviet proposal.[86] In November 1986, the US DOD released an unclassified report on Soviet BW facilities, high on illustration but insufficient in information (see Chapter 12).

Paradoxically, looking at Soviet developments in other areas in the period bracketing September 1986, perhaps one could have expected more movement by Soviet diplomats on BW. On January 15, 1986, General Secretary Gorbachev had made an unprecedented statement to the UN General Assembly regarding virtually every issue of arms control, *with one exception, BW.* By comparison, in reference to chemical weapons, he offered the following: "We are prepared to make, at the appropriate time, a declaration concerning the sites of enterprises producing chemical weapons and to cease their production, and we are ready to start developing procedures for destroying the relevant industrial base and to proceed, soon after the convention enters into force, with elimination of the stockpiles of chemical weapons. All these measures would be carried out under strict control, including international on-site inspections."[87]

Biological weapons were, however, not addressed in the entire statement. The two words appear only in the statement's unusually long, nine-line title, but never again in its text. However, making the decision in Moscow to offer this position in regard to chemical weapons in January 1986 was what allowed the Soviet Union to offer the infinitely more limited proposal at the Second BWC Review Conference.[88] In a second Soviet policy change, Gorbachev also offered "unequivocally" that the Soviet Union would accept "on-site inspections whenever necessary" if a moratorium on underground nuclear tests were agreed to. And in its third policy change, for the first time the Soviet Union accepted the principle of on-site inspection without the right of refusal. The principle appeared in the Stockholm Document of the Conference on Disarmament in Europe (CDE), the negotiations on confidence and security-building measures, which dealt with conventional arms control in Europe.[89] This occurred in September 1986, the very same month that the Second BWC Review Conference took place. The agreement was signed on September 22, 1986, during the final week of the Conference.

In the earlier negotiations for a CWC, the Soviet Union had been willing as of 1980 to accept that there should be some form of international intrusive on-site inspection, but only on a voluntary basis. The first change came in February 1984: the Soviet Union "indicated that they would be prepared to accept the continuous presence of inspection teams at sites where certain types of chemical weapons were to be destroyed."[90] The next step was Gorbachev's January 1986 speech. Following that, and most significant of all, after six months of staff preparation in Moscow, Soviet foreign minister Eduard A. Shevardnadze came to Geneva in August 1987 and accepted "anytime, anywhere" challenge inspections for the CWC. In October 1987 the Soviet Union invited multinational observers to visit the Shikhany CW test site. Finally, the fourth Soviet switch of positions on on-site verification took place during the Intermediate-Range Nuclear Force (INF) negotiations. The United States had proposed an "any time and any place" inspection provision in March 1986. When Gorbachev and Reagan met in Reykjavik in October 1986, the Soviet side accepted the proposal, much to the surprise of US officials.[91] The United States and the Soviet Union signed the INF agreement containing exceedingly intrusive verification provisions at the Washington Summit on December 8, 1987. At that summit the Soviet Union offered a proposal for on-site counting of each other's nuclear weapon consignments for strategic bombers. It was rejected by the United States: the Soviet Union had gone farther on a verification provision than the United States was willing to accept.[92]

All of these events and associated Soviet policy shifts took place within a period of 14 months straddling the Second BWC Review Conference in 1986, yet manifestation of the same willingness to accept on-site inspection in Soviet proposals for BW arms control was minimal. Gorbachev was anxious to *hasten* agreements in these other areas of strategic arms control, but the Soviet Union showed no hurry in regard to BW. Clearly the Soviet Union possessed chemical munitions, the SS-20, SS-22, and SS-23 category INF ballistic missiles, and strategic nuclear weapons. The existence of all of these major Soviet strategic weapon systems was known and acknowledged, and they did not impede the Soviet Union from reaching agreements on each respective category of weapons. In contrast, the existence of the secret Soviet BW program, which literally reached its peak between 1986 and 1990, was the reason for the anomalous omission of BW arms control from the series of agreements achieved between 1987 and 1992. What took place inside the Soviet policymaking machinery in regard to BW during these same years is discussed in Chapter 21.

But exactly what sort of provisions might the Soviet Union have been thinking of in September 1986 in its suggestion for an additional protocol to the BWC to concern verification and compliance? As indicated, as of that date, in the negotiations for a prospective CWC, the Soviet Union had accepted on-site inspection only to accompany the destruction of chemical weapon stocks, which was less than would be necessary for the effective verification of a CWC. The Soviet Union had not yet agreed to provisions for challenge or routine inspections of industrial chemical facilities, although these were implicit in Gorbachev's January 1986 General Assembly speech. Given what later transpired between 1990 and 1995 in the context of BW, it is difficult to imagine that Soviet policymakers had decided in 1986 to risk intrusion into the MOD BW facilities, or the disclosure of Biopreparat and the Soviet Union's mobilization capacity BW production facilities by their suggestion at the Second BWC Review Conference. There is no indication of any discussion regarding the Second BWC Review Conference in the Soviet Central Committee documents that we have obtained. Most likely then, given the precedent of 15 years of Swedish importuning for augmented consultative mechanisms, the Soviet Union would have accepted the earlier Swedish proposals. This would have contributed very little toward BW verification and compliance if one thinks of what was later elaborated after nearly 10 years of effort, between 1992 and 2001, for a BWC Verification Protocol.

What the Second BWC Review Conference did was to agree on four Confidence Building Measures. These were to be "politically binding," but not mandatory:

1. *The declaration of all high containment facilities and of defense facilities:* exchange data on high-security containment facilities (all BL-4 laboratories, and BL-3 ones at defense facilities), including providing data on their work programs.
2. *The declaration of unusual outbreaks of disease:* exchange information on unusual outbreaks of diseases (unusual in terms of the detection of a

new, possibly unique disease, and/or a disease at a location where it has never before been observed).

3. *The encouragement of the publication of the results of research:* encourage the open publication of results from bacteriological and biological research.

4. *The encouragement of international contacts between scientists:* actively promote international contacts between biological researchers, including promotion of joint projects between them directly related to the BWC.[93]

The first two of the above CBMs were composed largely, if not entirely, in direct response to the 1979 anthrax outbreak in Sverdlovsk.

Apparently there might have been a fifth. With the support of the Western Group, Ireland had proposed an exchange of information on vaccinations given to the military forces of BWC member states. The Soviet Union kept rejecting this suggestion, but Irish diplomats kept asking the Soviet Union to change its position. Finally a Soviet diplomat was authorized to say that the Soviet Union would not object to the proposal, at which point it was allegedly rejected by the US government.[94]

In April 1987, an ad hoc meeting of experts established the procedures for the information exchanges.[95] The first exchange of CBMs was to be completed by October 15, 1987. Subsequently, submissions were to be provided each year. The Third BWC Review Conference, to take place in 1991, would decide whether to make any changes in the procedures.

Further elaboration was also provided for the consultative provisions of Article V of the BWC, which Sweden had fought for at the First BWC Review Conference. It was decided that under Article V a consultative meeting would be promptly convened in order to consider a specific presumptive violation at the request of any signatory nation that asked for one. The Final Declaration of the Second Review Conference stressed "the need for all States to deal seriously with compliance issues and emphasizes that the failure to do so undermines the convention and the arms control process in general."[96]

The Soviet delegation also presented a paper to the Second BWC Review Conference. Following its presentation to delegates on September 10, 1986, Nikolai Antonov, a Soviet Ministry of Health official, replied to questions. He was asked if the Soviet Union had any secret high-containment facilities. He replied, "No, they are all under known organizations, and their personnel are all published."[97] This was not true. The initial set of Soviet CBMs submitted in 1987, which stated that the Soviet Union had only a defensive BW program, was of course grossly false, but remained unchanged in each succeeding Soviet CBM submission until 1992. In addition, during a small informal meeting, a member of the Soviet delegation provided a statement that ostensibly described a theoretical BW program that could either be offensive or defensive in nature. It turned out to be derived in minute detail from extracts of the annual reports of USAMRIID and the Walter Reed Army Institute of Research.[98]

At roughly the same time as the Soviet Ministry of Foreign Affairs was displaying a more accommodating posture at the Second BWC Review Conference, other Soviet agencies were displaying very different attitudes, and releasing quite different information. Vladimir Sergiyev, another Ministry of Health official who had been part of the Soviet delegation of experts to the Second BWC Review Conference, wrote a one-paragraph comment on the conference in the Soviet military publication *Voennyi Vestnik*. He stated that the Soviet Union had wanted the CBMs to require an exchange of information about work that took place in "hospitals and universities," in addition to that in high-containment facilities, because of "the persisting suspicion that at least 23 universities in the US are engaged in military-oriented bacteriological research."[99] This single paragraph served as the vehicle for a more extended "Commentary" in April 1987 by the editors of the publication, which was a classic piece of disinformation. Its title stated that the United States was "ready for . . . germ warfare in Europe," that "military-oriented biological research has not been discontinued in the United States." It identified five US DOD facilities and the "23 universities under contract" already referred to as the locations of the work. It claimed that the US Army has "adopted" 13 agents "since the US joined the Convention," and it made a particular claim that "work with the AIDS virus is being primarily carried out in military laboratories," the significance of which will become more obvious in a moment. To be certain that this was not simply an exercise in deceptive phrasing that did no more than describe permitted US defensive research, the article went on to refer to US military regulations for transportation of these 13 agents: "This deserves special attention also because the viruses and toxins are ready for transportation and use by the US Army as offensive weapons exactly on the European theatre."[100] Finally, it quoted a bogus US war plan that provided for "the use of chemical and biological munitions. They are to be employed by special-purpose forces (landing troops)."[101] All of this was an explicit charge of US violation of the BWC by continued production of BW weapons and preparation for their use—in 1987, and in the European theater. A year later another *Voennyi Vestnik* article accused USAMRIID of carrying out "a probable covert test contravening the biological Convention" because the old unused production Building 470 at Fort Detrick was being "totally decontaminated," which the Soviet military journal claimed could occur "only as a result of release of a large aerosol cloud."[102] Even earlier, in a patently propagandistic piece meant as a rebuttal of US charges regarding Sverdlovsk, a 1980 TASS article claimed: "The Carter Administration needed this dirty lie as a smokescreen for the manufacture of new barbarous means of warfare by the United States itself. . . . Following the reports on the 'Urals incident' it can be predicted that the Pentagon will ask for more billions for the manufacture of bacteriological weapons, the illegal production and stockpiling of which continues in NATO countries."[103] This was followed by two related statements in 1982. The first was a diatribe by Nikolai Antonov of the USSR Ministry of Public Health stating that "the United States needs to untie its hands so that it can continue its policy of developing new types of these weapons and of producing and stockpiling them."[104] The second claimed that "in accordance with the Reagan Administration's directions for building up stocks of chemical and biological weapons, the facilities producing these types of mass destruction weapons are being considerably expanded."[105]

The April 1987 *Voennyi Vestnik* "Commentary" was paired by a second publication in October 1987 in *Krasnaya Zvezda,* the newspaper of the Soviet military. It too referred to the Soviet proposals at the Second BWC Review Conference, which, it claimed, "would include on-site inspection," and stated that this had been rejected by the United States because "any form of inspection would have revealed that the conversion, announced by President Richard Nixon, of the Army bacteriological research laboratories at Fort Detrick (Maryland) to cancer research was in fact pure deception. . . . The conversion announced by Richard Nixon was a complete lie."[106] It went on to add that "it was precisely in the laboratories of Fort Detrick, which had been conducting large scale research into retroviri, that the virus NIU [HIV] was constructed, which turned out to be the cause of the viral disease AIDS which is presently presenting so many problems to health care throughout the world." Finally, the 1987 fourth edition of *When the Threat to Peace* wrote:

> Despite the decision officially announced by the US President in 1969 to stop developing biological weapons and the Convention . . . ratified by the US in 1975, the US Defense Department continues with an extensive biological program. Along with the further qualitative development of the existing types of biological weapons, the Pentagon's micro-

biological centers are working to develop new microbes—causing diseases occurring in humans, animals and plants. The latest genetic engineering methods are widely used to obtain modifications of microorganisms with affecting properties unknown before.[107]

Any Westerner would read all of these as pure propaganda, just as much so as the 1980 TASS dispatch, but presumably the publications in Soviet military periodicals would have been approved by senior Soviet military officials. What the Soviet General Staff really believed about the claims printed in these Soviet military publications will probably never be known.

However, it was the Soviet Union that was in gross violation of the BWC: for the preceding 15 years it had been doing exactly what its propaganda accused the United States of doing. Although the BWC CBMs were not legally binding, of the four CBMs agreed to at the Second BWC Review Conference in 1986, the Soviet Union consistently evaded compliance with three of them:

- The Soviet Union severely restricted international contacts between scientists. Soviet scientists in the Biopreparat portion of the Soviet BW program could hardly ever visit even their allied Warsaw Treaty states.
- Publication of work performed within Soviet research institutes engaged in the BW program was restricted to varying degrees.
- Most significantly, the Soviet declarations of facilities were severely distorted.

The Soviet Union provided its first set of CBMs on October 13, 1987. Not until 1989 did the Soviet Union add some of the Biopreparat facilities to the five MOD facilities it listed. And not until 1992 did the Russian CBM admit that the Soviet Union had maintained an offensive BW program, although that CBM would still turn out to be only minimally satisfactory.

In 1988, in response to the first submitted set of BWC CBMs, the Federation of American Scientists called for the United States and Soviet Union to open "their recently declared medical/biological defense facilities to reciprocal scientific exchange."[108] As if in reply, the Soviet counselor to the Soviet Permanent Mission to the UN stated in 1989 that the Soviet Union favored openness in research relevant to the BWC and that he expected that the Soviet Union "would invite and exchange experts."[109] It took exactly 12 more years before a single Western researcher was able to spend several months working in one of the Biopreparat facilities. As best as is known, no Western government official or civilian researcher has yet stepped inside any of the MOD BW institutes, and the institutes of the anti-plague system inside Russia are also closed to Westerners. Copies of the CBMs were in theory available from the UN, but no more than a very few academic scholars took advantage of this opportunity. In 1991, on one single occasion, all the CBMs for that year were published as an official document of the RevCon.[110] Beginning in 2001 with Australia, 11 countries made their CBMs publicly available, for varying years, until 2006. These countries included Australia, the United Kingdom, the United States, Sweden, Switzerland, and Germany. In 2006, Russia demanded that the CBMs should not be publicly released, and that they should be distributed only among BWC States Parties. This policy was accepted, with the exception that any country that wanted to release its CBMs publicly could do so.

By the time the Third BWC Review Conference convened in September 1991, there had been several significant developments. As already noted, the Soviet Union was being extremely cooperative in strategic arms control negotiations, and for the first time, provisions for on-site inspection had been written into the Stockholm CBMs in 1986 and into the INF Treaty by the end of 1987. By 1991 it was also more or less clear that the CWC, then under negotiation, was going to have rigorous verification provisions, including routine and challenge on-site inspections. In contrast, as far as BW and Soviet BWC compliance was concerned, the situation was exactly the inverse. Vladimir Pasechnik had defected to the United Kingdom in October 1989, and by September 1991 the most senior US, UK, and Soviet political leadership had been disputing the nature of the Soviet Union's BW program for 18 months. In addition, the Gulf War had just ended, and it had been feared that Iraq might use both biological and chemical weapons, and Iraq was a signatory of the BWC. Finally, the level of response by convention members to the voluntary CBMs was low.[111] There was, therefore, greater interest in BW proliferation, and given all of these factors combined, a substantial number of the States Parties attending the Third BWC Review Conference in 1991 were significantly interested in having stronger verification provisions in the BWC.

Seeing both the obvious need for strengthening and the opportunity provided by the changed international circumstances, there had been a good deal of thinking and preparation both by governments and NGOs in advance of the Third BWC Review Conference.[112] One of these preparatory efforts was instrumental in leading to the most important of the three additional CBMs that the Third BWC Review Conference would adopt. Sweden convened a meeting in 1990 with participants from Bulgaria, Canada, Czechoslovakia, France, the FRG, the GDR, the Netherlands, Norway, Poland, the United Kingdom, the United States, the Soviet Union, and Sweden. The conference's main objective was to give experts an opportunity to exchange views on research and also on ways to promote the CBMs agreed at the Second BWC Review Conference.[113] These countries therefore came to the Third Review Conference with some understanding of what their respective positions were. The most significant aspect of Soviet participation in these advance meetings in 1990 and 1991 will, however, be described below.

Soviet ambassador Serguei Batsanov's statement to the Third BWC Review Conference was important, and had effects that long outlasted the conference itself. After noting that "providing all its Parties with assurances that the Convention's provisions are being complied with" would strengthen the Convention, he said that the Soviet delegation "shares the ideas" of other delegations who had spoken "in favour of setting up a verification mechanism [for] the Convention." What followed was unquestionably fashioned in response to the ongoing secret Trilateral pressures by the United States and United Kingdom on the Soviet leadership for noncompliance with Article I of the BWC, as discussed in Chapter 21:

> For a verification mechanism to function effectively it is essential to identify clearly, on the basis of agreed criteria, what is specifically prohibited and what is not prohibited under the convention. . . . That is why it is necessary to draw a clear border-line, on the basis of objective criteria, between the area where legitimate activities, inter alia, for purposes of protection against biological weapons end up and the area where the work to create such weapons begins. The Soviet delegation urges States Parties to get down to work with the view to develop a verification mechanism. We believe that this work could comprise the following elements: elaboration of essential definitions of subjects of the prohibition, agreement on a list of microbiological or other biological agents and toxins which can have a potential use for creating weapons (such a list would be subject to a periodic review) as well as establishment of their threshold quantities, and concrete definition of activities, devices and equipment prohibited and non-prohibited under the Convention and their threshold values. We think that the experience in

solving similar problems within the framework of the convention on the prohibition of chemical weapons under elaboration in Geneva can prove to be quite valuable in this case. . . . I would only stress that we do everything possible in order to clarify concerns of certain States. Frankly speaking, we also have serious questions as to the compliance of certain states with their obligations under the Convention. However, we believe that these problems should be dealt with on the basis of dialogue in a calm and business-like manner. We cannot help noticing that in the absence of an agreed border-line between prohibited and non-prohibited activities there may be any misunderstanding, subjective interpretations, etc.[114]

These concepts were then maintained without revision as the standard Russian position between 1992 and 2000, after the dissolution of the Soviet Union. It is therefore important to note that they were composed during the Soviet period, before the Russian CBMs for 1992 admitted that there had been an offensive BW program under way in the Soviet Union for the entire life of the BWC. A former Soviet diplomat claimed that their meaning was different in 1991, although he admitted that these same suggestions were retrogressive in the decade that followed. He claimed that their purpose in 1991 was to indicate that the Soviet Union was prepared "to discuss practical things," basically just a message to say that "it was important to begin."[115] However, given what we learn below of the position of the Soviet MOD during 1990 and 1991 and in Chapter 21, one has to be skeptical that Batsanov's statement was just "a signal" of Soviet willingness, or that the MFA had much control of the situation. Regarding Article V of the BWC and consultation, the Soviet Union claimed that its agreement to participate in the work of the United Nations Special Commission (UNSCOM) "dealing with, among other things, Iraq's biological weapons," confirmed "its readiness to consult and cooperate with other States Parties in solving any problems which may arise in relation to the objective of, or in the appreciation of the provisions of the Convention."[116]

Instead of providing more details at the Third BWC Review Conference to explain the substance behind Batsanov's remarks, the Soviet Union had presented these ideas to a more restricted group of states in the private meetings in 1990 and 1991. At one such meeting in the Netherlands in February 1991, the Soviet MOD offered a remarkable outline of what it had in mind:

First of all, it would be advisable for the upcoming Third Review Conference on the Convention to adopt a decision to set up an International Committee of Experts to include military experts representing States Parties to the Convention with the aim of drafting supplements to the Convention similar to those existing in the draft Convention prohibiting chemical weapons. Firstly, it would be expedient to have these documents contain joint agreed definitions of "bacteriological (biological) and toxin weapons," "facilities for production and storage of biological and toxin weapons," "equipment for filling of biological and toxin weapons," "means of delivery of biological and toxin weapons," "munitions and devices specifically meant to kill or inflict other types of damage due to the properties of microbiological or other biological agents and toxins," and of other subjects of the prohibition.

Secondly, it would be advisable to prepare a list of microbiological and other biological agents and toxins that could be considered as biological agents with potential for military use, and also to define their threshold quantities the excess of which could be prohibited. It would be also useful to discuss both the methods for reviewing of the list and of the quantities, as well as ways of defining their infectious action and toxicity.

Thirdly, international experts could specify the types of activities, devices and equipment prohibited by the Convention. In our view the following Convention-covered subjects and types of activities could be referred to as prohibited:

- setting-up and funding of programs for development of biological and toxin weapons;
- carrying out research intended to create new, different from natural, pathogens and toxins that may cause previously unknown human, animal and plant diseases;
- development of pilot and industrial technologies for cultivation of microorganisms pathogenic to humans;
- storage of potential combat biological agents and toxins in quantities of more than 5 kilograms of each type, that according to the estimates exceed the quantitative level of dangerous biological materials necessary to assess the effectiveness of medical and technical means as well as methods of anti-biological protection and disinfection;

- availability of more than 2 fermenter-systems, with the capacity of more than 100 liters each in case of periodic cultivation, or of 4–6 systems with the capacity of more than 10 liters each in case of constant cultivation at facilities with P3-P4 protection levels, where pathogenic micro-organisms are available;
- developing, testing and production of biological ammunition and devices specially designed to inflict damage by combat biological agents;
- development of specialized equipment to fill ammunition with biological agents as well as of means of delivery of biological weapons;
- filling of ammunition with biological agents, storage of biological weapons ready for use in depots and in arsenals;
- availability of specialized military units equipped with means of transportation, delivery and use of biological weapons;
- elaboration of military doctrines envisaging the use of biological and toxin weapons;
- elaboration of regulations, manuals, instructions on storage, transportation and use of biological weapons;
- development and testing of means and ways of eliminating large quantities of micro-organisms pathogenic to humans.[117]

Of the 12 bulleted entries that the proposal suggested should be prohibited under the BWC, at least 10, and very likely all 12, existed or had existed in the Soviet BW program since the BWC entered into force in 1975. The list therefore implicates the installations and activities then existing in the Soviet Union. At the same time, the MOD was still not prepared to admit in its CBMs submitted since 1987 that it had maintained an offensive BW program, and it would still attempt to obscure that fact in its forthcoming CBM. The Russian Foreign Intelligence Service (FSB), the successor of the KGB, would release a second remarkable indicator list in 1993, again of 12 points, many of which overlapped with the 1991 MOD list (see Chapter 11). The FSB explicitly claimed that its list "identified on the basis of the following specific indicators . . . the development, production, stockpiling and possible use of biological weapons."[118] As we will see in Chapter 21, the Soviet-era KGB was arguing in 1991 that the Soviet Union should give up its offensive BW program. Despite the clear policy disagreement between the KGB and the MOD, the indicator lists that they each offered both clearly implicated the Soviet Union's own BW program. One has to be skeptical of the contention by the MFA that all of these particulars could have been overcome in negotiations. That proved to be the case in the next half dozen years.

The Third BWC Review Conference in 1991 first reaffirmed the four CBMs established in 1986. It then added three more: the declaration of national legislation related to the BWC; the declaration of past activities in offensive and defensive biological research and development programs, known as "Form F"; and the declaration of human vaccine production facilities.[119] The Soviet Union had played an essentially passive role in the elaboration of the first four CBMs in 1986, and the same was the case in 1991. Nevertheless, Soviet delegate Batsanov stated that "the USSR also stands for devising new and more radical confidence-building measures," and it did not attempt to impede any of the CBMs. Ironically, although a senior member of the US delegation at the Review Conference commented that, "The issue of verification became the single most contentious question at the 1991 BWC Review Conference,"[120] the problem was no longer the Soviet Union; it was now the United States.

In their major statements to the Third Review Conference, Sweden, the Netherlands, France, Germany, and Russia all referred to some kind of "Verification Protocol." Only the French statement referred specifically to on-site inspections, though it can be assumed that the other countries envisaged something along the same lines. All understood that an inspection regime would not produce absolute certainty of the absence of violation, but all felt that it was impossible to conceive of circumstances in which less information could be better than more information. In the mid-1980s, BW verification was not possible due to a combination of the traditional Soviet opposition to on-site inspection, and the anti-BW arms control animus of several senior US administration officials. The Reagan administration insisted as a matter of principle that BW verification was by definition impossible. Civilian DOD officials felt that the utility of the BWC was limited and denigrated it. By 1991–1992, with on-site verification in a BWC regime conceivable—albeit unquestionably difficult—the Bush administration adopted the same attitude and decided in advance that verification could not work, that it could not produce levels of *absolute* confidence, and it therefore opposed efforts to achieve any level of confidence whatsoever. A major barrier to verification was now the United States, and it would remain that way until the final US *coup de grâce* to the entire effort in 2001.[121] Therefore, despite the significant changes in Soviet attitudes to on-site verification between 1986 and 1988 discussed above, and despite US government expressions of uncertainty regarding the status of the Soviet and then the Russian BW program between 1975 and the present day, there was no US effort to negotiate BWC verification procedures as a way to attack the problem.

The irony was that US ambassador Ronald F. Lehman claimed that the United States possessed "firm evidence of noncompliance" by some countries to the BWC—almost certainly with primary reference to the Soviet Union—while the general position of the United States was that "technical and practical barriers to verification" would be impossible to overcome in any BWC verification regime involving on-site inspections.[122] The qualification here is that at least a substantial portion of the "firm evidence" available to the United States was the testimony of a major Soviet defector, Pasechnik. However, that same evidence was also in the hands of the British government, which took an absolutely opposite position to that of the United States on the value and potential for a BWC verification regime. When the Soviet Union finally acceded to the Trilateral discussions with the United States and United Kingdom in May 1990 regarding the Soviet BW program, Nicholas Sims later noted that this could be attributed to the years of international efforts to see the consultation and cooperation provisions of Article V implemented. That may be so, but due to the mounting high-level pressure from the United Kingdom and the United States, it was perhaps more the result of the risk to all of Gorbachev's strategic arms control efforts posed by the Soviet BW program. At the same time Sims warned in 1993 with unhappy accuracy that the United States might never allow a BWC verification protocol to be realized.[123]

There was no possibility that the Third BWC Review Conference could itself agree on a verification protocol in the few weeks of its existence. The "compromise" forced on the conference by the US position was the creation of an Ad Hoc Group of Governmental Experts. Its mandate was to investigate possible on-site and remote mechanisms for BWC treaty verification. It came to be known as the VEREX exercise, and its deliberations lasted for two years. In September 1994, it agreed to establish a new body, the Ad Hoc Group (AHG). Its mandate in turn was to "draft proposals to be included . . . in a legally binding instrument," which was frequently referred to as the BWC Verification Protocol. Russia did not expend any great effort between 1991 and 2001 battling for a BWC verification protocol, and the concerns that it did introduce were seen as unhelpful. Throughout five years of AHG discussions, Russia pressed issues that it was virtually alone in arguing for, and that nearly all other States Parties actively opposed and saw as obstructive. These were the aforementioned "definitions," "lists," and "thresholds" that the Soviet Union had first proposed in 1991. Russia asked for "clear definitions" and "objective criteria." Although the BWC had already been in force for 20 years, Russia now sought definitions of "biological weapon," "hostile purpose," and "biological agent." The lists requested were a subset of the definitions: which bacteria or viruses were covered by Article I prohibitions, with the corollary that those not on the list were not so covered. "Thresholds" was a request for specific quantities to be established as being prohibited under Article I.[124] Russia's argument continued to be that the establishment of lists of proscribed agents and thresholds of permissible materials would clarify which activities were permitted and which were prohibited under Article I of the BWC.

The Final Statements of all previous Review Conferences had repeatedly sought to reaffirm the basic prohibition against biological weapons and to strengthen what is referred to as the "General Purpose Criterion" of Article I of the BWC. This means that the Article I prohibition should be interpreted in the *broadest* and most *flexible* way possible. The repeated Russian calls from 1994 on for lists, definitions, and thresholds would, if realized, do exactly the opposite; they would *narrow* the prohibition. In an effort to "clarify" which activities were prohibited and which were permitted under Article I, the Russian proposals were therefore seen by virtually all other States Parties to the BWC as likely to undermine the General Purpose Criterion and therefore as retrogressive. They were opposed for that reason. Not coincidentally, they raised suspicions about Russian motives for seeking such specifications. Some saw them as a possible effort to retain an offensive BW program by setting aside things that one *could* do. And contrary to its earlier claims, Russia—together with China, Iran, India, Pakistan, and Cuba—also opposed the compliance measures being elaborated for the Protocol. The positions that Russia took only served to exacerbate the already strong opposition that many US officials expressed to the Verification Protocol.[125]

During his administration, President Clinton had withstood the resistance of his own negotiator in Geneva and officials from other US agencies during interagency deliberations and consistently supported the achievement of the Verification Protocol. In mid-May 2001, under the new George W. Bush administration, US diplomats informed major European allies that the United States would reverse the stated position of the former administration and would not support the BWC Verification Protocol. As for Russia, it was known that the MOD opposed the Protocol, and that even the Ministry of Foreign Affairs opposed it, but that the Russian government would support it if the United States did so, in order not to place Russia as the most prominent state in opposition. However, on July 25, 2001, the United States announced its opposition to the Verification Protocol under any circumstances—as it existed or if it were modified. The United States additionally proposed that the mandate for the AHG be abolished, a move that resulted in an abrupt halt to a process dating from the Third BWC Review Conference. After a year's suspension, the reconvened Fifth BWC Review Conference in November 2002 established a sequence of yearly meetings, and these were continued after the Sixth BWC Review Conference in 2006. However, at US insistence the issue of treaty compliance and verification was essentially banished from the discussions. Russia played no particularly meaningful role in these proceedings between 2002 and 2012.

At the Seventh BWC Review Conference held in December 2011, the Russian ambassador called for reopening negotiations for a mandatory verification regime.[126] It was a rather hypocritical position given the Russian record during the 1994–2000 years when the Verification Protocol was under negotiation. Diplomatic participants and observers noted that a group of five countries — Pakistan, Russia, India, Iran and China— acted in close coordination at the Review Conference to block any significant progress by rejecting a range of other incremental steps.[127]

Conclusion

The years following the signing and ratification of the BWC were taken up with an inefficient, slow-motion effort to fill the holes in the original treaty. Developments were essentially keyed to the occurrences of the five-year BWC Review Conferences. The Second BWC Review Conference coincided approximately with the first serious stirrings of change in Soviet arms control policy under Gorbachev, but their effect at the Conference was minimal. In the five years between the Second and Third BWC Review Conferences, 1986–1991, several major US-USSR strategic arms control treaties were achieved, and the Soviet Central Committee documents that we have tell us that the Politburo was considering slowing down the Soviet BW program. The most senior US and UK officials were pressing Gorbachev and Shevardnadze about the Soviet BW program between early 1990 and September 1991. Nevertheless, a verification and compliance regime for the BWC again escaped the Third BWC Review Conference. If the Soviet government was not prepared to admit the existence of an offensive BW program privately to the US president and British prime minister, it most certainly was not going to do so before the entire world at a BWC Review Conference. In the diplomatic world of BW arms control the pace was glacially slow, "consensus" diplomacy playing a key restrictive role. The Soviet Union and then Russia were satisfied to watch the years and decades pass as their MOD BW facilities remained closed to any international access.

And ironically, in 1991 the United States had become the major impediment. The Soviet Union and then Russia were never tested as they might have been if European efforts to strengthen the BWC had not been stymied. By 1994, Russian arms control policies had regressed as far as BW was concerned. The narrative of the US-UK-Russian Trilateral interactions and negotiations in 1990–1995 are dealt with in Chapter 21. Whether a BWC verification protocol containing the kind of on-site inspection of Russian BW facilities as exists in the CWC for chemical facilities could have been achieved will never be known. Despite the discovery of the enormous Soviet BW program, and the continued expression of uncertainty all through the 1990s as to whether it was all gone, the US government discarded the opportunity to obtain a regime that would undertake routine inspection of Russian biodefense facilities as well as those of any other nation that it had concerns about, and the opportunity to mount challenge inspections, primarily to protect its own biodefense program.

21

The Gorbachev Years: The Soviet Biological Weapons Program, 1985–1992

THE FIRST MAJOR QUESTION regarding the Soviet government's decision in 1972 to initiate a massive biological warfare (BW) program in violation of the Biological Weapons Convention (BWC) is why it decided to do so. There is extremely little direct information available that provides an answer. There is the obvious and primary motive, to develop an arsenal of biological weapons when the Western powers had none. There is also the evidence that senior figures in the USSR Academy of Sciences (USSR-AN) proposed the expansion of the existing BW program in order to obtain greater state resources. Given that this supplied an incremental boost, albeit a very large one, to an ongoing program, that second motive did no more than facilitate the primary one: to modernize, improve, and maintain a biological weapons capability.

Chapter 13 reviewed the history of the US covert disinformation campaign in the late 1960s and came to the conclusion that, as best as can be discerned, it did not in fact contribute to the 1972 Soviet Central Committee's decision to greatly increase the magnitude of the Soviet offensive BW program. As will be seen in this chapter, there was not a single reference to the US covert disinformation campaign in all of the Central Committee discussions of its own biological weapon program during the eight years of Gorbachev's tenure as general secretary and then as president of the Soviet Union. The numerous statements by Soviet spokesmen reviewed in other chapters, particularly the more strident ones claiming that the United States maintained an offensive BW program in the years after 1972, can fairly be assumed to have been gratuitous propaganda. Nevertheless, Central Committee documents dating from 1990 and quoted in this chapter clearly demonstrate that Soviet intelligence agencies supplied the same information to the most senior Soviet leadership, and in 1990 Gorbachev referred to the same claim in speaking with President George H. W. Bush.

The second task is to establish the composition of the program, its organization, its goals, and its achievements. Much of the first half of this book is devoted to providing that information. The third question is why the Soviet BW program was able to escape termination by Gorbachev after his 1985 ascendancy to power. He had displayed extraordinary political skill and achieved remarkable success in Moscow in reaching the major bilateral and multilateral arms control agreements that the Soviet Union undertook between 1987 and 1991 with the United States and with NATO. Despite its opposition and reluctance, the Soviet Ministry of Defense (MOD) eventually agreed to massive reductions in the central instruments of Soviet military power: tank armies, tactical strike aircraft, strategic nuclear weapon systems, and the entire category of nuclear-armed medium-range ballistic missiles. Gorbachev's arms control proposals had for the first time placed on the table substantial portions of the military's most prized assets, the long-range ballistic missiles of the Strategic Rocket Force.

All of these steps entailed policy changes of major significance for the Soviet Union, requiring the acquiescence of the major centers of power in the Soviet General Staff. They led to enormous operational consequences for the Soviet military, as well as shifting the alignment of power away from the military leadership in determining the course of Soviet security and defense policy in the final years of Gorbachev's tenure. In comparison, the BW program, for which the 15th Directorate of the General Staff was responsible, was a small component in the totality of Soviet military power, and the 15th Directorate itself was a relatively minor player in the overall Soviet military and political system. Nevertheless, though reduced and constrained to a degree that is still not altogether clear, the program survived in its essentials at least until after the disintegration of the Soviet Union on December 31, 1991, and for an unknown period of time after that. In addition, a corollary of this selective reservation of military autonomy continued through the post-Soviet period in the 1990s. It led to the ultimate failure of the Trilateral process, and the disinterest or inability of the highest levels of the Russian government—Yeltsin, Chernomyrdin, Putin, and their ministers of defense and foreign affairs—to force the MOD to clearly and verifiably comply with the BWC and to provide evidence of termination and transformation of its BW program. Stated in another way, it indicated their willingness to accept and tolerate the continuation of the status quo. Approaches by the United States to the Putin administration regarding BWC compliance issues were extremely limited and perfunctory, and the British government made no such approaches to Putin. The events following 1992 appear in Chapter 22.

Soviet Policymaking on Biological Warfare

An understanding of what transpired between the early 1970s—the years of the Central Committee decision to continue and enormously expand the Soviet Union's offensive BW program despite the Soviet signing and ratification of the BWC—and in 1987 to 1992, the period of intense strategic arms control negotiations with the United States, requires an introduction to the Soviet agencies and individuals who were responsible for formulating USSR defense and foreign policy. The events regarding the Soviet BW program between 1989 and 1992 in particular were played out against this broader background.

The policies of the Soviet Union were determined by the Politburo of the Central Committee of the CPSU and its Secretariat. However, both of these were agencies of the Party, and not of the "government," or "state." In nearly all cases, when one refers to "the Central Committee" one actually means its smaller Politburo; Politburo decisions were made in the name of the larger Central Committee. The Politburo was small to begin with, but decisions on security and foreign policy were relegated to an even smaller group, the Defense Council, which was nominally a state body. It is usually considered to have had seven members: the general secretary of the CPSU, the prime minister, the heads of the KGB, the MOD, the Ministry of Foreign Affairs (MFA), the General Staff, and the Military Industrial Commission (VPK). The Defense Council was not supported by any staff of its own. The Soviet General Staff supplied the staffing support for its work, at least until the ascendancy of Gorbachev, with additional participation of members of the Secretariat staff. When Gorbachev came to power, there already existed an interagency process to oversee the arms control negotiations with the United States. It had been established on November 11, 1969, as the Commission of the Politburo of the Central Committee. In this earlier period, the Commission again had a very small membership that substantially overlapped with the Defense Council. It was composed of a senior official from each of the MOD, represented by the head of the General Staff, the MFA, the VPK, the KGB, the USSR-AN, as well as a sixth member, the person who headed the Department of Defense Industries of the Central Committee, the Central Committee secretary for defense issues.[1] After 1979 the separate representation from the USSR-AN was discontinued and its representatives were integrated into those of the VPK. This left a group of five, which came to be known as the "*Pyatorka*," literally, the "five."[2] More formally, this was referred to as the "Higher" or "full" *Pyatorka*, which was seconded by a parallel "Lower" or "small" *Pyatorka*. (See Charts 21.1 and 21.2, and Table 21.1.) The substantive positions of three of the participating organizations—the General Staff, the VPK, and the Central Committee secretary for defense issues—were coordinated in advance, probably until late in the 1980s. More often than not the positions taken by the KGB were aligned with these three as well. This left the MFA as an outlier. The Commission was to reach its decisions by consensus; when consensus could not be reached the issue was referred to the Defense Council for resolution and decision. When Eduard Shevardnadze became the minister of foreign affairs, he arranged to be assisted by studies and position papers prepared by two institutes in the USSR-AN. In addition, Zaikov's office in the Politburo Secretariat also obtained permission to call in independent experts beginning on May 19, 1987, permission that had to be granted by Gorbachev. The organizational charts below were drawn up by Vitaly Kataev, a member of the Politburo Secretariat. It is evident that there was great overlap between membership in the Politburo, the Defense Council, and the renamed Commission for Arms Limitation in the Defense Council. The purpose of these consultation and advisory structures was primarily to deal with the negotiations with the United States on nuclear weapons.

The VPK regulated the weapon development process from the stage of applied research to that of preparation for factory production. The role of the VPK was crucial in the existence and maintenance of the Soviet BW program. In addition to the agency being a bureaucratic supervisor, its most senior officials were also extremely important policy actors. In its management role, it assured schedules, quality, and quantities produced.[3] In 1972 the senior VPK official responsible for BW programs and institutes was Danat Pavlovich Danotov, and his deputy was Gleb Vladimirovich Chuchkin. Danotov died in 1974 and was replaced by Chuchkin, who, with a newly

Organization for the
Preparation of proposals for military political issues

President of the USSR
(Gorbachev)

**Commission for Arms Limitation in the Defense Council
under the President of the USSR** (Zaikov)

Commission of the Politburo (Higher Pyatorka)
Zaikov, Kryuchkov (KGB), Shevardnadze (MFA), Yazov (MOD),
Maslyukov and Belousov (VPK)

Interagency Task Force Working Group (MRG)
Deputies level: Katayev (CC), Leonov (KGB),
Karpov, Petrovsky and Vorontsov (MFA),
Khromov (VPK), Akromeyev and Chervov (MOD),
Detinov and Serkin (VPK)

**Inter-
agency
Task
Force
Secretariat**

Problem-oriented subgroups (CBW here);
specialists: from ministries, design institutes,
standing working groups

Central Committee Secretaries for Defense Industry

Dmitry Ustinov:	1965–1976	Grigori Romanov:	1983–1985
Yakov Ryabov:	1976–1979	Lev Zaikov:	1985–1988
Andrei Kirilenko:	1979–1983	Oleg Baklanov:	1988–1991

CPSU Policymakers and Organization

Early Gorbachev

1985: With Gorbachev's accession as General Secretary, the name of the CPSU department was changed from "Defense Industries" to "Defense Department."

At the end of 1989

By 1991, Baklanov had replaced Zaikov as CPSU Committee Secretary, and the Department's name was again changed to "Department on the Issues of Defense and Security in the President's Administration of the USSR.

The "Higher *Pyatorka*"

1. Lev Nikolayevich Zaikov: CPSU Central Secretary, Committee on Defense Department
2. Viktor Mikhailovich Chebrikov
   Succeeded by Vladimir Alexandrovich Kryuchkov: Head, KGB
3. Eduard Abromosovich Shevardnadze: Minister of Foreign Affairs
4. Dimitri Timofievich Yazov: Ministry of Defense
4. Yuri Dimitrievich Maslyukov: Head, VPK (Succeeded by Igor S. Belousov)

Table 21.1 The Lower *Pyatorka*

CPSU Central Committee Department of the Defense Industry	Vitaly L. Kataev
	V. A. Popov
KGB	V. A. Kryuchkov
	Nikolai Sergeivich Leonov
Ministry of Foreign Affairs	Yuli Mikhailovich Vorontsov
	Succeeded by Vladimir Fyodorovich Petrovsky
	Viktor N. Karpov
	G. S. Stashevsky
Ministry of Defense	Marshal Sergei Fyodorovich Akhromeyev
	Col. Gen. Nikolai Fyodorovich Chervov
	Gen. Yuri V. Lebedev
VPK	Nikolai Nikolaevich Detinov
	G. K. Khronov
CPSU Central Committee, International Department (later combined with other Central Committee departments)	Georgi Markovich Kornienko (formerly MFA)
	General Victor Pavlovich Starodubov (formerly MOD)

expanded program, acquired four deputies: Kabanov, Bushko, Vadim, and Panov (a retired general). In April 1981, Chuchkin took one of Domaradsky's 11 assistants, Oleg Borisovich Ignatiev, who had been recommended to him by Domaradsky, as his deputy. In 1983 or 1984, when Chuchkin died, Ignatiev replaced him. From that time on until the present, Ignatiev appears to have played a significant role in both Soviet and, after 1992, Russian BW issues. Scientists such as Baroyan (KGB and Ministry of Health) and Zhdanov were advisors to the VPK and had a major role in writing the 1972 memo attributed to Ovchinnikov. The VPK was instrumental in getting Ovchinnikov his initial position as a member of the USSR-AN, and in 1970 he presented a report to the Central Committee on BW. Chuchkin also relied heavily on the advice of Baev and Skryabin, and he referred to Zhdanov, Baev, and Skryabin—all of whom served on visiting commissions to the MOD BW institutes for the VPK—as his "Gang of Three." He considered their opinions as "oracular," and the three held nearly the same status, with a slight shade of skepticism, for the Central Committee assistant, Rychkov.[4]

Issues concerning the Soviet Union's BW program were dealt with partly at the Central Committee Secretariat, and also in part, beginning in December 1986 or January 1987, in a separate interagency Special Working Group (SWG). A former Soviet diplomat and assistant to Shevardnadze stated that in 1986, at the time of the Second BWC Review Conference, the MFA, including the minister (by that time Shevardnadze), did not know of the 1972 Central Committee decisions, of Biopreparat, or of the three MOD BW facilities. They also had never heard of the US disinformation story dating from 1969–1971, nor were they informed of the MOD and KGB position that the United States was continuing an offensive BW program. As best as is known, the Department of International Organizations of the MFA, which dealt with arms control negotiations and treaties, was never briefed by the KGB on the BW program of the United States, nor was anyone else in the MFA.[5]

There was no separate section in the Central Committee that dealt with biological weapons; instead there was a small unit of two persons headed by Nikolai Alexandrovich Shakhov, whose responsibilities covered chemical and biological weapons and solid fuel for missiles. Shakhov served on the Secretariat staff from 1973–1974 to 1992, almost exactly overlapping with Kataev's tenure.[6] On the Secretariat he had first been someone else's deputy in that unit, then succeeded to its head. At the end of the 1970s or early 1980s, Shakhov in turn obtained a deputy, Alexander Sergeyevich Ivanov, who covered both CW and BW issues. Shakhov apparently also convened a working group of his own of specialists concerning BW, including Yevstigneev, Kalinin, and Grigory Glubkov from the Ministry of Chemical Industry. This was apparently apart from the biological weapons Special Working Group described below. Only a very limited number of people on the Secretariat staff were permitted to know about BW programs: Zaikov and Kataev, Shakhov and Ivanov, and, one has to presume, Belyakov, and following him Baklanov. But Kataev's knowledge was limited. Prior to 1985 all documents relevant to biological weapons went through Shakhov's hands. Kataev knew of the existence of *Ferment* but did not know details of the program. The subject entered his area of responsibilities because he had oversight over all bilateral and multilateral arms control negotiations. He did not deal with Lebedinsky or Yevstigneev at the 15th Directorate, or with the VPK regarding biological weapons issues; Shakhov and Ivanov did that. He also knew that Shakhov met with Ovchinnikov.

Others sources indicate that there were additional Central Committee assistants involved with biological programs in some way, whether overlapping in responsibilities with Shakhov and Ivanov or to what degree is not known. It is interesting to note that of these, at least two of the three directors of *Glavmikrobioprom* had earlier served on the Central Committee staff in this way in the 1970s. Vasily Belyaev headed *Glavmikrobioprom*, but it is not known if he had prior service on the Central Committee staff. R. S. Rychkov served on the Central Committee in the early 1970s and as director of *Glavmikrobioprom* from 1979 to late 1985. V. A. Bykov succeeded Rychkov and had served on the Central Committee up to 1979, and as *Glavmikrobioprom* director during 1984–1988. While on the Central Committee, Rychkov had an assistant trained in microbiology named Shiov, and Bykov had two assistants, Valeri Ambrosov, a military officer from the MOD BW facility at Zagorsk, and Yuri Kondrashin.

Pasechnik said that in addition to the VPK, Central Committee staffers were very active participants in BW affairs between 1977 and 1979. They used to review the construction of buildings, follow documentation, and "control" Central Committee decisions. Oleg G. Shirokov would accompany site-visiting "commissions" to SRCAM, IHPB, and other institutes, and held Pasechnik responsible if anything was not done right. Pasechnik also described Central Committee and VPK officials—Shirokov, Chuchkin, and Ignatiev— all scolding him in the same way: "You're lazy. You're not working hard enough. Work harder. Where is your Party card? Remember it; you'll lose it if something goes wrong." These were their sole interventions; not substantive issues. Distant from Central Committee policy considerations and VPK operations, this was all Pasechnik could witness of their concerns. They were interested in control, schedule, and scale. When Zaviyalov was deputy director of the IEI, Ignatiev came to visit the institute; however, he asked Zaviyalov only about his family history.

As for the VPK, Pasechnik visited their offices three or four times after 1985. Kalinin would prepare documents summarizing Biopreparat's yearly plan and present them to the Central committee, the VPK, and the 15th Directorate. The plans would be kept in their safes, and the three offices would consult with one another and compare the plans to the five-year plan and discuss issues of scale and timing. The manner of speaking of VPK officials was not very friendly: it was essentially "You follow our directions." Chuchkin had already passed away, and VPK deputy director Panov chaired the meetings where Kalinin was questioned about the documentary material that he had prepared. Panov would open the discussion and provide an introduction, and Ignatiev would take notes. No representative of the 15th Directorate was present.

The new attitude toward arms control began within days of Zaikov's arrival at the Secretariat in 1985, and by chance the Intermediate-Range Nuclear Force (INF) treaty was the first substantive problem tackled. By mid-1986, three standing working groups had been established, essentially within the "small *Pyatorka.*" They concerned, respectively, strategic weapons, chemical and biological weapons (with the same participants), and Afghanistan. CBW questions were frequently dealt with "on a lower level," as it was not considered "a global issue." The working groups would be able to resolve 70% of the issues themselves; the rest went to the full *Pyatorka.* Gorbachev had the final word. "It was the first time in the history of the Soviet Union that this happened. Everyone could say what they pleased, and it was much easier to resolve issues. When they were given the authority to resolve important issues, they most often did so." The decisions were turned into instructions; 70% of them went to the MFA, 30% to the MOD. They were called "Decisions of the Politburo," and there were two or three of them per week. Each ran to several dozen pages, because there were eight negotiations occurring simultaneously. Their work was largely concerned with policy issues: should the Soviet Union allow on-site inspection, conversion issues, secrecy issues, and can the working group decide problem X or Y on our own without a higher directive authorizing it. In May 1987 the Central Committee formalized the process to eliminate complaints about the authority of these groups to determine "such serious questions."[7] Zaikov also resisted being called "Director" in meetings; he preferred "coordinator." In previous times, as soon as there was a "Director," everyone had listened to *his* position and supported it. Now any member of the *Pyatorka* could call a meeting, even in his own office, and he was only the "coordinator," chair, of that meeting. Decisions became less "top-down" and were arrived at more by consensus. In reality, the big *Pyatorka* almost never met. Anywhere from 30 to 50 lower-ranking specialists, in the various working groups, usually participated in preparing recommendations. The working groups met in most cases in the office of the first deputy head of the General Staff, who acted as the "coordinator" but not its leader. Two colonels provided the staffing. When the big *Pyatorka* did meet, 19–20 people might be present, and the meetings took place in Zaikov's office. For a time, however, questions of "military policy" were still kept away from Zaikov if they were not explicitly "Questions on Negotiations."

Gorbachev considered Zaikov, who was referred to by his staff as "the velvet bulldozer," as his personal adviser on military-security issues. But while Gorbachev trusted Zaikov completely, substantive positions held by different members of the Secretariat staff diverged sharply. Shakhov, Belyakov, and Baklanov opposed arms control initiatives and were an "MOD-support clique" in Zaikov's office. Baklanov once told Kataev, "You and your Zaikov and Shevardnadze want to harm the country." Kataev described him as "principled of the old line." Baklanov could not even accept the new strategic arms control decision-making process, and he wrote a personal memo to Gorbachev opposing it. Gorbachev apparently wanted divided opinions in his staff, providing for adversarial positions to come up to him so that he could choose among them. On other occasions, he wanted compromises to be made in deciding on positions. If a paper was signed by either Baklanov or Zaikov, Gorbachev would sometimes give it to the other, who would give it to Kataev to find a resolution. But just as often, if Gorbachev received a memo signed by Zaikov, he would sign it, and if it came from Baklanov, he would sign it also. The signatures of all the members of the higher *Pyatorka* would be on the memos, and a note from Gorbachev's secretary would be appended saying "The Central Committee agrees with this." Gorbachev would then sign the memos.

The Beginning of Change

The SWG or "Interagency Committee" was established by a Politburo decision following the Second BWC Review Conference in 1986. Initially its main purpose was to prepare the Soviet submissions for the BWC confidence-building measures (CBMs). The main input for these came from the VPK and MOD. It also served as "a clearing house" to provide instructions for the Soviet delegation in Geneva, and to a small degree also to deal with questions arising from the 1979 Sverdlovsk anthrax incident. The SWG was headed by Deputy Foreign Minister Petrovsky. This was its first innovation, namely, that it was run by the MFA and not the MOD. The MFA set the agenda and determined what items should be discussed. However, the group was most often run by Petrovsky's deputy, Nikita Smidovich, who served as its staff. Members of the group included Petrovsky, Smidovich, Yevstigneev, Sergeev from the Ministry of Health, Sergeyev from the MOD, and Oleg Ignatiev, who took the place of Belousov, the director of the VPK. The former MFA official claimed that the MFA always wrote the papers for discussion at the "small *Pyatorka*" that dealt with CW and BW, but exceptions are noted below. The meetings took one hour maximum, because all the issues had been agreed upon in advance during interim "pre-meetings at the working level," otherwise it could never have been accomplished in one hour. "It was more important to have these negotiations than with the Americans," he said. The Geneva delegation reportedly sent the first draft to the MFA, and "the experts" were at the level of deputy heads of departments. The experts had the authority to decide issues, did not need approval from their home agencies, and there was no veto reserved to the VPK or the 15th Directorate. If there was no agreement, they would report to Shevardnadze and he would call Gorbachev. The risk for other agencies was that they might be ordered to agree to something "even worse" from their point of view and Shevardnadze might reproach the other ministers, "Your people are holding up the Soviet delegation."

By 1987 the MOD had arranged the visit to the Shikany CW facility by members of the Conference on Disarmament (CD) in Geneva. An Ad Hoc Committee on CW of the CD was negotiating the CWC. It was also felt that the MOD had made the error of previously keeping the Soviet MFA CWC negotiators essentially ignorant regarding Soviet CW facilities. In order not to repeat that mistake, it was decided to permit an MFA official to visit the three MOD BW sites. The trip took place in 1988 or 1989 over a period of two weeks, of which only two days were spent at each facility. The MFA official was accompanied by Colonel Nikifor Vasiliev of the 15th Directorate. The visits were "a courtesy" to him, he had no adviser with him, and he asked no questions. The names of no particular pathogens were mentioned while he was at any of the MOD sites; the purpose of the trip was to enable him "to look at facilities that were causing international concern." From the description given, it can scarcely have been a very useful exercise, except to show the official the MOD buildings that had already been reported in the Soviet Union's first BWC CBM submission in October 1987.[8] That submission listed 8 sites in the USSR, 5 of them belonging to the MOD.

The SWG discussed what might be done to prepare for verification on Soviet soil. Post-1986 changes in approach to policy began with CW, but after a year or two moved to BW as well. The first trial inspections under the CWC took place in September 1988 and March 1989 in the United Kingdom. It was plausible for someone in the SWG to ask if there could be a trial inspection of a BW facility. The two key themes were to treat accusations against the Soviet Union seriously, and that the Soviet Union was open to verification if it were not forced on the Soviet Union but was at its own initiative.[9] This at least was the view of the small cabal in the MFA seeking change, and would appear to be reflected at least in part in the series of five Central Committee decisions referred to below.

Alibek records his participation in the SWG, which he refers to as "the Inter-Agency Commission," and adds the USSR-AN to its membership. For a year or so prior to Alibek's appointment as Biopreparat deputy director in 1988, Vorobyov would have served as the Biopreparat representative. Alibek identifies the role of the group as primarily concerned with responding to US complaints of Soviet violations of the BWC. He states that neither Petrovsky nor Smidovich "was officially told of the existence of our program," and that when Smidovich reported US complaints about Soviet BW facilities at Kirov and Omutninsk, Yevstigneev replied that the US charge was "absolute nonsense," that Kirov only developed vaccines. Alibek added that Omutninsk made biopesticides. To which Smidovich allegedly replied: "I'm not stupid. . . . You guys really shouldn't bullshit me."[10] The meeting at which these comments were made took place prior to Pasechnik's defection. When a member of the MFA intimately involved in this work was asked why he did not phone Yevstigneev or Ignatiev and ask "What do you have?," the reply was threefold: "[First] Their culture was not to ask questions; [second] if the person being asked was not authorized to reply to his question he would answer 'I'm not authorized to discuss this with you'; [and finally] it was not his job." Despite the claim in Shevardnadze's July 1988 speech already quoted, it was not the MFA's responsibility to ask such questions. Their role was to suggest ways to make progress and reach agreement with the United States and United Kingdom.

Alibek claimed that Shevardnadze "was kept out of the loop" despite being a full Politburo member. The responses to the US complaints were written by the 15th Directorate and Biopreparat headquarters, and according to Alibek, "each was a lie from top to bottom."[11] At the same time, a "special task force" to coordinate all the deception plans for the MOD and Biopreparat institutes was established at the Moscow Institute of Applied Biochemistry, a "false-name" Biopreparat institute for the production of equipment for Biopreparat facilities. According to Alibek, this effort was in anticipation of the day when the Soviet BW institutes would face the presence of US and UK visitors. He reports that by 1988 an instruction manual for Biopreparat employees was prepared—in essence a catechism with questions and untruthful replies.[12] This is quite surprising if Alibek has not confused the dates when these advance preparations took place. US and UK officials did not at this time envision that such on-site visits to Soviet BW facilities would eventually take place. That was only conceivable after the high-level US and UK démarches in the spring of 1990, which followed Pasechnik's defection in October 1989.

As early as 1988, the SWG reportedly began to consider compliance issues—including Soviet BW compliance—and to prepare for the discussion of an anticipated BWC verification protocol, which, it correctly expected would be considered at the next BW Review Conference in 1991. It was presumed that the Soviet Union would submit a text for discussion in advance, so it could be considered at the Review Conference. It was nearly agreed to by all the SWG participants by the fall of 1990, and the 15th Directorate reportedly did not impede the work in any particular way. This was taking place during a period in which 14 rounds of bilateral US–Soviet discussions on CW took place. For six months, the MFA worked on the concept of unlimited challenge inspections in the CW context, anytime, anyplace, and in August 1987 Shevardnadze went to Geneva and announced Soviet acceptance of that concept. "The implications were obvious to the SWG members: if it was a good idea for one, CW, someone was going to suggest that was a good idea for the other, BW."

Documentary Evidence of Central Committee Deliberations

The first available document that provides evidence of Central Committee decisions regarding BW after Gorbachev took office contains some major surprises. The document (reproduced in full directly below) is a reference note, or *spravka*, that Kataev had written for himself as a record of five Central Committee decisions dating between November 1986 and March 1990. The full texts are not available, but three of them are mentioned in a subsequent memorandum by Zaikov to Gorbachev on May 15, 1990. The first three of these decisions predate Pasechnik's defection, which occurred in the last half of October 1989. There was no causal relationship, but by coincidence Pasechnik's defection, which would begin the unraveling of the Soviet Union's secret and illegal offensive BW program, came just as the Soviet occupation of Eastern Europe and its puppet regimes collapsed.

The first surprise in the Politburo decisions is the nature of the very first decision on November 18, 1986, as well as its date, and the claim that it was prompted by the MOD itself. All the subsequent decisions are essentially embellishments on or accelerations of the schedule of that original decision.

As we will see, these decisions came about for two reasons. The first was Soviet anticipation of pressure at the BWC Review Conferences, the most recent one having taken place in September 1986. That Review Conference focused on the new CBMs, two of which were designed with the 1979 Sverdlovsk anthrax incident in mind. The second was anticipation of the sort of on-site inspection provisions that were expected to come under the CWC. It is important to note the use of the phrases "special problems," "special sites," "special purpose product," "special production facilities," by the Politburo Secretariat for issues dealing with biological weapons. No euphemisms were used for chemical weapons.

On improvement of organization of works on special problems
1. Resolution of the CPSU CC and USSR Council of Ministers on Nov 18, 1986:
> For the goals of ensuring openness of work in conditions of international control, to agree with the suggestions of the USSR Defence Ministry on liquidation before 1992 of the stockpile of biological recipes and industrial capacities for production of biological weapons located at the sites of this Ministry.
2. Resolution of the CPSU CC and the USSR Council of Ministers of Oct 02, 1987:
> To ensure readiness of biological sites for international control for presence of chemical weapons there by January 01, 1989
3. Resolution of the CPSU CC of October 06, 1989:
> In conditions of possible introduction of international control over the compliance with the 1972 Convention: to recall standardization documentation [recipes] from all special sites connected with manufacturing of special-purpose product; to mobilize NIR [R&D] and OKR [full-scale development] to design new means of protection; to carry out works to modernize the facilities, keeping in mind their complete assimilation for manufacturing of protective *bio* agents.
> The proposed protective concept will allow the preservation, within the conditions of the 1972 Convention, of the achieved parity in the field of military biology.
4. CPSU CC decision of Dec 06, 1989:
> To prevent undesirable consequences for us (in connection with the possible leak of information thru Pasechnik) to instruct the USSR Ministry of Medical Industry (comrade Bykov V. A.) to reduce the

terms of assimilation of special production facilities and to ensure their readiness for international inspections from July 1, 1990
5. CPSU CC decision of March 16, 1990:

In connection with the progress at negotiations in Geneva, and the current domestic and international situation, to speed up the term of preparation of special sites of the USSR Defence Ministry and the USSR Council of Ministers' State Committee on Food and Provisions by reducing it by one year, and to ensure readiness for international control by January 1, 1991, instead of January 1, 1992.[13]

These Politburo resolutions appear to have been deliberately written using additional euphemistic or obscurantist phraseology. One would not ordinarily refer to "a stockpile of biological recipes;" "stockpiles" are composed of the product made by following the instructions in the recipe—namely, biological agents. (The Russian word used was *retsept.*) The Politburo decision to destroy BW stockpiles had no apparent effect on research at Biopreparat and MOD institutes to develop advanced agents. The period between 1986 and 1990 was precisely the time in which Biopreparat made its major advances.

One of the most difficult questions was to understand what kind of papers concerning biological weapons issues went to General Secretary Gorbachev in particular, irrespective of whether they concerned activities taking place in already existing facilities and programs, budgeting, construction, and so on. What did he see, what did he read, and what did he sign? Kataev claimed that any MOD reply to a question from the Central Committee secretary that went to Gorbachev had to be a true one, with one qualification: "If the Generals lied, they were under orders to." Following that, it was a political decision as to who else to tell the truth to. Lying to the Politburo was not permissible; lying to US Secretary of State Baker was permissible. "People in the government were used to lying, they had been doing it for years." Nevertheless he claimed, "No one lied to people in the Central Committee." In theory, beginning in 1985, Soviet diplomats were not supposed to provide false information to their foreign counterparts. If the circumstances required it, they were to remain silent and provide no information at all. If so, it was a precept thoroughly violated at the BWC Review Conference in September 1986 in regard to the 1979 Sverdlovsk anthrax events, and it was a precept violated after 1985 in regard to the Soviet BW program in other circumstances as well. Kataev knew nothing about Sverdlovsk until after 1985, and he claimed that Marshal Akhromeyev did not discover the truth about what had happened in Sverdlovsk in 1979 until 1987–1988.

A document such as the 1986 order to destroy BW stocks certainly went to Gorbachev. But he signed many documents in a single day, and he did not read them, certainly not each one. One of his assistants—Boldin, Lyukanov, or Chernyaev—would introduce each one as it was placed before him for signature, perhaps suggesting in his tone of voice something about the item in question. But someone like Chernyaev would not have seen the document or read it in advance; Lyukanov might have skimmed it. Authorization for the construction of new facilities would be in a budget plan, and would go to the general secretary and the chairman of the Council of Ministers. But the details of construction for chemical or biological weapons facilities would be in appendices that did not go to the general secretary, though his aides might mention them. Appendices dealing with facilities for nuclear, chemical, and biological weapons were only one or two pages each in length, and these were handled by specialists at the VPK and Gosplan and stored there. The general secretary signed a document that was for the overall general plan, not for each individual facility.

If the November 18, 1986, Central Committee Resolution truly was an MOD initiative, it is quite remarkable. Gorbachev's speech on May 23, 1986, contained strong implied criticisms of the policy positions held by the Soviet military. It was—and was intended by Gorbachev to be—a major shift in the power relations between the Soviet military leadership and the MFA. Nevertheless, the speech was not publicly reported in the USSR at the time; the military leadership still retained substantial support among other members of the Politburo. And in July 1988, speaking to the 19th All-Union CPSU Conference "Foreign Policy and Diplomacy," Shevardnadze referred to "the military sphere, which in the past was devoid of democratic control." He demanded in particular that "the Ministry of Foreign Affairs . . . must know literally everything that applies to their sphere of competency. Major innovations in defense development should be verified at the Ministry of Foreign Affairs to determine whether they correspond juridically to existing international agreements."[14] In other words, the MFA should be able to verify Soviet treaty compliance. In a 1989 speech to the Supreme Soviet, Gorbachev revealed that "his early sessions with the Defense Council were 'very painful' and marked by conflict with the marshals."[15] In March 1990, when Gorbachev became president while simultaneously remaining general secretary of the CPSU, he formed the Presidential Council as a replacement for the

Defense Council and altered the complexion of its membership by appointing to it more of his supporters among the senior political leadership. The move was a device to deliberately evade the constraints imposed by the military leadership in the Defense Council. However, when Gorbachev began to return his support to the military and the KGB in November 1990 the Presidential Council was abolished after a short lifetime of only eight months.

As late as June 1991, the US government could still see how little freedom Soviet diplomats had to negotiate. In one instance when Alexei Obukhov, the deputy foreign minister responsible for arms control, came to Washington to negotiate with a US team, he "was accompanied by Lieutenant-General Fyodor Ladygin, chief of the Treaty and Legal Directorate of the Soviet General Staff [General Chervov's successor] who clearly had the final say on any concessions that were to be made."[16] To overcome the opposition of the Soviet military leadership, Shevardnadze took initiatives in ways that had never been seen in Soviet policymaking.

> During the intense arms control negotiations with the Reagan Administration, the foreign minister had grown frustrated with the reflexive tendency of the Defense Ministry and the General Staff to block almost any modification of the Soviet negotiating position. He found that he could deliberately exceed his authority by short-circuiting the decision-making process in Moscow and bypassing the generals altogether.
>
> Shevardnadze had refined the practice of asking his own arms control experts to come up with new initiatives, which he would propose to the Americans himself. After they accepted his terms, he would take the breakthrough back to Gorbachev for his approval, and only then would he present it to the military—as a fait accompli. Precisely because this gambit worked so often and so well, Shevardnadze was despised in the highest ranks of the Soviet military.[17]

US Secretary of State Baker adopted the same tactic and for the same reason. When the START talks were deadlocked in mid-1991, Baker suggested that the remaining issues might be resolved by an exchange of correspondence between President Bush and Gorbachev in order to go over the heads of the Soviet military, a device that also had been used for problems with the Conventional Forces in Europe (CFE) treaty negotiations.[18] But none of these devices would produce any benefit on the subject of BW.

Given that all five of the decisions recorded in Kataev's *spravka* preceded the first US-UK démarche to the Soviet Union regarding its BW program on May 14, 1990, the second surprise is how unsatisfactory all the subsequent interactions on the problem between the United States, the United Kingdom, and the Soviet Union were between 1990 and 1996. The Soviet leadership was clearly prepared to dismantle—at least in part—the illegal Soviet offensive BW program, but it was not prepared to admit to the United States and the United Kingdom that it had ever had one or allow proof of its termination. The substance and timing of the successive decisions also make clear that later on Gorbachev, Shevardnadze, and their deputies lied in their dealings with their US and UK counterparts. Given what followed in 1992–1996, if the Politburo and Central Committee were prepared to make these decisions, it is fair to wonder whether the MOD intended to carry them out.

Many of the major players supported the continuation of the offensive BW program, as did their second-rank deputies. According to Alibek, Maslyukov at the VPK strongly supported it, as did his successor, Belousov, after Maslyukov moved to be the head of Gosplan in 1990–1992 for the last years of Gorbachev's tenure. Also according to Alibek, the most senior members of the General Staff, such as Akhromeyev and Moiseev, were "the biggest supporters" of the biological weapons program, and Yazov no less so.[19] Alibek's description of Maslyukov's opinions regarding BW appears to be at least partly inconsistent with Kataev's description of Maslyukov. He had been Zaikov's predecessor as head of the Central Committee's Department of Defense Industry. (Several years later, under President Yeltsin, he would serve as deputy prime minister to Primakov). According to Kataev, disarmament took off when Maslyukov moved to chair the VPK and Zaikov became secretary of the Central Committee Department. As allies, they were able to overcome the MOD's constant opposition to arms control, but if Alibek is correct perhaps BW was an exception for him.

In addition to information on the Central Committee decisions, there are also several pages of handwritten notes made by Kataev of meetings of the Politburo and Secretariat's *Pyatorka* groups.[20] The first of these unfortunately is undated, but notations in other documents suggest that it took place on October 2, 1987. Marshal Akhromeyev reported that a destruction plan has been developed, that in any case "defensive means" would remain, and that the schedule must not be shortened. He also noted that even if destruction is completed by January 1, 1989, any visiting specialists would see the rooms used for production, as they are hard to avoid. Maslyukov noted that the rooms used "for analysis" are not yet clean, but that a method to achieve this will be found by 1989. The equipment and storage areas of the "central military-medical institution" have been dismantled but a berm at the facility remains from 1972. Akhromeyev points out that it would require from 6 to 12 months to resume production, but Zaikov interjected that this is not the concern at the moment, rather it is what to do right now. Akhromeyev says that the situation is "OK concerning toxins," presumably indicating that there would be no noticeable indications of their having been produced or stockpiled. Shevardnadze noted that practical inspections will not "enter into force" until later, but that "we should go along with inspection." The page ends with a note saying, "Foreign Affairs Ministry [should] handle matters so that inspections do not occur before 1989."

Alibek claims that Biopreparat officials were told that the United States "had begun to demand entry to our labs as early as 1986," and that as one response to this "In 1988 . . . Gorbachev signed a decree, prepared by the Military-Industrial Commission [VPK], ordering the development of mobile production equipment to keep our weapons assembly lines one step ahead of inspectors."[21] This "decree" does not appear in the group listed by Kataev, but there were apparently other forms of administrative directives that could be categorized as decrees: *ukazenia* and *postavlenie*. In addition, BW issues came only partly within Kataev's responsibility on the Politburo Secretariat, and it is very likely that many, or even possibly most, papers on the subject available to Zaikov and Shakhov did not reach Kataev's notice.

A second set of notes by Kataev summarizes a presentation on July 27, 1989, by General Kalinin, "Deputy Minister of Medical Industry," before the Politburo Commission. Kalinin began with a set of figures to demonstrate the cost effectiveness of biological weapons. These are stated in dollars, although the area coverage is given in hectares (ha): conventional munitions, $2,000 per ha; nuclear weapons, $800 per ha; chemical weapons, $60 per ha; and biological weapons, $1 per ha. These figures are taken directly from the set of SIPRI volumes, *The Problem of Chemical and Biological Warfare,* which were considered classified information in the Soviet Union. In the SIPRI book, the figures are provided *per square kilometer,* for attack against a *civilian* target, and for the *payload alone,* that is, not counting the cost of the delivery systems.[22] Kalinin then stated that the "USA is hiding its bioweapons facilities," and that the bermed Soviet MOD facilities are ready for inspection. Rather astonishingly, he added that "berming indicates that they were for vaccine production." "Guarantees" would exist for visiting inspections, and that all research institutions—presumably a reference to Biopreparat facilities—have been given orders to prepare for inspections, but that it would require "1.5 years to bring the other two also into order," a possible reference to the MOD facilities at Zagorsk and Kirov.[23] In an obvious reference to Sverdlovsk, Kalinin says, "We are not finding spores now. But [they] might be in pockets," indicating that the MOD authorities had been carrying out a sampling and monitoring effort between 1979 and at least mid-1989 in the area covered by the plume of anthrax spores that had escaped from the MOD BW facility. Kalinin then added that an unnamed laboratory "does not contradict the convention," probably also a reference to the Sverdlovsk MOD facility. Shevardnadze asked, "Whether it is a violation or not, why are there legends? There will be [CWC] Convention one year from now. Any enterprise will be under monitoring." Kalinin replies—again in apparent reference to Sverdlovsk—that "the amount of production [is] not a contradiction. . . . But we will cease [production] in the agreed period, it will not be [in violation]." Notably, *"production" had not yet ended in mid-1989, and prior to Pasechnik's defection, it was not expected to end for another year and a half.* Zaikov notes that the deadlines proposed by the MOD are for one year, and by Bykov (minister of medical industry) is for 1.5 years.[24] On the subject of cleaning up former BW facilities and their conversion and re-utilization, Zaikov and Shevardnadze were urging accelerated cleanup but "the technical people" would respond, "No, we can't; we must use the appropriate technology and be sure that we get it right." Shevardnadze realized that when problems of an allegedly technological nature were introduced, it was used to slow down arms control.

Vladimir Pasechnik's Defection, and Soviet, US, and UK Responses

While on a trip sanctioned by Biopreparat officials to purchase equipment in France, in the second half of October 1989, Pasechnik defected (see Table 21.2). According to his own testimony, he had intended to defect to the Canadian Embassy, but their staff directed him to return with processed immigration application forms and then await notification of their decision. He therefore left and tried the British Embassy, which was within walking distance.[25] Several hours were required for British intelligence agencies in London to decide that he should quickly be brought to the United Kingdom, and several additional hours to obtain the required authorizations from several

Table 21.2 Chronology, 1989–1991

Date	Event
February 13, 1989	President Bush "pauses" US-USSR diplomacy
March 7, 1989	Vienna, Bush/Shevardnadze meeting
April 6, 1989	London, Gorbachev/Thatcher meeting
May 11, 1989	Moscow, Baker/Gorbachev meeting
September 21, 1989	Washington, Shevardnadze/Bush meeting
September 1989	Wyoming, Shevardnadze/Baker meeting
Late October 1989	Vladimir Pasechnik defects to the UK, debriefings begin in the UK
November 9, 1989	Berlin Wall is opened
December 2–3, 1989	Malta, Bush/Gorbachev Summit
February 9, 1990	Moscow, Baker/Gorbachev meeting
April 4–6, 1990	Washington, Baker/Shevardnadze meeting
May 14, 1990	Moscow, Matlock (US)/Braithwaite (UK) present démarche re: Soviet BW program to the Soviet Foreign Ministry[a]
May 2, 1990	Moscow, Baker/Shevardnadze meeting
May 17, 1990	Baker/Shevardnadze meeting
May 30, 1990	Washington, Bush/Gorbachev summit
June 8, 1990	Moscow, Thatcher/Gorbachev summit
July 16–18, 1990	Paris, Baker/Shevardnadze meeting
August 1, 1990	Irkutsk, Baker/Shevardnadze meeting
September 9, 1990	Helsinki, Bush/Gorbachev meeting
September 11, 1990	Paris, Baker/Shevardnadze meeting
September 14–15, 1990	Moscow, Hurd/Shevardnadze meeting
October 1990 to April 1991	Gorbachev aligns with "hardliners" and appoints a series of more reactionary individuals to major positions
November 19, 1990	Paris, Bush/Gorbachev meeting
December 9, 1990	Houston, Baker/Shevardnadze meeting
January 8–18, 1991	US/UK visits to Vector, Obolensk, IHPB, and Lyubuchany
March 5, 1991	Moscow, Major/Gorbachev meeting
June 2, 1991	Lisbon, Baker/Bessmyrtnykh meeting
July 17, 1991	London, Bush/Gorbachev meeting
July 29, 1991	Moscow, Bush/Gorbachev summit

(continued)

Table 21.2 (continued)

Date	Event
August 18–21, 1991	Failed coup attempt against Gorbachev in Moscow
October 30, 1991	Madrid, Bush/Gorbachev meeting
December 15, 1991	Moscow, Baker meets separately with Yeltsin and Gorbachev
December 1991	USSR visits Pine Bluff, USAMRIID, Dugway, Salk Institute (PA)

a. The Soviet Ministry of Foreign Affairs considered all UK-US-USSR interactions on this subject from May 1990, the date of the first transmission of a US-UK démarche to the USSR, as part of "the Trilaterals." The US and UK reserve the use of the term for the September 1992 negotiations that led to the signing of the Trilateral Statement in Moscow, and all the subsequent site visits and negotiations until the demise of the process in 1996.

British government ministries. Before the day's end, he was on his way to the United Kingdom.

The defection was, however, anything but the primary concern in Moscow at this time. Larger and larger demonstrations against the Communist government of East Germany had taken place in the preceding months, and the Hungarian government had decided to turn a blind eye to large numbers of East Germans fleeing across the Hungarian border to Austria and the West. Two weeks after Pasechnik's defection, on November 9, 1989, the Berlin Wall fell, and soon after that the entire Warsaw Pact disintegrated. By October 1990, the two halves of Germany were reunited.

A team from Biopreparat headquarters hurried to Leningrad and confiscated all the files in Pasechnik's office. They were searched in order to determine exactly what information had been available to Pasechnik, and how much detail about the Soviet BW program he might be able to divulge to Western intelligence. Surprisingly, according to Alibek, despite his own description of the work being done at Pasechnik's institute and knowing that Pasechnik had made multiple official visits to various Biopreparat facilities for over a dozen years, Biopreparat officials allegedly decided that "he didn't really know very much."[26] Mangold and Goldberg follow Alibek, and write that "Kalinin, the director of Biopreparat, was asked to prepare a confidential response for the Kremlin. After several working sessions with his staff to anticipate how much the West already knew, Kalinin decided to continue the bluffing. The reply would fully reject all accusations and claim that the nation possessed only a defensive biological programme."[27] Alibek also reported that the Politburo had earlier been misled by a previous memo that deemphasized the significance of Pasechnik's defection.

In the United Kingdom, Pasechnik—now codenamed TRUNCATE— was debriefed in several sessions through mid-November, and then intermittently apparently for two years. However, it was not until February 1990 that interim reports of the debriefings were given to senior British officials, and not until March 1990 that the first formal report on the information that Pasechnik had provided was completed. It is not clear at what point US intelligence agencies were informed of Pasechnik's defection, but they began to learn details of the debriefings in January and February 1990.

Another meeting took place on January 23, 1990, in Zaikov's office with an agenda point titled "On the instructions to the USSR representative at the Soviet-American consultations on the questions of the prohibition of bacteriological and toxin weapons." However, no notes are available for the discussion that took place on this topic, although at least minimal notes or decisions were recorded for the other four agenda topics on that day. Only a list of the 19 participants is recorded.[28] However, another meeting followed only a few days later, on January 31, 1990. It was now two months after Pasechnik's defection, and the United States and United Kingdom had not yet made any comment, but it was assumed that it would not be much longer in coming (However, it did not occur until May 14, 1990.) The meeting notes read like the script for a stage play, and are reproduced almost verbatim below:

Zaikov asks why "strict protection" [prohibiting access] is necessary.

Kalinin replies that 1.5 years will be needed for "protection . . . there is secrecy of development."

All recipes have been destroyed, and all stocks have been destroyed. "With the fulfillment of the decree political aspects will be removed." [This is presumably a euphemism for saying that the USSR would no longer be in violation of the BWC.] Multipurpose equipment is being retained; it is used for producing medicines. For the present time the equipment will be stored.

Shevardnadze: Why don't we discuss data for American companies?

Zaikov: "By January 1 [1991] destroy and dismantle equipment."

Kalinin: 121 countries have acceded [to the BWC], 24 have not.

Zaikov: Remove the documents. Estimate the tasks for a special period.

Chebrikov: Transfer permissible work to a laboratory

Belousov: There must be a document which brings everything into accord with the convention.

Kalinin: There is such a document.

Chebrikov: 24 countries did not accede: We must understand whether the Americans will monitor them. BW is more dangerous than nuclear strikes, because [it] does not have a response action. We must work without violating the convention.

Zaikov: Destroy the documentation: destroy it in three months.

Shevardnadze: A document should show what's in violation and what is not. Let them work. [i.e., have them prepare it]

Zaikov: This was discussed, it will be revised one more time. It will be considered at a closed meeting. The document will be "transferred from a defense into a political document;" also the title of the document will be changed. It will accord with the convention and contain a commentary.[29]

Zaikov's reiteration that all documentation should be destroyed implies that they have not been and suggests that he did not believe Kalinin's claim that "all recipes have been destroyed." Notes of another meeting that concerned only chemical weapons contain several striking comments, but it is difficult to know how to interpret these, although they seem to suggest a dangerous frame of mind: "Challenge inspections. Do not accept British proposal. They cannot verify hidden storage." "We accept verification but not Defense Ministry stocks." The British had not in fact made any "proposal" in 1990. However in the context of the ongoing CWC negotiations, the United Kingdom had carried out Practice Challenge Inspections, first at government-owned military sites and then at a British chemical plant in January 1991.[30]

More significantly, Alibek reports that following Pasechnik's defection KGB chairman Vladimir Kryuchkov had written a memorandum to Gorbachev "recommending the liquidation of our biological weapon production lines."[31] This memo was the very first initiative Kryuchkov had taken in the arms control process. On other issues he usually "finally" fell into line late, but here he was the one to suggest altering the status quo. Kryuchkov was intelligent, but perhaps more importantly Kryuchkov had a very intelligent deputy in the small *Pyatorka*, Nikolai Leonov, who very likely had influenced him. Kryuchkov took Leonov's advice, and took him along to meetings of the higher *Pyatorka*, and Leonov spoke there as well. Kataev could recall no meeting dealing with Kryuchkov's memo, but there need not have been one. In cases of an unusual position such as this one, there might just have been two or three people in Zaikov's office to talk about it. The memo would have been called "A Report to the Central Committee." However, Alibek places this alleged memo as following "our diplomatic reply to the U.S. and British governments," which would not occur until seven months after Pasechnik's defection. Supposedly, a decision on such "liquidation" had already been made in the sequence of five Central Committee decisions recorded by Kataev. It is nevertheless conceivable that Kruychkov and the KGB produced a memorandum during the months of March–April 1990, perhaps urging an acceleration of the "liquidation." In Alibek's description the rationale was to sacrifice the production facilities in order to preserve the BW research programs.

Pasechnik's defection did not cause any problem for the continued work of the SWG. The MOD and VPK representatives in the group were not protesting or vetoing. When a former Soviet diplomat was therefore asked why the subsequent discussions about BW with the United States and the United Kingdom did not go the way that negotiations about INF missiles or CW did, the reply was paradoxically that the latter were much bigger issues: "After all, Gorbachev had said on January 15, 1986, that *all* nuclear weapons should be dispensed with by the year 2000. At the small *Pyatorka* that dealt with the CWC, anywhere from five or six to a dozen generals starting with Lt. General Pikalov, might show up for a single meeting. Whereas in the SWG, there was one Major General. Kalinin was a Major General, and Yevstigneev was a Major General. There were thousands of Generals in the USSR. No one listened to the 15th Directorate."[32] If this reply means anything at all, it only makes the puzzle more intractable. If no one was listening to the 15th Directorate, why was the offensive BW program not shut down once it became a serious and irritating political issue in relations between the United States and the Soviet Union and then Russia?

Among the events spawned by Pasechnik's defection, Alibek describes a meeting in March 1990 at the VPK headquarters in the Kremlin. Its purpose was to think of ways to respond to the accusations expected from the United States and United Kingdom once they had been able to interrogate Pasechnik. The participants were Belousov, the head of the VPK, his deputy Alexei Arzhakov, Oleg Ignatiev, the head of VPK's Biological Weapons Directorate, which coordinated the development and production of biological weapons, and Yevstigneev.[34] Alibek describes the meeting as "ineffectual," but it was followed by a second episode that must be considered ludicrous. Two generals, one from the KGB and one from GRU, joined Alibek and Arzhakov and were tasked to produce information about facilities in the United

States that would indicate an active offensive US BW program. The two generals asked to be given several weeks time to gather the information. At the end of that period they returned, and in addition to Fort Detrick, which they had already mentioned at the first meeting, they mentioned Plum Island, the mothballed World War II Pfizer facility in Indiana, and several other locations that, Alibek pointedly noted, had all "been discounted as inactive," and about which masses of public information was easily available.[34]

Alibek follows this with an episode that he places in April 1990 following a planned government reorganization of the Ministry of Medical Industry. Alibek proposed to Kalinin that he would write a memorandum to Gorbachev's staff suggesting that the Soviet Union "stop all offensive biological research and production." Insertion of the words "offensive biological research" is a significant step beyond the five Central Committee resolutions and decisions for which we have Kataev's documentary record. Kalinin authorized Alibek to prepare a draft decree, and together with another military member of his staff, Colonel Pryadkin, Alibek did so. "There were just four paragraphs. The first announced that Biopreparat would cease to function as an offensive warfare agency. The final paragraph declared that it would be separated from the Ministry of Medical Industry."[35] The decree signed by Gorbachev arrived back in Kalinin's office on May 5, 1990. In addition to Alibek's four paragraphs, "an additional one had been tacked on at the end. It instructed Biopreparat 'to organize the necessary work to keep all of its facilities prepared for further manufacture and development.'" Alibek reports Kalinin saying, "With this paper, everyone gets to do what he wants to do."[36] Although this reportedly took place two weeks before the assumed date of Kataev's reference note, it is not listed in that compendium of five CPSU resolutions and decisions. As already indicated, it is possible that this too might have been an administrative order such as the *ukazenie* or *postavlenie* not requiring Central Committee authorization. Alibek states that one direct consequence of Gorbachev's decree was that "assembly lines were destroyed at Omutninsk, Berdsk, Stepnogorsk, Kurgan and Penza."[37]

Alibek also claims that Gorbachev signed an order in 1988–1989 for construction of two new BW *production* facilities, one at Yoshkar-Ola and the second "near Irkutsk," but that neither facility was ever built due to the lack of funds.[38] Budgeting for construction of facilities would again be incorporated into a larger *Gosplan* appropriations plan, and these were presumably mobilization capacity facilities and so they might not have been considered problematical even if they had explicitly been brought to Gorbachev's attention. They would have been analogous to the construction of the large small-pox production facility at Vector, which remained unfinished when the Soviet Union collapsed on December 31, 1991. Similarly, Kirov-200 was never fully equipped (see Chapter 3).

The description of Baklanov's substantive positions described earlier is relevant to the Alibek-Kalinin memo. Kataev's comment was that he could "see Baklanov's hand on that document." Kalinin had brought it to Aleksandr Galkin, the "postman" in the General Department of the Central Committee, but also the office where "Special Files" were kept.[39] If Kalinin was a frequent visitor to his office, it was presumably where "Special Problems" (BW) also resided. Galkin would have sent the memo to a small group: Zaikov, Kataev, Belyakov, and Baklanov. Gorbachev would not have read the document, and possibly neither would have Zaikov. If it came back to Gorbachev signed by the *Pyatorka*—which Alibek describes—Gorbachev would sign it and never see that the first four paragraphs and the last paragraph were contradictory. At roughly the same time in 1990, Alibek was informed at Gosplan that 300 million rubles were allotted toward Biopreparat's operations in 1990 and that he should submit his plans for its use.[40]

During January and February 1990, senior officials at the CIA were supplied with the details of Pasechnik's debriefings in the United Kingdom. Pasechnik's narrative was very specific: "This piece of equipment in institute X was used for purpose Y on date so and so."[41] Reportedly, the United States frequently had stored technical intelligence obtained in previous years, which could corroborate particular activities at a site and date. Aside from the overhead satellite photographs of each facility, these additional bits of information had always been isolated and fragmentary and carried no inherent meaning in themselves. They might simply be something like the presence of particular trucks at a particular site. In addition, the significance of these more detailed items had always been disputed within the intelligence community: there were those who had endowed them with significance relevant to BW, and others who had doubted such significance.[42] The Biopreparat facilities about which Pasechnik was providing information to his debriefers were, after all, the very same ones that the CIA had been publicly identifying repeatedly between 1976 and 1989, although it presumably knew little or nothing about what was taking place inside the buildings, with the possible exception of the MOD facility at Sverdlovsk.[43]

CIA officials went to President Bush's National Security Council (NSC) and argued that the United States had to approach the Soviets and resolve this question, otherwise the major strategic arms control treaties—SALT, START, and so forth—would be undermined if the information became known. The US Arms Control and Disarmament Agency (ACDA) was also required by law to report to Congress annually whether any treaty signatories were in violation of compliance with arms control treaties. Although the United States had already been charging the Soviet Union with noncompliance since at least 1986, Pasechnik's disclosures were too significant to be subsumed under the already existing US charges.

The administration had earlier established an ad hoc interagency panel within the NSC called the "un-group"—that is "no group." Despite its informal designation, it had major responsibilities in regard to all the arms-control negotiations being undertaken with the Soviet Union. It was directed by Arnold Kanter on the NSC staff. and included Reginald Bartholomew in the Department of State (DOS); Ronald Lehman, director of ACDA; General Howard Graves, who sat in for the chairman of the Joint Chiefs of Staff, General John Shalikashvilli; Paul Wolfowitz of the US Department of Defense (DOD), who usually sent Stephen Hadley; Douglas MacEachin of the CIA; and, toward the end of the process, Victor Alessi of the Department of Energy. The un-group now had a new problem to deal with: Pasechnik's disclosures about the Soviet offensive BW program. In the words of one of the members of the un-group, "the last thing we wanted was to allow this 'turd in a punch bowl' to sink the ship."[44] In early May 1990, the congressional leadership was also briefed: the House and Senate majority and minority leaders, and the heads of the "Big Six" committees: Foreign Affairs, Intelligence, and Armed Forces in both Senate and House. This was done after Baker had been to Moscow, due to the fear that someone would leak information pertaining to Pasechnik's disclosures so as to deliberately impede the strategic arms control negotiations. No one ever leaked the information.

The Malta summit early in December 1989 was too early to permit the United States to introduce the subject of the Soviet BW program. However, early in 1990, during a bilateral US-USSR consultation on CW weapons, the United States apparently did deliver some sort of message indicating concern about the Soviet BW program. The date of the interaction, and exactly what was said, is unknown. However, in response, and in anticipation of Shevardnadze's trip to Washington to meet with US Secretary of State Baker on April 4–6, 1990, the following instructions were provided to Shevardnadze in the event that Baker would bring up the subject:

Bacteriological Weapons. Confirm our positive evaluation of the bilateral consultations that have started in this area. To declare that we intend to pursue the matter until existing concerns are, to the extent possible, addressed prior to the Third Review Conference of the Convention on the Prohibition of Biological Weapons (September 1991). Propose to J. Baker to provide joint instructions on bilateral consultations to the delegations to prepare a draft agreement between the Governments of the USSR and the US on confidence-building measures and increasing transparency with regard to this convention by spring 1990 for his signature at the meeting between the Minister for Foreign Affairs of the USSR and the Secretary of State of the USA.

Do not object to routine consultations on questions of the prohibition of bacteriological weapons taking place within the framework of the second part of the 16th round of bilateral negotiations on the prohibition of chemical weapons.[45]

Baker apparently did not mention the subject of the Soviet BW program at their meetings during April 4–6 in Washington, and Shevardnadze apparently said nothing about it on that occasion. But Baker would do so a month later. It is known that the United States did pass some sort of note to Soviet diplomats sometime in April 1990, in addition to the May 14 US-UK démarche described further below. It is therefore possible that this was done during the April 4–6 meeting. It has been possible to ascertain at least some of the information that the United States asked Soviet officials to supply in April 1990 and in later notes because this information appears in a memorandum that was written in September 1992 for the senior US negotiator in Moscow in the deliberations that would produce the Trilateral Accords.[46] The document runs to 10 pages and is of particular interest because the information it contains regarding the Soviet BW program probably resembles to a substantial degree the contents of the successive notes that the United States passed to Gorbachev and Shevardnadze in the months following April 1990, none of which are publicly available. These 1990 notes were reportedly rather brief documents, and the information they contained was probably not overly detailed. The same is the case for the September 1992 US briefing document. The United States asked for clarification regarding the purpose of the Soviet Union's mobilization capacity BW production facilities, explicitly identifying Berdsk,

Omutninsk, Stepnogorsk, and several others by name. It should be recalled that the United States had been publicly naming these sites in a series of leaked and then official statements every year or two since 1976 (see Chapter 12).

We also know something about what took place in several of the lower-level bilateral diplomatic discussions from two documents obtained from US sources. In August 1989, US and Soviet diplomats drew up a draft proposal for a bilateral information exchange aside from the annual CBMs exchanged under the BWC. Each side would provide the other with the names and locations of facilities containing BSL-4 or BSL-3 laboratories that worked "under direction from or under contract with the Ministry/Department of Defense." They would also provide each other with lists of open-literature publications resulting from work in those facilities, or in BSL-3 and BSL-4 labs reported under the BWC CBMs. The exchange of information would begin by April 15, 1990. But in an early sign of an issue that would become critical four and five years later, the Soviet side wanted facilities not only on the territory of either party to be covered by the data exchange, but also *"under its jurisdiction or control anywhere,"* while the United States wanted only those *within the territory of the two sides* to be covered. The phrase "under contract with its Ministry/Department of Defense" was the only addition to the comparable 1986 CBMs.[47] A Soviet statement at another US-Soviet meeting of diplomats on February 20, 1990, noted that at the forthcoming Third BWC Review Conference in 1991, "it will be necessary to review the question of a possible system of international control and possible measures to safeguard the observance of the Convention," and it suggested that the United States and Soviet Union discuss issues relating to such control aimed at preparing "specific proposals" for the Review Conference.[48]

Based on interviews with members of the UK intelligence services, Mangold and Goldberg claim that following Pasechnik's debriefings, "many officials in Prime Minister Thatcher's government were urging that everything should be made public." This was in contrast to US wishes that Gorbachev and Shevardnadze should be approached in private: "The US also had to convince the British government to acquiesce with [the] quiet approach."[49] They also quote "a senior British official" saying that "Thatcher actually dragged a reluctant American president into a more forceful policy."[50] However, it is not clear that was the case. US policy makers were concerned with the diverse political pressures impacting Gorbachev and Shevardnadze at the moment. German reunification was already a major issue, and as always there were other priorities that took precedence.

The CIA prepared a paper built around Pasechnik's disclosures. It listed places, names, and for each the confirmatory sources and evidence that the CIA had had for years. The purpose of the additional information was to indicate to the Soviet leadership why the US government believed what Pasechnik said. When Baker and his assistant Dennis Ross were in Moscow to meet with Shevardnadze in on May 2, 1990, Baker handed Shevardnadze the paper while they were being driven to Zagorsk. Referring to the Soviet MOD BW facility in Zagorsk, Baker reportedly told Shevardnadze, "If you look out the window, you can see one of them." When they returned to Moscow, MFA officials Bessmyrtnykh and Batsanov, who had been informed of the US document by Shevardnadze, came into the room saying, "My God, My God; this is terrible. We didn't know." One week earlier, British foreign secretary Malcolm Rifkind had already presented similar information to Shevardnadze. The United Kingdom in fact saw itself as leading the effort with the Soviets on this issue. Yazov was in the room at the time and said, "Oh, you got that from Pasechnik." It is possible that Shevardnadze's deputies had not been informed of the substance of Rifkind's message; similar failure to communicate occurred at times on the US side as well. To an MFA observer it did not appear that the UK and US memoranda produced much concern or reaction on the Soviet side. In response, the MOD gave Shevardnadze a paper of five to six pages that began with a history of the Red Army's interest in BW in the 1930s, and at its end included a half page about Biopreparat. That was the only page of the MOD paper that remained among the Central Committee documents that were obtained. It is innocuous and portrays Biopreparat as a pharmaceutical concern. The MFA considered the paper useless.

The First US-UK Démarche and the Soviet Responses

On May 14, 1990, US ambassador Jack Matlock and British ambassador Rodric Braithwaite delivered a joint démarche to Aleksandr Bessmyrtnykh, Soviet deputy minister of foreign affairs. They also made the same presentation on the same day to Anatoly Chernyaev, special assistant to Gorbachev. Four days later, on May 18,

> at formal talks in Moscow between British Defence Minister Tom King and Soviet Minister of Defence, Dmitry Yazov, the hard-line Soviet Marshall dismissively told King that it was inconceivable that the Soviet Union would develop or possess biological weapons. In denying

everything, Yazov claimed that this issue had nothing to do with the Ministry of Defence. Any biological research by the military, he said, was intended only to collect intelligence about potential epidemics and to prevent animal diseases—like anthrax, cholera, and Plague—from breaching Soviet borders. Yazov added, for good measure, that the West's misinformation was coming from an "insane scientist" (Pasechnik) who was a liar with personal problems.[51]

It is possible to describe the substance of the joint US-UK démarche because Bessmyrtnykh produced a three-page memorandum recounting the presentation on the same day. It summarized the three major points of the US-UK document:

- Concerns regarding Soviet compliance with the BWC were expressed at the BWC RevCon in 1986, and "They acquire new resonance in connection with the new information received by us on specific Soviet facilities, people and programs in the given fields."
- "We have reasons to suppose that in the USSR a large-scale secret program in the field of biological weapons is being carried out and there exists significant stockpiles of such weapons far in excess of the reasonable requirements for research purposes. We also have information that bacteriological weapons are being manufactured and stockpiled in the USSR."
- "This démarche has a goal of closing this problem without bringing it to a high political level. We are interested in not burdening the contacts on a high and highest levels with discussions of the given question. We also intend to do everything possible so that information about this demarche and the data in our possession does not leak into the press. . . . both governments—the American and British—have in mind to resolve this question in a business-like fashion without public agitation around it. This approach in particular is motivated by the fact that numerous planned meetings at the highest level are approaching, and governments of these countries are not interested in bringing the question of the Soviet biological weapons to the political level. We would like, Braithwaite underlined, to solve it without additional fuss. . . . J. Matlock stressed the point that the USA and Great Britain do not intend to raise the given question in a confrontational context and do not intend to make it public. . . . Surely Matlock said, we are absolutely not interested in

burdening our relations with a new problem on the eve of the most important negotiations at the highest levels."[52]

Assuming Bessmyrtnykh's description is accurate, the degree to which Braithwaite and Matlock emphasized US and UK interest in not perturbing Gorbachev in this initial démarche is striking. After all, the Central Committee was certainly expecting to hear about it ever since Pasechnik's defection. Bessmyrtnykh added a short paragraph describing his disparaging reply to the US and UK ambassadors: "that there exists a claim which is by no means substantiated by anything yet, a claim about 'some violation.'"[53] Years later, in the United States, Alibek was informed of Chernyaev's reply to the US and UK ambassadors by Ambassador Matlock.[54] According to Matlock, Chernyaev said: "There are three possibilities one could assume about the information you are giving me. One is that the information is wrong; a second is that Gorbachev knows of this but hasn't told me; and a third is that neither he nor I know."[55]

According to Bessmyrtnykh's description, the United States and United Kingdom had not handed over anything specific in the démarches, none of the satellite photographs the United States by then had for approximately 14 years, no named locations, and so on. If Bessmyrtnykh's memo accurately represents the proportion of the US-UK message devoted to its final point, that situation would change in a very few months. President Bush and Prime Minister Thatcher would get directly involved, as would Prime Minister Major after that. So would Baker, UK Foreign Minister Hurd, and Gorbachev, Shevardnadze, and Yazov on the Soviet side.

On the very next day, Gorbachev was presented with a three-page memorandum "on the subject of biological weapons" by Zaikov. A copy of the memorandum was also delivered on the same day to Shevardnadze. Its major points were as follows:

- The US obtained biological weapons "immediately after WWII," but in the USSR their "development . . . began in the 1950s at . . . Kirov, Zagorsk and Sverdlovsk."
- "In 1971 they were joined in this work by another 12 organizations of the USSR Ministry of the Medical Industry and the former USSR State Agroindustrial Committee. By 1985 they had developed 12 recipes and means for using them. These were produced in suitable quantities, stored, and destroyed after the expiration of useful life (an average of 6 months)."

- "The Convention [BWC] . . . had no effective inspection mechanism for ensuring compliance, nor was there a precise definition of the difference between developing biological weapons and defensive means against them. According to some data, the NATO countries took advantage of the situation to engage in intensive development and production of especially aggressive biological infectious agents. Some of this work was done in third countries that had not signed the Convention."

- "Forced to respond, our country also carried out such work until 1989. However because of significant progress in negotiations on the Chemical Weapons Convention, which provided for inspection of any facility, including biological facilities, and the possible implementation of international inspection of compliance with the 1972 Biological Weapons Convention, the USSR Central Committee decided on October 6, 1989, that all research capacity for developing *biological* weapons be redirected and used to develop defensive means against these weapons so as not to contradict our international obligations."

- "In 1988 the stocks of special recipes were destroyed, production of active materials at industrial facilities was halted and special processing and munitions-assembly equipment was dismantled."

- "On December 6, 1989 the USSR Central Committee decided that eight biological research and production facilities of the USSR be prepared for international inspection by July 1, 1990. On March 16, 1990 the USSR Central Committee decided that three such facilities of the USSR Ministry of Defense and four facilities of the USSR Council of Ministers State Commission for Food and Procurements be prepared for inspection by January 1, 1991."

- Zaikov then noted, "It is possible that some Western circles have a heightened interest in our country's compliance with the 1972 Convention after the defection of V. A. Pasechnik in France in October 1989."

- "Pasechnik . . . had knowledge of the content of special biological research work as well as the locations of organizations involved in this work. However any possible leak of information by Pasechnik . . . will not cause major damage in revealing our scientific and technical achievements in this field but might provide a basis for Western countries to question the Soviet Union's compliance" with the BWC.

- "If the issue arises of visiting each other's biological facilities in order to lessen concerns about their activity, we could propose that the American visit facilities in Kirov, Novosibirsk and Obolensk. In return, Soviet specialists should visit the Baker Laboratory at Dugway Army Proving Ground, the National Toxicology Center (Pine Bluff, Arkansas), and the Cetus Corporation (Amityville, California) which were not on the list of biological facilities that the US declared to the UN."[56]

It is a strange document. Despite euphemistic language, inclusion of disinformation and outright falsification, taken together with the five Central Committee decisions it is very likely the most authoritative documentary "smoking gun" for the Soviet offensive BW program that will ever be seen. It refers successively to having "developed 12 recipes" by 1985, "production of active materials at industrial facilities," "produced in suitable quantities," "stocks of special recipes," the "means for using them," and "munitions assembly equipment." No evidence is offered that "NATO countries" ended the "intensive development" that the Soviet Union was supposedly only responding to, yet the Central Committee was abruptly deciding that the country should "not . . . contradict our international obligations," something that it had no reluctance to do for the preceding 15 years. The claim for 12 weaponized agents is actually more than Alibek describes in his book. In addition to the critical misinformation supplied to Gorbachev, there are implicit contradictions between various lines within the memorandum and also with statements in some of the other Central Committee materials. Zaikov's flat declaration that "stocks of special recipes were destroyed" and "production of active materials at industrial facilities" was halted in 1988 is contradicted by earlier remarks during discussions in the Central Committee, some of them made by Zaikov himself, others by Kalinin. The reference to "some western circles"—a hackneyed phrase used thousands of times in standard Soviet propaganda—seems an odd way to refer to President Bush and Prime Minister Thatcher and the US and UK foreign ministers and ambassadors in a memorandum to Gorbachev.

The information on which the memo was based would have been supplied by the MOD, intelligence agencies (KGB and GRU), and the VPK. If the MOD and intelligence agencies truly believed the statements introduced by phrases such as "According to some data" and "some data indicate," they were responsible for at least as great an intelligence failure as the US and the UK intelligence communities had been, albeit of exact opposite nature.[57] Between 1950 and 1976, the United States and United Kingdom did not see a program that was there, and Soviet intelligence agencies claimed to see a program that did not exist even through the 1990s. When the KGB formulated its secret reports, Kataev said that these were routinely "worst case analysis," exaggerated to make the subject seem more important. In a series of possible alternative interpretations, the approach was to pick the worst case, and to operate as if that were the reality. In case they had not obtained sufficient information, they nevertheless "defended their interests" in the information that they provided. "No one ever fired you for exaggeration; if you understated or underreported, you got demoted immediately. A KGB report might say, 'There are no new developments, but there could be,' and the senior leadership would read the words as 'There are.'" Kataev said that he received 10 such secret reports or cables per day. He was able to assess their credibility, but the same reports and cables went directly to the "higher ups" who were not able to make such assessments and accepted them as they were written. Kataev said that intelligence was also prepared by sections of the defense industry—and in the BW case, that would imply the VPK and Biopreparat headquarters—and they also produced worst-case analyses, "to produce more X or Y themselves, to increase their budget."

Did Shakhov, or other *Pyatorka* participants, believe that the United States had a covert, offensive BW program after 1972? Kataev had been very dissatisfied with KGB and GRU information delivered to him when he had still been a designer of strategic missiles in the years before he came to the Secretariat staff. He described their information-collecting methods as "a vacuum cleaner" with little discernment of significance. He realized that "their brief was to find the worst, and produce what their bosses wanted." He provided numerous examples of the military-scientific sector "producing what their bosses wanted" in the pre-1985 Soviet system, both in the way of interpretation and analysis as well as hardware. Kataev had never heard of the US BW disinformation operation, but in regard to the general question he replied that there was no open literature on the US program and that he and his colleagues could only evaluate what the KGB and GRU delivered to them. Therefore despite his own earlier personal experiences, he and his colleagues believed that there was such a program because "where there is smoke, there is fire."

When Pasechnik was recruited for the position as director of IHPB, he was provided with briefings by members of the staff of the Central Committee and the KGB. The Central Committee official at the time was Oleg G. Shirokov. Pasechnik was told that the United States and United Kingdom were developing biological weapons, although this was years after the US renunciation of BW in 1969, and even after the signing of the BWC in 1972. *No mention was made of the BWC.* As for Soviet intelligence agencies, Pasechnik thought that their basic assumption was that because the Soviet Union did both open and highly secret work, the United States therefore did the same.

The difference in testimony from civilian and military scientists involved in the Soviet BW program as regards their knowledge of the prohibitions of the BWC is striking. Alibek, a military officer and not a civilian scientist, provided a very different description. Alibek reports that, on being recruited to work at Omutninsk after his military medical education, he was given the following introduction: "You are aware that this isn't normal work . . . I have to inform you that there exists an international treaty on biological warfare, which the Soviet Union has signed. . . . According to that treaty no one is allowed to make biological weapons. But the United States signed it too, and we believe that the Americans are lying."[58]

Another high-ranking military officer in the BW program provided the same testimony as Alibek: of course they knew about the BWC, but they were told that it did not affect their work. It was of no interest to them, a matter for politicians, they had a job to do. Besides, the United States had an offensive BW program as well. The officer additionally mocked those scientists working in Biopreparat institutes who claimed not to have known of the BWC; he claimed that it was not secret and that anyone who cared to could read it.[59]

In yet another example, when Zaviyalov was working at SRCAM as a laboratory head and had been told that he would be made deputy director of a new institute, he was called to Moscow in 1978 to meet Colonel Victor Popov at Biopreparat. Up to that point, he had been told only the open legend. He had never heard of the BWC. In Moscow, Popov told him of the closed legend and told him, "We have information that our enemies, the US, UK are developing biological weapons." When Zaviyalov returned to SRCAM, a film about Fort Detrick was shown to a select group of laboratory heads. As he apparently had the best command of English in the group, he was asked to translate the captions. The film was quite detailed: how to do lab work, the organizational structure of the facility, the arrangement of the buildings, and so forth. Zaviyalov thought that it was an old film, very probably dating from before 1969 and intended for the training of incoming Fort Detrick staff. Nevertheless he accepted Colonel Popov's claim. On one single occasion in 1983, when he was still deputy director of IEI, Zaviyalov was given about 10 pages of GRU information about Fort Detrick and Porton Down. The pages claimed that "a program of biological weapons" continued in the United States. Zaviyalov described the text as "very general, strange general statements" about the pathogens being researched, without any specific evidence. As far as the BWC was concerned and Soviet scientists' understanding that they were involved in an offensive BW program even if they worked under the defensive "closed legend," Domaradsky's comment was that "the milk would not yet have dried in your mouth if you didn't understand what was going on."[60]

When Alibek was deputy director of Biopreparat, he had specifically asked the GRU to supply him with evidence of a US covert offensive BW program. They produced nothing of significance. Given this signal lack of evidence, the seeming conviction of Soviet intelligence authorities appears to have been either deliberate fabrication or, at best, simpleminded mirror-imaging of the Soviet Union's concealed program. The fact that they provided the same information to Zaikov and that it was quoted by Gorbachev indicates that it served for more than just a convenient story to tell the senior scientists who were being recruited for the Soviet BW program.

In describing Kalinin's reception at Biopreparat headquarters of the news about the US-UK démarche, Alibek repeats again that "Shevardnadze was not part of the small Kremlin circle that had been briefed about our biological weapons program. Only four members of the senior leadership—Gorbachev, KGB chairman Vladimir Kryuchkov, Defense Minister Dmitry Yazov, and Lev Zaikov—were fully aware of our secret."[61] The words "fully aware" very likely resolves the apparent inconsistency between Alibek's description and Shevardnadze's participation in the Politburo discussions already described and his knowledge of the Central Committee resolutions and decisions. It is plausible that Shevardnadze was not informed about many major and critical aspects of the BW program, such as the numbers of facilities involved and their size, precisely what they did, how many pathogens had been weaponized and produced, the size and location of stockpiles, any possible planning for contingencies for use, and so on. In one of the Politburo discussions described earlier, Zaikov refers to "a smaller group" that will meet to continue a particular discussion of the BW issue. But most importantly, if valid, Alibek's description undercuts Gorbachev's later claim that he did not know of the Soviet BW program. It seems doubtful, though, that Gorbachev would be physically present at the same time that Kryuchkov, Yazov, and Zaikov were briefed in some manner by the 15th Directorate. It is more likely that he would have been informed afterward by Zaikov. The CC Resolution of November 18, 1986, tells us that at least from that point on Gorbachev knew that a Soviet offensive BW program existed, but until the May 15, 1990, Zaikov memorandum, we cannot be certain about how detailed the information provided to him was. It is possible that Gorbachev was never as "fully aware" of details of the BW program as Zaikov, Yazov and the VPK were. What Gorbachev actually knew about the Soviet biological weapons program would depend on to what degree he questioned Zaikov privately, or Zaikov informed him privately, how closely he read the documents placed before him for signature, and whether or not those documents included euphemisms and inaccuracies as even Zaikov's May 1990 memorandum did.

Alibek's depiction should perhaps be qualified in another way as well. When Shevardnadze had to be given secret information about the Soviet BW program, Kataev wrote that the permission release had to be signed by Gorbachev. Kataev's description of this sequence is striking, but unclear as to exactly when it took place. His use of the term "negotiations" suggests that it followed the presentation of the first US-UK démarche. Despite the evidence already available that Shevardnadze knew of the Central Committee resolutions and decisions, he was not able to reply to his US and UK counterparts regarding specifics about the Soviet BW program, and so he asked for Zaikov's assistance. Zaikov replied that he could not authorize giving Shevardnadze the relevant information, that only Gorbachev could do that. Heretofore the directives had been that *no one* in the MFA should be allowed to receive *any* information on the Soviet BW program. But Shevardnadze was arriving at meetings with Baker and others without instructions and sending back panicky cables. Zaikov asked Kataev to write out a memo authorizing permission to provide Shevardnadze with BW information. Zaikov signed it, sent it to Gorbachev, who signed it. As a result "Shevardnadze got a little; not everything, but something." Pasechnik's claim that Shevardnadze had once approved the budget for all of Biopreparat in his role of Politburo member was based on information that he had been told by Kalinin at some point between 1986 and 1988.[62] In mid-1990, the United States reportedly obtained "a new human source in Moscow [who] confirmed that Shevardnadze had personally approved the allocation of funds for Biopreparat for 1991."[63] But it seems clear that this information, as well as Pasechnik's, was a misinterpretation of Shevardnadze's presence at Zaikov's Politburo meetings. To the degree that the US (and UK) policymakers accepted this "intelligence," they were misled at the time.[64] However, Mangold and Goldberg still misconstrued what was taking place in Moscow: Shevardnadze was not attempting to discover the details of Soviet expenditure on the offensive BW program; he was simply one of a small group of participants in these meetings. Shevardnadze's deputy, Petrovsky, was also granted some biological weapons–related documents from the VPK and MOD, among them the Soviet Union's 1987 BWC CBMs and later its 1991 CBMs. However, Shevardnadze was more fully informed than his deputies. Many years later, in a 2006 interview, Shevardnadze explained: "I had between 5,000 and 6,000 people working for me in the foreign ministry system. A third of them were KGB. I was very well informed."[65] Whether, and if so, precisely what, these KGB staffers working in the MFA provided in the way of accurate information on the nature and degree of the Soviet offensive BW system to Shevardnadze, Karpov, Petrovsky, and Smidovich is not known.

The permission, however, extended *only* to Shevardnadze, not to his deputies, and Kataev did not believe that he would have shared what he learned with them. Kataev described Shevardnadze as extremely cautious, and if he was not given carte blanche on a subject, he kept silent altogether. When Shevardnadze sent an emergency telegram to Zaikov, Zaikov would hand it to Kataev. Together with Anatoly Kovalyov, an older diplomat on Zaikov's staff, the two would draft the reply and give it to Zaikov. Zaikov would sign it, and the reply would go back to Shevardnadze with three signatures: Zaikov, Kataev, and Kovalyov. A copy would be sent to Yazov. Only very rarely were any of Kataev's replies altered. Once Zaikov, Akhromeyev, and Kataev were sitting together and Akhromeyev complained. Zaikov allowed a long pause, and pointing to Kataev replied, "He is the court of last resort about this." But Kataev also said that he never talked to Akhromeyev about biological weapons, but that "the generals like Akhromeyev, Yazov and Sokolov would support the development of any weapon, because they had lived through 1941." Kataev claimed that the MOD was absolutely against any disarmament or arms reductions, and "there never was enough of any weapon; arms control would harm the security of the Soviet Union. Kataev referred to their position as "the Leningrad syndrome," with reference to the German siege of Leningrad during World War II. Insofar as Akhromeyev was concerned, because he had been particularly helpful on CWC issues and even more so on strategic nuclear arms control, a senior US intelligence official was skeptical that he had been a BW supporter. This was despite the fact that Soviet documents declassified in 2007 demonstrated that Akhromeyev had strenuously protested some of the nuclear weapons agreements to Gorbachev.

Kataev mentioned one other problem in the "impossible effort to break through the secrecy" even in the Central Committee: KGB surveillance bugging. "The Central Committee staff couldn't talk about these [BW] programs to the Kremlin even with the very best telephone scramblers." BW remained "behind an iron curtain of secrecy, and the military utilized that. They wanted to keep something that the world did not know about."

Alibek writes that Belousov, the head of the VPK, was directed to prepare the reply to the US-UK démarche but that "Biopreparat wrote the bulk of the document." It declared "that the Soviet Union fully complied with every clause of the Biological Weapon Convention . . . [and] that all our research into biological warfare agents was conducted for the sole purpose of defending ourselves against potential aggressors."[66] The draft further offered to negotiate a schedule of visits to all sides, but Alibek claimed, "None of us really believed that the US government would take this suggestion seriously. It would force Americans to allow us inside their own bioweapons installations." Alibek again misdates this process, writing that the draft reply was completed by February 1990, when it can only have been drafted after May 15, 1990. Kryuchkov, Maslyukov, Belousov, Shevardnadze, and Yazov were asked to review and sign the document before it went to Gorbachev for his approval. Alibek claims that Shevardnadze refused to sign, but that eventually the signature of his deputy, Karpov, was accepted. Alibek reports Karpov's comment to him when he arrives to deliver the document: "I know who you are and I know what you do. And I know that none of what's written here is true."[67] When the formal reply was delivered from the MFA to the US and UK embassies, it carried Shevardnadze's signature.

High-Level US-Soviet Contacts

David Hoffman recounts a Gorbachev recollection of his conversation with Bush on June 2, 1990, at Camp David:

> "It was just the two of us and my interpreter," Gorbachev said.
>
> Bush told Gorbachev that the CIA was reporting that the Soviet Union had not destroyed all its biological weapons and production facilities.
>
> "I said," Gorbachev recalled, "my intelligence people report that *you* have not destroyed all your biological weapons. I believe you, I said, but why don't you believe me?"
>
> Bush: "Those are the reports I get."
>
> Gorbachev: "Well, you are not an expert on biological weapons. And I am not an expert on biological weapons. Let us have mutual verification, mutual verification of whether biological weapons have been destroyed.

Let your people come to our weapons facilities, we also know where your facilities are, and we will come to your country. Let's have an exchange."[68]

If Gorbachev's description is an accurate reflection of Bush's presentation of the problem, Bush was certainly not very effective or convincing. Whatever Gorbachev may have understood about the Soviet offensive BW program prior to May 1990, and with what level of clarity, detail, and absence of euphemisms, one at least knows what Zaikov's memo told him in May 1990. One can perhaps assume that more information may also have been provided to him at that time by Zaikov in private conversation. Finally, Alibek's testimony that "only four members of the senior leadership," Gorbachev, Kryuchkov, Yazov, and Zaikov, "were fully aware of our secret," explicitly includes Gorbachev.

On June 8, 1990, Prime Minister Margaret Thatcher met with Gorbachev in the Kremlin. She wrote in her memoirs that she had raised "with him the evidence which we had gleaned that the Soviet Union was doing research into biological weapons—something which he emphatically denied but nonetheless promised to investigate."[69] It was the same response that Gorbachev reportedly gave Bush several days before at Camp David. Percy Cradock, the chairman of the United Kingdom's Joint Intelligence Committee and hence the senior intelligence adviser to the British government, had prevailed upon Thatcher to take up the issue with Gorbachev, something that she was very unhappy to do. Thatcher was reluctant to have the BW charges interfere with her dealings with Gorbachev. Nevertheless she told him that they caused the United Kingdom "grave concern." Mangold and Goldberg claim that Thatcher "quietly threatened to put Pasechnik on international television if Gorbachev didn't cooperate and stop the programme."[70] Of course, much more was at issue than just "research." Thatcher strongly believed in Gorbachev's credibility and believed in his honesty in his dealings with her. The issue reportedly led to a subsequent serious disagreement with Cradock. Thatcher believed that Gorbachev was being deceived by his senior military leadership and that he did not know of the Soviet Union's illicit biological weapons program, nor of continued development of advanced nerve gases. Cradock flatly informed her that was impossible.

During the latter period of Gorbachev's tenure, there were relatively extensive direct contacts between the most senior US and Soviet military officials, mutual visits taking days at a time. It is interesting that during those interactions no one on the US side attempted to take up the issue of the Soviet BW program with their Soviet counterpart. Admiral Crowe, the chairman of the US Joint Chiefs of Staff, never spoke to Akhromeyev about the subject, nor to Yazov. Nor did anyone speak about it to General Shaposhnikov, who succeeded Yazov as minister of defense in the second half of 1991. However, an extremely important piece of information, with implications for understanding the MOD's role in controlling and defining the Soviet offensive BW program, did become available through these conversations. Akhromeyev told Admiral Crowe how much he envied the US Joint Chiefs of Staff (JCS) control over the entire DOD budget request, and that all he had responsibility for in the Soviet "MOD" budget was operations and maintenance, fuel, and training. The VPK had responsibility for all of the rest: weapons acquisition and military R&D.[71] Additionally, Akhromeyev further explained that military officers were not delegated to work at the VPK. The VPK therefore appears to have been the prime director of the Soviet offensive BW program for at least the preceding 3–4 decades. If not, it was a co-equal partner in that role with the MOD's 15th Directorate. If Ignatiev was the last VPK official responsible for the Soviet BW program during Gorbachev's tenure, his importance and that of the two VPK directors becomes all the more significant to the fact that the program survived destruction under Gorbachev and afterwards. The above also suggests that the MOD's 15th Directorate worked in collusion with the VPK, but somewhat independent from the General Staff as a whole. However, Pasechnik felt certain that Yevstigneev, and presumably his predecessors, reported to the defense minister—Yazov in this case—and sometimes to some other members of the General Staff (probably Petrov) and MOD senior hierarchy, and he believed that nothing was done by the 15th Directorate without authorization and approval by senior authorities.

On July 30, 1990, a meeting was held in Zaikov's office to discuss the draft of a reply to be given to Baker at the meeting between Shevardnadze and Baker in Irkutsk on August 1, 1990. Karpov made the presentation in a meeting in which Bykov, Belyakov and his deputy Arzhakov, and Shakhov and his assistant Ivanov were present. The draft reply noted that the Soviet Union's authority and prestige were at issue. Yet to maintain that authority and prestige denial would continue. "I can state that at present no activity is being carried out in the Soviet Union that would breach articles of the Convention on the Prohibition of Biological Weapons. We have no biological weapons. The issue of compliance with this Convention was examined by the political leadership of the country, and we are considering passing special legislation that would envisage criminal responsibility for people whose actions breach the Convention." Several draft replies were prepared, and one of the others makes no mention of consideration of criminal penalties, but in its place states that "special decisions were taken," a phrase that could have much broader implications. The draft reply then offered several proposals:

- to produce "a special Soviet-American agreement on measures of transparency within the Convention's framework, to be agreed to before the September 1991 BWC RevCon."
- "we are prepared to arrange visits to any biological facility named by the American side in the US memo, *that raised suspicions of breaching the Convention.*"
- to invite US "specialists and scientists to work at the Soviet biological facilities mentioned by the American side in the memo." Perhaps a scientific exchange could be arranged, but the US specialists could come "already this year."
- to build on a draft already handed to the United States, "a document . . . on provisions of an agreement between the USSR and the USA on confidence-strengthening measures and broadening transparency in connection with the Convention on biological weapons." "Joint works by the Soviet and American specialists and scientists in the sphere of defense from biological weapons" were suggested. The Soviet Union was prepared to work out a program for such cooperation before the main agreement was signed.[72]

On the very next day a second draft was prepared, which was exactly the same except that it omitted the last bullet above. There is no longer any reference to a draft document "on provisions of an agreement" given to the United States, nor to "joint work" on biodefense.[73] It is presumably the paper handed to Baker at the meeting in Irkutsk, which began on the same day.

At their meeting in Irkutsk on August 1, 1990, Shevardnadze gave Baker a written response to the memorandum Baker had handed him on May 2 on their drive to Zagorsk. According to a senior US official, it was one paragraph long and carefully worded. There was no mention of the past, of the period since 1972, or 1975. It simply said, "We are not doing this now." A very different description is provided by Mangold and Goldberg. They write that the joint US-UK memorandum that Baker gave Shevardnadze in Paris in July 1990 was "a written follow-up to the Bush and Thatcher summits with Gorbachev," and contained specific questions about the four major Bio-preparat facilities: SRCAM, Vector, IHPB, and IEI. At Irkutsk they claim that Shevardnadze stated that the Soviet reply covered all the preceding summit conversations, the Paris memo, and the earlier UK and US démarches. It denied any illegitimate activities, but as in the draft quoted, it offered the United States and United Kingdom the ability to visit the four sites, and even held out the possibility that American scientists could come and work at the four sites.[74] Perhaps the two accounts are reconcilable but it would seem difficult to fit all that into one paragraph. One day later, on August 2, Iraq invaded Kuwait, and the allied invasion of Iraq took place on January 16, 1991, freezing interactions with the Soviet Union for a brief period.

After Shevardnadze's reply at Irkutsk, the un-group focused the US approach on the most important objective: seeing to it that the Soviet BW program was terminated. If Soviet officials insisted that they had no offensive BW program and that US intelligence, and the information provided by their own defector, was mistaken, then US policy would attempt to turn their denial to use for US aims. The Soviet denial would be accepted for tactical purposes, and the US reply would be: "Fine, if you don't have a BW program, then we can exchange 'visits' and settle the issue." If the Soviets denied having anything, then there was no reason for them to deny a request by the United States and the United Kingdom to be allowed to see what was there.

In September, meeting again in Paris, Baker reportedly gave Shevardnadze the US response.

The US said that the Soviet plan, depending on the details, could offer a constructive approach to the whole BW problem. The Americans now produced a series of proposed guidelines for the Soviets, which would increase openness and build confidence in the new trilateral procedure. These basic principles of conduct included: a full description in advance of the organizational structure, research programmes, and personnel at each facility; access to the entire facility, including the insides of all buildings, laboratories, and bunkers; interviews with any staff scientists or technicians; access to financial records; and sampling and photography permitted where necessary and mutually agreed. This plan was intended to be the template for the future. . . .

Assuming these ground rules would be adopted and adhered to, the Americans were ready to start visits to the USSR by November. They would want to devote a minimum of three days to each site. Washington also placed the Soviets on notice with requests for inspections to seven additional Soviet BW facilities (beyond the original four). The new ones included three production plants—at Stepnogorsk, Berdsk, and Omutninsk; two military sites—at Zagorsk and Kirov; the outdoor test site at Vozrozhdeniye Island; and a biological equipment design plant in Moscow.[75]

It is useful to keep in mind the turmoil that was taking place at the top of the Soviet political and military hierarchy in these months, which would have been of far greater concern both to the military and to the civilian Soviet leadership. (See the Chronology, Table 21.2.) By the early spring of 1990, the military was infuriated by Shevardnadze's initiatives and compromises in several of the ongoing bilateral arms control negotiations taking place with the United States. Gorbachev substantially destroyed the political power of the Communist Party during the 28th Party Congress in July 1990. From that point on, KGB director Kryuchkov became the second most powerful figure in the Kremlin. After the party apparatus was dismantled, the KGB controlled the flow of information to Gorbachev, including reports from the MFA.[76] By the fall of 1990, Gorbachev had swung away from Shevardnadze and drawn closer to the military and security leadership. In December 1990, a new deputy defense minister slot was created to coordinate the operations of army units with those of the Ministry of Interior and the KGB in domestic events such as the use of Soviet special forces in the Baltic republics in January 1991. On March 31, 1991, the military agencies of the Warsaw Pact alliance were abolished, and in April the Soviet commander of the alliance was relieved of his duties. Following the failed coup in August 1991, Marshal Shaposhnikov replaced Yazov as minister of defense, and General Lobov replaced Moiseyev as chief of the General Staff.[77]

The first US-UK visits took place to Vector, SRCAM, IHPB, and IEI between January 8 and 18, 1991. In June 1991 Baker went to Lisbon and met with Bessmyrtnykh. Baker had reportedly remained somewhat skeptical about the Soviet BW story; but he was nevertheless requested to take up the issue again. The CIA and the DOD jointly prepared a second paper based on the same evidence that was contained in the first US paper. As indicated, the un-group had changed its approach in an important way; the primary US objective was to get the Soviet program terminated, rather than to emphasize obtaining an admission of past Soviet misdeeds. In an additional memorandum the US also proposed a 10-year "transparency" program of permanent scientific exchanges of US and Soviet scientists working in each other's research facilities. It is not clear if the papers were handed to Bessmyrtnykh, but Ambassador Matlock had already delivered the two papers in Moscow at the end of March 1991.

From the final three Soviet documents available we know that the Soviet Union received a memorandum from the United States on March 25, 1991, and that President Bush sent a letter to Gorbachev on June 19, 1991. The March 1991 memorandum followed the US-UK visit to the first Biopreparat facilities and "stated that [the] past visit did not remove, but has reinforced, [US-UK] concern regarding biological activity of the USSR."[78] It also demanded that the Soviet Union "should undertake practical measures including liquidation of a number of the sites of Biopreparat infrastructure." The United States also rejected the Soviet request that their experts visit US facilities before the Soviet Union "removed the noted concerns." The Soviets provided the United States with "detailed replies to the US memorandum" on May 14, 1991, but there is no publicly available record of what the replies said.

Bush's June 19 letter is also unavailable, but Gorbachev's reply was sent sometime between July 8—the date of a memorandum of advice to him by his aides—and July 17, 1991, when he met with Bush in London. The memo from Gorbachev's advisors notes that although a US-Soviet agreement was made in November 1990 for visits to both Soviet and US facilities, Bush's June 19 letter indicated that the United States would host Soviet visitors only after an experts' meeting "to discuss and remove" the concerns the United States had after visiting the Biopreparat sites. Gorbachev's advisers suggested that it would be "expedient" to agree to Bush's conditions provided the United States organize the reciprocal visit "immediately following," and "agree to an additional meeting of specialists to discuss the conclusions of the visit to the American sites."[79] They attached a draft reply for Gorbachev's use, which is quoted below. The primary Soviet emphasis was to make every aspect "reciprocal." However UK facilities are never mentioned in any of the Soviet documents. The memo to Gorbachev is signed by Baklanov, Zaikov, Yazov, Kryuchkov, Maslyukov, and a deputy of Bessmyrtnykh. Three of the six would be among the coup plotters within a month. The US agreement in 1990 to "reciprocity" with the primary aim of obtaining access to the Soviet facilities, no matter how well intentioned when the United States accepted it, provided the Russians with the wrecking tool that they would use to scuttle the entire process five years later.

In response to Bush's letter of June 19 noting the increase in American concerns after visiting Biopreparat sites, Gorbachev wrote: "I'd like to confirm that the USSR does not have the program of creation of biological and toxin weapons. We count on receiving confirmation that there is no such program in the United States either."[80] The first of these two lines is of course totally belied by the Trilateral Statement that would be agreed to in September 1992, and by the Russian BWC CBM for 1992 that would eventually be wrung out of Russia in the first months of the Yeltsin administration. The second line indicates that Gorbachev was personally willing to portray the issue as one of equality of concern, that the Soviet Union was just as suspicious that the United States had an offensive BW program and was violating the BWC as the United States and United Kingdom believed that the Soviet Union was. Gorbachev's letter continued disingenuously:

Until now, regretfully, there has been no agreement on where the boundary ends for activity permitted by the convention on defense from such weapons and where it begins on the banned activity. While such criteria do not exist, apparently, suspicions regarding the activity regulated by the convention will appear from time to time. In order to avoid it, it is necessary to jointly work out these objective guidelines that would take into account both the differences in the level of technological development and the different paths that biological science followed in our countries. This task is rather difficult, but without resolving it and creating a future on this basis of a control mechanism of the convention we will hardly make progress in removing mutual concerns.

Chapter 20 noted that Soviet diplomats were making these same points in preparatory meetings prior to the 1991 BWC Review Conference. They would continue to do so later on between 1994 and 2000 as well.[81] As the discussion in Chapter 11 demonstrates, this is a real problem, but it most certainly was not the problem with the Soviet BW program.

Gorbachev's letter continued:

An important step towards the same could be reciprocal visits of our experts to the American biological sites whose activity raises questions with us.

In this connection, we welcome the readiness confirmed by you to hold such a visit after the meeting of the experts.

For practical consideration, we consider it necessary to hold the meeting of the experts in the United States before Aug 15 and right after to hold a reciprocal visit of Soviet experts to the American facilities. . . .

. . . the experts must exchange opinions on such questions as the types of activity permitted and banned by the convention, the types and quantities of microbiological agents and toxins, instruments and equipment allowable for use in the defensive goals, as well as to get the answers of the American side to the questions of the USSR handed over in Houston in December 1990.[82]

Gorbachev also claimed that the US-UK team was granted "unrestricted access to any premises . . . the chance to talk with employees, explanations were given on all questions raised concerning the operation of these sites, opportunity was granted to photograph as well as take and export samples." As will be seen, this was the exact opposite of the view of by the arrived at US-UK team. It has proved impossible to determine if a meeting of experts took place in the United States in August 1991, and the Soviet team that visited US sites did not come to the United States until December 1991, shortly before the dissolution of the Soviet Union.

It is clear from Gorbachev's references to "the questions that we gave you in Houston" that the MOD and VPK were able to convince Zaikov and Gorbachev to continue to try and fend off the US and UK démarches on the question of Soviet BWC compliance by pretending that this subject was one of "equal" concern and that the Soviet Union harbored equal suspicion of the status of the US BW program. Shevardnadze and Baker held nine ministerial meetings in 1990, but as the year wore on, Shevardnadze's position progressively weakened. In 1989 and 1990, Gorbachev strengthened the role of the MOD in the several disarmament negotiations under way, and in addition to several other moves to mollify the military, he promoted Yazov to the rank of marshal. The military chiefs, including Akhromeyev, had been infuriated that Shevardnadze and Gorbachev had offered to include the new Soviet SS-23 (OTR-23- Oka) shorter range nuclear ballistic missile into the "double zero" INF negotiations with the United States. This would lead to the missile's withdrawal and dismantlement against the strong opposition of the MOD.[83] However, the most difficult and contentious issue was the effort by the military to evade the numerical limits for tanks and other heavy conventional arms set by the CFE treaty by moving these to sites east of the Urals. For example, 16,000 tanks alone were relocated so that they would escape destruction. These moves as well as others involving Army divisions to evade CFE Treaty limitations were made *with* the knowledge and approval of Gorbachev, and with the active pressure from Akhromeyev, Gorbachev's personal adviser on disarmament issues. They may perhaps be seen as an analogue of how the Soviet military chiefs dealt with BW as well. The Shevardnadze-Baker meeting in Houston on December 7, 1990, was the most difficult and contentious of all their ministerial meetings. It is very likely that Gorbachev's stubborn and even retrogressive position in defense of the Soviet BW program in July 1991 matched his transition from earlier support for Shevardnadze to supporting the military and intelligence agencies. It matched the change and turmoil in the balance of power among Gorbachev's immediate deputies in Moscow. Zaikov left his instrumental position as Central Committee secretary and was replaced by his deputy, Baklanov, someone who was aligned with the VPK and MOD, was unsympathic to arms-control measures, and who joined the coup plotters.

The MOD's main interest now was to gain US acceptance for the Soviet CFE evasions, and Shevardnadze's disagreements with the military came to a head over these.[84] The differences were openly exposed during the Houston proceedings, as was the fact that Shevardnadze no longer had Gorbachev's support on the issues. Two weeks after Houston he resigned as foreign minister. There is no public record of the questions about the US BW program that Shevardnadze handed over, and the document is not available. It can only have been another undesirable and irritating addition to a very difficult encounter. A year later, in 1991, Shevardnadze published a book that contained the following cryptic paragraph about the days immediately following his resignation: "If anything, Jim [Baker] could have had some doubts about my honesty, in connection with an unpleasant story I do not intend to tell here. Since I was not to blame for it, however, I preferred not to undermine our business alliance with mistrust. If things had continued as they were going, I would not have been able to look my partner in the eye. If you like, this is also one of the reasons for my resignation."[85]

It seems almost certain that the "unpleasant story" that Shevardnadze was still reluctant to explain was the continued covering up of the offensive Soviet BW program. There is ambiguous evidence as to whether Shevardnadze directly approached Gorbachev in 1990, or Zaikov, to express displeasure about the way in which the Soviet Union was handling the BW issue. As for Gorbachev, in an interview with David Hoffman held on June 4, 2004, he still refused to discuss any aspect of his knowledge of the offensive Soviet

BW program while he held office. He refused to discuss the Politburo deliberations on the Soviet BW program during his tenure, or his interactions with Bush, Thatcher, Hurd, Shevardnadze, or Baker on the subject.[86] Asked whether he had known of the existence of Biopreparat, his reply is an embarrassing combination of evasion and muddling. "No, I can't say I remember dealing with that organization . . . But there was medical research and they make vaccines against epidemics. Where is the line, the point where research becomes biological weapons and production? This is still controversial, even today, because you need cooperation, you need the kind of international relationship to make it possible to get rid of those weapons."[87] Then Gorbachev quickly changed the subject. Gorbachev had all the cooperation from the United States and the United Kingdom that he could have wanted at that time. Zaikov's memorandum had told Gorbachev that whatever "the line" was, the Soviet BW program had passed it by miles. If it was a matter of getting rid of biological weapons, then it does not concern vaccines. In addition, the United States and the United Kingdom did not have any biological weapons.

The First US-UK Visits to Soviet BW Facilities

Under US and UK pressure, Gorbachev in August 1990 had extended the invitation for visits to Soviet BW facilities. Following Soviet demands in September 1990 for reciprocity, time was then lost in Washington in disputes about whether the United States and United Kingdom should accede to that request. Additional months were lost in negotiations with Soviet diplomats on the parameters for the visits: the number of facilities to be visited, duration of the visits, conditions of access, site definitions, recording conditions, vaccination requirements, and team size. Gorbachev's simple standing invitation did not translate into easy access. Alibek has described the Soviet preparations in anticipation of the US-UK visits: "sanitizing" facilities, preparing detailed cover stories for individual pieces of equipment and experiments, to waste as much time as possible during the site visits on formal presentations by the host, to have long meals and lots of vodka on hand, and to absent staff on the days when the visitors were present. Alibek also states that "anxious debates raged inside the Military-Industrial Commission [VPK] and Ministry of Defense."[88]

A team from Biopreparat's Department of Security, Yermoshin, Zhavarnak, and one or two others, together with Alibek came to visit IEI in October

1990, some months before the US-UK team arrived in January 1991. Zaviyalov and a small number of his staff were told that US-UK team would be coming to visit. Alibek told him that the reason for the visit was due to "discussion on measures of trust." He did not mention the BWC, nor that the Soviet Union was being accused of violations and was being forced to comply with a request for visits to specific Biopreparat facilities. But Alibek did tell him that "the [BW] program will end," because of an agreement between the United States, United Kingdom and Soviet Union, and that "you cannot disclose the real purpose of the program." Zaviyalov and his staff were to respond to the visitors only with general statements. The discussion with the Biopreparat team was devoted to deciding on what to say and what to show under the open legend. The Biopreparat headquarters group designed the tour that the US-UK team would be given. In IEI's case, there were no facilities for working with dangerous pathogens and so all of the labs could be shown. All compromising papers were locked away.

Agreement was finally reached in November 1990 for a two-step process. US-UK visits would take place first, the results of the visits would be discussed with Soviet authorities, after which visits would be arranged to US and UK sites. The visits in the Soviet Union finally took place in January 1991 to the four major Biopreparat sites in the following sequence: the IEI in Lyubuchany; SRCAM in Obolensk; Vector in Koltsovo; and IHPB in Leningrad. Alibek guided the US-UK visitors during all visits. According to David Kelly, one of the UK inspectors:

> The visits did not go without incident. At Obolensk, access to parts of the main research facility—notably the dynamic aerosol test chambers and the plague research laboratories—was denied on the spurious grounds of quarantine requirements. Skirmishes occurred over access to an explosive aerosol chamber because the officials knew that closer examination would reveal damning evidence of offensive BW activities. At Koltsovo access was again difficult and problematic. The most serious incident was when senior officials contradicted an admission by technical staff that research on smallpox was being conducted there. The officials were unable to properly account for the presence of smallpox and for the research being undertaken in a dynamic aerosol test chamber on orthopoxvirus, which was capable of explosive dispersal. At the Institute of Ultrapure Preparations in Leningrad (Pasechnik's former workplace), dynamic and explosive test chambers were passed off

as being for agricultural projects, contained milling machines were described as being for the grinding of salt, and studies on plague, especially production of the agent, were misrepresented. Candid and credible accounts of many of the activities at these facilities were not provided. . . . Sampling was a matter of contention, discussion was stilted, site access was constrained, and quarantine restrictions were arbitrarily applied.[89]

When the US-UK team came to the IEI, it took hundreds of photos and left copies of them. Zaviyalov explained the work done in collaboration with SRCAM, and showed the visitors a publication on the capsular operon of *Yersinia pestis.* While in Zaviyalov's office with him, the US team leader, Ed Lacey, showed Zaviyalov Article 1 of the BWC, asked him to read it, and asked him whether he had any information about the Convention. Zaviyalov replied: "No, I have never seen this before."

The day after visiting the IEI, Zaviyalov served as the translator when the US-UK team visited SRCAM. He could see that Urakov's replies to questions were lies, but Zaviyalov nevertheless translated what Urakov said. Several of the Americans had spoken with Zaviyalov at his own institute in perfect Russian, so he already knew that they understood the language. As they walked down a corridor, Lacey asked him quietly: "Is Urakov's story true?" and Zaviyalov replied: "It is a lie." In the parking lot one of the US-UK team asked Alibek while Zaviyalov was standing alongside him why what they were hearing from Alibek was the open legend, and Alibek replied, "I cannot speak about the real aims." The cover stories that Alibek described as having been so carefully contrived were weak-to-ridiculous. Pasechnik said that he was shown a film of the US-UK visit to his own former institute when the UK team returned from the Soviet Union. He watched his former deputies who headed particular laboratories whose work he had described to his UK interrogators, not people that he disliked or disrespected, deny everything that they were asked: "We didn't do it; we didn't do it."[90] In addition very particular things were found. During the very first visit to IHPB in 1991 the equipment for experiments related to cruise missile BW dispersion was unexpectedly discovered.[91] This was a significant discovery, going beyond broad capabilities and general obfuscation. And while visiting Vector, senior institute officials reportedly claimed that their smallpox research program existed because the Soviet Union "believed the US had continued a secret BW program after 1972 to develop a smallpox weapon."[92]

Late in January 1991 the US-UK team drafted a 200-page report summarizing their conclusion that they had seen an

"offensive biological warfare programme run by Biopreparat and the military. . . . key indicators of offensive intent were the type and configuration of the equipment and the huge production capacity . . ." Soviet officials had done everything possible to limit the scope of the visits—through evasion, obfuscation, and prolonged negotiations. . . . During the entire tour, no Soviet official had been open, frank, or truthful about any aspects of the offensive programme. Whenever the Soviets were cornered and could not properly explain suspicious activities, they had resorted to excuses about doing purely "defensive" research against potential threats from the rest of the world.[93]

The results of the visits were shared with the Soviet MFA in March 1991. Eight points were emphasized that suggested that the offensive BW program had not been dismantled:

- Existence of new explosive aerosol test chambers
- Extensive production capacity
- Extensive biocontainment facilities/labs
- Unusual quarantine requirements
- Extensive research on nonindigenous threat agents
- Extensive new construction
- MOD funding
- Role of MOD personnel at sites[94]

In addition, delaying tactics, unusually high security, sanitized sites, poor cover stories, lack of candor, limits on access, and research with primates were all troubling indicators.

A second paper handed to Soviet diplomats listed 10 steps that the Soviet Union was asked to take to demonstrate that the offensive BW program had been closed.

- Dismantle all explosive test chambers
- Stop all work on smallpox except at the WHO-approved laboratory in Moscow
- Stop all open-air testing of dangerous pathogens

- Destroy all hardened bunkers at BW facilities
- Destroy all BW production buildings
- Destroy either Building 1 at Obolensk or Building 6A at Koltsovo
- Reduce production capacity to defensive standards at one BW facility
- Reduce biocontainment at any one site
- Reduce research at one site on pathogens that are not a public health risk
- Cut back significantly on the military's role in classified research on dangerous pathogens.[95]

Between March and July 1991, Bush, Major, Baker, and Braithwaite reportedly spoke to either Gorbachev or Bessmyrtnykh on 10 separate occasions in which they brought up the unsatisfactory results of the US-UK site visits in January 1991, making a mockery of Gorbachev's July 1991 letter to Bush quoted earlier. The visits had left the United States and the United Kingdom convinced that the Soviet Union continued an offensive BW program. Gorbachev and Bessmyrtnykh nevertheless continued to deny any Soviet violation of the BWC.[96]

In June 1991, US and Soviet negotiators were "crashing" to complete the START nuclear weapons treaty, and that subject occupied the total attention of the US administration's arms control specialists. The treaty was signed on July 30, 1991, at the Bush-Gorbachev Moscow summit. Nevertheless, a third paper on BW was prepared again in anticipation of that meeting. President Bush looked at it in advance of the meeting and said that he would discuss it with Gorbachev. However, he did not feel that he knew the subject matter sufficiently, and he told one of the authors of the paper to wait outside the room in which he would meet with Gorbachev. If he had the chance to raise the BW issue, he would call the individual in. But there was no call.

The coup attempt against Gorbachev took place three weeks later, on August 18–21 in Moscow. Late on the night of August 17, KGB, military, and "hard-line" political figures staged a coup to preempt the signing of a new Union treaty that was scheduled to take place on August 20. The coup attempt was bungled from its very start and collapsed within three days.[97] However, the consequences were disastrous for the Soviet Union. Latvia declared independence on August 21, the Ukraine on August 24, and most of the other former Soviet republics soon followed suit. Events in Moscow were equally dramatic: "The coup attempt snapped the last threads of authority of the Soviet government, and led directly to a countercoup by Yeltsin. The Communist Party was banned and Yeltsin began seizing the levers of power of the former central authority, including on August 28 the State Bank and Ministry of Finance. . . . Yeltsin moved quickly and adroitly to exploit the August 19 failed coup to destroy the central government and transfer to the Russian government—and himself—its authority and powers."[98]

Although unrelated in any way to any of the ongoing US-Soviet arms-control deliberations, the attempted coup in Moscow determined their nature for the next six to 12 months. The Soviet visits to the US facilities in fact took place in the very days that the Soviet Union was dissolved in December 1991. During the remaining months of 1991, though, Gorbachev could scarcely force through serious disclosures to the United States and United Kingdom regarding the Soviet BW program. In Washington, the coup suggested the desirability for greater US cooperation with Gorbachev's administration, rather than additional pressure. At the same time, the ungroup began to consider what to do next: "Where do we go from here?" Bush has said on several occasions that he "and Thatcher" approached Gorbachev on the Soviet BW issue, but they never met with Gorbachev together. Bush met with Gorbachev on four occasions prior to the July 1991 Moscow summit, and one more time afterward, in Madrid in October 1991. (At Bush's meeting with Gorbachev in Malta early in December 1989, the Russian BW program was not mentioned.) Once Gorbachev agreed to a first US-UK visit to Soviet sites, arranging those visits required extensive negotiations between lower-level US-UK and Soviet officials, composed of diplomats, scientists, and defense officials. One of the participants commented that "when the exchanges [about BW] at the highest levels occurred, they weren't on the agenda for the meetings; they always took place on the margins. For example, the April 1990 Ministerial meeting between Bush and Shevardnadze had a very big arms control agenda, but the Soviet BW program wasn't part of that agenda."

On September 1, 1991, quite soon after the coup attempt, Major met Gorbachev in Moscow and once again pressed him about the Soviet BW program. This time Gorbachev no longer denied its existence as he had for the previous 18 months. Now Gorbachev allegedly blamed Yazov and other of the coup plotters for having misled him in the past about the BW program.[99] Gorbachev promised to resolve the issue to the satisfaction of the United States and the United Kingdom. However, a meeting in Moscow in mid-October to discuss US and UK visits to Soviet sites at the end of 1991 again led nowhere. The VPK and the MOD were obviously able to follow their own agendas at this time. On November 18, the British ambassador in Moscow was allegedly informed "that Gorbachev had issued orders to end the

Soviet BW program."[101] There is no record of such an order in the Central Committee documents that we obtained, and given the ineffectiveness of simply "giving orders" in the Soviet system at any time, November 1991 was not a time in which an order from Gorbachev was likely to be acted on with any dispatch, if at all, by remaining BW supporters in the Biopreparat headquarters, the VPK, or the 15th Directorate. According to Alibek's description, of course, Gorbachev's "order" did not end the program at all.

Despite the decidedly problematic assessment of the site visits in the Soviet Union by the US-UK team, the meeting in Moscow in October 1991 did arrange for the return Soviet visits. The Soviet negotiators dispensed with visiting the United Kingdom and asked to visit four sites in the United States:

- Baker Test Facility, Dugway Proving Ground, Utah
- United States Army Medical Research Institute of Infectious Diseases (USAMRIID), Fort Detrick, Maryland
- National Center for Toxicological Research (Pine Bluff Arsenal), Jefferson, Arkansas
- Salk Institute, Government Services Division, Swiftwater, Pennsylvania[102]

Alibek states that in advance of leaving for the United States the 13-person Soviet team was provided with a briefing based on satellite photographs of the four sites that they were to visit. Pasechnik had reported that a KGB "Analytics" office also did satellite photography of the Soviet Union's own BW sites, and looked for telltale satellite signatures—as well as air and water effluents on the ground—that could presumably be applied by Soviet photoreconnaissance analysts to US facilities.

Pine Bluff had been the US BW production site prior to 1969, and the Salk facility was a contractor that made vaccines for the US military services. When the Soviet team came to Pine Bluff, the United States wanted to demonstrate that there was nothing there. Rather than holding the Soviet visiting team to the constraints that the Soviet Union had applied to the US-UK team when visiting Soviet sites, the Soviet team was explicitly told to video and record all that they cared to and that they could ask anything that they cared to and interview anyone they wanted to. The Soviet team included Colonel Vasiliev of the 15th Directorate, member of GRU; Alibek and Sherbakov of the Biopreparat directorate; and Biopreparat institute heads Urakov and Sandakhchiev. The nominal head of the team was Berdennikov of the MFA. The senior US hosting official was Lisa Bronson of DOD.

At the Dugway Proving Grounds, members of the Soviet team were reportedly allowed to take swipe samples and to pick bits of metal off the ground if they pleased.[102] Unfortunately, for many decades various US authorities had foolishly followed penny-wise and absent-minded policies, and facilities and components that should have been destroyed 30 years before were still present, if only in parts. At USAMRIID, the pre-1969 pilot plant, Building 470, had never been dismantled, so it contained much of its old equipment.[103] At Pine Bluff Arsenal all the fermenters had been removed, but 22 years on, an intact BW bomblet-filling machine was still sitting in one otherwise empty large hall, and the empty storage bunkers were still present. The cost to have destroyed these decades before would have been trivial, and it might have taken all of an hour's work for a crew with welding torches to slice up the filling machine and cart the segments to a metal recycler. The US side had reportedly made "dry runs" at each site in anticipation of the Soviet visitors, which makes the oversight of leaving in place any relevant equipment that had been sitting unused since 1969 even more egregious.[104] US Public Health Service officers wore uniforms, and the members of the Soviet team said, "I thought that you said all this was 'civilian'?" The Dugway Proving Ground still maintained open-air weapon test grids as part of the US biodefense program.

When Alibek returned to Moscow with the Soviet team, Colonel Vasiliev directed him to write a report stating that the United States had maintained an offensive BW program. He refused, and Vasiliev replied, "I will write it myself."[105] The Soviet report complained of limits on their access, excess production capacity, and the presence of an open-air test site. They claimed that the United States had a mothballed BW capability, a charge as close as they could approximate to their own massive infrastructure that was all intact except for filling lines that had been removed. According to Alibek, the report by the Soviet inspectors claimed that the gutted and derelict "8-ball" aerosol test chamber, anachronistically designated as a US national historical monument on the USAMRIID campus, remained in standby condition and could be reused.[106]

Even the very best of interlocutors on the Soviet side were apparently willing to accept very heavy doses of their own country's disinformation. Chernyaev, one of Gorbachev's closest advisers, wrote that the US-UK teams that visited the first four Soviet facilities in January 1991 "were granted unrestricted access to everything in the installations, they were given explanations about every question."[107] That was certainly not true, and the US-UK after-visit report that was handed to Soviet authorities said exactly the opposite. Later, in September 1992, US Under Secretary of State Frank Wisner told Russian negotiators in Moscow that the United States "knew that information was destroyed that would be incriminating; laboratories were cleaned to remove traces of plague bacteria; employees who knew what was going on were sent away; and microphones were installed to monitor every conversation." [108] As a result of that US-UK report, "Gorbachev had ordered an investigation, the results of which he'd reported to Bush in a letter a week before their meeting in London [on July 17, 1991]."[109] When Gorbachev met Bush in person, he repeated what he had written in the letter, "Gorbachev categorically denied all the accusations." The report he had asked for had been signed by Yazov: the violator had been asked to report on his own violations.

If Chernyaev's ostensibly verbatim narrative is to be trusted, Bush responded in an appalling manner, saying: "I don't know what's going on . . . It's hard for me to figure it out." Gorbachev replied, "I have it figured out. I can tell you with confidence we aren't making biological weapons . . . I suggest that we finish with this." Bush reportedly replied: "Let's do that. If our people are mistaken or misleading us, they're in trouble. But we need clarity. Maybe another meeting of experts would help."[110] However, it was Chernyaev who was concerned about "our people misleading us," on the Soviet side. He broached the subject in a memo to Gorbachev, asking him whether he "was sure that he wasn't being misled, as had happened with the Krasnoyarsk radar station and in some other cases." But Gorbachev remained "confident."[111] Two weeks after their meeting in London in July 1991, Bush was going to give Gorbachev a US paper yet again, but the coup intervened, with the result that the paper was later given to Kozyrev to pass on to Yeltsin.

Between the coup attempt in Moscow in August 1991 and the dissolution of the Soviet Union on December 31, 1991, there were in effect two governments: the Soviet government and Yeltsin's new government of "Russia." Andrei Kozyrev, the foreign minister of Russia, came to Washington during Thanksgiving week of November 1991. General John Gordon had now replaced Kanter as the head of the un-group. At a meeting between some members of the un-group and Kozyrev and the counsel of the Russian government embassy in Washington, Kozyrev was presented with the latest iteration of the US paper dealing with the Soviet BW program. He read it on the spot and reportedly replied, "I not only believe what is here, but there is probably a lot more as well that you don't know of." It is not likely that Ko-zyrev's remark indicated actual specific knowledge of "a lot more," but was more likely an assumption on his part based on his previous experience with the Soviet military. The NSC under Brent Scowcroft had decided that if there was no headway this time, they would leak the US memorandum to "Demo-cratic Russia," the grassroots movement that had come into being in 1990. That should have been done in any case, but unfortunately was not. After START, this was "issue #2." Kozyrev was told that the disputed Soviet offen-sive BW program could not continue under a new Russian government.

Gorbachev's tenure ended on December 31, 1991, together with the exis-tence of the Soviet Union. Essentially none of the key questions regarding the Soviet BW program had been resolved. The next day, Boris Yeltsin be-came the president of Russia and the target of US and UK attention, which is the subject of Chapter 22.

The Final Question

After reviewing Soviet BW policy between 1985 and December 1991, aided by substantial information that was not previously available, we return to the basic question that this chapter began with: Why was President Gorbachev unable to terminate the Soviet offensive BW program, particularly in view of his substantial success in achieving major nuclear and conventional arms control agreements with the United States between 1987 and 1992? Chapter 22 asks the same question in regard to why President Yeltsin probably failed at the same task in 1992–1996, if he even tried at all in any serious way.

Except for the comparatively minor instance of the Krasnoyarsk radar site, an explicit violation of the bilateral US-Soviet Anti-Ballistic Missile Treaty, which the Soviet Union eventually admitted to in 1989, the BWC was the sole example of a violation by the Soviet Union of an international arms con-trol treaty, bilateral or multilateral, in the post–World War II era. Admitting to that violation meant not only an admission to its treaty co-negotiators, the United States and United Kingdom, but to all other state parties to the treaty and to the entire world. Nevertheless, the record is abundantly clear that President Gorbachev had to overcome the consistent opposition of nearly all of the Soviet military leadership and even of some members of the Politburo to obtain the strategic arms control agreements with the United States during his tenure and that he succeeded in overcoming those objections. The Soviet offensive BW program was the obvious and very striking anomaly. Why?

The explanations that have been suggested are many. Some are complementary; others may be contradictory to one another at least in part. One should first note that the subject was not high on Gorbachev's list of priorities. Georgy Shakhnazarov, Gorbachev's main political advisor, noted that the agenda on Gorbachev's desk was enormous. His own domestic political policies had opened a great dam, and all the problems of 70 years had boiled up at once. At the international level, at one point during Gorbachev's tenure, the Soviet Union was reportedly involved in no less than 86 different negotiations simultaneously.[112]

Turning to the first of the substantive considerations, secrecy had worked for the Soviet Union in earlier decades in regard to strategic weapon systems. Khrushchev had attempted to fool the United States with manipulated bomber overflights over Moscow that were deliberately meant to mislead US officials in the viewing audience. He did the same with his claim of Soviet serial ICBM production a few years later. It is not known whether the Soviet leadership ever understood how counterproductive both deception attempts subsequently were for the Soviet Union. Although both of the attempted strategic deceptions were reportedly understood by US officials to be exactly that, they nevertheless contributed to massive US responses in strategic bomber and ICBM production. In the case of the offensive Soviet BW program, a very small number of generals and an equal number of colonels, estimated by a former MFA official as perhaps a half dozen of each, together with an equally small number of officials at the VPK, Biopreparat Headquarters, and the Central Committee staff, were capable of maintaining the program's secrecy and knowledge of the magnitude and details of the entire program. This total could be under 40 individuals. For the military overall, maintaining any weapon capability was primary. No senior military official would advocate relinquishing any existing capability, but would instead say "keep it." Even Marshal Akhromeyev, Gorbachev's personal military advisor, did not want to see the BW program abolished. In addition, the culture of many of the senior military was more than a little paranoid: not only should everything be kept secret, but the purpose of anything pressed for by the United States was obviously designed to hurt the Soviet Union. In a related example, the senior Russian military was still split in the mid-1990s on the question of destroying its chemical weapons. Some, working with their US counterparts, asked whether the still-intact Russian chemical arsenal was militarily usable, and answered "No." Others thought differently and replied "Yes, and we shouldn't destroy it so quickly before we think about it some more."[113] Interestingly, several who belonged to the second group, such as Kuntsevich and Petrov, were also involved in Soviet, and then Russian, BW policy.

A second suggestion, not inconsistent with the above, is that Gorbachev was essentially stonewalled by the MOD, that he may not have approved of the program either being in existence or being maintained, but that the MOD would present him with memoranda stating that the United States had also maintained an offensive BW program and therefore the Soviet Union had to do likewise.[114] However, in offering such a defense the MOD would explicitly be admitting that it did have an offensive BW program. The Central Committee documents and the Zaikov memorandum support this interpretation. Without access to Politburo documentation, Ambassador Matlock expressed the opinion in 1998 that he felt Gorbachev and Shevardnadze "did not know everything. There's plenty of evidence that shows these people were not able to get the information they wanted, because the system was so secret and the political authorities had so little control over the military and KGB. And they had no reliable way to check up on the information they did get."[115] For Matlock's view to be meaningful, however, one must recall both the BW program approvals that Gorbachev signed through 1991, as well as his letter delivered to the United States in July 1991 with its "questions" regarding US BW activities.

In a brief conversation in November 2011, apparently still not having seen any of the Central Committee documents, Matlock repeated two overlapping points: The MOD would have lied to Gorbachev about its own program, and at the same time it would have told him that the US had a covert, offensive BW program, and so it was only doing what the US did. It is very possible that Gorbachev accepted the MOD claims that the United States had maintained its offensive BW program; there are other stories of him believing wild conspiracy tales proffered to him by the KGB in late 1990: "During the dark winter of 1990–1991, Kryuchkov with the cooperation of Gorbachev's chief of staff, Valery Boldin, kept Gorbachev in an 'information aquarium,' . . . Alexander Yakovlev would recall that Gorbachev had actually believed, in March 1991, a preposterous KGB report that Yeltsin supporters were planning to put ladders against the Kremlin walls and mount an assault."[116] These are the same months when Gorbachev swung his support away from the MFA and to the military and the KGB.

Not only was Gorbachev apparently capable of believing such fantasies—at least during this period of intense internal crisis—but he fired his own appointee as minister of internal affairs, Vadim Bakatin, because the more accurate and more temperate reports from Bakatin's ministry conflicted with the dire and paranoid reports coming from the KGB. Claims alleging a US offensive BW program would therefore not have been the only such example.

Mangold and Goldberg quote Gary Crocker, a DOS official at the time, to introduce a new suggestion: that once Gorbachev was being pressed by his US and UK counterparts, he was "sold" a new defense of the Soviet BW program, "that it was needed to defend their homeland against 'the Chinese threat.' The Soviet generals claimed that this 'defensive' BW programme was the Soviet 'equalizer' which would prevent millions of Chinese from invading across the USSR's Southern border."[117] Mangold and Goldberg claim that the Soviet military had made this same argument "to the Kremlin" in previous years as well. This story seems extremely dubious. It places the military's suggestions after 1990, many years after any military pressures from China existed on the Soviet-Chinese border. In addition, it would of course have made explicitly clear to Gorbachev that the Soviet Union did have an offensive BW program. There are no known indications in classified Soviet military publications obtained by US intelligence agencies of any such conception.[118] There is a strong chance that Crocker's suggestion is a spurious concoction.

When Pasechnik was asked why he thought the Soviet Union had so stubbornly retained BW during the post-1987 US-USSR strategic arms control period, he offered two guesses. First, simply the inertia of continuing as before, from the "tons" of plague described by Babkin to those of Alibek. He also wondered if a cruise missile BW delivery system was one response to the Reagan administration's "Star Wars" conceptions. Because any cruise missile delivery system would obviously violate existing treaty-based provisions dating from SALT 2 in 1979 and INF in 1987, the Soviet Union could simply have added cruise missiles with nuclear warheads, which it had already deployed. The comments are of interest as an indication of the thoughts of a senior BW program administrator, but it is clear that these guesses from a participant not privy to the debates and deliberations in the Central Committee are far from what the documents tell us.

Nevertheless, the effort to find "a sensible reason" also led British intelligence analysts to argue that Gorbachev had actually encouraged the continuance of the BW program as the "asymmetric" response to the Reagan SDI program.[119] Whether the British analysts took this notion from Pasechnik, or arrived it on their own, is not known. As already discussed in Chapter 10, this conception is entirely implausible because the technical components of the

Soviet asymmetric responses to SDI were readily identified by strategic missile experts. It would no longer have been a sensible argument in 1990 to 1992, and there is no evidence for such an explanation in the Soviet documents.

Is it plausible that Gorbachev had not been properly informed to begin with, and then was severely embarrassed once he was being pressed about the Soviet BW program by Thatcher, Bush, Baker, and Hurd? There are known examples in the United States when the director of the National Security Agency did not know of all the programs being carried out by his agency, but this does not seem to be a comparable example. It is clear that the subject was discussed in the Politburo and there is Zaikov's three-page memorandum of May 15, 1990. Although it included false information about the West, and omitted crucial information about the Soviet offensive BW program, we know that Zaikov's memorandum told Gorbachev that the Soviet Union had "carried out such work until 1989." What more may have passed verbally between Zaikov and Gorbachev we do not know. It is very likely that Baklanov was not any more informative after Zaikov's departure. Gorbachev was faced with a Soviet weapons of mass destruction program carried out in secret that violated an international treaty for which the Soviet Union was a co-depository state. But is it plausible that he would not then have gotten to the bottom of the issue once being pressed? Gorbachev certainly confronted and acted upon a multitude of the most conflicted issues in Soviet domestic and foreign policy during his tenure. At the same time he was known to procrastinate and avoid at least some problems that presented him with uncomfortable dilemmas. On the other hand, if he did get to the bottom of the Soviet BW program, the implication is that he tolerated the status quo.

Anatoly Chernyaev, one of Gorbachev's closest assistants, claims that Gorbachev was misled. In an interview with David Hoffman in February 2005, he said: "Gorbachev was in favor of ending it. But he was being deceived. I don't remember when, but he was given a report [saying that] they were already closing down the military part of this program . . . Shevardnadze told him several times, 'They lie to us, Mikhail Sergeyevich,' on the subject of this program." When Hoffman asked Chernyaev who was deceiving Gorbachev, he replied, "The manufacturers of this weapon who dealt with this system. The military and the scientists who were involved."[120] Chernyaev should have replaced "the scientists" by the VPK, but he confirmed that "Gorbachev knew the Soviet Union was in violation of the biological weapons treaty. . . . Not even Gorbachev was fully informed about the activities of our military-industrial program."[121] When Berdennikov was asked why Gorbachev had been dishonest, he replied, "I can only speculate. Maybe it was the fact that it was in violation of an agreement," that is, the 1975 BWC.[122] Ironically, as late as April 1991, Gorbachev awarded the Lenin Prize to Generals Kuntsevich and Viktor Petrunin for the development of an advanced nerve gas, indicating the power of the status quo in these areas.

In Ambassador Braithwaite's memoirs of his years in Moscow, he described the common practice of Russian officials to lie at even the highest levels, writing that it was "an integral part of the conduct of business; junior officials lied to their seniors, the government lied to the public and to foreigners."[123] Certainly one of the most notorious cases was the message from local officials in the Ukraine to Moscow in the hours following the explosion and breaching of the Chernobyl nuclear reactor, reporting that the reactor was "under control."[124] Within a year of taking office, Gorbachev complained to the Politburo about "the impermissibility of distortions of the factual state of affairs in messages and informational reports sent to the Central Committee of the CPSU and other ruling bodies."[125] Although much of Gorbachev's letter of November 26, 1985, to the Politburo refers to reporting about domestic issues within the Soviet Union, he explicitly refers to misinformation dealing with the international affairs and the external relations of the Soviet Union as well: "Quite often our departments abroad fail to provide truthful information about the real political situation in this or that country. . . . [A]t the present moment when we are trying to achieve a turnaround in the development of the international situation, we especially need objective information showing not what we would like to see but what really is."[126] A few weeks later, in December 1985, KGB chairman Viktor Chebrikov met with his deputies to ensure that all elements of the KGB would "take all necessary measures to preclude sending to the KGB of the USSR all unreliable information and nonobjective evaluations of the state of affairs in concrete sectors and lines of operational service."

Garthoff points out that all the KGB "annual reports from 1985 through 1989 included reference to the role of the KGB in providing intelligence support to Gorbachev's summit meetings, and to other negotiations, as well as Soviet leadership consideration of international issues."[127] These "negotiations" and "issues" would of course have included the BWC, the CWC, and the Soviet BW program. In his 2010 memoir, Matlock notes that Gorbachev was often taken in by false reports from the KGB, one of which was noted earlier.[128] Specifically Matlock emphasizes the efforts by KGB head Kyruchkov to direct particular policies from 1989–1990 onward. Implicitly, then,

Gorbachev's entreaties in late 1985 that the Central Committee be supplied
with accurate information failed within four years. Matlock also notes that
"in the Soviet Union, the KGB had been allowed to become a state within a
state, and the political authorities had no mechanism to ensure that intelligence reports were accurate." It was not a peculiarity that applied only to the
KGB in the Soviet system: as we have also seen, the same held true for the
relationship between "the political authorities" and the 15th Directorate,
Biopreparat headquarters and the VPK.

In a review of Chernyaev's memoir describing events that took place in
Gorbachev's very office, the reviewer wrote: "There may be little new to say
about the sheer density of lying and unexamined stupidity on which the Soviet political system rested."[129] Chernayev had used the Chernobyl disaster as
an example: "Even our top leadership did not fully realize the difficulties and
dangers associated with nuclear energy. . . . The split between science and
morality in Soviet society, and the amorality of an elite part of the scientific
intelligentsia, bore their terrible fruit in Chernobyl. . . . Those who controlled the political system were kept in ignorance by the scientists."[130] At a
Politburo meeting that included a group of the scientific leaders of the Soviet
Union's nuclear power program, Gorbachev railed, "Everything was kept
secret from the Central Committee. Its apparat didn't dare to look into this
area."[131] Earlier Soviet leaders of course had established the Soviet administrative system of ignorance of details by the senior leadership together with
minimal oversight of the autonomy of important sectors of the government.

There was nothing new in this. Another of Gorbachev's personal aides,
Georgi Shakhnazarov, wrote in regard to the senior military officials: "They
reported to the leadership one thing, while thinking and doing something totally different. It was a cat and mouse game."[132] There are also recorded instances during this same period in which the most senior military leadership
circumvented both Gorbachev's and the Politburo's explicit orders. During
the protests in Georgia in early April 1989, the Politburo at Gorbachev's request had directed that no military response be made without its express
approval. On April 9, 1989, while Gorbachev and Shevardnadze were in
London, Defense Minister Yazov and General Igor Rodionov, the army
commander on the scene in Tbilisi, the Georgian capital, knowingly circumvented the Politburo's restrictions by pressuring Georgian officials to authorize a severe military crackdown. Not only did Yazov and Rodionov not seek
Politburo approval, the Politburo was not even informed.[133]

All of this was exacerbated by the myriad problems, dissension, conflict, and turmoil that was taking place by the beginning of 1989. By Gorbachev's final two years of 1990 and 1991, he was "desperate and distracted . . . a reviled and struggling Russian politician . . . a sad and rambling figure . . . while the Soviet Union was collapsing almost literally around his ears."[134] All these contributing factors were a powerful and disastrous combination: lying and overt deception by major segments of the government, only a superficial understanding of major military programs by the most senior political leadership of the Soviet Union, Gorbachev's domestic political preoccupations, and regarding the particular Soviet BW problem, irresolution, temporizing, and willingness to be misled. Perhaps he was also too embarrassed to admit a major national transgression, a violation of an international arms control treaty, to the United States, the United Kingdom, and the entire world. The result was that the status of the Soviet Union's offensive BW program was essentially unresolved when Gorbachev left office.

In his book Hoffman addresses the same question of Gorbachev's failure or inability to shut down the Soviet BW system and offers a similar suggestion. He quotes Chernyaev again saying, "He [Gorbachev] didn't know how to exercise his control," perhaps meaning that in his last two years, as his power waned at the same time as other problems multiplied, Gorbachev may have simply lacked the willpower or political capital to take on a new power struggle. Hoffman also offers the same possibility noted earlier that Gorbachev may have been unwilling to disclose the actual scope of the program out of embarrassment damage to "new thinking," or to his image.[135]

At the same time some have asked whether the United States in fact pushed the issue sufficiently. Braithwaite felt that sufficient pressure was not applied on the Soviet BW issue.[136] There were always "more important things" on the UK-US-Soviet agenda, and it is unquestionably true that there were issues that were considered more important and that were given primacy. The strategic nuclear arms control treaties were certainly given higher priority, as was the CFE treaty for the European continent. Managing the collapse of the Warsaw Treaty and the functional independence of its non-Soviet member states was certainly a greater priority, as was a "soft landing" for the disintegration of the Soviet Union itself. Gorbachev's domestic position was frequently tenuous from early 1990 to the end of 1991. The US government was concerned not to weaken or jeopardize his position further by external pressures that would require him to fight additional battles with the MOD.

The work of the un-group in the Bush administration certainly suggests a concerted effort on the part of the United States, however, President Bush appears to have been particularly inept in two different meetings with Gorbachev in regard to the Soviet BW program.

If we accept Chernyaev's testimony quoted earlier, the reality would appear to be somewhere in the middle of all these suggestions. Gorbachev came to power in 1985. In five years, he had ended the Cold War and transformed his country. The Warsaw Pact was gone, and the East European countries were free. The Soviet Union withdrew from Afghanistan. In contending with the Soviet military in the area of arms control, Gorbachev expended his most extensive efforts on nuclear weapons issues, with a fair amount of attention to chemical weapons. The Soviet Central Committee documents presented in the chapter tell us that there was some nominal movement on curtailing or ending the illegal offensive BW program, but in fact the achievements of the post-1972 Soviet BW program peaked in 1985 to 1990. Gorbachev was being misled and lied to on the subject of the Soviet offensive BW program by the senior military and the VPK and very likely even by some of the Central Committee staff. The US and UK pressure came only after 1990, following Pasechnik's defection, when Gorbachev was already riding a domestic whirlwind and beginning to lose control of the evolution of events within the Soviet Union. He was beset with severe political and economic problems between 1990 and 1992. Tackling the Soviet BW program at the end was one piece too many, with too little time to play, at the lowest point in his tenure. Despite the fact that the Politburo had started to take provisional steps as early as November 1986 to terminate at least some parts of the program, the MOD, its 15th Directorate, Biopreparat headquarters, and the VPK—Yevstigneev, Kalinin, and Ignatiev, together with a few others—defeated the five- or six-year effort to abolish the Soviet offensive BW program. Gorbachev too was defeated, although he himself had facilitated that defeat.

22

Boris Yeltsin to the Present

THE HIGH-LEVEL US-UK-USSR discussions that took place between 1990 and 1992 concerning an illegal Soviet BW program were not publicly known at the time. To the very great surprise of international observers of arms control, Russian president Boris Yeltsin referred in a speech on January 27, 1992, to a "lag in implementing" the 1972 Biological and Toxin Weapons Convention (BWC) by the former Soviet Union.[1] This began a series of public disclosures regarding the BW program of the former Soviet Union—and, in fact, of Russia as well—that continued until mid-September 1992. Much of it appeared in the Russian press. They were a continual surprise as one disclosure from Russian authorities followed another. Two days after his initial speech, on the eve of a trip to the United States, President Yeltsin granted an interview to the US television network ABC and its interviewer, Barbara Walters. Walters asked Yeltsin whether "right now," Russia was "still making chemical and biological weapons." The Russian President refused to answer. When pressed, he would only say, "In the next few months we're going to take steps to discontinue this type of activity in accordance with international agreements on chemical and biological weapons." He promised to have more to say on the matter in his private meetings with President George Bush.[2] On the same day, he also announced the Russian renunciation of the proviso to its ratification of the 1925 Geneva Protocol, which had maintained the right of reprisal using BW. But at the very same moment, Yevstigneev and Kalinin recommended to Yeltsin that Russia continue its offensive BW program—proving that it had not ended—on the grounds that the Soviet team's on-site visits to the United States in 1991 demonstrated that the United States maintained an offensive program.[3]

On January 20, 1992, Yeltsin met UK foreign minister Douglas Hurd and told him that Gorbachev and his defense minister had told him that the BW program had been terminated, but that it was not true. He promised to dismantle Biopreparat, retire Kalinin "immediately," and end the program.[4] Similarly on his return to Russia, Yeltsin was paraphrased in the press as having said that the "Union leadership" had "deceived the Americans, particularly on the issue of chemical and bacteriological weapons."[5] Because Gorbachev had reported that the Soviet Union had ceased producing *chemical* weapons in 1987, and the Soviet Union and the United States formally agreed to cease such production in 1990, this left biological weapons as the more probable likelihood for the substance of Yeltsin's remark. That was borne out by yet another interview Yeltsin gave in Russia in April 1992:

> When the three of us were alone—Bush, his interpreter and I . . . I said that I could not yet give firm guarantees of honest cooperation. Probably this is not the thing done among politicians but I said, "We are still swindling you, Mr. Bush. We promised to scrap bacteriological weapons. But some of our experts did everything possible to keep the truth from me. It was not easy, but I outsmarted them. I caught them red-handed. I found two test sites."[6]

In Washington on the day following the meeting of Yeltsin and Bush, Lieutenant General Dmitri Volkogonov, one of Yeltsin's top military advisers, also spoke to the press. According to the *Washington Post:* "Volkogonov also said Yeltsin had pledged for the first time to halt Russian research into biological weapons, an area where he suggested past military efforts had crossed the line set out by international treaties. He said Yeltsin disclosed that 'a number of centers dealing with this issue have been closed,' and said that 'from 1992 [forward], there will be no [military] budget allocations coming to that program.'"[7]

On February 28, 1992, Yeltsin established by decree a Committee on Convention Problems related to chemical and biological weapons. The committee's tasks were to resolve problems related to the Chemical Weapons Convention (CWC) and the BWC, to implement international and internal monitoring [Russian: *kontrol*], to prevent their development [Russian: *raz-*

rabotka], production, and stockpiling, and also to organize the elimination of stocks of chemical weapons. General Anatoly Kuntsevich, formerly deputy head of Soviet Chemical Troops and the Soviet military representative to the CW arms control negotiations, was appointed committee chairman, a highly unfortunate and counterproductive appointment.[8] It was the first sign that things would very quickly go wrong. On May 27, 1992, another interview with Yeltsin was published that made it explicit that BW R&D had continued in Russia *after* his February 28 decree. When asked when he first became aware during the Soviet years "of the development of biological weapons in [his old political headquarters] Sverdlovsk," and what his response to it had been, Yeltsin replied:

> When I learned that such development was under way, I visited Andropov . . . when an outbreak of anthrax occurred. . . . Andropov called [Defense Minister and member of the Politburo Dmitriy] Ustinov and ordered the liquidation of these production facilities completely. I believed it had been done this way. However, it turned out that the laboratories had simply been moved to another oblast, and the development of this weapon continued. And I told about this to Bush, Major and Mitterrand, i.e., this program is going on . . . I signed a decree to establish a special committee and banning the program. Only following this, experts flew there and put an end to the development.[9]

Finally, on April 11, 1992, President Yeltsin signed a decree committing Russia, as successor to the Soviet Union, to the BWC.[10] The signing followed Russian government assurances that it intended to strictly abide by the BWC. The assurance was prompted at least in part by conditions legislated by the US Congress for the expenditure of $400 million in US aid to dismantle nuclear and other weapons of mass destruction in the former Soviet Union. The condition stipulated that President Bush certify that the Soviet Union, and therefore subsequently Russia as the inheritor of the agreements, was *committed* to moving toward compliance with all arms control agreements. As late as March 30, 1992, in submitting its annual report to Congress, *Soviet Non-Compliance with Arms Control Agreements,* the administration had stated that the "Soviet Union continues to be in violation of the 1972 Biological and Toxin Weapons Convention."[11] Other pressures may have also contributed to forcing Yeltsin's disclosures: the public testimony of senior KGB and military officials in Moscow in November and December

1991 regarding the cause of the 1979 outbreak of anthrax in Sverdlovsk.[12] The greatest surprises were still to come.

Kuntsevich prepared a report for Yeltsin that "revealed that the military had illicitly developed aerial bombs and rocket warheads capable of carrying deadly anthrax, tularemia, and Q fever biological warfare agents." The report had not been released, but several months afterward Kuntsevich informed a *Washington Post* reporter "that the illicit weapons efforts was maintained at least through 1990 after being steadily scaled back during the six years of Gorbachev's presidency."[13] In September 1992 Kuntsevich stated in a Russian interview:

> Indeed these clear violations on the convention were only admitted after the totalitarian regime collapsed and duplicity in politics was abandoned. . . . The remnants of the offensive programs in the area of biological weapons were still around as recently as 1991. It was only in 1992 that Russia absolutely stopped this work.
>
> . . .
>
> We did not have stockpiles of biological weapons. The point is that they cannot be kept for a long time. Therefore, the question of their destruction does not come up.
>
> . . .
>
> Within the Russian Defence Ministry's structure the relevant directorate has been abolished and a directorate for radiological, chemical, and biological protection has been set up.[14]

It was a brief period in which Kuntsevich was, very surprisingly, partly truthful in public. Yeltsin's April 1992 decree ordering such work halted and its funding withdrawn followed the report that Kuntsevich had prepared for him. US intelligence sources were in agreement that the program had been scaled back, but could not determine if it had been eliminated. US officials also claimed that the Soviet Union had "stockpiled substantial germ weapons." Kuntsevich, however, "denied that such stockpiles existed and said that most development work was halted when weapons reached the prototype stage."

Russian Approaches to the BWC Confidence Building Measures

The Russian government was to have made its submission the BWC Confidence-Building Measures (CBMs) regarding its BW program to the

United Nations by April 14, 1992. Following the decisions of the Second BWC Review Conference in 1986, the Soviet Union had submitted its first CBM in October 1987. It named five laboratories under the jurisdiction of the Soviet MOD, as well as the Vozrozhdeniye Island testing site, and 14 civilian facilities. Some of the 14 belonged to the Biopreparat system, others to the anti-plague institutes. The Third BWC Review Conference in 1991 mandated three additional CBMs, the crucial one being "Form F," a declaration of past activities in offensive and defensive biological (weapon) research and development programs. Russia's submission for 1992 therefore would be of great significance and was eagerly anticipated.

There were, however, major difficulties with the draft submission. The document would have been prepared by the re-named 15th Directorate, the VPK, and Kalinin. US and UK officials charged that provisional drafts provided by the Russian government contained less information than had already been supplied by the Soviet Union in its initial CBMs in 1987. What all this strongly implied very early on was that the Yeltsin administration and Russian civilian political leadership did not yet have control, access, or knowledge of the BW facilities and program that it had inherited.[15] The credibility of the Russian Ministry of Defense (RF-MOD) was zero: its renamed Directorate for Bacteriological, Radiation and Chemical Defense told the Russian newspaper *Izvestia* that charges of an active Soviet germ warfare program were all lies, and that "all work on biological weapons stopped in 1975."[16] There was nothing to indicate that anything had been changed in the 15th Directorate except for a word change in its name. Yevstigneev remained its head, and its existing staff was retained. Despite the explicit admissions of BWC violation by Yeltsin and even Kuntsevich, the directors of individual laboratories continued to profess the total innocence of their respective institutions.

When the draft was first given to the United States and the United Kingdom privately, they considered it a travesty and they informed the Russian authorities that unless it was redone, the United States and the United Kingdom would make public their own description of the former Soviet program.[17] A revised version was apparently little better. It was six pages in length, for an offensive BW program lasting from the mid-1920s to at least the end of 1992, and it used most of its length to describe allegedly defensive BW aspects. It claimed that the offensive BW program was begun only in the late 1940s, and only "as a response measure" to foreign capabilities in BW.[18] However, the Soviet Union instituted its offensive BW program 20 years before the late

1940s, at a time when the Soviet Union faced no BW threat. The comparable US submission in 1992 for a program lasting only from 1942 to 1969, and probably a tenth or less in size compared to the Soviet program, was 10 pages and was expanded to 24 pages in 1996. The following deficiencies were present in the Russian CBMs:

- The locations of the three MOD facilities were given, but their proper identification is omitted. No description of their work is provided beyond their engagement in investigating "the feasibility of mass producing biological agents" and that they included "diked depots." It was claimed that no BW agents were produced or stored at these sites, and that no stockpiles were ever produced. All these claims are assumed to be false.
- It claimed that facilities of the MOD—not named—"began disassembling equipment and process lines involved in producing biological dispensing systems" in preparation for the Second BWC Review Conference in 1987. However, the Central Committee documents quoted in Chapter 21 demonstrate that to be false.
- It was claimed that the offensive BW program was terminated in March 1992, thereby admitting to the Soviet violation of the BWC between 1975 and 1992. Dates provided for other key decisions concerning the program are inaccurate, as are critical statements about other portions of the program.
- The statement that BW mobilization capacity production facilities, "industrial facilities with storage capabilities . . . were never provided with the infrastructure required to produce biological agents," is patently false.
- Biopreparat is described as a system of purely defensive research institutes, the basic cover story.

Despite its appalling inadequacy, Russia has never provided any expanded version of the 1992 Form F document in its CBM submissions in subsequent years, noting only "Nothing to Declare" year after year, or omitting the Form F entry entirely in many years.

On August 24, 1992, US Secretary of State Lawrence Eagleburger and UK Foreign Minister Douglas Hurd sent a five-page letter to their Russian counterpart, Andrei Kozyrev. The letter acknowledged that "President Yeltsin's forthright private and public statements acknowledging that the former Soviet Union had an illegal offensive biological warfare programme and undertaking to terminate it, have been extremely welcome."[19] Nevertheless the letter opened bluntly:

> Recent information which we are providing with this letter suggests that work on the offensive programme may nevertheless be continuing. This has potentially serious implications.
>
> We hope the Russian Government will now take determined steps to implement the assurances which President Yeltsin has given. We request that you bring these matters to President Yeltsin's personal attention.

It became clear that one or more additional defectors from Pasechnik's former institute in Leningrad, the IHPB, had reached the West. The letter reported that when the US-UK team visited the IHPB in January 1991, "this institute was then engaged in studying the cultivation process for antibiotic resistant strains of plague," and that by the spring of 1992

> research and development was completed and the question of its suitability for large-scale production resolved.
>
> Meanwhile, preparations have been underway for the Lakhta facility to carry out secret scale-up work for industrial production, including the development of legitimate production (Interleukin-II) as a cover to hide the secret activities.

The means by which this work had been observed when the US and UK inspectors visited the facility were itemized in the letter. It then went on to comment on the Russian draft BWC CBM for 1992, which had been shared with the United States and United Kingdom, and which was judged to be totally unsatisfactory:

> Although the draft Russian declarations to the United Nations acknowledged past offensive BW activity, they presented an incomplete and misleading picture of the size, scope and degree of maturity of the former Soviet programme. We will be obliged to explain publicly our reservations in this area if the text to be given to the UN is not corrected and amplified. It would be far preferable to avoid public recriminations on this subject while we press ahead together with the vital task of ending the offensive biological weapons programme.

Before concluding, the letter also explained the political consequences that would result in the United States from an unsatisfactory Russian response:

In the United States questions have arisen on this subject in the US Senate in the context of ratification of the START Treaty. The Senate's concerns and questions on this issue will need to be addressed in early September. In addition, cooperation under [the] Nunn-Lugar [Act] and consideration of the Freedom Support Act could be affected by this matter. Moreover, the US Executive Branch is obliged annually to certify to the Congress compliance of other signatories with existing arms control treaties.

These reports mentioned above underscore the need for a vigorous and visible campaign to dismantle once and for all the former Soviet Union's illegal offensive biological weapons programme and the entire apparatus—material and human—that has supported it.

We have frequently made it clear that we look for the Russian Government to take concrete steps to demonstrate that all aspects of the offensive programme are being terminated. In the past we have given you an illustrative list and other specific information on the programme indicating the kind of concrete measures which, if undertaken, would demonstrate to all concerned that it is being terminated.

We urge the Russian government not allow this essential process to be delayed or circumvented by actions designed to preserve an illegal programme in defiance of the decisions of the political leadership.

The last lines in the letter plainly told Yeltsin that he and his administration were being deceived by Kuntsevich and the renamed 15th Directorate.

September 1992: The Joint Statement and the Trilateral Negotiations

Several days after the letter was delivered in Moscow, "senior US officials" disclosed to the press that "the United States and Britain are worried that the Russian Government may not have fulfilled a six-month-old promise to shut down the Soviet Union's extensive program for making illicit germ weapons."[20] The Eagleburger-Hurd letter undoubtedly precipitated the Trilateral negotiations in Moscow in September 1992. The US delegation was led by Frank Wisner and Reginald Bartholomew. The British team was led by Paul Lever, assistant under-secretary in the FCO. On the Russian side, in addition to Deputy Foreign Minister Grigory Berdennikov, the senior Russian negotiator, and Yevstigneev, the former VPK staffers Oleg Ignatiev and Valery Spirande were both present among a team of 10 members.

On September 14, 1992, following negotiations in Moscow, the United Kingdom, the United States, and Russia signed the Trilateral Statement on the status of the Russian BW R&D program. The Statement was composed of three parts: the first section in which "the Russian Government stated that it had taken the following steps to resolve [BWC] compliance concerns" was elaborated in eight points. The second section listed four subsequent steps that Russia agreed to carry out. The third section, under which "the three governments agreed to create working groups, including experts," listed nine activities. (See the Annex for the full text of the Statement.) At a press conference that presented the Trilateral Statement to the Russian media in Moscow, Berdennikov stated: "The Soviet Union was violating this [BW] Convention and was running a program in the sphere of offensive biological research and development, which has been declared unlawful by the convention. . . . These activities were in progress from 1946 until March of 1992."[21] Perhaps the most significant Russian admission in the statement "Confirmed the termination of offensive research, *the dismantlement of experimental technological lines for the production of biological agents,*" and the closure of the biological weapons testing facility.[22] Although there was no mention of "stockpiles," the "experimental technological lines for the production of biological agents" seems a transparent but diplomatically worded admission of production, without identifying if and when the lines had been in operation and what quantities had been produced in the "experimental" program. The agreement also provided for inspection visits at any time to "any *non*-military biological site" and "visits to any *military* biological facility, on a reciprocal basis . . . on the basis of agreed principles."

Because of the consequence that the particular paragraphs in the Trilateral Statement concerning reciprocity in visits to facilities would have between 1994 and 1996, it is worth quoting them entirely:

Visits to any non-military biological site at any time in order to remove ambiguities, subject to the need to respect proprietary information on the basis of agreed principles. Such visits would include unrestricted access, sampling, interviews with personnel, and audio and video taping. After initial visits to Russian facilities there will be comparable visits to such U.S. and U.K. facilities on the same basis. . . .

Visits to any military biological facility, on a reciprocal basis, in order to remove ambiguities, subject to the need to respect confidential information on the basis of agreed principles. Such visits would include unrestricted access, sampling, interviews with personnel, and audio and video taping.[23]

The words alone were not the cause of the problem, but they would permit the subsequent manipulation and abuse that occurred. It appears likely that at least some members of the Russian negotiating team in September 1992 understood how particular wording they had demanded for the Trilateral Statement would be utilized by the Russian side later on, in 1994, 1995, and 1996, to bring the process to a halt. In Yazov's memorandum of January 10, 1990, to the Central Committee, reproduced in its entirety at the end of Chapter 15, he requested that the Ministry of Foreign Affairs (MFA) "not raise the question about the visit by American experts to the facility of the USSR Ministry of Defense in Sverdlovsk until the mechanisms of control over compliance with the mentioned international agreement are worked out."[24] In addition, Yevstigneev twice made the point during a Russian press conference following the signing of the statement that "we too have some questions to put to the British and US side," and "we have some complaints to make against the British and the Americans." These remarks repeated others made by Yazov in 1990. Referring to the Pine Bluff Arsenal in the United States, Yevstigneev claimed, "They have preserved it in a conserved form. As it had been prior to the signing of the [BWC] Convention."[25] That was certainly not the case, because all the fermenters had been removed.

In contrast to the United States, the members of the British negotiating team were not at all enthused as a matter of principle to accord equivalence to the Russians and accept the reciprocal visits to US/UK nonmilitary and military biological facilities that were the consequence. They felt that the purpose and parameters of the statement should have focused exclusively on the Russians to present convincing evidence that their offensive BW program was gone. Moreover, the UK team was largely taken by surprise by the US position and proposals, and agreed to them in line with the UK Foreign Office's primary concern to maintain a unified position with the United States.[26]

Although the absolute numbers were never provided, one of the points in the first section of the Trilateral Statement noted that the number of personnel working in Russian military biological programs would be cut in half, and funding would be reduced by 30%.[27] This partial reduction was demonstrably less of a curtailment than the zero budget allocation and the "halt [in] Russian research into biological weapons" that Volkogonov and Yeltsin had promised in February 1992. Further details made the reductions even less significant. In the post-Trilateral press conference, Yevstigneev provided the only known explanation on record of the composition of the 50% personnel and 30% funding reductions for what he claimed were "defensive biological programs":

> What is involved is the closure of a field test laboratory in the city of Aralsk and the abolition of the whole infrastructure supporting this division. Furthermore, the abolishing of related subdivisions at the RF Defense Ministry's Institute of Microbiology. There was a special research and test regiment which ensured the operation of this laboratory and also the 4 research subdivisions. Naturally, they will all be abolished as part of the general reductions of the RF Armed Forces. This will constitute precisely 50 percent.[28]

Not all of these lines are decipherable, but they suggest that fully 50 percent of all MOD BW R&D personnel had been involved in the testing program associated with Vozrozhdeniye Island. If that is correct it is further evidence that Yevstigneev's claim that nothing more than a few "toy" reproductions of US BW bomblet munitions were being tested at the island facility was nonsense. (See chapters 4 and 10)

This reduction is certainly less than might have been expected in the overall program of the RF-MOD BW institutes. The four "research subdivisions" are described as having functioned in direct support of the field testing program. There is no indication of any change in the nature of the research carried out at any of the RF-MOD BW facilities or in any reduction in their personnel numbers except for the end to field testing. Reconciling the February and September 1992 Russian announcements is difficult even if one assumes that the remaining programs were now to be wholly "defensive" in nature. Yeltsin had also privately promised senior US officials that he would remove generals such as Yevstigneev, Kalinin, and Petrov who had been intimately involved in the Soviet BW program. That did not happen.

Although both Berdennikov and Yevstigneev admitted in their press conference remarks that the Soviet Union and then Russia had violated the BWC "before March 1992," Yevstigneev went on to claim:

> The Defense Ministry's research services began to bring their activities in line with the Convention provisions beginning with 1985 under Gorbachev. This date coincides with the start of our new policy and with the beginning of preparations for the second conference on implementing the Convention . . . we prepared ourselves for visits by foreign delegations to our sites. Therefore the Defense Ministry already at the time took measures to dismantle the corresponding equipment which could be seen as in violation of the Convention. Actually by 1989 this work was completed.[29]

The Central Committee documents presented in the preceding chapter demonstrate Yevstigneev's claim to be false regarding both the 1985 starting date and the 1989 completion date. Central Committee documents show decisions stating that particular things should be done; none of them contain evidence as to when they were completed. On the contrary, the documents demonstrate the MOD's own requests for delays. "The work" that Yevstigneev refers to may not have been completed until after 1991 at best. The United States and United Kingdom would never obtain entry to any of the RF-MOD facilities, and what may or may not have actually been "completed" is unknown. When the United States was able to enter SNOPB in the newly independent Kazakhstan in 1994, the production facility was essentially intact. Finally, Yevstigneev took it upon himself to explain away the defector reports of continued offensive BW work at IHPB after March 1992 by saying that it was all a misunderstanding caused by a contract given to IHPB for production of a vaccine against chicken plague.[30]

As previously indicated, these events between late January and mid-September 1992 were a series of surprises. There are few instances in the years of post–World War II international arms control agreements in which any state has admitted to a deliberate violation of an arms control treaty that it had signed and ratified. In addition, the Russian admission should have led to the drastic reduction and conversion of the Soviet Union's BW R&D facilities within the RF-MOD, Biopreparat, and the other branches of the program. On January 19, 1993, the US government released its arms control treaty compliance report for the previous year. It stated:

The United States has determined that the Russian offensive biological warfare program, inherited from the Soviet Union, violated the Biological Weapons Convention through at least March 1992. The Soviet offensive BW program was massive, and included production, weaponization, and stockpiling. The status of the program since that time remains unclear. Despite the inadequate BWC declaration, and continued leadership by "old hands" of BW arms control negotiations and the BW defensive program, there has also been a marked increase in cooperation from President Yeltsin and other members of the Russian leadership to attempt to resolve compliance issues. We are now engaged in an effort to work with the Russian leadership to help terminate the illegal program and to pursue a number of measures to build confidence in Russian compliance with the BWC:

. . .

The modernization of biological agent capability and its toxin research and production in the territory of the former Soviet Union remains a concern.[31]

However it appeared by the beginning of 1993 that significant steps forward had already been taken: President Yeltsin's private admission of a past offensive Soviet BW program to his US and UK counterparts, the first Russian CBMs with an explicit acknowledgment of that program, and, despite the first indication of backsliding that caused it, the September 1992 Trilateral Accord. The incoming Clinton administration had an unbiased attitude to the Yeltsin government, which had not been the case four years before in the Bush administration's early approach to Gorbachev. There was also a strong interest to support Yeltsin as much as possible, just as the Bush administration had sought to support Gorbachev from 1989 onwards. In addition Yeltsin and his foreign minister were at first accommodating in their relationships with the West. In the next two years, US-UK and Russian teams would make site visits to each other's civilian facilities, and the United States and international partners would initiate a major grant-making initiative, the ISTC, to support former Soviet weapons of mass destruction (WMD) researchers, including those in the BW arena. It seemed a promising atmosphere.

In hindsight, we know that with the ultimate failure of the Trilateral process and the continued Russian refusal to open the RF-MOD facilities to the present day, neither the Yeltsin or Putin administrations ever carried out "a visible campaign to dismantle once and for all" the residual elements of the

Soviet BW program. The revised Russian CBM that was submitted for 1992 remained so minimal in its critical component, Form F, that it is difficult to imagine what the draft had been like. And because that key portion of the annual Russian CBM was never subsequently elaborated, and afterward was even informally renounced by various Russian officials, one wonders if it would not have been more effective for the United States and United Kingdom to have carried out their threat to make public all of their information on the Soviet offensive BW program in 1992. A chronology of events in the period 1992–1996 appears in Table 22.1.

1993 to mid-1996 were taken up with several activities:

- The US-UK-Russian Trilateral Working Group, which discussed past offensive programs and proposals for cooperation toward conversion of former Soviet BW institutes.
- The negotiations to arrange for the US-UK and Russian site visits, and carrying out the visits themselves.
- Negotiations between the United States, the United Kingdom, and Russia to obtain entry to the three still-closed RF-MOD BW facilities.
- Negotiations between the United States and Russia, inclusion of the continuing BW issues in meetings and correspondence between Clinton and Yeltsin, in the meetings of Albert A. Gore and Chernomyrdin in the Gore-Chernomyrdin Commission (GCC), and in a meeting between Secretary of State Christopher and Foreign Minister Primakov.

At the very first post–September 1992 meeting with Russian counterparts, the two US representatives were Edward Lacey and Donald Mahley of the US Department of State (DOS). In March 1993 US ambassador James Goodby was recalled from retirement to serve as the chief negotiator for the Nunn-Lugar CTR program for a period of one year, and in March 1994 he was asked to serve as the chair of the US group for the Trilateral follow-on negotiations. During 1994, US, UK, and Russian diplomats and other experts met during April 25–29 in London, May 25–28 in Moscow, June 6–7 in Vienna, October in Moscow, November 7–8 in Washington, and December 12–16 in Moscow. These meetings occurred in varying formats. Only the April and October 1994 meetings were formal sessions of the Working Group, and these had a broader agenda, including the past Soviet offensive BW program. A few were solely meetings between the senior US and Russian negotiators. The British Foreign and Commonwealth Office participants were

Table 22.1   Chronology, 1992–1996

January 1992: Transition to Russia, Yeltsin visits US, admits BW program, promises to shut it down

April 11, 1992: Yeltsin decree

August 24, 1992: Hurd/Eagleburger letter to Kozyrev

September 14, 1992: Trilateral meeting in Moscow and Statement

October 1992: Kanatjan Alibekov, former deputy director of Biopreparat, defects to US

April 1993: Clinton-Yeltsin meeting in Vancouver; BW is discussed (site visits)

May 1993: US-Russian meeting in Moscow

July 1993: Clinton, Major, and Yeltsin at G-7 summit

October 1–16, 1994: US/UK visit Pokrov, Berdsk

January 10–21, 1994: US/UK visit Omutninsk and Obolensk

February/March 1994: Russians visit 3 Pfizer sites and Plum Island

March 1994: Russians visit UK site

Spring 1994: Chernomyrdin suggests to Secretary of Defense Perry that GCC deal with BW

April 1994: Trilateral meeting in London

May 1994: First discussion of military site visits.

June 1994: Goodby/Kislyak meeting in Vienna; discussion of ground rules

October 1994: Trilateral meeting in Moscow; Russia wants "pre-BWC" sites included

November 1994: Clinton letter to Yeltsin

December 1994: Gore letter to Chernomyrdin

December 1994: GCC meeting—now, in definition of "military biological facility," Russia wants 3rd country as well as "pre-BWC" facilities included

May 1995: Yeltsin reneges on promises to Presidents Bush and Clinton

June 1995: Davis-Mamedov meet again; Russia suggests military-to-military contacts on 3rd country and "pre-BWC"; US says OK after a delay, but Russia reneges

September 1995: Davis-Mamedov meet again in DC before summit at Hyde Park

October 1995: Davis-Mamedov meet again in London, US proposal; Russia reneges

November 1995: Davis-Mamedov meet again, in London

March 1996: Secretary Christopher and Primakov take over from the GCC; Primakov proposes annual US letter on 3rd-country sites and Christopher provides first such letter

May 1996: Primakov responds US letter inadequate

September 1996: "US/UK" trilateral discussions

Ambassador Brian Donnelly, who was succeeded by Bruce Cleghorn, and John Walker. Their Russian counterparts were Sergei Kislyak and Georgy Mamedov. Lynn Davis and Timbie were additional members of the US negotiating team during different portions of the 1993 to 1996 period. Other sessions at which the US and UK ambassadors were not present dealt solely with the "Rules of the Road" document to obtain access to the RF-MOD facilities. The US-UK team at these sessions included Donald Mahley and James Timbie of the DOS, Elisa Harris of the National Security Council (NSC), and the United Kingdom's John Walker. The last of these particular meetings took place in December 1994.

Some UK government officials have argued that US formal acceptance of "reciprocity" in September 1992 was "the kiss of death" to the entire Trilateral enterprise, foretelling its destruction by the Russians. Ambassador Goodby thought not, but whether it was or not, it was a given, already an integral part of the process. Goodby believed that the issue of "ground rules" raised by the Russians was the crucial death wound, even if reciprocity had never existed. Yeltsin's clear and simple promise of access "anytime, anyplace" included no details and no parameters. But after that promise he washed his hands of the issue and allowed it to be torpedoed "lower down," by the military. By the end of 1993 and early 1994, Kremlin political figures realized that the "Grand Bargain," a "Marshall Plan" of massive economic assistance from the United States to Russia proposed by two Clinton administration officials, Graham Allison and Robert Blackwill, was not going to materialize. They therefore had no incentive to go to battle with the Russian military over the BW issue. The issue of thorough compliance with the BWC apparently held no intrinsic importance to Yeltsin or his Kremlin leadership, and they let it out of their hands.

A draft intelligence report prepared for President Clinton, presumably before his trip to Moscow in January 1994, stated that "Yeltsin has made some progress in curtailing the illicit [BW] effort since the Bush administration complained about it in a January 1993 report to Congress."[32] Clinton raised the subject in his meeting with Yeltsin, and was told that the existing program was benign, and that subsequent visits to Russian facilities would demonstrate the US concerns to be groundless. On April 7, 1994, Yeltsin dismissed Kuntsevich from his position as director of the Presidential Committee (on Problems of Chemical and Biological Disarmament) for "gross violation of his duties." On the very next day, the *Washington Post* published an article stating that the United States had evidence that Russia had not terminated the illegal BW program inherited from the Soviet Union despite Yeltsin's April 1992 decree outlawing offensive BW activities in Russia.[33] The press account was composed of interview remarks provided by what appeared to be four different government officials. The administration assessment was reportedly based on a composite of the conclusions drawn from the US-UK visits to former Soviet BW facilities as well as the account of yet an additional Russian defector in 1993, "a senior scientist in the program."

In response to the *Washington Post* story, the US Arms Control and Disarmament Agency prepared two pages of talking points for the use of DOS officials in responding to questions from the press.

- Russia was in violation of the BWC "through at least March 1992."
- The Soviet offensive BW program had included "production, weaponization, and stockpiling."
- "The status of the program since that time remains unclear and the U.S. remains concerned about the Russian BW program."
- The Trilateral Group was to meet later in April to review the results of the previous on-site facility visits and to discuss visits to Russian military BW facilities.
- In reference to Yeltsin's dismissal of Kuntsevich, who had reportedly been a hindrance to progress at the Trilaterals, the US has "never doubted President Yeltsin's personal commitment to ending the illegal biological weapons program of the former Soviet government."[34]

However, in speaking to a reporter in the preceding days, a US official phrased the final point less diplomatically: "No one disbelieves Yeltsin; but the wool does seem to have been pulled over his eyes."[35]

Russia agreed in the September 1992 Trilateral Agreement to accept:

- Visits to nonmilitary sites (subject to proprietary rights protection) to review measures to monitor compliance, to review potential modalities to test such measures, and to examine the physical infrastructure of the biological facilities in the three countries to determine whether there was specific equipment or capacity that was consistent with their stated purpose
- Cooperation in biological defence
- Ways of promoting cooperation and investment in conversion of facilities
- The exchange of information on a confidential, reciprocal basis concerning past offensive programmes

- The provision of periodic reports to legislatures and publics describing biological research and development (R&D) activities
- The encouragement of exchanges of scientists at biological facilities on a long-term basis[36]

Only the first of these six activities was to take place.[37]

In 1993–1994 visits by US-UK teams were made to the All-Union Scientific Research Institute of Veterinary Virology, Pokrov; the Chemical Plant, Berdsk; the Chemical Plant, Omutninsk; and SRCAM, Obolensk (for the second time). Disputes took place as to whether the US-UK team could see contiguous facilities at Berdsk, Omutninsk, and Pokrov. According to Kelly, "the visits to Pokrov, Berdsk and Omutninsk all revealed evidence of biological activity since 1975, such as large-scale production in hardened facilities, aerosol test chambers, excessive containment levels for current activity and accommodation for weapons-filling lines."[38] The US-UK team visiting Pokrov in October 1993 found a mobilization capacity production site for viral agents. It was assumed to have been intended primarily for producing variola virus. According to the UK team member, David Kelly, they found "nuclear hardened bunkers and incubators for thousands of eggs."[39] Because the infrastructure remained intact and also because the senior officials who all denied its purpose still remained in their positions of power, there was sufficient reason to suspect that everything continued as it had prior to 1992.[40]

There had been virtually no publicly available information in the 18 months between September 1992 and April 1994 on what was taking place inside the institutions that constituted the BW R&D program of the former Soviet Union. Once again, US and British qualms were based in part on information delivered by two new defectors from inside the Russian program, one in the winter of 1992 and the second in the fall of 1993. In addition, the US and British inspections in 1993 and 1994 "demonstrated that a 'substantial infrastructure with no commercial purpose' and with links to the Russian military remains largely intact."[41] These issues had again been brought to the attention of Yeltsin by Clinton during his visit to Moscow in January 1994, during US Secretary of Defense Perry's visit to Moscow in March 1994, and at the September 1994 Yeltsin-Clinton summit meeting. Russia had also submitted its annual BWC CBM declaration to the United Nations in April 1994, but it provided no additions to Russia's 1992 declaration of past offensive BW activities, the Form F submission that was to recount all past offensive programs going back to 1945. At that time US officials had complained that the 1992 Russian submission was even retrogressive in some respects compared to the one that the Soviet Union had submitted in 1988.

The Russian return visits took place in February 1994 to Pfizer US Pharmaceuticals, Vigo, Indiana; Pfizer US Pharmaceuticals, Groton, Connecticut; and Plum Island Animal Disease Center, US Department of Agriculture, Greenport, New York. In March 1994, they visited Evans Medical Limited in Liverpool in the United Kingdom, a facility that had only packaged anthrax vaccine and had been declared in the United Kingdom's CBMs. The Russians had assumed that the site produced the vaccine. The US facility in Vigo, Indiana, had been built for projected *B. anthracis* production in 1944–1945, but those plans were canceled well before World War II ended. It was then sold to commercial owners in 1946 for one dollar and had never been used at all. It had remained vacant and unused since then, but it afforded the Russians the opportunity to claim that it was a US mobilization capacity production facility. At the Pfizer facility in Connecticut the Russian team was allowed full access except for access to the sterile area in a clinical test facility, which they were able to video through a view port. Nevertheless the Russians protested that their access had been limited. With this unpromising record, discussion of the sequence of visits and their results now moved to the senior diplomatic level at the Trilateral meetings.

Zaviyalov reported that after the final Russian visits to US facilities, Colonel Sherbakov wrote a report stating that the US offensive BW program was in private commercial hands, and that the visiting Russian teams had therefore not been able to find it at Fort Detrick or at Pine Bluff. Sherbakov further claimed that Pfizer, itself a commercial entity, had also placed parts of the US program in private hands, and therefore Russia should follow the same device. Both claims were pure fabrications. Zaviyalov believed that once privatization of portions of the Biopreparat system began, a conspiracy was born in a collaboration between Kalinin and Morozov, their commercial purchaser: the facilities would be privatized, but all the mobilization production capacity would be retained.

Following the 1994 Russian visits to the United States and United Kingdom, a Trilateral meeting was held on the April 25–29, 1994, at the Foreign Office in London. The following subjects were discussed:

- Confidential disclosure of past American, British, and Soviet offensive programs
- An expression of concerns about current Russian activity

- Assessment of the trilateral visits undertaken
- "Rules of the Road" for future visits
- Access to military sites[42]

The United Kingdom and United States presented a confidential account of their former offensive activities, but Russia did not reciprocate. Kislyak introduced the issue of "ground rules," which he presented as a means of avoiding problems of access that had arisen in the first round of visits to non-military sites. The Russian side requested time limits of two days for site visits, a restricted definition of the area at a site that could be visited, and the need for mutually agreed objectives for visits. Goodby responded that it would be a great disadvantage for Russia if it used the ground rules issue to block an agreement. At their next meeting in June 1994 in Vienna, Goodby pointedly told Kislyak that Russia was using ground rules in that way, and that the eventual outcome would be no visits to the RF-MOD sites. Kislyak protested, "No, no." Did the United States have to agree to discuss "ground rules"? There was no alternative since the Trilateral Statement required that site visits be subject to "agreed principles." If the United States had not agreed to discuss them, Russia would never have accepted visits to the RF-MOD facilities at all. Nevertheless, the issue gave the Russians the means to block progress. "As soon as we solved one problem, Kislyak came up with another one." Kislyak and Mamedov differed in their behavior during the negotiations: "Kislyak's job was to stonewall."

Once the negotiations began to deteriorate, they deteriorated across the board to a degree that is scarcely conceivable. During the meeting in Moscow at the end of May 1994, the Russian negotiators withdrew Yeltsin's admission of an offensive Soviet BW program, despite the record of the 1992 Russian CBM submission and the admission in the Russian press conference in September 1992 after the signing of the Trilateral Statement. They also returned to the pre-1992 explanation for the cause of the 1979 anthrax outbreak in Sverdlovsk: they claimed that it had been caused by the sale of *B. anthracis*–infected meat. The recantation was made by a lieutenant colonel, but the Russian diplomat in the room, who was nominally leading the Russian team, said nothing to contradict him. Something similar occurred during one of the GCC meetings, at which a Russian military official denied that the Sverdlovsk outbreak ever took place at all. The speaker may very well have been Yevstigneev; Yazov had made the same remark to members of the Bush administration's team in Moscow in 1990. And following the Russian visits to Pfizer and Groton, Russian officials reiterated their alleged concerns regarding US compliance with the BWC.

While Kislyak claimed at the June 6, 1994, meeting in Vienna that Russia sought "complete implementation of the trilateral statement" and urged attention to "Rules of the Road" issues, the Russian side also presented a remarkable "Discussion Paper." It argued that

> building upon the agreements reached during the trilateral Moscow meeting (September 10–11, 1992) . . . it is necessary to develop guidelines for exchanging on a confidential and reciprocal basis information related to past offensive programs, not presented in detail in declarations for the United Nations.
>
> They should contain a list of information on past programs, including:
> (a) data on biological warfare agents developed in the past;
> (b) data on technologies for producing biological agents;
> (c) data on aerobiological research and testing;
> (d) data on program dismantling.
> The scope of data provided by the Parties should be as follows
> *under paragraph (a)*
> a list of agents of bacterial, viral, rickettsial and fungal nature and toxins;
> techniques for maintaining and storing infectious cultures;
> individual qualitative and quantitative criteria for the selection of bacterial, viral, rickettsial and fungal agents and toxins with a view to evaluating the possibility of using them as biological warfare agents;
> *under paragraph (b)*
> methods of growing biological bacterial, viral, rickettsial and fungal warfare agents and of toxin production;
> techniques for production of samples of biological warfare agents;
> description of equipment for producing biological agent samples;
> *under paragraph (c)*
> description of instruments, equipment and types of model animals for aerobiological research and testing;
> goals and objectives of aerobiological experiments;
> *under paragraph (d)*
> specific measures to eliminate organizational structures involved in the program . . .

The question of continuing the exchange of additional information to the F forms would be addressed after a justified request by one of the parties and approval by all parties to the Trilateral Statement of September 11, 1992.[43]

There are two astonishing things in this document. First, the very last line contradicts nearly two years of negotiations, as it would supply any one of the three parties with a veto, despite the fact that all the three parties had already signed the September 1992 Trilateral Statement two years earlier. This was the second occasion since the Trilateral Agreement in which Russian negotiators proposed new conditions to be agreed to by the United States and the United Kingdom that would give Russia unilateral veto rights. The word "justified" to modify "request" would provide additional grounds for refusal.

Second, most of the proposal is remarkably similar to the KGB cable appended to Chapter 2 that had been sent out to its external operatives in 1985 requesting that they obtain highly detailed information of direct benefit to the Soviet offensive BW program. It appears to be a Russian request for details of all the work done in the US and UK BW programs. The United States and United Kingdom had never made any comparable demand for such detailed information from Russia. A year later, in early 1995, the United Kingdom did present a paper to the Russians that suggested that Russia was not providing sufficient information about their past offensive BW program, and suggested that information could be provided, for example, about how the management structure of the Soviet BW program was organized, and what the Soviet concept for the use of variola virus had been. But no US-UK request included anything like the sort of detail that the Russian document requested. The language in the Trilateral Statement proposing exchange of information between the three parties was intended by the United States and United Kingdom to provide an opportunity for Russian officials to demonstrate that the Soviet offensive BW program was over. It was not meant to be a venue for Russia to request the kinds of detailed BW information that the Russian document asked for, nor did it request such information from Russia.

Because relatively little of the Russian request would have pertained to the UK offensive BW program when it existed between 1945 and the perhaps the 1960s, it was an excellent example of the Russian effort to turn the focus from their own illegal 1975–1992 offensive program to the then-legal pre-1969 US BW program. It is also extremely difficult to believe that the document was a serious proposal and that "Russia"—that is, whoever drafted the document—would have been prepared to supply the Russian answers to the information requested. Who would have written that Discussion Paper? Most likely a small team comprised of FSB staff, Vasiliev, Ignatiev, and perhaps a very few other collaborators. The MFA certainly did not write it.

Many decades before, between 1958 and 1963, the United States and Soviet Union had held long negotiations for a comprehensive nuclear test ban treaty. The negotiators began to approach the question of on-site inspections within such a treaty in order to assess disputed seismic events in 1961–1962. The Soviet Union had previously refused all discussion of on-site inspections on principle. There was therefore great apprehension on the US side that the Soviet Union would draw out the negotiations interminably over the minutiae of visits on Soviet territory. In the context of the Test Ban, these issues were referred to as the "modalities": how many inspectors there could be, how soon after a suspected nuclear test they could enter the country, what was the radius of the area from the suspected test epicenter that the visiting team could search, how long could they stay, what kind of samples could the visiting inspection team take away with them to test, and so on. Russian negotiating behavior in the Trilaterals was already showing the same elaborate replay of Soviet negotiating behavior. In essence, that is exactly what happened, and on a somewhat similar group of "modalities." This time it was the Russian insistence on "ground rules," or "rules of the road" as they were also referred to, that would be associated with prospective US-UK visits to RF-MOD facilities. The Russian negotiators claimed that it was necessary to take into account "lessons learned" from the visits to the nonmilitary biological sites, such as "the need for clear definitions and precise sampling rules." As a result, much of two years of Trilateral meetings was spent in trying to agree on language presented by the Russians on BW definitions, thresholds, definition of a military biological facility, and the sequence of visits. The similarity of all this to what Soviet diplomats had pressed for in a document presented at a preparatory meeting for the Third BWC Review Conference discussed earlier in Chapter 20 is obvious. Russian diplomats pressed for the same in the last half of the 1990s at the Ad-Hoc Group (AHG) negotiations for a BWC Verification Protocol. The same positions were constantly being recycled, and they did not suggest interest in reaching an agreement.

During the first and second working group meetings, presentations were made on each side's offensive BW programs, and on the results of visits to each other's nonmilitary facilities. As an example of the level of Russian response, their representatives claimed that the Soviet Union had only had an offensive *research* program, avoided answering questions about weaponization, and denied that the Sverdlovsk anthrax outbreak had anything to do with an accident at the MOD facility in the city. They would not reply to direct questions about their work with variola virus, nor would they answer questions about the role of the VPK in the BW program, even though two of its members, Ignatiev and Spirande, were participating in the meeting. They had been identified as members of the VPK in the Soviet delegation to the Third BWC Review Conference. Ignatiev and Spirande attended all of the working group meetings. It would have been simple for the Russian negotiators to respond to these questions and emphasize that the concerns were part of the pre-1992 Soviet era, but they did not do that. At the end of the October 1994 working group meetings, UK ambassador Brian Donnelly made a strong statement expressing his frustration with the uncooperative Russian behavior, the failure to address UK and US concerns, and the backsliding to ridiculous and long-discredited tales such as the contaminated meat explanation for Sverdlovsk. The Russian tactics might almost be seen as a purposeful display of scorn and contempt for the proceedings, and for their British and American counterparts.

Goodby believed that the December 1994 meeting in Moscow was the high point of the negotiations. Goodby, Timbie, and Davis composed the US negotiating team, Donnelly and Walker represented the United Kingdom, and Kislyak was their primary Russian interlocutor. The meeting was difficult, and involved the negotiation of a sequence of components to the "ground rules." At the conclusion of the discussions the US team thought that Kislyak was in agreement and was prepared to accept the result of their work. He said "I have to consult" and left the room, an indication that he did not know whether the tentative agreement would be acceptable to "others." If he had known that it was unacceptable, "no good," he would have said so. In the morning, a matter of hours later, he returned. In a further indication of his distance from the locus of decision in Moscow, his reply was, "I'm sorry, we can't do that . . . we have another problem." The new problem was an entirely separate issue, unrelated to the "ground rules" that had been the subject of the preceding day's discussion. Russian negotiators now demanded access to a group of US military medical research facilities located outside of the United States in exchange for US-UK access to the RF-MOD BW institutes. This request was almost certainly prompted by the RF-MOD and the security services, and very likely was designed to destroy or at least indefinitely stalemate the negotiations.

The US facilities in question comprised a large number of sites in third countries under a multiplicity of programs and acronyms. They were essentially field research laboratories whose work focused on diseases endemic to developing countries, but to which US military forces serving in those regions might also be exposed. There were three Naval Medical Research Units (NAMRU): NAMRU 1, in the Philippines, NAMRU 2 in Indonesia, and NAMRU 3 in Egypt. There was also a US Navy Medical Research Center, Lima, in Peru (NMRCD), which was a field outpost of the Naval Medical Research Institute (NMRI) in Bethesda, Maryland. In addition there were four US Army Medical Research Units (USAMRU), without numerical designations, in Brazil, Kenya, South Korea, and Thailand. The Thai facility again had its own designation, Armed Forces Research Institute of Medical Sciences (AFRIMS), which was the field facility of the Walter Reed Army Institute of Research (WRAIR) in Silver Spring, Maryland.[44] Notably, Russia never asked to visit the US-based parent organizations of the overseas institutes, WRAIR and NMRI, in any of its Trilateral inspections.

The Russian demand for access to these sites is universally considered to have been designed to foreclose the possibility of any agreement. NAMRU and USAMRU facilities had never been part of the US BW program, in direct contrast to the three RF-MOD facilities. They are essentially international public health research facilities, and they all include substantial numbers of scientists from the host countries on their staffs. Their research programs are public and the results of their work are frequently published in the research literature. The US government noted that the facilities were all on the sovereign territory of other states, and the United States was not in a position to speak for other countries or to negotiate Russian entry to them. Nevertheless, Goodby felt that the United States had no objections if the countries hosting the NAMRU and USAMRU facilities agreed to Russian site visits.

The Russians were trying to find "evidence" that the United States had retained a BW mobilization capacity after 1975 (and even that the United Kingdom had as well). They claimed that they needed access to the US military medical facilities in other countries in order to remove their concerns. This was not the position that Alibek reports, which was that prior to 1992 Soviet military intelligence claimed that the retained US capability was in the continental United States. That was also the charge they made in 1992 and 1995 after visiting facilities in the United States belonging to DOD and to US pharmaceutical corporations. Nor did the Russian Trilateral negotiators reintroduce the claim heard both before and after 1990 that the United States had "privatized" its BW program after 1975 to commercial entities. The Russian negotiators insisted not only on including "third party" facilities within the definition of military biological facilities that should be subject to visits, but also "pre-BWC facilities," that is, every former facility that was part of an offensive or defensive BW program after 1945. Once again, it is difficult to imagine that the Russian negotiators would have been willing to comply with that requirement on their own soil.

By the end of the Trilateral process, the meetings on the "rules of the road" document were dominated by the Russian military. The Russian team wanted very specific criteria for visits to its RF-MOD facilities based on simple yes/no answers to the presence of certain capabilities or the presence of agents in specified quantities. The United Kingdom saw such requirements as a way to constrain judgments about the nature of work being carried out at the sites, and strongly opposed them. During one of the final meetings, at the Russian Embassy in London, the US and UK negotiators believed they had just come to an agreement on a particular point with the MFA's Mamedov. However, he had to leave the meeting early, and as soon as he had left the room the two RF-MOD representatives present, Vasiliev and Kholstov, retracted what had just been agreed to.

Russia Defeats the Trilateral Process

The Russians established the principle of equivalence in the September 1992 Joint Statement. For the four years that followed they sought to shift the negotiations as much as possible onto a discussion of US activities and away from their own past BW programs and the continued withholding of US-UK access to the RF-MOD BW facilities. By the end of 1994 both Goodby and Donnelly were frustrated by what they believed to be deliberate Russian stonewalling, and Goodby requested to be transferred to other responsibilities. Goodby had no information from Washington or from the US embassy in Moscow regarding Russian BW-relevant decision making, and he was not involved in several subsequent meetings in 1995 and 1996 between Davis and Mamedov, including one in London in May 1995. These sessions primarily concerned other US-Russian arms control issues, and discussion of

BW occurred at the margin. Davis and Kislyak also met in March 1996. Finally, secretary of state Christopher and Primakov met on a single occasion. The details of these last meetings are unavailable. Goodby had no idea whether Yeltsin or Chernomyrdin even talked to the Russian military leadership about the closed RF-MOD BW facilities, the issues involved in the Trilateral negotiations, or Russia's Trilateral obligations. It was obvious why the Russians and Chernomyrdin suggested that the subject of BW be moved to the US-only GCC deliberations: the pressure on the Russians was stronger at the Trilaterals, with the British frequently taking more forceful positions than the United States.

As for Yeltsin, Goodby believed that "Yeltsin did not run his own government." The American diplomats referred to him as "the Wizard of Oz": Yeltsin would agree to do something, but nothing would happen. Goodby wrote about this in strong and explicit terms in the context of the negotiations that he was assigned to carry out the following year. In 1995 Goodby was given responsibility for negotiations with Russian officials for nuclear warhead dismantlement under the Nunn-Lugar program. He described the outcome in a portion of a book chapter published in 1999, which he titled "Reflections on Russian Government Policymaking:"

> Follow-on actions after important decisions were haphazard. Yeltsin seemed unable to prevent his government from reversing earlier presidential decisions or ignoring them.
>
> In nuclear matters several statements of intent were issued jointly by Presidents Clinton and Yeltsin that Russian officials chose to disregard. The most egregious example was their joint statement of May 10, 1995, [which was signed by Yeltsin] in which the two presidents in very precise terms endorsed early action on several important measures of transparency and irreversibility of nuclear weapons dismantlement, only to see the negotiations broken off at the urging of Russian officials six months later. In this particular instance there were detailed U.S.-Russian discussions at senior levels in the Ministry of Foreign Affairs and the Ministry of Atomic Energy about how to frame the two presidents' intent, and about its urgency, before and after the May 10, 1995, statement was issued. According to the Russians, interagency discussions had been held in Moscow that resulted in instructions to implement the May 10, 1995, statement. Still, neither the Russian president nor the prime minister was able or willing to enforce the decision when some officials in

the bureaucracy (probably inspired by the "security organs") concluded that transparency did not suit Russia.

For a time Prime Minister Chernomyrdin became one of the major discussion partners with the United States through the mechanism of the Gore-Chernomyrdin Commission. He was a competent and businesslike manager, but his authority over the "power ministries" in Moscow was limited. Only on September 10, 1996, as part of a temporary transfer of authority occasioned by his impending surgery, did President Yeltsin decree that these ministries should report to Chernomyrdin. His authority over the power ministries seemed to be limited even after that period.[45]

Only a few months after the May 1995 agreement mentioned above, someone at the Russian embassy in Washington telephoned Goodby at the DOS and informed him that to all intents and purposes, Russia was not going to abide by the agreement. They were "not ready" to engage in the discussions that were to have begun in December 1996. Russian officials never subsequently became "ready," and the May 1995 US-Russian agreement on nuclear weapon dismantlement was killed in Moscow.

There would be every reason to believe that the depiction provided by Goodby also reflected what happened to BW questions in Moscow between 1993 and 1996. In addition, the few generals and former VPK administrators who were presumably behind the effort to destroy the Trilateral Agreement and keep the RF-MOD BW facilities closed, an effort in which they succeeded, were presumably much weaker bureaucratic actors in Moscow than the Ministry of Atomic Energy. This example demonstrates again that although Russian obstruction regarding post-1992 BWC compliance may have been the most exceptional because it succeeded a WMD program that violated international treaty obligations between 1975 and at least late 1992, individuals in the RF-MOD were able to either overturn or frustrate major arms control efforts in at least two other areas as well. In the example provided by Goodby's narrative involving nuclear weapons, they were able to do this with the collaboration of Minatom and perhaps the FSB. In the area of chemical weapons destruction, mandated by the CWC, the RF-MOD generals did this on their own, as Chapter 19 demonstrates. And in the case of BWC compliance, they clearly had the assistance of officials whom Yeltsin had appointed to his "Conventions" Commission.

On November 26, 1996, Ambassador Grigori Berdennikov, the man who had signed the Trilateral Statement for Russia in September 1992, said at the

Fourth BWC Review Conference in Geneva that "Russia has never developed, produced, stockpiled or stored biological weapons."[46] Senior Russian officials had regressed a full 10 years, back to 1986.

The US Noncompliance Statements and Other US Intelligence Assessments

Based on the Yellow Rain allegations in Southeast Asia, the US government's annual reports on noncompliance with arms control treaties in 1984, 1985, and 1986 accused the Soviet Union of being in violation of the 1925 Geneva Protocol and the BWC. The operative sentence was often: "The Soviet Union . . . has maintained an offensive biological warfare program and capability in violation of its legal obligations under the Biological and Toxin Weapons Convention of 1972." In December 1987, following the submission of the first Soviet BWC CBM, the "in violation of" phrase was absent, but the document stated, "The Soviets have maintained a prohibited offensive biological warfare capability." In 1991 the wording was: "The United States has determined that the Soviet Union has maintained an active offensive program since the 1930's and continues to be in violation of the 1972 Biological and Toxin Weapons Convention (BWC)." In 1992 the phrase "the former Soviet Union's extensive ongoing offensive biological weapons program" was added to the 1991 lines. The 1994 statement made use of the developments during the two preceding years:

> The U.S. has determined that the offensive biological weapons (BW) program that Russia inherited from the Soviet Union violated the BWC through at least March 1992. An offensive research program was confirmed by Russian President Boris Yeltsin in March 1992. In April 1992, President Yeltsin issued a decree prohibiting activities inconsistent with the BWC. Following his decree, Russia claimed significant reductions in funding and personnel for biological R&D programs, closure of open-air BW test facilities and described other measures to bring Russia into compliance with the BWC. In August 1992, the Russian parliament passed a new law making participation in offensive BW research, development, production or weaponization a criminal offense. Following Yeltsin's decree, the actual status of the Russian offensive program was unclear.
>
> . . .

At the September 1994 summit, Presidents Yeltsin and Clinton agreed on the importance of full and continued implementation of the September 1992 Trilateral Statement as a means of gaining confidence that offensive BW programs have been terminated. The Presidents also agreed that their experts, along with those of the U.K., would meet without delay for a further working group meeting.

The U.S. continues to have concerns about Russia's compliance with the BWC. On the other hand, President Yeltsin, Prime Minister Chernomyrdin and other senior Russian officials have repeatedly expressed their commitment to compliance to their American counterparts. Under the September 1992 Trilateral Statement, Russia has carried out facility visits, information exchanges and experts meetings. These positive statements and actions demonstrate that the senior Russian leadership is committed to compliance with the BWC. However, Russia must still take concrete steps to follow through on this commitment and rectify existing problems. The U.S. will judge Russia's BWC compliance by its actions.[47]

The 1995 statement began to show the effects of Russian backsliding: "Previous assessments of Russian compliance have highlighted the dichotomy between what appears to be the commitment from President Yeltsin and other members of the Russian leadership in attempting to resolve BWC issues and the continued involvement of 'old hands' in trilateral BW discussions and in what Russia describes as a defensive BW program."[48]

Each of the compliance reports of 1996, 1997, 1998, 1999, 2000, and 2001 repeated the same formulations used in 1995, adding that no further information had been supplied by Russia regarding its former offensive BW program in its CBM for the preceding year. In the 2001 report, already drafted during the preceding Clinton administration, it was again stated, "The United States judges, based on available evidence, that Russia continues to maintain an offensive BW program in violation of the BWC."[49]

US administrations are required by law to present a noncompliance report every year. However, the Bush administration did so only once in its eight years in office, in 2005. (The report released in 2001 was a carryover from the previous Clinton administration.) The section that dealt with Russia and the BWC was quite different from previous years. Instead of being a paragraph or two in length, it was four and a half pages long. It repeated some of the core elements of statements from the previous years:

- That "the United States is concerned that Russia maintains a mature offensive BW program"
- That Russia's initial 1992 CBMs declaration was incomplete, that subsequent data declarations provide no additional information, and that the 1992 declaration "falsely denied past production and stockpiling of BW [and] . . . also failed to list all of the sites that supported the Soviet offensive BW program"
- That "the United States also assesses that Russia has the capability to mobilize BW production"[50]

An important new note that could now be added was that "public statements by Russian officials appear to retreat from the statements made by President Yeltsin in 1992. Some have asserted that Russia has never had an offensive BW program." This would of course contradict the Trilateral Statement that Russian signed. Similar retractions have previously been emphasized. On November 13, 2001, in a Joint Statement by President Bush and Vladimir Putin, now president of Russia, the United States and Russia agreed "to counter the threat of terrorist use of biological materials," and also "confirmed" their "strong commitment" to the BWC.[51] There is no indication, however, that the Bush administration used this venue to take up its contentions in the US noncompliance documents that Russia still maintained its offensive BW program.

There was, however, also a problematical element in the four pages, the mention of new Russian programs that US authorities found suspect. The Russian Pathogen Biodefense Initiative publicly initiated in 1999 was described as "ostensibly aimed at providing a unified government system to defend against human, animal and environmental pathogens, but could also potentially support or provide cover for offensive BW capabilities." Four particular experiments that were selected for mention were introduced by the following line: "A substantial amount of dual-use research conducted in recent years has legitimate biodefense applicability, but also could be used to further an offensive program."[52] Such provisional or conjectural statements cannot be denied, and unquestionably the Soviet Union had used Biopreparat and other agencies in its ministries of health and agriculture as a cover for its offensive BW program in the years prior to 1992. However, such statements regarding the risks of dual-use research would apply to no country in the world in the past decade as much as they would to the United States. One specialist who reviewed the four experiments remarked that "the US does them quicker, more, and better." In addition, similar experiments are carried out in countries all over the world, and some not even as part of biodefense programs but as research into the pathogenic mechanisms of microbial organisms. (See Chapter 11.)

The information used to draft a noncompliance report is provided by the US intelligence community, but the report itself is prepared with input from policy officials as well. There was *no* new reporting, just that the administration officials who received the draft report had changed, that is, senior officials in the Bush administration. This was notably the administration and its analytic cohort that had also produced the assessment that Iraq possessed mobile biological weapon production vehicles, an assessment of unprecedented and scandalous incompetence. The same approach was applied to the 2005 BWC compliance assessment of China, referring to "several BSL-3 laboratories and dual use capabilities in a facility identified as a vaccine producer," and stating that "facilities in China that may have legitimate public health and commercial uses could also offer access to additional BW-enabling capabilities." It is again an abstract statement that is indisputable, but in 2007 the United States had between 4,000 and 5,000 BSL-3 facilities, of which no fewer than 1,356 were licensed to work with "select agents," those considered of primary BW significance.[53] Such "capability" based statements would in the years after 2005 prove to have been a weakness in United States claims over many years about offensive BW programs in several other countries. It was unquestionable that RF-MOD and Ministry of Health institutes remained closed to Western observers, that Russia had essentially scuttled the Trilateral process, and that its BWC CBM was so dramatically insufficient that it had to generate extreme suspicion. However, to the degree that the "capability" and "dual use" elements were critical parts of the overall US assessment, they only served to undermine the credibility of the whole.

In addition to the compliance reports, the US intelligence community (IC) also produced a number of other intelligence assessments concerning the issue of Russian BW. In the fall of 1993, the US IC prepared a top-secret National Intelligence Estimate (NIE) describing what it knew about Russia's BW program, "including specific locations . . . everything the Americans knew."[54] Either this report, or another intelligence report in the same time period, "quoted Yeltsin himself as complaining that the biological weapons work was continuing at three facilities despite his decree."[55] Yeltsin was presumably referring to the three RF-MOD facilities. On November 1, 1993, in Bogota, Colombia, Aldrich Ames, a Soviet and then Russian spy within the CIA, turned that NIE over to Russian agents.[56] Given the description of Wisner's presentation to the Russian participants at the September 1992 Trilateral meeting in Moscow, it is impossible to gauge whether the NIE prepared just a year later included any significant additional information. At the time of the Trilaterals, the question had again been raised as to whether the United States and the United Kingdom should make public the details of the secret Soviet BW program. But Wisner believed in "quiet diplomacy rather than open confrontation. . . . 'Trying to force a public embarrassment, shock, confrontation wasn't going to get you a thing, and chipping away at the internal contradictions on the Russian side, nudging, pushing along was a better strategy.'"[57]

By 1996 Wisner would be proved grievously mistaken: "quiet diplomacy . . . , chipping away . . . , nudging, pushing . . . " had all failed dramatically. Despite the feeling in 1992–1993 that at least some progress was taking place, it was no longer a question of protecting Gorbachev. If there was ever an opportune moment to have publicly disclosed the history of the Soviet/ Russian program, it was probably lost in 1992 and 1993. Had the United States and United Kingdom released the memoranda that they had been handing to Shevardnadze, Gorbachev, and Yeltsin for three years, Russian authorities, primarily the RF-MOD, would no longer have been able to submit inconsequential CBMs and even retract the key admission of the 1992 one. Russian spokespersons like Yevstigneev could no longer have gone on blatantly lying. Kuntsevich, Yevstigneev, Kalinin, and some others might finally have been retired or dismissed—no small thing, given that the latter two remained active for another 15 years. But by 1995 and 1996, there were again very strong arguments for not making a public disclosure. First, to some in the administration it was by then a matter of protecting Yeltsin's political survival. Second, strategic nuclear arms control agreements with Russia would come under attack by opponents in the US Senate. Most immediately, the administration's effort to obtain Senate ratification of the Chemical Weapons Convention would very likely be defeated. Finally, US funding to Russia to secure fissionable nuclear material and related programs under the Nunn-Lugar legislation would risk being terminated because of a provision in the legislation that required certification by the president that Russia was "committed to" being in compliance with arms-control agreements, including the BWC. Although the US administration may have believed that Yeltsin was committed to complying with the BWC for perhaps two years after he entered office, after that it became an increasingly unrealistic assumption.

In 1995 the deputy director of the CIA and the director of the DIA appeared at the annual "Threat" briefing before the Senate Armed Services Committee. Senator Thurmond asked the following question:

> Russia appears to be maintaining an offensive biological weapons program despite the 1972 Biological Weapons Convention and the 1992 agreement with the United States and the United Kingdom to terminate such programs. On what evidence does the US base its claims that Russia is continuing to develop offensive biological weapons? Provide a detailed assessment of the Russian BW program, including a description of all facilities and a listing of all agents currently being maintained or developed.[58]

Virtually the entire reply of over a page was deleted, with the exception of a single paragraph:

> Despite repeated assurances that Russia has been in full compliance with the BWC since March 1992, the US Intelligence Community judges that some key offensive activities continue in Russia and that Yeltsin has been unable or unwilling to terminate them. We are confident that support for maintaining a mobilization base for wartime production and the scaled-down efforts aimed at developing new agents resides in the highest echelons of the Ministry of Defense. The continuing refusal of the Ministry to be open about past BW offensive activities, whether in declarations to the UN or in trilateral and bilateral discussions, only reinforces our doubts about its intent to terminate all offensive BW activities.[59]

In 1999 the US Senate requested the DOD to submit a report with answers for all the critical questions regarding the status of the Russian BW program. It requested:

1. an assessment of the extent of compliance by Russia with international agreements relating to the control of biological weapons (BW); and
2. a detailed evaluation of the potential political and military costs and benefits of collaborative biological pathogen research efforts by the United States and Russia. . . .

An evaluation of the extent of the control and oversight by the Government of Russia over the military and civilian-military biological warfare programs formerly controlled or overseen by states of the former Soviet Union.

- *The extent and scope of continued biological warfare research, development, testing and production in Russia, including the sites where such activity is occurring and the types of activity being conducted.*
- *An assessment of compliance by Russia with the terms of Biological Weapons Convention.*
- *An identification and assessment of the measures taken by Russia to comply with the obligations assumed under the Joint Statement on Biological Weapons, agreed to by the United States, the United Kingdom, and Russia on September 14, 1992.*
- *A description of the information provided by Russia about its biological weapons dismantlement efforts to date.*
- *An assessment of the accuracy and comprehensiveness of declarations by Russia regarding its biological weapons activities. . . .*

The responses by the DOD were very informative:

(U) We have little information on the extent of control and oversight by the Government of Russia over the military and civilian-military biological warfare programs formerly controlled or overseen by the Soviet Union. We are concerned, however, that the same generals who led the former Soviet offensive BW program are still in charge at military institutes that are said to be part of the greatly reduced defensive BW program. . . .

(U) Nevertheless, serious concerns about Russia's offensive BW capabilities remain. Key components of the former Soviet BW programs remain largely intact and may support a possible future mobilization capability for the production of biological agents and delivery systems. Moreover, work outside the scope of legitimate biological defense activity may be occurring now at selected sites. Some legitimate civilian research focusing on enhancing virulence, antibiotic resistance, or survivability of agents, could theoretically support a covert offensive BW program or help to maintain the capability to revive such a program.

(U) . . . Unless we can determine the intent behind various activities, distinguishing between permitted civilian or defensive work and illicit offensive activities is nearly impossible. . . .

(U) . . . The United States is concerned that such work may be occurring at selected Russian facilities. . . .

(U) . . . to address our concerns about continuing offensive BW work at Russian military facilities. . . .

(U) CTR and ISTC access to former soviet civilian BW sites has provided important insights into prior BW and current civilian activities at the facilities; this has created a more transparent working relationship with these facilities. . . .

(U) . . . the United States has been able, under CTR, the Department of Energy's Initiatives for Proliferation Prevention (IPP) Program, and ISTC activities, to achieve far more direct access to non-military former Russian BW facilities than was ever foreseen in the Trilateral process. . . .

(U) . . . During these visits, no direct evidence was observed that offensive activities were being conducted at the time of the visits. However, Russian lack of openness about past activities, the preservation of (and subsequent lack of explanation for) some of the physical infrastructure for BW research or production all heightened U.S. concerns that offensive activity had not ceased. . . .

(U) Where we have had access to former offensive BW research and production facilities, we have learned that research and production facilities specific to offensive BW work have fallen into considerable disrepair. For example, the high-level biological containment areas at Obolensk have been dramatically reduced in size. Our teams have found that the Biosafety Level Four (BSL-4) building number 6A at Vector has been unused for years, and that it would require a substantial investment of time and resources to be made operational.[60]

In another example, when US officials with the CTR program visited Pokrov in 2003, 10 years after the 1993 Trilateral visit, they found the facility "a shambles."

Yeltsin's Last Years

In December 1998, a three-day NATO Advanced Study Workshop was held in Moscow. Its aim was to induce a more cooperative approach from the Russian government at the AHG negotiations for a BWC Verification Protocol. The participants were mostly Western diplomats, plus several Russian officials and a few Western BW arms control specialists. Ignatiev repeatedly took the floor as the dominant Russian personality present to represent the Russian government position. Ignatiev was reasonably well informed of what took place at the proceedings in Geneva, both in VEREX and the AHG deliberations. Between the September 1991 Third BWC Review Conference and August 1997, he had participated in no fewer than 11 of the sessions as a member of the Russian delegation: three VEREX meetings, the Special Conference, the Fourth BWC Review Conference (1996), and six sessions of the AHG.[61] He stated that the Russian Federation obeyed all aspects of the BWC and had never produced or stored BW.[62] On the last day of the conference, when one of the academic participants timidly suggested that "some observers" had raised questions about whether the BW program of the Soviet Union might not have been offensive in nature, Ignatiev responded fiercely. He stated that "Russia has fully accounted for what the USSR did in the past." He referred to Russia's 1992 Form F CBM submission, adding that the Soviet Union had never made biological weapons, and that "This issue should be closed" and that he did not want to hear any further mention of it.

Ignatiev also stated that his office was the main coordinator of the Russian government's positions regarding the BWC Verification Protocol negotiations, as well as participating in the Russian delegation in Geneva. The Presidential Commission performed the function of a "National Authority" coordinating the Russian government's role regarding the BWC and the CWC. The MFA, he said, "takes care of the foreign policy of the country." The meaning of that last remark was more thoroughly explained in private by a Canadian diplomat who was present. When the Canadians visited the MFA in Moscow to speak to their counterparts, "It was just like the old days; they just threw up their hands." They were apparently cut out of any policy discussion regarding BW issues, wherever it was taking place in the Russian government. The MFA had no power, no ability to maneuver, and they were provided with convoluted directives. The Canadian observation was similar to a comment by US Ambassador Mahley: "There was nobody home at the MFA."[63] The Canadian diplomats had tried to arrange to meet with Ignatiev at the Commission, but the request was refused. Nor could they find anyone in the RF-MOD with responsibility for the subject, although more RF-MOD officials than MFA ones attended the 1998 NATO Workshop in Moscow. At the AHG negotiations in Geneva, the members of the Russian delegation rarely engaged, except to delay and deadlock those issues that they disagreed with.

As for substantive positions, an MFA representative, Gennady Lutay, stated that Russia did not support clarification visits to biological-related facilities, while Ignatiev added that "countries wouldn't report information that would produce suspicions to precipitate visits." Obviously missing the irony in his comments, Ignatiev also said that "many CBM submissions are very insufficient; some countries don't include all [necessary] information. Some countries pick and choose which portions to answer and disregard the rest," and that "natural outbreaks of disease should not be subject to the BWC." An RF-MOD representative, Anatoly Atrischenko, argued, "We should minimize visits associated with laboratories and make [the submission of] CBMs more voluntary," a position that was obviously contrary to Ignatiev's immediately preceding complaint that existing CBMs have been insufficient. When the deputy director of Vector began his presentation directly afterward by saying that he would describe the real-world experience of his institution when it hosted overseas visitors, Atrischenko showed his displeasure and conferred privately with Ignatiev.

Toward the end of Yeltsin's tenure, under his prime minister, Stepashin, the Presidential Commission on Conventional Problems was abolished. A newly created directorate in the equally new Munitions Agency took over its responsibilities. Zinovy Pak, an official formerly involved with directing the Russian defense industry, was appointed director of the Munitions Agency in May 1999. Ignatiev moved from the Commission staff to work under Pak as the head of the Directorate on BW issues. Kalinin became the chairman of the board of directors of National Biotechnologies, with *Gazprom*, a corporation closely associated with the Kremlin, as its main investor. According to Zaviyalov there had been minimal activity in the Biopreparat offices after 1992, no controls, no inspections of the IEI. However in 1998 and 1999, there was a renewal of security, with visits from the former 3rd Department of the KGB, now the FSB, which had not taken place since 1992. This renewal was coincident with Putin's placement in command of the FSB. The new Munitions Agency directorate under Ignatiev was to be responsible for implementing the BWC Verification Protocol that was still under negotiation in 1999. There had reportedly been "promising signals" to visiting US officials that if the BWC Verification Protocol came into being, then Russia would comply with it. The implication was that this was the *only* way that access to RF-MOD facilities would ever be achieved. If not, their situation would remain frozen.[64] The Bush administration rejected the BWC Verification Protocol in 2001, and the RF-MOD facilities remain closed to this day.

According to Kataev, when Yeltsin succeeded Gorbachev, "all logic went." Zaikov was gone, and Kuntsevich, Ivanov, and Ignatiev were initially the major players. "Anyone with sharp elbows got their way. In Yeltsin's period, people didn't work for the country, but for themselves." When Kozyrev was foreign minister and Igor Ivanov was his deputy, Kataev suggested that the *Pyatorka* should be resurrected. Ivanov replied, "No one would do that anymore; no one is interested in the country any more. It was no longer possible to impose constraints or limitations on some faction; they wouldn't accept it." Yeltsin could have fired people, but he could not have forced them to cooperate. Zaikov's "department" went to Yeltsin's Security Council staff, but without Zaikov. Shakhov moved to an office on defense industry conversion. The "Conventions Commission" came into being not because Yeltsin wanted it, but because Kuntsevich did and pushed the proposal through Yeltsin's staff director, Yurii Petrov. Kuntsevich's motives were that he was being retired from the army and he needed a position. He was able to argue that it was necessary to have a technical administration for both BW and CW inspections. Kataev could identify no "BW" person on Yeltsin's staff. There were no organized "working groups," and no formal requirement for "balance" or differing opinions. The individual with the most forceful and dominating presence took over in the old, pre-1985 way, and the others would follow that person. A direct personal experience with Kuntsevich in Moscow in November 1999 demonstrated that he was a very forceful advocate, even of a position composed totally of fabrications, preposterous arguments, and lies.[65] The position of the military leadership had not changed at all, and the result was that without any institutional opposition at a senior level, the position of the military and their ex-VPK colleagues was dominant.

Yeltsin's most important advisers on security and military affairs in the years between 1993 and 1996 were the minister of defense, General Pavel Grachev, Aleksandr Korzhakov, Alexei Ogarev, and Sergei Shakhrai. Shakhrai was the key individual during the early Yeltsin years on questions pertaining to national security, the former KGB, and military production. However, the two Yeltsin advisers who played the biggest role on questions of biological and chemical weapons were Kuntsevich and Yevstigneev. Once given charge of Yeltsin's "Commission," Kuntsevich apparently had a free hand. On November 25, 1992, he wrote a letter to Yeltsin saying that in contrast to US/UK claims, he had found no evidence that IHPB was carrying out any BW work "at the present time" and that the US/UK "anxiety" after their last visit to IHPB "has no objective basis." He went on to repeat Yevstigneev's preposterous tale that IHPB only "was working on a vaccine against bird plague for use in poultry farming in the Leningrad region."[66] Kuntsevich had no more hesitancy in lying to Yeltsin than the military had previously to lie to Gorbachev. And it must have been very much easier to lie to Yeltsin than it had been to Zaikov and Gorbachev. Despite the fact that Kuntsevich was removed from his post in late 1994 because of allegations that he had been involved in the illegal export of intermediate chemicals used for the production of chemical weapons, as well as for diverting US funds, he remained an influential figure. In the late 1990s he still served as an adviser for the communist deputies in the Duma, as well as for the ultranationalist deputies. Yeltsin's administration was also served by a Security Council in the mid-1990s, headed for a time by his rival, General Alexander Lebed. In July 1996 Yeltsin established a second nominal advisory body, the Defense Council, to offset Lebed, and Lebed was replaced in December 1996 by Ivan Rybkin. Zinovy Pak, who headed the Munitions Agency established by Yeltsin to supervise the dismantlement of both chemical munitions and installations as well as the conversion of the offensive BW program, served on both councils. However, it is not known whether either of these bodies, with substantially overlapping membership, ever addressed the question of the Russian BW program, or the appeals of the United States and United Kingdom as the Trilateral efforts collapsed exactly in those years.

"Other more important issues," above all the post-1992 Russian economic crisis, were certainly operative from the early Yeltsin years during the first Clinton administration through the years of meetings between Gore and Chernomyrdin. Despite the fact that Gore and Chernomyrdin reportedly discussed the BW issue on many occasions, both in person and through correspondence, when US government officials were asked if issues regarding Russia and BW had come up at the many meetings of the GCC, the reply was that the subject may have been on the agenda, but that the agenda was very long and that other bilateral issues had priority.[67] And of course, this was, once again true. In 1992 Yeltsin told senior US officials that he was unable to ascertain what was taking place in the Russian BW program; that his emissaries were being rebuffed and misled. But by January 1995 he sent a very different message: he rejected further questions from President Clinton and said that "it is time now to close the case."

The BW generals whom Yeltsin had promised in 1992 to remove all remained in their positions. As indicated, Ignatiev was Zinovy Pak's BW deputy; the triumvirate of Kuntsevich, Yevstigneev and Ignatiev remained in roles of influence.[68] Obviously the military were able to do as they pleased. Yeltsin and his senior government officials were neither interested in nor concerned with the issue. Yeltsin's rhetoric of early 1992 was long in the past, and the rhetoric had not produced the results that the United States and the United Kingdom had fought for. And although Biopreparat had been nominally placed under the control of the Russian Ministry of Health and Medical Industry, in 1995 a senior official of that ministry stated that as of that time they had never actually gained control over Biopreparat.[69] Both the RF-MOD and Kalinin continued to operate as independent actors, successfully fending off government control. A briefing by a RAND Corporation staffer in December 1996 that concerned the Russian administration of former Soviet BW facilities noted that Russian facility managers "deceive and deny," that Russian officials "have yet to identify all of their sites," that the "BW generals pursue [an] independent agenda without MOD oversight," that the Duma lacked oversight over defense programs and expenditures, and that "some relevant Russians still believe BW has a place in defense planning."[70] The suggestion that the "BW generals pursued an independent agenda without MOD oversight" was particularly striking. Was that done with the tacit agreement of the RF-MOD? Or was it a matter of essential insubordination of the RF-MOD in the same manner as it was of the civilian political leadership of Russia? Was that possible?

The key question was whether offensive activities continued, or whether it was simply that the remaining massive infrastructure supplied a latent capability that could be resurrected at a later time. Yeltsin almost certainly knew nothing more of what took place inside the RF-MOD facilities in January 1995 than he did in 1992 when he expressed the desire to shut down any prohibited activities. If anything, he probably knew less. Would the outcome have been any different if severe US pressure had been applied to Yeltsin on the BW issue between 1992 and the end of 1996? It seems very doubtful. There was never any indication that Yeltsin gave the subject any serious personal attention or effort. And once Yeltsin removed Kozyrev as foreign minister in 1994 and turned to the RF-MOD and the security services for support, as Gorbachev had in 1990–1991, it seems very doubtful that additional US pressure would have made any difference. But we will never know.

Yeltsin and his administration should have been considered problematic almost from the beginning. He issued empty paper decrees, relied on organizational name changes to paper over either no change at all or unknown degrees of change. When his deputies were telling him that they were unable to obtain entry to RF-MOD facilities, he informed US officials that "they," the Russian military, were fooling him. He relied on ex-cathedra statements by Berdennikov that "activities that would be running counter to the convention are not undertaken in this country," and he left the old foxes Kuntsevich and Yevstigneev in charge of the chickens. As for Yeltsin's "rule by decree" it meant nothing. By 1996 Yeltsin's government had issued no less than 12 decrees to secure payments for the Russian nuclear power industry. Not one of the 12 decrees had been implemented.[71]

The quite small community of Russian arms control experts has produced excellent work on strategic nuclear arms control, and even engaged the question of Russian chemical weapons dismantlement. But it has been essentially silent on the question of the former Soviet BW program, and if and to what degree it may continue in Russia. Two papers appeared over a span of 20 years. Although both were authored by seasoned observers, one in fact a former important official who dealt with the subject in the Yeltsin years as an assistant to Zinovy Pak in the Munitions Agency, both publications are appallingly deficient. The most significant aspect of both papers is their gaps and omissions, but in addition much of the information they do contain is misleading. The first was published in 1995 and does not identify or even allude to the 1992 Russian BWC CBM nor to the second admission of Russia's BWC violations in the September 1992 Trilateral Joint Statement signed by Russia.[72] Neither of these two critical documents is explored in any way. A full 10 years later a paper in the major Russian arms control annual followed the exact same pattern. It did not contain a single word about either the 1992 Russian CBM or the Trilateral Joint Statement, or the admissions of BWC violation in them.[73] In April 1993 Gorbachev established a foundation named Green Cross International. One of its major activities for the intervening 19 years has been to facilitate and monitor the destruction of Russia's chemical munitions. However, Green Cross did not engage the subject of the remnants of the Soviet biological weapon institutes at all.

When one thinks back to the stifled Trilateral negotiations in 1994 and 1995, it is remarkable to think of the degree of cynicism and disdain that was displayed toward the US and UK negotiators and to the entire Trilateral process by whoever was in effective control of the Russian negotiating posture. It was far from the heights of Clinton and Yeltsin, Gore and Chernomyrdin, and it was indulged in total impunity. Gorbachev bears the responsibility for not having abolished the Soviet BW program by 1992, and Yeltsin bears the same responsibility to the degree that it remained after that.

The Last Phase: Putin's Administration

During the years immediately preceding Putin's presidency, there were several Russian proposals to fund ostensibly biodefense research programs that would be performed by former Biopreparat institutes or ones closely associated with them. In 1995 Kalinin proposed a program to Yeltsin (who had promised to remove him three years earlier) described approximately as "Anti-biological warfare program for the citizens of Russia." Yeltsin agreed to fund it at a time of extremely constrained economic conditions in Russia, and did so for two or three years, after which it was discontinued.[74] In 1999, with Putin now the prime minister, the *Zashchita* for a similar annual work program titled "Defense Against Especially Dangerous Pathogens" had two parts, one part that was made public and a second part that remained secret. Putin signed it in the summer of 1999. Zaviyalov collaborated on the preparation of the open portion: diagnostic kits, vaccines, antibiotics, interferon, and cytokines against "especially dangerous pathogens." He assumed that the secret part provided for the work program of the RF-MOD institutes.

In early 2000, academician Aleksandr Spirin again proposed a new project dealing with "biological warfare," titled the "Biological Shield of Russia," to the new Putin administration.[75] The work would have been carried out mainly at institutes belonging to the Russian Academy of Sciences in the vicinity of Pushchino. Apparently the idea was not taken up, and in 2004 Spirin published a paper proposing his idea once more.[76] There was yet a fourth proposal, in 2005, to establish a Federal Agency for Biotechnology, which was never enacted.

When Putin took office, did he understand the impact of *non*-transparency on the perceptions of US officials, including senators who would be voting on the funding for WMD assistance to Russia? Was he even aware of this question? If he was, did it matter to him? As if to make this point, in 2003 Senator Lugar remarked that Russian "denials" and "evasiveness" about its biological weapons program could slow efforts to obtain US funding to destroy Russia's remaining chemical weapons stockpile.[77] Members of Congress assumed cheating in these circumstances, and they extrapolated it to other areas of strategic weapons agreements with Russia, existing or suggested.[78] Putin, however, was manifestly not a supporter of transparency regarding any aspect of Russian governance of domestic or foreign policy. Putin's main advisor on this subject was General Boris Sergeivich Ivanov, secretary of Putin's Security Council. Ivanov had a staff of approximately 175, not one of whom was known to follow the subject of BW. Two officials in the MFA,

Kislyak and Anatoly Antonov, dealt with US diplomats on questions regarding the RF-MOD BW program. Kislyak (who was soon promoted to Russian ambassador to the United States) was the veteran obstructionist at the Trilaterals, and neither had any record of sympathy with BW arms control. Other than possibly Ignatiev and Spirande, there was not a single individual with knowledge of the BW issue in the Russian government with access to senior Kremlin officials.

In November 2001, Presidents Putin and Bush met for a summit in Crawford, Texas. On the very first day of the meeting, the two presidents released a "Joint Statement on US-Russian Cooperation Against Bioterrorism." The last three sentences, which are included below, make three separate points that are of interest:

> We will continue to work to enhance the security of materials, facilities, expertise, and technologies that can be exploited by bioterrorists. We also confirm our strong commitment to the 1972 Convention on the Prohibition of the Development, Production and Stockpiling of Bacteriological (Biological) and Toxin Weapons and on Their Destruction.
>
> We have directed all of our officials and experts working on these critical matters to expand their cooperation and to consult on strengthening related international efforts.[79]

By coincidence, the meeting and the statement occurred at the height of the crisis in the United States following the distribution of a dry-powder preparation of *B. anthracis* spores through the US postal system (commonly referred to as the "Amerithrax" events). Nevertheless, the suggestion for this initiative was the result of discussions held much earlier among participants in a nongovernmental US-Russian working group brought together by William Schneider, the head of the Bush administration's DOD transition team, and then appointed as chair of the Defense Science Board. The initial suggestion that this issue be included in a summit statement came from the US side. The session that conceived of the proposal took place in Moscow. Russian participants included Yevgeni Velikhov (an important former adviser to Gorbachev on nuclear weapon issues), Sergei Rogov (director of the Institute for the USA and Canadian Studies in the Russian Academy of Sciences), General Viktor Yessin (the former head of the Russian Strategic Missile Forces from 1994 to 1996), and former Foreign Minister Bessmyrtnykh. The most knowledgeable US participant was former Ambassador Matlock. Schneider referred to the closed RF-MOD facilities during the group's discussion, labeling them an aberration, a remnant of the Cold War, and not part of the new Russia.[80] Velikhov and Schneider were the primary drafters of the material that was passed to government officials in the United States and Russia.

The results of this initiative were minimal. No joint US-Russian working groups were established, as had been the case in the Trilateral process during the early 1990s, an indication of both governments' lack of seriousness. The United States offered Russian authorities the opportunity to cooperate in the investigation of the Amerithrax events in 2001, and several Russian officials did visit Washington. The group included Aleksey Stepanov, a scientist who had worked on *B. anthracis* at SRCAM for many years.[81] In exchange the DOD asked the RF-MOD for the epidemiological data for the 1979 anthrax outbreak in Sverdlovsk. General Yuri Baluevsky (then chief of the Main Operations Directorate of the Russian General Staff, and also chief of its International Cooperation Directorate) replied to Douglas Feith that the information would be of no use to the United States because the 1979 outbreak involved only intestinal anthrax and not the airborne variety.[82] In Russia, however, a substantial number of documents were developed and approved for domestic application following the November 13, 2001, joint statement. Their purpose was to improve the safety and security of repositories of microbial strains, and new instructions were prepared for emergency response in case a bioterrorism incident took place in Russia.

Between 2000 and 2008, DOS officials Donald Mahley and Paula De-Sutter regularly presented their MFA counterparts with demands for US access to RF-MOD BW facilities. They also continued to urge the Russian MFA to provide a more credible account of the past Soviet BW program, as well as the current activities of the RF-MOD institutes.[83] There was no response from the Russian side. If one can judge by the reported uncommunicativeness of MFA officials on questions of the Russian CW destruction program, the degree of interaction on BW issues must have been very much poorer.[84] In 2003, Ignatiev and Spirande, the two ex-VPK officials now holding BW-relevant positions at the Russian Munitions Agency, wrote that "Russia has clearly established a functional legal and regulatory system, ensuring conformance with international treaties on the prohibition of biological weapons. It is not enough to simply establish a legal system; that system must function properly. Here there are certainly some problems, due to Russia's economic situation and a lack of coordination between authorities."[85]

It is a remarkable comment. For over a decade in the 1990s, Russian officials—particularly senior military officers—had explained Russia's extremely low rate of progress on chemical demilitarization as being caused by domestic economic constraints. But that was not the case in 2003, and it bore no relation to the biological weapon issue. "Russia's economic position" was totally irrelevant to whether the RF-MOD or other former BW facilities in Russia were carrying on activities in violation of the BWC in 2003. In the midst of a period of Russian economic surplus, economic issues were not involved. In fact, had they been, ending the programs would produce savings, as the continuation of such activities obviously incurred budgetary costs, even if they might not have been very large. In 1994, at one of the lowest points in the post-1992 Russian economic downturn, Alexei Arbatov had written, "The economic crisis and budgetary constraints will not affect compliance with the . . . [BWC]." Arbatov identified *the disintegration of centralized political control over state . . . organizations with vested interests in violating international agreements; the active domestic political opposition to treaty implementation and compliance*" as among the "main factors contributing to Russian compliance problems" [emphasis added].[86] Nothing is known to have changed in the years since his assessment. As for "a lack of coordination between the authorities," by 2003 "coordination" on the question had been taking place for 20 or more years, since at least the late 1980s. And deficient or not, Oleg Ignatiev, in one bureaucratic position or another, had been involved at the center of that "coordination" for the entire period.

In 2006, Russia headed the G-8 group. In the year before, Russian government agencies undertook a major interagency review to consider "whether to cooperate with the US on biological issues," that is, BW-relevant issues. It is assumed that Russia would never admit to having lied previously for many years, and the review apparently did not include consideration of opening up the three RF-MOD facilities to the United States and United Kingdom for visits. One result of its deliberations is, however, known. Russia approached the chair of the Australia Group (AG) and requested membership. Russian entities had sold some dual-use equipment in earlier years to countries under AG restrictions. It is not known whether Russia had been denied import requests of its own and wanted to remove any such impediments. More likely, Russia sought the membership as a means of establishing itself as being in good status under the BWC regime while bypassing the years of questions about any of its own facilities. However, Russia wanted a guarantee that their application for membership would be accepted before they made a formal application for membership. That demand was opposed by a broad majority of the AG members, and US diplomats also played a significant role in the rejection of Russia's request. Several "outreach" meetings between Russia and the AG led nowhere because Russia refused to accept the AG guidelines and demanded membership on its own terms.[87] In addition, Russia had been obstructive toward the AG since 2007 and threatened to obstruct issues in other export control regimes. Among the US government cables that were released by WikiLeaks in 2010, several recorded the proceedings of AG meetings.[88] Two of these, dated April 17, 2008, and June 29, 2009, nevertheless indicated Russia's continued interest in AG membership. At an AG meeting held on March 11, 2010, Russia now indicated that it was willing to accept all requirements for membership except for one. Its representatives would not discuss transparency in relation to its past BW programs or a continuing offensive program. They stated that these subjects were dealt with in forums dealing with the BWC, presumably a reference to Russia's deficient annual compliance statement delivered to the United Nations. Russia was not interested in any further meetings, and the AG would have to decide whether or not to accept the Russian terms at a plenary meeting in June 2010. Since many AG members would not accept the terms of the Russian ultimatum, which was accompanied by threats of negative consequences for the AG, the June plenary did not act on the issue in any way. Matters rested there, and Russia does not presently participate in AG activities.

In late 2008 the report of a congressionally mandated US commission wrote: "Increasingly, the Russian government has viewed biological CTR programs with disinterest and even suspicion, arguing that its growing economic strength obviates the need for continued assistance."[89] David Hoffman reported a somewhat different explanation: "Russian officials have insisted that since the country has no offensive biological weapons program, there is no need to cooperate."[90] Whichever the case may be, Chapter 23 explains that President Medvedev announced Russia's forthcoming withdrawal from a major component of these programs in 2011.

In a somewhat bizarre development in February and March 2012 Putin and Russian Minister of Defense Anatoly Serdyukov have publicly referred to 28 tasks that Putin established for the RF-MOD in order "to prepare for threats of the future." Putin wrote that Russia needed to be prepared for "quick and effective responses to new challenges," and one of the 28 tasks that Putin specified was "The development of weapons based on new physical principles: radiation, geophysical, wave, genetic, psychophysical, etc."[91]

"Genetic" weapons would obviously be forbidden by the Biological Weapons Convention, and the remainder are an arms control nightmare that would explicitly contravene another multilateral arms control treaty that was championed by the Brezhnev administration, the Convention on the Prohibition of Military or any other Hostile Use of Environmental Modification Technologies, signed on May 18, 1977 and entered into force on October 5, 1978.

Chapters 21 and 22 covered the events from 1985 to 2012, 27 years that saw the presumed dismantling of a substantial portion of the Soviet Union's offensive BW program, but that left an ambiguous and unsatisfactory situation still remaining. Through the tenures of Gorbachev and Yeltsin, a small coterie of the senior hierarchy of the Soviet and then Russian military together with several allied civilian officials successfully guarded the offensive BW program, prevented its eradication, and fought off all attempts to reveal its dimensions and purpose. As early as 1994, Russian officials participating in the Trilateral negotiations retracted the substance of the 1992 Russian BWC CBM submitted to the UN only two years earlier, denying that there had ever been an offensive Soviet BW program. One year later Yeltsin washed his hands of the issue in a letter to Clinton. Transparency was never achieved. The Putin years have essentially been 10 years of hibernation as far as Russia and BWC compliance is concerned. Since we do not actually know what is and has been taking place within the three RF-MOD facilities since 1992, perhaps the situation is better than might be feared. However as far as the rest of the world knows, everything remains as it was for Russia's Trilateral partners and the international arms control community—incomplete and unresolved.

23

United States and International Efforts to Prevent
Proliferation of Biological Weapons Expertise from
the Former Soviet Union

AFTER THE SOVIET UNION's dissolution, the United States and several
other countries took steps to prevent the dispersal of biological weapons expertise from former Soviet BW facilities. However, the level of funding
for biological weapons nonproliferation was much smaller than that allocated
to the nuclear and chemical weapons fields. Nevertheless, since approximately
1995, international assistance programs, including those of the United States,
have allocated over $1.5 billion to biological weapons nonproliferation efforts
in the former Soviet Union (see Tables 23.1 and 23.2).

In the future, other studies may provide a more detailed survey of the US
effort to restrain proliferation from the post-Soviet BW institutions through
the effort to "convert" these facilities to legitimate civilian R&D. This chapter
has the more limited purpose of taking a broad look at some of the policies
that affected those programs.[1]

Three basic purposes were to be served by these programs. The first was to
facilitate an end to research that directly served the offensive BW program
in Russia. Dismantlement or destruction of facilities was impossible within
Russia, because Russia would not permit such actions. It occurred extremely
rarely elsewhere, the only examples being the SNOPB production facility in
Kazakhstan, the Vozrozhdeniye Island test site in Uzbekistan, and a site in
Georgia. With that alternative unavailable, the remaining mechanism was
"conversion" or redirection of one kind or another.

Table 23.1 Funding, in Millions of Dollars, by Year and Agency/Program, for Biological Weapons Proliferation Prevention

Year	USDA	DOD	HHMI	EPA	HHS/ BTEP	IPP/ GIPP	BII	BTRP	ISTC	STC	Yearly total
1999	2	2	.570		4.8	3			34.6		46.97
2000	7	12	.833		11	7–8			85.8		124.633
2001	6	12	1.278		10	7–8			75.8		113.078
2002	5	17	1.201	2	9	7–8	30		84.6	30	156.801
2003	6	55	1.201	2–3	9	3.5	3	67.4	74.4	30	252.501
2004	5–6	55	1.201	2–3	8.5	3.5	3	67.8	56	30	228.001
2005	7	55		4	6	3.5	3	68.7	51.3	30.5	229
2006	6	60.8		1.5	7.6	3.6	10	69.8	50.6		209.9
2007	2	68.4		1.4	2.3	2.2	7	72.4			155.7
2008[a]		144.5					12.4				
2009[a]							8.9				
2010											
Total:	47	268.8	6.284	14.9	68.2	43.3	77.3	346.1	513.1	120.5	1,516.584 (partial)

a. Requested funds

Table 23.2   Selected US Programs to Assist Russia with Biological Weapons Nonproliferation

Agency	Program	Program objective
Department of Defense	Cooperative Threat Reduction Program, Biological Weapons Proliferation Prevention (BWPP)	Redirect BW scientists through collaborative research; improve safety at Russian BW facilities in preparation for collaborative research projects; improve security at Russian BW facilities by consolidating and restricting access to pathogens; eliminate BW infrastructure and equipment
Department of Energy	Initiative for Proliferation Prevention (IPP)	Redirect BW scientists through collaborative research; incorporate industry partners to identify market-driven projects that might produce commercial products and results
Department of State	International Science Centers Program (ISTC/STCU)	Provide grant funding to redirect BW scientists to nonmilitary research; provide support for the development, management, and auditing of projects sponsored by other US agencies
Department of Agriculture	Agricultural Research Service (ARS)—Former Soviet Union Scientific Cooperation Program	Redirect BW scientists through collaborative research on diseases that might affect plants and animals
Department of Health and Human Services	Biotechnology Engagement Program (BTEP)	Redirect BW scientists through collaborative research on public health problems
Environmental Protection Agency		Redirect BW scientists through collaborative research on environmental damage caused by biological weapons
Department of Commerce	Special American Business Internship Training Program (SABIT) Business Information Service for the Newly Independent States (BISNIS)	Facilitate business training and exchanges

Source: Michelle Stem Cook and Amy F. Woolf, *Preventing Proliferation of Biological Weapons: U.S. Assistance to the Former Soviet States,* CRS RL31368, Washington, D.C., April 10, 2010, 21.

The enhancement of transparency, the corollary of the conversion effort, was the second. In view of the failed Trilateral negotiations and Russia's refusal to permit access to its three RF-MOD facilities, it was a particular concern. Because that process had demonstrated continued Russian lying and deliberate obstruction, it raised substantial suspicion among US and UK policymakers. In the absence of the resolution of the Trilateral process, the utilization of "people to people" contacts in these programs provided substantial assurance that at least some of the former Soviet facilities involved in the offensive BW program, primarily those of the Biopreparat system, did not continue BWC-prohibited development programs.[2]

The third purpose was nonproliferation: to support the cadre of former Soviet BW research scientists so that they could continue to work in Russia and did not emigrate to countries of BW proliferation concern and take their knowledge with them. As we will see, this introduced the crucial question of what kind of research to support. Additionally, in the attempt to impede former Soviet BW scientists from emigrating to, and their home institutions from collaborating with, countries of concern, US assistance included a major condition that was strongly communicated to Russian institutes that were to be potential recipients of US grant funds. Their receipt of US and International Science and Technology Center (ISTC)/Science and Technology Center in Ukraine (STCU) funding was contingent on *zero* cooperation by their institutes with, or emigration of their scientists to, Iran.

The overall desirability and benefit of these programs was unquestionable. A report by the US National Academy of Sciences (NAS) in 2007 listed the three primary achievements:

> . . . BTRP [Biological Threat Reduction Program] activities have strengthened the containment of biological materials, technologies, equipment, and expertise that, if misused, could result in serious biological threats. Specific changes in the region that can be attributed at least in part to BTRP have included the following:
> - Unprecedented transparency at dozens of important facilities with dual-use capabilities that had not previously been open to foreign specialists
> - Dismantlement and/or conversion of production and research facilities established to support biological weapons activities, including transformation to civilian activities of more than a dozen important components of the weapons-oriented Biopreparat complex

- Redirection to civilian pursuits of hundreds of senior biological scientists, engineers, and technicians who were formerly engaged in defense programs.[3]

The opening portion of this chapter describes the political and policy concerns that attended this effort over the years. The relevant literature is already substantial, and only several points are made in this introduction, primarily focused on issues that might have been dealt with in other ways.[4] Over a period of 16 years these programs evolved and constantly changed, as new initiatives were devised, some were expanded and others were discontinued, and new US government agencies joined as participants, funders, and partners. The overall effort was at times motivated by cross-purposes, and the purposes sometimes changed in part over the duration of the programs. Some early missteps certainly could have been avoided; others possibly not, and would have to be considered a cost of the overall effort.

The earliest error occurred in a National Aeronautics and Space Administration (NASA) funded program in "Space Biotechnology" intended "to conduct biological research in space." The head of the Russian group within the grant committee established to distribute the funds was Kalinin. However, Kalinin was identified in documents only as "Dr. Kalinin," and as late as 2000, the head of NASA's grant programs in Russia, said that he had never heard of Biopreparat until the previous year, 1999, and that he had known nothing more about Kalinin.[5] The sum of the funding in its initial years was relatively small, but Kalinin had been able to steer it to institutions that he favored (see Chapter 6). When a delegation from the Department of Energy's (DOE) Initiatives for Proliferation Prevention (IPP) met with Kalinin in April 1997, he refused their requests to visit SRCAM, IEI, and *Biokhimmash*, despite the fact that the delegation had letters of invitation from all three institutions.[6]

The ISTC had to deal with—or accommodate—several irregularities, in one of which Kalinin unfortunately again played a role. The terms of agreement that were negotiated with Russian government authorities in order to allow the ISTC to operate in Russia again allowed Biopreparat to play a role. It was to serve as the initial recipient and intermediary in forwarding grant applications from Russian scientists to the ISTC for consideration. At a NATO Advanced Research Workshop in 1997 in Budapest, it was learned that Biopreparat—which was still headed by Kalinin—informed applying Russian scientists that it should be assigned 5% of each grant application as the supplier of reagents needed for the proposed research. If the applying scientist did not wish to agree to these terms, subsequent experience showed that his project application might be forwarded to the ISTC in 6, 12, or 18 months, or not at all. If he accepted the terms, it would be forwarded to the ISTC in one month.[7]

There were several additional problems with various grant programs. In the early years of the ISTC's operation, it also became apparent that in some cases Russian scientists were submitting grant applications, and had obtained grants, for research work that had already been accomplished during the Soviet period. A third irregularity the ISTC encountered was that the terms of ISTC grants, which forbade the parent institute of any scientist from diverting any portion of the salary of that investigator to be used for the support of other scientists at the institute, was violated in at least some cases. At a conference in Como, Italy, in December 1997, Vladimir Volkov, the deputy director of SRCAM, openly stated from the platform that his institution was doing exactly that.[8] A different problem was evidenced in the DOE's IPP program. Although data published by the US Government Accountability Office (GAO) in 2008 overwhelmingly concerned IPP grants to Russian nuclear scientists, more than half of 6,450 scientists in 97 IPP projects reported that they had never claimed to have had WMD experience. The GAO also stated, "Furthermore, according to officials at 10 nuclear and biological institutes in Russia and Ukraine, IPP program funds help them attract, recruit, and retain younger scientists and contribute to the continued operation of their facilities. This is contrary to the original intent of the program, which was to reduce the proliferation risk posed by Soviet-era weapons scientists."[9] Nevertheless, all of these might be considered relatively minor problems that occurred in the earliest years of the ISTC and the other related programs. Some may even have resulted in counter-proliferation benefits. They were soon understood, and those that could be remedied were remedied.

This left two really major and overlapping issues, which went to the core of all of the various programs. The first of these concerned the nature of the research to be supported. The first alternative was that the research funded be as far removed as possible from the pathogens that the former Soviet scientists had worked with. Instead it should be focused primarily on disease agents of actual significance to the concerns of Russian public health, and secondarily on those of international public health significance, or finally on other scientific problems in microbiology or virology which their professional competence would permit them to turn to, but excluding BW pathogens. This seemed closest to the early conceptions of "conversion." The second alternative was that the research funded could or should continue to hew closely to the pathogens that the Russian scientists had worked with previously, in essence those that came to be referred to as "select agents" or "dangerous pathogens" in the domestic US context. The second and closely related question was whether the support from the ISTC and its sister programs was enabling the continuation of, or contributing to, any offensive BW program that might still be continuing in Russia. Obviously, the more research the United States funded on the same pathogens that the Russian scientists had worked on during the Soviet period, the greater was the risk that the funds would support offensive purposes, either ongoing or at some future time.

It is simpler to address the second question first because the clearest expression of the dilemma appeared in GAO reports. According to an April 2000 report:

> The key risks include sustaining Russia's existing biological weapons infrastructure, maintaining or advancing Russian scientists' skills to develop offensive biological weapons, and the potential misuse of U.S. assistance to fund offensive research. Although seeking to add international transparency and compliance provisions to the Biological and Toxin Weapons Convention, the United States relies on safeguards implemented at the institute and project levels to mitigate risk. Such safeguards include (1) securing assurances from the institutes that they will abstain from offensive research or proliferation activities, (2) performing interagency reviews of all proposed projects, and (3) implementing a set of financial and programmatic oversight mechanisms for all projects. To mitigate risks associated with research on dangerous pathogens, the United States plans to use U.S. experts residing in Russia and—if Russia permits—at the institutes to monitor the projects. None of these measures, however, would prevent Russian project participants or institutes from potentially using their skills or research outputs to later work on offensive weapons activities at any of the Russian military institutes that remain closed to the United States.[10]

The hope to have foreign experts work in the Russian institutes receiving research grants was not achieved except for two cases of relatively brief duration. The first was Jens H. Kuhn, a young German scientist completing his doctoral thesis who was able to work on behalf of the US Defense Threat

Reduction Agency (DTRA) at Vector for just under six months in 2001 on a project dealing with Crimean-Congo hemorrhagic fever. He was followed by a US scientist working for roughly the same length of time at Vector with the same pathogen.[11]

No one in the United States, the ISTC or in any other international authority knew what was taking place in the three RF-MOD institutes, nor the intent of the renamed 15th Directorate in the decades after 1992, so it was impossible to know whether there was reason to harbor fears. As indicated in Chapters 21 and 22, the US government continued to express doubt regarding the degree of Russia's compliance with the BWC in the 20 years following 1992. However, this was primarily because the three RF-MOD institutes remained closed and it was impossible to know what their work consisted of. The GAO report cited above did go on to explain the basis for some degree of official confidence:

> Officials from the Departments of State, Defense, and Energy told us that through these collaborative research projects, the United States has achieved some access to more than 30 former Soviet biological weapons institutes in Russia, Kazakhstan, Ukraine, and Armenia. For example, the Science Center has funded projects at 29 institutes, including 19 primary institutes where projects were developed and managed and 10 institutes that provided support. In addition, the Initiatives for Proliferation Prevention program has funded contracts at 15 former Soviet biological weapons institutes, including 10 funded by the Science Center. Of particular significance is that projects funded by the two programs have provided some access to 15 of the 20 former Soviet biological weapons institutes in Russia that are considered key by the State Department.
>
> U.S. project officials said these projects have provided access and openness to facilities and scientists that would not have been available otherwise. The Department of Defense informed Congress in a January 2000 report that the access gained through the collaborative research programs has provided "high confidence" that Biopreparat institutes such as Vector and Obolensk [SRCAM] are not presently engaged in offensive activities. During our visits to six institutes in December 1999, institute officials invited us to tour buildings and laboratories associated with U.S.-funded projects. We talked with scientists participating in the programs and were allowed to take photographs. The institute directors

reported regular visits from the international community, including congressional delegations, U.S. executive branch officials, Science Center and Initiatives for Proliferation Prevention program and financial managers, scientific collaborators, auditors, and private sector officials.[12]

A possible note of disquiet was introduced in March 2000 when newly installed President Putin abolished the existing Ministry of Science and Technology and in its place established a much larger Ministry of Industry, Science and Technology, which oversaw "a vast network of weapons research and testing facilities."[13] Until a further reorganization in 2004, this ministry apparently had at least partial jurisdiction over some of the former Biopreparat facilities.[14] In 2006 Putin issued a decree that reestablished the VPK (Soviet-era Military Industrial Commission), which apparently once again oversees institutes in any way related to BW, presumably including defensive aspects.

The GAO report also made clear a change in US motivation in supporting these programs in addition to the initial and critical ones of conversion, transparency, and nonproliferation.[15] It noted that while half of about $220 million that Department of Defense (DOD) and Department of State (DOS) expected to spend between FY 2000 and 2004 "will be used to continue to redirect scientists toward peaceful civilian research," there was also a new "emerging area of emphasis. Defense and State plan to spend about $36 million to fund collaborative research with Russian institutes on dangerous pathogens. This research is intended to improve the U.S. defenses against biological weapons threats."[16] The strong interest of the CIA and DOD in obtaining knowledge from former Soviet BW researchers became evident in 1997. This of course required former Russian BW scientists to continue their work with the same "Select Agents" that had been the focus of their research during the Soviet offensive program, now for the benefit of US biodefense programs.

The evolution of the research program referred to in the GAO report provides a striking example of this development. In 1992 the US Agency for International Development (AID) supported an investigation by two major US vaccine producers into whether any of the significant Biopreparat facilities could be converted into centers for vaccine production in Russia under a joint venture that could meet good manufacturing practice (GMP) standards. Vector was considered in particular. After visiting Vector, the US vaccine manufacturers decided that the suggestion was impossible and that an entirely new facility would have to be built from scratch. The companies further proposed that the US government fund the construction of the vaccine production plant at an estimated cost of some $100 million. The proposal was dropped. In 1994 the Committee on International Security and Arms Control (CISAC), an arms control advisory group at the US NAS, began to reconsider ways in which the same former Biopreparat facilities could again be approached. The notion that a more limited vaccine production capability might still be feasible with much smaller US investment, based solely on upgrading existing Russian capabilities for production for the Russian market, was still initially considered. At the same time other forms of US-Russian research collaboration with Vector and other institutes on problems of significance to public health began to be considered. In these early US conceptualizations, the word "conversion" was used repeatedly. It was also suggested that US scientists should be involved in any projects that were developed, as this would ensure that research at the Russian facilities remained devoted to peaceful activities and that the conversion was successful.

Ideas continued to be elaborated during 1995, and in the fall of 1996 the NAS and Cooperative Threat Reduction (CTR) program initiated six pilot projects at Vector and SRCAM at a total cost of $420,000 as an initial stage to explore the feasibility of a much larger proposal being devised. Three of these projects concerned pathogens of public health interest (hepatitis C, TB, and opisthorchiasis, a parasitic disease prevalent in Siberia); two of "Select Agent" interest (monkeypox and anthrax); and one that straddled both categories (hantaviruses). It is notable that in selecting the pilot projects a NAS committee stated that "the Committee also made the judgment that each project's potential contributions to public health or U.S. national security interests outweigh the risk that the project might contribute to the development of improvement of offensive BW capabilities," demonstrating that the concern not yet expressed in GAO reports was not a contrived issue.[17] In October 1997 the NAS finally submitted the larger proposal, variously referred to as the Pathogens Initiative or the Project on Controlling Dangerous Pathogens, to DOD. It proposed a series of some 70 "joint" research projects to be funded over five years at a cost of approximately $38.5 million. It was now to concern "dangerous pathogens" and related fundamental research, and the first five of seven "program areas" were to be "anthrax, melioidosis/glanders, plague, orthopox virus, and viral hemorrhagic fevers . . . agents/diseases that have been linked with BW activities for many years. In each of these areas the Soviet government is believed to have invested large financial resources in carrying out research that has been largely unknown outside the country." Two additional program areas were proposed: "other dangerous pathogens and diseases of public health concern" and "cross-cutting basic research related to dangerous pathogens."[18] The selection of pathogens to be investigated under the project underwent an extraordinary evolution between 1994–95 and October 1997. Although the NAS report sets out an elaborate panoply of program goals and criteria for individual project selection, when Joshua Lederberg, the head of the NAS panel, was asked how this particular selection of "program areas" was arrived at, he replied that it was due to extreme pressure by certain US government agencies.[19] Other sources identified the agencies as the CIA and DOD. A staff member of ACDA commented that the decision had become "very political," and that "pressure from the intelligence community was very heavy" in regard to the selection of agents, to the point of threatening "otherwise you won't get the money."[20]

But were "select agents" the only choice that had to be made, even in terms of DOD interests, and certainly from the point of view of maintaining a high caliber of Russian research in molecular genetics? The clear answer is no. From the point of view of Russian public health, tuberculosis (TB), particularly drug-resistant TB, was a major problem in Russia. As one report explained: "Russia has one of the highest rates of TB in the world. In parts of its Far East, the infection rate is three times what the World Health Organization considers epidemic levels. . . . about a fifth of all TB patients here suffer from drug resistant strains—more than almost anywhere else in the world."[21] Work with the pathogen requires high-containment facilities, which both SRCAM and Vector had. In 1997, TB resulted in 3 million deaths worldwide, and an infection rate of 7 million cases per year. One of the pilot projects funded in 1996 at SRCAM was for work with TB.[22] After 1999 Vector initiated work with TB as well, under funding from the US Department of Health and Human Services (HHS). Vector continued working on the disease afterward under other funding by different Russian government sources and foundations, work that continues to the present day.[23]

But the story is far more interesting in terms of the DOD's interests. In April 1996, exactly when the NAS project was being elaborated, malaria vaccine development was listed as the very highest of 64 "DOD Medical Research and Development Science and Technology Objectives" (STOs), and malaria drug development was listed as the third highest.[24] Worldwide malaria produces 300–500 million clinical cases per year, and 2–3 million deaths per year. That is nearly as high a number of deaths each year as AIDS had produced, worldwide, in the 15 years prior to 1997. At the same time, a proposed international collaborative research effort, composed of international public health organizations, commercial vaccine producers, and private research institutes, to work on malaria and other tropical diseases had just collapsed.[25] Malaria vaccine research is of the very highest caliber in molecular genetics, involving the preparation of DNA vaccines. A special news report in *Science* on December 5, 1995, on DNA vaccines began with a description of the work being carried out on DNA vaccines for malaria at the Naval Medical Research Institute (NMRI) in Bethesda by Stephen Hoffman and his collaborators.[26] The same technique is currently being used to obtain vaccines for Ebola virus as well.

At the NATO Advanced Research Workshop on the Conversion of Former BW Facilities in Budapest in November 1997, one of the authors approached Lev Sandakchiev, Vector's director, and P. G. Sveshnikov, deputy director of the Research Center of Molecular Diagnostics and Therapy, Moscow. Each of them was asked separately if his institute would have any reason not to seek research funds in order to work on malaria. Both of them replied with the same phrase: "Why should we? Of course not." Sveshnikov added: "We would be happy to." Even more astonishing, Vector had in fact offered a proposal for work on malaria to the ISTC in 1993. Vector researchers had already isolated a fragment of DNA that they thought could be used in the development of a DNA vaccine. "But we were rejected, and so we have gone on to other things," was the comment of a senior Vector official.[27] The ISTC had promised to find a collaborator for the Vector proposal, but never did so. Vector officials were told that the project was "not of interest." A telephone call to Hoffman at NMRI in January 1998 found that he had never been contacted.

Less than three years later, a division of the National Institutes of Health awarded a seven-year $43.8 million contract to a team of nine US contractors to develop a malaria vaccine.[28] The ISTC had to do nothing more than initiate a Solicited Grant Program for malaria or TB, and the applications from Biopreparat institutes would have rolled in, as they always do in solicited grant competitions. It is a granting mechanism routinely used in the United States for decades both by federal agencies such as the National Science Foundation and by private foundations. But it was a mechanism that was never used for former Soviet BW researchers. Scientists go where funds are available, and that would most certainly have been the case in Russia in 1997–1998. Other alternative research areas could easily have been suggested, such as making rice, a basic food staple for major portions of the world's population, disease resistant through genetic engineering, in which the blight-resistant segment of the rice DNA was cloned in bacteria.[29]

Another perfect example is available. In June 1994 the chairman of the World Health Organization (WHO) Steering Committee on Diarrheal Diseases Vaccines (who was incidentally a US military officer at the Walter Reed Army Institute of Research), together with the director of the WHO's Global Program for Vaccines, wrote a letter to D. A. Henderson, then a deputy assistant secretary for health in the HHS.[30] The WHO committee had selected Vector as the site for testing recombinant candidate oral vaccines against diarrheal diseases of children: cholera, shigella, and those caused by enterohemorrhagic *E. coli*. It was to make use of Vector's BSL-3+ hospital. The program was to run for six years, therefore at least until the year 2000. A recombinant cholera vaccine had been developed at the Saratov Anti-plague Institute "*Mikrob*," but the clinical trials could take place only at Vector.[31] The WHO had funded the initiation of the project, and sought US funding of $5 million for the next six years to permit the project to continue. When the two senior officials at the DOD/CTR program and the DOS were asked in March 2008 why the United States did not take up the WHO request under any of its programs, it developed that they had never before heard of the proposal: Henderson had never forwarded the WHO letter to them.[32] Both officials stated that it was a mistake not to have funded the project. In 2010, India reported that it had made "the first" recombinant cholera vaccine and was seeking to license its production.

While acknowledging some level of risk of supporting work on Select Agents, Dr. Peter Jahrling, one of the members of the NAS panel that designed the Dangerous Pathogens proposal, commented, "Any one of these projects that doesn't entail looking at Paramecia in pond water has a certain level of risk." [33] As is clearly demonstrated by the three previous examples—involving a DNA malaria vaccine, TB, and a recombinant diarrheal vaccine for children—the statement is both wrong and misleading. It is obvious that it would have been easy to devise funding solutions of direct utility for the preventive health needs of the DOD as well as for the Russian population, and which would have affected a real conversion of the work of former Russian BW scientists away from work with pathogens of BW significance.[34] Supporting and maintaining research on "dual-threat agents," as they are sometimes also referred to, was the least desirable of all possible alternatives. It provided little or no conversion at all; it maintained Russian researchers working with the same pathogens of BW interest that they had been working on previously.[35] The most plausible route of conversion always was the production of pharmaceutical and medicinal products for domestic Russian and Commonwealth of Independent States (CIS) use, for which the need was enormous. However, when the DOS subsequently did support this direction, though, it first promoted the notion that the Russian producers should attempt to compete in the international market, a far more demanding task in terms of production and marketing, rather than again focusing on Russian domestic needs. Only after export-directed efforts failed did the DOS finally promote pharmaceutical production for domestic and CIS purchase and use.

Because of concerns about the security of pathogen collections and related facilities, in the late 1990s, DOD support programs began to shift toward several new areas: providing perimeter and portal security to former Biopreparat facilities, consolidating and replacing pathogen storage facilities at institutes, and building new and more secure version of these than had existed previously at these locations. As a corollary to upgrading the security of pathogen storage at Russian sites, DOD also sought access to the pathogen collections of the institutes that it was aiding.[36] DTRA's Threat Agent Detection and Response (TADR) program, which would establish epidemiological monitoring stations and central reference laboratories in Georgia, Uzbekistan, Kazakhstan, Azerbaijan and the Ukraine, was another new initiative. The new reference laboratories would also serve to consolidate the recipient countries' collection of extremely dangerous pathogens, and provide enhanced security for them in newly built facilities.[37] An NAS report stated that the TADR network, whose facilities would be interconnected and also connected with the CDC, "is well designed to support the U.S. government's strategy for strengthening BWC compliance while also supporting the mission of the DOD more broadly."[38] By 2007 it was estimated that 90% of DOD funds would be spent on these kinds of programs in the years that followed. DOD had never been able to conclude implementation agreements with the various Russian ministries with jurisdiction over the institutes whose researchers were receiving grants or in which these new programs were carried out, and therefore all these programs were implemented through the ISTC.[39] With time, fewer projects were carried out in Russia while an increasing number of projects were planned for and carried out in the various CIS countries. The 2007 NAS report again noted: "Russian policies that are unacceptable to DOD and lack of BTRP access to locations believed to be sites for repositories of dangerous pathogens limit the program, and no funding will be sought for FY2009 and beyond other than the possible continuation of smallpox-related research."[40] Both DOD and DOS also initiated programs in countries outside the CIS entirely, in Libya, Iraq, Pakistan, Indonesia and the Philippines.[41]

The DOD assistance programs in particular confronted new problems with the entry of the Bush administration in 2001. There were four issues on the basis of which either the executive or the Congress froze CTR funds at various times. Two were BW related and two were CW related:

- Russian refusal to supply the United States with a sample of its vaccine resistant strain of *B. anthracis*
- Russian refusal to permit access to its RF-MOD BW facilities
- Doubts about the level of Russia's CW stockpile tonnage
- The possession of unreported CW production sites, notification of which was required by the CWC and by the US/Russian bilateral CW information exchange agreements

The new administration's National Intelligence Estimate (NIE) on the Russian BW program led to the first delay by the executive branch. The NIE could not certify that the Russian Federation "was committed to" compliance with the BWC and the CWC. CTR program officials nevertheless hoped to obtain a waiver from the White House on national security grounds. However, obtaining the waiver took eight months, from early March 2002 to October 2002, and the waiver was for only a single year. At least some of the charges leveled against Russian compliance during the interagency review were not new, and had been faced previously during the Clinton administration. One of these, the allegation of financial diversions from ISTC grants to support prohibited RF-MOD work, was rejected when examined by an earlier Clinton administration interagency investigation.[42] The second delay followed a year later when the House Armed Services Committee included language in the National Defense Authorization Act of 2004 (Section 1304) that prevented spending any funds on any new CTR projects until the secretary of defense could certify that Russia was in compliance with the BWC and the CWC. The prohibition by the House Committee ended with that fiscal year, but the secretary of defense never provided a certification for Russia.

Although the ISTC continued to operate more or less without interference, other relevant events in Russia during these years were not of the best tenor either. Kalinin tried to maintain control of the mobilization capacity production facilities, or as many of them as he could, although several had freed themselves from his control to some degree by the fall of 2002. He or other officials in Moscow also were still able to exercise control of international travel by scientists working in various Biopreparat institutes. As late as 2000–2002, Kalinin was still attempting to regain some of the powers that he had lost during the late Yeltsin years. Onishchenko's motives at the Ministry of Health appear to be less sinister than their potential effects. In the early years of the ISTC's operation, he did everything that he could to keep the Anti-Plague system institutes from cooperating with it, and he succeeded. But once he broke Biopreparat control of its four main institutes and moved them under his own ministry's authority, significant conversion of lines of research took place. There is no longer any work with Marburg virus or Ebola virus at Vector, and the work program turned to significant work with influenza A viruses, and increased work with HIV/AIDS. However, Onishchenko has shown little interest in cooperation with the United States, or at least not more than absolutely necessary. As far as US access and the institute's transparency is concerned, he has moved Vector in the direction of the constraints that he imposed on the anti-plague system, such as reducing the access of Western visitors to Vector. US officials believe that the reasons have more to do with his decades as an old-style Soviet bureaucrat and a desire to maintain total control over the direction of work at the institutes, rather than provoking US concerns about "BW" intentions.[43] Onishchenko did, however, also maintain Kalinin as a personal advisor. In the summer of 2000, the FSB reportedly proposed a program estimated to cost $1 billion for "Non-traditional methods of fighting terrorists," including "biological" methods.[44] In the early 2000s, Onishchenko's name also began to appear on papers concerning the bioterrorist threat. In the spring of 2002 when CTR organized a conference in Russia, Onishchenko rejected an invitation to open the conference, refused to allow staff from some of the former Biopreparat institutes to attend, and rejected all Western visitors and Western grants.

NAS reports in 2006 and 2007 sought an additional redirection of the various biological engagement programs in order to enhance their sustainability in Russia once DTRA or other funding was ended. These reports now urged a greater emphasis on pathogens of primary public health concern to the countries in which these programs were situated rather than on the "select" or "dual use" agents that had been emphasized previously.

While a highly directed program based on the near-term security interests of the United States and tightly managed by American commercial contractors was appropriate during the 1990s, greater attention should now be given to having a program that serves the interests of the partner governments more broadly, as well as serving longer-term U.S. interests. This orientation will help (1) encourage cooperation of partner governments, institutions, and specialists, (2) enlist colleagues in common efforts that will continue for many years to help ensure that dual-use technologies are directed to peaceful pursuits, and (3) set the stage for sustainability of programs initiated through BTRP that should be maintained over the long term by partner institutions.[45]

The "highly directed programs based on the near-term security interests of the United States" were very likely as inappropriate in the 1990s as they were in 2006 and 2007.

In the course of 15 to 20 years, US government approaches had come nearly full circle, at least in conception, in thinking about these programs: from very early notions of "conversion," to collaborative research on "dual threat" pathogens of BW interest, to argumentation in favor of shifting focus to broader public health concerns of the recipient countries. Unfortunately the emphasis during that middle phase provided the opportunity for a very mixed appraisal of the Nunn-Lugar program by Valery Spirande, then a deputy at the Russian Munitions Agency. Asked in 2003 by a Russian journalist whether the Nunn-Lugar program was "still in effect," Spirande replied:

> Yes, it provides international help to Russia and CIS countries in preventing the proliferation of weapons of mass destruction. . . . One positive part of the program is the employment it provides for Russian scientists. Moreover, it helps to reinforce the physical protection and Biosafety at a number of sites (the Vector State Research Center, the Research Institute of Applied Microbiology, etc.). Those who work with the research institute receive modern scientific and communication equipment. We are worried by the fact that participants in the ISTC project are part of the U.S. military production complex. Essentially, through this scientific cooperation, about 30 Russian biological sites are externally controlled. The Russian "brain drain" has stopped, but now our brains are working to strengthen the defensive capacity of this foreign, well-paying "uncle."[46]

In August 2010, the Russian authorities began to act on the final lines of Spirande's 2003 commentary. The office of Russian President Dmitriy

Medvedev issued a decree saying that Russia would withdraw from the ISTC program within six months.[47] When the MFA finally sent a diplomatic note to the ISTC on July 13, 2011, it stated that Russia would withdraw from the ISTC by 2015. The date would allow all currently funded ISTC projects in Russia to be completed.[48]. One motive was reportedly the concern of the Russian security services that the United States was obtaining military secrets through collaborative research projects. This may have applied only to ISTC support to former Soviet nuclear weapon scientists, but if it should have referred to the former biological weapon scientists in 2011, the implications were obviously disturbing if it meant new military secrets rather than old ones. Russian government complaints had already led the European Union to stop funding new ISTC projects in Russia in 2010, although they continued in the Ukraine, Georgia, Belarus and other recipients.[49] Kazakhstan offered to host the ISTC headquarters when it leaves Moscow, and the six other ISTC/CIS recipients requested that ISTC grant funding should continue as at present and after 2015.

Writing in 1994, one author suggested that three conditions were absolute requirements for conversion of the former Soviet BW program in all of its components:

- The offensive BW program should be ended.
- The Biopreparat institutes should be removed from any control by the RF-MOD, not just in name. They should be under the total control of civilian ministries and civilian leadership. One should also seek the complete replacement of leading officials from the pre-1992 program in management positions.
- All of the institutes in question should be open to international scientific visitors, secrecy should be removed from any non-military institute, and the terms of the Trilateral Agreement should be fulfilled in regard to the three RF-MOD institutes.[50]

It remains unknown whether the first of these requirements has taken place. The 2010 iteration of the US "Non-Compliance" report, covering the years 2004 through 2008 still stated "Russia's annual BWC confidence-building measure declarations since 1992 have not satisfactorily documented whether this program was terminated. . . . It remains unclear . . . whether Russia has fulfilled its obligations under Article II of the BWC to destroy or divert to peaceful purposes the items specified in Article I of the Convention that it inherited."[51] The response by the Russian Ministry of Foreign Affairs (MFA) several days later was that "the lingering so-called uncertainty on the American side about whether Russia fulfills its obligations under Article 1 of the BWC . . . could have been eliminated a decade ago, if in 2001 the United States had not blocked multilateral negotiations on the development of a verification mechanism for the convention."[52] The implication was that Russia would have allowed full access to the RF-MOD institutes if a BWC Verification Protocol had been achieved. Russian authorities have never explained why access to these institutes has been denied without a BWC Verification Protocol. The MFA statement made no mention of Russia's commitments under the September 14, 1992, Trilateral Agreement. The second condition for the most part now exists, although the replacement of military and civilian officials occurred only gradually in the 20 years after 1992. Nonetheless, the process has not yet been completed. Several important bureaucrats from the pre-1992 period still play a significant role in overseeing the institutes that were involved in the former Soviet BW program. The third condition has been only partially achieved: the RF-MOD institutes remain closed.

Conclusion

THIS CHAPTER SUMMARIZES the most significant attributes of the Soviet BW program; its achievements in providing the Soviet military with a weapon; the reasons for its existence; and its lingering legacy in terms of possible threats to international security and weakening of international law.

Attributes

The 65-year duration of the Soviet offensive BW program, dating from 1928 or earlier to at least September 1992, made it the longest such program in the 20th century. For comparison, the second longest, the American program, had a 27-year duration (1942–1969); the British/Canadian program about 21 years (1939–1960); the Japanese BW program lasted 13 years (1932–1945); and the Iraqi program about 16 years (1975–1991). It was also the largest such program by many times. The Soviet Ministry of Defense (MOD) had more experience researching, developing, testing, and stockpiling biological weapons than any other national BW program. An important part of the infrastructure that supported that effort still exists in Russia, and is directly controlled by the Russian Ministry of Defense (RF-MOD).

During its lengthy existence the Soviet offensive BW program progressed through two overlapping generations; a "first generation," when classical microbiology methods were applied, and a "second generation," which utilized genetic engineering. During the first period, the MOD and its scientists, engineers, and technicians bore sole responsibility for offensive BW planning, R&D, laboratory and open field testing, and the engineering of munitions. The MOD supported three biological institutes where BW-related R&D was performed and agents were formulated, plus an extensive open-air testing facility and an unknown number of facilities for storing bulk BW agents and biological weapons.

The revolution in biotechnology that began in the early 1970s brought about drastic changes throughout the world's scientific, technical, and industrial infrastructures. In the Soviet Union, it did so in both the civilian and the military spheres. Sometime during 1970–1972, the new genetic engineering techniques became known to scientists in the Soviet Academies' biomedical institutes, ministry institutes, and institutions of higher learning (VUZ). Highly influential academicians recognized the significance of biotechnology, but were concerned that the government would not understand its implications and therefore would forego investing in the new field. As explained in Chapter 2, academicians for their own reasons convinced the military and Politburo of modern biotechnology's value for weapons-related R&D. That initiative led to the issuance of a top-secret decree by the Central Committee in 1972. The decree authorized a vastly expanded offensive BW program specifically designed to utilize genetic engineering for the weaponization of bacterial and viral pathogens.[1] The 1972 decree led to major changes, not only in the methods whereby BW-related R&D was to be performed in the Soviet Union, but also where it was performed and by whom. This initiated the second generation of the Soviet BW program, which continued until the Soviet Union dissolved in December 1991 and some indeterminate time after. Because the RF-MOD biological facilities remain closed to the rest of the world, the possibility exists that some portions of it remain in Russia today. There is simply no way to know.

After 1972 the MOD retained control over planning, open field testing, and munitions development, as well as overall management control. However the bulk of R&D and, possibly, laboratory testing was to be done in ostensibly civilian institutions and by civilian scientific workers. Although the focus in this book is on the Biopreparat system, whose governing agency nominally was *Glavmikrobioprom*, a host of other civilian ministries and agencies had important roles in the BW program, including the Ministry of Agriculture, Ministry of Health, elements of the USSR-Academy of Sciences and USSR-Academy of Medical Sciences, the anti-plague system, and the Ministry of Medical Industry (which came to supersede *Glavmikrobioprom*). As reported to Gorbachev in 1990, "in 1971 they [MOD institutes] were joined in this [BW] work by another 12 organizations of the USSR Ministry of the Medical Industry and the former USSR State Agroindustrial Committee."[2] This was a unique attribute of the Soviet BW program; no other national BW program has come close to involving such a wide scope of civilian agencies in its classified military-directed activities.

One of the attributes of the Soviet military-industrial complex was its affliction by incorrigible gigantism. Despite its great secrecy, the BW program was no exception. The 1972 decree led to the building and equipping of vast facilities, staffed by tens of thousands of scientists and support personnel and guarded by hundreds of Ministry of Interior troops. It utilized energy and utilities in prodigious quantities. The civilian BW system came to dwarf the MOD's BW program. Within a decade its Biopreparat component alone comprised five large R&D institutes and at least seven massive BW mobilization production facilities, which included adjacent weapon-filling stations and storage bunkers. Additional facilities, about which less is known, had important functions in supporting the program by designing and manufacturing special equipment and instrumentation; producing huge quantities of media, substrates, and biochemicals; and raising, feeding, and supplying the thousands of laboratory animals used for testing. Still other Biopreparat facilities did purely civilian work in order to provide cover for the entire enterprise.

A gigantic program required a huge workforce to operate it. Various estimates by previous authors on the number of individuals who worked in the Soviet BW program ranged from 40,000 to 65,000, including the *Ekologia* program in the Ministry of Agriculture. We lean toward the higher figure, recognizing that this number included all ranks of scientific and technical workers: scientists, engineers, technicians, and infrastructure support personnel. For comparison, based on estimates of historic BW programs made by others, the US program involved fewer than 8,000 people, the Japanese program probably had fewer than 5,000, the British and Canadian program fewer than 3,000, and the Iraqi program probably less than 500.

From what is known about the SNOPB production plant, it is reasonable to conclude that each mobilization production facility had carried through a series of production runs for whichever pathogen it was planned to manufacture. Additional production runs were done on a periodic basis to make certain that the mobilization production facility was ready to be fully mobilized within six weeks of receiving orders to do so. In view of the approximately

100–200 tons of poorly inactivated weaponized *B. anthracis* spores that were buried on Vozrozhdeniye Island by MOD personnel as part of the effort after 1988–1989 to conceal its BW program from future foreign inspectors, it also is reasonable to conclude that the MOD maintained stockpiles of at least some of its other BW agents in the years before 1992.

Recognizing that a biological weapon, rather than being simply a quantity of pathogens, is a system composed of formulated pathogen, munition, and dispersal mechanism (see Chapter 10), most of the effort in the second generation Soviet BW program was focused on weaponizing bacterial and viral pathogens. Unlike other national BW programs, which without exception used only classical or traditional applied microbiology techniques to weaponize agents, the post-1972 Soviet program had a futuristic aspect. By employing genetic manipulation and other molecular biology techniques, its scientists were able to breach barriers separating species and, even, disciplines, such as microbiology and protein chemistry. In doing so, Biopreparat scientists were able to undertake R&D that resulted in the creation of bacterial and viral strains that possessed characteristics not found in nature. One must assume that whatever genetically engineered bacterial and viral forms were created during the second generation Soviet BW program, they remain stored in the culture collections of the RF-MOD.

Accomplishments

A photograph from 1982 shows 64 men and women sitting or standing in a grand hall of the Kremlin Palace.[3] Some minutes before the photograph was taken, a senior Soviet official in the middle front row had passed out prizes and awards to each of the other 63 persons because he or she had made significant contributions to biotechnology, nominally in accordance with an open decree of the Central Committee in 1974. One of the characteristics of the group photographed is that it uniquely includes scientists from both closed and open institutes. The accompanying overlay to the photograph identifies prominent Biopreparat scientists with F clearance, such as Domaradsky, Pasechnik, and Zaviyalov, as well as internationally well-known scientists who had published in international journals and had collaborated with foreigners, such as Istvan Fodor and Alexandr Spirin. The photo was published at the time in prominent Soviet newspapers, but the awardees were not named, nor was their work described except in general terms.[4] However, none of the highest officials of the MOD and Biopreparat who directed the BW program were present in the photograph. Instead, at a top-secret ceremony in an adjacent hall, those military and Biopreparat officials were awarded the highest Soviet awards, such as the Lenin Prize, for their BW-related accomplishments.

While the achievements of scientists working in the open environment can be measured by objective criteria, such as their publication records and the regard with which they are held by their peers, those working in the closed system were of mostly unknown scientific quality. It is likely that the scientists of the closed system were rewarded for work that benefited the military R&D program rather than Soviet science or industry. How then can one assesses the accomplishments of the Soviet Union's huge second-generation BW program, which operated at least until 1993 at a tremendous cost? Did it, for example, make its military stronger and the Soviet state more secure? Did it spin off findings and applications that were useful to the Soviet population? Did it generate any other benefits for the Soviet state and its citizens?

Although the focus is on the BW program's second generation, the answer cannot be separated from what preceded it. During the first generation's long duration, several type-classified biological weapons were developed, some of which likely remained in the Soviet military's arsenal until at least 1992. These included spherical bomblets for delivery by aircraft carrying cluster bombs and potentially by missiles, as well as light bombers with medium-range carrying spray tanks for dispersal of BW formulations. The first generation BW agents that armed these weapons are listed in Chapter 1.

The accomplishments of the second generation BW program in bacteriology were the following:

- The first pathogen to be weaponized by *Ferment* was not genetically engineered. Institute of Engineering Immunology (IEI) researchers were able to coat *F. tularensis* cells with Protein A to protect them from human immunodefenses. Methods for the large-scale production of Protein A were developed at the Omutninsk Chemical Factory.
- All-Union Research Institute for Applied Microbiology (SRCAM) researchers strove to develop pathogens that were resistant to 10 antibiotics, but never reached this goal. However, in 1986 a strain of *B. anthracis* was genetically engineered to resist seven or eight antibiotics.[5] During 1987–1988, multiresistant antibiotic strains of *F. tularensis, B. mallei,* and *B. pseudomallei* were also created. Antibiotics in common use in NATO countries most likely would have been ineffective against biological weap-

ons armed with these creations. Attempts to create a multiresistant strain of *Y. pestis* failed.

- IEI scientists genetically engineered an F1-minus strain of *Y. pestis,* which altered the pathogen's surface antigenic presentation—a change that would have made Western countries unable to identify this strain using classical methods. Governments whose populations were attacked by biological weapons armed with this strain would therefore not have been able to begin timely treatment because of the delay that would take place in detection and identification of the pathogen.
- A SRCAM team successfully inserted virulence genes from *Bacillus cereus* into *Bacillus anthracis* that changed its antigenic presentation so that antibodies stimulated in test animals by the Russian live anthrax vaccine did not recognize them. When this work was published in 1997, some American scientists asserted that potentially all existing anthrax vaccines, including that used by the US armed forces, would be ineffective to prevent disease caused by the new strain.
- As part of the Bonfire program, *Legionella pneumophila* was genetically engineered at SRCAM to secrete peptides. This construct of pathogen and the peptides they secreted would stimulate the host's immunological defense system to eliminate the infection and, simultaneously, activate the immune cells capable of destroying myelin of nerve cells in those individuals who were infected by the genetically altered *L. pneumophila.* The destruction of myelin normally present in the human body induces an illness similar to multiple sclerosis, but with a quick death.

The accomplishments of the second-generation BW program in virology, as far can be identified, were the following:

- Military researchers at the Zagorsk Institute developed a new production methodology for variola virus using cell culture techniques rather than eggs. The development was completed at Vector by a virology team sent from the Zagorsk Institute. A new virus production building was in the course of being constructed at Vector in the mid- to late-1980s. The production line was to be equipped with a 630-liter fermenter. It would have considerably enhanced the Soviet Union's ability to mass-produce variola virus. Pasechnik estimated that its maximum yield of weaponized variola virus would have been about 2,000 kilograms annually. During the period at which this was taking place, construction was overtaken by the US-UK pressures on Gorbachev after 1990 to terminate the Soviet offensive BW program, and the building was never completed.

• Vector scientists developed methods for the large-scale production of a dry Marburg virus formulation that was effective when used for aerosol application. They also determined its efficacy on nonhuman primates using tests carried out in closed aerosol chambers. The results impressed the MOD sufficiently to provide its developers with awards. However, none of the variola virus or Marburg virus produced at Vector was genetically engineered in any way.

The newly created bacterial strains were taken over by the MOD for final stages of weaponization. These would have included, first, the testing of biological weapons armed with second generation agents in closed chambers and, if these were successful, the final step of open-air testing of the newly created weapons. However, the second generation BW program had reached the stage for these next steps just as CWC and BWC negotiations convinced the members of the Central Committee's Politburo that inspectors from Western states would soon be making site visits to Soviet CW and BW facilities. In preparation for visits, the Politburo and the MOD mandated the destruction of the existing Soviet BW agent and weapon stockpiles. Therefore, although it is probable that bomblets armed with second-generation agents would have undergone testing in the closed chambers of MOD institutes and apparently even at Biopreparat institutes, the final step of open-air testing was not taken.[6] Aralsk-7 by this time was either closing down or had already closed down, so there was no site at which to conduct open-air testing of new biological weapons.

MOD engineers may have worked continuously until 1992 to improve existing designs for biological weapons, such as biological bomblets and spray devices, but this would have involved incremental design and engineering changes with no radical or revolutionary developments or advances. In particular, there appear to have been no biological warheads for ICBMs or MRBMs that went beyond very early stages of development and none that was open-air tested. Therefore, no ICBM with a BW warhead was deployed. The development of a cruise missile system for BW delivery had also reached only a very early stage. By 1992, therefore, the second generation BW program does not appear to have enhanced the Soviet MOD's ability to conduct war to any significant degree. However, it is likely that type-classified weapons armed with second generation BW agents would have been realized relatively soon after 1992 if

Gorbachev's rise to power, Pasechnik's defection in late 1989, and the disintegration of the Soviet Union in December 1991 had not intervened.

As the second generation Soviet BW program appears to have developed some validated second generation BW agents, as well as others that were close to being validated, the critical question is: would pathogens whose properties had in some way been enhanced by genetic engineering have provided added benefits to Soviet use of biological weapons, had it taken place? Would they, for example, have made a substantial difference to the outcomes of battles or wars if the Soviet Union had placed hardier, more virulent, and/or antibiotic/antiviral-resistant pathogens in operational or strategic biological weapons, in comparison to arming them with first generation agents?

In general, it is reasonable to assume that much like any weapons system that is made more effective, imbuing BW agents with greater virulence, antibiotic resistance, and hardiness would have benefited Soviet forces if they had ever come to the point of using biological weapons. They would have killed or sickened more of the enemy than if the weapons had been filled with first-generation BW agents. In addition, the psychological damage to defenders exposed to biological agents that could not be detected or effectively treated might have been grave, producing hopelessness and panic among members of the attacked military forces or populations. For these reasons, genetically engineered enhancements to BW pathogens probably would have conveyed some advantages to second-generation Soviet biological weapons, though only open-air testing would have proved this. However, there is no way to estimate if these added characteristics would have been significant in determining the outcome of a military campaign or war, especially if either featured large-scale use of nuclear weapons. If the Cold War had been superseded by a "hot" war involving the substantial use of nuclear weapons, the destruction would have been so horrendous that the effects of all other weapon systems would likely have been trifling in comparison. A 1960 US intelligence report noted "Regarded in the context of a massive nuclear attack with consequent fallout, subsidiary clandestine biological and chemical attacks would be redundant."[7]

In the final analysis, we cannot assess the military accomplishments of the Soviet offensive BW program with any certainty. Twenty years of Biopreparat work did generate some validated second generation pathogens, but they were taken over by the MOD for final weaponization and thus disappeared from the purview of the Biopreparat scientists we interviewed. Pasechnik's defection and the resulting US-UK diplomatic efforts coincidentally intervened, and despite the opposition of the MOD, they led to the termination of the more active portions of the Soviet offensive BW program. It can be taken for granted that all recipes were retained at the Zagorsk and Kirov institutes, as well as at the RF-MOD archive should one exist, and that the validated strains remain in the culture collections of the RF-MOD biology facilities.

Details of the defensive BW program (Problem 5) that paralleled the offensive program were also mostly secret during the Soviet era. Some of its details are now known, however, as the more recent Russian literature has featured books, monographs, and articles describing accomplishments of the military and Biopreparat institutes related to the prevention and treatment of infectious diseases. For example, a major effort of the Soviet defensive BW program was the development of aerosol vaccines claimed to be safer, more efficient, easier to administer, and less expensive than classical vaccines administered by injection or ingestion.[8] Yet, to date none of the touted aerosol vaccines is marketed internationally. Similarly, claims have been made by Biopreparat officials that antisera, antibiotics, and antiviral substances were developed and produced by its institutions. The only such products that are known to have been sold on the internal Soviet market were vaccines against hepatitis A and hepatitis B, a recombinant interferon A preparation for antiviral use, and a "nootropic" peptide drug. Otherwise, by far most drugs sold in the later years of the Soviet Union and then in Russia were, and are, imported.[9] It therefore appears that the defensive BW program added very little value to *Glavmikrobioprom's* civilian industries. The reason for its meager output was probably that the R&D performed by Biopreparat for defensive or civilian applications was not done primarily to benefit the civilian sector, but to provide legends to shield the offensive BW program. Both the MOD and Biopreparat very likely had low expectations or intrinsic interest in seeing that products useful to civilians were generated.[10]

The Soviet offensive BW program was unquestionably detrimental to the Soviet Union as a whole. It drained very substantial, often scarce, human resources and funding away from USSR academic, industrial, and agricultural biotechnology R&D. One cannot blame only the Soviet BW program for the very slow development of a modern civilian biotechnology industry in the Soviet Union (and Russia). Nevertheless it is plausible to conclude that if the intense, expensive efforts to develop genetically engineered organisms and formulations for military purposes had instead been spent on civil R&D conducted at academy, ministry, and VUZ institutes, they would have resulted in applications meaningful to Soviet medicine, industry, and agriculture.

In conclusion, the Soviet offensive BW program did not benefit its military by meaningfully increasing its ability to wage war. Nor did it generate more than a very few products that would have helped the Soviet Union's civilian population to defend against disease, improve nutrition, and remediate the environment. At the same time it hindered the Soviet Union's economic development by impeding its civilian biotechnology R&D community and industry.

Rationale

There is virtually no confirmable information about the reason the Soviet government decided to pursue the development and acquisition of biological weapons, and particularly to do so after 1975. It is the subject in this book about which the least is known.

There are certain things, however, that can be said with confidence. The Soviet Union began its BW program around 1927, before it considered the United States to be its primary enemy. It continued that program after World War II, when the Geneva Protocol prohibited only the use of "bacteriological" weapons, but not the development, production, and stockpiling of agents and munitions. It did this before ICBMs existed and when its means of reaching the continental United States were extremely limited. And it is clear that the Soviet government and its military leadership wanted to have biological weapons after the BWC came into existence in 1975, despite the fact that this decision placed its country in violation of a major weapons of mass destruction disarmament treaty that mandated the abolition of all such weapons. The memorandum presented by scientists of both the Academy of Sciences and Academy of Medical Sciences to the Central Committee in 1971 that led to the enormous boost to the Soviet BW program was motivated primarily by parochial and professional bureaucratic reasons of competition with nuclear and missile scientists for the resources and priorities of the state. Finally, the institutional inertia that universally accompanies weapon development and acquisition programs was compounded in this instance by its extraordinary secrecy within the Soviet political system and the unusual characteristics of decision making in that system.

Everyone from the former Soviet Union who was interviewed was asked the same question: Why did the Soviet Union acquire such an enormous offensive BW program? None of the interviewees had been in a sufficiently high and critical position at the MOD to have been informed of such a highly classified policy decision, but each had opinions as to how it might be answered. Those opinions are essentially conjecture. The reasons for the Soviet BW program's existence might include a combination of what can be deduced from the paragraph above, the suggestions that follow, and others unknown to us.

- Despite Nixon's 1969 executive order and the public dismantlement of Fort Detrick and the Pine Bluff Arsenal, the Soviet government continued to believe—or at least elements in it claimed—that the United States continued to maintain a secret offensive BW program after 1972. By doing the same, it was following the Cold War logic of all-out competition for possession of weapons of mass destruction.

- As explained in Chapter 10, the Soviet military leadership presumably reckoned that biological weapons brought added benefits to its forces in the operational and/or strategic spheres. However, our interviewees, who were mostly scientists, mentioned primarily the strategic sphere. They expected that there would be several nuclear exchanges between the Soviet Union and the United States, the last of which would consist of Soviet missiles armed with biological warheads being used to decimate surviving Americans with deadly disease. With few exceptions, interviewees did not know that no type-classified Soviet missile had been developed for the delivery of BW agents.

- An entirely contrary suggestion was that the MOD believed that biological weapons were "seen as some kind of military asset, to be held in reserve, perhaps to compensate for other shortcomings in defense."[11] It is not clear what these perceived "shortcomings" might have been, but they could have been technological surprises that might be engineered by the technologically superior United States. The undefined nature of the imputed "shortcomings" highlights the highly speculative nature of many of these suggested alternative rationales.

- Soviet biological weapons were not to be used against NATO countries, but as strategic weapons against the Chinese, to decimate large numbers of forces attacking on the ground or, potentially its huge population.

- A last suggestion was that Soviet biological weapons were developed, not for military purposes, but for sabotage or terrorism. This hypothesis is based mostly on some objectives of the Bonfire and *Ekologia* programs. As recounted in Chapters 7 and 8, Bonfire scientists engineered both bacteria and viruses to produce peptides capable of stimulating destructive autoimmune reactions among victims ending in death after weeks had passed. *Ekologia* developed pathogens to destroy agriculturally important animals and plants and whose effects therefore would be to cause economic damage over months and, even, years, but would have no immediate military value.[12] However, the massive production capacity constructed by the Soviet Union to produce BW agents argues strongly against the notion of sabotage or terrorist use except as a minor, auxiliary potential. The fact that little or no research appears to have been devoted to weaponizing food-borne or water-borne pathogens also argues against sabotage as having been an aim of the program.

An interesting psychological dimension is introduced by the remarks of several relatively senior interviewees who claimed that they and their coworkers were convinced that Soviet biological weapons would never be used. Perhaps the reason for this conviction was that they had never heard of a doctrine for biological weapons deployment and use having been developed by the military. Assumedly, if such a doctrine existed, it would have been a closely held secret known to only a few of the most senior military officers in the 15th Directorate, not least because of its violation of the BWC. Nevertheless, if facilities such as SNOPB had orders to fill bomblets with prepared pathogens in time of war, someone in the higher echelons of the Soviet military command structure must have had an explicit idea of what would then be done with them. If a doctrine is developed and a military command structure has any expectation that it could be used, at least a portion of the officer corps has to be informed of it and appropriately trained.[13] Under these circumstances, it would seem reasonable that the existence of a doctrine, but not necessarily its details, might have become known to some of the highly placed individuals we interviewed. But except for Pasechnik, none indicated any knowledge of a doctrine for BW use. If it had been developed by the General Staff and its 15th Directorate, there is no knowledge of what it was, or whether and to what degree it was incorporated into Soviet military force planning. Certainly no evidence for that is known. If biological weapons were not a significant element of Soviet force planning, one wonders why the BW program was able to continue for so many years, outliving its earliest political, military, and academic supporters. The BW program appears to have been driven by internal bureaucratic inertia, a particularly compartmentalized and secretive MOD-VPK collaboration, and by a few of the Central Committee's leadership who directed the funds for its support to Gosplan using code words and euphemisms such as "special problems."

Legacy

Starting from March 26, 1975, when the Soviet government ratified the BWC, and despite the fact that the Soviet Union was one of the three co-depository states together with the United States and the United Kingdom, the Soviet offensive BW program was in continuous violation of the convention. Testimony by various former Soviet officials and scientists cited in this book provide extensive evidence of their direct roles in the program. The violation continued until the dissolution of the Soviet Union and for an indeterminate time after that. In its 1992 BWC confidence-building measures declaration, the Russian government admitted to the violation by the Soviet Union. The September 1992 Trilateral document, which Russia had signed, detailed the continued existence of incriminating facilities and equipment, and the fact that elements of the program continued at least as of that date. The individuals responsible for having directed and managed this illicit program during the time of the Soviet Union, as well as those who continued the deception afterward, have been clearly identified.

In view of this massive violation of the BWC, it is important to consider whether lasting damage was done to the convention and to what degree its continued operation has been compromised. Many security experts have noted that the BWC's greatest weakness is that it lacks provisions to ensure compliance by the nations that signed and ratified it. This book has not discussed the difficult and intertwined issues of BW treaty compliance and verification, other than to note that nations themselves try to assess whether real or potential adversaries possess BW programs by utilizing "national technical means." Briefly, this term refers to a nation using all technological intelligence methods available to it in attempts to ascertain another nation's capabilities and intentions in subjects relevant to its national security. Chapter 12 provides a detailed description and analysis of information made available to American and, less so, British leaders about the Soviet BW program by use of intelligence from 1945 on. The results of this effort for the greatest portion of those years were pitifully inadequate. Five years before Pasechnik's defection at the end of 1989, the intelligence community was convinced that the Soviet Union was using genetic engineering for offensive BW purposes. However, US-UK intelligence services were unable to discover any details about the second-generation Soviet BW program or the Soviet government's intentions for that program.

The only meaningful international law that seeks to prevent BW is the BWC. It clearly had no influence on the Soviet government's decision to acquire the largest, most expensive, and in terms of employing the biosciences, possibly the most sophisticated offensive BW program the world has ever experienced. The only effect that the BWC had on that decision was the institution of a system of legends to prevent the newly enhanced BW program from being discovered. Iraq, although it had not yet ratified the BWC, also initiated an offensive BW program, as did South Africa. In the instances that are known, the BWC did not dissuade nations from violating it.

The Soviet BW program's legacy as it affects the BWC still lingers in today's Russia. The major concern is the Russian military's residual ability to protect and maintain, to an unknown extent, the offensive BW program of the Soviet Union as represented by the three closed RF-MOD institutes. The military's interference with attempts by the Soviet political leadership to decisively terminate the BW program provides a disturbing history. The direct interventions by UK prime ministers Thatcher and Major, US president Bush, and their respective foreign and defense ministers and ambassadors did not lead to a definitive end to the Soviet program. The efforts by Gorbachev and Shevardnadze, while simultaneously denying the program's existence to their Western counterparts, were limited and in the end unsuccessful. Military and VPK intransigence succeeded. The similar failure by President Yeltsin and Prime Minister Chernomyrdin, under pressure by President Clinton, to effect civilian political control over a system being run by the RF-MOD without apparent oversight or control by the Russian executive or legislative branches of government was again due to RF-MOD intransigence. Although both the Soviet and Russian governments claim civilian control over their militaries, their civilian governments were not sufficiently concerned about this issue, and unable to either stop or open up what remained of the Soviet-era offensive BW program.

Russia's current official position is that no offensive BW program had existed in the Soviet Union, that the Sverdlovsk anthrax outbreak was a natural event, and that no weapons or weaponized agents had been tested on Vozrozhdeniye Island. It is also indicative that as of the time of this writing, no foreigner has been permitted to visit any of the RF-MOD's biological institutes that were vital components of the Soviet offensive BW program, nor, with one exception, any of the five Russian anti-plague institutes that had important roles in Problem 5 and lesser roles in the offensive BW program. The two key concerns are the continuing silence and/or disinformation regarding the former Soviet offensive BW program and the lack of transparency in the currently operating MOD research institutes. In regard to these two issues, one historical and one current, the level of secrecy is nearly as high now as it was in the Soviet Union. There is no available information as to why the Russian government is so intent on keeping its past BW program a secret, or why the veil of secrecy is maintained over current RF-MOD and anti-plague facilities and their operations. By continuing to maintain these positions, the Russian government violates both the letter and the spirit of the BWC, the Trialateral Agreement, and the political agreements reached in regards to the operation of the BWC's Confidence-Building Measures.

It is possible to end on a somewhat positive note. There were substantial fears, between 1992 and 2000 in particular, that former Soviet BW scientists might emigrate to countries of proliferation concern and/or that pathogens and technology developed as part of the Soviet offensive program might find their way to such countries. That essentially did not happen. Except for no more than a handful of individuals who went to Iran, there was no known proliferation of scientists, technology, or pathogens to countries of proliferation concern. Part of the reason for that was a program that the United States and international partners initiated to support research in the former Biopreparat institutes. More recently that same program has served to provide greatly enhanced external security for many of the Russian institutes, and within the institutes for their pathogen collections. During the mid- to late-1990s the United States has to date spent approximately $1.7 billion on this effort. The program might have been managed differently, so that it would have been of more benefit to Russian domestic needs, instead of focused on short-term parochial interests of the US intelligence and biodefense communities. Nevertheless, the program overall was highly beneficial and contributed very substantially to the reduction of the danger of BW proliferation from the former Soviet BW program. In 2011 the Russian government announced that it would cease cooperation with this program in 2015.

Annex A: Acronyms and Russian Terms

ACDA US Arms Control and Disarmament Agency.

AFMIC US Armed Forces Medical Intelligence Center.

AFRIMS US Armed Forces Research Institute for Medical Sciences.

AFRL US Air Force Research Laboratory.

AID US Agency for International Development.

All-Union National; an agency, enterprise, institute, or unit that existed throughout the Soviet Union.

ARS Agricultural Research Service of the US Department of Agriculture.

BDA Bilateral Destruction Agreement (1990), between the United States and the Soviet Union.

BII Bio-Industry Initiative by the US Department of State.

Biokhimmash *Institut Prikladnoy Biokhimii i Mashinostroeniya* (Institute for Biochemical Technological Development, part of Biopreparat, in Moscow).

Biopreparat An all union science production association established in 1974 under the Main Administration of Microbiological Industry (*Glavmikrobioprom*) for the purpose of heading and managing the ostensibly civilian component of the Soviet Union's biological warfare program. After the Soviet Union dissolved in 1991, Biopreparat was partially privatized and became RAO Biopreparat.

Biopribor *Vsesoyuzny Institut Biologicheskogo Priborostroeniya* (All-Union Institute for Biological Instrument Development, part of Biopreparat, in Moscow).

BNTS *Biopreparat Mezhvedomstvenny Nauchno-tekhnichesky Sovet* (Interbranch Scientific and Technical Council of Biopreparat).

BoNT Botulinum neurotoxin.

BRPC Biological Research and Production Centers, an element of the Cooperative Threat Reduction program.

BSL Biosafety level. There are four biosafety levels, BSL-1 through BSL-4. The lowest level, BSL-1, requires little more than a laboratory coat; BSL-4 requires working in a "space suit" with its own air supply.

BTEP Biotechnology Engagement Program, managed by the US Department of Health and Human Services.

BTRP Biological Threat Reduction Program of the US Department of Defense.

BW Biological warfare.

BWC 1972 Convention on the Prohibition of the Development, Production and Stockpiling of Bacteriological (Biological) and Toxin Weapons and on Their Destruction (Biological Weapons Convention for short).

BWPP Biological Weapons Proliferation Prevention, an element of the Cooperative Threat Reduction program.

CAMR Centre for Applied Microbiological Research, at Porton Down, United Kingdom.

CBMs Confidence Building Measures, associated with the BWC.

CBR Cooperative BioDefense Research, an element of the Cooperative Threat Reduction program.

CBW Chemical and biological warfare.

Central Committee Central Committee of the Communist Party of the Soviet Union.

CFE Conventional Forces in Europe treaty.

CIS Commonwealth of Independent States.

CISAC Committee on International Security and Arms Control of the National Academy of Sciences.

CNS James Martin Center for Nonproliferation Studies at the Monterey Institute of International Studies, Monterey, California.

COPERNICUS Community of Pan European Research Networks of Interdisciplinary Centres and Universities in Sciences.

CPSU *Kommunisticheskaya Partiya Sovetskogo Soyuza* (Communist Party of the Soviet Union).

CRDF Civilian Research and Development Foundation, Arlington, Virginia.

CTR Cooperative Threat Reduction program, managed by the US Department of Defense.

CW Chemical warfare.

CWC 1993 Convention on the Prohibition of the Development, Production, Stockpiling and Use of Chemical Weapons and on their Destruction (Chemical Weapons Convention for short).

CWPF Chemical Weapon Production Facility.

DARPA US Defense Advanced Research Products Agency.

DIA US Defense Intelligence Agency.

DNA Deoxyribonucleic acid.

DOD US Department of Defense.

DOE US Department of Energy.

DOS US Department of State.

Dokl.AN SSR *Doklady Akademii nauk SSSR (Proceedings of the USSR Academy of Sciences).*

DSWA US Defense Special Weapons Agency.

DTRA US Defense Threat Reduction Agency.

Ekologiya Code name for the Soviet BW program to R&D agents to harm and kill animals and plants (in English, Ecology).

ELISA Enzyme-linked immunosorbent assay, which is a rapid and sensitive means for identifying and quantifying small amounts of virus antigens or antiviral antibodies.

ENDC Eighteen Nation Disarmament Commission, in Geneva.

EU European Union.

FCO UK Foreign and Commonwealth Office.

FDA US Food and Drug Administration.

Ferment Code name for the Soviet BW program to R&D agents to harm and kill humans (in English, Enzyme).

15th Directorate *15-oe Glavnoe Upravlenie Ministerstvo Oborony* (Ministry of Defense's 15th Directorate).

FSB *Federalnaya Sluzhba Bezopasnosti* (Russian Federal Security Service).

FSU Former Soviet Union.

G8 The Group of Eight; the top eight most-industrialized countries: Canada, France, Germany, Italy, Japan, Russia, the United Kingdom, and the United States.

GAO US General Accounting Office.

GCC Gore-Chernomyrdin Commission;

GDR German Democratic Republic (East Germany).

Genshtab *Generalny shtab* (Soviet Army Headquarters; Command Center or the Counsel of Commanders).

GKNT *Gosudarstvenny Komitet Soveta Ministrov SSSR po Nauke I Tekhnike* (State Committee of Science and Technology).

GKO *Gosundarstvenny Komitet Oborony* (State Committee on Defense).

Glavmikrobioprom *Glavnoe Upravlenie Mikrobiologicheskoy Promyshlennosti* (Main Administration of Microbiological Industry).

GMP Good manufacturing practices.

Goskom *Gosudarstvenny Komitet* (state committee; usually the first two words of the name of a special committee).

GosNIIOKhT *Gosundarstvenny Nauchno-issledovatelsky Institut Organicheskoy Khimii i Tekhnologii* (State Research Institute of Organic Chemistry and Technology).

Gosplan *Gosudarstvenny Komitet po Planirovaniyu* (State Planning Commission of the Council of Ministers).

Gossanepidnadzor State Sanitary and Epidemiological Inspection, renamed *Rospotrebnadzor* in 2004.

GRU *Glavnoe Razvedovatelnoe Upravlenie* (Main Intelligence Directorate of the MOD).

Gulag *Glavnoe Upravlenie Ispravitelno-trudovykh Lagerey* (the Soviet penal system; more commonly, used as a general name for the network of forced labor camps in Siberia and other distant parts of the Soviet Union).

HEW US Department of Health, Education, and Welfare.

HHS US Department of Health and Human Services.

IC Intelligence community.

ICBM Intercontinental ballistic missile.

ICGEB International Centre for Genetic Engineering and Biotechnology, in Trieste, Italy.

IEI Institute of Engineering Immunology, part of Biopreparat, in Lyubuchany.

IHPB Institute of Highly Pure Biopreparations, part of Biopreparat, in Leningrad (eventually St. Petersburg); on July 8, 1997, renamed State Scientific Center Research Institute of Highly Pure Biopreparations.

INF Intermediate-Range Nuclear Force treaty.

INTAS International Association for the Promotion of Cooperation with Scientists from the Newly Independent States of the Former Soviet Union.

IPP Initiative for Proliferation Prevention program, US Department of Energy.

ISTC International Science and Technology Center, Moscow.

Izvestiya (*News*); nationwide daily newspaper once published by the Presidium of the Supreme Soviet of the USSR (contrast with *Pravda*). Current owner is National Media Group.

KGB *Komitet gosudarstvennoy bezopasnosti* (Committee on State Security).

Komsomol *Vsesoyuzny Leninsky kommunistichesky soyuz molodezhi* (All-Union Lenin Communist Youth League).

LACM Land-attack cruise missile.

MFA Soviet/Russian Ministry of Foreign Affairs.

MGB *Ministerstvo Gosudarstvennoy Bezopasnosti* (Ministry of State Security, a predecessor of the KGB).

MIC Military-Industrial Commission. See VPK.

Mikrob *Gosudarstvenny Nauchno-issledovatelsky Institut Mikrobiologii i Epidemiologii* (State Scientific Research Institute of Microbiology and Epidemiology of Southeast USSR, in Saratov).

MIHE Military Institute of Hygiene and Epidemiology, in Warsaw.

Minhimnefteprom *Ministerstvo Khimicheskoy i Neftepererabatyvayushchey Promyshlennosti* (USSR Ministry of Chemical and Oil Industries).

Ministry institute A general designation for an R&D facility controlled by a ministry, including *Glavmikrobioprom*.

MinMedprom *Ministerstvo Meditsinskoy i Mikrobiologicheskoy Promyshlennosti* (Ministry of the Medical and Microbiological Industry, *Glavmikrobioprom's* successor).

Minsredmash *Ministerstvo Srednego Mashinostroeniya* (Ministry for Medium Machine-Building; this was the Soviet ministry for the nuclear industry).

Minzdrav *Ministerstvo Zdravookhraneniya* (Ministry of Public Health).

MIRV Multiple independently targetable reentry vehicle.

MI-6 See SIS.

MNTS *Mezhvedomstvenny Nauchno-tekhnichesky Sovet* (Interagency Scientific and Technical Council for Molecular Biology and Genetics, part of *Glavmikrobioprom*).

MOD *Ministerstvo Oborony* (USSR Ministry of Defense).

MOH *Ministerstvo zdravookhraneniya SSSR* (USSR Ministry of Health).

MOU Memorandum of Understanding.

MRV Multiple reentry vehicle.

NAMRU-2 US Naval Medical Research Unit 2, in Indonesia.

NAS US National Academy of Sciences.

NASA US National Aeronautics and Space Administration.

NATO North Atlantic Treaty Organization.

NCTR US National Center for Toxicological Research.

NIE National Intelligence Estimate, created by the US intelligence community.

NIH US National Institutes of Health.

NII *Nauchno-issledovatelsky Institut* (scientific research institute).

NII Medstatistika Scientific Research Institute of Medical Statistics.

NIISI *Nauchno-issledovatelsky Ispytatelsky Sanitarny Institut Raboche-Krestyanskoy Krasnoy Armii* (Scientific Research and Testing Sanitation Institute of the Soviet Army).

NIL-1 *Nauchno-issledovatelskaya Laboratoriya-1* (Scientific Research Laboratory No. 1 of the MOD).

NKVD *Narodny Komissariat Vnutrennikh Del* (People's Commissariat of Internal Affairs).

NMRI US Naval Medical Research Institute.

Nomenklatura A list of posts and positions that could not be occupied or vacated without permission from the appropriate Communist Party committee.

Novosti *Agentstvo Pechati Novosti* (News Press Agency).

NPO *Nauchno-Proizvodstvennoe Obyedinenie* (Scientific Production Association).

NSC US National Security Council.

NSDM National Security Decision Memorandum.

NTI Nuclear Threat Initiative.

Oblast An administrative unit in the Soviet Union and later Russia akin to a province.

OGPU *Obyedinennoe Gosudarstvennoe Politicheskoe Upravlenie* (Unified State Political Administration, one of the several forerunners of the KGB).

OPCW Organisation for the Prohibition of Chemical Weapons, The Hague.

PCR Polymerase chain reaction.

PNIL *Polevaya Nauchno-issledovatelskaya Laboratoriya* (Field Scientific Research Laboratory at Aralsk-7).

Pravda *(Truth);* nationwide daily newspaper once published by the Central Committee of the CPSU (compare with *Izvestiya*). Current owner is Communist Party of the Russian Federation.

PSAC US President's Science Advisory Committee.

RAN *Rossiyskaya Akademiya Nauk* (Russian Academy of Sciences).

RAO *Rossiyskoe Aktsionernoe Obshchestvo* (joint stock company).

RCMDT State Research Center for Molecular Diagnostics and Therapy.

RCTHRB State Research Center for Toxicology and Hygienic Regulation of Biopreparations.

RF *Rossiyskaya Federatsiya* (Russian Federation).

RF-MOD *Ministerstvo Oborony Rossiyskoy Federatsii* (Russian Federation Ministry of Defense).

RF-MOH *Ministerstvo Zdravookhraneniya Rossiyskoy Federatsii* (Russian Federation Ministry of Health).

RKKA *Raboche-Krestyanskaya Krasnaya Armiya* (Worker's and Peasant's Red Army).

RMMA *Voenno-Meditsinskaya Akademiya Imeni S. M. Kirov* (S. M. Kirov Russian Military Medical Academy, in Leningrad).

Rosmedprom *Rossiyskaya Assotsiatsiya Proizvoditelei i Postavshchikov Lekarstvennykh Sredstv, Izdeliy i Tekhniki Meditsinskogo Naznacheniya* (Russian Association of Producers and Suppliers of Pharmaceuticals, Medical Products, and Technologies).

Rospotrebnadzor Federal Monitoring Service for the Protection of Consumer Rights and Well-Being.

RSA Russian Space Agency.

RSFSR *Rossijskaja Sovetskaja Federativnaja Sotsialisticheskaja Respublika* (Russian Soviet Federated Socialist Republic).

SALT Strategic Arms Limitation Talks.

SEB Staphylococcal enterotoxin B.

SGID *Gosudarstvenny Komitet po Delam Izobreteniy i Otkrytiy* (State Committee on Inventions and Discoveries).

SHAPE Supreme Headquarters Allied Powers Europe.

SIPRI Stockholm International Peace Research Institute, Solna, Sweden.

SIS British Secret Intelligence Service (MI-6).

SNOPB *Stepnogorskaya Nauchnaya Opytnopromyshlennaya Baza* (Stepnogorsk Scientific Experimental-Industrial Base, part of Biopreparat).

SPA *Nauchno-proizvodstvennoe Obyedinenie* (Scientific-Production Association).

SRCAM *Gosudarstvenny Nauchny Tsentr Prikladnoy Mikrobiologii* (State Research Center for Applied Microbiology, part of Biopreparat, in Obolensk).

SSR *Sovetskaya Sotsialisticheskaya Respublika* (Soviet Socialist Republic).

START Strategic Arms Reduction Talks Treaty.

STASI *Ministerium für Staatssicherheit* (GDR Ministry of State Security).

STCU Science and Technology Center in Ukraine, Kiev.

STI *Sanitarno-tekhnichesky Institut* (Medical-Technical Institute of the RKKA).

SVR *Sluzhba Vneshney Razvedki* (Russian Foreign Intelligence Service).

TADR Threat Agent Detection and Response program of the US Department of Defense.

UK United Kingdom.

UNMOVIC United Nations Monitoring, Verification, and Inspection Commission.

UNSCOM United Nations Special Commission (on Iraq).

US United States.

USAMRIID US Army Medical Research Institute for Infectious Diseases, Fort Detrick, Maryland.

USDA US Department of Agriculture.

USSR *Soyuz Sovetskikh Sotsialisticheskikh Respublik* (Union of the Soviet Socialist Republics).

USSR-AMN *Akademiya Meditsinskikh Nauk* (USSR Academy of Medical Sciences).

USSR-AN *Akademiya Nauk* (USSR Academy of Sciences).

VAK *Vysshaya Attestatsionnaya Komissiya* (Higher Accreditation Commission).

VASKhNIL *Vsesoyuznaya Akademiya Selsko-Khozyaystvennykh Nauk imeni V. I. Lenina* (V. I. Lenin All-Union Academy of Agricultural Sciences, in Leningrad).

Vector An all-inclusive name for the Biopreparat institute in Koltsovo, which had several names, including VNII-MB.

VEEV Venezuelan equine encephalitis virus.

VKM5 Russian Collection of Microorganisms.

VNII *Vsesoyuzny Nauchno-issledovatelsky Institut* (All-Union Research Institute . . . ; starting phrase for the names of many USSR research institutes).

VNII-MB *Vsesoyuzny Nauchno-issledovatelsky Institut Molekulyarnoy Biologii* (All-Union Research Institute of Molecular Biology [Vector], in Koltsovo).

VPK *Voenno-promyshlennaya Komissiya* (Military Industrial Commission of the USSR Council of Ministers).

VUZ *Vysshee Uchebnoe Zavedenie* (higher educational institution).

WHO World Health Organization.

WRAIR Walter Reed Army Institute of Research.

WTO Warsaw Treaty Organization (Warsaw Pact).

Annex B: Glossary of Biological Warfare-Related Words and Terms

Aerosol A colloidal suspension of liquid droplets or solid particles in air. For the purposes of this book, all aerosols we discuss are "bioaerosols"—aerosols whose components contain formulated bacteria, viruses, or toxins.

Amino acid Organic compounds containing a carboxyl group and an amino group. 20–22 particular amino acids are encoded by organisms. These are linked together in various combinations to form encoded peptides or proteins.

Antibody A specific protein molecule produced by an organism's immunological defense system when it is challenged by a foreign substance (the antigen). The antibody marks or neutralizes the antigen by binding to it.

Antigen A substance that when introduced into an organism elicits from it an immunological defensive response. Many living microorganism or chemical agents can, under appropriate circumstances, become antigens.

Applied research Experimental or theoretical work directed toward the application of scientific knowledge for the development, production, or utilization of some useful product or capability.

Basic research Experimental or theoretical work that is undertaken to acquire knowledge of fundamental principles of phenomena and observable facts and that might not be directed toward a specific application.

Bacteria One-celled organisms that generally lack a nucleus and have a plasma membrane cell wall. Bacteria can be aerobes or anaerobes; a small percentage of bacteria are pathogenic for humans or other animals. They store most of their DNA in one long looping molecule (chromosome), but can also contain plasmids, which are small, circular, double-stranded DNA molecules that replicate independently from their chromosome. See *Plasmids*.

Biomodulator A general term for biological or synthetic agents that are capable of eliciting specific and/or nonspecific effects on immunological or neurological

723

response systems for either positive or negative purposes. Thus, immunomodulators can (a) enhance the immune response that defends a host against pathogens, or (b) depress a host's immunological defense system, thereby making the host more susceptible to infection. Similarly, neuromodulators can improve a person's mood or, conversely, cause a person to suffer hallucinations and other irrational behavior.

Biosafety In activities involving life forms or their parts, the observance of precautions and preventive procedures that reduce the risk of adverse effects to the laboratory worker or the environment.

Biosecurity Activities designed to secure for humans, animals, and plants freedom from possible hazards attending biological activities, such as research, development, testing, and applications; measures taken by governments to guard against damage that may be brought about by accidental or intentional exposure to biological agents or toxins.

Biotechnology A collection of processes and techniques that involve the use of living organisms, or substances from those organisms, to make or modify products from raw materials for agricultural, industrial, or medical purposes.

Capability The ability to produce or apply a particular set of scientific techniques or technologies.

Cell culture The propagation of cells removed from a plant or animal in culture.

Clone A group of genetically identical cells or organisms asexually descended from a common ancestor. In case of a cloned organism, all cells making up that organism have the same genetic material and are almost exact copies of the original.

Cloning The use of genetic engineering to produce multiple copies of a single gene or a segment of DNA.

Contagious A contagious parasite can spread pathogens from an infected person to an uninfected person by direct or indirect contact. For BW purposes, the major contagious pathogens are variola virus and *Y. pestis*.

Culture The growth of cells or microorganisms in a controlled artificial environment.

Culture, batch A fermentation process that takes place within a fermenter, which is a closed culture system that contains an initial, limited amount of nutrients. The culture is seeded with a few microorganisms of choice, and these are allowed to propagate until a vital nutrient is used up or waste products accumulate to such an extent that they negatively affect the growth of microorganisms. After the fermentation ceases, the culture is removed from the fermenter and the microorganisms (biomass) are separated from the liquid culture medium. If the biomass is the desired product, it is formulated. If the bioproduct dissolved in the culture medium is the desired product, it is subjected to downstream processing.

Culture, continuous An open fermentation system in which a steady state is achieved by adding nutrients continuously to the culture and balancing the added material by removing cells constituting the biomass.

Cytokine Proteins, such as lymphokines and monokines, that are released by a host's immunodefense system (primarily primed T-lymphocytes) when it detects an antigen. Cytokines, while part of the immune defensive response to invaders, may also stimulate toxic or damaging actions to the host that produces them.

Database A collection of data, defined for one or more applications, that is physically located and maintained within one or more computers.

Development Progressive advance from a lower or simpler to a higher or more complex form; the process of applying scientific and technical knowledge to the practical realization or enhancement of a specific product or capability.

DNA Deoxyribonucleic acid; the carrier of genetic information found in all living organisms (except for a group of RNA viruses). Every inherited characteristic is coded somewhere in an organism's complement of DNA.

Doctrine In 1975, Soviet minister of defense Marshal Grechko defined military doctrine as "a system of views on the nature of war and methods of waging it, and on the preparation of the country and army for war, officially adopted in a given state and its armed forces."

Enzyme Special proteins produced by cells that catalyze the chemical processes of life.

Escherichia coli (E. coli) A bacterium that commonly inhabits the human lower intestine and the intestinal tract of most other vertebrates as well. Some strains are pathogenic, causing urinary tract infections and diarrheal diseases. Non-pathogenic strains are often used in laboratory experiments.

Expression The translation of a gene's DNA sequence via RNA into protein.

Fermentation The bioprocess in which yeasts, bacteria, or molds are grown, or propagated, within a closed container for one of three purposes: (1) maximum biomass production; (2) maximal production of by-products such as alcohols, antibiotics, organic acids, and proteins (including toxins); or (3) maximum nutrient consumption, as in waste treatment. There are two fermentation methods: see *Culture, batch* and *Culture, continuous.*

5-year Plans: First 5-year Plan, 1928–1932; Second 5-year Plan, 1933–1937; Third 5-year Plan, 1938–1941; Fourth and Fifth 5-year Plans, 1946–1950 and 1951–1955; Sixth 5-year Plan, 1956–1960; Seventh 5-year Plan, 1959–1965; Eighth 5-year Plan, 1966–1970; Ninth 5-year Plan, 1971–1975; Tenth 5-year Plan, 1976–1981; Eleventh 5-year Plan, 1981–1985; Twelfth 5-year Plan 1986–1990; Thirteenth 5-year Plan 1991.

Formulation (*spetsretseptura,* in Russian) A mixture of weaponized pathogens, or toxin, and additives. The additives are chemicals that serve to stabilize the mixture, protect the pathogen or toxin from environmental stresses, and lessen electrostatic attraction between aerosolized particles to prevent clumping. Each pathogen and toxin required its special formulation, the development of which was more of an artisanal endeavor than a scientific undertaking.

Gene The fundamental unit of heredity. Chemically a gene consists of ordered nucleotides that code for a specific product or control a specific function.

Gene splicing The use of site-specific enzymes that cleave and reform chemical bonds in DNA to create modified DNA sequences.

Genetic engineering A collection of techniques used to alter the hereditary apparatus of a living cell, enabling it to produce more or different chemicals. These techniques include chemical synthesis of genes, the creation of recombinant DNA or recombinant RNA, cell fusion, plasmid transfer, transformation, transfection, and transduction.

Genome An organism's complete set of genes and chromosomes.

Hazard The likelihood that an agent or substance will cause immediate or short-term adverse effects or injury under ordinary circumstances of use.

HEPA (High Efficiency Particulate Air) filters The highest efficiency filters readily available on the open market and used in the aerospace, biomedical, electronic, and nuclear fields. By definition, HEPA filters must capture 99.97% of contaminants at 0.3 microns in size.

Host An animal or plant whose tissues support the existence of one or more parasites; a cell whose metabolism is used for growth and reproduction of another organism.

Host-vector system Compatible host/vector combinations that may be used for the stable introduction of foreign DNA into host cells.

Hybridoma A special cell produced by joining a tumor cell (myeloma) and an antibody-producing cell (lymphocyte). Cultured hybridoma produce large quantities of a particular type of monoclonal antibodies.

ID$_{50}$ The number of microorganisms required to infect 50% of exposed individuals.

Immunomodulator See *Biomodulator.*

Infection The invasion and settling of a parasite within a host.

Infectious Capable of causing infection; spreading or capable of spreading to others.

Intellectual property The area of law encompassing patents, trademarks, trade secrets, copyrights, and plant variety protection.

Interferon A type of protein discovered in the 1950s having potential as anticancer and antiviral agents. Several major types of interferons are known, including alpha (IFN-α), beta (IFN-β), and gamma (IFN-γ). The gamma interferons are usually classified as cytokines.

LD$_{50}$ The dose, or amount, of a chemical needed to cause death to 50% of exposed individuals.

Legends "Facts" or plausible stories created by the KGB solely to mislead.

Log Shorthand for a "power of ten." Two logs (10^2) are 100, and six logs (10^6) are 1 million. If a scientist experiences a six-log reduction of virus viability in a solution, the titer has dropped 1 million times. An example of a six-log reduction would be a drop from 10^8 to 10^2.

Micron (µ) One millionth of a meter. The diameter of a human hair is approximately 100 microns.

Microorganism A microscopic living entity, including bacteria, fungi, protozoa, and viruses.

Monoclonal antibody An antibody produced by a hybridoma that recognizes only a specific antigen.

Morbidity The relative incidence of disease.

Munition An item of materiel used to carry a quantity of pathogens or chemicals to a chosen target; munitions include artillery shells, bombs, and missiles.

Mycotoxin A toxic protein produced by fungi such as members of the genus *Fusarium*.

Neuromodulator See *Biomodulator*.

Oligonucleotides Short DNA molecules, usually containing fewer than 100 bases.

Opportunistic pathogen A microorganism that is pathogenic only to immunocompromised persons.

Pathogen An organism that can cause disease.

Pathogenic Causing, or capable of causing, disease.

Peptide A linear polymer of two or more amino acids. A polymer consisting of many amino acids is called a polypeptide. Peptides are similar to proteins but smaller. By convention, small molecules that can be synthesized by joining individual amino acids are called peptides rather than proteins. The dividing line is at about 50 amino acids; i.e., if the polymer contains fewer than 50 amino acids it is a peptide, if more, it is a protein.

Plasmids Small, circular, self-replicating forms of DNA existing within bacteria. They are often used in recombinant DNA experiments as acceptors of foreign DNA.

Plasmid transfer The use of genetic or physical manipulation to introduce a foreign plasmid into a host cell.

Pleiotropic Manifesting more than one genic effect as a result of genetic engineering, with one of these effects usually having negative properties; specifically, having multiple phenotypic expressions.

Polymerase chain reaction (PCR) A technique used in laboratories to quickly create thousands to millions of copies of genetic material for purposes of analysis.

Production The conversion of raw materials into products, or components thereof, through a series of manufacturing processes.

Protein See *Peptide*.

Q$_{50}$ The quantity of an agent needed to achieve a 50% casualty rate via open-air exposure under ideal meteorological conditions in a 1 km^2 area.

Recipe Each biological weapons system deployed by the Soviet military was completely described in a specific recipe (*reglament* in Russian), including its weaponization process. Each recipe begins with a description and characterization of the agent in question and ends with a protocol for the mass production of the weaponized agent; a single recipe might require several book-length volumes. BW recipes were classified Top Secret. A recipe would be updated if, for example, the strain was considered for new weapons systems or if it was to be genetically engineered for special purposes.

Recombinant DNA (rDNA) The hybrid DNA resulting from joining pieces of DNA from different sources.

Redact To hide contents of a document by blacking out or otherwise making passages in it unreadable.

Reverse genetics Cutting-edge molecular technology used to, for example, create influenza A virus from plasmids.

Risk The probability of injury, disease, or death for persons or groups of persons undertaking certain activities or exposed to hazardous substances. Risk is sometimes expressed in numeric terms (in fractions) or qualitative terms (low, moderate, or high).

RNA Ribonucleic acid; found in many forms: genomic messenger, transfer, and ribosomal RNA are major types. RNA assists in translating the genetic code of a DNA sequence into its complementary protein.

Safe Not threatened by danger; or freed from harm, injury, or risk.

Secure Being secure from danger; freedom from fear and anxiety; measures taken by governments to guard against espionage, sabotage, and surprises.

Seed A bacterial or viral collection used as a "stock" for the large-scale production of the organism itself or products that it may synthesize.

Serological studies Laboratory immunological procedures that depend on interactions between antibodies and antigens to confirm or reject specific associations between them.

Siberian ulcer Russian name for anthrax.

Simulant An innocuous biological or chemical substance or material that can be used in place of a pathogenic or toxic agent in training, research, testing, or evaluation. For biological weapons purposes, it is vital that a simulant approximates the BW agent's aerosol diffusion and viability decay properties.

Spatial resolution A measure of the smallest object on a photo or the smallest interval between two objects that can be precisely determined.

Spore Some bacteria such as members of the genera *Bacillus* and *Clostridium,* possess two distinct morphologies: vegetative cell and spore. Spores are notable because they are extremely hardy, being able to withstand environmental, chemical, and physical stresses that would harm or kill a cell. Spores can be more infectious and pathogenic to animals than vegetative cells.

Synthesis The production of a compound by a living organism.

Technology The scientific and technical information, coupled with know-how, that is used to design, produce, and manufacture products or generate data.

Technology transfer The process of transferring intellectual property (intangible ideas such as algorithms, designs, and software) to organizations, including universities and commercial companies, to ensure that it is well utilized. For successful technology transfer, the intellectual property must be protected through means such as copyrights and patents.

Threat An indication of something impending and that is undesirable or dangerous to an individual, population, or environment.

Toxicity The quality of being poisonous or the degree to which a substance is poisonous.

Toxicology The scientific discipline concerned with the study of toxic chemicals and their effects on living systems.

Toxin A poisonous chemical by-product of microorganisms, animals, or plants.

Toxoid A toxin so modified that it is no longer toxic but is still able to induce antibody formation in a host.

Trait A characteristic that is coded for in the organism's DNA.

Transformation The introduction of new genetic information into a bacterial cell using naked DNA.

Type-classification Identification by US Department of Defense materiel status record action of an item or component to indicate its adoption for military service use. The equivalent term used by the Soviet and Russian MOD is *prinyatie na vooruzhenie*.

Validate In military terminology, validation of a weapons system refers to establishing documented evidence that the system, operated within established parameters, will perform effectively, reliably, and reproducibly to meet its predetermined specifications and attributes.

Vector A transmission agent, usually a plasmid or virus, used to introduce foreign DNA into a host cell.

Verification A policy function related to the process of judging compliance to an arms control treaty.

Virus A usually submicroscopic particle that consists of an RNA or DNA core with a protein coat, sometimes with external envelopes, and that is capable of infecting living organisms. Once a virus has gained entry into a host cell, it is able to subverting that cell's genetic mechanism to ensure its replication. A virus species is a polythetic class of viruses that constitutes a replicating lineage and occupies a particular ecological niche.

Weaponize The process of researching and developing a pathogen or toxin to the point where it becomes suitable for use in a weapons system.

Warhead The part of a bomb, missile, or shell that houses the explosive charge, or in the case of biological or chemical weapons, the pathogenic or toxic agent.

Zoonosis A disease communicable from animals to humans under natural conditions.

Annex C: A Joint Decree of the Central Committee of the Communist Party, USSR, and the USSR Council of Ministers, Dated 24 June 1981

The previous joint decree by the Central Committee of the Communist Party, USSR, and the USSR Council of Ministers in 1974, which called for an acceleration of the development of molecular biology and molecular genetics, has resulted in a certain success of Soviet scientists in the field of modern biology, including those areas mentioned above, as well as in the areas of bioorganic chemistry and immunology.

However, in spite of a certain success in this field, the development of modern biology in the Soviet Union is limited by the relatively small scale of the research, by the rather restricted list of chemicals and biochemicals which are produced industrially in the USSR, by the small selection of sophisticated biochemical equipment needed for modern studies, and by the unsatisfactory development of pilot plants and further scaling-up processes related to biochemical technology.

The Central Committee and the Council of Ministers consider the further development of fundamental studies in the field of physical chemistry of life as one of the most important tasks of Soviet science at the present time, and call for the development of a basis to achieve effective medical measures; production of pharmaceuticals, food and feed; and also the effective selection of crop plants in agriculture by means of using biotechnological methods.

The Academy of Science of the USSR, government ministries and departments, the State Committee of Science and Technology, the USSR Planning Committee (Gosplan) and the Councils of Ministers of National Republics have to provide effective conditions for the rapid development of the modern fields of biological sciences and for the wide use of the respective achievements in agriculture, medicine and industry for the benefit of the Soviet people.

The Central Committee and the Council of Ministers have considered and approved the main directions of fundamental and applied research and development in the fields of physiochemical biology and biotechnology, which were prepared by the USSR Academy of Sciences jointly with related ministries and departments. The State Committee of Science and-Technology has to accept the National Program in Biotechnology.

The supervisory, function in relation to the fundamental and applied research and development in the field of physiochemical biology and biotechnology, the control of those works and the respective co-ordination are assigned officially to the Interdepartmental Council on Physio-Chemical Biology and Biotechnology at the USSR State Committee on Science and Technology and at the Presidium of the USSR Academy of Sciences.

Special attention is focused on the education of graduate and post-graduate students for institutes and other organizations relative to the field of physiochemical biology and biotechnology.

Certain measures are undertaken to provide scientific equipment, computer techniques, chemicals and biochemicals, as well as to improve scientific and technical information for the research organizations working in the area of physiochemical biology and biotechnology.

(This translation of the decree should not be considered to be an exact transliteration.)

Annex D: Joint US/UK/Russian Statement of Biological Weapons

U.S. Department of State
Office of the Assistant Secretary/Spokesman
For Immediate Release
September 14, 1992

Joint US/UK/Russian Statement of Biological Weapons

Senior officials of the governments of the United States and the United Kingdom and the Russian Federation met in Moscow on 10 and 11 September to address concerns with regard to compliance with the 1972 Biological and Toxin Weapons Convention. The U.S. delegation was led by Under Secretary of State Frank G. Wisner, the United Kingdom delegation by Assistant Under Secretary of State Paul Lever, and the Russian Delegation was headed by the Deputy Foreign Minister Grigory Berdennikov. Senior Defense, Foreign Affairs, and other relevant officials also participated. The leaders of the United States and the U.K. delegations were received by the Russian Foreign Minister Andrei Kozyrev.

The three governments confirmed their commitment to full compliance with the Biological Weapons Convention and stated their agreement that biological weapons have no place in their armed forces.

During these meetings, the Russian government stated that it had taken the following steps to resolve compliance concerns:

A. Noted that President Yeltsin had issued on 11 April, 1992, a decree on securing the fulfillment of international obligations in the area of biological weapons. This affirms the legal succession of the Russian Federation to the obligations of the convention and states that the development and carrying out of biological programs in violation of the convention is illegal. Pursuant to that decree, the Presidential committee on convention related problems of chemical weapons and biological weapons was entrusted with the oversight of the implementation of the 1972 BWC in the Russian Federation.

B. Confirmed the termination of offensive research, the dismantlement of experimental technological lines for the production of biological agents, and the closure of the biological weapons testing facility.

C. Cut the number of personnel involved in military biological programs by fifty percent.

D. Reduced military biological research funding by thirty percent.

E. Dissolved the department in the MOD responsible for the offensive biological program and created a new department for radiological, biological and chemical defense.

F. Submitted the declaration to the United Nations under the terms of the confidence-building measures agreed at the BWC Third Review Conference in 1991.

G. President Yeltsin has ordered the conduct of an investigation into activities at the Institute of Ultrapure Biological Preparations at St. Petersburg, in response to concerns raised by the U.S. and the U.K. U.S., U.K. and other experts are invited to take part in the investigation, including a prompt visit to this facility, and the report will be made public.

H. The Russian Parliament has recommended to the President of the Russian Federation that he propose legislation to enforce Russia's obligations under the 1972 BWC.

As a result of these exchanges Russia has agreed to the following steps:

A. Visits to any non-military biological site at any time in order to remove ambiguities, subject to the need to respect proprietary information on the basis of agreed principles. Such visits would include unrestricted access, sampling, interviews with personnel, and audio and video taping. After initial visits to Russian facilities there will be comparable visits to such U.S. and U.K. facilities on the same basis.

B. The provision, on request, or information about dismantlement accomplished to date.

C. The provision of further clarification of information provided for in form F of its U.N. Declaration.

D. Prominent independent scientists will be invited to participate in the investigation of cases concerning compliance with the biological weapons convention.

In addition, the three governments agreed to create working groups, including experts, to address the following:

A. Visits to any military biological facility, on a reciprocal basis, in order to remove ambiguities, subject to the need to respect confidential information on the basis of agreed principles. Such visits would include unrestricted access, sampling, interviews with personnel, and audio and video taping.

B. A review of potential measures to monitor compliance with The Biological Weapons Convention and to enhance confidence in that compliance.

C. A review of potential modalities for testing such measures.

D. An examination of the physical infrastructure of biological facilities in the three countries to determine jointly whether there is specific equipment or excess capacity inconsistent with their stated purpose.

E. Consideration of cooperation in developing biological weapon defense.

F. Examination of ways to promote cooperation and investment in the conversion of biological weapons facilities, including visits to already converted facilities.

G. Consideration of an exchange of information on a confidential, reciprocal basis concerning past offensive programs not recorded in detail in the declarations to the U.N.

H. The provision of periodic reports to their legislatures and public describing biological research and development activities.

I. The encouragement of exchanges of scientists at biological facilities on a long-term basis.

Notes

Preface

Epigraphs: J. D. Bernal, "Speech Delivered at the Conference of the Soviet Partisans of Peace, in Moscow, August 27, 1949," *Science and Mankind* 2 (August 1949): 64–67; "Data for National Science Lecture, Atomic Power Series no. 7," Propaganda Department, Cultural Training Bureau, Democratic People's Republic of Korea, 1950; Oleg Bogdanov, *Stop the Arms Race Now* (Moscow, 1973), 39–40; V. N. Orlov, ed., *We Defended Russia* (in Russian) (Moscow, 2000); Valentin I. Yevstigneev, "Biological Weapons and Problems of Ensuring Biological Security" (in Russian), lecture at the Moscow Institute of Physics and Technology, April 4, 2003.

1. As of March 2012, 176 nations had signed the BWC, out of which 165 had also ratified the treaty.

2. "Weaponize" is the process of carrying out research and development with a pathogen to the point where it becomes suitable for use in a weapons system.

3. A. A. Baev, "Current Trends in Molecular Genetics: Genetic Engineering" (in Russian), *Vestnik Rossiyskoy Akademii Meditsinskikh Nauk* no. 7 (1976): 16–18.

4. V. D. Timakov and V. M. Zhdanov, "The Genetics of Microorganisms" (in Russian), *Vestnik Rossiyskoy Akademii Meditsinskikh Nauk* no. 7 (1976): 27. The 24th Congress of the Communist Party of the USSR was held between March 30 and April 8, 1971.

5. USSR Council of Ministers' Resolution 556, "Instructions for Maintaining the Regime of Secrecy in Ministries, Register Lists, Enterprises and Institutions, and Organizations of the USSR" (in Russian), approved on May 12, 1987. This resolution is classified and has to date not been published. According to one of our high-placed sources, who cannot be identified, Resolution 556 was replaced by a similar Russian resolution in 1992, which also is classified.

6. Murray Feshbach and Alfred Friendly Jr., *Ecocide in the USSR* (New York, 1992), 283.

7. Anders Åslund, "How Small Is the Soviet National Income?," in *The Impoverished Superpower: Perestroika and the Soviet Military Burden,* ed. Henry S. Rowen and Charles Wolf Jr. (San Francisco, 1998), 13–61, 288–305.

8. Ken Alibek with Stephen Handelman, *Biohazard: The Chilling True Story of the Largest Covert Biological Weapons Program in the World—Told from Inside by the Man Who Ran It* (New York, 1999), 43.

Introduction

1. Robert S. Norris and Hans M. Kristensen, "Global Nuclear Weapon Inventories, 1945–2010," *Bulletin of the Atomic Scientists* 66, no. 4 (July–August 2010): 77–83.

2. Lysenko was an agronomist who repudiated Mendelian genetics and instead followed the Lamarckian notion that structural changes in animals and plants brought about by environmental or agricultural forces are transmitted to offspring. This notion fitted Soviet ideology concerning how society can be changed, and it was adopted as state dogma, avowed by Stalin and Khrushchev. This had negative long-term effects on the biological sciences, because once discoveries made clear that genetic characteristics depended on information carried by DNA, Lysenkoists had to also repudiate these discoveries. For this reason, modern biotechnology had a slow start in the Soviet Union, not becoming a priority research subject until 1967.

3. In September 2001, the Russian press reported that the 1996 edict forbidding the divulging of pre-1992 secrets had been repealed by the Russian Supreme Court. We are unable to assess the practical results of this action. We believe that in practice the same restrictions apply now as before 2001. See note 5 below.

4. Our correspondence with Igor V. Domaradsky continued until just before his death on February 8, 2009.

5. A Council of Ministers decree that was issued on March 30, 1993, and signed by Prime Minister Viktor Chernomyrdin states that "information revealing the contents of work in the field of chemical or biological weapons conducted before or the essence of those works, results of the work achieved, information on formulas, recipes, technology of manufacturing or equipment of these devices" was to be added to the Temporary List of Pieces of Information of States Secrecy, which was adopted on September 18, 1992, by resolution of the Russian government no. 733–55. Both decrees are classified. Under these decrees, merely mentioning a secret program is sufficient cause to be arrested for "divulging state secrets." Quoted from Gale Colby and Irene Goldman, "When Will Russia Abandon Its Secret Chemical Weapons Program?," *Demokratizatsiya* 2, no. 1 (Winter 1994): 151.

6. After the international scientific community rallied to his cause, Mirzayanov's case was dismissed by decree on March 11, 1994, because of lack of evidence.

7. Ken Alibek with Stephen Handelman, *Biohazard: The Chilling True Story of the Largest Covert Biological Weapons Program in the World—Told from Inside by the Man Who Ran It* (New York, 1999).

8. Igor V. Domaradsky, *Troublemaker, or The Story of an "Inconvenient" Man* (in Russian), (Moscow, 1995). With English language and editing assistance from US author Wendy Orent, an expanded and updated version of this book is available in English; see Igor V. Domaradskij and Wendy Orent, *Biowarrior: Inside the Soviet/Russian Biological War Machine* (Amherst, N.Y., 2003).

9. Igor V. Domaradsky, "The History of One Risky Venture. Part I" (in Russian), *Snanie-Zila* (November 1996), 60–72; Igor V. Domaradsky, "The History of One Risky Venture. Part II" (in Russian), *Snanie-Zila* (December 1996), 54–64.

10. The *Ekologiya* program developed several types of viruses, bacteria, and fungi that were targeted to destroy animals and plants important to US agriculture. For animals, there were agents that caused diseases such as foot-and-mouth disease, African swine fever, and goatpox and sheeppox; for plants there were pathogens that attacked wheat, rye, and potatoes. Some information about Ministry of Agriculture institutes and their BW-related work appears in Chapter 16. To learn more about *Ekologiya*, see Anthony Rimmington, *Anti-Livestock and Anti-Crop Offensive Biological Warfare Programmes in Russia and the Newly Independent Republics*, Centre for Russian and East European Studies, University of Birmingham, June 1999.

1. The Soviet Union's Biological Warfare Program, 1918–1972

1. Hereafter, "Kirov Institute."

2. I. V. Darmov, I. P. Pogorelsky, and V. N. Velikanov, "To the Scientific-Research Institute of Microbiology of the Russian Federation Ministry of Defense at 70 years" (in Russian), *Voyenno Meditsinskiy Zhurnal* 18 (1999): 79–64.

3. Valentin Bojtzov and Erhard Geissler, "Military Biology in the USSR, 1920–45," in *Biological and Toxin Weapons: Research, Development and Use from the Middle Ages to 1945*, ed. Erhard Geissler and John E. van Courtland Moon, 153–167 (New York, 1999).

4. Hirsch was chief of Wa-prüf 9, which was the chemical research division of the Wehrmacht Ordnance Office; Kliewe served in section IIIc of the research division of the Surgeon General's Office (SJN/WiG/IIIc) and also in group VIIc, which was the weapons testing division of Wa-Prüf 9.

5. V. N. Orlov, ed., *We Defended Russia* (in Russian) (Moscow, 2000).

6. Ken Alibek with Stephen Handelman, *Biohazard: The Chilling True Story of the Largest Covert Biological Weapons Program in the World—Told from Inside by the Man Who Ran It* (New York, 1999).

7. Alfredo Morabia, " 'East Side Story': On Being an Epidemiologist in the Former USSR—An Interview with Marcus Klingberg," *Epidemiology* 17, no. 1 (2006): 115.

8. Ibid.

9. Bojtzov and Geissler, 1999. According to H. L. Gilchrist, chemical weapons killed 56,000 and wounded 419,340 Russians in World War I; see H. L. Gilchrist, *A Comparative Study of World War Casualties from Gas and Other Weapons* (Washington, D.C., 1928). Conversely, the Germans almost certainly employed biological weapons against the Allies; see Mark Wheelis, "Biological Sabotage during World War I," in Geissler and van Courtland Moon, 1999, 35–62.

10. We do not know when exactly this laboratory was built, but believe it came into existence in 1928 because of the celebration of, as noted above, the 70th anniversary of the Kirov Institute, which eventually grew out of this effort.

11. Article 61 of the new USSR constitution gave the OGPU the responsibility "to unite the revolutionary efforts of the Union Republics in the struggle against political and economic counter-revolution, espionage, and banditism." See Simon Wolin and Robert M. Slusser, "The Evolution of the Soviet Secret Police," in *The Soviet Secret Police,* ed. Wolin and Slusser (New York, 1957), 10.

12. Hirsch did not know the name of this facility. It was named in an article published in 1992; see A. Pasternak and O. Rubnikovich, "The Secret of Pokrovsky Monastery: Who Began Developing Bacteriological Weapons in the USSR, and When Did They Do So?" (in Russian), *Nezavisimaya Gazeta,* November 17, 1992.

13. Walter Hirsch, *Soviet BW and CW Preparations and Capabilities* ("The Hirsch Report") (Edgewood, Md., 1951).

14. Pasternak and Rubnikovich, 1992.

15. This person might have been M. M. Faybich, who later was recognized for his work in developing various vaccines.

16. These chemicals are common disinfectants that were found in most microbiological laboratories.

17. The two reporters who interviewed Parchina wrote that not all details of her story could be corroborated, particularly the parts dealing with human subjects. However, they also found that people who still live in the area, some of whom worked for the Special Purpose Bureau, are afraid to talk about the work that was done at the monastery and, possibly, some of them have been "coached" to discredit her testimony.

18. Bojtzov and Geissler, 1999. Also, there was an agreement signed in 1923 between the Soviet and German governments to establish a chemical plant, ostensibly for the manufacture of "superphosphates" for use as chemical fertilizer, but actually to produce the CW agents mustard and phosgene. In 1936 this plant, called Bersol, was already producing 4 tons of mustard daily. Most important, Bersol became the manufacturing basis for the Soviet CW program. See V. Zakharov and N. Yeliseyeva, "The Mystery of Bersol," *Soviet Soldier* (December 1991): 34–36.

19. Although BW and CW have often been linked, especially in international law, the entities are quite different in their characteristics and military utility. In the highly compartmentalized Soviet system, different departments were responsible for these two weapon systems and, as far as we are aware, there was very little interchange between them.

20. In fact, only France had an active BW program before 1930; Olivier Lepick, "French Activities Related to Biological Warfare, 1919–45," in Geissler and van Courtland Moon, 1999, 70–90.

21. Rimmington asserts that the "Military-Medical Institute" was created on April 10, 1930. He further states that it was renamed the "Red Army's Scientific-Research Experimental Medical Institute (or NIISI for short)" at some unspecified date. The latter, he believes, was eventually absorbed by the Kirov Military Medical Academy; see Anthony Rimmington, "Fragmentation and Proliferation? The Fate of the Soviet Union's Offensive Biological Weapons Programme," *Contemporary Security Policy* 20, no. 1 (April 1999): 86–110.

22. Order No. 2 of 1933 by the Revolutionary Military Council of the USSR (*Revvoensovet*).

23. The identities of the institute's directors over the years have been named by Orlov (2000). They were: I. F. Velikanov (1928–1937); from 1937–1939, when Stalin's purges were in full swing, there were three directors, L. M. Khatenever, N. A. Spitsyn, and A. A. Dorofeev; then N. F. Kopylov (1939–1940); N. I. Nikolayev (1949–1951); V. D. Neustroev (1951–1955); P. A. Ogurtsov (1955–1957); V. V. Skvortsov (1957–1973); V. N. Pautov (1973–1984); T. G. Abdullin (1984–1991); and Yevgeny V. Pimenov (1991–?).

24. Hirsch (1951) states that its code designation was Section V/2–1049.

25. The pathogen that causes plague was then called *Pasteurella pestis*. In 1944, it was proposed to change this name to *Yersinia pestis,* after its discoverer André Yersin. The name change became official in 1980. We use only the second hereafter. Further, following common scientific convention, we spell out the genera and species of microorganisms the first time they are named, but shorten them thereafter (for example, *Yersinia pestis* is shortened to *Y. pestis*).

26. Igor V. Domaradskij and Wendy Orent, *Biowarrior: Inside the Soviet/Russian Biological War Machine* (Amherst, N.Y., 2003). In the era before antibiotics, most people who contracted plague died.

27. Bojtzov and Geissler, 1999, 156–157.

28. Ibid.

29. Alibek with Handelman, 1999, 33.

30. The bacterium *B. anthracis* causes the disease called anthrax.

31. The bacterium *Crostridium botulinum* produces the most toxic substance in the world, botulinum neurotoxin (BoNT), which causes botulism.

32. The bacterium *Vibriocholerae* causes cholera.

33. Alibek changed his name after defecting from the Soviet Union in October 1992. His previous name was Kanatzhan Bayzakovich Alibekov.

34. Biopreparat was the ostensibly civilian facility dedicated to developing biological weapons after 1972; see Chapter 2.

35. The current name for the pathogen that causes endemic typhus is *Rickettsia typhi*.

36. Technical terms used in relation to biological weapons, such as"formulation," are defined in the Glossary and also explained in Chapter 10.

37. J. W. Barnes, C. Henze, W. J. Cromartie, and J. W. Hofer, *ALSOS Mission, Intelligence Report*, B-C-H-H/305 (Washington, D.C., 1945).

38. Kliewe made a mistake here; the last-named is not actually located in the Moscow region.

39. Possibly Fort Alexander I, which once was the home of a plague laboratory.

40. *Narodny Komissariat Vnutrennikh Del*, or People's Commissariat of Internal Affairs, was OGPU's successor and, accordingly, had the same responsibilities and powers.

41. A third island, Kugali Island in the Caspian Sea, might also have been a test site (see Chapter 12).

42. Hirsch, 1951.

43. We have information indicating that the Foot and Mouth Diseases Institute, operating under the auspices of the People's Commissariat of Agriculture, was established in 1932 on Gorodomlya Island. It was later renamed the Velikanov Institute and transferred to the authority of the Commissariat of Defense. This institute may have begun the first R&D on offensive biological weapons directed against animals.

44. Bojtzov and Geissler, 1999. Both Fishman and Ginsburg survived their imprisonment. Fishman was released in 1954, reinstated in the military, and died at the age of 75 with the rank of major general (ibid.). Ginsburg was released on an unknown date, retired from the Army with the rank of colonel of the medical service, then became director of the *Bacillus anthracis* laboratory at the Central Anti-plague Station in Moscow. He died on June 9, 1969, a day after completing the editing work for the monograph *Sibirskaya Yazva* (Anthrax), which was published in Moscow in 1975; see B. L. Cherkassky, *"Nikolay Nikolayevich Ginsburg: Developer of the STI Anthrax Vaccine"* (in Russian), in *Interesting Stories about the Activities and People of the Anti-Plague System of Russia and the Soviet Union* (in Russian), vol. 6 (Moscow, 1997), 211–226.

45. Igor V. Domaradsky, "Proscriptions" (in Russian), in *Interesting Stories About the Activities and People of the Anti-Plague System of Russia and the Soviet Union* (in Russian), vol. 3 (Moscow, 1994), 256–260.

46. Aleksandr I. Solzhenitsyn, *The First Circle* (New York, 1968).

47. Gaysky was the inventor of the Gaysky Live Vaccine, which is a preparation of *F. tularensis holarctica,* Strain 15; newer versions of this vaccine are still in use in the former Soviet Union.

48. W. Duranty, "Soviet Threatens to Use Gas in War," *New York Times,* February 23, 1938 (quoted in Stockholm International Peace Research Institute, *The Problem of Chemical and Biological Warfare.* Vol. 1, *The Rise of CB Weapons* (New York, 1971), 287.

49. Kei'ichi Tsuneishi, *The Germ Warfare Unit That Disappeared: The Kwantung Army's 731st Unit* (Tokyo, 1982); Peter Williams and David Wallace, *Unit 731: The Japanese Army's Secret of Secrets* (London, 1989); and Sheldon Harris, *Factories of Death: Japanese Biological Warfare, 1932–45, and the American Cover Up* (New York, 1994).

50. Lepick, 1999, 70–90.

51. Gradon B. Carter and Graham Pearson, "British Biological Warfare and Biological Defence, 1925–45," in Geissler and van Courtland Moon, 1999, 168–189.

52. Donald Avery, "Canadian Biological and Toxin Warfare Research, Development and Planning, 1925–45," in Geissler and van Courtland Moon, 1999, 190–214.

53. John van Courtland Moon, "US Biological Warfare Planning and Preparedness: The Dilemmas of Policy," in Geissler and van Courtland Moon, 1999, 215–254.

54. Erhard Geissler, "Biological Warfare Activities in Germany 1923–45," in Geissler and van Courtland Moon, 1999, 91–126.

55. Geissler and van Courtland Moon, 1999.

56. Ibid.

57. Orlov, 2000.

58. Igor Domaradsky, personal communication, 1999.

59. The term "recipe" refers to the written procedures followed by weapon scientists to research, develop, test, and produce a particular pathogen for weapons use (see Glossary and Chapter 10).

60. Orlov, 2000.

61. E. N. Shlyakhov and E. Rubinstein, "Human Live Anthrax Vaccine in the Former USSR," *Vaccine* 12, no. 8 (1994): 727–730; and Orlov, 2000.

62. Orlov, 2000.

63. It was the custom in the Soviet Union, and in other countries, to name an important strain after the institute where it was first developed.

64. Scarification involves the injection of the vaccine by puncturing the outermost layer of the skin (epidermis) with a needle, but without drawing more than a minimum of blood. This causes a local infection that stimulates antibody production by the immunological defense system of the recipient of the vaccine.

65. Orlov, 2000.

66. Shlyakhov and Rubinstein, 1994.

67. NIIEG is the Russian acronym for the Scientific Research Institute for Epidemiology and Hygiene, which was the name of the Medical-Technical Institute after 1942.

68. V. A. Lebedinsky, T. G. Abdullin, V. I. Yevstigneev, N. S. Garin, and Ye. P. Lukin, "Contribution Made by the Scientific Research Institute of Microbiology of the USSR Ministry of Defence to Research into the Problems of Infective Immunology" (in Russian), *Voenno-Meditsinskiy Zhurnal* 8 (1989): 67–71; and Orlov, 2000.

69. Work to improve the plague vaccine continued after the war. A team led by two military scientists, V. A. Lebedinsky and V. I. Ogarkov, is said to have developed a small-particle aerosol form of the dry EV vaccine that was administered by inhalation and showed marked advantage over all other vaccines in preventing pulmonary plague; see N. I. Nikolayev, "History of Development of Plague Prevention in the USSR" (in Russian), *Zhurnal Mikrobiologii, Epidemiologii i Immunobiologii,* no. 4 (1979): 110–115; and Orlov, 2000. As is described both of these military scientists became major figures in the Soviet BW program of the 1970s and 1980s.

70. Orlov, 2000.

71. Ibid.

72. Alibek with Handelman, 1999, 29–31; Eric Croddy, "Tularemia, Biological Warfare, and the Battle for Stalingrad (1942–1943)," *Military Medicine* 166, no. 10 (2001): 837–838; Erhard Geissler, "Alibek, Tularaemia and the Battle of Stalingrad," *The CBW Conventions,* nos. 69–70 (2005): 10–15.

73. Alibek with Handelman, 1999, 30.

74. Ibid., 31.

75. Alibek also makes the point that the Soviet high command learned something vital from this episode, namely, never to use a biological weapon in such a way that it could affect its own troops. After this, the strategy of the Soviet high command was to consider the use of biological weapons only for use against "deep targets," so far behind enemy lines that they could not possibly lash back at Soviet forces.

76. Natalya Yeliseyeva, "Rats of Mass Destruction: Americans Consider Tularemia a Biological Weapon, Russians Consider It a Disease that Is Treatable with Very Simple Antibiotics" (in Russian), *Moscow Strana.ru* (January 12, 2005).

77. Croddy, 2001, 838.

78. Robert Pollitzer, *History and Incidence of Tularemia in the Soviet Union: A Review* (Bronx, N.Y., 1967).

79. V. I. Agafonov and R. A. Tararin, "Some Organizational-Tactical Forms and Methods of Anti-Epidemiological Work in Troops of Stalingrad (Don) Front in 1942–43" (in Russian), *Zhurnal Mikrobiologii, Epidemiologii i Immunobiologii* 47,

no. 5 (May 1970): 6. This article and the Rogozin article cited next treat the tularemia outbreak as a natural one.

80. Quoted in I. I. Rogozin, "Prophylaxis of Tularemia during the Great Patriotic War" (in Russian), *Zhurnal Mikrobiologii, Epidemiologii i Immunobiologii* 47, no. 5 (May 1970): 23.

81. E. I. Smirnov, V. A. Lebedinsky, and N. S. Garin, *Wars and Epidemics* (in Russian) (Moscow, 1988), 122.

82. Igor Domaradsky, personal communication, 2001.

83. V. I. Agafonov and V. S. Perepelkin, "Experience in Protecting Troops against Epidemics during the Years of World War II" (in Russian), *Voenno-Meditsinskiy Zhurnal,* no. 5 (May 1985): 55.

84. "Validated" means that the agent has been weaponized to the point where it performs effectively, reliably, and reproducibly to meet its predetermined specifications and attributes (see Glossary and Chapter 10).

85. Morabia, 2006, 117.

86. M. A. Klingberg, "An Epidemiologist's Journey from Typhus to Thalidomide, and from the Soviet Union to Seveso," *JLL Bulletin: Commentaries on the History of Treatment Evaluation* (2010), http://www.jameslinglibrary.org.

87. Henry E. Sigerist, *Civilization and Disease* (Chicago, 1970), 122.

88. The term "Red Army" was discontinued in 1946, becoming "Soviet Army."

89. J. Hrušková, L. Daneš, and V. Klement, "Venezuelan Equine Encephalomyelitis Virus: Determination of Inhalation LD_{50} for Guinea Pigs and Mice," *Acta Virologica* 13 (1969): 202–209.

90. N. G. Olsufiev, O. S. Yemelyanova, and T. N. Dunayeva, "Comparative Study of Strains of *B. tularense* in the Old and New World and Their Taxonomy" (in Russian), *Zhurnal Mikrobiologii, Epidemiologii i Immunobiologii* 3 (1959): 138–149.

91. Ibid.

92. In an odd turnaround, in the 1950s the Soviets gave the United States some *F. tularensis* vaccine strains, one of which was developed by American scientists as the live vaccine strain (LVS). Although research and clinical studies by investigators at the US Army Medical Research Institute of Infectious Diseases evidenced that LVS vaccine was safe and efficient, it was never licensed in the United States; see Richard W. Titball and Anders Sjöstedt, "*Francisella tularensis:* An Overview," *ASM News* 69, no. 11 (November 2003): 562.

93. Ibid.

94. The case-fatality rate associated with natural tularemia is low, but weaponized *F. tularensis* dispersed as aerosol was a different story. According to Alibek, he was responsible for having developed a "lethal" weapon strain; i.e., a strain that when used against monkeys vaccinated against tularemia in open-air tests caused nearly all monkeys to die; Alibek with Handelman, 1999, 27.

95. See, in particular, four books: Union of Soviet Socialist Republics, *Materials on the Trial of Former Servicemen of the Japanese Army Charged with Manufacturing and Employing Bacteriological Weapons* (Moscow, 1950); Sheldon Harris, *Factories of Death* (New York, 1994); Tom Mangold and Jeff Goldberg, *Plague Wars: The Terrifying Reality of Biological Warfare* (New York, 1999); and James Yin, *The Rape of Biological Warfare: Japanese Carnage in Asia During World War II* (San Francisco, 2002).

96. Union of Soviet Socialist Republics, 1950, 7.

97. A Soviet scientist, Yelizaveta G. Livkina, who had an important role for the prosecution as an expert witness, has described details of trial proceedings and impressions of the defendants in a book; see Nikolay A. Ivanov and Vladislav V. Bogach, *Oruzhie Vne Zakona (Outlaw Weapon),* Khabarovsk Knizhnoe Izdatelstvo, 1989.

98. Boris G. Yudin, "A Historical and Ethical Examination of the Khabarovsk War Crimes Trial," *Knowledge. Understanding. Skill Journal* (February 21, 2008), http://www.zpu-journal.ru/en/articles/detail.php?ID=278.

99. Ibid.

100. A. S. Zakharov, "From the History of the Siberian Military District's State Public Health and Epidemiological Surveillance Center" (in Russian), *Voenno-Meditsinskiy Zhurnal* (September 30, 2002): 64.

101. V. V. Tomilin and R. V. Berezhnov, "Exposure of the Criminal Activities of the Japanese Militarists in Preparation for the Use of Bacteriological Warfare" (in Russian), *Voenno-Meditsinskiy Zhurnal,* no. 2 (September 1985): 28.

102. We say "presumably" because although we do not know for certain that this was the case, this agency was the predecessor of the 15th Directorate, which we know was in charge of the modern Soviet BW program.

103. "A High Reward" (in Russian), *Voenno-Meditsinskiy Zhurnal,* no. 4 (1978): 80–82.

104. T. F. Safonova and R. N. Lukina, "Ye. I. Smirnov: Creator of the System to Protect the Country against Epidemics during Emergencies," in *The 50 Years of the Ministry of Defense's Virology Center Deserve Recognition,* ed. Roza N. Lukina and Yevgeny P. Lukin (in Russian) (Sergiev Posad, 2004), 82.

105. The horrific but fascinating story of the "doctors-poisoners," including Smirnov's minor role, has been told by Jonathan Brent and Vladimir Naumov, *Stalin's Last Crime: The Plot against the Jewish Doctors, 1948–1953* (New York, 2004).

106. The Kirov Institute, like all closed Soviet facilities, had secret names that were changed over the years. We know just two of these names but do not know when they were in active use: Scientific Research Institute 48 (NII-48 [TsNII-48]) and Kirov-24.

107. Lukina and Lukin, 2004, 68.

108. Theodor Rosebury and Elvin A. Kabat, "Bacterial Warfare," *Journal of Immunology* 56 (1947): 7–96.

109. Theodor Rosebury, *Peace or Pestilence: Biological Warfare and How to Avoid It* (New York, 1949).

110. Union of Soviet Socialist Republics, 1950.

111. Quoted in Lukina and Lukin, 2004, 69.

112. Orlov, 2000. In a top-secret Central Committee document, this institute is called "USSR Defense Ministry Scientific Research Institute 44 (NII 44)."

113. The heads of the institute were as follows: N. F. Kopylov (1949–1952), Ye. I. Polosin (1952–1953), Yu. M. Volynkin (1954–1958), N. I. Nikolayev (1958–1960), V. N. Pavlovsky (1960–1969), I. I. Subbotin (1969), V. I. Ogarkov (1969–1973), V. V. Mikhaylov (1973–1980), V. Ya. Tereshchatov (1980–1987), and A. T. Kharechko (1987–?).

114. Lukina and Lukin, 2004, 69.

115. In the early 1980s, the US government accused the North Vietnamese of having used mycotoxins against the Hmong tribes as a weapon of terror and genocide. Furthermore, the Soviet Union was alleged to have supplied these toxins in contravention to international law. For an informed discussion on this subject, see Lisa D. Harris, "Sverdlovsk and Yellow Rain: Two Cases of Soviet Noncompliance?," *International Security* 11 (1987): 41–95.

116. We recognize that BoNT is a chemical and therefore technically is not a BW agent. In fact, after the Chemical Weapons Convention entered into force in 1997, all toxins fall under its purview. However, because BoNT was weaponized by both the US and the Soviet BW programs, and because it was covered by the BWC during 1975–1997, in this book we treat it as a BW agent.

117. Stephen S. Arnon et al., "Botulinum Neurotoxin as a Biological Weapon: Medical and Public Health Management," *Journal of the American Medical Association* 285 (2001): 1059–1070.

118. "Validating" refers to establishing documented evidence that an agent, used within established parameters, will perform effectively, reliably, and reproducibly to meet its predetermined specifications and attributes. Of the seven validated US biological weapons systems, four were based on bacteria *(Bacillus anthracis, Brucella suis, Coxiella burnetii, and Francisella tularensis),* one on a virus (VEEV), and two on toxins (BoNT A and staphylococcus enterotoxin B).

119. William C. Patrick III, "Analysis of Botulinum Neurotoxin, Type A, as a Biological Warfare Threat," unpublished study, May 1, 1998.

120. There are seven serotypes of BoNT, named A through G. Only serotypes A and B have so far been used for therapeutic and cosmetic purposes, but all serotypes can cause botulism.

121. Andrey Semenov, "Was There Anthrax in Sverdlovsk-19? Only President Boris Yeltsin and Our Interviewee, RAMS Academician Petr Burgasov, Know This Mystery" (in Russian), *Meditsinskaya Gazeta*, June 24, 1998, 4.

122. Lukina and Lukin, 2004, 147.

123. We have seen claims that the Zagorsk Institute researched *Burkholderia pseudomallei* (which causes glanders) and *Burkholderia mallei* (causes melioidosis), but have found no evidence to support these claims.

124. Evgeniya Kvitko, "Interview with Petr N. Burgasov: Smallpox - Also Not a Bad Weapon" (in Russian), *Moscovskie Novosti,* November 3, 2001; http://kungrad .com/aral/island/ospa/.

125. If the Soviet government had indeed done what Burgasov claims was done, the most likely method would have been to secretly include a formulation of botulinum toxoid in vials containing combination vaccines (such as the DTP vaccine) routinely administered to all young children. (We thank Dr. Stephen S. Arnon for this suggestion.)

126. Nikolay I. Aleksandrov and Nina Ye. Gefen, *Active Specific Prophylaxis of Infectious Diseases and Ways of Improvement* (in Russian), *Voennoe Izdatelstvo,* Soviet Ministry of Defense, Moscow, 1962.

127. Vorobyov was a highly regarded, high-ranking military scientist who will reappear in subsequent pages.

128. Defence Intelligence Staff, Directorate of Scientific and Technical Intelligence, *Soviet Studies on Botulinum Toxin,* DSTI Report No. 301, Ministry of Defence, London, August 1968 (Secret).

129. Ibid., para. 44.

130. V. I. Ogarkov and K. G. Gapochko, *Aerogenic Infection* (in Russian) (Moscow, 1975); and K. G. Gapochko, O. P. Misnikov, and K. K. Raevsky, *Methods and Resources for the Study of Microbial Aerosols* (in Russian) (Leningrad, 1985).

131. Gulbarshyn Bozheyeva, Yerlan Kunakbayev, and Dastan Yeleukenov, *Former Soviet Biological Weapons Facilities in Kazakhstan: Past, Present and Future,* CNS Occasional Paper No. 1 (Center for Nonproliferation Studies, Monterey, Calif., 1999), http://cns.miis.edu/pubs/opapers/op1/index.htm.

132. It is interesting to note that the Soviets might also have been the recipients of intelligence indicating that Western nations, including France, the United Kingdom, and the United States, were busy developing biological weapons; see Orlov, 2000, and Bojtzov and Geissler, 1999.

133. *Informatsionni Sbornik,* January 1941; quoted in Hirsch, 1951, 101.

134. Tomilin and Berezhnov, 1985.

135. Jacquard H. Rothschild, "Germs and Gas: The Weapons Nobody Dares Talk About," *Harper's Magazine* 218 (1959): 29–34; and Jacquard H. Rothschild, *Tomorrow's Weapons: Chemical and Biological* (New York, 1964).

136. George W. Merck, "Biological Warfare: Report to the Secretary of War by George W. Merck, Special Consultant for Biological Warfare, January 3, 1946," *Military Surgeon,* no. 98 (1946): 237–242.

137. A. M. Arkhangelsky, A. M. Kamorsky, and I. D. Nuzhdin, *Bacteriological Weapons and How to Defend against Them* (in Russian) (Moscow, 1967); and L. A.

Belikov, *The Bacteriological Weapon and Methods of Protection from It* (in Russian) (Moscow, 1960).

138. Igor Domaradsky, personal communication, 1999.

139. Raymond L. Garthoff, "Polyakov's Run," *Bulletin of the Atomic Scientists* 56, no. 5 (September/October 2000): 38.

140. Theodor Rosebury, "The Fuller Utilization of Scientific Resources for Total War," *Science*, 96:2504 (December 25, 1942): 571–575.

141. Theodor Rosebury and Elvin A. Kabat, with the assistance of Martin H. Boldt, "Bacterial Warfare, A Critical Analysis of the Available Agents, Their Possible Military Applications, and the Means for Protection Against Them," *Journal of Immunology* 55:1 (May 1947): 7–96.

142. United States Department of State, "Soviet International Fronts," August 1983, 4 pages; "International Communist Front Organizations," *CIA Report on Soviet Propaganda Operations*, reproduced in House of Representatives, Subcommittee on Oversight of the Permanent Select Committee on Intelligence, Hearings: *CIA and the Media*, Washington, DC: US Government Printing Office, 1978, pp. 621–624.

143. Henry DeWolf Smyth, *A General Account of the Development of Methods of Using Atomic Energy for Military Purposes Under the Auspices of the United States Government, 1940–1945*, Washington, DC: US Government Printing Office, 1945, and Henry DeWolf Smyth, *Atomic Energy for Military Purposes. The Official Report on the Development of the Atomic Bomb under the Auspices of the United States Government, 1940–1945*, Princeton, NJ: Princeton University Press, 1946.

144. Additional information about the Bush-Conant initiatives and Rosebury's efforts to provide public information about biological weapons is available from the authors upon request.

2. Beginnings of the "Modern" Soviet BW program, 1970–1977

1. Igor Domaradsky, personal communication, 2001.

2. The subheading is taken directly from the title of one of a series of six insightful articles written by William Kucewicz and published in the *Wall Street Journal* during April–May 1984; see William Kucewicz, "Lead Scientist in a Scourge Search," *Wall Street Journal,* May 1, 1984, 34.

3. V. T. Ivanov, ed., *Yu. A. Ovchinnikov, Selected Works: Chemistry of Life* (in Russian) (Moscow, 1990); and M. M. Shemyakin Institute of Bioorganic Chemistry, *Yury A. Ovchinnikov: Life and Scientific Activity* (in Russian) (Moscow, 1991).

4. See Table 2.1 for a listing of Soviet and Russian higher academic degrees and comparisons with US academic degrees.

5. Yury A. Ovchinnikov, "Biotechnology in the Forefront of Scientific-Technical Progress" (in Russian), *Kommunist* (July 1985): 20.

Table 2.1   Comparison of US, Soviet, and Russian Academic Degrees

United States	Soviet Union	Russia
BA/BS (4 years)	*Spetsialist* Diploma (ca. 5 years)	Level 2—*Bakalavr* (Baccalaureate) 4 years
MA/MS (1–2 years + thesis)		Level 3—*Magistr* (Master's) 2 years
PhD/ScD (3 years + dissertation)	*Kandidat Nauk*[a] • usually translated as "Candidate of Science" • awarded in scientific and professional disciplines	*Kandidat Nauk*
Higher than PhD = "Distinguished Professor"	*Doctor Nauk*[b] • usually translated as "Doctor of Science" • awarded in scientific disciplines only	*Doctor Nauk*
MD	*Vrach*[c]	*Vrach*

Source: Table developed by James W. Toppin, July 2005. Russian terms as recommended by the UNESCO European Center.

a. The *Kandidat Nauk* degree was introduced in Russia (USSR) in 1934. It is awarded to those who have completed graduate-level studies (usually 3 years), passed the degree examination, and defended a kandidat's dissertation.

b. The *Doctor Nauk* degree was in introduced in Russia in 1819, abolished in 1917, and revived in the Soviet Union in 1934. It is awarded to those who have accomplished independent research that elucidates theoretical principles and solves scientific problems representing an important contribution to scientific knowledge and practice. No fixed time period for completion. Public defense of doctoral dissertation is required.

c. Medical school is a 6-year program of higher education. Graduates of this program receive the title of "*vrach*" (medical doctor). However, in order to practice, they must complete further specialized training, for which four options are available:

Internatura (internship). A 1-year program that leads to certification in one of the basic specialties—bacteriology, infectious diseases, psychiatry, epidemiology, etc. In reference to infectious diseases, upon completion of the program the graduate would have the title *vrach bakteriolog* (doctor bacteriologist).

Ordinatura (residency). A 2-year program that leads to certification in a basic specialty or in a subspecialty.

Aspirantura (candidate of sciences). A 3-year program that awards the *Kandidat nauk* (candidate of sciences) degree in one of the medical specialties or subspecialties.

Dokturantura (doctor of sciences). A program that takes another 3 years beyond the *aspirantura* and leads to the *Doktor nauk* degree. Someone completing the *doktorantura* in the medical field would be a doctor (*vrach*) and would also have a doctorate degree (*Doktor nauk*).

The first two (*internatura* and *ordinatura*) denote practicing doctors, while *aspirantura* and *dokturantura* are indicative of research and teaching careers. However, in all four cases, the person could be referred to as "doctor bacteriologist," "doctor epidemiologist," etc.

6. M. M. Shemyakin and Yu. A. Ovchinnikov Institute of Bioorganic Chemistry, "History of Institute of Bioorganic Chemistry," 2009–2011, http://www.ibch .ru/en/about/history.

7. A good discussion on the properties and applications of valinomycin can be found in Wikipedia, "Valinomycin," http://en.wikipedia.org/wiki/Valinomycin.

8. A statue commissioned by Ovchinnikov from a Swiss sculptor that stands in front of the main building of the M. M. Shemyakin and Yu. A. Ovchinnikov Institute of Bioorganic Chemistry is a three-dimensional representation of valinomycin, which supposedly was the first molecule whose chemical structure was discovered by Ovchinnikov.

9. Dieter Oesterhelt and Walther Stoeckenius, "Functions of a New Photoreceptor Membrane," *Proceedings of the National Academy of Sciences USA* 70, no. 10 (October 1, 1973): 2853–2857.

10. Scientists who make significant contributions to science could be honored by being elected to membership in the USSR-AN. There were three types of membership: corresponding members, full members (Academicians), and foreign members. Being elected to membership was considered very prestigious. In 1974 the Academy had 237 full members and 439 corresponding members. After 1991 the USSR-AN was converted to the Russian Academy of Sciences (RAN). See Answers.com, Russian Academy of Sciences, 2011, http://www.answers.com/topic/russian-academy-of-sciences-1.

11. Briefly, Shemyakin graduated from Moscow State University in 1930, became a member of the Communist Party of the Soviet Union in 1951, and was named a corresponding member of the USSR-AS in 1953, a full academician in 1958, and a member of the Presidium in 1963. By the time of his death, Shemyakin was considered the Soviet Union's foremost bioorganic chemist.

12. Although DNA was discovered in 1869 by Friedrich Miescher, it was isolated in a pure state for the first time in 1935 by Belozersky. Further, in 1939 Belozersky found that both DNA and RNA are always present in bacteria.

13. This idea occurred to us as a result of having read Kucewicz, "Lead Scientist."

14. Nikolai Krementsov, *Stalinist Science* (Princeton, N.J., 1997), 4–5.

15. Ibid., 40–41.

16. Mark Williams, "Interview with Serguei Popov," at George Mason University, January 3, 2005. A variation of this quote was written by Kucewicz ("Lead Scientist"): "If we bring the Central Committee of the Communist Party of the Soviet Union vaccines, nobody will pay attention to it. But if we bring a virus, oh, then this will be recognized by all as a great victory."

17. Awarded anniversary medal "For exemplary work. In commemoration of the 100th anniversary of the birth of Vladimir Ilich Lenin."

18. Anthony Rimmington, "The Soviet Union's Offensive Program: The Implications for Contemporary Arms Control," in *Biological Warfare and Disarmament: New Problems/New Perspectives,* ed. Susan Wright (Maryland, 2002), 103–148.

19. An indication of Ovchinnikov's influence may be realized from what Joshua Lederberg wrote after having met him in June 1985: "Ovch. told me he had gotten Brezhnev's personal backing to modernize Soviet biology through molecular genetics, [fairly explicitly to get over the Lysenko blight] for its indispensable values for medicine and agriculture." In "Observations from Lederberg during his presence at the joint U.S.—U.S.S.R. CISAC meeting in Moscow in June 1985 (June 12, 1985)," Joshua Lederberg Papers, National Library of Medicine.

20. Anthony Rimmington, "Legacy of Biotechnology Visionary Lives On," *Microbiology Europe* 3, no. 3 (1995): 15.

21. Lederberg, 1985.

22. Marjorie Sun, "A Biotech Enterprise Soviet style: Collaborative Enterprise for Producing Biotechnology Products for Research," *Science* 241 (1988): 1154–1155.

23. In a top-secret Central Committee document, the 15th Directorate is called "Military Unit 26150."

24. The Soviet Union had many secret institutes that commonly were called "post office box institutes" because their classified names were P.O. Box numbers. Institutes and facilities whose P.O. Box numbers we know are listed in Table 2.2, as are Military Unit numbers.

Table 2.2   Post Office Box and Military Unit Numbers

All-Union Research Institute of Molecular Biology—P.O. Box V-8036

Aralsk-7 military support unit—Military Unit 25484

Biopreparat (also Ogarkov System)—P.O. Box A-1063

Design Bureau of Chemical Automation (involved in design and manufacturing of liquid fuel engines for rockets and missiles)—P.O. Box 20

Institute of Engineering Immunology (IEI)—P.O. Box G-4883

Institute of Highly Pure Biopreparations (IHPB)—not known

Interagency Scientific and Technical Council for Molecular Biology and Genetics (MNTS)—P.O. Box A-3092

Kirov-200—Post No. 992

Ministry of Defense 15th Directorate—P.O. Box A-1968; also Military Unit 26150

Ministry of Defense Scientific Research Institute for Sanitation—Military Unit 62992

Omutninsk Scientific and Production Base—P.O. Box B-8389

Shikhany-2 military support unit—Military Unit 74873

State Research Center for Applied Microbiology (SRCAM)—P.O. Box V-8724

Stepnogorsk Scientific Experimental-Industrial Base (SNOPB)—P.O. Box 2076

25. Igor V. Domaradskij and Wendy Orent, *Biowarrior: Inside the Soviet/Russian Biological War Machine* (Amherst, N.Y., 2003), 131, 134.

26. Genetic engineering had its origins during the late 1960s in experiments with plasmids, which are small, free-floating rings of DNA found in bacteria. A key discovery, made by Swiss microbiologist Werner Arber in 1968, was restriction enzymes, which are able to cut DNA into fragments during replication. The first experiments to combine DNA molecules from different sources were performed in Paul Berg's laboratory in the early 1970s and published in 1972 (he shared the 1980 Nobel Prize in Chemistry for this work). This is the birth of genetic engineering. Also in 1972, an expert with bacterial plasmids, Herbert Boyer, met with Stanley Cohen, an expert with restriction enzymes, and began a collaboration to use bacteria as tiny protein "factories." The following year, 1973, these two scientists reported having combined viral DNA and bacterial DNA in a plasmid, which was transferred to a bacterial cell, thus creating the first recombinant DNA organism. In short, the two scientists used genetic engineering to create a bacterium (host) that had some characteristics possessed by the virus (donor of DNA or gene). In 1976 Boyer established the first biotechnology company; its objective was to employ genetic engineering to produce proteins useful to medicine. The company's first success, in 1977, was to use genetic engineering to clone and manufacture a human protein, the hormone somatostatin. This achievement started the modern biotechnology "revolution."

27. Aleksandr A. Baev, "The Paths of My Life: Autobiography," *Comprehensive Biochemistry* 38 (1995): 439–479.

28. "New Technology and Biological Warfare: Testimony by Deputy Assistant Secretary of Defense for Negotiations Policy Douglas J. Feith before the Subcommittee on Oversight and Evaluation of the House Permanent Select Committee on Intelligence, Aug. 8, 1986." *Defense Issues* 1, no. 60 (September 8, 1986): 1.

29. M. A. Milstein and L. S. Semejko, "U.S. Military R&D through Soviet Eyes," *Bulletin of the Atomic Scientists* 33 (1977): 33–38.

30. Ibid., 36.

31. Ibid., 38.

32. There was a basis for this claim. In a report to Congress, the Department of the Army wrote that substantial support had been provided to the pre-1969 US BW program by non-DOD institutions. Specifically, "288 contracts were placed with 73 educational institutions and 440 contracts were awarded to 181 industrial firms." Office of the Secretary of the Army, "Information for Members of Congress: U.S. Army Activities in the U.S. Biological Warfare (BW) Program," Washington, D.C., March 8, 1977.

33. Vitaly Shlykov, "Fatal Mistakes of the U.S. and Soviet Intelligence: Part One," *International Affairs* (Moscow) 42, nos. 5–6 (1996): 159–178.

34. Ibid.

35. Domaradskij and Orent, 2003, 141–160.

36. The approximate US equivalent to "of special importance" would have been a category of "Sensitive Compartmented Information."

37. Some scholars refer to it as the 15th Directorate for Biological Protection of the General Staff. See Gulbarshyn Bozheyeva, Yerlan Kunakbayev, and Dastan Yeleukenov, *Former Soviet Biological Weapons Facilities in Kazakhstan: Past, Present and Future,* CNS Occasional Paper No. 1, Center for Nonproliferation Studies, Monterey, Calif., 1999.

38. Jonathan B. Tucker and Raymond A. Zilinskas, eds., *The 1971 Smallpox Epidemic in Aralsk, Kazakhstan, and the Soviet Biological Warfare Program,* Occasional Paper No. 9, Monterey, Calif., 2002.

39. Ken Alibek with Stephen Handelman, *Biohazard: The Chilling True Story of the Largest Covert Biological Weapons Program in the World—Told from Inside by the Man Who Ran It* (New York, 1999), 5, 297.

40. In 1990 the VPK was headed by Deputy Prime Minister Igor Belousov with Deputy Chairman Aleksei Arzhakov. Oleg Ignatiev was the head of its biological weapons directorate (Alibek with Handelman, 1999, 150, 180–181).

41. Domaradskij and Orent, 2003, 155–156.

42. Baroyan was a highly regarded scientist who had worked most of his professional career at the N. F. Gamaleya Institute of Epidemiology and Microbiology, Academy of Medical Sciences of the USSR, first on *Vibrio cholerae* and then on oncogenic viruses.

43. There is some confusion about the scope of "Enzymes" in the literature. It is sometimes described as the code word for the biological weapons program that was operated by Biopreparat. Alibek is unclear in his definition (Alibek with Handelman, 1999, 42). However, Domaradsky and Orent (2003, 141) are clear on the issue, asserting that "Enzymes" encompassed "the entire Soviet biological weapons program: research, design, weapons development." We use the Russian word *Ferment* throughout this book as the name of the Soviet offensive BW R&D program dedicated to harming and killing humans. We have information to the point that the USSR Council of Ministers approved a variety of top-secret R&D programs that addressed various aspects of chemical and biological weapons, many of which had code names beginning with the letter F. In addition to *Ferment* these included Fagot (unknown), Flask (unknown), Flora (military herbicides), Flute (immunotoxins for assassination), Foliant (next-generation nerve agents), and Fouette (unknown).

44. Domaradskij and Orent, 2003, 178.

45. Also translated as the Inter-Agency Scientific and Technical Council (Alibek with Handelman, 1999, 43).

46. Domaradskij and Orent, 2003, 301.

47. Like other noteworthy academicians such as Ovchinnikov, Bayev, and Skryabin, Zhdanov was adept at concealing from foreign colleagues his important role in the illegal Soviet BW program. A WHO executive who worked with him for a

long time wrote: "[Zhdanov was] a member of the WHO Executive Board and various WHO panels on infectious diseases. He was a dedicated supporter of efforts to establish a BWC which were often at variance with Soviet official policies. At WHO he strongly encouraged the development of a network of collaborating laboratories for communicable diseases, and the smallpox eradication program." Martin M. Kaplan, "The Efforts of WHO and Pugwash to Eliminate Chemical and Biological Weapons: A Memoir," *Bulletin of the World Health Organization* 77, no. 2 (1999): 153.

48. According to Domaradskij and Orent, 2003, 117, Belyaev had been instrumental in having *Glavmikrobioprom* established "as a cover for connections with the Ministry of Defense and the Military Industrial Commission."

49. Alikhanyan first headed the Microbiological Laboratory at the Radiobiological Department of the Kurchatov Institute of Atomic Energy and then later the Research Institute on the Genetics and Selection of Industrial Microorganisms (Vadim J. Birstein, *The Perversion of Knowledge* [Boulder, Colo., 2001]). In the MNTS he was later succeeded by V. Debabov.

50. G. K. Skryabin, then head of the Institute of Biochemistry and Physiology of Microorganisms; later he became the foreign secretary of the USSR-AN. (Not to be confused with his son, K. G. Skryabin.)

51. At that time Petrov was the chairman of the Department of Immunology, Second Moscow N. I. Pirogov Institute of Medicine.

52. Mirzabekov was a well-known chemist who was awarded the State Prize for Science and Technology in 1969 for studies on sequencing valine tRNA, and he rose to become the director of the Russian Academy of Sciences' Engelhardt Institute of Molecular Biology; he died in July 2003.

53. According to Pasechnik, the role of the USSR-AN in *Ferment* was delineated in a 1972 document. He paraphrased it as saying, "The Academy of Sciences will supply support for basic knowledge in molecular biology and bioengineering in support of the biological warfare program. The concrete plans of the Academy of Sciences will be presented to the MNTS."

54. Domaradskij and Orent, 2003, 145–146.

55. Established in 1966 to oversee the Soviet biotechnology industry.

56. Domaradskij and Orent, 2003, 169.

57. Ovchinnikov, 1985, 21.

58. Gus W. Weiss, *The Farewell Dossier*, (Center for the Study of Intelligence, Central Intelligence Agency, 1996), 1.

59. KGB in the Baltic States: Documents and Researches, http://www.kgbdocuments.eu/.

60. Major V. M. Shabalin, "List of Questions on Biological Weapons (Excerpt from Military-Industrial Complex Tasks chapter), Top Secret, Copy No. 2, No. 151/7-7672, Department 7, "T" Administration, USSR KGB First Main Adminis-

tration, January 22, 1985 (in Russian). We would like to thank Dr. Mark Kramer, Harvard University, who discovered this cable in November 2011 and made it available to us.

61. Anthony Rimmington, "Invisible Weapons of Mass Destruction: The Soviet Union's BW Programme and Its Implications for Contemporary Arms Control," *Journal of Slavic Military Studies* 13, no. 3 (2000): 1.

62. Alibek with Handelman, 1999, xii–xiii, 42, 303.

63. Ibid.

64. Ibid.

65. Ibid., 42.

66. Anthony Rimmington, "The Soviet Union's Offensive Program: The Implications for Contemporary Arms Control," in *Biological Warfare and Disarmament: New Problems/New Perspectives,* ed. Susan Wright (Maryland, 2002), 103–148.

67. Domaradskij and Orent, 2003.

68. Alibek with Handelman, 1999, 117; and Rimmington, 2002. Gosplan is an acronym for State Planning Committee of the USSR Council of Ministers. Its main responsibility was to draft economic plans for the nation and make certain they were implemented. In 1990, it was renamed Ministry of Economics and Forecasting.

69. Savva Yermoshin was the KGB commander in charge of headquarter security throughout Biopreparat's existence in the Soviet Union.

70. In the early 1980s it was headed by Dorogov; Alibek with Handelman, 1999, 100.

71. Ibid., 14 and 18.

72. The difficulties inherent to establishing and operating an ostensibly civilian institution dedicated to researching, developing, and testing biological weapons while under the control of the MOD are discussed in Chapter 6.

73. The following letters and numbers were assigned: F for psychotropic, behavior-altering biological agents; L for bacteria (L1: *Yersinia pestis,* L2: *Francisella tularensis,* L3: brucellae, L4: *Bacillus anthracis,* L5: *Burkholderia mallei,* L6: *Burkholderia pseudomallei*); N for viruses (N1: Variola virus, N2: Ebola virus, N3: Marburg virus, N4: Machupo virus). Alibek with Handelman, 1999, 20.

74. Ibid., 58 and 304.

75. Domaradsky asserts that in matters pertaining to *Ferment,* the KGB had the power to override the 3rd Directorate; see Domaradskij and Orent, 2003, 174.

76. The Soviet Union had three groupings for microorganisms according to the level of risk they posed to workers and environment, with Group 1 being the most dangerous and Group III the least dangerous (see Glossary).

77. Raymond A. Zilinskas and Burke K. Zimmerman, eds., *The Gene Splicing Wars: Reflections on the Recombinant DNA Controversy* (New York, 1986).

78. Domaradskij and Orent, 2003, 174.

79. Donald Fleming, "On Living in a Biological Revolution," *Atlantic Monthly,* February 1969, 64, 65–70.

3. USSR Ministry of Defense Facilities and Its
Biological Warfare Program

1. G. Labezov, "How to Defend Yourself against a Bacteriological Weapon" (in Russian), *Kryl'ya Rodiny* 12 (December 1, 1957); L. A. Belikov, *The Bacteriological Weapon and Methods of Protection from It* (in Russian) (Moscow, 1960); I. I. Rogozin, "Principles of Antibacterial Protection of Troops" (in Russian), *Military Thought* no. 3 (1966); A. M. Arkhangelskiy, A. M. Kamorskiy, and I. D. Nuzhdin, *Bacteriological Weapons and How to Defend against Them* (in Russian) (Moscow, 1967); and A. M. Myasnenko, G. M. Medinskiy, and M. I. Krasulin, "Part 5. Protection of Public against Bacteriological Warfare. Chapter 1. Principles of Antibacteriological Protection of Public and Rendering Medical Care to Victims of Bacteriological (Biological) Weapons," in *Handbook of Civil Defense Medical Service* (in Russian) (Moscow, 1983).

2. Belikov, 1960, 4.

3. V. I. Agafonov and V. S. Perepelkin, "Experience in Protecting Troops against Epidemics during the Years of World War II," in *The Experience of Soviet Medicine during World War II, 1941–1945* (in Russian) (Moscow, 1955), 2:17–24; Myasnenko et al., 1983.

4. Dmitriy Litovkin, "Russia Doesn't Have Biological Weapons, but Has Weapons against Biological Weapons" (in Russian), *Krasnaya Zvezda,* July 15, 1999; V. N. Orlov, ed., *We Defended Russia. 6.5. On Biological Weapons* (in Russian) (Moscow, 2000), 205–222; K. K. Rayevskiy and V. M. Dobrynin, "Most Important Results and Prospects of Scientific Work to Protect Naval Troops and Forces from Unfavorable Biological Factors" (in Russian), *Voyenno-Meditsinskiy Zhurnal* 321, no. 10 (October 1, 2000): 30–35; Victor Kholstov, "CBR Warfare Defense: New Solutions in Service of the Country" (in Russian), *Military Parade,* January 1, 2002; Anatoly A. Vorobyov, *Without Drawing a Line* (in Russian) (Moscow, 2003); and Roza N. Lukina, and Yevgeny P. Lukin, eds., *The 50 Years of the Ministry of Defense Virology Center Deserve to Be Known* (in Russian), Veterans' Council of the Virology Center of the Russian Federation Ministry of Defense's Scientific Research Institute for Microbiology, Publishing House Sergiyev Posad Ves, Sergiyev Posad, Russia, 2004. (Hereafter Lukina and Lukin, 2004.)

5. Vorobyov (1923–2006) made important contributions to the Soviet Union's military microbiological program and occupied senior positions within both the Soviet MOD and Biopreparat. In 1978 he was transferred to *Glavmikrobioprom,* where

he served as first deputy director of Biopreparat until 1988. In 2001 he was appointed a member of the Expert Council on Biosecurity under the State Duma, and in 2003, elected chairman of the Central Board and president of the Society for Russian Biotechnologists. (See "Biopreparat Head, Academician A.A. Vorobyov Dies at Age 83" (in Russian), *Immunologia* (May 2006): 192–193.

6. A. A. Vorobyov, "Current Problems in Microbiological Security" (in Russian), *Vestnik Rossiyskoy Akademii Meditsinskikh Nauk* no. 10 (2002): 9–12.

7. Problem 5 was the Soviet defensive BW program (see Chapter 5) and Fetish was a subprogram of the offensive BW program.

8. Orlov, 2000, 207.

9. "Kirov Region," *Kommersant Daily,* October 28, 2007, http://www.kommersant.com/t-47/r_5/n_390/Kirov_Region.

10. Google Earth imagery of Kirov city in June 2010 was of such poor quality that the Kirov Institute cannot be identified.

11. Anonymous, personal communication, 2001, 2003.

12. *Brucella suis* was weaponized by both the US and the Soviet BW programs. It is an effective BW agent because it is highly infectious via aerosol, is very difficult to treat, it causes a chronic debilitating disease, and at the time there was no vaccine.

13. Anonymous, personal communication, 2001, 2003.

14. *Y. pestis* is a BSL-3 pathogen in the US and most other countries, and even aerosol experiments would be done within BSL-3 facilities. However, in the USSR and its successor nations, *Y. pestis* is classified as a Group I pathogen, just like Ebola virus and therefore would require the same level of maximum BSL-4-like containment.

15. Mark Popovsky, *Manipulated Science: The Crisis of Science and Scientists in the Soviet Union Today* (New York, 1979), 156–158.

16. Orlov, 2000, 219.

17. Viktor Shalygin, "Kirov: Secret Scientific Research Institute Does Not Fear Even Meteorites" (in Russian), *Spaseniye,* August 30, 1992, 5. The reference to "meteorites" in the article's title refers to an assurance given by the director that the institute poses no hazard to the city's residents, not even if a meteorite were to hit it.

18. This facility is often misnamed Kirov-2000.

19. See the Kirov-200 site at Google Earth 58°25'12.85" N; 49°16'48.68" E.

20. Ken Alibek with Stephen Handelman, *Biohazard: The Chilling True Story of the Largest Covert Biological Weapons Program in the World—Told from Inside by the Man Who Ran It* (New York, 1999); Anthony Rimmington, "From Offence to Defence? Russia's Reform of Its Biological Weapons Complex and the Implications for Western Security," *Journal of Slavic Military Studies* 16, no. 1 (March 2003): 1–43.

21. Anonymous, personal communication, 2003.

22. Russian Ministry of Property Relations Order No. 451-R, August 25, 2000 (in Russian); Russian Ministry of Defense Order No. 2913, October 10, 2000 (in Russian).

23. I. Kuvaldina, "When Things Start Moving: Vyatka State University Is Becoming a Regional Biotechnology Center" (in Russian), *Pharmvestnik,* February 7, 2006, http://www.pharmvestnik.ru/cgi-bin/statya.pl?sid=10529%forprint=1.

24. Lukina and Lukin, 2004.

25. Other names were "Settlement 67," which is the number of kilometers on a road marker near the settlement's entry, and Zagorsk-6.

26. USSR Ministry of Defense Order No. 00180 of September 29, 1953, to implement the USSR Council of Ministers Decree of September 24, 1953, on creation of the Scientific Research Institute for Sanitation of the Ministry of Defense on the basis of the Scientific Research Institute for Sanitation of the Ministry of Health.

27. Zagorsk Institute's commanders during 1954–2004 were: Mikhail Ivanovich Kostyuchenok, major general of the Medical Service, 1954–1959; Vladimir Yakovlevich Podolyan, major general of the Medical Service, 1959–1966; Sergey Ivanovich Prigoda, lieutenant general of the Medical Service, 1966–1987; Viktor Nikolayevich Karpov, major general of the Medical Service, 1987–1990; Aleksandr Aleksandrovich Makhlay, major general of the Medical Service, 1990–1999; Vladimir Alekseyevich Maksimov, colonel of the Medical Service, July 1999 to 2004 (and perhaps beyond).

28. Lukina and Lukin, 2004, 141.

29. Ibid., xx.

30. Although *C. burnetii* is not closely related to rickettsiae, it was researched by rickettsiologists because it phenotypically resembles rickettsiae. Likewise, the institute researched rickettsiae because they phenotypically resemble viruses.

31. Ken Alibek, "Biological Weapons/Bioterrorism Threat and Defense," unpublished presentation, 2005.

32. The main scientists involved in rickettsia research were A. S. Bykov, Y. P. Lukin (who also researched VEE virus), and A. A. Vorobyov.

33. Anonymous, personal communication, 2003.

34. Lukina and Lukin, 2004, 224.

35. Ibid., 225.

36. Anonymous sources, personal communication, 2001, 2003. How this came about is discussed in Chapter 10.

37. Lukina and Lukin, 2004, 36.

38. Orlov, 2000, 221.

39. A great variety of VEEV strains exist in nature, so it is improbable that a single vaccine can protect against them all.

40. In contrast to some of the other encephalitis viruses, such as EEEV, which causes a localized infection of the brain, VEEV causes a systemic infection with viremia that also involves the brain.

41. The main scientists who undertook research on both the encephalitis viruses and the Langat and Sindbis viruses were Y. P. Lukin and T. M. Chernikova. V. N. Lebedev, who also worked on Ebola virus, researched RVF virus, while Vorobyov investigated VEEV.

42. Lukina and Lukin, 2004, 155.

43. The original work on the virus was done by R. Siegert and co-workers in Marburg, who also named the virus after the city.

44. The story of the first Marburg virus disease outbreak, including the BW allegations and transfer to the Soviet Union, is retold in detail in Mark Köppe, "Examination of the Events during the Marburg Virus Outbreak of 1967 in Marburg and Frankfurt" (in German) (diss. in Medicine, Department of Medicine, Philipps-Universität Marburg, Marburg an der Lahn, Germany, 2002).

45. These two Vector scientists were infected with Marburg virus, and Ustinov died (see Chapter 8).

46. Lukina and Lukin, 2004, 167.

47. Researchers who accomplished the "true scientific feat" and therefore were rewarded with high government prizes, included V. V. Mikhaylov, I. V. Borisevich, V. A. Markin, V. P. Krasnyanskiy, V. N. Gradovoyev, N. V. Portyvayeva, N. K. Chernikova, Ye. V. Lebedinskaya, and G. D. Timankova (Lukina and Lukin, 2004, 172).

48. Yu. Gladkevich, *Krasnaya Zvezda,* March 3, 1995.

49. During its existence, the Zagorsk Institute is said to have developed 10 vaccines and 30 types of immunoglobulins. However, Maksimov admitted in 2004 that of all vaccines against viral biological weapons, Russia had only one officially authorized vaccine, a yellow fever vaccine; see Vadim Udamtsev, "Virological center turns 50" (in Russian), *Voyenno-Promyshlennyy Kuryer,* April 28, 2004.

50. Judith Perera, "Health: Russian and U.S. Germ Warfare Troopers Fight Ebola virus," *Inter Press Service* (London), December 6, 1995.

51. O. V. Baroyan and A. F. Serenko, "Smallpox Outbreak in Moscow in 1959–1960" (in Russian), *Zhurnal Mikrobiologii, Epidemiologii i Immunobiologii* 32, no. 4 (1961): 72–79.

52. A. V. Eremiam, "The Clinical Picture and Differential Diagnosis of Smallpox (according to the Materials of the Epidemic of Imported Smallpox in Moscow in January 1960)" (in Russian), *Sovietskaia Meditsina* 25, no. 6 (1961): 40–51.

53. Yelena Mikhaylina, "Fever Zone: Secrets of the Numbered Zagorsks" (in Russian), *Moscovskiy Komsomolets,* December 8, 2004.

54. Anonymous, personal communication, 2003.

55. Lukina and Lukin, 2004, 235.

56. According to Mikhailina (2004), Zagorsk Institute had three zones – clean zone, technical zone, and virus center within the technical zone, with the third zone being the most secretive and thus well guarded.

57. Tatiana Mitkova, "TV on Russian Military Microbiologists" (in Russian), Moscow NTV broadcast on March 20, 1999.

58. Fedor Smirnov, "Taming Viruses: Center for Special Diagnosis and Treatment of Ultradangerous and Exotic Infectious Diseases" (in Russian), *Meditsinskaya Gazeta,* December 29, 1999, 10–11.

59. G. G. Onishchenko et al., "Center for Special Laboratory Diagnosis and Treatment of Dangerous and Exotic Infectious Diseases in System for Protecting Territory of Russian Federation against Epidemics" (in Russian), *Zhurnal Mikrobiologii, Epidemiologii I Immunobiologii* 78, no. 6 (December 31, 2001): 114–115.

60. Lena Norlander and Kristina S. Westerdahl, *The Role of the New Russian Anti-Bioterrorism Centres,* Umeå, Sweden: FOI—Swedish Defence Research Agency, June 2006.

61. Sergei Pluzhnikov and Aleksey Shvedov, "Investigation: Murder from a Test Tube" (in Russian), *Sovershenno Sekretno* no. 4 (1998): 12–14.

62. S. Bogomolov, "19th Post: A Reporter Is a Rare Guest Here" (in Russian), *Uralskiy Rabochiy* (Sverdlovsk), March 12, 1990.

63. Lidia Usacheva, "Nine Hours behind the Barbed Wire: Reporting from the 19th Military Installation from Which, Many Allege, Anthrax Broke Out in 1979" (in Russian), *Poisk* (Moscow), March 7–13, 1992, 5.

64. A. Pashkov, "Generals and Anthrax" (in Russian), video report on Russian Television Network (Moscow), broadcast on September 16, 1993.

65. Usacheva, 1992.

66. Andrey Semenov, "Was There Anthrax in Sverdlovsk-19? Only President Boris Yeltsin and Our Interviewee, RAMS Academician Pyotr Burgasov, Know This Mystery" (in Russian), *Meditsinskaya Gazeta,* June 24, 1998, 4.

67. Pashkov, 1993.

68. Pluzhnikov and Shvedov, 1998, 13.

69. We do not know how many biological weapons filling stations existed in the Soviet Union, but we believe there were more than the two we have so far named, Zima and Zlatoust.

70. Mathew M. Meselson et al., "The Sverdlovsk Anthrax Outbreak of 1979," *Science* 266 (1994): 1202–1208; Jeanne Guillemin, *Anthrax: The Investigation of a Deadly Outbreak* (Berkeley, Calif., 1999).

71. Anonymous sources, personal communications, 2001, 2003.

72. Meselson et al., 1994; Guillemin, 1999.

73. On this point, Yeltsin noted in a 1990 interview, "I knew about the existence of this post of a closed research center but had no information about what it was

doing specifically," and that after the outbreak had occurred, "a large group of military specialists and KGB people arrived. They did not inform me personally of the results of their work." Boris Yarkov, "The Disease Was in the Shoulder Straps" (in Russian), *Kuranty,* November 1, 1990.

74. Defense Intelligence Agency, *Chemical and Biological Warfare Capabilities – USSR (U),* Report DST-1600S-034-76-SUP 1, (Washington, D.C., March 1977), xxiii. (Secret)

75. Dmitriy Melman, "Historian of Death" (in Russian), *Moscovskiy Komsomolet,* April 7, 2006.

76. V. P. Nepranov et al., "The Analysis of Biological Terrorism Cases (for Last 10 Years) and Disinfection Actions on Liquidation of Their Consequences," in *Advanced Disinfectants and Safety Techniques Applied in Pathogen Treatment,* ed. G. N. Lepeshkin, 215–228, Proceedings of International Workshop, Kirov: RACEM Ltd, 2006, http://www.racem.org/.

77. Alibek with Handelman, 1999, 75.

78. Alibek's account differs from that of our sources; he writes that he was told by Lieutenant Colonel Gennady Lepeshkin that Chernichov was responsible for the accident, but that he was never punished; Alibek with Handelman, 1999, 83–84.

79. Anonymous, personal communication, 2003.

80. US Senate, Committee on Governmental Affairs and the Permanent Subcommittee on Investigations, *Hearings: Global Spread of Chemical and Biological Weapons* (Washington, D.C., 1990), 38.

81. Meselson et al., 1994, 1207.

82. Matthew Meselson, "Note regarding Source Strength," *ASA Newsletter* no. 87 (December 21, 2001): 1. In the original publication of this same note, in *ASA Newsletter* no. 48 (June 8, 1995) and in a still-earlier version that was privately distributed after the publication of the paper in *Science,* the line quoted in the text is not present.

83. Personal communication from three of the scientists present, 2000, and corroborated in April 2011.

84. Meselson et al., 1994, 1207.

85. Dean A. Wilkening, "Sverdlovsk Revisited: Modeling Human Inhalation Anthrax," *Proceedings of the National Academy of Sciences* 103, no. 20 (2006): 7590.

86. Definitions for ID_{50} and Q_{50} can be found in the Glossary.

87. See Guillemin, 1999, map 2, 261.

88. Steven Fetter, "Ballistic Missiles and Weapons of Mass Destruction: What Is the Threat? What Should be Done?," *International Security* 16, no. 1 (Summer 1991): 5–42. Fetter's assumptions do not explicitly appear in his published paper, but they were used as the basis for the calculations and results shown in the tables on pages 23 to 28 of his paper (Steven Fetter, personal communication, 1995).

89. Alibek with Handelman, 1999, 87.

90. Richard T. Okinaka et al., "Single Nucleotide Polymorphism Typing of *Bacillus anthracis* from Sverdlovsk Tissue," *Emerging Infectious Diseases* 14, no. 4 (April 2008): 653–656.

91. Paul Keim, personal communication, June 10, 2010.

92. Paul J. Jackson et al., "PCR Analysis of Tissue Samples from the 1979 Sverdlovsk Anthrax Victims: The Presence of Multiple *Bacillus anthracis* Strains in Different Victims," *Proceedings of the National Academy of Sciences, USA* 95, no. 3 (February 3, 1998): 1224–1229.

93. Okinaka et al., 2008.

94. Jackson relocated from Los Alamos to Lawrence Livermore National Laboratory in May 2005.

95. Paul J. Jackson, personal communication, January 21, 2010.

96. Lidiya Usacheva, "Nine Hours behind the Barbed Wire: Reporting from the 19th Military Installation from Which, Many Allege, Anthrax Broke Out in 1979" (in Russian), *Poisk,* March 7–13, 1992, 5; Bogomolov, 1990.

97. Usacheva, 1990, 5.

98. Bogomolov, 1990.

99. Aleksandr Korzun, "Everything That They're Saying about Us Is a Myth: Interview with Lt. Gen. Valentin Ivanovich Yevstigneyev" (in Russian), *New Izvestia,* March 3, 1998, 4.

100. Paul Quinn-Judge, "Of Breeding of Death: Fears Grow That a Secret Russian Germ Warfare Laboratory Is Once Again Making Biological Weapons," *Time,* February 16, 1998, http://www.time.com/time/magazine/1998/int/980216/europe .the_breeding_of_d6.html.

101. Ibid.

102. Rayevskiy and Dobrynin, 2000, 30.

103. Since its inception, the institute has been headed by a series of major generals of the Medical Service, including T. K. Dzharakyan, N. V. Savateyev, G. M. Starabykin, V. K. Kulagin, V. G. Vladimirov, S. A. Kutsenko, and since 1998, Nikolai N. Pluzhnikov.

104. Rayevskiy and Dobrynin, 2000, 30. We have no further information about *degmin* and R-405.

105. Anonymous, personal communication, 2003.

106. These studies were performed by, among others, V. P. Nikolayev, M. V. Shmidt, and S. Ya. Gaydamovich.

107. Similar to the IHPB, this Research Institute apparently was not allowed to work with Group I organisms because it was located within the city limits of Leningrad.

108. Joshua Lederberg, "Memo Regarding a Visit to the Military Medicine Research Institute in Leningrad," October 10, 1989, Joshua Lederberg Papers, National Library of Medicine.

109. Rayevskiy and Dobrynin, 2000, 35.

110. Aleksandr Viktorov, "Cheap but Terrifying Weapons That Terrorists Can Produce Just by Setting up a Small Laboratory: Interview with Lieutenant-General Valentin Yevstigneyev" (in Russian), *Nezavisimoye Voyennoye Obozreniye,* November 16, 2001 (Internet version).

4. Open-Air Testing of Biological Weapons by Aralsk-7 on Vozrozhdeniye Island

1. We follow military terminology in regard to open-air testing of biological weapons. Thus, the entire test facility, comprising the testing ranges and supportive facilities, is called "ground," as in the Aralsk-7 Testing Ground. An actual open-air test is performed on a "range," as in a test range.

2. "Aral" means "island," and if one examines a map from about 1853, it is clear that numerous islands were at that time situated off the Aral Sea's east coast;

3. Named after Grand Duke Konstantin N. Romanov (1827–1892), president of the Russian Geographical Society.

4. A wonderful map of the Aral Sea was published by Commander A. Butshoff in 1853, a copy of which can be seen at the University of Texas Library, http://www.lib .utexas.edu/maps/historical/aral_1853.jpg.

5. The Syr Darya river is Central Asia's longest river (2,200 kilometers), and before it was dammed it was the second largest by volume.

6. *Kulaks* were moderately well-off peasants who in the late 1920s and early 1930s were accused by the Stalin administration of having overexploited the land and oppressed poor peasants and farm workers. Millions of *kulaks* were arrested and either quickly executed or deported to *gulags* in distant parts of the Soviet Union.

7. A fascinating and revealing study of Soviet decision making in the environmental field, including that related to seas and rivers, is David F. Duke's "Unnatural Union: Soviet Environmental Policies, 1950–1991" (PhD diss., Department of History and Classics, University of Alberta, Edmonton, Alberta, Spring 1999).

8. See Central Asia Regional Water Information Base (CAREWIB) Project, Database of the Aral Sea, "CAREWIB" 2004–2007, http://www.cawater-info.net/aral /data/index_e.htm.

9. The Kazakh name for the island is *Barsakelmes.*

10. World Bank, "Syr Darya Control & Northern Aral Sea Phase I Project," The World Bank Group, April 5, 2010; http://web.worldbank.org/external/projects /main?pagePK=64312881&piPK=64302848&theSitePK=40941&Projectid =P046045.

11. Source: Christopher Pala, "In Northern Aral Sea, Rebound Comes with a Catch," *Science* 334:303 (October 21, 2011).

12. Gulbarshyn Bozheyeva, Yerlan Kunakbayev, and Dastan Yeleukenov, *Former Soviet Biological Weapons Facilities in Kazakhstan: Past, Present and Future,* CNS Occasional Paper No. 1, Center for Nonproliferation Studies, Monterey, Calif., 1999.

13. Walter Hirsch, *Soviet BW and CW Preparations and Capabilities* ("The Hirsch Report") (Edgewood, Md., 1951).

14. This incident is discussed in Chapter 1.

15. The first names and patronymics of these individuals are not known.

16. There is an imprecision about this list that is disconcerting. In particular, several strains of *Shigella* can cause dysentery; and pyemia, a disease condition characterized by septicemia, can be caused by a number of pus-forming bacteria such as staphylococci and streptococci (or other bacteria); so it is not at all clear which bacteria were in fact tested.

17. Bozheyeva et al., 1999.

18. Anonymous scientist, personal communication, 2004.

19. We have seen two other forms of this city's name: Kontubek and Kantyubek.

20. Bozheyeva et al., 1999.

21. Information used to reconstruct life, activities, and facilities during approximately 1970–1992 on Vozrozhdeniye Island, as well as its current configuration, originates from several different primary sources, mainly interviews with persons who at one time or another lived and worked there as civilians or soldiers. The following is a listing of these sources in chronological order with brief explanations as needed:

Damir Safulin, "Will the Secret Laboratory Not Move from Kazakhstan to Russia? The Bacteriological 'Sand Dune' on Vozrozhdeniye Island Continues to Alarm the Public" (in Russian), *Nezavisimaya Gazeta* (Moscow), July 1, 1992. [Safulin's son served in Unit 25484 and described his life as a soldier on the island in 1991–1992.]

Judith Miller, "Poison Island: A Special Report—At Bleak Asian Site, Killer Germs Survive," *New York Times,* June 2, 1999, A1.

Olga Malakhova, "Death from Vozrozhdeniye Island" (in Russian), *Novoe Pokolenie* (Almaty), August 6, 1999, 1.

Nina Moskvina, "Where Anthrax Is Buried" (in Russian), *Stringer-agency* (Moscow), April 9, 2002. [The article contains a lengthy interview with an anonymous soldier who served on the island in the "early 1990s."]

Zhumabay Zhaqyp, "There Is No Secret in the Secret Island Now, but It Has Many Mysteries We Do Not Know" (in Kazakh), *Zhas Alash* (Almaty), June 18, 2002. [Article contains interviews with Tolganbek Tiyshev, a Kazakh ship maintenance worker who traveled between Aralsk and the island to tend to ships and boats during 1980s, and with Yelubay Orazov, chief of the weather station in Aralsk, who was one of the first Kazakhs to visit the island in 1996.]

Yuri P. Grigorashkin, "Barkhan: Concerning the Television Broadcast of 'Top Secret' and Also the Agreement between Tashkent and Washington on the Vozrozhdeniye Island Test Area" (in Russian), *Scientific Problems and Their Solution,* part 2 (n.p., 2003), 195–205. [Grigorashkin was a colonel who spent several years on Vozrozhdeniye Island as a military scientist.]

Christopher Pala, "Anthrax Island," *New York Times,* January 12, 2003, http://cscs.umich.edu/~crshalizi/sloth/2003-01-17.html. [Pala, a freelance reporter based in Almaty, visited the island in 2002 and interviewed Colonel Gennady Lepeshkin, a military scientist who claims to have spent 18 summers on the island performing field testing.]

Christopher Pala, "A Trip to Abandoned Anthrax Island," *Moscow Times,* January 14, 2003, 1. [A follow-up to the preceding article, Pala describes a visit to Vozrozhdeniye Island when he was guided by a team of looters.]

Olga Malakhova, "Ali Murzaliev: The One Who Survived Hell" (in Russian), *Novoe Pokolenie* (Almaty), January 20, 2003, http://www.centrasia.ru/newsA .php4?st=1043011860. [In Soviet times, Murzaliev worked on the island as an animal keeper.]

22. Bozheyeva et al., 1999.

23. We understand that the military city and the laboratory complex had separate P.O. Box numbers, but do not know why or their numbers.

24. Grigorashkin was an expert on biological aerosols, and Donchenko was a virologist. Both came from the Zagorsk Institute.

25. Google Earth, Latitude 45° 8'9.87"N; longitude 59°18'37.13"E, as seen from an altitude of approximately 1,600 feet; accessed January 19, 2008. V61 is located in the northeast corner of the compound; V60 is in the opposite corner.

26. Pala, January 12, 2003.

27. Eman P. Fridman, *Medical Primatology: History, Biological Foundations and Applications* (London, 2002).

28. Anonymous, personal communication, 2003.

29. Dmitriy Melman, "Historian of Death" (in Russian), *Moscovskiy Komsomolet* (April 7, 2006).

30. Vadim J. Birstein, *The Perversion of Knowledge: The True Story of Soviet Science,* (Boulder 2001), 107.

31. The biological bomblet most commonly used by the Soviet military was the *Gshch*-304, which is described in Chapter 10.

32. This important factor is called ID_{50} (Infectious Dose 50). This tells the bioweaponeers how many bacteria or viruses are needed to infect 50% of the target population. For example, $ID_{50} = 1$ would be very favorable because it would mean that just one

particle each would infect each of 50 persons out of a total population of 100. *Bacillus anthracis* spores have an $ID_{50} = 8,000$, which is not so favorable for military purposes, but these spores have other properties that more than make up for the high ID_{50}. For weapons developers it is important to test each weapons system with different animals because the ID_{50} vary considerably as different animals are more or less susceptible to infection by pathogens. Only by determining the ID_{50} of many kinds of animals, including nonhuman primates, is it possible to estimate the likely ID_{50} for humans.

33. Sergey Gerasimenko, "'Everything They Are Saying about Us Is a Hoax': Lieutenant General Valentin Yevstigneev, Deputy Chief of Radiation, Chemical and Biological Defense Troops for Biological Defense, Claims That Russia Had Not Supplied Iraq with Equipment for Production of Bacteriological Weapons" (in Russian), *Novye Izvestia,* March 3, 1998, 4.

34. The Soviet Union is likely to have received superficial information about the American 4-pound M114 biological bomblet and the M33 cluster bomb from interrogations of Colonel Walter M. Mahurin by his Chinese and North Korean captors. See: Walter M. Mahurin, *Depositions of Nineteen Captured US Airmen on Their Participation in Germ Warfare in Korea* (Peking, December 1, 1953), 11–21.

35. The authors consider it judicious not to reproduce the precise identification of the source document.

36. Alibek with Handelman, 1999, 26–28.

37. Jonathan B. Tucker and Raymond A. Zilinskas, eds., *The 1971 Smallpox Epidemic in Aralsk, Kazakhstan, and the Soviet Biological Warfare Program,* CNS Occasional Paper No. 9 (Monterey, Calif., 2002).

38. Named after Lev S. Berg (1876–1950), a leading Soviet ichthyologist and geographer.

39. Alan P. Zelicoff, "An Epidemiological Analysis of the 1971 Smallpox Outbreak in Aralsk, Kazakhstan," in Tucker and Zilinskas, 2002, 12–21.

40. O. Misaleva, *Report on Measures Taken to Contain and Eradicate the Smallpox Outbreak Locale in the City of Aralsk (September/October, 1971)* (in Russian) (Aralsk, October 18, 1971). (Top Secret)

41. Zelicoff, 2002.

42. Evgeniya Kvitko, Interview with Petr N. Burgasov: "Smallpox–Also Not a Bad Weapon" (in Russian), *Moscovskie Novosti,* November 3, 2001; http://kungrad.com/aral/island/ospa/.

43. Richard P. Strong, ed., *Report of the International Plague Conference Held at Mukden, April 1911* (Manila, Philippines, 1912).

44. A translation of Burgasov's interview became available in the United States only after Zelicoff's study was published.

45. Corona was a joint program between the CIA and the United States Air Force. Sources: National Reconnaissance Office, "Corona Facts," http://www.nro

.gov/corona/facts.html; David T. Lindgren, *Trust but Verify: Imagery Analysis in the Cold War* (Naval Institute Press: Annapolis, 2000).

46. Jeffrey Richelson, *The Wizards of Langley: Inside the CIA's Directorate of Science and Technology* (Boulder, CO, 2002), 102–130.

47. The Google Earth version 5.0.11337.1968 (beta), and presumably later versions, has a very interesting and useful function, namely "Historical Imagery," which can be found under the View button. It allows the viewer to see imagery of the subject being viewed taken at different dates. For example, Google Earth has imagery from as early as December 1973 of the Vozrozhdeniye Island region, and as recent as August 2008. By comparing the various images taken at different times, the dessication of the Aral Sea is made dramatically clear.

48. Under the new 1992 Constitution of Uzbekistan, the Republic of Karakalpakstan was established as an integral part of Uzbekistan with its sovereignty guaranteed by the Republic of Uzbekistan. The Republic of Karakalpakstan has an autonomous status and its own constitution. David and Sue Richardson, "Government of Karakalpakstan," March 9, 2007, http://www.karakalpak.com/stangov.html.

49. Former U.S. official, personal communication, 2007.

50. See CNS Branch Office, Washington, D.C., "Briefing Series: Biological Decontamination of Vozrozhdeniye Island: The U.S.-Uzbek Agreement, January 18, 2002," http://cns.miis.edu/pubs/dc/briefs/011802.htm.

51. The sources of information that follow on the decontamination project are: VIPDO Project Manager, *Vozrozhdeniye Island (VI) Pathogenic Destruction Operation (VIPDO) Final Report,* Cooperative Threat Reduction Program, June 6, 2002; VIPDO Mission Commander, *Voz Island Pathogen Destruction Operation (VIPDO) Post Mission Report,* Defense Threat Reduction Agency, July 30, 2002; and Christopher Pala, "Old Weapon Buried for Good: U.S. Team Sterilizes Site of Soviet Anthrax Testing," *Washington Times,* March 22, 2003.

52. An alternative approach would be for the Russian government to convert part of an existing or defunct chemical weapons test site to a biological test site. The most likely candidates for such conversion would be the Volsk-18 complex in Shikhany, Saratov Region, which probably evolved from the Tomka Central Army Chemical Proving Ground; Shikhany-1, which harbors the State Institute for Organic Synthesis Technologies; or Shikhany-2, which incorporates the Central Scientific-Research Experimental Institute and Military Unit 74873.

5. Soviet Civilian Sector Defenses against Biological Warfare and Infectious Diseases

1. Raymond A. Zilinskas, "The Anti-plague System and the Soviet Biological Warfare Program," *Critical Reviews in Microbiology* 32, no. 1 (2006): 7–64.

2. The Biological and Toxin Weapons Convention Website, http://www.opbw.org.

3. Sonia Ben Ouagrham-Gormley, Alexander Melikishvili, and Raymond A. Zilinskas, "The Soviet Anti-plague System: An Introduction," *Critical Reviews in Microbiology* 32, no. 1 (2006): 15–14; Alexander Melikishvili, "Genesis of the Anti-plague System: The Tsarist Period," *Critical Reviews in Microbiology* 32, no. 1 (2006): 19–31; Sonia Ben Ouagrham-Gormley, "Growth of the Anti-plague System during the Soviet Period," *Critical Reviews in Microbiology* 32, no. 1 (2006): 33–46; Sonia Ben Ouagrham-Gormley, Alexander Melikishvili, and Raymond A. Zilinskas, "What Non-proliferation Policy for the Soviet Anti-plague System?," *Critical Reviews in Microbiology* 32, no. 1 (2006): 65–67; Zilinskas, 2006. These articles are also available at http://cns.miis.edu/research/antiplague/index.htm.

It is important to note that in 1996–2002, a 12-volume history of the anti-plague system was published in Russia. It has not been translated into English as of this writing. We possess a copy of the set and have had translated parts of it that are relevant to this book. See Moisey I. Levi, ed., *Interesting Stories about the Activities and People of the Anti-plague System of Russia and the Soviet Union* (in Russian), vols. 1–12 (Moscow: Informika, 1996–2002). We refer to this source as the "Levi volumes."

4. B. Velimirovic, "Plague and Glasnost: First Information about Human Cases in the Soviet Union in 1989 and 1990," *Infection* 18, no. 6 (1990): 72/388–77/393.

5. A. I. Dyatlov, "Tracking Down the Answer to the Riddle of Plague Enzoosis," in Levi, vol. 3, 141.

6. V. Yu. Litvin, "Sapronotic Aspects of Plague Enzootic" (in Russian), *Spekhi Sovremennoy Biologii* (December 31, 2003): 543.

7. Igor V. Domaradsky, *Troublemaker, or The Story of an "Inconvenient" Man* (in Russian) (Moscow, 1995).

8. Ken Alibek with Stephen Handelman, *Biohazard: The Chilling True Story of the Largest Covert Biological Weapons Program in the World—Told from Inside by the Man Who Ran It* (New York, 1999); Taisia Belousova, "Fifth problem: Comments from Russian scientists (in Russian)," *Sovershenno Sekretno*, no. 11 (2001): 16–17.

9. Zilinskas, 2006.

10. Ben Ouagrham-Gormley, Melikishvili, and Zilinskas, 2006; anti-plague scientist, personal communication, 2003.

11. Igor Domaradsky, personal communication, 2001.

12. Igor V. Domaradskij and Wendy Orent, *Biowarrior: Inside the Soviet/Russian Biological War Machine* (Amherst, N.Y., 2003).

13. Ben Ouagrham-Gormley, 2006.

14. All three of these institutes were USSR-AMN institutes and accordingly were not under the authority of the MOH. Thus, Problems 1–4 were the responsibility of the MOH's 2nd Directorate, but Problem 5 was supported by the MOD, guided by the USSR-AMN, and operated by the 2nd Directorate. There probably were some difficult jurisdictional issues involved in this setup.

15. Anti-plague scientist, personal communication, 1999.

16. Igor Domaradsky, personal communication, September 2002.

17. Ben Ouagrham-Gormley, 2006.

18. Vaccine research and development in the Soviet Union presents an odd dichotomy as to secrecy. Work done under Problem 5 on vaccines was classified, so its results were not openly published. However, much work on, for example, plague vaccines done at anti-plague institutes was open and its results published. It might be that work to investigate and improve known vaccine strains, such as EV, was permitted to be done openly, while research on new or unique strains was kept secret. For an early review of Soviet plague R&D, see Robert Pollitzer, *Plague and Plague Control in the Soviet Union: History and Bibliography through 1964*, Institute of Contemporary Russian Studies, Fordham University, 1966.

19. Leonid F. Zykin, "Volgograd Anti-plague Institute: From Sunrise to Sunset" (in Russian), in Levi, vol. 8 (1998), 37–52.

20. Boris G. Valkov, "Northwest Caspian Plague Focus and Several Aspects of Activity in It" (in Russian), in Levi, vol. 12, pt. 2, (2002), 4–39.

21. In Soviet times, *Burkholderia mallei* and *Burkholderia pseudomallei* were respectively called *Pseudomonas mallei* and *Pseudomonas pseudomallei*.

22. Zykin, 1998, 42.

23. Ibid., 46.

24. Byelorussian scientist, personal communication, 2003.

25. Igor Domaradsky, personal communication, 2001.

26. Similar classified volumes might well exist at the Ivanovsky and Chumakov Institutes.

27. Igor Domaradsky, personal communication, 2001. Domaradsky described General Pautov as a very cautious man (he later became director of the Institute of Experimental Hygiene in Kirov).

28. Information for this section was derived mostly from interviews conducted by one of the authors (Zilinskas), who visited Lviv in May 2003. Because the Ukraine government indicated sensitivity about this visit, we do not name those he interviewed.

29. The SES provided traditional public health services—such as communicable disease surveillance, prevention, and control, and the maintenance of environmental health—to all parts of the Soviet Union.

30. Brill-Zinsser disease is a recrudescent case of typhus. After a patient is treated with antibiotics and the disease has seemingly been cured, rickettsiae may linger in body tissues. Months, years, or even decades after treatment, organisms may re-emerge and cause a recurrence of typhus. How rickettsiae linger silently in a person and by what mechanism recrudescence is mediated are unknown. The presentation of Brill-Zinsser disease is less severe and lethality is much lower than in epidemic typhus. Risk factors that may predispose a person to recrudescence include improper or incomplete antibiotic therapy and malnutrition.

31. See Waclaw Szybalski, "The Genius of Rudolf Stefan Weigl (1883–1957), a Lvovian Microbe Hunter and Breeder—in Memoriam," paper presented at the International Weigl Conference "Microorganisms in Pathogenesis and Their Drug Resistance," Programme and Abstracts, September 11–14, 2003, Lviv, Ukraine.

32. Ben Ouagrham-Gormley, Melikishvili, and Zilinskas, 2006; Melikishvili, 2006; and Ben Ouagrham-Gormley, 2006.

6. Biopreparat's Role in the Soviet Biological Warfare Program and Its Survival in Russia

1. This organization went through several name changes over its existence. In addition to its first official name, All-Union Science Production Association Biopreparat, we have learned of the following open names: The Ogarkov Organization, the Ogarkov System, Special Directorate of the Main Administration of Microbiological Industry, the Main Directorate Biopreparat of the USSR Ministry of Medical Industry, the State Concern Biopreparat, the Joint Stock Company (RAO) Biopreparat, and, informally, the System. Its classified name was P.O. Box A-1063. For the sake of simplicity, we call it "Biopreparat" throughout this book.

2. Ken Alibek with Stephen Handelman, *Biohazard: The Chilling True Story of the Largest Covert Biological Weapons Program in the World—Told from Inside by the Man Who Ran It* (New York, 1999); Igor V. Domaradskij and Wendy Orent, *Biowarrior: Inside the Soviet/Russian Biological War Machine* (Amherst, N.Y., 2003).

3. Anthony Rimmington, "The Soviet Union's Offensive Program: The Implications for Contemporary Arms Control," in *Biological Warfare and Disarmament: New Problems/New Perspectives,* ed. Susan Wright (New York, 2002), 110.

4. See Alibek with Handelman, 1999, 117; Rimmington, 2002.

5. It remains difficult to draw a distinct line separating Biopreparat from the other secret Soviet BW subprograms because they shared plans, funding, facilities, and personnel. The two men who headed Biopreparat from 1972 to 2001 (Ogarkov and his successor, Yury T. Kalinin) both held the rank of lieutenant general and had previously worked at BW facilities under the MOD. Their deputy Vorobyov held

the rank of major general and his successor, Kanatzhan B. Alibekov, that of colonel. Major General Urakov, former deputy director of the MOD's Kirov Institute, became the successor of the first head of the All-Union Scientific-Research Institute of Applied Microbiology in Obolensk, Major General Vinogradov-Volzhinsky, who came from the Zagorsk Institute. Lieutenant Colonel Yevgeny A. Stavsky graduated together with Alibekov from the Tomsk Military Academy. He joined the 15th Directorate and later worked at the Zagorsk Institute, but then transferred to Vector, where he worked under Colonel Yevgeny P. Lukin, who together with his deputy Vladimir Shishkov had come from the Zagorsk Institute. Lukin soon was appointed deputy director general of Vector and, together with Stavsky and Shishkov, was placed in charge of a project to manufacture smallpox virus on an industrial scale for BW purposes; see Alibek with Handelman, 1999, 4.

6. Ibid., 14, 18, and 20.

7. Pasechnik informed us that there was a second council that operated in parallel with the MNTS that was called the Biopreparat Interbranch Scientific and Technical Council (BNTS). The BNTS was also headquartered at Ulitsa Samokatnaya, and its chairman was Kalinin. As its name suggests, it dealt with issues of importance to all Biopreparat institutes and facilities.

8. The membership of the MNTS, established in 1973, besides these two, included Anatoly A. Skladnev (head of the technical directorate of *Glavmikrobioprom*), S. I. Alikhanyan (head of *Glavmikrobioprom's* Institute of Genetics and Selection of Microorganisms), Vladimir A. Lebedinsky (Smirnov's deputy), Rem V. Petrov (USSR-AN), Yu. A. Ovchinnikov (USSR-AN), A. I. Burnazyan (deputy minister of health and head of its 3rd Directorate), G. K. Skryabin (USSR-AN), A. A. Baev (USSR-AN), V. Morozov (deputy minister of agriculture). The appointment of these men to MNTS was the responsibility of the Politburo *nomenklatura*, although we understand that Brezhnev (general secretary of the CPSU) and Kosygin (chairman of the Council of Ministers) personally confirmed their appointments.

9. Domaradskij and Orent, 2003, 177.

10. Ibid., 146–147, 177–178.

11. Ibid., 178. The MOD laboratories continued to develop, test, and produce first generation biological weapons as Bonfire was implemented and would continue to do so until newly created or enhanced pathogens were validated and thus could be used to replace classical pathogens.

12. Immunological research has shown that an individual's immune system is triggered to fight off pathogens, such as bacteria and viruses, when specific components of the immune defense system—antibodies, B-cells, and T cells—recognize parts of the pathogen's surface called epitopes. Past vaccinations to protect against the pathogen prepare an individual's immune defense system's ability to recognize

those epitopes, and once mobilized help prevent future infections. Deliberately changing epitopes may render the vaccines possessed and used by a target population useless.

13. Sergei Popov, personal communication, 2005.

14. Domaradskij and Orent, 2003, 154.

15. We have found a variety of names for this institute, including Institute of Biological Instrumentation, Institute for Biological Instrument Design, All-Union Scientific-Research Institute of Medical Instrument Design, State Research Institute of Biological Instrument-Making, Institute of Biological Instrument-Making, and Special Design Bureau for Biological Instrument Development. Further, the acronym *Biopribor* is also used for a similar type institute located in Pushchino.

16. We would like to make clear that Domaradsky was an eminent scientist rather than a bureaucrat. His record is very impressive – author of 17 books and monographs, more than 300 scientific articles, and 51 inventions; he also trained 13 doctors and 57 candidates of science. See "In Memory of Igor Valerianovich Domaradskiy" (in Russian), *Zhurnal Mikrobiologii Epidemiologii i Immunologii,* (May 1, 2006).

17. Igor V. Domaradsky, "The History of One Risky Venture. Part I" (in Russian), *Znanie-Sila,* November 1996, 60.

18. Domaradskij and Orent, 2003, 169.

19. Zilinskas heard him give a talk at the only international conference sponsored by Biopreparat and noted at that time, "Ogarkov's talk was a disappointment to me because it only dealt with generalities and provided no data. It sounded like a set speech probably given to every worker's delegation Ogarkov is asked to address." Raymond A. Zilinskas, "Metabolic Plasmids Conference. Trip Report: USSR, October 17–28, 1982," unpublished paper, 1982.

20. V. I. Ogarkov and K. G. Gapochko, *Aerogenic Infection* (in Russian) (Moscow, 1975).

21. Alibek with Handelman, 1999, 23.

22. Ibid, 23.

23. Ibid, 62–69.

24. Igor V. Domaradsky, December 1996, 58.

25. Prominent foreign scientists who attended the conference included Irwin C. Gunsalus (US), Clarence I. Kado (US), Daniel Kunz (US), John Cullum (UK), Johannes Doehmer (FRG), and David Dubnau (US).

26. Office of Technology Assessment, *Commercial Biotechnology: An International Analysis* (Washington, D.C., 1984); Raymond A. Zilinskas, "Biotechnology in the USSR, Part I," *Bio/Technology* 2 (July 1984): 610–615; Zilinskas, "Biotechnology in the USSR, Part II," *Bio/Technology* 2 (August 1984): 686–692; Zilinskas, "Biotechnology in the USSR, Corrigendum," *Bio/Technology* 2 (September 1984): 744.

27. Director of Central Intelligence, *Soviet Genetic-Engineering Capabilities* (Washington, D.C., December 1983) (Secret). See especially pages 4–7.

28. Before this appointment, Bykov served as the director of the biochemical plant in Kirishi during 1971–1976 (see below), the first secretary of Kirishi's committee of the USSR Communist Party (1976–1979), and head of sector of the Department of Chemical Industry of the Central Committee of USSR Communist Party (1979–1985). Bykov was the successor of *Glavmikrobioprom's* previous head, R. S. Rychkov. Rychkov, in turn, had succeeded Belyayev.

29. Alibek with Handelman, 1999, 44.

30. Vladimir Pasechnik, personal communication, October 1998.

31. Ibid.; Alibek with Handelman, 1999, 299–300.

32. Vladimir Pasechnik, personal communication, October 1998.

33. Alibek with Handelman, 1999, 300.

34. Ibid.

35. This institute also has a variety of names, including Institute *Biokhimmashproekt* for Technological Development, Scientific-Research Design Institute of Applied Biochemistry, All-Union Research-and-Development Design-and-Engineering Institute of Applied Biochemistry, and Scientific-Research Machine-Building Institute. Its current name in Russia is Institute of Applied Biochemistry and Machine Building (*JSC Biochimmash*).

36. Alibek with Handelman, 1999, xii, 146–147, 300

37. Brochure "Institute of Applied Biochemistry and Machine Building (*JSC Biochimmash*)" (in English), March 15, 2010.

38. Anthony Rimmington, "Fragmentation and Proliferation? The Fate of the Soviet Union's Offensive Biological Weapons Programme," *Contemporary Security Policy* 20, no. 4 (April 1999): 95, citing *Biotechnology Directory Eastern Europe,* ed. E. M. Lucke and E. Poetzsch (Berlin, 1993).

39. Pasechnik, 1998.

40. Anthony Rimmington, *Technology and Transition: A Survey of Biotechnology in Russia, Ukraine and the Baltic States* (London, 1992).

41. Raymond A. Zilinskas, "Biotechnology Industry Survives with a Struggle in the Baltic Republics," *Genetic Engineering News* 13, no. 17 (October 1, 1993): 11.

42. Ilene Schneider, "Fermentas Learned Fast How to Go Global," *Genetic Engineering News* 28, no. 6 (March 15, 2008): 20.

43. Sonia Ben Ouagrham and Kathleen M. Vogel, *Conversion at Stepnogorsk: What the Future Holds for Former Bioweapons Facilities,* Occasional Paper #28, Peace Studies Program, Cornell University, 2003, 12.

44. Alibek with Handelman, 1999, x, 43.

45. Vitaly Kaysyn, "Top Secret: Drugs—A Defense, or a Weapon?" (in Russian), *Pravda,* October 15, 1992, 4.

46. Vitaly Kondratyev, "How One Citizen Outsmarted the Government: Strange Things Are Going on in Russia's Medical Industry" (in Russian), *Komsomolskaya Pravda,* December 7, 2000, 14–15.

47. Igor Khripunov, "Soviet BW Offensive Program and Its Residual Capacity in Russia (part II)," unpublished paper, April 21, 2000.

48. Business Information Service for the Newly Independent States (BISNIS), "Search for Partners—Medical/Health Care," August 1996; http://www.iep.doc .gov/bisnis/bisnis.html (accessed in 2003 but on June 20, 2008, it was unavailable; BISNIS was supported by the US Department of Commerce but appears to have closed in 1996.)

49. Pharmaceutical Technology, "Izvarino Medications Production Plant, Russia" (2000), http://www.pharmaceutical-technology.com/projects/moscow/.

50. John Fialka, "Old Soviet Biological-Weapons Labs Lend a Hand to U.S.: Research Holds Promise for Buffalo Disease, Vaccine Techniques and Bacteria Detectors," *Wall Street Journal,* November 2, 2000, A16. We do not keep track of commercial activities in Russia beyond those involving Biopreparat, so we suggest that readers interested in this field access *Kommersant,* which is the major Russian business newspaper published in English and Russian (http://kommersantuk.com /?lang=en).

51. Biopreparat scientist, personal communication, 2000.

52. Kondratyev, 2000, 14.

53. Ibid., 15.

54. Miller et al. are referring to a meeting that was held in September 1997 between Kalinin and a high-placed US official named Andrew C. Weber. It did not go well because of Kalinin's resistance to the Americans dealing directly with individual institutes. Weber probably was not aware of the secret 1997 decree.

55. Judith Miller, Stephen Engelberg, and William Broad, *Germs: Biological Weapons and America's Secret War* (New York, 2001), 221.

56. Zaviyalov might not have been aware of the secret 1997 decree.

57. Judith Miller, "U.S. Aid Is Diverted to Germ Warfare, Russian Scientists Say," *New York Times,* January 25, 2000.

58. Unattributed, "Infectious Money" (in Russian), *Izvestia,* January 26, 2000; Aleksey Khodorych, "Pharmacists Suspected of Producing Weapons" (in Russian), *Kommersant Daily,* February 2, 2000.

59. Roberta L. Gross, Inspector General of the National Aeronautics and Space Administration, Statement before the Subcommittee of Space and Aeronautics, House Committee on Science, March 16, 2000.

60. Ibid.

61. George W. S. Abbey, *Verification of Payments to Biopreparat.* Report, March 28, 2000. Houston: National Aeronautics and Space Administration.

62. Office of Inspector General, *NASA Oversight of Russian Biotechnology Research 1994–1997, G-00-007,* Washington, D.C., October 13, 2000, 19.

63. At a NATO Advanced Research Workshop in 1997 in Budapest, participants were informed that Biopreparat's "overhead" was 5%; see Chapter 23.

64. At the same NATO Advanced Research Workshop in 1997, participants were told that if the overhead was not included in the budget, the project would be delayed 12 or 18 months, or would not be funded at all.

65. Judith Miller, "Russia: Germ-Warfare Expert Replaced," *New York Times,* April 5, 2001.

66. Oleg Volkov and Anastasiya Naryshkina, "Products List Change" (in Russian), *Vremya Novostey,* April 6, 2001, 5.

67. Biopreparat, "Biopreparat: Russian Joint Stock Company" (brochure, in Russian) (n.p., n.d.). Our source gained possession of the brochure in 2005 and was told it was published that year.

68. "Fradkov Fires Roszdravnadzor Chief," *Kommersant Daily,* March 5, 2007, http://www.kommersant.com/p-10247/ouster_beneficial_medicaments/.

69. Mikhail Rabinovich, "History of Biotech in Russia," *Biotechnology Journal* 2 (2007): 776.

70. "Special: Biotech in Russia," *Biotechnology Journal* 2 (2007): 775–789.

71. The Bioprocess Group, "History," http://www.bioprocess.ru/38/.

72. In March 2010, Zilinskas participated in a Gordon Research Conference and at that time had an opportunity to converse with two British bacteriologists who worked at the Health Protection Agency laboratories at Porton Down. Neither had heard of the BWC.

73. "USSR Statute on Discoveries, Inventions and Rationalization Proposals of 1973," *Industrial Property,* July 1974, 298–319.

74. In practice, in Soviet times patents were granted only to foreign entities.

75. V. Meshcheryakov, "'Classification' lives on in Russia" (in Russian), *Izobretatel i Ratsionalizator,* no. 11 (1994): 14.

76. It bears noting that the US government was, and is, empowered to issue secret patents when it believes this is necessary for national security; see Invention and Secrecy Act of 1951, 35 U.S.C. 181.

77. Meshcheryakov, 1994.

7. Biopreparat's State Research Center for Applied Microbiology (SRCAM)

1. Igor V. Domaradskij and Wendy Orent, *Biowarrior: Inside the Soviet/Russian Biological War Machine* (Amherst, N.Y., 2003), 148.

2. N. N. Urakov, "The 25th Anniversary of the State Research Center of Applied Microbiology: Results and Perspectives" (in Russian), *Prikladnaya Biokhimiya i*

Mikrobiologiya 36, no. 6 (2000): 626–630. The years 1974 and 1975 were particularly important, because during this time decisions were made and funding was allocated to construct and equip most of the major Biopreparat institutes, including the All-Union Research Institute for Applied Microbiology in Obolensk, the All-Union Research Institute of Molecular Biology in Koltsovo, the Stepnogorsk Scientific Experimental-Industrial Base, the Institute of Biological Instrumentation in Moscow, the *Biokhimmashproekt* for Technological Development in Moscow, as well as lesser facilities at Omutninsk, Yoshkar-Ola, and Penza.

3. Ken Alibek with Stephen Handelman, *Biohazard: The Chilling True Story of the Largest Covert Biological Weapons Program in the World—Told from Inside by the Man Who Ran It* (New York, 1999), 159.

4. Igor Domaradsky, personal communication, 1999.

5. Dmitri V. Vinogradov-Volzhinsky was born in Leningrad in the 1920s. He earned his medical doctorate at the S. M. Kirov Military Medical Academy in Leningrad, but then decided to specialize in parasitology. During 1954–1965, he worked at the Zagorsk Institute, developing mosquitoes and other insects as vectors for BW agents. After the MOD lost interest in this line of BW, he returned to the Military Medical Academy and researched natural focus infections. In 1973 he became the director of SRCRAM and was responsible for its construction and equipping. In 1982, Vinogradov-Volzhinsky was appointed secretary of the MNTS, where he worked for several years. He retired as a major general of the medical service. The last information we have of him is that in the 1990s he worked at the All-Union Scientific Research Institute of Biochemical Mechanical Engineering, studying methods of plant protection. (Source: Former Biopreparat scientist, 2008.)

6. Obolensk is named after a Russian noble family, Obolensky, which once owned property in the area. The family fled to England after the Russian 1917 revolution. The last survivor of the family, Prince Alexander Obolensky, was killed at the age of 24 while practicing landings in a Hawker Hurricane on March 29, 1940. See Brendan Gallagher, "The Day a Russian Prince in an England Shirt Beat the All Blacks," *The Telegraph* (London), March 11, 2006. In the Soviet system there were closed cities and secret cities. Closed cities, of which the most noteworthy for our purposes was Sverdlovsk, were cities that foreigners were not allowed to enter without special permission. Secret cities were known only to persons with the right clearances and did not appear on ordinary maps. The secret cities we discuss in this book, like Obolensk, typically had two subdivisions: one that contained the closed facility like SRCAM, and the second that was a settlement where the facility's workers and their families were housed. Usually, several kilometers separated the subdivisions because of safety and security considerations.

7. Domaradskij and Orent, 2003, 197.

8. In Soviet times, *Coxiella burnetii* was called *Rickettsia burnetii*.

9. Two of the five Biopreparat institutes we address—SRCAM and SNOPB— were from their beginnings directed by military officers.

10. Pushchino was one of the Soviet Union's most important "science" cities, home to dozens of Academy and ministry research institutions and a settlement where their scientists and families lived.

11. Former Biopreparat scientist, personal communication, 2004.

12. Igor Domaradsky, personal communication, 2001.

13. Nikolai Tyurin, "Forty Years of High-Energy Physics in Protvino," *CERN Courier,* November 1, 2003, http://cerncourier.com/cws/article/cern/28958.

14. Urakov, 2000.

15. Vorobyov (at times spelled Vorobyev) studied at the Military-Naval Medical Academy (VMMA). In 1956 he joined the Zagorsk Institute. Vorobyov and Igor P. Ashmarin may well have been the foremost military scientists in the Soviet Union during the 1972–1992 period. For his biography, see "Anatoly Andreevich Vorobyov (on His 80th birthday)" (in Russian), *Vestnik Rossiyskoy Akademii Meditsinskikh Nauk,* January 31, 2003, 3–5.

16. State Research Center of Russia, State Research Center for Applied Microbiology, [Untitled brochure in English describing the Center's history, organization, and work program], 2000.

17. Organisation for Economic Cooperation and Development, *The OECD Megascience Forum. Unique Research Facilities in Russia. Volume 2. Laboratory Complex of P-3 Level of Physical Protection for Studies on the Agents of Severe Infections, Static-Climatic; Horizontal Dynamic Device (SC-10; HDD-600), State Research Center of the Russian Federation, State Research Center for Applied Microbiology, Ministry of Health and Medical Industry,* Paris, OECD Publication Service, 1997; http://web.archive.org/web/20001212153100/www.oecd.org/dsti/sti/s_t/ms/prod/russia/1ch5.htm.

18. Organisation for Economic Cooperation and Development, 1997.

19. Vitaly Kaysyn, "Visiting a Caged Beast" (in Russian), *Pravda,* February 4, 992.

20. SRCAM workers often claim that the center was a safe place to work, with not a single serious accident from the time it opened until 2004 (see below). As far as we can discern, this statement is correct.

21. Domaradskij and Orent, 2003, 185.

22. Peter Nichols, "The Invisible Weapon," *Rutgers Magazine,* Spring 2002.

23. State Research Center of Russia, State Research Center for Applied Microbiology, 2000.

24. Ibid.

25. Domaradskij and Orent, 2003, 195.

26. Since about 1993, the United States government has instituted restrictions on the purchase and transport of so-called Select Agents. Before this time, most microorganisms, even pathogens, usually were easily procured by legitimate researchers.

27. Problems faced by Soviet scientists at that time are discussed in Raymond A. Zilinskas, "Biotechnology in the USSR, Part I," *Bio/Technology* 2, no. 1 (July 1984): 610–615; Zilinskas, "Biotechnology in the USSR, Part II," *Bio/Technology* 2, no. 2 (August 1984): 686–692; and Zilinskas, "Biotechnology in the USSR, Corrigendum," *Bio/Technology* 2, no. 3 (September 1984): 744.

28. In Soviet times, the scientific names of *B. mallei* and *B. pseudomallei* were, respectively, *Pseudomonas mallei* and *Pseudomonas pseudomallei*.

29. The term "holarctic" means "related to the northern regions of the world in Europe and Asia."

30. In 1984 the MOH gave SRCAM permission to work with virulent non-holarctic strains, such as the Schu strain.

31. As noted in Chapter 1, weaponized *F. tularensis* disseminated as aerosol was considered a lethal agent by the Soviet BW program.

32. Alibek with Handelman, 1999, 62–68.

33. Ibid., 204.

34. Domaradskij and Orent, 2003, 21. (Emphasis in the original.)

35. For Domaradsky to be transferred from "real" work to open-legend work was an obvious demotion.

36. Domaradskij and Orent, 2003, 218.

37. Ibid., 216.

38. Former Biopreparat scientist, personal communication, 2003.

39. Sergei Popov, personal communication, 2007.

40. Scientists at the Kirov Institute might have taken an alternative approach that depended on developing two strains of *B. anthracis,* with each being resistant to five different antibiotics, and then mixing these two strains in one formulation.

41. A. P. Pomerantsev, Yu. V. Mockov, L. I. Marinin, A. V. Stepanov, and L. G. Podinova. "Anthrax Prophylaxis by Antibiotic Resistant Strain STI-AR in Combination with Urgent Antibiotic Therapy," Centre for Applied Microbiology and Research, Porton Down, England, 1995.

42. One of the Soviet Union's foremost plague experts has asserted that he and his colleagues had attempted to genetically engineer *Yersinia pestis* so it would be resistant to 10 antibiotics. In this they were only partially successful—they succeeded in developing two strains, each of which resisted the actions of five antibiotics (Sergei Popov, personal communication, 2000).

43. The failed attempt by Russian scientists to develop strains of bacterial pathogens resistant to 10 antibiotics demonstrates that the more antibiotic resistance one attempts to imbue an organism with, the larger the technical barriers that have to be overcome. It must be noted, however, that the Russian work on this subject was done before 1992. Since that time there have been remarkable advances in the biosciences so what was not doable by the Russians probably is possible today.

44. A. P. Pomerantsev, N. A. Staritsin, Yu. V. Mockov, and L. I. Marinin, "Expression of Cereolysine AB Genes in *Bacillus anthracis* Vaccine Strain Ensures Protection against Experimental Hemolytic Anthrax Infection," *Vaccine* 15, nos. 17–18 (December 1997): 1846–1850.

45. *B. cereus* is a common microbial contaminant of various kinds of food and when ingested by humans can cause serious food poisoning. Its cereolysine genes code for the production of cereolysine A and B, which have powerful cytotoxic properties that destroy red blood cells and some tissue cells.

46. Robert M. DeBell, "Progress in Research with the plcR Gene in *Bacillus anthracis*," *ASA Newsletter,* issue no. 102, March 2004, http://www.asanltr.com/news letter/04-3/articles/043c.htm.

47. William J. Broad, "Gene-Engineered Anthrax: Is It a Weapon?" *New York Times,* March 14, 1998, D1, D4.

48. Natural *B. anthracis* strains do not have the capability to hemolyze red blood cells.

49. Paul Keim, personal communication, May 2011.

50. For a useful review article, see Edward J. Bottone, *"Bacillus cereus,* a Volatile Human Pathogen," *Clinical Microbiology Reviews* 23, no. 2 (April 2010): 382–398.

51. For an overview of the methods whereby *B. anthracis* can be genetically engineered, we refer the reader to Brian K. James and Scott Stibitz, "Genetic Manipulation Methods in *Bacillus anthracis,"* in *Bacillus anthracis and Anthrax,* ed. Nicholas H. Berman (Hoboken, N.J., 2011), 53–66.

52. According to Popov, the name "Factor" was derived from that program's objective of adding virulence *factors* to BW agents.

53. D. Michael Gill, "Bacterial Toxins: A Table of Lethal Amounts," *Microbiological Reviews* 46, no. 1 (March 1982): 86.

54. Domaradskij and Orent, 2003, 231.

55. Volkovoy was one of the few remaining Lysenkoists at SRCAM. He believed that *Y. pseudotuberculosis* could be converted into pathogenic *Y. pestis* if the right environmental stresses were applied to it or if it were passed through multiple animals. We understand that Volkovoy was always strongly supported by Urakov.

56. Igor P. Ashmarin (1925–June 23, 2007) was by several accounts the MOD's brightest bioscientist. He graduated from the Kirov Military Medical Academy and then spent his whole life in the military, retiring in 1986 with the rank of major general. He apparently spent many years on weaponizing rickettsiae and variola virus at the Zagorsk Institute before becoming interested in neuropeptides. He was given the unusual privilege for a military scientist to head a laboratory at the open Moscow State University, which provided a base for him to publish open-source articles and books.

57. Nootropic drugs supposedly improve human cognitive abilities.

58. Semax International Inc.: "SEMAX® is a neuropeptide developed by the Institute of Molecular Genetics; Russian Academy of Sciences, Moscow, Russia and 'Lomonosov' University, Moscow. Research started in 1982 and involved over 30 scientists in the fields of Neurochemistry, Neurobiology, Neurology and Biochemistry from the Russian Federation." Source: http://www.semaxint.com/history.htm.

59. It bears noting that the world's first peptide drug introduced into clinical practice was insulin, discovered in 1921 by Fredrick G. Banting. In 2010 it remains the leading peptide therapeutic drug in terms of sales.

60. Roza N. Lukina and Yevgeny P. Lukin, eds., *The 50 Years of the Ministry of Defense Virology Center Deserve to Be Known* (in Russian), Sergiev Posad, Russia, Veterans Council of the Virology Center of the Russian Federation Ministry of Defense's Scientific Research Institute for Microbiology and the publishing house Ves Sergiev Posad, January 10, 2004, 112. Ashmarin is listed as a co-inventor in one Soviet inventor's certificates and three Russian patents related to peptides: "Heptapeptide as prolonged action memory stimulator" (SU 939440, 1982); "Neuropeptides showing behavioral activity" (SU 1623166, 1994); "Heptapeptide with adaptogenic and anxiolytic activity" (RU 2161500, 2001); and "Peptide family eliciting neurotropic property" (RU 2206573, 2003).

61. Homeland Defense, "Interview—Serguei Popov," *Journal of Homeland Security,* November 1, 2000, updated November 19, 2002, http://www.homelandsecurity.org/journal/Interviews/PopovInterview_001107.htm.

62. Sergei Popov, personal communication, 2007.

63. Ibid.

64. A promoter is a segment of DNA that is located upstream of a gene. When exposed to specific stimulus, the promoter "turns on" the gene; i.e., it causes the gene to start producing the protein it encodes.

65. Sergei Popov, personal communication, 2000.

66. Researchers from the Swedish Defence Research Agency published a report on SRCAM in 2004 that provides a fine overview of its activities since 1992, including an analysis of the articles its researchers have published. See Britta Häggström, Åke Forsberg, and Lena Norlander, *Conversion of a Former Biological Weapon Establishment,* report FOI-R-1316-SE, September 2004. Our account here deals with developments and activities not covered by the Swedes, including machinations by Urakov and SRCAM interactions with other institutes and agencies.

67. Most of the nonhuman primates used at SRCAM came from the Sukhumi Primate Center in Georgia, but sometimes there was a need for such a large number of animals that Sukhumi was unable to supply them, thus necessitating the direct ordering of nonhuman primates from foreign suppliers.

68. Former Biopreparat scientist, personal communication, 2007.

69. Ibid.

70. Ibid.

71. Sergei Popov, personal communication, 2000.

72. Former Biopreparat scientist, personal communication, 2007.

73. Rita Mokhel, "Death Lab" (in Russian), *Moskovsky Komsomolets,* March 1, 005.

74. Former Biopreparat scientist, personal communication, 2007; Sergei Popov, personal communication, 2000.

75. Former Biopreparat scientist, personal communication, 2007.

76. Ibid.

77. At the height of its existence, SRCAM employed approximately 4,000 persons. This number went down to 2,904 in 1990; 2,249 in 1992; 1,580 in 1994; and 1,326 in 1996. Source: State Research Center of Russia, State Research Center for Applied Microbiology, [Untitled brochure in English describing the Center's history, organization, and work program], 2000. SRCAM's workforce in 2006 numbered approximately 550.

78. The ISTC is an internationally funded donor organization that supports former weapon scientists (see Chapter 23).

79. Urakov, 2000, 626.

80. Mokhel, 2005.

81. Urakov, 2000, 629.

82. We would like to make clear that SRCAM's indebtedness to utility companies was not unique. In 2002 the Moscow weekly magazine *Profil* interviewed the heads of seven regions and republics and found that all had military facilities within their jurisdictions that were indebted to utilities; see "View from the Gallery" (in Russian), *Profil,* February 4, 2002.

83. Some of these companies are listed on the website http://obolensk.chat.ru /index.htm. However, like many, perhaps most, websites in Russia, this one is dated; the last entry is July 2004.

84. Mokhel, 2005.

85. "Custodians of Anthrax and Plague Were Cut Off from Power Supplies" (in Russian), *Strana.ru,* August 15, 2002, http://strana.ru. Although the claim is made in this article that the power was cut off and these measures instituted, when Zilinskas visited SRCAM in 2003 and 2004 there was no indication that this had occurred.

86. Sergey Ptichkin, "Disco on plague: Only here, in Obolensk, Our Scientists Can Organize Russia's Effective Protection against the Most Ominous Epidemics, but . . ." (in Russian), *Rossiyskaya Gazeta,* March 19, 2002.

87. "Deadly Viruses from a Moscow Oblast Depository Threaten Moscow" (in Russian), *Izvestia,* March 18, 2002.

88. These are called ZAO "Konpo," AO "Ekovet," the Biotechnical Innovation Center, AO Bioruss, and AO Bellar. Anthony Rimmington, "Fragmentation and Proliferation? The Fate of the Soviet Union's Offensive Biological Weapons Programme," *Contemporary Security Policy* 20, no. 1 (April 1999): 86–110.

89. State Research Center for Applied Microbiology, "Center Information," 2008, http://obolensk.org/eng/index.htm. The English-language part of the SR-CAM site was last updated in April 2008, but the Russian-language part is up-to-date as of 2011 and is more informative and complete.

90. The circumstances of Boldyreva's death are described by Mokhel, 2005.

8. All-Union Research Institute of Molecular Biology and Scientific-Production Association "Vector"

1. Vector, "History of SRC VB VECTOR," 2003, http://www.vector.nsc.ru /DesktopDefault.aspx?lcid=9&tabid=280&tabindex=1.

2. "Especially dangerous" was Soviet-era terminology, but which is still used in Russia.

3. At the time, Klyucharev was Domaradsky's deputy; Igor V. Domaradskij and Wendy Orent, *Biowarrior: Inside the Soviet/Russian Biological War Machine* (Amherst, N.Y., 2003), 148. Later, Klyucharev became head of Biopreparat's Scientific Directorate, a position he held for many years. He was eventually replaced by Colonel Grigory Shcherbakov about 1991.

4. In the early 1920s, Koltsov was at the forefront of world genetics research. In the Soviet Union, he initiated work on phenogenetics (the genetic basis of the development of an organism), the rules of mutagenesis, and theoretical genetics (the basis of molecular genetics). See Vadim A. Ratner, "Nikolay Vladimirovich Timofeef-Ressovsky (1900–1981): Twin of the Century of Genetics," *Genetics* 158 (July 2001): 933–939.

5. Koltsovo's longitude and latitude on Google Earth are: 54° 56' 28.98" N; 83° 11' 07.77" E, while those of Vector are: 54° 56' 28.35" N; 83° 13' 47.97" E. Specifically, Vector's administration building is at: 54° 57' 05.52" N; 83° 12' 24.48" E.

6. Oddly enough, after SRCAM opened up to foreign visitors in 1994, its scientists would take an almost perverse pleasure in telling them that the level of workmanship here, supplied by military units, was markedly lower than was the case of Biopreparat institutes, such as Vector, which were built by convicts. Scientists at Vector would state the opposite.

7. Damansky Island (or Zhēnbǎo Dǎo in Chinese) is located in the Ussuri River, which delineates the border between northeastern China and the Soviet Union's Siberian Far East. Starting March 2, 1969, tensions that had simmered between China and the Soviet Union since Stalin's death boiled over into a series of violent border clashes, which for a time threatened to set off widespread conventional, or even nuclear, war. See Bruce Kennedy, "Centuries-Old Dispute Became Open Combat during Cold War," CNN Perspectives Series, No. 15, 1998, http://www.cnn .com/SPECIALS/cold.war/episodes/15/spotlight/.

8. Ectromelia virus causes mousepox, which is deadly to mice but does not affect humans. It is a distant relative of variola virus. Polydnaviruses parasitize the larval

stage of gypsy moths and therefore may be used as a biopesticide to eradicate this pest.

9. Sergeev (also spelled Sergeyev) had previously been a military physician and had moved with his family to Koltsovo from Zagorsk in 1979. He had worked under Vorobyov at the Zagorsk Institute, specializing in hemorrhagic fever viruses and variola major. At Vector he was one of a very few specialists who had experience with biological weapons production.

10. Cherny was also a virologist and Zagorsk Institute alumnus.

11. SPAs were large components of the Soviet military-industrial complex that specialized in the production of specific weapons systems. Each was composed of a research institute and an associated production facility. The production facility at times had separate components located at different sites. Each SPA also served as a type of social agent in that it was responsible for the creation of housing and leisure space for its employees.

12. Ken Alibek with Stephen Handelman, *Biohazard: The Chilling True Story of the Largest Covert Biological Weapons Program in the World—Told from Inside by the Man Who Ran It* (New York, 1999), 117.

13. Berdsk, with a population of approximately 90,000, is located approximately 20 km south of Koltsovo; see Google Earth at 54° 45′ 29.93″ N, 83° 5′ 32.08″ E.

14. Sergey V. Netesov, "The Scientific and Production Association Vector: The Current Situation," in *Control of Dual-Threat Agents: The Vaccines for Peace Programme,* ed. E. Geissler and J. P. Woodall, SIPRI Chemical and Biological Warfare Studies, vol. 15. Stockholm International Peace Research Institute, Solna, Sweden, 1994, 133–138.

15. Anthony Rimmington, "Invisible Weapons of Mass Destruction: The Soviet Union's BW Programme and Its Implications for Contemporary Arms Control," *Journal of Slavic Military Studies* 13, no. 3 (2000): 38, endnote 60.

16. Ibid.

17. Ibid.

18. Sergey V. Netesov, "The State Research Center of Virology and Biotechnology VECTOR for the Prevention of Misuse of Biological Sciences," in *First Forum of the International Scientific Panel on the Possible Consequences of the Misuse of Biological Sciences, Science for Peace Series,* vol. 6, UNESCO Venice Office, 1997, 125–139.

19. The Google Earth locations for these three important buildings are as follows: Building 1 at 54° 56′ 28.65″ N, 83° 13′ 31.97″ E; Building 6 at 54° 56′ 31.35″ N, 83° 13′ 46.24″ E; and Building 6A at 54° 56′ 32.70″ N, 83° 13′ 47.18″ E.

20. In 2007–2008, Chepurnov was a scientist at the Michigan Nanotechnology Institute for Medicine and Biological Sciences, Ann Arbor, Michigan.

21. Organisation for Economic Cooperation and Development, *The OECD Megascience Forum: Unique Research Facilities in Russia. Volume 2. P-4 Biocontainment Virological Laboratory Experimental Building,* Paris, OECD Publication Service,

1997, http://web.archive.org/web/20001213001400/http:/www.oecd.org/dsti/sti /s_t/ms/prod/russia/russia2.htm.

22. Ibid.

23. Organisation for Economic Cooperation and Development, *The OECD Megascience Forum. Unique Research Facilities in Russia. Volume 2. Unique Climatic Static-Dynamic Unit UKSD-25,* Paris, OECD Publication Service, 1997, http://web .archive.org/web/20001213001400/http:/www.oecd.org/dsti/sti/s_t/ms/prod /russia/russia2.htm.

24. Ibid. The OECD has archived the three volumes of *Unique Research Facilities in Russia* and, most unfortunately, has removed many of the photographs that illustrated the first editions of these volumes. The photographs of Vector facilities, including UKSD-25, were exceptionally interesting and therefore the OECD should restore them.

25. Organisation for Economic Cooperation and Development, *The OECD Megascience Forum. Unique Research Facilities in Russia. Volume 2. Laboratory Animals Farm,* Paris, OECD Publication Service, 1997, http://web.archive.org/web /20001213001400/http:/www.oecd.org/dsti/sti/s_t/ms/prod/russia/russia2.htm.

26. Biopreparat scientist, personal communication, 1999.

27. According to a currently active virologist, some of the findings stated by the Vector scientist need to be modified in light of more recent research findings.

28. There is much confusion about Marburg virus being contagious or noncontagious. It is not contagious in terms of the virus being transmitted person-to-person via aerosol, but it is readily spread by body fluids. A CDC information note states: "Droplets of body fluids, or direct contact with persons, equipment, or other objects contaminated with infectious blood or tissues are all highly suspect as sources of disease." Centers for Disease Control and Prevention, "Questions and Answers about Marburg Hemorrhagic Fever," May 03, 2005, http://www.cdc.gov/ncidod/dvrd/spb /mnpages/dispages/marburg/qa.htm.

29. According to a filovirus expert with whom we consulted, in nature Marburg virus does not experience loss of virulence by passage through humans. However, it is not possible to determine whether this also is true for humans who are infected via the "unnatural" aerosol route. The Vector virologists we interviewed were certain that Marburg virus does lose virulence as it sequentially passes through one host after another.

30. What the Soviet scientists came up against is typical of the problems besetting vaccine development. Because virus–host interactions are specific, it can be very difficult for vaccine developers to come up with a cell line that would be efficiently infected and hence produce high titers of virus. As far as vaccine production goes, it is a similar issue; i.e., many killed vaccines are not able to stimulate an effective antibody response and hence prove to be unsatisfactory vaccine candidates. This can be caused by any of a number of problems pertaining to, for example, the

method of killing the virus, the antigens themselves not being antigenic enough to stimulate an antibody response, the antigenic material being unstable, and the antigenic material not being present in the proper form to produce an antibody response. (Source: Alan J. Mohr, personal communication, 2008.)

31. Alibek describes the two viral propagation techniques very well; see Alibek with Handelman, 1999, 111–115.

32. N. I. Gonchar describes the three stages of hemorrhagic fever virus research at the Zagorsk Institute in some detail; see Nikolay I. Gonchar, "They Were the First: Stages in the Study of Exotic Hemorrhagic Fevers," in *The 50 Years of the Ministry of Defense's Virology Center Deserves Recognition* (in Russian), ed. Roza N. Lukina and Yevgeny P. Lukin (Sergiev Posad, 2004), 165–172 (see Chapter 3).

33. This information was provided by a Biopreparat scientist. However, because no challenge testing allegedly was done on humans in the Soviet Union, we do not know how this scientist can be certain about this statement's accuracy.

34. In 2000, a long article in the *Dallas Observer* described a collaboration between the University of Texas Southwestern Medical Center's Center for Biomedical Inventions (CBI) and Vector on developing a vaccine against Ebola virus disease. The collaboration was funded by the US Defense Advance Research Projects Agency. The Vector team was headed by Aleksandr Chepurnov, who was described as the head of Vector's Biosafety Level 4 virus laboratory. On his first visit to CBI, Chepurnov brought with him the entire genome of the Ebola virus broken into RNA fragments. These were to be tested for vaccine potential by CBI scientists, and promising candidates would be transported to Vector for animal testing in guinea pigs. See Joe Pappalardo, "From Russia with Bugs," *Dallas Observer,* June 22, 2000, http://www .dallasobserver.com/2000-06-22/news/from-russia-with-bugs.

35. It is worth noting that since that time virologists in the United States and other countries have done similar vaccine experiments and published extensively on them.

36. This "rule" was only loosely enforced. In general, Vector managers attempted to make certain that work on related viruses was confined to one floor so one would not see, for example, variola virus and hemorrhagic fever virus research on the same floor.

37. At Vector it is now possible to work on several agents on one floor, but it has to be done in different "boxes" (a "box" is a laboratory unit). The one-floor, one-pathogen rule still stands for the vivarium.

38. As discussed in Chapter 3, variola virus R&D for military purposes may have been started as early as 1956 by Valerian D. Neustroyev at the Zagorsk Institute, although the period of highest intensity of this work was after 1963. See Lukina and Lukin, 2004, 96.

39. Lukin was a leading scientific associate of the Zagorsk Institute and held the rank of colonel in the Soviet Army. His first research interest was BoNT, and his secret candidate thesis in 1961 was on this topic. He then worked for a short time on VEEV, but his most important research was done on rickettsiae, including his secret

doctoral thesis, which he defended in 1971. Russia's Higher Certification Commission awarded Lukin the title of professor in 1996; that same year he was elected a full member of the Academy of Military Sciences and Academy of Medical and Technical Sciences. He has been listed as co-author of articles published in Russian as late as 2008. We know little about Shishkov. He worked as a scientific associate at the Zagorsk Institute, specializing in the study of hemorrhagic fevers. His secret dissertation was also on this topic and was awarded sometime during 1969–1979.

40. Biopreparat scientist, personal communication, 1999.

41. Ibid.

42. Alibek with Handelman, 1999, 122.

43. We learned from a Vector scientist that a mobilization production plant was constructed at the Ministry of Agriculture's Pokrov Institute of Veterinary Virology that was capable of large-scale production of validated variola virus should war be imminent.

44. Vladimir Ye. Repin et al., "Permafrost as a Potential Source for Replenishing Collections with Pathogenic Microorganisms," *Hydrological Science and Technology* 16, nos. 1–4 (2000): 38.

45. "Has Smallpox Really Been Conquered?" (in Russian), *Radikal* (Moscow), no. 43, November 1992, 11.

46. Vector scientist, personal communication, 2009.

47. Vladimir Pokrovsky, "National 'Virus Property'" (in Russian), *Obshchaya Gazeta,* May 8, 1997.

48. Richard Stone, "Is Live Smallpox Lurking in the Arctic?," *Science* 295 (March 15, 2002): 2002.

49. Repin et al., 2000.

50. Ibid.

51. For reasons not known to us, soon after Drozdov took over as Vector's new director, he canceled all work on variola virus in permafrost regions.

52. Jonathan B. Tucker, *Scourge: The Once and Future Threat of Smallpox* (New York, 2001), 135–136.

53. Ibid., 174.

54. World Health Organization, Department of Communicable Disease Surveillance and Response, *Report of the Meeting of the Ad Hoc Committee on Orthopoxvirus Infections. Geneva, Switzerland, 14–15 January 1999,* report WHO/CDS/CSR/99.1.

55. E. N. Starkov, "Measures to Provide Biosafety at the Research Center of Virology and Biotechnology 'Vector,'" in *Maximising the Security and Development Benefits from the Biological and Toxin Weapons Convention,* ed. Malcolm R. Dando, Graham S. Pearson, Cyril Klement, and Marian Negut, NATO Science Series: 1. Disarmament Technologies, vol. 36, Dordrecht, Netherlands, October 2002, 247–252.

56. A chimera (or recombinant) is an organism that contains genetic constructs from two or more other organisms.

57. Actually, scientists at the USSR-AN Institute of the Biochemistry and Physiology of Microorganisms in Pushchino were the first in the Soviet Union to construct recombinant vaccinia virus, which was accomplished in 1986. For this task they needed special plasmids, which were developed by a Hungarian scientist who had been trained in the United States. When this work was reported, Vector scientist Vladimir Blinov contacted scientists at the Pushchino institute and asked for these plasmids to be sent to him, which was done.

58. Alibek with Handelman, 1999, 259–260; Homeland Defense, "Interview—Serguei Popov," *Journal of Homeland Security,* November 1, 2000, updated November 19, 2002, http://www.homelandsecurity.org/journal/Interviews/PopovInterview _001107.htm.

59. Tucker, 2001, 158.

60. According to Pasechnik, during the winter of 1988 and the spring of 1989, the BNTS had a series of internal discussions on the value of testing peptides on human subjects. The decision was that it should be done, so a formal request was made to the VPK and Central Committee for permission to do so. In 1989, just before Pasechnik's departure, permission was granted to conduct testing of peptides on no more than 3–5 human test subjects from "mental/psychiatric" institutions. He did not know if these tests were actually done.

61. Others who had trained at Zagorsk were Sergeyev and Cherny.

62. Alibek with Handelman, 1999, 131.

63. The pre-1969 US BW program did something similar. During its existence, three scientific workers were infected with *B. anthracis;* two of them died. Samples of blood were taken from all three and analyzed for virulence. One of them, named the Vollum 1B strain, was eventually weaponized; see Scott Shane, "Army Harvested Victims' Blood to Boost Anthrax: Ex-Scientists Detail Detrick Experiments," *Baltimore Sun,* December 23, 2001, 1A.

64. Alibek with Handelman, 1999, 131–132.

65. We do not know whether the immunoglobulin helped Vedishchev survive (it was administered much past 24 hours after exposure) or if Marburg virus variant U was indeed less virulent than the original strain that killed Ustinov.

66. Reportedly, yet another scientist, named O. A. Kostyrev, was present at Ustinov's autopsy and was exposed to Marburg virus. However, he did not develop the disease, but died in 1991 due to unrelated kidney disease.

67. V. V. Nikiforov, Yu. I. Turovsky, P. P. Kalinin, et al., "Case of Laboratory Marburg Fever Infection" (in Russian), *Zhurnal Mikrobiologii, Epidemiologii i Immunobiologii* 71, no. 3 (May/June 1994): 104–106.

68. "Science Scope," *Science* 304 (May 28, 2004): 1225.

69. L. A. Akinfeeva et al., "A Case of Ebola Hemorrhagic Fever" (in Russian), *Infectious Disease* 3, no. 1 (2005): 85–88.

70. In Soviet times there were no "paychecks." Instead there were lists on which each Biopreparat payee signed across his printed name and then was given his salary in cash. For military scientists, there was a second list.

71. Former Biopreparat scientist, personal communication, 2003.

72. Janet R. Gilsdorf and Raymond A. Zilinskas, "New Considerations in Infectious Disease Outbreaks: The Threat of Genetically Modified Microbes," *Clinical Infectious Diseases* 40 (2005): 1160–1165.

73. In the early days of genetic engineering, scientists often employed the "black box approach" to conducting experiments. This involved conducting, for example, a genetic engineering experiment without the investigators having a real understanding of the mechanisms of what they were doing or what its end product would be. The black box approach thus would be taken to find out what the end product would be and, based on its characteristics, the investigators would attempt to deduce the mechanism to explain its creation.

74. This first visit by a US-UK team, mentioned in foregoing chapters, is discussed in detail in Chapter 21.

75. Decisions as to where to go and what to see were made by the visitors on an ad hoc basis while visits were taking place. In effect, the visitors did not know in which buildings or laboratories BW-related work had been, or was being, done, so they had to guess. Further, the visitors had only a few hours to conduct their visits, which was clearly insufficient for covering such large facilities as Vector.

76. "Self-financed" refers to funding that Vector administrators raised from other sources than Biopreparat and MOD.

77. Vector homepage, http://www.vector.nsc.ru/DesktopDefault.aspx?lcid=9&tabindex=0&tabid=50. The Russian-language part of the Vector website is much more informative and up-to-date than the English part.

78. Decree No. 247 of the Government of the Russia Federation (March 29, 1994).

79. Russian Ministry of Public Health and Medical Industry, Order No. 210 (October 21, 1994).

80. Irina Samakhova, "Ebola Virus Research Continues at Vector State Virology and Biotechnology Center" (in Russian), *Literaturnaya Gazeta,* June 15, 1995, 13.

81. Sergey V. Netesov and Lev S. Sandakhchiev, "Possible Participation of the State Research Center for Virology and Biotechnology 'Vector' in a National and Global Network for Distinguishing Outbreaks," paper presented at the NATO-Advance Research Workshop "The Role of Biotechnology in Countering BTW Agents," October 21–23, 1998, Prague; L. S. Sandakhchiev, S. V. Netesov, and V. B. Loktev, "The Proposal to Establish an International Center for Emerging Diseases at the State Research Center for Virology and Biotechnology 'VECTOR,'" 5. Medizinische B-Schutz-Tagung des BMVg, October 28–29, 1998, Munich, Bavaria,

Germany; L. S. Sandakhchiev, "The Need for International Cooperation to Provide Transparency and to Strengthen the BWC," in *Conversion of Former BTW Facilities,* ed. E. Geissler, L. Gazsó, and E. Buder, NATO Science Series, Kluwer Academic Publishers, Netherlands, 1998, 149–156.

82. Pasechnik told us that this was an old idea of Sandakhchiev's. In 1985 Sandakhchiev had proposed to Kalinin that Vector be made an international center for dangerous viral pathogens and be opened for deposit of dangerous pathogens from anywhere in the world. He had argued that this development would be beneficial to Soviet security, the KGB, and even Kalinin himself. Kalinin had disagreed strongly, and this led to heated discussions between the two. The matter was discussed at both MNTS and BNTS meetings, but in the end Kalinin won out.

83. Starting in 1995, Vector has been a major recipient of funding from the Cooperative Threat Reduction Program to undertake a series of research projects under the heading of "Pathogens Initiative." These are considered in Chapter 23.

84. Richard Stone, "Russia, NIH Float Big Plan for Former Soviet Bioweapons Lab," *Science* 291 (2001): 2288–2289.

85. Lev S. Sandakhchiev, "Proposal to establish an International Laboratory for Emerging Infections at State Research Center of Virology and Biotechnology 'Vector,'" unpublished presentation made in 2000.

86. Irina Samakhova, "Vector Does Not Hex Neighboring Gardens: Their Concern Is Preservation of Unique Collection of Viruses—Interview with Academician Lev Sandakhchiev" (in Russian), *Obshchaya Gazeta,* July 20, 2000, http://www.vector.nsc.ru/DesktopDefault.aspx?lcid=9&tabid=352.

87. Vector, "History of Vector," 2003, http://www.vector.nsc.ru.

88. Lev S. Sandakhchiev, "State Research Center of Virology and Biotechnology 'Vector'" (in Russian), *Vestnik Rossiyskoy Akademii Meditsinskikh Nauk* no. 3 (1998): 3–5.

89. These are the Service Plant (directed by Ivan A. Pochtar), the Transportation Department (directed by Vladimir Yu. Sivay), and the Animal Breeding Farm (directed by Viktor N. Bondarenko).

90. These are the Daughter Unitary Energy-Producing Unit "Promtekhenergo" (directed by Nikolay I. Sklyarevsky), the Daughter State Unitary Production Unit "Vector-Farm" (directed by Sergey N. Targonsky), the Daughter State Unitary Pilot Production Unit "Vektor-BiAlgam" (directed by Leonid G. Nikulin), and the Daughter State Unitary Pilot Production Agricultural Enterprise "Vector-PPAE" (directed by D. N. Loktionov).

91. These include the ZAO "Vector-Best" in Novosibirsk, ZAO "Vector-Best-Baltika" in St. Petersburg, and, in Koltsovo, AO Vektor-BioProdukt, ZAO Vektor-MaiStar, and TOO "Delta." Anthony Rimmington, "Fragmentation and Proliferation? The Fate of the Soviet Union's Offensive Biological Weapons Programme," *Contemporary Security Policy,* Vol. 20, No. 1 (April 1999), 96.

92. Sergey V. Netesov and Lev S. Sandakhchiev, "The Development of the Network of International Centers to Combat Infectious Diseases and Bioterrorism Threat," in *Proceedings of the CB Medical Treatment Symposium Industry I—Eco-Terrorism, Chemical and BW without Chemical and Biological Weapons,* October 25–31, 1998, Ministry of Defense, Republic of Croatia, and Applied Science and Analyses, Inc., Zagreb-Dubrovnik, Croatia, 38/213–38/218.

93. Ibid.

94. Vector-Best, "About Company," February 6, 2007, http://www.vector-best.com/head_e.htm.

95. Former Vector scientist, October 2011.

96. Sandakhchiev, who was a heavy smoker all his adult life, died on June 29, 2006, after a long bout with heart disease; see Joby Warrick, "Lev Sandakhchiev: Led Russian Arms Shift," *Washington Post,* June 30, 2006, B6.

97. Ilya G. Drozdov was born on October 16, 1953, in Andijan, Uzbek SSR. In 1977 he graduated from the Saratov State Medical Institute. From 1977 to 2005 he worked at the Mikrob Anti-plague Research Institute in Saratov. During this time he advanced from graduate student to assistant director of science. In 1995 he became a doctor of medicine, and in 1996 a professor of microbiology.

98. Netesov left Vector in 2006 and became a vice dean at Novosibirsk State University.

99. In April 2008, the rather weighty official name of Vector and its acronym are as follows: Federal State Unitary Enterprise State Research Center for Virology and Biotechnology Vector of the Federal Service for Surveillance in the Area of Protection of Consumer Rights and Human Welfare (FGUN GNTs VB Vektor Rospotrebnadzora).

100. Vector scientists, personal communication, March 2008.

101. Losing ISTC funding would have been a heavy blow to Vector, as is demonstrated by the fact that it had received $31 million during 1995 and 2000. (Source: Vector scientist, personal communication, March 2011).

102. Gennady G. Onishchenko is Russia's chief medical officer and head of the Ministry of Health's Federal Service for Supervision in the Sphere of Protection of Consumer Rights and Well-Being of the Person. As part of his duties, he is in charge of the Biopreparat system and thus is able to formulate policy for its employees' working conditions.

103. Personal communication, 2011.

104. "A 'Laundry' Marked 'Secret'? Millions of Budget Rubles Dissolved at the Vektor Virology Center in Siberia." Open letter to Russian president Dmitry Anatolyevich Medvedev from Pavel Korchagin, deputy of the settlement council of the Koltsovo science city in Novosibirsk *Oblast,* preceded by *Novaya Gazeta* editorial introduction (in Russian), *Novaya Gazeta Online,* April 7, 2010, http://www.novaya-gazeta.ru/.

105. Ibid.

106. Personal communication, 2011.

107. Fredrik Westerlund, "Russian Intelligence Gathering for Domestic R&D: Short Cut or Dead End for Modernisation?," FOI Memo 3126, Swedish Defense Research Agency, April 2010.

108. Tetracycline, or one of its many derivatives, at that time was the antibiotic of choice for the treatment of plague.

109. Sergei Popov, personal communication, August 2007.

9. Biopreparat Facilities at Leningrad, Lyubuchany, and Stepnogorsk

1. This institute's name has been translated in several different ways, including Institute of Ultra-pure Compounds and Institute of Ultra-pure Biopreparations. We use the official name as spelled out on the Institute's homepage and descriptive brochure: State Scientific Center—Research Institute of Highly Pure Biopreparations (IHPB), *Illustrated Brochure in Russian and English,* St. Petersburg (2003).

2. Mark Urban, *UK Eyes Alpha: Inside British Intelligence* (London, 1996), 129–132; James Adams, "The Red Death: The Untold Story of Russia's Secret Biological Weapons," *Sunday Times* (London), March 27, 1994, sec. 4, 1–4; James Adams, *The New Spies: Exploring the Frontiers of Espionage* (London, 1994), 270–283.

3. Simon Cooper, "Life in the Pursuit of Death," *Seed,* January/February 2003, 67–107.

4. IHPB's three buildings can be seen on Google Earth at 59° 57'55.58" N and 30°17'32.45" E.

5. The IHPB's homepage is at http://www.hpb-spb.com/. The homepage has a nonfunctioning button for an English version; in addition, there is an uninformative website in English at http://biistate.net/docs/profiles/srihpb.pdf.

6. Interview with Vladimir Pasechnik, July 7, 2000. Adams (March 1994) states that Pasechnik told him that the IHBP employed 2,500 persons. Assuming that he is correct, this large number could include all persons who worked for IHBP, including those in the main building where the secret work was done, the Problem 5 laboratories, and some open work by, for example, the Group of Genetics headed by Vladimir Larionov. Our smaller number of 600 may include only workers at the main building.

7. The two officers made it clear that they were "Ogarkov's eyes and ears" at IHPB.

8. The standard Soviet definition of Q_{50} was: the amount of a BW agent formulation that when spread evenly over one square kilometer would cause 50% casualties among the population inhabiting that area.

9. On July 7, 2000, Pasechnik told us that he knew only that project Metol existed but not about its details.

10. Colonel Babkin was a strong proponent of wet *Y. pestis* formulations. In his zeal for this approach, he came to extend the wet versus dry argument from the Kirov Institute to the IHPB.

11. Cooper, 2003, 72.

12. Pasechnik quoted in Urban, 131.

13. Cooper, 2003, 72–73.

14. The source of all information in this paragraph was Vladimir Pasechnik, personal communication, July 7, 2000.

15. N. A. Polikarpov and M. P. Bragina, "Sensitivity to Antibiotics of Opportunistic Human Indigenous Microorganisms before and after Isolation in an Airtight Environment" (in Russian), *Kosmicheskaya Biologiyai Aviakosmicheskaya Meditsina* 23, no. 3 (1989): 62–65.

16. For a comprehensive review of the Soviet space program, including its biological aspects, see Brian Harvey with Olga Zakutnyaya, *Russian Space Probes: Scientific Discoveries and Future Missions* (Chichester, UK, 2011).

17. Under Gorbachev, a new law called Law of Cooperatives of May 1988 allowed private enterprises in the Soviet Union.

18. David C. Kelly, "The Trilateral Agreement: Lessons for Biological Weapons Verification," in *Verification Yearbook 2002,* ed. Trevor Findlay and Oliver Meier (London, 2002), 95.

19. The Yeltsin administration established the Committee on the Conventional Problems of Chemical and Biological Weapons Conversion in 1992 and made it responsible for the oversight of treaty provisions as spelled out in the BWC and Geneva Protocol (see Chapter 22). The Committee's first head was the former commander of the Russian chemical troops, Major General Anatoly Kuntsevich.

20. Nikolay Krupenik, " 'No Grounds' for Allegations Found" (in Russian), *ITAR-TASS,* November 21, 1992.

21. Sergey Leskov, "Contrary to Rumors, They Are Not Breeding Plague in St. Petersburg" (in Russian), *Izvestia,* November 25, 1992, 2.

22. Dmitry Frolov, "Interview with General Valentin Yevstigneev: We Never Filled Our Models with Live Cultures: The Biological Protection Service Will Engage Only in Protection" (in Russian), *Nezavisimaya Gazeta,* December 2, 1992, 6.

23. John Barry, "Planning a Plague? A Secret Soviet Network Spent Decades Trying to Develop Biological Weapons," *Newsweek,* February 1, 1993, 40–41.

24. Mikhail Leshchinsky (host), "Inside the Soviet Biological Center" (in Russian), *Moscow Ostankino Television First Channel Network,* 1455 GMT, April 15, 1993.

25. The man who replaced Pasechnik as director, Yevgeny N. Sventitsky, certainly has done his sharing of misinforming about the IHPB's past, but nevertheless the institute's work program and association with foreigners are more open than other Biopreparat institutes.

26. Russian Federation Government Decree No. 846, dated 8 July 1997: "Concerning Awarding the State Institute for Scientific Research on High-Purity Biologicals the Status of a Russian Federation State Scientific Center" (in Russian).

27. State Scientific Center—Research Institute of Highly Pure Biopreparations (IHPB), illustrated brochure in Russian and English (no date, but probably 2004).

28. For some odd reason, many articles we have read identify Lyubuchany's location incorrectly, stating that it is located north of Moscow.

29. BIOCAD was established in 2000 by one of Russia's first biotech entrepreneurs, Dmitry Morosov. Somehow he was able to receive $1.7 million in funding in 2003 from the US government's BioIndustries Initiative, which supposedly supports former weapons scientists undertaking peacefully directed research (see Chapter 23). Sabine Loët, "Profile: Dmitry Morosov," *Nature Biotechnology* 23 (December 6, 2005): 1465.

30. We have seen various spellings of his last name, the most common being Zaviyalov and Zav'yalov.

31. Privalov has been called the creator of modern protein thermodynamics; since 1999 he has been a professor at John Hopkins University, holding joint appointments in the departments of biology and biophysics.

32. Domaradsky describes Volkovoy as being "engaged in recruiting staff for the institute (SRCAM). The selection of good younger staff can be directly credited to him." Igor V. Domaradskij and Wendy Orent, *Biowarrior: Inside the Soviet/Russian Biological War Machine* (Amherst, N.Y., 2003), 200.

33. Harvey with Zakutnyaya, 2011, 349.

34. The last time Zaviyalov and Pasechnik met was in 1996 in Porton Down, England, where they discussed developing a joint proposal for the European Community research program.

35. Over the life of its existence, the institute had three names: the Institute of Immunology, then the Institute of Engineering Immunology (IEI), and the current name Institute of Immunological Engineering. We use the second throughout because during its time the institute was heaviest involved in offensive BW R&D.

36. The entire IEI complex can be clearly observed on Google Earth. The IEI Administration Building is located at 55 15' 29.34 N, 37 33' 34.92 E. The main laboratory building is the first building northeast of the Administration Building.

37. The three were colonels from the Zagorsk Institute—Stanislav S. Afanasyev, Vladimir A. Andreyev, and Yury I. Morozov.

38. The first-level legend for Protein A production was that it was to be used for large-scale manufacture of affinity chromatography and immune-enzyme assay equipment.

39. Later she worked as a professor at Mount Sinai School of Medicine, New York.

40. We do not know whether Skryabin was aware of the purpose of this tasking.

41. We believe that the work done at IEI was based on earlier, openly published research performed at USSR-AN and MOD institutes by medical researchers such as N. I. Aleksandrov, N. Y. Gefen, N. S. Garin, K. G. Gapochko, and V. I. Ogarkov.

42. Although this aerosol vaccine could have been satisfactory to the MOD, it might not have passed the scrutiny of civilian authorities responsible for licensing vaccines. In any case, currently no tularemia aerosol vaccine is licensed anywhere in the world.

43. USPTO Application #20060165654, Peptides and Recombinant Proteins Mimicking Interferons (July 27, 2006); US Patent #7326684, Peptides for Enhancing Resistance to Microbial Infections (February 5, 2008); European Patent EP0981359, Compositions for Enhancing Immunosuppressants' Pharmacological Activities (March 19, 2003); European Patent EP1551441, Peptides and Recombinant Proteins Mimicking Interferons (December 13, 2006).

44. An epitope is a region on the surface of a bacterium or virus that induces the synthesis of specific antibodies against it by the infected host.

45. Each *Y. pestis* cell is surrounded by a capsule composed of Fraction 1 (F1) protein. F1 is fully expressed only at 37°C, which is the normal human body temperature. Thus, when *Y. pestis* invades the human host and is exposed to its 37°C environment, it mobilizes F1, whose major effect is to protect the pathogen from phagocytosis (ingestion by white blood cells).

46. Subsequently professor at Kingston University, UK.

47. Subsequently a reader at the University of Leicester, UK.

48. Newsletters published by the Federation of European Biochemical Societies for the express purpose of rapid scientific communication.

49. Lentiviruses can be used in cancer research for delivering genes into non-dividing cells.

50. This institute, named Scientific-Research Agricultural Institute of the Ministry of Agriculture, developed BW agents against both animals and plants.

51. Its official name in Soviet times was Central Asian Scientific Research Anti-plague Institute.

52. Anthony Rimmington, "Conversion of BW Facilities in Kazakhstan," in *Conversion of Former BTW Facilities,* ed. Erhard Geissler, Lajos Gazsó, and Ernst Buder (Dordrecht, Netherlands, 1998), 167–186.

53. Gulbarshyn Bozheyeva, Yerlan Kunakbayev, and Dastan Yeleukenov, *Former Soviet Biological Weapons Facilities in Kazakhstan: Past, Present and Future,* Center for Nonproliferation Studies, Monterey Institute of International Studies, Occasional Paper no. 1, June 1999, http://www.cns.miis.edu/pubs/opapers/op1/op1.pdf.

54. Sonia Ben Ouagrham and Kathleen M. Vogel, *Conversion at Stepnogorsk: What the Future Holds for Former Bioweapons Facilities,* Cornell University Peace Studies

Program, Occasional Paper no. 28, February 2003, http://einaudi.cornell.edu/
PeaceProgram/publications/occasional_papers/Stepnogorsk-28.pdf.

55. Ken Alibek with Stephen Handelman, *Biohazard: The Chilling True Story of the Largest Covert Biological Weapons Program in the World—Told from Inside by the Man Who Ran It* (New York, 1999), 87–106.

56. For readers who wish to know more about SNOPB, we particularly recommend Bozheyeva et al. (1999) and Ben Ouagrham and Vogel (2003) because their completeness, utilization of recent information, and ready availability on the Web.

57. The name Stepnogorsk probably stems for a combination of the Russian words *stepnoy* (steppe) + *gora* (mountain) + *-sk* (grammatical ending); i.e., "Steppe Mountain."

58. SNOPB can be clearly seen on Google Earth. Building 600 is located at 52°26'17.40"N and 72°01'42.52"E.

59. Ben Ouagrham and Vogel, 2003, 16.

60. These pesticides were based on *Bacillus thuringiensis,* which is closely related to *Bacillus anthracis* and could be applied as a *B. anthracis* simulant.

61. "Bitoxibacillin to Combat Colorado Beetle" (in Russian), *Pravda,* May 14, 1984.

62. Bozheyeva et al., 1999, 9.

63. A former Progress scientist informed Zilinskas about the secret decree in 2000.

64. Some of Lepeshkin's accomplishments are described as follows: "Gennady Nikolayevich Lepeshkin is the former head of the military programs for the production of bacteriological weapons in Stepnogorsk, Doctor of Medical and Biological Sciences, professor of biology, and Full Member of the Russian Academy of Medical and Technical Sciences; he has been awarded the Order of the Red Star, three USSR Defense Ministry medals, and the Vernadsky Star, First Degree; he is a colonel in the medical service reserve." Tatyana Novik, "A Story of Mass Destruction: Interview with Microbiologist Gennadiy Lepeshkin" (in Russian), *Ekspress K* (Almaty), May 7, 2002, 3.

65. Bozheyeva et al., 1999, 11.

66. Former SNOPB scientist, personal communication, 2000. The fact that no large-scale production was done at SNOPB was also verified by US experts sent in the early 1990s to help with the converting of the plant to peaceful uses.

67. Novik, 2002, 3.

68. For a thorough description of the travails and eventual demise of Biomedpreparat, we suggest that readers peruse the excellent report by Ben Ouagrham and Vogel (2003).

10. Soviet Biological Weapons and Doctrines for Their Use

1. Iraqi biological weapons might have had a terrorizing effect on its adversary's troops and, additionally forced them into protective postures that would have carried a heavy logistic and battlefield burden.

2. The term "type-classified" was developed by the US Department of Defense. The equivalent term used by the Soviet and Russian MOD is *prinyatie na vooruzhenie* принятие на вооружение). For convenience, we hereafter use the American term.

3. W. C. Anderson III and J. M. King, *Vaccine and Antitoxin Availability for Defense against Biological Warfare Threat Agents,* Final Report 83-003, U.S. Army Health Services Command, Fort Sam Houston, Texas, September 1983, 3–4.

4. Defense Intelligence Agency, *Chemical and Biological Warfare Capabilities – USSR (U)*, Report DST-1600S-034-76-SUP 1, (Washington, D.C., March 1977), xxiii. (Secret)

5. Paul J. Jackson, personal communication, February 7, 2012.

6. Former Biopreparat scientist, personal communication, 1999.

7. Formulations are to this day one of the most secret components of biological weapons developed by both the US and Soviet BW programs. We have chosen not to provide how-to information about formulations and fillers in this book beyond what is minimally necessary for explanatory purposes.

8. The authors consider it judicious not to reproduce the precise identification of the source document.

9. M. V. Walter, B. Marthi, V. P. Fieland, and L. M. Ganio, "Effect of Aerosolization On Subsequent Bacterial Survival," *Applied and Environmental Microbiology* 56, no. 11 (1990): 3468–3472.

10. The sensitivity of natural (not weaponized) cells to environmental stress varies among bacteria. Thus, the causative bacterium of Q fever, *Coxiella burnetii,* is very hardy (able to survive for more than half an hour); *F. tularensis* cells are somewhat hardy (able to survive 10–20 minutes); and *Y. pestis* is relatively fragile (able to survive for only a few minutes).

11. The process described here is for a bacterial pathogen; the weaponization process for a virus would differ somewhat.

12. One of the authors (Zilinskas) was able to visit the Bakanas natural plague focus and the Bakanas Anti-plague Station in 2001 and observe its field and laboratory operations. Bakanas is located approximately 200 km due north of Almaty, Kazakhstan.

13. The main natural hosts for *Y. pestis* in Central Asia are gerbils, marmots, and susliks and the ectoparasites they carry.

14. Sonia Ben Ouagrham-Gormley, "Growth of the Anti-plague System during the Soviet Period," *Critical Reviews in Microbiology* 32, no. 1 (2006): 33–46.

15. The Soviet Union had a carefully developed set of regulations pertaining to biosafety that specified, among other things, how dangerous pathogens were to be transported. When visiting several anti-plague stations and institutes in the new republics as Belarus, Kazakhstan, Kyrgyzstan, Moldova, and Ukraine, Zilinskas noted that biosafety regulations, dated 1972 and signed by Petr N. Burgasov, USSR Deputy Minister of Health and Chief Sanitary Physician during 1965–1986, were still in loose-leaf binders and were being followed by the scientific staffs.

16. After approximately 1975, the Kirov Institute scientists also employed genetic engineering techniques for these purposes.

17. In a published interview Alibek provided a highly dubious description of the bomblets' operation: "The bomblets were developed for dissemination of biological weapons at certain altitudes, such as 25 meters, 50 meters, 75 meters, 100 meters, sometimes up to 200 meters. The optimal altitude for release was between 25 and 100 meters." Jonathan B. Tucker, "Biological Weapons in the Former Soviet Union: An Interview with Dr. Kenneth Alibek," *Nonproliferation Review* 6, no. 3 (Spring 1999): 3. Alibek's explanation is puzzling because the design of the Soviet bomblet does not indicate that it contains either a barometric or a proximity fuse. In addition, a barometric fuse would be unlikely to distinguish differences of 25 meters in altitude. Time-delay fuses also exist, but due to technical aspects of their functioning, their presence in these BW bomblets is even less plausible. The fuse in the most dependable US bomblet's was armed after a set number of rotations was achieved by the bomblet as it was falling.

Alibek also told a US contractor that the Soviet bomblet would detonate "at 50 feet" (as best as the individual could now recall). In this case he referred only to a single altitude and said that the bomblet was "pressure fused," that is, dependent on *a barometric fuse.* (Source: Personal communication, September 2010.) Not only is Alibek's first description implausible, but the two descriptions, the first in the Tucker interview and the second to a Department of Defense contractor, are different.

18. The military technical term for a weapon designed to bounce is "bounding."

19. Julian Perry Robinson, personal communication, 2010.

20. Personal communication, December 31, 2011.

21. Former Biopreparat scientist, personal communication, 2001.

22. We asked an American biological weapons expert to evaluate the *Gshch-304* design. He made these comments: "The engineering and components of this bomblet are the most sophisticated that I have seen. It appears that their intentions were to minimize inactivation of the payload by shielding it from the force of the explosion. It would be interesting to know what they used to blow the bomblet apart; it looks like they were using a shaped charge that would also direct the energy (probably to minimize force on the payload and to disperse it more efficiently) away from the payload. Aluminum is fairly common for biological bomblets because it is easily

blown apart and has a high heat content to bleed heat away." Alan J. Mohr, personal communication, 2009.

23. "Biological Warfare Capabilities—Warsaw Pact [U]. A Defense S&T Intelligence Study," DST 16105-123-90, March 1990, 53. (Secret)

24. M. Ye. Levin et al., *Defense against Agents of Mass Destruction*, (Moscow, 1960), 23.

25. *Russia's Arms and Technologies: The XXI Century Encyclopedia*. Vol. 10: *Aircraft Armament and Avionics* (Moscow: 2005), 230–231.

26. The authors consider it judicious not to reproduce the precise identification of the source document.

27. The authors consider it judicious not to reproduce the precise identification of the source document.

28. William J. Broad, "US Sells Papers on Making Germ Weapons," *New York Times,* January 13, 2002.

29. Tucker, 1999, 3. The Ilyushin-28 is better described as a light bomber, though the word "medium" in the quotation refers to its range and not its payload.

30. Venturi effect—as the aircraft moves through air, wind blows over the top of the container, thus increasing the air pressure at its front side (side facing the wind), but reducing the air pressure at back side, which results in a vacuum being created over that container that draws out its contents. The formulation is then dispersed by the aircraft's slipstream.

31. Ken Alibek, "Biological Weapons/Bioterrorism Threat and Defense: Past, Present and Future," presentation at the National Center for Biodefense at the George Mason University, 2005.

32. L. Zaikov, "To the President of the Union of Soviet Socialist Republics, Comrade M. S. Gorbachev" (in Russian), May 15, 1990. (From Kataev Archives—see Chapter 21.)

33. Alibek, 2005. We do not know when burkholderiae were validated, but we estimate that it was done in the early 1980s after the Volgograd Anti-plague Institute had been functioning for some years.

34. Vladimir Pasechnik, personal communication, 1998.

35. Vladimir Pasechnik, interviewed by Mark Urban on *BBC Newsnight,* January 21, 1993.

36. Foreign Intelligence Service of the Russian Federation, *A New Challenge after the Cold War: The Proliferation of Weapons of Mass Destruction* (in Russian), (Moscow, 1993), 15. (JPRS-TND-93-007)

37. J. H. Rothschild, *Tomorrow's Weapons: Chemical and Biological* (New York, 1964).

38. Tucker, 1999, 3. As with other questions concerning actual Soviet plans for BW use, none of Alibek's interviewers apparently ever asked him how he knew of these details.

39. Herbert L. Abrams and William E. Von Kaenel, "Medical Problems of Survivors of Nuclear War: Infection and the Spread of Communicable Disease," *New England Journal of Medicine* 305, no. 20 (1981):1226–1232.

40. Carsten M. Haaland, Conrad V. Chester, and Eugene P. Wigner, *Survival of the Relocated Population of the U.S. After a Nuclear Attack. Final Report,* (Oakridge National Laboratory, June 1976).

41. Ibid., 1231.

42. The US military continued vaccination against smallpox for all recruits entering into the services until 1990; after this date they vaccinated only those service persons who were deemed likely to be exposed to smallpox, such as those involved in Desert Storm, the allied invasion of Iraq in 1991.

43. In 1985 the CDC maintained 19 million doses of smallpox vaccine in storage. If this stockpile would not have been wholly or mostly destroyed immediately by Soviet nuclear missiles and some of the smallpox vaccine survived the initial onslaught, the loss of electricity following a nuclear attack of the magnitude used in the scenario would have led to their deterioration within a few weeks. In addition, no mechanism for its distribution would have survived.

We do not know when the Soviet Union ceased to vaccinate its civilian population; perhaps this date was a state secret. However, the Soviet military stopped vaccinating service personnel in 1979, but resumed vaccinating them in 1983, supposedly because "immunization was continuing in the armed forces of the countries of Western Europe." V. I. Yevstigneev, A. I. Polozov, Ye. G. Zezerov, S. I. Rybak, and C. B. Fedorov, "From the Pages of the Foreign Medical Press" (in Russian), *Voyenno-Meditsinskiy Zhurnal,* no. 11 (November 1991):68–70.

44. Ken Alibek with Stephen Handelman, *Biohazard: The Chilling True Story of the Largest Covert Biological Weapons Program in the World—Told from Inside by the Man Who Ran It* (New York, 1999), 3–8, 78.

45. Ibid., 5.

46. Sergey Pluzhnikov and Aleksey Shvedov, "The Murderer from the Test Tube" (in Russian), *Sovershenno Sekretno* (Moscow), no. 4 (April 1998): 12–14.

47. Ken Alibek, personal communication, August 4, 1998.

48. Jonathan Tucker, *Scourge: The Once and Future Threat of Smallpox* (New York, 2001), 141–142. In the second edition of his book, Tucker removed the mention of the SS-13 and SS-17 missiles.

49. Tom Mangold and Jeff Goldberg, *Plague Wars: A True Story of Biological Warfare* (New York, 1999), 95–96, 413 (nn. 13 and 14).

50. Information on the Soviet ICBM and strategic bomber systems discussed in the text can be found in *Russian Strategic Nuclear Forces,* ed. Pavel Podvig (Cambridge, Mass., 2001). For the SS-18, see pp. 215–220; for the SS-11, see pp. 201–205; for the T4-95 "Bear" strategic bomber, see pp. 379–385. The Ilyushin 28 light bomber was a "Eurostrategic" system whose flight radius did not permit it to reach

the United States from bases in the Soviet Union. See Ray Bonds, ed., *The Illustrated Directory of Modern Soviet Weapons* (New York, 1986), 366–367.

51. Mangold and Goldberg, 1999, 96–97.

52. Ibid., 413.

53. Alibek with Handelman, 1999, 297–298. Alibek has identified "Zima" as "Usolye-Sibirskoye in Irkutsk Oblast," and as the site labeled "Malta" by the United States.

54. Ken Alibek, personal communication, 2001.

55. Alibek with Handelman, 1999, 298; Mangold and Goldberg, 1999, 94.

56. Ken Alibek, personal communication, August 2001.

57. The Soviet Air Force took delivery of the first Ilyushin Il-28 jet bomber in 1950, and withdrew it from service in the 1980s. It had a three-man crew, range of 2,180 km, maximum speed of 900 km/hr, and maximum carrying capacity of 3,000 kg.

58. Personal communications, 2008 and 2009.

59. Former US government officials, personal communications, 2007 and 2008. In interviews, Alibek has described Soviet proposals for BW agents production in space stations, a conception that can only be considered bizarre. Interviews with his former colleague Pasechnik produced similar descriptions, with the two ex-Soviet BW scientists disputing which of the two was the originator or champion of the conceptions. This is, however, irrelevant to the issue of Soviet ICBM delivery of BW agents.

60. Ken Alibek, "The Former Soviet Union/Russia's Offensive Biological Warfare Program [U]," SRS 97-6675, December 20, 1996 (Secret). This report has not been declassified as of the time of editing this book.

61. Vitaly Kataev, personal communication, 2000.

62. "DIA Official Notes Uncertainty about 'Mod-4' of Soviet's SS-11 ICBM," *Aerospace Daily,* December 18, 1979, 239.

63. Bruce S. Grim, "Biological Agent Delivery by ICBM," US Army Dugway Proving Ground, Utah, April 1981 (Secret).

64. Jack Anderson and Dale Van Atta, "How Russia Fights with Poison and Plague," *Reader's Digest,* October 1984, 61. Much of the rest of this Anderson/Van Atta story is a maze of disinformation on other aspects of alleged Soviet BW or CW.

65. "Washington Roundup," *Aviation Week and Space Technology* 120P4 (January 30, 1984): 15.

66. Mangold and Goldberg, 1999, 83–85.

67. Ibid.

68. Ibid.

69. Pavel Podvig, personal communication, 2008.

70. Former senior US government official, personal communication.

71. Pavel Podvig, personal communication, 2008. Nevertheless, the US Department of Defense publication *Soviet Military Power* still listed 335 SS-11s as deployed in 1990, and they remained in service until 1991.

72. Mangold and Goldberg, 1999, 97.

73. It is conceivable that the authors simply were imprecise, and meant to say that tests with simulants had shown what percentage of *B. anthracis* spores would survive, etc. In any case, the warheads would have had to be recovered to establish the percentage of simulant survival.

74. In a long essay in *New Yorker* magazine in 1999 (Richard Preston, "The Demon in the Freezer," *New Yorker,* July 12, 1999, 44–61), Preston wrote that he attempted to corroborate Alibek's ICBM description with "certain government sources." Two unidentified individuals whom he quotes replied to him in the affirmative. One refers to Soviet ICBM tests "over the Pacific Ocean" before 1991, and the second describes warheads weirdly spinning because they carried "an active refrigeration system." Queried in August 2010, one of the most senior US intelligence officials with responsibility for this subject matter in the first Bush administration replied that he had never seen "a single piece of evidence to support Preston's claims."

A Russian author wrote in 2005, "It is public knowledge that, after Boris Yeltsin issued his decree of 11 April 1992, stockpiles of BW missile warheads were resited from Sverdlovsk (Yekaterinburg) to Kizner, Udmurtia, to the CW missile and artillery depot. They did not remain there for very long and, in anticipation of international inspections, they were transferred to a new location." L. A. Fedorov, *Soviet Biological Weapons: History, Ecology, Politics* (Moscow, 2005), 205. It is not known what kind of "BW missile warheads" Fedorov is referring to. As best as is known, there were no such warheads.

75. Mangold and Goldberg, 1999, 96–97 and reference 414. In an extended interview with Christopher Davis made by Mangold and Goldberg for a TV documentary based on their book, Davis makes no mention of Soviet BW-bearing ICBMs.

76. Christopher Davis, personal communication, June 3, 2002. In a paper of his own Davis wrote, "Intercontinental ballistic missiles with MIRVed warheads containing plague were available for launch even before 1985, and SS-11 and SS-18 missiles have been mentioned in this connection." Christopher J. Davis, "Nuclear Blindness: An Overview of the Biological Weapons Programs of the Former Soviet Union and Iraq," *Emerging Infectious Diseases* 5, no. 4 (July–August 1999): 509–512.

As already indicated, the SS-11 is not a MIRVed ICBM. Davis said that there was "some confusion" in his sentences quoted above, and that his reference to "available for launch" was "a theoretical statement." Christopher Davis, personal communication, 2002.

77. Our own interviews with Pasechnik totaled around 35 hours over four days plus correspondence for a period of a year. Davis reportedly spent two years debriefing him; at first intensively and then at intervals.

78. Vladimir Pasechnik, personal communication, June 1999.

79. Ibid.

80. Ibid., September 1998.

81. Davis, 1999, 509–512.

82. Vladimir Pasechnik, personal communication, June 1999.

83. Defense Intelligence Agency, 1985, 7.

84. M.T. Cagle, *History of the Sergeant Weapon* System, Historical Monograph AMC 55M, US Army Missile Command, Redstone Arsenal, Alabama, 1971, and Reid Kirby, personal communications, November 2011.

Sergeant missiles were deployed to Europe between 1962 and 1977, but they carried M-139 chemical bomblets.

85. This was the Aerojet MQM-58A; See *Jane's All the World Aircraft 1965–66,* 35.

86. Rex Kiziah, "Assessment of the Emerging Biocruise Threat," in *The Counter-Proliferation Papers,* Future Warfare Series No. 6, Air War College, Maxwell Air Force Base, Alabama, August 2000, 25.

87. Dennis Gormley and Richard Speier, Carnegie Endowment for International Peace, Proliferation Roundtable, "Cruise Missile Proliferation: Threat, Policy, and Defenses," Washington, D.C., October 9, 1998, 9.

11. Distinguishing between Offensive and Defensive Biological Warfare Activities

1. "Convention on the Prohibition of the Development, Production and Stockpiling of Bacteriological (Biological) and Toxin Weapons and on Their Destruction," in United States Arms Control and Disarmament Agency, *Arms Control and Disarmament Agreements: Texts and Histories of the Negotiations* (Washington, D.C., 1996), 94–104.

2. ENDC 255, July 10, 1969, reprinted in *Documents on Disarmament,* US Arms Control and Disarmament Agency (Washington, D.C., 1969), 324–326.

3. Milton Leitenberg, "Background Paper," presented at the 10th International Microbiology Congress of the International Association of Microbiological Societies, Mexico City, August 1970.

4. "Testimony of Dr. David Huxsoll," before the US Senate, Committee on Governmental Affairs, Hearings: *Global Spread of Chemical and Biological Weapons,* 101st Congress, 1st Session, May 1989, 199–203. Huxsoll appeared, however, also to rely on the presence of BSL-4 facilities and "program intent" as two key discriminanda. In 1989, Huxsoll's testimony need not have been cleared by higher officials in the US Department of Defense, or in other government agencies, as became the case in later years. As late as the mid-1990s, congressional testimony by a later director of USAMRIID did not require clearance beyond the US Army Materiel Command. Personal communication, April 2011.

5. "Testimony of Dr. Barry Erlick in US Senate," *Global Spread of Chemical and Biological Weapons,* 33–40.

6. Raymond A. Zilinskas and Tazewell Wilson, "Introduction," in *The Microbiologist and Biological Defense Research: Ethics, Politics and International Security, Annals of the New York Academy of Sciences,* ed. Raymond A Zilinskas, vol. 666 (New York: 1992), xi–xii.

7. R. Jeffrey Smith, "The Dark Side of Biotechnology: Experts Say That Recent Scientific Achievements Threaten an International Treaty Banning Biological Warfare," *Science* 224 (June 15, 1984): 1215–1216. A recent unclassified document by the US intelligence community defines "Offensive Biological Warfare Programs" as follows: "Offensive BW programs are those whose objective is to research, develop, produce, and weaponize biological agents for overt or covert delivery against civilian or military targets, including personnel and agricultural targets." A definition based on "objective" is 100% intent. The implied corollary is that any activity would be permissible as long as the stated intent were "defensive."

8. Milton Leitenberg, *The Problems of Biological Weapons* (Stockholm, 1984), 180–184; Judith Miller, "When Is Bomb Not a Bomb? Germ Experts Confront US," *New York Times,* September 5, 2001.

9. National Security Decision Memorandum 35, "United States Policy on Chemical Warfare Program and Bacteriological/Biological Research Program," November 25, 1969. It is questionable whether the Soviet government knew of this phrasing. The first declassified version of the document, with partial deletions, appeared in September and October 1977. Although that version does contain the sentence quoted, it is not known to whom the release was made, or what circulation it was given. Sometime after 1988, apparently around 1990, the National Security Archive, a private research organization in Washington, D.C., obtained a copy, and it would have been available to researchers visiting its library. This version is available at http://www.gwu.edu/~nsarchiv/NSAEBB/NSAEBB58/RNCBW8.pdf. A declassified version of the memorandum became available on November 7, 1995.

10. "HAK Talking Points: Briefing for Congressional Leadership and Press," http://www.gwu.edu/~nsarchiv/NSAEBB/NSAEBB58/RNCBW11.pdf.

11. "US Policy on Chemical and Biological Warfare and Agents: Report to the National Security Council," submitted to the Interdepartmental Political-Military Group in response to NSSM [National Security Study Memorandum] 59 (November 10, 1969), 26. (Top Secret)

12. Forrest Russell Frank, *U.S. Arms Control Policymaking: The 1972 Biological Weapons Convention Case* (PhD diss., Stanford University, California, November 1974), 239.

13. Brent Scowcroft, "U.S. Compliance with the Biological Weapons Convention," December 23, 1975. Reproduced in *Chemical and Biological Weapons Convention Bulletin* 57, no. 2 (September 2002), http://fas-www.harvard.edu/~hsp/bulletin/cbwcb57.pdf.

14. See Glossary.

15. Darryl Howlett and John Simpson, "Dangers in the 1990s: Nuclear, Chemical and Biological Weapons and Missile Proliferation," in *Disarmament: Topical Paper 6: Confidence Building Measures in the Asia Pacific Region* (New York, 1991), 38.

16. Ken Alibek, testimony to the Joint Economic Committee, US Senate, May 20, 1998.

17. Personal communication, November 7, 1998, and July 2002.

18. Personal communication, November 1998. It is not altogether clear what the rationale behind production of such a molecular genetic "chimera" of two pathogens would have been, as against simply combining the two independent pathogens and delivering them simultaneously. One suggestion has been that it would provide a mechanism to enclose a more lethal but noncontagious pathogen inside the genome of a less lethal but more contagious pathogen to obtain the combination of high contagiousness and high lethality. However, this explanation does not fit the two organisms involved in the alleged work. Another suggestion was that it would prevent disease identification by automated detection and identification devices. However, rapid identification devices did not exist when the supposed "chimera" development took place (and they are only now in development, 20–25 years later). In addition, the strategic rationale that Alibek has described for the potential circumstances in which Soviet military planners conceived of using these agents offered little reason to be concerned with whether the attacked party could identify the disease agent rapidly or not. Nevertheless, as indicated, the project almost certainly did exist.

19. Sergei Popov, interview with PBS TV *NOVA* program "Bioterror," November 17, 2001.

20. B. Moss, "Use of Vaccinia Virus for the Development of Live Vaccines," in *Genetically Altered Viruses and the Environment* (New York, 1985), 291–298; G. Thomas et al., "Expression and Cell Type-Specific Processing of Human Preproenkephalin with a Vaccinia Recombinant," *Science* 232 (1986): 1641–1643; B. Roizman and F. J. Jenkins, "Genetic Engineering of Novel Genomes of Large DNA Viruses," *Science* 229 (1985): 1208–1214; Dale Short and Kathleen Blount, "Microscopic Missiles: Revamping Viruses to Demolish Disease," *UAB* (University of Alabama-Birmingham) 22, no. 1 (Winter 2002): 3–9; O. I. Serpinski et al., "Design of Orthopoxvirus Recombinant Variants by Foreign Gene Insertion into an Intergene Region of Viral Genome" (in Russian), *Molecular Biology* 30, no. 5 (1996): 1055–1065.

21. W. Wayt Gibbs, "Bioterrorism: Innocence Lost-Is Enough Being Done to Keep Biotechnology Out of the Wrong Hands?," *Scientific American* 285 (January 2002): 14–15.

22. A. Lucht et al., "Production of Monoclonal Antibodies and Development of the Antigen Capture ELISA Directed against the Envelope Glycoprotein GP of Ebola Virus," *Medical Microbiology and Immunology* (Berlin), October 31, 2003.

23. David Huxsoll, "In Memoriam: Joel M. Dalrymple," in *The Microbiologist and Biological Defense Research: Ethics, Politics and International Security,* ed.

Raymond A. Zilinskas, vol. 666 (1992), ix; Laurence K. Altman, "Vaccine for Hanta Virus Found Safe in Early Test," *New York Times,* May 23, 1995.

24. Severin Carrell, "Porton Down Makes New Plague and Pox," *Independent,* February 10, 2002. "Porton Down" is essentially a misnomer, as there were two separate research establishments at the site—CAMR under the UK Department of Health, and the Chemical and Biological Defence Sector of DERA (Ministry of Defence, Defence Evaluation and Research Agency) at which most of the work referred to was taking place. In July 2001, DERA/CBDS was renamed the DSTL Biomedical Sciences.

25. A. N. Bennet et al., "Recombinant Vaccinia Viruses Protect against *Clostridium perfringens* a-toxin," *Viral Immunology* 12 (1991): 97–105.

26. Jack Melling, personal communication, February 2002.

27. S. D. Miller, "A Virus Induced Molecular Mimicry Model of Multiple Sclerosis," *Abstracts of the 41st Interscience Conference on Antimicrobial Agents* (2001). See also D. J. Theil et al., "Viruses Can Silently Prime For and Trigger Central Nervous System Autoimmune Disease," *Journal of Neurovirology* 7, no. 3 (June 2001): 220–227. This research used a recombinant vaccine virus as a nonspecific inducer of multiple sclerosis.

28. Jack Melling, personal communication, February 2002.

29. Stockholm International Peace Research Institute, "The Problems of Inspection Concerned with BW Agents," in *Technical Aspects of Early Warning and Verification,* vol. 6 in *The Problem of Chemical and Biological Warfare* (Stockholm, 1975), 39–60, 89–103.

30. Executive Summary, Solicitation Number DAAD13-02-R-0016, US Army Robert Morris Acquisition Center (RMAC), 2002.

31. Personal communication, April 2011.

32. Personal communication, April 2002.

33. US Government Accounting Office, *Arms Control: US and International Efforts to Ban Biological Weapons,* GAO/NSIAD-93-113, Washington, D.C., December 1992, 21.

34. Russian Federation Foreign Intelligence Service, *Proliferation Issues: A New Challenge after the Cold War—Proliferation of Weapons of Mass Destruction,* Russian Federation Foreign Intelligence Service Report, 1993.

35. Armed Forces Medical Intelligence Center, *Signatures for Biological Warfare Facilities,* Fort Detrick: Armed Forces Medical Intelligence Center (unclassified), n.d.

36. Source agency is unidentified.

37. US Government, *The Worldwide Biological Warfare Weapons Threat* (2001), 45.

38. Milton Leitenberg, "The Conversion of Biological Warfare Research and Development Facilities to Peaceful Uses," in *SIPRI Chemical and Biological Warfare Studies,* Vol. 15, *Control of Dual Threat Agents: The Vaccines for Peace Programme,* ed. Erhard Geissler and John P. Woodall (Stockholm, 1994), 77–105.

39. Its current name is Defence Science and Technology Laboratory (DSTL).

40. Personal communications, April 2002.

41. Ken Alibek, quoted in Miller et al., 2001, 310.

We asked a former Soviet weapons scientist what, in his opinion, Western intelligence agencies could have done to discover whether the facility where he worked—it happened to be SRCAM—was involved in secret work. After pondering the question for a short time he answered: they simply could have written a letter. His point was that a well-known scientist in a Western country could have written an official letter to the facility director and asked whether he could come and visit, for example, to discuss possible collaboration. Such a letter would have thrown the facility and Biopreparat administrators into confusion, with the immediate response being no response; the Western scientist most likely would not have received any answer. If he persisted in making queries, he eventually would receive a reply to the effect that no visit was possible and giving some reason that made little sense. A similar letter to an "open" institute would have elicited an immediate reply, welcoming the visit and possible collaboration. So the lack of transparency even at this low level of a letter exchange should immediately have raised suspicions about the first institute's responsibilities. As far as we know, no such letter was ever written.

42. Officials of the Sanitätsakademie der Bundeswehr, Institut für Mikrobiologie, personal communications, 1999, 2000, 2001.

43. US General Accounting Office, *Biological Weapons: Effort to Reduce Former Soviet Threat Offers Benefits, Poses New Risks,* GAO-NSIAD-00-138, Washington, D.C., April 28, 2000.

44. For example, as discussed in Chapter 18 in greater detail, it is known that Russian scientists trained PhD-level molecular biology students at the Pasteur Institute in Tehran at least between 1996 and 2002, and possibly longer. The Russian scientists were members of the staff of institutes belonging to the RF-AN. In addition, several other Russian scientists who appear to have had closer links to the former Soviet BW program were known to be working elsewhere in Iran. Since 1988, the United States has identified Iran as maintaining an offensive BW program, although the phrasing for this determination was relaxed considerably in 2007. See Judith Miller and William J. Broad, "Bioweapons in Mind, Iranians Lure Needy Ex-Soviet Scientists," *New York Times,* December 8, 1998.

12. Assessments of Soviet Biological Warfare Activities by Western Intelligence Services

1. Richard K. Betts, "Strategic Intelligence Estimates: Let's Make Them Useful," *Studies in Intelligence* 25, no. 9 (Spring 1981) (Secret).

2. A National Intelligence Estimate is defined by the Defense Technical Information Center as "a strategic estimate of the capabilities, vulnerabilities, and

probable courses of action of foreign nations that is produced at the national level as a composite of the views of the intelligence community." Special National Intelligence Estimates (SNIEs) address special, limited subjects, often of topical interest.

3. Anthony Cave Brown, ed., *DROPSHOT: The United States Plan for War with the Soviet Union in 1957* (New York, 1978).

4. Ibid., 11.

5. Ibid., 12. "Methods of introduction would probably include infection of food and water supplies, detonation of small bombs at predetermined times, use of natural vectors such as fleas and lice, contamination of the air either directly or via ventilating systems, smearing agents on equipment, counters, and handrails. Animals, crops, and humans could be subjected to biological or chemical agents by coverts methods without great difficulty to the saboteur."

6. Raymond L. Garthoff, *Soviet Strategy in the Nuclear Age* (New York, 1958), 104. An original copy of Marshall Zhukov's remark was obtained by SIPRI in August 1968. On that occasion, Oleg Reutov, a member of the USSR Academy of Sciences provided a semi-official interpretation of the Zhukov statement that SIPRI had solicited over a period of months. It said that Zhukov was *not* making a statement of Soviet intentions, but that he was making a flat observation of what could be anticipated.

One of the earliest widely circulated English translations read: "Future war, should it be unleashed" rather than "Future war, if they [i.e., the West] unleash it." *Current Digest of the Soviet Press* 8 (1956): 10–11.

7. Director of Central Intelligence, *Soviet Chemical and Biological Warfare Capabilities,* National Intelligence Estimate 11-11-69, February 13, 1969, 9.

8. Malcolm McIntosh, Raymond Garthoff, and Michael McGwire, personal communications, during the 1980s. See also C. N. Donnelly, "Winning the NBC War: Soviet Army Theory and Practice," *International Defense Review* 14, no. 8 (1981): 996.

9. The name "Kugali" is most probably incorrect; the correct name should be Kulaly Island.

10. Chemical Warfare Research Department, "Chemical Report. Russia. Bacteriological Warfare," Report CX/9767 (Secret), September 17, 1926. British National Archives WO 188/784.

11. J. Davidson Pratt, "Comments of the Chemical Warfare Research Department," D. 7969, (December 7, 1926) British National Archives WO 188/784. (Pratt was an industrial chemist by training who later wrote a book on the UK chemical industry.)

12. Chemical Warfare Research Department, "Soviet Russia: Bacteriological Warfare," Report CX/9767 (Secret), January 24, 1927. British National Archives WO 188/784.

13. Ibid.

14. Ibid.

15. J. Davidson Pratt, "Comments of the Chemical Warfare Research Department," Report D.10606, (February 28, 1927) British National Archives WO 188/784.

16. P. Warburton, *Note by the Joint Secretary: Extract of Information Received up to the 21st October, 1936, regarding the Development of Bacteriological Warfare in Germany,* Committee of Imperial Defence, Sub-committee on Bacteriological Warfare, Whitehall Gardens, S.W.1. C.B.W. 4 (1936).

17. Ibid.

18. The Spanish "Reds" refers to the Spanish Republican government and its forces, which were supported by the Soviet Union during the Spanish Civil War.

19. W. Elliot, *Note by the Joint Secretary: Biological Warfare Activities in Russia,* Committee of Imperial Defence, Sub-committee on Emergency Public Health Laboratory Services, London, Richmond Terrace (1938) S.W.1., C.B.W. 40.

20. Military Intelligence Division, War Department, *Biological Warfare: Activities & Capabilities of Foreign Nations* (Washington, D.C., March 30, 1946) (Top Secret).

21. Ibid., 18.

22. Ibid., 19.

23. Ibid., Annex H, 1 and 4.

24. Ibid., 19–20.

25. Joint Biological Warfare Intelligence Committee, *Estimate of the Situation in BW Intelligence in the USSR,* OSI/SR-8/49-1 (Washington, D.C., 1949) (Top Secret).

26. Ibid., 3.

27. Theodore Rosebury and Elvin A. Kabat, "Bacterial Warfare," *Journal of Immunology* 56 (1947): 7–96.

28. Theodore Rosebury, *Peace or Pestilence* (New York, 1949).

29. Union of the Soviet Socialist Republics, *Materials on the Trial of Former Servicemen of the Japanese Army Charged with Manufacturing and Employing Biological Weapons* (Moscow, 1950).

30. Ad Hoc Committee on Biological Warfare, *Report of the Secretary of Defense's Ad Hoc Committee on Biological Warfare* (Washington, D.C., 1949), 6 (Secret).

31. Intelligence Advisory Committee, *National Intelligence Estimate: The Probability of Soviet Employment of BW and CW in the Event of Attacks upon the US,* NIE-18 (Washington, D.C., 1950) (Top Secret).

32. Department of the Army, *US Army Activity in the U.S. Biological Warfare Program.* Vol. 2: *Annexes,* February 15, 1977 (Secret).

33. Intelligence Advisory Committee, *National Intelligence Estimate: Soviet Capabilities for Clandestine Attack against the US with Weapons of Mass Destruction and the Vulnerability of the US to Such Attack (mid-1951 to mid-1952),* NIE-31 (Washington, D.C., 1951) (Top Secret).

34. Ibid., 7.

35. In 1957 the JIC moved to the Cabinet Office. Since then, it has maintained a dedicated staff who prepare draft intelligence assessments for the JIC to consider.

36. Joint Intelligence Committee, "Estimate of Availability of Soviet Weapons of Mass Destruction and Scientific Developments, 1950–1952," report J.I.C. 435/52 (February 7, 1951) (Top Secret).

37. Those numbers were substantially inflated. A compilation published in 2010 provided estimates of 1 in 1949, 5 in 1950, 25 in 1951, and 50 in 1952. The latter numbers are educated guesses and may also be overestimates. They were based on assumptions about available Soviet delivery systems at that time, and not on Soviet availability of fissile material or the fabrication of warheads per se. Soviet or Russian sources have never released numbers of nuclear weapons that the Soviet Union possessed in the years in question. See Robert S. Norris and Hans M. Kristensen, "Global Nuclear Weapons Inventories, 1945–2010," *Bulletin of the Atomic Scientists* 66, no. 4 (July/August 2010): 77–83.

38. Joint Intelligence Committee, "Estimate of Sino-Soviet Capabilities in the Far East with Respect to Japan," report J.I.C. 1924/61 (August 31, 1951) (Top Secret).

39. Joint Intelligence Group, "Intelligence on Soviet Capabilities for Chemical and Bacteriological Warfare," report J.I.C. 156/12 (June 16, 1952) (Secret).

40. Anthony Rimmington, "Soviet Biotechnology: The Case of Single Cell Protein," in *Technical Progress and Soviet Economic Development,* ed. Ronald Amann and Julian Cooper (New York, 1986), 75–93.

41. Joint Intelligence Group, 1952.

42. Joint Intelligence Committee, "Intelligence on Soviet Capabilities for Waging Biological and Chemical Warfare," report J.I.C. 558/197 (April 23, 1953) (Top Secret).

43. Ibid., answer number 15.

44. Intelligence Advisory Committee, *National Intelligence Estimate: Soviet Bloc Capabilities through 1957,* NIE-65 (Washington, D.C., 1953), 10 (Top Secret). (A footnote states that three members of the Intelligence Advisory Committee disagreed with the conclusion about the crystallization of viruses.)

45. Intelligence Advisory Committee, *Special Estimate: Soviet Capabilities for Attack on the US through mid-1955,* SE-36/1 (Washington, D.C., 1953), 2 (Top Secret).

46. Intelligence Advisory Committee, *Special National Intelligence Estimate: Soviet Capabilities for Attack on the US through 1957,* SNIE-11-2-54 (Washington, D.C., 1954) (Top Secret).

47. Intelligence Advisory Committee, *National Intelligence Estimate: Soviet Capabilities and Probable Courses of Action through mid-1959,* NIE 11-4-54 (Washington, D.C., 1954) (Top Secret); Intelligence Advisory Committee, *National Intelligence Estimate: Soviet Gross Capabilities for Attacks on the US and Key Overseas Installations and Forces through 1 July 1958,* NIE 11-7-55 (Washington, D.C., 1955) (Top Se-

cret); and Director of Central Intelligence, *National Intelligence Estimate Number 11-4-59: Main Trends in Soviet Capabilities and Policies, 1959–1964,* NIE 11-4-59 (Washington, D.C., 1959) (Top Secret).

48. Intelligence Advisory Committee, 1954, *Special National Intelligence Estimate,* 3.

49. Joint Intelligence Committee, Scientific and Technical Intelligence Sub-Committee, *Soviet Biological Warfare,* S.T.I.S. Report No. 36, London, September 1960 (Secret). We have found only one British report dated later than 1960, which is the report discussed in Chapter 1 on the Soviet Union's interest in botulinum toxin; see Defence Intelligence Staff, Directorate of Scientific and Technical Intelligence, *Soviet Studies on Botulinum Toxin,* DSTI Report No. 301, Ministry of Defence, London, August 1968 (Secret).

50. Intelligence Advisory Committee, *National Intelligence Estimate: Soviet Capabilities and Intentions with Respect to Biological Warfare,* NIE 11-6-64 (Washington, D.C., 1964), 5–6 (Secret).

51. Wilton E. Lexow and Julian Hoptman, "The Enigma of Soviet BW," *Studies in Intelligence* 9 (Spring 1965): 15–20 (Secret).

52. Ibid.

53. A former intelligence analyst suggested that there could be another explanation for this kind of finding. Apparently, in any intelligence organization there is a reluctance of its leadership to admit to its client that there are important things they are not able to do (unless they suggest "If you give us more money we will be able to do it"). In cases where there is no evidence of something, this could mean either that something does not exist or that it exists but the intelligence organization is unable to find or detect it. When a "no finding" occurs, it would be up to the head of the organization or agency, and not the analysts, to make the ultimate determination as to its meaning, and such a determination might be made on political grounds. In this case, a finding of "no biological weapons in the USSR" could have been made in support of the many previous negative findings set forth in earlier NIEs.

54. Lexow and Hoptman, 1965, 20.

55. US House of Representatives, *Chemical, Biological and Radiological Warfare Agents: Hearings before the Committee on Science and Astronautics,* Washington, DC, June 16–22, 1958. This and the four citations that follow are all to be found in Stockholm International Peace Research Institute, *The Problem of Chemical and Biological Warfare.* Vol. 2: *CB Weapons Today* (Stockholm, 1973), 183.

56. US House of Representatives, *Department of Defense Appropriations for 1963: Hearings before a Subcommittee of the Committee on Appropriations,* Washington, DC, March 1962, 175–184.

57. US Senate, *Authorization for Military Procurement 1970: Hearings before the Committee on Armed Services* (Washington, D.C., 1969), 536.

58. US House of Representatives, *Department of Defense Appropriations for 1970: Part 6. Hearings before a Subcommittee of the Committee on Appropriations* (Washington, D.C., 1969), 104–144.

59. US House of Representatives, *Hearings on Military Posture 1970 before the Committee on Armed Services(* Washington, D.C., 1969), 3923.

60. A *Washington Post* journalist wrote, "Another complication for the military is the growing dispute among US intelligence agencies over Russia's biological warfare capabilities . . . the fact is that the State Department's intelligence agencies [*sic*] have reported for a number of years that there is no evidence whatsoever of any significant Russian activity in biological warfare. . . . 'We've been asking them [the Army] for years to find the Russian biological test facility,' one source told me, 'and they can't.'" S. M. Hersh, "Pentagon's Gas Plans Spring a Leak," *Washington Post,* June 29, 1969.

61. Henry A. Kissinger, "U.S. Policy on Chemical and Biological Warfare and Agents," National Security Study Memorandum 59 (Washington, D.C., 1969).

62. Interdepartmental Political-Military Group, *U.S. Policy on Chemical and Biological Warfare and Agents,* report submitted to the National Security Council in response to NSSM 59 (Washington, D.C., 1969) (Top Secret).

63. Interdepartmental Political-Military Group, 1969, 8.

64. Interdepartmental Political-Military Group, *Annual Review of United States Chemical Warfare and Biological Research Programs as of 1 November 1970,* NSC Under Secretaries Committee, The Under Secretary of State, Washington, D.C., February 4, 1971 (Top Secret).

65. Intelligence Advisory Committee, *National Intelligence Estimate: Soviet Military Research and Development,* NIE 11-12-72, Central Intelligence Agency, Washington, D.C., 19 September 1972. (Top Secret); Intelligence Advisory Committee, *National Intelligence Estimate: The Soviet Assessment of the US,* NIE 11-5-75, Central Intelligence Agency, Washington, D.C., 9 October 1975 (Secret); Intelligence Advisory Committee, *Trends in Soviet Military Programs,* Interagency Intelligence Memorandum, NIO IIM 76-039J, Central Intelligence Agency, Washington, D.C., October 1976 (Top Secret).

66. Interagency Intelligence Memorandum, 1976.

67. Ibid.

68. It bears noting that the first two open publications in the Soviet Union reporting on genetic engineering achievements appeared in December 1975, authored by, respectively, Aleksandr A. Baev (recombinant gamma phage) and Vladimir G. Debabov (recombinant plasmid).

69. Defense Intelligence Agency, *Soviet Genetic Engineering—Status and Threat: A Comparative Analysis,* DIATIR 4–76, August 23, 1976, Washington, D.C., Defense Intelligence Agency (Secret).

70. United States Army Intelligence Threat Analysis Detachment, *Military Operations of the Soviet Army,* 14-U-76, 1976, Arlington, Virginia; Department of the Army, United States Army Intelligence and Security Command, United States Army Intelligence and Threat Analysis Center, *Soviet Army Operations,* April 1978 (n.p.).

71. Defense Intelligence Agency, *Chemical and Biological Warfare Capabilities—USSR (U),* DST-1600S-034-76-SUP 1, March 1977, Washington, D.C. (Secret).

72. Ibid., 324. In Chapters 3 and 10, we make note of estimates made by the DIA in its 1977 report including that the Soviet Union had applied "genetic molecular biology research . . . to have already modified BW agents which only they can identify, treat, and control" (Ibid., xxiii). We received this information very late in the editing process, on February 6, 2012, and therefore have not been able to incorporate it fully in this book.

73. Brian Jones, *Failing Intelligence: The True Story of How We Were Fooled into Going to War in Iraq* (London, 2010), 18–19.

74. Brian Jones was head of the Nuclear, Biological, Chemical Technical Intelligence Branch, Defence Intelligence Staff, during 1987–2003.

75. Former senior British intelligence official, personal communication, 2004.

76. Director of Central Intelligence, *Prospects for Soviet Military Technology and R&D,* NIE 11-12-80, July 31, 1980 (Top Secret). The 16 technologies were computers, microelectronics, signal processing, production technology, communications, directed energy, guidance/navigation, power sources, structural materials, propulsion, nuclear weapons, chemical explosives, acoustic sensors (antisubmarine warfare), nonacoustic sensors (antisubmarine warfare), radar, and electro-optical sensors.

77. Director of Central Intelligence, 1980, 12.

78. Joseph Finder, "Biological Warfare, Genetic Engineering and the Treaty That Failed," *Washington Quarterly* 9, no. 2 (Spring 1986): 5–14.

79. National Foreign Assessment Center, *Soviet Biological Warfare Agents: Probable Cause of the Anthrax Epidemic in Sverdlovsk—An Intelligence Policy Analysis,* date and place of publication redacted but probably 1981, 7. (Classification level redacted, but probably Secret.)

80. Ibid., 8.

81. DAMO-NCC Report, *Alleged Biological Warfare Agent Incident at Sverdlovsk,* October 23, 1981 (classification redacted).

82. Defense Intelligence Agency, *Chemical and Biological Warfare Capabilities—USSR,* DST-1600S-D34-82, February 1982 (Secret), 251.

83. Scientific and Technical Intelligence Committee, *Soviet Genetic-Engineering Capabilities,* Director of Central Intelligence, August 1983 (Secret).

84. Ibid., 13–14.

85. Scientific and Technical Intelligence Committee, *Soviet Genetic-Engineering Capabilities,* Director of Central Intelligence, August 1983. Special Analysis. USSR: Genetic Engineering. March 9, 1984 (Top Secret).

86. Scientific and Technical Intelligence Committee, *Soviet Genetic-Engineering Capabilities,* Director of Central Intelligence, August 1983. USSR: Genetically Engineered Biological Warfare. August 5, 1987 (Top Secret).

87. Director of Central Intelligence, *New Directions in Soviet BCW Agent Development and Their Implications: Key Judgments,* SNIE 11/17-84/C, 1984 (Top Secret).

88. *United States Chemical and Biological Weapons Arms Control Policy,* National Security Decision Directive Number 18, January 4, 1982 (Unclassified).

89. U.S. Department of State, "Legal Issues Associated with Formally Charging the Soviet Union with Violation of the BWC (as well as the Geneva Protocol of 1925 and Related Rules of Customary International Law)," ca. 1982 (Unclassified).

90. "Prepared Statement by Max M. Kampelman, Chairman, U.S. Delegation CSCE," in *Hearings: Department of Defense Authorization for Appropriations for Fiscal Year 1983,* Committee on Armed Services, United States Senate, March 22, 1982, Washington, D.C., 1982, 5030.

91. "Soviet non-compliance with arms control agreements," *Fact Sheet,* issued in conjunction with a classified National Security Council report to Congress on that subject, January 23, 1984.

92. US Department of Defense, *Soviet Military Power 1984,* Washington, D.C., April 10, 1984.

93. Secretary Weinberger's letter has apparently never been published. However it was apparently obtained from Senator Sasser's office and is quoted by Charles Piller and Keith R. Yamamoto in their book, *Gene Wars, Military Control over New Genetic Technologies* (New York, 1988), 141–142, 275.

94. "Soviet Noncompliance with Arms Control Agreements," National Security Decision Directive Number 121, January 14, 1984 (Unclassified).

95. "Soviet Noncompliance with Arms Control Agreements," National Security Decision Directive Number 161, February 6, 1985 (Unclassified).

96. "Soviet Noncompliance with Arms Control Agreements," National Security Decision Directive Number 202, December 20, 1985 (Unclassified). (Although the paragraphs are otherwise identical, we cannot be certain of the contents of the two redacted lines. In 1987, the lines read "continued activity during 1986 at suspect biological and toxin weapon facilities in the Soviet Union, and reports that a Soviet BW program may now include investigation of new classes of BW agents.")

97. "Soviet Noncompliance with Arms Control Agreements," National Security Decision Directive Number 260, February 17, 1987 (Unclassified).

98. See Chapter 16. This conclusion by the US government was almost certainly incorrect.

99. Office of Public Affairs and the Bureau of Verification and Intelligence, *Soviet Noncompliance,* ACDA Publication 120, March 1986, Washington, D.C., US Arms Control and Disarmament Agency, 14.

100. Personal communication, December 2010.

101. Second Review Conference of the Parties to the Convention on the Prohibition of the Development, Production and Stockpiling of Bacteriological (Biological) and Toxin Weapons and on their Destruction, "Summary Record of the 3rd Meeting," BWC/CONF.II/SR.3, September 18, 1986, 5. Lowitz's previous remarks had focused solely on the allegation of the use of toxins. The remarks by the UK ambassador, speaking for the 12 member states of the European Community, were much more limited and referred only, by implication, to Soviet inadequacy in explaining the Sverdlovsk events.

102. Defense Intelligence Agency, *Soviet Biological Warfare Threat,* DST-1610F-057-86, Washington, D.C., 1986, US Department of Defense.

103. Ibid., 1–2. There is no evidence that the Soviet Union ever developed cholera bacteria for BW purposes.

104. Ibid., v.

105. Douglas J. Feith, "New Technology and Biological Warfare," Testimony before the Subcommittee on Oversight and Evaluation of the House Permanent Select Committee on Intelligence, August 8, 1986, in *Defense Issues* 1, no. 60 (September 8, 1986): 1–3.

106. Ibid., 3.

107. Arkady N. Shevchenko, *Breaking with Moscow* (New York, 1985).

108. Office of Public Affairs and the Bureau of Verification and Intelligence, *Soviet Noncompliance,* ACDA Publication 120.

109. There were two versions of the ACDA report, unclassified and classified. We have not seen the classified version, and it is possible that it contained even more explicit substantive information than the unclassified version.

110. Central Intelligence Agency, *Soviet Chemical and Biological Warfare Program,* NIE 11-17-86/S, August 1986, Washington, D.C., Central Intelligence Agency (Top Secret).

111. Ibid., 1–4.

112. Ibid., 3.

113. Thomas D. Sizemore, Kathleen A. Bailey, George E. Pierce, and Donna T. Palmer, *Methodology for the Analysis of Foreign Bioactive Peptide Research,* Report no. 0002BF, Columbus, Ohio, Battelle, March 10, 1988, iv.

114. Defense Intelligence Agency, *Biological Warfare Capabilities—Warsaw Pact (U): A Defense S&T Intelligence Study,* DST 16108-123-90, Washington, D.C., March 1990 (Secret).

115. Ibid., 20–21.

116. Some of the most important information found in this report appears to have been provided by a knowledgeable source or sources, and in March 1990 the only known individual who fits that category was Pasechnik. However, the report's information page notes: "Information Cutoff Date: 1 January 1989."

Because Pasechnik defected at the end of October 1989, information he divulged could not have been included in this report.

117. Central Intelligence Agency, *Declassified National Intelligence Estimates on the Soviet Union and International Communism,* 2008, http://www.foia.cia.gov/doc _list_soviet_communism.htm.

118. The primary source for the information in this paragraph was the interview with Pasechnik carried out in June 1999. It was supplemented by a personal communication from former UK intelligence officials in 2004 and additional information from another former UK intelligence official in 2010.

119. Jones, 2010, 20.

120. Pasechnik related his initial experience with the CIA: "I first told them who I was and my responsibilities, and then I described to them the Biopreparat system. After about an hour I noticed how the Americans were looking at me very oddly. They looked at me like I was the biggest liar in the world." Vladimir Pasechnik, personal communication, July 10, 1998.

121. Ken Alibek, *The Former Soviet Union/Russia's Offensive Biological Warfare Program (U),* SRS 97-6675, publisher and place of publication not given, December 20, 1996 (Secret).

122. Stockholm International Peace Research Institute, 1973, 181–185.

123. Ibid., 182. Quote is reprinted from "Russ Reported Producing 'Disease Agents' for Germ War," *San Francisco Examiner,* June 2, 1952, 9.

124. Stockholm International Peace Research Institute, 1973, 184.

125. William Beecher, "Soviets Feared Violating the Weapons Ban," *Boston Globe,* September 28, 1975.

126. Nicholas Wade, "Biological Warfare: Suspicions of Soviet Activity," *Science* 192 (1976): 38–40.

127. Associated Press, "Russia: 6 'Germ' Plants?," dispatch to Scripps-Howard newspapers, June 15, 1976.

128. Robert C. Toth, "Russ Believed Plunging into Gene Study," *Los Angeles Times,* February 20, 1977.

129. Ibid.

130. Ibid. Toth was quoting from A. A. Baev, "Current Trends in Molecular Genetics-Genetic Engineering" (in Russian), *Vestnik Akademii Meditsinskikh Nauk SSSR* 7 (1976): 8–18.

131. Mark Popovsky, "In Secret Laboratories the Soviets Are Incubating Biological Weapons: Privileges, Rubles and Good Provisions—Rewards for Outlawed Research" (in German), *Die Welt,* May 6, 1978.

132. Ibid.

133. Approximately two years after the publication of the *Die Welt* article, Popovsky testified before the House Subcommittee on Oversight on the subject of Soviet compliance with the BWC. His testimony dealt mostly with the 1979 anthrax

outbreak in Sverdlovsk, as did most of the questions posed to him by the committee members. See "Testimony by Mark Popovskiy," in *The Sverdlovsk Incident: Soviet Compliance with the Biological Weapons Convention?*, Hearing before the Subcommittee on Oversight of the Permanent Select Committee on Intelligence, House of Representatives, 96th Congress, Second Session, May 29, 1980, Washington, D.C., U.S. Government Printing Office, 1980, http://lawlibrary.rutgers.edu/gdoc/hearings/80603451/80603451.html.

134. William Kucewicz, personal communication, 2003.

135. William Kucewicz, "Soviet Search for Eerie New Weapons: Beyond 'Yellow Rain,'" *Wall Street Journal*, April 23, 1984.

136. William Kucewicz, "The Science of Snake Venom," *Wall Street Journal*, April 25, 1984.

137. William Kucewicz, "Surveying the Lethal Literature," *Wall Street Journal*, April 27, 1984.

138. William Kucewicz, "Lead Scientist in a Scourge Search," *Wall Street Journal*, May 1, 1984.

139. The fifth deals with the abysmal safety record of Soviet science as exemplified by a major nuclear accident near Kyshtym in 1957, a major spill of highly concentrated nuclear waste into the Dniester River in 1983, and the 1979 Sverdlovsk anthrax outbreak. (William Kucewicz, "Accident Prone and Asking for Calamity," *Wall Street Journal*, May 3, 1984.) The sixth describes the troubles that David Goldfarb, one of the Soviet Union's most respected molecular biologists, encountered when he attempted to emigrate to Israel. (William Kucewicz, "The Gates Slam Shut on a Microbiologist," *Wall Street Journal*, May 8, 1984.) The seventh article recounts the history of the Soviet BW program from 1919 to the present (1984), describes the Hirsh report, and contains an interview with Popovsky. (Mark Popovsky quoted in William Kucewicz, "The Non-stop Russian Response to WWI," *Wall Street Journal*, May 11, 1984.)

140. William Kucewicz, "Beyond 'Yellow Rain'—An Update—The Threat Of Soviet Genetic Engineering: Word from behind the Iron Curtain," *Wall Street Journal*, December 28, 1984.

141. An insightful rejoinder to the third article was written in a Letter to the Editor; see Elkan R. Blout, "Research, Pestilence and War," *Wall Street Journal*, May 8, 1984, 38. Blount's main point was that there are "many sound reasons for the work on toxins" and at least 60 laboratories in the United States, Soviet Union, and other countries were performing research of the type deemed suspicious in Kucewicz's third article but were clearly not involved in biological warfare research. Blount wrote, "Without hard evidence, a similar article could have been written by a Soviet editorial writer about my research."

142. Jack Anderson, "Soviets Plotting Biotech War, President Told," *Washington Post*, February 21, 1984.

143. Jack Anderson, "Upgrading Germ-Warfare Intelligence," *Washington Post,* November 30, 1984.

144. Jack Anderson, "Soviets Push Biological-Weapons Work," *Washington Post,* December 4, 1984. The third point is probably based on a confusion of biological and chemical weapons, as it goes on to speak of "psychochemicals."

145. Jack Anderson and Dale Van Atta, "Sanitation Institute a Soviet Front," *Washington Post,* August 3, 1989.

146. Ken Alibek with Stephen Handelman, *Biohazard: The Chilling True Story of the Largest Covert Biological Weapons Program in the World—Told from Inside by the Man Who Ran It* (New York, 1999), 297–300.

147. There is also a smattering of disinformation in the stories passed along by the administration sources, particularly in an earlier 1981 Anderson story, "Cuba Reported to Store Deadly Chemical Arms," *Washington Post,* September 21, 1981.

148. Intelligence Advisory Committee, 1954, *Special National Intelligence Estimate,* 3.

149. Before the BWC came into effect in March 1975, all steps taken to acquire biological weapons were legal under international law.

150. Beecher 1975; Associated Press, 1976.

151. Brent Scowcroft, "Intelligence Is Not a Crystal Ball," *Washington Post,* January 12, 2000.

152. Ambassador James Leonard, personal communications, December 2010 and January 2012.

153. British official, personal communication, 2010.

154. John R. Walker, *Britain and Disarmament: The UK and Nuclear, Biological and Chemical Arms Control, 1955–1975* (Farnham, UK, 2012).

13. United States Covert Biological Warfare Disinformation

1. It has not been possible to ascertain which office she belonged or was assigned to.

2. The available sources on this series of tests include:

- "DOD Releases Project SHAD Fact Sheets," News Release No. 264-02, May 23, 2002, US Department of Defense, and Deployment Link, to Project SHAD.

- US Senate, Committee on Armed Services, Subcommittee on Personnel, *Hearing: The Department of Defense's Inquiry into Project 112/Shipboard Hazard and Defense (SHAD) Tests,* October 10, 2002, Washington, D.C., 2003.

- *2003 Report to Congress, Disclosure of Information on Project 112 to the Department of Veterans' Affairs, As Directed by PL 107-314,* US Department of Defense, undated.

- US General Accounting Office, *Chemical and Biological Defense: DOD Needs to Continue to Collect and Provide Information on Tests and on Potentially Exposed Personnel,* GAO-04-410, May 2004.
- *Under Secretary for Health's Information Letter: Evaluation of Veterans Involved in Project Shad, Autumn Gold, Copperhead, and Other Related Tests for Possible Occupational Health Exposure,* US Department of Defense, December 1, 2000, IL 10-2000-012.
- Edward Regis, *The Biology of Doom: The History of America's Secret Germ Warfare Project* (New York, 1999), 198–206.

As far as the BW portion of these tests is concerned, the designation for the entire test series, SHAD, standing for Shipboard Hazard and Defence, is a euphemism and a misnomer.

3. U.S. Offensive BW Program (1941–1972); Test and Evaluation, page VI-12, in *1996 Biological Weapon Convention Confidence Building Measures, Annex 6, Declaration of Past Acts in Offensive and/or Defensive Biological R and D Programs, USA: April 1996,* US Arms Control and Disarmament Agency. Chapter 20 provides a more complete explanation of the origins and content of the BWC CBMs.

4. Regis, 1999, 201–204.

5. Office of the Special Assistant to the Under Secretary of Defense (Personnel and Readiness) for Gulf War Illnesses, Medical Readiness and Military Deployments, "Project Shipboard Hazard and Defense (SHAD): Shady Grove," September 13, 2001, http://fhp.osd.mil/CBexposures/pdfs/shady_grove.pdf.

6. Tom Mangold and Jeff Goldberg, *Plague Wars: The Terrifying Reality of Biological Warfare* (New York, 1999), 40. In 1999 a former member of the British Defence Intelligence staff described the US BW over-ocean test series as follows: "You could take all the ships that were devoted to (BW) trials in the US system before 1969, and (it) would make . . . the fifth largest Navy in existence at that time." Christopher Davis, Interview for "Plague War," PBS-TV *Frontline* presentation, 1999. This claim is grossly in error. Exactly 21 US naval vessels took part in the tests, all of them comparatively small ships. None were capital ships. The claim could have been plausible only if the US aircraft involved in the spray tests were launched from aircraft carriers, because US carriers do not operate alone, but have submarine and destroyer escorts. The aircraft used in the tests were A4D Skyhawks and F-4 Phantoms. The tests between 1964 and 1968 used land-based A4D Skyhawk aircraft flying from the Johnston Island airbase. The 1968 tests at Eniwetok Atoll used USAF F-4 aircraft. It is presumed that they were also land-based, because no carrier is named among the participating US naval vessels.

7. H. B. Fletcher, Memorandum: "Biological Warfare—Sabotage," August 4, 1949, section (c) Double Agent Program, in *FBI File: Bacteriological Warfare in the United States,* 3, http://www.thememoryhole.org/biowar.htm.

8. Fletcher, 1949, 3.

9. Ibid.

10. The chemical weapons half of this overall deception program was disclosed in a book written by David Wise, *Cassidy's Run: The Secret Spy War over Nerve Gas* (New York, 2000). The biological part was mentioned only fleetingly on pages 58–61.

11. Raymond L. Garthoff, "Polyakov's Run," *Bulletin of the Atomic Scientists* 56, no. 5 (September/October 2000): 37–40; Garthoff, "Correction," *Bulletin of the Atomic Scientists* 57, no. 1 (January/February 2001): 73. In a 2002 publication, Jeanne Guillemin wrote that Garthoff's paper was written "using declassified documents." Jeanne Guillemin, "The 1979 Anthrax Epidemic in the USSR: Applied Science and Political Controversy," *Proceedings of the American Philosophical Society* 146, no. 1 (March 2002): 30. That is not correct: Garthoff possessed no declassified (or classified) documents regarding the affair. Raymond Garthoff, personal communication, May 17, 2008.

12. Personal communication, 2001.

13. Ibid.

14. Garthoff, 2000, 39. Garthoff had written that he thought the US disinformation program had ended "probably in the mid-1970s." He is now less certain of that, and essentially agrees with the description provided in this chapter. Raymond Garthoff, personal communication, May 14, 2008.

15. Garthoff, 2000, 40.

16. Raymond Garthoff, personal communication, May 17, 2008.

17. The Forty Committee was established by National Security Decision Memorandum 40, in February 1970, to approve and control covert actions. The committee was also to annually review any covert actions previously approved, and the director of Central Intelligence was assigned the responsibility for coordinating and controlling covert operations, and submitting them to the Forty Committee for approval. See Emmanuel Adler, "Executive Command and Control in Foreign Policy: The CIA's Covert Activities," *Orbis* 23 (Fall 1979): 677–678.

18. Wise, 2000, 46.

19. Garthoff was referring to both chemical and biological Soviet weapons: Ben Fenton, "US Blunder Triggered Global Germ Bomb Race," *Electric Telegraph* (UK), March 12, 2001.

20. Ken Alibek with Stephen Handelman, *Biohazard: The Chilling True Story of the Largest Covert Biological Weapons Program in the World—Told from Inside by the Man Who Ran It* (New York, 1999).

21. Mangold and Goldberg, 1999, 136.

22. Cited in "US CBW Facilities, Use, Program Described," Radio Moscow, March 24, 1982.

23. Andrey Semenov, "Burgasov Denies Anthrax Claims," interview with RAMS Academician Petr Nikolayevich Burgasov; "Was There Anthrax in Sverdlovsk-19?

Only President Boris Yeltsin and Our Interviewee, RAMS Academician Pyotr Burgasov, Know This Mystery" (in Russian), *Meditsinskaya Gazeta,* June 24, 1998.

The suggestion that the "Council for *Defense Against . . .*" may also have directed parts of the Soviet offensive BW program in the late 1960s is of interest as well.

14. Soviet Allegations of the Use of Biological Weapons by the United States

1. "Pravda Lays Plague Blame on America," Reuters, June 11, 1950.

2. Memorandum, US Department of State, OIR/CPI (March 20, 1952).

3. Erhard Geissler, *Schwarzer Tod und Amikäfer: Biologische Waffen und Ihre Geschichte, Anmerkungen Zu Einer Ausstellung* [Plague and 'American Beetles:' Biological Weapons and Their History. Comments for an Exhibition] (July 2000), 14, 16–17, 25–28.

4. Ibid.

5. Lt. Col. MR Konrad Kluge et. al., *Forschungsergebnisse zum Thema Die Biologischen Mittel* [Research Report on the Subject of Biological Means], Ministerrat Der Deutschen Demokratischen Republik, Ministerium Für Staatssicherheit, CVS JHS 001-32/81. In 1967 the Soviet KGB and the East German (GDR) Stasi launched a major disinformation campaign against West Germany. It included the defection of Dr. Ehrenfried Petras, a West German scientist whom the Stasi had recruited as early as 1950 and had been able to place inside a West German aerobiology institute. The GDR accused West Germany of carrying out an offensive BW program. The charges were false. These were not, however, allegations made against the United States, nor were they allegations of BW use. See Erhard Geissler, "Biowaffen für die Bundeswehr, Dr. Petras und die Entlarvung der westdeutschen B-Waffen-Rüstung durch das MFS" [Biological Weapons for the Bundeswehr, Dr. Petras and the Exposure of West German Biological Weapon Armament through the MFS], Schweizerische Vereinigung des Pugwash (December 2006); and Jens Gieseke, *Der Mielke-Konzern: Die Geschichte der Stasi, 1945–1990* [The Mielke "Company:" The History of the Stasi] (Munich, 2006).

6. "Fury of the People" (in Russian), *Pravda,* May 30, 1952, 4.

7. "Blue-Prints for BW," *FAS Newsletter,* October 23, 1952 (citing *New York Times* article of October 3, 1952).

8. This record, including the initial Chinese and Soviet Korean War BW allegations, was published in a monograph, three journal publications, and a book chapter: Milton Leitenberg, "The Korean War Biological Warfare Allegations Resolved," Occasional Paper 36, Stockholm University, May 1998; Leitenberg, "Resolution of the Korean War Biological Warfare Allegations," *Critical Reviews in Microbiology* 24, no. 3 (Fall 1998): 169–194; Leitenberg, "New Russian Evidence on Korean War Biological Warfare Allegations: Background and Analysis," *Cold War International History*

Project Bulletin, issue 11 (Winter 1998): 185–200, and 180–185 for the documents in full (English translation); Leitenberg, "The Korean War Biological Weapons Allegations: Additional Information and Disclosures," *Asian Perspectives* 24, no. 3 (2000): 159–172; Leitenberg, "False Allegations of US Biological Weapons Use during the Korean War," in *Terrorism, War, or Disease? Unraveling the Use of Biological Weapons,* ed. Anne L. Clunan, Peter R. Lavoy, and Susan B. Martin (Stanford, Calif., 2008).

9. Resolution of the Presidium of the USSR Council of Ministers about Letter to the Ambassador of the USSR to the PRC, V. V. Kuznetsov, and to the Chargé d'Affaires of the USSR in the DPRK. S. P. Suzdalev, May 2, 1953.

10. Personal communication, spring 2003.

11. Maarten Schneider, "Bacteria as Propaganda Weapon," *International Spectator,* May 8, 1957.

12. Mose Harvey, "Briefing on Soviet Developments following the Death of Stalin (April 24, 1953)," in US House of Representatives, Committee on Foreign Affairs, *Selected Executive Session Hearings of the Committee, 1952–56,* vol. 14 (Washington, D.C., 1980), 459.

13. *Report of the Secretary General, Chemical and Bacteriological (Biological) Weapons and the Effects of Their Possible Use* (New York, 1969). The fact that Japan was not a party to the 1925 Geneva Protocol does not at all affect the statement to which the Soviet Union agreed.

14. A. M. Arkhangelskiy et al., *Bacteriological Weapons and How to Defend against Them* (in Russian) (Moscow, 1967).

15. In 1985, on the 40th anniversary of the end of World War II, the Novosti Press Agency published a small book, *Recalling the Past for the Sake of the Future: The Causes, Results, and Lessons of World War II.* Japan's wartime BW program and the use of BW by Japan "in China and Mongolia" are reviewed in the book's pages 112–113. No mention is made of the Korean War, although the book goes on to discuss various "lessons" until the 1980s.

16. General E. I. Smirnov et al., *Wars and Epidemics* (in Russian) (Moscow, 1988).

17. Yelena Solomonovna Levina, "Experimental Biology in the System of Russian Security of the Second Half of the Twentieth Century: Biological Weapons or Health Care?" (in Russian), in *Nauka I bezopasnost Rossii: Istoriko-nauchniye, metodologicheskiye, istorico-tekhnicheskiye aspekty* (Moscow, 2000), 367–394, 574. In 1989, a book about biological weapons was published in Khabarovsk that included a chapter repeating the Korean War BW allegations, as well as those involving Cuba. Nikolay A. Ivanov and Vlaidslav V. Bogach, *Oruzhie Vne Zakone* [Outlaw Weapons] (Khabarovsk, 1989).

18. US Department of State, ed., *Documents on Disarmament: 1945–1959,* vol. 1: *1945–1956* (Washington, D.C., 1970), 402.

19. At roughly this same time, Soviet military authors also accused the United States of using chemical agents: "The American press has called attention to the

widespread use of psychochemical 'OV' in dealing with people who are leading national liberation movements." The reference to items in "the American press" is apparently spurious. Col. B. Timofeyev, "The Criminal Weapon of the Pentagon," *Agitator's Notebook* (in Russian), no. 17 (1967): 30–32.

20. "WHO-Supported Collaborative Research Projects in India: The Facts," *WHO Chronicle* 30, no. 4 (1976): 131–139.

21. Vasiliy Mitrokhin, "KGB Active Measures in Southwest Asia in 1980–82," *Cold War International History Project Bulletin,* nos. 14–15 (Winter 2003–Spring 2004): 201–202.

22. "CIA's Lahore Mosquito Project," TASS, March 24, 1982; and "US CBW Facilities, Use Program Described," Radio Moscow, March 24, 1982.

23. Michael Kaufman, "Pakistanis Expel a Malaria Expert," *New York Times,* February 10, 1982; John Schidlovsky, "University of Maryland Malaria Lab Chief Ousted by Pakistan: Mosquito Research Drew Soviet Attack," *Baltimore Sun,* February 9, 1982; "Foreign Labs Shut," *Nature* 296 (March 11, 1982): 104–105; and "A Strange Visit," *Hindustan Times,* February 28, 1982; *Literaturnaya Gazeta,* February 3, 1982; and *Moscow Times,* February 4, 1982.

24. Raymond Zilinskas, "Cuban Allegations of Biological Warfare by the United States: Assessing the Evidence," *Critical Reviews in Microbiology* 25, no. 3 (1999): 173–228; Charles Calisher, "Scientist in a Strange Land: A Cautionary Tale," *Nonproliferation Review* 16, no. 3 (November 2009): 509–519.

25. Richard Beeston, "US Plans to Protest at Summit on Soviet Disinformation Efforts," *Washington Times,* May 17, 1988.

26. Lt. General Mikhail Kiryan, "Biological Weapons and US Plans," *Strategic Studies,* Spring 1982, 59.

27. Herbert Romerstein, "Disinformation as a KGB Weapon in the Cold War," *Journal of Intelligence History* 1, no. 1 (Summer 2001): 60–61.

28. "World Stands on the Brink of Biological War" (in Russian), *Pravda,* May 15, 2009. The opinions were attributed to the "doctor . . . expert, and political consultant, Sergey Markelov."

29. Igor Makarov, "A Biological Bomb at Our Borders: Dangerous Experiments in Secret Georgian Laboratories Equipped by American Specialists" (in Russian), *Pravda,* December 3, 2009.

30. See *Krasnaya Zvezda,* April 18, 1984.

31. See, for example, *Soviet News,* no. 6019, April 22, 1980.

32. Christopher Andrew and Vasili Mitrokhin, *The Sword and the Shield: The Mitrokhin Archive and the Secret History of the KGB* (New York, 1999), 244–245, 484.

33. Ibid., appendix D, 569, 224.

34. Thomas Boghardt, "Operation INFEKTION: Soviet Bloc Intelligence and Its AIDS Disinformation Campaign," *Studies in Intelligence* 53, no. 4 (December

2009): 5. See also David A. Spetrino, "Soviet Active Measures: AIDS Disinformation," *Studies in Intelligence* 32 (Winter 1988): 9–14.

35. Valentin Zapevalov, "Panic in the West, or What Is Hiding behind the Sensation Surrounding AIDS" (in Russian), *Literaturnaya Gazeta,* October 30, 1985.

36. Oleg Kalugin, *The First Directorate: My 32 Years in Intelligence and Espionage against the West* (New York, 1994), 158.

37. This was a standard technique of Soviet BW disinformation campaigns. The KGB would first place the story with an overseas newspaper that it had close dealings with. The Indian *Patriot* and a Kenyan daily were repeated favorites. The story would then be picked up in the Soviet press, citing the Third World source. In a final step, the story in the Soviet press would then be transmitted worldwide by the Soviet press agency TASS or by Novosti. See David B. Ottoway, "US Links Soviets to Disinformation," *Washington Post,* January 17, 1988.

38. The HVA had its own disinformation unit, Department X, or HVA-X. In 1992, a book by two former Stasi officers explained how their agency had also been involved in furthering the AIDS disinformation story: Peter Richter and Klaus Rösler, *Wolfs West-Spione: Ein Insider Report* [Wolf's Spies in the West: An Insider Report] (Berlin, 1992). See also Boghardt, 2009; Erhard Geissler, "The AIDS Disinformation Campaign Continues and Bears Rotten Fruit: Part I, An Overview," *ASA Newsletter,* February 26, 2010, 14; and Part II, manuscript, courtesy of Dr. Geissler. Geissler has also published two book chapters in German on the subject, in 2009 and 2010.

39. Andrew and Mitrokhin, 1999, 245.

40. James Brooke, "In Cradle of AIDS Theory, a Defensive Africa Sees a Disguise for Racism," *New York Times,* November 19, 1987.

41. Richard Beeston, "US Plans to Protest at Summit on Soviet Disinformation Efforts," *Washington Times,* May 17, 1988; Don Oberdorfer, "State Dept. Hails Moscow for 'Disavowal' on AIDS: Propaganda Had Blamed Disease on US," *Washington Post,* November 3, 1987. The Active Measures Analysis and Response Office of the DOS' Bureau of Intelligence and Research released three studies: "Soviet Influence Activities: A Report on Active Measures and Propaganda, 1986–1987," August 1987; "Soviet Influence Activities: A Report on Active Measures and Propaganda, 1987–1988," August 1989; and "Soviet Active Measures and Propaganda during the Gorbachev Era: 'New Thinking' and Influence Activities," March 1992. All of these publications provided additional extensive evidence of the KGB's role in purveying the AIDS disinformation.

42. Bill Keller, "American Outraged by Soviet Article," *New York Times,* June 6, 1987.

43. Romerstein, 2001, citing *Izvestia* in October 1987; P. Phillippov, "Criminal Laboratories at Work: The Biological Convention and the Hypocrisy of the USA" (in Russian), *Krasnaya Zvezda,* October 4, 1987.

44. Brooke, 1987.

45. Herbert Romerstein, "The Role of Forgeries in Soviet Active Measures," *Survey* 30 (October 1998): 3, quoting Al-Qabas (Kuwait), January 29, 1987. This fabrication was amazingly clumsy. It included a photograph of a tank purportedly firing the ethnic weapon, "the germ bomb," and accusing the United States of taking over biological weapons research from the Japanese, a charge going back nearly 40 years to 1949 and 1950.

46. Brooke, 1987.

47. Boghardt, 2009, 6.

48. Constance Holden, "Curbing Soviet Disinformation," *Science* 242 (November 4, 1988): 665.

49. Boghardt, 2009, 16.

50. Ibid.

51. Ibid. The countries include India, Pakistan, Brazil, the Soviet Union, West Germany, Panama, Yugoslavia, Turkey, Peru, the United Kingdom, and others. As a result of GDR assistance in the disinformation effort, a West German TV documentary based on the disinformation was aired as late as 1989, and on the United Kingdom's Channel 4 in 1990.

52. Former Soviet Foreign Ministry official, personal communication, 1999.

53. Romerstein, 2001, citing *Izvestia*, March 19, 1992.

54. Romerstein, 2001, citing *Moskovskaya Pravda*, August 15, 1992.

55. Public opinion polls in the late 1990s continued to show that a very large proportion of the African-American community in the United States claimed to believe that HIV-1 had been released by US government agencies to target their population. The disinformation has been championed by Louis Farrakhan, the head of the US black Muslim organization, and in the spring of 2008 it became an issue in the presidential primary campaign of the US Democratic Party because of the pronouncements of the pastor of the church of presidential candidate Obama. It is continually propagated by books sold on the Web and by dedicated websites. And on September 26, 2007, the BBC reported that Archbishop Francisco Chimoio, the head of the Catholic Church in Mozambique, stated that countries in Europe were deliberately delivering HIV-1 to his country via condoms and retroviral drugs "in order to finish quickly the African people. . . . They want to finish with the African people. This is the programme." BBC News, September 26, 2007, http://news.bbc.co/uk/go/pr/fr/-/2/hi/africa/7014335.stm.

56. Sergey Lesov, "U.S. Military-Biological Research on Foreign Soil: Leaks of Up-to-Date Technology Can Lead to Deplorable Consequences" and "U.S. Hit over Alleged BW Experiments Abroad" (in Russian), *Nezavasimaya Gazeta*, October 24, 1995.

57. Sergei Gerasimenko, "Everything That They Are Saying about Us Is a Lie" (in Russian), *New Izvestia*, March 3, 1998. Most of the interview is a

resurrection of Soviet-era denials of the cause of the anthrax epidemic in Sverdlovsk in 1979.

58. Dmitry Litovkin, "Interview: Valentin Yevstigneev on Issues Relating to Russian Biological Weapons," *Yaderny Kontrol* (Nuclear Control), no. 11 (Summer 1999): 43–51 in the English edition, 15–25 in the Russian edition.

59. BBCSWB (Summary of the World Broadcasts), "Russia: Military Bacteriological Centre Short of Funds (Transmission of Moscow NTV, November 22, 1995)," November 27, 1995.

60. Interview with General Valentin Yevstigneev, "Biological Weapons Are the Cheapest Kind of WMD: An Interview" (in Russian), Moscow, November 26, 2001.

61. Ken Alibek with Stephen Handelman, *Biohazard: The Chilling True Story of the Largest Covert Biological Weapons Program in the World—Told from Inside by the Man Who Ran It* (New York, 1999), 274; Ken Alibek, personal communication, June 1998.

62. Vladimir Pasechnik, personal communication, June 1999.

63. Evgeniya Kvitko, "Interview with Petr N. Burgasov: Smallpox—Also Not a Bad Weapon" (in Russian), *Moscovskie Novosti,* November 3, 2001; http://kungrad .com/aral/island/ospa/.

64. Dmitry Butrin et al., "Russia Warily Eyes Human Samples: In the Name of Fighting Bioterrorism, Export of Biological Materials Prohibited" (in Russian), *Kommersant,* May 30, 2007. In a peculiar evolution, a book published in 2005 by a former Soviet intelligence agent who had emigrated from Russia to New Zealand continued this tradition. According to him, "almost every outbreak of a new or emerging infectious disease in the past 15 years—including the outbreak of foot-and mouth-disease in Britain in 2001 and the severe acute respiratory syndrome (SARS) pandemic in 2003—may have been either a deliberate bioweapons attack or an accidental release of a genetically engineered microbe from a bioweapons facility." He also implied that "the causative agents of hantavirus pulmonary syndrome were genetically engineered specifically to attack Native Americans." Jens H. Kuhn et al., "Russia's Secret Weapons," a review of *Biological Espionage: Special Operations of the Soviet and Russian Foreign Intelligence Services in the West,* by Alexander Kouzminov, *Nature* 436 (August 4, 2005): 628–629.

65. *Krasnaya Zvezda,* November 13, 2007, http://www.redstar.ru/2007/11/13 _11/1_02.html.

15. Sverdlovsk 1979: The Release of *Bacillus anthracis* Spores from a Soviet Ministry of Defense Facility and Its Consequences

1. Les Aspin was quoted in a lengthy press examination of the Sverdlovsk events and their US political consequences, in Leslie H. Gelb, "Keeping an Eye on Russia:

A Mysterious Event in Sverdlovsk Has Raised Serious Doubts about Arms-Treaty Surveillance," *New York Times Magazine,* November 29, 1981.

2. Permanent Select Committee on Intelligence, House of Representatives, "The Sverdlovsk Incident: Soviet Compliance with the Biological Weapons Convention," Washington, D.C., May 29, 1980. This Hearing contained the testimony of Mark Popovsky, a Soviet émigré author with contacts in the Soviet Union who was responsible for the first reports of the events in Sverdlovsk (see Chapter 12).

3. Committee on Foreign Affairs, US House of Representatives, *Congress and Foreign Policy—1980* (Washington, D.C., 1981), 21. An April 1980 CIA report concluded that there was "strong evidence that a biological production or storage site is at the Sverdlovsk facility. It shows that an extremely large number of anthrax spores were released—effectively negating any assessment of peaceful or defensive research being conducted there. This flies in the face of the 1972 convention." The lines quoted were leaked by the CIA to a journalist in 1984; see Jack Anderson and Dale Van Atta, "Poison and Plague: Russia's Secret Terror Weapons," *Reader's Digest,* September 1984, 54–58.

4. Annual Report, Pursuant to Clause 1(d) Rule XI of the Rules of the House of Representatives, Report By the Permanent Select Committee on Intelligence (Washington, D.C., 1980), 7.

5. Following the Soviet invasion of Afghanistan on December 24, 1979, the Carter administration did not press for Senate ratification of SALT II and the treaty was never ratified, although both parties agreed to abide by its numerical limitations for strategic weapons.

6. BWC Review Conference document BWC/Conf.I/SR.12, paragraph 29.

7. "Anthrax Propaganda Used to Poison World Situation," Moscow, TASS, March 24, 1980; and David K. Willis, "Soviets: US Double-Crossed Us on Germ Warfare Charges," *Christian Science Monitor,* March 28, 1980.

8. US Department of State cable to Ambassador Flowerree, EO12065, March 26, 1980 (Secret).

9. National Archives (TNA) Kew FCO 66, Washington tel no 3757 to FCO, August 13, 1980.

10. Ibid.

11. National Archives (TNA) Kew FCO 66, Record of a meeting between Mr. Ralph Earle, Director of ACDA, and Mr. Douglas Hurd, September 9, 1980, Sverdlovsk.

12. In September 1980, Secretary of Defense Harold Brown testified that "DOD is supporting the Administration in attempting to initiate technical consultations with the Soviets, on a bilateral basis—under the terms of the BWC—to gain a better understanding of this very serious incident. The Administration is determined to pursue this problem to a satisfactory resolution." US Senate, Committee on Armed

Services, Hearing: *Chemical Warfare,* September 4, 1980 (Washington, D.C., 1981), 3.

13. "Alleged Biological Warfare Agent Incident at Sverdlovsk," DAMO-NCC, October, 23, 1981, US Department of State Cable, E.O. 12065: RDS-1.

14. John R. Walker, *Britain and Disarmament: The UK and Nuclear, Biological and Chemical Weapons Arms Control and Programmes, 1956–1975* (Farnham, UK, 2012).

15. Ambassador H. Allen Holmes, assistant secretary, US Department of State, in *Global Spread of Chemical and Biological Weapons,* Hearings before the Committee on Governmental Affairs, US Senate, February 9, 1989 (Washington, D.C., 1990), 184.

16. Harald Muller, "Specific Approaches: Nuclear, Chemical and Biological Proliferation," in *Disarmament and Arms Limitation Obligations: Problems of Compliance and Enforcement,* ed. Serge Sur, UNIDIR (Geneva, 1994), 258.

17. Ibid. Article VI of the BWC allows any member state to bring a compliance concern to the United Nations Security Council, which could, in theory, then decide to launch an investigation. Since the Soviet Union had the power to veto any UNSC resolution calling for an investigation, this was a fruitless path and was never attempted.

18. Transmittal letter, "Soviet Submission to US on Sverdlovsk—1988," LS No./126894, JS/AO (in Russian). In April 1987 the Soviet Union gave DOS representatives a briefer report presumably written by, and signed by, Burgasov on May 25, 1979. "Report on Measures Taken in Sverdlovsk in Connection with an Outbreak of Anthrax," LS No. 121846, JS/AO (in Russian).

19. S. Bezdenezhnykh and V. N. Nikiforov, "An Epidemiological Analysis of Incidences of Anthrax in Sverdlovsk" (in Russian), *Zh. Mikrobiol. Immunol. Epidemiol* (USSR), no. 5 (May 1980): 111–113; and Bezdenezhnykh and Nikiforov, "Strict Observance of Veterinary Regulations" (in Russian), *Chelovek I Zakon* (Man and the Law) (USSR), September 9, 1980. The 1988 paper (unpublished manuscript) is titled "Epidemiological Analysis of Anthrax Outbreak in Sverdlovsk" (in Russian) and is authored by Bezdenezhnykh, Burgasov, and Nikiforov. See also Milton Leitenberg, "A Return to Sverdlovsk: Allegations of Soviet Activities Related to Biological Weapons," *Arms Control and Contemporary Security Policy* 12, no. 2 (September 1991): 161–190; and Leitenberg, "Anthrax in Sverdlovsk: New Pieces to the Puzzle," *Arms Control Today* 22, no. 3 (April 1992): 10–13.

20. Personal communication.

21. Remarks by Soviet ambassador Israelyan, Summary Record of the Fifth Meeting, BWC/CONF./11/SR.5, September 19, 1986; R. Jeffrey Smith, "Soviets Offer Account of '79 Anthrax Outbreak," *Washington Post,* October 9, 1986.

22. Personal communication.

23. Eliot Marshall, "Sverdlovsk: Anthrax Capitol? Soviet Doctors Answer Questions about an Unusual Anthrax Epidemic Once Thought to Have Been Triggered by a Leak from a Weapons Lab," *Science* 240 (April 22, 1988): 383–385; Matthew S. Meselson, "The Biological Weapons Convention and the Sverdlovsk Anthrax Outbreak of 1979," *Federation of American Scientists Public Interest Report* 41. no. 7 (September 1988): 1–6; R. Jeffrey Smith and Philip J. Hilts, "Soviets Deny 1979 Outbreak Involved Germ Lab: Tainted Meat Caused Anthrax Deaths, Officials Say in Most Detailed Account to Date," *Washington Post,* April 13, 1988; Lois Ember, "Soviet Anthrax Dispute: Details of 1979 Outbreak Presented," *Chemical and Engineering News* 66. no. 16 (April 18, 1988): 4–5; Joseph Palea, "Anthrax Outbreak in Soviet Union Due to Natural Causes," *Nature* 322 (April 21 1988): 674; R. Jeffrey Smith, "Despite Soviet Account of Anthrax Outbreak, Questions Remain," *Washington Post,* April 14, 1988.

24. "Burgasov Denies Anthrax Claims" (in Russian), *Meditsinskaya Gazeta,* June 24, 1998.

25. Serguei Popov and Marina Voronova, "Russian Bioweapons: Still the Best-Kept Secret" *Nonproliferation Review* 11, no. 3 (Fall 2004): 1–14 (review of *Ya Veril* [I Believed], by Petr N. Burgasov [Moscow, 2000]); Dmitriy Melman, "Historian of Death—Interview with Peter Nikolayevich Burgasov" (in Russian), *Moskovsky Komsomolets,* April 7, 2006, http://www.mk.ru/newshop/bask.sap?artid=127351.

26. "Soviet Now Mentioning Foot-and-Mouth Disease," *New York Times,* March 27, 1980.

27. Sergei Kulik, "'Bacteriological Weapons' Forgery Is Used to Conceal USA's Own Unsavory Plans," *Soviet News,* March 25, 1980, 101. See also Leonid Krashov, "Anthrax Propaganda Used to Poison World Situation," *International Affairs* (USSR), March 25, 1980.

28. Personal communication, January 4, 2008.

29. Former Soviet diplomat, personal communication, July 28, 1999.

30. Leitenberg, 1991, 1992. Two additional papers that supply a useful guide to the pre-1990 literature on the Sverdlovsk events are Julian Perry Robinson, "The Soviet Union and the Biological Weapon Convention and a Guide to Sources on the Sverdlovsk Incident," *Arms Control* 3, no. 3 (1982): 41–56; and Nicholas Sims, "The Sverdlovsk Incident," in *The Diplomacy of Biological Disarmament: Vicissitudes of a Treaty in Force, 1975–1985* (London, 1988), 226–254.

31. A. Pashkov, "How We Have Been 'Inoculated' with Anthrax: Military in White Lab Coats Are Still Potentially Dangerous for the Society" (in Russian), *Izvestia,* November 11, 1991; A. Pashkov, "I Know Where the Anthrax in Sverdlovsk Came From: The Late General of Counterespionage Informed the Editor's Desk" (in Russian), *Izvestia,* November 23, 1991; and A. Pashkov, "End to Legend of Anthrax in the Urals" (in Russian), *Izvestia,* December 11, 1991, in JPRS-ULS-92-008, February 28, 1992, 27–29.

32. "Head of Chemical Weapons Directorate on 1979 Sverdlovsk Anthrax Outbreak," Interview with General V. I. Yevstigneev, *BBC Summary of World Broadcasts,* SU/1367, C2/5,6, April 29, 1992; also in FBIS-Sov-92-082, April 28, 1992. Both reproduce an article originally published in Russian in *Izvestia,* April 12, 1992.

33. D. Muratov et al., "Boris Yeltsin: I Am Not Hiding the Difficulties as I Want the People to Understand This" (in Russian), *Komsomolskaya Pravda,* May 27, 1992, FBIS-SOV-92-103, May 28, 1992, 28.

34. Martin Walker, "Yeltsin Says USSR Held US Airmen," *The Guardian,* June 17, 1992; "Germ Weapon Killed Scores, Yeltsin Says," *Chicago Tribune* [Associated Press, from Moscow], June 17, 1992. Both press accounts say that Yeltsin attributed the Sverdlovsk anthrax to "germ warfare experiments." The translation used in the text rendered the key words as "military developments." D. Muratov et al., *Komsomolskaya Pravda,* May 27, 1992.

35. US Department of State, "Press Guidance: Biological Weapons in Russia," June 17, 1992.

36. Personal communication, 1992.

37. Former US government official, personal communication, February 1999.

38. Kataev archive at Hoover Institution of War, Revolution and Peace, Stanford, California; translated by Natalia Alexandrova and David Hoffman.

39. Vitaly Kataev, personal communication.

40. Vitaly Kataev, handwritten notes, Kataev archive, Hoover Institution of War, Revolution and Peace, Stanford, Calif.; translated by John Hart.

41. This document was labeled "#2/upovr of January 5, 1990," and it is identified as a Ministry of Foreign Affairs response to the December 19, 1989, memorandum.

42. "On the Draft Resolution of the TsK KPSS 'On Directives to the USSR Delegation at the Soviet-American Consultations on Issues of Banning Bacteriological and Toxin Weapons,'" Kataev archive, Hoover Institution of War, Revolution and Peace, Stanford, Calif.; translated by Natalia Alexandrova and David Hoffman.

43. "To Comrade Lazarev V. F., V. Karpov, 11 Jan 1990, #03/upovr," Kataev archive, Hoover Institution of War, Revolution and Peace, Stanford, Calif.; translated by Natalia Alexandrova and David Hoffman.

44. Excerpt from a memo by Central Committee Defense Department staffers Oleg Belyakov and Vitaly Kataev to Lev Zaikov, January 11, 1990, included in National Security Archive document set, *Cracking Open the Soviet Biological Weapons System,* 2010.

45. "Secretariat of the Central Committee," "Additional Directives. Appendix 3: Informational material about the Sverdlovsk facility," prepared for consultations with US/UK in April 1990, classified, n.d.

46. L. P. Mishustina, People's Deputy of the Russian Federation, 1990–1995, "To the President of the Russian Federation, B. N. Yeltsin." The Soviet government's position was that the deaths in Sverdlovsk had not occurred due to any act by

any government agency, so it is unknown on what grounds the compensation was made.

47. Natalya Zenova, "Continuing a Topic: Once Again on Military Secrets" (in Russian), *Literaturnaya Gazeta,* November 13, 1991, JPRS-TND-91-019, December 2, 1991, 37. In 1992, after President Yeltsin named General Kuntsevich to head his commission overseeing both BW and CW matters (see Chapter 22), Kuntsevich expressed doubt that Compound 19 had anything to do with the anthrax outbreak and declared that his commission would investigate the question. If any such investigation was ever carried out, no one, even in Russia, has ever seen any evidence of it. L. Chemenko, "In Order to Live We Should Destroy the Deadly Weapons Stockpiles" (in Russian), *Rossiyskiye Vesti,* September 22, 1992, FBIS-SOV-92-186, September 24, 1992, 2.

48. A. V. Yablokov and S. K. Revina, "Information," December 6, 1991.

49. L. A. Fedorov, *Soviet Biological Weapons: History, Ecology, Politics* (in Russian) (Moscow, 2005), 150–151; translated by the Multilingual Division of the Translation Bureau, Government of Canada (Ottawa, March 17, 2008).

50. Matthew Meselson et al., "The Sverdlovsk Anthrax Outbreak of 1979," *Science* 266 (November 18, 1994): 1201–1208; Jeanne Guillemin, *Anthrax: The Investigation of a Deadly Outbreak* (Berkeley, Calif., 1999); Faina A. Abramova et al., "Pathology of Inhalational Anthrax in 42 Cases from the Sverdlovsk Outbreak of 1979," *Proceedings of the National Academy of Sciences,* 90 (March 1993): 2291–2294; Philip J. Hilts, "US and Russian Researchers Tie Anthrax Deaths to Soviets," *New York Times,* March 15, 1993; Michael D. Gordon, "The Anthrax Solution: The Sverdlovsk Incident and the Resolution of a Biological Weapons Controversy," *Journal of the History of Biology* 30 (1997): 441–480; and Jeanne Guillemin, "The 1979 Anthrax Epidemic in the USSR: Applied Science and Political Controversy," *Proceedings of the American Philosophical Society* 146, no. 1 (March 2002): 18–36.

51. Martin Hugh-Jones, personal communication, June 2, 2003.

52. S. I. Dzupina, *Forecasting Epizootic Situations on the Epizootic Aspects of Siberian Ulcer* (in Russian), Institute of Experimental Veterinary of Siberia and Far East, Siberian Branch of the Russian Academy of Agricultural Sciences (Novosibirsk, 1996).

53. Dean A. Wilkening, "Sverdlovsk Revisited: Modeling Human Inhalation Anthrax," *Proceedings of the National Academy of Sciences* 103, no. 20 (May 16, 2006): 7590.

54. E. V. Pimenov, *Siberskaya Yazva* (Moscow, 1999), 218–219, 236–237, referred to in Jeanne Guillemin, *Biological Weapons: From the Invention of State-Sponsored Programs to Contemporary Bioterrorism* (New York, 2005), 143, 229.

55. Sergey N. Volkov, *Yekaterinburg: Man and City* (in Russian) (Yekaterinburg, Yekaterinburgsky (G)umanitarno—Ekologichesky Litsey, 1997). Available excerpts from the book indicate that its description of the accident at Compound 19 is not very reliable.

56. B. N. Mishankin, "Anthrax Outbreak in Sverdlovsk" (in Russian), in *Interesting Stories about the Activities and People of the Anti-Plague System of Russia and the Soviet Union* (in Russian), vol. 9 (Moscow, 1999), 89–113. (Presentations at the scientific conference on the 20th anniversary of the Sverdlovsk events held at the Rostov-on-Don Anti-Plague Research Institute.) Both Vladimir Volkov and Mishankin describe the cause of the anthrax release as "a munitions explosion" at "an underground experimental production facility" for anthrax at "Military Town 19 (P.O. Box 47051)."

57. Personal communication, January 6, 2008.

58. Wilkening, 2006.

59. Personal communication, March 2005.

60. David Franz, personal communication, 2004.

61. Zaviyalov, personal communication.

62. Lederberg learned that a Moscow epidemiologist and infectious disease specialist told her son at that time that the disease outbreak was caused by the combination of the drying of a large quantity of *B. anthracis,* an accident, and the filter in the exhaust mechanism not being in place. Joshua Lederberg to Alexis Shelokov, Memorandum: "Anthrax Outbreak in Sverdlovsk," March 24, 1994.

63. Stanislav Petrov et al., "Biological Subversive Activity in the Urals" (in Russian), *Nezavisimaya Gazeta,* May 23, 2001. The paper was apparently written by one of the co-authors, Mikhail Supotnitskiy. Personal communication, 2001.

64. Adelaida Sigida, "Not Everyone Will Die, and Not from the Ulcer" (in Russian), *Kommersant-Daily,* October 16, 2001.

65. Petr Burgasov, "Report on Measures Taken in Sverdlovsk in Connection with an Outbreak of Anthrax" (in Russian), May 5, 1979.

66. Burgasov, 1998.

67. Melman, 2006. Burgasov is apparently capable of saying two different things at the same time. When he was asked in an interview "whether the 1979 outbreak in Sverdlovsk was biological warfare? No, he said, in short." Yevgeniya Kvitko, "Anthrax Is Not Bacterial Warfare in America; It's Psychological Warfare" (in Russian), *Moscovskie Novosti,* 2001, http://kungrad.com/aral/island/ospa/.

68. A. Pashkov, "End to Legend of Anthrax in the Urals" (in Russian), *Izvestia,* December 11, 1991, in JPRS-ULS-92-008, February 28, 1992, 27–29.

69. K. Belyaninov et al., "Komsomolskaya Pravda Investigation: Our Expedition Tracked the Clues of a Secret Biological War" (in Russian), *Komsomolskaya Pravda,* June 10, 1992, in JPRS-ULS-92-018, June 23, 1992, 17–21.

70. Stanislav Petrov and Mikhail Supotnitskiy "The Sverdlovsk Twin of the American 'White Powder'" (in Russian), *Nesavisimaya Voyennoye Obozveniye,* July 18, 2009, and *Nesavisimaya Gazeta,* July 17, 2009. Because Petrov and Supotnikskiy claimed that the Sverdlovsk outbreak could not have been caused by a single aerosol release, Fedorov sarcastically noted that this required that the supposed US sabo-

teurs were wandering the streets of Sverdlovsk for several months spraying an aerosol without being apprehended; Fedorov, 2005, 166.

71. Kvitko, 2001.

72. Personal communication, November 2007.

73. H. A. Holmes, "Testimony," in *Global Spread of Chemical and Biological Weapons,* Hearings before the Committee on Governmental Affairs and Its Permanent Subcommittee on Investigations, US Senate (Washington, D.C., 1989), 190–191.

74. International Atomic Energy Agency, *"Report on a Radiological Accident in the Southern Urals on 29 September 1957,"* Information Circular, INFCIRC/368, July 28, 1989; Zhores Medvedev, *Nuclear Disaster in the Urals* (New York, 1979).

16. Soviet Research on Mycotoxins

1. US Department of State, "Chemical Warfare in Southeast Asia and Afghanistan," Report to the Congress from Secretary of State Alexander M. Haig Jr. (Special Report No. 98), March 22, 1982. See also: US Department of State, "Chemical Warfare in Southeast Asia and Afghanistan: An Update," Report from Secretary of State George P. Shultz (Special Report No. 104), November 1982.

2. Special Director of Central Intelligence, National Intelligence Estimate, *Implications of Soviet Use of Chemical and Toxin Weapons for US Security Interests,* SNIE 11-17-83, September 13, 1983; Director of Central Intelligence, Special National Intelligence Estimate, *Use of Toxins and Other Lethal Chemicals in Southeast Asia and Afghanistan,* SNIE 11/50/37-82, March 2, 1983.

3. Once the CWC came into force, toxins fell under the purview of both the BWC and the CWC.

4. Lawrence S. Eagleburger, "Yellow Rain: The Arms Control Implications," Statement to a subcommittee of the Senate Foreign Relations Committee, February 24, 1983, printed as US Department of State, "Current Policy," No. 458. Fifteen months earlier, Richard Burt, director of the Bureau of Politico-Military Affairs in the DOS had been slightly more expansive before the same Senate subcommittee: Richard Burt, "Use of Chemical Weapons in Asia," Statement to a subcommittee of the Senate Foreign Relations Committee, November 10, 1981, printed as US Department of State "Current Policy No. 342."

5. General Eugene T. Tighe, "Testimony," in *Chemical Warfare,* Hearing, US Senate, Committee on Armed Services (DC, 1981), 22.

It is very possible that this suggestion was correct and that the agents used by Vietnam were from the large stocks of riot control agents left behind in the country at the time of the US withdrawal in 1975.

6. *Foreign Policy and Arms Control Implications of Chemical Weapons,* Hearings, Committee on Foreign Affairs, House of Representatives, March and July 1982 (Washington, D.C., 1982).

7. Special National Intelligence Estimate, *Use of Toxins and Other Lethal Chemicals in Southeast Asia and Afghanistan,* Memorandum to Holders, Directorate of Central Intelligence, March 2, 1983. This US National Intelligence estimate argued that "the comprehensive assessment of the CW evidence that the United States has published and briefed worldwide in classified and unclassified form has helped to persuade many governments that lethal agents, including toxins, are being used and that the Soviet Union is implicated. There is reluctance on the part of most governments, however, to levy such charges publicly. Governments are loath to take a public position on the issue because to acknowledge that the USSR has violated its international commitments is to call into question the trustworthiness of the USSR as a party to arms limitation agreements. Even the most conclusive and incontrovertible intelligence evidence is unlikely to galvanize other governments into forceful public positions on an issue that has such politically unpleasant implications."

8. Matthew S. Meselson and Julian Perry Robinson, "The Yellow Rain Affair: Lessons Learned from a Discredited Allegation," in *Terrorism, War, or Disease? Unraveling the Use of Biological Weapons,* ed. Anne L. Clunan et al. (Stanford, Calif., 2008), 72–96. See also Joan W. Nowicke and Matthew Meselson, "Yellow Rain—A Palynological Analysis," *Nature* 309 (May 17, 1984): 205–206; Thomas D. Seeley et al., "Yellow Rain," *Scientific American* 253, no. 3 (September 1985): 128–137; and Julian Perry Robinson et al., "Yellow Rain: The Story Collapses," *Foreign Policy,* no. 68 (Fall 1987): 100–117. In addition to the published US government sources and the declassified documents already quoted, the following publications provide a wider oversight into the contested claims:

- Grant Evans, *The Yellow Rainmakers: Are Chemical Weapons Being Used in Southeast Asia?* (London, 1983).
- Elisa D. Harris, "Sverdlovsk and Yellow Rain: Two Cases of Soviet Noncompliance," *International Security* 11, no. 4 (Spring 1987): 41–95.
- Jonathan B. Tucker, "The 'Yellow Rain' Controversy: Lessons for Arms Control Compliance," *Nonproliferation Review* 8, no. 1 (Spring 2001): 25–42.
- Rebecca L. Katz, "Yellow Rain Revisited: Lesson Learned for the Investigation of Chemical and Biological Weapons Allegations" (PhD thesis, Princeton University, May 2005).

9. United Nations General Assembly, *Chemical and Bacteriological (Biological) Weapons: Report of the Secretary-General,* A/36/613, November 20, 1981; United Nations General Assembly, *Chemical and Bacteriological (Biological) Weapons: Report of the Secretary-General,* A/37/259, December 1, 1982.

10. Director of Central Intelligence, Special National Intelligence Estimate, 1983, 6.

11. United States Department of State, March 22, 1982, 30.

12. Anthony Rimmington, "The Soviet Union's Offensive Program: The Implications for Contemporary Arms Control," in *Biological Warfare and Disarmament: New Problems/New Perspectives,* ed. Susan Wright (Lanham, Md., 2002), 103–148.

13. "Russia: 6 'Germ Plants'?," AP dispatch, in Scripps Howard newspapers, June 15, 1976. See also Nicholas Wade, "Biological Warfare: Suspicions of Soviet Activity," *Science* 172 (April 2, 1976): 38–40; R. C. Tóth, "Russia Believed to Be Plunging into Gene Study: New Labs Could Lead to Development Of Biological Weapons," *Los Angeles Times,* February 20, 1977.

14. Director of Central Intelligence, Attached Question and Answer Paper, Memorandum for Members, CBW/Toxin Working Group, September 17, 1982.

15. Sharon Watson, *Intelligence Appraisal: Southeast Asia—Mycotoxins and the Soviet Connection,* DIAIAPPR 149A-81, Defense Intelligence Agency, September 27, 1981, 4 and 5. (Copy obtained courtesy of Dr. Rebecca Katz.) A MEDLINE search done on August 27, 2005, produced the titles of 69 Russian-language publications dealing with *Fusaria* published between 1970 and 1979. Judging solely from the titles of the publications, and in a few cases, abstracts, 23 dealt with mycotoxins, and of those, only six appeared to deal with the conditions of synthesis, and three were literature reviews. An analogous search in PubMed for the same years, 1970 to 1979, produced 637 papers in English for the key word "fusarium," and 230 with the words "fusarium" and "toxin" in the same title. Without having a copy of each of the 230 papers, it is not possible to identify how many of the 230 were published in the United States. It is clear that in at least some cases work on mycotoxins was published in Western journals before analogous studies appear to have been investigated in the Soviet Union.

16. G. B. Carter, *The Large-Scale Production of Fusaria and Trichothecenes for Civil Purposes in the USSR,* Ministry of Defense (UK), unpublished report, n.d.

17. Armed Forces Medical Intelligence Center, *Yellow Rain—Separating Fact from Fiction,* Letter/Report, ACSI Task: 84-056, AFMIC-SA, June 18, 1984.

18. Personal communication, August 2005.

19. Watson, 1981, 13.

20. Ibid., 4.

21. Director of Central Intelligence, National Intelligence Estimate, *Implications of Soviet Use of Chemical and Toxin Weapons,* B-1. Dr. Joffe's book on mycotoxins, *Fusarium Species: Their Biology and Toxicology,* was published by John Wiley in 1986.

22. Ken Alibek and Sergei Popov, personal communications.

23. Personal communication, 2005.

24. Personal communication, 2005.

25. Ibid.

26. US Department of State cable (R01120bZ July 97) regarding USDA/DOD/DOS visit to Tashkent in July 1997.

27. Igor Domaradsky, personal communication, June 1999.

28. Russian Federation, Confidence-Building Measure "F," 1992 Submission of the Russian Federation to the Biological Weapons Convention (Spring 1993). The sentence in the original Russian document reads "Mikotoksiny, pootsenke ekspertov, voennogo znacheniya ne umeyut."

17. Assistance by Warsaw Pact States in the Soviet Union's Biological Warfare Program

1. A chapter that appeared in the important historical volume on national BW programs in 2006 unfortunately contains virtually no useful information. Lajos Rozsa and Kathryn Nixdorff, "Biological Weapons in Non-Soviet Warsaw Pact Countries," in *Deadly Cultures: Biological Weapons since 1945,* ed. Mark Wheelis et al. (Cambridge, Mass., 2006), 157–168, 442–423.

The Warsaw Treaty Organization (WTO), more commonly called the Warsaw Pact, was a mutual defense alliance established under a treaty signed in Warsaw, Poland, in 1955 by Albania, Bulgaria, Czechoslovakia, the GDR, Hungary, Poland, Romania, and the Soviet Union. The organization was the Soviet bloc's equivalent of NATO. A unified military command with headquarters in Moscow directed the WTO united armed forces, which included Soviet divisions stationed in some of the member nations prior to the signing of the treaty. After the collapse of the Communist governments in Eastern Europe after 1989, the treaty became inactive, and it was formally dissolved in June 1991.

2. Ken Alibek with Stephen Handelman, *Biohazard: The Chilling True Story of the Largest Covert Biological Weapons Program in the World—Told from Inside by the Man Who Ran It* (New York, 1999), 273.

3. Defense Intelligence Agency, *Biological Warfare Capabilities: Warsaw Pact* (U), DST 1610S-123-90, DIA Task Unit PT 1610-01-021, US March 1990, 4. There were other portions of General Sejna's description that suggest that despite the senior key position that he had held in the Czech Defense Ministry, the information that he was providing on the role of CW and BW in Soviet/WTO plans in the 1960s and 1970s was not accurate.

4. Defense Intelligence Agency, 1990, 4.

5. Former GDR source, personal communication, October 1999.

6. Former GDR and Hungarian sources, personal communications, 1998, 2000.

7. Timothy V. Brac, *Collateral Analysis of Warsaw Pact Neurotoxin Publications,* Contract Report #34/90, Suffield, Canada: Defence Research Establishment, June 1990.

8. Polish source, personal communication, November 1999.

9. Hungarian Defense Forces, personal communication, Budapest, Hungary, July 8, 2000.

10. Alibek with Handelman, 1999, 275.

11. Notably, by providing only the area of the floor space, the description omits inclusion of the total volume of these units. The problem, however, appears to be the fault of the formulators of the BWC CBM, and not the Czechs, as the request is explicitly for "size" in square meters, i.e., floor space, and provides no indication of their volume, which is of additional significance.

12. "Draft Annex to Final Declaration on Confidence Building Measures," BWC/CONF. III/22/Add.3, September 27, 1991. The internal citation is from P. Propper and M. Splino, "Defence Program in Czechoslovakia," presented at the Symposium on Improving Confidence-Building Measures for the BW-Convention, Umeå, Sweden, May 27–30, 1990. Propper was one of Těchonín's co-directors. A copy of the Czech draft annex, as well as the 1990 Propper-Splino paper, was supplied to the author by Czech government authorities in 2000, but copies of both had been obtained privately several years earlier.

13. Ales Macela, "Why Tularemia: The Truth about the Institute of Immunology at Těchonín," Purkyne Military Medical Academy, Hradec Kralove, 1994, unpublished paper. These same points were enumerated in the paper by Propper and Splino referred to in the Czech CBM. Its actual title was "BW-Defence Program in Czechoslovakia." The Czech CBM omitted the "BW" in the paper's title.

14. Personal communication, 2000.

15. Igor Domaradsky, *Troublemaker: Or the Story of an Inconvenient Man* (in Russian) (Moscow, 1995).

16. Igor V. Domaradskij and Wendy Orent, *Biowarrior: Inside the Soviet/Russian Biological War Machine* (Amherst, N.Y., 2003), 134.

17. Vladimir Pasechnik, personal communication, June 1999.

18. WTO source, personal communications.

19. Transmission from Colonel Vladimir Radovnicky, Central Military Health Institute, Prague, January 24, 2000.

20. Personal communication, 2000.

21. These appeals were made successively to the chief of the Medical Service in the Ministry of Defense and the head of the Central Military Health Institute. The first official did not reply at all. The second, Colonel Radovnicky, who the author had met with at a NATO biodefense meeting in 1999, stated that an invitation to come to Prague would be possible after a formal letter of request was submitted. However, when that request was submitted, it was rejected. These requests were made directly and not through diplomatic channels, which may or may not have made a difference to the outcome. We have no knowledge that any independent scholar or analyst has subsequently examined these records

22. "The Czech Republic Recently Destroyed Two Sets of Viral Strains," *Arms Control Reporter,* April 1994, Entry 701.B.125. The short summary provided in this source is based on four FBIS-EEU translations of Czech newspaper articles. See also

Benjamin C. Garrett, "Czech BW/CW Stocks?," *CBIAC Newsletter* 8, nos. 1–2 (Winter/Spring 1994): 1, 9.

23. "The Czech Republic Recently Destroyed Two Sets of Viral Strains," *Arms Control Reporter.*

24. Personal communications from members of the visiting Swedish team, 1998, 1999, 2011.

25. Brac, 1990, 89.

26. Rosa N. Lukina and Yevgeniy P. Lukin, eds., *The 50 Years of the Ministry of Defense Virology Center Deserve to Be Known* (in Russian) (Sergiev Posad, 2004), 37.

27. Ernst-Jürgen Finke, "The Research Program of the Institute for Field Epidemiology and Microbiology of the Military Medical Section of the Ernst-Mortiz-Arndt University, Greifswald" (in German), in *The Medical Service of the GDR Army—Part 1* (in German), ed. Franz-J. Lemmoens and Wolfgang G. Locher (Bonn, 2008).

28. Ernst Buder, personal communication, April 5, 2001. Because 60 is probably a larger number of fermenters than the two sites contained, it implies that some of those fermenters were very likely transferred to other Biopreparat or MOD facilities. The first information regarding these exports came from a member of a team from the German Academy of Sciences that visited Berdsk and Omutninsk in 1996. In addition to interviews with Alibek, this led to assistance by academic colleagues in Germany in tracking down the GDR company.

29. Ken Alibek, personal communication, April 2001.

30. Personal communication.

31. Personal communication, May 2008. It has not been possible to verify this information.

32. Personal communication, June 18, 2001.

33. Personal communication, 2005.

34. Erhard Geissler, "Conversion of the BTW Facilities: Lessons from German History," in *Conversion of Former BTW Facilities,* ed. E. Geissler, Lajos Gazso, and Ernst Buder (Dordrecht, 1998), 61–62.

35. Erhard Geissler, "The Role of German Bioweapon Experts in the Post World War II Period" (in German), in *Post-World War II Policies in Medical Schools* (in German), ed. S. Oehler-Klein and V. Roelcke (Stuttgart, 2007), 9–11.

36. Personal communication, 1999.

37. Ibid.

38. Erhard Geissler, personal communications, April–May 2008. Two of these publications were also translated into Russian and published in the Soviet Union in the Soviet journal *Mir Nauki (Scientific World)* in 1982 and 1983. Interestingly, we have been able to determine that the Russian translation of the journal existed in the library of at least some of the Soviet Biopreparat institutes, in particular SR-CAM in Obolensk. Without a line-by-line examination of the Russian text, that

would tell us little, because Soviet authorities routinely deleted lines that they considered politically compromising in journals that were distributed in the Soviet Union in Russian translation. The Russian translation of one of these papers (Erhard Geissler, "On the Misuse of Results of Research in Molecular and Cellular Biology: Facts and Myths" [in Russian], *Mir Nauki* no. 1 [1982]) was obtained, and the relevant paragraph, following a discussion of the possible misuse of genetic engineering for the purposes of producing biological weapons, reads as follows:

> In 1971 an international legal barrier to this misuse of scientific achievements was put forth as a proposal by the Soviet Union and other parties to the Convention on the Prohibition of the Development, Production and Stockpiling of Bacteriological (Biological) and Toxin Weapons and on Their Destruction. The Convention entered into force in 1975 and by the end of 1978 it had been ratified by 80 governments, including Great Britain, the GDR, the USSR and the USA. The effectiveness of the Convention was confirmed by signatory countries at a special conference held under the auspices of the UN in March 1980.

Aside from the self-serving characterization of the origin of the BWC, only the title of the treaty, containing all the key words, is present. But that is the same way in which the German original was written.

39. Erhard Geissler, personal communications, May 2008.

40. Personal communication, 2008.

41. Piotr Koscielniak, "Method for Fighting Bioterrorism: Daily Describes Poland's First Biological Warfare Lab, Bio-Safety System," *Warsaw Rzeczpospolita,* January 16, 2002.

42. Former WTO source, personal communication, 2000.

43. Reply of the Government of the Republic of Bulgaria, Addressed to the Secretary General of the United Nations in Accordance with UNGA Resolution 46/35C (valid for 1991) May 26, 1992. Not all forms of field testing are carried out in designated test areas that have regular topographical features that would be detectable by satellite.

44. Brac, 1990, 87–89, iv–v.

45. Rozsa and Nixdorf, 2006, 158–159.

46. Personal communication, 2000.

47. Brac, 1990, 89–91.

18. The Question of Proliferation from the USSR Biological Warfare Program

1. Boris Yeltsin, "Decree on Ensuring the Implementation of International Pledges in the Sphere of Biological Weapons" (in Russian), April 11, 1992. See Dmitriy

Frolov, "Russia Promises to Discontinue Production of Bacteriological Weapons: Military Maintains That Americans Confused Them with Veterinary Science" (in Russian), *Nezavisimaya Gazeta* (Moscow), September 15, 1992, 1; and Anonymous, "President Yeltsin Has Signed a Decree Banning Research Programmes Which Violate the Biological Weapons Convention," *Oxford Analytica East Europe Brief,* June 9, 1992.

2. Personal communication, 2002.

3. Personal communication, November 1997.

4. Personal communication, 1993.

5. Personal communications, 2000, 2001, and 2002.

6. Valentin Tikhonov, *Russia's Nuclear and Missile Complex: The Human Factor in Proliferation,* Carnegie Endowment for International Peace, Washington D.C. 2002, 64–67.

Specialists' countries of destination, percentage of total number who have emigrated:

Country of Destination	%
Germany	33
Israel	32
Sweden	12
United States	11
Finland	5
France	3
India	3
Unknown	1
Total Sampling	100

7. "Brain Drain from Russia: A New Proliferation Threat," *Security Issues, Executive Intelligence Newsletter* 4 (June 2000): 12. Available figures for the number of "scientists" in the Soviet Union vary substantially, but in 2000 the Russian Ministry of Science and Technology stated that of 1.6 million people "working in science" in 1990, 800,000, or exactly half, had left the field by 2000. For these figures to have any plausibility whatsoever, the 500,000 that allegedly emigrated would have to come from the 800,000 that the Russian Ministry claimed had left the field— and not from the 800,000 that remained in Russia. Amelia Gentleman, "Russian Suffering from Another Brain Drain: Scientific Labor Being Sold to West at Discount Prices," *San Francisco Examiner,* July 30, 2000.

8. Angela Charlton, "Once-Revered Russian Scientists Protest at Government Headquarters to Demand More Funding," Associated Press, July 27, 2001.

9. Untitled, IIR 2 762 0018 88, June 30, 1987.

10. Jonathan B. Tucker, *Scourge: The Once and Future Threat of Smallpox* (New York, 2001), 205.

11. Personal communications, 2001 and 2002. It has so far been impossible to corroborate this from a second source.

12. Reuters. "Iraq Reportedly to Let 1,000 Soviets Leave: Aeroflot Officials Say Nearly a Third of Expatriates to Go Home," *Washington Post,* December 4, 1990.

13. An obituary for Vladimir Pasechnik claimed that after he defected to the United Kingdom in 1989 he informed his British debriefers that Iraq had obtained some of the knowledge for its BW program from the Soviet Union. Pearce Wright, "Vladimir Pasechnik: Defector Who Alerted the West to the Dangers of Soviet Biological Weapons Production," *Guardian,* November 28, 2001. The claim was incorrect: Pasechnik did not relay such information. Personal communication, 2009.

Another former Biopreparat official, Colonel Gennady Lepeshkin, was quoted in a Russian press interview saying that Iraq had "anthrax weapons technology . . . because some former Soviet scientists settled there." "A History of Mass Destruction," *Ekspress K,* no. 83, May 7, 2002. In this instance, a US government official discounted the remark, believing both that Lepeshkin would not know if it were in fact the case, and that he was most likely repeating rumors printed in the international press, which turned out to be exactly the case. No less a presumed authority than Richard Perle, then chairman of the Defense Policy Board that reports to the US Secretary of Defense, stated in a 2002 TV interview that "it is likely that chemical weapons, biological weapons in the possession of the Iraqis derived during the Cold War from the Soviet Union" (PBS TV, *Wide Angle,* July 12, 2002). Perle's claim is almost totally wrong except for several items explained in the chapter text, and it was not corroborated by the US Iraq Survey Group report in 2004 following the US occupation of Iraq.

14. US Defense Intelligence Agency, *Russian Biological Warfare Technology,* IIR 2 201 0910 94, April 1994.

15. Barton Gellman, "4 Nations Thought to Possess Smallpox: Iraq, North Korea Named, Two Officials Say," *Washington* Post, November 5, 2002. A *New York Times* story of September 8, 2002, refers to an Iraqi defector, identified only as "Shemri," who stated that "Iraq had received assistance in its chemical, germ, and nuclear programs *from Russian scientists who are still working in Iraq"* (emphasis added), Michael R. Gordon and Judith Miller, "U.S. Says Hussein Intensifies Quest for A-Bomb Parts," *New York Times,* September 8, 2002. It soon became known that many of the claims in *New York Times* stories by Miller and colleagues during this period derived from fraudulent disinformation provided by members of Adnan Chalabi's Iraqi National Congress.

16. WINPAC was responsible for errors that were far more serious in this same time period. WINPAC was the group within the CIA responsible for the false claim that Iraq possessed mobile biological weapon production vehicles, a claim that was used as one of the prime justifications for invading Iraq.

17. Peter Nichols, "The Invisible Weapon," *Rutgers Magazine,* Spring 2002. The phrasing is ambiguous, but Smithson presumably interviewed Russian scientists at

former Biopreparat institutes in Russia, and not at their supposed locations in "Syria, Iraq, Libya, China, and North Korea among other countries." The "other countries" also referred to by Smithson are presumably meant to refer to non-Western countries.

18. Personal communications, 2002. Other presumed disinformation appeared in two *Newsweek* press accounts alleging relations between former Soviet BW specialists and al Qaeda. The first, in December 2001, alleged that "one or more Russian scientists were working inside Afghanistan . . . helping Al-Qaeda to develop anthrax." The second report, in February 2002, claimed only that "some Russian experts traveled to Kandahar for interviews" but returned home. Jeffrey Bartholet et al., "Al-Qaeda Runs for the Hills," *Newsweek*, December 17, 2001; and Fred Guterl and Eve Conant, "The Former Soviet Union Had Huge Stocks of Biological Agents: Assessing the Real Risks," *Newsweek International*, February 25, 2002. Both of these stories were described by a US government specialist on the former Soviet BW program as "journalistic invention."

19. Ken Alibek, personal communication, 2000.

20. Margaret Coker, "Russian Cash Crisis Unleashes Bio Threat," *Atlanta Journal-Constitution*, October 19, 2002.

21. Judith Miller, "CIA Hunts Iraq Tie to Soviet Smallpox," *New York Times*, December 3, 2002.

22. Jonathan B. Tucker and Raymond A. Zilinskas, eds., *The 1971 Smallpox Epidemic in Aralsk, Kazakhstan, and the Soviet Biological Warfare Program*, Occasional Paper No. 9 (Monterey, Calif., 2002).

23. Martin Enserink, "Did Bioweapons Test Cause a Deadly Smallpox Outbreak?," *Science* 296 (June 21, 2002): 2116–2117.

24. Personal communications, December 2002

25. Tatyana Bateneva, "Russian Scientist Accused of Selling Biological Weapons" (in Russian), *Izvestia*, December 5, 2002.

26. Former UNSCOM officials, personal communications, 1995, 2001, 2003.

27. Ibid.

28. Ken Alibek, personal communication, 1999. Alibek only used the words "technological assistance," so it may have been no more than supplying a fermenter.

29. Personal communication, 2002.

30. It would, of course, be easiest for an intelligence service to know such details if some of its nationals were working with the program, but this cannot be taken as proof that that was the case.

31. Ken Alibek with Stephen Handelman, *Biohazard: The Chilling True Story of the Largest Covert Biological Weapons Program in the World—Told from Inside by the Man Who Ran It* (New York, 1999), 275. Alibek also wrote, "We spent decades building institutes and training scientists in India, Iraq, Iran." Exactly what Alibek was referring to is not known; they may have been entirely civilian scientific institutes unrelated to BW.

Alibek also describes a general "type of proliferation involv[ing] scientists from other countries being brought to the proliferating country for training in biotechnology, microbiology, and genetic engineering techniques. For instance, for years Moscow State University provided such training to scientists from dozens of countries, including Cuba, North Korea, Eastern Bloc nations, Iran, Iraq, Syria, and Libya." [Testimony of Kenneth Alibek, "Chemical/Biological Defense for U.S. Forces," Before the House Armed Services Committee, Subcommittees on Military Procurement and on Military Research and Development, October 15, 1999.]

So long as the education was basic scientific training in "biotechnology, microbiology, and genetic engineering techniques," it would be no different than if the students had attended universities and graduate schools in Western countries. Students from some of these countries of course did exactly that, Iraq being the most notorious example in terms of relevance to its BW program. It is also known that military medical officers from the Soviet Union's allied Warsaw Pact nations, as well as from several of the countries named by Alibek in the above example, also received more specialized training at the Russian Military Medical Academy in Leningrad. Interviews with former Warsaw Pact military officers that attended such a year-long course suggest that the schooling was confined to military microbiology and defensive aspects of BW. [Personal communication, November 1999. This is discussed further in Chapter 17.

Alibek also testified to "having unconfirmed information that some scientists from the Kirov facility visited North Korea in the early 1990s" [Alibek, October 1999]. In this case Alibek's source of information was a Russian press item [Ken Alibek, personal communication, July 2002]. It is not known whether Alibek was the "former Soviet scientist" referred to in the 1994 DIA and CIA intelligence reports referred to earlier. It has also proved impossible for us to trace a report cited in a draft paper written by a Russian author for SIPRI that stated, "Illegal exports in 1991–2 of large quantities of chemical and biological weapons to Iraq have been reported by the BBC in 1996." Given the years in question, 1991–1992, this claim seems highly unlikely. No such BBC item could be discovered. The draft paper was written for the SIPRI volume *Russia and the Arms Trade* (1998), but it does not appear in the published volume, and the author provided no source for the statement. Again, it has so far proved impossible to corroborate any of the above reports.

32. Ekéus described this incident during the Leo Zeftel Memorial Lecture, Chemical and Biological Arms Control Institute, Washington, D.C., February 6, 2001.

33. These press accounts coincided with the debate within the WHO as to whether the remaining variola cultures at CDC and at Vector should finally be destroyed, as had been decided by WHO some years earlier. Both the United States and Russia now argued that they should be retained for further research.

34. Personal communications, 2001 and 2002.

35. Milton Leitenberg, "Deadly Unknowns about Iraq's Biological Weapons Programs," *Asian Perspective* 24, no. 1 (2001): 217–223.

36. Statement of Richard O. Spertzel, testimony, Committee on International Relations, US House of Representatives, December 5, 2001.

37. R. Jeffrey Smith, "Russians Admit Firms Met Iraqis: Plant That Could Make Germ Weapons at Issue," *Washington Post,* February 18, 1998.

38. Judith Miller, "The Russians: Official Confirms 1995 Russian-Iraq Deal," *New York Times,* February 18, 1998.

39. R. Jeffrey Smith, "Did Russia Sell Iraq Germ Warfare Equipment? Document Seized by U.N. Inspectors Indicates Illicit Deal; Moscow Has Yet to Explain," *Washington Post,* February 12, 1998. The initial story contained several marginal errors; it referred to only a single document, and reported that the negotiations concerned the delivery of a single 5,000-liter fermenter, which was actually only one-tenth of the fermentation capacity of 50,000 liters that was being negotiated.

40. Steven Erlanger, "Suspicious: Russian's Deny Report of '95 Deal with Iraq," *New York Times,* February 13, 1998.

41. Personal communications, February 2001 and July 2002.

42. Ken Alibek, personal communication, July 2001; Alibek with Handelman, 1999, 275.

43. Alibek with Handelman, 1999, 275.

44. Ibid.

45. Personal communication, October 2002.

46. Richard Z. Chesnoff, "Bad Chemistry: A Mystery at a Pesticide Plant," *U.S. News and World Report,* October 25, 1999, 42.

47. Aleksey Nikolskiy, "Russian Official Denies Russia Implicated in Iraqi Biological Weapons," *Vedomosti,* on BBC Monitoring International Reports, April 7, 2003. This affair may implicate then FSB head Primakov and Prime Minister Chernomyrdin.

48. *Vremya Novostey,* April 23, 2003.

49. Personal communication, 1994.

50. Personal communication, November 1997.

51. The figure of $10,000 came from personal communications in 1999 and 2000. See also Joby Warrick, "Russia's Poorly Guarded Past: Security Lacking at Facilities Used for Soviet Bioweapons Research," *Washington Post,* June 17, 2002.

52. Personal communication, October 1998.

53. Personal communication, March 30, 2010.

54. Personal communication, April 2010.

55. Ibid.

56. Warrick, 2002.

57. David R. Franz and Murray P. Hamlet, Trip Report, May 1 to May 13, 2004, in Support of the National Defense Authorization Act of FY04, SEC.1304, *Limita-*

tion on Use of Funds for Biological Research in the Former Soviet Union, 7. See also
*Biological Weapons: Effort to Reduce Former Soviet Threat Offers Benefits, Poses New
Risks,* GAO/NSIAD-00-138, April 2000, 15.

58. Ibid., 14.

59. Personal communication, November 1997. Another anecdote seems somewhat similar, but it is not possible to corroborate any of these descriptions. Zaviyalov reported that Grigori Sherbakov, head of the Department of Science at Biopreparat, visited Iran several times, at least twice in 1997–1998, for a week each time.
Sherbakov does not speak English. He was reportedly taken to visit "a biotechnology center . . . of high quality." The interesting aspect of this report is that it would
indicate Iranian contacts with senior members of Biopreparat's administration. It
may explain how Iran obtained access to Vector in particular.

60. Personal communication, 1999.

61. Judith Ingram and Sergei Shargorodsky, "Russians Help Bioterrorism Defense," *Washington Times,* January 29, 2002.

62. Judith Miller and William Broad, "Bio-Weapons in Mind, Iranians Lure
Needy Ex-Soviet Scientists," *New York Times,* December 8, 1998.

63. Personal communications, 2001.

64. The authors would like to thank Mark Gorwitz for supplying the Iranian
journal papers.

65. There are reports that Bakaev accepted "a teaching position" in Iran around
1990–1991. Information regarding these dates may not be correct and is contradicted by other information. As the years indicated are still in the Soviet era, Bakaev
presumably would not have been permitted to leave at that time if he had been a
participant in the Soviet BW program.

66. Domaradsky was quoted in January 2002 as saying, "I know that in the mid-
'90s, several quite prominent scientists—genetic scientists whom I do not want to
name—prepared personnel for Iran. But I think that ended seven years ago" (Judith Ingram, 2002).

67. John A. Lauder, Testimony to the Committee on Foreign Relations, US Senate, November 5, 2000.

68. Unclassified Responses to the Questions for the Record from the Worldwide
Threat Hearing on February 6, 2002, Central Intelligence Agency, to Senator Bob
Graham, Chairman, Select Committee on Intelligence, US Senate, April 8, 2002.

69. Personal communication, June 2002. In January 2003, an Iranian microbiologist working at the Faculty of Veterinary Medicine at the University of Tehran
wrote to a Vector scientist, asking to work in his laboratory to learn about "gene or
protein manipulation" of Marek's disease virus (MDV), a herpes virus that affects
chickens. The Vector scientist did not work on MDV at the time, but prior to 1996
he had worked on orthopox viruses (personal communication, 2010). The significance of this incident is unknown.

70. Dana Priest, "Iran's Emerging Nuclear Plant Poses Test for US," *Washington Post,* July 29, 2002.

71. Ibid.

72. Yevgenia Albats, "Our Man in Teheran," *Novaya Gazeta,* March 16, 1998; Michael Dobbs, "A Story of Iran's Quest for Power: A Scientist Details the Role of Russia," *Washington Post,* January 13, 2002; and Michael Dobbs, "Collapse of Soviet Union Proved Boon to Iranian Missile Program," *Washington Post,* January 13, 2002.

73. James Adams, presentation at Chemical and Biological Arms Control Institute (CBACI), April 1996. It is likely that Adams's sources were members of the US intelligence community.

74. S. G. Gwynne and Larry Gurwin, "The Russia Connection," *Time,* July 8, 1996, 32–36.

75. Lila Shevtsova, *Yeltsin's Russia: Myths and Realities* (Washington, D.C., 1999), 17.

76. Tadashi Shirakawa, "Coup d'etat Plan of Aum Found in Hayakawa's Note" (in Japanese), *Bungei Shunjyu* (June 1995), 10; Fumiya Ichinashi, "A Truth of the Aum Empire" (in Japanese), *Shicho* 45 (May 1996), 160. Japanese press sources apparently obtained Vorobyov's name from a portion of a memo written by a senior Aum member, Dr. Kiyohide Hayakawa. It was leaked to the press by the police following Hayakawa's arrest. The leaked portion does not specify that the Aum actually met with Vorobyov and the remainder remains undisclosed. Personal communications, December 2011 and April 2012 from Dr. Masaaki Sugishima.

77. Milton Leitenberg, "Aum Shinrikyo's Efforts to Produce Biological Weapons: A Case Study in the Serial Propagation of Misinformation," in *The Future of Terrorism,* ed. Max Taylor and John Horgan (London, 2000), 149–158; this article appeared earlier in *Terrorism and Political Violence* 11, no. 4 (Winter 1999): 149–158. See also Leitenberg, "The Experience of the Japanese Aum Shinrikyo Group and Biological Agents," in *Hype or Reality? The "New Terrorism" and Mass Casualty Attacks,* ed. Brad Roberts (Alexandria, Va., 2000), 159–172.

78. Personal communications, 2000 and 2001. An attempt was made to verify this allegation by contacting Aum officials in Japan, but no response was obtained.

79. M. Leitenberg, 2000, "Aum Shinrikyo's Efforts to Produce Biological Weapons: A Case Study in the Serial Propagation of Misinformation."

80. Paul Keim et al, "Molecular Investigation of the Aum Shinrikyo Anthrax Release in Kameido, Japan," *Journal of Clinical Microbiology* 39:12 (2011): 4566–4567.

81. Personal communications, 2001, 2002.

82. Alibek with Handelman, 273–275.

83. Personal communication, September 2002.

84. Alibek with Handelman, 275.

85. Personal communication, September 2002.

86. P. R. Kumaraswamy, "Has Israel Kept Its BW Options Open?," *Jane's Intelligence Review* 10, no. 3 (1998): 23. Israel reportedly requires that a person have Israeli citizenship and an extensive period of residency in Israel before being hired to work at Nes Ziona. Nevertheless, anecdotal information from one interviewee in Europe indicates that a researcher from one of the former East European biodefense programs was working at Nes Ziona.

87. Yossi Melman, "I Spy," *Ha'aretz,* April 15, 2008; and Yitzhak Laor, "Not Afraid to Go All the Way," *Ha'aretz,* April 15, 2008.

88. Personal communication, 1999.

89. Personal communication, June 1999.

90. Alibek with Handelman, 273.

91. Milton Leitenberg, "Assessing the Threat of Bioterrorism," in Benjamin H. Friedman, *Terrorizing Ourselves,* 161–184, Washington, D.C.: 2010.

19. Recalcitrant Russian Policies in a Parallel Area

1. Jonathan B. Tucker, *War of Nerves* (New York, 2006), 230.

2. Russian propaganda agencies reciprocated in kind, claiming that "Western experts" estimated the size of the US CW stockpile "at 150–300,000 tons." Gennadi Stashevsky, *Chemical Weapons Disarmament: The View from Moscow* (Moscow, 1988), 6. At the time that this publication appeared, Stashevsky was deputy head of the Office for Arms Limitation and Disarmament of the USSR Ministry of Foreign Affairs.

3. Jesse James, "Soviet Union Declares Size of Chemical Arsenal," *Arms Control Today* 18, no. 1 (1988): 26. The United States declared that its CW stockpile was 29,000 metric tons of agents.

4. Rodney McElroy (*Briefing Book on Chemical Weapons,* Boston, Council for a Livable World Education Fund, October 1989) summarized that diplomatic history as follows:

> In 1968, as co-chairs of the Eighteen Nation Disarmament Committee, the United States and the Soviet Union supported a Swedish proposal to place chemical and biological warfare on the Committee's agenda. When subsequent efforts to ban both chemical and biological weapons proved impossible, the United States and the Soviet Union agreed to postpone action on chemicals to facilitate conclusion of the 1972 Biological and Toxin Weapons Convention.
>
> President Nixon and General Secretary Leonid Brezhnev pledged a "joint initiative" on chemical disarmament at their July 1974 summit in Moscow, reaffirmed in November at Vladivostok by President Ford and Secretary Brezhnev. A series of bilateral talks was held, starting in August 1976 and continuing throughout the Carter administration. Despite considerable progress, by 1980 the atmosphere for the talks had soured due to Soviet intransigence

over verification, the Soviet invasion of Afghanistan, and US allegations of Soviet chemical and biological warfare activities. The Reagan administration decided not to renew the bilateral discussions in 1981.

Bilateral consultations to work out specific technical issues were reestablished in 1984. These led to Soviet acceptance of US proposals on verification during 1986 and 1987. Further progress was made in 1989 when the United States and the Soviet Union reached agreement on some of the key elements still to be resolved in the draft Chemical Weapons Convention, including a timetable for weapons destruction and procedures for surprise inspections. On September 23, 1989 at Jackson Hole, Wyoming, US Secretary of State James Baker and Soviet Foreign Minister Eduard Shevardnadze signed an agreement to exchange data on their chemical weapons stockpiles, and to conduct mutual inspections of stockpiles and production facilities, in order to build confidence and gain experience for the CWC.

In an address to the United Nations General Assembly on September 25, 1989, President Bush proposed that, while working to complete the CWC, the United States and the Soviet Union reduce their stockpiles to a level equal to twenty percent of the existing US stockpile. He also stated that the United States would destroy ninety-eight percent of its current stockpiles within eight years after the Convention enters into force, provided the Soviet Union is a party to it. (17)

5. US General Accounting Office, *Arms Control: Status of U.S.-Russian Agreements and the Chemical Weapons Convention,* GAO Report, 1994, GAO/NSIAD-94-136.

6. US General Accounting Office, *Arms Control: US and International Efforts to Ban Chemical Weapons,* GAO/NSAID-91-317, September 1991.

7. Address by Vil Mirzayanov to the CBRNe World Convergence 2010, http://vilmirzayanov.blogspot.com/ [Russian Chemical Weapons Program].

8. *US Capability to Monitor Compliance with the Chemical Weapons Convention,* Report of the Select Committee on Intelligence, United States Senate (Washington, D.C., 1994), 26–30.

9. Derek Averre and Igor Khripunov, "Chemical Weapons Disposal: Russia Tries Again," *Bulletin of Atomic Scientists* 57, no. 5 (September/October 2001): 57–63.

10. Douglas L. Clarke, "Chemical Weapons in Russia," *Radio Free Europe/Radio Liberty Research Report* 2, no. 2 (1993): 47–53.

11. R. Jeffrey Smith, "Estimate of Soviet Arms Is Cut: U.S. Revises Figure on Chemical Weapons," *Washington Post,* November 9, 1989.

12. Jesse James, "'Glasnost' Spreads to Chemical Weapons," *Arms Control Today* 17, no. 9 (November 1987): 23. Aleksey Yablokov, then chairman of the Russian Security Council's Interdepartmental Commission for Ecological Safety, still disputed

the 40,000 ton figure in March 1994, and suggested that it was "possibly a whole order of magnitude more"; see Radio Moscow Rossi Network, "Expert Terms Official Data on Toxics 'Very Conservative'" (in Russian), March 10, 1994. A month earlier the chief of the General Staff of the Russian Armed Forces, General Mikhail Kolesnikov, had stated that Russia's chemical weapon stockpile was "under 40,000 tons"; see "Defense Ministry Substantiates Chemical Arms Destruction" (in Russian), ITAR-TASS, February 26, 1994.

13. Clarke, 1993, 51.

14. Marcus Warren, "Russian Admits Deception on Chemical-Arms Stocks," *Washington Times,* March 21, 1994.

15. Lev A. Fedorov, *Chemical Armament in the War against People: The Russian's Tragic Experience* (Moscow, 2009).

16. Amy Smithson et al., *Chemical Weapons Disarmament in Russia: Problems and Prospects,* Stimson Center, report no. 17 (Washington, D.C.: 1995); John Hart and Cynthia D. Miller, eds., *Chemical Weapon Destruction in Russia: Political, Legal, and Technical Aspects,* SIPRI Chemical and Biological Warfare Studies, no. 17 (1998); Sonia Ben Ouagrham, "Conversion of Russian Chemical Weapons Production Facilities: Conflicts with the CWC," *Nonproliferation Review* 7, no. 2 (2000): 44–62; Averre and Khripunov, 2001; Yevgenia Borisova, "The Long Wait for US Cash to Destroy Arms," *Moscow Times,* November 21, 2001; "Russia Seen Unwilling to Fund Scrapping Chemical Weapons," *Gateway to Russia,* September 24, 2003; and Judith Perera, "Russia Finally Faces Up to Its CW Legacy," *Jane's Intelligence Review,* April 1999, 23–27. The Russian Munitions Agency maintains a website on its chemical weapon demilitarization/destruction program: http://www.munition.gov.ru/eng/hstchw.htm.

17. Clarke, 1993; Gale Colby, "Fabricating Guilt," *Bulletin of Atomic Scientists* 49, no. 8 (October 1993): 12–13; and Derek L. Averre, "The Mirzayanov Affair: Russia's 'Military-Chemical Complex,'" *European Security* 4, no. 2 (1995): 273–305.

18. Igor Khripunov, "The Human Element in Russia's Chemical Weapons Disposal Efforts," *Arms Control Today* 25, no. 6 (1995): 16–21; and Jonathan B. Tucker, "Russia's New Plan for Chemical Weapons Destruction," *Arms Control Today* 31, no. 6 (2001): 9–13.

19. Averre and Khripunov, 2001.

20. Until 2001, the Russian government was simply not appropriating the funds necessary to approach any of the goals established by the CWC treaty, despite sizable Western (US, EU, Japanese) donations for that purposes. In 1998 the Russian Federal budget listed 500 million rubles for CW destruction, but only 3.9% of that was actually appropriated. For CWPF destruction and conversion, the Finance Ministry requested 113.5 million rubles, but only 25 million rubles of that sum was budgeted, and only 4.4 million rubles were actually appropriated; see Ben Ouagrham, 2000.

21. Natalya Kalinina, "Chemical Weapons: Arms Control and Demilitarization," Address to the Global Green Seventh Annual Legacy Forum, Washington, D.C., April 25, 2001.

22. "Russia May Quit Pact," *Moscow Times,* October 8, 2002; "Russia Might Suspend Its Membership in Convention Banning Chemical Weapons," Interfax News Agency, October 7, 2002.

23. US General Accountability Office, "Russia Faces Significant Challenges in Destroying Its Chemical Weapons," in *Nonproliferation: Delays in Implementing the Chemical Weapons Convention Raise Concerns about Proliferation,* GAO-04-361, March 2004, 20–25.

24. Green Cross—Russia, *National Dialogue Forum* (Moscow, 2007), 16, 33.

25. The Weapons of Mass Destruction Commission, *Weapons of Terror: Freeing the World of Nuclear, Biological and Chemical Arms* (Stockholm, 2006), 90.

26. US Department of State and US Department of Defense, "U.S. Request to Extend CWC Deadline for Complete Destruction of Chemical Weapons Stocks," Washington, D.C., April 17, 2006.

27. Chris Schneidmiller, "Nations Get CW Treaty Extensions," *Global Security Newswire,* December 16, 2006, http://www.nti.org/d_newswire/issues/2006_12_11 .html#263C85C9.

28. Joe Bauman, "45% of US Chemical, Nerve Weapons Stockpile Destroyed," *Deseret Morning News,* June 30, 2007.

29. Lois Ember, "US Can't Eliminate Arsenal until 2017: Even with Allowable Five-Year Extension, US Won't Be Able to Comply with Treaty," *Chemical and Engineering News* 84, no. 17 (April 24, 2006): 9; and Associated Press, "Senate OKs Deadline, Money to Destroy Chemical Weapons," September 18, 2007, http:// www.kentucky.com/471/story/179926.html.

30. Sergey Oznobistchev and Alexander Saveliev, "Russia and the Chemical Disarmament Process," SIPRI monograph no. 33 (Stockholm, August 2005); and Global Security Newswire, "Russian CW Destruction Lags, OPCW Chief Says," May 20, 2005.

31. RIA Novosti, "Failure to Comply with Chemical Weapons Liquidation Program Will Cost Russia Dearly," July 22, 2005.

32. Resolution no. 639, dated October 24, 2005; John Hart, "Assistance for the Destruction of Chemical Weapons in the Russian Federation: Political and Technical Aspects," conference on Strengthening European Action on WMD Non-proliferation and Disarmament: "How Can Community (EU) Instruments Contribute?," background paper 5, Brussels, Belgium, December 7–8, 2005.

33. Paul Walker, personal communications, October 21, 2007; July 1, 2010; and May 11, 2011.

34. S. Utkina et al., "Russian Views on Conversion of Former Chemical Weapons Production Facilities," *OPCW Synthesis,* issue 5 (November–December, 1999): 13–15. A declassified US agency description of the Soviet chemical weapon produc-

tion complex became available in the spring of 1987. US Defense Intelligence Agency, *The Soviet Chemical Weapons Threat* (Washington, D.C., 1985).

35. Jonathan B. Tucker and Alexander Pikaev, eds., "Eliminating a Deadly Legacy of the Cold War: Overcoming Obstacles to Russian Chemical Disarmament," Executive Summary of Monterey-Moscow Study Group Report (Moscow, January 1998).

36. US General Accountability Office, 2004, 25.

37. "Russia Eliminates Over 15% of Chemical Wpns Stockpile: Official," ITAR-TASS, December 6, 2006, http://www.itar-tass.com/eng/level2.html?NewsID=11056743&PageNum=0.

38. "Russia Disposes of Over 19% of Its Chemical Weapons Stock," Interfax-AVN, January 23, 2007 (World News Connection, Item CEP200701239502251).

39. Rogelio Pfirter, statement to the Conference on Disarmament, Geneva, Switzerland, August 7, 2007.

40. Martin Matishak, "Russia Restricts Transparency at Major Chemical Weapons Sites, Group Says," Global Security Newswire, August 14, 2009.

41. "Global Green USA Congratulates South Korea for Abolishing Chemical Weapons," Press Advisory, October 17, 2008.

42. "Opening Statement by the Director General to the Executive Council at Its Fifty-Seventh Session," OPCW document EC-57/DG.15*, July 14, 2009.

43. Matishak, 2009.

44. "Opening Statement by the Director-General to the Conference of the States Parties at Its Fourteenth Session," OPCW document C-14/DG.13, November 30, 2009.

45. "Global Green USA Congratulates US for Chemical Weapons Destruction Milestone," Global Green, July 6, 2010.

46. "Opening Statement by the Director General to the Executive Council at Its Sixty-First Session," OPCW document EC-61/DG.17, June 29, 2010.

47. Martin Matishak, "One Year to US, Russian Chemical Weapons Disposal Deadline," Global Security Newswire, April 29, 2011.

48. Central Intelligence Agency, "CIA Responses to Congressional Queries," March 9, 1995, Document #1460142262 (Secret), http://www.foia.cia.gov/docs/DOC_0001239709/DOC_0001239709.pdf.

49. US Congress, Committee on Armed Services, *Worldwide Threat to the United States*, S.HRG., January 17, 1995, 45–47.

50. US Arms Control and Disarmament Agency, *Adherence to and Compliance with Arms Control Agreements: 1996 Annual Report* (Washington, D.C., 1996), http://dosfan.lib.uic.edu/acda/reports/annual/comp.htm.

51. Central Intelligence Agency, 1995.

52. Masha Katsva, "'Our Chemical Weapons May Be Kept for Another Forty Years, and They Do Not Disturb Anyone': Interview with Colonel-General Albert Makashov," *Yaderny Kontrol Digest*, no. 3 (Winter 1996): 21–22.

53. Ibid., 22.

54. "Legal, Scientific and Technical Basis for Strengthening the BTWC through a Verification Protocol," NATO Advanced Research Workshop, Moscow, December 9–11, 1998. One of the authors (Leitenberg) was a participant in the NATO workshop.

55. Viktor Yuzbashev, "Lack of Funds Impedes CW Convention Commitments" (in Russian), *Moscow Vremya,* November 18, 2000.

56. "On the Interdepartmental Scientific Council for Conventional Problems of Chemical and Biological Weapons within the Presidium of the Russian Academy of Sciences and the Russian Munitions Agency" (in Russian), Resolution #32/70, Moscow, May 4–7, 2001. The "Provisions" of the new Council note that its establishment follows in part from a "Recommendation #2, dated May 23, 1999," and ironically it appears possible that this in turn was an adaptation of a recommendation made by the Monterey panel in 1998. See endnote number 35.

57. Military News Agency, Moscow, July 26, 2001.

58. Burak Ersemiz, "Twenty Containers of Mustard Gas Seized" (in Turkish), *Istanbul Hurriyet,* August 25, 1996; and Burak Ersemiz, "Sarin Gas Reported among Seized Mustard Gas Containers" (in Turkish), *Istanbul Hurriyet,* August 27, 1996.

59. For another review of these same events between 1998 and 2001, see Alexander Pikaev, "Russian Implementation of the CWC," in Jonathan B. Tucker, ed. *The Chemical Weapons Convention: Implementation Challenges and Solutions,* Monterey Institute of International Studies, April 2001, 31–38.

60. N. Kalinina, "Existing Challenges for the Global Partnership on Nonproliferation of Weapons of Mass Destruction," in Green Cross—Russia, *National Dialogue Forum* (Moscow, 2007), 16. Kalinina was deputy director of Inspection Audit, Chamber of the Russian Federation, at that time. See also remarks by Valery Biryukov of the Russian Ministry of Foreign Affairs, in Green Cross—Russia, *National Dialogue Forum* (Moscow, 2007), 30–33. .

61. Paul F. Walker, "Looking Back: Kananaskis at Five—Assessing the Global Partnership," *Arms Control Today* 37, no. 7 (September 2007): 48–49. See also Oliver Thränert and Jonathan B. Tucker, *Freeing the World of Chemical Weapons: The Chemical Weapons Convention at the Ten-Year Mark,* SWP Research Paper 8 (Berlin, 2007), 15–16

62. US Department of State, "Condition (10) (C) Report. Compliance with the Convention on the Prohibition of the Development, Production, Stockpiling and Use of Chemical Weapons and on Their Destruction," Unclassified, August 2011, 13–15.

20. The Soviet Union, Russia, and Biological Warfare Arms Control

1. James M. Naughton, "Nixon Renounces Germ Weapons, Orders Destruction of Stocks; Restricts Use of Chemical Arms Step Unilateral: Use of Defoliants in

Vietnam War Will Be Continued," *New York Times,* November 26, 1969; National
Security Decision Memorandum 35, November 25, 1969. Archived in National
Security Archive Electronic Briefing Book No. 58, October 25, 2001, "The Nixon
Administration's Decision to End U.S. Biological Warfare Programs," http://www
.gwu.edu/~nsarchiv/NSAEBB/NSAEBB58/.

2. James M. Naughton, "Nixon Widens Ban on Germ Warfare to Include Tox-
ins: Bans Production and Use of the Poisonous Weapons Derived from Bacteria—
Sees a Move for Peace—White House Says Unilateral Action Is Significant Step
toward Arms Control," *New York Times,* February 15, 1970; and National Security
Decision Memorandum 44, "United States Policy on Toxins," February 20, 1970,
National Security Archive Electronic Briefing Book No. 58.

3. Between November 1955, when US secretary of the army Wilber M. Brucker
approved an important report, and the early 1960s, US BW policy underwent a series of important changes. *The Law of Land Warfare* (US Army Field Manual, FM-
10, July 1956) noted, "The United States is not a Party to any treaty, now in force,
that prohibits or restricts the use in warfare of toxic or non-toxic gases, of smoke or
incendiary materials, or of bacteriological warfare." During World War II, chemical
herbicides had been categorized as biological weapons. However, around 1960 another US Army field manual moved them to the category of chemical weapons, although plant pathogens clearly remained within the domain of biological weapons.
Robin Romero and Milton Leitenberg, "Chemical and Biological Warfare: History
of International Control and US Policy," *Scientist and Citizen,* August–September
1967, 130–140.

4. Stockholm International Peace Research Institute, "1961–1970: Indochina,"
in *The Problem of Chemical and Biological Warfare.* Vol. 1: *The Rise of CB Weapons*
(Stockholm, 1971), 162–210.

5. "Statement on the Use of Chemical Agents in the Vietnam War," January 11,
1966. The petition effort was actually carried out in three steps: the 29 signatories of
January 11, 1966, 22 of whom went on in September 1966 to sponsor the third and
larger petition effort. The petition effort was conceived of and carried out by one of
the authors (Leitenberg), with the assistance of the Federation of American Scientists, the Physicians for Social Responsibility, and several other academic and professional groups. The spokespersons for both petitions were Dr. John Edsall and
Dr. Matthew Meselson, both of Harvard University. "22 Scientists Bid Johnson Bar
Chemical Weapons in Vietnam," *New York Times,* September 20, 1966; and "Press
Release: U.S. Scientists Ask Review of Chemical and Biological Weapons Policy,"
February 14, 1967.

6. Donald F. Hornig, Science Advisor to the President, Memorandum for the
President, Subject: Use of Biological Weapons, December 8, 1966; and Donald F.
Hornig, Science Advisor to the President, Memorandum for the President, Subject:
Scientists Petition on Chemical and Biological Weapons, February 14, 1967.

7. W. W. Rostow, Memorandum for Secretary of State, Secretary of Defense, Director of ACDA, "Draft Presidential Public Statement," March 10, 1967.

8. Seymour M. Hersh, *Chemical and Biological Warfare: America's Hidden Arsenal* (Indianapolis, 1969); Richard D. McCarthy, *The Ultimate Folly: War by Pestilence, Asphyxiation, and Defoliation* (New York, 1969).

9. Robin Clarke, *We All Fall Down: The Prospect of Biological and Chemical Warfare* (London, 1968); Steven Rose, ed., *CBW, Chemical and Biological Warfare* (Boston, 1968).

10. US House of Representatives, Committee on Foreign Affairs, *Hearings: Chemical-Biological Warfare: U.S. Policies and International Effects,* 91st Congress, First Session, 1970; US Senate, Committee on Foreign Relations, *Hearing: Chemical and Biological Warfare,* 91st Congress, 1st Session, 1969. Between July and November 1969 the US Senate also made a symbolic and tentative move to "eliminate . . . funds requested by the military for development of offensive uses of lethal and incapacitating chemical and biological warfare agents." The effort was ineffectual and came to naught. John W. Finney, "Pentagon Denied Fund to Develop Chemical Arms," *New York Times,* July 14, 1979; Warren Weaver, "Germ Warfare Curb Voted in Senate," *New York Times,* August 12, 1969; "Conferees Back Weapons Budget with Few Trims," *New York Times,* November 5, 1969. The three sources were kindly supplied by Dr. Martin Furmanski.

11. *Report of the Secretary General: Chemical and Bacteriological (Biological) Weapons and the Effects of Their Possible Use* (New York, 1968); *Report of a WHO Group of Consultants: Health Aspects of Chemical and Biological Weapon* (Geneva, 1970). The Soviet scientist appointed to the UN secretary-general's expert group was a chemical weapons specialist, Academician O. A. Reutov, who arrived, however, with a sizable staff of assistants. The Soviet scientist sent to the WHO working group was Dr. O. V. Baroyan, director of the Gamaleya Institute and also a KGB major general. The Gamaleya was heavily involved with Problem 5 in the Soviet BW program.

12. Personal communication, November 2007. As early as 1966, Senator Clifford P. Case II, a Republican, had proposed a ban on biological weapons.

13. Report by Secretary of State Rogers to President Nixon: "Convention on the Prohibition of the Development, Production, and Stockpiling of Bacteriological (Biological) and Toxin Weapons, and on Their Destruction," June 21, 1972, US Department of State, *Foreign Relations,* 1969–1976, Volume E-2, Documents on Arms Control, 1969–1972.

14. The questions by Congressman Richard McCarthy in March, 1969, a memorandum from the Joint Chiefs of Staff on April 23, 1969, and from the secretary of defense's staff on April 29, 1969, are all currently under declassification review. Nevertheless, Congressman McCarthy's questions, all or in part, as well as the answers, appeared in March and April 1969 in releases from the congressman's office: "Congressman McCarthy Asks Secretary Laird for Answers to Public Policy Ques-

tions about Chemical and Biological Warfare," Release, March 7, 1969; "Statement of Congressman Richard D. McCarthy on Chemical and Biological Warfare and Practices," Release, April 21, 1969. The longest of these memoranda is also included in Congressman McCarthy's book, *The Ultimate Folly* (1969) and in US House of Representatives, Committee on Foreign Affairs, Hearings: *Chemical-Biological Warfare*, 347–367.

15. Stockholm International Peace Research Institute, *The Problem of Chemical and Biological Warfare*, vols. 1–6 (Stockholm, 1971–1973).

16. Report by Secretary of State Rogers to President Nixon. A review of BW programs in the DOD had been undertaken in October 1961, and policy reviews before that took place in the mid-1950s. It appears that between 1963 and 1965, before the US use of herbicides and gases became a national policy issue, there were several suggestions within US government agencies for a CBW policy review. The suggestions were all very tentative and no review occurred until 1969.

17. National Security Study Memorandum 59, National Security Council, May 18, 1969.

18. Forrest R. Frank, "U.S. Arms Control Policymaking: The Biological Weapons Convention Case" (PhD diss., Stanford University, November 1974), 109, 118.

19. "Annual Review of United States Chemical Warfare and Biological Research Programs as of 1 November 1970," submitted by the Interdepartmental Political-Military Group, 19.

20. "U.S. Policy on Chemical and Biological Warfare and Agents," Report to the National Security Council, Submitted by the Interdepartmental Political Military Group in response to NSSM 59 (November 10, 1969), 8.

21. House of Representatives, Committee on Foreign Affairs, Hearings: *Chemical-Biological Warfare*, 38–39.

22. In addition to the document set produced by National Security, Archive Electronic Briefing Book No. 58, "The Nixon Administration's Decision to End U.S. Biological Warfare Programs," the following are the most informative studies available dealing with the formulation of the Nixon administration's decisions: Frank, 1974; Paul G. Conway, "An Analysis of Decision Making on U.S. Chemical and Biological Warfare Policies" (PhD thesis, Purdue University, 1972), 141–155, 192–196; and Jonathan B. Tucker, "A Farewell to Germs: The U.S. Renunciation of Biological and Toxin Warfare, 1969–70," *International Security* 27, no. 1 (Summer 2002): 107–148. Tucker's article had the advantage of access to the documents declassified in 2001.

23. National Security Decision Memorandum 35, National Security Archive Electronic Briefing Book No. 58, "The Nixon Administration's Decision to End U.S. Biological Warfare Programs."

24. James M. Naughton, "Nixon Asks Senate to Back Germ War Ban," *New York Times*, August 20, 1970.

25. Secretary of Defense Melvin Laird, "Subject: Chemical Warfare and Biological Research—Terminology," Memorandum for the Secretary of State, Assistant to the President, for National Security Affairs, Director Central Intelligence Agency, 1969.

26. For a history of the U.S. biological weapons program, see Ed Regis, *The Biology of Doom: The History of America's Secret Germ Warfare Project* (New York, 1999); and John Van Courtland Moon, *The American Biological Warfare Program* (Cambridge, Mass., forthcoming).

27. *Pentagon Press Briefing on the Biological Demilitarization Program,* mimeo; US Department of Defense, "Demilitarization of Biological Agents and Weapons," Press Release no. 1025-70, December 18, 1970.

28. Roy Reed, "Army Is Destroying Biological Weapons," *New York Times,* July 14, 1971; "Destroying the Germs of War," *Life Magazine,* July 30, 1971; and editorial, "The Art of Penetrating a Forbidden Buildup," *Life Magazine,* July 30, 1971.

29. Melvin R. Laird, Secretary of Defense, Memorandum for the President, Re National Security Decision Memoranda 35 and 44, July 6, 1970.

30. US Army, "Demilitarization" (annex L), in *US Army Activity in the US Biological Warfare Program,* vol. 2, Washington, D.C., February 24, 1977, L-1-L-11.

31. Annual Review of the United States Chemical Warfare and Biological Programs of July 1, 1972.

32. US Senate, Select Committee to Study Governmental Operations with Respect to Intelligence Activities, *Intelligence Activities: Senate Resolution 21.* Vol. 1: *Unauthorized Storage of Toxic Agents,* 94th Congress, 1st Session, Washington, D.C., September 1975, 388–389.

33. "Department of Defense Semi-Annual Report on Chemical and Biological Warfare Programs," *Congressional Record,* November 2, 1973, S-19818-S-19830. In September 2001, it would be learned that these reports did not include secret research, "black" biodefense projects that were either illicit or whose treaty compliance was disputed. Milton Leitenberg, *The Problem of Biological Weapons,* National Defense College, Sweden, 1994, 181–182; and Milton Leitenberg, *Assessing the Biological Weapons and Bioterrorism Threat,* Strategic Studies Institute, US Army War College (Carlisle, PA, 2005), 69–70.

34. Nicholas Wade, "Russians Reserve Doubts: Is Fort Detrick Really De-Tricked?" *Science* 117 (August 11, 1972): 500; Stuart Auerbach, "Russians See Army's Labs Now Used in Cancer Work," *Washington Post,* August 4, 1972; "An Exemplary Transition . . . : Fort Detrick Converting to Major Medical Research Center," *Army Research and Development News Magazine,* July–August 1973, 16–18.

35. It should be recalled that Soviet scientists, unquestionably with official approval, had requested and obtained a sample of Lassa virus from the United States in 1972 (see Chapter 2).

36. The 1984 study for the United Nations (by Leitenberg) was included in a larger publication 10 years later: Milton Leitenberg, "The Conversion of Biological Warfare Research and Development Facilities to Peaceful Uses," in *SIPRI Chemical and Biological Warfare Studies,* ed. E. Geissler and J. P. Woodall, vol. 15 (Oxford, 1994), 77–108.

37. Personal communication, April 18, 1999.

38. Vladimir Pasechnik, personal communication, June 1999. The purpose was presumably to see what the United States would see using its own satellites.

39. United Nations, *The United Nations and Disarmament: 1945–1970* (New York, 1970), 28, 349.

40. Ibid., 352–353.

41. Ibid., 78–125, 354.

42. ACDRU had been established by the Labor government of Harold Wilson in 1965 to provide detailed contributions to the formation of arms control policy within the FCO.

43. FCO 10/179 Biological and Chemical Weapons folio 90 Record of Mulley's discussion in Washington (ACDA) 2 July 1968, and FCO 10/181 Biological and Chemical Weapons 1967–1968 folio 88A Sir Edward Peck comments on draft submission 5 July 1968.

44. The National Archives, Kew, FCO 10/181 Biological and Chemical Weapons 1967–1968, Cabinet Defence and Oversea Policy Committee OPD (68) 13th Meeting 12 July 1968 Item 2 Further Measures on Disarmament. The authors would like to thank Dr. John R. Walker for drawing their attention to the sources in references no. 43–44, 48–51 and 54. See also John R. Walker, *Britain and Disarmament: The UK and Nuclear, Biological and Chemical Weapons Arms Control and Programmes, 1956–1975* (Farnham, UK, 2012).

45. Disarmament Conference Documents, ENDC/231, August 6, 1968. The Eighteen Nation Disarmament Commission (ENDC) was established in 1962. Its name was changed to the Conference of the Committee on Disarmament (CCD) in 1970 when the size of the group was enlarged. In 1979 the name was again changed, to the Committee on Disarmament (CD).

46. Stockholm International Peace Research Institute, *The Problem of Chemical and Biological Warfare.* Vol. 4: *CB Disarmament Negotiations, 1920–1970* (Stockholm, 1971), 254–250; Robert W. Lambert and Jean E Mayer, *International Negotiations on the Biological-Weapons and Toxin Convention,* US Arms Control and Disarmament Agency, US Department of State, publication no. 78, Washington, D.C., May 1975.

47. James Leonard, personal communications, May 20 and May 23, 2004.

48. Supplement for 1969, Document DC/232, Annex C (ENDC/253 and Rev. 1); ENDC 255, July 10, 1969.

49. Official Records of the General Assembly, Twenty-Fourth Session, Annexes, Agenda item 104, document A/7655.

50. Department of State, Telegram 078171, Subject: CCD: Consultations With UK on BW Convention, May 14, 1971.

51. The National Archives, Kew, FCO 66/298 UK policy on chemical and biological warfare and draft Biological Warfare Convention 1981, UKDis Geneva telegram No. 43 to FCO, 3 May 1971 Draft BW Convention.

52. Stephen S. Rosenfeld, "Russian Capability for Chemical, Biological War," *Washington Post,* July 19, 1969.

53. United Nations, 1970, 366.

54. National Archives, Kew, FCO66/302 UK policy on chemical and biological warfare and draft Biological Warfare Convention 1981, FCO telegram No. 21 to UKDis Geneva 27 August 1971 Draft Biological Warfare Convention.

55. Official Records of the Disarmament Commission, Supplement for 1971, CCD/337 and CCD/338.

56. James Leonard, personal communication, November 2007.

57. U.S. Department of State, *Foreign Relations of the United States, 1969–1976.* Volume E-2: *Documents on Arms Control, 1969–1972,* document no. 256, http://www .state.gov/r/pa/ho/frus/nixon/e2/83722.htm. The "jackass" remark was made to Secretary Connolly on April 11, 1972, and the "silly" remark to Kissinger on April 10, 1972.

58. Thomas C. Schelling and Morton H. Halperin, *Strategy and Arms Control* (New York, 1961).

59. Conference of the Committee on Disarmament, Verbatim record, CCD/ PV.542, September 28, 1971.

60. "Ponomarev, Others Hail Ban on Bacteriological Weapons," TASS, February 3, 1975.

61. Decree of Presidium of the Supreme Soviet of USSR on Ratification of the Convention on the Prohibition of the Development, Production, and Stockpiling of Bacteriological (Biological) and Toxin Weapons and on their Destruction, 11 February 1975; "Soviet Ratifies Convention Banning Germ-War Arms," *New York Times,* February 11, 1975. By the time of the Soviet ratification, there were 109 signatories, and 37 other countries, including the United States, had already ratified the BWC.

62. Statement by A. A. Roshchin, *Conference of the Committee on Disarmament,* Verbatim Records 1975, Meetings 666 to 687, CCD/PV.666 (June 24, 1975), 13.

63. Former Soviet diplomat, personal communication, 2007.

64. Victor Israelyan, *On the Battlefields of the Cold War: A Soviet Ambassador's Confession* (University Park, Pa., 2003), 341.

65. Arkady N. Shevchenko, *Breaking with Moscow* (New York, 1985), 230. Unfortunately the Central Committee documents that we obtained do not go back far enough to confirm this.

66. Andrei Malosolov, "Unlike the USA, Russia Will Not Produce Bacteriological Weapons," *RIA Novosti,* September 6, 2001. The comment added by *RIA Novosti* to its interview, which had been put to the defense minister and elicited his remark, was also disinformation. It can only have referred to the *New York Times* report of September 4, 2001, which included reference to Project Bacchus at the Nevada Test Site, which did not involve "production of new types of bacteriological weapons," but was a production signature emission test using a standard simulant for *B. anthracis.*

67. "Domestic Legislation for the BTWC Implementation in the Russia Federation," BWC/MSP.2003/MX/WP.31, prepared for the Meeting of Experts, August 19, 2003. Lev Fedorov refers, however, to "Article 67-2 of the Criminal Code of the RSFSR," that is, pre-1992 Soviet legislation. In an ambiguous sentence he implies that it required observance of the conditions of Article I of the BWC.

68. L. A. Fedorov, *Soviet Biological Weapons: History, Ecology, Politics* (in Russian) (Moscow, 2005), 160 (translated by the Multilingual Division of the Translation Bureau, Government of Canada, Ottawa, March 17, 2008).

69. The Second BWC Review Conference was held six years after the first. This delay was caused by a clash of dates in the disarmament calendar in Geneva.

70. Nicholas A. Sims, "Sweden's Campaign at the First Review Conference," in *The Diplomacy of Biological Disarmament: Vicissitudes of a Treaty in Force, 1975– 1985* (New York, 1988), 169–196. See also his following chapter, "Unfinished Business: The Clarification of Article Five," 199–225.

71. J. Christian Kessler, *Verifying Non Proliferation Treaties: Obligation, Process, and Sovereignty* (Washington, D.C., 1995), 56–57.

72. Julian Perry Robinson, "East-West Fencing at Geneva," *Nature* 284 (April 3, 1980): 393.

73. Robinson, 1980. It should be noted that two of the most well-informed and seasoned observers of issues surrounding the BWC, Robinson and Sims, were suspicious and skeptical of the US démarche to Moscow in relation to the Sverdlovsk anthrax events in the middle of the First BWC Review Conference. They saw them as harming the BWC. Sims went so far as to wonder whether they were not "a wrecking operation," and Robinson felt that they "paradoxically strengthened the position of the USSR."

74. Jonathan B. Tucker, *Strengthening Consultative Mechanisms Under Article V to Address BWC Compliance Concerns,* Harvard Sussex Program Occasional Paper, Issue 01 (Brighton, UK: May 2011), 7–8.

75. UN General Assembly Resolution 37/98C, 1982. See also UN General Assembly Resolutions 37/98D and 39/65E.

76. Rolf Ekéus, personal communication, December 10, 2007.

77. US Department of State Cable, from US Mission Geneva, to US Secretary of State, "Second Biological and Toxin Weapons Convention Review Conference (BW-CRC): Soviet Offer to Discuss Sverdlovsk," Geneva 08160, September 16, 1986.

Because this exchange took place in the meeting of the Committee of the Whole, it is not recorded in the official documentary record of the Review Conference.

78. "Statement by Ambassador Victor L. Israelyan, Head of the Delegation, Member of the Collegium of the Ministry of Foreign Affairs of the USSR," USSR Delegation to the Second Review Conference of the Parties to the Convention on the Prohibition of the Development, Production and Stockpiling of Bacteriological (Biological) and Toxin Weapons and on their Destruction, September 15, 1986. I have chosen to quote directly from a copy of Ambassador Israelyan's presentation as distributed on September 15, 1968. The English in the summation in the conference record was better, but also contained some altered wording. The conference record text appears in Second Review Conference of the Parties to the Convention on the Prohibition of the Development, Production and Stockpiling of Bacteriological (Biological) and Toxin Weapons and on Their Destruction, "Summary Record of the 7th Meeting," BWC/CONF.II/SR.7, September 22, 1986, 13–14.

79. Former Soviet diplomat, personal communication, December 2007. According to this information, *all* proposals by the Socialist states were Soviet proposals, and given to their partners to introduce or join with.

80. "Proposal by the German Democratic Republic, the Hungarian People's Republic and the Soviet Union," Second Review Conference of the Parties to the Convention on the Prohibition of the Development, Production and Stockpiling of Bacteriological (Biological) and Toxin Weapons and on Their Destruction: Summary Record of the 9th Meeting, BWC/CONF.II/SR.9, held at the Palais des Nations, Geneva, on Monday, 22 September 1986, 3.

81. Barbara Hatch Rosenberg, personal communication, December 2007, from notes taken at the conference.

82. Former Soviet diplomat, personal communication, December 10, 2007.

83. Ibid.

84. The conference record text appears in Second Review Conference of the Parties to the Convention on the Prohibition of the Development, Production and Stockpiling of Bacteriological (Biological) and Toxin Weapons and on Their Destruction, "Background Document on Compliance by States Parties with All Their Obligations under the Convention on the Prohibition of the Development, Production and Stockpiling of Bacteriological (Biological) and Toxin Weapons and on Their Destruction: Addendum," BWC/ CONF.II/3, add.2 (August 29, 1986), 2.

85. Ibid. President Reagan's first use of the "Trust but Verify" slogan occurred in November 1985.

86. Barbara Hatch Rosenberg, "Updating the Biological Weapons Ban," *Bulletin of the Atomic Scientists* 43, no. 1 (January/February 1987): 40–43; and Nicholas A. Sims, "The Second Review Conference on the Biological Weapons Convention," in *Preventing a Biological Arms Race,* ed. Susan Wright (Cambridge, 1990), 266–288.

87. UN General Assembly, "Letter dated 21 January 1986 from the Permanent Representative of the Union of Soviet Socialist Republics addressed to the Secretary-General," [Statement by M. S. Gorbachev to the Central Committee of the Communist Party of the USSR, January 15, 1986] A/41/9 (January 22, 1986), 9.

88. Former Soviet diplomat, personal communication, December 10, 2007.

89. Stockholm International Peace Research Institute, *SIPRI Yearbook 1987: World Armaments and Disarmament* (Oxford, 1987), 339–371, appendix 10A, "Stockholm Document."

90. John R. Walker, *Chemical Weapons Convention Negotiations, 1972–92* (London, July 1993), 8, 11, and 17. However, in 1988–1990, the United States began to backtrack on "anywhere, anytime" challenge inspection under the CWC so as to protect nuclear or other US defense installations unrelated to CW from unwanted inspections. This resulted in some limitation to the CWC challenge inspection provisions. This evolution was a forerunner of the sequential US dilution of the facility and field investigations (that is, challenge inspection) provisions in the BWC Verification Protocol negotiations between 1995 and 2000, and of its final total rejection by the United States in 2001.

91. *The INF Treaty and the Washington Summit: 20 Years Later,* National Security Archive Electronic Briefing Book (December 10, 2007), introduction, 3.

92. "Record of Conversation between S. F. Akhromeev and P. Nitze at the US State Department, December 8, 1987," declassified in *The INF Treaty and the Washington Summit: 20 Years Later,* National Security Archive Electronic Briefing Book, doc. no. 26 (December 10, 2007), 14.

93. Second Review Conference of the Parties to the Convention on the Prohibition of the Development, Production and Stockpiling of Bacteriological (Biological) and Toxin Weapons and on Their Destruction, BWC/CONF.II.

94. Former Soviet diplomat, personal communication, 2007.

95. "Final Document," Second Review Conference of the Parties to the Convention on the Prohibition of the Development, Production, and Stockpiling of Bacteriological (Biological) and Toxin Weapons and on Their Destruction, BW/CONF. II/13, September 30, 1986.

96. Ibid.

97. Barbara Hatch Rosenberg, personal communication, December 2007, from notes taken at the conference.

98. C. J. Peters, personal communication, May 15, 2005.

99. "Vladimir Sergiyev, Head of the Administration for Quarantine Inspections, Ministry of Public Health of the USSR: The Need for Specific Steps to Build Up Trust" (in Russian), *Voennyi Vestnik* 9, no. 15 (April 1987): 4. *Voennyi Vestnik* (Military Herald), the journal of the Soviet ground forces, is a Soviet MOD publication.

100. "Commentary by the *Military Herald:* Europeans Have Every Reason for Concern—United States Ready for Chemical and Germ Warfare in Europe," *Voennyi Vestnik* 9, no. 15 (April 1987): 5–8. 13 was the number of validated Soviet pathogens.

101. The alleged US military plan was named "Annex K" to COMSOTFE OPLAN NR. 10-1, "Employment of Chemical and Biological Munitions," undated. This appears to be a classic example of a Soviet "Active Measures" forgery. Several former US military officers directly involved with US Special Operations in Europe during the mid- and late-1980s all stated that they had never heard of any such plan. Personal communications, December 2007. It has also proved impossible to trace any "February 1977 report of the House Science and Astronautics Committee of the US Congress" that the *Voennyi Vestnik* "Commentary" purports to quote.

102. "Military Bulletin Commentary: Dugway US Army Test Range—Biological Material Used on a Growing Scale," *Voennyi Vestnik,* October 1988, 3–5.

103. Sergei Kulik, "'Bacteriological Weapons' Forgery Is Used to Conceal USA's Own Unsavory Plans," *Soviet News,* March 25, 1980. 11 years after the end of the US offensive BW program, and five years after entry into force of the BWC, Soviet propaganda still had "production and stockpiling" of BW taking place in the United States and in unnamed "NATO" countries.

104. *Ban Chemical Weapons,* Moscow: Novosti Press Agency Publishing House, March 11, 1982.

105. *When the Threat to Peace,* 2nd ed. (Moscow, 1982), 64.

106. P. Phillippov, "Criminal Laboratories at Work: The Biological Convention and the Hypocrisy of the USA," *Krasnaya Zvezda,* October 4, 1987.

107. *When the Threat to Peace,* 4th ed. (Moscow, 1987), 60.

108. "A New Approach to Compliance with the CBW Treaties," *F.A.S. Public Interest Report* 41, no. 7 (September 1988): 1.

109. Yuri Antipov, "Commentary on Verifying International Approaches," at the Friedrich Ebert Foundation Roundtable Discussion on the International Control of Chemical and Biological Weapons, New York City, February 10, 1989.

110. Iris Hunger, "Confidence Building Needs Transparency: A Summary of Data Submitted under the Bioweapons Convention's Confidence Building Measures 1987–2003," Austin, TX: The Sunshine Project, September 2005; and Nicolas Isla, *Transparency in Past Offensive Biological Weapon Programmes: An Analysis of Confidence Building Measure Form R 1992–2003,* Occasional Paper no. 1, Hamburg Centre for Biological Arms Control, June 2006.

111. The record of submission of the voluntary CBM declarations was poor. Only 13 states submitted CBM declarations in 1987, 24 in 1988, 28 in 1989, 36 in 1990, 41 in 1991, and 35 in 1992. Many of these were no more than a single line stating that the country in concern was in compliance. It took five years before one-third of the States Parties to the BWC provided declarations.

112. Erhard Geissler, ed., *Strengthening the Biological Weapons Convention by Confidence-Building Measures,* SIPRI Chemical and Biological Warfare Studies, no. 10 (Oxford, 1990); S. J. Lundin, ed., *Views on Possible Verification Measures for the Biological Weapons Convention,* SIPRI Chemical and Biological Warfare Studies, no. 12 (Oxford, 1991); and The Netherlands Ministry of Foreign Affairs, *Collected Papers: Seminar on the Biological Weapons Convention* (Noordwijk, The Netherlands, February 1991).

113. Symposium on Improving Confidence-Building Measures for the BW Convention, National Research Establishment, Umeå, Sweden, May 1990.

114. Statement by Ambassador Serguei B. Batsanov, Head of the USSR Delegation to the Third Review Conference of the Biological Weapons Convention, Geneva, September 12, 1991.

115. Former Soviet diplomat, personal communication, December 2007.

116. Third Review Conference of the Parties to the Convention on the Prohibition of the Development, Production, and Stockpiling of Bacteriological (Biological) and Toxin Weapons and on Their Destruction, BWC/CONF.III/3, add.1 (September 10, 1991).

117. Colonel N. T. Vasiliev (Ministry of Defense of the USSR), "A Few Proposals on Strengthening the 1972 Convention and Establishing a Verification Mechanism," Seminar on the Biological Weapon Convention in the Perspective of the Forthcoming BW Convention Third Review Conference, Noordwijk, The Netherlands, February 6–8, 1991.

118. "Proliferation Issues: A New Challenge after the Cold War—Proliferation of Weapons of Mass Destruction," Russian Federation Foreign Intelligence Service Report, March 3, 1993, JPRS-TND-93-007, 15–16. It is likely that the pre-1992 KGB also had a hand in drafting the earlier 1991 list presented by the MOD.

119. Third Review Conference of the Parties to the Convention on the Prohibition of the Development, Production, and Stockpiling of Bacteriological (Biological) and Toxin Weapons and on Their Destruction, BW/CONF.III/22, add. 2 (September 27, 1991).

120. Quoted in Michael Moodie, "Bolstering Compliance with the Biological Weapons Convention: Prospects for the Special Conference," *Chemical Weapons Convention Bulletin,* no. 25 (September 1994): 1–3.

121. Leitenberg, *The Problem of Biological Weapons* (Stockholm, 2004), 97–114.

122. Statement by Ronald Lehman II, head of the US Delegation to the Third Review Conference of the Biological Weapons Convention, Geneva, September 10, 1991. Lehman stated: "So far, no persuasive case has been made for the effectiveness of either routine or challenge inspections of biological facilities. Ineffective verification regimes and measures that adversely impact biological defense programs and other peaceful biological activities are not acceptable. Nor are regimes that foster a false sense of confidence."

123. Nicholas A. Sims, "The Biological Weapons Convention: Progress since Its Agreement," Wilton Park Arms Control Seminar IV: Controlling Biological Weapons, September 24–26, 1993.

124. Iris Hunger, *Biological Weapons Control in a Multipolar World: The Function of Trust in International Relations* (in German) (Frankfurt, 2005).

125. See Milton Leitenberg, *Biological Weapons Arms Control,* PRAC Paper no. 16, College Park, Md., May 1996, 59–69; Leitenberg, *The Problem of Biological Weapons* (Stockholm, 2004), 97–114; Nicholas Sims, *The Evolution of Biological Disarmament,* SIPRI Chemical and Biological Warfare Series, no. 19 (Oxford, 2001); and Jez Littlewood, *The Biological Weapons Convention: A Failed Revolution* (Aldershot, UK, 2005).

126. Permanent Mission of the Russian Federation to the Conference on Disarmament in Geneva, "Statement by H.E. Mr. Gennady Gatilov, Deputy Minister of Foreign Affairs of the Russian Federation, at the 7th Review Conference for the Biological and Toxin Weapons Convention," Geneva, December 5, 2011; and ITAR-Tass, "Russia Urges Verification Powers be Added to Bioweapons Treaty Regime, December 7, 2011.

127. Personal communications from multiple participants at the Seventh Review Conference, December 2011.

21. The Gorbachev Years

1. A summary of the sequence between 1969 and 1985 regarding this Commission was written by Vitaly Kataev, a staff member of the Central Committee Secretariat and Lev Zaikov's assistant:

> Coordination in the USSR of Questions on the Control of Arms Prior to 1985
> Bodies were created by decisions of the Politburo of the CC [Central Committee] of the CPSU which were charged with questions on arms control:
> 21.11.69 The establishment of the Commission for Oversight of Soviet-American Negotiations in Helsinki: ". . . Comrades D. F. Ustinov, Yu.V. Andropov, and XX [sic] were charged with systematically following negotiations in Helsinki."
> 21.03.74 Decision "On the Commission for Oversight of Soviet-American Negotiations" taken: "In order to oversee negotiations on the question of restraining the strategic weapons arms race, Comrades D. F. Ustinov (on invitation), Yu.V. Andropov, A. A. Grechko, A. A. Gromyko, L. V. Smirnov, M. V. Keld'sh are charged with systematically following negotiations and to submit recommendations to the CC of the CPSU as necessary."
> 26.05.77 As a consequence of the negotiations between A. A. Gromyko and C. Vance it is decided: "To charge the Commission of the Politburo of the CC of

the CPSU (Comrades Gromyko, Ustinov, Andropov, Ryabov and Smirnov) to submit . . . recommendations related to further negotiations with the USA on the limitation of strategic offensive weapons . . . To charge this same Commission to periodically, as necessary, prepare and present to the CC of the CPSU instructions for the Soviet delegation in Geneva . . ."

21,06.79 It is decided "To charge the previously established Commission consisting of Comrades Gromyko, Ustinov, Andropov and Smirnov to continue to daily consider questions concerning the entry-into-force and the practical realization of the signed documents on the limitation of strategic weapons, as well as questions on the preparation for follow-on negotiations . . ."

13.04.83 The decision "On the Commission of the Politburo of the CC of the CPSU on the Oversight of Soviet-American Negotiations" is taken: "In partial modification of the decision of the Politburo of the CC of the CPSU dated 21 June 1979 (p155/1) to charge the Commission consisting of A. A. Gromyko, D. F. Ustinov, L. V. Smirnov and V. M. Chebrikov to continue to daily consider questions related to Soviet-American negotiations on the limitation of nuclear weapons."

23.04.84 "The Commissions of the Politburo of the CC of the CPSU on China, the Near East, on Negotiations on the Limitation of Nuclear Weapons and others [commissions] are to submit to the CC of the CPSU concrete proposals on questions, by directive in speech by Comrade K. U. Chernenko."

2. Aleksandr' G. Savel'yev and Nikolay N. Detinov, *The Big Five: Arms Control Decision-Making in the Soviet Union* (Westport, Conn., 1995). See also discussions of "the *Pyatorka*" in Oleg A. Grinevsky, "Disarmament: The Road to Conversion," in *The Anatomy of Russian Defense Conversion,* ed. Vlad E. Genin (Walnut Creek, Calif., 2001), 158–207; Vitaly L. Kataev, "MIC: The View from Inside," in Genin, 2001, 52–88; "Policy Formation in the USSR on the INF Treaty: A Nuclear History Program Oral History Transcript Interview with Alexei Arbatov, Milton Leitenberg and Ivo Daalder," NHP Oral History Transcript #3, Center for International Security Studies, School of Public Affairs, University of Maryland, June 1991. For an unusual earlier, although limited, paper by a Soviet author who had held important institute positions before he defected to the United States, see Igor S. Glagolev, "The Soviet Decision-Making Process in Arms Control Negotiations," *Orbis,* Winter 1978, 767–776. See also Pavel Podvig, "The Structure and Operations of Strategic Nuclear Forces," chap. 2 in *Russian Strategic Nuclear Forces,* ed. Pavel Podvig (Cambridge, Mass., 2001), 33–49; Jeremy R. Azrael, *The Soviet Civilian Leadership and the Military High Command, 1976–1986,* RAND R-3521-AF, June 1987; Jan Sejna and Joseph D. Douglas Jr., *Decision-Making in Communist Countries: An Inside View* (Washington, D.C., 1986).

3. As one minor aspect of its role in the BW arena, the VPK sent teams of two or three scientists on "control" visits to both MOD and Biopreparat institutes.

4. This chapter is unique in that a large portion of the narrative is based on very extensive interviews, in some cases lasting several days each, with three individuals who were directly involved at a very senior level with the events that took place between 1985 and 1992. One of these individuals was Vitaly Kataev. A second was a senior Soviet diplomat. The third was a senior US official. These three interviews resulted in 80 pages of single-spaced notes. Interviews were carried out with one additional former Soviet diplomat and with 10 additional US and UK officials who also participated directly in the events, particularly from the time of Pasechnik's defection in Paris at the end of October 1989 to mid-1995. Individual items that contribute to the chapter derived from these interviews will not be further identified by source. In addition, 15 Soviet Central Committee documents, dating from May 19, 1987, to July 1991, were obtained and provide important information on processes within the Central Committee on the BW issue. We are of course missing innumerable Central Committee documents that pertained to the offensive BW program: memoranda from the VPK and/or MOD, Central Committee approvals of projects and budgets, etc., and most importantly, those dating from the early years after 1972–1973 until 1987.

5. Other departments of the MFA, particularly the Department of the USA and Canada in the case of the SALT nuclear weapon negotiations, were also involved in arms control questions.

6. Shakhov had been a chemical engineer at the Kazan Institute of Chemical Technology, then worked in a missile solid fuel plant in Perm and was recruited to the Central Committee staff. His specialty was the "recipes" for solid fuels.

7. "On the Arrangement for Preparing Documents on Military-Political Questions for the Report of the CC (Central Committee) of the CPSU," Submitted to the Central Committee by L. Zaikov, V. Chebrikov, E. Shevardnadze, S. Sokolov, A. Dobrynin, Yu. Maslyukov, May 7, 1987; Consented to by the CC of the CPSU, May 19, 1987. The document established among whom documents should be distributed (the big *Pyatorka*, plus two other offices), the functioning of the working groups (small *Pyatorka*), and who would consider the prepared recommendations (the big *Pyatorka*). A former member of the MFA provided further elaboration: "Decisions of the Central Committee" were made in the 1980s by the Politburo, and came in two parts—a "decision," in one page, to do something, and recording those who approved. Attached would be a text, "*Direktiva*" (Directives) and "*Ukazanye*" (Guidelines), both carrying equal weight. Those who wanted to submit an item for consideration, a "*Zapiske*," or note to the Central Committee, provided a maximum 1.5-page submission with annexes. However, Politburo members would never read the annexes.

8. The CBMs were only agreed at the BWC Second Review Conference in 1986, and the modalities worked out by an expert group from March 31–April 21, 1987. The first Soviet BWC CBMs were submitted to the UN in October 1987.

9. As part of taking accusations "seriously," the MFA had arranged that there should be a response to the Sverdlovsk allegations, and a direct meeting on a diplomatic level had been held with the United States in Geneva. However, as already indicated in the previous chapter, the first of these presentations by Soviet officials continued all the standard lies, and the second was ineffectual. The MFA also arranged the two meetings between committees of the US and Soviet Academies of Sciences to discuss the Sverdlovsk anthrax episode, but the individuals on the Soviet side at these sessions were the same as those in Geneva, and again repeated the same lies. Meselson was also permitted two visits to Moscow and allowed to meet with Yevstigneev. The MFA was able to initiate new meetings, but it could not alter the substance of what Soviet representatives presented on these occasions.

10. Ken Alibek with Stephen Handelman, *Biohazard: The Chilling True Story of the Largest Covert Biological Weapons Program in the World—Told from Inside by the Man Who Ran It* (New York, 1999), 146.

11. Ibid.

12. Ibid., 147–148.

13. Vitaly Kataev, *"SPRAVKA,"* undated but obviously written after March 16, 1990, and very likely on May 14–15, 1990. This translation was provided courtesy of David Hoffman. The Russian term for the first three is *postanovleniye*—"instruction" or "resolution"—and for the last two it is *resheniye*—"decision."

14. Eduard Shevardnadze, "The 19th All-Union CPSU Conference," *International Affairs,* October 1988, 19.

15. John Van Oudenaren, *The Role of Shevardnadze and the Ministry of Foreign Affairs in the Making of Soviet Defense and Arms Control Policy,* RAND Report R-3898-USDP, July 1990, 10–11, quoting Paul Quinn-Judge, "Gorbachev Hints at Troubles in the Military," *Christian Science Monitor,* July 12, 1989.

16. Michael R. Beschloss and Strobe Talbott, *At the Highest Levels: The Inside Story of the End of the Cold War* (Boston, 1993), 403.

17. Ibid., 118. Shevardnadze became minister of foreign affairs on June 29, 1985, and held office until December 20, 1990. He was succeeded by Alexander Bessmertynykh, who served between January and August 1991. Bessmertynykh was removed by Gorbachev for not opposing the coup plotters. His replacement was Boris Pankin, a career diplomat but an incompetent one, who was quickly removed in November 1991. Shevardnadze then returned, but only until December 31, 1991, when the Soviet Union was dissolved.

18. Bechloss and Talbott, 1993, 402.

19. Ken Alibek, personal communication, 1999.

20. Kataev's notes were not recorded in precise detail and at times required a word or two to be interpolated. The original wording was retained as much as possible in the descriptions provided, but particularly important phrases were emphasized by placing them within quotation marks.

21. Alibek with Handelman, 1999, 145. There is no known diplomatic record of such a US request before 1990. Alibek also claimed that *in mid-1990*, Biopreparat authorized the procurement of "new railcars for the mobile deployment of biological production plants" (191). This would have been a remarkable development if the claim was accurate; however, it has not been possible to corroborate it from any other source.

22. Stockholm International Peace Research Institute, *The Problem of Chemical and Biological Warfare*, 2:135.

23. Kalinin's meaning of "Guarantees" is unclear. It might have referred to the protection of proprietary information or possibly agreement on the modalities that would be established for inspections.

24. Questions for Consideration at CPSU CC at Comrade L. N. Zaikov's, July 27, 1989, "On Measures to Improve Organization of Works on Special Problems," Report by Comrade Kalinin, Yury Tikhonovich.

25. Vladimir Pasechnik, personal communications, June 1999.

26. Ken Alibek, personal communications, 1998; and Alibek with Handelman, 1999, 138–144.

27. Tom Mangold and Jeff Goldberg, *Plague Wars: A True Story of Biological Warfare* (New York, 1999), 107–108.

28. "Materials for the meeting of the Central Committee of the Communist Party of the Soviet Union at Comrade L. N. Zaikov's office, January 23, 1990, at 16:00 hours."

29. Kataev, handwritten meeting notes, January 31, 1980.

30. The results were reported to the CCD in CD/1012 in July 1990, and CD/1080 on June 5, 1991.

31. Alibek with Handelman, 1999, 177–178. No record of such a KGB memorandum appears in the relatively small number of Soviet BW documents that we have obtained.

32. Former Soviet MFA official, personal communication, March 1995.

33. Alibek with Handelman, 1999, 180–181.

34. Ibid., 181–182. Alibek incorrectly refers to the Pfizer facility as being "in Illinois." Russian inspectors would in fact request to visit it four years later.

35. Ibid., 187–190.

36. Ibid. It notably echoes Akhromeyev's "renewed production."

37. Ibid., 263. Presumably weapon filling lines.

38. Ken Alibek, personal communication, fall 1998.

39. Galkin was a member of the Central Committee's General Department, headed by Boldin at that time. Two Western scholars have suggested that the Central Committee designation, which translates literally to "special files," would approximate "sensitive compartmentalized information," "especially secret," or "super top secret."

40. Alibek with Handelman, 1999, 183.

41. Pasechnik believed that the US officials who came to London to speak with him in 1990 thought that he was not telling the truth, lying, , and that they would not rely on what he told them. He also believed that Gorbachev ordered all offensive BW activities and programs to be hidden after his defection: not ended, but hidden. It is not clear how Pasechnik would arrive at that opinion. At the time when he left in 1989, Pasechnik said that everything in the Biopreparat system was still "in full go." He never heard that production had been stopped. Kalinin's testimony indicates that he was correct. However, the recipe for a dry *Y. pestis* formulation had still not been completed.

42. Douglas Hogg, later minister of state in the UK Foreign Office, commented that Pasechnik's disclosures "reinforced a whole range of suspicions and information that we already had, but the information he gave us was very significant." As indicated, the reaction in the US intelligence community was very similar—to match Pasechnik's new information to information gathered over the previous decades. At the same time, there were individuals in both governments who still maintained some skepticism. Mark Urban, *UK Eyes Alpha: Inside British Intelligence* (London, 1996), 130.

43. A supposedly well-informed author and former US DOD official, Richard Danzig, has repeated a common but grossly misinformed view: "Our vast and intensely committed Cold War intelligence establishment overlooked a Soviet biowarfare program that employed 50,000 people over two decades." See Richard Danzig, *Preparing for Catastrophic Bioterrorism* (National Defense University, May 2008), 30.

Of much greater significance are the comments by one of Secretary of State Baker's deputies, Richard Clarke. Clarke was one of Baker's assistant secretaries of state during 1989–1990 and describes himself as being one of the five people in the Department of State allowed to read Pasechnik's testimony. He claims that Pasechnik "told [of] something that the US intelligence community had believed did not exist, a massive Soviet program to develop and deploy biological weapons". Given the official US government publication only three years earlier in 1986 accusing the Soviet Union of an offensive BW program, the statement is difficult to comprehend. If accepted literally, it indicates the existence of widely divergent assessments of that program within the US intelligence community and other government departments. Clarke continues:

> It was not the kind of news that any of us had wanted to hear, but it was definitely not what Secretary of State Jim Baker needed. Baker had told the Pentagon, the Congress, and the President that we could safely sign several major arms-control agreements with the Soviets. He had said it was highly unlikely that these Soviet leaders would risk getting caught violating an international

arms-control agreement and, moreover, if they did, US intelligence would catch a violation using "national technical means."

But at least the first of these predictions had proved wrong, and to some degree, the second.

Clarke also wrote, "The friendly senior Soviet officials with whom we were negotiating arms-control treaties had known all about the illegal program and the efforts to keep it secret from us." That may have been true for MOD officials, but not for those in the MFA, and even there, only in part for Shevardnadze.

In a gloss that covers many months and a far more complicated process that was to follow, Clark wrote:

> Baker's first reaction had been to keep the knowledge about the Soviet program restricted, until he could get the Soviet leadership to admit it existed and promise to destroy the program in front of US observers. Unfortunately, the Soviets were not quite so ready to cooperate when confronted. They claimed that the US must have such a program too. They wanted to inspect our facilities.

Clarke expressed the position that "the Soviets had [never] given us the two things we really needed: first, a complete list of everything they had developed (and destroyed), and second, the antidotes they had developed to whatever new strains of disease had festered up in their pots".

Richard A. Clarke, *Against All Enemies: Inside America's War on Terror* (New York, 2004), pp. 159–160.

44. Personal communication, November 2009.

45. "Instructions for Forthcoming Meeting with US Secretary of State James Baker on Warsaw Pact-NATO-Related Matters," undated.

46. Victor Alessi, Briefing paper for Frank Wisner, US Department of State, September 1992.

47. "Rudimentary Draft, MOU Discussed during RD [Round] 12, US-USSR Bilats," August 1989.

48. "USSR Statement at Opening Plenary, RD 14, US-USSR Bilats," February 20, 1990.

49. Mangold and Goldberg, 1999, 104. They quote US Department of State official Gary Crocker as saying, "The British were hot to get going. They wanted to accuse the Soviets of violations and to shut down the Soviet programme. They were more aggressive than the US."

50. Ibid.

51. Ibid., 416, ref. #12.

52. Memo of Conversation: Between the US Ambassador to the USSR J. Matlock and the British Ambassador to the USSR R. Braithwaite, May 14, 1990. Mb-

01203-oc, A. Bessmyrtnykh, Deputy Minister, Ministry of Foreign Affairs, USSR.

53. *Ibid.*

54. Personal communication, June 2008.

55. Alibek with Handelman, 1999, 149.

56. L. Zaikov, "To the President of the Union of Soviet Socialist Republics, Comrade M. S. Gorbachev," May 15, 1990. When referring to the three Central Committee decisions, Zaikov uses the same words that appear in Kataev's reference note, which are *postanovleniye* and *resheniye.*

57. The "Cetus Corporation" existed in Berkeley, California, during 1971–1991. In the end, the USSR never did request to visit the "Cetus Corporation."

58. Alibek with Handelman, 1999, 53.

59. Personal communication, March 2005.

60. Igor Domaradsky, personal interview, 1999.

61. Alibek with Handelman, 1999, 149–150. The VPK would be included.

62. Pasechnik apparently told his interrogators that the Biopreparat budget, or "plan," was on one occasion "submitted to" or "approved by" Shevardnadze sitting in the CPSU general secretary's "chair." As we will see, this was very likely a misinterpretation of what had taken place.

63. Mangold and Goldberg, 1999, 111.

64. Ibid., 112–113.

65. Paul Quinn-Judge, "Shevardnadze the Survivor," *Washington Post,* March 19, 2006. In the interview, Shevardnadze was asked what basis he had for his warning, when he resigned in December 1990, that a coup against Gorbachev was being prepared. At that time, he had offered no proof, but stated that he knew of the assembly of tanks and troops 100 kilometers from Moscow.

66. Alibek with Handelman, 1999, 151.

67. Ibid., 150.

68. David E. Hoffman, *The Dead Hand: The Untold Story of the Cold War Arms Race and Its Dangerous Legacy* (New York, 2009), 350.

69. Urban, 1994, 129–134.

70. Mangold and Goldberg, 1999, 111. Their description is that "Thatcher . . . bluntly asked Gorbachev if the Soviets were or were not making new biological weapons. 'Are you hiding secret research to develop weapons of mass destruction.' . . . The General Secretary replied that the Soviets had no programmes to develop BW or toxins. He repeated his pledge to question the military officials in charge."

71. This incidentally explains why the official Soviet "defense budget" was always about one-fourth of what the United States estimated to be true Soviet military expenditure.

72. "Draft Response to J. Baker's Memo to E. A. Shevardnadze on the Subject of the Soviet Program in the Field of Biological Warfare for the Soviet-American Minister's Summit in Irkutsk on August 1, 1990," July 30, 1990.

73. "Draft Response to J. Baker's Memo to E. A. Shevardnadze on the Subject of the Soviet Program in the Field of Biological Warfare for the Soviet-American Minister's Summit in Irkutsk on August 1, 1990," August 1, 1990.

74. Mangold and Goldberg, 1999, 114; Hoffman, 2009, 351.

75. Mangold and Goldberg, 1999, 115–116.

76. Alexander Rahr, "KGB Chief Said to Have Masterminded 1991 Putsch," *Research Bulletin* (RFE/RL Research Institute) 10 (August 17, 1993): 16; Alexander Rahr, "Kryuchkov, the KGB, and the 1991 Putsch," *RFE/RL Research Report* 2 (July 30, 1993): 31.

77. Stephen Foye, "Personnel Changes in the High Command," *Reports on the USSR* (RFE/RL Research Institute) 3, no. 39 (September 27, 1991): 1–6.

78. "Biological Weapons," n.d.

79. To the President of the Union of Soviet Socialist Republics, Comrade Gorbachev, M. S., "On the Reply to the US President on the Question of Biological Weapons," July 8, 1991.

80. Untitled, n.d.; either the draft for or the letter from Gorbachev to Bush prior to July 17, 1991.

81. Russian diplomats reiterated these points for a third time in the negotiations in 1994 and 1995 following the September 1992 signing of the Trilateral Agreement between Russia, the United States, and the United Kingdom, and for a fourth time after the BWC Protocol negotiations began in 1995. It is very likely that the authors of all these different Soviet documents were the same individuals.

82. Untitled, n.d. (supra 81)

83. Thomas Blanton and Svetlana Savranskaya, *The Last Superpower Summits: Reagan, Gorbachev, Bush and the End of the Cold War* (Budapest, forthcoming 2012).

84. Carolyn M. Ekedal and Melvin A. Goodman, *The Wars of Eduard Shevardnadze* (University Park, Pa., 1997), 124–127.

85. Eduard Shevardnadze, *The Future Belongs to Freedom* (New York, 1991), 72.

86. Hoffman, 2009, and personal communication.

87. Ibid., 350–351.

88. Alibek with Handelman, 1999, 195–200.

89. David C. Kelly, "The Trilateral Agreement: Lessons for Biological Weapons Verification," *Verification Yearbook, 2002* (London, 2002). See also Alibek with Handelman, 1999, 198–200.

90. Vladimir Pasechnik, personal communication, June 1999.

91. Personal communication, 2009.

92. Mangold and Goldberg, 1999, 136, 423. The authors claim that Sandakhchiev repeated this explanation in a 1998 interview.

93. Ibid., 138–139. The lines quoted are included in five paragraphs stated to be extracted directly from the conclusion of the report.

94. Ibid., 424.

95. Ibid., 424–425.

96. Ibid., 141, 424–425. Their itemization lists only eight occasions.

97. Beschloss and Talbott, 1993, 421–441; and Robert M. Gates, *From the Shadows* (New York, 1996), 521–525.

98. Ibid., 524.

99. Mangold and Goldberg, 1999, 142.

100. Ibid., 143.

101. Kelly, 2002, 96.

102. Mangold and Goldberg, 1999, 148.

103. It was in fact finally dismantled, down to the ground, in 2003–2004.

104. Mangold and Goldberg, 1999, 145.

105. Ken Alibek, personal communication, 1999.

106. Mangold and Goldberg, 1999, 157.

107. Anatoly S. Chernyaev, *My Six Years with Gorbachev* (University Park, Pa., 2000), 358.

108. Hoffman, 1999, 431.

109. Chernyaev, 2000, 358.

110. Ibid.

111. Ibid., 358–359.

112. Archie Brown, Presentation at the conference "The Road Taken: Twenty Years After the Fall of the Soviet Union," Kennan Institute, Washington, DC, November 16, 2011.

113. Former MFA official, personal communication, March 1995.

114. Ibid.

115. Mangold and Goldberg, 1999, 109. Matlock overlooked the VPK.

116. Scott Shane, *Dismantling Utopia: How Information Ended the Soviet Union* (Chicago, 1994), 248. Yakovlev had studied at Columbia University in the United States in 1958–1960 with KGB cognizance. But in 1991 the KGB was suggesting that Yakovlev was a CIA agent.

117. Mangold and Goldberg, 1999, 109, 417 n. 17.

118. Personal communication, 2012. Crocker is the same DOS official who championed the Yellow Rain allegations and is an unreliable authority.

119. Urban, 1994, 134. We have been able to verify that this conception was in fact held by British intelligence analysts.

120. David Hoffman, personal communication, July 11, 2009.

121. Hoffman, 1999, 302.

122. Urban, 1994, 134.

123. Rodric Braithwaite, *Across the Moscow River: The World Turned Upside Down* (New Haven, Conn., 2003), 29.

124. Ann MacLachlan, "What the Experts Learned from Chernobyl Post-Accident Review," *Nucleonics Week,* September 4, 1986.

125. Raymond L. Garthoff, "The KGB Reports to Gorbachev," *Intelligence and National Security* 11, no. 2 (April 1996): 224–244.

126. "Gorbachev: Letter to the Politburo of November 26, 1985, on Distortion of Facts in Reports and Information Coming to the CPSU Central Committee," Fond 3, Opis 111, Delo 144, papkas 39–41, archive unknown.

127. Garthoff, 1996, 230.

128. Jack Matlock, *Superpower Illusions: How Myths and False Ideologies Led America Astray . . . And How to Return to Reality* (New Haven, Conn., 2010), 96–98.

129. Robert Cottrell, "Founding Father" (review of *My Six Years with Gorbachev,* by Anatoly S. Chernyaev), *New York Review of Books,* April 26, 2001, 20–22.

130. Cottrell, 2001.

131. Chernayev, 2000, 66. Chernayev continued: "The system was plagued by servility, bootlicking, window dressing . . . persecution of critics, boasting, favoritism and clannish management." The nuclear power program was, of course, public. It is not known if this description is applicable to the BW program, which was secret.

132. Georgi Shakhnazarov, 1993, quoted in Hoffman, 2009, 212, 519.

133. Mark Kramer, "The Collapse of East European Communism and the Repercussions within the Soviet Union (Part 2)," *Journal of Cold War Studies* 6, no. 4 (Fall 2004): 27–31.

134. Cottrell, 2001.

135. Hoffman, 2009, 302–303. US author Gregory Koblentz concluded that "Gorbachev played a two-level game. He persisted in denying the existence of an offensive program to the West to avoid embarrassment and a confrontation with the military while he and Shevardnadze engaged in a bureaucratic struggle to rein in the offensive program." Gregory D. Koblentz, *Living Weapons: Biological Warfare and International Security* (Ithaca, N.Y., 2009), 120.

136. Former UK government official, personal communication, 2007.

22. Boris Yeltsin to the Present

1. Statement on Disarmament by Russian Federation President Boris Nikolayevich Yeltsin on January 29, 1992, Moscow Teleradiakompaniya Ostankino Television, First Program Network, January 27, 1992, Text. There were reports that Yeltsin made this public statement because he was told by the Bush administration that he could not come to Washington unless he publicly acknowledged the Soviet BW program.

2. ABC News, *20/20,* January 31, 1992.

3. Ken Alibek with Stephen Handelman, *Biohazard: The Chilling True Story of the Largest Covert Biological Weapons Program in the World—Told from Inside by the Man Who Ran It* (New York, 1999), 242–243.

4. Tom Mangold and Jeff Goldberg, *Plague Wars: The Terrifying Reality of Biological Warfare* (New York, 1999), 158.

5. A. Devroy and R. J. Smith, "US, Russia Pledge New Partnership," *Washington Post,* February 2, 1992, and *Nezavisimaya Gazeta,* February 5, 1992, translated in Foreign Broadcast Information Service, *Daily Report—Central Eurasia* (FBIS-SOV), FBIS-SOV-92-031, February 14, 1992, 26.

6. M. Zakharov, "A Visit to the President" (in Russian), *Izvestia,* April 23, 1992, in FBIS-SOV-92-079, April 23, 1992, 26–29. Yeltsin's reference to "two test sites" may or may not be an impromptu misstatement.

7. Devroy and Smith, 1992.

8. *Rossiyskaya Gazeta,* Moscow, February 28, 1992, quoted in BBC-SWB, SU/1317 C3/1, February 29, 1992.

9. President Yeltsin's interview in *Komsomolskaya Pravda,* May 27, 1992.

10. "Yeltsin Commits to Germ Warfare Ban," *Washington Post,* April 17, 1992.

11. White House, Office of the Press Secretary, *Soviet Non-Compliance with Arms Control Agreements, March 30, 1992,* Washington, D.C., April 9, 1992.

12. Milton Leitenberg, "A Return to Sverdlovsk: Allegations of Soviet Activities Related to Biological Weapons," *Arms Control* 12, no. 2 (September 1991): 161–190, esp. 166; Milton Leitenberg, "Anthrax in Sverdlovsk: New Pieces to the Puzzle," *Arms Control Today* 22, no. 3 (April 1992): 10–13; and R. J. Smith, "Yeltsin Blames '79 Anthrax on Germ Warfare Efforts," *Washington Post,* June 16, 1992.

13. R. J. Smith, "Russia Fails to Detail Germ Arms," *Washington Post,* August 31, 1992. See also editorial, "Cheating on Biological Weapons," *Washington Post,* September 11, 1992.

14. Interview with General Kuntsevich (in Russian), *Rossiyskiye Vesti,* September 22, 1992, in FBIS-SOV-92-186, September 24, 1992.

15. In testimony to Congress in 2002, Constantine Menges, a retired US defense official, commented: "I do recall in one of my visits to Russia being in the Kremlin with an adviser to President Yeltsin in 1992 right at the start of the post-Soviet era, and this individual said to me that one of their greatest concerns is that they know they have so many chemical, biological, and nuclear weapons and facilities scattered all over the former Soviet republics, and they also know they do not have control over them or even a good inventory." US House of Representatives, Committee on International Relations, Hearing: *Loose Nukes, Biological Terrorism, and Chemical Warfare: Using Russian Debt to Enhance Security,* July 25, 2002 (Washington, D.C., 2002), 37.

16. M. R. Gordon, "U.S. Asking Russia to Show It Has Ended Germ Weapons Program," *New York Times,* September 1, 1992. The name of the "new" directorate appears in varying versions in English translation, with the word "protection" appearing at times in place of "defense."

17. As in Chapter 21, this chapter contains information, at times within quotation marks, derived from personal interviews with participants in the events described. As in Chapter 21, identification of the sources has been withheld.

18. Russian Federation, "Declaration of Past Activity in regard to Offensive and Defensive Programs of Biological Research and Development," United Nations Form F, DDA/4-92/BWIII, 1992. See also Gregory D. Koblentz, *Living Weapons, Biological Warfare and International Security* (Ithaca, N.Y., 2009), 123–124.

19. Letter from Lawrence Eagleburger and Douglas Hurd to Andrei Kozyrev, August 24, 1992.

20. R. J. Smith, "Russia Fails to Detail Germ Arms"; see also "Cheating on Biological Weapons."

21. J. T. Dahlburg, "Russia Admits Violating Biological Warfare Pact," *Los Angeles Times,* September 15, 1992.

22. *Joint Statement on Biological Weapons by the Governments of the United Kingdom, the United States, and the Russian Federation,* September 14, 1992 (emphasis in text added).

23. Ibid., 2, 3.

24. D. Yazov, "On the Draft Resolution of the CPSU CC 'On Directives to the USSR Delegation at the Soviet-American Consultations on Issues of Banning Bacteriological and Toxin Weapons,'" January 10, 1990.

25. "Press Briefing of Deputy Foreign Minister Grigory Berdennikov," Official Kremlin International News Broadcast, September 14, 1992, 2, 5.

In September 1992, Russian officials informally raised questions concerning US implementation of the BWC, questioning the capability of former US BW facilities based on the pre-1992 visits to US sites by Soviet teams. See the section titled "Allegations of U.S. Noncompliance," in US Arms Control and Disarmament Agency, *Adherence to and Compliance with Arms Control Agreements and the President's Report to Congress on Soviet Noncompliance with Arms Control Agreements,* January 14, 1993, 5.

26. Personal communications, 2011.

27. See Dahlburg, 1992; M. R. Gordon, "Russia and West Reach Accord on Monitoring Germ Weapon Ban," *New York Times,* September 15, 1992; and R. J. Smith, "Russia Agrees to Inspection of Its Biological Research Facilities," *Washington Post,* September 15, 1992.

28. "Press Briefing of Deputy Foreign Minister Grigory Berdennikov," 5.

29. Ibid.

30. Ibid.

31. *Text of a Letter from the President to the Speaker of the House of Representatives and the President of the Senate,* Pursuant to Public Law 99-145; 22 U.S.C. 2592a as amended, and section 52 of the Arms Control and Disarmament Act, Washington, DC: White House, Office of the Press Secretary, January 19, 1993.

32. R. Jeffrey Smith, "U.S. Officials Allege That Russians Are Working on Biological Arms," *Washington Post,* April 8, 1994.

33. Ibid.

34. Arms Control and Disarmament Agency, "Russia: Biological Weapons Program," April 8, 1994.

35. Smith, 1994.

36. David C. Kelly, "The Trilateral Agreement: Lessons for Biological Weapons Verification," in *Verification Yearbook 2002,* ed. Trevor Findlay and Oliver Meier (London, 2002), 97.

37. There were a few desultory exchanges on conversion issues at the first and second working group meetings. Before visits could take place, there had to be agreement on a second document on the protection of confidential information. The Russians would not agree to visits until this had been worked out, which was not accomplished until May 1993. The document was titled "Procedures for Respecting Proprietary Information during Visits to Non-military Biological Sites pursuant to Paragraph 4(A) of the Joint US-UK Russian Statement on Biological Weapons."

38. Kelly, 2002, 99.

39. Joby Warrick, "Russia's Poorly Guarded Past: Security Lacking at Facilities Used for Soviet Bioweapons Research," *Washington Post,* June 17, 2002.

40. Personal communication, November 2009.

41. R. Jeffrey Smith, "US Wary of Russian Germ Arms: Despite Assurances from Yeltsin, Effort May Be Continuing," *Washington Post,* April 8, 1994.

42. Ibid., 101.

43. "Discussion Paper" [Russia], June 6, 1994, unofficial translation.

44. An undated briefing document by the US Army Medical Research and Development Command showed additional USAMRU units located in Malaysia and Germany. Russian diplomats did not seek access to a network maintained by the US Air Force Department of Defense Global Emerging Infections System, which included an Influenza Surveillance Program with three sites in Europe and seven in Asia. The US government also maintained numerous non-DOD international collaborative field sites under the jurisdiction of the US National Institutes of Health, comprising seven different programs with facilities in 17 countries. The major programs were the International Collaboration in AIDS Research (ICAR) with sites in six countries, the International Collaboration in Infectious Disease Research (ICIDR), with sites in five countries, the Tropical Medicine Research Centers

(TMRC), with sites in three countries, and the Epidemic Intelligence Service, with sites in three countries.

45. James Goodby, "Transparency and Irreversibility in Nuclear Warhead Dismantlement," in *The Nuclear Turning Point: A Blueprint for Deep Cuts and De-alerting of Nuclear Weapons,* ed. Harold A. Feiveson (Washington, D.C., 1999), 189.

46. Plenary Meeting of the Fourth Review Conference of the States Party to the BWC, Geneva, November 27, 1996.

47. United States Arms Control and Disarmament Agency, *Adherence to and Compliance with Arms Control Agreements,* Washington, D.C.: May 30, 1994, 14.

48. Ibid.

49. US Department of State, *Adherence to and Compliance with Arms Control Agreements and Nonproliferation Agreements and Commitments,* 2002, 12.

50. US Department of State, *Adherence to and Compliance with Arms Control Agreements,* Washington, D.C.: 2005, 27, 28, 30.

51. "Joint Statement by President George W. Bush and President Vladimir V. Putin on Cooperation against Bioterrorism," November 13, 2001, Office of the Press Secretary, http://avalon.law.yale.edu/sept11/joint_003.asp.

52. The third experiment is incorrectly described. Russian scientists did not have the ability to carry out the procedure until five years after the date indicated, but that is beside the point.

53. US Government Accountability Office, *High-Containment Biosafety Laboratories,* GAO-08-108T, Washington, D.C., October 4, 2007.

54. David E. Hoffman, *The Dead Hand: The Untold Story of the Cold War Arms Race and Its Dangerous Legacy* (New York, 2009), 437.

55. Ibid., 436.

56. Ibid., 437. Hoffman claims US intelligence sources for this information. Personal communication, November 2009.

57. Ibid., 432. Wisner would have been on firmer ground if he had referred to the potential damage to the Nunn-Lugar legislation.

58. US Senate, Committee on Armed Services, *Worldwide Threat to the United States,* Hearing (Washington, D.C., 1995), 36. In contrast, substantial information was supplied to the Committee in regard to Russian backsliding on its commitments to carry out a program of destruction of its chemical munitions. (See Chapter 19).

59. US Senate, Committee on Armed Services, *Worldwide Threat to the United States.* In a second presentation before the Senate Select Committee on Intelligence, the director of the DIA, general James R. Clapper Jr., was asked: "In your written testimony, you state that Russia has '. . . active biological and chemical warfare programs. . . .' How robust are Russia's biological and chemical warfare programs?" Clapper's reply regarding the biological portion of the question was:

Russia's biological warfare (BW) program involves more than 20 facilities. This infrastructure involves facilities subordinate to the Ministries of Defense, Health, Agriculture, and the biotechnology consortium called BIOPRE-PARAT. These facilities support the full spectrum of research through production of weaponization. Dual-use facilities for wartime agent production of large quantities of BW agents are found at multiple sites belonging to BIO-PREPARAT. These facilities produce legitimate pharmaceutical products in peacetime but are designed to convert to wartime BW agent production. The open air BW test facility on Vozrozhdeniye island in the Aral Sea is on Kazakh territory and has been shut down.

Staffing of the program is assessed to have been affected by the recent upheaval in [the] Russian scientific sector. Figures of between 6,500 and 25,000 dedicated scientific workers have been reported. The former figures were cited by the Russian defector from BIOPREPARAT, Vladimir Pasechnik, and are very close to those described by Russia's 1992 Biological Weapons Convention (BWC) declaration as supporting offensive BW work.

In Russia's 1993 BWC declaration, there was no mention of any offensive BW activities. Instead there was a description of a defensive BW program currently centered at 5 primary facilities supported by 7 others, with a staff of at least 6,000. This new Russian version of a defensive program undoubtedly incorporated a significant portion of the facilities and personnel of the earlier offensive program. The size of the resulting entity is inordinately large for its purported purpose.

US Senate, Select Committee on Intelligence, Hearing: *Worldwide Intelligence Review* (Washington, D.C., 1995), 160.

60. "Section 1308: Report on Biological Weapons Programs in Russia," Report from the US Department of Defense to Congress, January 11, 2000.

61. The author would like to thank Dr. Iris Hunger for providing this information.

62. One of the authors (Leitenberg) attended the workshop, and all quotations and observations are from his notes.

63. Mahley's remark was made during a seminar presentation in Washington, D.C., in the late 1990s.

64. US Senate official, personal communication, December 2000.

65. One of the authors (Leitenberg) was a participant in the NATO Advanced Study Workshop in Moscow at which the Russian co-convener had invited Kuntsevich to make a presentation. (See Chapter 21.)

66. Personal communication.

67. Former US government official, personal communication, mid- and late-1990s.

68. Ignatiev's position as Pak's senior deputy for BW issues included the oversight of the former biological weapon institutes.

69. Koblentz, 2009, 124–125; quoting RF-MOH official Yuri Doshchitsyn.

70. John E. Tedstrom, "Russia's Biological Weapons System: Policy Options for U.S. Security Planners," RAND Briefing document, December 23, 1996.

71. Artiom Ustinov, "Russian Atomic Energy Reaches a Critical Mass," *Forum for Applied Research and Public Policy* 11:1 (Spring 1996): 110–112.

72. Alexandre Kaliadine, "Prohibition of Biological Weapons," in *Russian Arms Control: Compliance and Implementation,* ed. Alexei G. Arbatov, Report no. 14, Center for Geopolitical and Military Forecasts, Moscow, Russian Federation (Washington, D.C., 1995), 75–80.

73. Natalya Kalinina and Elina Kirichenko, "Compliance with the Biological and Toxin Weapons Convention: The Russian Perspective," in *Russia: Arms Control, Disarmament and International Security,* IMEMO Supplement to the Russian Edition of the *SIPRI Yearbook, 2004* (Moscow, 2004), 65–75. Kalinina had served as an assistant to Zinovy Pak in the Munitions Agency.

74. Former Soviet official, personal communication, 2009.

75. Vadim Birstein, *The Perversion of Knowledge: The True Story of Soviet Science* (Boulder, Colo., 2001), 304.

76. A. S. Spirin, "Basic Science and the Problems of Biological Security" (in Russian), *Vestnik Rossiyskoy Akademii Nauk* 74, no. 11 (2004): 963–972. Spirin apparently took the main ideas in this paper from one published the year before by three members of the US DIA: J. B. Petro, T. R. Plasse, and J. A. McNulty, "Biotechnology: Impact on Biological Warfare and Biodefence," *Biosecurity and Bioterrorism* 1 (2003): 161–163.

77. Steve Gutterman, "Sen.: Russia Too Evasive over Bioweapons," Associated Press, August 15, 2003.

78. US Senate official, personal communication, December 2000.

79. "Joint Statement on US-Russian Cooperation against Bioterrorism," in CD/1655, December 20, 2001, 2.

80. Personal communication from one of the participants, January 2010.

81. Personal communication, February 2010. It could not be ascertained if additional Russian scientists were also in the group.

82. Personal communication, US government official, January 2010.

83. US Department of Defense official, personal communication, July 2008. In the last few years, Russia has issued annual "non-compliance" statements of its own directed at the United States.The first appeared on August 7, 2010, and in it Russia reintroduced its old claim from the Trilateral negotiations, stating that the United States excludes part of its biodefense establishment from its CBM declarations. In particular, Russia argued that the United States should declare in its annual CBMs the presence of US "military medical research facilities" in, among other states, Egypt, Indonesia, Kenya, Peru and Thailand. (Russian Ministry of Foreign Affairs, "The Facts of the Violation by the USA of its Obligations in the Sphere of Non-Proliferation of Weapons of Mass Destruction and Arm Control," August 7,2010;

cited in John Hart and Peter Clevestig, "Reducing Security Threats from Chemical and Biological Materials," *SIPRI Yearbook 2011: Armaments, Disarmament and International Security* (Stockholm, 2011), p. 393.)

The second such statement on September 2, 2011, commented "As for the Biological and Toxin Weapons Convention, all the doubts relayed by the American side about Russia's compliance with the BTWC could long ago have been dispelled . . . if they had not torpedoed ten years ago the negotiation process to seek and develop on a multilateral basis a verification mechanism for the convention . . . Instead of agreeing on an effective mechanism for verifying compliance with the BTWC, they pursue a line on raising the so-called transparency of bioresearch, which can in no way substitute for full verification (Ministry of Foreign Affairs of the Russian Federation, "Russian MFA Press and Information Department Comment in Relation to the Publication of the US State Department Reports on Adherence to and Compliance with Arms Control, Nonproliferation and Disarmament Agreements and Commitments," September 2, 2011).

84. US Department of State official, personal communication, December 2000.

85. Valery V. Spirande and Oleg B. Ignatiev, "Strengthening the BTWC: An Important Factor for the Non-proliferation of Weapons of Mass Destruction" (in Russian), *Khimicheskaya I biologischeskaya bezopasnost* 9–10 (2003):3–6, cited in Jan T. Knoph and Kristina S. Westerdahl, "Re-evaluating Russia's Biological Weapons Policy, as Reflected in the Criminal Code and Official Admissions: Insubordination Leading to a President's Subordination," *Critical Reviews in Microbiology* 32, no. 1 (2006): 1–13. Also available at http://www.cbsafety.ru/rus/saf_9_10_01.pdf.

86. Arbatov, 1995, iv–vi.

87. Personal communication, government representative of an AG member state, December 2009. The Australia Group was a voluntary group of exporting states of CW and BW relevant equipment.

88. "Australia Group: 2008 Information Exchange (IE)," April 17, 2008, Ref ID: 08PARIS735, see paragraph 44, and "Viewing cable 09STATE67207, Australia Group: Promoting Participation In," June 29, 2009, see paragraph 5. Interestingly, at the June 2009 AG meeting, the US delegation to the AG asked member states for "any information you can share on the current state of Russia's CBW-related programs," this despite the fact that the United States probably had the largest presence inside Russia of any AG member state.

89. *World at Risk: The Report of the Commission on the Prevention of WMD Proliferation and Terrorism,* Washington, D.C., December 2008, 77.

90. Hoffman, 2009, 481.

91. David Hoffman, "Genetic Weapons, you say?" *Foreign Policy,* http://hoffman.foreignpolicy.com, in reference to an essay by Putin published in *Rossiiskaya Gazeta,* February 20, 2012, and a transcript of a Putin meeting with his cabinet ministers on March 22, 2012.

23. United States and International Efforts to Prevent Proliferation of Biological Weapons Expertise from the Former Soviet Union

1. Information about the various programs that were initiated by governments to aid this effort, the United States in particular, the US agencies managing them, and the funds expended for them will be placed on a website dedicated to this book. We wish to convey our gratitude to CNS Graduate Research Assistants Paula Humphrey and Charlotte Savidge for their assistance in producing the material that will be placed on the dedicated website.

2. See the discussion of offensive and defensive R&D in Chapter 11.

3. National Research Council/National Academies of Science, *The Biological Threat Reduction Program of the Department of Defense: From Foreign Assistance to Sustainable Partnerships* (Washington D.C., 2007), 2.

4. Milton Leitenberg, "The Conversion of Biological Warfare Research and Development Facilities to Peaceful Uses," in *Control of Dual-Threat Agents: The Vaccines for Peace* Program, ed. Erhard Geissler and John P. Woodall (Oxford, 1994), 77–105; Milton Leitenberg, "The Possibilities and Limitations of Biological Weapons Conversion: Personnel and Facilities," in *The Conversion of Former BTW Facilities*, ed. Erhard Geissler (Dordrecht, 1998), 119–133; Erhard Geissler, ed., *The Conversion of Former BTW Facilities* (Dordrecht, 1998); Ernst Buder, ed., *Möglichkeiten und Grenzen der Konversion von B-Waffen-Einrichtungen* (Munster, 2000); Petra Lilya, Roger Roffey, and Kristina Westerdahl, *Disarmament or Retention: Is the Soviet Biological Weapons Program Continuing in Russia?*, FOA-R-99-01366-865-SE, Umeå, Sweden, December 1999; Roger Roffey and Kristina S. Westerdahl, *Conversion of Former Biological Weapon Facilities in Kazakhstan: A Visit to Stepnogorsk, July 2000*, FOI-R-0082-SE, Umeå, Sweden, May 2001; Roger Roffey et al., *Support to Threat Reduction of the Russian Biological Weapons Legacy: Conversion, Biodefence and the Role of Biopreparat*, FOI-R-0841-SE, Umeå, Sweden, April 2003; Britta Hagström, Åke Forsberg, and Lena Norlander, *Conversion of a Former Biological Weapon Establishment*, FOI-R-1316-SE, Umeå, Sweden, September 2004; Kristina S. Westerdahl and Lena Norlander, *The Role of the New Russian Anti-Bioterrorism Centres*, FOI-R-1971-SE, June 2006; Glenn E. Schweitzer, *Moscow DMZ: The Story of the International Effort to Convert Russian Weapons Science to Peaceful Purposes* (Armonk, N.Y., 1996); National Research Council/National Academies of Science, *Biological Science and Biotechnology in Russia: Controlling Diseases and Enhancing Security* (Washington, D.C., 2006); and Sonia Ben Ouagrham and Kathleen Vogel, *Conversion at Stepnogorsk: What the Future Holds for Former Bioweapons Facilities*, Occasional Paper no. 28, Cornell University Peace Studies Program, February 2003.

5. Judith Miller, "U.S. Aid Is Diverted to Germ Warfare, Russian Scientists Say," *New York Times*, January 25, 2000.

6. Leitenberg, 1998.

7. One of the authors (Leitenberg) attended the NATO Advanced Research Workshop on Conversion of Former BTW Facilities: Development and Production of Prophylactic, Diagnostic and Therapeutic Measures for Countering Diseases, Budapest, Hungary, November 1997.

8. First Forum of the International Scientific Panel on the Possible Consequences of the Misuse of Biological Sciences, Landau Network–Centro Volta, Como, Italy, December 1997. Both authors attended this conference.

9. General Accounting Office, *Nuclear Nonproliferation: DOE Needs to Reassess Its Program to Assist Weapons Scientists in Russia and Other Countries,* GAO-08-434T, January 23, 2008.

10. General Accounting Office, *Biological Weapons: Effort to Reduce Former Soviet Threat Offers Benefits, Poses New Risks,* GAO/NSIAD-00-138, April 2000, 6. See also other GAO and CRS reports: *Cooperative Threat Reduction: DOD Has Improved Its Management and Internal Controls, but Challenges Remain,* GAO-05-329, June 2005; *Weapons of Mass Destruction: Nonproliferation Programs Need Better Integration,* GAO-05-157, January 2005; "Weapons of Mass Destruction: Observations on U.S. Threat Reduction and Nonproliferation Programs in Russia," Statement of Joseph A. Christoff, Director, International Affairs and Trade, GAO-03-526T, March 2003; *Weapons of Mass Destruction: Additional Russian Cooperation Needed to Facilitate U.S. Efforts to Improve Security at Russian Sites,* GAO-03-482, March 2003; *Weapons of Mass Destruction: State Department Oversight of Science Centers Program,* GAO-01-582, May 2001; and Michelle Stem Cook and Amy F. Woolf, *Preventing Proliferation of Biological Weapons: U.S. Assistance to the Former Soviet States,* Congressional Research Service, RL 31368, April 10, 2002. See also Amy Smithson, *Toxic Archipelago: Preventing Proliferation from the Former Soviet Chemical and Biological Complexes,* Stimson Center Report no. 32, 1999.

11. Several European graduate students were also able to spend a few weeks each at Biopreparat institutes in the vicinity of Moscow. However, their purview would presumably have been extremely limited.

12. General Accounting Office, 2000, 24.

13. Mark Kramer, "Demilitarizing Russian Weapons Scientists: The Challenge," in *Beyond Nunn-Lugar: Curbing the Next Wave of Weapons Proliferation Threats from Russia,* ed. H. D. Sokolski and T. Riisager, Strategic Studies Institute, 2002, 115–177. See, in particular, 146, 150–152.

14. Personal communication, July 2010.

15. In 1996 the US Senate passed legislation mandating that no DOD funds could be used to support "defense industry conversion" in Russia, of any portion of the former Soviet Union's weapons production infrastructure. This did not affect US funding to support the destruction of Russia's chemical stockpile, but it did cause some small problems afterward for CTR's engagement with Russian BW facilities.

16. General Accounting Office, 2000, 6.

17. National Academy of Sciences/Institute of Medicine/National Research Council, *Controlling Dangerous Pathogens: A Blueprint for U.S.-Russian Cooperation,* A report to the Cooperative Threat Reduction Program of the US Department of Defense, October 1997, 5.

18. Christopher P. Howson, "Controlling Dangerous Pathogens: A Blueprint for U.S.-Russian Cooperation," in Geissler, 1998, 135–148.

19. Personal communication, Joshua Lederberg, April 1997.

20. Personal communication, April 1998.

21. Sarah Shafer, "Russia Bracing for Spread of Dangerous TB Strains," *Washington Post,* August 24, 2009.

22. Howson, 1998, 142.

23. Personal communications, 2008 and 2010.

24. DOD Malaria Research Programs, PowerPoint Briefing Charts, April 17, 1996, at the Naval Medical Research Institute.

25. Richard Gallagher, "Global Initiative Takes Shape Slowly," *Science* 277 (July 18, 1997): 309; Nigel Williams, "Consensus on African Research Projects," *Science* 278 (November 21, 1997): 1393; Nigel Williams, "Drug Companies Decline to Collaborate," Science 278 (December 5, 1997): 1704; and Daniel Greenberg, "A Pittance to Fight Malaria," *Washington Post,* January 4, 1998.

26. Gary Taubes, "Salvation in a Snippet of DNA?," *Science* 278 (December 5, 1997): 1711–1714. See also "Malaria Vaccine Studies," in *Activity Report, 1999,* International Centre for Genetic Engineering and Biotechnology, 49–54; and ICGEB 2000 course, "Molecular Approaches to Malaria: Implications for Vaccine and Drug Development."

27. Personal communication, January 1998.

28. Terence Chea, "Md. Biotech Firms Attack Malaria: Team Led by SAIC Awarded $43.8 Million Contract to Develop Vaccine," *Washington Post,* October 26, 2000.

29. Pamela C. Ronald, "Making Rice Disease Resistant," *Scientific American* 277, no. 5 (November 1997): 101–107.

30. Letter from Dr. J. W. Lee, WHO, and Dr. Jerald C. Sadoff, Walter Reed Army Institute of Research, to D. A. Henderson, Department of Health and Human Services, GPV/V27/181/1, June 26, 1994.

31. A. V. Osin et al., "Expression Traits of a Recombinant Plasmid with the Genes of the Cholera Toxin in the Cells of an Avirulent Strain of Vibrio Cholerae 0139 Serotype," *Biotechnology,* no. 3 (2004): 12–18.

32. Personal communications, Andrew Weber and Anne Harrington, March 2008.

33. Richard Stone, "Russia: An Antidote to Bioproliferation," *Science* 278 (November 14, 1997): 1222.

34. Leitenberg, 1994, contains a detailed catalog of Soviet and Russian statements between 1990 and 1994 concerning capabilities, intentions, and plans for conversion of BW facilities and research. It also contains a list of major categories of commercial microbiological products that these institutes could turn to. Several of these products are used for environmental remediation. Interestingly, the RF-MOD facility in Yekaterinburg stated that it would be producing one of these, widely used for the remediation of oil pollution.

35. It can be argued that grants for work with BW pathogens reached the Russian scientists of greatest proliferation concern, and personal contact with that group again provided reassurance that they were not occupied in improper activities.

36. "Lugar Discusses Upcoming Elections, Calls on Ukraine to Share Bio Strains," *The Lugar Trip Report,* August 2004, 6.

37. Boris Ivanov, "Pentagon Funding Construction of Reference Laboratory in Almaty: Americans Archiving Viruses" (in Russian), *Kursiv,* April 10, 2009.

38. National Research Council/National Academies of Science, 2007, 90.

39. Amy F. Woolf, *Nonproliferation and Threat Reduction Assistance: US Programs in the Former Soviet Union,* RL31957, Congressional Research Service, July 31, 2009, 20–21; National Research Council/National Academies of Science, 2007, 67–69, 90.

40. National Research Council/National Academies of Science, 2007, 68.

41. Department of State, Office of Cooperative Threat Reduction (CTR), "Combating Biological Threats Globally," nd [ca 2008].

The expansion occurred under expanded congressional authority and two newer Presidential Directives (NSPD 33/HSPD 10 and NSPD 17). The programs in these additional countries are also supported by additional international assistance from the WHO, the OIE, the United Kingdom, Canada and Japan.

42. Personal communication, November 2004.

43. Personal communications, December 2009.

44. Personal communication, 2004.

45. National Research Council/National Academies of Science, 2007, 69. See also National Academy of Sciences, 2006.

46. Nikolai Poroskovy, "We Did Not Plan to Use Biological Weapons" (in Russian), interview with Valery Spirande, *Vremya Novosti,* April 23, 2003.

47. "Russia Rejects Western Aid Program of $1 Billion US," *Torgovo-Promyshlennyye Vedomosti,* April 22, 2011.

48. "Statement of the 54th Governing Board of the International Science and Technology Center," December 9, 2011.

49. Geoff Brumfiel, "Curtain Falls on Collaborative Work," *Nature* 468 (November 1, 2010), 16.

50. Leitenberg, 1998.

51. US Department of State, *Adherence to and Compliance with Arms Control, Nonproliferation and Disarmament Agreements and Commitments,* July 2010, 23–24.

The 2011 statement modifies the key line slightly: "Russia's annual BWC confidence-building measure declarations since 1992 have not satisfactorily documented whether this program was completely destroyed or diverted to peaceful purposes in accordance with Article II of the BWC." US Department of State, *Adherence to and Compliance with Arms Control, Nonproliferation and Disarmament Agreements and Commitments,* August 2011, 12–13.

52. Ministry of Foreign Affairs of the Russian Federation, "Comment of the Russian MFA Press and Information Department Following the Publication of the US State Department Report on Adherence to and Compliance with Arms Control, Nonproliferation, and Disarmament Agreements and Commitments," July 29, 2010. The MFA document was a rebuttal of the US report, listing its own compendium of US arms control treaty violations. It included a section on the BWC containing three categories: (1) violations by the United States of the BWC Article I obligations; (2) violations of the US requirements of Article IV of the BWC and UNSC Resolution 1540; and (3) violations of US obligations under the BWC Confidence Building Measures. Under the first of these three categories, the first words read "Without formally violating its obligations . . . ," paradoxically implying that there were *no* "formal" charges of US BWC violations. The remaining pages were an extremely incompetent hodgepodge of various US laboratory accidents involving Select Agent pathogens that had all been well aired in the US media and websites between 2004 and 2010. The Russian rendition of these included several notable and tendentious inaccuracies. The last paragraph of the document repeated the issues concerning US DOD laboratories in Asia and Africa raised by Russia in 1994–1996 that helped cripple the Trilateral negotiations. However the MFA document now suggested that the United States needed only to have reported those laboratories in its CBMs.

Conclusion

1. As described in Chapter 2, there was also an open and widely published 1974 decree that spelled out the necessity for advancing biotechnology in the civilian sphere.

2. L. Zaikov, "To the President of the Union of Soviet Socialist Republics, Comrade M. S. Gorbachev," May 15, 1990. (Kataev archive at the Hoover Institute.)

3. The photo has been cropped to disclose as much detail as possible of award recipients. The original photo shows the group in an extravagant setting that included artful wall panels, grandiose chandeliers, and intricate parquet flooring.

4. One interviewee stated that the KGB had inserted several individuals unconnected with the event in the group to confuse Western intelligence agencies that may have attempted to identify its members.

5. Scientists at the Kirov Institute might have taken an alternative approach that depended on developing two strains of *B. anthracis,* with each being resistant to five different antibiotics, and then mixing these two strains in one formulation.

6. The US-UK Trilateral inspection teams noticed that explosive test chambers at IHPB, SRCAM and Vector showed dents on their inner metal walls, suggesting that munitions had been detonated in tests within them.

7. "Soviet Capabilities and Intentions with Respect to the Clandestine Introduction of Weapons of Mass Destruction into the US," National Intelligence Estimate number 11-7-60, May 14, 1960, 4.

8. Raymond A. Zilinskas and Hussein Alramini, "Aerosol Vaccines" in *Innovation, Dual Use, and Security: Managing the Risks of Emerging Biological and Chemical Technologies,* Jonathan B. Tucker, editor. (MIT Press, Cambridge, Mass., 2012).

9. There is a vast pharmaceutical market internal to Russia that offers drugs that outsiders know little about. It is therefore possible that some drugs developed during Soviet times by Biopreparat or MOD institutes are available to Russians. However, Russians who can afford it purchase Western or Japanese drugs because they are produced according to internationally recognized Good Manufacturing Practices (GMP). Very few, if any, Russian drugs are produced according to GMP.

10. As discussed in Chapter 5, the strictly civilian work done by the anti-plague system was probably efficient in terms of preventing exotic diseases from entering the Soviet Union and dangerous indigenous diseases from causing catastrophic damage.

11. David E. Hoffman, *The Dead Hand: The Untold Story of the Cold War Arms Race and Its Dangerous Legacy* (New York, 2010), 303.

12. As noted in Chapter 12, the US IC largely agreed with this reason; i.e., several NIEs that dealt with BW concluded that the United States' greatest vulnerability was to sabotage or terrorism that utilized biological weapons. However, the NIEs in question were written long before the US IC knew anything about Soviet BW production capacity, as well as any of the particulars regarding the Soviet program. In addition, when the United States developed anti-plant BW agents after World War II against food grains such as wheat, rye, and rice, these were intended to be used as strategic weapons.

13. If the plans for use were relegated to an extremely few senior military officers, and particularly if the conception involved use after a nuclear weapon exchange, those few individuals would almost certainly have died in the very first nuclear strike if they had been located in Moscow.

Acknowledgments

Many individuals contributed greatly to the success of this project, and we wish to thank all of them for their assistance. In particular, we are indebted to the numerous scientists of the former Soviet Union, as well as non-Russian experts, who provided crucial information during interviews and in less formal discussions. In spite of our desire to recognize these individuals for their contributions to this work, a large number of them wish to remain anonymous. Although not named, we are enormously thankful to them for their assistance.

Igor Domaradsky, Vladimir Pasechnik, Sergei Popov, and Vladimir P. Zaviyalov, as well as other Russian scientists who cannot be named, spent many days with us while explaining the operations of Biopreparat, its institutes, and its relationships with other Soviet agencies. Vitaly Kataev was a source of information on processes of decision making at the highest political level of the Soviet Union, the Central Committee of the Communist Party. His valuable contributions to our book continued after his death, when his personal records became available to researchers. David E. Hoffman shared information relevant to our book that he uncovered while working with the Kataev document collection at the Hoover Institute, as well as in British government archives. Andrew Weber described his work in the former Soviet Union to implement the Cooperative Threat Reduction program. This brought him into direct contact with many of the major Soviet BW scientists whose names appear in this book. James W. Toppin was our highly skilled translator, who also undertook specialized research. Raymond Garthoff and John Walker kindly read and commented on many of the chapters in the second half of the book. Lastly, this book would not have been completed without the assistance of Nicole Ball.

Valuable contributions to our understanding of various subjects directly treated in the book, by directing us to important sources, were made by Ken Alibek, Richard Beedham, Istvan Fodor, David Franz, Martin Furmanski, Dennis Gormley, Mark Gorwitz, Elisa D. Harris, John Hart, Paul Jackson, Paul Keim, Mark Kramer, James Leonard, Jack Melling, Matthew Meselson, Allan Jeff Mohr, Natasha Pasechnik, Francesca Perry, Julian Perry Robinson, Roger Roffey, Nikita Smidovich, Mitchell Fadem, John van Courtland Moon, and Marina Voronova.

At Harvard University Press, its executive editor Michael Fisher provided unfailing support since we submitted our manuscript. We are particularly grateful for his guidance as the manuscript was prepared in its final form. The actual production of the book was supervised by production editor Michael Haggett, who we thank for meeting our last minute requests with unfailing patience. We would also like to extend special thanks to the two anonymous reviewers for the Harvard University Press and to Jonas Siegal who edited half of the book manuscript.

Finally, producing this book would not have been possible without the initial support we received from the Smith-Richardson Foundation. We thank the Foundation for that support and convey our special appreciation to Nadia Schadlow for her patience during the many extra years that were required to complete the book following the Foundation grant.

Index

vaccine against, 220–221, 330, 786n34; Vector accidents involving, 232–233; Soviet allegations on US use of, 419

Economy of production, 284

Ectromelia virus, 208, 783n8

Edgewood Arsenal, 451

Edsall, John, 853n5

Eighteen Nation Disarmament Commission (ENDC), 525, 532, 533, 535, 536, 537, 857n45

Eisenhower, Dwight D., 403, 411

Ekéus, Rolf, 483–484, 485, 487, 490, 543

Ekologiya program, 9, 210, 275, 700, 708–709, 739n10

Elsey, George, 50

Emigration of Soviet BW personnel, 476–478, 480, 840n6; to Israel, 477, 478, 500–501, 840n6; proliferation concerns in, 682

Encapsulation technology, 290

Endorphins, 193, 229, 236, 237

Endo, Seichi, 55

Engelhardt, Vladimir A., 262, 264

Eniwetok Atoll, open-air testing of BW agents at, 398

Enkephalins, 192, 193, 236, 237

Enniatine, 53

Enterotoxin, 288, 372, 398

Entomology in Zagorsk Institute, 90

Enzyme development and production in Biopreparat, 164

Enzymes programs, 67, 164, 754n43. See also *Ferment* programs

Epitopes, 271, 795n44

Erlick, Barry, 107

Escherichia coli, 262, 331; genetic engineering research on, 191, 193, 199, 366, 499; Vector research on, 236, 237, 247

Estaviev, Gennady, 483–484, 487

F clearance in Biopreparat system, 69–70, 154

F Form in Confidence Building Measures, 635, 636, 644, 648

Facilities and equipment: in Shemyakin Institute, 59–60; in Sverdlovsk, 100–101; in Aralsk-7, 124–127; in Field Scientific Research Laboratory (PNIL), 125, 766n25; in SRCAM, 180–184, 198; in Vector, 211–215; in IHPB, 251–252; in IEI, 266; German production of, 276, 278, 458, 469–470, 488; in SNOPB, 277–279; as indicator of offensive program, 337, 339, 340; mass media reports on, 380–381; from Warsaw Pact states, 458, 459; in Czechoslovakia, 462, 464, 465–466, 467; in Iraq, 481–482, 487, 488, 489, 505; in China, 499; in Cuba, 500; for chemical weapons,

514, 516–517, 518; in United States, 528–529, 530, 531

Factor program, 68, 69, 190–197, 229, 332, 780n52; goals of, 157, 177, 178, 190; peptide research in, 178, 192–194; genetic engineering in, 190–196; intelligence community assessment of, 368

Fagot program, 754n43

Falin, Valentin, 415, 416

Falk, Richard, 326

Farm facilities: of Zagorsk Institute, 96; of Vector, 214

Farrakhan, Louis, 825n55

Faybich, M. M., 19, 28, 29, 740n15

Fayzullin, Leonid Z., 228

Federal Bureau of Investigation (FBI) disinformation effort, 399–401, 404

Federal Security Service (FSB), 246, 417, 421, 483, 694

Fedorov, Lev A., 440, 510, 540, 802n74, 831n49, 832n70, 849n15, 859n67, 859n68

Feith, Douglas, 373–374, 390, 441, 675

Ferment programs, 7, 9–10, 67–69, 153, 155, 754n43; institutes involved in, 71; objective of, 71; Bonfire, 156–157, 177, 184–190, 772n11; Factor, 177, 178, 190–197; Metol, 177, 178; accomplishments of, 197, 702; IHPB in, 252, 265. *See also specific programs*

Fetish program, 68, 69, 81, 758n7

Fetter, Steven, 110

Field Scientific Research Laboratory (PNIL), 124–126

Fifth Problem Commission, 143. *See also* Problem 5 program

Fildes, Paul, 55

Filippov, Vladimir I., 421

Filler substances, 290

Filoviruses, 253

First generation of Soviet BW program, 8, 16–50, 156, 247, 698–699; conclusions on, 17, 43–47; in years 1920–1946, 17, 18–34; in years 1946–1972, 17, 34–43; US/UK intelligence community assessments of, 18, 43, 346–360, 389–390; accomplishments of, 702

First International Conference on Metabolic Plasmids, 159

First Problem Commission, 142

Fishman, Yakov M., 18, 20–21, 24, 55, 742n44

Flask program, 754n43

Fleming, Donald, 73

Flora program, 754n43

Flute program, 68, 69, 73, 754n43

Fodor, Istvan, 701, 890